The Longman Anthology of British Literature

VOLUME 2A

The Longman Anthology of British Literature

Fifth Edition

◄—┼—═◊═—┼—►

David Damrosch and Kevin J. H. Dettmar
General Editors

VOLUME 2A

THE ROMANTICS AND THEIR CONTEMPORARIES
Susan Wolfson *and* Peter Manning

Amelia Klein
Associate Editor

PEARSON

Boston Columbus Indianapolis New York San Francisco Upper Saddle River
Amsterdam Cape Town Dubai London Madrid Milan Munich Paris Montreal Toronto
Delhi Mexico City São Paulo Sydney Hong Kong Seoul Singapore Taipei Tokyo

Editor-in-Chief: *Joseph Terry*
Development Editor: *Erin Reilly*
Editorial Assistant: *Kelly Carroll*
Executive Marketing Manager: *Joyce Nilsen*
Senior Supplements Editor: *Donna Campion*
Production Manager: *Ellen MacElree*
Project Coordination, Text Design, and Page Makeup: *PreMediaGlobal, Inc.*
Cover Designer/Manager: *John Callahan*
Image Permission Coordinator: *Debbie Latronica*
Senior Manufacturing Buyer: *Dennis J. Para*
Printer and Binder: *RR Donnelley Crawfordsville, In*
Cover Printer: *Lehigh-Phoenix Color/Hagerstown*

For permission to use copyrighted material, grateful acknowledgment is made to the copyright holders on pages 1215–1216, which are hereby made part of this copyright page.

Library of Congress Cataloging-in-Publication Data

The Longman anthology of British literature / David Damrosch and Kevin J. H. Dettmar, general editors.—5th ed.
　　p. cm.
　Includes bibliographical references and index.
　ISBN 978-0-205-22316-9 (v. 2A)
　1. English literature.　2. Great Britain—Literary collections.　I. Damrosch, David.
II. Dettmar, Kevin J. H., 1958–
　PR1109.L69 2012
　820.8—dc23
　　　　　　　　　　　　　　　　　　　　　　　　　　　　　　2011032696

10 9 8—DOC—15 14

On the cover: *The Burning of the Houses of Lords and Commons*, October 16, 1834 (detail). The Philadelphia Museum of Art / Art Resource, NY

ISBN-10:　　0-205-22316-8
ISBN-13: 978-0-205-22316-9

CONTENTS

The Romantics and Their Contemporaries

⇒⊹ PERSPECTIVES ⊹⇐
The Abolition of Slavery and the Slave Trade   229

🍳 PERCY BYSSHE SHELLEY   868

ADDITIONAL RESOURCES

Longman Cultural Editions

These major texts, with a generous selection of contextual material, reveal the conversations and controversies of the historical moment. One Longman Cultural Edition is available at no additional cost when packaged with the anthology. For a complete list of titles, go to www.pearsonhighered.com/literature. Contact your local Pearson Publisher's Representative for packaging details. Some titles of interest for this volume include:

Austen. *Emma*, ed. Ferguson
ISBN-10: 0-321-22504-X
ISBN-13: 978-0-321-22504-7

Austen. *Northanger Abbey*, ed. Gaull
ISBN-10: 0-321-20208-2
ISBN-13: 978-0-321-20208-6

Austen. *Persuasion*, ed. Galperin
ISBN-10: 0-321-19822-0
ISBN-13: 978-0-321-19822-8

Austen. *Pride and Prejudice*, ed. Johnson and Wolfson
ISBN-10: 0-321-10507-9
ISBN-13: 978-0-321-10507-3

Brontë. *Wuthering Heights*, ed. Booth
ISBN-10: 0-321-21298-3
ISBN-13: 978-0-321-21298-6

Conrad and Kipling. *The Heart of Darkness, The Man Who Would Be King and Other Works on Empire*, ed. Damrosch
ISBN-10: 0-321-36467-8
ISBN-13: 978-0-321-36467-8

Dickens. *Hard Times*, ed. Nunokawa and McWeeney
ISBN-10: 0-321-10721-7
ISBN-13: 978-0-321-10721-3

Forster. *Howards End*, ed. Mao
ISBN-10: 0-205-53737-5
ISBN-13: 978-0-205-53737-2

Joyce. *Dubliners*, ed. Latham
ISBN-10: 0-205-53736-7
ISBN-13: 978-0-205-53736-5

John Keats, ed. Wolfson
ISBN-10: 0-321-23616-5
ISBN-13: 978-0-321-23616-6

Kipling. *Kim*, ed. Krebs and Lootens
ISBN-10: 0-321-43583-4
ISBN-13: 978-0-321-43583-5

Shelley. *Frankenstein*, ed. Wolfson
ISBN-10: 0-321-39953-6
ISBN-13: 978-0-321-39953-3

Percy Bysshe Shelley, ed. Behrendt
ISBN-10: 0-321-20210-4
ISBN-13: 978-0-321-20210-9

Stevenson, Conrad, and Shelley. *Dr Jekyll and Mr. Hyde*, *The Secret Sharer*, and *Transformation: Three Tales of Doubles*, ed. Wolfson and Qualls
ISBN-10: 0-321-41561-2
ISBN-13: 978-0-321-41561-5

Stoker. *Dracula*, ed. Elfenbein
ISBN-10: 0-205-63263-7
ISBN-13: 978-0-205-63263-3

Walpole and MacKenzie. *The Castle of Otranto* and *The Man of Feeling*, ed. Mandell
ISBN-10: 0-321-39892-0
ISBN-13: 978-0-321-39892-5

Wilde. *The Picture of Dorian Gray*, ed. Elfenbein
ISBN-10: 0-321-42713-0
ISBN-13: 978-0-321-42713-7

Wollstonecraft. *A Vindication of the Rights of Woman and The Wrongs of Woman; or Maria*, ed. Mellor and Chao
ISBN-10: 0-321-18273-1
ISBN-13: 978-0-321-18273-9

Dorothy Wordsworth, ed. Levin
ISBN-10: 0-321-27775-9
ISBN-13: 978-0-321-27775-6

WEB SITE FOR *THE LONGMAN ANTHOLOGY OF BRITISH LITERATURE*

www.myliteraturekit.com

The fifth edition makes connections beyond its covers as well as within them. The Web site we have developed for the course provides a wealth of resources:

- **An Archive of Additional Texts.** Our online archive contains a wealth of selections that could not fit within the bounds of the print anthology. The following selections are available for the Romantic period:

  - **William Wordsworth**
    from *The Wanderer*, 1845 Version
    Response to *The Excursion*. John Wilson: "But is it Christianity? . . . Was Margaret a Christian?" from "On Sacred Poetry" Blackwood's *Edinburgh Magazine*, 1828

  - **Percy Bysshe Shelley**
    The Cenci
    "Julian and Maddalo"
    "The Sensitive Plant"
    Letter to Maria Gisborne
    Response to "The Mask of Anarchy." Leigh Hunt: Introduction to "The Mask of Anarchy"
    Response to "To a Sky-Lark." Thomas Hardy: Shelley's Skylark
    Response. Mary Shelley: Introductions to the Works of Percy Bysshe Shelley (1824, 1839)

- **Discussion Questions for Major Selections and Perspectives Sections.** Designed to prepare students for the kind of deeper-level analysis expected in class discussions, these compelling prompts are available for each period introduction and for major selections and Perspectives groupings.

- **Self-Grading Multiple Choice Practice Questions.** Available for each period introduction and for all major authors and Perspectives groupings, these objective practice quizzes are designed to help students review their basic understanding of the reading.

- **An Interactive Timeline.** Our interactive timeline helps students visualize the key literary, political, and cultural events of an era. Each event is accompanied by a detailed explanation, usually including references to relevant texts that can be found in the anthology, and colorful pictures and illustrations.

- **Links to Valuable British Literature Resources.** Our Online Research Guide provides a wealth of annotated links to excellent Web resources on major authors, texts, and related historical and cultural movements and events.

PREFACE

Literature has a double life. Born in one time and place and read in another, literary works are at once products of their age and independent creations, able to live on long after their original world has disappeared. The goal of *The Longman Anthology of British Literature* is to present a wealth of poetry, prose, and drama from the full sweep of the literary history of Great Britain and its empire, and to do so in ways that will bring out both the works' original cultural contexts and their lasting aesthetic power. These aspects are in fact closely related: form and content, verbal music and social meanings, go hand in hand. This double life makes literature, as Aristotle said, "the most philosophical" of all the arts, intimately connected to ideas and to realities that the writer transforms into moving patterns of words. The challenge is to show these works in the contexts in which, and for which, they were written, while at the same time not trapping them within those contexts. The warm response this anthology has received from the hundreds of teachers who have adopted it in its first four editions reflects the growing consensus that we are not forced to choose between the literature's aesthetic and cultural dimensions. Our users' responses have now guided us in seeing how we can improve our anthology further, so as to be most pleasurable and stimulating to students, most useful to teachers, and most responsive to ongoing developments in literary studies. This preface can serve as a road map to this book's goals and structure.

NEW TO THIS EDITION

We have added more than 170 pages of literature to this edition of Volume 2A: *The Romantics and Their Contemporaries*, providing readers with the deeper perspective necessary for courses focusing on the Romantic era, as well as a more robust selection for survey courses. These new works include the following selections:

- John Ruskin
  from Modern Painters

- Samuel Taylor Coleridge
  from Jacobinism
  from Once a Jacobin Always a Jacobin

- William Blake
  All Religions Are One
  There is No Natural Religion [a]
  There is No Natural Religion [b]

- Charles Lamb
  from The Praise of Chimney-Sweepers

LITERATURE IN ITS TIME—AND IN OURS

When we engage with a rich literary history that extends back over a thousand years, we often encounter writers who assume their readers know all sorts of things that are little known today: historical facts, social issues, literary and cultural references. Beyond specific information, these works will have come out of a very different literary culture than our own. Even the contemporary British Isles present a cultural situation— or a mix of cultures—very different from what North American readers encounter at home, and these differences only increase as we go farther back in time. A major emphasis of this anthology is to bring the works' original cultural moment to life: not because the works simply or naively reflect that moment of origin, but because they do refract it in fascinating ways. British literature is both a major heritage for modern

North America and, in many ways, a very distinct culture; reading British literature will regularly give an experience both of connection and of difference. Great writers create imaginative worlds that have their own compelling internal logic, and a prime purpose of this anthology is to help readers to understand the formal means—whether of genre, rhetoric, or style—with which these writers have created works of haunting beauty. At the same time, as Virginia Woolf says in *A Room of One's Own*, the gossamer threads of the artist's web are joined to reality "with bands of steel."

The Longman Anthology pursues a range of strategies to bring out both the beauty of these webs of words and their points of contact with reality and to bring related authors and works together in several ways:

☞ PERSPECTIVES: **Broad groupings that illuminate underlying issues in a variety of the major works of a period.**

☞ AND ITS TIME: **A focused cluster that illuminates a specific cultural moment or a debate to which an author is responding.**

☞ RESPONSES: **One or more texts in which later authors in the tradition respond creatively to the challenging texts of their forebears.**

These groupings provide a range of means of access to the literary culture of each period. The Perspectives sections do much more than record what major writers thought about an issue: they give a variety of views in a range of voices, to illustrate the wider culture within which the literature was being written. Passionate voices on both sides of the debate over slavery; fiction and essays exploring the development of popular prose; these and many other vivid readings featured in Volume 2A give rhetorical as well as social contexts for the poems, plays, and stories around them. Perspectives sections typically relate to several major authors of the period, as with a section on the rights of man and the revolution controversy that brings the essays of Edmund Burke and Mary Wollstonecraft into conversation with less widely read figures such as Helen Maria Williams and William Godwin. Most of the writers included in Perspectives sections are important figures of the period who might be neglected if they were listed on their own with just a few pages each; grouping them together has proved to be useful pedagogically as well as intellectually. Perspectives sections may also include work by a major author whose primary listing appears elsewhere in the period; thus, a Perspectives section on the Sublime, the Beautiful, and the Picturesque features a selection by Mary Wollstonecraft, so as to give a rounded presentation of the issue in a way that can inform the reading of that author in his or her individual section.

When we present a major work "And Its Time," we give a cluster of related materials to suggest the context within which the work was written. Thus Coleridge's lectures on Shakespeare are accompanied by additional contemporary critical views from Charles Lamb, William Hazlitt, and Thomas De Quincey, suggesting the wealth of ways Shakespeare mattered in the Romantic era. Some of the writers in these groupings and in our Perspectives sections have not traditionally been seen as literary figures, but all have produced lively and intriguing works, such as the aesthetic philosophy of Immanuel Kant's *Critique of Judgement*, or articles from the *Anti-Jacobin* and the *Edinburgh Review*. We also include "Responses" to significant texts in the British literary tradition, demonstrating the sometimes far-reaching influence these works have had over the decades and centuries, and sometimes across oceans and continents.

What Is British Literature?

Stepping back from the structure of Volume 2A: *The Romantics and Their Contemporaries*, let us define our basic terms: What is "British" literature? What is literature itself? And just what should an anthology of this material look like at the present time? The term "British" can mean many things, some of them contradictory, some of them even offensive to people on whom the name has been imposed. If the term "British" has no ultimate essence, it does have a history. The first British were Celtic people who inhabited the British Isles and the northern coast of France (still called Brittany) before various Germanic tribes of Angles and Saxons moved onto the islands in the fifth and sixth centuries. Gradually the Angles and Saxons amalgamated into the Anglo-Saxon culture that became dominant in the southern and eastern regions of Britain and then spread outward; the old British people were pushed west, toward what became known as Cornwall, Wales, and Ireland, which remained independent kingdoms for centuries, as did Celtic Scotland to the north. By an ironic twist of linguistic fate, the Anglo-Saxons began to appropriate the term "British" from the Britons they had displaced, and they took as a national hero the early, semimythic Welsh King Arthur. By the seventeenth century, English monarchs had extended their sway over Wales, Ireland, and Scotland, and they began to refer to their holdings as "Great Britain." Today, Great Britain includes England, Wales, Scotland, and Northern Ireland, but does not include the Republic of Ireland, which has been independent since 1922.

This anthology uses "British" in a broad sense, as a geographical term encompassing the whole of the British Isles. For all its fraught history, it seems a more satisfactory term than to speak simply of "English" literature, for two reasons. First, most speakers of English live in countries that are not the focus of this anthology (for instance, the United States and Canada); second, while the English language and its literature have long been dominant in the British Isles, other cultures in the region have always used other languages and have produced great literature in these languages. Important works by Irish, Welsh, and Scots writers appear regularly in the body of this anthology, some of them written directly in their languages and presented here in translation, and others written in an English inflected by the rhythms, habits of thought, and modes of expression characteristic of these other languages and the people who use them.

We use the term "literature" in a similarly capacious sense to refer to a range of artistically shaped works written in a charged language, appealing to the imagination at least as much as to discursive reasoning. It is only relatively recently that creative writers have been able to make a living composing poems, plays, and novels, and only in the past hundred years or so has creating "belles lettres" or high literary art been thought of as a sharply separate sphere of activity from other sorts of writing that the same authors would regularly produce. The past two decades have seen the lowly "comic book" reemerge as the respectable "graphic novel" and, in the process, bring the immediacy and dynamism of visual form to contemporary British fiction in a new and powerful fashion.

Varieties of Literary Experience

Above all, we have strived to give as full a presentation as possible to the varieties of great literature produced from the eighth to the twenty-first centuries in the British

Isles, by women as well as men, in outlying regions as well as in the metropolitan center of London, and in prose, drama, and verse alike. We hope that this anthology will show that the great works of earlier centuries can speak to us compellingly today, their value only increased by the resistance they offer to our views of ourselves and our world. To read and reread the full sweep of this literature is to be struck anew by the degree to which the most radically new works are rooted in centuries of prior innovation.

ILLUSTRATING VISUAL CULTURE

Another important context for literary production has been a different kind of culture: the visual. This edition includes a suite of color plates in each volume, along with hundreds of black-and-white illustrations throughout the anthology, chosen to show artistic and cultural images that figured importantly for literary creation. Sometimes, a poem refers to a specific painting, or more generally emulates qualities of a school of visual art. At other times, more popular materials like advertisements may illuminate scenes in modern writing. In some cases, visual and literary creation have merged, as in William Blake's illustrations. Thumbnail portraits of many major authors mark the beginning of author introductions.

AIDS TO UNDERSTANDING

We have attempted to contextualize our selections in suggestive rather than exhaustive ways, trying to enhance rather than overwhelm the experience of reading the texts themselves. Thus, when difficult or archaic words need defining in poems, we use glosses in the margins, so as to disrupt the reader's eye as little as possible; footnotes are intended to be concise and informative, rather than massive or interpretive.

Important literary and social terms are defined when they are used. For convenience of reference, Period at a Glance features appear at the beginning of each volume, providing a thumbnail sketch of daily life during the period. With these informative, illustrated features readers can begin to connect with the world that the anthology is illuminating. Sums of money, for instance, can be understood better when one knows what a loaf of bread cost at the time; the symbolic values attached to various articles of clothing are sometimes difficult for today's readers to decipher, without some information about contemporary apparel and its class associations. And the gradual shift of the Empire's population from rural regions to urban centers is graphically presented in charts for each period.

There is also an extensive glossary of literary and cultural terms available at the end of the book. For further reading, carefully selected, up-to-date bibliographies for each period and for each author can be found there as well.

TEACHING BRITISH LITERATURE

For instructors, we have revised and expanded our popular companion volume, *Teaching British Literature*, written directly by the anthology editors, 600 pages in length, available free to everyone who adopts the anthology.

ACKNOWLEDGMENTS

In planning and preparing the fifth edition of our anthology, the editors have been fortunate to have the support, advice, and assistance of many committed and gifted people. Our editor, Joe Terry, has been unwavering in his enthusiasm for the book and his commitment to it; he and his associates Roth Wilkofsky, Mary Ellen Curley, and Joyce Nilsen have supported us in every possible way throughout the process, ably assisted by Kelly Carroll. Our developmental editor Erin Reilly guided us and our manuscript from start to finish with unfailing acuity and seemingly unwavering patience. Our copyeditor Stephanie Magean seamlessly integrated the work of a dozen editors. Virginia Creeden cleared our many permissions, and Rona Tucillo tracked down and cleared our many illustrations. Finally, Nancy Wolitzer and Ellen MacElree oversaw the production with sunny good humor and kept the book successfully on track on a very challenging schedule, working closely with Doug Bell at PreMediaGlobal, Inc.

Our plans for the new edition have been shaped by comments and suggestions from many faculty who have used the book over the years. We would like to thank Lucien Agosta (California State University, Sacramento), Jesse T. Airaudi (Baylor University), Anne W. Astell (Purdue University), Derek Attridge (Rutgers University), Linda Austin (Oklahoma State University), Arthur D. Barnes (Louisiana State University), Robert Barrett (University of Pennsylvania), Candice Barrington (Central Connecticut State University), Joseph Bartolomeo (University of Massachusetts, Amherst), Mary Been (Clovis Community College), Stephen Behrendt (University of Nebraska), Todd Bender (University of Wisconsin, Madison), Bruce Boehrer (Florida State University), Bruce Brandt (South Dakota State University), Joel J. Brattin (Worcester Polytechnic Institute), James Campbell (University of Central Florida), J. Douglas Canfield (University of Arizona), Paul A. Cantor (University of Virginia), George Allan Cate (University of Maryland, College Park), Philip Collington (Niagara University), Linda McFerrin Cook (McLellan Community College), Thomas Crofts (East Tennessee State University), Eugene R. Cunnar (New Mexico State University), Earl Dachslager (University of Houston), Elizabeth Davis (University of California, Davis), Andrew Elfenbein (University of Minnesota), Hilary Englert (New Jersey City University), Margaret Ferguson (University of California, Davis), Lois Feuer (California State University, Dominguez Hills), Sandra K. Fisher (State University of New York, Albany), Sandra C. Fowler (University of Alabama), Allen J. Frantzen (Loyola University, Chicago), Daniel P. Galvin (Clemson University), Kevin Gardner (Baylor University), Kate Gartner Frost (University of Texas), S. E. Gontarski (Florida State University), Leon Gottfried (Purdue University), Leslie Graff (University at Buffalo), Mark L. Greenberg

(Drexel University), Peter Greenfield (University of Puget Sound), Natalie Grinnell (Wofford College), James Hala (Drew University), Wayne Hall (University of Cincinnati), Donna Hamilton (University of Maryland), Stephen Harris (University of Massachusetts), Wendell Harris (Pennsylvania State University), Richard H. Haswell (Washington State University), Susan Sage Heinzelman (University of Texas, Austin), Standish Henning (University of Wisconsin, Madison), Noah Heringman (University of Missouri—Columbia), Jack W. Herring (Baylor University), Carrie Hintz (Queens College), Romana Huk (University of Notre Dame), Maurice Hunt (Baylor University), Mary Anne Hutchison (Utica College), Patricia Clare Ingham (Indiana University), Kim Jacobs (University of Cincinnati Clermont College), Carol Jamison (Armstrong Atlantic State University), Eric Johnson (Dakota State College), Mary Susan Johnston (Minnesota State University), Eileen A. Joy (Southern Illinois University—Edwardsville), Colleen Juarretche (University of California, Los Angeles), George Justice (University of Missouri), Roxanne Kent-Drury (Northern Kentucky University), R. B. Kershner (University of Florida), Lisa Klein (Ohio State University), Adam Komisaruk (West Virginia University), Rita S. Kranidis (Radford University), Leslie M. LaChance (University of Tennessee at Martin), John Laflin (Dakota State University), Lisa Lampert (University of California, San Diego), Dallas Liddle (Augsburg College), Paulino Lim (California State University, Long Beach), Elizabeth B. Loizeaux (University of Maryland), Ed Malone (Missouri Western State College), John J. Manning (University of Connecticut), William W. Matter (Richland College), Evan Matthews (Navarro College), Michael Mays (University of Southern Mississippi), Lawrence McCauley (College of New Jersey), Michael B. McDonald (Iowa State University), James J. McKeown Jr. (McLennan Community College), Kathryn McKinley (Florida International University), Peter E. Medine (University of Arizona), Darin A Merrill (Brigham Young University—Idaho), David G. Miller (Mississippi College), Barry Milligan (Wright State University), Celia Millward (Boston University), Charlotte Morse (Virginia Commonwealth University), Mary Morse (Rider University), Thomas C. Moser Jr. (University of Maryland), Crystal L. Mueller (University of Wisconsin Oshkosh), James Najarian (Boston College), Deborah Craig Nester (Worcester State College), Jude V. Nixon (Baylor University), Richard Nordquist (Armstrong Atlantic State University), Daniel Novak (Tulane University), John Ottenhoff (Alma College), Violet O'Valle (Tarrant County Junior College, Texas), Joyce Cornette Palmer (Texas Women's University), Leslie Palmer (University of North Texas), Richard Pearce (Wheaton College), Rebecca Phillips (West Virginia University), Renée Pigeon (California State University, San Bernardino), Tadeusz Pioro (Southern Methodist University), Deborah Preston (Dekalb College), William Rankin (Abilene Christian University), Sherry Rankin (Abilene Christian University), Luke Reinsma (Seattle Pacific University), Elizabeth Robertson (University of Colorado), Deborah Rogers (University of Maine), David Rollison (College of Marin), Brian Rosenberg (Allegheny College), Charles Ross (Purdue University), Kathryn Rummel (California Polytechnic), Harry Rusche (Emory University), Laura E. Rutland (Berry College), Gary Schneider (University of Texas—Pan American), Kenneth D. Shields (Southern Methodist University), R. G. Siemens (Malaspina University-College), Clare A. Simmons (Ohio State University), Sally Slocum (University of Akron), Phillip Snyder (Brigham Young University), Isabel Bonnyman Stanley (East Tennessee University), Brad Sullivan (Florida Gulf Coast University), Margaret Sullivan (University of California, Los Angeles), Herbert Sussmann

(Northeastern University), Mary L. Tanter (Tarleton State University), Ronald R. Thomas (Trinity College), Theresa Tinkle (University of Michigan), William A. Ulmer (University of Alabama), Jennifer A. Wagner (University of Memphis), Anne D. Wallace (University of Southern Mississippi), Brett Wallen (Cleveland Community College), Jackie Walsh (McNeese State University, Louisiana), Daniel Watkins (Duquesne University), John Watkins (University of Minnesota), Martin Wechselblatt (University of Cincinnati), Arthur Weitzman (Northeastern University), Bonnie Wheeler (Southern Methodist University), Jan Widmayer (Boise State University), Dennis L. Williams (Central Texas College), William A. Wilson (San Jose State University), Paula Woods (Baylor University), and Julia Wright (University of Waterloo).

Other colleagues brought our developing book into the classroom, teaching from portions of the work-in-progress. Our thanks go to Lisa Abney (Northwestern State University), Charles Lynn Batten (University of California, Los Angeles), Brenda Riffe Brown (College of the Mainland, Texas), John Brugaletta (California State University, Fullerton), Dan Butcher (Southeastern Louisiana University), Lynn Byrd (Southern University at New Orleans), David Cowles (Brigham Young University), Sheila Drain (John Carroll University), Lawrence Frank (University of Oklahoma), Leigh Garrison (Virginia Polytechnic Institute), David Griffin (New York University), Rita Harkness (Virginia Commonwealth University), Linda Kissler (Westmoreland County Community College, Pennsylvania), Brenda Lewis (Motlow State Community College, Tennessee), Paul Lizotte (River College), Wayne Luckman (Green River Community College, Washington), Arnold Markely (Pennsylvania State University, Delaware County), James McKusick (University of Maryland, Baltimore), Eva McManus (Ohio Northern University), Manuel Moyrao (Old Dominion University), Kate Palguta (Shawnee State University, Ohio), Paul Puccio (University of Central Florida), Sarah Polito (Cape Cod Community College), Meredith Poole (Virginia Western Community College), Tracy Seeley (University of San Francisco), Clare Simmons (Ohio State University), and Paul Yoder (University of Arkansas, Little Rock).

As if all this help weren't enough, the editors also drew directly on friends and colleagues in many ways, for advice, for information, sometimes for outright contributions to headnotes and footnotes, even (in a pinch) for aid in proofreading. In particular, we wish to thank David Ackiss, Marshall Brown, James Cain, Cathy Corder, Jeffrey Cox, Michael Coyle, Pat Denison, Tom Farrell, Andrew Fleck, Jane Freilich, Laurie Glover, Lisa Gordis, Joy Hayton, Ryan Hibbet, V. Lauryl Hicks, Nelson Hilton, Jean Howard, David Kastan, Stanislas Kemper, Andrew Krull, Ron Levao, Carol Levin, David Lipscomb, Denise MacNeil, Jackie Maslowski, Richard Matlak, Anne Mellor, James McKusick, Melanie Micir, Michael North, David Paroissien, Stephen M. Parrish, Peter Platt, Cary Plotkin, Desma Polydorou, Gina Renee, Alan Richardson, Esther Schor, Catherine Siemann, Glenn Simshaw, David Tresilian, Shasta Turner, Nicholas Watson, Michael Winckleman, Gillen Wood, and Sarah Zimmerman for all their guidance and assistance. The pages on the Restoration and the eighteenth century are the work of many collaborators, diligent and generous. Michael F. Suarez, S. J. (Campion Hall, Oxford) edited the Swift and Pope sections; Mary Bly (Fordham University) edited Sheridan's *School for Scandal*; Michael Caldwell (University of Chicago) edited the portions of "Reading Papers" on *The Craftsman* and the South Sea Bubble. Steven N. Zwicker (Washington University) co-wrote the period introduction, and the headnotes for the Dryden section. Bruce Redford

(Boston University) crafted the footnotes for Dryden, Gay, Johnson, and Boswell. Susan Brown, Janice Cable, Christine Coch, Marnie Cox, Tara Czechowski, Susan Greenfield, Mary Nassef, Paige Reynolds, and Andrew Tumminia helped with texts, footnotes, and other matters throughout; William Pritchard gathered texts, wrote notes, and prepared the bibliography. Doug Thomson (Georgia Southern University) prepared The Romantics: At a Glance.

For this landmark fifth edition of *The Romantics and Their Contemporaries*, Susan Wolfson and Peter Manning are happy to welcome Amelia Klein as Associate Editor. More than an Associate Editor, Amelia Klein has been the infrastructure of a production that would not have been possible without her reliable, savvy, conscientious involvement.

To all, abiding thanks. It has been a pleasure to work with these colleagues in the ongoing collaborative process that has produced this book and brought it to this new stage of its life and use. *The Longman Anthology of British Literature* exists for its readers, whose reactions and suggestions we warmly welcome, as these will in turn reshape this book for later users in the years to come.

ABOUT THE EDITORS

David Damrosch is Professor of Comparative Literature at Harvard University. He is past president of the American Comparative Literature Association and has written widely on world literature from antiquity to the present. His books include *What Is World Literature?* (2003), *The Buried Book: The Loss and Rediscovery of the Great Epic of Gilgamesh* (2007), and *How to Read World Literature* (2009). He is the founding general editor of the six-volume *The Longman Anthology of World Literature* (2009), and the editor of *Teaching World Literature* (2009).

Kevin J. H. Dettmar is W. M. Keck Professor and Chair of the Department of English at Pomona College, and past president of the Modernist Studies Association. He is the author of *The Illicit Joyce of Postmodernism* and *Is Rock Dead?*, and the editor of *Rereading the New: A Backward Glance at Modernism; Marketing Modernisms: Self-Promotion, Canonization, and Rereading; Reading Rock & Roll: Authenticity, Appropriation, Aesthetics*; the Barnes & Noble Classics edition of James Joyce's *A Portrait of the Artist as a Young Man* and *Dubliners; The Blackwell Companion to Modernist Literature and Culture*; and *The Cambridge Companion to Bob Dylan*.

Christopher Baswell is A.W. Olin Chair of English at Barnard College, and Professor of English and Comparative Literature at Columbia University. His interests include classical literature and culture, medieval literature and culture, and contemporary poetry. He is author of *Virgil in Medieval England: Figuring the "Aeneid" from the Twelfth Century to Chaucer*, which won the 1998 Beatrice White Prize of the English Association. He has held fellowships from the National Endowment for the Humanities, the National Humanities Center, and the Institute for Advanced Study, Princeton.

Clare Carroll is Director of Renaissance Studies at the Graduate Center, City University of New York and Professor of Comparative Literature at Queens College, CUNY. Her research is in Renaissance Studies, with particular interests in early modern colonialism, epic poetry, historiography, and translation. She is the author of *The Orlando Furioso: A Stoic Comedy*, and editor of Richard Beacon's humanist dialogue on the colonization of Ireland, *Solon His Follie*. Her most recent book is *Circe's Cup: Cultural Transformations in Early Modern Ireland*. She has received Fulbright Fellowships for her research and the Queens College President's Award for Excellence in Teaching.

Andrew Hadfield is Professor of English at the University of Sussex. He is the author of a number of books, including *Shakespeare and Republicanism* (2005), which was awarded the 2006 Sixteenth-Century Society Conference Roland H. Bainton Prize for Literature; *Literature, Travel and Colonialism in the English Renaissance, 1540–1625* (1998); and *Spenser's Irish Experience: Wild Fruyt and Salvage Soyl* (1997). He has also edited a number of texts, most recently, with Matthew Dimmock, *Religions of* the *Book: Co-existence and Conflict, 1400–1660* (2008), and with Raymond Gillespie, *The Oxford History of the Irish Book, Vol. III: The Irish Book in English, 1550–1800* (2006). He is a regular reviewer for the *Times Literary Supplement*.

Heather Henderson is a freelance writer and former Associate Professor of English Literature at Mount Holyoke College. A specialist in Victorian literature, she is the recipient of a fellowship from the National Endowment for the Humanities. She is the author of *The Victorian Self: Autobiography and Biblical Narrative*. Her current interests include homeschooling, travel literature, and autobiography.

Peter J. Manning is Professor of English at Stony Brook University. He is the author of *Byron and His Fictions* and *Reading Romantics*, and of numerous essays on the British Romantic poets and prose writers. With Susan J. Wolfson, he has coedited *Selected Poems of Byron*, and *Selected Poems of Beddoes, Hood, and Praed*. He has received fellowships from the National Endowment for the Humanities and the John Simon Guggenheim Memorial Foundation, and the Distinguished Scholar Award of the Keats-Shelley Association.

Anne Schotter is Professor of English at Wagner College. She is the coeditor of *Ineffability: Naming the Unnamable from Dante to Beckett* and author of articles on Middle English poetry, Dante, and medieval Latin poetry. Her current interests include the medieval reception of classical literature, particularly the work of Ovid. She has held fellowships from the Woodrow Wilson and Andrew W. Mellon foundations.

William Sharpe is Professor of English Literature at Barnard College. A specialist in Victorian poetry and the literature of the city, he is the author of *Unreal Cities: Urban Figuration in Wordsworth, Baudelaire, Whitman, Eliot, and Williams*. He is also co-editor of *The Passing of Arthur* and *Visions of the Modern City*. He is the recipient of Guggenheim, National Endowment of the Humanities, Fulbright, and Mellon fellowships, and he has recently published *New York Nocturne: The City After Dark in Literature, Painting, and Photography*.

Stuart Sherman is Associate Professor of English at Fordham University. He received the Gottschalk Prize from the American Society for Eighteenth-Century Studies for his book *Telling Time: Clocks, Diaries, and English Diurnal Form, 1660–1775*, and is currently at work on a study called "News and Plays: Evanescences of Page and Stage, 1620–1779." He has received the Quantrell Award for Undergraduate Teaching, as well as fellowships from the American Council of Learned Societies and the Chicago Humanities Institute.

Susan J. Wolfson is Professor of English at Princeton University and is general editor of Longman Cultural Editions. She has also produced editions of Felicia Hemans, Lord Byron, Thomas L. Beddoes, William M. Praed, and Thomas Hood. She is the editor of the innovative Longman Cultural Editions of John Keats, and of Mary Shelley's *Frankenstein*, and coeditor (with Barry V. Qualls) of *Three Tales of Doubles*, and (with Claudia Johnson) of Jane Austen's *Pride and Prejudice*. She is author of *The Questioning Presence* (1986), *Formal Charges: The Shaping of Poetry in British Romanticism* (1997), and *Borderlines: The Shiftings of Gender* (2007).

ABOUT THE COVER

THE BURNING OF THE HOUSES OF LORDS AND COMMONS BY J.M.W. TURNER (1835)

The very painting is an event of Romantic "spontaneity." Turner painted it in a burst of energy on "varnishing day," when the canvas was already hung at the Royal Institution. Reminding us that Romantic sublimity had urban sites as well as natural ones, the apocalyptic vista suggests the passing of an old order: 1834 marks the New Poor Law, the first major piece of legislation to come from the new parliament of the 1832 Reform Bill. This fire was the most massive one since the "Great London Fire" of 1666, and it became a spectacle, with crowds gathering to witness it. Firefighters were unable to stop it from consuming the House of Commons, and it menaced Westminster Hall, its 14th-century roof spared only by the concerted efforts of firefighters and a citizens' brigade to keep it dampened with river water.

Charles Dickens related

an old, indisputable, very well-known story, which has so pointed a moral at the end of it, that I will substitute for it a new case, by doing of which I may avoid, I hope, the sacred wrath of St. Stephen's [the House of Commons was located in the former St. Stephen's chapel]. Ages ago, a savage mode of keeping accounts on notched sticks was introduced into the Court of Exchequer, and the accounts were kept much as Robinson Crusoe kept his calendar on the desert island. In the course of considerable revolutions of time, . . . [s]till official routine inclined to these notched sticks, as if they were pillars of the constitution, and still the Exchequer accounts continued to be kept on certain splints of elm wood, called "tallies." In the reign of George III., an inquiry was made by some revolutionary spirit, whether, pens, ink, and paper, slates and pencils being in existence, this obstinate adherence to an obsolete custom ought to be continued, and whether a change ought not to be effected. All the red tape in the country grew redder at the bare mention of this bold and original conception; and it took till 1826 to get these sticks abolished. In 1834, it was found that there was a considerable accumulation of them; and the question then arose, What was to be done with such worn-out, wormeaten, rotten, old bits of wood? I dare say, there was a vast amount of uninviting memoranduming and despatch-boxing on this mighty subject. The sticks were housed at Westminster, and it would naturally occur to any intelligent person that nothing could be easier than to allow them to be carried away for firewood by the miserable people who live in the neighborhood. However, they never had been useful, and official routine required that they never should be; and so the order went forth that they were to be privately and confidently burned. It came to pass that they were burned in a stove in the House of Lords. The stove, over-gorged with these preposterous sticks, set fire to the pannelling; the panelling set fire to the House of Lords; the House of Lords set fire to the House of Commons; the two houses were reduced to ashes; architects were called in to build others; we are now in the second million of the cost thereof; the national pig is not nearly over the stile yet; and the little old woman, Britannia, hasn't got home to-night.[1]

---

1. Blanchard Jerrold, "Charles Dickens, In Memoriam," in *The Best of All Good Company*, 1874.

Thomas Girtin, *Tintern Abbey*, c. 1793. A famously "picturesque" ruin, a favorite of tourists, sketchers, painters and poets.

THE ROMANTIC PERIOD

POPULATION[1]

NATIONAL POPULATIONS (IN MILLIONS)

Year	England and Wales	Scotland	Ireland
1791	8.3	1.4	4.8
1801[2]	9.0	1.6	5.2
1811	10.3	1.8	6.0
1821	12.1	2.1	6.8
1831	14.0	2.4	7.8

URBAN POPULATIONS

Year	London	Manchester	Edinburgh
1801	959,310	70,409	83,000
1811	1,139,355	98,573	103,143
1821	1,379,543	108,016	138,235
1831	1,878,229	142,026	162,403

LIFE EXPECTANCY[3]

Life expectancy in 1801 is 37; by 1831 it has increased to 39. Common diseases include smallpox, typhus, typhoid, influenza, and syphilis. The first cholera epidemic strikes Britain in 1831. Dysentery and diarrhea are notorious in poorer sections of cities because of the lack of sanitation. Air pollution in cities, especially "pea-soupers" resulting from coal burning, causes tuberculosis, bronchitis, and anthracosis (the 19th-century term for pneumoconiosis or miner's lung).

DAILY LIFE[4]

DISTRIBUTION OF THE BRITISH LABOR FORCE IN MILLIONS (PLUS PERCENTAGE)

	1801	1811	1821	1831
Agriculture, fisheries, and forestry	1.7 (35.4)	1.8 (32.7)	1.8 (29.0)	1.8 (25.0)
Manufactures, mining, and industry	1.4 (29.1)	1.7 (30.9)	2.4 (38.7)	3.0 (41.7)
Trade and transport	0.5 (10.4)	0.6 (12.7)	0.8 (12.9)	0.9 (12.5)
Domestic and personal	0.6 (12.5)	0.7 (12.7)	0.8 (12.9)	0.9 (12.5)
Public service and professional	0.3 (6.3)	0.4 (7.3)	0.3 (4.8)	0.3 (4.2)
Total	4.8	5.5	6.2	7.2

AVERAGE ANNUAL INCOMES C. 1800[5]

£4,000   Wealthy gentry; maintains a house in London for the social season and a country house
£700–1000   Upper professional; affords a horse and carriage
£200   Lower gentry; lives without manual labor but can maintain only a single servant

1. Unless otherwise noted, the source for the information gathered below is Eric J. Evans, *The Forging of the Modern State: Early Industrial Britain 1783–1870* (New York: Longman, 2001).
2. Beginning with the Census Act of 1800, England undertook a count of its population, partly in response to T. R. Malthus' *Principles of Population* (1798), which argued that population growth exceeded the ability of the nation to feed its people, and partly to determine the number of men who could be summoned to fight in the wars with France. Yet, these early censuses must be viewed with an extremely critical eye.
3. Mary J. Dobson, *Contours of Death and Disease in Early Modern England* (Cambridge, England: Cambridge UP, 2003).
4. The National Archive, http://www.nationalarchives.gov.uk/currency, "The Value of Money in 18th and Early 19th Century Britain." *The Georgian Index*. http://www.georgianindex.net/fd/index.html
5. G. E. Mingay, *English Landed Society in the Eighteenth Century* (London: Routledge and Paul, 1963) and Edward Copeland, "Money," *The Cambridge Companion to Jane Austen*, ed. Edward Copeland and Juliet McMaster (New York: Cambridge University Press, 1997). Courtesy of *Longman Cultural Editions*.

£150	Shopkeepers
£120	Clergy, farm owners, and schoolmasters
£55	Skilled laborers
£30	Agricultural workers
£40	Miners
£20	Seamstresses
£12–20	Governesses

CURRENCY[6]

4 farthings	1d. (1 penny)	One penny in 1800 would be worth 20 U.S. cents today.
12d.	1s. (1 shilling)	One shilling in 1800 would be worth $2.44 today.
5s.	1 crown	One crown in 1800 would be worth $12.20 today.
20s.	1£ (1 pound)	One pound in 1800 would be worth $48.80 today.
21s.	1 guinea (last minted in 1813)	One guinea in 1800 would be worth $51.24 today.

COST OF GOODS

11s. 7d.	4-pound loaf of bread, 1804 (compared to 5s.1d. in 1750)
2s. 3d.	1 chicken in London, 1785
10d.	1 pound of butter, 1785
8d.	1 pound of bacon, 1795–1796
4.5d.	1 pound of wheat flour, 1795
6d.	1 pound of tobacco, 1795
7d.	1 pound of sugar, 1795–1796
12s.	1 pound of high-quality tea, early 1790s
15s.	Average monthly grocer's bill for Didsbury laborer, 1780s
£59 13s.	Food expenditure for household of Rev. Laurie of Newburn, Fifeshire, 1795

Bread prices rise sharply toward the end of the 18th-century, due to a number of poor harvests, the growing population, and the wars with France, which hamper the import of grain. Wheat prices (based on yearly average price per imperial quarter) rise from 45s.1d. in 1780–1789 to 126s. in 1812 (the 19th-century peak). Expenditure on poor relief in England and Wales rises from £2,004,000 in 1783–1785 to £6,788,000 in 1819–1823. The Speenhamland System is devised in 1795 to provide parish-subsidized relief to the poor based on the price of bread and the size of a family.

FOOD AND DRINK

Working-class Britons subsist on a diet of bread, oysters, potatoes, bacon, cheese, puddings, and a hot meal on Sundays cooked at the local bake shop because individual households do not have ovens of their own. Middle-class diets are enhanced with mutton and root vegetables. Prepared by cooks, upper-class meals are ornate, consisting of multiple courses and avoiding the items associated with lower- and middle-class dining. Water is unpotable until boiled; therefore, ale, beer, and tea are the main beverages for all classes.

APPAREL[7]

For the upper classes, fashion between 1795 and 1820 in Britain witnesses the end of the brocades, lace, periwigs, and powder that were the vogue of the earlier 18th-century. Women's fashion turns to a more natural, relaxed look based on the garments loosely draping classical statues. High-waisted gowns, made of silk or thin muslin, signal the end of the tight-fitting corsets of the earlier era and allow women to dress in both comfort and the latest fashion. Hairstyles follow suit, with a preference for loose, flowing masses of curls worn over the forehead and ears.

In men's fashion Beau Brummel leads the way, with an emphasis on meticulous personal grooming and high-quality tailoring. This style favors

6. Historical equivalences for the purchasing power of a given sum are very approximate. Different types of calculation provide quite different results. A calculation based on wages, for instance, yields a different figure from a calculation based on the prices of basic consumer goods; and those consumer goods thought essential to daily life change drastically over time. These conversions, then, are meant to be only approximations.
7. Venetia Murray, *High Society: A Social History of the Regency Period, 1788–1830* (New York: Viking, 1998).

trousers (instead of breeches), coats with tall-standing collars, linen shirts (also with high collars), and tall, conical hats. Hairstyles are shorter, and mutton chops become a fashionable style for facial hair.

Members of the lower classes make do with one set of clothing that they wear until worn out. Servants, who often dress in their master's castoffs (and later uniforms) are also often allowed to keep "rag bags" in which they collect valuable scraps from the house to sell into the large second-hand market.

RULERS

MONARCHS	PRIME MINISTERS
George III (1760–1820)	Lord North (28 January 1770–22 March 1782), Tory
	Marquess of Rockingham (27 March 1782–1 July 1782), Whig
	Earl of Shelburne (4 July 1782–2 April 1783), Whig
	Duke of Portland (2 April 1783–19 December 1783), Whig
	William Pitt the Younger (19 December 1783–14 March 1801), Tory
	Henry Addington (17 March 1801–10 May 1804), Tory
	William Pitt the Younger (10 May 1804–23 January 1806), Tory
	Lord Grenville (11 February 1806–31 March 1807), Whig
	Duke of Portland (31 March 1807–4 October 1809), Tory
	Spencer Perceval (4 October 1809–11 May 1812), Tory
George IV (1820–1830)	Lord Liverpool (8 June 1812–9 April 1827), Tory
	George Canning (10 April 1827–8 August 1827), Tory
	Viscount Goderich (31 August 1827–21 January 1828), Tory
William IV (1830–1837)	Duke of Wellington (22 January 1828–16 November 1830), Tory
	Earl Grey (22 November 1830–9 July 1834), Whig
	Viscount Melbourne (16 July 1834–14 November 1834), Whig
	Duke of Wellington (14 November 1834–10 December 1834), Tory

William Pitt

George IV

TIMELINE

1760 George III succeeds his grandfather George II.
1765 Horace Walpole's *The Castle of Otranto*, often regarded as the first gothic novel, is published.
1765 James Macpherson, *The Works of Ossian* (page 394)
1772 Slavery is effectively outlawed within England (the slave trade with colonies continues).
1773 Anna Letitia Aikin (later Barbauld), *Poems* (page 65)
1776 The American colonies declare their independence.
1778 Parliament passes the Catholic Relief Act, removing many restrictions on Catholic worship. This bill precipitates the destructive Gordon Riots of 1780, an eruption of anti-Catholic sentiment. ⊢
1779 Samuel Crompton creates the spinning mule; in 1784 Edward Cartwright invents the first power loom. These and other developments mark the beginning of the Industrial Revolution, generally dated between 1760 and 1832.
1781 The British lose a pivotal battle to the Americans at Yorktown, ending the American War for Independence.
1781 One hundred thirty three Africans are thrown overboard from the slave ship *Zong*.
1784 Charlotte Smith's, *Elegiac Sonnets and Other Poems* (page 85)
1787 The first fleet of convicts is transported to Australia.
1788 Abolitionist Thomas Clarkson and parliamentary spokesman William Wilberforce lead the case against the slave trade.
1789 A bill to repeal Test and Corporations Act (granting rights to Dissenters) fails.

1789 The fall of the Bastille launches the French Revolution.

✒ **1789** Olaudah Equiano's *The Interesting Narrative of the Life of Olaudah Equiano* (page 230)

✒ **1790** Edmund Burke's *Reflections on the Revolution in France* (page 113); Mary Wollstonecraft's *A Vindication of the Rights of Men* (page 123)

1791 Parliament rejects Wilberforce's bill to abolish the slave trade. Joseph Priestley's house is attacked by anti-reforming mob.

✒ **1791** Thomas Paine's *The Rights of Man* (Part I) (page 132)

1792 George III issues a Royal Proclamation banning seditious writings; radical artisans form the London Corresponding Society and the Whig Friends of the People.

✒ **1792** Mary Wollstonecraft's *A Vindication of the Rights of Woman* (page 304)

1793 France declares war against England.

1793 British troops attempt to suppress Toussaint L'Ouverture's uprising in Haiti.

✒ **1793** William Godwin's *An Enquiry Concerning Political Justice* (page 144)

1794 Pitt suspends *habeas corpus* (the right of trial before imprisonment).

✒ **1794** William Blake's *Songs of Innocence and of Experience* (page 176)

1795 Speenhamland poor relief system begins. Pitt introduces Treasonable Practices and Seditious Meetings Act.

1797 Naval mutinies occur at Spithead and the Nore.

1798 Society of United Irish rebel against British rule.

✒ **1798** William Wordsworth's and Samuel Coleridge's *Lyrical Ballads* (page 412)

1801 The Act of Union joins Great Britain (England, Scotland, Wales) with Ireland to create the United Kingdom.

✒ **1802** Writing of Wordsworth's "Immortality" Ode (page 552) and Coleridge's *Dejection: An Ode* (page 674).

1802 The Peace of Amiens ends fighting between England and France.

1804 Napoleon crowns himself emperor of France.

1805 The Royal Navy defeats French and Spanish fleets at the Battle of Trafalgar.

✒ **1805** Wordsworth completes 13-book version of *The Prelude, or Growth of a Poet's Mind* (page 477).

1807 Slave trade is abolished aboard British ships.

1811 Prince George assumes title of Prince Regent.

✒ **1811** Anna Letitia Barbauld's *Eighteen Hundred and Eleven* (page 72)

1812 Widespread economic distress; during the Luddite rebellion textile workers attack industrial machinery in protest of job losses.

✒ **1812** Lord Byron's first two cantos of *Childe Harold's Pilgrimage* (page 765)

1814 Hostilities between Americans and British ended by Treaty of Ghent.

1815 The Corn Laws are introduced to protect British agriculture by imposing heavy tariffs on imported grain.

1815 Napoleon is defeated at the Battle of Waterloo.

✒ **1816** Samuel Taylor Coleridge's *Christabel* (written in 1800) is published (page 652).

✒ **1816** The Shelley Circle, including Percy, Mary, and Byron, at Villa Diodati, Geneva, hold a ghost-story telling contest. Percy Shelley publishes *Alastor, or the Spirit of Solitude* and writes *Mont Blanc* (page 871).

✒ **1817** Samuel Taylor Coleridge's *Biographia Literaria* (page 683)

✒ **1818** Anonymous publication of Mary Shelley's *Frankenstein* (page 757); Jane Austen's *Northanger Abbey* (page 1148) is published.

✒ **1819** Percy Shelley writes *The Mask of Anarchy* (page 878) and Byron writes first two cantos of *Don Juan* (page 781).

1819 Eleven citizens are killed at the "Peterloo Massacre" in Manchester, where a crowd had peaceably gathered to protest government policies and high food prices.

1820 After a long period of intermittent mental illness, George III dies and is succeeded by George IV.

✒ **1820** John Keats's *Lamia, Isabella, The Eve of St. Agnes*, and other poems (including the great odes) (page 973)

1825 The first steam locomotive passenger service begins.

1829 Roman Catholic emancipation is granted.

1830 George IV dies and is succeeded by William IV.

✒ **1831** *The History of Mary Prince, a West Indian Slave* (page 240)

1832 The third version of the Reform Bill passes, extending the vote to landed men with a specific amount of property.

1833 The Factory Act limits work hours for women and children and provides some mandatory schooling for children.

1833 The Abolition of Slavery Act frees all slaves in the British empire.

1834 The Poor Law Amendment Act passes and establishes a national commission to oversee the system of aiding the poor.

The Romantics and Their Contemporaries

LITERATURE AND THE AGE: "NOUGHT WAS LASTING"

Reviewing Mary Shelley's *Frankenstein* in 1818, the *Edinburgh Magazine* remarked that "never was a wilder story imagined." Even so (the reviewer went on) "like most of the fictions of this age, it has an air of reality attached to it, by being connected with the favourite projects and passions of the times. The real events of the world have, in our day, too, been of so wondrous and gigantic a kind,—the shiftings of the scenes in our stupendous drama have been so rapid and various, that Shakespeare himself, in his wildest flights, has been completely distanced by the eccentricities of actual existence." The turbulent world and whirl of real events shaped the years of the "Romantic" period. It was marked on the one end by the revolutions in America and France, and on the other by the reform of Parliament to extend the vote and reconfigure representation, by the emergence of the modern industrial state, and by the abolition of slavery in British colonies. In the early 1820s, Lord Byron protested:

> Talk not of seventy years as age; in seven
>   I have seen more changes, down from monarchs to
> The humblest individual under heaven,
>   Than might suffice a moderate century through.
> I knew that nought was lasting, but now even
>   Change grows too changeable without being new:
> Nought's permanent among the human race... (*Don Juan* 11.81)

As the nod toward monarchs indicates, the French Revolution of the 1790s cast a long shadow across British consciousness. Its events had announced a radical break in historical continuity—a sudden, cataclysmic overthrow of a monarchy surrounded by high culture, and the eruption of a new social order that no one knew how to "read." New, challenging, and often contradictory energies reverberated across Britain and Europe. Enthusiasts heralded the fall of an oppressive aristocracy and the birth of democratic and egalitarian ideals, a new era, shaped by "the rights of man" rather than the entailments of wealth and privilege, while skeptics and reactionaries rued the end of chivalry, lamented the erosion of order, and foresaw the decline of civilization.

    Yet whatever side one took, the upheaval bore a stark realization: politically, socially, economically, and philosophically, an irrevocable tide of new ideas had risen against seemingly entrenched structures. "It was now known," as historian E. J. Hobsbawm puts it, "that revolution in a single country could be a European phenomenon, that its doctrines could spread across the frontiers....It was now known that social revolution was possible, that nations existed as something independent of states, peoples as something independent of their rulers, and even that the poor existed as something independent of the ruling classes." Other challenges appeared, framed in the rhetoric of the

Revolution debate and animated by appeals to moral law and natural principle. There were arguments for and against the rights of women (not for the vote, but for better principles of education and improved social attitudes); debates over the abolition of Britain's slave trade and of slavery in its colonies (a moral blight but also a source of enormous and widespread commercial profit); movements for social and political remedies for the poor (versus the traditional spiritual consolations); and a newly emergent class consciousness among discontented workers in Britain's fields, mines, factories, and mills.

Polemical essays and pamphlets helped shape the controversies, and so did various forms of literary writing: sonnets and songs, ballads and poetic epistles, tales and plays, the sensationally turned narrative and the didactic novel. Even literature not forged in the social and political turbulence was caught by a sense of revolution. The first generation of writers (those who made their marks in the 1790s and the first decade of the new century) included William Blake, William Wordsworth, Samuel Taylor Coleridge, and Walter Scott, as well as several remarkable women: Anna Barbauld, Charlotte Smith, Hannah More, Mary Wollstonecraft, Ann Radcliffe, Joanna Baillie, and Mary Robinson. The second generation (emerging before 1820) adds the younger voices and visions of Percy Shelley, Mary Shelley, John Keats, Lord Byron, and John Clare. It also witnesses the emergence of international literary celebrity, first and foremost in the charismatic figure of Lord Byron, then extending in the 1820s to the adored Felicia Hemans and at last to

...awakening the mind's attention from the lethargy of custom.

venerable Wordsworth, who would become a beloved Poet Laureate in 1843. All these writers were invigorated by a sense of participating in the modern world, of defining its values, and of claiming a place for writers as its instructors, prophets, critics, and inspirers. In 1792 Wollstonecraft urged "a REVOLUTION in female manners," and at the end of the decade, Wordsworth's Preface to the second edition of *Lyrical Ballads* announced his break with "known habits of association" in the genre of poetry—a program, as his collaborator Coleridge later said, of "awakening the mind's attention from the lethargy of custom" (*Biographia Literaria*, 1817). The post-Revolutionary poet "strips the veil of familiarity from the world," declared Shelley in *A Defence of Poetry*, a document he concluded by designating poets the "unacknowledged legislators of the world." This enthusiasm inspired innovations in content and literary form. Lyric, epic, and autobiography became radically subjective, spiraling inward to psychological dramas of mind and memory, or projecting outward into prophecies and visions of new worlds formed by new values. Other hybrid forms, such as political ballads and polemical narrative, emerged to address pressing issues of the day, while novelists were producing new kinds of female heroines and new narrative structures to represent family and social life. Still other writers developed forms such as the personal essay, the travelogue, or the journal, to join the personal and the political, the social and the domestic, the world of feeling to the world of thought, and both to the world of action.

ROMANCE, ROMANTICISM, AND THE POWERS OF THE IMAGINATION

In this vibrant culture of new imaginative possibilities, "Imagination" itself became a subject of reflection, and often debate. Eighteenth-century philosophy and science had argued for objective, verifiable truth and the common basis of our experience in a world of concrete, measurable physical realities. Over the century, however, there emerged a competing interest in individual variations, subjective filterings, and the mind's independence of physical realities, or even creative transformation of them: not just a recorder or mirror, the mind was an active, synthetic, dynamic, even vision-ary power—of particular importance to poets. Poets tended to define "Imagination" against what it was not, even categorically the opposite of: thus, imagination vs. reality; imagination vs. reason; vs. science; vs. the understanding (especially its "fixities" and "certainties"); vs. mere "fancy"; even vs. religious truth. Blake declared its priority: "What is now proved was once, only imagin'd" (*The Marriage of Heaven and Hell*); it is imagination that can "see a World in a Grain of Sand / And a Heaven in a Wild Flower" (*Auguries of Innocence*). Deeming Wordsworth too wedded to observation and description, he scribbled in the margin of Wordsworth's 1815 *Poems*, "One Power alone makes a Poet.—Imagination The Divine

> *. . . see a World in a Grain of Sand / And a Heaven in a Wild Flower.*

Vision." Yet Wordsworth had moods in which he shared Blake's sense of imagination as most potent when severed from ordinary senses and experiences: "Imagination— here the Power so called / Through sad incompetence of human speech— / That awful Power rose from the Mind's abyss / Like an unfathered vapour" (1850 *Prelude* Book 6, 593–96), he writes at a pivotal moment in a work that is the story of imagination, celebrated in his conclusion as the ultimate synthesizing power: "Imagination . . . in truth, / Is but another name for absolute strength / And clearest insight, and amplitude of mind, / And reason in her most exalted mood" (1805 *Prelude* 13.167–70).

Coleridge defined "Primary Imagination" as "the living Power and prime Agent of all human Perception," analogous to but a lesser power than divine creation. Poetry is written by the "secondary Imagination," an "echo" of the Primary "coexisting with con-scious will": it dissolves and diffuses the materials of perception "in order to recreate," and thus shows itself "in the balance or reconciliation of opposite or discordant qualities," among these, the general and the individual, the new and the familiar, emo-tion and order, judgment and enthusiasm, rationality and passion, the artificial and the natural (*Biographia Literaria* chs. 13, 14). Percy Shelley, who also liked binaries, con-trasted "Imagination" to "Reason" in the first paragraph of his *Defence of Poetry,* and following Coleridge, coordinated their powers: "Reason is to imagination as the instru-ment to the agent, as the body to the spirit, as the shadow to the substance." Byron, when he wasn't dramatizing the torments of imagination, was inclined to look wryly: "Imagination droops her pinion, / And the sad truth which hovers o'er my desk / Turns what was once romantic to burlesque" (*Don Juan* 4.3); "And as for other love, the illusion's o'er; / And money, that most pure imagination, / Gleams only through the dawn of its creation" (12.2). Keats proposed the imagination as a link to the ideal world at the dawn of creation: "The Imagination may be compared to Adam's dream—he awoke and found it truth," he suggested, referring to the dream of Eve. But he was ulti-mately more interested in the way imagination operates on real perception: "probably every mental pursuit takes its reality and worth from the ardour of the pursuer—being in itself a nothing." And like his contemporaries, he was drawn by the involvement of imagination with disease, deviance, delusion, egotism, escapism.

As Keats's analogy of Adam's dream suggests, male imagination often projects an eroticized female or feminized object. How did women writers address the imagination? They were prone to a skeptical bias, accenting dangers, a corruption of rational capacity and moral judgment, an alliance with destructive (rather than creative) passion. This view was not just resistance to male schemes of gender; it was also fueled by a discourse of rational education and intellectual dissent that included both men and women. "The imagination should not be allowed to debauch the understanding before it has gained strength, or vanity will become the forerunner of vice," cautioned Wollstonecraft in *A Vindication of the Rights of Woman;* the best books are those "which exercise the understanding and regulate the imagination." When Jane Austen describes Emma's vain, egotistical illusions, she pointedly terms her an "imaginist...on fire with speculation and foresight!—especially with such a ground-work of anticipation as her mind had already made" (*Emma* vol. 3, ch. 3).

In her widely read *Plays on the Passions* Joanna Baillie summons the word to name trouble and torment: "strange imaginations," "dark imaginations...frightful.../ The haunt of damned spirits," "the worst imagination" of a "madden'd brain," "a wild imagination / Which has o'erreach'd...judgment." Mary Robinson recognized how, Hamlet-wise, "pall'd imagination, sick'ning, spurns / The sanity of reason!" (*The Sicilian Lover* 15.23–24). When Mary Shelley recalls, "My imagination, unbidden, possessed and guided me, gifting the successive images that arose in my mind with a vividness far beyond the usual bounds of reverie," the gift was *Frankenstein.* Men often wrote about these dangers, but usually in a pattern of alternation with enthusiastic, idealizing, visionary projections. And women were not always or only cautionary. Like Byron, Robinson could wax satiric, especially

> My *imagination, unbidden,*
> *possessed and guided me, gifting*
> *the successive images that arose*
> *in my mind with a vividness*
> *far beyond the usual bounds of*
> *reverie....*

when her object is a self-styled male poet, his garret "the airy throne / Of bold Imagination, rapture-fraught / Above the herds of mortals" (*The Poet's Garret*). Yet of the women poets, she is probably the most enthusiastic: enchanted by Coleridge's opium-inspired *Kubla Khan*, she addresses him as "Spirit Divine!" and offers to "trace / Imagination's boundless space" with him (*To the Poet Coleridge*); writing a poem for his infant son, she celebrates his fortune in being born among "Romantic mountains! from whose brows sublime / Imagination might to frenzy turn."

Imagination was a heady romance—an inspiring force, a dangerous seduction. Not coincidentally, the issues often took shape in the language of romance. The rapid changes, new demands, and confusions of the age often pressed writers into imagining worlds elsewhere, the impulse of the mode from which the "Romantic" era gets its name: the "Romance." In 1755 Samuel Johnson's great *Dictionary* defined it thus: "A military fable of the middle ages; a tale of wild adventures in war and love." Under this appeal, the subtitle "A Romance" graced a host of titles in the Romantic era. Radcliffe perfected the gothic romance novel; Scott elaborated the poetic romance and virtually defined the historical romance, while Byron made his name and fame in exotic quest romance: his first success, *Childe Harold's Pilgrimage* (1812), was subtitled "A Romaunt" (an old "romance" spelling), confirming the aura of the main title. In a variety of genres—ballad, narrative poem, novel—Romance turned to other places and times, or shaped timeless, ahistorical tales of quest and desire, love and adventure. A medieval idiom, which flourished into a "gothic" vogue, supplied vivid language for Radcliffe's novels, Coleridge's *Christabel* and

The Rime of the Ancyent Marinere (in the patently antiqued version of 1798), Scott's *Lay of the Last Minstrel* (1805), Byron's *Childe Harold*, Keats's *La Belle Dame* and *The Eve of St. Agnes* (1820), and Hemans's many poems of the age of the Crusades. Romance could inhabit the even more distant pasts of Anglo-Saxon legend or classical mythology. Percy Shelley and Keats turned to the landscapes and myths of ancient Greece as resources of imagination before the age of Christian "truth." As the settings of many of these works indicate, Romance is also fascinated with foreign worlds. *Childe Harold*, Coleridge's *Kubla Khan*, and Hemans's *Tales, and Historic Scenes* testify to the vogue of Eastern materials. Byron intrigued readers with a lexicon of "jelicks" and "baracans," "giaours" and "viziers" (*Don Juan*). "Queen of far-away!" Keats hailed "Romance" itself.

In various forms, Romances shared a feature that Victorians would take as exemplary of the literary (if not the polemical) imagination of the age: a turn, even an escape, from the tumultuous and confusing here-and-now. The appeal lay not only in exotic settings and remote ages but also in the freedom these licensed to explore superstitions and customs that had been dismissed by the Enlightenment faith in "Reason," progress, and universal truths. These historically distant worlds were often sites for prophecy of renewed worlds and alternative values. Defined against "neoclassical" values of proportion, rational order, balanced harmony, and a reverence for the traditions that conveyed these values, "romantic" had long stood for a recurrent impulse in the history of the arts: a passion for the wild, the unfamiliar, the irregular, the irrational, even anti-rational. Johnson's *Dictionary* offered a suggestive cluster for "romantick": "1) resembling the tales of romances; wild. 2) Improbable; false. 3) Fanciful; full of wild scenery." All these senses infuse one powerful model for the male Romantic poet: the enraptured, entranced "bard" (see Color Plate 1). Descended from the Old Testament prophet, Englished by Milton and elaborated in the eighteenth-century ode, the bard emerged in the Romantic era as an electrically visionary poet and prophet for the age. Poets as various and as different from one another as Blake, Wordsworth, Coleridge, Shelley, and Keats assume a bardic stance to credit their dreams, hopes, and visions, even as socially oriented reformists, such as Wollstonecraft advocating "the rights of woman" or Wilberforce arguing for the abolition of slavery, adopt bardic tones to project a better, more moral world.

There was another landscape in the Romantic age that overlapped with these exotic worlds: the psychic terrain of imagination. Here a second definition Johnson supplies for "romance"—"A lie; a fiction"—casts its shadow. Romance is the genre not only of enchanted dreams and inspired visions, but also of superstitions and spells, delusions and nightmares. Coleridge said that his work for *Lyrical Ballads* was devoted to "persons and characters supernatural, or at least romantic"; hence the nightmare worlds and sensations of demonic possession in *The Rime of the Ancyent Marinere* and *Christabel*. Infused with sensations of supernatural power, or fed by opiated fantasies, the magical mystery tours of supernatural romance may hold the keys to paradise or the passage to hell, or both by turns—as they do in Thomas De Quincey's bizarrely romantic autobiography, *Confessions of an English Opium Eater*. The genre of romance fairly bristles with complexities. Acutely aware of the chaos of their historical moment, writers often make attraction to another world a critical

Charm'd magic casements, opening on the foam / Of perilous seas, in faery lands forlorn.

theme: "magic casements," said Keats, "opening on the foam / Of perilous seas, in faery lands forlorn" (*Ode to a Nightingale*). The dubiously magic casements, moreover, may turn into mirrors: Romances often reflect, and reflect on, the world seemingly escaped or effaced from consciousness. The most celebrated romancers were hardly uncritical practitioners. Byron casts *Childe Harold* as a quest romance, but its path turns repeatedly to modern life, in particular the Napoleonic wars ravaging Europe.

At the same time, the prestige of "romance" and "romanticism" posed problems for women writers. Keats suggests one of these when he casts "Romance" as a danger-ous seductress (a "Queen of far-away," a "Fair plumed Syren") and opposes her allure to the demands of epic and tragedy (by which male poets claimed their fame). The sexist critique of "Romance" is ironic, since many women writers were inclined to criticize the genre. If Clara Reeve, Wollstonecraft, Barbauld, and Hannah More divided, often sharply, on a variety of political and social issues, they found common ground on the dangers of "Romance." Especially in the popular form of the novel, it encouraged too much "sensibility"—the cultivation of emotional refinement over rational intellect—and fed an appetite for fantasy over sound judgment. "Romances" deal in "the wild and extravagant," worried Reeve in *The Progress of Romance* (1785); they are "dangerous" for young readers: "they create and encourage the wildest ex-cursions of imagination." "Novels...tend to make women the creatures of sensation," warned Woll-stonecraft's *Rights of Woman* (1792); "their charac-ter is thus formed in the mould of folly." Enfeebled reason courted illusions about "romantic love," with perilous social consequences. By 1810, Barbauld was willing to argue that good nov-els could teach good values, but she was still cautious about the power of "romances...to impress false ideas on the mind." Urging women to cultivate the Enlightenment values of "Reason" and mental strength, these female critics also challenged romance stereotypes proffered as universal truth: the ideals of "feminine" silence, self-sacrifice, passivity, and unquestioning obedience; the ideology of female life contained in the domestic sphere.

> Novels...*tend to make women the creatures of sensation...their character is thus formed in the mould of folly.*

There were still more ways that Romance exoticism intersected with the socially immediate world. Encounters with outcasts of all kinds—refugees, the poor, aban-doned and fallen women, discharged soldiers, sailors, vagrants, peasants, north-country shepherds and smallholders, abject slaves—supplied the unusual and unexpected, and at the same time provoked social self-reflection. Foreign cultures might be close to home, as in the ballads enthusiastically collected by Scott in *Minstrelsy of the Scot-tish Border* (1802–1803) and his subsequent use of Highland materials in the series of novels begun with *Waverley*. Scots poet Robert Burns packaged himself as a primi-tive bard: the son of a tenant-farmer and tenant-farmer himself, a heavy-drinking, illegitimate-child-siring, native genius whose dialect verse and egalitarian sentiments seemed to make him the very voice of the people. William Wordsworth produced incidents from rural life in *Lyrical Ballads*, and his sister Dorothy Wordsworth cap-tured the dialects in her journal. John Clare wrote of rural life in a rural idiom and himself embodied the figure of the peasant poet. Meanwhile, the "wild scenery" of Johnson's definition was caught in new travel books and records of "tours," while "tourists"—a word that emerged around 1800—began to delight in locales ignored by previous generations, or thought unpleasantly rough. Once-isolated Wales became so flooded by tourists that by 1833 a Welsh grammar carried an appendix of useful phrases: "I long to see the monastery"; "Is there a waterfall in this neighbourhood?"

This romance of novelty interplays with a powerful sense of a past that might be renewed. Writers created hybrid forms, building on models anywhere from the middle ages through the eighteenth century. Byron remained loyal to neoclassic poets such as Pope and Dryden, even as he gave their forms new vibrancy and reveled in contemporary political satire. Literary tradition was a cherished, if daunting, national heritage. Many admired Chaucer's tale-telling and descriptive detail; others worked variations on Spenser's allegorical epic, *The Faerie Queene*. Hazlitt honored Spenser as "the poet of our waking dreams," and the Spenserian stanza that conveyed these dreams shaped more than a few new "romances"—among them, Byron's *Childe Harold*, Hemans's *Forest Sanctuary*, Keats's *Eve of St. Agnes*, Shelley's *Revolt of Islam* and his homage to Keats, *Adonais*. Shakespeare and Milton were the great progenitors. Shakespeare was admired for the intensity of his imagery, his spectacular versatility, his unparalleled characterizations, as well as his mastery of "organic" (as opposed to "mechanical") aesthetic form, a concept elaborated in the criticism of Coleridge. He was an early inspiration for Coleridge's lectures and poetry; Wordsworth, Byron, and Hemans could hardly write without alluding to him; Keats named him his "Presider," and De Quincey wrote vivid essays about him. For this generation of writers, Milton's revolutionary politics provided an example of antimonarchical courage, and *Paradise Lost* was indisputably the most important poem in English literature. Milton's Eve focuses the feminist grievances of Wollstonecraft's *Rights of Woman*, while for poets, as Byron declares in *Don Juan*, "the word 'Miltonic' mean[s] 'sublime,'" stimulating epic ambitions in works as diverse as Blake's *Milton* and *Jerusalem*, Charlotte Smith's *Emigrants*, Wordsworth's *Prelude*, Percy Shelley's *Prometheus Unbound*, Keats's *Hyperion*, and Byron's *Don Juan*. Milton's Satan, an epitome of the "sublime," is echoed and doubled everywhere, and along with Milton's God and Adam, casts his shadow across the fable of masculine ambition and heroic alienation that Wollstonecraft's daughter Mary Shelley creates for *Frankenstein*.

At the same time, Romantic creativity also defined itself—often defiantly—against tradition, experimenting with new forms and genres. Blake writes visionary epics; Wordsworth spends half a century on his poetic autobiography, "a thing unprecedented in Literary history," he said. Mary Shelley fuses several myths into a complex, interlocking structure of tales and tellers to form *Frankenstein*. Byron interplays stand-up patter with a tale of adventure to shape his burlesque *Don Juan*, "a poem totally of its own species...at once the stamp of originality and a defiance of imitation," Percy Shelley exclaimed to him. Individual experience, simultaneously the most exotic and most common region of all, led to excavations of the depths of the single self—which is to say, the unfolding of a self conceived as having depths and mysterious recesses. Reading Wordsworth's *Tintern Abbey*, Keats found "Genius" in its "dark Passages." In the Prospectus to *The Recluse* (1814), Wordsworth himself proclaimed

> Not Chaos, not
> The darkest pit of lowest Erebus,
> Nor aught of blinder vacancy—scooped out
> By help of dreams, can breed such fear and awe
> As fall upon us often when we look
> Into our Minds, into the Mind of Man,
> My haunt, and the main region of my Song.

Byron jibed that Keats's *Sleep and Poetry* was "an ominous title," but when Wordsworth named "the Mind" as his subject, Keats understood completely, and even women poets participated. This post-Enlightenment, bourgeois Protestant individualism moved beyond the rhetorical first-person of eighteenth-century poetry to produce the "I" as an individual authority, for whom the mind, in all its creative powers and passionate testimony of deeply registered sensations, became a compelling focus. The "I" could sponsor extravagant self-display (Robinson and Byron), prophetic self-elevation (Blake and Shelley), poignant song (Hemans), internal debate (Keats), or what Keats, thinking of Wordsworth, called the "egotistical sublime." Many of its forms defined a radical or alienated subjectivity. Wollstonecraft wrote as a nonconformist, Cowper and Hemans were famous for the melancholy autobiography that haunts their poetry, while poets such as Byron, Coleridge, and Shelley cultivated the "I" as antihero: the exile, the damned visionary, the alienated idealist, the outcast, whose affiliates were Cain, Satan, even the paradoxical figure of Napoleon—all joined by the passion of mind and the torments of imagination.

Whether cast as experiment and innovation or allied with liberty and revolution, these new expressive forms were sharpened by a sense of modernity, the writers often viewing old forms and traditions as tyranny or, at the very least, as the strictures of custom and habit. Revoking the neoclassical argument of Dryden (in the seventeenth century) that the poet is responsible for "putting bounds to a wilde over-flowing Fancy," Wordsworth asserted in the Preface to *Lyrical Ballads* (1800) that poetry is a "spontaneous overflow of powerful feelings," in which (he explained in a later version) "the feeling...gives importance to the action and situation, and not the action and situation to the feeling." Framing "incidents of common life," he gave importance to the feeling of such socially disenfranchised figures as children, bereft mothers, impoverished shepherds, beggars, and old veterans. In a lecture "On the Living Poets" (1818), William Hazlitt satirized this "mixed rabble of...convicts, female vagrants, gipsies,...ideot boys and mad mothers... peasants, pedlars," but Wordsworth's revolution was to treat them all as vehicles of worthy imagination and passion. Hazlitt had no trouble linking this program to "the sentiments and opinions which produced the French revolution" as well as its "principles and events":

> *...rhyme was looked upon as a relic of the feudal system, and regular metre was abolished along with regular government.*

> The change in the belles-lettres was as complete, and...as startling, as the change in politics, with which it went hand in hand....According to the prevailing notions, all was to be natural and new. Nothing that was established was to be tolerated....Kings and queens were dethroned from their rank and station in legitimate tragedy or epic poetry, as they were decapitated elsewhere; rhyme was looked upon as a relic of the feudal system, and regular metre was abolished along with regular government.

THE FRENCH REVOLUTION AND ITS REVERBERATIONS

In the 1780s, the American Revolution was a recent memory for the British, at once an inspiration to political progressives, an embarrassment for the prestige of the Empire, and a worry to a conservative ruling class concerned about the arrival of democratic ideas on British shores. When the next Revolution exploded in France just a few miles across the Channel, rather than a hemisphere away, the press of radical, violent, and inevitable change seemed imminent. With the fall of the Bastille prison, a symbol of royal tyranny, on 14 July 1789, and the *Declaration of the Rights of Man* that soon followed, British consciousness was dominated by French events. Conservatives were alarmed, while liberals welcomed the early phase as a repetition of England's "Glorious Revolution" of 1688, an overdue end to feudal abuse and the inauguration of constitutional government. Radicals hoped for a more thorough-going renovation: "Bliss was it in that dawn to be alive, / But to be young was very heaven!" Wordsworth said in retrospect, in a passage from his poetic autobiography that he published in 1809, and again in 1815 under the title *French Revolution as it Appeared to Enthusiasts at its Commencement*. Everything was infused with "the attraction of a country in Romance!" He was not the only one in rapture. Southey recalled how "a visionary world seemed to open.... Old things seemed passing away, and nothing was dreamt of but the regeneration of the human race." Burns was certain that "man to man the world o'er / Shall brithers be for a' that." In their own idioms, Wollstonecraft, Blake, and Charles Lamb joined the chorus, and in subsequent generations, Byron and Percy Shelley continued to hope that what was started in France could be continued elsewhere with better consequences.

> ...*man to man the world o'er /*
> *Shall brithers be for a' that.*

Better consequences, because millenarian dreams were soon undermined by harsh developments: the overthrow of the monarchy in August 1792 and in the next month, the massacre of more than a thousand prisoners by a Paris mob. When extremist Jacobins prevailed over moderate Girondins, the Revolution fragmented into the Reign of Terror. Louis XVI was guillotined in January 1793, Queen Marie Antoinette in October. In February, France declared war on Britain and Britain reciprocated, throwing the political ideals of Wordsworth and his generation into sharp conflict with their love of country. Except for the brief interlude of the deceptive Peace of Amiens (1802–1803: "Peace in a week, war in a month," a British diplomat commented), Britain was at war with France until the final defeat of Napoleon at Waterloo in 1815. The shock of these events lasted for decades and lent retroactive credit to the conservative polemic of Edmund Burke's *Reflections on the Revolution in France*, published in 1790, after the arrest and imprisonment of the royal family. In 1790 Burke seemed a sentimental hysteric to political opponents and was quickly subject to sarcastic challenge in Wollstonecraft's *Vindication of the Rights of Men* (1790) and Tom Paine's *Rights of Man* (1791). In 1793 radical philosopher William Godwin's *Political Justice*, though not directly about the Revolution, offered a vision of a society governed by individual reason, without the oppression of social institutions or private property. But the course of the Revolution confirmed Burke's alarm.

Under the systematic Terror of Robespierre (1793–1794), thousands of aristocrats, their employees, the clergy, and ostensible opponents of the Revolution were guillotined, the violence swallowing up Robespierre himself in 1794. British unease increased when France offered to support all revolutions abroad, and then invaded the Netherlands and the German states in 1794, Italy in 1796, and republican Switzerland in 1798. Now "Oppressors in their turn," Wordsworth wrote, "Frenchmen had changed a war of self-defense / For one of conquest, losing sight of all / Which

THE CONTRAST

1792

BRITISH LIBERTY.

FRENCH LIBERTY.

RELIGION.   MORALITY.
LOYALTY OBEDIENCE TO THE LAWS
INDEPENDANCE PERSONAL SECURITY
JUSTICE INHERITANCE PROTECTION
PROPERTY INDUSTRY NATIONAL PROSPERITY
HAPPINESS

ATHEISM   PERJURY
REBELLION TREASON ANARCHY MURDER
EQUALITY MADNESS CRUELTY INJUSTICE
TREACHERY INGRATITUDE IDLENESS
FAMINE NATIONAL & PRIVATE RUIN.
MISERY

WHICH IS BEST

Thomas Rowlandson, after a drawing by Lord George Murray, *The Contrast, 1792*. British propaganda against the revolution in France.

they had struggled for" (1805 *Prelude* 10.791–94). In 1799 Napoleon, a general who consolidated his power in the Italian and Swiss campaigns, staged a *coup d'état* and was named First Consul for life. The Revolution had evolved into a military dictatorship, its despotism confirmed when Napoleon crowned himself Emperor in 1804. A complex personality—a challenger of entrenched monarchies; a charismatic military genius; a ruthless, egotistical imperialist—he generated nearly two decades of war that ravaged the Continent. Although war barely reached Britain, it was a constant threat, cost thousands of British lives and sent its economy into turmoil.

When Napoleon invaded the Iberian Peninsula in 1807, British support for the spontaneous resistance of the Portuguese and Spanish peoples enabled former radicals to return to the patriotic fold, to see their country as the champion of liberty against French imperialism. Napoleon's actions, claimed Coleridge, produced a "national unanimity unexampled in our history since the reign of Elizabeth...and made us all once more Englishmen." English self-definition was energized, the contest with France drawing on historical antagonisms that went back for centuries. Unlike the English, the French rejected their monarchy; if France could thus claim to be the first modern nation in the old world, Britain could feel superior to a country defined by the Terror and then Napoleon. National self-definition had strong literary manifestations. Hemans began her career with patriotic anthems celebrating Britain's support for the "noble" (and highly "romantic") Spanish resistance, and across these decades she published *Welsh Melodies, Greek Songs, Songs of Spain, National Lyrics*, and even the canonical American anthem, "The Landing of the Pilgrim Fathers" (our "Thanksgiving" hymn). Thomas Moore wrote *Irish Melodies* (1807–1834) and championed the grievances of Ireland. Byron wrote *Hebrew Melodies* (1815), got involved with Italian liberation movements, and in his last real-life romance, died in Greece where he had gone to aid the revolution against the Ottoman Empire.

Yet even as class differences blended into a general culture of songs for the salon, and made nationalism a vivid "romance," continuing disturbances pointed to those excluded from Coleridge's ideal of "us all...Englishmen." With ever fresh fears of invasion, the government clamped down on any form of political expression that hinted at French ideas. Efforts to reform Parliament begun in the 1780s were stifled, as was the movement to abolish the slave trade, and even moderates were silenced by accusations of "Jacobinism" (sympathy with Revolutionary extremists). In 1791 authorities in Birmingham connived at three days of riots by a loyal "Church and King" mob against Dissenters who had held a dinner to commemorate the Fall of the Bastille. When his house and laboratory were sacked, the eminent chemist and nonconformist Joseph Priestley fled to London and then emigrated to America. In 1792 Paine fled to France; he was tried and convicted in absentia of sedition for *The Rights of Man*, and his publishers and booksellers were regularly prosecuted. In 1794, twelve London radicals were arrested, including a novelist and playwright, Thomas Holcroft, and Horne Tooke, a philologist whose publications seemed a dangerous attempt to democratize language. Charged with high treason, they were defended by Godwin and acquitted, but the trial was a harbinger.

In 1794 the government suspended the long-established right of habeas corpus, which required the state to show cause for imprisonment and to conduct trials in a timely fashion; now anyone suspected of a crime could be jailed indefinitely. The Gagging Acts of 1795 targeted radical lecturers and societies, defining any criticism of the monarchy as treason and squelching political organization by limiting the size of meetings called to discuss reform. The Combination Act of 1799 forbade workmen, under penalty of conspiracy charges, to unionize or even to associate for purposes of collective bargaining. All these laws were enforced by government spies. Coleridge and Wordsworth, walking and conversing on the coastal hills of the Bristol Channel and plotting nothing more revolutionary than poems for *Lyrical Ballads*, looked suspicious enough to warrant tailing by a government informer. Coleridge was amused that their talk of the philosopher Spinoza was reported as references to "Spy Nozy," but actual radicals suffered severer consequences, for the government was also deploying *agents provocateurs* to incite them into capital offences. These infiltrators played a major role in plotting the Pentridge Rising of 1817 and the Cato Street Conspiracy of 1820, a scheme to murder cabinet ministers (a prime minister had been assassinated in 1812) and stage a coup d'état. "Cato Street" was "exposed" and its radical conspirators hanged or sent to prison in Australia, but the ultimate conspirator had been the government. Policy was still more severe outside England: in Edinburgh, delegates to the first British Convention of reformers were arrested for sedition and doomed to sentences in Australia; in Ireland, where Britain had more troops than on the Continent, a peasants' rebellion was crushed in a bloodbath (1798). Rather than international "fraternity," it was repression at home and wars abroad that defined the legacy of the French Revolution. When Napoleon was finally defeated in 1815 and the Bourbons were restored to the throne of France, the result was to reinforce reactionary measures and despotic monarchies all over Europe.

In the England of 1815, a further affliction was visited on the poor, among whom were many veterans, by Parliament's passage of the Corn Laws. Because importing grain had been impossible during the war years, prices for native grain soared; the Corn Laws now restricted imports in order to sustain the artificially high prices, a boon for landlords and a disaster for the poor, for whom bread was a chief article of diet. Bad harvests further raised costs. For the first time, in the estimate of the *Morning Chronicle,* protests and petitions erupted from "a majority of the adult male population of England," igniting food riots across the country. Under the unreformed electoral system, petitions to Parliament were the only recourse for those without representatives. In 1800 only males, and only five percent of them, were allowed to vote; only Anglicans, members of the state Church, could serve in the House of Lords. Workers did not have a vote, or even a representative in Parliament. The worker-populated cities of Leeds, Manchester, Birmingham, and Sheffield did not have a vote, whereas depopulated "rotten boroughs," consisting of one or two houses owned by a single landlord, enjoyed one or even two representatives in Parliament. As the Prince Regent returned from the opening of Parliament in January 1817, he found his carriage surrounded by a hostile crowd and stoned.

Workers were also being displaced by new machinery; they sometimes retaliated with attacks on the machines themselves, actions punishable by death. (Byron's first speech in the House of Lords was against such a measure, the Frame-breaking Bill provoked by weavers' riots.) Throughout the 1820s, farmworkers, angry at their degraded conditions, erupted into sporadic violence, culminating in a great uprising in 1830, in which barns burned across the countryside, and laborers again attacked machinery. The unemployed starved to death. Men scrambled for employment, while women and children, because they were deemed tractable and obedient, found it at pitiful wages. Prevailing attitudes and institutions were inadequate to ameliorate the misery and consequent disruptions. Since Elizabethan times, England had relied on a network of parishes and justices of the peace: local notables, serving in a largely volunteer capacity that enhanced their status, who kept records, assisted the needy, and administered everyday justice. Indigent newcomers to the cities could not easily be returned to their home parishes for support; they were needed as workers. And the parish system left out many: Irish Catholic immigrants, members of dissenting sects, and those lapsed from an Anglicanism that had failed to build churches for the new populations and at worst seemed remote from their concerns. When Lord John Manners declared that "the only means of Christianizing Manchester" was to revive the monasteries, he made clear the inadequacy of the current state Church to supply moral authority, social structure, and needed assistance.

No wonder that it was in Manchester that the modern vocabulary of class struggle emerged. The eighteenth-century ideal of stable social "orders" and "ranks" was challenged by a growing antagonism between successful capitalist entrepreneurs and their workers. In August 1819, nearly a hundred thousand mill-workers and their families gathered at nearby St. Peter's Field for a peaceful demonstration with banners and parades, capped by an address by the radical "Orator" Hunt calling for parliamentary reform. Alarmed by the spectacle, the local ruling class sent their drunken, sabre-wielding militia to charge the rally and arrest Hunt. Hunt offered no resistance, but the militia struck out at the jeering though unarmed crowd and, backed by mounted Hussars, in ten minutes left an official toll of eleven dead, including one trampled child, and more than four hundred injured, many from sabre wounds. Unreported injuries and later deaths from injury undoubtedly added to the official toll. This pivotal event in nineteenth-century economic and political strife was immediately dubbed "Peterloo" by the left press—a sardonic echo of the celebrated British triumph over Napoleon at Waterloo, four years before. Parliament did not reform, but instead consolidated the repressive measures of previous decades into the notorious Six Acts at the end of 1819. These Acts outlawed demonstrations, empowered magistrates to enter private houses in search of arms, prohibited meetings of more than fifty unless all participants were residents of the parish in which the meeting was held, increased the prosecution of blasphemous or seditious libel (defined as language "tending to bring into hatred or contempt" the monarchy or government), and raised the newspaper tax, thus constricting the circulation of William Cobbett's radical *Political Register* by tripling its price.

THE MONARCHY

Outraged by the situation summed by "Peterloo," Percy Shelley mordantly surveyed *England in 1819*, the title of a sonnet whose language rendered it unpublishable, even in a radical newspaper such as his friend Leigh Hunt's *Examiner*. It began:

> An old, mad, blind, despised, and dying King,
> Princes, the dregs of their dull race, who flow
> Through public scorn,—mud from a muddy spring,—
> Rulers who neither see, nor feel, nor know...

The Lear-like king who inspired this contempt was George III, Washington's antagonist in the American Revolution. He had had an episode of mental instability in 1765 and another in 1788: he talked incessantly and rarely slept, and once his eldest son tried to throttle him. The episode at once epitomized their antagonism and reflected the political conflicts of the late Georgian era. The King lived a domestic life and his successive administrations were firmly Tory—that is, socially and politically "conservative," committed to the constitutional power of the monarchy and the Church, and opposed to concessions of greater religious and political liberties. The Prince lived extravagantly at taxpayers' expense, with a devout Roman Catholic mistress whom he secretly and unconstitutionally married. In 1787 he obtained an extra £10,000 from the King, a relief from Parliament of £100,000 to pay his debts, and an additional £60,000 to build his residence, Carlton House—a total equivalent to almost seven million dollars today. But because his comparative political flexibility held out the hope of some reforms, he was backed by the opposition party, the liberal Whigs. He expected the crown in 1788, but the King unexpectedly recovered, hanging on until November 1810, when he relapsed and became permanently mad. In January 1811 the Prince was appointed "Regent."

In this new position of power, he focused all the contradictions and tensions of the time. In 1812, the *Morning Post* addressed him in the loyalist hyperbole that earned it the nickname of the "Fawning Post": "You are the glory of the People... You breathe eloquence, you inspire the Graces—You are an Adonis in loveliness." Leigh and John Hunt replied in *The Examiner*, denouncing "this Adonis in Loveliness" as "a corpulent gentleman of fifty...a man who had just closed half a century without one single claim on the gratitude of his country or the respect of posterity." Their scathing rejoinder earned them two-year sentences for libel and fines of £500 each, but Leigh Hunt continued to edit *The Examiner* from his prison cell, which he

Thomas Lawrence, *Coronation Portrait of the Prince Regent* (*George IV*), 1820. Thomas Lawrence (1769–1830) succeeded Sir Joshua Reynolds as painter-in-ordinary to George III when still in his twenties, and he remained attached to the monarchy ever afterward. He had painted portraits for the Regent of Frederick William of Prussia and Tsar Alexander and their generals when they visited London after the overthrow of Napoleon in 1814, was knighted in 1815, and was dispatched in 1818 to Europe to complete the Regent's collection of portraits of the restored sovereigns. This image of the Prince Regent in his Coronation robes (1821) was developed from an earlier portrait in Garter robes that had become the Prince's favorite representation of himself.

transformed into a gentleman's parlor, where he was visited as a hero by Byron, Moore, Keats, and Lamb.

Meanwhile, the Prince Regent was transforming the face of London. He and his architects recreated Regent's Park in the north and St. James's Park in the south, linking them by extending Regent Street, built Trafalgar Square, elevated Buckingham House into Buckingham Palace, and erected the Hyde Park arch. The "metropolitan improvements" bespoke impressive city planning, but also demarcated the boundaries between rich and poor. The Gothic/Chinese/Indian fantasy of his beloved retreat, the Brighton Pavilion, spoke even more loudly of his distance from the everyday life of his subjects. By 1815, when £150 a year provided a comfortable living for many, he was £339,000 in debt, an extravagance that brought contempt on the monarchy. The pity many still felt for George III did not extend to the son. On his accession to power, he abandoned his Whig friends, separated his estranged Queen Caroline from their daughter Charlotte, and was absent from Charlotte when she died in childbirth in 1817. In 1820, when George III died and he at last became King, he attempted to divorce Caroline by initiating a sordid investigation of her escapades abroad. The scandal rebounded on a man excoriated, in the Hunts' words, as "a libertine over head and heels in debt and disgrace, a despiser of domestic ties," and provided yet another handle for attacks upon him. The personal elegance that had made him "the first gentleman of Europe" had dissipated; already in 1813, Beau Brummell, an aristocratic "dandy" whose impeccable style and social assurance made him a paragon of the era, responded to a slight by the Regent by loudly inquiring of a fellow dandy, "Who's your fat friend?" The Prince was too fat to mount his horse by 1816; by 1818 it was reported that "Prinny has let loose his belly which now reaches his knees." Of his official Coronation portrait, Moore acidly noted that it was "disgraceful both to the King & the painter—a lie upon canvas." It was inevitable that satiric sketches would compete for fame.

...Who's your fat friend?

INDUSTRIAL ENGLAND AND "NEVER-RESTING LABOUR"

In the decades of this royal extravagance, the general population was rapidly expanding, accompanied by grim social misery. By 1750, the population of England and Wales was around five-and-a-half million; at the turn of the century, when the first census was taken, it was about eight million, with most of the increase in the last two decades. Scotland registered another million and a half, Ireland more than five million. Traditionally viewed as an index to a nation's wealth, population now loomed as a danger, inspiring the dire prophecy of Thomas Malthus's *On the Principle of Population As It Affects the Future Improvement of Society* (1798): "population, when unchecked, increases in a geometrical ratio. Subsistence increases only in an arithmetical ratio. A slight acquaintance with numbers will show the immensity of the first power in comparison of the second." The increase continued: by 1831 the population of Great Britain neared fourteen million.

...population, when unchecked, increases in a geometrical ratio.

The numbers tell only part of the story. Ever since the end of the eighteenth century and then with postwar acceleration, the economic base had begun to shift from agriculture, controlled by wealthy aristocrats (the landlords), to manufacture, controlled by new-money industrialists. The war against France fueled a surge: "A race of merchants and manufacturers and bankers and loan jobbers and contractors" was born, remarked Cobbett in 1802. Factories and mills invaded the countryside, pumped small towns into burgeoning cities, and cities into teeming metropolises. In 1800 only London—with about ten percent of the population of England and Wales—had more than a hundred thousand people. By 1837, when Victoria was crowned, there were five such cities, and London was growing by as much as twenty percent a decade. Even more staggering was the growth of the new industrial cities of the north. Manchester's population increased fivefold in fifty years, to 142,000 in 1831. Cobbett denounced these developments as "infernal," and many of his contemporaries, alarmed by the new populations and their demands for wages, food, and housing, feared a repetition at home of the mob violence of France.

This unprecedented concentration was the result of several converging factors. Poor harvests afflicted the countryside in the 1790s, and again in 1815. Scarcities were aggravated by the Corn Laws and ever more "Enclosure acts"—the consolidation and privatization of old common fields into larger, more efficient farms. The modernizing did improve agricultural yield and animal husbandry, offsetting in some measure Malthus's prediction of an inadequate food supply, but it also produced widespread dislocation and misery. The pattern of country landholding changed. Smallholders, from independent, modest farmers to proprietors of estates up to a thousand acres, fell away, while the great estates prospered in size and number: "the big bull frog grasps all," Cobbett pungently remarked. Meanwhile, the farmers and herdsmen rendered landless by enclosure had to settle for meager subsistence wages in the country or migrate to the cities. The census of 1811 revealed that for the first time a majority of families had nonagricultural employment. The yeomen who had represented the mythic heart of sturdy English freedom became day laborers, while others sank into poverty, and centuries-old social structures eroded. Sending the Whig leader in Parliament a copy of *Lyrical Ballads* that he hoped might stir sympathy for the rural poor, Wordsworth lamented that without a "little tract of land" as "a kind of permanent rallying point" in their hardships, "the bonds of domestic feeling… have been weakened, and in innumerable instances entirely destroyed."

…the bonds of domestic feeling…have been weakened, and in innumerable instances entirely destroyed.

Uprooted families were pulled by hopes of employment to the new factory towns. Cotton made modern Manchester. By 1802 there were more than fifty spinning mills, and the once-provincial city had become one of the commercial capitals of Europe. Textiles produced in vast quantities by power looms eliminated skilled hand-weavers, and extinguished the traditional supplement to the income of the cottager. The city did not incorporate until 1838, and no regulations controlled manufacture, sanitation, or housing; the unchecked boom enriched the few master manufacturers and immiserated the workers. The factories required a workforce disciplined to the constant output of the machines they tended; families accustomed to the ebb and flow of agricultural rhythms found themselves plunged into a world of industrial clock-time. Twelve- to fifteen-hour shifts, strict discipline, capricious firings, dangerous and unsanitary conditions, injuries, and ruined health were the rule of the day. Children were the preferred staff for the mills, and youngsters of five worked in the mines, their little bodies ideal for hauling coal in the narrow shafts. Workers were often further victimized by debts to their employers for housing and food. There was no philosophy of government restraint and regulation of these practices; all was "laissez-faire," the doctrine associated with Adam Smith's enormously influential *Wealth of Nations* (1777) that national wealth would flourish if businesses were left to operate with unfettered self-interest. By the 1780s there was a measurable gulf between rich and poor, ever more apparent in Manchester in the contrast between the homes of the wealthy in the suburbs and the slums by the polluted city river. "The town is abominably filthy," declared a visitor in 1808, "the Steam Engine is pestiferous, the Dyehouses noisome and offensive, and the water of the river as black as ink or the Stygian lake."

The twin agricultural and industrial revolutions recast both the town and the country and altered the relationship between them. To obtain waterpower, early mills and factories were set by rivers, thereby converting peaceful valleys into sites of production. Gas lighting, first used in such buildings, made possible twenty-four-hour operation, and the resulting spectacle affected contemporaries as a weird and

ominous splendor. In regions that were once the "assured domain of calm simplicity /
And pensive quiet," wrote Wordsworth in *The Excursion* (1814):

> an unnatural light,
> Prepared for never-resting Labour's eyes,
> Breaks from a many-windowed Fabric huge;
> And at the appointed hour a Bell is heard—
> Of harsher import than the Curfew-knoll
> That spake the Norman Conqueror's stern behest,
> A local summons to unceasing toil!
> Disgorged are now the Ministers of day;
> And, as they issue from the illumined Pile,
> A fresh Band meets them, at the crowded door,—
> And in the Courts—and where the rumbling Stream,
> That turns the multitude of dizzy wheels,
> Glares, like a troubled Spirit, in its bed
> Among the rocks below. Men, Maidens, Youths,
> Mother and little Children, Boys and Girls,
> Enter, and each the wonted task resumes
> Within this Temple—where is offered up
> To Gain—the Master Idol of the Realm,
> Perpetual sacrifice. (8.169–87)

Industry invaded the most picturesque quarters of the British Isles. A center of tourism,
Wales was also home to oppressive slate mines. Richard Pennant of North Wales epitomized the fortunes made in the trade in slaves and new-world commodities. Using the
profits from his family's Jamaican sugar plantations, Pennant developed and mechanized the slate quarries on his estates. Elected to Parliament from Liverpool in 1783, he
led the planters' defense of the slave trade while boosting the market for slate at home.
Slate was an ideal roofing material, and the spread of education created a need for slate
blackboards; at Port Penrhyn, the town Pennant established to ship slate, a hundred
thousand writing slates were manufactured each year. In the eighteenth century, the
quarries employed six hundred and the manufactory thirty more; by 1820 the workforce
was a thousand, and it expanded rapidly over the next two decades. The concurrent
discovery on the estate of minerals useful to the manufacture of Herculaneum pottery
in Liverpool generated still more income. The profits underwrote Penrhyn Castle, a
lush Norman fantasy constructed (from 1821) by Pennant's heir.

The rhetoric of an 1832 history of Wales obscures the dislocations entailed by
the progress it lauds: "About forty years ago, this part of the country bore a most
wild, barren, and uncultivated appearance, but it is now covered with handsome villas, well-built farm houses, neat cottages, rich meadows, well-cultivated fields, and
flourishing plantations; bridges have been built, new roads made, bogs and swampy
grounds drained and cultivated, neat fences raised, and barren rocks covered with
woods." At Portmadoc, about twelve miles south of the sublime scenery of Mount
Snowdon in Wales, William Madocks was performing one of the celebrated technological feats of the day, building a massive embankment (1808–1811), draining the
tidal estuary behind it, enlarging the harbor, and founding a model village named
after himself, Tremadoc—a project on which Percy Shelley enthusiastically collaborated, until he and his household fled from Wales in 1813 in the wake of a murderous

attack. Popular biography ascribed the incident to Shelley's propensity to hallucination, but underlying it were genuine conflicts between idealist radicalism, paternalistic planning, local privilege, and labor unrest.

If Romantic poetry is famous for celebrating "Nature," this affection coincides with the peril to actual nature by modern industry. "Our feeling for nature," wrote Friedrich Schiller in the 1790s, "is like the feeling of an invalid for health." Industry scarred previously rural communities. Visiting Scotland in 1803 with her brother, Dorothy Wordsworth noted of one village: "a pretty place it once has been, but a manufactory is established there; and a townish bustle and ugly stone houses are fast taking the place of the brown-roofed thatched cottages." Of the famous Carron Iron-works, "seen at a distance," she noted, "the sky above them was red with a fiery light." Industry ringed even their beloved Lake District, and on its coast the shafts of the coal mines owned by the employer of Wordsworth's father, Sir James Lowther, ran ever deeper and longer, until they extended under the sea and even caused the collapse of houses in Whitehaven, the planned port city from which the coal was shipped.

The need to bring coal and iron into conjunction spurred improvements in transport. In 1759 the Duke of Bridgewater cut an eleven-mile canal between his colliery at Worsley and Manchester; two years later an extension linked Manchester to the sea. Soon canals transected the country; between 1790 and 1794 alone, eighty-one acts for the construction of canals were passed. The cost of carriage was drastically cut, and the interior of England opened for commerce. By 1811 there were steamboats on the rivers; by 1812 locomotives were hauling coal. Large-scale road-building followed, including arteries between Shrewsbury and Holyhead (the port of departure for Ireland) and another between Carlisle and Glasgow in Scotland. During these years, a Scotsman, John Macadam, developed the road surface that bears his name. Across the country, distant regions were joined by a web of new roads and the Royal Mail coaches that ran along them on regular schedules. Decades later, remembering coach travel as it was in 1812, De Quincey recalled the new sensation of speed: "we saw it, we felt it as a thrilling; and this speed was not the product of blind insensate agencies, that had no sympathy to give, but was incarnated in the fiery eyeballs of an animal, in his dilated nostril, spasmodic muscles, and echoing hoofs" (*The English Mail-Coach, or the Glory of Motion*, 1849).

In this age of acceleration, the British Empire was expanding, too. Economically and politically, it had become the preeminent world power. The American colonies had been lost, but Canada and the West Indies remained, and Australia, New Zealand, and India marked a global reach. British forces subjugated natives, defeated rival French ambitions, and held the Turks and Russians in check, while the East India Company, originally a trading organization, gradually assumed administrative control of the subcontinent, even to the point of collecting taxes to protect British interests. The Company penetrated every aspect of British life: Warren Hastings, the first governor-general of India, was tried for cruelty and corruption, having amassed a fortune of over £400,000 in India. His trial, lasting from 1788 to 1795, was a *cause célèbre*, establishing the fame of the prosecutors even though he was acquitted. While his profits were exceptional, they marked a trend of great numbers of younger sons seeking fortunes in India. In a pattern common to north-country boys with the right connections, Wordsworth's family destined his younger brother John for service with the East India Company. "I will work for you," he said to William, "and you shall attempt to do something for the world." Although John lost his life in 1805 in the wreck of a tradeship, so widespread was the phenomenon of English fortunes based on Indian gain that "nabob," Hindi for "vicegerent" or "governor," entered the vernacular as a synonym for a wealthy man.

CONSUMERS AND COMMODITIES

Even more remarkable was the role of the East India Company as the prototype for later colonial rule. At a time when Oxford and Cambridge graduates were preparing for clerical orders, the Company college at Haileybury trained its students for their foreign service. Malthus taught there; both James Mill and son John Stuart Mill worked for the Company; Lamb was a clerk in the home office in London. And thousands more indirectly derived livelihoods or pleasures from the Company's activities. Napoleon sneered at Britain as "a nation of shopkeepers," taking this phrase from Smith's *Wealth of Nations*: "To found a great empire for the sole purpose of raising up a people of customers, may at first sight appear a project fit only for a nation of shopkeepers." But Smith's mercantile empire was a perspicacious forecast, confirmed in 1823 by Byron when he named England's pride as its "haughty shopkeepers, who sternly dealt / Their goods and edicts out from pole to pole, / And made the very billows pay them toll" (*Don Juan* 10.65).

> *To found a great empire for the sole purpose of raising up a people of customers, may at first sight appear a project fit only for a nation of shopkeepers.*

Cotton and tea were major goods. So was opium, and behind the dreams of Coleridge's *Kubla Khan*, Keats's *Ode to a Nightingale* (whose poet compares his state of sensation to intoxication by "some dull opiate"), and De Quincey's *Confessions of an English Opium Eater* were grim realities. Laudanum, opium dissolved in alcohol, was widely prescribed for a variety of complaints; it was the chief ingredient in a host of sedatives for children, especially of the poor, whose families had to leave them at home while they worked. It was also a cheap intoxicant. When Marx said that "religion was the opium of the masses," he was not using a random metaphor. Opium virtually defined foreign profiteering. De Quincey's uncle was a colonel in Bengal, in the military service of the East India Company, which reaped enormous profits from producing opium and smuggling it into China against the prohibition of the Chinese government. A Member of Parliament remarked: "If the Chinese are to be poisoned by opium, I would rather they were poisoned for the benefit of our Indian subjects than for the benefit of any other Exchequer." But the profits accrued less to Indian subjects than to the ruling British, even as the Opium Wars served the larger purpose of opening China to Lancashire cotton, as India had been opened earlier: the Wars concluded with the annexation of Hong Kong, and the opening of five treaty ports to British commerce. Meanwhile, the persistence of slave labor in British colonial plantations (not abolished until 1833) continued to raise ethical questions about the traffic in their commodities. International affairs inescapably cast their shadow on national life: "By foreign wealth are British morals chang'd," charged Barbauld in 1791, "And Afric's sons, and India's, smile aveng'd."

> *By foreign wealth are British morals chang'd, / And Afric's sons, and India's, smile aveng'd.*

As morals adjusted in relation to economic opportunities, the empire also fed a growing appetite for the exotic among those shut up in urban squalor, or merely in an increasingly routinized commercial life. For those who had the wherewithal, the era proffered a new world of objects, which had begun to proliferate in the late eighteenth century. An exemplary instance of the success of marketing joined to new technological advance is Josiah Wedgwood (1730–1795), whose cream-colored earthenware became known as "Queen's ware" because of Queen Charlotte's patronage in 1765, and, aided by that éclat, soon enjoyed a worldwide sale. In the 1770s he discovered how quickly high art could be transformed into status commodity, and began to produce imitation Greek vases, in vogue because of recent excavations at Herculaneum and Pompeii. The Wedgwood fortune enabled Josiah's sons to offer Coleridge an annuity of £150 so that he could devote himself to literature.

Alfred Bird, inventor of "Bird's Custard," pinned up in his Birmingham shop a telling motto mixing morality and the new imperatives of trade: "Early to bed. Early to rise / Stick to your work…And Advertise." From the late eighteenth century on, fashion magazines with colored plates advertised to provincial residents the latest styles of the capital. Even as she denounced the enslavement of women by "the perpetual fluctuation of fashion," Mary Hays conceded that "this constant variation of mode is serviceable to commerce, and promotes a brisk circulation of money" (*Letters and Essays*, 1793). This stimulus reached its acme with the arrival of *Forget Me Not, a Christmas and New Year's Present for 1823*. More than sixty annuals emerged to capitalize on this pioneering venture, bearing such titles as *The Book of Beauty*. Partly because they targeted female readers, they were hospitable to female authors, including Shelley and Hemans. And because they paid so well, they also attracted male writers: Wordsworth, Coleridge, Southey, Lamb, and Scott published in them, even though literary contributions were subordinated to the engravings that were their most compelling feature. The elegantly produced annuals were best-sellers (*The Literary Souvenir* attained a circulation of fifteen thousand); copies were shipped across the empire months in advance.

Not only women and city-dwellers were seduced by the lure of shop windows, magazines, and circulating catalogues. Cobbett hurled jeremiads at the prosperous farmers who aspired to a gentility that set them apart from the workers they had once fed as part of the family:

> Everything about this farm-house was formerly the scene of *plain manners* and *plentiful living*. … But all appeared to be in a state of decay and nearly of disuse. There appeared to have been hardly any *family* in that house, where formerly there were, in all probability, from ten to fifteen men, boys, and maids: and, which was the worst of all, there was a *parlour*. Aye, and a *carpet* and a *bell-pull* too!… And, there were the decanters, the glasses, the "dinner-set" of crockery-ware, and all just in the true stock-jobber style. And I dare say it has been 'Squire Charington and the Miss Charingtons; and not plain Master Charington, and his son Hodge, and his daughter Betty Charington, all of whom this accursed system has, in all likelihood, transmuted into a species of mock gentlefolks, while it has ground the labourers down into real slaves. (*Rural Rides*, 20 October 1825)

This revolution in manners and family structure reduced "family" to its biological nucleus, replacing the economic unit that enfolded laborers, servants, and dependents. This was but one manifestation of the "acceleration" and "agitation" that, in De Quincey's words, characterized the period well before the French Revolution.

Color Plate 1 **"Ruin seize thee, ruthless king!"** John Martin, *The Bard,* 1817. According to the legend retold in Thomas Gray's 1757 ode *The Bard,* in the thirteenth century Edward I attempted to stamp out Welsh resistance to English power by ordering the court poets, bards, put to death. Martin's large canvas captures the sublime moment at which the last bard denounced the invading monarch before leaping into the River Conway below. (*Laing Art Gallery, Tyne and Wear Museums.*)

Color Plate 2 Actress, Celebrity, Prince's Mistress, Poet.   Thomas Gainsborough, *Mrs. Mary Robinson: "Perdita,"* c. 1781. Gainsborough was one of the most fashionable portraitists of his day, surpassed only by his rival Sir Joshua Reynolds. His elegant depiction of the actress and poet Mary Robinson is witness to her social triumph. The locket in Robinson's hand reveals a portrait of the Prince of Wales, whose infatuation with her was the cause of her first celebrity. *(The Wallace Collection, London.)*

Color Plate 3 Byron as Byronic Hero.   Thomas Phillips, *Lord Byron,* 1814. Byron himself was the premier model for the "Byronic Hero." The character type was as theatrical as it was mysterious. He wrote to his mother in 1809, full of admiration for Albanian dress: "the most magnificent in the world, consisting of a long <u>white kilt,</u> old worked cloak, crimson velvet gold laced jacket & waistcoat, silver mounted pistols & daggars." He purchased some outfits for himself: "the only expensive articles in this country they cost 50 guineas each & have so much gold they would cost in England two hundred." *(Copyright © National Portrait Gallery, London.)*

Color Plate 4 Former Slave, Now British Gentleman.   Portrait traditionally identified as Olaudah Equiano, 18th century. The recent challenge to the identification of this figure as Equiano adds to the questions of veracity and verisimilitude that the *Interesting Narrative* raises. Whoever the sitter, the vivid image testifies to the respectability attainable by some blacks in 18th-century Britain. (*The Bridgeman Art Library International.*)

Color Plate 5 The Horrific Sublime of Human Misery. J. M. W. Turner, *Slavers Throwing the Dead and Dying Overboard, Typhoon Coming On*, 1840. Turner depicts a notorious incident that galvanized the abolition movement. In 1781 the captain of the slave ship *Zong* ordered 133 weak and diseased slaves ejected into shark-infested waters, planning to collect on a policy that held the insurer liable for cargo jettisoned in order to salvage the remainder. In 1783 Olaudah Equiano brought the incident to the attention of the abolition movement; the resulting trial (which debated not the captain's criminal liability but the insurer's financial liability), presided over by Lord Mansfield, sided with the captain. (*Museum of Fine Arts, Boston. Henry Lillie Pierce Fund; 99.22. All Rights Reserved. Photograph © 2003, Museum of Fine Arts, Boston.*)

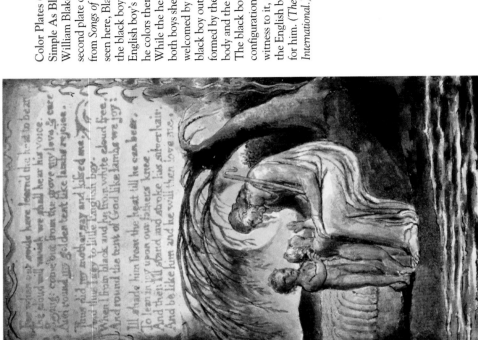

For when our souls have learn'd the heat to bear
The cloud will vanish we shall hear his voice.
Saying: come out from the grove my love & care,
And round my golden tent like lambs rejoice.

Thus did my mother say and kissed me,
And thus I say to little English boy.
When I from black and he from white cloud free,
And round the tent of God like lambs we joy:

I'll shade him from the heat till he can bear,
To lean in joy upon our fathers knee.
And then I'll stand and stroke his silver hair,
And be like him and he will then love me.

Color Plates 6 and 7   Not As Simple As Black and White. William Blake, two versions of the second plate of *The Little Black Boy*, from *Songs of Innocence*. As can be seen here, Blake sometimes tints the black boy's skin as light as the English boy's (near left); in others, he colors them differently (far left). While the heavenly scene portrays both boys sheltered by the tree and welcomed by Christ, it also puts the black boy outside the inner circle formed by the curve of Christ's body and the praying English boy. The black boy is not part of this configuration of prayer, but rather a witness to it, stroking the hair of the English boy, who has no regard for him. (*The Bridgeman Art Library International.*)

Color Plate 8   Fearful Symmetry?   (far left) William Blake, *The Tyger*, from *Songs of Experience*. In some copies, Blake colors the tyger in lurid tones; in others, the tyger is colored in pastels. Strangely, the unmenacing, sideways image of the tyger not only fails to display the "fearful symmetry" that alarms the poem's speaker, but also seems no cause for the horrified tone of address. (*The Bridgeman Art Library International*.)

Color Plate 9   Blake's Diagnosis, in Pictures and Words.   (near left) William Blake, *The Sick Rose*, from *Songs of Experience*. The sickness of the rosebush is conveyed not only by its trailing on the ground but also by several particulars: the encircling thorns; the quite visible worm wrapped around the naked body emerging (in joy? in pain?) from the rose; the caterpillars devouring the leaves; a second naked body constricted by a snakelike worm. (*Courtesy of the Library of Congress*.)

Color Plate 10   A Romance of Modern Life.   Joseph Wright, *An Iron Forge Viewed from Without*, 1773. Derby was a center of the Industrial Revolution, and Wright (1734–1797), a native, gained fame for his treatment of scientific and industrial subjects. He was particularly renowned for his handling of artificial light, and the dramatic contrast of fire and dark in this painting illustrates the romantic effects that could be drawn from technology. The contrast between the lurid forge and the picturesque background also suggests the contemporary spread

AUTHORSHIP, AUTHORITY, AND "ROMANTICISM"

In this fast-moving world, the fortunes of writers, too, began to rise and fall with new speed. Writing in the *Edinburgh Review* in 1829, the critic Francis Jeffrey meditated on "the perishable nature of modern literary fame":

> Since the beginning of our critical career, we have seen a vast deal of beautiful poetry pass into oblivion, in spite of our feeble efforts to recall or retain it in remembrance. The tuneful quartos of Southey are already little better than lumber:—And the rich melodies of Keats and Shelley,—and the fantastical emphasis of Wordsworth,—and the plebeian pathos of Crabbe, are melting fast from the fields of our vision. The novels of Scott have put out his poetry. Even the splendid strains of Moore are fading into distance and dimness, except where they have been married to immortal music; and the blazing star of Byron himself is receding from its place of pride.... The two who have the longest withstood this rapid withering of the laurel, and with the least marks of decay on their branches, are Rogers and Campbell; neither of them, it may be remarked, voluminous writers, and both distinguished rather for the fine taste and consummate elegance of their writings, than for the fiery passion, and disdainful vehemence, which seemed for a time to be so much more in favour with the public.... If taste and elegance, however, be titles to enduring fame, we might venture securely to promise that rich boon to the author before us.

The author before Jeffrey as he wrote was Felicia Hemans, a poet widely admired on both sides of the Atlantic but by the end of the century forgotten, except for a few anthology favorites. Meanwhile, with nearly three decades of reviewing experience, Jeffrey was unable to predict the durable fame of some of the writers who by the century's end would be deemed quintessential "romantics": Byron, Wordsworth, Keats, and Shelley. And he misguessed about Rogers and Campbell, though it is clear he would have attributed their demise to degraded public taste rather than intrinsic faults. What Jeffrey helps us see is that naming a literary canon is a matter of selection from a wide field, motivated by personal values. Other than Hemans, for instance, he thinks of English literary tradition as defined by men—even though Jane Austen and Mary Shelley proved to have as much durability as anyone in his census (Austen's novels and Shelley's *Frankenstein* have never been out of print). He also prefers literature of "fine taste" and "elegance" to the fiery passion and disdainful vehemence that other readers would admire in Byron and Shelley.

It was the conservative Jeffrey who first attempted to assess the "new poets," in the inaugural issue of the *Edinburgh Review* (1802). Here he castigates Southey as a member of a heretical "sect of poets, that has established itself in this country within these ten or twelve years, and is looked upon, we believe, as one of its chief champions and apostles." His polemical intent was to brand with all the excesses of the French Revolution a group he called "the Lakers" (from their residence in the Lake District): Southey, Wordsworth, and Coleridge. Well before Hazlitt, Jeffrey was blaming "the revolution in our literature" on "the agitations of the French revolution, and the discussion as well as the hopes and terrors to which it gave occasion." "A splenetic and idle discontent with the existing institutions of society, seems to be at the bottom of all their serious and peculiar sentiments"; "the ambition of Mr. Southey and some of his associates" is not "of that regulated and manageable sort which

A splenetic and idle discontent with the existing institutions of society, seems to be at the bottom of all their serious and peculiar sentiments.

usually grows up in old established commonwealths," but "of a more undisciplined and revolutionary character which looks, we think with a jealous and contemptuous eye on the old aristocracy of the literary world."

By the Regency, the revolutionary "Lake School" was joined by the upstart "Cockney School," a term of insult fixed on Londoners Hazlitt, Hunt, and Keats by the Scotsman John Gibson Lockhart, writing in *Blackwood's* in 1817, partly in response to Hunt's celebration of a vigorous school of "Young Poets" in essays he was writing for *The Examiner*. Hunt was a radical; Lockhart despised his politics. In 1821 ex-Laker and now Poet Laureate Southey identified still a third school. His youthful radicalism well behind him, he denounced the men "of diseased hearts and depraved imaginations" who formed "the Satanic School...characterized by a Satanic spirit of pride and audacious impiety." Provoked by the allusion to himself and Percy Shelley, Byron responded with satiric attacks against both Southey personally and the establishment politics he had come to espouse. All these classifications were politically motivated—in most cases sneers at innovators and nonconformists or class-inflected put-downs. The designation of a "Romantic School" was not a product of the age itself, but was applied much later in the century—by literary historians with their own Victorian motivations and nostalgia.

With no sense of a monolithic movement that could be called "Romanticism," the polemical terms of the age itself mark a field animated by differences of location, class, gender, politics, and audience. The boundaries that appear rigid at one moment re-form when the perspective shifts: to Lockhart, Lakers (whom he respected) and Cockneys were distinct; to Byron, a champion of Pope, Keats was both "a tadpole of the Lakes" and a Cockney brat who "abused Pope and Swift." And except for Hunt and Scott, most of these men bonded across class and political lines in their contempt of "Blue Stockings" (intellectual women) and female writers, even as these women were defining themselves for and against the stigmatized precedent of Wollstonecraft. Liberals, conservatives, and radicals; Byron and Shelley, self-exiled aristocrats in Italy; Wordsworth, Coleridge, and Southey praising domesticity in the Lakes; Keats, Hazlitt, and Hunt, an apprentice surgeon and working journalists, all precariously middle-class Londoners; women novelists, poets, and essayists, Blue Stockings and Wollstonecraftians, moralizers and rebels: the array is diverse and engaged in a contest for attention too keen to call debate or conversation.

The difficulty of specifying the term "Romantic" arises in part because it hovers between chronological and conceptual references. Its literature emerges in the social and literary ferment of the 1780s, a benchmark being the publication of Blake's *Songs of Innocence* in the climactic year of 1789. The period's close is usually seen in the 1830s—the decade in which George IV died, as did several writers who defined the age: Scott, Lamb, Coleridge, Hemans. By this time, too, Keats, Byron, and Percy Shelley, Austen, and most of the first generation were dead. In the same decade, Alfred Lord Tennyson's poetic career began, and Victoria was crowned Queen. Yet the temporal boundaries are fluid: "Romantic" Keats and "Victorian" Thomas Carlyle were born the same year, 1795, and Wordsworth's major poem, *The Prelude*, though he worked on it for a half century beginning in 1797 or so, was not published until the year of his death, 1850, the same year that Tennyson's quintessentially Victorian

In Memoriam appeared. Much of Keats's poetry appeared for the first time after 1848, reviving interest in him among a new generation of readers.

Yet even with these ambiguous boundaries, the "Romantic" movement, from its first description in the nineteenth century until the mid-1980s, was characterized by men's writing. In the age itself, the powers of literary production—publishers, booksellers, reviews, and the press—were men's domains and not always open to female authors, and the culture as a whole was not receptive to female authority. Wollstonecraft's *Rights of Woman* (1792) was one of the first analyses to define "women" as an oppressed class that cut across national distinctions and historical differences—oppressed by lack of education, by lack of legal rights and access to gainful employment, as well as by a "prevailing opinion" about their character: that women were made to feel and be felt, rather than to think; their duty was to bear children and be domestic drudges, to obey their fathers and their husbands without complaint.

Women writers faced more than a few challenges. One was the pervasive cultural attitude that a woman who presumed to authority, published her views, and even aspired to make a living as an author was grossly immodest, decidedly "unfeminine," and probably a truant from her domestic calling. Many women published anonymously, under male pseudonyms, with the proper title "Mrs." or, as in Austen's case, under an anonymous and socially modest signature, "by a Lady" (not one of Austen's novels bore her name). They also maintained propriety by hewing to subjects and genres deemed "feminine"—not political polemic, epic poetry, science or philosophy but children's books, conduct literature, travel writing (if it was clear they had proper escorts), household hints, cookbooks, novels of manners, and poems of sentiment and home, of patriotism and religious piety. Women who transgressed provoked harsh discipline. When Barbauld ventured an anti-imperialist poem, *Eighteen Hundred and Eleven*, the Tory *Quarterly Review* exercised reproof precisely in terms of the gender-genre transgression:

> Mrs. Barbauld turned satirist!...We had hoped, indeed, that the empire might have been saved without the intervention of a lady-author....Her former works have been of some utility; her "Lessons for Children," her "Hymns in Prose," her "Selections from the Spectator,"...but we must take the liberty of warning her to desist from satire...writing any more pamphlets in verse. (June 1812)

Barbauld took this advice to heart, and desisted from satire. About fifteen years earlier, Anglican arbiter Richard Polwhele viciously listed a whole set of contemporary female writers in his poem *The Unsex'd Females*, with virulent animosity to Wollstonecraft. They are "unsex'd" by their public stance, parading what "ne'er our fathers saw."

The Tory *British Critic*, on the occasion of praising Hemans's excellence "in painting the strength and the weaknesses of her own lovely sex" and the "womanly nature throughout all her thoughts and her aspirations," kept up the surveillance, taking the opportunity to despise anything that advertised the intellectual and critical authority of women. It opened its review of Hemans (1823) not with a discussion of the work at hand but with an assault on the world that was changing before its

> ...We had hoped, indeed, that the empire might have been saved without the intervention of a lady-author....

eyes, against which it invokes every counterauthority, from divine creation, to modern science, to Shakespeare, to the language of ridicule and disgust:

> We heartily abjure Blue Stockings. We make no compromise with any variation of the colour, from sky-blue to Prussian blue, blue stockings are an outrage upon the eternal fitness of things. It is a principle with us to regard an Academicienne of this Society, with the same charity that a cat regards a vagabond mouse. We are inexorable to special justifications. We would fain make a fire in Charing-Cross, of all the bas bleus in the kingdom, and albums, and commonplace books, as accessaries [sic] before or after the fact, should perish in the conflagration.
>
> Our forefathers never heard of such a thing as a Blue Stocking, except upon their sons' legs; the writers of Natural History make no mention of the name....Shakspeare, who painted all sorts and degrees of persons and things, who compounded or created thousands, which, perhaps, never existed, except in his own prolific mind, even he, in the wildest excursion of his fancy never dreamed of such an extraordinary combination as a Blue Stocking! No!

The extraordinary combination, however, was there to stay, and even with all these constraints, women writers thrived. More, Barbauld, Robinson, Charlotte Smith, and Maria Edgeworth stand out among those who earned both reputation and a living through poetry, novels, and tracts on education and politics, freely crossing the borders between public and private spheres, male and female realms.

POPULAR PROSE

When the *Edinburgh Review* was founded in 1802 as an organ of liberal political opinion, it raised the status of periodical writing. "To be an Edinburgh Reviewer," opined Hazlitt, who freelanced in the journal, "is, I suspect, the highest rank in modern literary society." By the end of the decade, the rival Tory *Quarterly Review* arrived on the scene. The quarterlies favored an authoritative, anonymous voice, while new monthly magazines revived the lighter manner of the eighteenth-century "familiar essay." *Blackwood's* (founded 1817) printed raffish conversations set in a nearby tavern, and the *London* (founded 1820) hosted Lamb's essays and De Quincey's *Confessions of an English Opium Eater*. Whether the topic was imaginative literature, social observation, science, or political commentary, the personality of the essayist and the literary performance—by turns meditative, autobiographical, analytical, whimsical, terse and expansive—were what commanded attention. "All the great geniuses of the day are Periodical," declared John Wilson, writing in *Blackwood's* in 1829—a self-interested judgment, but true insofar as it acknowledges the new importance of the periodical essay. Meanwhile, beneath the realm of the respectable journals, though not out of their anxious sight, thrived Cobbett, who published a weekly newspaper, the *Political Register* (founded 1802), its price low enough to evade the stamp tax (thus becoming known as "The Two-Penny Trash"). It reached a circulation of forty or fifty thousand and helped make him the most widely read writer of his era, and surely the most prolific, with an output estimated at more than twenty million words.

If later decades tended to represent "Romanticism" largely as an age of poetry, in the age itself, poetry, traditionally the genre of prestige, had to compete with prose, and not just the engaging new essay form, but also, and quite emphatically, the once-disreputable novel. The novel had begun to command new attention after the success of Godwin's political romance from the 1790s, *Caleb Williams*, and new respect after the critical and popular success of Scott's *Waverley* (1814). With dozens of works of narrative fiction over the next two decades, Scott perfected the genre of historical "romance"—"the interest of which turns upon marvelous and uncommon incidents," he said in a review of Austen. As the occasion indicates, the novel was also a genre in which women achieved considerable success—perhaps why, in addition to its status as a "low" form, Sir Walter kept his authorship of the *Waverley* novels anonymous. In *Waverley*, Scott spoofed the gothic devices that animated Ann Radcliffe's sensational "gothic" novels. But Radcliffe was remarkably popular; the genre that she perfected in the 1790s caught everyone's attention, including publishers'. She received the unheard of sum of £500 for *The Mysteries of Udolpho* (1794), topped by £600 for *The Italian* (1797), and achieved unprecedented fame for a novelist of any sex. Edgeworth's regional-historical novels, their career launched in 1800 with *Castle Rackrent* and extending over a quarter century, also caught the attention of Scott, who dubbed her "the great Maria" both out of admiration for a genre that shaped his own ventures and in recognition of her considerable financial success. Hannah More's only novel, *Coelebs in Search of a Wife* (1808), ran through twelve editions in its first year, and before her death in 1833 had sold thirty thousand copies in America alone. Shelley produced a durable masterpiece with *Frankenstein* (1818 and 1831), while Austen's novels caught public interest with their sharp social observation and stories of heroines coming of age in a world of finely calibrated social codes and financial pressures. With Scott, she would be deemed one of the major figures in the genre.

Throughout the years, social turmoil and technological change fostered a proliferation of writing. In the Preface to *Lyrical Ballads* (1800) Wordsworth deplored the "multitude of causes unknown to former times… now acting with a combined force to blunt the discriminating powers of the mind," and diagnosed the most virulent as "the great national events which are daily taking place, and the encreasing accumulation of men in cities, where the uniformity of their occupations produces a craving for extraordinary incident which the rapid communication of intelligence hourly gratifies." Newspapers, daily and Sunday, multiplied to meet this craving. In 1814 the London *Times* converted to a steam press, and doubled circulation. Newspaper sales reached thirty million, with yet more readers in the coffee-houses and subscription reading-rooms that took papers that taxes rendered too expensive for individual purchase. Parliamentary commissions and boards of review collected information and compiled statistics and summaries as never before on every aspect of the nation's economy and policies, and the press disseminated them. Cobbett ceaselessly lambasted the fund-holders who profited from the debts incurred by the war, even as those who had fought suffered from the postwar depression; John Wade investigated sinecures, aristocratic incomes, pluralism in the Church, corruption in Parliament, and the expenditures of the civil list, and published his findings in the sensational *Black Book* (1820), available in sixpenny installments that sold ten thousand copies each.

The explosion of readers at once liberated authors from patronage and exposed them to the turbulent and precarious world of the literary marketplace. In 1812 Jeffrey reckoned that among "the higher classes" there were twenty thousand readers, but at least "two hundred thousand who read for amusement and instruction, among the middling classes of society," defining "middling" as those "who do not aim at distinction or notoriety beyond the circle of their equals in fortune or station." Faced with an audience fissured along class lines, he thought that it was "easy to see" which group an author should please. But others looked to the growing number of literate

THE PRESS, invented much about the same time with the *Reformation,* hath done more mischief to the discipline of our Church, than all the doctrines can make amends for. 'Twas an happy time, when all learning was in manuscript, and some little officer did keep the key of the library! Now, since PRINTING came into the world, such is the mischief, that *a man cannot write a book but presently he is answered!* There have always been ways found out to *fine* not the people, but even the *grounds and fields where they assembled:* but no art yet could prevent these SEDITIOUS MEETINGS OF LETTERS! Two or three brawny fellows in a corner, with meer ink and elbow-grease, do more harm than an *hundred systematic divines.* Their ugly printing *letters,* that look but like so many rotten teeth, how oft have they been pulled out by the public tooth-drawers! And yet these rascally operators of the press have got a trick to fasten them again in a few minutes, that they grow as firm a set, and as biting and talkative as ever! O PRINTING! how thou hast "*disturbed the peace!*" Lead, when moulded into bullets, is not so mortal as when founded into *letters!* There was a mistake sure in the story of Cadmus; and the *serpent's teeth* which he sowed, were nothing else but the *letters* which he invented.

Marvell's Rehearsal transposed, 4to, 1672.

Being marked only with *four and twenty letters,—variously transposed* by the help of a PRINTING PRESS,—PAPER works miracles. The Devil dares no more come near a *Stationer's* heap, or a *Printer's Office,* than *Rats* dare put their noses into a Cheesemonger's Shop.

A Whip for the Devil, 1669, p. 92.

George Cruikshank, *The Press,* from the satirical pamphlet *The Political Showman—at Home!* by William Hone, 1821. We transcribe the text that was originally printed on this pamphlet.

poor who lacked traditional education, vast numbers whose allegiance was fought over by radicals like Cobbett and Paine and conservatives such as More, whose *Cheap Repository Tracts* (1795–1799) were circulated by the millions.

Such journalism diffused and intensified troubled perceptions of the functioning of society and one's place in it. "The beginning of Inquiry is Disease," intoned Carlyle; he inveighed against "the diseased self-conscious state of Literature" but this self-consciousness was its character. Uncertain of the audience(s) by whom they would be read, writers resorted to an ironic wavering that sought to forestall being pinned down to a position and dismissed, or devised various strategies to seduce assent: the development of the authorial "I" whom readers might come to trust as an authentic percipient, personae that insiders would be able to penetrate, and codings that would deepen a sense of solidarity among a constituency. Wordsworth had made his name with the highly personal, but culturally resonant, lyric outpouring of "Lines, written a few miles above Tintern Abbey, On Revisiting the Banks of the Wye during a Tour, July 13, 1798" (*Lyrical Ballads, 1798*); he celebrated his return from France in 1802 with a sonnet "Composed in the Valley, near Dover, On the Day of Landing," rejoicing in familiar sights of rivers and boys at play: "All, all are English." In a neighboring sonnet in the same collection, though, he complained, "The world is too much with us," running our lives with "getting and spending" and alienating our hearts from "Nature."

Wordsworth remained ambivalent about developing a voice and a literature that would gain popular reception, and continued to resent those, such as Scott, who were more successful in these terms. But the new world and the new literatures were finding remarkable sympathy in many quarters. Scott's first romance, *The Lay of the Last Minstrel* (1805), sold well over 2,000 copies within a year of publication, and nearly 10,000 more by 1807. His publisher offered him 1,000 guineas, sight unseen, for his next poetic romance, *Marmion* (1808). Scott said the sum "made men's hair stand on end," but the bargain was a good one on both sides: by 1811 it had sold 28,000 copies. These figures were topped by Byron, who, Scott good-naturedly conceded, drove him from the field of poetry, while his own *Waverley* novels proved still more popular. Over his lifetime, Scott made about £80,000 from his writing. That Byron's *Corsair* (1814) could sell 10,000 copies on the day of publication testifies to the mechanisms of production, publicity, and sales the book trade commanded. Byron was not embarrassed to seek £2600 for *Childe Harold IV* (1818). It must have galled Wordsworth that his publisher gave Thomas Moore 3,000 guineas for *Lalla Rookh*, more than had ever been offered for a single poem. Yet along with these stunning successes, other careers were more modestly compensated, and poets, at least, did not often enjoy the degree of prosperity that the novelists did.

The volatility of the market and of public taste points to salient qualities of the period: a heightened awareness of differences and boundaries, and of the energies generated along their unstable edges, and even more, a heightened awareness of time and history, public and cultural as well as personal. "Romanticism" denotes less a unified concept, or even a congeries of ideas, than an era and a literature of clashing systems, each plausibly claiming allegiance, in a world of rapid change.

⇥ PERSPECTIVES ⇥
The Sublime, the Beautiful, and the Picturesque

No reader of the eighteenth century and Romantic periods proceeds very far without recognizing the prevalence of the terms *sublime*, *beautiful* and *picturesque* in literature and art, and in the critical discourses they inspired. An encounter at the famous destination of Cora Linn, the Falls of the River Clyde, recorded by Dorothy Wordsworth in the journal describing her tour of Scotland with William and Coleridge in 1803 exemplifies their salience:

> We sat upon a bench, placed for the sake of one of these views, whence we looked down upon the waterfall, and over the open country, and saw a ruined tower (called Wallace's Tower), which stands at a very little distance from the fall, and is an interesting object. A lady and gentleman, more expeditious tourists than we, came to the spot; they left us at the seat, and we found them again at another station above the Falls. C., who is always good-natured enough to enter into conversation with anybody whom he meets in his way, began to talk with the gentleman, who observed that it was a "*majestic* waterfall." Coleridge was delighted with the accuracy of the epithet, particularly as he had been settling in his own mind the precise meaning of the words grand, majestic, sublime, etc., and had discussed the subject with Wm. at some length the day before. "Yes sir," says Coleridge, "it *is* a majestic waterfall." "Sublime and beautiful," replied his friend. Poor C. could make no answer, and, not very desirous to continue the conversation, came to us and related the story, laughing heartily.

More than a decade later Coleridge inserted the episode in one of his own essays, *On the Principles of Genial Criticism*: "Many years ago, the writer, in company with an accidental party of travelers, was gazing on a cataract of great height, breadth, and impetuosity, the summit of which appeared to blend with the sky and clouds, while the lower part was hidden by rocks and trees, and, on his observing, that it was, in the strictest sense of the word, a sublime object, a lady present assented with warmth to the remark, adding—'Yes! and it is not only sublime, but beautiful and absolutely pretty.'" The joke in both versions is the indifference of his tourist interlocutor to distinctions that the philosopher wishes to make "precise." The published text, by dispensing with "majestic," focuses it more finely on the couple of "sublime" and "beautiful." By transposing the respondent from male to female Coleridge invidiously genders the contrast between philosophic rigor and casual conversation: "pretty," a condescending term, made still more ludicrously inappropriate by conjunction with the force of "absolutely," marks the distance of this "warm" woman from intellectual pursuits.

And yet, as his laughter in the first version suggests, the joke tells against Coleridge too, for trying to demarcate terms that inevitably implicated one another and gained currency through the easy looseness of their application. The concept of the *beautiful* had a long pedigree, whether reaching back to the Platonic identification of the beautiful with the true and the good or merely characterizing that which is pleasing to the senses. The concept of the *sublime* derived from the first-century rhetorician Longinus, whose treatise *Peri Hupsous*, rediscovered in the Renaissance, was variously translated into English in the seventeenth century as *Of the Height of Eloquence* and *Of the Loftiness or Elegancy of Speech* and into French by Boileau as *Du Sublime* (1674). As the English titles suggest, the term initially characterized literary style, where the sublime was understood as "the echo of a great soul," but its use rapidly spread to cover those features of landscape that inspired profound sensations. The third key term, the *picturesque*, was the most recent and problematic; absent from both versions of Coleridge's encounter, it saturates Dorothy's journal entry and motivates the whole.

In its most general signification meaning "that which is suitable for painting," the picturesque carried more specific qualities. As early as 1748, in his Spenserian *Castle of Indolence*,

London. Pub. Feb.º 1 1817 at R. Ackermann's Repository of Arts, 101. Strand.

Dr SYNTAX SKETCHING THE LAKE.

Drawn & Etched by Rowlandson

Thomas Rowlandson, *Dr. Syntax Sketching by the Lake,* from *The Tour of Dr. Syntax in Search of the Pictur-esque,* 1812. The first issue of Rudolf Ackermann's *Poetical Magazine* contained *The Schoolmaster's Tour,* a couplet satire written by William Combe (1749–1823) and illustrated by Thomas Rowlandson (1756–1827). The pedantic Dr. Syntax and the caricatures proved so popular that in 1812 Ackermann published *Doctor Syntax in Search of the Picturesque,* which was followed by *Doctor Syntax in Search of Consolation* (1820) and yet a further sequel, *Doctor Syntax in Search of a Wife* (1821). Dr. Syntax, shown sketching near Keswick in this plate, is shortly to be thrown into the lake by his carelessly grazing horse.

James Thomson identified the painters whose works were to influence British representations of landscape for decades to come: "Whate'er *Lorrain* light-touched with softening Hue, / Or savage *Rosa* dash'd, or learned *Poussin* drew" (I.38). Connoisseurs with tastes formed on the seventeenth-century artists Claude Lorrain, Salvator Rosa, Nicolas Poussin, and his brother Gaspard Dughet sought in nature the compositions and colors they knew from art, generating an endlessly oscillating loop between the two realms. If picturesque nature served as a counter-aesthetic to neoclassical correctness and regularity, to the proprieties of social man, it was always in danger of revealing itself as just another form of artifice.

Before that self-defeating moment was manifest, however, the concept of the picturesque animated several fields. As a quality said to inhere in the world, it fueled the search for it, substantially contributing to the contemporary transformation of travel into touring and tour-ism. The picturesque traveler became a recognized type, equipped with his Claude glass—a folding pocket mirror tinted brown, the preeminent color of the picturesque, that enabled the viewer to frame the scene by turning his back on it, to look at its composed reflection rather than directly. Tinted glasses were also popular, making it possible to alter the color balance of the viewed scene into cool morning or warm evening hues. Remote spots such as Wales and Scotland drew travelers such as the Wordsworths and Coleridge in expeditions codified and publicized in guidebooks, spawning an industry of roads, lodgings, transportation, and local agents. Each particular spot, moreover, soon developed a favored observation point, the place from which the attraction, be it mountain, gorge, valley, or castle, could be best appreciated.

Dorothy's journal entry is replete with the material trappings that accompanied the nexus of the sublime, the beautiful, and the picturesque. The visit to Cora Linn is only the first

Joseph Mallord William Turner, *The Passage of the St. Gothard*, 1804. This large watercolor, over 3 feet high by 2 feet wide, stems from the sketchbooks Turner (1775–1851) made on his first trip to the Continent in 1802 during the Peace of Amiens. The craggy Alpine scene, dwarfing the pack animals, their path disappearing into the chasm obscured by the rising cloud, exemplifies the romantic sublime. John Constable (1776–1837), his fellow artist, observed years later of Turner's developed style: Turner "seems to paint with tinted steam, so evanescent, and so airy."

testimony to the social power of this discourse. The "bench, placed for the sake of one of these views," marks the careful management of the scene—the analogy between landscape viewing and stage sets is recurrent in the period—and the "ruined tower (called Wallace's Tower)... an interesting object" furnishes the virtually indispensable prompt to ruminations on personal and historical mutability. To undertake the tour in which Cora Linn prominently figures signaled participation in contemporary aesthetic discourse and the possession of the leisure (and usually the means) to realize it for oneself. Access to the experience depended on the relations of property: in this public space, one needed to follow the paths provided by the landlord, who required remuneration for the privilege; when the famous spot stood on a noble-man's estate, access required the appearance of gentility, and the senior servant who showed one round expected a tip for the favor, such gratuities being among the cherished perquisites of his position. Major theorists of the picturesque, such as Uvedale Price (*Essays on the Pictur-esque*, 1794) and his friend and neighboring squire Richard Payne Knight (*Analytical Inquiry into the Principles of Taste*, 1805), were substantial landowners who transformed their estates according to their aesthetic principles.

Inexact as the relations between the sublime, the beautiful, and the picturesque might be in common parlance, and infinitely repetitive as their combinations and permutations might become—for example, the composer Charles Avison's characterization of the rugged landscape of the Lake District, cited by Gilpin, "Here is beauty indeed—Beauty lying in the lap of Horrour!"—the very buzzing confusion of this discourse attests to the energy of a phenomenon at once pictorial, literary, cultural, economic, and psychological. The selections that follow illustrate its features and its staying power.

Edmund Burke
1729–1797

Edmund Burke was not yet thirty when *A Philosophical Enquiry into the Origin of Our Ideas of the Sublime and Beautiful* appeared in 1757. Educated at Trinity College, Dublin, he entered the Middle Temple in 1750 to study law. Publication was a means to attract attention and the patronage he needed; he wrote for the *Annual Register,* became a founding member of the Club surrounding Dr. Johnson, and by 1765 attained the post of secretary to the Whig prime minister, the Marquis of Rockingham, and entered Parliament. The *Enquiry* set the terms of subsequent discussion, less by subtlety than by the rhetorical brilliance that distinguished Burke's political career. From the outset Burke's bold formulations provoked resistance from more cautious thinkers; Payne Knight noticed that Burke's derivation of sublimity from "whatever is fitted in any sort to excite the ideas of pain, and danger" required the vague qualification of "at certain distances, and with certain modifications," left unspecified. He was equally skeptical of Burke's linkage of astonishment and the sublime:

> If during this period [of Burke's celebrated indictment of Warren Hastings and the abuses of the East India Company] he had walked up St. James's Street without his breeches, it would have occasioned great and universal *astonishment;* and if he had, at the same time, carried a loaded blunderbuss in his hands, the astonishment would have been mixed with no small portion of terror; but I do not believe that the unified effects of these two powerful passions would have produced any sensation approaching to sublime, even in the breast of those who had the strongest sense of self-preservation.

Funny as this riposte is, and exemplary of the exuberant *ad hominem* character of eighteenth-century debate, it misses the point. If Burke can be dismayingly positivist in connecting physical objects to mental states, he is far subtler than Knight is here about the mind's capacity to respond to its own fantasies, figures, and fictions.

For more selections by Burke, see Perspectives: The Rights of Man and the Revolution Controversy (page 113).

from A Philosophical Enquiry into the Origin of Our Ideas of the Sublime and Beautiful

Of the Sublime

Whatever is fitted in any sort to excite the ideas of pain and danger, that is to say, whatever is in any sort terrible, or is conversant about terrible objects, or operates in a manner analogous to terror, is a source of the *sublime;* that is, it is productive of the strongest emotion which the mind is capable of feeling. I say the strongest emotion, because I am satisfied the ideas of pain are much more powerful than those which enter on the part of pleasure. Without all doubt, the torments which we may be made to suffer, are much greater in their effect on the body and mind, than any pleasures which the most learned voluptuary could suggest, or than the liveliest imagination,

Benjamin Robert Haydon, *Study after the Elgin Marbles*, from *Annals of the Fine Arts*, 1819. The painter
Benjamin Haydon (1786–1846), Keats's friend, tirelessly promoted the Elgin Marbles (see note to Keats's
On Seeing the Elgin Marbles, page 987), here in the periodical he dominated, the *Annals of the Fine Arts*,
and elsewhere. In this "comparison between the Venetian Horse's Head, said to be by Lysippus, and the
Horse's Head from the Parthenon, in the Elgin Collection," the realism and vigor of the Parthenon horse,
with his prominent eye and flaring nostril, recall the passage from Job that Burke had cited as an instance
of the sublime (see page 40). Haydon proclaimed that "in as much as the Elgin Horse's head differs in
form and is superior to the head of Lysippus so do the rest of the Elgin marbles differ from and are superior
to all other statues of this, and every subsequent age."

and the most sound and exquisitely sensible body, could enjoy. Nay I am in great
doubt whether any man could be found who would earn a life of the most perfect
satisfaction, at the price of ending it in the torments, which justice inflicted in a
few hours on the late unfortunate regicide in France.[1] But as pain is stronger in its
operation than pleasure, so death is in general a much more affecting idea than
pain; because there are very few pains, however exquisite, which are not preferred
to death; nay, what generally makes pain itself, if I may say so, more painful, is,
that it is considered as an emissary of this king of terrors. When danger or pain
press too nearly, they are incapable of giving any delight, and are simply terrible;
but at certain distances, and with certain modifications, they may be, and they
are delightful, as we every day experience. The cause of this I shall endeavour to
investigate hereafter.

1. Robert-François Damiens was publicly tortured and executed by quartering in March 1757 for his attempt on the life
of Louis XV.

Of the passion caused by the Sublime

The passion caused by the great and sublime in *nature*, when those causes operate most powerfully, is astonishment; and astonishment is that state of the soul, in which all its motions are suspended, with some degree of horror. In this case the mind is so entirely filled with its object, that it cannot entertain any other, nor by consequence reason on that object which employs it. Hence arises the great power of the sublime, that, far from being produced by them, it anticipates our reasonings, and hurries us on by an irresistible force. Astonishment, as I have said, is the effect of the sublime in its highest degree; the inferior effects are admiration, reverence, and respect.

from *Terror*

No passion so effectually robs the mind of all its powers of acting and reasoning as fear. For fear being an apprehension of pain or death, it operates in a manner that resembles actual pain. Whatever therefore is terrible, with regard to sight, is sublime too, whether this cause of terror be endued with greatness of dimensions or not; for it is impossible to look on any thing as trifling, or contemptible, that may be dangerous.

from *Obscurity*

To make any thing very terrible, obscurity seems in general to be necessary. When we know the full extent of any danger, when we can accustom our eyes to it, a great deal of the apprehension vanishes. Every one will be sensible of this, who considers how greatly night adds to our dread, in all cases of danger, and how much the notions of ghosts and goblins, of which none can form clear ideas, affect minds which give credit to the popular tales concerning such sorts of beings. *** No person seems better to have understood the secret of heightening, or of setting terrible things, if I may use the expression, in their strongest light by the force of a judicious obscurity, than Milton. His description of Death in the second book is admirably studied; it is astonishing with what a gloomy pomp, with what a significant and expressive uncertainty of strokes and colouring, he has finished the portrait of the king of terrors:

> The other shape,
> If shape it might be call'd that shape had none
> Distinguishable, in member, joint, or limb;
> Or substance might be call'd that shadow seemed;
> For such seemed either; black he stood as night;
> Fierce as ten furies; terrible as hell;
> And shook a deadly dart. What seem'd his head
> The likeness of a kingly crown had on.[2]

In this description all is dark, uncertain, confused, terrible, and sublime to the last degree.

***

In nature, dark, confused, uncertain images have a greater power on the fancy to form the grander passions, than those have which are more clear and determinate. *** I am sensible that this idea has met with opposition, and is likely still to be rejected by several. But let it be considered that hardly any thing can strike the mind

---

2. Satan encounters Sin and Death, in an infernal parody of the Trinity (*Paradise Lost*, 2.666–73).

with its greatness, which does not make some sort of approach towards infinity; which nothing can do whilst we are able to perceive its bounds; but to see an object distinctly, and to perceive its bounds, is one and the same thing. A clear idea is therefore another name for a little idea.

from *Power*

Besides those things which *directly* suggest the idea of danger, and those which produce a similar effect from a mechanical cause, I know of nothing sublime, which is not some modification of power. And this branch rises as naturally as the other two branches, from terror, the common stock of every thing that is sublime. *** Look at a man, or any other animal of prodigious strength, and what is your idea before reflection? Is it that this strength will be subservient to you, to your ease, to your pleasure, to your interest in any sense? No; the emotion you feel is, lest this enormous strength should be employed to the purposes of rapine and destruction. That power derives all its sublimity from the terror with which it is generally accompanied, will appear evidently from its effect in the very few cases, in which it may be possible to strip a considerable degree of strength of its ability to hurt. When you do this, you spoil it of every thing sublime, and it immediately becomes contemptible. An ox is a creature of vast strength; but he is an innocent creature, extremely serviceable, and not at all dangerous; for which reason the idea of an ox is by no means grand. A bull is strong too; but his strength is of another kind; often very destructive, seldom (at least amongst us) of any use in our business; the idea of a bull is therefore great, and it has frequently a place in sublime descriptions, and elevating comparisons. Let us look at another strong animal in the two distinct lights in which we may consider him. The horse in the light of an useful beast, fit for the plough, the road, the draught; in every social useful light, the horse has nothing of the sublime; but it is thus that we are affected with him, *whose neck is cloathed with thunder, the glory of whose nostrils is terrible, who swalloweth the ground with fierceness and rage, neither believeth that it is the sound of the trumpet?*[3] In this description the useful character of the horse entirely disappears, and the terrible and the sublime blaze out together. *** In short, wheresoever we find strength, and in what light soever we look upon power, we shall all along observe the sublime the concomitant of terror, and contempt the attendant on a strength that is subservient and innoxious. The race of dogs in many of their kinds, have generally a competent degree of strength and swiftness; and they exert these, and other valuable qualities which they possess, greatly to our convenience and pleasure. Dogs are indeed the most social, affectionate, and amiable animals of the whole brute creation; but love approaches much nearer to contempt than is commonly imagined; and accordingly, though we caress dogs, we borrow from them an appellation of the most despicable kind, when we employ terms of reproach; and this appellation is the common mark of the last vileness and contempt in every language.

from *Privation*

All *general* privations are great, because they are all terrible; *Vacuity, Darkness, Solitude,* and *Silence.*

3. Job 39.19–24.

from *Vastness*

Greatness of dimension is a powerful cause of the sublime. This is too evident, and the observation too common, to need any illustration; it is not so common, to consider in what ways greatness of dimension, vastness of extent, or quantity, has the most striking effect. Extension is either in length, height, or depth. Of these the length strikes least; an hundred yards of even ground will never work such an effect as a tower an hundred yards high, or a rock or mountain of that altitude. I am apt to imagine likewise, that height is less grand than depth; and that we are more struck at looking down from a precipice, than at looking up at an object of equal height: but of that I am not very positive. A perpendicular has more force in forming the sublime, than an inclined plane; and the effects of a rugged and broken surface seem stronger than where it is smooth and polished.

from *Infinity*

Another source of the sublime, is *Infinity*; if it does not rather belong to the last. Infinity has a tendency to fill the mind with that sort of delightful horror, which is the most genuine effect, and truest test of the sublime.

from *Difficulty*

Another source of greatness is *Difficulty*. When any work seems to have required immense force and labour to effect it, the idea is grand. Stonehenge,[4] neither for disposition nor ornament, has any thing admirable; but those huge rude masses of stone, set on end, and piled on each other, turn the mind on the immense force necessary for such a work. Nay, the rudeness of the work increases this cause of grandeur, as it excludes the idea of art and contrivance; for dexterity produces another sort of effect, which is different enough from this.

from *Perfection not the cause of Beauty*

There is another notion current, pretty closely allied to the former; that *Perfection* is the constituent cause of beauty. This opinion has been made to extend much farther than to sensible objects. But in these, so far is perfection, considered as such, from being the cause of beauty; that this quality, where it is highest, in the female sex, almost always carries with it an idea of weakness and imperfection. Women are very sensible of this; for which reason, they learn to lisp, to totter in their walk, to counterfeit weakness, and even sickness.[5] In all this they are guided by nature. Beauty in distress is much the most affecting beauty. Blushing has little less power; and modesty in general, which is a tacit allowance of imperfection, is itself considered as an amiable quality, and certainly heightens every other that is so.

4. The monumental Druid stone circle.
5. Burke echoes Hamlet's denunciation of women to Ophelia: "You jig and amble, and you lisp; you nickname God's creatures and make your wantonness your ignorance" (3.1.146–48).

from *Beautiful objects small*

The most obvious point that presents itself to us in examining any object, is its extent or quantity. And what degree of extent prevails in bodies that are held beautiful, may be gathered from the usual manner of expression concerning it. I am told that, in most languages, the objects of love are spoken of under diminutive epithets. It is so in all the languages of which I have any knowledge.

from *Smoothness*

The next property constantly observable in such objects is *Smoothness*: A quality so essential to beauty, I do not now recollect any thing beautiful that is not smooth. In trees and flowers, smooth leaves are beautiful; smooth slopes of earth in gardens; smooth streams in the landscape; smooth coats of birds and beasts in animal beauties; in fine women, smooth skins; and in several sorts of ornamental furniture, smooth and polished surfaces.

from *Gradual Variation*

But as perfectly beautiful bodies are not composed of angular parts, so their parts never continue long in the same right line. They vary their direction every moment, and they change under the eye by a deviation continually carrying on, but for whose beginning or end you will find it difficult to ascertain a point. *** Observe that part of a beautiful woman where she is perhaps the most beautiful, about the neck and breasts; the smoothness; the softness; the easy and insensible swell; the variety of the surface, which is never for the smallest space the same; the deceitful maze, through which the unsteady eye slides giddily, without knowing where to fix, or whither it is carried. Is not this a demonstration of that change of surface, continual, and yet hardly perceptible at any point, which forms one of the great constituents of beauty?

from *The physical cause of Love*

When we have before us such objects as excite love and competency, the body is affected, so far as I could observe, much in the following manner. The head reclines something on one side; the eyelids are more closed than usual, and the eyes roll gently with an inclination to the object, the mouth is a little opened, and the breath drawn slowly, with now and then a low sigh: the whole body is composed, and the hands fall idly to the sides. All this is accompanied with an inward sense of melting and languor. These appearances are always proportioned to the degree of beauty in the object, and of sensibility in the observer. And this gradation from the highest pitch of beauty and sensibility, even to the lowest of mediocrity and indifference, and their correspondent effects, ought to be kept in view, else this description will seem exaggerated, which it certainly is not. But from this description it is almost impossible not to conclude, that beauty acts by relaxing the solids of the whole system. There are all the appearances of such a relaxation; and a relaxation somewhat below the natural tone seems to me the cause of all positive pleasure.

from *How Words influence the passions*

In painting we may represent any fine figure we please; but we never can give it those enlivening touches which it may receive from words. To represent an angel in a picture, you can only draw a beautiful young man winged: but what painting can furnish any thing so grand as the addition of one word, "the angel of the *Lord?*" It is true, I have here no clear idea; but these words affect the mind more than the sensible image did; which is all I contend for. A picture of Priam dragged to the altar's foot, and there murdered, if it were well executed, would undoubtedly be very moving; but there are very aggravating circumstances which it could never represent:

> *Sanguine faedantem* quos ipse sacraverat *ignes.*[6]

As a further instance, let us consider those lines of Milton, where he describes the travels of the fallen angels through their dismal habitation,

> —O'er many a dark and dreary vale
> They pass'd, and many a region dolorous;
> O'er many a frozen, many a fiery Alp;
> Rocks, caves, lakes, fens, bogs, dens, and shades of death,
> A universe of death.[7]

Here is displayed the force of union in

> Rocks, caves, lakes, dens, bogs, fens, and shades——;

which yet would lose the greatest part of the effect, if they were not the

> *Rocks, caves, lakes, dens, bogs, fens, and shades*——
> ——*of* Death.

This idea or this affection caused by a word, which nothing but a word could annex to the others, raises a very great degree of the sublime; and this sublime is raised yet higher by what follows, a "*universe of Death.*" Here are again two ideas not presentable but by language; and an union of them great and amazing beyond conception; if they may properly be called ideas which present no distinct image to the mind:—but still it will be difficult to conceive how words can move the passions which belong to real objects, without representing those objects clearly. This is difficult to us, because we do not sufficiently distinguish, in our observations upon language, between a clear expression, and a strong expression. These are frequently confounded with each other, though they are in reality extremely different. The former regards the understanding; the latter belongs to the passions. The one describes a thing as it is; the other describes it as it is felt. *** The truth is, all verbal description, merely as naked description, though never so exact, conveys so poor and insufficient an idea of the thing described, that it could scarcely have the smallest effect, if the speaker did not call in to his aid those modes of speech that mark a strong and lively feeling in himself. Then by the contagion of our passions, we catch a fire already kindled in another, which probably might never have been struck out by the object described. Words, by strongly conveying the passions, by those means which we have already mentioned, fully compensate for their weakness in other respects.

1747–1754   1757, 1759

---

6. Aeneas recounts the sight of Priam "polluting with his blood the fires he / himself had hallowed" (Virgil, *Aeneid*   2.502, trans. by Allen Mandelbaum).
7. *Paradise Lost*, 2.618–22.

Immanuel Kant
1724–1804

The Critique of Pure Reason, published at Riga in 1781, quickly established the stature of the German philosopher Immanuel Kant. By the 1790s his name had begun to appear in British journals; reviews and essays on his system multiplied, including a significant piece by Coleridge's friend the physician Thomas Beddoes in *The Monthly Magazine* (1796), followed by books, translations, and courses of lectures. Coleridge declared in Chapter 9 of the *Biographia Literaria* (1817) that

> the writings of the illustrious sage of Köningsberg, the founder of the Critical Philosophy, at once invigorated and disciplined my understanding. The originality, the depth, and the compression of the thoughts, the novelty and subtlety, yet solidity and importance, of the distinctions; the adamantine chain of the logic; and I will venture to add (paradox as it will appear to those who have taken their notion of IMMANUEL KANT, from Reviewers and Frenchmen) the *clearness* and *evidence*.... took possession of me as with a giant's hand.

Declaring that after fifteen years' familiarity he "still read" Kant "with undiminished delight and increasing admiration," Coleridge became the chief propagator of Kant's reputation in England. As the sneer at "Frenchmen" suggests, the increasing importance of German culture (for example, Carlyle's devotion to Goethe) flagged a shift away from what had come to seem for many the shallow and dangerous rationalism of the French enlightenment. When in *Confessions of an English Opium-Eater* (1821) De Quincey charged that Hazlitt had "not read Plato in his youth (which most likely was only his misfortune) but neither has he read Kant in his manhood (which is his fault)" the invocation marked a conservative's rebuke to a radical. The *"all-to-nothing-crushing* KANT," as Coleridge translated the epithet coined by Moses Mendelssohn, became the foundation of a new conception of ethics and polity.

In the *Critique of Judgement*, published at Leipzig in 1790, Kant acknowledges that Burke "deserves to be called the foremost" of those who have developed "a merely empirical exposition of the sublime and beautiful," but rejects the sensationist approach to ground the experience of the sublime in the operations of the mind itself. His account of the unease that the sublime arouses and the resurgent sense of the superiority of the mind it provokes should be compared to Wordsworth's staging of the "spots of time" in *The Prelude*.

The Critique of Judgement

from *Book 2, Analytic of the Sublime*
A. The Mathematically sublime
from SECTION 25, DEFINITION OF THE TERM "SUBLIME"

Sublime is the name given to what is *absolutely great*. But to be great and to be a magnitude are entirely different concepts (*magnitudo* and *quantitas*). In the same way to *Assert without qualification* (*simpliciter*) that something is great, is quite a different thing from saying that it is *absolutely great* (*absolute, non comparative magnum*). The latter is *what is beyond all comparison great*. *** If, however, we call anything not alone great, but, without qualification, absolutely, and in every respect (beyond all comparison) great, that is to say, sublime, we soon perceive that it is not permissible to seek an appropriate standard outside itself, but merely in itself. It is a greatness comparable to itself alone. Hence it comes that the sublime is not to be looked for in things of nature, but only in our own ideas. *** But precisely because there is a striving in our imagination towards progress *ad infinitum*, while reason demands absolute totality, as a real idea, that same inability on the part of our faculty for the estimation of the magnitude of things of the world of sense to attain to this idea, is the awakening of a feeling of a supersensible faculty[1] within us, and it is the use to which judgment naturally puts particular objects on behalf of this latter feeling, and not the object of sense, that is absolutely great, and every other contrasted employment small. Consequently it is the disposition of soul evoked by a particular representation engaging the attention of the reflective judgement, and not the Object, that is to be called sublime.

The forgoing formulae defining the sublime may, therefore, be supplemented by yet another: *The sublime is that, the mere capacity of thinking which evidences a faculty of mind transcending every standard of sense.*

from SECTION 27, QUALITY OF THE DELIGHT IN OUR ESTIMATE OF THE SUBLIME

The feeling of the sublime is, therefore, at once a feeling of displeasure, arising from the inadequacy of the imagination in the aesthetic estimation of magnitude to attain to its estimation by reason, and a simultaneously awakened pleasure, arising from this very judgement of inadequacy of the greatest faculty of sense being in accord with ideas of reason, so far as the effort to attain to these is for us a law. *** Therefore the inner perception of the inadequacy of every standard of sense to serve for the rational estimation of magnitude is a coming into accord with reason's laws, and a displeasure that makes us alive to the feeling of the supersensible side of our being, according to which it is final, and consequently a pleasure, to find every standard of sensibility falling short of the ideas of reason.

The mind feels itself *set in motion* in the representation of the sublime in nature; whereas in the aesthetic judgment upon what is beautiful therein it is in *restful* contemplation. This movement, especially in its inception, may be compared with a vibration, i.e. with a rapidly alternating repulsion and attraction to the same Object. The point of excess for the imagination (towards which it is driven in the apprehension of the intuition) is like an abyss in which it fears to lose itself; yet again for the rational idea of the supersensible it is not excessive, but conformable to law, and directed to drawing out such an effort on the part of the imagination: and so in turn as much a source of attraction as it was repellent to mere sensibility.

B. The Dynamically Sublime in Nature
from SECTION 28, NATURE AS MIGHT

Might is a power which is superior to great hindrances. It is termed *dominion* if it is also superior to the resistance of that which itself possesses might. Nature considered in an aesthetic judgement as might that has no dominion over us, is *dynamically sublime*.

---

1. Above and beyond the senses; not sensual; intellectual.

If we are to estimate nature as dynamically sublime, it must be represented as a source of fear (though the converse, that every object that is a source of fear is, in our aesthetic judgement, sublime, does not hold). For in forming an aesthetic estimate (no concept being present) the superiority to hindrances can only be estimated according to the greatness of the resistance. Now that which we strive to resist is an evil, and, if we do not find our powers commensurate to the task, an object of fear. ***

Bold, overhanging, and as it were, threatening rocks, thunderclouds piled up the vault of heaven, borne along with flashes and peals, volcanoes in all their violence of destruction, hurricanes leaving desolation in their track, the boundless ocean rising with rebellious force, the high waterfall of some mighty river, and the like, make our power of resistance of trifling moment in comparison with their might. But, provided our own position is secure, their aspect is all the more attractive for its fearfulness; and we readily call these objects sublime, because they raise the forces of the soul above the height of vulgar commonplace, and discover within us a power of resistance of quite another kind, which gives us courage to be able to measure ourselves against the seeming omnipotence of nature.

In the immeasurableness of nature and the incompetence of our faculty for adopting a standard proportionate to the aesthetic estimation of the magnitude of its *realm*, we found our own limitation. But with this we also found in our rational faculty another non-sensuous standard, one which has that infinity itself under it as a unit, and in comparison with which everything in nature is small, and so found in our minds a pre-eminence over nature even in its immeasurability. Now in just the same way the irresistibility of the might of nature forces upon us the recognition of our physical helplessness as beings of nature, but at the same time reveals a faculty of estimating ourselves as independent of nature, and discovers a pre-eminence above nature that is the foundation of a self-preservation of quite another kind from that which may be assailed and brought into danger by external nature. This saves humanity in our own person from humiliation, even though as mortal men we have to submit to external violence. In this way external nature is not estimated in our aesthetic judgement as sublime so far as exciting fear, but rather because it challenges our power (one not of nature) to regard as small those things of which we are wont to be solicitous (worldly goods, health, and life), and hence to regard its might (to which in these matters we are no doubt subject) as exercising over us and our personality no such rude dominion that we should bow down before it, once the question becomes one of our highest principles and of our asserting or forsaking them. Therefore nature is here called sublime merely because it raises the imagination to a presentation of those cases in which the mind can make itself sensible of the appropriate sublimity of the sphere of its own being, even above nature. ***

Sublimity, therefore, does not reside in any of the things of nature, but only in our own mind, in so far as we may become conscious of our superiority over nature within, and thus also over nature without us (as exerting influence upon us). Everything that provokes this feeling in us, including the *might* of nature which challenges our strength, is then, though improperly, called sublime, and it is only under presupposition of the idea within us, and in relation to it, that we are capable of attaining to the sublimity of that Being which inspires deep respect in us, not by the mere display of its might in nature, but more by the faculty which is planted in us of estimating the might without fear, and of regarding our estate as exalted above it.

1790

William Gilpin
1724–1804

No name is more associated with the fashion of the picturesque than that of William Gilpin, from 1777 the vicar of Boldre. He traveled throughout the British Isles, and the records of his tours, illustrated with pen and wash drawings, circulated widely in manuscript before publication made them the handbooks of picturesque travel and picturesque sketching. Such works as his *Observations on the River Wye, and Several Parts of South Wales, relative chiefly to Picturesque Beauty; made in the Summer of 1770* (1782), read by Thomas Gray, who left a journal of his tour in the Lake District, before his death in 1771, *Observations relative chiefly to Picturesque Beauty, Made in the Year 1772, on several Parts of England; particularly the Mountains, and Lakes of Cumberland, and Westmoreland* (1786), and *Observations, relative chiefly to Picturesque Beauty, Made in the Year 1776, on Several Parts of Great Britain; particularly the High-Lands of Scotland* (1789) promoted travel to hitherto neglected regions and fixed the discourse of appreciation. *Three Essays,* excerpted below, contained aquatints precisely illustrating how the addition of detail and management of lighting could convert a smoothly regular landscape into an appealingly varied picturesque prospect. How closely Gilpin's taste accorded with and in turn shaped artistic practice may be gauged by comparing his description of Tintern Abbey with the images of Thomas Girtin and Edward Dayes:

No part of the ruins of Tintern is seen from the river, except the abbey-church. It has been an elegant Gothic pile; but it does not make that appearance as a *distant* object, which we expected.... No ruins of the tower are left, which might give form, and contrast to the walls, and buttresses, and other inferior parts. Instead of this, a number of gabel-ends hurt the eye with their regularity; and disgust it by the vulgarity of their shape. A mallet judiciously used (but who durst use it?) might be of service in fracturing some of them.... But if *Tintern-abbey* be less striking as a distant object, it exhibits, on a *nearer* view (when the whole together cannot be seen, but the eye settles on some of its nobler parts,) a very inchanting piece of ruin. Nature has now made it her own. Time has worn off all traces of the rule: it has blunted the sharp edges of the chissel, and broken the regularity of opposing parts. The figured ornaments of the east window are gone; those of the west-window are left. Most of the other windows, with their principal ornaments, remain. To these are superadded the ornaments of time. Ivy, in masses uncommonly large, has taken possession of many parts of the wall; and gives a happy contrast to the grey-coloured stone, of which the building is composed. Nor is this undecorated. Mosses of various hues, with lychens, maiden-hair, penny-leaf, and other humble plants, overspread the surface, or hang from every joint, and crevice.... Such is the beautiful appearance, which Tintern-abbey exhibits on the *outside.*... But when we *enter it,* we see it in most perfection.... The roof is gone, but the walls, pillars, and abutments, which supported it, are intire. A few of the pillars indeed have given way; and here, and there, a piece of the facing of the wall: but in correspondent parts, one always remains to tell the story.... When we stood at one end of this awful piece of ruin; and surveyed the whole in one view—the elements of air, and earth, its only covering, and pavement, and the grand, and venerable remains, which terminated both—perfect enough to form the perspective, yet broken enough to destroy the regularity; the eye was above measure delighted with the beauty, the greatness, and the novelty of the scene.

Edward Dayes, *Tintern Abbey from across the Wye*, 1794. The draftsman Edward Dayes (1763–1804),
to whom Thomas Girtin was apprenticed (see page 2), made this drawing of Tintern Abbey in 1794.
William Gilpin had commented in his *Observations on the River Wye* (1782): "were the building ever so
beautiful, incompassed as it is with shabby houses, it could make no appearance from the river." The presentation of the building amid the surrounding scenery was nonetheless attractive enough for the drawing
to be reproduced.

from Three Essays on Picturesque Beauty, on Picturesque Travel, and on Sketching Landscape

from *Essay 1, on Picturesque Beauty*

Disputes about beauty might perhaps be involved in less confusion, if a distinction
were established, which certainly exists, between such objects as are *beautiful*, and
such as are *picturesque*—between those, which please the eye in their *natural state*;
and those, which please from some quality, capable of being *illustrated by painting*.

Ideas of beauty vary with the objects, and with the eye of the spectator. The
stone-mason sees beauties in a well-jointed wall, which escape the architect, who
surveys the building under a different idea. And thus the painter, who compares his
object with the rules of his art, sees it in a different light from the man of general
taste, who surveys it only as simply beautiful.

As the difference therefore between the *beautiful*, and the *picturesque* appears really to exist, and must depend upon some peculiar construction of the object; it may be
worth while to examine, what that peculiar construction is. We inquire not into the
general sources of beauty, either in nature, or in representation. This would lead into a
nice, and scientific discussion, in which it is not our purpose to engage. The question
simply is, *What is that quality in objects, which particularly marks them as picturesque?*

In examining the *real object*, we shall find one source of beauty arise from that
species of elegance, which we call *smoothness*, or *neatness*; for the terms are nearly
synonymous. The higher the marble is polished, the brighter the silver is rubbed, and

the more the mahogany shines, the more each is considered as an object of beauty: as if the eye delighted in gliding smoothly over a surface. ***

But in *picturesque representation* it seems somewhat odd, yet perhaps we shall find it equally true, that the reverse of this is the case; and that the ideas of *neat* and *smooth*, instead of being picturesque, in reality strip the object, in which they reside, of all pretensions to *picturesque beauty*.—Nay, farther, we do not scruple to assert, that *roughness* forms the most essential point of difference between the *beautiful* and the *picturesque*; as it seems to be that particular quality which makes objects chiefly pleasing in painting.—I use the general term *roughness*; but properly speaking roughness relates only to the surfaces of bodies: when we speak of their delineation, we use the word *ruggedness*. ***

A piece of Palladian[1] architecture may be elegant in the last degree. The proportion of its parts—the propriety of its ornaments—and the symmetry of the whole may be highly pleasing. But if we introduce it in a picture, it immediately becomes a formal object, and ceases to please. Should we wish to give it picturesque beauty, we must use the mallet, instead of the chisel: we must beat down one half of it, deface the other, and throw the mutilated members around in heaps. In short, from a *smooth* building we must turn it into a *rough* ruin. No painter, who had the choice of the two objects, would hesitate which to choose.

Again, why does an elegant piece of garden-ground make no figure on canvas? The shape is pleasing; the combination of the objects, harmonious; and the widening of the walk in the very line of beauty. All this is true, but the *smoothness* of the whole, tho right, and as it should be in nature, offends in picture. Turn the lawn into a piece of broken ground: plant rugged oaks instead of flowering shrubs: break the edges of the walk give it the rudeness of a road; mark it with wheel-tracks; and scatter around a few stones, and brushwood; in a word, instead of making the whole *smooth*, make it rough; and you make it also *picturesque*. ***

That lovely face of youth smiling with all its sweet, dimpling charms, how attractive is it in life! How beautiful in representation! It is one of those objects, that please, as many do, both in nature, and on canvas. But would you see the human face in its brightest form of *picturesque beauty*, examine that patriarchal head. What is it, which gives that dignity of character; that force of expression; those lines of wisdom, and experience; that energetic meaning, so far beyond the rosy hue, or even the bewitching smile of youth? What is it, but the forehead furrowed with wrinkles? The prominent cheek-bone, catching the light? The muscles of the cheek strongly marked, and losing themselves in the shaggy beard? And, above all, the austere brow, projecting over the eye—the feature which particularly struck Homer in his idea of Jupiter, and which he had probably seen finely represented in some statue; in a word, what is it, but the *rough* touches of age? ***

from *Essay 2, on Picturesque Travel*

The first source of amusement to the picturesque traveler, is the *pursuit* of his object—the expectation of new scenes continually opening, and arising to his view. We suppose the country to have been unexplored. Under this circumstance the mind is kept constantly in an agreeable suspense. The love of novelty is the foundation of this pleasure. Every distant horizon promises something new; and with this pleasing expectation we follow her through all her walks. We pursue her from hill to dale; and hunt after those various beauties, with which she everywhere abounds. ***

1. The designs of Italian neoclassical architect Andrea Palladio (1518–1580) were influential in England.

After the pursuit we are gratified with the *attainment* of the object. Our amusement, on this head, arises from the employment of the mind in examining the beautiful scenes we have found. Sometimes we examine them under the idea of a *whole*: we admire the composition, the colouring, and the light, in one *comprehensive view*. When we are fortunate enough to fall in with scenes of this kind, we are highly delighted. But as we have less frequent opportunities of being thus gratified, we are more commonly employed in analyzing the *parts of scenes*; which may be exquisitely beautiful, tho unable to produce a whole. We examine what would amend the composition; how little is wanting to reduce it to the rules of our art; how trifling a circumstance sometimes forms the limit between beauty, and deformity. Or we compare the objects before us with other objects of the same kind: or perhaps we compare them with the imitations of art. From all these operations of the mind results great amusement.

But it is not from this *scientifical* employment, that we derive our chief pleasure. We are most delighted, when some grand scene, tho perhaps of an incorrect composition, rising before the eye, strikes us beyond the power of thought—when the *vox faucibus haeret*;[2] and every mental operation is suspended. In this pause of intellect; this deliquium of the soul, an enthusiastic sensation of pleasure overspreads it, previous to any examination by the rules of art. The general idea of the scene makes an impression, before any appeal is made to the judgment. We rather *feel*, than *survey* it.

*** From this correct knowledge of objects arises another amusement; that of representing, by a few strokes in a sketch, those ideas, which have made the most impression upon us. *** There may be more pleasure in recollecting, and recording, from a few transient lines, the scenes we have admired, than in the present enjoyment of them. If the scenes indeed have *peculiar greatness*, this secondary pleasure cannot be attended with those enthusiastic feelings, which accompanied the real exhibition. But, in general, tho it may be a calmer species of pleasure, it is more uniform, and uninterrupted. It flatters us too with the idea of a sort of creation of our own; and it is unallayed with that fatigue, which is often a considerable abatement to the pleasures of traversing the wild, and savage parts of nature. ***

We are in some degree, also amused by the very visions of fancy itself. Often, when slumber has half-closed the eye, and shut out all the objects of sense, especially after the enjoyment of some splendid scene; the imagination, active, and alert, collects its scattered ideas, transposes, combines, and shifts them into a thousand forms, producing such exquisite scenes, such sublime arrangements, such glow, and harmony of colouring, such brilliant lights, such depth, and clearness of shadow, as equally foil description, and every attempt of artificial colouring. ***

The more refined our taste grows from the *study of nature*, the more insipid are the *works of art*. Few of its efforts please. The idea of the great original is so strong, that the copy must be pure, if it do not disgust. But the varieties of nature's charts are such, that, study them as we can, new varieties will always arise: and let our taste be ever so refined, her works, on which it is formed (at least when we consider them as *objects*), must always go beyond it; and furnish fresh sources both of pleasure and amusement.

from *Essay 3, on The Art of Sketching Landscape*

Your intention in taking *views from nature*, may either be to *fix them in your own memory*—or to *convey, in some degree, your ideas to others*.

---

2. Stunned by the image of his lost wife Creusa, Aeneas finds his "voice held fast within / [his] jaws" (Virgil, *Aeneid*, 2.774); see also Turnus's horror (12.868).

Two William Gilpin pen and wash drawings from his *Three Essays*, 1792. "In a mountain-scene what composition could arise from the corner of a smooth knoll coming forward on one side, intersected by a smooth knoll on the other; with a smooth plain perhaps in the middle, and a smooth mountain in the distance? The very idea is disgusting. Picturesque composition consists in uniting in one whole a variety of parts; and these parts can only be obtained from rough objects. If the smooth mountains, and plains were broken by different objects, the composition might be good, on a supposition the great lines of it were so before . . . From *rough* objects also he [the painter] seeks the *effect of light and shade*. . . . One uniform light, or one uniform shade produces no effect. It is the various surfaces of objects, sometimes turning to the light in one way, and sometimes in another, that give the painter his choice of opportunities in massing, and graduating both his lights, and shades."—from William Gilpin's *Essay I, On Picturesque Beauty;* from *Three Essays,* 2nd ed. (1794), 99.19–20.

With regard to the former, when you meet a scene you wish to sketch, your first consideration is to get it in the best point of view. A few paces to the right, or left, make a great difference. The ground, which folds awkwardly here, appears to fold more easily there: and that long black curtain of the castle, which is so unpleasing a circumstance, as you stand on one side, is agreeably broken by a buttress on another. ✳✳✳

But when a sketch is intended *to convey in some degree, our ideas to others*, it is necessary, that it should be somewhat more adorned. To *us* the scene, familiar to our recollection, may be suggested by a few rough strokes: but if you wish to raise the idea, *where none existed before*, and to do it *agreeably*, there should be some *composition* in your sketch—a degree of *correctness, and expression* in the out-line—and some *effect of light*. A little *ornament* also from figures, and other circumstances may be introduced. In short, it should be so far dressed, as to give some idea of a picture. I call this an *adorned sketch*; and should sketch nothing that was not capable of being thus dressed. ✳✳✳

But the *composition*, you say, is already fixed by the *original sketch*.

It is true, but still it may admit many little alterations, by which the forms of objects may be assisted; and yet the remembrance not disfigured: as the same piece of music, performed by different masters, and graced variously by each, may yet continue still the same. We must ever recollect that nature is most defective in composition; and *must* be a little assisted. Her ideas are too vast for picturesque use, without the restraint of rules. ✳✳✳

In a hasty transcript *from nature*, it is sufficient to take the lines of the country just as you find them: but in your *adorned sketch* you must grace them a little, where they run false. You must contrive to hide offensive parts with wood; to cover such as are too bald, with bushes; and to remove little objects, which in nature push themselves too much in sight, and serve only to introduce too many parts into your *composition*.

1794

✦ ❧✦❧ ✦

Mary Wollstonecraft
1759–1797

Mary Wollstonecraft's *A Vindication of the Rights of Men*, published anonymously in 1790, was one of the first replies to Burke's *Reflections on the Revolution in France*. By joining her attack on Burke's reactionary politics to a severe critique of the invidious gendering that operates in his *Philosophical Enquiry into the Origin of Our Ideas of the Sublime and Beautiful*, Wollstonecraft not only discloses the continuities between Burke's aesthetics and his politics, but also confirms the continuing currency of the aesthetic theory. Despite political differences from Burke, Wollstonecraft's own treatment of nature in her fiction and in *Letters Written During a Short Residence in Sweden, Norway, and Denmark* (1796) remained imbued with Burkean categories.

For more on Wollstonecraft, see the entry in *Perspectives: The Rights of Man and the Revolution Controversy* (page 122) and the main entry under her name (page 302).

from **A Vindication of the Rights of Men**

Where is the dignity, the infallibility of sensibility, in the fair ladies, whom, if the voice of rumour is to be credited, the captive negroes curse in all the agony of bodily pain, for the unheard of tortures they invent? It is probable that some of them, after the sight of a flagellation, compose their ruffled spirits and exercise their tender feelings by the perusal of the last imported novel.——How true these tears are to nature, I leave you to determine. But these ladies may have read your Enquiry concerning the origin of our ideas of the Sublime and Beautiful, and, convinced by your arguments, may have laboured to be pretty, by counterfeiting weakness.[1]

You may have convinced them that *littleness* and *weakness* are the very essence of beauty; and that the Supreme Being, in giving women beauty in the most supereminent degree, seemed to command them, by the powerful voice of Nature, not to cultivate the moral virtues that might chance to excite respect, and interfere with the pleasing sensations they were created to inspire. Thus confining truth, fortitude, and humanity, within the rigid pale of manly morals, they might justly argue, that to be loved, woman's high end and great distinction! They should "learn to lisp, to totter in their walk, and nick-name God's creatures." Never, they might repeat after you, was any man, much less a woman, rendered amiable by the force of those exalted qualities, fortitude, justice, wisdom, and truth; and thus forewarned of the sacrifice they must make to those austere, unnatural virtues, they would be authorized to turn all their attention to their persons, systematically neglecting morals to secure beauty.——Some rational old woman indeed might chance to stumble at this doctrine, and hint, that in avoiding atheism you had not steered clear of the mussulman's [Muslim's] creed; but you could readily exculpate yourself by turning the charge on Nature, who made our idea of beauty independent of reason. Nor would it be necessary for you to collect, that if virtue has any other foundation than worldly utility, you have clearly proved that one half of the human species, at least, have not souls; and that Nature, by making women *little, smooth, delicate, fair* creatures, never designed that they should exercise their reason to acquire the virtues that produce opposite, if not contradictory, feelings. The affection they excite, to be uniform and perfect, should not be tinctured with the respect which moral virtues inspire, lest pain should be blended with pleasure, and admiration disturb the soft intimacy of love. This laxity of morals in the female world is certainly more captivating to a libertine imagination than the cold arguments of reason, that give no sex to virtue. If beautiful weakness be interwoven in a woman's frame, if the chief business of her life be (as you insinuate) to inspire love, and Nature has made an eternal distinction between the qualities that dignify a rational being and this animal perfection, her duty and happiness in this life must clash with any preparation for a more exalted state. So that Plato and Milton were grossly mistaken in asserting that human love led to heavenly, and was only an exaltation of the same affection; for the love of the Deity, which is mixed with the most profound reverence, must be love of perfection, and not compassion for weakness.

To say the truth, I not only tremble for the souls of women, but for the good natured man, whom every one loves. The *amiable* weakness of his mind is a strong argument against its immateriality, and seems to prove that beauty relaxes the *solids* of the soul as well as the body.[2]

It follows then immediately, from your own reasoning, that respect and love are antagonist principles; and that, if we really wish to render men more virtuous, we must

<hr>

1. See the excerpt from the section "Perfection not the cause of Beauty," in Burke's *Enquiry* (page 41).

2. See the excerpt from the section "The physical cause of Love," in Burke's *Enquiry*, above (page 42).

endeavour to banish all enervating modifications of beauty from civil society. We must, to carry your argument a little further, return to Spartan regulations, and settle the virtues of men on the stern foundation of mortification and self-denial; for any attempt to civilize the heart, to make it humane by implanting reasonable principles, is a mere philosophic dream. If refinement invariably lessens respect for virtue, by rendering beauty, the grand tempter, more seductive; if these relaxing feelings are incompatible with the nervous exertions of morality, the sun of Europe is not set; it begins to dawn, when cold metaphysicians try to make the head give laws to the heart.[3]

But should experience prove that there is a beauty in virtue, a charm in order which necessarily implies exertion, a depraved sensual taste may give way to a more manly one—and *melting* feelings to rational satisfactions. Both may be equally natural to man; the test is their moral difference, and that point reason alone can decide.

Such a glorious change can only be produced by liberty.

1790   1790

Jane Austen
1775–1817

Pride and Prejudice (1813) is Jane Austen's most famous novel. Before this passage, heroine Elizabeth Bennet had angrily refused a proposal of marriage from Mr. Darcy, believing him to be an arrogant snob and the cause of misery to her sister. Darcy then sent a letter, with new information that has altered her view of him. Not having seen him since, she is now on a tour of Derbyshire with her aunt and uncle and, believing Darcy to be absent, she agrees to a visit of his estate.

from Pride and Prejudice

Vol. III, Ch. 1

Elizabeth, as they drove along, watched for the first appearance of Pemberley Woods with some perturbation; and when at length they turned in at the lodge,[1] her spirits were in a high flutter.

The park[2] was very large, and contained great variety of ground. They entered it in one of its lowest points, and drove some time through a beautiful wood, stretching over a wide extent.

Elizabeth's mind was too full for conversation, but she saw and admired every remarkable spot and point of view. They gradually ascended for half a mile, and then found themselves at the top of a considerable eminence, where the wood ceased, and the eye was instantly caught by Pemberley House, situated on the opposite side of a valley, into which the road with some abruptness wound. It was a large, handsome, stone building, standing well on rising ground, and backed by a ridge of high woody hills;—and in front, a stream of some natural importance was swelled into greater, but without any artificial appearance. Its banks were neither formal, nor falsely adorned.

---

3. See Burke's paean to Marie Antoinette and chivalry in the excerpt from *Reflections on the Revolution in France* (page 118).

1. An out-building for use by recreational hunters.
2. A vast estate of land, of hundreds of acres. (Darcy is one of the richest men in England.)

Elizabeth was delighted. She had never seen a place for which nature had done more, or where natural beauty had been so little counteracted by an awkward taste.[3] They were all of them warm in their admiration; and at that moment she felt, that to be mistress of Pemberley might be something!

1813

from **Northanger Abbey, Chapter 14**[1]

The Tilneys were *** viewing the country with the eyes of persons accustomed to drawing, and decided on its capability of being formed into pictures, with all the eagerness of real taste. Here Catherine was quite lost. She knew nothing of drawing— nothing of taste: and she listened to them with an attention which brought her little profit, for they talked in phrases which conveyed scarcely any idea to her. The little which she could understand, however, appeared to contradict the very few notions she had entertained on the matter before. It seemed as if a good view were no longer to be taken from the top of an high hill, and that a clear blue sky was no longer a proof of a fine day. She was heartily ashamed of her ignorance. A misplaced shame. Where people wish to attach, they should always be ignorant. To come with a well-informed mind is to come with an inability of administering to the vanity of others, which a sensible person would always wish to avoid. A woman especially, if she have the misfortune of knowing anything, should conceal it as well as she can.

The advantages of natural folly in a beautiful girl have been already set forth by the capital pen of a sister author;[2] and to her treatment of the subject I will only add, in justice to men, that though to the larger and more trifling part of the sex, imbecility in females is a great enhancement of their personal charms, there is a portion of them too reasonable and too well informed themselves to desire anything more in woman than ignorance. But Catherine did not know her own advantages—did not know that a good-looking girl, with an affectionate heart and a very ignorant mind, cannot fail of attracting a clever young man, unless circumstances are particularly untoward. In the present instance, she confessed and lamented her want of knowledge, declared that she would give anything in the world to be able to draw; and a lecture on the picturesque immediately followed, in which his instructions were so clear that she soon began to see beauty in everything admired by him, and her attention was so earnest that he became perfectly satisfied of her having a great deal of natural taste. He talked of foregrounds, distances, and second distances—side-screens and perspectives—lights and shades; and Catherine was so hopeful a scholar that when they gained the top of Beechen Cliff, she voluntarily rejected the whole city of Bath as unworthy to make part of a landscape. Delighted with her progress, and fearful of wearying her with too much wisdom at once, Henry suffered the subject to

3. If, as scholars suppose, the model for Pemberley is the great estate of the Dukes of Devonshire, Chatsworth, what Elizabeth sees as "nature" was the result of extensive, expensive reshaping by landscape architect Lancelot "Capability" Brown. Austen's language exquisitely hints at the paradoxes of the picturesque project: the stream has been swelled; natural beauty has been aesthetically curated.
1. First drafted in the late 1790s as a spoof of the popular "gothic novel," *Northanger Abbey* was not published until 1818, the year after Austen's death. In this excerpt, heroine

Catherine Morland, a newcomer to the resort town of Bath, has been invited on a rural excursion with her new friends, brother and sister Henry and Eleanor Tilney. Austen lightly satirizes the aesthetics of female beauty, the "Picturesque" landscape, and the urban sublime, with inflections from the Reign of Terror in France, 1792–1794.
2. The narrator's satire on the prevailing advice that young women should not display learning if they want to attract a man; the sister author is Lady Mary W. Montagu, advising her daughter about how to raise her own daughter.

decline, and by an easy transition from a piece of rocky fragment and the withered oak which he had placed near its summit, to oaks in general, to forests, the enclosure of them, waste lands, crown lands and government, he shortly found himself arrived at politics; and from politics, it was an easy step to silence. The general pause which succeeded his short disquisition on the state of the nation was put an end to by Catherine, who, in rather a solemn tone of voice; uttered these words, "I have heard that something very shocking indeed will soon come out in London."

Miss Tilney, to whom this was chiefly addressed, was startled, and hastily replied, "Indeed! And of what nature?"

"That I do not know, nor who is the author. I have only heard that it is to be more horrible than anything we have met with yet."

"Good heaven! Where could you hear of such a thing?"

"A particular friend of mine had an account of it in a letter from London yesterday. It is to be uncommonly dreadful. I shall expect murder and everything of the kind."

"You speak with astonishing composure! But I hope your friend's accounts have been exaggerated; and if such a design is known beforehand, proper measures will undoubtedly be taken by government to prevent its coming to effect."

"Government," said Henry, endeavouring not to smile, "neither desires nor dares to interfere in such matters. There must be murder; and government cares not how much."

The ladies stared. He laughed, and added, "Come, shall I make you understand each other, or leave you to puzzle out an explanation as you can? No—I will be noble. I will prove myself a man, no less by the generosity of my soul than the clearness of my head. I have no patience with such of my sex as disdain to let themselves sometimes down to the comprehension of yours. Perhaps the abilities of women are neither sound nor acute—neither vigorous nor keen. Perhaps they may want observation, discernment, judgment, fire, genius, and wit."

"Miss Morland, do not mind what he says; but have the goodness to satisfy me as to this dreadful riot."

"Riot! What riot?"

"My dear Eleanor, the riot is only in your own brain. The confusion there is scandalous. Miss Morland has been talking of nothing more dreadful than a new publication which is shortly to come out, in three duodecimo volumes,[3] two hundred and seventy-six pages in each, with a frontispiece to the first, of two tombstones and a lantern—do you understand? And you, Miss Morland—my stupid sister has mistaken all your clearest expressions. You talked of expected horrors in London—and instead of instantly conceiving, as any rational creature would have done, that such words could relate only to a circulating library, she immediately pictured to herself a mob of three thousand men assembling in St. George's Fields, the Bank attacked, the Tower threatened, the streets of London flowing with blood, a detachment of the Twelfth Light Dragoons (the hopes of the nation) called up from Northampton to quell the insurgents, and the gallant Captain Frederick Tilney, in the moment of charging at the head of his troop, knocked off his horse by a brickbat from an upper window.[4] Forgive her stupidity. The fears of the sister have added to the weakness of the woman; but she is by no means a simpleton in general."

3. A very inexpensive format, in which *Pride and Prejudice,* among many other novels, was published.
4. Although this seems a fantasy importing of the Parisian Terror to England's capital, during the 1790s, there had been a number of riots in London, over food shortages and in confrontations with the government over "unlawful" assembly and publication.

Maria Jane Jewsbury
1800–1833

Witty poet, novelist, incisive essayist, and penetrating reviewer, Maria Jane Jewsbury became an intimate of the Wordsworth family, and one of Felicia Hemans's closest friends. She began publishing poetry in the newspapers, and like many women, found an outlet for her poems and sketches in the literary annuals of the 1820s; by 1830 she was a frequent contributor to the new urban weekly, *The Athenaeum*. Her alternately satirical and bitter novella, *The History of an Enthusiast* (1830) not only refused to punish her lovelorn, successful female poet with social abjection or death (the paradigm of the day), but unembarrassedly allied her with Mary Wollstonecraft in an era when Wollstonecraft's name was scarcely mentionable in polite society. In a kind of "old maid" panic, Jewsbury married William Kew Fletcher in August 1832, and accompanied him to India, where he was posted as chaplain to the East India Company, and where she died in the cholera epidemic of 1833. Her first book, a compendium of tales, poems, and essays titled *Phantasmagoria; or Sketches of Life and Literature* (1825), the author given as "M.J.J." (who some reviewers thought had to be male), was admired by William and Dorothy Wordsworth, among others, for its sharp yet not mean-spirited wit. *A Rural Excursion*, laced with witty literary allusions and riffs on picturesque culture, is from *Phantasmagoria*, as is the satire in Perspectives: Popular Prose and the Problems of Authorship (page 1151).

A Rural Excursion
Communicated by a Young Bachelor

Hortensio.	Mistress, what cheer?
Katharine.	'Faith, as cold as can be.

SHAKESPEARE[1]

I don't know, I hope I am sensible of all my good qualities, I am sure I am very willing to palliate my bad ones, but on one point my mind misgives me;—I fear, notwithstanding my poetical tastes, and long residence in a romantic country, that I have no right and proper taste for fine scenery. I like a jaunt in search of the picturesque, I admire cascades, and ruins, and spreading trees, and autumnal tints; and I think a summer day spent amongst woods and wilds, and fair ladies, very delightful,—but somehow, it is a dreadful thing to confess, no person of refinement will ever endure me afterwards—on these occasions, I never *can* help thinking about my dinner! I never can have a due regard to the beauties in the distance, unless I may also have something comfortable in the foreground; provision for the mouth, as well as food for that chameleon member, the eye! I have not the slightest objection to run, ride, or walk, in quest of the sublime and beautiful; but, forgive me sentimental reader—I cannot *starve*! It is my weakness, my misfortune, perhaps my fault,—that while others are packing up poetry, and sketch books, and pencils, and parasols, and spy-glasses, as the chief requisites for a rural excursion, my thoughts should wander to the prog basket;—mine alone be an Israelitish imagination, and the "victualling department" be the one in which I generally crave an office.[2]

---

1. In *The Taming of the Shrew* (4.3.37), shrewish Katharine is being starved into submission by her husband Petruchio (Hortensio's friend).

2. Prog: victuals. The Old Testament set strict dietary laws and protocols.

What then were my feelings, when beguiled by fair weather and fairer promises, I consented to become *le cavalier seul* in a Rural Excursion set on foot by young ladies, and for which—shade of Sancho Panza!—the caterers were old maids![3]

It is unnecessary to inform the enlightened reader that these arrangements took place—"quite in the country"; there, only, would they have been tolerated; there, only, would six ladies have set forth contentedly with a single beau; and there, only, would he, poor unfortunate! have undertaken to escort six ladies. No sooner had they cajoled me into acquiesence, than my mind misgave me as to the main point, the eligibility of our purveyors; but when the eventful morning actually arrived, and I saw the party and the provision basket in juxta-position, utter dismay took possession of my spirit. Six mouths in addition to my own, and that of a great lubberly gormandising lad, one of those interesting beings called "fine children"—whom his mother had smuggled into the party on the plea of his "being useful!" I knew better; my prophetic eye perceived, that his only "use" would be to make our "little less." To mend matters, the ladies, as usual on such occasions, could eat "no breakfast,"—but one and all declared, what excellent appetites they should have for the "cold collation." Unfortunately the more clearly I perceived that starvation awaited me, the more impossible it was I saw to escape. There was not time to get up a tooth-ach, or head-ach, or indeed an available ache of any kind, and I was too well watched to be able to have recourse to any of the thousand manœuvers common in such a case of distress;—no convenient friend could arrive from a distance;—no summons of urgent business could be received;—I was embarked for better for worse;—"the fates had fast bound me"—with six ladies "round me,"[4] and patient submission was my only alternative. The village shandry,[5] a vehicle that might have been a land carriage when Noah's Ark was a water one, deep, and high, and wide, and poling forwards; with a head that arched over you like a dungeon, and an apron that came under your chin like a pinafore,—and shafts made to reach Land's End,—and a horse just fresh from plough,—"dragged their slow length" to the front door.[6] Into this elegant carriage, the connecting link between a cart and a washing tub, the three presiding spinsters, (the Parcae[7] of the party), myself, and the provision basket, were wedged without loss of time. Carefully indeed did I plant this last, and with *one* exception, most interesting part of the group, but care was needless;—no bottles chattered! no gravy threatened to "mar the white beauty" of the damask coverings! no culinary fragrance exhaled through the wicker work! All was dry, and silent, and light, far lighter than my heart. "Smack went the whip, round went the wheels," and we jolted on our way;[8]—behind us trotted a donkey cart, conveying the matron of our party and her son, whom for the time being I wished with Sancho amongst the birch trees; and after them followed our two hoyden belles, one on a skittish colt, the other on a one eyed pony, and closed the procession.

---

3. The only knight. Sancho Panza is the practical-minded comrade of idealistic knight Don Quixote; old maids are women over 30, considered unlikely to marry.

4. Echoing Alexander Pope, *Ode for Music on St. Cecilia's Day* (1708), with Young Bachelor self-cast as Euridyce in Hell: "Tho' fate had fast bound her, / With Styx nine times round her" (90–91); Styx is the river of the underworld. See also Hazlitt's riff on this line (page 1102).

5. A rickety vehicle.

6. "A needless Alexandrine ends the song, / That like a wounded snake, drags its slow length along" (Alexander Pope, *An Essay on Criticism* 358–59); an alexandrine is a line of six iambs, at odds with the five-foot pattern.

7. The three Fates of Roman mythology.

8. William Cowper, *The Diverting History of John Gilpin; Shewing How he Went Farther than Intended, And Came Home Safe Again* (41).

The object of our "Rural Excursion" was to see three mounds of a remarkably odd shape, *supposed* to have been used by the Romans as burying places;—to clamber up into a ruined tower, from which it was *believed* we could see three counties;—and as a finish, to walk two miles to a cascade and a labyrinth, *said* to be very wonderful! Now admitting that, under the "happiest attitude" of circumstances, these "views" were worth seeing, were they (I ask the candid reader) worth starving for?—I should not have been half so much mortified, had not my companions been obstinately enchanted with every thing that crossed their path; and as I was their only gentleman, conceived it a duty to pay me attention. My neck had no peace—at the bidding of some one or other of my fair plagues, it was continually turning from side to side like a Chinese shaking figure—"Dear Mr.———just observe the tints on that tree"—cried one; and "do admire that little cloud just behind you"—exclaimed another; and "Oh Mr.———" said the belles, panting like their ponies—"*do* look at yonder love of a cottage, shouldn't you like to live there?" Of course I looked, and admired, and liked, as they bade me, but I could have parodied poor Burns' lines[9] and told them—

> My heart's in the kitchen, my heart is not here,
> My heart's in the kitchen, though following the dear,
> Thinking on the roast meat, and musing on the fry,
> My heart's in the kitchen whatever I spy.

The reader will not surely (under these circumstances) expect me to describe any of the beauties of nature which passed under my observation on the day in question. It is true I was obliged to circumvallate[1] the hills, and join in the intellectual "wonder" of the young ladies, as to what was "inside them";—to climb the ruin and there listen to those moral reflections put forth by all who are "past their prime"; but these were endurable evils, inasmuch as I was free to *hear* or not, as I chose. The two miles walk to the cascade and the labyrinth, I was determined to set aside; and accordingly conjured up such visions of spoiled pelisses, scratched arms, and approaching thunder storms, that I eventually carried my point, and we descended the ruined tower—to dine!

> What hids't thou in thy treasure caves and cells,
> Thou *hollow sounding* and mysterious main?[2]

said I to myself whilst *unpinning* the damask napkins and writing paper, in which, like Egyptian mummies, the viands were enveloped. Banish I beseech you, reader, all visions of good cheer—let not the civic pasty, the baronial ham, the regal sirloin, haunt your fancy, for neither lot nor part had they in our "table of contents." Instead of these "nobler substances," I drew forth the demure, delicate chicken, peering through wreaths of parsley, like beauty through a green veil;—wee wee patés, calculated to increase rather than diminish hunger;—the transparent jelly—the tantalizing custard—shrimps, sandwiches, and "little cakes"—whereof a legion fill not a square inch of

9. My heart's in the highlands, my heart is not here,
  My heart's in the highlands a following the deer,
  A following the wild deer and chasing the roe,
  My heart's in the highlands wherever I go.
  [M.J.J.'s footnote]
Robert Burns's much beloved song, based on an old ballad and published, with music, in the 1790s.

1. Surround with ramparts.
2. The opening lines of *The Treasures of the Deep* (1823), by Felicia Hemans; Jewsbury began to correspond with her in 1827 and they finally met in 1828 and became close friends.

appetite, with many similar nonentities, and mathematical points of food! "Slowly and sadly I laid them down,"[3] and when spread upon the grass in dinner array, they were indeed calculated to strike terror into the heart of a hungry man like myself.

Not so our spinster[4] hostesses. They had gauged our stomachs by their own, and utterly unconscious of the scantiness of their stores, pressed us with hospitable importunity "to help ourselves,"—to "feel perfectly at home,"—to "stand upon no ceremony,"— delightful invitations when addressed to one at a well furnished board, but in the present case absolute insults.—Heaven help *le cavalier seul!* said I to myself, as with smiles that ill concealed my sorrow, I performed my office of carver to the chicken, and distributor of shrimps and sandwiches, secretly grumbling at that custom of civilized life, which ordains that ladies shall be helped first. So would you too, polite reader, had you seen as I did, a probable chance of having to make a Nebuchadnessar's meal on the parsley garnish.[5] I could have borne *this* patiently, had not my self-denial chiefly benefited the young cub, whose presence I had from the first deplored;—but was it not too much for human nature, to see the little wretch wedged in by his mother's side, stuffing,—whilst I sat opposite, starving!—and she, unnatural creature! if his great ugly mouth did for one instant cease opening and shutting, wearying him with maternal importunities to re-commence his atrocities! "My dear Charles, now you know you eat no breakfast this morning, do love take this leg of chicken, it is not much."

In two seconds it was "with the" chicken legs "before the flood,"[6]—and the lady mother resumed. "That was such a little bit, you must have some sandwiches my dear, just those three that are left."

The sandwiches disappeared with the speed of thought.

"Wont you take a few of these little cakes love?" said one of the spinsters who began to entertain a well grounded fear of famine;—"they are *quite* common, your mamma need not fear their hurting you; or one of these *nice hard* crackers to nibble at."

Neither Charles nor his mamma were to be put off with common cakes and hard crackers. "Why, I believe," said the judicious matron, "the poor thing *longs* for that paté,"—Mr.———may I trouble you to give it him."

I had fixed my own mind on this identical paté, nevertheless with a hearty wish that it might choke the "poor thing," I surrendered it.

"But I don't like it though," said the young barbarian, laying it down after he had bitten a large piece from the side.

If words were but whips, and wishes blows, your bones should ache for a month, thought I.

"Don't eat it then, darling," said his mother soothingly; "take something else, this jelly love, you don't know how good it is, now *try*, just to oblige me."

"I can't eat mother I'm so dry"—said the interesting creature.

"Here is some nice fresh water," said the spinster aforesaid, quite the most sensible of the sisterhood:—"Thank you," replied mamma, "but my poor Charles is so delicate, and after all these good things—Mr.———I'll thank you for just one glass

3. An outrageous riff on the last stanza of Irish poet Charles Wolfe's widely admired ballad, *The Burial of Sir John Moore at Corunna* (1817): "Slowly and sadly we laid him down, / From the field of his fame fresh and gory; / We carved not a line, we raised not a stone— / But we left him alone with his glory"); Moore was a hero in the Peninsular War against Napoleon. Wolfe had died recently, in 1823, at the age of 32.
4. An old maid, from the assumption that she has no other occupation than to work at her spinning wheel.
5. A fast by Jews to commemorate the siege of Jerusalem in 588 B.C.E. by Nebuchadnezzar, King of Babylon, himself famed for sumptuous feasting.
6. That is, as gone as the world before Noah's flood.

of wine for him";—and the delicate little monster swallowed the last drop of our one bottle of cowslip wine.

Now to prove that I am not censorious, I will make the *amende honorable,*[7] and confess, that the moment all the eatables had vanished, every one, not excepting the matron, began to fear I had "taken care of every one but myself,"—that "I had made a poor dinner,"—that "they did not recollect having seen me eat any thing," &c. &c. Then followed histories of wine left behind by mistake; and good things destroyed by the cat; of a tongue that would not go into the basket; and a pigeon pie spoiled in the baking;—but if the mind can exist upon remembrance, the body cannot, nor is anticipation a whit more solid food; for despite the "comfortable cup of tea" promised me on our return, I remained as hungry as ever.

Of the rest of the day I retain but a dim recollection. I was sad, spiritless, and ill tempered; so blind to the beauties of nature, that I would have given the whole range of the blue sky for a beef steak; and equally insensible to the charms of poetry in praise of rural life. Was it indeed likely, that a dinnerless creature like myself, should comprehend the beauty of that sentiment—

> Man wants but little here below,
> Nor wants that little long;—

or, acknowledge that the necessaries of life consist in—

> A script with herbs and fruits supplied,
> And water from the spring;[8]—

No—the only time for writing or speaking in praise of abstemiousness, is immediately after an excellent dinner!

It is time, however, to close this dolorous history. We returned home in safety; and once arrived within sight of that loveliest "view," the smoke of my own kitchen chimney, I resigned the reins to my companions,—excused myself from any further experience of their hospitality,—sprang from the shandry,—and never rested, until my hunger and my ire were alike satisfied;—the former, by a good though too late dinner;—the latter, by committing to paper these "simple annals" of a day's sufferings in search of the picturesque.

John Ruskin
1819–1900

John Ruskin's first book, *Modern Painters,* if one can call a book a project published over more than a decade and a half (1843–1860) and running in the end to five volumes, was an impassioned defense of the greatness of the art of J. M. W. Turner. In the excerpt below one sees the continuing uses of the term "picturesque," and the metamorphoses it could take in the hands of a brilliant critic and fierce moralist. The Reverend Gilpin acknowledged the paradox that "moral and picturesque ideas do not always coincide," but shied away from exploring its implications: "In a moral view, the industrious mechanic is a more pleasing object than the loitering peasant. But in a picturesque light, it is otherwise. The arts of industry are rejected; and even idleness,

---

7. Honorable compensation; an honorable public apology.

8. Thus says a Hermit of his humble repast in Oliver Goldsmith's *Edwin and Angelina* (31–32, 27–28).

if I may so speak, adds dignity to a character" (*Observations relative chiefly to Picturesque Beauty*, 1786). Ruskin turns and turns the paradox, first criticizing the callousness of the hunter after ruin and misery, then conceding the possibility of increased sympathy. More: if the endurance that Ruskin attributes to Calais Church and the innate dignity of the unconsciously suffering laborer (think of Wordsworth's Michael) that he finds in the noble picturesque cannot be neatly cordoned-off from the condescension of the "low school of the surface-picturesque," Ruskin's wielding of his distinction is urgent. The picturesque had begun as a counter to eighteenth-century ideals of symmetry, harmony, and regularity; in Ruskin's mid-nineteenth century deepening it is a weapon against a rootless, industrializing, utilitarian modernity.

from Modern Painters

from Of the Turnerian Picturesque[1]

And the most interesting of these subjects of inquiry, with which, therefore, it may be best to begin, is the precise form under which he has admitted into his work the modern feeling of the picturesque, which, so far as it consists in a delight in ruin, is perhaps the most suspicious and questionable of all the characters distinctively belonging to our temper, and art. ***

The essence of picturesque character has already been defined to be a sublimity not inherent in the nature of the thing, but caused by something external to it; as the ruggedness of a cottage roof possesses something of a mountain aspect, not belonging to the cottage as such. And this sublimity may be either in mere external ruggedness, and other visible character, or it may lie deeper, in an expression of sorrow and old age, attributes which are both sublime; not a dominant expression, but one mingled with such familiar and common characters as prevent the object from becoming perfectly pathetic in its sorrow, or perfectly venerable in its age.

For instance, I cannot find words to express the intense pleasure I have always in first finding myself, after some prolonged stay in England, at the foot of the old tower of Calais church. The large neglect, the noble unsightliness of it; the record of its years written so visibly, yet without sign of weakness or decay; its stern wasteness and gloom, eaten away by the Channel winds, and overgrown with the bitter sea grasses; its slates and tiles all shaken and rent, and yet not falling, its desert of brickwork full of bolts, and holes, and ugly fissures, and yet strong, like a bare brown rock; its carelessness of what any one thinks or feels about it, putting forth no claim, having no beauty nor desirableness, pride, nor grace; yet neither asking for pity; not, as ruins are, useless and piteous, feebly or fondly garrulous of better days; but useful still, going through its own daily work,—as some old fisherman beaten gray by storm, yet drawing his daily nets: so it stands, with no complaint about its past youth, in blanched and meagre massiveness and serviceableness, gathering human souls together underneath it; the sound of its bells for prayer still rolling through its rents; and the grey peak of it seen far across the sea, principal of the three that rise above the waste of surfy sand and hillocked shore,— the lighthouse for life, and the belfry for labour, and this for patience and praise.

I cannot tell the half of the strange pleasures and thoughts that come about me at the sight of that old tower, for, in some sort, it is the epitome of all that makes the Continent of Europe interesting, as opposed to new countries; and, above all, it completely expresses that agedness in the midst of active life which binds the old and the new into harmony. We, in England, have our new street, our new inn, our green shaven lawn, and our piece of ruin emergent from it,—a mere *specimen* of the

1. From vol. 4, part 5, "Of Mountain Beauty."

middle ages put on a bit of velvet carpet to be shown, which, but for its size, might as well be on a museum shelf at once, under cover. But, on the Continent, the links are unbroken between the past and present, and in such use as they can serve for, the greyheaded wrecks are suffered to stay with men; while, in unbroken line, the generations of spared buildings are seen succeeding each in its place. And thus in its largeness, in its permitted evidence of slow decline, in its poverty, in its absence of all pretence, of all show and care for outside aspect, that Calais tower has an infinite of symbolism in it, all the more striking because usually seen in contrast with English scenes expressive of feelings the exact reverse of these. ***

Now, I have insisted long on this English character, because I want the reader to understand thoroughly the opposite element of the noble picturesque; its expression, namely, of *suffering* of *poverty*, or *decay*, nobly endured by unpretending strength of heart. Nor only unpretending, but unconscious. If there be visible pensiveness in the building, as in a ruined abbey, it becomes, or claims to become, beautiful; but the picturesqueness is in the unconscious suffering,—the look that an old labourer has, not knowing that there is anything pathetic in his grey hair, and withered arms, and sunburnt breast; and thus there are the two extremes, the consciousness of pathos in the confessed ruin, which may or may not be beautiful, according to the kind of it; and the entire denial of all human calamity and care, in the swept proprieties and neatnesses of English modernism: and, between these, there is the unconscious confession of the facts of distress and decay, in the by-words; the world's hard-work being gone through all this while, and no pity asked for, nor contempt feared. And this is the expression of that Calais spire, and of all picturesque things, in so far as they have mental or human expression at all.

I say, in so far as they have mental expression, because their merely outward delightfulness—that which makes them pleasant in painting, or, in the literal sense, picturesque—is their actual variety of colour and form. A broken stone has necessarily more various forms in it than a whole one; a bent roof has more various curves in it than a straight one; every excrescence or cleft indicates some additional complexity of light and shade, and every stain of moss on eaves or wall adds to the delightfulness of colour. Hence, in a completely picturesque object, as of an old cottage or mill, there are introduced, by various circumstances not essential to it, but, on the whole, generally somewhat detrimental to it as cottage or mill, such elements of sublimity—complex light and shade, varied colour, undulatory form, and so on—as can generally be found only in noble natural objects, woods, rocks, and mountains. This sublimity, belonging in a parasitical manner, to the building, renders it, in the usual sense of the word, "picturesque."

Now, if this outward sublimity be sought for by the painter, without any regard for the real nature of the thing, and without any comprehension of the pathos of character hidden beneath it, it forms the low school of the surface-picturesque; that which fills ordinary drawing-books and scrap-books, and the most popular living landscape painters of France, England, and Germany. But if these same outward characters be sought for in subordination to the inner character of the object, every source of pleasurableness being refused which is incompatible with that, while perfect sympathy is felt at the same time with the object as to all that it tells of itself in those sorrowful by-words, we have the school of true or noble picturesque; still distinguished from the school of pure beauty or sublimity, because, in its subjects, the pathos and sublimity are all *by the way,* as in Calais old spire,—not inherent, as in a lovely tree or mountain; while it is distinguished still more from the schools of the lower picturesque by its tender sympathy, and its refusal of all sources of pleasure inconsistent with the perfect nature of the thing to be studied. ***

It is mainly because the one painter has communion of heart with his subject, and the other only casts his eyes upon it feelinglessly, that the work of the one is greater than that of the other.[2] And, as we think farther over the matter, we shall see that this is indeed the eminent cause of the difference between the lower picturesque and the higher. For, in a certain sense, the lower picturesque ideal is eminently a *heartless* one; the lover of it seems to go forth in the world in a temper as merciless as its rocks. All other men feel some regret at the sight of disorder and ruin. He alone delights in both; it matters not of what. Fallen cottage—desolate villa—deserted village—blasted heath—mouldering castle—to him, so that they do but show jagged angles of stone and timber, all are sights equally joyful. Poverty, and darkness, and guilt, bring in their several contributions to his treasury of pleasant thoughts. The shattered window, opening into black and ghastly rents of wall, the foul rag or straw wisp stopping them, the dangerous roof, decrepit floor and stair, ragged misery or wasting age of the inhabitants,—all these conduce, each in due measure, to the fulness of his satisfaction. What is it to him that the old man has passed his seventy years in helpless darkness and untaught waste of soul? The old man has at last accomplished his destiny, and filled the corner of a sketch, where something of an unshapely nature was wanting. What is it to him that the people fester in that feverish misery in the low quarter of the town, by the river? Nay, it is much to him. What else were they made for? what could they have done better? The black timbers, and the green water, and the soaking wrecks of boats, and the torn remnants of clothes hung out to dry in the sun;—truly the fever-struck creatures, whose lives have been given for the production of these materials of effect, have not died in vain.

Yet, for all this, I do not say the lover of the lower picturesque is a monster in human form. He is by no means this, though truly we might at first think so, if we came across him unawares, and had not met with any such sort of person before. Generally speaking, he is kind-hearted, innocent of evil, but not broad in thought; somewhat selfish, and incapable of acute sympathy with others; gifted at the same time with strong artistic instincts and capacities for the enjoyment of varied form, and light, and shade, in pursuit of which enjoyment his life is passed, as the lives of other men are, for the most part, in the pursuit of what *they* also like,—be it honour, or money, or indolent pleasure,—very irrespective of the poor people living by the stagnant canal. And, in some sort, the hunter of the picturesque is better than many of these; inasmuch as he is simple-minded and capable of unostentatious and economical delights, which, if not very helpful to other people, are at all events utterly uninjurious, even to the victims or subjects of his picturesque fancies; while to many others his work is entertaining and useful. And, more than all this, even that delight which he *seems* to take in misery is not altogether unvirtuous. Through all his enjoyment there runs a certain undercurrent of tragical passion,—a real vein of human sympathy;—it lies at the root of all those strange morbid hauntings of his; a sad excitement, such as other people feel at a tragedy, only less in degree, just enough, indeed, to give a deeper tone to his pleasure, and to make him choose for his subject the broken stones of a cottage wall rather than a roadside bank, the picturesque beauty of form in each being supposed precisely the same: and, together with this slight tragical feeling, there is also a humble and romantic sympathy; a vague

---

2. Before this point Ruskin has paired and contrasted studies of windmills by Turner and Clarkson Stanfield, "the first master of the lower picturesque, among our living artists."

desire, in his own mind, to live in cottages rather than palaces; a joy in humble things, a contentment and delight in makeshifts, a secret persuasion (in many respects a true one) that there is in these ruined cottages a happiness often quite as great as in kings' palaces, and a virtue and nearness to God infinitely greater and holier than can commonly be found in any other kind of place; so that the misery in which he exults is not, as he sees it, misery, but nobleness, "poor, and sick in body, and beloved by the Gods." And thus, being nowise sure that these things can be mended at all, and very sure that he knows not how to mend them, and also that the strange pleasure he feels in them *must* have some good reason in the nature of things, he yields to his destiny, enjoys his dark canal without scruple, and mourns over every improvement in the town, and every movement made by its sanitary commissioners, as a miser would over a planned robbery of his chest; in this being not only innocent, but even respectable and admirable, compared with the kind of person who has *no* pleasure in sights of this kind, but only in fair façades, trim gardens, and park palings, and who would thrust all poverty and misery out of his way, collecting it into back alleys, or sweeping it finally out of the world, so that the street might give wider play for his chariot wheels, and the breeze less offence to his nobility.

Therefore, even the love for the lower picturesque ought to be cultivated with care, wherever it exists; not with any special view to artistic, but to merely humane, education. It will never really or seriously interfere with practical benevolence; on the contrary, it will constantly lead, if associated with other benevolent principles, to a truer sympathy with the poor, and better understanding of the right ways of helping them; and, in the present stage of civilization, it is the most important element of character, not directly moral, which can be cultivated in youth; since it is mainly for the want of this feeling that we destroy so many ancient monuments, in order to erect "handsome" streets and shops instead, which might just as well have been erected elsewhere, and whose effect on our minds, so far as they have any, is to increase every disposition to frivolity, expense, and display.

1868

➤ END OF PERSPECTIVES: THE SUBLIME, THE BEAUTIFUL, AND THE PICTURESQUE ➤

Anna Letitia Barbauld
1743–1825

Anna Barbauld's long career exemplifies that of the professional woman of letters: a respected poet (and not only on conventionally feminine themes), a writer on radical causes throughout the 1790s, an early welcomer of Coleridge (who presented her with a prepublication copy of *Lyrical Ballads*), and a friend of Priestley, Hannah More, and Joanna Baillie. The daughter of John Aikin, master of Warrington Academy, a celebrated institution of English Dissenting culture where she lived between the ages of fifteen and thirty, Anna Letitia Aikin is said to have learned to read English by age three, Italian and French not long after, and Greek and Latin while still a child. Her first volume, *Poems* (1773), went through five editions in four years; in the same year, she published *Miscellaneous Pieces in Prose* with her brother John, later editor of the *Monthly Magazine*, an influential radical journal. In 1774 she married Rochemont Barbauld, a Dissenting clergyman, with whom she ran a school. Samuel Johnson derided the activity as the waste of a fine education, but it led to her often reprinted *Lessons for Children* (1778) and

Hymns in Prose for Children (1781). When her husband's increasing mental instability forced them to close their school, she undertook ambitious editorial projects. In 1794 she produced an edition of Akenside, one of Collins in 1797, and in 1804 a six-volume *Correspondence of Samuel Richardson*, followed by a fifty-volume set of *The British Novelists* (1810), with biographical introductions and a sophisticated preface arguing for the instructive value of a genre depreciated as mere entertainment, as well as a popular anthology for young women, *The Female Speaker* (1811). Like Wollstonecraft, she believed young women should be educated to become responsible wives and mothers. Our selection, ranging from the lively domestic realism of *Washing-Day* (1797) to the apocalyptic vision of England in decay, *Eighteen Hundred and Eleven* (1812), displays her versatility as a poet. *Washing-Day* moves from mock-epic to personal recollection to a recent scientific advance, Montgolfier's balloon ascent, effortlessly crossing the conventional boundaries of private and public, feminine and masculine, realms. *The First Fire* likewise surprisingly joins a celebration of the domestic hearth to a vista of geological process. The stark vision of *Eighteen Hundred and Eleven* marks the cultural pessimism that, after decades of war, had succeeded the Enlightenment optimism of her youth; though she continued writing until the 1820s, the harsh review its stern anti-imperialism provoked from John Wilson Croker in the conservative *Quarterly Review* nearly brought her career of publication to an end. His alarm over a woman daring to write about politics and his dismissal, as feminine illogic, of the bold transitions and startling prospects of the poem witness the force of Barbauld's achievement.

Selections by Barbauld also appear in Perspectives: Abolition of Slavery and the Slave Trade, page 259, and Responses: Wollstonecraft, page 326.

The Mouse's Petition to Dr. Priestley[1]

O hear a pensive prisoner's prayer,
    For liberty that sighs;
And never let thine heart be shut
    Against the wretch's cries!

5   For here forlorn and sad I sit,
        Within the wiry grate;
And tremble at the approaching morn,
    Which brings impending fate.

If e'er thy breast with freedom glowed,
10   And spurned a tyrant's chain,
Let not thy strong oppressive force
    A free-born mouse detain!

O do not stain with guiltless blood
    Thy hospitable hearth;
15 Nor triumph that thy wiles betrayed
    A prize so little worth.

The scattered gleanings of a feast
    My frugal meals supply;
But if thine unrelenting heart
20   That slender boon deny,—

1. The title in early editions is *The Mouse's Petition, Found in the trap where he had been confined all night*, accompanied by a motto from Virgil's *Aeneid* (6.853): "Parcere subjectis & debellare superbos" [To spare the conquered, and subdue the proud]. Joseph Priestley (1733–1804), political radical and eminent chemist who discovered oxygen, had been testing the properties of gases on captured household mice. Tradition has it that Barbauld's petition succeeded, and this mouse was released.

The cheerful light, the vital air,
　　Are blessings widely given;
Let nature's commoners enjoy
　　The common gifts of heaven.

25　The well-taught philosophic mind
　　To all compassion gives:
Casts round the world an equal eye,
　　And feels for all that lives.

If mind,—as ancient sages taught,—
30　　A never-dying flame,
Still shifts through matter's varying forms,
　　In every form the same;

Beware, lest in the worm you crush
　　A brother's soul you find;
35　And tremble lest thy luckless hand
　　Dislodge a kindred mind.

Or, if this transient gleam of day
　　Be *all* of life we share,
Let pity plead within thy breast
40　　That little *all* to spare.

So may thy hospitable board
　　With wealth and peace be crowned;
And every charm of heartfelt ease
　　Beneath thy roof be found.

45　So when destruction lurks unseen,
　　Which men, like mice, may share,
May some kind angel clear thy path,
　　And break the hidden snare.

1771　　　　　　　　　　　　　　　　1773

On a Lady's Writing

Her even lines her steady temper show,
Neat as her dress, and polished as her brow;
Strong as her judgment, easy as her air;
Correct though free, and regular though fair:
5　And the same graces o'er her pen preside,
That form her manners and her footsteps guide.

1773

Inscription for an Ice-House[1]

Stranger, approach! within this iron door
Thrice locked and bolted, this rude arch beneath

---

1. The ice-house, where blocks of ice were kept cold in the warmer months, was the commonest form of refrigeration before the twentieth century.

That vaults with ponderous stone the cell; confined
By man, the great magician, who controuls
5   Fire, earth and air, and genii of the storm,
And bends the most remote and opposite things
To do him service and perform his will,—
A giant sits; stern Winter; here he piles,
While summer glows around, and southern gales
10   Dissolve the fainting world, his treasured snows°   sherberts
Within the rugged cave.—Stranger, approach!
He will not cramp thy limbs with sudden age,
Nor wither with his touch the coyest flower
That decks thy scented hair. Indignant here,
15   Like fettered Sampson[2] when his might was spent
In puny feats to glad the festive halls
Of Gaza's wealthy sons; or he who sat
Midst laughing girls submiss, and patient twirled
The slender spindle in his sinewy grasp;[3]
20   The rugged power, fair Pleasure's minister,
Exerts his art to deck the genial board;
Congeals the melting peach, the nectarine smooth,
Burnished and glowing from the sunny wall:
Darts sudden frost into the crimson veins
25   Of the moist berry; moulds the sugared hail:
Cools with his icy breath our flowing cups;
Or gives to the fresh dairy's nectared bowls
A quicker zest. Sullen he plies his task,
And on his shaking fingers counts the weeks
30   Of lingering Summer, mindful of his hour
To rush in whirlwinds forth, and rule the year.

c. 1793   1825

To a Little Invisible Being
Who Is Expected Soon to Become Visible

Germ of new life, whose powers expanding slow
For many a moon their full perfection wait,—
Haste, precious pledge of happy love, to go
Auspicious borne through life's mysterious gate.

5   What powers lie folded in thy curious frame,—
Senses from objects locked, and mind from thought!
How little canst thou guess thy lofty claim
To grasp at all the worlds the Almighty wrought!

2. Judges 16 relates the imprisonment of the blinded
Samson in Gaza, forced to make "sport" for the Philistines; the story forms the subject of Milton's tragedy,

Samson Agonistes (1671).
3. In his term as slave to Queen Omphale, Hercules performed women's tasks.

And see, the genial season's warmth to share,
10   Fresh younglings shoot, and opening roses glow!
Swarms of new life exulting fill the air,—
Haste, infant bud of being, haste to blow!°   *bloom*

For thee the nurse prepares her lulling songs,
The eager matrons count the lingering day;
15   But far the most thy anxious parent longs
On thy soft cheek a mother's kiss to lay.

She only asks to lay her burden down,
That her glad arms that burden may resume;
And nature's sharpest pangs her wishes crown,
20   That free thee living from thy living tomb.

She longs to fold to her maternal breast
Part of herself, yet to herself unknown;
To see and to salute the stranger guest,
Fed with her life through many a tedious moon.

25   Come, reap thy rich inheritance of love!
Bask in the fondness of a Mother's eye!
Nor wit nor eloquence her heart shall move
Like the first accents of thy feeble cry.

Haste, little captive, burst thy prison doors!
30   Launch on the living world, and spring to light!
Nature for thee displays her various stores,
Opens her thousand inlets of delight.

If charmed verse of muttered prayers had power,
With favouring spells to speed thee on thy way,
35   Anxious I'd bid my beads° each passing hour,   *tell my rosary*
Till thy wished smile thy mother's pangs o'erpay.
c. 1795   1825

To the Poor[1]

Child of distress, who meet'st the bitter scorn
Of fellow men to happier prospects born,
Doomed art and nature's various stores to see
Flow in full cups of joy,—and not for thee,
5   Who seest the rich, to heaven and fate resign'd,
Bear *thy* afflictions with a patient mind;
Whose bursting heart disdains unjust controll,
Who feel'st oppression's iron in thy soul,
Who drag'st the load of faint and feeble years,
10   Whose bread is anguish and whose water tears—

---

1. Barbauld wrote that this poem was "inspired by indignation on hearing sermons in which the poor are addressed in a manner which evidently shows the design of making religion an engine of government."

Bear, bear thy wrongs, fulfil thy destined hour,
Bend thy meek neck beneath the foot of power!
But when thou feel'st the great deliverer nigh,
And thy freed spirit mounting seeks the sky,
15   Let no vain fears thy parting hour molest,
No whispered terrors shake thy quiet breast,
Think not their threats can work thy future woe,
Nor deem the Lord above, like Lords below.
Safe in the bosom of that love repose
20   By whom the sun gives light, the ocean flows,
Prepare to meet a father undismayed,
Nor fear the God whom priests and kings have made.

1795   1825

Washing-Day

"… And their voice,
Turning again towards childish treble, pipes
And whistles in its sound."[1]

The Muses are turned gossips; they have lost
The buskined° step, and clear, high-sounding phrase,   *tragic*
Language of gods. Come, then, domestic Muse,
In slipshod measure° loosely prattling on[2]   *loose meters*
5   Of farm or orchard, pleasant curds and cream,
Or drowning flies, or shoe lost in the mire
By little whimpering boy, with rueful face;
Come, Muse, and sing the dreaded Washing-day.
Ye who beneath the yoke of wedlock bend,
10   With bowed soul, full well ye ken the day
Which week, smooth sliding after week, brings on
Too soon;—for to that day nor peace belongs,
Nor comfort; ere the first gray streak of dawn,
The red-armed washers come and chase repose.
15   Nor pleasant smile, nor quaint device of mirth,
E'er visited that day: the very cat,
From the wet kitchen's scared and reeking° hearth,   *smoking*
Visits the parlor,—an unwonted guest.
The silent breakfast-meal is soon despatched;
20   Uninterrupted, save by anxious looks
Cast at the lowering° sky, if sky should lower.   *threatening*
From that last evil, O preserve us, heavens!
For should the skies pour down, adieu to all
Remains of quiet: then expect to hear
25   Of sad disasters,—dirt and gravel stains

---

1. See Shakespeare, *As You Like It*, 2.7.161–63, the 6th age in Jaques's description of the seven ages of man. Barbauld has changed "his big manly voice" to "And their voice," and "his sound" to "its sound."

2. Though loose shoes slip off and hobble this domestic Muse, Barbauld's verse line consists of well-fitted iambs (feet).

Hard to efface, and loaded lines at once
Snapped short,—and linen-horse° by dog thrown down,   *drying rack*
And all the petty miseries of life.
Saints have been calm while stretched upon the rack,
30   And Guatimozin³ smiled on burning coals;
But never yet did housewife notable°   *efficient*
Greet with a smile a rainy washing-day.
But grant the welkin° fair, require not thou   *the heavens*
Who call'st thyself perchance the master there,
35   Or study swept, or nicely dusted coat,
Or usual 'tendance,—ask not, indiscreet,
Thy stockings mended, though the yawning rents
Gape wide as Erebus;⁴ nor hope to find
Some snug recess impervious: shouldst thou try
40   The 'customed garden-walks, thine eyes shall rue
The budding fragrance of thy tender shrubs,
Myrtle or rose, all crushed beneath the weight
Of coarse checked apron,—with impatient hand
Twitched off when showers impend: or crossing lines
45   Shall mar thy musings, as the wet, cold sheet
Flaps in thy face abrupt. Woe to the friend
Whose evil stars have urged him forth to claim
On such a day the hospitable rites!
Looks, blank at best, and stinted courtesy,
50   Shall he receive. Vainly he feeds his hopes
With dinner of roast chicken, savory pie,
Or tart, or pudding:—pudding he nor tart
That day shall eat; nor, though the husband try,
Mending what can't be helped, to kindle mirth
55   From cheer deficient, shall his consort's brow
Clear up propitious: the unlucky guest
In silence dines, and early slinks away.
I well remember, when a child, the awe
This day struck into me; for then the maids,
60   I scarce knew why, looked cross, and drove me from them:
Nor soft caress could I obtain; nor hope
Usual indulgences; jelly or creams,
Relic of costly suppers, and set by
For me their petted one, or buttered toast,
65   When butter was forbid; or thrilling tale
Of ghost or witch or murder,—so I went
And sheltered me beside the parlor fire:
There my dear grandmother, eldest of forms,
Tended the little ones, and watched from harm,
70   Anxiously fond, though oft her spectacles

---

3. Cuauhtemoc, last Aztec emperor of Mexico, tortured
and executed by Cortés in 1525.   4. In Greek myth, the dark passage through which souls
enter Hades.

With elfin cunning hid, and oft the pins
Drawn from her ravelled stockings, might have soured
One less indulgent.—
At intervals my mother's voice was heard,
75 Urging despatch: briskly the work went on,
All hands employed to wash, to rinse, to wring,
To fold, and starch, and clap, and iron, and plait.
Then would I sit me down, and ponder much
Why washings were. Sometimes through hollow bowl
80 Of pipe amused we blew, and sent aloft
The floating bubbles; little dreaming then
To see, Montgolfier,[5] thy silken ball
Ride buoyant through the clouds,—so near approach
The sports of children and the toils of men.
85 Earth, air, and sky, and ocean hath its bubbles,
And verse is one of them,—this most of all.

1797

Eighteen Hundred and Eleven[1]

Still the loud death-drum, thundering from afar,
O'er the vext nations pours the storm of war:
To the stern call still Britain bends her ear,
Feeds the fierce strife, the alternate hope and fear;
5 Bravely, though vainly, dares to strive with Fate,
And seeks by turns to prop each sinking state.
Colossal power with overwhelming force
Bears down each foot of Freedom in its course;
Prostrate she lies beneath the despot's° sway,   *Napoleon's*
10 While the hushed nations curse him—and obey.

Bounteous in vain, with frantic man at strife,
Glad Nature pours the means—the joys of life;
In vain with orange-blossoms scents the gale,
The hills with olives clothes, with corn the vale;
15 Man calls to Famine, nor invokes in vain,
Disease and Rapine follow in her train;
The tramp of marching hosts disturbs the plough,
The sword, not sickle, reaps the harvest now,
And where the soldier gleans the scant supply,
20 The helpless peasant but retires to die;
No laws his hut from licensed outrage shield,
And war's least horror is the ensanguined field.

Fruitful in vain, the matron counts with pride
The blooming youths that grace her honored side;

---

5. In 1783, in France, the Montgolfier brothers launched the first hot-air balloon.
1. This dark satire was published as a quarto pamphlet. Its somber tone reflects the times: Britain had been at war with France almost continuously since 1793. At home, the economy had sunk, and distress was widespread; Napoleon controlled the Continent and blockaded British trade; George III had lapsed into madness; conditions with America were strained and verging on war, which broke out the following year.

25   No son returns to press her widowed hand,
        Her fallen blossoms strew a foreign strand.
        —Fruitful in vain, she boasts her virgin race,
        Whom cultured arts adorn and gentlest grace;
        Defrauded of its homage, Beauty mourns
30   And the rose withers on its virgin thorns.
        Frequent, some stream obscure, some uncouth name,
        By deeds of blood is lifted into fame;
        Oft o'er the daily page some soft one bends
        To learn the fate of husband, brothers, friends,
35   Or the spread map with anxious eye explores,
        Its dotted boundaries and pencilled shores,
        Asks where the spot that wrecked her bliss is found,
        And learns its name but to detest the sound.

        And think'st thou, Britain, still to sit at ease,
40   An island queen amidst thy subject seas,
        While the vext billows, in their distant roar,
        But soothe thy slumbers, and but kiss thy shore?
        To sport in wars, while danger keeps aloof,
        Thy grassy turf unbruised by hostile hoof?
45   So sing thy flatterers;—but, Britain, know,
        Thou who hast shared the guilt must share the woe.
        Nor distant is the hour; low murmurs spread,
        And whispered fears, creating what they dread;
        Ruin, as with an earthquake shock, is here,
50   There, the heart-witherings of unuttered fear,
        And that sad death, whence most affection bleeds,
        Which sickness, only of the soul, precedes.
        Thy baseless wealth dissolves in air away,
        Like mists that melt before the morning ray:[2]
55   No more on crowded mart or busy street
        Friends, meeting friends, with cheerful hurry greet;
        Sad, on the ground thy princely merchants bend
        Their altered looks, and evil days portend,
        And fold their arms, and watch with anxious breast
60   The tempest blackening in the distant West.°   the United States

        Yes, thou must droop; thy Midas dream is o'er;
        The golden tide of Commerce leaves thy shore,
        Leaves thee to prove the alternate ills that haunt
        Enfeebling Luxury and ghastly Want;
65   Leaves thee, perhaps, to visit distant lands,
        And deal the gifts of Heaven with equal hands.
        Yet, O my Country, name beloved, revered,
        By every tie that binds the soul endeared,
        Whose image to my infant senses came
70   Mixt with Religion's light and Freedom's holy flame!

2. Echoing Shakespeare's Prospero, on the vanishing of the illusions he has wrought; *The Tempest* 4.1.150–56.

If prayers may not avert, if 't is thy fate
To rank amongst the names that once were great,
Not like the dim, cold Crescent[3] shalt thou fade,
Thy debt to Science and the Muse unpaid;
75   Thine are the laws surrounding states revere,
Thine the full harvest of the mental year,
Thine the bright stars in Glory's sky that shine,
And arts that make it life to live are thine.
If westward streams the light that leaves thy shores,
80   Still from thy lamp the streaming radiance pours.
Wide spreads thy race from Ganges° to the pole,   *river in India*
O'er half the Western world thy accents roll:
Nations beyond the Apalachian hills[4]
Thy hand has planted and thy spirit fills:
85   Soon as their gradual progress shall impart
The finer sense of morals and of art,
Thy stores of knowledge the new states shall know,
And think thy thoughts, and with thy fancy glow;
Thy Lockes, thy Paleys,[5] shall instruct their youth,
90   Thy leading star direct their search for truth;
Beneath the spreading platane's° tent-like shade,   *Asian plane-tree*
Or by Missouri's rushing waters laid,
"Old Father Thames" shall be the poet's theme,
Of Hagley's woods[6] the enamored virgin dream,
95   And Milton's tones the raptured ear enthrall,
Mixt with the roaring of Niagara's fall;
In Thomson's glass the ingenuous youth shall learn
A fairer face of Nature to discern;
Nor of the bards that swept the British lyre
100   Shall fade one laurel, or one note expire.
Then, loved Joanna,[7] to admiring eyes
Thy storied groups in scenic pomp shall rise;
Their high-souled strains and Shakespeare's noble rage
Shall with alternate passion shake the stage.
105   Some youthful Basil from thy moral lay
With stricter hand his fond desires shall sway;
Some Ethwald, as the fleeting shadows pass,
Start at his likeness in the mystic glass;
The tragic Muse resume her just control,
110   With pity and with terror purge the soul,
While wide o'er transatlantic realms thy name

3. Symbol of the Muslim empire.
4. The United States had begun to expand westward with the Louisiana Purchase of 1803.
5. John Locke, author of *An Essay Concerning Human Understanding* (1690) and *Two Treatises on Civil Government* (1690); William Paley, author of *The Principles of Moral and Political Philosophy* (1785), *Evidences of*

Christianity (1794), and *Natural Theology* (1802).
6. The estate of Lord Lyttelton, celebrated in *The Seasons* (1726–1730), a poem by James Thomson ("Thomson's glass," i.e., mirror, line 97).
7. Joanna Baillie, whose *Plays on the Passions* include *Count Basil* (1798) and *Ethwald* (1802).

Shall live in light and gather all its fame.

Where wanders Fancy down the lapse of years,
Shedding o'er imaged woes untimely tears?
115   Fond, moody power! as hopes—as fears prevail,
She longs, or dreads, to lift the awful veil,
On visions of delight now loves to dwell,
Now hears the shriek of woe or Freedom's knell:
Perhaps, she says, long ages past away,
120   And set in western wave our closing day,
Night, Gothic night, again may shade the plains
Where Power is seated, and where Science reigns;
England, the seat of arts, be only known
By the gray ruin and the mouldering stone;
125   That Time may tear the garland from her brow,
And Europe sit in dust, as Asia now.

Yet then the ingenuous youth whom Fancy fires
With pictured glories of illustrious sires,
With duteous zeal their pilgrimage shall take
130   From the Blue Mountains,° or Ontario's lake,   *in Pennsylvania*
With fond, adoring steps to press the sod
By statesmen, sages, poets, heroes, trod;
On Isis'° banks to draw inspiring air,   *river in Oxford*
From Runnymede[8] to send the patriot's prayer;
135   In pensive thought, where Cam's° slow waters wind,   *Cambridge river*
To meet those shades that ruled the realms of mind;
In silent halls to sculptured marbles bow,
And hang fresh wreaths round Newton's awful brow.[9]
Oft shall they seek some peasant's homely shed,
140   Who toils, unconscious of the mighty dead,
To ask where Avon's winding waters[1] stray,
And thence a knot of wild flowers bear away;
Anxious inquire where Clarkson,[2] friend of man,
Or all-accomplished Jones[3] his race began;
145   If of the modest mansion aught remains
Where Heaven and Nature prompted Cowper's strains;[4]
Where Roscoe, to whose patriot breast belong
The Roman virtue and the Tuscan song,
Led Ceres to the black and barren moor
150   Where Ceres never gained a wreath before:[5]
With curious search their pilgrim steps shall rove
By many a ruined tower and proud alcove,
Shall listen for those strains that soothed of yore

---

8. The meadow on the banks of the Thames where King
John signed the Magna Carta in 1215.
9. Sir Isaac Newton (1642–1727), philosopher, physicist,
and mathematician, was professor at Cambridge University.
1. In Stratford, home of Shakespeare.
2. Abolitionist Thomas Clarkson.
3. Sir William Jones (1746–1794), distinguished scholar
of Indian language and law.

4. The poet William Cowper, here cited as author of *Olney
Hymns* (1779).
5. William Roscoe (1753–1831), noted agricultural im-
prover, a scholar, and opponent of the war. The claim that
he led Ceres, Roman goddess of agriculture, where she
had never succeeded before, alludes to his achievement of
growing high-quality crops on moorland.

Thy rock, stern Skiddaw, and thy fall, Lodore;[6]
155 Feast with Dun Edin's° classic brow their sight,   *Edinburgh's*
And "visit Melross by the pale moonlight."[7]

But who their mingled feelings shall pursue
When London's faded glories rise to view?
The mighty city, which by every road,
160 In floods of people poured itself abroad
Ungirt by walls, irregularly great,
No jealous drawbridge, and no closing gate;
Whose merchants (such the state which commerce brings)
Sent forth their mandates to dependent kings;
165 Streets, where the turbaned Moslem, bearded Jew,
And woolly Afric, met the brown Hindu;
Where through each vein spontaneous plenty flowed,
Where Wealth enjoyed, and Charity bestowed.
Pensive and thoughtful shall the wanderers greet
170 Each splendid square, and still, untrodden street;
Or of some crumbling turret, mined by time,
The broken stairs with perilous step shall climb,
Thence stretch their view the wide horizon round,
By scattered hamlets trace its ancient bound,
175 And, choked no more with fleets, fair Thames survey
Through reeds and sedge pursue his idle way.

With throbbing bosoms shall the wanderers tread
The hallowed mansions of the silent dead.
Shall enter the long aisle and vaulted dome°   *St. Paul's Cathedral*
180 Where Genius and where Valor find a home;
Awe-struck 'midst chill sepulchral marbles breathe,
Where all above is still, as all beneath;
Bend at each antique shrine, and frequent turn
To clasp with fond delight some sculptured urn,
185 The ponderous mass of Johnson's form to greet,
Or breathe the prayer at Howard's sainted feet.[8]

Perhaps some Briton, in whose musing mind
Those ages live which Time has cast behind,
To every spot shall lead his wondering guests
190 On whose known site the beam of glory rests;
Here Chatham's[9] eloquence in thunder broke,
Here Fox persuaded, or here Garrick[1] spoke;
Shall boast how Nelson,[2] fame and death in view,

---

6. Skiddaw, a mountain, and Lodore, the site of a waterfall, are two tourist spots in the Lake District.
7. Sir Walter Scott, *The Lay of the Last Minstrel* 2.1. The
ruined abbey was famously picturesque.
8. Statues of critic and lexicographer Samuel Johnson
(1709–1784) and prison reformer John Howard (1726–
1790) stand in the nave of St. Paul's Cathedral.
9. William Pitt, first Earl of Chatham (1708–1778), a famous orator and the dominant political figure of his time.

1. Charles James Fox (1749–1806), leader of the Whig
opposition; David Garrick (1717–1779), celebrated
Shakespearean actor.
2. "Every reader will recollect the sublime telegraphic
dispatch, 'England expects every man to do his duty'"
[Barbauld's note], sent by Admiral Horatio Nelson
(1758–1805), to his fleet, just before he was killed in the
victory of the Battle of Trafalgar.

To wonted victory led his ardent crew,
195 In England's name enforced, with loftiest tone,
Their duty,—and too well fulfilled his own:
How gallant Moore,[3] as ebbing life dissolved,
But hoped his country had his fame absolved.
Or call up sages whose capacious mind
200 Left in its course a track of light behind;
Point where mute crowds on Davy's[4] lips reposed,
And Nature's coyest secrets were disclosed;
Join with their Franklin, Priestley's injured name,[5]
Whom, then, each continent shall proudly claim.

205 Oft shall the strangers turn their eager feet
The rich remains of ancient art to greet,
The pictured walls with critic eye explore,
And Reynolds be what Raphael was before.[6]
On spoils from every clime their eyes shall gaze,
210 Egyptian granites and the Etruscan vase;
And when 'midst fallen London they survey
The stone where Alexander's ashes lay,[7]
Shall own with humbled pride the lesson just
By Time's slow finger written in the dust.

215 There walks a Spirit o'er the peopled earth,
Secret his progress is, unknown his birth;
Moody and viewless° as the changing wind,   *invisible, unseeing*
No force arrests his foot, no chains can bind;
Where'er he turns, the human brute awakes,
220 And, roused to better life, his sordid hut forsakes:
He thinks, he reasons, glows with purer fires,
Feels finer wants, and burns with new desires:
Obedient Nature follows where he leads;
The steaming marsh is changed to fruitful meads;
225 The beasts retire from man's asserted reign,
And prove his kingdom was not given in vain.
Then from its bed is drawn the ponderous ore,
Then Commerce pours her gifts on every shore,
Then Babel's towers and terraced gardens rise,
230 And pointed obelisks invade the skies;
The prince commands, in Tyrian purple drest,
And Egypt's virgins weave the linen vest.
Then spans the graceful arch the roaring tide,
And stricter bounds the cultured fields divide.
235 Then kindles Fancy, then expands the heart,

3. "I hope England will be satisfied," were the last words of General Moore [Barbauld's note]. Sir John Moore died while commanding the British retreat at the Battle of Coruña (1809).
4. Sir Humphry Davy (1778–1829), inventor of the miner's safety lamp, gave public lectures on chemistry at the Royal Institution.
5. Benjamin Franklin (1706–1790) and Joseph Priestley corresponded about their work on electricity.

6. Sir Joshua Reynolds (1723–1792), leading British portrait painter and first president of the Royal Academy; Raffaelo Sanzio (1483–1520), great Italian Renaissance artist.
7. A sarcophagus brought for display at the recently opened British Museum in 1802 was thought to be that of Alexander the Great; among the "Egyptian granites" was the Rosetta stone.

Then blow° the flowers of Genius and of Art;   bloom
Saints, heroes, sages, who the land adorn,
Seem rather to descend than to be born;
While History, 'midst the rolls consigned to fame,
240   With pen of adamant inscribes their name.

The Genius now forsakes the favored shore,[8]
And hates, capricious, what he loved before;
Then empires fall to dust, then arts decay,
And wasted realms enfeebled despots sway;°   rule
245   Even Nature's changed; without his fostering smile
Ophir° no gold, no plenty yields the Nile;   region famed for gold
The thirsty sand absorbs the useless rill,
And spotted plagues from putrid fens distil.
In desert solitudes then Tadmor sleeps,
250   Stern Marius then o'er fallen Carthage weeps;[9]
Then with enthusiast love the pilgrim roves
To seek his footsteps in forsaken groves,
Explores the fractured arch, the ruined tower,
Those limbs disjointed of gigantic power;
255   Still at each step he dreads the adder's sting,
The Arab's javelin, or the tiger's spring;
With doubtful caution treads the echoing ground,
And asks where Troy or Babylon is found.
And now the vagrant Power no more detains
260   The vale of Tempe or Ausonian plains;[1]
Northward he throws the animating ray,
O'er Celtic nations bursts the mental day;
And, as some playful child the mirror turns,
Now here, now there, the moving lustre burns;
265   Now o'er his changeful fancy more prevail
Batavia's dykes than Arno's purple vale;[2]
And stinted suns, and rivers bound with frost,
Than Enna's plains or Baia's viny coast;
Venice the Adriatic weds in vain,
270   And Death sits brooding o'er Campania's plain;[3]
O'er Baltic shores and through Hercynian groves,°   the Black Forest
Stirring the soul, the mighty impulse moves;
Art plies his tools, and Commerce spreads her sail,
And wealth is wafted in each shifting gale.
275   The sons of Odin° tread on Persian looms,   Norsemen

---

8. See Milton's elegy, *Lycidas*, 183.

9. Tadmor is the biblical name for Palmyra, an ancient Syrian city. Roman consul Gaius Marius (157–86 B.C.E.), vanquished by Sulla, fled to Africa, where he was denied entry. Plutarch records his lament to the governor: "Tell him, then, that thou hast seen Marius a fugitive, seated amid the ruins of Carthage" (a city destroyed by the Romans in 146 B.C.E.).

1. Tempe is in Greece; Ausonia is Virgil's name for Italy: hence, the realms of classical literature.

2. Batavia is the Netherlands; the Arno flows through Florence.

3. Enna is a valley in Sicily; Baia is a Roman resort on the Bay of Naples. In a grand annual ceremony, Venice symbolically wed the Adriatic. The infamous swamps of Campania enclose Capua and Naples.

And Odin's daughters breathe distilled perfumes;
Loud minstrel bards, in Gothic halls, rehearse
The Runic rhyme, and "build the lofty verse."[4]
The Muse, whose liquid notes were wont to swell
280   To the soft breathings of the Æolian shell,
Submits, reluctant, to the harsher tone,
And scarce believes the altered voice her own.
And now, where Cæsar saw with proud disdain
The wattled hut and skin of azure stain,[5]
285   Corinthian columns rear their graceful forms,
And light verandas brave the wintry storms,
While British tongues the fading fame prolong
Of Tully's eloquence and Maro's song.[6]
Where once Bonduca[7] whirled the scythed car,
290   And the fierce matrons raised the shriek of war,
Light forms beneath transparent muslins float,
And tutored voices swell the artful note.
Light-leaved acacias and the shady plane
And spreading cedar grace the woodland reign;
295   While crystal walls the tenderer plants confine,
The fragrant orange and the nectared pine;
The Syrian grape there hangs her rich festoons,
Nor asks for purer air or brighter noons:
Science and Art urge on the useful toil,
300   New mould a climate and create the soil,
Subdue the rigor of the Northern Bear,
O'er polar climes shed aromatic air,
On yielding Nature urge their new demands,
And ask not gifts, but tribute, at her hands.

305   London exults:—on London Art bestows
Her summer ices and her winter rose;
Gems of the East her mural crown adorn,
And Plenty at her feet pours forth her horn.°   *cornucopia*
While even the exiles her just laws disclaim,
310   People a continent, and build a name:
August she sits, and with extended hands
Holds forth the book of life to distant lands.

But fairest flowers expand but to decay;
The worm is in thy core, thy glories pass away;
315   Arts, arms, and wealth destroy the fruits they bring;
Commerce, like beauty, knows no second spring.
Crime walks thy streets, Fraud earns her unblest bread,

4. Milton, *Lycidas* (1637): "Who would not sing for Lycidas? he knew / Himself to sing, and build the lofty rhyme"
(10–11). Runic: mysteriously lettered.
5. In *Gallic Wars*, Julius Caesar noted that the ancient
Scots wore blue warpaint.

6. Marcus Tullius Cicero (106–43 B.C.E.) won renown for
his denunciations of the traitor Catiline; "Maro" is the
surname of Virgil (70–19 B.C.E.), author of the *Aeneid*.
7. Celtic queen who revolted against the Romans, and
took her own life when she was finally defeated (61 C.E.).

O'er want and woe thy gorgeous robe is spread,
And angel charities in vain oppose:
320   With grandeur's growth the mass of misery grows.
For, see,—to other climes the Genius soars,
He turns from Europe's desolated shores;
And lo! even now, 'midst mountains wrapt in storm,
On Andes' heights he shrouds his awful form;
325   On Chimborazo's summits treads sublime,
Measuring in lofty thought the march of Time;
Sudden he calls: "'Tis now the hour!" he cries,
Spreads his broad hand, and bids the nations rise.
La Plata hears amidst her torrents' roar;
330   Potosi hears it, as she digs the ore:[8]
Ardent, the Genius fans the noble strife,
And pours through feeble souls a higher life,
Shouts to the mingled tribes from sea to sea,
And swears—Thy world, Columbus, shall be free.[9]

1811   1812

RESPONSE

John Wilson Croker: from *A Review of* Eighteen Hundred and Eleven[1]

Our old acquaintance Mrs. Barbauld turned satirist! The last thing we should have expected, and, now that we have seen her satire, the last thing that we could have desired.

May we (without derogating too much from that reputation of age and gravity of which critics should be so chary) confess that we are yet young enough to have had early obligations to Mrs. Barbauld; and that it really is with no disposition to retaliate on the fair pedagogue of our former life, that on the present occasion, we have called her up to correct her exercise?

But she must excuse us if we think that she has wandered from the course in which she was respectable and useful, and miserably mistaken both her powers and her duty, in exchanging the birchen for the satiric rod, and abandoning the superintendance of the "ovilia" [lambs] of the nursery, to wage war on the "reluctantes dracones" [struggling lawgivers], statesmen, and warriors, whose misdoings have aroused her indignant muse.

We had hoped, indeed, that the empire might have been saved without the intervention of a lady-author: we even flattered ourselves that the interests of Europe

---

8. The first of a series of references to the spreading resistance to colonialism in South America: the Andes are mountains in Peru; Chimborazo is a mountain in Equador; La Plata, a city in Argentina; Potosi, a city in Bolivia, celebrated for its silver.
9. Landing in the Caribbean islands in 1492, Columbus claimed Central and South America for Spain.
1. Published in 1812 in the seventh issue of the *Quarterly Review*. Croker established a reputation in his native Ireland as an academic, man of letters, and lawyer. He entered Parliament in 1806 and served until the Reform Bill of 1832, which he opposed. His knowledge of Irish affairs

quickly drew Tory favor: he was backed by Arthur Wellesley, later the Duke of Wellington, and in 1810 became secretary to the admiralty, a crucial post in wartime Britain that he held until 1830. Croker was an authority on the French Revolution and an editor of 18th-century memoirs and letters, but his notoriety rests on his writing for the *Quarterly Review*, from its founding in 1809 until 1845. His reviews include a savaging of Keats's *Endymion* (1818), and he was particularly harsh on works by women. His biases were repaid in kind. William Hazlitt, wielding an ethnic slur, called him "a talking potato"; Thomas Babington Macaulay "detested [him] more than cold boiled veal."

and of humanity would in some degree have swayed our public councils, without the descent of (dea ex machina)[2] Mrs. Anna Letitia Barbauld in a quarto, upon the theatre where the great European tragedy is now performing. Not such, however, is her opinion; an irresistible impulse of public duty—a confident sense of commanding talents—have induced her to dash down her shagreen[3] spectacles and her knitting needles, and to sally forth. ***

The poem, for so out of courtesy we shall call it, is entitled Eighteen Hundred and Eleven, we suppose, because it was written in the year 1811; but this is a mere conjecture, founded rather on our inability to assign any other reason for the name, than in any particular relation which the poem has to the events of the last year. We do not, we confess, very satisfactorily comprehend the meaning of all the verses which this fatidical [prophetic] spinster has drawn from her poetical distaff;[4] but of what we do understand we very confidently assert that there is not a topic in "Eighteen Hundred and Eleven" which is not quite as applicable to 1810 or 1812, and which, in our opinion, might not, with equal taste and judgment, have been curtailed, or dilated, or transposed, or omitted, without any injustice whatever to the title of the poem, and without producing the slightest discrepancy between the frontispiece and the body of the work. ***

Upon this melancholy night, however, a bright day dawns, and all the little sense with which Mrs. Barbauld set out, now dissolves away in blissful visions of American glory. This Genius of her's which "walks the *peopled* earth," "viewless and secret," suddenly *appears* walking on the summit of Chimberaço, (which never was nor can be *peopled*,) displays his "*viewless*" form on the Andes, and "*secretly*" arouses, by loud exclamations, all the nations of the western continent.

> 'Ardent the Genius fans the noble strife,
> And pours through feeble souls a higher life;
> Shouts to the mingled tribes from sea to sea,
> And *swears*—Thy world, Columbus, shall be free.' [331–34]

And with this oath concludes "Eighteen Hundred and Eleven," upon which we have already wasted too much time. One word, however, we must seriously add. Mrs. Barbauld's former works have been of some utility; her "Lessons for Children," her "Hymns in Prose," her "Selections from the Spectator," et id genus omne [works of that kind], though they display not much of either taste or talents, are yet something better than harmless: but we must take the liberty of warning her to desist from satire, which indeed is satire on herself alone; and of entreating, with great earnestness, that she will not, for the sake of this ungrateful generation, put herself to the trouble of writing any more party pamphlets in verse. We also assure her, that we should not by any means impute it to want of taste or patriotism on her part, if, for her country, her fears were less confident, and for America her hopes less ardent; and if she would leave both the victims and the heroes of her political prejudices to the respective judgment which the impartiality of posterity will not fail to pronounce.

---

2. God(dess) from a machine, a device of Greek drama that became a term for a sudden, magical resolution.
3. An untanned leather.

4. The slur as spinster (unmarriageable woman) was nasty—Barbauld had recently been widowed. A distaff holds wool for spinning.

The First Fire
October 1st, 1815

Ha, old acquaintance! many a month has past
Since last I viewed thy ruddy face; and I,
Shame on me! had mean time well nigh forgot
That such a friend existed. Welcome now!—
5   When summer suns ride high, and tepid airs
Dissolve in pleasing langour; then indeed
We think thee needless, and in wanton pride
Mock at thy grim attire and sooty jaws,
And breath sulphureous, generating spleen,—
10   As Frenchmen say; Frenchmen, who never knew
The sober comforts of a good coal fire.
—Let me imbibe thy warmth, and spread myself
Before thy shrine adoring:—magnet thou
Of strong attraction, daily gathering in
15   Friends, brethren, kinsmen, variously dispersed,
All the dear charities of social life,
To thy close circle. Here a man might stand,
And say, This is my world! Who would not bleed
Rather than see thy violated hearth
20   Prest by a hostile foot? The winds sing shrill;
Heap on the fuel! Not the costly board,
Nor sparkling glass, nor wit, nor music, cheer
Without thy aid. If thrifty thou dispense
Thy gladdening influence, in the chill saloon
25   The silent shrug declares th' unpleased guest.
—How grateful to belated traveller
Homeward returning, to behold the blaze
From cottage window, rendering visible
The cheerful scene within! There sits the sire,
30   Whose wicker chair, in sunniest nook enshrined,
His age's privilege,—a privilege for which
Age gladly yields up all precedence else
In gay and bustling scenes,—supports his limbs.
Cherished by thee, he feels the grateful warmth
35   Creep through his feeble frame and thaw the ice
Of fourscore years, and thoughts of youth arise.
—Nor less the young ones press within, to see
Thy face delighted, and with husk of nuts,
Or crackling holly, or the gummy pine,
40   Feed thy immortal hunger: cheaply pleased
They gaze delighted, while the leaping flames
Dart like an adder's tongue upon their prey;

Or touch with lighted reed thy wreaths of smoke;
Or listen, while the matron sage remarks
45   Thy bright blue scorching flame and aspect clear,
Denoting frosty skies. Thus pass the hours,
While Winter spends without his idle rage.

—Companion of the solitary man,
From gayer scenes withheld! With thee he sits,
50   Converses, moralizes; musing asks
How many eras of uncounted time
Have rolled away since thy black unctuous° food   *oily*
Was green with vegetative life, and what
This planet then: or marks, in sprightlier mood,
55   Thy flickering smiles play round the illumined room,
And fancies gay discourse, life, motion, mirth,
And half forgets he is a lonely creature.

—Nor less the bashful poet loves to sit
Snug, at the midnight hour, with only thee
60   Of his lone musings conscious. Oft he writes,
And blots, and writes again; and oft, by fits,
Gazes intent with eyes of vacancy
On thy bright face; and still at intervals,
Dreading the critic's scorn, to thee commits,
65   Sole confidant and safe, his fancies crude.

—O wretched he, with bolts and massy bars
In narrow cell immured, whose green, damp walls,
That weep unwholesome dews, have never felt
Thy purifying influence! Sad he sits
70   Day after day till in his youthful limbs
Life stagnates, and the hue of hope is fled
From his wan cheek. And scarce less wretched he,—
When wintry winds blow loud and frosts bite keen,—
The dweller of the clay-built tenement,
75   Poverty-struck, who, heart[h]less,[1] strives to raise
From sullen turf, or stick plucked from the hedge,
The short-lived blaze; while chill around him spreads
The dreary fen, and Ague, sallow-faced,
Stares through the broken pane;—assist him, ye
80   On whose warm roofs the sun of plenty shines,
And feel a glow beyond material fire!

1815   1825

---

1. The word in the 1825 *Poems*, "heartless," is an error for "hearthless." This usage predates, by two years, the first entry in OED.

On the Death of the Princess Charlotte[1]

Yes, Britain mourns, as with electric touch,[2]
For youth, for love, for happiness destroyed.
Her universal population melts
In grief spontaneous, and hard hearts are moved,
5   And rough unpolished natures learn to feel
For those they envied, leveled in the dust
By fate's impartial stroke; and pulpits sound
With vanity and woe to earthly goods,
And urge and dry the tear—Yet one[3] there is
10   Who midst this general burst of grief remains
In strange tranquillity; whom not the stir
And long-drawn murmurs of the gathering crowd,
That by his very windows trail the pomp
Of hearse, and blazoned arms, and long array
15   Of sad funeral rites, nor the long groans
And deep-felt anguish of a husband's heart
Can move to mingle with this flood one tear:
In careless apathy, perhaps in mirth,
He wears the day. Yet is he near in blood,
20   The very stem on which this blossom grew,
And at his knees she fondled in the charm
And grace spontaneous which alone belongs
To untaught infancy:—Yet O forbear!
Nor deem him hard of heart; for awful, struck
25   By heaven's severest visitation, sad,
Like a scathed oak amidst the forest trees,
Lonely he stands; leaves bud, and shoot, and fall;
He holds no sympathy with living nature
Or time's incessant change. Then in this hour,
30   While pensive thought is busy with the woes
And restless change of poor humanity,
Think then, O think of him, and breathe one prayer,
From the full tide of sorrow spare one tear,
For him who does not weep!

1818   1819, 1825

---

1. Charlotte Augusta, daughter of the Prince Regent and wife of Leopold of Saxe-Coburg, died in childbirth on 6 November 1817; the baby was stillborn. She was 21, widely popular, and the presumptive heiress to the throne. The mourning for her was general, a combination of sincere grief and political manipulation.
2. Electricity was the new science (and pseudoscience). Mesmerism, based on the theory of animal magnetism propounded by F. A. Mesmer (1737–1815), enjoyed a vogue; the demonstration of electric response in a frog by Luigi Galvani (1737–1798) and the invention of the battery in 1800 by his friend Alessandro Volta (1745–1827) enabled dramatic advances in chemistry by Humphry Davy and other scientists.
3. George III had again lapsed into madness (now thought to be porphyria) in 1810, necessitating the creation of the regency in 1811; shortly afterward he lost his sight. Barbauld had written a sympathetic poem on his afflictions at the time. William McCarthy, one of her modern editors, reads "one" as referring to the Regent, criticized for his indifference to his daughter; he did not attend her funeral.

Charlotte Smith
1749–1806

Charlotte Smith was already famous for her *Elegiac Sonnets* when Cambridge student William Wordsworth sought her out in Brighton on his way to France in 1791. In addition to Wordsworth (who would read her sonnets in 1802 to encourage his own exercise in the form) her admirers included Samuel Taylor Coleridge, who credited her and W. L. Bowles (see page 626) for the sonnet-revival in his generation. Bowles's influence flowed from Smith's success. Wordsworth was impressed by her "true feeling for rural nature," so he reflected in the 1830s. In the 1790s, Coleridge cited her sonnets as an "exquisite" example of how "moral Sentiments, Affections, or Feelings" could be "deduced from, and associated with, the scenery of Nature." Smith's poetry involves literary associations, too, full of echoes of, quotations of, and allusions to a host of English poets, as well as Petrarch and Goethe.

Their emotional tone was proved on the pulses of her mostly miserable life. Charlotte Turner was born into a world of comfortable elegance, and although her mother died in childbirth three years later, her youth passed pleasantly enough between her father's London townhouse and Sussex estate. She read avidly and was tutored in landscape painting, dancing, and acting—all evident in her poetic art. This girlhood life came to a sharp conclusion just before her sixteenth birthday, with an arranged marriage to twenty-one-year-old Benjamin Smith, spendthrift heir to a West Indian business and prone to womanizing and temper tantrums. Knowing his son's failings, Benjamin's father wrote a complicated will of inheritance, but the result was decades of litigation, not sorted out until long after the deaths of Benjamin and Charlotte in 1806. By late 1783, Benjamin had landed in debtors' prison, where Charlotte, leaving their children with her brother, joined him for seven months. On his release in 1784, they fled to France. Pregnant with her twelfth child (she had fourteen in all, three dying in early childhood), Charlotte then moved the entire family to France. By 1785, she had had enough, and legally separated from her husband and returned to England to earn a living as a writer (the deadbeat continued to press legal claims to her income for years afterward). Much earlier than this, Smith realized she would have to support herself and her children, and she found immediate success with her first publication, its title marked by her misery, her lost life of luxury, and her determination to make a name for herself: *Elegiac Sonnets, and Other Essays by Charlotte Smith of Bignor Park, in Sussex*. Its popularity led to eight more, ever-expanding editions over the next sixteen years (we use the ninth [1800], the last she supervised). She also proved a prodigious novelist. Of the ten, *The Old Manor House* (1793) was popular through the nineteenth century, and *Desmond* (1792), a romance set amidst the French Revolution, has attracted fresh attention today. She also published two long, remarkable poems in blank verse. *The Emigrants* (1793), a complex meditation on Britain's relationship to France in the wake of the Revolution (1793 saw the Terror and Britain's entry into war against France), ultimately evolves into a passionate, maternal indictment of warfare. Her ideals of social justice, which she esteemed in poet Robert Burns (see her sonnet page 405), endured.

Smith's long-twinned interests in pedagogy and in nature—not transcendent "visionary nature" or material transformed by the sublime self, but a realm of phenomena to be studied and classified—shape her *Conversations, Introducing Poetry; chiefly on subjects of natural history, for the use of children and young persons* (1804). In these exchanges a mother enlists poetry to educate her children's response to, and understanding of, the natural world. Smith's final work, *Beachy Head* (published posthumously in 1807 by radical bookseller Joseph Johnson) is also a generic mixture: in blank verse punctuated by rhymed lyrics, she produces autobiographical reminiscence, topographical description, geological speculation, reflections on history and natural science (botany and zoology), small narratives, and a final tale of pathos. The Advertisement to *Beachy Head and Other Poems* remarks that the title poem was "not completed according to the original design" because of "the increasing debility of its author."

from ELEGIAC SONNETS AND OTHER POEMS

Sonnet IV: To the Moon

QUEEN of the silver bow![1]—by thy pale beam,
    Alone and pensive, I delight to stray,
And watch thy shadow trembling in the stream,
    Or mark the floating clouds that cross thy way.
5   And while I gaze, thy mild and placid light
    Sheds a soft calm upon my troubled breast;
And oft I think—fair planet of the night,
    That in thy orb, the wretched may have rest:
The sufferers of the earth perhaps may go,
10   Releas'd by death—to thy benignant sphere,
And the sad children of despair and woe
    Forget in thee, their cup of sorrow here.
Oh! that I soon may reach thy world serene,
Poor wearied pilgrim—in this toiling scene!

Sonnet XXVII

SIGHING I see yon little troop at play;
    By sorrow yet untouch'd; unhurt by care;
While free and sportive they enjoy to-day,
    "Content and careless of to-morrow's fare!"[1]
5   Oh happy age! when Hope's unclouded ray
    Lights their green path, and prompts their simple mirth,
Ere yet they feel the thorns that lurking lay
    To wound the wretched pilgrims of the earth,
Making them rue the hour that gave them birth,
10   And threw them on a world so full of pain,
Where prosperous folly treads on patient worth,
    And to deaf pride, misfortune pleads in vain!
Ah! for their future fate how many fears
    Oppress my heart—and fill mine eyes with tears![2]

---

1. Diana, the goddess of the moon, is an archer.
1. Thomson [Smith's note]. In James Thomson's *Autumn* (1730), "lovely young Lavinia," favored by "Fortune" then betrayed to poverty, withdraws with her "widow'd mother, feeble, old" (181) into a secluded vale, to avoid the scorn of the world, and "Almost on Nature's common bounty fed; / Like the gay birds that sung them to repose, / Content, and careless of to-morrow's fare" (189–91).
2. A knowing reprise of Thomas Gray's famous *Ode on a Distant Prospect of Eton College* (1747), which sighs even of privileged Eton schoolboys, "Alas, regardless of their doom, / The little victims play! / No sense have they of ills to come, / Nor care beyond today" (51–54).

Plate 1.   Sonnet 4.

Arbould del   Milton sculp.

Publish'd Jan.ʳ 1 1789 by T. Cadell, Strand.

Queen of the Silver Bow, &c.

Engraving for Sonnet IV: "To the Moon," frontispiece to volume 1 of Smith's *Elegiac Sonnets and Other Poems*, 8th ed. (1797). Courtesy of Princeton University Library.

To melancholy. Written on the banks of the Arun October, 1785

When latest Autumn spreads her evening veil,
    And the grey mists from these dim waves arise,
    I love to listen to the hollow sighs,
Thro' the half-leafless wood that breathes the gale:
5 For at such hours the shadowy phantom pale,
    Oft seems to fleet before the poet's eyes;
    Strange sounds are heard, and mournful melodies,
As of night-wanderers, who their woes bewail!
Here, by his native stream, at such an hour,
10 Pity's own Otway I methinks could meet,[1]
    And hear his deep sighs swell the sadden'd wind!
O Melancholy!—such thy magic power,
    That to the soul these dreams are often sweet,
    And soothe the pensive visionary mind!

                                            1800

Far on the sands

Far on the sands, the low, retiring tide,
    In distant murmurs hardly seems to flow,
And o'er the world of waters, blue and wide,
    The sighing summer-wind forgets to blow.
5 As sinks the day star° in the rosy West,   *sun*
    The silent wave, with rich reflection glows;
Alas! can tranquil nature give *me* rest,
    Or scenes of beauty, soothe me to repose?
Can the soft lustre of the sleeping main,°   *sea*
10 Yon radiant heaven, or all creation's charms,
"Erase the written troubles of the brain,"[1]
    Which Memory tortures, and which Guilt alarms?
Or bid a bosom transient quiet prove,
That bleeds with vain remorse, and unextinguish'd love!

                                            1800

To tranquillity

In this tumultuous sphere, for thee unfit,
    How seldom art thou found—Tranquillity!
    Unless 'tis when with mild and downcast eye
By the low cradles, thou delight'st to sit
5 Of sleeping infants—watching the soft breath,
    And bidding the sweet slumberers easy lie;

---

1. Thomas Otway (1652–1685), a dramatist known for pathos.
1. When Macbeth asks his wife's doctor, "Canst thou not minister to a mind diseased, / Pluck from the memory of a rooted sorrow, / Raze out the written troubles of the brain?" he replies, "Therein the patient / Must minister to himself" (*Macbeth* 5.3.39–46).

Or sometimes hanging o'er the bed of death,
    Where the poor languid sufferer—hopes to die.
O! beauteous sister of the halcyon peace![1]
10   I sure shall find thee in that heavenly scene
       Where Care and Anguish shall their power resign;
    Where hope alike, and vain regret shall cease,
      And Memory—lost in happiness serene,
    Repeat no more—that misery has been mine!

1789   1800

Written in the church-yard at Middleton in Sussex

Press'd by the Moon, mute arbitress of tides,
    While the loud equinox its power combines,
    The sea no more its swelling surge confines,
But o'er the shrinking land sublimely rides.
5   The wild blast, rising from the Western cave,
    Drives the huge billows from their heaving bed;
    Tears from their grassy tombs the village dead,
And breaks the silent sabbath of the grave![1]
With shells and sea-weed mingled, on the shore
10   Lo! their bones whiten in the frequent wave;
    But vain to them the winds and waters rave;
They hear the warring elements no more:
While I am doom'd—by life's long storm opprest,
To gaze with envy, on their gloomy rest.

1789   1800

On being cautioned against walking on an headland overlooking the sea, because it was frequented by a lunatic[1]

Is there a solitary wretch who hies
    To the tall cliff, with starting pace or slow,
And, measuring, views with wild and hollow eyes
    Its distance from the waves that chide below;
5   Who, as the sea-born gale with frequent sighs
    Chills his cold bed upon the mountain turf,
With hoarse, half-utter'd lamentation, lies
    Murmuring responses to the dashing surf?
In moody sadness, on the giddy brink,
10   I see him more with envy than with fear;

1. When her husband perished in a shipwreck, Halcyone threw herself into the sea; in pity the gods changed the two into kingfishers and calmed the sea for a brief interval each year so they could mate. A halcyon peace is a blessed interval of calm amid adversity.
1. Middleton is a village on the margin of the sea. [...] There were formerly several acres of ground between its small church and the sea, which now, by its continual encroachments, approaches within a few feet of this half-ruined and humble edifice. The wall, which once surrounded the church-yard, is entirely swept away, many of the graves broken up, and the remains of bodies interred washed into the sea; whence human bones are found among the sand and shingles on the shore [Smith's note, 1800].
1. First published in *The Old Manor House* (1793).

He has no *nice felicities* that shrink[2]
   From giant horrors; wildly wandering here,
He seems (uncursed with reason) not to know
   The depth or the duration of his woe.

1793   1800

The sea view[1]

The upland Shepherd, as reclined he lies
   On the soft turf that clothes the mountain brow,
Marks the bright Sea-line mingling with the skies;
   Or from his course celestial, sinking slow,
5   The Summer-Sun in purple radiance low,
Blaze on the western waters; the wide scene
   Magnificent, and tranquil, seems to spread
Even o'er the Rustic's breast a joy serene,
   When, like dark plague-spots by the Demons shed,
10 Charged deep with death, upon the waves, far seen,
   Move the war-freighted ships; and fierce and red,
   Flash their destructive fires—The mangled dead
And dying victims then pollute the flood.
Ah! thus man spoils Heaven's glorious works with blood!

1797   1800

The Dead Beggar

An Elegy, Addressed to a Lady, who was affected at seeing the Funeral of a nameless Pauper, buried at the Expence of the Parish, in the Church-Yard at Brighthelmstone, in November 1792.[1]

Swells then thy feeling heart, and streams thine eye
   O'er the deserted being, poor and old,
Whom cold, reluctant, Parish Charity[2]
   Consigns to mingle with his kindred mold?

---

2. "'Tis delicate felicity that shrinks / When rocking winds are loud." Walpole [Smith's note, 1800], echoing Milton's *Il Penseroso*: "while rocking winds are piping loud" (126); The reference to Walpole is uncertain.
1. Suggested by the recollection of having seen, some years since, on a beautiful evening of Summer, an engagement between two armed ships, from the high down called the Beacon Hill, near Brighthelmstone [Smith's note, referring to modern Brighton].
1. I have been told that I have incurred blame for having used in this short composition, terms that have become obnoxious to certain persons. Such remarks are hardly worth notice; and it is very little my ambition to obtain the suffrage of those who suffer party prejudice to influence their taste; or of those who desire that because they have themselves done it, every one else should be willing to sell their best birth-rights, the liberty of thought, and of expressing thought, for the *promise* of a mess of pottage.

It is surely not too much to say, that in a country like ours, where such immense sums are annually raised for the poor, there ought to be some regulation which should prevent any miserable deserted being from perishing through want, as too often happens to such objects as that on whose interment these stanzas were written.

It is somewhat remarkable that a circumstance exactly similar is the subject of a short poem called the Pauper's Funeral, in a volume lately published by Mr. Southey [Smith's note]. The "obnoxious" terms refer to "rights of Man" (20), Smith's endorsement of the principles of the French Revolution. In Genesis (25.27–34), Esau sells his birthright, his inheritance as eldest son, to Jacob, his younger brother, for a meal. Robert Southey's *Poems* (1797) contained *The Pauper's Funeral*.
2. Each parish (that is, district Church of England) was responsible for its indigent residents, and some resorted to quite stringent economies.

5   Mourn'st thou, that *here* the time-worn sufferer ends
      Those evil days still threatening woes to come;
  Here, where the friendless feel no want of friends,
      Where even the houseless wanderer finds an home!

  What tho' no kindred croud in sable° forth,   *mourning clothes*
10   And sigh, or seem to sigh, around his bier;
  Tho' o'er his coffin with the humid earth
      No children drop the unavailing tear?

  Rather rejoice that *here* his sorrows cease,
      Whom sickness, age, and poverty oppress'd;
15 Where Death, the Leveller,[3] restores to peace
      The wretch who living knew not where to rest.

  Rejoice, that tho' an outcast spurn'd by Fate,
      Thro' penury's rugged path his race he ran;
  In earth's cold bosom, equall'd with the great,
20   Death vindicates the insulted rights of Man.

  Rejoice, that tho' severe his earthly doom,
      And rude, and sown with thorns the way he trod,
  Now, (where unfeeling Fortune cannot come)
      He rests upon the mercies of his GOD.

1797

THE EMIGRANTS Charlotte Smith contends with the immigration crisis of the early 1790s. In May 1792 the French revolutionary regime required clergy to leave the Roman Church and join the Constitutional Church, or be deported—or worse. In September massacres claimed three bishops, 220 priests, and hundreds of lesser clergy. Surviving clergy, and others dispossessed and imperiled by the Revolution—from high aristocrats to lowly laborers on their estates—soon sought refuge in nearby England, not only from civil violence but also an emerging pan-European war. *The Emigrants* reflects Smith's struggle with her conflicting impulses: reflexive sympathy for those abjected by turns of social and political fate, and a sense of responsibility in caring for fellow Christian outcasts, whatever their deserts; English Protestant distaste for Roman Catholicism in general and the Church's complicity with tyrannical regimes in France; bitter grievances against the British legal system, which left her and her dozen children in poverty; and her horror at an emerging world war, and its peril to her family.

Writing at the end of a century in which epic-minded poets typically wrote in heroic couplets, Smith was impressed by William Cowper's popular, meditative blank verse in *The Task* (1785) as well as by his fearless liberal voice in an era of state repressions. She decided on blank verse, sharpened by its heritage from Milton, famous poet of lost paradises and champion of British liberty. Her opening sentence—sustained for eight lines, by enjambments that gesture toward the play of morning light on the waves that break along the shore and bear the French emigrants to England—reflects her careful attention to the formal resources. Miltonic blank verse is the form William Wordsworth would use at the end of the decade, for his epic autobiography. At the end of each book Smith appended notes, perhaps a strategic displacement, given the incendiary political remarks in more than a few. We intersperse her notes with ours.

---

3. Death-the-Leveller is an old image, referring not just to the leveling of human life, but also to the "democracy" where all are equal.

TO WILLIAM COWPER, ESQ.

DEAR SIR,

THERE is, I hope, some propriety in my addressing a Composition to you, which would never perhaps have existed, had I not, amid the heavy pressure of many sorrows, derived infinite consolation from your Poetry, and some degree of animation and of confidence from your esteem.

The following performance is far from aspiring to be considered as an imitation of your inimitable Poem, "THE TASK;" I am perfectly sensible, that it belongs not to a feeble and feminine hand to draw the Bow of Ulysses.[1]

The force, clearness, and sublimity of your admirable Poem; the felicity, almost peculiar to your genius, of giving to the most familiar objects dignity and effect, I could never hope to reach; yet, having read "The Task" almost incessantly from its first publication to the present time, I felt that kind of enchantment described by Milton, when he says,

> The Angel ended, and in Adam's ear
> So charming left his voice, that he awhile
> Thought him still speaking.[2]——

And from the force of this impression, I was gradually led to attempt, in Blank Verse, a delineation of those interesting objects which happened to excite my attention, and which even pressed upon an heart, that has learned, perhaps from its own sufferings, to feel with acute, though unavailing compassion, the calamity of others.

A Dedication usually consists of praises and of apologies; my praise can add nothing to the unanimous and loud applause of your country. She regards you with pride, as one of the few, who, at the present period, rescue her from the imputation of having degenerated in Poetical talents; but in the form of Apology, I should have much to say, if I again dared to plead the pressure of evils, aggravated by their long continuance, as an excuse for the defects of this attempt.

Whatever may be the faults of its execution, let me vindicate myself from those, that may be imputed to the design.—— In speaking of the Emigrant Clergy, I beg to be understood as feeling the utmost respect for the integrity of their principles; and it is with pleasure I add my suffrage to that of those, who have had a similar opportunity of witnessing the conduct of the Emigrants of all descriptions during their exile in England; which has been such as does honour to their nation, and ought to secure to them in ours the esteem of every liberal mind.

Your philanthropy, dear Sir, will induce you, I am persuaded, to join with me in hoping, that this painful exile may finally lead to the extirpation of that reciprocal hatred so unworthy of great and enlightened nations; that it may tend to humanize both countries, by convincing each, that good qualities exist in the other; and at length annihilate the prejudices that have so long existed to the injury of both.

Yet it is unfortunately but too true, that with the body of the English, this national aversion has acquired new force by the dreadful scenes which have been acted in France during the last summer[3]—even those who are the victims of the Revolution, have not escaped the odium, which the undistinguishing multitude annex to all the natives of a country where such horrors have been acted: nor is this the worst effect those events have had on the minds of

1. Besieged by suitors during her husband Ulysses' long absence during the Trojan War and return voyage, Penelope challenges them to prove their strength by drawing the bow Ulysses had since his childhood; only Ulysses himself, on his return, can manage it.

2. Archangel Raphael spends a day in Eden, conversing with Adam (*Paradise Lost* 8.1–3).

3. The French Revolution turned massively violent in late summer 1792, first with the arrest of King Louis XVI and his family in August, then with the "September Massacres."

the English; by confounding the original cause with the wretched catastrophes that have followed its ill management; the attempts of public virtue; with the outrages that guilt and folly
have committed in its disguise, the very name of Liberty[4] has not only lost the charm it used
to have in British ears, but many, who have written, or spoken, in its defence, have been
stigmatized as promoters of Anarchy, and enemies to the prosperity of their country. Perhaps even the Author of "The Task," with all his goodness and tenderness of heart, is in the
catalogue of those, who are reckoned to have been too warm in a cause, which it was once
the glory of Englishmen to avow and defend—The exquisite Poem, indeed, in which you
have honoured Liberty, by a tribute highly gratifying to her sincerest friends, was published
some years before the demolition of regal despotism in France, which, in the fifth book, it
seems to foretell—All the truth and energy of the passage to which I allude, must have been
strongly felt, when, in the Parliament of England, the greatest Orator of our time[5] quoted
the sublimest of our Poets—when the eloquence of Fox did justice to the genius of Cowper.

I am, dear SIR,
    With the most perfect esteem,
        Your obliged and obedient servant,

CHARLOTTE SMITH.

Brighthelmstone,[6] May 10, 1793.

from THE EMIGRANTS, A POEM, IN TWO BOOKS

Book I

SCENE, on the Cliffs to the Eastward of the Town of Brighthelmstone in Sussex.
TIME, a Morning in November, 1792.

SLOW in the Wintry Morn, the struggling light
Throws a faint gleam upon the troubled waves;
Their foaming tops, as they approach the shore
And the broad surf that never ceasing breaks
5   On the innumerous pebbles, catch the beams
Of the pale Sun, that with reluctance gives
To this cold northern Isle, its shorten'd day.
Alas! how few the morning wakes to joy!
How many murmur at oblivious night
10   For leaving them so soon; for bearing thus
Their fancied bliss (the only bliss they taste!),
On her black wings away!—Changing the dreams
That sooth'd their sorrows, for calamities

---

4. The Task Book V champions "Liberty," byword of
the French Revolution and an antimonarchal principle. Prime Minister William Pitt exploited the crisis in
France to institute brutally repressive laws in England,
making any antigovernment sentiment, publication, or
speech actionable as treason.
5. Charles James Fox, leader of the Whig opposition in
the House of Commons, opposed Britain's entry into war
against France.
6. Brighton, on the coast across from France, was
also the site of the Prince's elaborate pleasure palace.
Smith's preface was written after Louis XVI had been
tried and executed; Marie Antoinette was in prison and
awaiting trial.

(And every day brings its own sad proportion)
15   For doubts, diseases, abject dread of Death,
And faithless friends, and fame and fortune lost;
Fancied or real wants; and wounded pride,
That views the day star,° but to curse his beams.   *sun*
    Yet He, whose Spirit into being call'd
20   This wond'rous World of Waters; He who bids
The wild wind lift them till they dash the clouds,
And speaks to them in thunder; or whose breath,
Low murmuring, o'er the gently heaving tides,
When the fair Moon, in summer night serene,
25   Irradiates with long trembling lines of light
Their undulating surface; that great Power,
Who, governing the Planets, also knows
If but a Sea-Mew falls, whose nest is hid
In these incumbent cliffs;[1] He surely means
30   To us, his reasoning Creatures, whom He bids
Acknowledge and revere his awful° hand,   *awe-inspiring*
Nothing but good: Yet Man, misguided Man,
Mars the fair work that he was bid enjoy,
And makes himself the evil he deplores.
35   How often, when my weary soul recoils
From proud oppression, and from legal crimes[2]
(For such are in this Land, where the vain boast
Of equal Law is mockery, while the cost
Of seeking for redress is sure to plunge
40   Th' already injur'd to more certain ruin
And the wretch starves, before his Counsel° pleads)   *lawyer*
How often do I half abjure Society,
And sigh for some lone Cottage, deep embower'd
In the green woods, that these steep chalky Hills
45   Guard from the strong South West;[3] where round their base
The Beach° wide flourishes, and the light Ash   *beech-tree*
With slender leaf half hides the thymy turf!—
There do I wish to hide me; well content
If on the short grass, strewn with fairy flowers,
50   I might repose thus shelter'd; or when Eve
In Orient crimson lingers in the west,
Gain the high mound, and mark these waves remote
(Lucid tho' distant), blushing with the rays
Of the far-flaming Orb, that sinks beneath them;

---

1. An echo of Matthew 10.29, familiar from Pope's *Essay on Man*: "Who sees with equal eye, as God of all, / A hero perish, or a sparrow fall" (1.87–88).
2. To some readers, Smith's repeated references to her legal ordeals are wearisomely self-centered. But her readers were her only court of appeal. Her ceaseless "toil in the affairs of my childrens Grandfather" (in her words) was the stuff of legend, prompting her in preface after preface, and thinly coded autobiography in novels and tales, to rant about the law's delay and women's utter dependency on insolent, ignorant, unfeeling male trustees.
3. Atlantic Ocean winds, from the southwest. Like the white hills of Dover, Brighton's coastal hills were comprised of lime-chalk.

55 For I have thought, that I should then behold
The beauteous works of God, unspoil'd by Man
And less affected then, by human woes
I witness'd not; might better learn to bear
Those that injustice, and duplicity
60 And faithlessness and folly, fix on me:
For never yet could I derive relief,
When my swol'n heart was bursting with its sorrows,
From the sad thought, that others like myself
Live but to swell affliction's countless tribes!
65 —Tranquil seclusion I have vainly sought;
Peace, who delights solitary shade,
No more will spread for me her downy wings,
But, like the fabled Danaïds[4]—or the wretch,
Who ceaseless, up the steep acclivity,
70 Was doom'd to heave the still rebounding rock,[5]
Onward I labour; as the baffled wave,
Which yon rough beach repulses, that returns
With the next breath of wind, to fail again.—
Ah! Mourner—cease these wailings: cease and learn,
75 That not the Cot° sequester'd, where the briar   *cottage*
And wood-bine wild, embrace the mossy thatch,
(Scarce seen amid the forest gloom obscure!)
Or more substantial farm, well fenced and warm,
Where the full barn, and cattle fodder'd round
80 Speak rustic plenty; nor the statelier dome
By dark firs shaded, or the aspiring pine,
Close by the village Church (with care conceal'd
By verdant foliage, lest the poor man's grave
Should mar the smiling prospect of his Lord),
85 Where offices[6] well rang'd, or dove-cote stock'd,
Declare manorial residence; not these
Or any of the buildings, new and trim
With windows circling towards the restless Sea,
Which ranged in rows,° now terminate my walk,   *terraced*
90 Can shut out for an hour the spectre Care,
That from the dawn of reason, follows still
Unhappy Mortals, 'till the friendly grave
(Our sole secure asylum) "ends the chace."[7]
        Behold, in witness of this mournful truth,
95 A group approach me, whose dejected looks,
Sad Heralds of distress! proclaim them Men

---

4. A loaded allusion to the Greek legend of 50 daughters of Danaüs who ordered them to murder their husbands on their wedding night, and were condemned to an eternity, in the underworld, of drawing water in a sieve.
5. King Sisyphus, condemned in Hell to push a boulder up a hill, watch it roll back down, and repeat his labor for eternity.

6. Various outbuildings on a farm, such as barns, stables, henhouses, dairies.
7. Smith's first endnote cites a probable source in Edward Young's poetry that she cannot locate. "Death ends the Chase" is the grim wisdom of *Simonides on Human Life Paraphrased* (32), by Thomas Cooke (*Poems*, 1742).

Banish'd for ever and for conscience sake
From their distracted Country,[8] whence the name
Of Freedom misapplied, and much abus'd
100   By lawless Anarchy, has driven them far
To wander; with the prejudice[9] they learn'd
From Bigotry (the Tut'ress of the blind),
Thro' the wide World unshelter'd; their sole hope,
That German spoilers, thro' that pleasant land
105   May carry wide the desolating scourge
Of War and Vengeance;[1] yet unhappy Men,
Whate'er your errors, I lament your fate:
And, as disconsolate and sad ye hang
Upon the barrier of the rock, and seem
110   To murmur[2] your despondence, waiting long
Some fortunate reverse that never comes;
Methinks in each expressive face, I see
Discriminated anguish; there droops one,
Who in a moping cloister long consum'd
115   This life inactive, to obtain a better,
And thought that meagre abstinence, to wake
From his hard pallet with the midnight bell,
To live on eleemosynary bread,°   alms, charity
And to renounce God's works, would please that God.
120   And now the poor pale wretch receives, amaz'd,
The pity, strangers give to his distress,
Because these strangers are, by his dark creed,
Condemn'd as Heretics—and with sick heart
Regrets° his pious prison, and his beads.[3]—   laments
125   Another, of more haughty port,° declines   aspect
The aid he needs not; while in mute despair
His high indignant thoughts go back to France,
Dwelling on all he lost—the Gothic dome,
That vied with splendid palaces;[4] the beds
130   Of silk and down, the silver chalices,
Vestments with gold enwrought for blazing altars;
Where, amid clouds of incense, he held forth
To kneeling crowds the imaginary bones

---

8. In summer 1793, Smith's daughter married an emigrant French aristocrat, to whom Smith had given shelter the previous winter. Her novel *The Banished Man* (1794) begins in 1792 after the September Massacres, and is much more sympathetic to French Catholic refugees.
9. Anti-English, anti-Protestant.
1. In 1792, when the Austro-Prussian army invaded France as an ally of the deposed monarchy, many French loyalists and emigrants joined it; although the invasion was repelled, it announced a continuing threat (or hope).
2. In the 1790s, *murmur* had a connotation of political unrest.
3. Lest the same attempts at misrepresentation should now be made, as have been made on former occasions, it is necessary to repeat, that nothing is farther from my thoughts, than to reflect invidiously on the Emigrant

Clergy, whose steadiness of principle excites veneration, as much as their sufferings compassion. Adversity has now taught them the charity and humility they perhaps wanted, when they made it a part of their faith, that salvation could be obtained in no other religion than their own [Smith's note].
4. Let it not be considered as an insult to men in fallen fortune, if these luxuries (undoubtedly inconsistent with their profession) be here enumerated—France is not the only country, where the splendour and indulgences of the higher, and the poverty and depression of the inferior Clergy, have alike proved injurious to the cause of Religion [Smith's note, implying England too]. The wealth, power, and luxury of the higher orders of the Church (which, like the aristocracy, paid no taxes), impelled the revolution, and its confiscation of Church properties.

Of Saints suppos'd, in pearl and gold enchas'd,°   *encased*
135 And still with more than living Monarchs' pomp
Surrounded; was believ'd by mumbling bigots
To hold the keys of Heaven, and to admit
Whom he thought good to share it—Now alas!
He, to whose daring soul and high ambition
140 The World seem'd circumscrib'd; who, wont to dream,
Of Fleuri, Richelieu, Alberoni, men
Who trod on Empire, and whose politics
Were not beyond the grasp of his vast mind,[5]
Is, in a Land once hostile, still prophan'd
145 By disbelief, and rites un-orthodox,
The object of compassion—At his side,
Lighter of heart than these, but heavier far
Than he was wont, another victim comes,
An Abbé—who with less contracted brow
150 Still smiles and flatters, and still talks of Hope;
Which, sanguine as he is, he does not feel,
And so he cheats the sad and weighty pressure
Of evils present;————Still, as Men misled
By early prejudice (so hard to break),
155 I mourn your sorrows; for I too have known
Involuntary exile;[6] and while yet
England had charms for me, have felt how sad
It is to look across the dim cold sea,
That melancholy rolls its refluent° tides   *back-flowing*
160 Between us and the dear regretted land
We call our own—as now ye pensive wait
On this bleak morning, gazing on the waves
That seem to leave your shore; from whence the wind
Is loaded to your ears, with the deep groans
165 Of martyr'd Saints and suffering Royalty,
While to your eyes the avenging power of Heaven
Appears in aweful anger to prepare
The storm of vengeance, fraught with plagues and death.
Even he of milder heart, who was indeed
170 The simple shepherd in a rustic scene,
And, 'mid the vine-clad hills of Languedoc,
Taught to the bare-foot peasant, whose hard hands
Produc'd[7] the nectar he could seldom taste,
Submission to the Lord[8] for whom he toil'd;
175 He, or his brethren, who to Neustria's° sons   *Normandy's*
Enforc'd religious patience, when, at times,

---

5. Powerful cardinals: the first was tutor to Louis XV (Louis XVI's father) and chief administrator of France from 1726 to 1743; the second, a power in the administration of Louis XIII in the early 17th century; the third (an Italian), chief administrator of Spain between 1715–1719.
6. When Benjamin Smith fled to France to escape debtors' prison, he insisted that Charlotte and their many children join him; they spent a miserable, life-threatening winter there in 1784–1785.
7. Smith cites "finely descriptive Verses written at Mont auban in France in 1750, by Dr. Joseph Warton." These begin noting the alienation of "bare-foot sun-burnt peasants" from the (literal) fruits of their labors: "No cups nectareous shall their toils repay."
8. Landlord, with a sarcasm about religion.

On their indignant hearts Power's iron hand
Too strongly struck; eliciting some sparks
Of the bold spirit of their native North;
180   Even these Parochial Priests, these humbled men;
Whose lowly undistinguish'd cottages
Witness'd a life of purest piety,
While the meek tenants were, perhaps, unknown
Each to the haughty Lord of his domain,
185   Who mark'd them not; the Noble scorning still
The poor and pious Priest, as with slow pace
He glided thro' the dim arch'd avenue°   *tree-lined path*
Which to the Castle led; hoping to cheer
The last sad hour of some laborious life
190   That hasten'd to its close—even such a Man
Becomes an exile; staying not to try
By temperate zeal to check his madd'ning flock,
Who, at the novel sound of Liberty
(Ah! most intoxicating sound to slaves!),
195   Start into licence—Lo! dejected now,
The wandering Pastor mourns, with bleeding heart,
His erring people, weeps and prays for them,
And trembles for the account that he must give
To Heaven for souls entrusted to his care.—
200   Where the cliff, hollow'd by the wintry storm,[9]
Affords a seat with matted sea-weed strewn,
A softer form reclines; around her run,
On the rough shingles, or the chalky bourn,[1]
Her gay unconscious children, soon amus'd;
205   Who pick the fretted stone, or glossy shell,
Or crimson plant marine: or they contrive
The fairy vessel, with its ribband sail
And gilded paper pennant:° in the pool,   *banner*
Left by the salt wave on the yielding sands,
210   They launch the mimic navy—Happy age!
Unmindful of the miseries of Man!—
Alas! too long a victim to distress,
Their Mother, lost in melancholy thought,
Lull'd for a moment by the murmurs low
215   Of sullen billows, wearied by the task
Of having here, with swol'n and aching eyes
Fix'd on the grey horizon, since the dawn
Solicitously watch'd the weekly sail
From her dear native land, now yields awhile
220   To kind forgetfulness, while Fancy brings,

9. Although *The Emigrants* proved too controversial for republication in Smith's lifetime, as Britain went to war against France, this passage on the forlorn mother was much admired in the reviews; thus excerpted, it appeared as "The Female Exile" in later editions of *Elegiac Sonnets and Other Poems.*
1. Stony beach, and the back edge against the chalk-cliffs.

In waking dreams, that native land again!
Versailles[2] appears—its painted galleries,
And rooms of regal splendour, rich with gold,
Where, by long mirrors multiply'd, the crowd
225 Paid willing homage—and, united there,
Beauty gave charms to empire—Ah! too soon
From the gay visionary pageant rous'd,
See the sad mourner start!—and, drooping, look
With tearful eyes and heaving bosom round
230 On drear reality—where dark'ning waves,
Urg'd by the rising wind, unheeded foam
Near her cold rugged seat:—To call her thence
A fellow-sufferer comes: dejection deep
Checks, but conceals not quite, the martial air,
235 And that high consciousness of noble blood,
Which he has learn'd from infancy to think
Exalts him o'er the race of common men:
Nurs'd in the velvet lap of luxury,
And fed by adulation—could *he* learn,
240 That worth alone is true Nobility?
And that *the peasant* who, "amid[3] the sons
Of Reason, Valour, Liberty, and Virtue,
Displays distinguish'd merit, is a Noble
Of Nature's own creation!"—If even here,
245 If in this land of highly vaunted Freedom,
Even Britons controvert the unwelcome truth,
Can it be relish'd by the sons of France?
Men, who derive their boasted ancestry
From the fierce leaders of religious wars,
250 The first in Chivalry's emblazon'd page;
Who reckon Gueslin, Bayard, or De Foix,[4]
Among their brave Progenitors? *Their* eyes,
Accustom'd to regard the splendid trophies
Of Heraldry° (that with fantastic hand   *family coat of arms*
255 Mingles, like images in feverish dreams,
"Gorgons and Hydras, and Chimeras dire,"[5]
With painted puns, and visionary shapes;),
See not the simple dignity of Virtue,

2. Famed for its hall of mirrors, the splendid palace of Louis XVIII (built by Louis XIV), from which the royal family was arrested in October 1790 (see Edmund Burke, page 113).
3. These lines are Thomson's, and are among those sentiments which are now called (when used by living writers), not common-place declamation, but sentiments of dangerous tendency [Smith's note]. In James Thomson's mid-century *Coriolanus*, Roman general Cominius, heading a delegation to exiled Coriolanus to petition for a halt to his vengeful war-making, chastises his arrogant refusal: it ill suits "one who sits / In the grave senate of a free republic, /

To talk so high, and as it were to thrust / Plebeians from the native rights of man.———" (3.3). Then follows Smith's quotation. In 1789, and again in 1792, John Philip Kemble barred performances of *Coriolanus* in Covent Garden, fearing the effect on British plebeians.
4. Renowned French warriors (especially against England) from the 14th, 15th, and early 16th centuries. Bayard was famed as the perfect knight.
5. The creatures, "worse / Than fables yet have feigned," that Satan encounters in the outer regions of Hell (*Paradise Lost* 2.628).

But hold all base, whom honours such as these
260   Exalt not from the crowd[6]—As one, who long
Has dwelt amid the artificial scenes
Of populous City,[7] deems that splendid shows,
The Theatre, and pageant pomp of Courts,
Are only worth regard; forgets all taste
265   For Nature's genuine beauty; in the lapse
Of gushing waters hears no soothing sound,
Nor listens with delight to sighing winds,
That, on their fragrant pinions, waft the notes
Of birds rejoicing in the trangled° copse;   rod-like
270   Nor gazes pleas'd on Ocean's silver breast,
While lightly o'er it sails the summer clouds
Reflected in the wave, that, hardly heard,
Flows on the yellow sands: so to *his* mind,
That long has liv'd where Despotism hides
275   His features harsh, beneath the diadem°   crown
Of worldly grandeur, abject Slavery seems,
If by that power impos'd, slavery no more:
For luxury wreathes with silk the iron bonds,
And hides the ugly rivets with her flowers,
280   Till the degenerate triflers, while they love
The glitter of the chains, forget their weight.
But more the Men,[8] whose ill acquir'd wealth
Was wrung from plunder'd myriads, by the means
Too often legaliz'd by power abus'd,
285   Feel all the horrors of the fatal change,
When their ephemeral greatness, marr'd at once
(As a vain toy that Fortune's childish hand
Equally joy'd to fashion or to crush),
Leaves them expos'd to universal scorn
290   For having nothing else; not even the claim
To honour, which respect for Heroes past
Allows to ancient titles; Men, like these,
Sink even beneath the level, whence base arts

6. It has been said, and with great appearance of truth, that the contempt in which the Nobility of France held the common people, was remembered, and with all that vindictive asperity which long endurance of oppression naturally excites, when, by a wonderful concurrence of circumstances, the people acquired the power of retaliation. Yet let me here add, what seems to be in some degree inconsistent with the former charge, that the French are good masters to their servants, and that in their treatment of their Negro slaves, they are allowed to be more mild and merciful than other Europeans [Smith's note with a criticism of Britain; even so, the Smith family fortunes, which she was trying to secure for her children, were involved with West Indian plantation slavery].

7. The pattern is from a famous epic simile in *Paradise Lost*, in which Satan "as one who has been long in populous city pent" feels the delights of Eden on the morning when he will seduce Eve (9.445 ff); Satan's city is Hell's Pandemonium.

8. *The Financiers and Fermiers Generaux* are here intended. In the present moment of clamour against all those who have spoken or written in favour of the first Revolution of France, the declaimers seem to have forgotten, that under the reign of a mild and easy tempered Monarch, in the most voluptuous Court in the world, the abuses by which men of this description were enriched, had arisen to such height, that their prodigality exhausted the immense resources of France: and, unable to supply the exigencies of Government, the Ministry were compelled to call *Le Tiers Etat*; a meeting that gave birth to the Revolution, which has since been so ruinously conducted [Smith's note]. Louis XVI was not regarded as a tyrant, though his court and the aristocracy were lavishly self-indulgent; *fermiers*, or *fermiers generaux* to be true to Smith's term (the usual one), were not really bankers. They were put in charge of collecting taxes, with a substantial commission to themselves.

Alone had rais'd them;—unlamented sink,
295 And know that they deserve the woes they feel.
　　　Poor wand'ring wretches! whosoe'er ye are,
That hopeless, houseless, friendless, travel wide
O'er these bleak russet downs;[9] where, dimly seen,
The solitary Shepherd shiv'ring tends
300 His dun discolour'd flock (Shepherd, unlike
Him, whom in song the Poet's fancy crowns
With garlands, and his crook with vi'lets binds);
Poor vagrant wretches! outcasts of the world!
Whom no abode receives, no parish owns;
305 Roving, like Nature's commoners, the land
That boasts such general plenty: if the sight
Of wide-extended misery softens yours
Awhile, suspend your murmurs!—here behold
The strange vicissitudes of fate—while thus
310 The exil'd Nobles, from their country driven,
Whose richest luxuries were their's, must feel
More poignant anguish, than the lowest poor,
Who, born to indigence, have learn'd to brave
Rigid Adversity's depressing breath!—
315 Ah! rather Fortune's worthless favourites!
Who feed on England's vitals—Pensioners
Of base corruption, who, in quick ascent
To opulence unmerited, become
Giddy with pride, and as ye rise, forgetting
320 The dust ye lately left, with scorn look down
On those beneath ye (tho' your *equals* once
In fortune, and *in worth superior still*.
They view the eminence, on which ye stand,
With wonder, not with envy; for they know
325 The means, by which ye reach'd it, have been such
As, in all honest eyes, degrade ye far
Beneath the poor dependent, whose sad heart
Reluctant pleads for what your pride denies);
Ye venal, worthless hirelings of a Court!
330 Ye pamper'd Parasites! whom Britons pay
For forging fetters for them; rather here
Study a lesson that concerns ye much;
And, trembling, learn, that if oppress'd too long,
The raging multitude, to madness stung,
335 Will turn on their oppressors; and, no more
By sounding titles and parading forms
Bound like tame victims, will redress themselves!
Then swept away by the resistless torrent,
Not only all your pomp may disappear,

---

9. Shakespeare's banished King Lear is shocked by the world outside his castle: "Poor naked wretches, wheresoe'er you are, / That bide the pelting of this pitiless storm, / How shall your houseless heads and unfed sides, / Your loop'd and window'd raggedness, defend you / From seasons such as these?" (3.4.26–32). In sentimental pastoral tradition, shepherds live in happy harmony with nature, in contrast to the urbane poets who romanticize (or condescend to) them.

340   But, in the tempest lost, fair Order sink
       Her decent head, and lawless Anarchy
       O'erturn celestial Freedom's radiant throne;—
       As now in Gallia; where Confusion, born
       Of party rage and selfish love of rule,
345   Sully the noblest cause that ever warm'd
       The heart of Patriot Virtue[1]—There arise
       The infernal passions; Vengeance, seeking blood,
       And Avarice; and Envy's harpy fangs
       Pollute the immortal shrine of Liberty,
350   Dismay her votaries, and disgrace her name.
       Respect is due to principle; and they,
       Who suffer for their conscience, have a claim,
       Whate'er that principle may be, to praise.
       These ill-starr'd Exiles then, who, bound by ties,
355   To them the bonds of honour; who resign'd
       Their country to preserve them, and now seek
       In England an asylum—well deserve
       To find that (every prejudice forgot,
       Which pride and ignorance teaches), we for them
360   Feel as our brethren; and that English hearts,
       Of just compassion ever own the sway,
       As truly as our element, the deep,
       Obeys the mild dominion of the Moon—
       This they *have* found; and may they find it still!
365   Thus may'st thou, Britain, triumph!—May thy foes,
       By Reason's gen'rous potency subdued,
       Learn, that the God thou worshippest, delights
       In acts of pure humanity!—May thine
       Be still such bloodless laurels! nobler far
370   Than those acquir'd at Cressy or Poictiers,[2]
       Or of more recent growth, those well bestow'd
       On him who stood on Calpe's blazing height
       Amid the thunder of a warring world,[3]
       Illustrious rather from the crowds he sav'd
375   From flood and fire, than from the ranks who fell
       Beneath his valour!—Actions such as these,
       Like incense rising to the Throne of Heaven,
       Far better justify the pride, that swells
       In British bosoms, than the deafening roar
380   Of Victory from a thousand brazen throats,
       That tell with what success wide-wasting War
       Has by our brave Compatriots thinned the world.

1792–1793   1793

---

1. This sentiment will probably *renew* against me the indignation of those, who have an interest in asserting that
no such virtue any where exists [Smith's note]; "noblest"
reclaims the adjective from the "Noble" classes that
assume their innate virtue.

2. Two key battles in Edward III's campaign to claim
France for England in the mid-14th century.
3. City in Gibraltar; its celebrated military commander,
G. A. Eliott, in his 60s, courageously held out against a vigorous Spanish siege on the territory, between 1779–1783.

from **Beachy Head**[1]

An early worshipper at Nature's shrine;[2]
I loved her rudest scenes—warrens, and heaths,
And yellow commons, and birch-shaded hollows,
And hedge rows, bordering unfrequented lanes
350 Bowered with wild roses, and the clasping woodbine
Where purple tassels of the tangling vetch[3]
With bittersweet, and bryony inweave,[4]
And the dew fills the silver bindweed's[5] cups—
I loved to trace the brooks whose humid banks
355 Nourish the harebell, and the freckled pagil;[6]
And stroll among o'ershadowing woods of beech,
Lending in Summer, from the heats of noon
A whispering shade; while haply there reclines
Some pensive lover of uncultur'd flowers,
360 Who, from the tumps° with bright green mosses clad,   hillock *(local usage)*
Plucks the wood sorrel,[7] with its light thin leaves,
Heart-shaped, and triply folded; and its root
Creeping like beaded coral; or who there
Gathers, the copse's pride, anémones,[8]
365 With rays like golden studs on ivory laid
Most delicate: but touch'd with purple clouds,
Fit crown for April's fair but changeful brow.
Ah! hills so early loved! in fancy still
I breathe your pure keen air; and still behold
370 Those widely spreading views, mocking alike
The Poet and the Painter's utmost art
And still, observing objects more minute,
Wondering remark the strange and foreign forms
Of sea-shells; with the pale calcareous[9] soil
375 Mingled, and seeming of resembling substance.[1]

---

1. In crossing the Channel from the east coast of France, Beachy Head is the first land made [Smith's note]. This massive headland is the southernmost point of Sussex, directly across the English Channel from the French port of Dieppe.

2. Compare Wordsworth's *Tintern Abbey*. "I, so long / A worshipper of nature" (152–53).

3. Vetch. *Vicia sylvatica* [Smith's note].

4. Bittersweet. *Solanum dulcamara*. Bryony, *Bryonia alba* [Smith's note].

5. Bindweed. *Convolvulus sepium* [Smith's note].

6. Harebell. *Hyacinthus non scriptus*. pagil. *Primula veris* [Smith's note].

7. Sorrel. *Oxalis acetosella* [Smith's note].

8. Anémones. *Anemóne nemorosa*. It appears to be settled on late and excellent authorities, that this word should not be accented on the second syllable, but on the penultima. I have however ventured the more known accentuation, as more generally used, and suiting better the nature of my verse [Smith's note].

9. Limestone.

1. Among the crumbling chalk I have often found shells, some quite in fossil state and hardly distinguishable from chalk. Others appeared more recent; cockles, muscles [mussels], and periwinkles, I well remember, were among the number; and some whose names I do not know. A great number were like those of small land snails. It is now many years since I made these observations. The appearance of sea-shells so far from the sea excited my surprise, though I then knew nothing of natural history. I have never read any of the late theories of the earth, nor was I ever satisfied with the attempts to explain many of the phenomena which call forth conjecture in those books I happened to have had access to on this subject [Smith's note].

Tho' surely the blue Ocean (from the heights
Where the downs westward trend, but dimly seen)
Here never roll'd its surge. Does Nature then
Mimic, in wanton mood, fantastic shapes
380   Of bivalves, and inwreathed volutes,° that cling   *spiral shells*
To the dark sea-rock of the wat'ry world?
Or did this range of chalky mountains, once[2]
Form a vast bason,° where the Ocean waves   *basin*
Swell'd fathomless? What time these fossil shells,
385   Buoy'd on their native element, were thrown
Among the imbedding calx:° when the huge hill   *lime*
Its giant bulk heaved, and in strange ferment
Grew up a guardian barrier, 'twixt the sea
And the green level of the sylvan weald.
390   Ah! very vain is Science' proudest boast,
And but a little light its flame yet lends
To its most ardent votaries; since from whence
These fossil forms are seen, is but conjecture,
Food for vague theories, or vain dispute,
395   While to his daily task the peasant goes,
Unheeding such inquiry; with no care
But that the kindly change of sun and shower,
Fit for his toil the earth he cultivates.
As little recks the herdsman of the hill,
400   Who on some turfy knoll, idly reclined,
Watches his wether[3] flock; that deep beneath
Rest the remains of men, of whom is left[4]
No traces in the records of mankind,
Save what these half obliterated mounds
405   And half fill'd trenches doubtfully impart
To some lone antiquary; who on times remote,
Since which two thousand years have roll'd away,
Loves to contemplate. He perhaps may trace,
Or fancy he can trace, the oblong square
410   Where the mail'd legions, under Claudius,[5] tear'd,

2. The theory here slightly hinted at, is taken from an idea started by Mr. White [Smith's note]. Gilbert White (1720–1793) published *The Natural History of Selborne* in 1789.
3. Male sheep, kept on high ground.
4. These Downs are not only marked with traces of encampments, which from their forms are called Roman or Danish; but there are numerous tumuli [burial mounds] among them. Some of which having been opened a few years ago, were supposed by a learned antiquary to contain the remains of the original natives of the country [Smith's note].
5. That the legions of Claudius were in this part of Britain appears certain. Since this emperor received the submission of Cantii, Atrebates, Irenobates, and Regni, in which later denomination were included the people of Sussex [Smith's note]. Roman emperor Claudius invaded Britain in 43 C.E. and made it a province.

The rampire,° or excavated fossé° delved;   *rampart / trench or moat*
What time the huge unwieldy Elephant[6]
Auxiliary reluctant, hither led,
From Afric's forest glooms and tawny sands,
415   First felt the Northern blast, and his vast frame
Sunk useless; whence in after ages found,
The wondering hinds, on those enormous bones
Gaz'd;[7] and in giants[8] dwelling on the hills
Believed and marvell'd—

* * *

Just beneath the rock[9]
Where Beachy overpeers the channel wave,
Within a cavern mined by wintry tides
Dwelt one,[1] who long disgusted with the world
675   And all its ways, appear'd to suffer life
Rather than live; the soul-reviving gale,
Fanning the bean-field, or the thymy heath,
Had not for many summers breathed on him;
And nothing mark'd to him the season's change,
680   Save that more gently rose the placid sea,
And that the birds which winter on the coast
Gave place to other migrants; save that the fog,
Hovering no more above the beetling cliffs

6. In the year 1740, some workmen digging in the park at Burton in Sussex, discovered, nine feet below the surface, the teeth and bones of an elephant; two of the former were seven feet eight inches in length. There were besides these, tusks, one of which broke in removing it, a grinder not at all decayed, and a part of the jaw-bone, with bones of the knee and thigh, and several others. Some of them remained very lately at Burton House, the seat of John Biddulph, Esq. Others were in possession of the Rev. Dr. Langrish, minister of Petworth at that period, who was present, when some of these bones were taken up, and gave it as his opinion, that they had remained there since the universal deluge [the time of Noah's Ark]. The Romans under the Emperor Claudius probably brought elephants into Britain. Milton, in the Second Book of his History, in speaking of the expedition, says that "He [...] like a great eastern king, with armed elephants, marched through Gallia" [John Milton published *The History of Britain* in 1670]. This is given on the authority of Dion Cassius, in his Life of the Emperor Claudius [Dio Cassius., c. 150–235, wrote an 80-book history of Rome]. It has therefore been conjectured, that the bones found at Burton might have been those of one of these elephants, who perished there soon after its landing; or dying on the high downs, one of which, called Duneton Hill, rises immediately above Burton Park, the bones might have been washed down by the torrents of rain, and buried deep in the soil. They were not found together, but scattered at some distance from each other. The two tusks were twenty feet apart. I had often heard of the elephant's bones at Burton, but never saw them; and I have no books to refer to. I think I saw, in what is now

called the National Museum at Paris, the very large bones of an elephant, which were found in North America: though it is certain that this enormous animal is never seen in its natural state, but in the countries under the torrid zone of the old world. I have, since making this note, been told that the bones of the rhinoceros and hippopotamus have been found in America [Smith's note].
7. Compare the famous lines from Virgil's *Georgics*. "Surely a time will come when in those regions / The farmer heaving the soil with his curved plough / Will come on spears all eaten up with rust / Or strike with his heavy hoe on hollow helmets / And gape at the huge bones in the upturned graves" (1.490; trans. by L. P. Wilkinson).
8. The peasants believe that the large bones sometimes found belonged to giants, who formerly lived on the hills. The devil also has a great deal to do with the remarkable forms of hill and vale: the Devil's Punch Bowl, the Devil's Leaps, and the Devil's Dyke, are names given to deep hollows, or high and abrupt ridges, in this and the neighbouring county [Smith's note].
9. The concluding passage.
1. In a cavern almost immediately under the cliff called Beachy Head, there lived, as the people of the country believed, a man of the name of Darby, who for many years had no other abode than this cave, and subsisted almost entirely on shell-fish. He had often administered assistance to ship-wrecked mariners; but venturing into the sea on this charitable mission during a violent equinoctial storm, he himself perished. As it is above thirty years since I heard this tradition of Parson Darby (for so I think he was called): it may now perhaps be forgotten [Smith's note].

Betray'd not then the little careless sheep[2]
685   On the brink grazing, while their headlong fall
Near the lone Hermit's flint-surrounded home,
Claim'd unavailing pity; for his heart
Was feelingly alive to all that breath'd;
And outraged as he was, in sanguine youth,
690   By human crimes, he still acutely felt
For human misery.
                              Wandering on the beach,
He learn'd to augur from the clouds of heaven,
And from the changing colours of the sea,
And sullen murmurs of the hollow cliffs,
695   Or the dark porpoises,[3] that near the shore
Gambol'd and sported on the level brine
When tempests were approaching: then at night
He listen'd to the wind; and as it drove
The billows with o'erwhelming vehemence
700   He, starting from his rugged couch,° went forth   bed
And hazarding a life, too valueless,
He waded thro' the waves, with plank or pole
Towards where the mariner in conflict dread
Was buffeting for life the roaring surge;
705   And now just seen, now lost in foaming gulphs,
The dismal gleaming of the clouded moon
Shew'd the dire peril. Often he had snatch'd
From the wild billows, some unhappy man
Who liv'd to bless the hermit of the rocks.
710   But if his generous cares were all in vain,
And with slow swell the tide of morning bore
Some blue swol'n corse to land; the pale recluse
Dug in the chalk a sepulchre–above
Where the dank sea-wrack[4] mark'd the utmost tide,
715   And with his prayers perform'd the obsequies
For the poor helpless stranger.
                                        One dark night
The equinoctial wind blew south by west,
Fierce on the shore;—the bellowing cliffs were shook
Even to their stony base, and fragments fell
720   Flashing and thundering on the angry flood.
At day-break, anxious for the lonely man,
His cave the mountain shepherds visited,
Tho' sand and banks of weeds had choak'd their way—

2. Sometimes in thick weather the sheep feeding on the summit of the cliff, miss their footing, and are killed by the fall [Smith's note].

3. *Delphinus phocœna* [Smith's note; the zoological term].
4. Line of refuse (seaweed, shells, and driftwood).

He was not in it; but his drowned cor'se
725 By the waves wafted, near his former home
Receiv'd the rites of burial. Those who read
Chisel'd within the rock, these mournful lines,
Memorials of his sufferings, did not grieve,
That dying in the cause of charity
730 His spirit, from its earthly bondage freed,
Had to some better region fled for ever.

1806   1807

➤◄ PERSPECTIVES ◄➤
The Rights of Man and
the Revolution Controversy

"The Revolution in France," wrote Percy Shelley, "overthrew the hierarchy, the aristocracy, and the monarchy, and the whole of that peculiarly insolent and oppressive system on which they were based." Celebrated international center of high culture and progressive philosophy, eighteenth-century France was also a country of profound social inequalities and oppression. Dissatisfaction had been growing against the corrupt and inefficient aristocracy, who relentlessly taxed the lower classes (the "Third Estate": peasants, serfs, yeomen, industrial workers and economically independent bourgeoisie) without granting them political power. Tensions mounted in the 1780s as the government went bankrupt and tried to hold on with more taxation and the imprisonment of dissidents, without trial, in the Bastille prison in Paris. Open rebellion broke out with the storming of the Bastille in 1789 and radiated into a series of cataclysmic events watched from across the English Channel, and witnessed by some English visitors to France, with a mixture of interest, sympathy, and horror.

Support for the Revolution was a coterie enthusiasm in England rather than widespread, but it was still of concern to the government and allied institutions. Following the American Revolution, and close to the centenary of Britain's "Glorious Revolution" of 1688, this latest upheaval underscored to European monarchies the insecurity of long-standing alliances of church, state, and aristocracy, and seemed to advance "the spirit of the age" toward liberalism and democracy. Political idealists took fire, excited by the bold reformation of French life: not only a new government but also new street names, a new calendar (Year I beginning 21 September 1792) with new month names, new deities (goddesses Reason, Liberty), and new national festivals to replace the old religious holidays. "Bliss was it in that dawn to be alive!" exclaimed William Wordsworth in a retrospect published in 1809 (*Prelude* 10.689). But the dawn darkened as the French Republic descended into factionalism, extremist purges, internal violence, terrorism, and imperialist war-mongering: the monarchy was overthrown in August 1792, thousands of artistocrats and suspected sympathizers were massacred in September, Louis XVI was guillotined in January 1793, and Queen Marie Antoinette in October. Wordsworth and others fell into disenchantment and despair ("The scenes that I witnessed during the earlier years of the French Revolution when I was resident in France," he wrote in 1835, "come back on me with appalling violence"). Conservatives sounded the alarm and, warning of a French invasion, the British government enacted a series of repressive measures in the 1790s—suspending civil rights, spying on and harassing political groups, outlawing and vigorously prosecuting some kinds of assembly and publication. France and Britain declared war, and peace was not secured until the defeat of Napoleon, at Waterloo in 1815. The Revolution and its sequels had such a profound effect on British political life that in 1823 Samuel Taylor Coleridge could say, "We are not yet aware of the consequences of that event. We are too near it."

For William Wordsworth's conflicted retrospect on this tumultuous era, see *The Prelude* 6:339–421 (pages 505–06) and the excerpts from Books 9 and 10 (pages 514–27).

⊶ ▰◆▰ ⊷

Helen Maria Williams
1762–1827

When Helen Maria Williams died in Paris in 1827, England's *Gentleman's Magazine* remembered her as "pre-eminent among the violent female devotees of the Revolution." Of Scots and Welsh descent, Williams entered the London literary scene with *Edwin and Eltruda* (1782).

Her reputation as a poet of liberal opinions was fixed by subsequent works, among them *Peru* (1784), a critique of imperialism, and *A Poem on the Bill lately passed for regulating the Slave Trade* (1788). A poem on the Bastille in her only novel, *Julia* (1790), signaled her enthusiasm for the Revolution. She visited Paris in 1790, returned in 1791, and settled there in 1792. A close friend of moderate Girondins, she was imprisoned in 1793, but her faith in the principles of the Revolution never wavered. The salon she ran until 1816 was a magnet for expatriates, including Paine and Wollstonecraft; Wordsworth bore a letter of introduction to her from Charlotte Smith when he arrived in 1791. Her *Letters Written in France, in the Summer of 1790* were followed by further volumes of *Letters from France* (1792–1796), and *A Tour in Switzerland* (1798), which recorded the impact of the Revolution on the Swiss Republic. Her admiration for Napoleon dimmed only when he crowned himself Emperor in 1804. Her disillusion can be seen in two later works, published in 1815 and 1819, which carry her account of French life through to the restoration of Louis XVIII, but by then her identification with radicalism was set. Such sentiments, joined with her enduring affair with Unitarian radical John Hurford Stone, tarnished her standing at home, provoking Horace Walpole to call her "a scribbling trollop." But Williams's devotion had produced an unparalleled eyewitness narrative of more than twenty-five turbulent years; perhaps no English subject knew so many of those who shaped the course of the Revolution.

from **Letters Written in France, in the Summer of 1790,**
to a Friend in England, Containing Various Anecdotes Relative to the French Revolution[1]

[ARRIVAL IN PARIS]

I arrived at Paris, by a very rapid journey, the day before the federation;[2] and when I am disposed to murmur at the evils of my destiny, I shall henceforth put this piece of good fortune into the opposite scale, and reflect how many disappointments it ought to counterbalance. Had the packet which conveyed me from Brighton to Dieppe failed a few hours later; had the wind been contrary; in short, had I not reached Paris at the moment I did reach it, I should have missed the most sublime spectacle which, perhaps, was ever represented on the theatre of this earth.

[A DEPICTION OF A FEDERATION]

I promised to send you a description of the federation: but it is not to be described! One must have been present, to form any judgment of a scene, the sublimity of which depended much less on its external magnificence than on the effect it produced on the minds of the spectators. "The people, sure, the people were the sight!" I may tell you of pavilions, of triumphal arches, of altars on which incense was burnt, of two hundred thousand men walking in procession; but how am I to give you an adequate idea of the behaviour of the spectators? How am I to paint the impetuous feelings of that immense, that exulting multitude? Half a million people assembled at a spectacle, which furnished every image that can elevate the mind of man; which connected the enthusiasm of moral sentiment with the solemn pomp of religious ceremonies; which addressed itself at once to the imagination, the understanding, and the heart!

The Champ de Mars[3] was formed into an immense amphitheatre, round which were erected forty rows of seats, raised one above another with earth, on which wooden forms were placed. Twenty days['] labour, animated by the enthusiasm of the

---

1. Selections from volume 1, letters 1, 2, 4, and 5.
2. The Festival of the Federation was held in Paris on 14 July 1790, the first anniversary of the fall of the Bastille

and the new constitution.
3. "The Field of Mars," the former military parade ground on the left bank of the Seine.

people, accomplished what seemed to require the toil of years. Already in the Champ de Mars the distinctions of rank were forgotten; and, inspired by the same spirit, the highest and lowest orders of citizens gloried in taking up the spade, and assisting the persons employed in a work on which the common welfare of the state depended. Ladies took the instruments of labour in their hands, and removed a little of the earth, that they might be able to boast that they also had assisted in the preparations at the Champ de Mars; and a number of old soldiers were seen voluntarily bestowing on their country the last remains of their strength. A young Abbé of my acquaintance told me, that the people beat a drum at the door of the convent where he lived, and obliged the Superior to let all the Monks come out and work in the Champ de Mars. The Superior with great reluctance acquiesced, "Quant à moi," said the young Abbé, "je ne demandois pas mieux" ["As for me, I desired nothing better"].[4]

At the upper end of the amphitheatre a pavilion was built for the reception of the King, the Queen, their attendants, and the National Assembly,[5] covered with striped tent-cloth of the national colours, and decorated with streamers of the same beloved tints, and fleur de lys. The white flag was displayed above the spot where the King was seated. In the middle of the Champ de Mars L'Autel de la Patrie[6] was placed, on which incense was burnt by priests dressed in long white robes, with sashes of national ribbon. Several inscriptions were written on the altar, but the words visible at the greatest distance were, La Nation, la Loi, et le Roi [The Nation, the Law, and the King].

At the lower end of the amphitheatre, opposite to the pavilion, three triumphal arches were erected, adorned with emblems and allegorical figures.

The procession marched to the Champ de Mars, through the central streets of Paris. At La Place de Louis Quinze, the escorts, who carried the colours, received under their banners, ranged in two lines, the National Assembly, who came from the Tuilleries. When the procession passed the street where Henry the Fourth was assassinated,[7] every man paused as if by general consent: the cries of joy were suspended, and succeeded by a solemn silence. This tribute of regret, paid from the sudden impulse of feeling at such a moment, was perhaps the most honourable testimony to the virtues of that amiable Prince which his memory has yet received.

In the streets, at the windows, and on the roofs of the houses, the people, transported with joy, shouted and wept as the procession passed. Old men were seen kneeling in the streets, blessing God that they had lived to witness that happy moment. The people ran to the doors of their houses loaded with refreshments, which they offered to the troops; and crouds of women surrounded the soldiers, and holding up their infants in their arms, and melting into tears, promised to make their children imbibe, from their earliest age, an inviolable attachment to the principles of the new constitution.

[A VISIT TO THE BASTILLE PRISON]

Before I suffered my friends at Paris to conduct me through the usual routine of convents, churches, and palaces, I requested to visit the Bastille; feeling a much stronger desire to contemplate the ruins of that building than the most perfect edifices in Paris. When we got into the carriage, our French servant called to the coachman, with an air of triumph, "A la Bastille—mais nous n'y resterons pas" ["To the Bastille,—but we shall not remain there"]. We drove under that porch which so many wretches have

---

4. The translations are by Williams, who wanted her work to reach as broad an audience as possible.
5. The legislative assembly made up of the third estate, or commons, that by declaring itself the governing body of the nation had precipitated the revolution in 1789.

6. The Altar of the Fatherland.
7. Henry of Navarre (1533–1610) became king in 1589, and was known for his love of his subjects. He was assassinated in 1610 by a Catholic extremist.

entered never to repass, and alighting from the carriage descended with difficulty into the dungeons, which were too low to admit of our standing upright, and so dark that we were obliged at noon-day to visit them with the light of a candle. We saw the hooks of those chains by which the prisoners were fastened round the neck, to the walls of their cells; many of which being below the level of the water, are in a constant state of humidity; and a noxious vapour issued from them, which more than once extinguished the candle, and was so insufferable that it required a strong spirit of curiosity to tempt one to enter. Good God! and to these regions of horror were human creatures dragged at the caprice of despotic power. What a melancholy consideration, that

> ———Man! proud man,
> Drest in a little brief authority,
> Plays such fantastic tricks before high heaven,
> As make the angels weep.[8]

There appears to be a greater number of these dungeons than one could have imagined the hard heart of tyranny itself would contrive; for, since the destruction of the building, many subterraneous cells have been discovered underneath a piece of ground which was inclosed within the walls of the Bastille, but which seemed a bank of solid earth before the horrid secrets of this prison-house were disclosed. Some skeletons were found in these recesses, with irons still fastened on their decaying bones.

After having visited the Bastille, we may indeed be surprized, that a nation so enlightened as the French, submitted so long to the oppressions of their government; but we must cease to wonder that their indignant spirits at length shook off the galling yoke.

Those who have contemplated the dungeons of the Bastille, without rejoicing in the French revolution, may, for aught I know, be very respectable persons, and very agreeable companions in the hours of prosperity; but, if my heart were sinking with anguish, I should not fly to those persons for consolation. Sterne[9] says, that a man is incapable of loving one woman as he ought, who has not a sort of an affection for the whole sex; and as little should I look for particular sympathy from those who have no feelings of general philanthropy. If the splendour of a despotic throne can only shine like the radiance of lightning, while all around is involved in gloom and horror, in the name of heaven let its baleful lustre be extinguished for ever. May no such strong contrast of light and shade again exist in the political system of France! but may the beams of liberty, like the beams of day, shed their benign influence on the cottage of the peasant, as well as on the palace of the monarch! May liberty, which for so many ages past has taken pleasure in softening the evils of the bleak and rugged climates of the north, in fertilizing a barren soil, in clearing the swamp, in lifting mounds against the inundations of the tempest, diffuse her blessings also on the genial land of France, and bid the husbandman rejoice under the shade of the olive and the vine!

[THE ARISTOCRACY]

I am just returned from a visit to Madame Sillery, whose works on education are so well known and so justly esteemed in England[1] *** Mons. d'Orléans[2] has certainly

8. A compression of Isabella's tirade against the tyranny of Angelo, the agent of the Duke, in Shakespeare's *Measure for Measure* 2.2.117–22.
9. In Laurence Sterne's *A Sentimental Journey* (1768), the narrator Yorick makes this statement.
1. The Marquise de Sillery, better known as Mme. de Genlis, was the author of *Adele et Theodore, ou Lettres sur l'education* (London ed., 1782); when the Jacobins

triumphed in 1793, her husband was guillotined and she and her pupil Mlle. d'Orléans fled to Switzerland.
2. Louis Philippe Joseph, Duke of Orléans (1747–1793), the richest man in France, earned the name Philippe Egalité for his liberal convictions; elected a deputy from Paris to the Convention, he voted for the king's death, but when his eldest son, the Duke of Chartres, deserted to the Austrians, he was arrested and guillotined.

conferred a most essential obligation upon his children, by placing them under the care of this lady. I never met with young people more amiable in their dispositions, or more charming in their manners, which are equally remote from arrogance, and from those efforts of condescension which I have seen some great people make, with much difficulty to themselves, and much offence to others. The Princess, who is thirteen years of age, has a countenance of the sweetest expression, and appears to me to be Adelaide, the heroine of Madame Sillery's Letters on Education, personified. The three princes, though under Madame Sillery's superintendence, have also preceptors who live in the house, and assist in their education. The eldest prince, Mons. de Chartres, is nearly eighteen years of age, and his attentive politeness formed a striking contrast in my mind, to the manners of those fashionable gentlemen in a certain great metropolis, who consider apathy and negligence as the test of good-breeding. But if I was pleased with the manners of this young Prince, I was still more delighted to find him a confirmed friend to the new constitution of France, and willing, with the enthusiasm of a young and ardent mind, to renounce the splendour of his titles for the general good. When he heard that the sacrifice of fortune also was required, and that the immense property, which he had been taught to consider as his inheritance, was to be divided with his brothers, he embraced them with the utmost affection, declaring that he rejoiced in such a division. To find a democratic Prince, was somewhat singular:[3] I was much less surprized that Madame Sillery had adopted sentiments which are so congenial to an enlarged and comprehensive mind. This lady I have called Sillery, because it is the name by which she is known in England; but, since the decree of the National Assembly, abolishing the nobility, she has renounced with her title the name of Sillery, and has taken that of Brulart.

She talked to me of the distinctions of rank, in the spirit of philosophy, and ridiculed the absurdity of converting the rewards of personal merit into the inheritance of those who had perhaps so little claim to honours, that they were a sort of oblique reproach on their character and conduct. There may be arguments against hereditary rank sufficiently convincing to such an understanding as Madame Brulart's: but I know some French ladies who entertain very different notions on this subject; who see no impropriety in the establishments of nobility; and who have carried their love of aristocratical rights so far as to keep their beds, in a fit of despondency, upon being obliged to relinquish the agreeable epithets of Comtesse or Marquise, to which their ears had been so long accustomed.

But let me do justice to the ladies of France. The number of those who have murmured at the loss of rank, bears a very small proportion to those who have acted with a spirit of distinguished patriotism; who, with those generous affections which belong to the female heart, have gloried in sacrificing titles, fortune, and even the personal ornaments, so dear to female vanity, for the common cause. It was the ladies who gave the example of le don patriotique [the patriotic donation], by offering their jewels at the shrine of liberty; and, if the women of ancient Rome have gained the applause of distant ages for such actions, the women of France will also claim the admiration of posterity.

The women have certainly had a considerable share in the French revolution: for, whatever the imperious lords of the creation may fancy, the most important events which take place in this world depend a little on our influence; and we often act in human affairs like those secret springs in mechanism, by which, though invisible, great movements are regulated.

---

3. Under the old system of primogeniture, the Prince (as eldest son) would have been sole heir. See also Wollstonecraft's critique of primogeniture as a corruption of virtue (page 126, n. 9).

But let us return to Madame Brulart, who wears at her breast a medallion made of a stone of the Bastille polished. In the middle of the medallion, *Liberté* was written in diamonds; above was marked, in diamonds, the planet that shone on the 14th of July; and below was seen the moon, of the size she appeared that memorable night. The medallion was set in a branch of laurel, composed of emeralds, and tied at the top with the national cockade, formed of brilliant stones of the three national colours.

Edmund Burke
1729–1797

A political writer and Irish member of Parliament for nearly thirty years, famous for electrifying oratory, Edmund Burke embodied the debates of his century. Although he was allied with the Whigs and not the Tories, and with them often advocated liberal and reform clauses, his politics were never of a piece. The son of a Protestant minister and a Catholic mother, he castigated Britain's handling of Ireland, urging the emancipation of Irish trade, the Irish Parliament, and Irish Catholics. He endorsed William Wilberforce's movement for the abolition of the slave trade, worked for the reform of the East India Company's abuses in India, and argued for better treatment of and greater autonomy for the American colonies. Yet he also supported Britain's right to tax the colonies and was a celebrated opponent of the French Revolution, denouncing it as an unparalleled disaster in modern history.

"Burke never shows his powers, except he is in a passion. The French Revolution was alone a subject fit for him," remarked Samuel Taylor Coleridge. Burke's best known work is *Reflections on the Revolution in France*, published in November 1790, a year after the arrest and imprisonment of Louis XVI and Marie Antoinette but before the Terror and their execution. (Wordsworth, who as a young man saw the Revolution heralding a new golden age in human history, was horrified by the Terror and later praised the "Genius of Burke.") Selling quickly and widely (7,000 copies the first week and 30,000 over the next few years), *Reflections* provoked strong reactions, pro and con. Framed as a letter to a young gentleman, it was championed throughout Europe for a principled conservatism that revered an idealized past and historical continuity, and on this basis defended the moral authority of a nation's institutions: the monarchy, the aristocracy, the church, and the constitution that guaranteed their power. A famous passage dramatized the arrest and imprisonment of the royal family, with a dignified queen as tragic heroine. Sympathizers with the Revolution immediately produced rebuttals, among the first, Mary Wollstonecraft's *Vindication of the Rights of Men*, and the most influential, Tom Paine's *Rights of Man*.

from Reflections on the Revolution in France
["THIS STRANGE CHAOS"]

All circumstances taken together, the French Revolution is the most astonishing that has hitherto happened in the world. The most wonderful things are brought about in many instances by means the most absurd and ridiculous; in the most ridiculous modes; and, apparently, by the most contemptible instruments. Everything seems out of nature in this strange chaos of levity and ferocity, and of all sorts of crimes jumbled together with all sorts of follies. In viewing this monstrous tragicomic scene, the most opposite passions necessarily succeed, and sometimes mix with each other in the mind; alternate contempt and indignation; alternate laughter and tears; alternate scorn and horror.

James Gillray, *Smelling out a Rat;———or The Atheistical Revolutionist disturbed in his Midnight Calculations*, 1790. The picture on the wall depicts *Death of Charles I, or the Glory of Britain*, the King was
beheaded in the English Civil Wars of the 1640s. Burke, wielding the symbols of the monarchy and the
established Church and bearing his *Reflections* on his brow, detects a "Rat" at his desk writing *The Benefits
of Anarchy, Regicide & Atheism*; at his feet are Dr. Richard Price's *Sermon to the Revolution Society* (1789,
Burke's incitement to *Reflections*) and *Treatise on the ill effects of order and government on society, and the
absurdity of serving GOD and honoring the KING*.

It cannot however be denied, that to some this strange scene appeared in quite
another point of view. Into them it inspired no other sentiments than those of exultation and rapture. They saw nothing in what has been done in France, but a firm and
temperate exertion of freedom; so consistent, on the whole, with morals and with
piety as to make it deserving not only of the secular applause of dashing Machiavelian
politicians,[1] but to render it a fit theme for all the devout effusions of sacred eloquence.

[THE CONSTITUENT PARTS OF A STATE]

The constituent parts of a state are obliged to hold their public faith with each other,
and with all those who derive any serious interest under their engagements, as much
as the whole state is bound to keep its faith with separate communities. Otherwise
competence and power would soon be confounded, and no law be left but the will
of a prevailing force. On this principle the succession of the crown has always been
what it now is, an hereditary succession by law: in the old line it was a succession by
the common law; in the new by the statute law, operating on the principles of the
common law, not changing the substance, but regulating the mode, and describing

1. Florentine statesman Niccolo Machiavelli (1469–1527) was famous for *The Prince*, a handbook on power; "Machiavelian" came to refer to a cynical politics of cunning, manipulation, and duplicity.

the persons. Both these descriptions of law are of the same force, and are derived from an equal authority, emanating from the common agreement and original compact of the state, *communi sponsione reipublicae*,[2] and as such are equally binding on king and people too, as long as the terms are observed, and they continue the same body politic.

[LIBERTIES AS AN ENTAILED INHERITANCE]

You will observe, that from Magna Charta to the Declaration of Right,[3] it has been the uniform policy of our constitution to claim and assert our liberties, as an *entailed inheritance* derived to us from our forefathers, and to be transmitted to our posterity; as an estate specially belonging to the people of this kingdom, without any reference whatever to any other more general or prior right. By this means our constitution preserves a unity in so great a diversity of its parts. We have an inheritable crown; an inheritable peerage; and a House of Commons[4] and a people inheriting privileges, franchises, and liberties, from a long line of ancestors.

This policy appears to me to be the result of profound reflection; or rather the happy effect of following nature, which is wisdom without reflection, and above it. A spirit of innovation is generally the result of a selfish temper, and confined views. People will not look forward to posterity, who never look backward to their ancestors. Besides, the people of England well know, that the idea of inheritance furnishes a sure principle of conservation, and a sure principle of transmission; without at all excluding a principle of improvement. It leaves acquisition free; but it secures what it acquires. Whatever advantages are obtained by a state proceeding on these maxims, are locked fast as in a sort of family settlement; grasped as in a kind of mortmain[5] for ever. By a constitutional policy, working after the pattern of nature, we receive, we hold, we transmit our government and our privileges, in the same manner in which we enjoy and transmit our property and our lives. The institutions of policy, the goods of fortune, the gifts of providence, are handed down to us, and from us, in the same course and order. Our political system is placed in a just correspondence and symmetry with the order of the world, and with the mode of existence decreed to a permanent body composed of transitory parts; wherein, by the disposition of a stupendous wisdom, moulding together the great mysterious incorporation of the human race, the whole, at one time, is never old, or middle-aged, or young, but, in a condition of unchangeable constancy, moves on through the varied tenor of perpetual decay, fall, renovation, and progression. Thus, by preserving the method of nature in the conduct of the state, in what we improve, we are never wholly new; in what we retain, we are never wholly obsolete. By adhering in this manner and on those principles to our forefathers, we are guided not by the superstition of antiquarians, but by the spirit of philosophic analogy. In this choice of inheritance we have given to our frame of polity the image of a relation in blood; binding up the constitution of our country with our dearest domestic ties; adopting our fundamental laws into the bosom of our family affections; keeping inseparable, and cherishing with the warmth of all their combined and mutually reflected charities, our state, our hearths, our sepulchres, and our altars.

2. Common compact of the state (Latin). Burke invokes classical Roman republican authority for the principle of rule based on mutual agreement.
3. The Magna Carta (Great Charter) of 1215 was forced on King John by the nobles, clergy, and merchants to protect them from taxation without consent and from the seizure of property and persons without due process. The Declaration of Right, a result of the Glorious Revolution of 1688, provided civil liberties for the nobility and subjected the monarchy to the rule of law and the consent of Parliament.
4. Lower house of Parliament, to which those without aristocratic titles could be elected as representatives by their home districts.
5. Dead hand (French), the perpetual possession of property by a corporate entity.

Through the same plan of a conformity to nature in our artificial institutions, and by calling in the aid of her unerring and powerful instincts, to fortify the fallible and feeble contrivances of our reason, we have derived several other, and those no small benefits, from considering our liberties in the light of an inheritance. Always acting as if in the presence of canonized forefathers, the spirit of freedom, leading in itself to misrule and excess, is tempered with an awful gravity. This idea of a liberal descent inspires us with a sense of habitual native dignity, which prevents that upstart insolence almost inevitably adhering to and disgracing those who are the first acquirers of any distinction. By this means our liberty becomes a noble freedom. It carries an imposing and majestic aspect. It has a pedigree and illustrating ancestors. It has its bearings and its ensigns armorial. It has its gallery of portraits; its monumental inscriptions; its records, evidences, and titles. We procure reverence to our civil institutions on the principle upon which nature teaches us to revere individual men; on account of their age, and on account of those from whom they are descended. All your sophisters cannot produce anything better adapted to preserve a rational and manly freedom than the course that we have pursued, who have chosen our nature rather than our speculations, our breasts rather than our inventions, for the great conservatories and magazines[6] of our rights and privileges.

[Levellers Can Never Equalise]

Your present confusion, like a palsy, has attacked the fountain of life itself. Every person in your country, in a situation to be actuated by a principle of honour, is disgraced and degraded, and can entertain no sensation of life, except in a mortified and humiliated indignation. But this generation will quickly pass away. The next generation of the nobility will resemble the artificers and clowns, and money-jobbers, usurers, and Jews, who will be always their fellows, sometimes their masters. Believe me, Sir, those who attempt to level,[7] never equalise. In all societies, consisting of various descriptions of citizens, some description must be uppermost. The levellers therefore only change and pervert the natural order of things.

[The Real Rights of Men]

Far am I from denying in theory, full as far is my heart from withholding in practice, (if I were of power to give or to withhold,) the *real* rights of men.[8] In denying their false claims of right, I do not mean to injure those which are real, and are such as their pretended rights would totally destroy. If civil society be made for the advantage of man, all the advantages for which it is made become his right. It is an institution of beneficence; and law itself is only beneficence acting by a rule. Men have a right to live by that rule; they have a right to do justice, as between their fellows, whether their fellows are in public function or in ordinary occupation. They have a right to the fruits of their industry; and to the means of making their industry fruitful. They have a right to the acquisitions of their parents; to the nourishment and improvement of their offspring; to instruction in life, and to consolation in death. Whatever each man can separately do, without trespassing upon others, he has a right to do for himself; and he has a right

---

6. Storehouses, particularly for arms.
7. An allusion to the Levellers, the radical republicans of the English Civil War period of the 1640s, who advocated principles that were to shape democratic movements in Burke's day: universal suffrage for men, a written constitution, proportional representation in a single governing body, and abolition of the monarchy and class privileges.
8. Alluding to the French Revolutionary Declaration of the Rights of Man.

to a fair portion of all which society, with all its combinations of skill and force, can do in his favour. In this partnership all men have equal rights; but not to equal things. He that has but five shillings in the partnership, has as good a right to it, as he that has five hundred pounds has to his larger proportion. But he has not a right to an equal dividend in the product of the joint stock; and as to the share of power, authority, and direction which each individual ought to have in the management of the state, that I must deny to be amongst the direct original rights of man in civil society.

THE ARREST AND IMPRISONMENT OF THE KING AND QUEEN

History will record, that on the morning of the 6th of October, 1789, the king and queen of France, after a day of confusion, alarm, dismay, and slaughter, lay down, under the pledged security of public faith, to indulge nature in a few hours of respite, and troubled, melancholy repose. From this sleep the queen was first startled by the voice of the sentinel at her door, who cried out to her to save herself by flight—that this was the last proof of fidelity he could give—that they were upon him, and he was dead. Instantly he was cut down. A band of cruel ruffians and assassins, reeking with his blood, rushed into the chamber of the queen, and pierced with a hundred strokes of bayonets and poniards the bed, from whence this persecuted woman had but just time to fly almost naked, and, through ways unknown to the murderers, had escaped to seek refuge at the feet of a king and husband, not secure of his own life for a moment.

This king, to say no more of him, and this queen, and their infant children, (who once would have been the pride and hope of a great and generous people,) were then forced to abandon the sanctuary of the most splendid palace in the world, which they left swimming in blood, polluted by massacre, and strewed with scattered limbs and mutilated carcases. Thence they were conducted into the capital of their kingdom. Two had been selected from the unprovoked, unresisted, promiscuous slaughter, which was made of the gentlemen of birth and family who composed the king's body guard. These two gentlemen, with all the parade of an execution of justice, were cruelly and publicly dragged to the block, and beheaded in the great court of the palace. Their heads were stuck upon spears, and led the procession; whilst the royal captives who followed in the train were slowly moved along, amidst the horrid yells, and shrilling screams, and frantic dances, and infamous contumelies, and all the unutterable abominations of the furies of hell, in the abused shape of the vilest of women. After they had been made to taste, drop by drop, more than the bitterness of death, in the slow torture of a journey of twelve miles, protracted to six hours, they were, under a guard, composed of those very soldiers who had thus conducted them through this famous triumph, lodged in one of the old palaces of Paris, now converted into a bastile for kings.

Is this a triumph to be consecrated at altars? to be commemorated with grateful thanksgiving? to be offered to the divine humanity with fervent prayer and enthusiastic ejaculation? ***

Such treatment of any human creatures must be shocking to any but those who are made for accomplishing revolutions. But I cannot stop here. Influenced by the inborn feelings of my nature, and not being illuminated by a single ray of this new sprung modern light, I confess to you, Sir, that the exalted rank of the persons suffering, and particularly the sex, the beauty, and the amiable qualities of the descendant of so many kings and emperors, with the tender age of royal infants, insensible only through infancy and innocence of the cruel outrages to which their parents were exposed, instead of being a subject of exultation, adds not a little to my sensibility on that most melancholy occasion.

I hear that the august person,[9] who was the principal object of our preacher's triumph, though he supported himself, felt much on that shameful occasion. As a man, it became him to feel for his wife and his children, and the faithful guards of his person, that were massacred in cold blood about him; as a prince, it became him to feel for the strange and frightful transformation of his civilized subjects, and to be more grieved for them than solicitous for himself. It derogates little from his fortitude, while it adds infinitely to the honour of his humanity. I am very sorry to say it, very sorry indeed, that such personages are in a situation in which it is not becoming in us to praise the virtues of the great.

I hear, and I rejoice to hear, that the great lady[1] the other object of the triumph, has borne that day, (one is interested that beings made for suffering should suffer well,) and that she bears all the succeeding days, that she bears the imprisonment of her husband, and her own captivity, and the exile of her friends, and the insulting adulation of addresses, and the whole weight of her accumulated wrongs, with a serene patience, in a manner suited to her rank and race, and becoming the offspring of a sovereign distinguished for her piety and her courage: that, like her, she has lofty sentiments; that she feels with the dignity of a Roman matron;[2] that in the last extremity she will save herself from the last disgrace; and that, if she must fall, she will fall by no ignoble hand.[3]

It is now sixteen or seventeen years since I saw the queen of France, then the dauphiness, at Versailles;[4] and surely never lighted on this orb, which she hardly seemed to touch, a more delightful vision. I saw her just above the horizon, decorating and cheering the elevated sphere she just began to move in,—glittering like the morning-star, full of life, and splendour, and joy. Oh! what a revolution! and what a heart must I have to contemplate without emotion that elevation and that fall! Little did I dream when she added titles of veneration to those of enthusiastic, distant, respectful love, that she should ever be obliged to carry the sharp antidote against disgrace concealed in that bosom; little did I dream that I should have lived to see such disasters fallen upon her in a nation of gallant men, in a nation of men of honour, and of cavaliers. I thought ten thousand swords must have leaped from their scabbards to avenge even a look that threatened her with insult. But the age of chivalry is gone. That of sophisters, economists, and calculators, has succeeded; and the glory of Europe is extinguished for ever. Never, never more shall we behold that generous loyalty to rank and sex, that proud submission, that dignified obedience, that subordination of the heart, which kept alive, even in servitude itself, the spirit of an exalted freedom. The unbought grace of life, the cheap defence of nations, the nurse of manly sentiment and heroic enterprise, is gone! It is gone, that sensibility of principle, that chastity of honour, which felt a stain like a wound, which inspired courage whilst it mitigated ferocity, which ennobled whatever it touched, and under which vice itself lost half its evil, by losing all its grossness.

This mixed system of opinion and sentiment had its origin in the ancient chivalry; and the principle, though varied in its appearance by the varying state of human affairs, subsisted and influenced through a long succession of generations, even to

---

9. Louis XVI. The preacher is Richard Price (1723–1791), to whose *Discourse on the Love of Our Country* Burke is replying.

1. Queen Marie Antoinette.

2. The women of ancient Rome were famous for dignified self-possession in adversity; Marie Antoinette's mother was the Empress of Austria, Maria Theresa.

3. In ancient Roman custom, the action of honor in defeat was suicide (see below: "the sharp antidote to disgrace concealed in that bosom"—a small knife or poison). This hope was not realized for Marie Antoinette, who was beheaded in a noisy public event in 1793.

4. The royal palace outside Paris from 1682 until the arrest of this royal family; dauphiness: princess.

the time we live in. If it should ever be totally extinguished, the loss I fear will be great. It is this which has given its character to modern Europe. It is this which has distinguished it under all its forms of government, and distinguished it to its advantage, from the states of Asia, and possibly from those states which flourished in the most brilliant periods of the antique world. It was this, which, without confounding ranks, had produced a noble equality, and handed it down through all the gradations of social life. It was this opinion which mitigated kings into companions, and raised private men to be fellows with kings. Without force or opposition, it subdued the fierceness of pride and power; it obliged sovereigns to submit to the soft collar of social esteem, compelled stern authority to submit to elegance, and gave a dominating vanquisher of laws to be subdued by manners.

But now all is to be changed. All the pleasing illusions, which made power gentle and obedience liberal, which harmonized the different shades of life, and which, by a bland assimilation, incorporated into politics the sentiments which beautify and soften private society, are to be dissolved by this new conquering empire of light and reason.[5] All the decent drapery of life is to be rudely torn off. All the super-added ideas, furnished from the wardrobe of a moral imagination, which the heart owns, and the understanding ratifies, as necessary to cover the defects of our naked, shivering nature, and to raise it to dignity in our own estimation, are to be exploded as a ridiculous, absurd, and antiquated fashion.

On this scheme of things, a king is but a man, a queen is but a woman; a woman is but an animal, and an animal not of the highest order. All homage paid to the sex[6] in general as such, and without distinct views, is to be regarded as romance and folly. Regicide, and parricide, and sacrilege, are but fictions of superstition, corrupting jurisprudence by destroying its simplicity. The murder of a king, or a queen, or a bishop, or a father, are only common homicide; and if the people are by any chance, or in any way, gainers by it, a sort of homicide much the most pardonable, and into which we ought not to make too severe a scrutiny.

On the scheme of this barbarous philosophy, which is the offspring of cold hearts and muddy understandings, and which is as void of solid wisdom as it is destitute of all taste and elegance, laws are to be supported only by their own terrors, and by the concern which each individual may find in them from his own private speculations, or can spare to them from his own private interests. In the groves of *their* academy,[7] at the end of every vista, you see nothing but the gallows. Nothing is left which engages the affections on the part of the commonwealth. On the principles of this mechanic philosophy, our institutions can never be embodied, if I may use the expression, in persons; so as to create in us love, veneration, admiration, or attachment. But that sort of reason which banishes the affections is incapable of filling their place. These public affections, combined with manners, are required sometimes as supplements, sometimes as correctives, always as aids to law. The precept given by a wise man, as well as a great critic, for the construction of poems, is equally true as to states:—*Non satis est pulchra esse poemata, dulcia sunto.*[8] There ought to be a system of manners in every nation, which a well-formed mind would be disposed to relish. To make us love our country, our country ought to be lovely.

---

5. A sarcastic reference to the Enlightenment ideology of Reason championed by political reformers and revolutionaries alike.
6. The female sex (a common usage).

7. In ancient Greece, philosophers and students met outside under the shade of the trees.
8. "It is not enough that poems be beautiful, they must be sweet [tender, touching]" (Horace, *Ars Poetica*).

But power, of some kind or other, will survive the shock in which manners and opinions perish; and it will find other and worse means for its support. The usurpation which, in order to subvert ancient institutions, has destroyed ancient principles, will hold power by arts similar to those by which it has acquired it. When the old feudal and chivalrous spirit of *fealty*,[9] which, by freeing kings from fear, freed both kings and subjects from the precautions of tyranny, shall be extinct in the minds of men, plots and assassinations will be anticipated by preventive murder and preventive confiscation, and that long roll of grim and bloody maxims, which form the political code of all power, not standing on its own honour, and the honour of those who are to obey it. Kings will be tyrants from policy, when subjects are rebels from principle.

When ancient opinions and rules of life are taken away, the loss cannot possibly be estimated. From that moment we have no compass to govern us; nor can we know distinctly to what port we steer. Europe, undoubtedly, taken in a mass, was in a flourishing condition the day on which your revolution was completed. How much of that prosperous state was owing to the spirit of our old manners and opinions is not easy to say; but as such causes cannot be indifferent in their operation, we must presume, that, on the whole, their operation was beneficial.

We are but too apt to consider things in the state in which we find them, without sufficiently adverting to the causes by which they have been produced, and possibly may be upheld. Nothing is more certain, than that our manners, our civilization, and all the good things which are connected with manners and with civilization, have, in this European world of ours, depended for ages upon two principles; and were indeed the result of both combined; I mean the spirit of a gentleman, and the spirit of religion. The nobility and the clergy, the one by profession, the other by patronage, kept learning in existence, even in the midst of arms and confusions, and whilst governments were rather in their causes, than formed. Learning paid back what it received to nobility and to priesthood; and paid it with usury,[1] by enlarging their ideas, and by furnishing their minds. Happy if they had all continued to know their indissoluble union, and their proper place! Happy if learning, not debauched by ambition, had been satisfied to continue the instructor, and not aspired to be the master! Along with its natural protectors and guardians, learning will be cast into the mire, and trodden down under the hoofs of a swinish multitude.[2]

["THIS GREAT DRAMA"]

[W]hen kings are hurled from their thrones by the Supreme Director[3] of this great drama, and become the objects of insult to the base, and of pity to the good, we behold such disasters in the moral, as we should behold a miracle in the physical, order of things. We are alarmed into reflection; our minds (as it has long since been observed) are purified by terror and pity;[4] our weak, unthinking pride is humbled under the dispensations of a mysterious wisdom. Some tears might be drawn from me, if such a spectacle were exhibited on the stage. I should be truly ashamed of finding in myself that superficial, theatric sense of painted distress, whilst I could exult over it in real life. With such a perverted mind, I could never venture to show my face at a

---

9. Medieval ideal of a vassal's fidelity to his lord; by extension, the allegiance that secures social order both from violent revolt and from preventive lordly tyranny.
1. Interest; here, a positive term.
2. Among the several rebuttals provoked by *Reflections* was *The Reply of the Swinish Multitude to Mr. Burke*.

3. A metaphor for God.
4. In his extended metaphor of the "great drama," Burke refers to Aristotle's argument in *Poetics* for the salutary effect of drama in its controlled release of sensations of pity and fear. See also Barbauld, *Eighteen Hundred and Eleven*, line 110.

tragedy. People would think the tears that Garrick formerly, or that Siddons not long since, have extorted from me, were the tears of hypocrisy;[5] I should know them to be the tears of folly.

Indeed the theatre is a better school of moral sentiments than churches, where the feelings of humanity are thus outraged. Poets who have to deal with an audience not yet graduated in the school of the rights of men, and who must apply themselves to the moral constitution of the heart, would not dare to produce such a triumph as a matter of exultation. There, where men follow their natural impulses, they would not bear the odious maxims of a Machiavelian policy, whether applied to the attainment of monarchical or democratic tyranny. They would reject them on the modern, as they once did on the ancient stage, where they could not bear even the hypothetical proposition of such wickedness in the mouth of a personated tyrant, though suitable to the character he sustained. No theatric audience in Athens would bear what has been borne, in the midst of the real tragedy of this triumphal day; a principal actor weighing, as it were in scales hung in a shop of horrors,—so much actual crime against so much contingent advantage,—and after putting in and out weights, declaring that the balance was on the side of the advantages. They would not bear to see the crimes of new democracy posted as in a ledger against the crimes of old despotism, and the book-keepers of politics finding democracy still in debt, but by no means unable or unwilling to pay the balance. In the theatre, the first intuitive glance, without any elaborate process of reasoning, will show, that this method of political computation would justify every extent of crime. They would see, that on these principles, even where the very worst acts were not perpetrated, it was owing rather to the fortune of the conspirators, than to their parsimony in the expenditure of treachery and blood. They would soon see, that criminal means once tolerated are soon preferred. They present a shorter cut to the object than through the highway of the moral virtues. Justifying perfidy and murder for public benefit, public benefit would soon become the pretext, and perfidy and murder the end; until rapacity, malice, revenge, and fear more dreadful than revenge, could satiate their insatiable appetites. Such must be the consequences of losing, in the splendour of these triumphs of the rights of men, all natural sense of wrong and right.

[THE CONTRACT OF SOCIETY]

To avoid therefore the evils of inconstancy and versatility, ten thousand times worse than those of obstinacy and the blindest prejudice, we have consecrated the state, that no man should approach to look into its defects or corruptions but with due caution; that he should never dream of beginning its reformation by its subversion; that he should approach to the faults of the state as to the wounds of a father, with pious awe and trembling solicitude. By this wise prejudice we are taught to look with horror on those children of their country, who are prompt rashly to hack that aged parent in pieces, and put him into the kettle of magicians, in hopes that by their poisonous weeds, and wild incantations, they may regenerate the paternal constitution, and renovate their father's life.[6]

---

5. David Garrick (1717–1779) and Sarah Siddons (1755–1831) were celebrated actors of Shakespeare's tragedies; "hypocrisy" is derived from a Greek word for "stage-acting."

6. Manipulated by the sorceress Medea, the daughters of Pelias, King of Thessaly, took this course of action, not realizing that Medea was in league with Pelias's dispossessed half-nephew, Jason.

Society is indeed a contract. Subordinate contracts for objects of mere occasional interest may be dissolved at pleasure—but the state ought not to be considered as nothing better than a partnership agreement in a trade of pepper and coffee, calico or tobacco, or some other such low concern, to be taken up for a little temporary interest, and to be dissolved by the fancy of the parties. It is to be looked on with other reverence; because it is not a partnership in things subservient only to the gross animal existence of a temporary and perishable nature. It is a partnership in all science; a partnership in all art; a partnership in every virtue, and in all perfection. As the ends of such a partnership cannot be obtained in many generations, it becomes a partnership not only between those who are living, but between those who are living, those who are dead, and those who are to be born. Each contract of each particular state is but a clause in the great primaeval contract of eternal society, linking the lower with the higher natures, connecting the visible and invisible world, according to a fixed compact sanctioned by the inviolable oath which holds all physical and all moral natures, each in their appointed place. This law is not subject to the will of those, who by an obligation above them, and infinitely superior, are bound to submit their will to that law. The municipal corporations of that universal kingdom are not morally at liberty at their pleasure, and on their speculations of a contingent improvement, wholly to separate and tear asunder the bands of their subordinate community, and to dissolve it into an unsocial, uncivil, unconnected chaos of elementary principles. It is the first and supreme necessity only, a necessity that is not chosen, but chooses, a necessity paramount to deliberation, that admits no discussion, and demands no evidence, which alone can justify a resort to anarchy. This necessity is no exception to the rule; because this necessity itself is a part too of that moral and physical disposition of things, to which man must be obedient by consent or force: but if that which is only submission to necessity should be made the object of choice, the law is broken, nature is disobeyed, and the rebellious are outlawed, cast forth, and exiled, from this world of reason, and order, and peace, and virtue, and fruitful penitence, into the antagonist world of madness, discord, vice, confusion, and unavailing sorrow.

Mary Wollstonecraft
1759–1797

Mary Wollstonecraft was living on her own in London on Bastille Day, 14 July 1789, writing for and serving on the staff of the *Analytical Review*, enjoying a lively circle of artists, writers, and intellectuals gathered around Joseph Johnson, its politically radical publisher. *A Vindication of the Rights of Men* (published by Johnson) appeared on 29 November 1790, leading a flood of responses to Burke's *Reflections on the Revolution in France*, which had appeared only weeks before. Her title refers to the Declaration of the Rights of Man voted by the French Constituent Assembly in August 1789. Caustic, trenchant, and frequently sarcastic, *Rights of Men* made her reputation when the second edition, nineteen days later, bore her name. Concerned chiefly to refute Burke's arguments for the hereditary succession of the crown, the inviolability of a national constitution, and the necessary alliance of church and state, Wollstonecraft also drew notice for her collateral arguments about the property of the poor, and for her bitter critiques of naval impressment, antipoaching laws, slavery, and Burke's attitudes about women and gender, which had already irritated her in his widely influential *A Philosophical Enquiry into the Origin of Our Ideas of the Sublime and Beautiful* (1757); see page 52.

For more about Wollstonecraft, see her principal listing, page 302.

from A Vindication of the Rights of Men
in a Letter to the Right Honourable Edmund Burke; Occasioned by his Reflections on the Revolution in France

Mr. Burke's Reflections on the French Revolution first engaged my attention as the transient topic of the day. *** My indignation was roused by the sophistical arguments, that every moment crossed me, in the questionable shape[1] of natural feelings and common sense. *** I have confined my strictures, in a great measure, to the grand principles at which he has levelled many ingenious arguments in a very specious garb.

[SENSIBILITY]

Sensibility is the *manie* of the day,[2] and compassion the virtue which is to cover a multitude of vices, whilst justice is left to mourn in sullen silence, and balance truth in vain.

In life, an honest man with a confined understanding is frequently the slave of his habits and the dupe of his feelings, whilst the man with a clearer head and colder heart makes the passions of others bend to his interest; but truly sublime is the character that acts from principle. *** All your pretty flights arise from your pampered sensibility; and that, vain of this fancied pre-eminence of organs, you foster every emotion till the fumes, mounting to your brain, dispel the sober suggestions of reason. It is not in this view surprising, that when you should argue you become impassioned, and that reflection inflames your imagination, instead of enlightening your understanding.

Quitting now the flowers of rhetoric, let us, Sir, reason together.[3]***

The birthright of man, to give you, Sir, a short definition of this disputed right, is such a degree of liberty, civil and religious, as is compatible with the liberty of every other individual with whom he is united in a social compact, and the continued existence of that compact.[4]

Liberty, in this simple, unsophisticated sense, I acknowledge, is a fair idea that has never yet received a form in the various governments that have been established on our bounteous globe; the demon of property has ever been at hand to encroach

---

1. A sardonic allusion to Hamlet's first address to his father's ghost: "Angels and ministers of grace defend us! / Be thou a spirit of health or goblin damned, / Bring with thee airs from heaven or blasts from hell, / Be thy intents wicked or charitable, / Thou com'st in such a questionable shape / That I will speak to thee" (*Hamlet* 1.4.39–44).

2. The "Cult of Sensibility," elevating feelings over rationality, was associated with poets and novelists of both sexes, but with a sense that such culture is "feminine" in character. *Manie*, a quasi-medical term, blends the senses of emotional hyperactivity and mania, a cultural craze. See the opening of Lockhart's *Cockney School of Poetry*, page 982.

3. A parody of Isaiah: "Come now, and let us reason together, saith the Lord: though your sins be as scarlet, they

shall be as white as snow" (1.18). Rhetoric, an ornamental art, may displace reason; see Wollstonecraft's remarks on her style in *Rights of Woman*, pages 305–09.

4. John Locke's *Two Treatises on Civil Government* (1690) defines the "*original Compact*," whereby every man "with others incorporates into *one Society*," with "an obligation to every one of that Society, to submit to the determination of the *majority*, and to be concluded by it" (2.97). Jean-Jacques Rousseau's *Social Contract* (1762) argues that a free acceptance of this contract involves the surrender of the individual to the State, their reciprocal obligations, and their legal equality. Although Rousseau distrusted democracy and preferred monarchy, this work would be blamed for inspiring the "democratic despotism" fostered by the French Revolution.

on the sacred rights of men, and to fence round with awful pomp laws that war with justice. *** I perceive from the whole tenor of your Reflections, that you have a moral antipathy to reason; but, if there is any thing like argument, or first principles, in your wild declamation, behold the result:—that we are to reverence the rust of antiquity, and term the unnatural customs, which ignorance and mistaken self-interest have consolidated, the sage fruit of experience: nay, that, if we do discover some errors, our *feelings* should lead us to excuse, with blind love, or unprincipled filial affection, the venerable vestiges of ancient days. These are gothic notions of beauty[5]—the ivy is beautiful, but, when it insidiously destroys the trunk from which it receives support, who would not grub it up? ***

The civilization which has taken place in Europe has been very partial, and, like every custom that an arbitrary point of honour has established, refines the manners at the expence of morals, by making sentiments and opinions current in conversation that have no root in the heart, or weight in the cooler resolves of the mind.—And what has stopped its progress?—hereditary property—hereditary honours. The man has been changed into an artificial monster by the station in which he was born, and the consequent homage that benumbed his faculties like the torpedo's touch;[6]—or a being, with a capacity of reasoning, would not have failed to discover, as his faculties unfolded, that true happiness arose from the friendship and intimacy which can only be enjoyed by equals; and that charity is not a condescending distribution of alms, but an intercourse of good offices and mutual benefits, founded on respect for justice and humanity.

[AUTHORITY, SLAVERY, AND NATURAL RIGHTS]

Are we to seek for the rights of men in the ages when a few marks were the only penalty imposed for the life of a man, and death for death when the property of the rich was touched? when—I blush to discover the depravity of our nature—when a deer was killed![7] Are these the laws that it is natural to love, and sacrilegious to invade?—Were the rights of men understood when the law authorized or tolerated murder?—or is power and right the same in your creed? ***

It is necessary emphatically to repeat, that there are rights which men inherit at their birth, as rational creatures, who were raised above the brute creation by their improvable faculties; and that, in receiving these, not from their forefathers but, from God, prescription can never undermine natural rights.

A father may dissipate his property without his child having any right to complain;—but should he attempt to sell him for a slave, or fetter him with laws contrary to reason; nature, in enabling him to discern good from evil, teaches him to break the ignoble chain, and not to believe that bread becomes flesh, and wine blood, because his parents swallowed the Eucharist[8] with this blind persuasion.

There is no end to this implicit submission to authority—some where it must stop, or we return to barbarism; and the capacity of improvement, which gives us a

---

5. The "gothic" aesthetic of the 18th century admired the gloomy, wild, and untamed, and adored ivied ruins (preferably of medieval Gothic architecture); ivy is a parasite.
6. The numbing electric discharges of the torpedo, a ray fish; *torpedo* in Latin means *numbness*.
7. From 1389 to 1831, British law restricted the right to kill game to wealthy landlords and leaseholders; poaching, a

theft often motivated by desperate hunger, was punishable by death.
8. Catholic theology stressed that the communion bread and wine are inwardly transformed into Christ's body and blood. Wollstonecraft was religious; her contempt issues from a general English disdain of Roman Catholicism as well as from her Enlightenment deism, which distrusted the authority of an established Church.

natural sceptre on earth, is a cheat, an ignis-fatuus,[9] that leads us from inviting meadows into bogs and dunghills. And if it be allowed that many of the precautions, with which any alteration was made, in our government, were prudent, it rather proves its weakness that substantiates an opinion of the soundness of the stamina, or the excellence of the constitution.

But on what principle Mr. Burke could defend American independence, I cannot conceive;[1] for the whole tenor of his plausible arguments settles slavery on an everlasting foundation. Allowing his servile reverence for antiquity, and prudent attention to self-interest, to have the force which he insists on, the slave trade ought never to be abolished;[2] and, because our ignorant forefathers, not understanding the native dignity of man, sanctioned a traffic that outrages every suggestion of reason and religion, we are to submit to the inhuman custom, and term an atrocious insult to humanity the love of our country, and a proper submission to the laws by which our property is secured.—Security of property! Behold, in a few words, the definition of English liberty. And to this selfish principle every nobler one is sacrificed.—The Briton takes place of the man, and the image of God is lost in the citizen! But it is not that enthusiastic flame which in Greece and Rome consumed every sordid passion: no, self is the focus; and the disparting rays rise not above our foggy atmosphere. But softly—it is only the property of the rich that is secure; the man who lives by the sweat of his brow has no asylum from oppression. *** It is a farce to pretend that a man fights *for his country, his hearth, or his altars,* when he has neither liberty nor property.—His property is in his nervous arms—and they are compelled to pull a strange rope at the surly command of a tyrannic boy, who probably obtained his rank on account of his family connections, or the prostituted vote of his father, whose interest in a borough, or voice as a senator, was acceptable to the minister.[3] ***

Misery, to reach your heart, I perceive, must have its cap and bells;[4] your tears are reserved, very *naturally* considering your character, for the declamation of the theatre, or for the downfall of queens, whose rank alters the nature of folly, and throws a graceful veil over vices that degrade humanity; whilst the distress of many industrious mothers, whose *helpmates* have been torn from them, and the hungry cry of helpless babes, were vulgar sorrows that could not move your commiseration, though they might extort an alms. ***

The game laws are almost as oppressive to the peasantry as press-warrants to the mechanic.[5] In this land of liberty what is to secure the property of the poor farmer when his noble landlord chooses to plant a decoy field near his little property?[6] Game devour the fruit of his labour; but fines and imprisonment await him if he dare to kill any—or lift up his hand to interrupt the pleasure of his lord. How many families have been plunged, in the *sporting* countries, into misery and vice for some paltry transgression of these coercive laws, by the natural consequence of that anger which a man feels when he sees the reward of his industry laid waste by unfeeling luxury?— when his children's bread is given to dogs!

9. Latin for false/foolish fire: nighttime lights over marsh-lands supposedly caused by spontaneous combustion of gases released by the decay of organic material; a deceptive guiding light, an illusory ideal.
1. Burke's *Speech on Conciliation with America* (22 March 1775) defended the American Revolution on principles of traditional British liberties (e.g., taxation by consent and representation).
2. The institution of slavery in ancient Greece and Rome poses a contradiction to Burke's support in the 1780s of the parliamentary movement to abolish the slave trade.
3. "Nervous" means "well strung, vigorous." The italics tweak at Burke (see page 115).
4. A court-jester's bell-tipped hat; hence, amusements.
5. Game laws criminalized any killing of a protected herd; a mechanic is a skilled laborer. To meet wartime needs, warrants of impressment forced men into military service.
6. As bait.

You have shewn, Sir, by your silence on these subjects, that your respect for rank has swallowed up the common feelings of humanity; you seem to consider the poor as only the live stock of an estate, the feather of hereditary nobility.

A brutal attachment to children has appeared most conspicuous in parents who have treated them like slaves, and demanded due homage for all the property they transferred to them, during their lives. It has led them to force their children to break the most sacred ties; to do violence to a natural impulse, and run into legal prostitution to increase wealth or shun poverty.[7] *** It appears to be a natural suggestion of reason, that a man should be freed from implicit obedience to parents and private punishments, when he is of an age to be subject to the jurisdiction of the laws of his country; and that the barbarous cruelty of allowing parents to imprison their children, to prevent their contaminating their noble blood by following the dictates of nature when they chose to marry, or for any misdemeanor that does not come under the cognizance of public justice, is one of the most arbitrary violations of liberty.[8]

Who can recount all the unnatural crimes which the *laudable*, *interesting* desire of perpetuating a name has produced? The younger children have been sacrificed to the eldest son; sent into exile, or confined in convents, that they might not encroach on what was called, with shameful falsehood, the *family* estate.[9] Will Mr Burke call this parental affection reasonable or virtuous?—No; it is the spurious offspring of overweening, mistaken pride—and not that first source of civilization, natural parental affection, that makes no difference between child and child, but what reason justifies by pointing out superior merit.

Another pernicious consequence which unavoidably arises from this artificial affection is, the insuperable bar which it puts in the way of early marriages. It would be difficult to determine whether the minds or bodies of our youth are most injured by this impediment. Our young men become selfish coxcombs. ***

The same system has an equally pernicious effect on female morals.—Girls are sacrificed to family convenience, or else marry to settle themselves in a superior rank, and coquet, without restraint, with the fine gentleman whom I have already described.

[PROPERTY AND VIRTUE]

Property, I do not scruple to aver it, should be fluctuating, which would be the case, if it were more equally divided amongst all the children of a family; else it is an everlasting rampart, in consequence of a barbarous feudal institution, that enables the elder son to overpower talents and depress virtue.[1]

Besides, an unmanly servility, most inimical to true dignity of character is, by this means, fostered in society. Men of some abilities play on the follies of the rich, and mounting to fortune as they degrade themselves, they stand in the way of men of superior talents, who cannot advance in such crooked paths, or wade through the filth which *parasites* never boggle at. Pursuing their way straight forward, their spirit

---

7. Marriage for financial reasons—a term, used by Daniel Defoe in *Conjugal Lewdness: or, Matrimonial Whoredom* (1727), and again by Wollstonecraft, in *Rights of Woman*.
8. In *Letters Written in France, in the Summer of 1790*, Helen Maria Williams tells of one family that suffered such injustice (chs. 16–22); until 1791, a "lettre de cachet" signed by the king permitted imprisonment without trial.

Wordsworth tells a story, based on Williams, of French parental tyranny against young lovers at the end of Book 9 of the 1805 *Prelude* (556–935).
9. The system of primogeniture, abolished in the French Revolution, preserved the estate by restricting inheritance to the first-born son. See H. M. Williams, page 112.
1. So Locke argued in *Treatises on Government* (2.25–51).

is either bent or broken by the rich man's contumelies[2] or the difficulties they have to encounter.

The only security of property that nature authorizes and reason sanctions is, the right a man has to enjoy the acquisitions which his talents and industry have acquired; and to bequeath them to whom he chooses. *** Overreaching, adultery, and coquetry, are venial offences, though they reduce virtue to an empty name, and make wisdom consist in saving appearances.

"On this scheme of things[3] a king *is* but a man; a queen *is* but a woman; a woman *is* but an animal, and an animal not of the highest order."—All true, Sir; if she is not more attentive to the duties of humanity than queens and fashionable ladies in general are. I will still further accede to the opinion you have so justly conceived of the spirit which begins to animate this age.—"All homage paid to the sex in general, as such, and without distinct views, is to be regarded as *romance* and folly." Undoubtedly; because such homage vitiates them, prevents their endeavouring to obtain solid personal merit; and, in short, makes those beings vain inconsiderate dolls, who ought to be prudent mothers and useful members of society. "Regicide and sacrilege are but fictions of superstition corrupting jurisprudence, by destroying its simplicity. The murder of a king, or a queen, or a bishop, are only common homicide."—Again I agree with you; but you perceive, Sir, that by leaving out the word *father,* I think the whole extent of the comparison invidious.[4]

[Romance and Chivalry]

Whether the glory of Europe is set, I shall not now enquire; but probably the spirit of romance and chivalry is in the wane; and reason will gain by its extinction.

From observing several cold romantic characters I have been led to confine the term romantic to one definition—false, or rather artificial, feelings. Works of genius are read with a prepossession in their favour, and sentiments imitated, because they were fashionable and pretty, and not because they were forcibly felt.

In modern poetry the understanding and memory often fabricate the pretended effusions of the heart, and romance destroys all simplicity; which, in works of taste, is but a synonymous word for truth. This romantic spirit has extended to our prose, and scattered artificial flowers over the most barren heath; or a mixture of verse and prose producing the strangest incongruities. The turgid bombast of some of your periods[5] fully proves these assertions; for when the heart speaks we are seldom shocked by hyperbole, or dry raptures. *** I am led very often to doubt your sincerity, and to suppose that you have said many things merely for the sake of saying them well. *** The mock dignity and haughty stalk, only reminds me of the ass in the lion's skin.

A sentiment of this kind glanced across my mind when I read the following exclamation. "Whilst the royal captives, who followed in the train, were slowly moved along, amidst the horrid yells, and shrilling screams, and frantic dances, and infamous contumelies, and all the unutterable abominations of the furies of hell, in the abused shape of the vilest of women."[6] Probably you mean women who gained a livelihood by selling vegetables or fish, who never had any advantages of education; or their

---

2. Insults and abuses; a phrase from Hamlet's world-weary soliloquy (3.1).
3. As you ironically observe [Wollstonecraft's note]. Here and following, she applies her emphases to statements in Burke's *Reflections*.

4. Burke actually wrote "Regicide, and parricide, and sacrilege" (see page 119).
5. Sentences.
6. See Burke's *Reflections*, page 117.

vices might have lost part of their abominable deformity, by losing part of their gross-ness. The queen of France—the great and small vulgar, claim our pity; they have almost insuperable obstacles to surmount in their progress towards true dignity of character; still I have such a plain downright understanding that I do not like to make a distinction without a difference. But it is not very extraordinary that *you* should, for throughout your letter you frequently advert to a sentimental jargon, which has long been current in conversation, and even in books of morals, though it never received the *regal* stamp of reason. A kind of mysterious instinct is *supposed* to reside in the soul, that instantaneously discerns truth, without the tedious labour of ratiocination. This instinct, for I know not what other name to give it, has been termed *common sense,* and more frequently *sensibility,* and, by a kind of *indefeasible* right, it has been *supposed,* for rights of this kind are not easily proved, to reign paramount over the other faculties of the mind, and to be an authority from which there is no appeal. *** It is to this instinct, without doubt, that you allude, when you talk of the "moral constitution of the heart."

In the name of the people of England, you say, "*** In England we have not yet been completely emboweled of our natural entrails; we still feel within us, and we cherish and cultivate those inbred sentiments which are the faithful guard-ians, the active monitors of our duty, the true supporters of all liberal and manly morals."—What do you mean by inbred sentiments? From whence do they come? How were they bred? Are they the brood of folly, which swarms like the insects on the banks of the Nile, when mud and putrefaction have enriched the languid soil? Were these *inbred* sentiments faithful guardians of our duty when the church was an asylum for murderers, and men worshipped bread as a God? when slavery was authorized by law to fasten her fangs on human flesh, and the iron eat into the very soul? If these sentiments are not acquired, if our passive dispositions do not expand into virtuous affections and passions, why are not the Tartars in the first rude horde endued with sentiments white and *elegant* as the driven snow? Why is passion or heroism the child of reflection, the consequence of dwelling with intent contemplation on one object? The appetites are the only perfect inbred powers that I can discern; and they like instincts have a certain aim, they can be satisfied—but improveable reason has not yet discovered the perfection it may arrive at—God forbid!

[THE RICH AND THE POOR]

The rich and weak, a numerous train, will certainly applaud your system, and loudly celebrate your pious reverence for authority and establishments—they find it pleas-anter to enjoy than to think; to justify oppression than correct abuses.—*The rights of men* are grating sounds that set their teeth on edge; the impertinent enquiry of philosophic meddling innovation. If the poor are in distress, they will make some *benevolent* exertions to assist them; they will confer obligations, but not do justice. Benevolence is a very amiable specious quality; yet the aversion which men feel to accept a right as a favour, should rather be extolled as a vestige of native dignity, than stigmatized as the odious offspring of ingratitude. The poor consider the rich as their lawful prey; but we ought not too severely to animadvert on[7] their ingrati-tude. When they receive an alms they are commonly grateful at the moment; but old habits quickly return, and cunning has ever been a substitute for force. ***

---

7. Censure.

Among all your plausible arguments, and witty illustrations, your contempt for the poor always appears conspicuous, and rouses my indignation. The following paragraph in particular struck me, as breathing the most tyrannic spirit, and displaying the most factitious feelings. "Good order is the foundation of all good things. To be enabled to acquire, the people, without being servile, must be tractable and obedient. The magistrate must have his reverence, the laws their authority. The body of the people must not find the principles of natural subordination by art rooted out of their minds. They *must* respect that property of which they *cannot* partake. *They must labour to obtain what by labour can be obtained; and when they find, as they commonly do, the success disproportioned to the endeavour, they must be taught their consolation in the final proportions of eternal justice.* Of this consolation, whoever deprives them, deadens their industry, and strikes at the root of all acquisition as of all conservation. He that does this, is the cruel oppressor, the merciless enemy, of the poor and wretched; at the same time that, by his wicked speculations, he exposes the fruits of successful industry, and the accumulations of fortune, (ah! there's the rub)[8] to the plunder of the negligent, the disappointed, and the unprosperous."

This is contemptible hard-hearted sophistry, in the specious form of humility, and submission to the will of Heaven.—It is, Sir, *possible* to render the poor happier in this world, without depriving them of the consolation which you gratuitously grant them in the next. They have a right to more comfort than they at present enjoy; and more comfort might be afforded them, without encroaching on the pleasures of the rich: not now waiting to enquire whether the rich have any right to exclusive pleasures. What do I say?—encroaching! No; if an intercourse were established between them, it would impart the only true pleasure that can be snatched in this land of shadows, this hard school of moral discipline.

I know, indeed, that there is often something disgusting in the distresses of poverty, at which the imagination revolts, and starts back to exercise itself in the more attractive Arcadia of fiction.[9] The rich man builds a house, art and taste give it the highest finish. His gardens are planted, and the trees grow to recreate the fancy of the planter, though the temperature of the climate may rather force him to avoid the dangerous damps they exhale, than seek the umbrageous retreat. Every thing on the estate is cherished but man;—yet, to contribute to the happiness of man, is the most sublime of all enjoyments. But if, instead of sweeping pleasure-grounds, obelisks, temples, and elegant cottages, as *objects* for the eye,[1] the heart was allowed to beat true to nature, decent farms would be scattered over the estate, and plenty smile around. Instead of the poor being subject to the griping hand of an avaricious steward, they would be watched over with fatherly solicitude, by the man whose duty and pleasure it was to guard their happiness, and shield from rapacity the beings who, by the sweat of their brow, exalted him above his fellows.

I could almost imagine I see a man thus gathering blessings as he mounted the hill of life; or consolation, in those days when the spirits lag, and the tired heart finds no pleasure in them. It is not by squandering alms that the poor can be relieved, or

---

8. The flaw in the argument, echoing *Hamlet* 3.1.65, on the attraction of suicide thwarted by fear of the afterlife.
9. Ancient Greek region famed for pastoral simplicity, beauty, and harmony.

1. A reference to the 18th-century vogue on aristocratic estates, which frequently involved vast relandscaping, picturesquely enhanced by pillars, classical temples, instant ruins, and quaint cottages.

improved—it is the fostering sun of kindness, the wisdom that finds them employments calculated to give them habits of virtue, that meliorates their condition. ***

Why cannot large estates be divided into small farms? these dwellings would indeed grace our land. Why are huge forests still allowed to stretch out with idle pomp and all the indolence of Eastern grandeur? Why does the brown waste meet the traveller's view, when men want work? But commons cannot be enclosed without *acts of parliament* to increase the property of the rich![2] Why might not the industrious peasant be allowed to steal a farm from the heath? This sight I have seen;—the cow that supported the children grazed near the hut, and the cheerful poultry were fed by the chubby babes, who breathed a bracing air, far from the diseases and the vices of cities. Domination blasts all these prospects; virtue can only flourish amongst equals, and the man who submits to a fellow-creature, because it promotes his worldly interest, and he who relieves only because it is his duty to lay up a treasure in heaven,[3] are much on a par, for both are radically degraded by the habits of their life.

In this great city, that proudly rears its head, and boasts of its population and commerce, how much misery lurks in pestilential corners, whilst idle mendicants assail, on every side, the man who hates to encourage impostors, or repress, with angry frown, the plaints of the poor! How many mechanics, by a flux of trade or fashion, lose their employment; whom misfortunes, not to be warded off, lead to the idleness that vitiates their character and renders them afterwards averse to honest labour! Where is the eye that marks these evils, more gigantic than any of the infringements of property, which you piously deprecate? Are these remediless evils? And is the humane heart satisfied with turning the poor over to *another* world, to receive the blessings this could afford? ***

What were the outrages of a day[4] to these continual miseries? Let those sorrows hide their diminished head before the tremendous mountain of woe that thus defaces our globe![5] Man preys on man; and you mourn *** for the empty pageant of a name, when slavery flaps her wing, and the sick heart retires to die in lonely wilds, far from the abodes of men. Did the pangs you felt for insulted nobility, the anguish that rent your heart when the gorgeous robes were torn off the idol human weakness had set up, deserve to be compared with the long-drawn sigh of melancholy reflection, when misery and vice are thus seen to haunt our steps, and swim on the top of every cheering prospect? Why is our fancy to be appalled by terrific perspective of a hell beyond the grave?—Hell stalks abroad;—the lash resounds on the slave's naked sides; and the sick wretch, who can no longer earn the sour bread of unremitting labour, steals to a ditch to bid the world a long good night—or, neglected in some ostentatious hospital, breathes his last amidst the laugh of mercenary attendants.

Such misery demands more than tears—I pause to recollect myself; and smother the contempt I feel rising for your rhetorical flourishes and infantine sensibility.

Second edition, 1790

2. Eastern: Asian. "Brown waste" is arable but untilled land. Lancelot "Capability" Brown, a famous landscaper of aristocratic estates, devised, among other "improvements," idle, though picturesque, stretches of forests and plains. In the 18th century, Parliament enacted a series of extreme "enclosure" acts, deeding to private ownership formerly public lands (the "commons" being the least arable of these), on which the poor lived, grew crops, and pastured livestock.
3. Jesus preaches, "lay up for yourselves treasures in heaven, where neither moth nor rust doth corrupt, and

where thieves do not break through nor steal" (Matthew 6.20). Wollstonecraft's sarcasm on self-interested charity, the belief that such acts will count in one's favor in the judgment of Heaven.
4. The 6th of October (1789) [Wollstonecraft's note]; see Burke, *Reflections*, page 117.
5. In *Paradise Lost*, Satan notes how "all the Stars / Hide thir diminisht heads" at the sight of the noonday sun, "with surpassing Glory crown'd" (4.32–33).

Letter to Joseph Johnson, from Paris, December 27, 1792.[1]

I should immediately on the receipt of your letter, my dear friend, have thanked you for your punctuality, for it highly gratified me, had I not wished to wait till I could tell you that this day was not stained in blood. Indeed the prudent precautions taken by the National Convention to prevent a tumult, made me suppose that the dogs of faction would not dare to bark, much less to bite, however true to their scent; and I was not mistaken; for the citizens, who were all called out, are returning home with composed countenances, shouldering their arms. About nine o'clock this morning, the king passed by my window, moving silently along (excepting now and then a few strokes on the drum, which rendered the stillness more awful) through empty streets, surrounded by the national guards, who, clustering round the carriage, seemed to deserve their name. The inhabitants flocked to their windows, but the casements were all shut, not a voice was heard, nor did I see any thing like an insulting gesture.—For the first time since I entered France, I bowed to the majesty of the people, and respected the propriety of behaviour so perfectly in unison with my own feelings. I can scarcely tell you why, but an association of ideas made the tears flow insensibly from my eyes, when I saw Louis sitting, with more dignity than I expected from his character, in a hackney coach,[2] going to meet death, where so many of his race have triumphed. My fancy instantly brought Louis XIV[3] before me, entering the capital with all his pomp, after one of the victories most flattering to his pride, only to see the sunshine of prosperity overshadowed by the sublime gloom of misery. I have been alone ever since; and, though my mind is calm, I cannot dismiss the lively images that have filled my imagination all the day.—Nay, do not smile, but pity me; for, once or twice, lifting my eyes from the paper, I have seen eyes glare through a glass-door opposite my chair, and bloody hands shook at me. Not the distant sound of a footstep can I hear.—My apartments are remote from those of the servants, the only persons who sleep with me in an immense hotel, one folding door opening after another.—I wish I had even kept the cat with me!—I want to see something alive; death in so many frightful stages has taken hold of my fancy—I am going to bed—and, for the first time in my life, I cannot put out the candle.

M.W.

Thomas Paine
1737–1809

"These are the times that try men's souls," declared Tom Paine in a pamphlet that was read to George Washington's suffering and discouraged troops before the battle of Trenton. Paine was already famous for *Common Sense* (1776), urging the colonies to revolt from Britain; selling

---

1. Written during the trial of Louis XVI for treason before the National Convention (he would be executed on 21 January), this letter was first published in William Godwin's posthumous edition (1798). Publisher Joseph Johnson had hired Wollstonecraft to write for *Analytical Review* in 1788, and in 1792 he sent her to France as a foreign correspondent.

2. A hired four-wheeled coach, drawn by two horses.

3. The "Sun King" (reigned 1643–1715), the infamous autocrat, who bankrupted France through his extravagances, among them, the lavish palace of Versailles, royal residence and seat of power.

briskly, more than 100,000 copies in three months, it was a critical inspiration for the Declaration of Independence and the American Revolution. Born in England, and with only a grammar-school education, Paine endured various unsatisfactory jobs until he met Ben Franklin in London. At thirty-seven, with letters of introduction from Franklin, he sailed to America, where he launched his career as a writer, with articles on women's rights and the abolition of slavery. After he returned to England in 1787, he shuttled back and forth to France, and when Burke's *Reflections on the Revolution in France* appeared in 1790, he quickly began his rebuttal, *The Rights of Man*, published early the next year. Burke wrote eloquent prose for the educated elite; Paine's simple, electric style was framed for the common reader, and his tract, priced cheaply, was an immediate and widespread success, selling 200,000 copies by 1793—but not without cost. Paine's incitement to revolution over reform and his attack on monarchies sent his bookseller to jail and led to his own indictment for treason. Fleeing to France in 1792 (just after the September Massacres), he was warmly received, elected to the National Assembly and given honorary citizenship. But he soon got into trouble for criticizing the execution of Louis XVI. Imprisoned by the Jacobins, he only narrowly escaped the guillotine himself through the intercession of James Monroe, then American ambassador to France. Convicted in absentia in England, he could not return without imprisonment, so he went back to America. There he completed *The Age of Reason* (1792–1795), a case for Deism begun during his imprisonment in France. Its strident denunciation of institutionalized Christianity and the Bible cost Paine sympathetic readers, however, and his reputation fell further in 1796 when he attacked Washington and federalism. He died in 1809, impoverished, angry, and ostracized. Denounced as an atheist, he was denied a consecrated burial, but in 1819, William Cobbett, a sympathetic English radical, exhumed his remains and took them to England.

from The Rights of Man
Being an answer to Mr. Burke's attack on the French Revolution
["MAN HAS NO PROPERTY IN MAN"]

There never did, there never will, and there never can, exist a Parliament, or any description of men, or any generation of men, in any country, possessed of the right or the power of binding and controuling posterity to the *"end of time."* *** Every age and generation must be as free to act for itself *in all cases* as the ages and generations which preceded it. The vanity and presumption of governing beyond the grave is the most ridiculous and insolent of all tyrannies. Man has no property in man; neither has any generation a property in the generations which are to follow. The Parliament or the people of 1688,[1] or of any other period, had no more right to dispose of the people of the present day, or to bind or to controul them *in any shape whatever*, than the Parliament or the people of the present day have to dispose of, bind or controul those who are to live a hundred or a thousand years hence. Every generation is, and must be, competent to all the purposes which its occasions require. It is the living, and not the dead, that are to be accommodated. When man ceases to be, his power and his wants cease with him; and having no longer any participation in the concerns of this world, he has no longer any authority in directing who shall be its governors, or how its Government shall be organised, or how administered.

I am not contending for nor against any form of Government, nor for nor against any party, here or elsewhere. That which a whole Nation chooses to do, it has a right

---

1. The year of the Glorious Revolution, when Parliament deposed Catholic James II.

to do. Mr. Burke says, No. Where, then does the right exist? I am contending for the rights of the *living*, and against their being willed away, and controuled and contracted for, by the manuscript assumed authority of the dead; and Mr. Burke is contending for the authority of the dead over the rights and freedom of the living. There was a time when Kings disposed of their Crowns by will upon their death-beds, and consigned the people, like beasts of the field, to whatever successor they appointed. This is now so exploded as scarcely to be remembered, and so monstrous as hardly to be believed; but the Parliamentary clauses upon which Mr. Burke builds his political church are of the same nature.

The laws of every country must be analogous to some common principle. In England no parent or master, nor all the authority of Parliament, omnipotent as it has called itself, can bind or controul the personal freedom even of an individual beyond the age of twenty-one years. On what ground of right, then, could the Parliament of 1688, or any other Parliament, bind all posterity for ever?

Those who have quitted the world, and those who are not yet arrived at it, are as remote from each other as the utmost stretch of mortal imagination can conceive. What possible obligation, then, can exist between them; what rule or principle can be laid down that of two non-entities, the one out of existence and the other not in, and who never can meet in this world, the one should controul the other to the end of time? *** It is the nature of man to die, and he will continue to die as long as he continues to be born. But Mr. Burke has set up a sort of political Adam, in whom all posterity are bound for ever; he must, therefore, prove that his Adam possessed such a power, or such a right. *** It requires but a very small glance of thought to perceive that altho' laws made in one generation often continue in force through succeeding generations, yet that they continue to derive their force from the consent of the living. A law not repealed continues in force, not because it *cannot* be repealed, but because it *is not* repealed; and the non-repealing passes for consent.

[PRINCIPLES, NOT PERSONS]

Mr. Burke shows that he is ignorant of the springs and principles of the French Revolution. It was not against Louis XVI, but against the despotic principles of the government, that the Nation revolted. These principles had not their origin in him, but in the original establishment, many centuries back; and they were become too deeply rooted to be removed, and the Augean stable of parasites and plunderers too abominably filthy to be cleansed,[2] by anything short of a complete and universal Revolution. When it becomes necessary to do a thing, the whole heart and soul should go into the measure, or not attempt it. That crisis was then arrived, and there remained no choice but to act with determined vigour, or not to act at all. The King was known to be the friend of the Nation, and this circumstance was favourable to the enterprise.[3] Perhaps no man bred up in the style of an absolute King, ever possessed a heart so little disposed to the exercise of that species of power as the present King of France. But the principles of the Government itself still remained the same.

---

2. One of Hercules's labors was to purge the notoriously filthy stables of King Augeas—hence, a place of entrenched corruption.
3. In the 1770s and 1780s, Louis XVI tried unsuccessfully to initiate some reforms, including moderate taxation of the nobility. After the Revolution, he withdrew his troops, reinstated his reform-minded director of the treasury (ousted by reactionary factions), and outwardly accepted the Republic.

The Monarch and the Monarchy were distinct and separate things; and it was against the established despotism of the latter, and not against the person or principles of the former, that the revolt commenced, and the Revolution has been carried.

Mr. Burke does not attend to the distinction between *men* and *principles*; and, therefore, he does not see that a revolt may take place against the despotism of the latter, while there lies no charge of despotism against the former.

The natural moderation of Louis XVI contributed nothing to alter the hereditary despotism of the Monarchy. All the tyrannies of former reigns, acted under that hereditary despotism, were still liable to be revived in the hands of a successor. It was not the respite of a reign that would satisfy France, enlightened as she then was become. A casual discontinuance of the *practice* of despotism, is not a discontinuance of its *principles*; the former depends on the virtue of the individual who is in immediate possession of the power; the latter, on the virtue and fortitude of the nation. In the case of Charles I and James II of England, the revolt was against the personal despotism of the men;[4] whereas in France, it was against the hereditary despotism of the established government. But men who can consign over the rights of posterity for ever on the authority of a mouldy parchment, like Mr. Burke, are not qualified to judge of this Revolution. It takes in a field too vast for their views to explore, and proceeds with a mightiness of reason they cannot keep pace with.

But there are many points of view in which this Revolution may be considered. When despotism has established itself for ages in a country, as in France, it is not in the person of the King only that it resides. It has the appearance of being so in show, and in nominal authority; but it is not so in practice and in fact. It has its standard everywhere. Every office and department has its despotism, founded upon custom and usage. Every place has its Bastille, and every Bastille its despot.[5] The original hereditary despotism resident in the person of the King, divides and subdivides itself into a thousand shapes and forms, till at last the whole of it is acted by deputation. This was the case in France; and against this species of despotism, proceeding on through an endless labyrinth of office till the source of it is scarcely perceptible, there is no mode of redress. It strengthens itself by assuming the appearance of duty, and tyrannises under the pretence of obeying.

When a man reflects on the condition which France was in from the nature of her Government, he will see other causes for revolt than those which immediately connect themselves with the person or character of Louis XVI. There were, if I may so express it, a thousand despotisms to be reformed in France, which had grown up under the hereditary despotism of the monarchy, and became so rooted as to be in great measure independent of it. Between the Monarchy, the Parliament, and the Church, there was a *rivalship* of despotism; besides the feudal despotism operating locally, and the ministerial despotism operating everywhere. But Mr. Burke, by considering the King as the only possible object of a revolt, speaks as if France was a village, in which everything that passed must be known to its commanding officer, and no

---

4. Charles I, son of James I (successor of Elizabeth I), was unpopular for exorbitant taxes, suspending Parliament, and harshly oppressing religious dissent; defeated in the 1640s Civil War with Parliament, he was beheaded for "high treason and other high crimes" in 1649. The monarchy was restored in 1660, and his Roman Catholic son became King James II in 1685, but was soon forced from office for his attempt to restore absolute monarchy and Catholicism as the state religion. Seven powerful nobles,

with the consent of Parliament, invited William III of Orange (grandson of Charles I) to "invade" England to protect its liberties and become joint monarch with Charles's Protestant daughter, Mary; William advanced bloodlessly to London with 15,000 troops, and Parliament proclaimed him and Mary monarchs in 1689.

5. France's infamous prison, holding many political prisoners, mostly without trial, was the icon of tyranny, stormed by revolutionaries on 14 July 1789.

oppression could be acted but what he could immediately controul. Mr. Burke might have been in the Bastille his whole life, as well under Louis XVI as Louis XIV,[6] and neither the one nor the other have known that such a man as Mr. Burke existed. The despotic principles of the Government were the same in both reigns, though the dispositions of the men were as remote as tyranny and benevolence.

What Mr. Burke considers as a reproach to the French Revolution (that of bringing it forward under a reign more mild than the preceding ones) is one of its highest honours. The Revolutions that have taken place in other European countries, have been excited by personal hatred. The rage was against the man, and he became the victim. But, in the instance of France we see a revolution generated in the rational contemplation of the rights of man, and distinguishing from the beginning between persons and principles.

But Mr. Burke appears to have no idea of principles when he is contemplating Governments. "Ten years ago," says he, "I could have felicitated France on her having a Government, without inquiring what the nature of that Government was, or how it was administered." Is this the language of a rational man? Is it the language of a heart feeling as it ought to feel for the rights and happiness of the human race? On this ground, Mr. Burke must compliment all the Governments in the world, while the victims who suffer under them, whether sold into slavery, or tortured out of existence, are wholly forgotten. It is power, and not principles, that Mr. Burke venerates. * * *

As to the tragic paintings by which Mr. Burke has outraged his own imagination, and seeks to work upon that of his readers, they are very well calculated for theatrical representation, where facts are manufactured for the sake of show, and accommodated to produce, through the weakness of sympathy, a weeping effect. But Mr. Burke should recollect that he is writing history, and not *plays*, and that his readers will expect truth, and not the spouting rant of high-toned exclamation.

When we see a man dramatically lamenting in a publication intended to be believed that "*The age of chivalry is gone! that The glory of Europe is extinguished for ever! that the unbought grace of life* (if any one knows what it is), *the cheap defence of nations, the nurse of manly sentiment and heroic enterprise is gone!*" and all this because the Quixote age of chivalry nonsense is gone, what opinion can we form of his judgment, or what regard can we pay to his facts?[7] In the rhapsody of his imagination he has discovered a world of windmills, and his sorrows are that there are no Quixotes to attack them. But if the age of Aristocracy, like that of Chivalry, should fall (and they had originally some connection), Mr. Burke, the trumpeter of the order, may continue his parody to the end, and finish with exclaiming: "*Othello's occupation's gone!*"[8]

Notwithstanding Mr. Burke's horrid paintings, when the French Revolution is compared with the Revolutions of other countries, the astonishment will be that it is marked with so few sacrifices; but this astonishment will cease when we reflect that *principles*, and not *persons*, were the meditated objects of destruction. The mind of the nation was acted upon by a higher stimulus than what the consideration of persons could inspire, and sought a higher conquest than could be produced by the

---

6. Louis XVI's ancestor (1638–1715), the Sun King, a notorious spendthrift, advocate of the divine right of kings, and patron of the arts.
7. Quoting Burke's *Reflections*, page 118. Cervantes's Don Quixote, a country gentleman who, fed on chivalric romances, sets out in search of knightly adventure and winds up tilting at windmills.
8. Othello utters this cry, when, falsely convinced of his wife's infidelity, he feels he has nothing more to live for (*Othello* 3.3.354).

downfall of an enemy. Among the few who fell there do not appear to be any that were intentionally singled out. They all of them had their fate in the circumstances of the moment. *** From his violence and his grief, his silence on some points and his excess on others, it is difficult not to believe that Mr. Burke is sorry, extremely sorry, that arbitrary power, the power of the Pope[9] and the Bastille, are pulled down.

Not one glance of compassion, not one commiserating reflection that I can find throughout his book, has he bestowed on those who lingered out the most wretched of lives, a life without hope in the most miserable of prisons. It is painful to behold a man employing his talents to corrupt himself. Nature has been kinder to Mr. Burke than he is to her. He is not affected by the reality of distress touching his heart, but by the showy resemblance of it striking his imagination. He pities the plumage, but forgets the dying bird.[1] Accustomed to kiss the aristocratical hand that hath purloined him from himself, he degenerates into a composition of art, and the genuine soul of nature forsakes him. His hero or his heroine must be a tragedy-victim expiring in show, and not the real prisoner of misery, sliding into death in the silence of a dungeon.

[THE DOCTRINE OF EQUAL RIGHTS]

If the mere name of antiquity is to govern in the affairs of life, the people who are to live an hundred or a thousand years hence, may as well take us for a precedent, as we make a precedent of those who lived an hundred or a thousand years ago. The fact is, that portions of antiquity, by proving everything, establish nothing. It is authority against authority all the way, till we come to the divine origin of the rights of man at the creation. Here our inquiries find a resting-place, and our reason finds a home. If a dispute about the rights of man had arisen at the distance of an hundred years from the creation, it is to this source of authority they must have referred, and it is to this same source of authority that we must now refer.

Though I mean not to touch upon any sectarian principle of religion, yet it may be worth observing, that the genealogy of Christ is traced to Adam. Why then not trace the rights of man to the creation of man? I will answer the question. Because there have been upstart Governments, thrusting themselves between and presumptuously working to *un-make* man.

If any generation of men ever possessed the right of dictating the mode by which the world should be governed for ever, it was the first generation that existed; and if that generation did it not, no succeeding generation can show any authority for doing it, nor can set any up. The illuminating and divine principle of the equal rights of man (for it has its origin from the Maker of man) relates, not only to the living individuals, but to generations of men succeeding each other. Every generation is equal in rights to the generations which preceded it, by the same rule that every individual is born equal in rights with his contemporary.

Every history of the creation, and every traditionary account, whether from the lettered or unlettered world, however they may vary in their opinion or belief of certain particulars, all agree in establishing one point, *the unity of man*; by which I mean that men are all of *one degree*, and consequently that all men are born equal, and with

---

9. Pre-Revolutionary France was Catholic (like Burke's Ireland), and so answerable to the Pope.
1. The most famous sentence in this tract. Royalty frequently ornamented itself with elaborate plumage

(feathers); Paine's point is that Burke is so wrapped up in the disgrace of the royal family that he neglects the misery of the state that sustains it, and which itself is dying from poverty and corruption.

equal natural rights, in the same manner as if posterity had been continued by *creation* instead of *generation*, the latter being only the mode by which the former is carried forward; and consequently every child born into the world must be considered as deriving its existence from God. The world is as new to him as it was to the first man that existed, and his natural right in it is of the same kind.

The Mosaic account of the creation,[2] whether taken as divine authority or merely historical, is fully up to this point, *the unity or equality of man*. The expressions admit of no controversy. "And God said, Let us make man in our own image. In the image of God created he him; male and female created he them." The distinction of sexes is pointed out, but no other distinction is even implied. If this be not divine authority, it is at least historical authority, and shows that the equality of man, so far from being a modern doctrine, is the oldest upon record. ***

It is not among the least of the evils of the present existing Governments in all parts of Europe that man, considered as man, is thrown back to a vast distance from his Maker, and the artificial chasm filled up by a succession of barriers, or sort of turnpike gates, through which he has to pass. I will quote Mr. Burke's catalogue of barriers that he has set up between Man and his Maker. Putting himself in the character of a herald, he says: *We fear God—we look with* AWE *to kings—with affection to Parliaments—with duty to magistrates—with reverence to priests, and with respect to nobility.* Mr. Burke has forgotten to put in "*chivalry.*" He has also forgotten to put in Peter.[3]

The duty of man is not a wilderness of turnpike gates, through which he is to pass by tickets from one to the other. It is plain and simple, and consists but of two points. His duty to God, which every man must feel; and with respect to his neighbour, to do as he would be done by. If those to whom power is delegated do well, they will be respected; if not, they will be despised; and with regard to those to whom no power is delegated, but who assume it, the rational world can know nothing of them.

[THE REPUBLICAN SYSTEM]

When we survey the wretched condition of Man, under the monarchical and hereditary systems of Government, dragged from his home by one power, or driven by another, and impoverished by taxes more than by enemies, it becomes evident that those systems are bad, and that a general Revolution in the principle and construction of Governments is necessary.

What is Government more than the management of the affairs of a Nation? It is not, and from its nature cannot be, the property of any particular man or family, but of the whole community, at whose expence it is supported; and though by force and contrivance it has been usurped into an inheritance, the usurpation cannot alter the right of things. Sovereignty, as a matter of right, appertains to the Nation only, and not to any individual; and a Nation has at all times an inherent, indefeasible right to abolish any form of Government it finds inconvenient, and to establish such as accords with its interest, disposition, and happiness. The romantic and barbarous distinction of men into Kings and subjects, though it may suit the conditions of courtiers, cannot that of citizens; and is exploded by the principle upon which Governments are now founded. Every citizen is a member of the sovereignty, and, as such, can acknowledge no personal subjection: and his obedience can be only to the laws.

---

2. Moses was thought to be the author of Genesis. Paine patches his quotation from Genesis 1.26–27.

3. In Christian lore, St. Peter is Heaven's gatekeeper.

*** In this view of Government, the Republican system, as established by America and France, operates to embrace the whole of a Nation. *** What we formerly called Revolutions, were little more than a change of persons, or an alteration of local circumstances. They rose and fell like things of course, and had nothing in their existence or their fate that could influence beyond the spot that produced them. But what we now see in the world, from the Revolutions of America and France, are a renovation of the natural order of things, a system of principles as universal as truth and the existence of man, and combining moral with political happiness and national prosperity.

Helen Maria Williams
1762–1827

The selections from this later edition of *Letters* reflect Helen Maria Williams's difficult challenge in giving a candid report of the horrific course of the Revolutionary government while maintaining fidelity to the principles of "Liberty" on which the Revolution was founded. See pages 108–13 for selections from her letters of summer 1790, when republican romance was high.

from Letters from France, 1796[1]
[THE EXECUTION OF THE KING]

Paris, Feb. 10, 1793

The faction of the anarchists desired that the French king should be put to death without the tedious forms of a trial. This opinion, however, was confined to the summit of the Mountain,[2] that elevated region, where, aloof from all the ordinary feelings of our nature, no one is diverted from his purpose by the weakness of humanity, or the compunction of remorse; where urbanity is considered as an aristocratical infringement of les grands principes, and mercy as a crime de leze-nation [high treason].

The trial of the king was decreed by the National Convention, and the eleventh of December was fixed upon for that purpose. Lewis the sixteenth had supported his long imprisonment with fortitude; and, when he heard that the day for his trial was fixed, he said with great calmness, "Eh bien! qu'on me guillotine si on veut; je suis preparé." ["Well! let them *guillotine* me if they will; I am prepared."]

A short time after the taking of the Bastille the king was observed reading the history of Charles the first.[3] "Why, sire," said an attendant, "do you read that history? it will make you melancholy." "Je me mets dans l'esprit," replied the king, "qu'un jour je finirai comme lui." ["I feel an impression on my mind, that one day I shall end like him."] It appears that the French queen has also chosen a model for her behaviour, in the last scene of life, from the English annals; for since her imprisonment she has been employed in reading the history of Mary queen of Scots.[4] Marie Antoinette, however, is in no danger of sharing the same fate: if she were, her haughty indignant spirit, which preferred the chance of losing empire and life to the certainty of retaining any thing less than absolute dominion, would probably meet death with becoming dignity, feeling, that "to be weak is to be miserable, doing or suffering."[5] ***

---

1. Volume 4, letters 1 and 5.
2. The radical Jacobin deputies, who sat on the high benches in the left of the National Convention.
3. In the English Revolution of the 1640s, Charles I was executed (30 January 1649).
4. Daughter of James V of Scotland, Mary became queen as an infant; in 1558 she married the Dauphin of France;

a romantic figure, for the next three decades, she was the Roman Catholic threat to England's Queen Elizabeth. Imprisoned from 1569 and tried for treason in 1586, she was beheaded in 1587.
5. So Milton's Satan lectures his defeated allies; *Paradise Lost* 1.156–57.

History will, indeed, condemn Lewis the sixteenth. The evidence of his guilt is clear; and the historian will fulfil his duty in passing sentence upon his memory; for the historian has not, like the judge, the prerogative to pardon. But Lewis the six-teenth will not stand alone at the bar of posterity. His judges also must appear at that tribunal; on them, also, the historian will pass sentence. He will behold the same men acting at once as accusers, party, and judge; he will behold the unfortunate monarch deprived, not only of his inviolability as a king, but of his rights as a citizen; and per-haps the irrevocable decree of posterity may reverse that of the National Convention.

The detail of the interrogation which the French king underwent at the bar of the National Convention is too well known to need repetition.—He was conducted back to the Temple about six in the evening: the night was dark; but the town was illuminated; and those objects which appeared only half formed, and were seen in-distinctly, imagination finished and filled up, as best suited the gloomy impressions of the moment. By the way, since the second of September, when the whole town was lighted up for security, an illumination at Paris appears no gaudy pageant, which beams the symbol of public festivity; but is considered as the harbinger of danger— the signal of alarm—the tocsin of night. A considerable number of horse as well as foot-guards formed the escort of the king; and the trampling of the horses' feet—the hoarse sounds of the collected multitude—the beating of drums—the frequent report of fire-arms—all conspired to excite the most solemn emotions. The long page of human history rushed upon the mind—age after age arose to memory, in sad suc-cession, like the line of Banquo;[6] and each seemed disfigured by crimes or darkened by calamity. The past was clouded with horror—a great experiment was about to be made for the future; but it was impossible to reflect, without trembling anxiety, that the stake was human happiness, and that the issue was doubtful, while all that could be calculated with certainty was, that millions must perish in the trial. It is asserted that the philosophers of France produced the revolution; I believe this to be an error. They, indeed, have disseminated the principles which form the basis of the new fab-ric of French government; but the ancient system was overthrown, not because it was unphilosophical, but because it could be upheld no longer. The revolution was the effect of imperious necessity; for, whatever permanent good may result from a change of government, the temporary evil is so certain, that every age is disposed to leave that work to a succeeding generation. The instinct of the people teaches them, that in framing a new government they can only hope, like Moses, to see the promised land, but not to enter it. They may plant the seeds of general prosperity, sown with toil and trouble, and bathed in blood;[7] but the blooming vegetation and the golden fruit belong to another race of men.

The defence of Lewis the sixteenth *** though it failed to prove his innocence, at least interested the humane part of the audience in behalf of his misfortunes: and such of that audience as reflected, that he who now stood an arraigned criminal at the bar of the Convention, had, four years ago, the destiny of twenty-five millions of people at the disposal of his will, felt that, whatever were his sins against the na-tion, he was already punished enough. *** The attention of all Europe was fixed in anxious suspense on the issue of this important trial; and the situation of Lewis the sixteenth excited universal sympathy. But at Paris it cast a peculiar horror—a sort of local gloom over the whole city; it seemed as if the National Convention had chosen

---

6. See Shakespeare, *Macbeth*, 4.1.112–24. Banquo is mur-dered by the king's assassins, but his descendants eventu-ally claim the Scottish throne.

7. The witches who inspire Macbeth's murderous ambi-tions to the throne chant of "toil and trouble." For the allusion to Moses, see Deuteronomy 34.4.

the very means most proper to re-kindle the dying flame of loyalty. We remembered that the king had betrayed his people, till, by the rigour of their resentment, they made us lose the sense of his guilt in the greatness of his calamities. They wished us to feel indignation at his offence, and they compelled us to weep for his misfortunes. They called on our abhorrence of the ungenerous use he had made of the power with which he was entrusted, and we saw how little magnanimous was the use which they made of theirs. Their decision seemed at once so cruel and so impolitic, that it is not surprising if, instead of appearing to foreign nations in the light of a painful sacrifice made to public security, it bore the aspect of public security sacrificed to inhumanity and vengeance. It were, however, an error to believe, either that Lewis the sixteenth fell the victim of that barbarous thirst for his blood displayed by the chiefs of the Mountain, or that he was devoted to death by the pusillanimity of those who were influenced by considerations of their own personal safety. No; while we admire the heroic courage of such as, in defiance of the popular outcry, pleaded with pathetic eloquence the cause of mercy; while we love the humanity of Brissot, the philosophy of Condorcet, we must admit, that amongst those who voted for the death of Lewis the sixteenth are found men equally incapable of being actuated by fear or by vengeance; men, who, considering the king's death as essential to security of the republic, pronounced the fatal sentence in the bitterness of their souls, and as the performance of a cruel duty which their country imperiously required.

The proposition of an appeal to the departments was rejected, because it was apprehended, that such an appeal might lead to civil war. *** The French king received the intelligence of his approaching fate without dismay. He displayed far more firmness upon the scaffold than he had done upon the throne, and atoned for the weakness and inconsistency of his conduct in life, by the calmness and fortitude of his behaviour in death. The evening before his execution, his family, from whom he had been separated since the commencement of his trial, were conducted to the tower of the Temple, and allowed the sad indulgence of a last interview, unmolested by the presence of his guards. *** Ah, surely, amidst the agonies of final separation from those to whom we are bound by the strongest ties of nature and affection! surely when we cling to those we love, in the unutterable pang of a last embrace—in such moments the monarch must forget his crown, and the regrets of disappointed ambition must be unfelt amidst the anguish which overwhelms the broken heart. ***

The king had sufficient firmness to avoid seeing his family on the morning of his execution! He desired the queen might be told that he was unable to bear the sight of her and his children in those last moments! he took a ring off his finger, which contained some of his own hair, of the queen's, and of his two children, and desired it might be given to the queen. He called the municipal officers round him, and told them, it was his dying request, that Clery, his valet-de-chambre, might remain with his son. He then said to Santerre, "Marchons" ["Let us go"]; and after crossing, with a hurried pace, the inner court of the Temple, he got into the mayor's carriage, which was in waiting, and was attended by his confessor.

It is certain that many of those acts of illegal power, which brought the unhappy monarch to the scaffold, were dictated by the fanatical and discontented clergy which swarmed about his palace; by non-juring bishops and archbishops; men who, having lost their wealth and their influence by the revolution, prompted the king to run all risks in order to gratify their own resentment. ***

The calmness which Lewis the sixteenth displayed on this great trial of human fortitude, is attributed not only to the support his mind received from religious faith, but also to the hope which it is said he cherished, even till his last moment, that the people, whom he meant to address from the scaffold, would demand that his life might be spared. And his confessor, from motives of compassion, had encouraged him in this hope. After ascending the scaffold with a firm step, twice the unhappy monarch attempted to speak, and twice Santerre prevented him from being heard, by ordering the drums to beat immediately. *** Then it was that despair seized upon the mind of the unfortunate monarch—his countenance assumed a look of horror— twice with agony he repeated, "Je suis perdu! je suis perdu!" ["I am undone! I am un- done!"] His confessor mean time called to him from the foot of the scaffold, "Louis, fils de St. Louis, montez au ciel" ["Son of St. Louis, ascend to heaven!"]; and in one moment he was delivered from the evils of mortality.

The executioner held up the bleeding head, and the guards cried "Vive la Repub- lique!" ["Long live the Republic!"] Some dipt their handkerchiefs in the blood—but the greater number, chilled with horror at what had passed, desired the commandant would lead them instantly from the spot. The hair was sold in separate tresses at the foot of the scaffold.

["WHAT THEN IS THE CONCLUSION OF THE WHOLE MATTER?"[8]]

Paris, March 1793

*** The destruction of the monarchy in France on the 10th of August—the hor- rors of the massacre of the 2d of September,[9] and then the death of the king, finally alienated the minds of Englishmen from the French revolution; rendered popular a war, which otherwise no minister would have dared to undertake; disgusted all wise, and shocked all humane men; and left to us, and all who had espoused the cause, no hope but that Heaven, which knows how to bring good out of evil, would watch over an event so interesting to the welfare of mankind as the French revolution; nor suf- fer the folly and vice of the agents concerned in it, to spoil the greatest and noblest enterprise ever undertaken by a nation.

A variety of secondary causes operated, in conjunction with these primary ones, to alienate the minds of our countrymen from the French revolution. It is curious, and may be useful to trace a few of them.

Those who have long held the first rank in any society are always reluctant to yield up their place, or suffer others, who were below, to be raised above them. Ac- customed to regard their own constitution as the perfection of civil polity, the Eng- lish found a new source of disapprobation of the French institution: they forgot that their dearest privileges, trial by jury, the liberty of the press, and other advantages, had once been regarded by foreign nations as audacious novelties; and had scandal- ized the despots of Europe and their degraded subjects, as much as the new experi- ments of the French did at present. It was a common saying in France, under the old system, that "Le roi d'Angleterre / Regne dans l'enfer" ["The king of England / reigns

8. Critic Stephen Blakemore (*Crisis in Representation*, 1997) reports that this letter was written by Williams's friend Thomas Christie.

9. 1792, when more than a thousand aristocrats, priests, and other suspected royalists were slaughtered. The king was executed January 1793.

in hell"] and the freedom of speech, and of writing on public affairs, the dearest rights of Englishmen, were constantly represented as absurd and noxious privileges, that occasioned eternal commotion in the state, and *disturbed the peace of government*. In spite of these facts, when circumstances arose that hurt their national vanity, by exalting a rival people, many of our countrymen appear to have forgotten the ancient history of England—the nations seemed to have changed sides, and Englishmen talked of France as Frenchmen were wont to talk of England. But truth changes not with the fashions of the times. It was not to be forgotten, that the English had been the first *bold experimenters* in the science of government in modern Europe—the first who carried into practical execution the calumniated principle of EQUALITY— the first people who formally brought a monarch to the scaffold—the first asserters of the neglected *rights of man*. In the common law of England, and the commentaries of the older lawyers on it, I have found all the fundamental principles of the French declaration des droits de l'homme [of the rights of man].

But, said some, we made our revolution without bloodshed, and theirs has been a continued scene of confusion and murder. It is true, the revolution of 1688 was accomplished with little trouble; but it produced the wars of 1715 and 1745, in the last of which the metropolis very nearly fell into the hands of the enemy; a circumstance that would have placed a popish despot on the throne, and annihilated the liberties of England. And it is to be observed, that the revolution of 1688 was but one of many events that formed the English constitution. That system was the fruit of the labours of ages of struggle and confusion. The establishment of our liberties cost us many wars—and amidst the civil dissensions caused by the contest of principles against ancient error, our history records a sad catalogue of crimes and cruelties committed on all sides. Whoever, Madam, will examine these annals, will soon be convinced, that we have not much ground to reproach our neighbours. In France, indeed, a greater number of events have been crowded into a shorter space of time; and the enormities in France have been committed at a period, when, by means of the facility of communication, all public events are more widely and rapidly circulated than in former ages; circumstances that alter the appearance, but not the reality, of the case. We now enjoy the blessings of freedom, and have forgotten the price it cost our ancestors to obtain it. But no people ever travelled to the temple of Liberty by a path strewed with roses; nor has established tyranny ever yielded to reason and justice, till after a severe struggle. I do not pretend to justify the French, but I do not see much right that we at least have to condemn them. We cannot even reproach them with the fate of Louis the sixteenth, without calling up to remembrance that of Charles the first. ***

If the destruction of the monarchy was absolutely necessary, certainly the death of the king was not; and France might have struck surrounding nations with reverence at her sublime clemency, in place of shocking all Europe by a condemnation, the justice of which was at best doubtful, and which the generality of them at present consider as an atrocious crime. *** However much indisposed our countrymen were to the French from preceding reasons, it is certain that the death of the king alone prepared their minds for war, and completed the triumph of the enemies of France in England. ***

Whether France will finally be able to extricate herself from an intestine, as well as external war, which now assail her at once—whether she will be able to support her republic; or, fatigued with anarchy, repose herself in limited monarchy; or finally, overwhelmed by her foes, be forced to accept that constitution which they choose to give her, are points that surpass my powers to decide. Were I to conjecture, I would say, that she will succeed in maintaining her own freedom, but not in communicating it to her neighbours. But should she even be overpowered by her enemies, and should continental despots wish to load her with the most galling chains, I cannot forget, Madam, that Britain is concerned in this transaction! And this recollection cheers my mind; for a free and generous people cannot condemn twenty-five millions of men to be slaves! No: the severest sentence that England can suffer to be pronounced, even on her rival, would be, "Let France be delivered from the dominion of a ferocious mob—let her be delivered from anarchy, and restored to reason and lawful sway!" Thus terminate how it will, I trust the French revolution will promote the good of France, and this prospect consoles me amidst the present evils. ***

When I said that the French revolution began in wisdom, I admitted that it came afterwards into the hands of fools. But *the foundation was laid in wisdom*. I must intreat you to mark that circumstance; for if even the superstructure should fall, the foundation would remain. The BASTILLE, though honoured by Mr. Burke with the title of the *king's castle* (a shocking satire on every humane and just prince), will never be rebuilt in France; and the declaration of the rights of man will remain eternal, as the truths it contains. In the early ages of the world, the revolutions of the states, and the incursions of barbarians, often overwhelmed knowledge, and occasioned *the loss of principles:* but since the invention of printing has diffused science over Europe, and accumulated the means of extending and preserving truth, PRINCIPLES can no more be lost. Like vigorous seeds committed to the bosom of the fertile earth, accidental circumstances may prevent their vegetation for a time, but they will remain alive, and ready to spring up at the first favourable moment.

What then is the conclusion of the whole matter? This, surely, that PRINCIPLES are never to be abandoned, however unsuccessful may be the attempt to carry them into *practice*. We in England, however, have had practical experience of the good effects of right principles: our maxims of liberty have proved their intrinsic worth, by counteracting even the natural defects of our country. They have made, as Addison happily expresses, "our bleak rocks and barren mountains smile"; and on the careful preservation of these maxims depends the continuance of the blessings they have procured us. But I must conclude:

> O Liberty! expand thy vital ray,
> O'er the dark globe diffuse celestial day;
> Glad distant regions by thy blissful voice,
> Till India's wilds and Afric's sands rejoice;
> Thy spirit breathe, wide as creation's space;
> Exalt, illume, inspire the human race;
> As heaven's own æther thro' expansion whirl'd,
> Attracts, sublimes, and animates the world.[1]

Thus wishes a worthy member of the British Senate, and such are your wishes and mine.

ADIEU

---

1. Attributed by Williams to John Courtenay (1738–1816), dissenter, abolitionist, supporter of the French Revolution. The prior reference is to Joseph Addison (1672–1719), poet, Whig statesman, and essayist.

⊷ ⊰✦⊱ ⊷

William Godwin
1756–1836

Husband of Mary Wollstonecraft and father of Mary Wollstonecraft Shelley, William Godwin has his own claim to fame as the author of *An Enquiry Concerning Political Justice*, an intellectually if not politically influential work published in the wake of the execution of Louis XVI of France. The son of a dissenting minister, Godwin entered this profession in 1778, but under the sway of Enlightenment philosophy, he was beset by religious doubts, and in 1782 he left the calling for political writing. *Political Justice*, begun in 1791 and published in 1793, is one of the most emphatic English statements of "anarchist" political philosophy: the disdain of governmental institutions and their legal apparatus as the source of manifold evils and corruptions. In a kind of radical Protestantism, Godwin placed faith in the capacity of man to be guided by private judgment, arguing that rational men, pursuing common good, would cease to need government, law, and religion. He went so far as to abolish marriage and private property. This work appalled conservatives but for a time had a strong following, including William Wordsworth, Samuel Taylor Coleridge, Lord Byron, and Percy Shelley. "No work in our time gave such a blow to the philosophical mind of the country," wrote William Hazlitt in *The Spirit of the Age* (1825); "Tom Paine was considered for the time as Tom Fool to him;... Edmund Burke a flashy sophist." For Wordsworth's account of his romance and disillusionment with Godwinian philosophy, see *The Prelude* 10.805–65, (1805 text). *Political Justice* was revised and expanded in 1796 and saw a third edition in 1798, in an atmosphere of increasing censorship of "seditious" writing. Excerpts are from the first edition, the one that blazed on the scene of English debate in the wake of the Terror.

from An Enquiry Concerning Political Justice and Its Influence on General Virtue and Happiness
from Of Justice

If justice have any meaning, it is just that I should contribute every thing in my power to the benefit of the whole. *** Justice is a rule of conduct originating in the connection of one percipient being with another. A comprehensive maxim which has been laid down upon the subject is, "that we should love our neighbour as ourselves."[1] But this maxim, though possessing considerable merit as a popular principle, is not modelled with the strictness of philosophical accuracy.

In a loose and general view I and my neighbour are both of us men; and of consequence entitled to equal attention. But in reality it is probable that one of us is a being of more worth and importance than the other. A man is of more worth than a beast; because, being possessed of higher faculties, he is capable of a more refined and genuine happiness. In the same manner the illustrious archbishop of Cambray was of more worth than his chambermaid, and there are few of us that would hesitate to pronounce, if his palace were in flames, and the life of only one of them could be preserved, which of the two ought to be preferred.[2]

---

1. The second of the great Commandments, according to Jesus (Mark 12.31).
2. In a later edition, Godwin changed "chambermaid" to "valet" (a male personal attendant). Archbishop of Cambrai; François Fénelon lost favor in the court of Louis XIV upon the publication of *Télémaque* (1699), a didactic romance that indirectly criticized the king's policies by urging humane internationalism and stressing the king's obligations to the welfare of his subjects. In the paragraphs below, "wife" and "mother" were later changed to "brother" and "father" and "prostitute" to "profligate," with other correspondent gender-adjustments.

But there is another ground of preference, beside the private consideration of one of them being farther removed from the state of a mere animal. We are not connected with one or two percipient beings, but with a society, a nation, and in some sense with the whole family of mankind. Of consequence that life ought to be preferred which will be most conducive to the general good. In saving the life of Fenelon, suppose at the moment when he was conceiving the project of his immortal Telemachus, I should be promoting the benefit of thousands, who have been cured by the perusal of it of some error, vice and consequent unhappiness. Nay, my benefit would extend farther than this, for every individual thus cured has become a better member of society, and has contributed in his turn to the happiness, the information and improvement of others.

Supposing I had been myself the chambermaid, I ought to have chosen to die, rather than that Fenelon should have died. The life of Fenelon was really preferable to that of the chambermaid. But understanding is the faculty that perceives the truth of this and similar propositions; and justice is the principle that regulates my conduct accordingly. It would have been just in the chambermaid to have preferred the archbishop to herself. To have done otherwise would have been a breach of justice.

Supposing the chambermaid had been my wife, my mother or my benefactor. This would not alter the truth of the proposition. The life of Fenelon would still be more valuable than that of the chambermaid; and justice, pure, unadulterated justice, would still have preferred that which was most valuable. Justice would have taught me to save the life of Fenelon at the expence of the other. What magic is there in the pronoun "my," to overturn the decisions of everlasting truth? My wife or my mother may be a fool or a prostitute, malicious, lying or dishonest. If they be, of what consequence is it that they are mine?

"But my mother endured for me the pains of child bearing, and nourished me in the helplessness of infancy." When she first subjected herself to the necessity of these cares, she was probably influenced by no particular motives of benevolence to her future offspring. Every voluntary benefit however entitles the bestower to some kindness and retribution. But why so? Because a voluntary benefit is an evidence of benevolent intention, that is, of virtue. It is the disposition of the mind, not the external action, that entitles to respect. But the merit of this disposition is equal, whether the benefit was conferred upon me or upon another. I and another man cannot both be right in preferring our own individual benefactor, for no man can be at the same time both better and worse than his neighbour. My benefactor ought to be esteemed, not because he bestowed a benefit upon me, but because he bestowed it upon a human being. His desert will be in exact proportion to the degree, in which that human being was worthy of the distinction conferred. Thus every view of the subject brings us back to the consideration of my neighbour's moral worth and his importance to the general weal, as the only standard to determine the treatment to which he is entitled. Gratitude therefore, a principle which has so often been the theme of the moralist and the poet, is no part either of justice or virtue. ***

Now the same justice, that binds me to any individual of my fellow men, binds me to the whole. If, while I confer a benefit upon one man, it appear, in striking an equitable balance, that I am injuring the whole, my action ceases to be right and becomes absolutely wrong. But how much am I bound to do for the general weal, that is, for the benefit of the individuals of whom the whole is composed? Every thing in my power. What to the neglect of the means of my own existence? No; for I am myself a part of the whole. Beside, it will rarely happen but that the project of doing for others every thing in my power, will demand for its execution the preservation of my own existence; or in other words, it will rarely happen but that I can do more good in twenty years than in one. If the extraordinary case should occur in which I can promote the general good by my death, more than by my life, justice requires that I should be content to die. *** I hold my person as a trust in behalf of mankind. I am bound to employ my talents, my understanding, my strength and my time for the production of the greatest quantity of general good. Such are the declarations of justice, so great is the extent of my duty. ***

Society is nothing more than an aggregation of individuals. Its claims and its duties must be the aggregate of their claims and duties, the one no more precarious and arbitrary than the other. What has the society a right to require from me? The question is already answered: every thing that it is my duty to do. *** What is it that the society is bound to do for its members? Every thing that can contribute to their welfare. But the nature of their welfare is defined by the nature of mind. That will most contribute to it, which enlarges the understanding, supplies incitements to virtue, fills us with a generous consciousness of our independence, and carefully removes whatever can impede our exertions.

Should it be affirmed, "that it is not in the power of any political system to secure to us these advantages," the conclusion I am drawing will still be incontrovertible. *** There is one thing that political institutions can assuredly do, they can avoid positively counteracting the true interests of their subjects.

from *Of Revolutions*

No question can be more important than that which respects the best mode of effecting revolutions. Before we enter upon it however, it may be proper to remove a difficulty which has suggested itself to the minds of some men, how far we ought generally speaking to be the friends of revolution; or, in other words, whether it be justifiable in a man to be the enemy of the constitution of his country.

"We live," it will be said, "under the protection of this constitution; and protection, being a benefit conferred, obliges us to a reciprocation of support in return."

To this it may be answered, first, that this protection is a very equivocal thing; and, till it can be shown that the vices, from the effects of which it protects us, are not for the most part the produce of that constitution, we shall never sufficiently understand the quantity of benefit it includes. *** Affection to my countrymen will be much better proved, by my exertions to procure them a substantial benefit, than by my supporting a system which I believe to be fraught with injurious consequences. ***

The true instruments for changing the opinions of men are argument and persuasion. The best security for an advantageous life is free and unrestricted discussion. In that field truth must always prove the successful champion. If then we would improve the social institutions of mankind, we must write, we must argue, we must converse. To this business there is no close; in this pursuit there should be no pause. Every method should be employed,—not so much positively to allure the attention of mankind, or persuasively to invite them to the adoption of our opinions—as to remove every restraint upon thought, and to throw open the temple of science and the field of enquiry to all the world. *** The phalanx of reason is invulnerable; it advances with deliberate and determined pace; and nothing is able to resist it. But when we lay down our arguments, and take up our swords, the case is altered. Amidst the barbarous pomp of war and the clamorous din of civil brawls, who can tell whether the event[3] shall be prosperous or miserable?

We must therefore carefully distinguish between informing the people and inflaming them. Indignation, resentment and fury are to be deprecated; and all we should ask is sober thought, clear discernment and intrepid discussion. Why were the revolutions of America and France a general concert of all orders and descriptions of men, without so much (if we bear in mind the multitudes concerned) as almost a dissentient voice; while the resistance against our Charles the first divided the nation into two equal parts?[4] Because the latter was the affair of the seventeenth century, and the former happened in the close of the eighteenth. Because in the case of America and France philosophy had already developed some of the great principles of political truth, and Sydney and Locke and Montesquieu and Rousseau had convinced a majority of reflecting and powerful minds of the evils of usurpation.[5] If these revolutions had happened still later, not one drop of the blood of one citizen would have been shed by the hands of another, nor would the event have been marked so much perhaps as with one solitary instance of violence and confiscation.

There are two principles therefore which the man who desires the regeneration of his species ought ever to bear in mind, to regard the improvement of every hour as essential in the discovery and dissemination of truth, and willingly to suffer the lapse of years before he urges the reducing his theory into actual execution. With all his caution it is possible that the impetuous multitude will run before the still and quiet progress of reason. *** But, if his caution be firmly exerted, there is no doubt that he will supersede many abortive attempts, and considerably prolong the general tranquility.

from *Of the Enjoyment of Liberty*
["EVILS OF COHABITATION—AND MARRIAGE"]

Cohabitation is not only an evil as it checks the independent progress of mind; it is also inconsistent with the imperfections and propensities of man. It is absurd to expect that the inclinations and wishes of two human beings should coincide through any long period of time. To oblige them to act and to live together, is to subject them to some inevitable portion of thwarting, bickering, and unhappiness. This cannot be otherwise, so long as man has failed to reach the standard of absolute perfection. The

3. Outcome.
4. The Civil Wars of the 1640s, concluding in the execution of Charles I.
5. Algernon Sydney, English politician who took Parliament's side. After the Restoration, he joined the opposition to Charles II; he was executed in 1683. In 1698, his influential liberal *Discourses Concerning Government* was published. John Locke's *Two Treatises on Civil Government* (1690), in part a justification of the Glorious Revolution of 1688, set forth the qualified rights of revolution, of property, the rights to the products of one's labor, and a system of governmental checks and balances. Influenced by Locke, Charles Montesquieu wrote *The Spirit of the Laws* (1748), an analysis of three types of government—monarchy, republic, despotism— also advocating a separation and balance of powers. The political philosophy of Rousseau is best known from *The Social Contract* (1762), an argument for the voluntary submission of social subjects to a common good, determined by rational reflection.

supposition that I must have a companion for life, is the result of a complication of vices. It is the dictates of cowardice, and not of fortitude. It flows from the desire of being loved and esteemed for something that is not desert.

But the evil of marriage as it is practised in European countries lies deeper than this. The habit is, for a thoughtless and romantic youth of each sex to come together, to see each other for a few times and under circumstances full of delusion, and then to vow to each other eternal attachment. What is the consequence of this? In almost every instance they find themselves deceived. They are reduced to make the best of an irretrievable mistake. They are presented with the strongest imaginable temptation to become the dupes of falsehood. They are led to conceive it their wisest policy to shut their eyes upon realities, happy if by any perversion of intellect they can persuade themselves that they were right in their first crude opinion of their companion. The institution of marriage is a system of fraud; and men who carefully mislead their judgments in the daily affair of their life, must always have a crippled judgment in every other concern. We ought to dismiss our mistake as soon as it is detected; but we are taught to cherish it. We ought to be incessant in our search after virtue and worth; but we are taught to check our enquiry, and shut our eyes upon the most attractive and admirable objects. Marriage is law, and the worst of all laws. Whatever our understandings may tell us of the person from whose connexion we should derive the greatest improvement, of the worth of one woman and the demerits of another, we are obliged to consider what is law, and not what is justice.

Add to this, that marriage is an affair of property, and the worst of all properties. So long as two human beings are forbidden by positive institution to follow the dictates of their own mind, prejudice is alive and vigorous. So long as I seek to engross one woman to myself, and to prohibit my neighbor from proving his superior desert and reaping the fruits of it, I am guilty of the most odious of all monopolies. Over this imaginary prize men watch with perpetual jealousy, and one man will find his desires and his capacity to circumvent as much excited, as the other is excited to traverse his projects and frustrate his hopes. As long as this state of society continues, philanthropy will be crossed and checked in a thousand ways, and the still augmenting stream of abuse will continue to flow.

The abolition of marriage will be attended with no evils. We are apt to represent it to ourselves as the harbinger of brutal lust and depravity. But it really happens in this as in other cases, that the positive laws which are made to restrain our vices, irritate and multiply them. Not to say, that the same sentiments of justice and happiness which in a state of equal property would destroy the relish for luxury, would decrease our inordinate appetites of every kind, and lead us universally to prefer the pleasures of intellect to the pleasures of sense.

The intercourse[6] of the sexes will in such a state fall under the same system as any other species of friendship. Exclusively of all groundless and obstinate attachments, it will be impossible for me to live in the world without finding one man of worth superior to that of any other whom I have an opportunity of observing. To this man I shall

---

6. Here, social interaction, but over the paragraph, the sexual sense is included.

feel a kindness in exact proportion to my appreciation of his worth. The case will be precisely the same with respect to the female sex. I shall assiduously cultivate the intercourse of that woman whose accomplishments shall strike me in the most powerful manner. "But it may happen that other men will feel for her the same preference that I do." This will create no difficulty. We may all enjoy her conversation; and we shall all be wise enough to consider the sensual intercourse as a very trivial object. This, like every other affair in which two persons are concerned, must be regulated in each successive instance by the unforced consent of either party. It is a mark of the extreme depravity of our present habits, that we are inclined to suppose the sensual intercourse [of] any wife material to the advantages arising from the purest affection. Reasonable men now eat and drink, not from the love of pleasure, but because eating and drinking are essential to our healthful existence. Reasonable men then will propagate their species, not because a certain sensible pleasure is annexed to this action, but because it is right the species should be propagated; and the manner in which they exercise this function will be regulated by the dictates of reason and duty.

Such are some of the considerations that will probably regulate the commerce of the sexes. It cannot be definitively affirmed whether it will be known in such a state of society who is the father of each individual child. But it may be affirmed that such knowledge will be of no importance. It is aristocracy, self love and family pride that teach us to set a value upon it at present. I ought to prefer no human being to another, because that being is my father, my wife, or my son, but because, for reasons which equally appeal to all understandings, that being is entitled to preference. One among the measures which will successively be dictated by the spirit of democracy, and that probably at no great distance, is the abolition of surnames.

━━◄◆►━━

The Anti-Jacobin, or Weekly Examiner

In thirty-six numbers, November 1797 to July 1798, The Anti-Jacobin, edited by William Gifford, defended Pitt's government by brilliantly lampooning any and all signs of radical opposition. Claiming to combat the spread of subversive ideas, George Ellis, John Hookham Frere, George Canning, and their fellows deployed a wit as pointed as it was exuberant against political figures and at writers such as Wordsworth and Charles Lamb suspected of dangerous sympathies. Robert Southey's The Widow (1796) offered an irresistible target: Frere and Canning derided its classical Sapphic meter as an "absurdity" in true English verse, even as they denounced Southey's "new topics of invective against the pride of property"—a characteristic juxtaposition of abstract republican philanthropy with Jacobin conduct, real or imagined. Their burlesque, The Friend of Humanity and the Knife-Grinder, appeared on 27 November 1797, illustrated by the leading caricaturist of the day, James Gillray (see another cartoon by Gillray on page 114), with an instantly recognizable portrait of James Tierney, Member of Parliament and of the reformist society, The Friends of the People. The piece caused a sensation. As late as 1890, an editor could say, "perhaps no lines in the English language have been more effective, or oftener quoted." They endure as a vivid index of the charged climate in which the poems of the Romantics emerged.

from The Anti-Jacobin
The Friend of Humanity and the Knife-Grinder

In the specimen of JACOBIN POETRY which we gave in our last number was developed a principle, perhaps one of the most universally recognised in the Jacobin creed; namely, "that the animadversion of *human law* upon *human actions* is for the most part nothing but *gross oppression;* and that, in all cases of the administration of *criminal justice*, the truly benevolent mind will consider only the *severity of the punishment*, without any reference to the *malignity of the crime*." This principle has of late years been laboured with extraordinary industry, and brought forward in a variety of shapes, for the edification of the public. It has been inculcated in bulky quartos, and illustrated in popular novels. It remained only to fit it with a poetical dress, which had been attempted in the INSCRIPTION for CHEPSTOW CASTLE, and which (we flatter ourselves) was accomplished in that for MRS. BROWNRIGG'S CELL.[1]

Another principle, no less devoutly entertained, and no less sedulously disseminated, is the *natural and eternal warfare of the* POOR *and the* RICH. In those orders and gradations of society, which are the natural result of the original difference of talents and of industry among mankind, the Jacobin sees nothing but a graduated scale of violence and cruelty. He considers every rich man as an oppressor, and every person in a lower situation as the victim of avarice, and the slave of aristocratical insolence and contempt. These truths he declares loudly, not to excite compassion, or to soften the consciousness of superiority in the higher, but for the purpose of aggravating discontent in the inferior orders.

A human being, in the lowest state of penury and distress, is a treasure to the reasoner of this cast. He contemplates, he examines, he turns him in every possible light, with a view of extracting from the variety of his wretchedness new topics of invective against the pride of property. He, indeed (if he is a true Jacobin), refrains from *relieving* the object of his compassionate contemplation; as well knowing that every diminution from the general mass of human misery must proportionably diminish the force of his argument.

This principle is treated at large by many authors. It is versified in sonnets and elegies without end. We trace it particularly in a poem by the same author from whom we borrowed our former illustration of the Jacobin doctrine of crimes and punishments. In this poem, the pathos of the matter is not a little relieved by the absurdity of the metre. *** The learned reader will perceive that the metre is SAPPHIC, and affords a fine opportunity for his *scanning* and *proving*, if he has not forgotten them.

The Widow
Sapphics

> Cold was the night wind; drifting fast the snows fell;
> Wide were the downs, and shelterless and naked;
> When a poor wand'rer struggled on her journey,
>   Weary and way-sore.

---

1. The first *Anti-Jacobin,* 20 November 1797, parodied Southey's sympathetic *Inscription for the Apartment in Chepstow Castle,* where Henry Marten, the Regicide, *was imprisoned 30 years* with an *Inscription for the Door of the Cell in Newgate,* where *Mrs. Brownrigg,* the *"Prentice-cide," was confined previous to her Execution.* Henry Marten was a republican who signed the death warrant of Charles I; he was imprisoned at the Restoration in 1660. Mrs. Brownrigg was infamous for sadistic treatment of young female apprentices. She was executed for her crimes in 1767.

Sapphics

The FRIEND of HUMANITY and the KNIFE-GRINDER, — Scene. The Borough.
in Imitation of Mr. Southey's Sapphics. — Vide. Anti Jacobin. p. 15.

To the Independant Electors of the Borough of Southwark, this Print is most respectfully dedicated ———

Friend of Hum? — "Needy Knife-grinder! whither are you going?
Rough is the road, your Wheel is out of order—
Bleak blows the blast; — your Hat has got a hole in't,
                              So have your Breeches!

"Weary Knife-grinder! little think the proud ones,
Who in their coaches roll along the turnpike-
—road, what hard work 'tis crying all day 'Knives and
                              Scissars to grind O!'"

"Tell me, Knife-grinder, how came you to grind knives?
Did some rich man tyrannically use you?
Was it the Squire? or Parson of the Parish?
                              Or the Attorney?

"Was it the 'Squire for killing of his Game? or
Covetous Parson for his Tythes distraining?
Or roguish Lawyer made you lose your little
                              All in a law-suit?

"(Have you not read the Rights of Man, by Tom Paine?)
Drops of compassion tremble on my eye-lids,
Ready to fall, as soon as you have told your
                              Pitiful story"

Knife-grinder. — "Story! God bless you! I have none to tell, Sir,
Only last night a-drinking at the Chequers,
This poor old Hat and Breeches, as you see, were
                              Torn in a scuffle.

"Constables came up, for to take me into
Custody; they took me before the Justice;
Justice Oldmixon put me in the Parish-
                              Stocks for a Vagrant.

"I should be glad to drink your Honour's health in
A Pot of Beer, if you would give me Sixpence;
But for my part, I never love to meddle
                              With Politics, Sir."

Friend of Hum? I give thee Sixpence! I will see thee damn'd first
Wretch! whom no sense of wrongs can rouse to ven—
Sordid, unfeeling, reprobate, degraded,
                              Spiritless outcast!

(Kicks the Knife-grinder, overturns his Wheel, and exit in
a transport of republican enthusiasm and universal—
                              —Philanthropy)

James Gillray, *The Friend of Humanity and the Knife-Grinder,* 1797.

Drear were the downs, more dreary her reflections;
Cold was the night wind, colder was her bosom:
She had no home, the world was all before her,[2]
    She had no shelter.

Fast o'er the heath a chariot rattled by her:
"Pity me!" feebly cried the poor night wanderer.
"Pity me, strangers! lest with cold and hunger
    Here I should perish.

Once I had friends—but they have all forsook me!
Once I had parents—they are now in heaven!
I had a home once—I had once a husband—
    Pity me, strangers!

I had a home once—I had once a husband—
I am a widow, poor and broken-hearted!"
Loud blew the wind, unheard was her complaining;
    On drove the chariot.

Then on the snow she laid her down to rest her;
She heard a horseman: "Pity me!" she groaned out.
Loud was the wind, unheard was her complaining;
    On went the horseman.

Worn out with anguish, toil, and cold and hunger,
Down sunk the wanderer; sleep had seized her senses:
There did the traveller find her in the morning—
    God had released her.

                        —*Robert Southey* [1796]

We proceed to give our IMITATION, which is of the *Amoeboean* or *Collocutory* kind.[3]

Hannah More
1745–1833

Mocked by William Cobbett as an "old bishop in petticoats," Hannah More was a formidable figure who earned her opponents by her achievements. Educated at home in Gloucestershire with her sisters by her father, a High Anglican schoolmaster, More and her five sisters founded a successful school at Bristol for the daughters of the middle class, joining education in mathematics, history, and literature to religious instruction and training in traditional female "accomplishments" (languages, dancing, music, sketching). More also became a visible presence in local society. At seventeen she published a pastoral drama intended for the edification of young ladies, and in 1774 she moved to London, where she found friends in prominent women of letters, the "Bluestockings," as well as Edmund Burke, Samuel Johnson, Horace Walpole,

---

2. Echoing Milton, *Paradise Lost* 12.646–47, on Adam and Eve's prospects after their expulsion from Eden.

3. A poem with alternating speakers; a dialogue.

and the leading actor of the times, David Garrick. She wrote two dramas but after Garrick's death in 1779 she withdrew from the urban society in which she had figured prominently, and turned to the Evangelical circle associated with William Wilberforce. *Sacred Dramas* (1782) and *Slavery: A Poem* (1788) mark the philanthropic and moral concerns of her subsequent work.

In 1792 the Bishop of London persuaded More to write *Village Politics* to counter the "wild impressions of liberty and equality" among "the lower order of people." "It is as vulgar as heart could wish," More said of her effort, but the appeal to the working classes in the language that they were presumed to speak had immense ramifications. The government distributed *Village Politics* by the thousands, and its success forecast the *Cheap Repository Tracts* that More and her sisters undertook in 1795. By 1799 the series had grown to more than a hundred titles; priced at a penny or less, and often disseminated free by churchmen, gentry, and aristocrats hoping to inculcate obedience in the restive lower classes, the tracts spread literacy across the land. Even as they condemned revolutionary ideas, they preached sobriety to the upper classes; by 1796 more than two million had sold, and the numbers continued to rise, aided by an organization that grew into the Religious Tract Society. These publications were an extension of More's educational activities. In the 1790s she and her sisters established a series of schools for the poor in the area south of Bristol. "My plan for instructing the poor is very limited and strict," she wrote to John Bowdler in 1799. "They learn of weekdays such coarse work as may fit them for servants. I allow of no writing. My object has not been to teach dogmas and opinions, but to form the lower class to habits of industry and virtue." Confined as this program now seems, it aroused bitter opposition from the clergy, who accused her of Methodism, and the farmers, who feared that any education of the poor would ruin them for agricultural labor.

Although More criticized Wollstonecraft's *Vindication of the Rights of Woman* (1792), her own career demonstrated the influence a woman could wield in reshaping the education of women and the poor. Vowing, after the unhappy termination of an engagement in 1781, never to marry, she led a life that seems to allegorize the transition from the eighteenth-century world, in which a provincial schoolgirl might still compose a pastoral drama and become friends with Samuel Johnson and the Bluestockings, to an indefatigable and productive Victorian philanthropy. By the time of her death at eighty-eight, More had earned more than £30,000 from her writings, and become the object of pilgrimages by reformers inspired by her example.

Additional works by More appear in the Perspectives sections The Abolition of Slavery and the Slave Trade (page 263), and The Wollstonecraft Controversy and the Rights of Women (page 361).

Village Politics

Addressed to all the Mechanics, Journeymen and Day Labourers, in Great Britain, By WILL CHIP, A Country Carpenter

A DIALOGUE between JACK ANVIL the Blacksmith, and TOM HOD the Mason.

JACK: What's the matter, Tom? Why dost look so dismal?

TOM: Dismal indeed! Well enough I may.

JACK: What's the old mare dead? or work scarce?

TOM: No, no, work's plenty enough, if a man had but the heart to go to it.

JACK: What book art reading? Why dost look so like a hang dog?

TOM [*looking on his book*]: Cause enough. Why I find here that I'm very unhappy, and very miserable; which I should never have known if I had not had the good luck to meet with this book. O 'tis a precious book!

JACK: A good sign tho'; that you can't find out you're unhappy without looking into a book for it. What is the matter?

TOM: Matter? Why I want liberty.

JACK: Liberty! What has any one fetched a warrant for thee? Come man, cheer up, I'll be bound for thee.—Thou art an honest fellow in the main, tho' thou dost tipple and prate a little too much at the Rose and Crown.

TOM: No, no, I want a new constitution.

JACK: Indeed! Why I thought thou hadst been a desperate healthy fellow. Send for the doctor then.

TOM: I'm not sick; I want Liberty and Equality, and the Rights of Man.

JACK: O now I understand thee. What thou art a leveller and a republican I warrant.

TOM: I'm a friend to the people. I want a reform.

JACK: Then the shortest way is to mend thyself.

TOM: But I want a *general reform*.

JACK Then let every one mend one.

TOM: Pooh! I want freedom and happiness, the same as they have got in France.

JACK: What, Tom, we imitate them? We follow the French! Why they only begun all this mischief at first, in order to be just what *we* are already. Why I'd sooner go to the Negers to get learning, or to the Turks to get religion, than to the French for freedom and happiness.

TOM: What do you mean by that? ar'n't the French free?

JACK: Free, Tom! aye, free with a witness. They are all so free, that there's nobody safe. They make free to rob whom they will, and kill whom they will. If they don't like a man's looks, they make free to hang him without judge or jury, and the next lamp-post does for the gallows; so then they call themselves free, because you see they have no king to take them up and hang them for it.

TOM: Ah, but Jack, didn't their king formerly hang people for nothing too? and besides, wer'n't they all papists before the Revolution?

JACK: Why, true enough, they had but a poor sort of religion, but bad is better than none, Tom. And so was the government bad enough too, for they could clap an innocent man into prison, and keep him there too as long as they would, and never say with your leave or by your leave, Gentlemen of the Jury. But what's all that to us?

TOM: To us! Why don't our governors put many of our poor folks in prison against their will? What are all the jails for? Down with the jails, I say; all men should be free.

JACK: Harkee, Tom, a few rogues in prison keep the rest in order, and then honest men go about their business, afraid of nobody; that's the way to be free. And let me tell thee, Tom, thou and I are tried by our peers as much as a lord is. Why the *king* can't send me to prison if I do no harm, and if I do, there's reason good why I should go there. I may go to law with Sir John, at the great castle yonder, and he no more dares lift his little finger against me than if I were his equal. A lord is hanged for hanging matter, as thou or I shou'd be; and if it will be any comfort to thee, I myself remember a Peer of the Realm being hanged for killing his man, just the same as the man wou'd have been for killing *him*. [Lord Ferrers was hanged in 1760, for killing his steward; More's note]

TOM: Well, that is some comfort.—But have you read the Rights of Man?

JACK: No, not I. I had rather by half read the *Whole Duty of Man*.[1] I have but little
time for reading, and such as I should therefore only read a bit of the best.

TOM: Don't tell me of those old fashioned notions. Why should not we have the
same fine things they have got in France? I'm for a *Constitution*, and *Organization*,
and *Equalization*.

JACK: Do be quiet. Now, Tom, only suppose this nonsensical equality was to take
place; why it wou'd not last while one cou'd say Jack Robinson; or suppose it cou'd—
suppose, in the general division, our new rulers were to give us half an acre of ground
a-piece; we cou'd to be sure raise potatoes on it for the use of our families; but as every
other man would be equally busy in raising potatoes for *his* family, why then you see if
thou wast to break thy spade, I should not be able to mend it. Neighbour Snip wou'd
have no time to make us a suit of cloaths, nor the clothier to weave the cloth, for
all the world would be gone a digging. And as to boots and shoes, the want of some
one to make them for us, wou'd be a greater grievance than the tax on leather. If we
shou'd be sick, there wou'd be no doctor's stuff for us; for doctor wou'd be digging too.
We cou'd not get a chimney swept, or a load of coal from pit, for love or money.

TOM: But still I shou'd have no one over my head.

JACK: That's a mistake: I'm stronger than thou; and Standish, the exciseman,[2] is a
better scholar; so we should not remain equal a minute. I shou'd out-*fight* thee,
and he'd out-*wit* thee. And if such a sturdy fellow as I am, was to come and break
down thy hedge for a little firing, or to take away the crop from thy ground, I'm
not so sure that these new-fangled laws wou'd see thee righted. I tell thee, Tom,
we have a fine constitution already, and our fore-fathers thought so.

TOM: They were a pack of fools, and had never read the Rights of Man.

JACK: I'll tell thee a story. When Sir John married, my Lady, who is a little fantastical, and likes to do every thing like the French, begged him to pull down yonder
fine old castle, and build it up in her frippery way. No, says Sir John; what shall I
pull down this noble building, raised by the wisdom of my brave ancestors; which
outstood the civil wars, and only underwent a little needful repair at the Revolution; and which all my neighbours come to take a pattern by—shall I pull it all
down, I say, only because there may be a dark closet or an inconvenient room or
two in it? My lady mumpt and grumbled; but the castle was let stand, and a glorious building it is, though there may be a trifling fault or two, and tho' a few decays
may want stopping; so now and then they mend a little thing, and they'll go on
mending, I dare say, as they have leisure, to the end of the chapter, if they are let
alone. But no pull-me-down works.[3] What is it you are crying out for, Tom?

TOM: Why for a perfect government.

JACK: You might as well cry for the moon. There's nothing perfect in this world, take
my word for it.

TOM: I don't see why we are to work like slaves, while others roll about in their
coaches, feed on the fat of the land, and do nothing.

---

1. Tom Paine's *The Rights of Man* was published in 1791;
The Whole Duty of Man was a popular devotional work by
Richard Allestree (1619–1681), a royalist divine in the
Civil Wars.

2. Tax collector.
3. Throughout his *Reflections*, Burke employs this architectural figure to contrast the evolving British constitution to the French demolition.

JACK: My little maid brought home a storybook from the Charity-School[4] t'other day, in which was a bit of a fable about the Belly and the Limbs. The hands said, I won't work any longer to feed this lazy belly, who sits in state like a lord, and does nothing. Said the feet, I won't walk and tire myself to carry him about; let him shift for himself; so said all the members; just as your levellers and republicans do now. And what was the consequence? Why the belly was pinched to be sure; but the hands and the feet, and the rest of the members suffered so much for want of their old nourishment, that they fell sick, pined away, and wou'd have died, if they had not come to their senses just in time to save their lives, as I hope all you will do.[5]

TOM: But the times—but the taxes, Jack.

JACK: Things are dear, to be sure: but riot and murder is not the way to make them cheap. And taxes are high; but I'm told there's a deal of old scores paying off, and by them who did not contract the debt neither, Tom. Besides things are mending, I hope, and what little is done, is for us poor people; our candles are somewhat cheaper, and I dare say, if the honest gentleman [George III] is not disturbed by you levellers, things will mend every day. But bear one thing in mind: the more we riot, the more we shall have to pay. Mind another thing too, that in France the poor paid all the taxes, as I have heard 'em say, and the quality paid nothing.

TOM: Well, I know what's what, as well as another; and I'm as fit to govern—

JACK: No, Tom, no. You are indeed as good as another man, seeing you have hands to work, and a soul to be saved. But are all men fit for all kinds of things? Solomon says, "How can he be wise whose talk is of oxen?"[6] Every one in his way. I am a better judge of a horse-shoe than Sir John; but he has a deal better notion of state affairs than I; and I can no more do without him than he can do without me. And few are so poor but they may get a vote for a parliament-man, and so you see the poor have as much share in the government as they well know how to manage.

TOM: But I say all men are equal. Why should one be above another?

JACK: If that's thy talk, Tom, thou dost quarrel with Providence and not with government. For the woman is below her husband, and the children are below their mother, and the servant is below his master.

TOM: But the subject is not below the king; all kings are "crowned ruffians": and all governments are wicked. For my part, I'm resolved I'll pay no more taxes to any of them.

JACK: Tom, Tom, this is thy nonsense; if thou didst go oftner to church, thou wou'dst know where it is said, "Render unto Cesar the things that are Cesar's"; and also, "Fear God, honour the king."[7] Your book tells you that we need obey no government but that of the people, and that we may fashion and alter the government according to our whimsies; but mine tells me, "Let every one be subject to the higher powers, for all power is of God, the powers that be are ordained of God; whosoever therefore resisteth the power, resisteth the ordinance of God."[8] Thou sayst, thou wilt pay no taxes to any of them. Dost thou know who it was that work'd a miracle, that he might have money to pay tribute with, rather than set you and me an example of disobedience to government?

---

4. A school funded by private or religious donations for the education of the poor.
5. Menenius Agrippa tells this fable to quiet the rebellious plebeians in Shakespeare's *Coriolanus* (1.1.90–149).

6. Ecclesiasticus 38.25.
7. Mark 12.17; 1 Peter 2.17.
8. Romans 13.1–2.

TOM: I say we shall never be happy, till we do as the French have done.

JACK: The French and we contending for liberty, Tom, is just as if thou and I were to pretend to run a race; thou to set out from the starting post, when I am in already: why we've got it man; we've no race to run. We're there already. Our constitution is no more like what the French one was, than a mug of our Taunton beer is like a platter of their soup-maigre.[9]

TOM: I know we shall be undone, if we don't get a new *constitution*—that's all.

JACK: And I know we shall be undone if we *do*. I don't know much about politicks, but I can see by a little, what a great deal means. Now only to shew thee the state of public credit, as I think Tim Standish calls it. There's Farmer Furrow: a few years ago he had an odd 50£ by him; so to keep it out of harm's way, he put it out to use, on government security I think he calls it. Well; t'other day he married one of his daughters, so he thought he'd give her that 50£ for a bit of a portion. Tom, as I'm a living man, when he went to take it out, if his fifty pounds was not grown almost to an hundred! and wou'd have been a full hundred, they say, by this time, if the gentleman had been let alone.

TOM: Well, still, as the old saying is—I shou'd like to do as they do in France.

JACK: What shou'dst like to be murder'd with as little ceremony as Hackabout, the butcher, knocks down a calf? Then for every little bit of tiff, a man gets rid of his wife. And as to liberty of *conscience*, which they brag so much about, why they have driven away their parsons, (aye and murdered many of 'em) because they wou'd not swear as they would have them. And then they talk of liberty of the press; why, Tom, only t'other day they hang'd a man for printing a book against this pretty government of theirs.

TOM: But you said yourself it was sad times in France, before they pull'd down the old government.

JACK: Well, and suppose the French were as much in the right as I know them to be in the wrong; what does that argue for *us*? Because neighbour Furrow t'other day pulled down a crazy, old barn, is that a reason why I must set fire to my tight cottage?

TOM: I don't see why one man is to ride in his coach and six, while another mends the highway for him.

JACK: I don't see why the man in the coach is to *drive over* the man on foot, or hurt a hair of his head. And as to our great folks, that you levellers have such a spite against; I don't pretend to say they are a bit better than they should be; but that's no affair of mine; let them look to that; they'll answer for that in another place. To be sure, I wish they'd set us a better example about going to church, and those things; but still *hoarding's* not the sin of the age; they don't lock up their *money*— away it goes, and every body's the better for it. They do spend too much, to be sure, in feastings and fandangoes, and if I was a parson I'd go to work with 'em in another kind of a way; but as I am only a poor tradesman, why 'tis but bringing more grist to my mill. It all comes among the people—Their coaches and their furniture, and their buildings, and their planting, employ a power of tradespeople and labourers.—Now in this village; what shou'd we do without the castle? Tho' my Lady is too rantipolish,[1] and flies about all summer to hot water and cold water, and fresh water and salt water, when she ought to stay at home with Sir John; yet when

---

9. Thin soup.   1. Unruly.

she does come down, she brings such a deal of gentry that I have more horses than I can shoe, and my wife more linen than she can wash. Then all our grown children are servants in the family, and rare wages they have got. Our little boys get something every day by weeding their gardens, and the girls learn to sew and knit at Sir John's expence; who sends them all to school of a Sunday.

TOM: Aye, but there's not Sir Johns in every village.

JACK: The more's the pity. But there's other help. 'Twas but last year you broke your leg, and was nine weeks in the Bristol 'Firmary, where you was taken as much care of as a lord, and your family was maintained all the while by the parish. No poor-rates in France, Tom; and here there's a matter of two million and a half paid for them, if 'twas but a little better managed.

TOM: Two million and a half!

JACK: Aye, indeed. Not translated into ten-pences, as your French millions are, but twenty good shillings to the pound. But, when this levelling comes about, there will be no 'firmaries, no hospitals, no charity-schools, no sunday-schools, where so many hundred thousand poor souls learn to read the word of God for nothing. For who is to pay for them? *equality* can't afford it; and those that may be willing won't be able.

TOM: But we shall be one as good as another, for all that.

JACK: Aye, and bad will be the best. But we must work as we do now, and with this difference, that no one will be able to pay us. Tom! I have got the use of my limbs, of my liberty, of the laws, and of my Bible. The two first, I take to be my *natural* rights; the two last my *civil* and *religious*; these, I take it, are the *true Rights of Man*, and all the rest is nothing but nonsense and madness and wickedness. My cottage is my castle; I sit down in it at night in peace and thankfulness, and "no man maketh me afraid." Instead of indulging discontent, because another is richer than I in this world, (for envy is at bottom of your equality works,) I read my bible, go to church, and think of a treasure in heaven.

TOM: Aye; but the French have got it in *this* world.

JACK: 'Tis all a lie, Tom. Sir John's butler says his master gets letters which *say* 'tis all a lie. 'Tis all murder and nakedness, and hunger; many of the poor soldiers fight without victuals, and march without clothes. These are your *democrats!* Tom.

TOM: What then, dost think all the men on our side wicked?

JACK: No—not so neither—they've made fools of the most of you, as I believe. I judge no man, Tom; I hate no man. Even republicans and levellers, I hope, will always enjoy the protection of our laws; though I hope they will never be our *law-makers.* There's many true dissenters, and there's hollow churchmen; and a good man is a good man, whether his church has got a steeple to it or not. The new fashioned way of proving one's religion is to *hate* somebody. Now, tho' some folks pretend that a man's hating a Papist, or a Presbyterian, proves him to be a good *Churchman,* it don't prove him to be a good *Christian,* Tom. As much as I hate republican works, I'd scorn to *live* in a country where there was not liberty of conscience; and where every man might not worship God his own way. Now that they had not in France: the Bible was shut up in an unknown heathenish tongue. While here, thou and I can make as free use of our's as a bishop; can no more be sent to prison unjustly than a judge; and are as much taken care of by the laws as the parliament man who makes them. And this leveling makes people so dismal. These poor French fellows used to be the merriest dogs in the world; but since equality come in, I don't believe a Frenchman has ever laughed.

TOM: What then dost thou take French *liberty* to be?

JACK: To murder more men in one night, than ever their poor king did in his whole life.

TOM: And what dost thou take a *Democrat* to be?

JACK: One who likes to be governed by a thousand tyrants, and yet can't bear a king.

TOM: What is *Equality?*

JACK: For every man to pull down every one that is above him, till they're all as low as the lowest.

TOM: What is *the new Rights of Man?*

JACK: Battle, murder, and sudden death.

TOM: What is it to be an *enlightened people?*

JACK: To put out the light of the gospel, confound right and wrong, and grope about in pitch darkness.

TOM: What is *Philosophy,* that Tim Standish talks so much about?

JACK: To believe that there's neither God, nor devil, nor heaven, nor hell.—To dig up a wicked old fellow's[2] rotten bones, whose books, Sir John says, have been the ruin of thousands; and to set his figure up in a church and worship him.

TOM: And what mean the other hard words that Tim talks about—*organization* and *function,* and *civism,* and *incivism,* and *equalization,* and *inviolability,* and *imperscriptible?*

JACK: Nonsense, gibberish, downright hocus-pocus. I know 'tis not English; Sir John says 'tis not Latin; and his valet de sham[3] says 'tis not French neither.

TOM: And yet Tim says he shall never be happy till all these things are brought over to England.

JACK: What into this Christian country, Tom? Why dost know they have no *sabbath?* Their mob parliament meets of a Sunday to do their wicked work, as naturally as we do to go to church. They have renounced God's word and God's day, and they don't even date in the year of our Lord. Why dost turn pale man? And the rogues are always making such a noise, Tom, in the midst of their parliament-house, that their speaker rings a bell, like our penny-postman, because he can't keep them in order.

TOM: And dost thou think our Rights of Man will lead to all this wickedness?

JACK: As sure as eggs are eggs.

TOM: I begin to think we're better off as we are.

JACK: I'm sure on't. This is only a scheme to make us go back in every thing. 'Tis making ourselves poor when we are getting rich.

TOM: I begin to think I'm not so very unhappy as I had got to fancy.

JACK: Tom, I don't care for drink myself, but thou dost, and I'll argue with thee in thy own way; when there's all equality there will be no *superfluity;* when there's no wages there'll be no drink; and levelling will rob thee of thy ale more than the malt-tax does.

TOM: But Standish says if we had a good government there'd be no want of any thing.

---

2. Voltaire [More's note].

3. A *valet de chambre*, or manservant and here, a creditable detector of "sham" sloganeering.

JACK: He is like many others, who take the king's money and betray him. Tho' I'm no scholar, I know that a good government is a good thing. But don't go to make me believe that *any* government can make a bad man good, or a discontented man happy.—What art musing upon man?

TOM: Let me sum up the evidence, as they say at 'sizes[4]—Hem! To cut every man's throat who does not think as I do, or hang him up at a lamp-post!—Pretend liberty of conscience, and then banish the parsons only for being conscientious!—Cry out liberty of the press, and hang up the first man who writes his mind!—Lose our poor laws!—Lose one's wife perhaps upon every little tiff!—March without clothes, and fight without victuals!—No trade!—No bible!—No sabbath nor day of rest!—No safety, no comfort, no peace in this world—and no world to come!—Jack, I never knew thee tell a lie in my life.

JACK: Nor wou'd I now, not even against the French.

TOM: And thou art very sure we are not ruined.

JACK: I'll tell thee how we are ruined. We have a king so loving, that he wou'd not hurt the people if he cou'd; and so kept in that he cou'd not hurt the people if he wou'd. We have as much liberty as can make us happy, and more trade and riches than allows us to be good. We have the best laws in the world, if they were more strictly enforced; and the best religion in the world, if it was but better followed. While Old England is safe, I'll glory in her and pray for her, and when she is in danger, I'll fight for her and die for her.

TOM: And so will I too, Jack, that's what I will.

[sings] "O the roast beef of Old England!"[5]

JACK: Thou art an honest fellow, Tom.

TOM: This is Rose and Crown night, and Tim Standish is now at his mischief; but we'll go and put an end to that fellow's work.

JACK: Come along.

TOM: No; first I'll stay to burn my book, and then I'll go and make a bonfire and—

JACK: Hold, Tom. There is but one thing worse than a bitter enemy, and that is an imprudent friend. If thou wou'dst shew thy love to thy king and country, let's have no drinking, no riot, no bonfires; but put in practice this text, which our parson preached on last Sunday, "Study to be quiet, work with your own hands, and mind your own business."

TOM: And so I will, Jack—Come on.

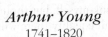

Arthur Young
1741–1820

"Give a man the secure possession of a bleak rock, and he will turn it into a garden; give him a nine years' lease of a garden, and he will convert it into a desert." At a time when agriculture, the engine of the British economy, was undergoing a revolution in productivity, Arthur Young was the most famous authority. Editor for twenty-five years of *Annals of Agriculture* and secretary to the Board of Agriculture, he increased his influence with his *Tours. Tour in Ireland*

---

4. Assizes, a circuit court held several times a year.   5. A popular patriotic song.

(1780) showed the powers of detailed observation and matter-of-fact analysis that distinguish *Travels in France During the Years 1787–1788, and 1789* (1792), a work quickly reprinted and widely translated. Unenchanted by the aspirations of the French radicals and skeptical of philosophical abstraction, firmly committed to the British values of property and commerce, seeming only a commonsense recorder of what daily experience presented, Young accumulated the evidence that initially led British moderates to welcome the Revolution as an overdue righting of cruel injustices. His bluff and often prickly manner contributes to his persuasive power: none could accuse him of Jacobin or democratic sympathies, and no contemporary could ignore the weight of his testimony. In the debate over the Revolution, Young's plain documentary style, built on first-hand knowledge, spoke as forcefully as the polemics of Paine and Burke in arousing British sympathy for the Revolution. Yet *The Example of France, A Warning to Britain*, which appeared in February 1793, reveals how quickly the Revolution had distressed liberal British opinion. Hopes that France was evolving toward a British-style constitutional monarchy, devoted to the preservation of property, were dashed when on 10 August 1792 a popular insurrection overthrew the monarchy and the Constitution of 1791. The moderate Girondins soon fell to the Jacobins, radicals who alienated middle-class British supporters. As a former advocate, Young was an influential voice of disillusion.

from Travels in France During the Years 1787–1788, and 1789
["BEGGARS"]

[*June 1787*] Pass Payrac, and meet many beggars, which we had not done before. All the country, girls and women, are without shoes or stockings; and the ploughmen at their work have neither sabots nor feet to their stockings. This is a poverty, that strikes at the root of national prosperity; a large consumption among the poor being of more consequence than among the rich: the wealth of a nation lies in its circulation and consumption; and the case of poor people abstaining from the use of manufactures of leather and wool ought to be considered as an evil of the first magnitude. It reminded me of the misery of Ireland.

["DULNESS AND STUPIDITY"]

[*July 1789*] The 4th. To Chateau Thiery, following the course of the Marne. The country is pleasantly varied, and hilly enough to render it a constant picture, were it inclosed. Thiery is beautifully situated on the same river. I arrived there by five o'clock, and wished, in a period so interesting to France, and indeed to all Europe, to see a newspaper. I asked for a coffee-house, not one in the town. Here are two parishes, and some thousands of inhabitants, and not a newspaper to be seen by a traveller, even in a moment when all ought to be anxiety.—What stupidity, poverty, and want of circulation! This people hardly deserve to be free; and should there be the least attempt with vigour to keep them otherwise, it can hardly fail of succeeding. To those who have been used to travel amidst the energetic and rapid circulation of wealth, animation, and intelligence of England, it is not possible to describe, in words adequate to one's feelings, the dulness and stupidity of France. I have been to-day on one of their greatest roads, within thirty miles of Paris, yet I have not seen one diligence,[1] and met but a single gentleman's carriage, nor anything else on the road that looked like a gentleman.

---

1. A public stagecoach.

["A POOR WOMAN"]

[*July 1789*] The 12th. Walking up a long hill, to ease my mare, I was joined by a poor woman, who complained of the times, and that it was a sad country; demanding her reasons, she said her husband had but a morsel of land, one cow, and a poor little horse, yet they had a *franchar* (42 lb.) of wheat, and three chickens, to pay as a quick-rent to one Seigneur; and four *franchar* of oats, one chicken and 1 *sou* to pay to another, besides very heavy tailles and other taxes. She had seven children, and the cow's milk helped to make the soup. But why, instead of a horse, do not you keep another cow? Oh, her husband could not carry his produce so well without a horse; and asses are little used in the country. It was said, at present, that *something was to be done by some great folks for such poor ones, but she did not know who nor how*, but God send us better, *car les tailles & les droits nous écrasent* [Because the taxes and the feudal duties crush us].—This woman, at no great distance, might have been taken for sixty or seventy, her figure was so bent, and her face so furrowed and hardened by labour,—but she said she was only twenty-eight. An Englishman who has not travelled, cannot imagine the figure made by infinitely the greater part of the countrywomen in France; it speaks, at the first sight, hard and severe labour: I am inclined to think, that they work harder than the men, and this, united with the more miserable labour of bringing a new race of slaves into the world, destroys absolutely all symmetry of person and every feminine appearance. To what are we to attribute this difference in the manners of the lower people in the two kingdoms? To GOVERNMENT.

["SCARCELY ANY POLITICS"]

[*August 1789*] Before I leave Clermont, I must remark, that I dined, or supped, five times at the table d'hôte, with from twenty to thirty merchants and tradesmen, officers, & c.; and it is not easy for me to express the insignificance,—the inanity of the conversation. Scarcely any politics, at a moment when every bosom ought to beat with none but political sensations. The ignorance or the stupidity of these people must be absolutely incredible; not a week passes without their country abounding with events that are analyzed and debated by the carpenters and blacksmiths of England. The abolition of tythes, the destruction of the *gabelle* [salt tax], game made property, and feudal rights destroyed, are French topics, that are translated into English within six days after they happen, and their consequences, combinations, results, and modifications, become the disquisition and entertainment of the grocers, chandlers, drapers, and shoemakers, of all the towns of England; yet the same people in France do not think them worth their conversation, except in private. Why? because conversation in private wants little knowledge; but in public, it demands more, and therefore I suppose, for I confess there are a thousand difficulties attending the solution, they are silent.

from The Example of France, a Warning to Britain

Having resided a good deal in France during the progress of the Revolution, to which I was, for some time, a warm friend; having passed through every province of the kingdom; examined all her principal manufactures; gained much instruction, relative to the state of her commerce, and attended minutely to the situation of her people, it was natural for me, on my return to England, to consult with attention the legislative acts of the new government; and to procure, by correspondence and conversation, with persons on whom I could depend, such intelligence as was necessary to enable me to satisfy my curiosity concerning the result of the most singular Revolution recorded in the annals of mankind. I should consider myself as a bad subject of Britain, if I did not use every endeavour to render the knowledge, thus acquired, of use to my countrymen. ***

But in attempting to give expressions inadequate to the indignation every one must feel at the horrible events now passing in France, I am sensible that I may be reproached with changing my politics, my "principles," as it has been expressed.— My principles I certainly have not changed, because if there is one principle more predominant than another in my politics, it is the *principle of change*. I have been too long a farmer to be governed by any thing but events; I have a constitutional abhorrence of theory, of all trust in abstract reasoning; and consequently I have a reliance merely on experience, in other words, on events, the only principle worthy of an experimenter. ***

The Revolution before the 10th of August, was as different from the Revolution after that day as light from darkness; as clearly distinct in principle and practice as liberty and slavery; for the same man to approve therefore of both, he must either be uncandid or changeable; uncandid in his approbation before that period—changeable in his approbation after it. How little reason therefore for reproaching me with sentiments contrary to those I published before the 10th of August! I am not changeable, but steady and consistent; the same principles which directed me to approve the Revolution, in its commencement (the principles of real liberty), led me to detest it after the 10th of August. The reproach of changeableness, or *something worse*, belongs entirely to those who did *not* then change their opinion, but approve the *republic*, as they had approved the *limited monarchy*.

***

The old government of France, with all its faults, was certainly the best enjoyed by any considerable country in Europe, England alone excepted; but there were many faults in it which every class of the people wished to remedy. This natural and laudable wish made democrates in every order, amongst the possessors of property, as well as among those who had none. At the commencement of the Revolution, France possessed a very flourishing commerce; the richest colonies in the world; the greatest currency of solid money in Europe; her agriculture was improving; and her people, though from too great population much too numerous for the highest degrees of national prosperity, yet were more at their ease than in many other countries of Europe; the government was regular and mild; and, what was of as much consequence as the rest, her benignant sovereign, with a patriotism unequalled, was really willing to improve, by any reasonable means, the constitution of the kingdom. All these circumstances, if compared with England, would not make the proper impression. They are to be compared alone with what has since ensued; and her present state may thus, with truth, be correctly described.—Her government an anarchy, that values neither life nor property. Her agriculture fast sinking; her farmers the slaves of all; and her people starving. Her manufactures annihilated. Her commerce destroyed; and her colonies absolutely ruined. Her gold and silver disappeared; and her currency paper so depreciated, by its enormous amount of 300 millions, besides incredible forgeries, that it advances, with rapid strides, to the entire stagnation of every species of industry and circulation. Her national revenue diminished three-fourths. Her cities scenes of revolt, massacre, and famine; and her provinces plundered by gangs of banditti. Her future prospect of peace and settlement, depending on a constitution that is to be *formed* by a convention of rabble, and *sanctioned* by the *sans culottes*[2] of the kennel. It is not a few insulated crimes on some undeserving men; it is a series of horrid proscription, spreading far and near; pervading every quarter of the kingdom; it is the annihilation of rank, of right, of property; it is the destruction of the possessors of more than half France; it is the legislation of wolves, that govern only in destruction: and all these massacres, and plunderings, and burnings, and horrors of every denomination, are so far from being necessary for the establishment of liberty, that they have most effectually destroyed it. In one word, France is at present absolutely without government; anarchy reigns; the poniard and the pike of the mob give the law to all that once formed the higher classes, and to all that at present mocks with the shew of legislation. The mob of Paris have been long in the actual possession of unrivalled power; they will never freely relinquish it: if the Convention presumes to be free, it will be massacred; and, after a circle of new horrors, will sink (should foreign aid fail) into the despotism of triumvirs or dictators: the change will be from a Bourbon[3] to a butcher!

"All former Revolutions," says Paine, "till the American, had been worked within the atmosphere of a court, and never on the great floor of a nation;"[4] unfortunately for this miserable copy, she worked on a floor broad enough; her basis was the blood and property of France. The picture has no resemblance in "the *insipid* state of hereditary government." She found in "scenes of horror and perfection of iniquity," what "man is up to." It is easy to see what they have lost; as to their gains, they have assignats, cockades, and the music of *ça ira;*[5] it may be truely said, that they have made a wise barter: they have given their gold for paper; their bread for a ribbon; and their blood for a song. Heaven preserve us from the phrenzy of such exchanges! and leave Revolutions for the "order of the day," for "the morning of reason rising upon man" in France.

* * *

There is a party in this kingdom who call loudly for a reform in the representation of the people, and who would have such reformation give a right of election indiscriminately to all mankind: I am myself in the number of those who wish a reform, but not of such a complexion, nor at a moment like this; I wish the middle classes of landed property better represented; I wish a new member for every county, elected by men who possess not less than an hundred a year in land, and not more than a thousand;[6] and an equal number of members deducted from the most objectionable boroughs.[7] But I would live at Constantinople rather than at Bradfield, if the wild and preposterous propositions founded on the Rights of Man, were to become effective in this kingdom. In other words, I have property; and I do not choose to live where the first beggar I met, may, the sabre in one hand, and *Rights of Man* in the other, demand a share of that which a good government tells me is *my own.*

* * *

---

2. "Without breeches": a term of scorn by the upper classes for the working-class dress of the radicals.
3. The hereditary monarchs of France.
4. *Rights of Man* [Young's note]. The other quotations in this paragraph are from the same work.
5. Assignats were the new currency issued by the revolutionary government, quickly devalued; the cockade was the tricolor (red, white, and blue) emblem of the revolution, replacing the white of the Bourbon monarchy; *Ça ira*

(We shall succeed) was the Revolutionary anthem.
6. The property qualification of more than £100 in land excludes lesser freeholders and all those who derived their wealth from other sources, such as trade.
7. "Rotten boroughs," which retained the right to send members to Parliament despite declines in population that made them easy to control, were an abuse singled out by those wishing to reform the system of representation.

If there is truth in the representation I have given of our danger—if the field of that danger is at home—and if in this war with France we have to fight, not thro' ambition or for conquest, but for the preservation of our lives and properties against foreign and domestic foes, combined for our destruction; it then surely behooves every man that wishes well to his country, to give firmness and vigour to that government by which alone we can hope for defence and security; by as great unanimity as our enemies will admit,—by rejecting, reprobating, and holding up to abhorrence, every idea of altering, reforming, or tampering, at so dangerous a crisis, with the constitution to which we owe the prosperity that is so hateful an object to the Jacobins of France;—by exerting ourselves, every man in his individual and collective capacity, with all vigour, to promote the views of government in an energic conduct of the war, by which alone we can hope for a continuance of those blessings which belong to us Britons. The public conduct which this kingdom at present holds, is paternal to the dearest interests of the people, and ought to render it popular and respected. Success under God depends on the people bearing the burthens, which the necessity of war may impose on them, with patience and chearfulness; convinced as they must be, that the war is not only just, but absolutely and essentially necessary to the salvation of all that makes life desirable; the peace of families,—the surety of dwellings,—the safety of life,—the security of property:—they will consider its expence as the sacrifice of a little, for the preservation of the whole.

Samuel Taylor Coleridge
1772–1834

Samuel Taylor Coleridge contributed to the *Morning Post*, an important London newspaper, from 1798 to 1803. *Jacobinism* was published in the *Post* on Saturday, 14 January 1800. *Once a Jacobin Always a Jacobin* appeared almost three years later on 21 October 1802. As the second essay makes clear, in England the term had come to refer to the cause of radical political reform in general.

See also the principal Coleridge listing on page 624.

from Jacobinism

The last campaign has checked the views of France, and our reverses in Switzerland must have checked the views of the allies also.[1] Neither party has great cause of joy at the result. This temper of mind, neither elated nor depressed, is of all others the most favourable to negotiation. From the commencement of the war till now, France has been either insolent and flushed with victory, or thrown under the power of the Jacobins by defeats. Now for the first time her ambition has been checked; and Jacobinism, if not mortally wounded, yet requires all the aids of a war against France, to its resuscitation.[2] As events vary, so our ministers vary their tone! Are we successful? The object of the war is to extirpate Jacobinism.—Are we beaten in all points? It then becomes necessary to check the progress of French ambition. It is melancholy that the war has produced, with rapid alternation, the two evils, for the prevention of which it is carried on and justified. We profess to wage the war against Jacobinism

1. The French defeated an allied army at Zurich in September 1799 and were in turn defeated in Italy by an Austro-Russian army.

2. By 1800 Coleridge had been antagonized by Napoleon's wars of aggression.

and ambition: and the moment France is threatened by our successes, Jacobinism revives and flourishes. The war began with Austria and Prussia, May 1792, and on the 10th of August following, royalty was overthrown, and the Brissotine republicanism substituted.[3] In February 1793, we joined the allies; and the war was triumphant in every quarter. In the West the Chouans, who brought at once 80,000 men into the field; General Wurmser[4] in the East; the English on the South; and the Anglo-Austrians on the North. We took Toulon, Valenciennes and Condé. What was the effect? The Brissotine party, comparatively at least humane and enlightened, was overturned by the faction of Robespierre, and the furies of Jacobinism were let loose on the devoted country. In May 1794, the Duke of York took Landrecy, and in imagination we were already the conquerors of France. Jacobinism still predominated, till in June the weathercock of success shifted. The French conquered Flanders, drove back Austria, and even foiled the Duke of York; and in this flush of victory Robespierre and his party were annihilated. Then victories flowed in upon France in full tide; and the public opinions became more temperate, as the nation was less and less in danger from foreign enemies. The last constitution was framed; our ministerial papers, and then the minister himself, spoke of the existing government in France as a power that might be treated with. We endeavoured to treat; France was insolent and vindictive; and the succeeding campaigns effected a reverse of fortune. The conquests of France in Italy were reconquered. Her armies ill organized and ill supported, and her frontiers threatened. What was the effect? The clubs were re-opened. Jacobinism was again brought into play, and became active and powerful in exact proportion to the degree of our success. Hence it appears that the war against France as a republic, produces in the French republic ambition and insolence by its failure, and Jacobinism by its success; nor is this difficult of explanation. When a nation is in safety, men think of their private interests; individual property becomes the predominating principle, the lord of the ascendant; and all politics and theories inconsistent with property and individual interest give way, and sink into a decline, which, unless unnaturally stimulated, would end in speedy dissolution. But is the nation in danger? Every man is called into play; every man feels his interest as a citizen predominating over his individual interests; the high, and the low, and the middle classes become all alike politicians; the majority carry the day; and Jacobinism is the natural consequence. Let us not be deceived by words. Every state, in which all the inhabitants without distinction of property are roused to the exertion of a public spirit, is for the time a Jacobin state. France at present is only preparing to become so.—If the present consulate can conclude a peace, the glory attached to it will, for a while, reconcile the people to an Oligarchy,[5] which can only exist while it is popular; and as manufactures and commerce revive, the spirit of property will regain its ascendency, and the government of France will be modified accordingly.

from Once a Jacobin Always a Jacobin

This charitable adage was at one time fashionable in the ministerial circles; and Mr. Pitt[1] himself, in one of his most powerful speeches, gave it every advantage that is derivable from stately diction. What he thus condescended to decorate, it were well,

---

3. Jacques-Pierre Brissot (1754–1793) was a leader of the Girondins, a moderate bourgeois faction opposed to the extremist Jacobins. He was guillotined on Robespierre's orders during the Terror.

4. Commander of the Austrian army 1793–1794.
5. Government by a small, dominant class or clique.
1. William Pitt, the Tory Prime Minister from 1783–1801.

if he had attempted to prove. But no! he found it a blank assertion, and a blank assertion he suffered it to remain. What *is* a Jacobin? Perhaps the best answer to this question would be, that it is a term of abuse, the convenient watchword of a faction. ***
But though we should find it difficult to determine, what a Jacobin *is*, we may however easily conjecture, what the different sects of Anti-Jacobins have meant by the word. The base and venal creatures, and the blind and furious bigots, of the late ministry, comprehended under that word all, who from whatever cause opposed the late war, and the late ministry, and whom they hate for this opposition with such mortal hatred, as is usual with bigots alarmed, and detected culprits. *"Once a Jacobin always a Jacobin,"* signifies no more in the minds of these men, than *"such a one is a man, whom I shall never cease to hate."* With other men, honest and less violent Anti-Jacobins, the word implies a man, whose affections have been warmly and deeply interested in the cause of general freedom, who has hoped all good and honourable things both *of,* and *for,* mankind. In this sense of the word Jacobin, the adage would affirm, that no man can ever become altogether an apostate to liberty, who has at any time been sincerely and fervently attached to it. His hopes will burn like the Greek fire, hard to be extinguished, and easily rekindling. Even when he despairs of the cause, he will yet *wish,* that it had been successful. And even when private interests have warped his public character, his convictions will remain, and his wishes often rise up in rebellion against his outward actions and public avowals. Thus interpreted, the assertion, *"Once a Jacobin always a Jacobin,"* is so favourable a representation of human nature, that we are willing, too willing perhaps, to admit it even without proof. There is yet a third class of Anti-Jacobins, and of this class we profess ourselves to be, who use the word *Jacobin,* as they use the word, *Whig,* and both words only for want of better; who confess, that Jacobin is too often a word of vague abuse, but believe, that there are certain definite ideas, hitherto not expressed in any single word, which may be attached to this word; and who in consequence uniformly use the word, Jacobin, with certain definite ideas attached to it, those ideas, and no other. A Jacobin, in *our* sense of the term, is one who believes, and is disposed to act on the belief, that all, or the greater part of, the happiness or misery, virtue or vice, of mankind, depends on forms of government; who admits no form of government as either good or rightful, which does not flow directly and formally from the persons governed; who,—considering life, health, moral and intellectual improvement, and liberty both of person and conscience, as blessings which governments are bound as far as possible to increase and secure to every inhabitant, whether he has or has not any fixed property, and moreover as blessings of infinitely greater value to each individual, than the preservation of property can be to any individual,—does consequently and consistently hold, that every inhabitant who has attained that age of reason, has a natural and inalienable right to an *equal* share of power in the choice of the governors. In other words, the Jacobins affirm that no legislature can be rightful or good, which did not proceed from universal suffrage. In the power, and under the controul, of a legislature so chosen, he places all and every thing, with the exception of the natural rights of man, and the means appointed for the preservation and exercise of these rights, by a direct vote of the nation itself—that is to say, by a constitution. Finally, the Jacobin deems it both justifiable and expedient to effect these requisite changes in faulty governments, by absolute revolutions, and considers no violences as properly rebellious or criminal, which are the *means* of giving to a nation the power of declaring and enforcing its sovereign will. In brief, therefore, a Jacobin's creed is this: 1. A government is the organ, by which form and publicity are given to the sovereign will of the people; and by which that will is

enforced and exercised. 2. A government is likewise the instrument and means of purifying and regulating the national will by its public discussions, and by direct institutions for the comforts and instruction of the people. 3. Every native of a country has an equal right to that quantity of property, which is necessary for the sustenance of his life and health. 4. All property beyond this, not being itself a right, can confer no right. Superior wisdom, with superior virtue, would indeed confer a right of superior power; but who is to decide on the possession? Not the person himself, who makes the claim: and if the people, then the right is given, and not inherent. Votes, therefore, *cannot* be *weighed* in this way, and they *must not* be weighed in any other way. Nothing therefore remains possible, but that they must be *numbered*. No form of electing representatives is rightful, but that of universal suffrage. Every individual has a *right* to elect, and a capability of being elected. 5. The legislature has an absolute power over all other property, but that of article 3: unless the people shall have declared otherwise in the constitution. 6. All governments not constituted on these principles are unjust governments. 7. The people have a right to overturn them, in whatever way it is possible, and any means necessary to this end become, *ipso facto*, right means. 8. It is the right and duty of each individual, living under that government, as far as in him lies, to impel and enable the people to exercise these rights.—The man who subscribes to *all* these articles is a complete Jacobin; to many, but not to all of them, a Semi-Jacobin, and the man who subscribes to any one article (excepting the second, which the Jacobin professes only in common with every other political sect not directly an advocate of despotism), may be fairly said to have a *shade* of Jacobinism in his character. If we are not greatly deceived we could point out more than one or two celebrated Anti-Jacobins, who are not slightly infected with some of the worst symptoms of the madness, against which they are raving; and one or two acts of parliament which are justifiable only upon Jacobin principles. These are the ideas which we attach to the word Jacobin; and no other single word expresses them. Not republican; Milton was a pure republican, and yet his notions of government were highly aristocratic; Brutus was a republican, but he perished in consequence of having killed the Jacobin, Caesar. Neither does Demagogue express that which we have detailed; not yet Democrat. The former word implies simply a mode of conduct, and has no reference to principles; and the latter does of *necessity* convey no more than that a man prefers in any country a form of government, without monarchy or aristocracy, which in any country he *may* do, and yet be no Jacobin, and which in some countries he can do without any impeachment of good sense or honesty: for instance, in the purely pastoral and agricultural districts of Switzerland, where there is no other property but that of land and cattle, and that property very nearly equalized. Whoever builds a government on personal and natural rights, is so far a Jacobin. Whoever builds on social rights, that is, hereditary rank, property, and long prescription, is an Anti-Jacobin, even though he should nevertheless be a republican, or even a democrat.

If we have been prolix, let the importance of the subject induce our readers to consider it as a venial fault. Concerning a term, which nine-tenths of the nation have been in the habit of using, either as a name of glory, or a name of reproach and abhorrence, it is not only our advantage but even our duty to have clear, correct, and definite conceptions. *** From what other source that alarm concerning peace, because we should flock to Paris, and all come back *Jacobins?* In the name of all that is sacred, of all that is great and honourable, in the name of Briton, unless this alarmist and his faction believe the truth of Jacobinism, although from self-interest they oppose it, what, do they imagine we have done with our common sense and common feelings? Is Jacobinism an absurdity—and have we no reason to detect it with? Is it productive of all misery, and all horrors? and have we no natural humanity to make us turn away with indignation and loathing from it? Uproar and confusion, personal insecurity, insecurity of property, the tyranny of mobs, or the domination of a soldiery; private houses changed to brothels, the very ceremony of marriage only an initiation to harlotry, while marriage itself is degraded to mere concubinage—these Mr. W. and his friends, have said, and truly said, are the effects of Jacobinism! An insufferable licentiousness in their houses, and abroad an insufferable despotism. These are the effects of Jacobinism; and these, the whole English nation was to be clapped under hatches, lest they should see and fall in love with! "Once a Jacobin, always a Jacobin!" And why? Is it because the creed which we have stated, is dazzling at first sight to the young, the innocent, the disinterested, and to those who, judging of men in general, from their own uncorrupted hearts, judge erroneously, and expect unwisely? Is it because it deceives the mind in its purest and most flexible period? Is it because it is an error that every day's experience aids to detect? an error against which all history is full of warning examples? Or, is it because the experiment has been tried before our eyes, and the error made palpable? From what source are we to derive this strange phaenomenon, that the young, and the inexperienced, who, we know by regular experience, are deceived in their religious antipathies, and grow wiser; in their friendships, and grow wiser; in their modes of pleasure, and grow wiser; should, if once deceived in a question of abstract politics, cling to the error for ever and ever! though, in addition to the natural growth of judgment and information with increase of years, they live in the age, in which the tenets had been unfortunately acted upon, and the consequences, deformities, at which every good man's heart sickens, and head turns giddy? We were never at any period of our life converts to the system of French politics. As far back as our memory reaches, it was an axiom in politics with us, that in every country in which property prevailed, property must be the grand basis of the government; and that that *government was the best, in which the power was the most exactly proportioned to the property.* Yet we do not feel the less shocked by those who would turn an error in speculative politics into a sort of sin against the Holy Ghost, which in some miraculous and inexplicable manner shuts out not only mercy but even repentance!—and who now, that religious bigotry is dying away, would substitute in its place dogmas of *election* and *reprobation* in politics.

⊰⊱ END OF PERSPECTIVES: THE RIGHTS OF MAN AND THE REVOLUTION CONTROVERSY ⊰⊱

⊷ ⊰⊱ ⊶

William Blake
1757–1827

It was from William Blake's *Marriage of Heaven and Hell* that a sensationally transgressive rock band of the 1960s, The Doors, took their name:

> If the doors of perception were cleansed
> every thing would appear to man as it is: In-
> > finite.

But unlike The Doors, Blake needed no pharmaceutical assistance in cleansing his vision. His eccentricity and imaginative intensity, which seemed like madness to more than a few contemporaries, emerged from a childhood punctuated by such events as beholding God's face pressed against his window, seeing angels among the haystacks, and being visited by the Old Testament prophet Ezekiel. When his favorite brother died in 1787, Blake claimed that he saw his "released spirit ascend heavenwards, clapping its hand for joy." Soon after, he reports, this spirit visited him with a critical revelation of the method of "Illuminated Printing" that he would use in his major poetical works.

Rebellious, unconventional, fiercely idealistic, Blake became a celebrity in modern counterculture—Allen Ginsberg and many of the Beat poets of the 1950s and 1960s cited him as a major influence. But for a good part of the nineteenth century, he was known only to a coterie. He did not support himself as a poet but got by on patronage and commissions for engraving and painting. His projects included the Book of Job and other scenes from the Bible; Chaucer's Canterbury Pilgrims; characters in Spenser's *Faerie Queene*; Milton's *L'Allegro, Il Penseroso, Paradise Lost*, and *Paradise Regained*; Gray's *The Bard*; Young's *Night Thoughts*; and Blair's *The Grave*. His obscurity as a poet was due in part to the difficulty of his work after the mid-1790s but chiefly to the very limited issue of his books, a consequence of the painstaking and time-consuming process of "Illuminated Printing." He hoped to reach a wider audience with a private exhibition of his illustrations in 1809, but his adventurous originality, coupled with his cantankerous and combative personality, left him ignored, except for one vicious review in *The Examiner*, which called him a lunatic. He died impoverished and almost entirely unknown except to a small group of younger painters. Only in 1863 did interest begin to grow, thanks to Alexander Gilchrist's biography, *The Life of William Blake: Pictor Ignotus*, its second volume a selection of poems edited by Dante Gabriel Rossetti. The revival was fanned by the enthusiasm of the Pre-Raphaelite circle and subsequent essays by Algernon Charles Swinburne, William Michael Rossetti (Dante Gabriel's brother), and William Butler Yeats.

Although Blake had no formal education, he was an avid reader, immersing himself in English poetry, the Bible, and works of mysticism and philosophy, as well as a study of Greek, Latin, and Hebrew. With precocious talent as a sketcher, he hoped to become a painter, but his father could not afford the tuition, and so apprenticed him at age fourteen as an engraver. During this seven-year term, Blake found time to write the poems gathered into his first publication, *Poetical Sketches* (1783), his only unilluminated volume. The later illuminated books were not products of the letter-press, but of a process of hand-etching designs onto copper plates, using these plates to ink-print pages that were then individually hand-colored and hand-bound into volumes. So labor-intensive a method was not adaptable to any production of quantity: there are, for instance, only twenty-seven known copies of *Songs of Innocence and of Experience* and only nine of *The Marriage of Heaven and Hell*. Yet Blake's commitment to involving his verbal text with pictures and pictorial embellishments created books of extraordinary beauty and an innovative "composite art" of word and image. In this art, the script conveys meaning—flowing versus starkly blocked letters, for instance—and the pictorial elements are significant, sometimes illustrating, sometimes adding another perspective or an ironic comment on the verbal text, sometimes even presenting contradictory information. Our selection of plates shows these dynamics, and our transcriptions of the poetry in all cases follow the linear arrangement on the plates.

Blake's popularity is based chiefly on his earlier and most accessible works from the 1790s. *Songs of Innocence and of Experience* (1789–1794) was much admired in his own day by Samuel Taylor Coleridge, Charles Lamb, and William Wordsworth (even though Blake deemed him too enamored of "Natural Piety"—faith in the natural world as spiritual and poetic resource: "I see in Wordsworth the Natural man rising up against the Spiritual Man Continually, & then he is No Poet but a heathen Philosopher at Enmity against all true Poetry or Inspiration"). *Songs* is compelling not only for a concern with the different ways children and adults see and understand their world (a theme that would occupy Wordsworth, too) but also for its acid critiques of social evils, political injustice, and their agents, the triumvirate of "God & his Priest & King" (in the voice of a too-experienced chimney sweeper). Reflecting Blake's familiarity with the range of freethinking contemporary biblical commentary that became the "Higher Criticism," *The Marriage of Heaven and Hell* (1790) brings visionary energy and poetic extravagance to a trenchant argument for imaginative freedom over psychological inhibition, conventional morality, and institutionalized authority. It is also one of the first Romantic-era rethinkings of Milton *Paradise Lost,* the archetypal story of right and wrong, sin and punishment. Blake takes as an important effect a common reaction (including even Alexander Pope): that Satan and the scenes in Hell provide far more exciting and imaginatively powerful reading than the Angels and God's court in Heaven. "The reason Milton wrote in fetters when / he wrote of Angels & God, and at liberty when of / Devils & Hell," proposes Blake's "Voice of the Devil," is "because he was a true Poet and / of the Devils party without knowing it." Unfettering himself from Milton's moral machinery with this outrageously subversive commentary, Blake presents devils who are a lot more fun than his angels. The *Proverbs of Hell* offer their wisdom with a kind of transgressive glee, sarcastic levity, and diabolical wit that anticipates the sly aphorisms of Oscar Wilde and the exuberance of American Beat poetry.

Visions of the Daughters of Albion (1793), a potent commentary on the tyranny of rape and sexual possession, reflects Blake's admiration for Mary Wollstonecraft's *Vindication of the Rights of Woman,* published the year before. These works and others of the 1790s emerge from Blake's involvement with the London circle of bookseller Joseph Johnson, including Wollstonecraft, William Godwin, Tom Paine, and Dr. Joseph Priestley—a group of artists and religious dissenters joined by progressive politics and support of the French Revolution. Like many of this group, Blake regarded the revolutions in America and France as heralds of a new millennium, and thus inspired, he produced a sequence of (sometimes abstruse) visionary works celebrating the overthrow of tyranny: *The French Revolution* (1791), *America: A Prophecy* (1793), *Europe: A Prophecy* (1794), and *The Book of Urizen* (1794). His later "prophetic" works—*Milton* (1804) and *Jerusalem* (1804–1820)—develop some of these themes with an increasingly esoteric vocabulary and elaborate personal mythology, and are notoriously difficult to read, although they contain passages of impressive energy and imagination.

An emblematic episode from 1803 suggests the real-life consequences of Blake's uncompromising visions. When a drunken dragoon urinated on his cottage garden and refused to leave, Blake vigorously ejected him, and was arrested for seditious threats against the crown. With England at war with France, this was a capital offense for which the penalty could have been death. Blake's trial ended in an acquittal loudly applauded by the spectators, but the ordeal exacerbated his memory of having been arrested in 1780 under the suspicion of being a spy for France while on a riverboat sketching excursion, and it crystallized his anger at state authority. Energizing all Blake's works is his commitment to imagination and the potency of visionary idealism, sharpened by resistance to psychological, ideological, institutional, and political tyrannies.

For Blake's poem on Wollstonecraft, see page 329.

[Plate 1]   The voice of one crying in the
                                        Wilderness[1]

[Plate 2]   **All Religions Are One**[2]

[Plate 3]   The Argument
                        As the true meth-
                        -od of knowledge
                        is experiment,
                        the true faculty
                        of knowing must
                        be the faculty which
                        experiences. This
                        faculty I treat of.

[Plate 4]   PRINCIPLE 1ST

                        That the Poetic Genius is
                        the true Man, and that
                        the body or outward form
                        of Man is derived from the
                        Poetic Genius. Likewise
                        that the forms of all things
                        are derived from their
                        Genius, which by the
                        Ancients was called an
                        Angel & Spirit & Demon.

[Plate 5]   PRINCIPLE 2D

                        As all men are alike in
                        outward form, So (and
                        with the same infinite
                        variety) all are alike in
                        the Poetic Genius

[Plate 6]   PRINCIPLE 3D

                        No man can think
                        write or speak from his

---

1. The prophecy of Isaiah 40.3, which Matthew 3.3 takes
to refer to John the Baptist.
2. Blake did not sign his name to this potentially heretical

declaration, but presents its argument and principles in the
voice of a biblical prophet speaking to the modern age.

heart, but he must intend
truth. Thus all sects of
Philosophy are from the
Poetic Genius, adapted
to the weaknesses of
every individual.

[Plate 7]   PRINCIPLE 4TH

As none by trave
ling over known
lands can find out
the unknown, So,
from already ac
quired knowledge,
Man could not ac
quire more; there
fore an universal
Poetic Genius exists.

[Plate 8]   PRINCIPLE 5TH

The Religions of all Nat-
-ions are derived from each
Nations different reception
of the Poetic Genius which
is every where call'd the Spi
rit of Prophecy

[Plate 9]   PRINCIPLE 6TH

The Jewish & Chris-
tian Testaments are
An original derivati-
-on from the Poetic Ge-
nius: this is necessary
from the confined natu
re of bodily sensation

[Plate 10]   PRINCIPLE 7TH

As all men are alike
(tho' infinitely vari
ous) So all Religions:
& as all similars have
one source,
The true Man is the
source, he being the
Poetic Genius

There Is No Natural Religion [a][1]

[Plate a3]

The Argument

Man has no notion of moral
fitness but from Education.
Naturally he is only a natu
ral organ subject to Sense.

[Plate a4]

I

Man cannot naturally Per-
cieve but through his natural
or bodily organs

[Plate a5]

II

Man by his reason-
ing power can only
compare & judge of
what he has already
perciev'd.

[Plate a6]

III

From a perception of
only 3 senses or 3 ele
ments none could de-
duce a fourth or fifth

[Plate a7]

IV

None could have other
than natural or organic
thoughts if he had none
but organic perceptions

[Plate a8]

V

Mans desires are
limited by his percepti
ons. none can de-
sire what he has not
prciev'd

[Plate a9]

VI

The desires & percepti
-ons of man untaught by

---

1. Blake did sign this tract "The Author and Printer W. Blake." Like contemporary Deists, he rejects the authority of any particular sect, but he does not accept the Deist's "natural religion," the view that knowledge of God is acquired by reason, working with the information reported by the bodily, or natural, senses. [a] presents the Deist "Argument," and [b] is Blake's refutation.

any thing but organs of
sense, must be limited
to objects of sense.

There Is No Natural Religion [b]

[Plate b3]   I

Mans percepti-
-ons are not bound
-ed by organs of
perception. he per-
-cieves more than
sense (tho' ever
so acute) can
discover

[Plate b4]   II

Reason or the ra-
-tio[1] of all we have
already known is
not the same that
it shall be when
we know more

[Plate b6][2]   IV

The bounded is
loathed by its pos-
-sessor. The same
dull round even
of a univer[s]e, would
soon become a
mill with complica-
-ted wheels.

[Plate b7]   V

If the many bec-
-ome the same as
the few, when pos-
-sess'd, More! More!
is the cry of a mista-
-ken soul, less than
All cannot satisfy
Man

---

1. In Latin *ratio* means "reason" and "sum."   2. Plate 5 (III) is missing, either lost or never composed.

[Plate b8]   VI

                              If any could de-
                              -sire what he is in-
                              -capable of posses-
                              sing, despair must
                              be his eternal
                              lot

[Plate b9]   VII

                              The desire of
                              Man being Infi-
                              -nite the possession
                              is Infinite & him-
                              -self Infinite

[Plate b10]   Application
                              He who sees the In-
                              -finite in all things
                              sees God. He who
                              sees the Ratio only
                              sees himself only

[Plate b11]   Conclusion
                              If it were not for the
                              Poetic or Prophetic
                              character, the Philo-
                              -sophic& Experimen-
                              -tal would soon be
                              at the ratio of all
                              things, & stand still,
                              unable to do other
                              than repeat the same
                              dull round over a-
                                        -gain

[Plate b12]   Therefore
                              God becomes as
                              we are that we
                              may be as he
                              is

SONGS OF INNOCENCE AND OF EXPERIENCE   Blake's most popular work appeared in two phases. In 1789 he published *Songs of Innocence;* five years later he bound these poems with a set of new poems in a volume titled *Songs of Innocence and of Experience Shewing the two contrary States of the Human Soul.* "Innocence" and "Experience" are definitions of consciousness that rethink Milton's existential-mythic states of "Paradise" and the "Fall." Blake's categories are modes of perception that tend to coordinate with a chronology that would become standard in Romanticism: childhood is a time and a state of protected "innocence," but not immune to the fallen world and its institutions. This world sometimes impinges on childhood itself, and in any event becomes known through "experience," a state of being marked by the loss of childhood vitality, by fear and inhibition, by social and political corruption, and by the manifold oppression of Church, State, and the ruling classes. The volume's "Contrary States" are sometimes signaled by patently repeated or contrasted titles: in *Innocence, Infant Joy,* in *Experience, Infant Sorrow;* in *Innocence, The Lamb,* in *Experience, The Fly* and *The Tyger.*

William Blake, frontispiece
for *Songs of Innocence*.

These contraries are not simple oppositions, however. Unlike Milton's narrative of the Fall from Paradise, Blake shows either state of soul possible at any moment. Some children, even infants, have already lost their innocence through a soiling contact with the world; some adults, particularly joyously visionary poets, seem able to retain vitality even in experience. Moreover, the values of "Innocence" and "Experience" are themselves complex. At times, an innocent state of soul reflects a primary, untainted vitality of imagination; at other times, Blake, like Mary Wollstonecraft, implicates innocence with dangerous ignorance and vulnerability to oppression. In rhetorical structure, the songs may present an innocent singer against dark ironies that a more experienced reader, alert to social and political evil, will grasp. But just as trickily, experience can also trap a soul in its own "mind-forg'd manacles." Blake's point is not that children are pure and adults fallen, or that children are naive and adults perspicacious. Contrary possibilities coexist, with different plays and shades of emphasis in different poems. These values are often further complicated by the illustrations that accompany and often frame the song-texts. Sometimes these sustain the singer's tone and point of view (e.g., *The Lamb*), and sometimes (e.g., *The Little Black Boy*) they offer an ironic counter-commentary.

SONGS of
INNOCENCE
and of
EXPERIENCE
Shewing the Two Contrary States
of the Human Soul

from SONGS of INNOCENCE

Introduction

Piping down the valleys wild
Piping songs of pleasant glee
On a cloud I saw a child
And he laughing said to me.

5 Pipe a song about a Lamb:
So I piped with merry chear,
Piper, pipe that song again—
So I piped, he wept to hear.

Drop thy pipe thy happy pipe
10 Sing thy songs of happy chear,
So I sang the same again
While he wept with joy to hear

Piper sit thee down and write
In a book that all may read—
15 So he vanish'd from my sight
And I pluck'd a hollow reed

And I made a rural pen,
And I stain'd the water clear,
And I wrote my happy songs,
20 Every child may joy to hear

The Shepherd.

How sweet is the Shepherds sweet lot,
From the morn to the evening he strays:
He shall follow his sheep all the day
And his tongue shall be filled with praise.

5 For he hears the lambs innocent call.
And he hears the ewes tender reply,
He is watchful while they are in peace,
For they know when their Shepherd is nigh.

The Ecchoing Green

The Sun does arise,
And make happy the skies.
The merry bells ring

To welcome the Spring.
5   The sky-lark and thrush,
The birds of the bush,
Sing louder around,
To the bells chearful sound
While our sports shall be seen
10 On the Ecchoing Green.

Old John with white hair
Does laugh away care,
Sitting under the oak,
Among the old folk,
15 They laugh at our play,
And soon they all say,
Such such were the joys
When we all girls & boys,
In our youth time were seen,
20 On the Ecchoing Green.

Till the little ones weary
No more can be merry
The sun does descend,
And our sports have an end:
25 Round the laps of their mothers
Many sisters and brothers,
Like birds in their nest,
Are ready for rest:
And sport no more seen,
30 On the darkening Green.

The Lamb

Little Lamb who made thee
Dost thou know who made thee
Gave thee life & bid thee feed,
By the stream & o'er the mead;
5   Gave thee clothing of delight,
Softest clothing wooly bright;
Gave thee such a tender voice,
Making all the vales rejoice:
Little Lamb who made thee
10 Dost thou know who made thee

Little Lamb, I'll tell thee.
Little Lamb, I'll tell thee;
He is called by thy name
For he calls himself a Lamb:
15 He is meek & he is mild,
He became a little child:
I a child & thou a lamb,

William Blake, *The Lamb*, from *Songs of Innocence*. Blake pictures the boy in a natural state of nakedness among the lambs, all embraced by twining branches.

We are called by his name.
    Little Lamb God bless thee
20   Little Lamb God bless thee

The Little Black Boy[1]

My mother bore me in the southern wild,
And I am black, but O! my soul is white
White as an angel is the English child:
But I am black as if bereav'd of light.

5   My mother taught me underneath a tree
And sitting down before the heat of day,
She took me on her lap and kissed me,
And, pointing to the east, began to say.

Look on the rising sun: there God does live
10 And gives his light and gives his heat away.
And flowers and trees and beasts and men recieve
Comfort in morning joy in the noon day.

---

1. See Color Plates 6 and 7. In Plate 7 the black boy's skin is as light as the English boy's; other versions use contrasting hues. The plates show both boys sheltered by the tree and welcomed by Christ, but also put the black boy outside the inner circle formed by the curve of Christ's body and the praying English boy. He is not part of this configuration, but rather a satellite of the English boy.

And we are put on earth a little space
That we may learn to bear the beams of love.
15   And these black bodies and this sun-burnt face
Is but a cloud, and like a shady grove.

For when our souls have learn'd the heat to bear
The cloud will vanish we shall hear his voice
Saying: come out from the grove, my love & care,
20   And round my golden tent like lambs rejoice.

Thus did my mother say, and kissed me.
And thus I say to little English boy.
When I from black and he from white cloud free,
And round the tent of God like lambs we joy:

25   Ill shade him from the heat till he can bear,
To lean in joy upon our fathers knee
And then Ill stand and stroke his silver hair,
And be like him and he will then love me.

The Blossom.

Merry Merry Sparrow
Under leaves so green
A happy Blossom
Sees you swift as arrow
5   Seek your cradle narrow
Near my Bosom.

Pretty Pretty Robin
Under leaves so green
A happy Blossom
10   Hears you sobbing sobbing
Pretty Pretty Robin
Near my Bosom.

The Chimney Sweeper[1]

When my mother died I was very young
And my father sold me while yet my tongue
Could scarcely cry weep weep weep weep.[2]
So your chimneys I sweep & in soot I sleep.

5   Theres little Tom Dacre, who cried when his head
That curl'd like a lambs back, was shav'd, so I said:
Hush Tom never mind it, for when your head's bare
You know that the soot cannot spoil your white hair

1. Chimney-cleaning was done by young boys, whose impoverished parents sold them into the business, or who were orphans, outcasts, or illegitimate children with no other means of living. It was filthy, health-ruining labor, aggravated by overwork and inadequate clothing, food, and shelter. Among the hazards were burns, permanently blackened skin, deformed legs, black lung disease, and cancer of the scrotum. Protective legislation passed in 1788 was never enforced. Blake's outrage also sounds in "London." Charles Lamb sent this poem to James Montgomery (a topical poet and radical-press editor) for inclusion in *The Chimney-Sweeper's Friend, and Climbing Boy's Album* (1824), which he was assembling for the Society for Ameliorating the Condition of Infant Chimney-Sweepers.
2. The lisping street cry of advertisement ("sweep! sweep!").

William Blake, *The Little Boy lost,* from *Songs of Innocence.*

And so he was quiet, & that very night,
10   As Tom was a sleeping he had such a sight,
That thousands of sweepers Dick, Joe, Ned & Jack
Were all of them lock'd up in coffins of black,

And by came an Angel who had a bright key,
And he open'd the coffins & set them all free.
15   Then down a green plain leaping laughing they run
And wash in a river and shine in the Sun.

Then naked & white, all their bags left behind,
They rise upon clouds, and sport in the wind
And the Angel told Tom if he'd be a good boy,
20   He'd have God for his father & never want joy

And so Tom awoke and we rose in the dark
And got with our bags & our brushes to work.
Tho' the morning was cold, Tom was happy & warm
So if all do their duty they need not fear harm.[3]

The Little Boy lost

Father, father, where are you going
O do not walk so fast.
Speak father, speak to your little boy
Or else I shall be lost,

3. A conduct homily.

William Blake, *The Little Boy found*, from *Songs of Innocence*.

5   The night was dark no father was there
       The child was wet with dew.
       The mire was deep, & the child did weep
       And away the vapour flew.

The Little Boy found

       The little boy lost in the lonely fen,°   *swamp*
       Led by the wand'ring light,[1]
       Began to cry, but God ever nigh,
       Appeard like his father in white.

5   He kissed the child & by the hand led
       And to his mother brought,
       Who in sorrow pale thro' the lonely dale
       Her little boy weeping sought.

The Divine Image.

       To Mercy Pity Peace and Love,
       All pray in their distress:
       And to these virtues of delight
       Return their thankfulness.

1. Phosphorescent marsh.

5   For Mercy Pity Peace and Love
Is God our father dear:
And Mercy Pity Peace and Love,
Is Man his child and care.

For Mercy has a human heart
10   Pity, a human face:
And Love, the human form divine,
And Peace, the human dress.

Then every man, of every clime
That prays in his distress,
15   Prays to the human form divine
Love Mercy Pity Peace.

And all must love the human form,
In heathen, turk or jew.
Where Mercy, Love & Pity dwell,
20   There God is dwelling too.

HOLY THURSDAY[1]

Twas on a Holy Thursday their innocent faces clean
The children walking two & two in red & blue & green[2]
Grey headed beadles[3] walkd before with wands as white as snow
Till into the high dome of Pauls they like Thames waters flow

5   O what a multitude they seemd these flowers of London town
Seated in companies they sit with radiance all their own
The hum of multitudes was there but multitudes of lambs
Thousands of little boys & girls raising their innocent hands

Now like a mighty wind they raise to heaven the voice of song
10   Or like harmonious thunderings the seats of heaven among
Beneath them sit the aged men wise guardians of the poor
Then cherish pity lest you drive an angel from your door[4]

Nurses Song

When the voices of children are heard on the green
And laughing is heard on the hill,
My heart is at rest within my breast
And everything else is still

---

1. One of the poems with a companion in *Experience* (see page 190). Holy Thursday celebrated the Ascension; it was customary to conduct the children in London's charity schools, many of them orphans, to services at St. Paul's, the chief Anglican cathedral.

2. The colors of school uniforms.
3. Minor officials for ushering and preserving order.
4. See Hebrews 13.1–2: "Let brotherly love continue. Be not forgetful to entertain strangers: for thereby some have entertained angels unawares."

5 Then come home my children the sun is gone down
And the dews of night arise
Come come leave off play, and let us away
Till the morning appears in the skies

No no let us play, for it is yet day
10 And we cannot go to sleep
Besides in the sky the little birds fly
And the hills are all coverd with sheep

Well well go & play till the light fades away
And then go home to bed
15 The little ones leaped & shouted & laugh'd
And all the hills ecchoed

Infant Joy

I have no name.
I am but two days old—
What shall I call thee?
I happy am
5 Joy is my name—
Sweet joy befall thee!

Pretty joy!
Sweet joy but two days old.
Sweet joy I call thee:
10 Thou dost smile,
I sing the while,
Sweet joy befall thee

A Dream

Once a dream did weave a shade,
O'er my Angel-guarded bed,
That an Emmet° lost it's way   ant
Where on grass methought I lay.

5 Troubled wilderd and folorn
Dark benighted travel-worn,
Over many a tangled spray
All heart-broke I heard her say.

O my children! do they cry
10 Do they hear their father sigh.
Now they look abroad to see,
Now return and weep for me.

Pitying I drop'd a tear;
But I saw a glow-worm near:
15 Who replied. What wailing wight°   creature
Calls the watchman of the night.

I am set to light the ground,
While the beetle goes his round:
Follow now the beetles hum,
20   Little wanderer hie thee home.

On Anothers Sorrow

Can I see anothers woe.
And not be in sorrow too.
Can I see anothers grief,
And not seek for kind relief.

5   Can I see a falling tear,
And not feel my sorrows share,
Can a father see his child,
Weep, nor be with sorrow fill'd.

Can a mother sit and hear,
10   An infant groan an infant fear—
No no never can it be.
Never never can it be.

And can he who smiles on all
Hear the wren with sorrows small,
15   Hear the small birds grief & care
Hear the woes that infants bear—

And not sit beside the nest
Pouring pity in their breast.
And not sit the cradle near
20   Weeping tear on infants tear.

And not sit both night & day.
Wiping all our tears away.
O! no never can it be.
Never never can it be.

25   He doth give his joy to all.
He becomes an infant small.
He becomes a man of woe
He doth feel the sorrow too.

Think not, thou canst sigh a sigh,
30   And thy maker is not by,
Think not, thou canst weep a tear,
And thy maker is not near.

O! he gives to us his joy,
That our grief he may destroy
35   Till our grief is fled & gone
He doth sit by us and moan

❧

COMPANION READING

Charles Lamb from *The Praise of Chimney-Sweepers*[1]

I like to meet a sweep; understand me,—not a grown sweeper, (old chimneysweepers are by no means attractive,) but one of those tender novices, blooming through their first nigritude, the maternal washings not quite effaced from the cheek: such as come forth with the dawn, or somewhat earlier, with their little professional notes sounding like the *peep peep* of a young sparrow; or liker to the matin lark should I pronounce them, in their aërial ascents not seldom anticipating the sun-rise?

I have a kindly yearning toward these dim specks—poor blots—innocent blacknesses.

I reverence these young Africans of our own growth,—these almost clergy imps, who sport their cloth without assumption; and from their little pulpits, (the tops of chimneys,) in the nipping air of a December morning, preach a lesson of patience to mankind.

When a child, what a mysterious pleasure it was to witness their operation! to see a chit no bigger than one's-self, enter, one knew not by what process, into what seemed the *fauces Averni*,[2]—to pursue him in imagination, as he went sounding on through so many dark stifling caverns, horrid shades!—to shudder with the idea that "now, surely, he must be lost for ever!"—to revive at hearing his feeble shout of discovered day-light—and then (O fulness of delight!) running out of doors, to come just in time to see the sable phenomenon emerge in safety, the brandished weapon of his art victorious like some flag waved over a conquered citadel! I seem to remember having been told that a bad sweep was once left in a stack with his brush, to indicate which way the wind blew. It was an awful spectacle certainly; not much unlike the old stage direction in Macbeth, where the "Apparition of a child crowned, with a tree in his hand, rises."[3]

Reader, if thou meetest one of these small gentry in thy early rambles, it is good to give him a penny. It is better to give him twopence. If it be starving weather, and to the proper troubles of his hard occupation a pair of kibed[4] heels (no unusual accompaniment) be superadded, the demand on thy humanity will surely rise to a tester.[5] * * *

In one of the state-beds at Arundel Castle,[6] a few years since, under a ducal canopy, (that seat of the Howards is an object of curiosity to visitors, chiefly for its beds, in which the late duke was especially a connoisseur,) encircled with curtains of delicatest crimson, with starry coronets inwoven, folded between a pair of sheets whiter and softer than the lap where Venus lulled Ascanius,[7] was discovered by chance, after all methods of search had failed, at noon-day, fast asleep, a lost chimney-sweeper. The little creature, having somehow confounded his passage among the intricacies of those lordly chimneys, by some unknown aperture had alighted upon this magnificent chamber; and, tired with his tedious explorations, was unable to resist the delicious invitement to repose, which he there saw exhibited; so creeping between the sheets very quietly, laid his black head upon the pillow, and slept like a young Howard.

1. From *London Magazine*, May 1822, under the pseudonym "Elia." For more by Lamb, see listings under William Wordsworth (page 472), Coleridge's "Lectures" and Their Time (page 702), and Popular Prose and the Problems of Authorship (page 1087).
2. The Jaws of Avernus (a phrase from Vergil's *Aeneid*, 6.201); Lake Avernus, near Naples, was thought to lead to the underworld.

3. Cf. *Macbeth* 4.1; the crowned child is a sign that a line other than childless Macbeth's will become Scotland's kings. Awful: awe-inspiring.
4. Ulcerated and inflamed from exposure to the cold.
5. Sixpence.
6. Home of the Howard family, Dukes of Norfolk.
7. Aeneas's young son (*Aeneid* bk. 1) who, protected by Venus, escaped with his father from burning Troy.

Such is the account given to the visitors at the Castle. But I cannot help seeming to perceive a confirmation of what I had just hinted at in this story. A high instinct was at work in the case, or I am mistaken. Is it probable that a poor child of that description, with whatever weariness he might be visited, would have ventured, under such a penalty as he would be taught to expect, to uncover the sheets of a Duke's bed, and deliberately to lay himself down between them, when the rug, or the carpet, presented an obvious couch still far above his pretensions? Is this probable, I would ask, if the great power of nature, which I contend for, had not been manifested within him, prompting to the adventure? Doubtless this young nobleman (for such my mind misgives me that he must be) was allured by some memory, not amounting to full consciousness, of his condition in infancy, when he was used to be lapped by his mother, or his nurse, in just such sheets as he there found, into which he was now but creeping back as into his proper *incunabula* [cradle clothes] and resting-place. By no other theory than by this sentiment of a pre-existent state (as I may call it), can I explain a deed so venturous, and indeed upon any other system, so indecorous, in this tender but unseasonable sleeper.

My pleasant friend Jem White[8] was so impressed with a belief of metamorphoses like this frequently taking place, that in some sort to reverse the wrongs of fortune in these poor changelings, he instituted an annual feast of chimney-sweepers, at which it was his pleasure to officiate as host and waiter. *** O it was a pleasure to see the sable younkers lick in the unctuous meat, with *his* more unctuous sayings—how he would fit the tit-bits to the puny mouths, reserving the lengthier links for the seniors—how he would intercept a morsel even in the jaws of some young desperado, declaring it "must to the pan again to be browned, for it was not fit for a gentleman's eating"—how he would recommend this slice of white bread, or that piece of kissing-crust,[9] to a tender juvenile, advising them all to have a care of cracking their teeth, which were their best patrimony,—how genteelly he would deal about the small ale, as if it were wine, naming the brewer, and protesting, if it were not good, he should lose their custom; with a special recommendation to wipe the lip before drinking. Then we had our toasts—"The King,"—"the Cloth,"—which, whether they understood or not, was equally diverting and flattering;—and for a crowning sentiment, which never failed, "May the Brush supersede the Laurel!" All these, and fifty other fancies, which were rather felt than comprehended by his guests, would he utter, standing upon tables, and prefacing every sentiment with—"Gentlemen, give me leave to propose so and so," which was a prodigious comfort to those young orphans; every now and then stuffing into his mouth (for it did not do to be squeamish on these occasions) indiscriminate pieces of those reeking sausages, which pleased them mightily, and was the savouriest part, you may believe, of the entertainment.

> Golden lads and lasses must,
> As chimney-sweepers, come to dust.[1]

James White is extinct, and with him these suppers have long ceased. He carried away with him half the fun of the world when he died—of my world at least. His old clients look for him among the pens; and missing him, reproach the altered feast of St. Bartholomew, and the glory of Smithfield departed for ever.

8. Lamb's schoolmate at Christ's Hospital, a London school for orphans and poor children, also attended by Coleridge and Leigh Hunt.
9. Overhanging crust that touches, or kisses, the crust of another loaf of bread during baking.
1. A couplet from a song in Shakespeare's *Cymbeline* (4.2.262–63); "dust" is the chimney-sweepers' soot and the body after death.

❧

from SONGS of EXPERIENCE

Introduction.

Hear the voice of the Bard!
Who Present, Past, & Future sees
Whose ears have heard,
The Holy Word,
5   That walk'd among the ancient trees.¹
Calling the lapsed Soul
And weeping in the evening dew:
That might controll
The starry pole:²
10   And fallen fallen light renew!

O Earth O Earth return!³
Arise from out the dewy grass:
Night is worn.
And the morn
15   Rises from the slumberous mass.

Turn away no more
Why wilt thou turn away
The starry floor
The watry shore
20   Is givn thee till the break of day.

EARTH'S *Answer*¹

Earth rais'd up her head.
From the darkness dread & drear.
Her light fled:
Stony dread!
5   And her locks cover'd with grey despair.

Prison'd on watry shore
Starry Jealousy does keep my den
Cold and hoar
Weeping o'er
10   I hear the Father of the ancient men.²

---

1. Adam and Eve (the first lapsed souls), "heard the voice of the Lord God walking in the garden in the cool of the day" and "hid themselves from the presence of the Lord God amongst the trees of the garden" (Genesis 3.8).
2. The star above the North Pole (the North Star), its fixed position a symbol of steadfastness and a focus for navigation; the pivot of celestial order.
3. God exhorts his erring people: "O Earth, earth, earth, hear the word of the Lord" (Jeremiah 22.29). The place-

ment of "return" at the turn of the verse line is a poet's pun (*versus* in Latin means *turn*) replayed in *turn* in lines 16 and 17.
1. Blake's plate design surrounds and penetrates the text with sinewy plant stems, which along the bottom turn into a prone serpent, its head slightly raised, with an open mouth and flickering tongue. One effect is to suggest that "Earth's answer" comes from this tongue.
2. On some plates "Father" is "father."

Selfish father of men
Cruel jealous selfish fear
Can delight
Chain'd in night
15   The virgins of youth and morning bear

Does spring hide its joy
When buds and blossoms grow?
Does the sower?
Sow by night?
20   Or the plowman in darkness plow?

Break this heavy chain.
That does freeze my bones around
Selfish! vain!
Eternal bane!
25   That free Love with bondage bound

The CLOD & the PEBBLE

Love seeketh not Itself to please,
Nor for itself hath any care;
But for another gives its ease,
And builds a Heaven in Hells despair.[1]

5   So sung a little Clod of Clay
           Trodden with the cattles feet:
           But a Pebble of the brook,
           Warbled out these metres meet.

Love seeketh only Self to please
10   To bind another to Its delight:
Joys in anothers loss of ease,
And builds a Hell in Heavens despite.[2]

HOLY THURSDAY[1]

Is this a holy thing to see,
In a rich and fruitful land
Babes reducd to misery
Fed with cold and usurous hand?

5   Is that trembling cry a song?
Can it be a song of joy?
And so many children poor?
It is a land of poverty!

---

1. I Corinthians 13.4: "Charity suffereth long, and is kind; charity envieth not; charity vaunteth not itself, is not puffed up."
2. In Hell Satan declares, "The mind is its own place, and in itself / Can make a Heaven of Hell, a Hell of Heaven" (*Paradise Lost* 1.254–55).
1. See *Holy Thursday* in *Songs of Innocence* (page 184).

And their sun does never shine,
10   *And their fields are bleak & bare,*
And their ways are fill'd with thorns
It is eternal winter there.

For where-e'er the sun does shine,
And where-e'er the rain does fall:
15   *Babe can never hunger there,*
Nor poverty the mind appall.

The Little Girl Lost[1]

In futurity
I prophetic see.
That the earth from sleep.
(Grave the sentence deep)

5   Shall arise and seek
For her maker meek:
And the desart wild
Become a garden mild.[2]

In the southern clime,
10   Where the summers prime.
Never fades away;
Lovely Lyca[3] lay.

Seven summers old
Lovely Lyca told,°   °tallied
15   She had wanderd long.
Hearing wild birds song.

Sweet sleep come to me
Underneath this tree;
Do father, mother weep.—
20   Where can Lyca sleep.

Lost in desert wild
Is your little child.
How can Lyca sleep,
If her mother weep.

25   If her heart does ake,
Then let Lyca wake;

1. This and The Little Girl Found were in Songs of Innocence in 1789, where they followed A Dream and were followed by The Little Boy Lost. In Experience, Holy Thursday comes before and The Chimney Sweeper after. The first plate of Lost shows a young naked man and flimsily veiled young woman kissing and embracing under willow branches, as she points to a soaring dove. On the opposite margin are climbing vines, which curl across the plate, entwined with an open-mouthed snake, between the first two and next eight stanzas.
2. The prophecy of Isaiah: "The desert shall rejoice and blossom as the rose" (35.1).
3. A name suggesting affinity with lykos, the Greek word for "wolf."

If my mother sleep,
Lyca shall not weep.

Frowning frowning night,
30   O'er this desert bright,
Let thy moon arise,
While I close my eyes.

Sleeping Lyca lay:
While the beasts of prey,
35   Come from caverns deep,
View'd the maid asleep

The kingly lion stood
And the virgin view'd,
Then he gambold round
40   O'er the hallowd ground;

Leopards, tygers play,
Round her as she lay;
While the lion old,
Bow'd his mane of gold.

45   And her bosom lick,
And upon her neck,
From his eyes of flame,
Ruby tears there came;

While the lioness,
50   Loos'd her slender dress,
And naked they convey'd
To caves the sleeping maid.[4]

The Little Girl Found

All the night in woe,
Lyca's parents go:
Over vallies deep
While the desarts weep.

5   Tired and woe-begone,
Hoarse with making moan:
Arm in arm seven days.
They trac'd the desert ways.

Seven nights they sleep,
10   Among shadows deep:

4. On the next plate, depicted beneath the last three stanzas is a woman clad, seated alone under a leafless tree in the woods, looking up.

And dream they see their child
Starv'd in desert wild.

Pale thro' pathless ways
The fancied image strays.[1]

15   Famish'd, weeping, weak
With hollow piteous shriek

Rising from unrest,
The trembling woman prest,
With feet of weary woe;
20   She could no further go.

In his arms he bore,
Her arm'd with sorrow sore:
Till before their way,
A couching lion lay.

25   Turning back was vain,
Soon his heavy mane.
Bore them to the ground;
Then he stalk'd around,

Smelling to his prey.
30   But their fears allay,
When he licks their hands:
And silent by them stands.

They look upon his eyes
Fill'd with deep surprise:
35   And wondering behold.
A spirit arm'd in gold.

On his head a crown
On his shoulders down,
Flow'd his golden hair.
40   Gone was all their care.

Follow me he said,
Weep not for the maid;
In my palace deep,
Lyca lies asleep.

45   Then they followed,
Where the vision led:
And saw their sleeping child,
Among tygers wild.[2]

---

1. The title and lines 1–14 are on the bottom half of the plate on which *The Little Girl Lost* ends, as if a two-part song. Next to this verse is a lioness under a tree, with her nose in the air (scenting prey?).

2. The plate with the rest of the song shows intertwined elm trunks, and at their base a small child nestling with a resting lion, two young children playing on the back of a reposing lioness, next to whom a naked woman sleeps, face down.

To this day they dwell
50   In a lonely dell
Nor fear the wolvish howl,
Nor the lions growl.

THE Chimney Sweeper

A little black thing among the snow:
Crying weep, weep, in notes of woe!
Where are thy father & mother? say?
They are both gone up to the church to pray.

5   Because I was happy upon the heath
And smil'd among the winters snow:
They clothed me in the clothes of death,
And taught me to sing the notes of woe.

And because I am happy & dance & sing,
10   They think they have done me no injury:
And are gone to praise God & his Priest & King
Who make up a heaven of our misery.[1]

NURSES Song

When the voices of children, are heard on the green
And whisprings are in the dale:
The days of my youth rise fresh in my mind,
My face turns green and pale.

5   Then come home my children, the sun is gone down
And the dews of night arise
Your spring & your day, are wasted in play
And your winter and night in disguise.

The SICK ROSE[1]

O Rose thou art sick.
The invisible worm,
That flies in the night
In the howling storm:

5   Has found out thy bed
Of crimson joy:
And his dark secret love
Does thy life destroy.[2]

1. Construct their happiness from the elements of our misery; create an illusion of heavenly will in our misery.
1. See Color Plate 9.
2. There are two manuscript versions of 7–8: "O dark secret love / Does life destroy"; "And her dark secret love / Does thy life destroy."

William Blake, *THE Chimney Sweeper,* from *Songs of Experience.* The contrasting colors of soot-burdened sweep and snowstorm also involve a moral recognition: in the adverse winter world where effective home heating requires clean chimneys, the warm homes are closed to the sweep.

William Blake, THE FLY, from *Songs of Experience*. How should we read? The activities depicted seem "innocent": a girl bats a shuttlecock; a nurse guides a boy's early steps. But the poem-text provokes a view of the girl as a potential flyswatter, and in another frame of reference, of both little ones as analogues to the "little fly."

Although in a manuscript notebook, Blake numbered the stanzas 1–5 in the order of top left to bottom right, his plate design—without numbers—makes the sequence ambiguous. Should we read down or across? This is the only column-arrangement in *Songs*.

THE FLY

Little Fly
Thy summer's play,
My thoughtless hand
Has brush'd away.[1]

Am not I
A fly like thee?
Or art not thou
A man like me?

For I dance
And drink & sing:
Till some blind hand
Shall brush my wing.

If thought is life
And strength & breath:[2]
And the want
Of thought is death;

Then am I
A happy fly,
If I live,
Or if I die.

---

1. Cf. the blinded Gloucester's bitterly rueful comment in *King Lear*: "As flies to wanton boys, are we to th' gods, / They kill us for their sport" (4.1.36–37).
2. Descartes famously said, "I think, therefore I am."

The Angel

I Dreamt a Dream! what can it mean?
And that I was a maiden Queen:
Guarded by an Angel mild:
Witless woe, was ne'er beguil'd!

5 And I wept both night and day
And he wip'd my tears away
And I wept both day and night
And hid from him my hearts delight

So he took his wings and fled:
10 Then the morn blush'd rosy red:
I dried my tears & armd my fears,
With ten thousand shields and spears.

Soon my Angel came again;
I was arm'd, he came in vain:
15 For the time of youth was fled
And grey hairs were on my head

The Tyger[1]

Tyger Tyger, burning bright,
In the forests of the night;[2]
What immortal hand or eye,
Could frame thy fearful symmetry?

5 In what distant deeps or skies,
Burnt the fire of thine eyes?
On what wings dare he aspire?[3]
What the hand dare sieze the fire?

And what shoulder & what art,
10 Could twist the sinews of thy heart?
And when thy heart began to beat,
What dread hand? & what dread feet?[4]

What the hammer? what the chain,
In what furnace was thy brain?
15 What the anvil? what dread grasp,
Dare its deadly terrors clasp!

When the stars threw down their spears
And water'd heaven with their tears:[5]
Did he smile his work to see?[6]
20 Did he who made the Lamb make thee?[7]

1. See Color Plate 8.
2. A time of day and a metaphysical location, characterized by forest mazes—the terrain that conducts to Hell in Dante's *Inferno*. Cf. "midnight streets" in *London*, line 13.
3. Icarus, with his father Daedalus, fashioned wings of feathers and wax to escape from prison. Icarus, ignoring his father's cautions, soared too close to the sun; the wax melted and he fell to his death in the sea.
4. One engraving has, "What dread hand Formd thy dread feet?"

5. In the war in Heaven, *Paradise Lost* (bk. 6), Satan is defeated and driven down to Hell. Blake's verb leaves it undecidable whether the stars "threw down their spears" in desperate surrender or in defiance.
6. In a notebook draft, Blake wrote "did he laugh his work to see."
7. An allusion to Jesus, "The Lamb of God" (John 1.29 and 1.36) and, indirectly, to the poem in *Songs of Innocence*, with Blake as the maker.

Tyger Tyger burning bright,
In the forests of the night:
What immortal hand or eye,
Dare frame thy fearful symmetry?

My Pretty ROSE TREE[1]

A flower was offerd to me;
Such a flower as May never bore.
But I said I've a Pretty Rose-tree:
And I passed the sweet flower o'er.

5   Then I went to my Pretty Rose-tree;
To tend her by day and by night.
But my Rose turnd away with jealousy:
And her thorns were my only delight.

AH! SUN-FLOWER[1]

Ah Sun-flower! weary of time,
Who countest the steps of the Sun:
Seeking after that sweet golden clime
Where the travellers journey is done

5   Where the Youth pined away with desire,
And the pale Virgin shrouded in snow:
Arise from their graves and aspire
Where my Sun-flower wishes to go.

The GARDEN of LOVE

I went to the Garden of Love.
And saw what I never had seen:
A Chapel was built in the midst,
Where I used to play on the green.

5   And the gates of this Chapel were shut,
And Thou shalt not, writ over the door;[1]
So I turnd to the Garden of Love,
That so many sweet flowers bore.

And I saw it was filled with graves,
10   And tomb-stones where flowers should be:
And Priests in black gowns, were walking their rounds,
And binding with briars, my joys & desires.[2]

---

1. This song and *Ah! Sun-Flower* are on the same plate.
1. In Ovid's *Metamorphoses* (4.192), a nymph spurned by Apollo, the sun god, so pined for him that she turned into a sunflower, a heliotrope (turning its face to follow the sun).
1. A parody of the syntax of the Ten Commandments.
2. A crown of thorns tortured Jesus.

LONDON

I wander thro' each charter'd street,[1]
Near where the charter'd Thames does flow
And mark in every face I meet
Marks of weakness, marks of woe.

5   In every cry of every Man,
In every Infants cry of fear,
In every voice; in every ban,[2]
The mind-forg'd manacles I hear[3]

How the Chimney-sweepers cry
10   Every blackning Church appalls.[4]
And the hapless Soldiers sigh
Runs in blood down Palace walls

But most thro' midnight streets I hear
How the youthful Harlots curse[5]
15   Blasts the new-born Infants tear[6]
And blights with plagues the Marriage hearse

The Human Abstract.

Pity would be no more,
If we did not make somebody Poor:
And Mercy no more could be,
If all were as happy as we:

5   *And mutual fear brings peace:*
Till the selfish loves increase.
Then Cruelty knits a snare,
And spreads his baits with care.

He sits down with holy fears,
10   *And waters the ground with tears:*
Then Humility takes its root
Underneath his foot.

Soon spreads the dismal shade
Of Mystery over his head;

---

1. A charter is a grant of liberty or privilege, as in Magna Carta (1215). Exclusive: granted to some, it forbids others. Whether rights were chartered or natural was contested in the 1790s.
2. Several meanings: political prohibition, public condemnation, curse, announcement of marriage.
3. The forgers are the authorities of Church and State (Blake first wrote "german forged," referring to the German-born King George III) and the individuals who fetter themselves in fear or compliance. Between this "hear" and its rhyming repetition at the end of line 13, is an acrostic of the first letters of the third stanza H E A R.

4. The capital C makes it clear that this is the institutional Church of England; "blackning" involves soot with the imagery of moral evil; "appalls" continues the indictment, by drawing into the sense of "dismay" (to which the Church is immune) the literal meaning, "make pale"—that is, clean the soot out of; this color-moral extends into the next stanza's "blasts" and "blights."
5. Many prostitutes were desperately poor girls barely out of childhood, abandoned or disowned by their families.
6. Prenatal blindness caused by sexually transmitted diseases.

15   And the Catterpiller and Fly,
      Feed on the Mystery.

      And it bears the fruit of Deceit,
      Ruddy and sweet to eat:
      And the Raven his nest has made
20   In its thickest shade.

      The Gods of the earth and sea,
      Sought thro' Nature to find this Tree
      But their search was all in vain:
      There grows one in the Human Brain

INFANT SORROW

      My mother groand! my father wept.
      Into the dangerous world I leapt:
      Helpless naked piping loud:
      Like a fiend hid in a cloud.

5   Struggling in my fathers hands:
      Striving against my swadling bands
      Bound and weary I thought best
      To sulk upon my mothers breast.

A Little BOY Lost

      Nought loves another as itself
      Nor venerates another so.
      Nor is it possible to Thought
      A greater than itself to know:

5   And Father, how can I love you,
      Or any of my brothers more?
      I love you like the little bird
      That picks up crumbs around the door.

      The Priest sat by and heard the child.
10   In trembling zeal he siez'd his hair:
      He led him by his little coat:
      And all admir'd the Priestly care.

      And standing on the altar high,
      Lo what a fiend is here! said he:
15   One who sets reason up for judge
      Of our most holy Mystery.°   religion

      The weeping child could not be heard.
      The weeping parents wept in vain:
      They strip'd him to his little shirt.
20   And bound him in an iron chain.

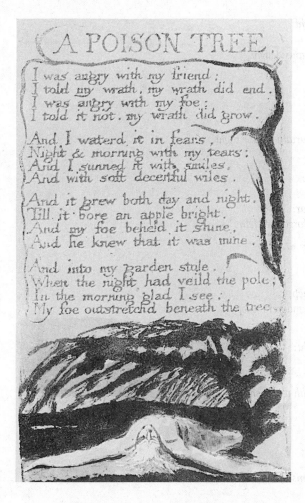

William Blake, A POISON TREE. The poem was originally titled "Christian Forbearance." We present this Song only in the image of this plate. How does this invite you to read? The tail of the "y" in "My" at the beginning of the last line becomes a clockwise frame of the whole, as a branch of the poison tree. The outstretched body is in the posture of a crucifixion.

And burn'd him in a holy place,
Where many had been burn'd before:
The weeping parents wept in vain.
Are such things done on Albions° shore.   England's

A Little GIRL Lost

Children of the future Age,
Reading this indignant page;
Know that in a former time.
Love! sweet Love! was thought a crime.

In the Age of Gold,
Free from winters cold:[1]

1. In classical myth, the first idyllic era of existence (always spring), analogous to Adam and Eve in unfallen Eden; here imagined in a visionary present by force of "delight" as verb.

Youth and maiden bright,
To the holy light,
5   Naked in the sunny beams delight.[2]

Once a youthful pair
Fill'd with softest care:
Met in garden bright.
Where the holy light.
10   Had just removd the curtains of the night.

There in rising day.
On the grass they play:
Parents were afar:
Strangers came not near:
15   And the maiden soon forgot her fear.

Tired with kisses sweet
They agree to meet,
When the silent sleep
Waves o'er heavens deep;
20   And the weary tired wanderers weep.

To her father white
Came the maiden bright:
But his loving look,
Like the holy book,
25   All her tender limbs with terror shook.

Ona! pale and weak!
To thy father speak:
O the trembling fear!
O the dismal care!   *hair*[3]
30   That shakes the blossoms of my hoary

The School-Boy[1]

I love to rise in a summer morn,
When the birds sing on every tree;
The distant huntsman winds° his horn,   *blows*
And the sky-lark sings with me.
5   O! what sweet company.

But to go to school in a summer morn
O! it drives all joy away;
Under a cruel eye outworn
The little ones spend the day,
10   In sighing and dismay.

---

2. Ambiguous or double grammar (noun/verb): "beam's delight" / "Youth and maiden…delight."
3. On the right side of Blake's plate, the curve of a tree-trunk design compels him to etch "hair" above the end of line 30.
1. This song was originally placed in *Songs of Innocence,* then transferred to *Songs of Experience.*

Ah! then at times I drooping sit,
And spend many an anxious hour.
Nor in my book can I take delight,
Nor sit in learnings bower
15 Worn thro' with the dreary shower.

How can the bird that is born for joy,
Sit in a cage and sing,
How can a child when fears annoy,
But droop his tender wing.
20 And forget his youthful spring.

O father & mother, if buds are nip'd,
And blossoms blown away,
And if the tender plants are strip'd
Of their joy in the springing day,
25 By sorrow and cares dismay.

How shall the summer arise in joy.
Or the summer fruits appear   (troy[2]
Or how shall we gather what griefs des
Or bless the mellowing year
30 When the blasts of winter appear.

A DIVINE IMAGE

Cruelty has a Human Heart
And Jealousy a Human Face
Terror, the Human Form Divine
And Secrecy, the Human Dress

5 The Human Dress, is forged in Iron
The Human Form, a fiery Forge.
The Human Face, a Furnace seal'd
The Human Heart, its hungry Gorge.

THE MARRIAGE OF HEAVEN AND HELL   In his first, though hardly systematic, attempt to present a philosophical vision, Blake's aim is to challenge, even outrage, conventional ideologies of good and evil and the moral rewards of Heaven and Hell. His immediate target is the teachings of Emanuel Swedenborg (1688–1772), a visionary theologian whom he had initially admired: it is Swedenborg's *Memorable Relations*, solemn reports of encounters with angels and devils in his *Treatise Concerning Heaven and Hell* (1778), that are satirized in Blake's *Memorable Fancies*. Most of Blake's targets are still recognizable: scientific materialists such as Locke who value reason and the information of the senses over imagination; pious moral philosophies that regard the body and soul as distinct, antithetical entities; conventional strictures, keyed to such philosophies, that shame the body and sexuality. Although Blake assails orthodox

---

2. On Blake's plate, the word *destroy* is broken into its two syllables, with the second one placed on the line above, its connection to the first indicated by a left parenthesis. While this is a printer's device when page space does not allow the whole line to be printed straight out, Blake's plate shows that he might have had plenty of space after "des" had the syllable not met the tree-trunk of his pictorial design; he displays a destruction of the very word.

Christian pieties, his argument is not with religion per se: he is intensely spiritual, believing in visionary prophecy, presenting the prophets Isaiah and Ezekiel as inspirational allies and fellow poets, and admiring Jesus, not as the enforcer of the Ten Commandments but as a compassionate rebel whose "virtue" is precisely that he "acted from im-/-pulse and not from rules." Blake's poem wields the allied genres of satire, enlightenment treatise, and prophecy (of spiritual revolution, signaled by political revolution). The verse lines in the text below vary from standard editorial transcriptions: we follow the linear arrangement of Blake's plates. Square brackets to the left give the plate number in Blake's illuminated book.

[Plate 1]

THE
MARRIAGE
of
HEAVEN
and
HELL

[Plate 2]

The Argument.[1]

Rintrah[2] roars & shakes his fires in the burdend air;
Hungry clouds swag° on the deep   *lie heavily*

Once meek, and in a perilous path,
The just man[3] kept his course along
5   The vale of death.
Roses are planted where thorns grow.
And on the barren heath
Sing the honey bees.

Then the perilous path was planted:
10 And a river, and a spring
On every cliff and tomb;
And on the bleached bones[4]
Red clay brought forth.[5]

Till the villain left the paths of ease,
15 To walk in perilous paths, and drive
The just man into barren climes.
Now the sneaking serpent walks
In mild humility.
And the just man rages in the wilds[6]
20 Where lions roam.

1. Normally a thematic prose summary of a verse passage to follow. The verse that follows is hardly a simple summary.
2. A punning Blake-name for a ranting, wrathful poet-prophet of the Old-Testament type and (like John the Baptist) herald of a new era, this figure rebukes present aridity and predicts restorative revolution.
3. The spiritual pilgrim and prophet, trying to keep faith after the Fall.
4. See Ezekiel 37, an account of the resurrection of life from a valley of bones ("can these bones live?").
5. A literal translation of "Adam"; also the blood of violence. Isaiah 5 prophesies assault by devouring fire and

a "roaring" army (30), and chapters 34–35, to which Blake refers on plate 3, prophesy "the day of the Lord's vengeance" on Edom—the destruction of the armies, the dominion of wild beasts, and a land reduced to deserts and thorns and then restored to fertility and the rebirth of faith: "the desert shall...blossom as the rose...in the wilderness shall waters break out...And an highway shall be there...called The way of holiness."
6. Compare the epigraph for *All Religions Are One*. The voice from the wilderness is prophesied in Isaiah 40.3 and taken by Matthew (3.3) to refer to John the Baptist.

Rintrah roars & shakes his fires in the
    burdend air;
Hungry clouds swag on the deep.

[Plate 3]

As a new heaven is begun, and it is now thir-
-ty-three years since its advent:[7] *the Eternal Hell*[8]
revives. And lo! Swedenborg is the Angel sitting
at the tomb: his writings are the linen clothes folded
up.[9] *Now is the dominion of Edom,*[1] *& the return of*
Adam into Paradise; see Isaiah XXXIV & XXXV Chap:[2]

Without **Contraries** *is no progression. Attraction*
and Repulsion, Reason and Energy, Love and
Hate, are necessary to **Human existence.**

From these contraries spring what the religious call
Good & Evil. Good is the passive that obeys Reason
Evil is the active springing from Energy.

Good is Heaven. Evil is Hell.

[Plate 4]

The voice of the
Devil[3]

All Bibles or sacred codes, have been
the causes of the following Errors.
    1. That Man has two real existing princi-
ples Viz: a Body & a Soul.
    2. That Energy, calld Evil, is alone from the
Body, & that Reason, calld Good, is alone from
the Soul.
    3. That God will torment Man in Eternity
for following his Energies.
    But the following Contraries to these are True
    1. Man has no Body distinct from his Soul
for that calld Body is a portion of Soul discernd
by the five Senses, the chief inlets of Soul in this
age.
    2. Energy is the only life and is from the Body
and Reason is the bound or outward circumference
of Energy.

---

7. In 1757, 33 years before he began this poem in 1790, Blake was born and Swedenborg claimed to have witnessed the Last Judgment and the advent of "New Heaven." At age 33, Christ was crucified and resurrected, hence Blake's sly reference to himself as a Christ-like prophet.

8. Any prophecy of "a new heaven" brings forth a new Hell. Blake's anti-Swedenborgian writing is his "Bible of Hell" (see Plate 24).

9. See John 20.4–14 for Christ's empty sepulchre, the empty burial linens folded and two angels sitting where the body was. Swedenborg is in the ironic situation of announcing his teachings are empty.

1. See Genesis 27.40: "Edom" is another name for Esau, the honest brother duped out of his inheritance by the trickery of Jacob; their father Isaac assures Esau that "it shall come to pass when thou shalt have the dominion, that thou shalt break [Jacob's] yoke from off thy neck." Isaiah 63 presents the allegory of an Edomite (Esau's descendant) "red in apparel"—bloodspattered from a vengeful war with rebellious Israelites. "Edom," like "Adam," means "red earth," a pun that in the 1790s would evoke bloody political revolution to regain paradise.

2. In addition to these chapters and verses, Blake is also, defiantly, satirizing Isaiah 5.20: "Woe unto them that call evil good and good evil."

3. An opponent of "sacred codes"—"what the religious call Good & Evil"—the Devil argues that Good is only a synonym for sterility unto death and that Evil is energy, freedom, and life.

3. Energy is Eternal Delight

[Plate 5]   *Those who restrain desire, do so because theirs is weak enough to be restrained; and the restrainer or reason usurps its place & governs the unwilling.*

And being restraind it by degrees becomes passive till it is only the shadow of desire.

The history of this is written in Paradise Lost. & the Governor or Reason is call'd Messiah.[4]

And the original Archangel or possessor of the command of the heavenly host is call'd the Devil or Satan and his children are call'd Sin & Death[5]

But in the Book of Job Miltons Messiah is call'd Satan.[6]

For this history has been adopted by both parties

It indeed appear'd to Reason as if Desire was cast out, but the Devil's account is, that the Messi-

[Plate 6]   *ah fell. & formed a heaven of what he stole from the Abyss*

This is shewn in the Gospel, where he prays to the Father to send the comforter or Desire that Reason may have Ideas to build on,[7] the Jehovah of the Bible being no other than he   who dwells in flaming fire.

Know that after Christs death, he became Jehovah.

But in Milton; the Father is Destiny, the Son, a Ratio of the five senses.[8] & the Holy-ghost, Vacuum![9]

Note. The reason Milton wrote in fetters when he wrote of Angels & God, and at liberty when of Devils & Hell, is because he was a true Poet and of the Devils party[1] without knowing it

A Memorable Fancy

As I was walking among the fires of hell, delighted with the enjoyments of Genius; which to Angels look like torment and insanity. I collected some of their Proverbs: thinking that as the sayings used in a nation, mark its character, so the Proverbs of Hell, shew the nature of Infernal wisdom better than any description of buildings or garments

When I came home, on the abyss of the five senses, where a flat sided steep frowns over the pre-

---

4. In Paradise Lost, "Reason" is knowledge of God, and thus the governor of "lower" faculties such as passion and appetite.

5. Satan was Archangel Lucifer before his fall from Heaven along with the rebels against God (Paradise Lost 6.824ff.). Milton provides a lurid account of the birth of Satan's children: first his daughter Sin, and then their incestuous son, Death (2.746–814).

6. God tests Job's faith by allowing Satan to torment him.

7. Doubting Christ's assurance that after his earthly death he will send the Holy Ghost as comforter; see John 14.16–17.

8. As in There Is No Natural Religion, Blake puns on the Latin meanings of "sum" and "Reason."

9. Milton was skeptical of the Trinitarian completion of divinity by the Holy Ghost.

1. The Devil's point of view and the political faction he led against God. This "Note" is a famous instance of "Romantic Satanism" and the practice of reading Paradise Lost against Milton's "Argument."

-sent world. I saw a mighty Devil folded in black
clouds hovering on the sides of the rock, with cor-
                                                    -or
[Plate 7]   -roding fires[2] he wrote the following sentence now per-
-cieved by *the minds of men, & read by them on earth.*
     How do you know but ev'ry Bird that cuts the airy way,
Is an immense world of delight, clos'd by your senses five?[3]

Proverbs of Hell.[4]

In seed time learn, in harvest teach, in winter enjoy.
Drive your cart and your plow over the bones of the dead.
The road of excess leads to the palace of wisdom.
Prudence is a rich ugly old maid courted by Incapacity.
5   He who desires but acts not, breeds pestilence.
The cut worm forgives the plow.
Dip him in the river who loves water.
A fool sees not the same tree that a wise man sees.
He whose face gives no light, shall never become a star.
10   Eternity is in love with the productions of time.
The busy bee has no time for sorrow.
The hours of folly are measur'd by the clock, but of wis-
          -dom: no clock can measure.
All wholsom food is caught without a net or a trap.
15   Bring out number weight & measure in a year of dearth
No bird soars too high. if he soars with his own wings.
A dead body. revenges not injuries.
The most sublime act is to set another before you.
If the fool would persist in his folly he would become
20   Folly is the cloke of knavery.   (wise
Shame is Prides cloke.

[Plate 8]   Proverbs of Hell
Prisons are built with stones of Law, Brothels with
          bricks of Religion.
The pride of the peacock is the glory of God.
5   The lust of the goat is the bounty of God.
The wrath of the lion is the wisdom of God.
The nakedness of woman is the work of God.
Excess of sorrow laughs. Excess of joy weeps.
The roaring of lions, the howling of wolves the raging

---

2. Casting himself and other poets as Devils, Blake refers
to his process of page production: he etched designs on
copper plates with an acid-resistant fluid, then washed
the plate in acid so that the designs emerge in relief.
Hand-colored, this relief plate was used to print the
pages. See Plate 14 for a reference to the symbolic value
of this method.
3. These lines allude to verses by Thomas Chatterton:
"How dydd I know that eve'ry darte, / That cutte the

Airie waie, / Myghte nott find passage toe my harte, /
And close myne eyes for aie?" (*Bristowe Tragedie*). Chatterton's suicide at age 17 in despair of success made him
a Romantic icon of martyred genius (see Wordsworth's
Resolution and Independence, 43–50).
4. A satire of the Old Testament's Book of Proverbs as
well as the *Aphorisms* of Kaspar Lavater (1788), Swiss
moralist and friend of Henry Fuseli, an artist who was also
Blake's friend.

10   of the stormy sea, and the destructive sword, are
portions of eternity too great for the eye of man.
The fox condemns the trap. not himself.
Joys impregnate. Sorrows bring forth.
Let man wear the fell of the lion. woman the fleece of
15   the sheep.
The bird a nest, the spider a web, man friendship.
The selfish smiling fool. & the sullen frowning fool. shall
be both thought wise, that they may be a rod.
What is now proved was once, only imagin'd.
20   The rat, the mouse, the fox, the rabbet; watch the roots,
the lion, the tyger, the horse, the elephant, watch
the fruits.
The cistern contains: the fountain overflows
One thought. fills immensity.
25   Always be ready to speak your mind, and a base man
will avoid you.
Every thing possible to be believ'd is an image of truth.
The eagle never lost so much time. as when he submit-
-ted to learn of the crow.

The

[Plate 9]   Proverbs of Hell

The fox provides for himself. but God provides for the lion.
Think in the morning. Act in the noon, Eat in the even-
-ing, Sleep in the night.
He who has sufferd you to impose on him knows you.
5   As the plow follows words, so God rewards prayers.
The tygers of wrath are wiser than the horses of in-
Expect poison from the standing water.   (-struction
You never know what is enough unless you know what is
more than enough.
10   Listen to the fools reproach! it is a kingly title!
The eyes of fire, the nostrils of air, the mouth of water,
the beard of earth.
The weak in courage is strong in cunning.
The apple tree never asks the beech how he shall grow,
15   nor the lion, the horse, how he shall take his prey.
The thankful reciever bears a plentiful harvest.
If others had not been foolish. we should be so.
The soul of sweet delight. can never be defil'd,
When thou seest an Eagle, thou seest a portion of Ge
20   -nius. lift up thy head!
As the catterpiller chooses the fairest leaves to lay
her eggs on, so the priest lays his curse on
the fairest joys.
To create a little flower is the labour of ages.
25   Damn, braces: Bless relaxes.
The best wine is the oldest. the best water the newest

Prayers plow not! Praises reap not!
Joys laugh not! Sorrows weep not!

[Plate 10]   Proverbs of Hell

The head Sublime, the heart Pathos, the genitals Beauty
    the hands & feet Proportion.
As the air to a bird or the sea to a fish, so is contempt
    to the contemptible.
5   The crow wish'd every thing was black, the owl, that eve-
    -ry thing was white.
Exuberance is Beauty.
If the lion was advised by the fox. he would be cunning.
Improvent makes strait roads, but the crooked roads
10   without Improvement. are roads of Genius.
Sooner murder an Infant in its cradle than nurse unact
    -ed desires
Where man is not nature is barren.
Truth can never be told so as to be understood and
15   not be believd.

Enough! or Too much

[Plate 11]   *The ancient Poets animated all sensible objects
with Gods or Geniuses, calling them by the names and
adorning them with the properties of woods, rivers,
mountains, lakes, cities, nations, and whatever their
enlarged & numerous senses could percieve.*

*And particularly they studied the genius of each
city & country. placing it under its mental deity.*

*Till a system was formed, which some took ad-
vantage of & enslav'd the vulgar by attempting to
realize or abstract the mental deities from their
objects: thus began Priesthood.*

*Choosing forms of worship from poetic tales.
And at length they pronouncd that the Gods
had orderd such things.*

*Thus men forgot, that All deities reside
in the human breast.*

[Plate 12]   *A Memorable Fancy.*

*The Prophets Isaiah and Ezekiel dined with
me, and I asked them how they dared so roundly to
assert. that God spake to them; and whether they
did not think at the time, that they would be mis-
-understood, & so be the cause of imposition.*

*Isaiah answer'd. I saw no God, nor heard
any, in a finite organical perception; but my sen-
-ses discover'd the infinite in every thing, and as I
was then perswaded, & remain confirmd; that the
voice of honest indignation is the voice of God, I
cared not for consequences but wrote.*

Then I asked: does a firm perswasion that a thing is so, make it so?

He replied. All poets believe that it does. & in ages of imagination this firm perswasion remo ved mountains; but many are not capable of a firm perswasion of any thing.

Then Ezekiel said. The philosophy of the east taught the first principles of human perception some nations held one principle for the origin & some another; we of Israel taught that the Poetic Genius (as you now call it) was the first principle and all the others merely derivative, which was the cause of our despising the Priests & Philosophers of other countries. and prophecying that all Gods would

[Plate 13]   would at last be proved to originate in ours & to be the tributaries of the Poetic Genius, it was this. that our great poet King David desired so fervently & invokes so patheticly, saying by this he conquers enemies & governs kingdoms; and we so loved our God. that we cursed in his name all the deities of surrounding nations, and asserted that they had rebelled; from these opinions the vulgar came to think that all nati -ons would at last be subject to the jews.

This said he, like all firm perswasions, is come to pass, for all nations believe the jews code and wor- -ship the jews god, and what greater subjection can be

I heard this with some wonder. & must confess my own conviction. After dinner I ask'd Isaiah to fa- vour the world with his lost works, he said none of equal value was lost. Ezekiel said the same of his.

I also asked Isaiah what made him go naked and barefoot three years?[5] he answerd, the same that made our friend Diogenes the Grecian.

I then asked Ezekiel. why he eat dung, & lay so long on his right & left side?[6] he answerd, the desire of raising other men into a perception of the infinite this the North American tribes practise. & is he hon- est who resists his genius or conscience. only for the sake of present ease or gratification?

[Plate 14]   The ancient tradition that the world will be con- -sumed in fire at the end of six thousand years[7]

5. God instructs Isaiah to walk "naked and barefoot" (Isa- iah 20.2).
6. See Ezekiel 4. Ezekiel is instructed to act out with his body the siege of Jerusalem by lying on his left side for 390 days to represent the years of Israel's iniquity and for 40 days on his right side for the years of the iniquity of the house of Judah; he is also ordered to eat barley cakes mixed with dung. Diogenes, famous for searching in daylight with a lantern for one honest man, was a

4th-century Greek Cynic philosopher who led a severely ascetic life. Blake alludes to these extraordinary actions to reflect the eccentricity often associated with visionary prophets.
7. This prophetic tradition is represented in the Book of Revelation and based on the translation of the six days of creation into six millennia (see 2 Peter 3.8); Blake relates this symbolism to the American and French revolutions.

is true. as I have heard from Hell.

For the cherub with his flaming sword is hereby commanded to leave his guard at tree of life,[8] and when he does, the whole creation will be consumed and appear infinite. and holy whereas it now appears finite & corrupt.

This will come to pass by an improvement of sensual enjoyment.

But first the notion that man has a body distinct from his soul, is to be expunged; this I shall do, by printing in the infernal method, by corrosives, which in Hell are salutary and medicinal, melting apparent surfaces away, and displaying the infinite which was hid.

If the doors of perception were cleansed every thing would appear to man as it is: Infinite.

For man has closed himself up, till he sees all things thro' narrow chinks of his cavern.[9]

[Plate 15]

A Memorable Fancy[1]

*I was in a **Printing house** in Hell & saw the method in which knowledge is transmitted from generation to generation.*

In the first chamber was a Dragon-Man, clearing away the rubbish from a caves mouth; within, a number of Dragons were hollowing the cave.

In the second chamber was a Viper folding round the rock & the cave, and others adorning it with gold silver and precious stones.

In the third chamber was an Eagle, with wings and feathers of air, he caused the inside of the cave to be infinite, around were numbers of Eagle like men, who built palaces in the immense cliffs.

In the fourth chamber were Lions of flaming fire raging around & melting the metals into living fluids.

In the fifth chamber were Unnam'd forms, which cast the metals into the expanse.

There they were reciev'd by Men who occupied

---

8. See Genesis 3.24. Evicting Adam and Eve from Eden, God "placed at the east of the garden of Eden cherubims, and a flaming sword which turned every way, to keep the way of the tree of life" (one of the last images in *Paradise Lost*).

9. Plato's allegory of the Cave (*Republic 7*) compares the mind to a cavern where men sit with backs to the aperture of daylight, apprehending only shadows cast by firelight on the wall. Locke's *Essay Concerning Human Understanding* (1690–1700) describes "external and internal sensation" as "the windows by which light is let into [the] dark room" of the mind: "understanding is not much unlike a closet wholly shut from light, with only some little openings left, to let in external visible resemblances, or ideas of things without" (2.11.17).

1. The cryptic allegory involves restored caverns. In the first, a figure of diabolic energy is clearing away the rubbish of wasted systems; the second chamber is undergoing artistic restoration; the third is being made into a place for liberated imagination; in the fourth and fifth chambers, the metal plates for Blake's printing are being formed; in the sixth, men take possession of books, as energy is submitted to system.

the sixth chamber, and took the forms of books &
were arranged in libraries.

[Plate 16] The Giants who formed this world into its
sensual existence and now seem to live in it
in chains; are in truth. the causes of its life
& the sources of all activity, but the chains
are, the cunning of weak and tame minds which
have power to resist energy. according to the pro-
-verb, the weak in courage is strong in cunning.

Thus one portion of being, is the Prolific. the
other, the Devouring: to the devourer it seems as
if the producer was in his chains, but it is not so;
he only takes portions of existence and fancies
that the whole.

But the Prolific would cease to be Prolific
unless the Devourer as a sea recieved the excess
of his delights.

Some will say, Is not God alone the Prolific?
I answer. God only Acts & Is, in existing beings
or Men.

These two classes of men are always upon
earth. & they should be enemies: whoever tries
to

[Plate 17] to reconcile them seeks to destroy existence.
Religion is an endeavour to reconcile the two.

Note. Jesus Christ did not wish to unite
but to separate them, as in the Parable of sheep and
goats! & he says I came not to send Peace but a
Sword.²

Messiah or Satan or Tempter was formerly
thought to be one of the Antediluvians³ who are our
Energies.

A Memorable Fancy⁴

An Angel came to me and said. O pitiable foolish
young man! O horrible! O dreadful state! consider
the hot burning dungeon thou art preparing for thyself
to all eternity, to which thou art going in such career.

I said. perhaps you will be willing to shew me
my eternal lot & we will contemplate together upon it
and see whether your lot or mine is most desirable.

---

2. The Prolific (diabolical creators) and the Devourers
(sterile pious reasoners) accord with the parable in Matthew 25.32–33: Jesus, the Shepherd, separates the sheep
on his right hand, admitting them to his kingdom, and
the goats on his left, condemning them to everlasting fire:
"think not that I am come to send peace on earth: I came
not to send peace, but a sword" (10.34).
3. Those living "before the flood" survived by Noah.

4. Blake wages an elaborately comic argument with a
pious Swedenborgian Angel, the voice of conventional
morality and religion. Their fantastic tour follows the decline of Christianity, beginning in the stable of Christ's
birth and the church founded in His name, and descending into the vault, the cave, the mill, and the abyss
(institutional religion).

So he took me thro' a stable & thro' a church
& down into the church vault at the end of which
was a mill: thro' the mill we went, and came to a
cave. down the winding cavern we groped our tedi-
-ous way till a void boundless as a nether sky ap-
-peard beneath us & we held by the roots of trees
and hung over this immensity: but I said, if you
please we will commit ourselves to this void, and
see whether providence is here also, if you will not
I will? but he answerd, do not presume O young-
man but as we here remain behold thy lot which
will soon appear when the darkness passes away
So I remaind with him sitting in the twisted

[Plate 18]

root of an oak; he was suspended in a fungus
which hung with the head downward into the deep:
By degrees we beheld the infinite Abyss, fiery
as the smoke of a burning city; beneath us at an
immense distance was the sun, black but shining
round it were fiery tracks on which revolv'd vast
spiders, crawling after their prey; which flew or
rather swum in the infinite deep, in the most ter-
-rific shapes of animals sprung from corruption.
& the air was full of them, & seemd composed
of them; these are Devils. and are called Powers
of the air. I now asked my companion which was my
eternal lot? he said, between the black & white spiders
But now, from between the black & white spiders
a cloud and fire burst and rolled thro the deep
blackning all beneath, so that the nether deep grew
black a sea & rolled with a terrible noise: be-
-neath us was nothing now to be seen but a black
tempest, till looking east between the clouds & the
waves, we saw a cataract of blood mixed with fire
and not many stones throw from us appeard and
sunk again the scaly fold of a monstrous serpent.
at last to the east, distant about three degrees[5] ap-
-peard a fiery crest above the waves slowly it rear-
-ed like a ridge of golden rocks till we discoverd
two globes of crimson fire, from which the sea
fled away in clouds of smoke, and now we saw, it
was the head of **Leviathan.**[6] *his forehead was di-*
vided into streaks of green & purple like those on
a tygers forehead: soon we saw his mouth & red
gills hang just above the raging foam, tinging the

5. The longitudinal position of Paris, heart of the French Revolution, relative to London.
6. A beast described in the Bible (Job 41.1, Isaiah 27.1, Psalms 104.26), and alluded to by Thomas Hobbes (1588–1679) in his famous treatise on government, *Leviathan, or the Matter, Form, and Power of a Commonwealth,* *Ecclesiastical and Civil* (1651), written during the commonwealth and defending a secular monarchy; Hobbes argues that appetitive self-interest must be controlled only by the laws and institutions of government, whose authority is agreed upon by common contract. In Blake's view, this vision of the state is monstrous.

black deep with beams of blood, advancing toward
                                                    us

[Plate 19] *us with all the fury of a spiritual exsitence.*

  My friend the Angel climb'd up from his station into the mill; I remain'd alone, & then this
appearance was no more, but I found myself sitting on a pleasant bank beside a river by moon
light hearing a harper who sung to the harp. &
his theme was, The man who never alters his
opinion is like standing water, & breeds reptiles
of the mind.

  But I arose, and sought for the mill &
there I found my Angel, who surprised asked
me, how I escaped?

  I answerd. All that we saw was owing to your
metaphysics: for when you ran away, I found myself
on a bank by moonlight hearing a harper, But
now we have seen my eternal lot, shall I shew you
yours? he laughd at my proposal; but I by force
suddenly caught him in my arms, & flew westerly
thro' the night, till we were elevated above the
earths shadow: then I flung myself with him directly into the body of the sun, here I clothed myself in
white,[7] & taking in my hand Swedenborgs volumes
sunk from the glorious clime, and passed all the
planets till we came to saturn, here I staid to rest
& then leap'd into the void, between saturn & the
fixed stars.

  Here said I! is your lot, in this space, if space
it may be calld. Soon we saw the stable and the
church, & I took him to the altar and open'd the
Bible, and lo! it was a deep pit, into which I de-
-scended driving the Angel before me, soon we saw
seven houses of brick,[8] one we enterd: in it were a
                                                    num

[Plate 20] number of monkeys, baboons, & all of that species
chaind by the middle, grinning and snatching at
one another, but witheld by the shortness of their
chains:[9] however I saw that they sometimes grew nu
merous, and then the weak were caught by the strong
and with a grinning aspect first coupled with & then
devourd, by plucking off first one limb & then ano-
-ther till the body was left a helpless trunk. this after
grinning & kissing it with seeming fondness they de-
-vourd too; and here & there I saw one savourily pic-
-king the flesh off of his own tail; as the stench ter-

7. In Revelation 7.9, the redeemed appear before the throne of Christ in white robes.

8. The seven churches to whom John addresses the Book of Revelation (1.4).

9. Blake's satire of theological dispute. "Witheld" may be a pun.

-ribly annoyd us both we went into the mill, & I in my hand brought the skeleton of a body, which in the mill was Aristotles Analytics.[1]

So the Angel said: thy phantasy has imposed upon me & thou oughtest to be ashamed.

I answerd: we impose upon one another. & it is but lost time to converse with you whose works are only Analytics

Opposition is true Friendship[2]

[Plate 21]   I have always found that Angels have the vani--ty to speak of themselves as the only wise; this they do with a confident insolence sprouting from systema--tic reasoning:

Thus Swedenborg boasts that what he writes is new: tho' it is only the Contents or Index of already publish'd books

A man carried a monkey about for a shew, & be--cause he was a little wiser than the monkey, grew vain, and conciev'd himself as much wiser than se--ven men. It is so with Swedenborg: he shews the folly of churches & exposes hypocrites, till he im--agines that all are religious, & himself the single one

[Plate 22]   one on earth that ever broke a net.

Now hear a plain fact: Swedenborg has not writ--ten one new truth: Now hear another: he has written all the old falshoods.

And now hear the reason. He conversed with Angels who are all religious. & conversed not with Devils who all hate religion for he was incapable thro' his conceited notions.

Thus Swedenborgs writings are a recapitulation of all superficial opinions, and an analysis of the more sublime. but no further.

Have now another plain fact: Any man of mechani--cal talents may from the writings of Paracelsus or Ja--cob Behmen,[3] produce ten thousand volumes of equal value with Swedenborg's, and from those of Dante or Shakespear, an infinite number.

But when he has done this, let him not say that he knows better than his master, for he only holds a can--dle in sunshine.

A Memorable Fancy
Once I saw a Devil in a flame of fire, who arose be

---

1. A "skeleton" is a bare-bones abstract summary. "Analytics" treats logic as the highest mental discipline.
2. This motto appears in three of the nine known copies of the poem.

3. Paracelsus (1493–1541) was a Swiss physician, occultist, and alchemist; German mystic Jakob Boehme (1575–1624), believed that God was knowable from the unity of the natural world.

fore an Angel that sat on a cloud, and the Devil ut-
-terd these words.

The worship of God is. Honouring his gifts in other men each according to his genius. and loving the great

[Plate 23] greatest men best, those who envy or calumniate great men hate God, for there is no other God.

The Angel hearing this became almost blue but mastering himself he grew yellow, & at last white pink & smiling. and then replied,

Thou Idolater, is not God One? & is not he visible in Jesus Christ? and has not Jesus Christ given his sanction to the law of ten commandments and are not all other men fools sinners & nothings?

The Devil answer'd; bray a fool in a morter with wheat yet shall not his folly be beaten out of him[4] if Jesus Christ is the greatest man, you ought to love him in the greatest degree; now hear how he has given his sanction to the law of ten command--ments: did he not mock at the sabbath, and so mock the sabbaths God? murder those who were murderd because of him? turn away the law from the woman taken in adultery? steal the labor of others to support him? bear false witness when he omitted making a defence before Pilate? covet when he pray'd for his disciples, and when he bid them shake off the dust of their feet against such as refused to lodge them? I tell you, no virtue can exist without breaking these ten command-ments: Jesus was all virtue, and acted from im--pulse

[Plate 24] -pulse: not from rules.[5]

When he had so spoken, I beheld the Angel who stretched out his arms embracing the flame of fire & he was consumed and arose as Elijah.[6]

Note. This Angel, who is now become a Devil, is my particular friend: we often read the Bible to--gether in its infernal or diabolical sense which the world shall have if they behave well.

I have also: **The Bible of Hell:**[7] which the world shall have whether they will or no.

One Law for the Lion & Ox is Oppression

1790–1793   1793–1825

4. Proverbs 27.22: "Though thou shouldest bray [crush] a fool in a mortar among wheat with a pestle, yet will not his foolishness depart from him."

5. For Jesus's breaking of Jewish law, see John 8.2–11, and Matthew 9.14–17, 12.1–8, and 27.11–14.

6. 2 Kings 2.11: "there appeared a chariot of fire, and horses of fire, and...Elijah went up by a whirlwind into heaven."

7. Blake's own scripture—that is, his illuminated poems.

William Blake, Plate i,
from *Visions of the Daughters
of Albion*.

VISIONS OF THE DAUGHTERS OF ALBION   Although "Albion," a mythical name for England, gives this poem the aura of a fable, its immediate context is Wollstonecraft's *Rights of Woman* (1792). Blake presents a chorus comprised of the Daughters of Albion (oppressed English-women) and three characters: Oothoon, "the soft soul of America," that is, freedom and new hope; Theotormon ("God Torment"), her lover; and Bromion, who rapes her. Theotormon, paralyzed by jealousy (sexual possessiveness), binds Bromion and Oothoon back-to-back in his cave, and sits at the entry weeping. The remainder of the poem consists of the monologues of the three characters in this unchanging situation. Bromion expresses the tyrant's creed of violent oppression and terror; Theotormon laments debilitating religious strictures; Oothoon inveighs against egotism and envisions love free from sexual and economic oppression. Like Wollstonecraft, Blake means to shock the sons of Albion by linking sexual oppression to slav-ery, including the ravages of colonialism and the exploitation of children. *Visions* concludes with the Daughters echoing Oothoon's woe, but its subtitle, "The Eye sees more than the Heart knows," invites a regard of Oothoon's long soliloquy not only as a potent detailing of the oppression her heart knows well, but also as a visionary hymn to unfettered love, infused with a passionate hope for transformation. But at the end of Plate 7, part of Oothoon's generosity involves procuring girls for Theotormon's pleasures.

VISIONS
of [1]
the Daughters of
Albion

[Plate ii]   *The Eye sees more than the Heart knows.*

[Plate iii]   *The Argument*[2]
       I loved Theotormon
       And I was not ashamed
       I trembled in my virgin fears
5   *And I hid in Leutha's vale!*

       I plucked Leutha's flower,[3]
       And I rose up from the vale;
       But the terrible thunders tore
       My virgin mantle in twain.

[Plate 1]   **Visions**

ENSLAV'D,[4] *the Daughters of Albion weep: a trembling lamentation*
Upon their mountains; in their valleys. sighs toward America.[5]

For the soft soul of America, Oothoon[6] *wandered in woe,*
5   *Along the vales of Leutha seeking flowers to comfort her;*
And thus she spoke to the bright Marygold of Leutha's vale

   Art thou a flower! art thou a nymph! I see thee now a flower:
   Now a nymph! I dare not pluck thee from thy dewy bed!

       The Golden nymph replied; pluck thou my flower Oothoon the mild
10   *Another flower shall spring, because the soul of sweet delight*
       Can never pass away. she ceas'd & closd her golden shrine.

Then Oothoon pluck'd the flower saying, I pluck thee from thy bed,
Sweet flower, and put thee here to glow between my breasts
And thus I turn my face to where my whole soul seeks.

15 *Over the waves she went in wing'd exulting swift delight;*
And over Theotormons reign, took her impetuous course.

Bromion rent her with his thunders.[7] *on his stormy bed*
Lay the faint maid, and soon her woes appalld his thunders hoarse

Bromion spake. behold this harlot[8] *here on Bromions bed*
20 *And let the jealous dolphins sport around the lovely maid:*

---

1. Are the Daughters bearers or objects of visions?
2. Oothoon's description of herself before being raped.
3. Traditional image for sexual initiation.
4. Blake's large letters advertise the affinity of sexual slavery and chattel slavery, a theme in Wollstonecraft's *Rights of Woman* (1792) and Thompson and Wheeler's *Appeal* (1825).
5. A country that has already revolted against tyranny.
6. An evocation of Oi-thona, the "virgin of the waves" in James Macpherson's *Ossian*, kidnapped and raped by a

rejected suitor. For Ossian, see page 393.
7. His wrath and the physical violence of rape.
8. The common contempt of a rape victim as fallen, soiled, blamable. In *Rights of Woman*, Wollstonecraft observes, "A woman who has lost her honour, imagines that she cannot fall lower, and as for recovering her former station, it is impossible; no exertion can wash this stain away. Losing thus every spur, and having no other means of support, prostitution becomes her only refuge."

Thy soft American plains are mine, and mine thy north & south:
Stampt with my signet are the swarthy children of the sun:[9]
They are obedient, they resist not, they obey the scourge:
Their daughters worship terrors and obey the violent:[1]

[Plate 2]   Now thou maist marry Bromions harlot, and protect the child
Of Bromions rage, that Oothoon shall put forth in nine moons
                                                              (time

Then storms rent Theotormons limbs; he rolled his waves around.
5   And folded his black jealous waters round the adulterate pair
Bound back to back in Bromions caves[2] Terror & meekness dwell
At entrance Theotormon sits wearing the threshold hard
With secret tears; beneath him sound like waves on a desart shore
The voice of slaves beneath the sun, and children bought with money,
10   That shiver in religious caves beneath the burning fires
Of lust, that belch incessant from the summits of the earth

Oothoon weeps not: she cannot weep! her tears are locked up;
But she can howl incessant, writhing her soft snowy limbs.
And calling Theotormons Eagles to prey upon her flesh.

15   I call with holy voice! kings of the sounding air,
Rend away this defiled bosom that I may reflect.
The image of Theotormon on my pure transparent breast.

The Eagles at her call descend & rend their bleeding prey;
Theotormon severely smiles. her soul reflects the smile;
20   As the clear spring mudded with feet of beasts grows pure & smiles

The Daughters of Albion hear her woes, & eccho back her sighs.

Why does my Theotormon sit weeping upon the threshold;
And Oothoon hovers by his side, perswading him in vain:
I cry arise O Theotormon for the village dog
25   Barks at the breaking day, the nightingale has done lamenting,
The lark does rustle in the ripe corn, and the Eagle returns
From nightly prey, and lifts his golden beak to the pure east;
Shaking the dust from his immortal pinions to awake
The sun that sleeps too long. Arise my Theotormon I am pure.
30   Because the night is gone that clos'd me in its deadly black.
They told me that the night & day were all that I could see;
They told me that I had five senses to inclose me up.
And they inclos'd my infinite brain into a narrow circle.
And sunk my heart into the Abyss, a red round globe hot burning
35   Till all from life I was obliterated and erased.
Instead of morn arises a bright shadow, like an eye
In the eastern cloud; instead of night a sickly charnel house;

9. The branding of African slaves.
1. A tyrant's self-sustaining myth.
2. As in *The Marriage of Heaven and Hell*, caves image the
mind—a prison evident in Theotormon's jealous regard

of the rapist and his victim as "the adulterate pair" and
his susceptibility to Bromion's taunting presentation of
rape-impregnated Oothoon to him for marriage, pregnant
by Bromion; jealous: sexually possessive.

That Theotormon hears me not! to him the night and morn
Are both alike: a night of sighs, a morning of fresh tears;

[Plate 3]   And none but Bromion can hear my lamentations.

With what sense is it that the chicken shuns the ravenous hawk
With what sense does the tame pigeon measure out the expanse?
With what sense does the bee form cells? have not the mouse & frog
5   Eyes and ears and sense of touch? yet are their habitations,
And, their pursuits, as different as their forms and as their joys:
Ask the wild ass why he refuses burdens: and the meek camel
Why he loves man: is it because of eye ear mouth or skin
Or breathing nostrils? No, for these the wolf and tyger have.
10   Ask the blind worm the secrets of the grave, and why her spires
Love to curl round the bones of death! and ask the rav'nous snake
Where she gets poison: & the wing'd eagle why he loves the sun
And then tell me the thoughts of man, that have been hid of old.

Silent I hover all the night, and all day could be silent.
15   If Theotormon once would turn his loved eyes upon me;
How can I be defild when I reflect thy image pure?

                                                    (woe

Sweetest the fruit that the worm feeds on. & the soul prey'd on by
The new wash'd lamb ting'd with the village smoke & the bright swan
By the red earth of our immortal river: I bathe my wings.
20   And I am white and pure to hover round Theotormons breast.

Then Theotormon broke his silence. and he answered.

Tell me what is the night or day to one oerflowd with woe?
Tell me what is a thought? & of what substance is it made?
Tell me what is a joy? & in what gardens do joys grow?
25   And in what rivers swim the sorrows? and upon what mountains
[Plate 4]   Wave shadows of discontent? and in what houses dwell the wretched
Drunken with woe forgotten, and shut up from cold despair.

Tell me where dwell the thoughts forgotten till thou call them forth
Tell me where dwell the joys of old? & where the ancient loves?
5   And when will they renew again & the night of oblivion past?
That I might traverse times & spaces far remote and bring
Comforts into a present sorrow and a night of pain
Where goest thou O thought? to what remote land is thy flight?
If thou returnest to the present moment of affliction
10   Wilt thou bring comforts on thy wings. and dews and honey and balm;
Or poison From the desart wilds, from the eyes of the envier.
Then Bromion said: and shook the cavern with his lamentation

Thou knowest that the ancient trees seen by thine eyes have fruit;
But knowest thou that trees and fruits flourish upon the earth
15   To gratify senses unknown? trees beasts and birds unknown:
Unknown, not unpercievd, spread in the infinite microscope,
In places yet unvisited by the voyager, and in worlds

Over another kind of seas, and in atmospheres unknown?
Ah! are there other wars, beside the wars of sword and fire!
20 And are there other sorrows, beside the sorrows of poverty?
And are there other joys, besides the joys of riches and ease?
And is there not one law for both the lion and the ox?[3]
And is there not eternal fire, and eternal chains?
To bind the phantoms of existence from eternal life?

25 Then Oothoon waited silent all the day, and all the night,
[Plate 5] But when the morn arose, her lamentation renewd.
The Daughters of Albion hear her woes, & eccho back her sighs.

O Urizen! Creator of men! mistaken Demon of heaven:[4]
Thy joys are tears! thy labour vain, to form men to thine image.
5 How can one joy absorb another? are not different joys
Holy, eternal, infinite! and each joy is a Love.

Does not the great mouth laugh at a gift? & the narrow eyelids mock
At the labour that is above payment, and wilt thou take the ape
For thy councellor? or the dog for a schoolmaster to thy children?
10 Does he who contemns poverty, and he who turns with abhorrence
From usury: feel the same passion or are they moved alike?
How can the giver of gifts experience the delights of the merchant?
How the industrious citizen the pains of the husbandman.
How different far the fat fed hireling with hollow drum;
15 Who buys whole corn fields into wastes, and sings upon the heath:
How different their eye and ear! how different the world to them!
What are his nets & gins & traps, & how does he surround him
With cold floods of abstraction, and with forests of solitude,
To build him castles and high spires, where kings & priests may dwell.
20 Till she who burns with youth and knows no fixed lot; is bound
In spells of law to one she loaths: and must she drag the chain
Of life, in weary lust! must chilling murderous thoughts, obscure
The clear heaven of her eternal spring! to bear the wintry rage
Of a harsh terror driv'n to madness, bound to hold a rod
25 Over her shrinking shoulders all the day; & all the night
To turn the wheel of false desire: and longings that wake her womb
To the abhorred birth of cherubs in the human form
That live a pestilence & die a meteor & are no more.
Till the child dwell with one he hates, and do the deed he loaths
30 And the impure scourge force his seed into its unripe birth
E'er yet his eyelids can behold the arrows of the day.
Does the whale worship at thy footsteps as the hungry dog?
Or does he scent the mountain prey, because his nostrils wide
Draw in the ocean? does his eye discern the flying cloud
35 As the ravens eye? or does he measure the expanse like the vulture?

3. See the last line of *The Marriage of Heaven and Hell*.
4. Oothoon wonders if the limitations of both Bromion and Theotormon are the work of Urizen, a creator of men in his own image: his name sounds like "your reason" (sterile rationality) and "horizon" (derived from the Greek word for outward limit, or boundary circle).

Does the still spider view the cliffs where eagles hide their young?
Or does the fly rejoice, because the harvest is brought in?
Does not the eagle scorn the earth & despise the treasures beneath?
But the mole knoweth what is there, & the worm shall tell it thee.
40 Does not the worm erect a pillar in the mouldering church yard?
[Plate 6] And a palace of eternity in the jaws of the hungry grave
Over his porch these words are written. Take thy bliss O Man!
And sweet shall be thy taste, & sweet thy infant joys renew!

Infancy, fearless, lustful, happy! nestling for delight
5 In laps of pleasure; Innocence! honest, open, seeking
The vigorous joys of morning light; open to virgin bliss.
Who taught thee modesty, subtil modesty! child of night & sleep
When thou awakest. wilt thou dissemble all thy secret joys
Or wert thou not awake when all this mystery was disclos'd!
10 Then comst thou forth a modest virgin knowing to dissemble
With nets found under thy night pillow, to catch virgin joy,
And brand it with the name of whore: & sell it in the night,
In silence, ev'n without a whisper, and in seeming sleep:
Religious dreams and holy vespers, light thy smoky fires:
15 Once were thy fires lighted by the eyes of honest morn
And does my Theotormon seek this hypocrite modesty!
This knowing, artful, secret, fearful, cautious, trembling hypocrite.
Then is Oothoon a whore indeed! and all the virgin joys
Of life are harlots: and Theotormon is a sick mans dream
20 And Oothoon is the crafty slave of selfish holiness.

But Oothoon is not so, a virgin fill'd with virgin fancies
Open to joy and to delight where ever beauty appears
If in the morning sun I find it: there my eyes are fix'd
[Plate 7] In happy copulation; if in evening mild wearied with work,
Sit on a bank and draw the pleasures of this free born joy.

The moment of desire! the moment of desire! The virgin
That pines for man; shall awaken her womb to enormous joys
5 In the secret shadows of her chamber; the youth shut up from
The lustful joy, shall forget to generate. & create an amorous image
In the shadows of his curtains and in the folds of his silent pillow.
Are not these the places of religion? the rewards of continence?
The self enjoyings of self denial? Why dost thou seek religion?
10 Is it because acts are not lovely, that thou seekest solitude,
Where the horrible darkness is impressed with reflections of desire.

Father of Jealousy,[5] be thou accursed from the earth!
Why hast thou taught my Theotormon this accursed thing?
Till beauty fades from off my shoulders, darken'd and cast out,
15 A solitary shadow wailing on the margin of non-entity.
I cry, Love! Love! Love! happy happy Love! free as the mountain wind!

---

5. Urizen, who creates men with this passion of possessiveness.

William Blake, Plate 8,
from *Visions of the Daughters
of Albion*.

Can that be Love, that drinks another as a sponge drinks water?
That clouds with jealousy his nights, with weepings all the day:
To spin a web of age around him, grey and hoary! dark!
20 Till his eyes sicken at the fruit that hangs before his sight.
Such is self-love that envies all! a creeping skeleton
With lamplike eyes watching around the frozen marriage bed.

But silken nets and traps of adamant will Oothoon spread,
And catch for thee girls of mild silver, or of furious gold:
25 I'll lie beside thee on a bank & view their wanton play
In lovely copulation bliss on bliss with Theotormon:
Red as the rosy morning, lustful as the first born beam,
Oothoon shall view his dear delight, nor e'er with jealous cloud
Come in the heaven of generous love; nor selfish blightings bring.

30 Does the sun walk in glorious raiment. on the secret floor
[Plate 8] Where the cold miser spreads his gold? or does the bright cloud drop

On his stone threshold? does his eye behold the beam that brings
Expansion to the eye of pity? or will he bind himself
Beside the ox to thy hard furrow? does not that mild beam blot
The bat, the owl, the glowing tyger, and the king of night.
The sea fowl takes the wintry blast, for a cov'ring to her limbs:
And the wild snake, the pestilence to adorn him with gems & gold.
And trees & birds, & beasts, & men, behold their eternal joy.
Arise you little glancing wings. and sing your infant joy!
Arise and drink your bliss, for every thing that lives is holy![6]

Thus every morning wails Oothoon. but Theotormon sits
Upon the margind ocean conversing with shadows dire.

The Daughters of Albion hear her woes, & eccho back her sighs.

The End

1793

LETTERS

To Dr. John Trusler[1]

23 August 1799

Rev'd Sir,

I really am sorry that you are fall'n out with the Spiritual World, Especially if
I should have to answer for it. I feel very sorry that your Ideas & Mine on Moral
Painting differ so much as to have made you angry with my method of Study. If I
am wrong, I am wrong in good company. I had hoped your plan comprehended All
Species of this Art, & Especially that you would not regret that Species which gives
Existence to Every other, namely, Visions of Eternity. You say that I want somebody
to Elucidate my Ideas. But you ought to know that What is Grand is necessarily obscure to Weak men. That which can be made Explicit to the Idiot is not worth my
care. The wisest of the Ancients considered what is not too Explicit as the fittest
for Instruction, because it rouses the faculties to act. I name Moses, Solomon, Esop,
Homer, Plato.

But as you have favor'd me with your remarks on my Design, permit me in return
to defend it against a mistaken one, which is, That I have supposed Malevolence
without a Cause.[2] Is not Merit in one a Cause of Envy in another, & Serenity &
Happiness & Beauty a Cause of Malevolence? But Want of Money & the Distress of
A Thief can never be alleged as the Cause of his Thieving, for many honest people
endure greater hardships with Fortitude. We must therefore seek the Cause elsewhere
than in want of Money, for that is the Miser's passion, not the Thief's.

6. In some printings of *The Marriage of Heaven and Hell*, Blake appended "A Song of Liberty," with this declaration as the concluding line.
1. Rev. Dr. John Trusler (1735–1820), clergyman and minor man of letters, hoped Blake would illustrate his

books, but found Blake's designs too much "in the other world, or the World of Spirits, which accords not with my Intentions, which, whilst living in This World, Wish to follow *the Nature of it.*"
2. One of Blake's illustrations for Trusler.

I have therefore proved your Reasonings Ill-proportion'd, which you can never prove my figures to be; they are those of Michael Angelo, Rafael & the Antique, & of the best living Models. I perceive that your Eye is perverted by Caricature Prints, which ought not to abound so much as they do. Fun I love, but too much Fun is of all things the most loathsome. Mirth is better than Fun, & Happiness is better than Mirth. I feel that a Man may be happy in This World. And I know that This World Is a World of IMAGINATION & Vision. I see Every thing I paint In This World, but Everybody does not see alike. To the Eyes of a Miser a Guinea is more beautiful than the Sun, & a bag worn with the use of Money has more beautiful proportions than a Vine filled with Grapes. The tree which moves some to tears of joy is in the Eyes of others only a Green thing that stands in the way. Some See Nature all Ridicule & Deformity, & by these I shall not regulate my proportions; & Some Scarce see Nature at all. But to the Eyes of the Man of Imagination, Nature is Imagination itself. As a man is, So he Sees. As the Eye is formed, such are its Powers. You certainly Mistake, when you say that the Visions of Fancy are not to be found in This World. To Me This World is all One continued Vision of Fancy or Imagination & I feel Flattered when I am told so. What is it sets Homer, Virgil & Milton in so high a rank of Art. Why is the Bible more Entertaining & Instructive than any other book? Is it not because they are addressed to the Imagination, which is Spiritual Sensation, & but mediately to the Understanding or Reason? Such is True Painting and such [was] alone valued by the Greeks & the best modern Artists. Consider what Lord Bacon says: "Sense sends over to Imagination before Reason have judged, & Reason sends over to Imagination before the Decree can be acted." See Advancem[ent] of Learning Part 2, P. 47 of first Edition.[3]

But I am happy to find a Great Majority of Fellow Mortals who can Elucidate My Visions & Particularly they have been Elucidated by Children, who have taken a greater delight in contemplating my Pictures than I even hoped. Neither Youth nor Childhood is Folly or Incapacity. Some Children are Fools & so are some Old Men. But There is a vast Majority on the side of Imagination or Spiritual Sensation.

To Engrave after another Painter is infinitely more laborious than to Engrave ones own Inventions. And of the Size you require my price has been Thirty Guineas & I cannot afford to do it for less. I had Twelve for the Head I sent you as a Specimen, but after my own designs I could do at least Six times the quantity of labour in the same time which will account for the difference of price as also that Chalk Engraving is at least six times as laborious as Aqua tinta. I have no objection to Engraving after another Artist. Engraving is the profession I was apprenticed to, & should never had attempted to live by any thing else, If orders had not come in for my Designs & Paintings, which I have the pleasure to tell you are Increasing Every Day. Thus If I am a Painter it is not to be attributed to Seeking after. But I am contented whether I live by painting or Engraving.

I am Revd Sir, Your very obedient servant,

WILLIAM BLAKE

---

3. Francis Bacon's *Advancement of Learning* (1605). Blake liked this sentiment, but despised Bacon's commitment to patronage, scientific reason, and the monarchy. In his later works, "Bacon & Newton & Locke" are an infernal trinity of materialism.

To Thomas Butts[1]

22 November 1802

Dear Sir,

*** I will bore you more with some Verses which My Wife desires me to Copy out & send you with her kind love & Respect; they were Composed above a twelve-month ago, while walking from Felpham to Lavant to meet my Sister:

> With happiness stretch'd across the hills
> In a cloud that dewy sweetness distills,
> With a blue sky spread over with wings
> And a mild Sun that mounts & sings,
> 5   With trees & fields full of Fairy elves
> And little devils who fight for themselves,
> Rememb'ring the Verses that Hayley sung[2]
> When my heart knock'd against the root of my tongue,
> With Angels planted in Hawthorn bowers
> 10   And God himself in the passing hours,
> With Silver Angels across my way
> And Golden Demons that none can stay,
> With my Father hovering upon the wind
> And my Brother Robert just behind
> 15   And my Brother John the evil one
> In a black cloud making his moan;[3]
> Tho' dead, they appear upon my path,
> Notwithstanding my terrible wrath;
> They beg, they intreat, they drop their tears,
> 20   Fill'd full of hopes, fill'd full of fears;
> With a thousand Angels upon the Wind
> Pouring disconsolate from behind
> To drive them off, & before my way
> A frowning Thistle implores my stay.
> 25   What to others a trifle appears
> Fills me full of smiles or tears;
> For double the vision my Eyes do see,
> And a double vision is always with me.[4]

---

1. Thomas Butts (1757–1845), a government worker and real estate entrepreneur, was a lifelong friend and patron. Blake produced 80 biblical illustrations for him from 1800 to 1805, and 21 watercolors of the Book of Job from 1805 to 1810. Altogether, Butts purchased about 200 pictures and ten illuminated books, a collection that spilled out of his home and into his greenhouse. We have added line numbers to the poetry.

2. William Hayley (1745–1820), minor poet and patron of art, was Blake's patron and neighbor in Felpham (on the English Channel) from 1800 to 1803. He commissioned him to illustrate his *Life of Cowper* and his *Essay on Sculpture*. Disapproving of Blake's visionary bent, he urged him toward more conventional modes. As with

Trusler, the relationship proved uncongenial, and the two had a falling out. When, however, Blake was arrested for treason (the cottage garden episode related on page 170), Hayley contributed to his defense.

3. The spirits of Blake's father (d. 1784); his favorite brother Robert (1767–1787); and brother John (b. 1760), who had enlisted in the army, was once apprenticed to a gingerbread maker, but fell into poverty and alcoholism, and died young.

4. "Single vision" (line 88) is mere sense perception or "Newton's sleep"—the sleep of imagination in the domain of mathematical reason; "double" or twofold vision is perception infused with individual imagination.

With my inward Eye 'tis an old Man grey;
30   With my outward, a Thistle across my way.
"If thou goest back," the thistle said,
"Thou art to endless woe betray'd;
For here does Theotormon lower,°   brood
And here is Enitharmon's bower,
35   And Los the terrible thus hath sworn,[5]
Because thou backward dost return,
Poverty, Envy, old age & fear
Shall bring thy Wife upon a bier;
And Butts shall give what Fuseli gave,[6]
40   A dark black Rock & a gloomy Cave."

I struck the Thistle with my foot,
And broke him up from his delving root.
"Must the duties of life each other cross?
Must every joy be dung & dross?
45   Must my dear Butts feel cold neglect
Because I give Hayley his due respect?
Must Flaxman look upon me as wild,
And all my friends be with doubts beguil'd?[7]
Must my Wife live in my Sister's bane,[8]
50   Or my Sister survive on my Love's pain?
The curses of Los, the terrible shade,
And his dismal terrors make me afraid."

So I spoke & struck in my wrath
The old man weltering upon my path.
55   Then Los appeared in all his power;
In the Sun he appear'd, descending before
My face in fierce flames; in my double Sight[9]
'Twas outward a Sun, inward Los in his might.

"My hands are labour'd day and night,
60   And Ease comes never in my sight.
My Wife has no indulgence given
Except what comes to her from Heaven.
We eat little, we drink less;
This Earth breeds not our happiness.

5. Theotormon is the son of Enitharmon and Los, both figures in Blake's later poetry. Enitharmon, the spirit of Beauty, is the twin of Los, the spirit of poetry and imagination.
6. Henry Fuseli, a neoclassical painter and lifelong friend, frequently employed Blake to engrave his own paintings, and like almost everyone else, had a falling out over matters of artistic vision, and ceased to employ him by 1802—hence the snippiness and worry that Butts will turn out the same way, forcing Blake into a gloomy Cave devoid of imagination.

7. John Flaxman (1755–1826), one of England's major sculptors, was a close friend and supporter of Blake in his early career, subsidizing the printing of his first, unillustrated, volume, *Poetical Sketches* (1783). Like Hayley, he urged Blake to devote himself to drawing and engraving and to forgo his grand visionary paintings and prophetic illuminated poems.
8. Blake's sister was living with him and his wife at Felpham while he worked for Hayley, and did not get along with his wife.
9. See "double vision," line 28.

65   Another Sun feeds our life's streams,
     We are not warmed with thy beams;
     Thou measurest not the Time to me,
     Nor yet the Space that I do see;
     My Mind is not with thy light array'd.
70   Thy terrors shall not make me afraid."

     When I had my Defiance given,
     The Sun stood trembling in heaven;
     The Moon that glowed remote below,
     Became leprous & white as snow;
75   And every soul of men on the Earth
     Felt affliction & sorrow & sickness & dearth.
     Los flam'd in my path, & the Sun was hot
     With the bows of my Mind & the Arrows of Thought.
     My bowstring fierce with Ardour breathes;
80   My arrows glow in their golden sheaves;
     My brothers & father march before;
     The heavens drop with human gore.

     Now I a fourfold vision see,
     And a fourfold vision is given to me;
85   'Tis fourfold in my supreme delight
     And threefold in soft Beulah's night
     And twofold Always. May God us keep
     From Single vision & Newton's sleep![1]

    I also enclose you some Ballads by Mr. Hayley,[2] with prints to them by Your H[mble] Serv[t]. I should have sent them before now but could not get any thing done for You to please myself; for I do assure you that I have truly studied the two little pictures I now send, & do not repent of the time I have spent upon them.

    God bless you.

Yours,

W. B.

P.S. I have taken the liberty to trouble you with a letter to my Brother, which you will be so kind as to send or give him, & oblige yours, W. B.

1. In Blake's hierarchy, fourfold vision is pure visionary inspiration, with no reliance on the physical senses and the material world; threefold vision is the deep source of poetic vision: the subconscious, the world of dreams, figuratively "Beulah's night." Beulah, which means "married," is an important spiritual location in Blake's later poetry. In Isaiah, 62.4, it is the name given to Zion when it is restored to God's favor. In John Bunyan's dream allegory, *Pilgrim's Progress from This World to That Which* *Is to Come* (1678–1684), Beulah is the Earthly Paradise, gained by wayfaring Christians after toils and challenges, where they abide until they cross the River of Death into the Celestial City. "Newton's sleep" is the dormancy of imagination in the scientific (empirical) mind, referring to Isaac Newton (1642–1727), formulator of the laws of modern physics.

2. *Designs to a Series of Ballads written by William Hayley* (1802), for which Blake did 14 engravings.

⇒ PERSPECTIVES ⇐
The Abolition of Slavery and the Slave Trade

Slavery and the slave trade provoked sharp controversy in the age of Romanticism, and literary writing played a major role in shaping public opinion. From 1783 to 1793 more than 300,000 slaves were sold in the British colonies, at a value of over £15,000,000. A "triangular trade" flourished, whereby British investors financed expeditions to the African Gold Coast to buy or kidnap human cargo, to be shipped (the "Middle Passage") under brutal conditions to New-World markets. About thirteen percent of this cargo died, while the survivors suffered heat, cramped filthy quarters, fettering, physical abuse, and disease. With the profits, which usually exceeded a hundred percent of the initial investment, the ships were filled with exotic colonial goods—tobacco, sugar, molasses, rum, spices, cotton—to be sold in Europe, also at tremendous profits. Moral opposition to this trade, spearheaded by the Quakers and Evangelical Christian sects, was invigorated by Lord Mansfield's ruling in 1772 declaring the absence of any legal basis for slavery in England. Over the 1770s, several abolitionist tracts appeared, and by the end of the decade, bills were introduced in Parliament to regulate the trade. National attention was galvanized by the scandal of the slave ship *Zong* (1781) whose captain ordered 133 weak and diseased slaves ejected into shark-infested waters in order to collect on a policy that held the insurer liable for cargo jettisoned in order to salvage the remainder. Color Plate 5 shows J. M. W. Turner's famous painting of this event.

In the 1780s the Quakers continued to petition Parliament and distribute pamphlets, while other abolitionists wrote tracts challenging the scriptural as well as economic justifications for slavery, and reformed slave-traders published memoirs detailing the horrors of the trade. By the end of the decade, William Wilberforce was heading a parliamentary investigation and the former slave Olaudah Equiano's *Interesting Narrative* quickly became a best-seller. But the advent of the French Revolution in 1789 increased fear of slave revolts, and Wilberforce's first bill for abolition was defeated in 1791.

Even so, the abolition movement persisted. In 1792 Edmund Burke's *Sketch of a Negro Code* gave a plan for orderly abolition and emancipation, and in 1793 Wilberforce's second bill for abolition at least won in the House of Commons. By the decade's end, the British treasury was reeling under the cost of regulating the trade and defending the plantation owners. The abolition movement achieved its first major success in 1807, when Parliament abolished British slave-trading. Wilberforce's stirring *Letter on the Abolition of the Slave Trade* (1807), praising the moral importance of the event, helped sustain the movement for abolishing slavery itself (still legal in the colonies)—as did Thomas Clarkson's gripping *History of the Abolition of the African Slave-Trade by the British Parliament* (1808), which detailed the horrors of the trade both for the slaves and the seamen. By the 1820s, the movement was benefiting from the increasing involvement of women, who were horrified by the often violent and sexually abusive treatment of female slaves. In 1823 Clarkson and Wilberforce founded the influential *Anti-Slavery Monthly Reporter*, which relentlessly publicized all the horrors, and Parliament seriously addressed the issue, with Foreign Secretary George Canning declaring that "the spirit of the Christian religion is hostile to slavery." The year 1831 was a critical one, marked not only by a massive slave rebellion in Jamaica, with severe reprisals against slaves and sympathetic missionaries, but also by the publication of former slave Mary Prince's autobiography, with searing reports of atrocities, especially to female slaves. The Reform Parliament of 1832 proved hospitable to emancipation, and in 1833 it passed the Emancipation Bill, liberating 800,000 slaves in British colonies and compensating the owners with more than £20,000,000.

It was the plantation-owners and investors in Bristol and Liverpool, enjoying immense profits, who opposed abolition. Supported by their Standing Committee in Parliament, they justified slavery by arguing that Africans had already enslaved each other; that they were mental and moral primitives, animals and heathens, to whom plantation life brought a work ethic, civilized behavior, and the grace of Christian religion; and finally, that British abolition would not end the trade, only leave the profits to other nations. Their literary propaganda tended toward the genre of "romance," pastoral stories with happy endings in which slaves are grateful and masters benevolent. The appeal to social stability was amplified by alarm at the French Revolution, and in 1791 a massive slave revolt in Santo Domingo made it possible to link abolitionism to Jacobinism and to embarrass at least the Evangelical abolitionists, who tended to be critical of the Revolution.

Abolitionists came from differing, often opposed political groups: Tory, Evangelical, Quaker, Unitarian, Dissenter, Nonconformist, radical. Some, such as Anna Barbauld, Mary Wollstonecraft, and Tom Paine, energized abolitionism with commitments to social reform and the new philosophies of "the rights of man" and "the rights of woman." Wordsworth's excoriation of slavery in *The Prelude* Book 10 powerfully sounds this note. But others, including the Parliamentarians Burke and Wilberforce and most Evangelical Christians, were politically conservative, often wealthy; wanting to avoid political arguments, the Evangelicals condemned slavery as a moral blight on a Christian nation and advocated parliamentary reform. They refuted the planters' claims of kind treatment on slave-ships and plantations, and vividly purveyed what amounts to a pornography of atrocities, even as the moral stress was on common humanity and Christian values. With their own version of African primitivism, their fables evoked sympathy for the slaves' childlike simplicity and the pathos of their destroyed families, their physical tortures and suffering. In these narratives, redemption for the slaves appears not through rebellion, but through the salvational processes of Christian conversion, forbearance, and an appeal to enlightened authority.

Many well-known writers entered the debate, rallying support by using vivid stories to exemplify the broad social and ethical issues involved. The texts that follow show the range of literary resources, and the range of viewpoints, employed by writers who composed poems, essays, and stories as part of the protracted struggle over abolition.

+—+ ⟨◊⟩ +—+

Olaudah Equiano
1745–1797

In the parliamentary inquiry into the condition of the slave trade between 1788 and 1789, evidence came almost exclusively from the traders. A very different perspective is seen in *The Interesting Narrative of the Life of Olaudah Equiano, or Gustavus Vassa, the African. Written by Himself*, published in London in 1789. The force of the account drew in part from this claim of authoritative witness to the harrowing experiences of slavery. Equiano presented himself as born to a high-ranking, prosperous, slave-owning family of the Ebo tribe, in the region of modern Nigeria. At age ten, he says, he was stolen from his village by freelance slavers, and served masters in Africa before being shipped first to Barbados and then to North America.

The disorienting effects are reflected in the series of names given by successive owners: on the slave-ship he was "Michael," then renamed "Jacob" by a Virginia plantation owner, and then dubbed "Gustavus Vassa" after the Swedish hero of a recent play when he was purchased by Lieutenant Michael Pascal of the British navy. Pascal took him to England in 1757, and then to Canada where he fought in the Seven Years' War. He was baptized in London in 1759, and worked for the British navy in the Mediterranean as a servant and gunner's mate, eventually rising to the rank of able seaman. In 1762 Pascal broke his promise to free Equiano and sold him to Captain James Doran. In the West Indies he was sold, again, to an American Quaker merchant, Robert King, on whose trading ships he worked. With profits from private trade conducted by his own initiative and entrepreneurial skill, he earned enough from the system he abhorred to purchase his freedom, for £70, in 1766. Subsequent adventures took him to the Caribbean and even to the Arctic (seeking a polar route to India), where a shipmate was young Horatio Nelson, later the hero of the Battle of Trafalgar. At various times, Equiano managed a plantation in Central America, earned a living as a hairdresser in London, and worked for the Sierra Leone project (a planned colony for freed slaves in Africa), until he protested against financial mismanagement and was dismissed.

Once settled in England, he rediscovered Christianity and worked with the Evangelicals, campaigned tirelessly for abolition, and met the founder of the radical working-class London Corresponding Society. His celebrity stemmed from his *Interesting Narrative*, which movingly renders the cruelty of the Middle Passage, the violence of slavery, and the uncertain status of even the free black; at the same time it is a vivid picaresque adventure, a religious conversion narrative, and a testimony to surprising social mobility. In his own time critics in the slaveholder camp challenged the truthfulness of Equiano's claim to an African origin, and recently historian Vincent Carretta has brought forward documents suggesting that Equiano was born in Carolina. Though Carretta's research confirms the accuracy of Equiano's story of his adult life, doubts of historical fact redouble the literary fascination of the *Interesting Narrative*.

"Olaudah Equiano" may be not the narrator's original name but the persona of the writer, crafted under the influence of Evangelicals and radicals to appeal to their audience and promote abolition. His seemingly artless document raises questions of the artifice of autobiography, the intricacies of identity, and the status of the "author" as a fiction cooperatively produced by writer, publisher, and readers. The *Interesting Narrative*, of which Mary Wollstonecraft published the first review, was an immediate sensation, selling five thousand copies the first year, and going through thirty-six editions over the next half century, including numerous editions in the United States and others as far afield as Germany and Russia. Equiano remained a speaker devoted to abolition, and an emblem of the rise from humble beginnings to middle-class success. In 1792 he married an Englishwoman with whom he had two daughters, and he was well enough off at his death, in 1797, to leave his surviving daughter £950 to inherit on her twenty-first birthday in 1816. A story of triumph as well as of oppression, the *Interesting Narrative* has a complexity the more compelling for its apparent transparency. His portrait (Color Plate 4) suggests the complexities of his African-American-British identity.

from The Interesting Narrative of the Life of Olaudah Equiano
or Gustavus Vassa, the African
[THE SLAVE SHIP AND ITS CARGO]

The first object that saluted my eyes when I arrived on the coast was the sea, and a slave ship, which was then riding at anchor, and waiting for its cargo.[1] These filled me with astonishment, that was soon converted into terror, which I am yet at a loss to describe, and much more the then feelings of my mind when I was carried on board. I was immediately handled and tossed up to see if I was sound, by some of the crew; and I was now persuaded that I had got into a world of bad spirits, and that they were going to kill me. Their complexions too, differing so much from ours, their long hair, and the language they spoke, which was very different from any I had ever heard, united to confirm me in this belief. Indeed such were the horrors of my views and fears at the moment, that if ten thousand worlds had been my own, I would have freely parted with them all to have exchanged my condition with the meanest slave in my own country. When I looked

---

1. Captured by slavers along with his sister, Equiano was soon separated from her and sold to different masters over a period of several months before reaching the African coast for shipment to Barbados.

round the ship too, and saw a large furnace or copper boiling and a multitude of black people, of every description, chained together, every one of their countenances expressing dejection and sorrow, I no longer doubted of my fate; and, quite overpowered with horror and anguish, I fell motionless on the deck, and fainted. When I recovered a little, I found some black people about me, who I believed were some of those who brought me on board, and had been receiving their pay: they talked to me in order to cheer me, but all in vain. I asked them if we were not to be eaten by those white men with horrible looks, red faces, and long hair. They told me I was not: and one of the crew brought me a small portion of spirituous liquor in a wine glass; but, being afraid of him, I would not take it out of his hand. One of the blacks therefore took it from him and gave it to me, and I took a little down my palate, which, instead of reviving me, as they thought it would, threw me into the greatest consternation at the strange feeling it produced, having never tasted any such liquor before.

Soon after this the blacks who brought me on board went off, and left me abandoned to despair. I now saw myself deprived of all chance of returning to my native country, or even the least glimpse of gaining the shore, which I now considered as friendly; and I even wished for my former slavery, in preference to my present situation, which was filled with horrors of every kind, still heightened by my ignorance of what I was to undergo. I was not long suffered to indulge my grief. I was soon put down under the decks, and there I received such a salutation in my nostrils as I had never experienced in my life: so that, with the loathsomeness of the stench, and with my crying together, I became so sick and low that I was not able to eat, nor had I the least desire to taste any thing. I now wished for the last friend, death, to relieve me; but soon, to my grief, two of the white men offered me eatables; and, on my refusing to eat, one of them held me fast by the hands, and laid me across, I think, the windlass, and tied my feet, while the other flogged me severely. I had never experienced any thing of this kind before, and although, not being used to the water, I naturally feared that element the first time I saw it, yet nevertheless, could I have got over the nettings, I would have jumped over the side, but I could not; and besides the crew used to watch us very closely, who were not chained down to the decks, lest we should leap into the water. I have seen some of these poor African prisoners most severely cut for attempting to do so, and hourly whipped for not eating. This indeed was often the case with myself. In a little time after, amongst the poor chained men, I found some of my own nation, which in a small degree gave ease to my mind. I inquired of these what was to be done with us. They gave me to understand we were to be carried to these white people's country to work for them. I was then a little revived, and thought if it were no worse than working, my situation was not so desperate. But still I feared I should be put to death, the white people looked and acted, as I thought, in so savage a manner; for I had never seen among any people such instances of brutal cruelty: and this is not only shewn towards us blacks, but also to some of the whites themselves. One white man in particular I saw, when we were permitted to be on deck, flogged so unmercifully with a large rope near the foremast, that he died in consequence of it; and they tossed him over the side as they would have done a brute. This made me fear these people the more; and I expected nothing less than to be treated in the same manner. I could not help expressing my fearful apprehensions to some of my countrymen; I asked them if these people had no country, but lived in this hollow place, the ship. They told me they did not, but came from a distant one. "Then," said I, "how comes it, that in all our country we never heard of them?" They told me, because they lived so very far off. I then asked, where their women were: had they any like themselves. I was told they had. "And why," said I, "do we not see them?" They answered, because they were left behind. I asked how the vessel could go. They told me they could not tell; but that there was cloth put upon the masts by the help of the ropes I saw, and then the vessel went on; and the white men had some spell or magic they put in the water, when they liked, in order to stop the vessel. I was exceedingly amazed at this account, and really thought they were spirits. I therefore wished much to be from amongst them, for I expected they would sacrifice me; but my wishes were in vain, for we were so quartered that it was impossible for any of us to make our escape.

[EQUIANO, AGE 12, REACHES ENGLAND]

One morning, when I got upon deck, I perceived it covered over with the snow that fell overnight. As I had never seen any thing of the kind before, I thought it was salt; so I immediately ran down to the mate and desired him, as well as I could, to come and see how somebody in the night had thrown salt all over the deck. He, knowing what it was, desired me to bring some of it down to him; accordingly I took up a handful of it, which I found very cold indeed; and when I brought it to him he desired me to taste it. I did so, and was surprised above measure. I then asked him what it was; he told me it was snow; but I could not by any means understand him. He asked me if we had no such thing in our country; and I told him "No." I then asked him the use of it, and who made it; he told me a great man in the heavens, called God: but here again I was to all intents and purposes at a loss to understand him; and the more so, when a little after I saw the air filled with it, in a heavy shower, which fell down on the same day.

After this I went to church; and having never been at such a place before, I was again amazed at seeing and hearing the service. I asked all I could about it; and they gave me to understand it was "worshiping God, who made us and all things." I was still at a loss, and soon got into an endless field of inquiries, as well as I was able to speak and ask about things. However, my dear little friend Dick[2] used to be my best interpreter; for I could make free with him and he always instructed me with pleasure. And from what I could understand by him of this God, and in seeing that these white people did not sell one another as we did, I was much pleased: and in this I thought they were much happier than we Africans. I was astonished at the wisdom of the white people in all things which I beheld; but I was greatly amazed at their not sacrificing, not making any offerings, and at their eating with unwashen hands, and touching of the dead. I also could not help remarking the particular slenderness of their women, which I did not at first like, and I thought them not so modest and shamefaced as the African women.

I had often seen my master Dick employed in reading; and I had a great curiosity to talk to the books, as I thought they did; and so to learn how all things had a beginning. For that purpose I have often taken up a book and talked to it, and then put my ears to it, when alone, in hopes it would answer me; and I have been very much concerned when I found it remaining silent.

[READING THE BIBLE; FINDING A "FATHER"; SOLD AGAIN INTO SLAVERY]

There was also one Daniel Queen, about forty years of age, a man very well educated, who messed with me on board this ship,[3] and he likewise dressed and attended the captain. Fortunately this man soon became very much attached to me, and took great

---

2. Richard Baker, an American boy four or five years older than Equiano.

3. The *Etna*, of which Pascal had been given command in 1759; messed: ate.

pains to instruct me in many things. He taught me to shave, and dress hair a little, and also to read in the Bible, explaining many passages to me, which I did not comprehend. I was wonderfully surprised to see the laws and rules of my own country written almost exactly here; a circumstance which, I believe, tended to impress our manners and customs more deeply on my memory. I used to tell him of this resemblance, and many a time we have sat up the whole night together at this employment. In short, he was like a father to me; and some used even to call me after his name: they also styled me "the black Christian." Indeed I almost loved him with the affection of a son. Many things I have denied myself, that he might have them; and when I used to play at marbles or any other game, and won a few halfpence, or got some money for shaving any one, I used to buy him a little sugar or tobacco, as far as my stock of money would go. He used to say that he and I never should part, and that when our ship was paid off, as I was free as himself or any other man on board, he would instruct me in his business, by which I might gain a good livelihood. This gave me new life and spirits; and my heart burned within me, while I thought the time long till I obtained my freedom. For though my master had not promised it to me, yet, besides the assurances I had often received that he had no right to detain me,[4] he always treated me with the greatest kindness, and reposed in me an unbounded confidence. He even paid attention to my morals, and would never suffer me to deceive him, or tell lies, of which he used to tell me the consequences; and that if I did so, God would not love me. So that from all this tenderness I had never once supposed, in all my dreams of freedom, that he would think of detaining me any longer than I wished.

In pursuance of our orders we sailed from Portsmouth for the Thames, and arrived at Deptford the 10th of December, where we cast anchor just as it was high water. The ship was up about half an hour, when my master ordered the barge to be manned; and, all in an instant, without having before given me the least reason to suspect any thing of the matter, he forced me into the barge, saying, I was going to leave him, but he would take care that I did not. I was so struck with the unexpectedness of this proceeding, that for some time I did not make a reply, only I made an offer to go for my books and chest of clothes, but he swore I should not move out of his sight; and if I did, he would cut my throat, at the same time taking out his hanger.[5] I told him that I was free, and he could not by law serve me so. But this only enraged him the more; and he continued to swear, and said he would soon let me know whether he would or not, and at that instant sprung himself into the barge, from the ship, to the astonishment and sorrow of all on board.

The tide, rather unluckily for me, had just turned downward, so that we quickly fell down the river along with it, till we came among some outwardbound West Indiamen; for he was resolved to put me on board the first vessel he could get to receive me. The boat's crew, who pulled against their will, became quite faint at different times, and would have gone ashore, but he would not let them. Some of them strove then to cheer me, and told me he could not sell me, and that they would stand by me, which revived me a little, and I still entertained hopes; for as they pulled me along he asked some vessels to receive me, and they refused.

But, just as we had got a little below Gravesend, we came alongside of a ship going away the next tide for the West-Indies; her name was the Charming Sally, Captain James Doran. My master went on board and agreed with him for me; and in little

---

4. Even before the Mansfield Decision of 1772, contemporary opinion held that Royal Navy ships were British territory, on which slavery was inappropriate.
5. Short sword.

time I was sent for into the cabin. When I came there Captain Doran asked me if I knew him; I answered I did not: "Then," said he, "you are now my slave." I told him my master could not sell me to him nor to any one else. "Why," said he, "did not your master buy you?" I confessed he did. "But I have served him," said I, "many years, and he has taken all my wages and prize-money,[6] for I only got one sixpence during the war. Besides this I have been baptized; and, by the laws of the land, no man has a right to sell me." And I added, that I had heard a lawyer, and others, at different times tell my master so. They both then said, that those people who told me so, were not my friends: but I replied—it was very extraordinary that other people did not know the law as well as they. Upon this, Captain Doran said I talked too much English, and if I did not behave myself well and be quiet, he had a method on board to make me. I was too well convinced of his power over me to doubt what he said; and my former sufferings in the slave-ship presenting themselves to my mind, the recollection of them made me shudder. However, before I retired I told them, that as I could not get any right among men here, I hoped I should hereafter in Heaven, and I immediately left the cabin, filled with resentment and sorrow.

The only coat I had with me my master took away with him, and said, "if your prize-money had been £10,000, I had a right to it all, and would have taken it." I had about nine guineas, which, during my long sea-faring life, I had scraped together from trifling perquisites and little ventures; and I hid it that instant, lest my master should take that from me likewise, still hoping that, by some means or other, I should make my escape to the shore. Indeed some of my old shipmates told me not to despair, for they would get me back again; and that, as soon as they could get their pay, they would immediately come to Portsmouth to me, where this ship was going. But, alas, all my hopes were baffled, and the hour of my deliverance was, as yet, far off. My master, having soon concluded his bargain with the captain, came out of the cabin, and he and his people got into the boat and put off. I followed them with aching eyes as long as I could, and when they were out of sight I threw myself on the deck, with a heart ready to burst with sorrow and anguish.

[EMPLOYMENT IN THE WEST INDIES]

I had the good fortune to please my master[7] in every department in which he employed me; and there was scarcely any part of his business, or household affairs, in which I was not occasionally engaged. I often supplied the place of a clerk, in receiving and delivering cargoes to the ships, in tending stores, and delivering goods; and, besides this, I used to shave and dress my master, when convenient, and take care of his horse; and when it was necessary, which was very often, I worked likewise on board of his different vessels. By these means I became very useful to my master, and saved him, as he used to acknowledge, above a hundred pounds a year. Nor did he scruple to say I was of more advantage to him than any of his clerks; tho' their usual wages in the West-Indies are from sixty to a hundred pounds current a year.

I have sometimes heard it asserted that a negro cannot earn his master the first cost; but nothing can be further from the truth. I suppose nine tenths of the mechanics throughout the West-Indies are negro slaves; and I well know the coopers[8] among them earn two dollars a-day; the carpenters the same, and oftentimes more; also the

6. Profits from an enemy ship and its cargo seized during war, traditionally shared among the victorious crew.
7. In 1763 Equiano was sold to Robert King, a Quaker merchant, and thereafter served in the West Indies in one of his ships under Captain Thomas Farmer.
8. Barrel-makers.

masons, smiths, and fishermen, &c. and I have known many slaves whose masters would not take a thousand pounds current for them. But surely this assertion refutes itself: for, if it be true, why do the planters and merchants pay such a price for slaves? And, above all, why do those, who make this assertion, exclaim the most loudly against the abolition of the slave trade? So much are men blinded, and to such inconsistent arguments are they driven by mistaken interest! I grant, indeed, that slaves are sometimes, by half-feeding, half-clothing, over-working, and stripes,[9] reduced so low, that they are turned out as unfit for service, and left to perish in the woods, or to expire on a dunghill.

My master was several times offered by different gentlemen one hundred guineas[1] for me; but he always told them he would not sell me, to my great joy: and I used to double my diligence and care for fear of getting into the hands of these men, who did not allow a valuable slave the common support of life. Many of them used to find fault with my master for feeding his slaves so well as he did; although I often went hungry, and an Englishman might think my fare very indifferent: but he used to tell them he always would do it, because the slaves thereby looked better and did more work.

While I was thus employed by my master, I was often a witness to cruelties of every kind, which were exercised on my unhappy fellowslaves. I used frequently to have different cargoes of new negroes in my care for sale; and it was almost a constant practice with our clerks, and other whites, to commit violent depredations on the chastity of the female slaves; and to these atrocities I was, though with reluctance, obliged to submit at all times, being unable to help them. When we have had some of these slaves on board my master's vessels to carry them to other islands, or to America, I have known our mates commit these acts most shamefully, to the disgrace not of christians only, but of men. I have even known them gratify their brutal passion with females not ten years old; and these abominations some of them practised to such a scandalous excess, that one of our captains discharged the mate and others on that account. And yet in Montserrat[2] I have seen a negro-man staked to the ground, and cut most shockingly, and then his ears cut off, bit by bit, because he had been connected with a white woman, who was a common prostitute! As if it were no crime in the whites to rob an innocent African girl of her virtue; but most heinous in a black man only to gratify a passion of nature, where the temptation was offered by one of a different colour, though the most abandoned woman of her species.

[THE PERILS OF BEING A FREEMAN]

I have since often seen in Jamaica and other islands, free men, whom I have known in America, thus villainously trepanned[3] and kept in bondage. I have heard of two similar practices even in Philadelphia: and were it not for the benevolence of the Quakers in that city, many of the sable race, who now breathe the air of liberty, would, I believe, be groaning under some planter's chains. These things opened my mind to a new scene of horror, to which I had been before a stranger. Hitherto I had thought only slavery dreadful; but the state of a free negro appeared to me now equally so at least, and in some respects even worse; for they live in constant alarm

---

9. Lashings and the welts they leave.
1. The guinea coin, first struck in 1663 by a company of merchants chartered by the British crown to obtain slaves from the Guinea coast of Africa (hence the name), was
worth 21 shillings; made of gold, it often traded for more than its face value and connoted a certain prestige.
2. Island in the British West Indies.
3. Betrayed.

for their liberty, which is but nominal; and they are universally insulted and plundered without the possibility of redress; such being the equity of the West-Indian laws, that no free negro's evidence will be admitted in their courts of justice. * * *

I determined to make every exertion to obtain my freedom, and to return to Old England. For this purpose I thought a knowledge of Navigation might be of use to me; for, though I did not intend to run away unless I should be ill used, yet, in such a case, if I understood navigation, I might attempt my escape in our sloop, which was one of the swiftest sailing vessels in the West-Indies, and I could be at no loss for hands to join me. Had I made this attempt, I had intended to go in her to England; but this, as I said, was only to be in the event of my meeting with any ill usage. I therefore employed the mate of our vessel to teach me Navigation, for which I agreed to give him twenty-four dollars, and actually paid him part of the money down; though when the captain, some time after, came to know that the mate was to have such a sum for teaching me, he rebuked him, and said it was a shame for him to take any money from me. However, my progress in this useful art was much retarded by the constancy of our work.

Had I wished to run away I did not want opportunities, which frequently presented themselves; and particularly at one time, soon after this. When we were at the island of Guadaloupe there was a large fleet of merchantmen bound for Old France; and seamen then being very scarce, they gave from fifteen to twenty pounds a man for the run. Our mate and all the white sailors left our vessel on this account, and went aboard of the French ships. They would have had me also to go with them, for they regarded me, and swore to protect me, if I would go: and, as the fleet was to sail the next day, I really believe I could have got safe to Europe at that time. However, as my master was kind, I would not attempt to leave him; still remembering the old maxim, that *honesty is the best policy*, I suffered them to go without me. Indeed my captain was much afraid of my leaving him and the vessel at that time, as I had so fair an opportunity: but, I thank God, this fidelity of mine turned out much to my advantage hereafter, when I did not in the least think of it; and made me so much in favour with the captain, that he used now and then to teach me some parts of Navigation himself. But some of our passengers, and others, seeing this, found much fault with him for it, saying it was a very dangerous thing to let a negro know Navigation; and thus I was hindered again in my pursuits.

[MANUMISSION][4]

When we had unladen the vessel, and I had sold my venture,[5] finding myself master of about forty-seven pounds, I consulted my true friend, the Captain, how I should proceed in offering my master the money for my freedom. He told me to come on a certain morning, when he and my master would be at breakfast together. Accordingly, on that morning I went, and met the Captain there, as he had appointed. When I went in I made my obeisance to my master, and with my money in my hand, and many fears in my heart, I prayed him to be as good as his offer to me, when he was pleased to promise me my freedom as soon as I could purchase it. This speech seemed to confound him; he began to recoil; and my heart that instant sunk within me. "What," said he, "give you your freedom? Why, where did you get the money? Have you got forty pounds sterling?" "Yes, sir," I answered. "How did you get it?" replied he. I told him, "very honestly." The Captain then said he knew I got the

---

4. The formal liberation of a slave.   5. The stock he was permitted to trade for himself.

money very honestly and with much industry, and that I was particularly careful. On which my master replied, I got money much faster than he did; and said he would not have made me the promise which he did, had he thought I should have got the money so soon. "Come, come," said my worthy Captain, clapping my master on the back, "Come, Robert, (which was his name[6]) I think you must let him have his freedom. You have laid your money out very well; you have received good interest for it all this time, and here is now the principal at last. I know GUSTAVUS has earned you more than a hundred a year, and he will still save you money, as he will not leave you. Come, Robert, take the money." My master then said, he would not be worse than his promise; and, taking the money, told me to go to the Secretary at the Register Office, and get my manumission drawn up.

These words of my master were like a voice from heaven to me: in an instant all my trepidation was turned into unutterable bliss, and I most reverently bowed myself with gratitude, unable to express my feelings, but by the overflowing of my eyes, and a heart replete with thanks to God; while my true and worthy friend, the Captain, congratulated us both with a peculiar degree of heartfelt pleasure. As soon as the first transports of my joy were over, and that I had expressed my thanks to these my worthy friends in the best manner I was able, I rose with a heart full of affection and reverence, and left the room, in order to obey my master's joyful mandate of going to the Register Office. As I was leaving the house I called to mind the words of the Psalmist, in the 126th Psalm, and like him, "I glorified God in my heart, in whom I trusted."[7] These words had been impressed on my mind from the very day I was forced from Deptford[8] to the present hour, and I now saw them, as I thought, fulfilled and verified.

My imagination was all rapture as I flew to the Register Office; and in this respect, like the apostle Peter (whose deliverance from prison was so sudden and extraordinary, that he thought he was in a vision)[9] I could scarcely believe I was awake. Heavens! who could do justice to my feelings at this moment? Not conquering heroes themselves, in the midst of a triumph—Not the tender mother who has just regained her long-lost infant, and presses it to her heart—Not the weary, hungry mariner, at the sight of the desired friendly port—Not the lover, when he once more embraces his beloved mistress, after she has been ravished from his arms!—All within my breast was tumult, wildness, and delirium! My feet scarcely touched the ground; for they were winged with joy, and, like Elijah, as he rose to Heaven, they "were with lightning sped as I went on."[1] Every one I met I told of my happiness, and blazed about the virtue of my amiable master and Captain. * * *

In short, the fair as well as black people immediately styled me by a new appellation,—to me the most desirable in the world,—which was "Freeman," and, at the dances I gave, my Georgia superfine blue clothes made no indifferent appearance, as I thought. Some of the sable females, who formerly stood aloof, now began to relax and appear less coy; but my heart was still fixed on London, where I hoped to be ere long. So that my worthy Captain, and his owner, my late master, finding that the bent of my mind was towards London, said to me, "We hope you won't leave us,

6. Robert King; see n. 7, page 235.
7. Psalm 126 celebrates release from captivity; the phrase Equiano quotes does not appear there, though it echoes several other psalms (28, 33, 86, 125).
8. See excerpt above.
9. Acts 12.9 [Equiano's note].
1. In 2 Kings (2.11), Elijah has a vision of a chariot of fire and is carried to Heaven in a whirlwind.

but that you will still be with the vessels." Here gratitude bowed me down; and none but the generous mind can judge of my feelings, struggling between inclination and duty. However, notwithstanding my wish to be in London, I obediently answered my benefactors that I would go in the vessel, and not leave them; and from that day I was entered on board as an able-bodied seaman, at thirty-six shillings per month, besides what perquisites I could make.[2] My intention was to make a voyage or two, entirely to please these my honoured patrons; but I determined that the year following, if it pleased God, I would see Old England once more, and surprise my old master, Captain Pascal, who was hourly in my mind: for I still loved him, notwithstanding his usage to me, and I pleased myself with thinking of what he would say when he saw what the Lord had done for me in so short a time, instead of being, as he might perhaps suppose, under the cruel yoke of some planter.

Mary Prince
c. 1788–after 1833

The History of Mary Prince, a West Indian Slave, Related by Herself is the earliest known slave narrative by a woman. Sponsored by the Anti-Slavery Society to galvanize support for abolition, especially from Britain's women, its saga of overwork, abuse, and sexual violence was chronicled in unprecedented depth and detail. Mary Prince's *History* was a sensation, reaching a third edition the year it was published, 1831.

Prince was born a slave on a farm in Bermuda, a British colony whose major industries were shipbuilding and salting, and whose population was half slave. In her childhood, she was treated with relative kindness, but at age twelve, she was sold to sadistic, sexually abusive new owners. After several years of brutality, she was sold to an even more ghastly situation in the "cruel, horrible" salt ponds of Turks Island, about 200 miles northeast of Bermuda, where her labor left her legs covered with boils and eventually crippled her with rheumatism. Perpetually beaten, and sexually assaulted by an "indecent master," she requested to be sold to a merchant from Antigua, who was impressed by her reputation as a good worker. Overworked and exhausted, she began to rebel, and suffered imprisonment and repeated beatings and floggings. With the help of abolitionists, she escaped from her owners, when they took her to London in 1827. Thomas Pringle, a Methodist and secretary of the Anti-Slavery Society, employed her as a domestic servant. He also edited her *History* as publicity for the movement; it sparked a national controversy when attacked in *Blackwood's Edinburgh Magazine* and *The Glasgow Courier* as fraudulent propaganda by a loose-moraled liar. Libel suits erupted, Prince's owner suing Pringle, and Pringle suing *Blackwood's*. *Blackwood's* declined to cross-examine her, letting her statement stand, but Pringle lost the other case because he couldn't produce witnesses from the West Indies to substantiate the allegations of *The History*. Even so, *The History* commanded wide readership, influencing the cause not only in its representation of general atrocities, but also in its image of Prince's individual resilience and determination. "All slaves want to be free," she declared in the final paragraph; "to be free is very sweet. . . . I can tell by myself what other slaves feel, and by what they have told me. The man that says slaves be quite happy in slavery—that they don't want to be free—that man is either ignorant or a lying person. I never heard a slave say so."

---

2. Equiano has the right to trade for himself and to receive tips.

from The History of Mary Prince, a West Indian Slave
Related by Herself

It was night when I reached my new home. The house was large, and built at the bottom of a very high hill; but I could not see much of it that night. I saw too much of it afterwards. The stones and the timber were the best things in it; they were not so hard as the hearts of the owners.[1]

Before I entered the house, two slave women, hired from another owner, who were at work in the yard, spoke to me, and asked who I belonged to? I replied, "I am come to live here." "Poor child, poor child!" they both said; "you must keep a good heart, if you are to live here."—When I went in, I stood up crying in a corner. Mrs. I——came and took off my hat, a little black silk hat Miss Pruden[2] made for me, and said in a rough voice, "You are not come here to stand up in corners and cry, you are come here to work." She then put a child into my arms, and, tired as I was, I was forced instantly to take up my old occupation of a nurse.—I could not bear to look at my mistress, her countenance was so stern. She was a stout tall woman with a very dark complexion, and her brows were always drawn together into a frown. I thought of the words of the two slave women when I saw Mrs. I——, and heard the harsh sound of her voice.

The person I took the most notice of that night was a French Black called Hetty, whom my master took in privateering[3] from another vessel, and made his slave. She was the most active woman I ever saw, and she was tasked to her utmost. A few minutes after my arrival she came in from milking the cows, and put the sweet-potatoes on for supper. She then fetched home the sheep, and penned them in the fold; drove home the cattle, and staked them about the pond side;[4] fed and rubbed down my master's horse, and gave the hog and the fed cow[5] their suppers; prepared the beds, and undressed the children, and laid them to sleep. I liked to look at her and watch all her doings, for hers was the only friendly face I had as yet seen, and I felt glad that she was there. She gave me my supper of potatoes and milk, and a blanket to sleep upon, which she spread for me in the passage before the door of Mrs. I——'s chamber.

I got a sad fright, that night. I was just going to sleep, when I heard a noise in my mistress's room; and she presently called out to inquire if some work was finished that she had ordered Hetty to do. "No, Ma'am, not yet," was Hetty's answer from below. On hearing this, my master started up from his bed, and just as he was, in his shirt, ran down stairs with a long cow-skin in his hand.[6] I heard immediately after, the cracking of the thong, and the house rang to the shrieks of poor Hetty, who kept crying out, "Oh, Massa! Massa! me dead. Massa! have mercy upon me—don't kill me outright."— This was a sad beginning for me. I sat up upon my blanket, trembling with terror, like a frightened hound, and thinking that my turn would come next. At length the house became still, and I forgot for a little while all my sorrows by falling fast asleep.

The next morning my mistress set about instructing me in my tasks. She taught me to do all sorts of household work; to wash and bake, pick cotton and wool, and wash floors, and cook. And she taught me (how can I ever forget it!) more things

---

1. These strong expressions, and all of a similar character in this little narrative, are given verbatim as uttered by Mary Prince [Thomas Pringle's note].
2. Prince's first owner, Mrs. Williams, had fallen on hard times and hired her out at age 12 to Mrs. Pruden; with Mrs. Williams's death, she was sold to "Captain I—."
3. Sanctioned raiding of enemy ships by armed private

vessels.
4. The cattle on a small plantation in Bermuda are, it seems, often thus staked or tethered, both night and day, in situations where grass abounds. [Pringle's note].
5. A cow fed for slaughter. [Pringle's note].
6. A thong of hard twisted hide, known by this name in the West Indies [Pringle's note].

than these; she caused me to know the exact difference between the smart of the rope, the cart-whip, and the cow-skin, when applied to my naked body by her own cruel hand. And there was scarcely any punishment more dreadful than the blows I received on my face and head from her hard heavy fist. She was a fearful woman, and a savage mistress to her slaves.

There were two little slave boys in the house, on whom she vented her bad temper in a special manner. One of these children was a mulatto,[7] called Cyrus, who had been bought while an infant in his mother's arms; the other, Jack, was an African from the coast of Guinea, whom a sailor had given or sold to my master. Seldom a day passed without these boys receiving the most severe treatment, and often for no fault at all. Both my master and mistress seemed to think that they had a right to ill-use them at their pleasure; and very often accompanied their commands with blows, whether the children were behaving well or ill. I have seen their flesh ragged and raw with licks.—Lick—lick—they were never secure one moment from a blow, and their lives were passed in continual fear. My mistress was not contented with using the whip, but often pinched their cheeks and arms in the most cruel manner. My pity for these poor boys was soon transferred to myself; for I was licked, and flogged, and pinched by her pitiless fingers in the neck and arms, exactly as they were. To strip me naked—to hang me up by the wrists and lay my flesh open with the cow-skin, was an ordinary punishment for even a slight offence. My mistress often robbed me too of the hours that belong to sleep. She used to sit up very late, frequently even until morning; and I had then to stand at a bench and wash during the greater part of the night, or pick wool and cotton; and often I have dropped down overcome by sleep and fatigue, till roused from a state of stupor by the whip, and forced to start up to my tasks.

Poor Hetty, my fellow slave, was very kind to me, and I used to call her my Aunt; but she led a most miserable life, and her death was hastened (at least the slaves all believed and said so), by the dreadful chastisement she received from my master during her pregnancy. It happened as follows. One of the cows had dragged the rope away from the stake to which Hetty had fastened it, and got loose. My master flew into a terrible passion, and ordered the poor creature to be stripped quite naked, notwithstanding her pregnancy, and to be tied up to a tree in the yard. He then flogged her as hard as he could lick, both with the whip and cow-skin, till she was all over streaming with blood. He rested, and then beat her again and again. Her shrieks were terrible. The consequence was that poor Hetty was brought to bed before her time, and was delivered after severe labour of a dead child. She appeared to recover after her confinement, so far that she was repeatedly flogged by both master and mistress afterwards; but her former strength never returned to her. Ere long her body and limbs swelled to a great size; and she lay on a mat in the kitchen, till the water burst out of her body and she died. All the slaves said that death was a good thing for poor Hetty; but I cried very much for her death. The manner of it filled me with horror. I could not bear to think about it; yet it was always present to my mind for many a day.

After Hetty died all her labours fell upon me, in addition to my own. I had now to milk eleven cows every morning before sunrise, sitting among the damp weeds; to take care of the cattle as well as the children; and to do the work of the house. There was no end to my toils—no end to my blows. I lay down at night and rose up in the morning in

7. A person of mixed African and Caucasian descent, frequently the issue of rape.

fear and sorrow; and often wished that like poor Hetty I could escape from this cruel bondage and be at rest in the grave. But the hand of God whom then I knew not, was stretched over me; and I was mercifully preserved for better things. It was then, however, my heavy lot to weep, weep, weep, and that for years; to pass from one misery to another, and from one cruel master to a worse. But I must go on with the thread of my story.

One day a heavy squall of wind and rain came on suddenly, and my mistress sent me round the corner of the house to empty a large earthen jar. The jar was already cracked with an old deep crack that divided it in the middle, and in turning it upside down to empty it, it parted in my hand. I could not help the accident, but I was dreadfully frightened, looking forward to a severe punishment. I ran crying to my mistress, "O mistress, the jar has come in two." "You have broken it, have you?" she replied; "come directly here to me." I came trembling; she stripped and flogged me long and severely with the cow-skin; as long as she had strength to use the lash, for she did not give over till she was quite tired.—When my master came home at night, she told him of my fault; and oh, frightful! how he fell a swearing. After abusing me with every ill name he could think of, (too, too bad to speak in England,) and giving me several heavy blows with his hand, he said, "I shall come home to-morrow morning at twelve, on purpose to give you a round hundred." He kept his word—Oh sad for me! I cannot easily forget it. He tied me up upon a ladder, and gave me a hundred lashes with his own hand, and master Benjy[8] stood by to count them for him. When he had licked me for some time he sat down to take breath; then after resting, he beat me again and again, until he was quite wearied, and so hot (for the weather was very sultry), that he sank back in his chair, almost like to faint. While my mistress went to bring him drink, there was a dreadful earthquake.[9] Part of the roof fell down, and every thing in the house went—clatter, clatter, clatter. Oh I thought the end of all things near at hand; and I was so sore with the flogging, that I scarcely cared whether I lived or died. The earth was groaning and shaking; every thing tumbling about; and my mistress and the slaves were shrieking and crying out, "The earthquake! the earthquake!" It was an awful day for us all. * * *

Some little time after this, one of the cows got loose from the stake, and eat one of the sweet-potatoe slips.[1] I was milking when my master found it out. He came to me, and without any more ado, stooped down, and taking off his heavy boot, he struck me such a severe blow in the small of my back, that I shrieked with agony, and thought I was killed; and I feel a weakness in that part to this day. The cow was frightened at his violence, and kicked down the pail and spilt the milk all about. My master knew that this accident was his own fault, but he was so enraged that he seemed glad of an excuse to go on with his ill usage. I cannot remember how many licks he gave me then, but he beat me till I was unable to stand, and till he himself was weary.

After this I ran away and went to my mother, who was living with Mr. Richard Darrel.[2] My poor mother was both grieved and glad to see me; grieved because I had been so ill used, and glad because she had not seen me for a long, long while. She dared not receive me into the house, but she hid me up in a hole in the rocks near, and brought me food at night, after every body was asleep. My father, who lived at Crow-Lane, over the salt-water channel, at last heard of my being hid up in the

8. Captain I——'s son, about Prince's age.
9. An earthquake shook Bermuda on 19 February 1801.
1. A cutting, rooted and planted.

2. Captain Darrell had purchased Prince and her mother, and then gave Prince to his daughter-in-law, Mrs. Williams.

cavern, and he came and took me back to my master. Oh I was loth, loth to go back; but as there was no remedy, I was obliged to submit.

When we got home, my poor father said to Cap. I——, "Sir, I am sorry that my child should be forced to run away from her owner; but the treatment she has received is enough to break her heart. The sight of her wounds has nearly broke mine.—I entreat you, for the love of God, to forgive her for running away, and that you will be a kind master to her in future." Capt. I——said I was used as well as I deserved, and that I ought to be punished for running away. I then took courage and said that I could stand the floggings no longer; that I was weary of my life, and therefore I had run away to my mother; but mothers could only weep and mourn over their children, they could not save them from cruel masters—from the whip, the rope, and the cow-skin. He told me to hold my tongue and go about my work, or he would find a way to settle me. He did not, however, flog me that day. * * *

For five years after this I remained in his house, and almost daily received the same harsh treatment. At length he put me on a sloop, and to my great joy sent me away to Turk's Island. I was not permitted to see my mother or father, or poor sisters and brothers, to say good bye, though going away to a strange land, and might never see them again. Oh the Buckra [white] people who keep slaves think that black people are like cattle, without natural affection. But my heart tells me it is far otherwise. * * *

My new master was one of the owners or holders of the salt ponds, and he received a certain sum for every slave that worked upon his premises, whether they were young or old. This sum was allowed him out of the profits arising from the salt works. I was immediately sent to work in the salt water with the rest of the slaves. The work was perfectly new to me. I was given a half barrel and a shovel, and had to stand up to my knees in the water from four o'clock in the morning till nine, when we were given some Indian corn boiled in water, which we were obliged to swallow as fast as we could for fear the rain should come on and melt the salt. We were then called again to our tasks, and worked through the heat of the day; the sun flaming upon our heads like fire, and raising salt blisters in those parts which were not completely covered. Our feet and legs, from standing in the salt water for so many hours, soon became full of dreadful boils, which eat down in some cases to the very bone, afflicting the sufferers with great torment. We came home at twelve; ate our corn soup, called *blawly*, as fast as we could, and went back to our employment till dark at night. We then shovelled up the salt in large heaps, and went down to the sea, where we washed the pickle from our limbs, and cleaned the barrows and shovels from the salt. When we returned to the house, our master gave us each our allowance of raw Indian corn, which we pounded in a mortar and boiled in water for our suppers.

We slept in a long shed, divided into narrow slips, like the stalls used for cattle. Boards fixed upon stakes driven into the ground, without mat or covering, were our only beds. On Sundays, after we had washed the salt bags, and done other work required of us, we went into the bush and cut the long soft grass, of which we made trusses for our legs and feet to rest upon, for they were so full of the salt boils that we could get no rest lying upon the bare boards.

Though we worked from morning till night, there was no satisfying Mr. D——. I hoped, when I left Capt. I——, that I should have been better off, but I found it was but going from one butcher to another. There was this difference between them: my former master used to beat me while raging and foaming with passion; Mr. D——was usually quite calm. He would stand by and give orders for a slave to be cruelly whipped, and assist in the punishment, without moving a muscle of his face, walking about and taking snuff with the greatest composure. Nothing could touch his hard heart—neither sighs, nor tears, nor prayers, nor streaming blood: he was deaf to our cries, and careless of our sufferings.—Mr. D——has often stripped me naked, hung me up by the wrists, and beat me with the cow-skin with his own hand, till my body was raw with gashes. Yet there was nothing very remarkable in this; for it might serve as a sample of the common usage of slaves on that horrible island.

Thomas Bellamy
1745–1800

Thomas Bellamy had various careers, as a hosier, a bookseller's clerk, magazine publisher, writer, and proprietor of a circulating library. In 1789 he wrote *The Benevolent Planters* in support of the anti-emancipation West Indian lobby. Staged at the Theatre Royal, Haymarket, with some of the leading actors of the day, his playlet presents a world of kindly paternal masters whose slaves proclaim their happiness and gratitude.

The Benevolent Planters
A Dramatic Piece

Scene, Jamaica

Characters

Planters: GOODWIN, STEADY, HEARTFREE
Slaves: ORAN, SELIMA
Archers, &c. &c.

Prologue (By a Friend)[1]

AN AFRICAN SAILOR:
>   To Afric's torrid clime, where every day
>   The sun oppresses with his scorching ray,
>   My birth I owe; and here for many a year,
>   I tasted pleasure free from every care.
> 5   There 'twas my happy fortune long to prove
>   The fond endearments of parental love.
>   'Twas there my Adela, my favourite maid,
>   Return'd my passion, love with love repaid.
>   Oft on the banks where golden rivers flow,
> 10   And aromatic woods enchanting grow,
>   With my lov'd Adela I pass'd the day,
>   While suns on suns roll'd unperceiv'd away.

---

1. Spoken by Stephen George Kemble, a leading tragic actor, as "An African Sailor." In the play Kemble performed Oran, whose beloved, Selima, was performed by his wife. The anti–slave trade, pro-liberty prologue is not disputed by the playlet, which instead presents a humane, anti-emancipation image of plantation life.

But ah! this happiness was not to last,
Clouds now the brightness of my fate o'ercast;
15 For the white savage fierce upon me sprung,
Wrath in his eye, and fury on his tongue,
And dragg'd me to a loathsome vessel near,
Dragg'd me from every thing I held most dear,
And plung'd me in the horrors of despair.
20 Insensible to all that pass'd around,
Till, in a foreign clime, myself I found,
And sold to slavery!—There with constant toil,
Condemn'd in burning suns to turn the soil.
Oh! if I told you what I suffer'd there,
25 From cruel masters, and the lash severe,
Eyes most unus'd to melt, would drop the tear.
But fortune soon a kinder master gave,
Who made me soon forget I was a slave,
And brought me to this land, this generous land,°   *Jamaica*
30 Where, they inform me, that an hallow'd band,
Impelled by soft humanity's kind laws,
Take up with fervent zeal the Negroe's cause,
And at this very moment, anxious try,
To stop the widespread woes of slavery.
35 But of this hallow'd band a part appears,
Exult my heart, and flow my grateful tears.
Oh sons of mercy! whose extensive mind
Takes in at once the whole of human kind,
Who know the various nations of the earth,
40 To whatsoever clime they owe their birth,
Or of whatever colour they appear,
All children of one gracious Parent are.
And thus united by paternal love,
To all mankind, of all the friend you prove.
45 With fervent zeal pursue your godlike plan,
And man deliver from the tyrant man!
What tho' at first you miss the wish'd-for end,
Success at last your labours will attend.
Then shall your worth, extoll'd in grateful strains,
50 Resound through Gambia's and Angola's plains.[2]
Nations unborn your righteous zeal shall bless,
To them the source of peace and happiness.
Oh mighty Kannoah, thou most holy power,
Whom humbly we thy sable race adore!
55 Prosper the great design—thy children free
From the oppressor's hand, and give them liberty!

---

2. Gambia: northwest African country, with a strong British colonial presence; Angola: Portuguese colony on the south-west coast.

Scene 1

A Room in Goodwin's House; Enter Goodwin, meeting Steady and Heartfree.

GOODWIN: Good morrow, neighbours, friend Steady,[3] is your jetty tribe ready for the diversions?

STEADY: My tribe is prepared and ready to meet thine, and my heart exults on beholding so many happy countenances. But an added joy is come home to my bosom. This English friend, who, some time since, came to settle among us, in order that he might exhibit to his brother Planters, the happy effects of humanity, in the treatment of those who, in the course of human chance, are destined to the bonds of slavery, has honoured my dwelling with his presence, and gladdened my heart with his friendship.

HEARTFREE: A cause like the present, makes brothers of us all, and may heaven increase the brothers of humanity—Friend Steady informs me, that we are to preside as directors of the different diversions.

GOODWIN: It is our wish to prevent a repetition of disorders, that last year disturbed the general happiness. They were occasioned by the admission of one of those games, which, but too often, begin in sport, and end in passion. The offenders, however, were soon made sensible of the folly of attacking each other without provocation, and with no other view than to shew their superior skill, in an art, which white men have introduced among them.[4]

HEARTFREE: If that art was only made use of as a defence against the attacks of an unprincipled and vulgar violence, no man could with propriety form a wish of checking its progress. But while it opens another field where the gambler fills his pocket at the expence of the credulous and unsuspecting, whose families too often mourn in poverty and distress the effects of their folly; every member of society will hold up his hand against it, if his heart feels as it ought. I am sorry likewise to add, that too many recent instances of its fatal effects among my own countrymen, have convinced me of the guilt and folly of venturing *a life* to display *a skill*.

GOODWIN: We are happy to find our union strengthened by corresponding sentiments.

HEARTFREE: The sports, I find, are to continue six days; repeat your design, respecting the successful archers.

STEADY: The archers, friend, to the number of twelve, consist of selected slaves, whose honest industry and attachment have rendered them deserving of reward. They are to advance in pairs, and the youth who speeds the arrow surest, is to be proclaimed victor.

HEARTFREE: And what is his reward?

STEADY: A portion of land for himself, and his posterity—freedom for his life, and the maiden of his heart.

HEARTFREE: Generous men! humanity confers dignity upon authority. The grateful Africans have hearts as large as ours, and shame on the degrading lash, when it can be spared—Reasonable obedience is what we expect, and let those who look for more, feel and severely feel the sting of disappointment.

STEADY: Will your poor fellow attend the festival?

HEARTFREE: He will. I respect your feelings for the sorrows of the worthy Oran.

---

3. "Friend" evokes the Quaker term of address; Bellamy may be suggesting that not all Quakers were adamant abolitionists.

4. Perhaps boxing or dueling.

GOODWIN: Oran, did you say? What know you of him; pardon my abruptness, but relate his story, it may prove a task of pleasure.

HEARTFREE: By the fate of war,[5] Oran had been torn from his beloved Selima. The conquerors were on the point of setting fire to the consuming pile to which he was bound, while the partner of his heart, who was devoted[6] to the arms of the chief of the adverse party, was rending the air with her cries; at this instant a troop of Europeans broke in upon them, and bore away a considerable party to their ships; among the rest was the rescued Oran, who was happily brought to our mart, where I had the good fortune to become his master—he has since served me well and affectionately. But sorrow for his Selima is so deeply rooted in his feeling bosom, that I fear I shall soon lose an excellent domestic and as valuable a friend, whose only consolation springs from a sense of dying in the possession of Christian principles, from whence he acknowledges to have drawn comforts inexpressible.

GOODWIN: And comfort he shall still draw from a worldly as well as a heavenly source. For know, I can produce the Selima he mourns. She has told me her story, which is indeed a tale of woe. Inward grief has preyed upon her mind, and like her faithful Oran, she is bending to her grave. But happiness, love, and liberty shall again restore them.

HEARTFREE: When the mind has made itself up to misery—discoveries admitting of more than hope, ought ever to be made with caution. But you have a heart to feel for the distress of another, and conduct to guide you in giving relief to sorrow; leave me to my poor fellow, and do you prepare his disconsolate partner.

GOODWIN: I'll see her immediately, and when we take our seats on the plain of sports, we will communicate to each other the result of our considerations.

STEADY: Till then, my worthy associates, farewell. [*Exeunt*]

Scene II

Another Apartment in Goodwin's house. Enter Goodwin and Selima.

GOODWIN: Come, my poor disconsolate, be composed, and prepare to meet your friends on those plains, where you never shall experience sorrow; but on the contrary, enjoy every happiness within the power of thy grateful master to bestow; you once told me, Selima, that my participation of your griefs abated their force; will you then indulge me with that pleasing tho' mournful Song you have made, on the loss of him, who, perhaps, may one day be restored?

SELIMA: Good and generous Master! ever consoling me with hope, can I deny you who have given me mind, taught me your language, comforted me with the knowledge of books, and made me every thing I am? Prepared too, my soul for joys, which you say are to succeed the patient bearing of human misery. Oh, Sir, with what inward satisfaction do I answer a request in every way grateful to my feelings!

SONG. SET TO MUSIC BY MR. REEVE[7]

How vain to me the hours of ease,
When every daily toil is o'er;

---

5. Tribal warfare in Africa.
6. Destined.

7. William Reeve (1757–1815), actor and composer.

In my sad heart no hope I find,
> For Oran is, alas! no more.

Not sunny Africa could please,
> Nor friends upon my native shore,
To me the dreary world's a cave,
> For Oran is, alas! no more.

In bowers of bliss beyond the moon,
> The white man says, his sorrow's o'er,
And comforts me with soothing hope,
> Tho' Oran is, alas, no more.

O come then, messenger of death,
> Convey me to yon starry shore,
Where I may meet with my true love,
> And never part with Oran more.

GOODWIN: There's my kind Selima! and now attend to a discovery, on which depends your future happiness; not only liberty, but love awaits you.

SELIMA: The first I want not—the last can never be! for where shall I find another Oran?

GOODWIN: O my good girl, your song of sorrow shall be changed into that of gladness. For know—the hours of anguish are gone by, your Oran lives, and lives but to bless his faithful Selima.

SELIMA [after a pause]: To that invisible Being who has sustained my suffering heart, I kneel, overwhelmed with an awful[8] sense of his protecting power. But how?

GOODWIN: As we walk on, I will explain every thing. You soon will embrace your faithful Oran, and his beloved Selima shall mourn no more. [Exeunt.]

Scene III

An open Plain.

> [On one side a range of men-slaves; on the other a range of women-slaves—at some distance, seated on decorated chairs, Heartfree, Goodwin, and Steady—twelve archers close the line on the men-side, meeting the audience with Oran at their head, distinguished from the rest by a rich dress—Oran, advancing to the front of the stage, stands in a dejected posture.]

HEARTFREE: Now let the air echo to the sound of the enlivening instruments, and beat the ground to their tuneful melody; while myself and my two worthy friends, who since our last festival have reaped the benefit of your honest labours, in full goblets drink to your happiness.

> [Flourish of music, and a dance.]

HEARTFREE: Now let the archers advance in pairs, and again, in replenished cups, health and domestic peace to those who surest speed the arrow.

> [Flourish. Here the archers advance in pairs to the middle of the Stage, and discharge their arrows through the side wings—the victor is saluted by two female slaves, who

8. Awe-filled.

present to him the maiden of his choice—then a flourish of music, and the parties fall back to the side. After the ceremony has been repeated five times to as many pair of archers, and Oran and Almaboe only remain to advance as the sixth pair, Oran appears absorbed in grief, which is observed with evident concern by Heartfree.]

HEARTFREE: Why Oran, with looks divided between earth and heaven, dost thou appear an alien among those who are encompassed with joy and gladness? Though your beloved Selima is torn from your widowed arms, yet it is a duty you owe yourself, as a man, an obligation due to me, as your friend, to take to your bosom one whom I have provided for you. A contest with Almaboe is needless; he has fixed on his partner, to whom, according to your request, he is now presented. [*A flourish of music—two female slaves advance with a third, who is presented to Almaboe—the parties embrace.*] It remains, therefore, for you to comply with the wishes of those who honour your virtues, and have respected your sorrows.

ORAN: Kind and benevolent masters; I indeed came hither unwillingly, to draw the bow, with a heart already pierced with the arrow of hopeless anguish. You have done generously by my friend, to whom I meant to have relinquished the victor's right, had the chance been mine. For alas, Sirs! Selima was my first and only love; and when I lost her, joy fled from a bosom it will never again revisit. The short date of my existence is therefore devoted alone to that Power whom you have taught me to revere. Sacred to gratitude, and sacred to her whose beckoning spirit seems at this moment to call on me from yonder sky—

GOODWIN: What say you, Oran, if I should produce a maiden whose virtues will bring you comfort, and whose affection you will find as strong as hers, whose loss you so feelingly deplore?

ORAN: O Sirs! had you but known my Selima, you would not attempt to produce her equal! Poor lost excellence! Yes, thy spirit, released from all its sufferings, is now looking down upon its Oran! But let not imagination too far transport me: perhaps she yet lives, a prey to brutal lust. [*Turns to Almaboe.*] Brother of my choice, and friend of my adverse hour, long may your Coanzi be happy in the endearments of her faithful Almaboe. And O my friend! when thy poor Oran is no more, if [it] chance that Selima yet lives, if blessed Providence *should* lead her to these happy shores, if she should escape the cruel enemy, and be brought hither with honour unsullied;[9] tell her how much she owes to these generous men; comfort her afflicted spirit, and teach her to adore the God of truth and mercy.

ALMABOE: Oran must himself endeavour to live for that day, and not by encouraging despair, sink self-devoted to the grave.[1] The same Providence, my friend, which has turned the terrors of slavery into willing bondage, may yet restore thy Selima.

ORAN: The words of Almaboe come charged with the force of truth, and erring Oran bends to offended Heaven! Yet erring Oran must still feel his loss, and erring Oran must for ever lament it.

GOODWIN: It is true, Oran, our arguments to urge thee to be happy, have hitherto proved fruitless. But know, thou man of sorrow, we are possessed of the means which will restore thee to thyself and to thy friends. Hear, then, the important secret, and know, that thy Selima yet lives!

---

9. As a virgin.   1. By suicide; "devoted" means "doomed."

ORAN [*after a pause*]: Yet lives! Selima yet lives! what my Selima! my own dear angel! O speak again, your words have visited my heart, and it is lost in rapture.

HEARTFREE: Nay, Oran, but be calm.

ORAN: I am calm—Heaven will permit me to support my joy, but do you relieve me from suspence.

GOODWIN: Let the instruments breathe forth the most pleasing strains—Advance, my happy virgins, with your charge, and restore to Oran his long-lost Selima. You receive her pure as when you parted, with a mind released from the errors of darkness, and refined by its afflictions.

[*Soft music—Selima comes down the stage, attended by six virgins in fancied dresses, who present her to Oran—the lovers embrace—flourish of music, and a shout.*]

ORAN: Lost in admiration, gratitude, and love, Oran has no words, but can only in silence own the hand of Heaven; while to his beating heart he clasps his restored treasure. And O my masters! for such, though free, suffer me still to call you; let my restored partner and myself bend to such exalted worth; while for ourselves, and for our surrounding brethren, we declare, that you have proved yourselves *The Benevolent Planters*, and that under subjection like yours,

SLAVERY IS BUT A NAME

SONG. TO THE TUNE OF *RULE BRITANNIA*.[2]

In honour of this happy day,
    Let Afric's sable sons rejoice;
To mercy we devote the lay,
    To heaven-born mercy raise the voice.
Long may she reign, and call each heart her own,
And nations guard her sacred throne.

Fair child of heaven, our rites approve,
    With smiles attend the votive song,
Inspire with universal love,
    For joy and peace to thee belong.
Long may'st thou reign, and call each heart thy own,
While nations guard thy sacred throne.

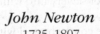

John Newton
1725–1807

In 1748, John Newton, a former sailor and then captain in the slave trade, converted to evangelical Christianity, and became a rector. In *An Authentic Narrative of Some Remarkable and Interesting Particulars in the Life of John Newton* (1764) he related his adventures in a narrative of divine salvation, and so reinforced the spiritual argument for the abolition of the slave trade. His memoirs, *Thoughts Upon the African Slave Trade* (1788), more starkly detailed the "business at which my heart now shudders," publicizing the horrors of capture

---

2. A famous song, written by James Thomson in 1740, with music by Thomas Arne. Its last stanza: "Blest Isle! with matchless beauty crowned / And manly hearts to guard the fair. / Rule Britannia, rule the waves, / Britons never will be slaves!"

and the Middle Passage. (Newton guessed that on the voyages he captained, one-fourth of the slave cargo was lost.) As a charismatic minister, Newton championed abolition. His famous hymn of personal salvation, now known as *Amazing Grace*, was originally titled *Faith's Review and Expectation*, and was keyed (as was the practice) to a biblical text, I Chronicles 17.16–17. It was written some time between 1760 and 1770 and first published in 1779.

Amazing Grace!

   AMAZING grace! how sweet the sound!
      That saved a wretch like me!
   I once was lost, but now am found,
      Was blind, but now I see.

5   'Twas grace that taught my heart to fear,
      And grace my fears relieved;
   How precious did that grace appear
      The hour I first believed!

   Through many dangers, toils, and snares,
10   I have already come;
   'Tis grace has brought me safe thus far,
      And grace will lead me home.

   The Lord has promised good to me,
      His Word my hope secures;
15   He will my shield and portion be,
      As long as life endures.

   Yes, when this flesh and heart shall fail,
      And mortal life shall cease,
   I shall possess, within the veil,
20   A life of joy and peace.

   The earth shall soon dissolve like snow;
      The sun forbear to shine;
   But God, who call'd me here below,
      Will be for ever mine.

1760–1770   *1779, Olney Hymns*

Ann Cromartie Yearsley
?1756–1806

One of the most bitterly ironic voices of abolition poetry was Ann Yearsley, a Bristol dairymaid and milkseller whose career was launched by Hannah More. The daughter of a day laborer and a dairywoman, Ann Cromartie lacked formal education; she learned to read and write from her brother and developed a passion for poetry. She married John Yearsley in 1774, bore six children in six years, and suffered near starvation with her family during the brutal winter of 1783–1784. Learning of her plight, More read her poems and was impressed by them and their author, whom she described as "industrious in no common degree, pious, unambitious, simple and unaffected." With the assistance of Elizabeth Montagu (another woman of letters), she secured a printer, developed an impressive subscription list, and served as editor, proofreader, and publicist for Yearsley's first volume, *Poems on Several Occasions* (1785). She also tried to control the proceeds—eventually £600—by placing Yearsley on a small annual allowance and establishing a trust fund for her children. Yearsley insisted on controlling the money herself and when More refused, concerned that she might set her sights "out of her station," Yearsley broke with her and lambasted her treatment of her in a prefatory "Autobiographical Narrative" to the fourth edition (1786), which she reprinted in *Poems on Various Subjects* (1787). Although such "ingratitude" appalled More's friends (see Polwhele, page 349, n. 8), Yearsley continued to earn praise for "genius," and an "unusually sound masculine understanding." A passionate sense of social injustice infuses *Poem on the Inhumanity of the Slave-Trade* (1788), a rival to More's *Slavery: A Poem* (1788). Strategically addressing the citizens of Bristol, a hub of the trade, Yearsley details the rending apart of African families, the physical degradation, suffering, and torture of the slaves, and the affront to Christian conscience, but she departs from the salvational model of Evangelical narratives by presenting a rebellious protagonist who is martyred for his resistance. For Yearsley's poem on women's freedom in staying unmarried, see page 327.

from A Poem on the Inhumanity of the Slave-Trade

> Go seek the soul refin'd and strong;
> Such aids my wildest pow'r of song:
> For those I strike the rustic lyre
> Who *share* the transports *they inspire.*

To the Right Hon. and Right Rev. Frederick, Earl of Bristol, Bishop of Derry, &c. &c.

My Lord,

Being convinced that your Ideas of Justice and Humanity are not confined to *one* Race of Men, I have endeavoured to lead you to the Indian Coast.[1] My Intention is not to cause that Anguish in your Bosom which powerless Compassion ever gives; yet, my Vanity is flattered, when I but *fancy* that your Lordship feels as I do.

> With the highest Reverence, I am,
> My Lord
> Your Lordship's much obliged,
> And obedient Servant,
> ANN YEARSLEY.

> BRISTOL,[2] thine heart hath throbb'd to glory.—Slaves,
> E'en Christian slaves, have shook their chains, and gaz'd
> With wonder and amazement on thee. Hence
> Ye grov'ling souls, who think the term I give,
> 5   Of Christian slave, a paradox! to *you*
> I do not turn, but leave you to conception
> Narrow; with that be blest, nor dare to stretch
> Your shackled souls along the course of *Freedom.*
>
> * * *
>
> But come, ye souls who feel for human woe,
> Tho' drest in savage guise! Approach, thou son,
> Whose heart would shudder at a father's chains,

---

1. West Indies.
2. With Liverpool, one of the chief ports in England from

which slave traders, financed by local merchants, departed to procure Africans.

And melt o'er thy lov'd brother as he lies
35 Gasping in torment undeserv'd. Oh, sight
Horrid and insupportable! far worse
Than an immediate, an heroic death;
Yet to this sight I summon thee. Approach,
Thou slave of avarice!

* * *

Luco[3] is gone; his little brothers weep,
115 While his fond mother climbs the hoary rock
Whose point o'er-hangs the main. No Luco there,
No sound, save the hoarse billows. On she roves,
With love, fear, hope, holding alternate rage
In her too anxious bosom. Dreary main!
120 Thy murmurs now are riot, while she stands
List'ning to ev'ry breeze, waiting the step
Of gentle Luco. Ah, return! return!
Too hapless mother, thy indulgent arms
Shall never clasp thy fetter'd Luco more.
125 See Incilanda! artless maid, my soul
Keeps pace with thee, and mourns.

* * *

A father comes,
But not to seek his son, who from the deck
Had breath'd a last adieu: no, he shuts out
The soft, fallacious gleam of hope, and turns
170 Within upon the mind: horrid and dark
Are his wild, unenlighten'd pow'rs: no ray
Of *forc'd* philosophy to calm his soul,
But all the anarchy of wounded nature.

* * *

Where now shall Incilanda seek him? Hence,
195 Defenceless mourner, ere the dreary night
Wrap thee in added horror. Oh, Despair,
How eagerly thou rend'st the heart! She pines
In anguish deep, and sullen: Luco's form
Pursues her, lives in restless thought, and chides
200 Soft consolation. Banished from his arms,
She seeks the cold embrace of death; her soul
Escapes in one sad sigh. Too hapless maid!

* * *

Luco is borne around the neighb'ring isles,
Losing the knowledge of his native shore
215 Amid the pathless wave; destin'd to plant
The sweet luxuriant cane.[4] He strives to please,
Nor once complains, but greatly smothers grief.
His hands are blister'd, and his feet are worn,

---

3. A boy kidnapped into slavery; Incilanda is his beloved.
4. Sugarcane, a chief West Indian crop, was processed into rum, molasses, and refined sugar, for sale in England and Europe.

Till ev'ry stroke dealt by his mattock° gives   *hoe*
220 Keen agony to life; while from his breast
The sigh arises, burthen'd with the name
Of Incilanda. Time inures the youth,
His limbs grow nervous, strain'd by willing toil;
And resignation, or a calm despair,
225 (Most useful either) lulls him to repose.

A Christian renegade, that from his soul
Abjures the tenets of our schools, nor dreads
A future punishment, nor hopes for mercy,
Had fled from England, to avoid those laws
230 Which must have made his life a retribution
To violated justice, and had gain'd,
By fawning guile, the confidence (ill placed)
Of Luco's master. O'er the slave he stands
With knotted whip, lest fainting nature shun
235 The task too arduous, while his cruel soul,
Unnat'ral, ever feeds, with gross delight,
Upon his suff'rings. Many slaves there were,
But none who could suppress the sigh, and bend,
So quietly as Luco: long he bore
240 The stripes,° that from his manly bosom drew   *lashes*
The sanguine° stream (too little priz'd); at length   *bloody*
Hope fled his soul, giving her struggles o'er,
And he resolv'd to die. The sun had reach'd
His zenith—pausing faintly, Luco stood,
245 Leaning upon his hoe, while mem'ry brought,
In piteous imag'ry, his aged father,
His poor fond mother, and his faithful maid:
The mental group in wildest motion set
Fruitless imagination; fury, grief,
250 Alternate shame, the sense of insult, all
Conspire to aid the inward storm; yet words
Were no relief, he stood in silent woe.

   Gorgon,[5] remorseless Christian, saw the slave
Stand musing, 'mid the ranks, and, stealing soft
255 Behind the studious Luco, struck his cheek
With a too-heavy whip, that reach'd his eye,
Making it dark for ever. Luco turn'd,
In strongest agony, and with his hoe
Struck the rude Christian on the forehead. Pride,
260 With hateful malice, seize[d] on Gorgon's soul,
By nature fierce; while Luco sought the beach,
And plung'd beneath the wave; but near him lay

---

5. The Gorgons of Greek mythology were monstrous snake-haired sisters whose gaze turned men to stone.

A planter's barge, whose seamen grasp'd his hair,
Dragging to life a wretch who wish'd to die.

265   Rumour now spreads the tale, while Gorgon's breath
Envenom'd, aids her blast: imputed crimes
Oppose the plea of Luco, till he scorns
Even a just defence, and stands prepared.
The planters, conscious that to fear alone
270 They owe their cruel pow'r, resolve to blend
New torment with the pangs of death, and hold
Their victims high in dreadful view, to fright
The wretched number left. Luco is chain'd
To a huge tree, his fellow-slaves are ranged
275 To share the horrid sight; fuel is plac'd
In an increasing train, some paces back,
To kindle slowly, and approach the youth,
With more than native terror. See, it burns!
He gazes on the growing flame, and calls
280 For "water, water!" The small boon's deny'd.
E'en Christians throng each other, to behold
The different alterations of his face,
As the hot death approaches. (Oh, shame, shame
Upon the followers of Jesus! shame
285 On him that dares avow a God!) He writhes,
While down his breast glide the unpity'd tears,
And in their sockets strain their scorched balls.
"Burn, burn me quick! I cannot die!" he cries:
"Bring fire more close!" The planters heed him not,
290 But still prolonging Luco's torture, threat
Their trembling slaves around. His lips are dry,
His senses seem to quiver, e'er they quit
His frame for ever, rallying strong, then driv'n
From the tremendous conflict. Sight no more
295 Is Luco's, his parch'd tongue is ever mute.

                    * * *

                Must our wants
365 Find their supply in murder? Shall the sons
Of Commerce shiv'ring stand, if not employ'd
Worse than the midnight robber? Curses fall
On the destructive system that shall need
Such base supports! Doth England need them? No;
370 Her laws, with prudence, hang the meagre thief
That from his neighbour steals a slender sum,
Tho' famine drove him on. O'er *him* the priest,
Beneath the fatal tree, laments the crime,
Approves the law, and bids him calmly die.
375 Say, doth this law, that dooms the thief, protect
The wretch who makes another's life his prey,
By hellish force to take it at his will?

Is this an English law, whose guidance fails
When crimes are swell'd to magnitude so vast,

380 That *Justice* dare not scan them? Or does *Law*
Bid *Justice* an eternal distance keep
From England's great tribunal, when the slave
Calls loud on *Justice only?* Speak, ye few
Who fill Britannia's senate, and are deem'd

385 The fathers of your country! Boast your laws,
Defend the *honour* of a land so fall'n,
That Fame from ev'ry battlement is flown,
And Heathens start, e'en at a Christian's name.

* * *

Oh, social love,

415 Thou universal good, thou that canst fill
The vacuum of immensity, and live
In endless void! thou that in motion first
Set'st the long lazy atoms, by thy force
Quickly assimilating, and restrain'd

420 By strong attraction; touch the soul of man;
Subdue him; make a fellow-creature's woe
His own by heart-felt sympathy, whilst wealth
Is made subservient to his soft disease.

And when thou hast to high perfection wrought
425 This mighty work, say, *"such is Bristol's soul."*

—+ ⟩⟨◆⟩⟨ +—

William Cowper
1731–1800

The son of a rector and a mother who traced her descent to Henry III and John Donne, William Cowper was beset through his life with manic, sometimes suicidal, depressions, aggravated by his attraction to sects emphasizing man's original sin. He studied law but found poetry more congenial, and with the Evangelical minister and abolitionist John Newton published a volume of hymns in 1779, including Newton's great hymn *Amazing Grace*. He followed with a series of moral satires in the early 1780s, and his most famous poem, *The Task* (1785), whose second book opens with a strong critique of slavery. Feeling deeply the moral blight of slavery as an institution sustained only by greed, Cowper responded to Newton's call for popular abolitionist literature with four ballads in 1788 that would be widely reprinted. The poet of *The Morning Dream* envisions the goddess Britannia sailing west to a "slave-cultured island" to confront the cruel "Demon" of slave-ownership, who sickens and dies at her sight; the balladeer of *Pity for Poor Africans,* insisting that he is "shock'd at the purchase of slaves," justifies his participation by arguing that foreigners will not give up the trade: "He shar'd in the plunder, but he pitied the man." *Sweet Meat Has Sour Sauce: or, The Slave-Trader in the Dumps* is the ditty of a trader lamenting the inevitable abolition of his business and trying to unload his gear. *The Negro's Complaint,* the most popular of the group in part because of its stark wood-cut illustrations, doubly refutes the view of slaves as subhuman: its slave-speaker not only expresses his own profound humanity but also exposes the inhumanity of the "iron-hearted" masters, whom he calls "slaves of gold." Cowper grew so depressed with his involvement in the slavery issue that eventually he had to stop writing about it. His last poem, written shortly before his death, is the beautifully melancholy *The Castaway* (see page 650).

Sweet Meat Has Sour Sauce
or, The Slave-Trader in the Dumps

A trader I am to the African shore,
But since that my trading is like to be o'er,
I'll sing you a song that you ne'er heard before,
    Which nobody can deny, deny,
5   Which nobody can deny.

When I first heard the news it gave me a shock,
Much like what they call an electrical knock,
And now I am going to sell off my stock,
    Which nobody can deny.

10 'Tis a curious assortment of dainty regales,°   *choice pieces*
To tickle the Negroes with when the ship sails—
Fine chains for the neck, and a cat with nine tails,[1]
    Which nobody can deny.

Here's supple-jack plenty, and store of rat-tan,[2]
15 That will wind itself round the sides of a man,
As close as a hoop round a bucket or can,
    Which nobody can deny.

Here's padlocks and bolts, and screws for the thumbs,
That squeeze them so lovingly till the blood comes;
20 They sweeten the temper like comfits or plums,
    Which nobody can deny.

When a Negro his head from his victuals withdraws,
And clenches his teeth and thrusts out his paws,
Here's a notable engine to open his jaws,[3]
25   Which nobody can deny.

Thus going to market, we kindly prepare
A pretty black cargo of African ware,
For what they must meet with when they get there,
    Which nobody can deny.

30 'Twould do your heart good to see 'em below
Lie flat on their backs all the way as we go,[4]
Like sprats on a gridiron, scores in a row,[5]
    Which nobody can deny.

1. Cat-o'-nine-tails, a whip of nine knotted lashes.
2. Both supple-jack (a woody vine) and rattan (a climbing palm) were used to make whips, canes, and ropes.
3. Force-feeding of a slave meaning to starve to death.
4. A reference to the torturous tight-packing of slave
cargo; see illustration, page 280.
5. Sprats are herrings (metaphorically, insignificant people); a gridiron is a griddle—an image of slaves cooking in hot cargo-holds.

But ah! if in vain I have studied an art
35   So gainful to me, all boasting apart,
I think it will break my compassionate heart,
      Which nobody can deny.

For oh! how it enters my soul like an awl!
This pity, which some people self-pity call,
40   Is sure the most heart-piercing pity of all,
      Which nobody can deny.

So this is my song, as I told you before;
Come, buy off my stock, for I must no more
Carry Caesars and Pompeys to Sugar-cane shore,[6]
45   Which nobody can deny, deny,
      Which nobody can deny.

1788

The Negro's Complaint

FORCED from home and all its pleasures,
    Afric's coast I left forlorn,
To increase the stranger's treasures,
    O'er the raging billows borne.
5   Men from England bought and sold me,
    Paid my price in paltry gold;
But, though slave they have enroll'd me,
    Minds are never to be sold.

Still in thought as free as ever,
10   What are England's rights, I ask,
Me from my delights to sever,
    Me to torture, me to task?
Fleecy locks and black complexion
    Cannot forfeit Nature's claim;
15   Skins may differ, but affection
    Dwells in white and black the same.

Why did all creating Nature
    Make the plant for which we toil?
Sighs must fan it, tears must water,
20   Sweat of ours must dress the soil.
Think, ye masters, iron-hearted,
    Lolling at your jovial boards,
Think how many backs have smarted
    For the sweets your cane° affords.   *sugarcane*

25   Is there, as ye sometimes tell us,
    Is there One who reigns on high?
Has He bid you buy and sell us,
    Speaking from his throne, the sky?

---

6. Caesar and Pompey were famous ancient Romans (many slaves were royalty in their African cultures); "Sugar-cane shore" is the West Indies.

Ask Him, if your knotted scourges,°   *whips*
30 Matches, blood-extorting screws,°   *thumbscrews*
Are the means that duty urges
     Agents of his will to use?

Hark! He answers!—Wild tornadoes
     Strewing yonder sea with wrecks,
35 Wasting towns, plantations, meadows,
     Are the voice with which he speaks.
He, foreseeing what vexations
     Afric's sons should undergo,
Fix'd their tyrants' habitations
40 Where his whirlwinds answer—No.[1]

By our blood in Afric wasted,
     Ere our necks received the chain;
By the miseries that we tasted,
     Crossing in your barks° the main;°   *ships / sea*
45 By our sufferings, since ye brought us
     To the man-degrading mart,
All sustain'd by patience, taught us
     Only by a broken heart!

Deem our nation brutes no longer,
50 Till some reason ye shall find
Worthier of regard and stronger
     Than the colour of our kind.
Slaves of gold, whose sordid dealings
     Tarnish all your boasted powers,
55 Prove that you have human feelings
     Ere you proudly question ours!

1788   1793

Anna Letitia Barbauld
1743–1825

In 1780 bookseller Joseph Johnson published *The Master and the Slave* (1780), a dialogue by Anna Barbauld and her brother John Aikin, in which a plantation slave urges his emancipation into paid labor by appealing to the master's economic self-interest. On 17 April 1791, William Wilberforce's bill for the abolition of the slave trade was defeated in the House of Commons by a vote of 163 to 88. To excoriate his adversaries, Barbauld fired off an *Epistle*, in the heroic couplets of eighteenth-century public poetry, and Johnson rushed it into print as a fourteen-page, one-shilling pamphlet (our text). Barbauld assails the conscience of English women, casting England as a female country shamed by its slave trade, twin to the plantation mistress—a picture of "barbarity and voluptuousness" that Hannah More found "striking" (A. L. Le Breton, *Memoir*). For more about Barbauld, see her principal listing on page 65.

---

1. Tornados and other natural catastrophes were taken to be signs of divine anger and retribution.

Epistle to William Wilberforce, Esq.
On the Rejection of the Bill for Abolishing the Slave Trade

CEASE, Wilberforce, to urge thy generous aim!
Thy Country knows the sin, and stands the shame!
The Preacher, Poet, Senator in vain
Has rattled in her sight the Negro's chain;
5   With his deep groans assail'd her startled ear,
And rent the veil that hid his constant tear;
Forc'd her averted eyes his stripes° to scan,   *lashes*
Beneath the bloody scourge laid bare the man,
Claimed Pity's tear, urged Conscience' strong controul,
10   And flash'd conviction on her shrinking soul.
The Muse, too soon awak'd, with ready tongue
At Mercy's shrine applausive peans° rung;   *praising hymns*
And Freedom's eager sons, in vain foretold
A new Astrean reign, an age of gold:[1]
15   She knows and she persists—Still Afric bleeds,
Uncheck'd, the human traffic° still proceeds;   *trade*
She stamps her infamy to future time,
And on her harden'd forehead seals the crime.

    In vain, to thy white standard[2] gathering round,
20   Wit, Worth, and Parts and Eloquence are found:
In vain, to push to birth thy great design,
Contending chiefs, and hostile virtues join;
All, from conflicting ranks, of power possest
To rouse, to melt, or to inform the breast.[3]
25   Where seasoned tools of Avarice prevail,[4]
A Nation's eloquence, combined, must fail:
Each flimsy sophistry° by turns they try;   *reasoning*
The plausive° argument, the daring lye,   *speciously plausible*
The artful gloss,° that moral sense confounds,   *explanation*
30   Th' acknowledged thirst of gain that honour wounds:
Bane of ingenuous minds, th' unfeeling sneer,
Which, sudden, turns to stone the falling tear:
They search assiduous, with inverted skill,
For forms of wrong, and precedents of ill;
35   With impious mockery wrest the sacred page,°   *Scripture*
And glean up crimes from each remoter age:
Wrung Nature's tortures, shuddering, while you tell,
From scoffing fiends bursts forth the laugh of hell;
In Britain's senate, Misery's pangs give birth

---

1. In the Greek mythology of the Golden Age (an era of peace and prosperity) Astrea is the goddess of justice. She abandoned humanity as it grew unjust; "golden age" is now the modern age of commercial gold.
2. Another bitter punning: "standard" means *flag* and *ethical principle*. A white standard is a traditional emblem of virtue, defaulted on by the white race.

3. Usual political antagonists (Whigs such as Edmund Burke and Charles James Fox, and Tories such as Prime Minister William Pitt) opposed Britain's participation in the slave trade.
4. The argument that the slave system is necessary to Britain's commercial preeminence.

40   To jests unseemly, and to horrid mirth[5]—
       Forbear!—thy virtues but provoke our doom,
       And swell th' account of vengeance yet to come;
       For, not unmark'd in Heaven's impartial plan,
       Shall man, proud worm, contemn° his fellow-man?   *scorn*
45   And injur'd Afric, by herself redrest,°   *avenged*
       Darts her own serpents at her Tyrant's breast.
       Each vice, to minds deprav'd by bondage known,
       With sure contagion fastens on his own;
       In sickly languors melts his nerveless frame,
50   And blows to rage impetuous Passion's flame:
       Fermenting swift, the fiery venom gains
       The milky innocence of infant veins;
       There swells the stubborn will, damps learning's fire,
       The whirlwind wakes of uncontroul'd desire,
55   Sears the young heart to images of woe,
       And blasts the buds of Virtue as they blow.°   *bloom*

         Lo! where reclin'd, pale Beauty courts the breeze,
       Diffus'd on sofas of voluptuous ease;
       With anxious awe, her menial train around,
60   Catch her faint whispers of half-utter'd sound;
       See her, in monstrous fellowship, unite
       At once the Scythian, and the Sybarite;[6]
       Blending repugnant vices, misally'd,
       Which *frugal* nature purpos'd to divide;
65   See her, with indolence to fierceness join'd,
       Of body delicate, infirm of mind,
       With languid tones imperious mandates urge;
       With arm recumbent wield the household scourge;
       And with unruffled mien, and placid sounds,
70   Contriving torture, and inflicting wounds.

         Nor, in their palmy walks and spicy groves,
       The form benign of rural Pleasure roves;
       No milk-maid's song, or hum of village talk,
       Sooths the lone Poet in his evening walk:
75   No willing arm the flail unweary'd plies,
       Where the mix'd sounds of cheerful labour rise;
       No blooming maids, and frolic swains are seen
       To pay gay homage to their harvest queen:
       No heart-expanding scenes their eyes must prove
80   Of thriving industry, and faithful love:
       But shrieks and yells disturb the balmy air,
       Dumb sullen looks of woe announce despair,
       And angry eyes thro' dusky features glare.
       Far from the sounding lash the Muses fly,
85   And sensual riot drowns each finer joy.

---

5. Editors W. McCarthy and E. Kraft note that during the debate in Parliament, there was laughter at the story of a slave forced to throw the body of her dead child overboard.

6. Ancient peoples epitomizing, respectively, savagery and decadent luxury.

Nor less from the gay East,° on essenc'd wings,   *India*
Breathing unnam'd perfumes, Contagion springs;
The soft luxurious plague alike pervades
The marble palaces, and rural shades;
90   Hence, throng'd Augusta° builds her rosy bowers,   *London*
And decks in summer wreaths her smoky towers;
And hence, in summer bow'rs, Art's costly hand
Pours courtly splendours o'er the dazzled land:
The manners melt—One undistinguish'd blaze
95   O'erwhelms the sober pomp of elder days;
Corruption follows with gigantic stride,
And scarce vouchsafes his shameless front to hide:
The spreading leprosy taints ev'ry part,
Infects each limb, and sickens at the heart.
100 Simplicity! most dear of rural maids,
Weeping resigns her violated shades:
Stern Independence from his glebe° retires,   *plot of land*
And anxious Freedom eyes her drooping fires;
By foreign wealth are British morals chang'd,
105 And Afric's sons, and India's, smile aveng'd.

For you, whose temper'd ardour long has borne
Untir'd the labour, and unmov'd the scorn;
In Virtue's fasti° be inscrib'd your fame,   *calendar of festivals*
And utter'd your's with Howard's honour'd name,[7]
110 Friends of the friendless—Hail, ye generous band!
Whose efforts yet arrest Heav'n's lifted hand,
Around whose steady brows, in union bright,
The civic wreath, and Christian's palm unite:
Your merit stands, no greater and no less,
115 Without, or with the varnish of success;
But seek no more to break a Nation's fall,
For ye have sav'd yourselves—and that is all.
Succeeding times your struggles, and their fate,
With mingled shame and triumph shall relate,
120 While faithful History, in her various page,
Marking the features of this motley° age,   *various*
To shed a glory, and to fix a stain,
Tells how you strove, and that you strove in vain.

Hannah More and *Eaglesfield Smith*
1745–1833   c. 1770–1838

Poet and essayist Hannah More published 114 *Cheap Repository Tracts* between 1795 and 1798. With simple language cast into stories, ballads, poems, dialogues, sermons, prayers, parables, and moral tales, she strove, with an Evangelical view, "to improve the habits, and raise

7. Prison reformer John Howard (1726–1790).

the principles of the common people . . . not only to counteract vice and profligacy on the one hand, but error, discontent, and false religion on the other." Among her concerns were quelling political discontent and class antagonisms (see *Village Politics*, page 153) and shaping public opinion in favor of abolition. Priced at a halfpenny, and marketed not only in shops but also at fairs and on street corners, the *Tracts* sold quickly and widely, over two million in the first year alone. They were purchased in bulk by preachers for their congregations, landlords for their tenants and laborers, and missionaries for their work in Africa and India, and disseminated in hospitals, prisons, the armed forces, and the workhouses. More had first treated the issue in *Slavery: A Poem* (1788), a 356-line polemical oration aimed at creating support for Wilberforce in Parliament. Eager to involve a popular audience, she devoted four of her *Tracts* to slavery. The most popular were *The Black Prince* (perhaps co-authored with More's mentor John Newton) and *The Sorrows of Yamba*, which critic Alan Richardson reports was co-authored with Eaglesfield Smith. We also thank him for helping us establish this text.

Additional work by More appears in Perspectives: The Wollstonecraft Controversy and the Rights of Women, pages 360–66.

The Sorrows of Yamba
or, The Negro Woman's Lamentation

"IN St. Lucie's distant isle,[1]
    Still with Afric's love I burn;
Parted many a thousand mile,
    Never, never to return.

5   Come, kind death! and give me rest;
    Yamba has no friend but thee;
Thou can'st ease my throbbing breast,
    Thou can'st set the Prisoner free.

Down my cheeks the tears are dripping,
10   Broken is my heart with grief;
Mangled my poor flesh with whipping,
    Come, kind death! and bring relief.

Born on Afric's Golden Coast,[2]
    Once I was as blest as you;
15   Parents tender I could boast,
    Husband dear, and children too.

Whity man he came from far,
    Sailing o'er the briny flood,
Who with help of British Tar,°   *seaman*
20   Buys up human flesh and blood.

With the baby at my breast
    (Other too were sleeping by)
In my Hut I sat at rest
    With no thought of danger nigh.

1. Santa Lucia, in the British West Indies.
2. An evocation of an idyllic world and ironically, the

"Gold Coast," a British West African colony (now Ghana) trading chiefly in gold and slaves.

25   From the Bush at even tide,
        Rushed the fierce man-stealing crew;
    Seiz'd the Children by my side,
        Seiz'd the wretched Yamba too.

    Then for love of filthy Gold,
30   Strait they bore me to the Sea,
    Cramm'd me down a Slave Ship's hold,
        Where were Hundreds stow'd like me.

    Naked on the Platform lying,
        Now we cross the tumbling wave;
35   Shrieking, sickening, fainting, dying;
        Deed of shame for Britons brave.

    At the savage Captain's beck,
        Now like Brutes they make us prance:
    Smack the Cat° about the Deck,   *whip*
40   And in scorn they make us dance.

    Nauseous horse-beans they bring nigh,
        Sick and sad we cannot eat;
    Cat must cure the Sulks, they cry,
        Down their throats we'll force the meat.[3]

45   I, in groaning passed the night,
        And did roll my aching head;
    At the break of morning light,
        My poor Child was cold and dead.

    Happy, happy, there she lies,
50   Thou shalt feel the lash no more.
    Thus full many a Negro dies
        Ere we reach the destin'd shore.

    Thee, sweet infant, none shall sell,
        Thou hast gained a wat'ry Grave;
55   Clean escap'd the Tyrants fell,°   *fierce*
        While thy mother lives a Slave.

    Driven like Cattle to a fair,
        See they sell us, young and old;
    Child from Mother too they tear,
60   All for love of filthy Gold.

    I was sold to Massa° hard,   *Master*
        Some have Massas kind and good:
    And again my back was scarr'd,
        Bad and stinted was my food.

---

3. Forced feeding; horse-beans are food for horses.

65   Poor and wounded, faint and sick,
        All exposed to burning sky,
    Massa bids me grass to pick,
        And I now am near to die.

    What and if to death he send me,
70   Savage murder tho' it be,
    British Law shall not befriend me,
        They protect not Slaves like me."

    Mourning thus my wretched state,
        (Ne'er may I forget the day)
75   Once in dusk of evening late
        Far from home I dar'd to stray;

    Dared, alas! with impious haste
        Towards the roaring Sea to fly;
    Death itself I longed to taste,
80   Long'd to cast me in and Die.

    There I met upon the Strand°   *shore*
        English Missionary Good;
    He had Bible book in hand,
        Which poor me no understood.

85   Led by pity from afar,
        He had left his native ground;
    Thus, if some inflict a scar,
        Others fly to cure the wound.

    Strait he pull'd me from the shore,
90   Bid me no self-murder do;
    Talk'd of state when life is o'er,
        All from Bible good and true.

    Then he led me to his Cot,°   *cottage*
        Soothed and pitied all my woe;
95   Told me 'twas the Christian's lot
        Much to suffer here below.

    Told me then of God's dear Son,
        (Strange and wondrous is the story;)
    What sad wrong to him was done,
100   Tho' he was the Lord of Glory.

    Told me too, like one who knew him,
        (Can such love as this be true?)
    How he died for them that slew him,
        Died for wretched Yamba too.

105   Freely he his mercy proffered,
        And to Sinners he was sent;

E'en to Massa pardons offered;
   O if Massa would repent!

Wicked deed full many a time
110   Sinful Yamba too hath done;
But she wails to God her crime,
    But she trusts his only Son.

O ye slaves whom Massas beat,
    Ye are stained with guilt within;
115 As ye hope for Mercy sweet,
    So forgive your Massas' sin.

And with grief when sinking low,
    Mark the Road that Yamba trod;
Think how all her pain and woe
120 Brought the Captive home to God.

Now let Yamba too adore
    Gracious Heaven's mysterious Plan;
Now I'll count thy mercies o'er,
    Flowing thro' the guilt of man.

125 Now I'll bless my cruel capture,
    (Hence I've known a Saviour's name)
Till my Grief is turn'd to Rapture,
    And I half forget the blame.

But tho' here a convert rare
130   Thanks her God for Grace divine,
Let not man the glory share,
    Sinner, still the guilt is thine.

Here an injured Slave forgives,
    There a Host for vengeance cry;
135 Here a single Yamba lives,
    There a thousand droop and die.

Duly now baptiz'd am I,
    By good Missionary Man:
Lord my nature purify
140   As no outward water can!

All my former thoughts abhorr'd
    Teach me now to pray and praise;
Joy and Glory in my Lord,
    Trust and serve him all my days.

145 Worn indeed with Grief and Pain,
    Death I now will welcome in:
O the Heavenly Prize to gain!
    O to 'scape the power of Sin!

True of heart, and meek and lowly,
150   Pure and blameless let me grow!

Holy may I be, for Holy,
    Is the place to which I go.

But tho' death this hour may find me,
    Still with Afric's love I burn;
155   (There I've left a spouse behind me)
      Still to native land I turn.

And when Yamba sinks in death,
    This my latest° prayer shall be,   *last*
While I yield my parting breath,
160   *O that Afric might be free.*

Cease, ye British Sons of murder!
    Cease from forging Afric's chain:
Mock your Saviour's name no further,
    Cease your savage lust of gain.

165 Ye that boast *"Ye rule the waves,"*
    Bid no Slave Ship soil the sea;
Ye, that *"never will be slaves,"*
    Bid poor Afric's land be free.[4]

Where ye gave to war it's birth,
170   Where your traders fix'd their den,
There go publish *"Peace on Earth,"*
    Go, proclaim *"good-will to men."*[5]

Where ye once have carried slaughter,
    Vice, and Slavery, and Sin;
175 Seiz'd on Husband, Wife, and Daughter,
    Let the Gospel enter in.

Thus, where Yamba's native home,
    Humble Hut of Rushes stood,
Oh if there should chance to roam
180   Some dear Missionary good;

Thou in Afric's distant land,
    Still shalt see the man I love;
Join him to the Christian band,
    Guide his Soul to the Realms above.

185 There no Fiend again shall sever
    Those whom God hath join'd and bless'd;
There they dwell with Him for ever,
    There *"the weary are at rest."*[6]

1795

---

4. Quoting James Thomson's imperialist hymn, *Rule Britannia*. See also page 250.
5. The angels' heralding of the birth of Jesus (Luke 2.14).
6. Job, tormented by Satan on a mission from God as a test of his faith, longs for death, where "the wicked cease from troubling; and . . . the weary be at rest" (3.17).

⊷ ⊷≋⊷ ⊷

Robert Southey
1774–1843

Author of the children's story *The Three Bears*, Robert Southey was savaged, as Poet Laureate, for his Tory politics by Byron in *Don Juan* and *The Vision of Judgment* (1822). In younger days he had been a political radical with friends William Wordsworth and Samuel Taylor Coleridge, fellow "Lake Poets." In 1794 he and Coleridge planned a utopian community, Pantisocracy, on the banks of the Susquehanna in Pennsylvania. The poets agreed to abolish private property, but the plan fell apart on a disagreement over whether to have servants. Throughout the 1790s and into the next decade, Southey wrote several political works, including *Wat Tyler* (1794), a drama about the leader of the English Peasants' Revolt of 1381, and *Joan of Arc* (1796), an epic about the French heroine as martyred champion of liberty. His abolitionist *Poems Concerning the Slave-Trade*, six sonnets and a ballad, written in 1798 and published in 1799, emphasize the moral and physical effects of the trade on the slave-ship crews, themselves often kidnapped like slaves and pressed into service.

For Southey's poem on Wollstonecraft, see page 328.

from Poems Concerning the Slave-Trade

Sonnet III

Oh he is worn with toil! the big drops run
    Down his dark cheek; hold—hold thy merciless hand,
    Pale tyrant! for, beneath thy hard command
O'er wearied Nature sinks. The scorching Sun,
5   As pityless as proud Prosperity,
    Darts on him his full beams; gasping he lies
    Arraigning with his looks the patient skies,
While that inhuman trader lifts on high
    The mangling scourge. O ye who at your ease
10   Sip the blood-sweetened beverage![1] thoughts like these
Haply ye scorn: I thank thee Gracious God,
    That I do feel upon my cheek the glow
Of indignation, when beneath the rod
    A sable brother writhes in silent woe.

Sonnet IV

'Tis night: the mercenary tyrants sleep
    As undisturb'd as Justice! but no more
    The wretched Slave, as on his native shore,
Rests on his reedy couch: he wakes to weep!
5   Tho' thro' the toil and anguish of the day
    No tear escap'd him, not one suffering groan
    Beneath the twisted thong, he weeps alone
In bitterness; thinking that far away
Tho' the gay negroes join the midnight song,
10   Tho' merriment resounds on Niger's shore,

---

1. Tea, with plantation sugar.

She whom he loves far from the chearful throng
   Stands sad and gazes from her lowly door
With dim grown eye, silent and woe-begone,
   And weeps for him who will return no more.

Sonnet V

Did then the Slave rear at last the Sword
   Of Vengeance? drench'd he deep its thirsty blade
In the cold bosom of his tyrant lord?
   Oh! who shall blame him?[1] thro' the midnight shade
5 Still o'er his tortured memory rush'd the thought
   Of every past delight; his native grove,
   Friendship's best joys, and Liberty and Love,
All lost for ever! Then remembrance wrought
His soul to madness; round his restless bed
10 Freedom's pale spectre stalk'd, with a stern smile
   Pointing the wounds of slavery, the while
She shook her chains and hung her sullen head:
No more on Heaven he calls with fruitless breath,
But sweetens with revenge, the draught of death.

Sonnet VI

High in the air expos'd the Slave is hung,
   To all the birds of Heaven, their living food!
He groans not, tho' awaked by that fierce Sun
   New torturers live to drink their parent blood!
5 He groans not, tho' the gorging Vulture tear
   The quivering fibre! hither gaze O ye
   Who tore this Man from Peace and Liberty!
Gaze hither ye who weigh with scrupulous care
The right and prudent; for beyond the grave
10 There is another world! and call to mind,
   Ere your decrees proclaim to all mankind
Murder is legalized, that there the Slave,
Before the Eternal "thunder-tongued shall plead
Against the deep damnation of your deed."[1]

1794

The Sailor Who had Served in the Slave-Trade

In September, 1798, a dissenting minister of Bristol[1] discovered a
sailor, in the neighborhood of that city, groaning and praying in a
cow-house. The circumstance which occasioned his agony of mind
is detailed in the annexed ballad, without the slightest addition or
alteration. By presenting it as a poem, the story is made more public; and such stories ought to be made as public as possible.

---

1. Vengeance is a mortal sin.
1. The murder of the king in Shakespeare's *Macbeth* (1.7.19–20).

1. In this hub of the slave trade, dissenting sects (refusing the authority of the Church of England) were active in the abolition movement.

It was a Christian minister,[2]
   Who, in the month of flowers,
Walked forth at eve amid the fields
   Near Bristol's ancient towers,—

5   When, from a lonely out-house° breathed,   *cowshed*
   He heard a voice of woe,
And groans which less might seem from pain
   Than wretchedness to flow.

Heart-rending groans they were, with words
10   Of bitterest despair,
Yet with the holy name of Christ
   Pronounced in broken prayer.

The Christian minister went in:
   A Sailor there he sees,
15   Whose hands were lifted up to heaven;
   And he was on his knees.

Nor did the Sailor, so intent,
   His entering footsteps heed;
But now "Our Father"° said, and now   *the Lord's Prayer*
20   His half-forgotten creed,—

And often on our Saviour called
   With many a bitter groan,
But in such anguish as may spring
   From deepest guilt alone.

25   The miserable man was asked
   Why he was kneeling there,
And what had been the crime that caused
   The anguish of his prayer.

"I have done a cursed thing!" he cried:
30   "It haunts me night and day;
And I have sought this lonely place
   Here undisturbed to pray.

Aboard I have no place for prayer;
   So I came here alone,
35   That I might freely kneel and pray,
   And call on Christ, and groan.

If to the mainmast-head I go,
   The Wicked One is there;
From place to place, from rope to rope,
40   He follows everywhere.

I shut my eyes,—it matters not;
   Still, still the same I see;
And, when I lie me down at night,
   'Tis always day with me.

2. Southey wrote this ballad of a haunted sailor after reading Coleridge's balladlike *Rime of the Ancyent Marinere* (1798),
echoed in the opening line. Though dated "1798" at the close, the text here is the version first published in 1815.

45   He follows, follows everywhere;
          And every place is hell:[3]
      O God! and I must go with him
          In endless fire to dwell!

      He follows, follows everywhere;
50   He's still above, below:
      Oh, tell me where to fly from him!
          Oh, tell me where to go!"

      "But tell thou," quoth the stranger then,
          "What this thy crime hath been;
55   So haply I may comfort give
          To one who grieves for sin."

      "Oh, cursed, cursed is the deed!"
          The wretched man replies;
      "And night and day, and everywhere,
60   'Tis still before my eyes.

      I sailed on board a Guinea-man,[4]
          And to the slave-coast went:
      Would that the sea had swallowed me
          When I was innocent!

65   And we took in our cargo there,—
          Three hundred negro slaves;
      And we sailed homeward merrily
          Over the ocean-waves.

      But some were sulky of the slaves,
70   And would not touch their meat;
      So therefore we were forced by threats
          And blows to make them eat.

      One woman, sulkier than the rest,
          Would still refuse her food:
75   O Jesus God! I hear her cries!
          I see her in her blood!

      The captain made me tie her up,
          And flog while he stood by;
      And then he cursed me if I stayed
80   My hand to hear her cry.

      She shrieked, she groaned: I could not spare;
          For the captain he stood by:
      Dear God! that I might rest one night
          From that poor creature's cry!

3. The curse of Milton's Satan: "Me miserable! which way
shall I fly / Infinite wrath, and infinite despair? / Which
way I fly is Hell; myself am Hell" (*Paradise Lost* 4.73–75).

4. An armed vessel used for slave-trading, named for
Guinea, an old term for the west coast of Africa, and
main source of slave cargo.

85 What woman's child a sight like that
        Could bear to look upon?
    And still the captain would not spare,
        But made me still flog on.

    She could not be more glad than I
90   When she was taken down:
    A blessed minute! 'twas the last
        That I have ever known.

    I did not close my eyes all night,
        Thinking what I had done:
95 I heard her groans, and they grew faint
        Towards the rising sun.

    She groaned and moaned, but her voice grew
        Fainter at morning tide;
    Fainter and fainter still it came,
100   Until, at noon, she died.

    They flung her overboard: poor wretch!
        She rested from her pain;
    But when, O Christ! O blessed God!
        Shall I have rest again?

105 I saw the sea close over her:
        Yet she is still in sight;
    I see her twisting everywhere;
        I see her day and night.

    Go where I will, do what I can,
110   The Wicked One I see:
    Dear Christ, have mercy on my soul!
        O God, deliver me!

    Oh, give me comfort, if you can!
        Oh, tell me where to fly!
115 Oh, tell me if there can be hope
        For one so lost as I!"

    What said the Minister of Christ?
        He bade him trust in Heaven,
    And call on Him for whose dear sake
120   All sins shall be forgiven.

    He told him of that precious blood°   *Christ's martyrdom*
        Which should all sins efface
    Told him that none are lost but they
        Who turn from proffer'd grace.

125 He bade him pray, and knelt with him,
        And joined him in his prayers;
    And some who read the dreadful tale
        Perhaps will aid with theirs.

1798   1815

◆►▣◄◆

Dorothy Wordsworth
1771–1855

Dorothy Wordsworth was an ardent advocate of abolition, and closely followed parliamentary events, writing to a friend in May 1792, "I hope you were an *immediate* abolitionist and are angry with the House of Commons for continuing the traffic in human flesh so long as till 96 but you will also rejoice that so much has been done. I hate Mr. Dundas" (the member of Parliament who created the plan to delay abolition until 1796). Her Grasmere journal records the story of a slave-ship sailor, whom she views as a collateral victim of the trade; her brother William touches obliquely on this issue in Book 4 of *The Prelude*, in his recollection of his encounter with a gaunt veteran of service in "the Tropic isles."

For more about Dorothy Wordsworth, see her principal listing, page 592.

from **The Grasmere Journals**

Monday Morning [March 15, 1802]. . . . . a sailor who was travelling from Liverpool[1] to Whitehaven called he was faint & pale when he knocked at the door, a young Man very well dressed. We sate by the kitchen fire talking with him for 2 hours—he told us most interesting stories of his life. His name was Isaac Chapel—he had been at sea since he was 15 years old. He was by trade a sail-maker. His last voyage was to the Coast of Guinea.[2] He had been on board a slave ship the Captain's name Maxwell where one man had been killed a Boy put to lodge with the pigs & was half eaten, one Boy set to watch in the hot sun till he dropped down dead. He had been cast away in North America & had travelled 30 days among the Indians where he had been well treated—He had twice swum from a King's ship in the Night & escaped, he said he would rather be in hell than be pressed.[3] He was now going to wait in England to appear against Captain Maxwell. "O he's a Rascal, Sir, he ought to be put in the papers!" The poor man had not been in bed since Friday Night—he left Liverpool at 2 o'clock on Saturday morning, he had called at a farm house to beg victuals & had been refused. The woman said she would give him nothing. "Won't you? Then I can't help it." He was excessively like my Brother John.[4]

◆►▣◄◆

Thomas Clarkson
1760–1846

"The grand mover of the main efforts for the abolition of the Slave Trade," in Dorothy Wordsworth's phrase, Thomas Clarkson was the hero of the movement. In 1785, while a student at Cambridge University, he wrote a prize-winning essay, *On the Slavery and Commerce of the Human Species*, its moral arguments supported with a litany of atrocities documented in the West Indies. When it was published in 1786, one slave owner protested, "I declare to God, I do not believe that a series of more abominable falsehoods ever blotted a page in the wide history of

1. Another hub of the slave trade.
2. West coast of Africa.
3. Kidnapped and forced into service, a kind of white

male slavery.
4. John Wordsworth was captain of a merchant vessel; he would drown in a shipwreck in 1805.

human depravity!" The next year, Clarkson joined with the English Quakers' Anti-Slavery Society, and at its behest began an arduous investigation of atrocities, centering his research in Bristol and Liverpool, where investors were financing and thriving on the trade. Often at great personal risk, Clarkson gathered detailed information, from the devastating effects on the seamen impressed into the brutal service, to the abuse of the slaves and the conditions aboard ship, to the conduct of the slave-markets. His labor supplied William Wilberforce with material for his parliamentary campaign. In the 1790s, Clarkson traveled to France to urge the Revolutionary government to abolish its slave trade and colonial slavery, agitated in England for a boycott of West Indian sugar and tea, and continued to document the atrocities that the planters' lobby continued to deny and excoriate as falsehoods, working himself into physical collapse in 1794. His most famous work, the *History of . . . the Abolition of the African Slave-Trade* (1808), helped fuel the movement for the abolition of slavery itself, a cause in which Clarkson remained active.

from The History of the Rise, Progress, & Accomplishment of the Abolition of the African Slave-Trade by the British Parliament

["THE NATURE OF THE EVIL"]

To see it as it has been shown to arise in the first case, let us suppose ourselves on the Continent [Africa]. Well then: We are landed; we are already upon our travels; we have just passed through one forest; we are now come to a more open place, which indicates an approach to habitations. And what object is that, which first obtrudes itself upon our sight? Who is that wretched woman, whom we discover under that noble tree, wringing her hands, and beating her breast, as if in the agonies of despair? Three days has she been there at intervals to look and to watch, and this is the fourth morning, and no tidings of her children yet. Beneath its spreading boughs they were accustomed to play: But alas! the savage man-stealer interrupted their playful mirth, and has taken them for ever from her sight.

But let us leave the cries of this unfortunate woman, and hasten into another district: And what do we first see here? Who is he that just now started across the narrow pathway, as if afraid of a human face? What is that sudden rustling among the leaves? Why are those persons flying from our approach, and hiding themselves in yon darkest thicket? Behold, as we get into the plain, a deserted village! The rice-field has been just trodden down around it. An aged man, venerable by his silver beard, lies wounded and dying near the threshold of his hut. War, suddenly instigated by avarice, has just visited the dwellings which we see. The old have been butchered, because unfit for slavery, and the young have been carried off, except such as have fallen in the conflict, or have escaped among the woods behind us. * * *

Let us examine the state of the unhappy Africans, reduced to slavery in this manner, while on board the vessels, which are to convey them across the ocean to other lands. And here I must observe at once, that, as far as this part of the evil is concerned, I am at a loss to describe it. Where shall I find words to express properly their sorrow, as arising from the reflection of being parted for ever from their friends, their relatives, and their country? Where shall I find language to paint in appropriate colours the horror of mind brought on by thoughts of their future unknown destination, of which they can augur nothing but misery from all that they have yet seen? How shall I make known their situation, while labouring under painful disease, or while struggling in the suffocating holds of their prisons, like animals inclosed in an exhausted receiver?[1] How

---

1. Emptied tank.

shall I describe their feelings as exposed to all the personal indignities, which lawless appetite or brutal passion may suggest? How shall I exhibit their sufferings as determining to refuse sustenance and die, or as resolving to break their chains, and, disdaining to live as slaves, to punish their oppressors? How shall I give an idea of their agony, when under various punishments and tortures for their reputed crimes? Indeed every part of this subject defies my powers, and I must therefore satisfy myself and the reader with a general representation, or in the words of a celebrated member of Parliament [Wilberforce], that "Never was so much human suffering condensed in so small a space."

I come now to the evil, * * * the situation of the unhappy victims of the trade, when their painful voyages are over, or after they have been landed upon their destined shores. And here we are to view them first under the degrading light of cattle.[2] We are to see them examined, handled, selected, separated, and sold. Alas! relatives are separated from relatives, as if, like cattle, they had no rational intellect, no power of feeling the nearness of relationship, nor sense of the duties belonging to the ties of life! We are next to see them labouring, and this for the benefit of those, to whom they are under no obligation, by any law either natural or divine, to obey. We are to see them, if refusing the commands of their purchasers, however weary, or feeble, or indisposed, subject to corporal punishments, and, if forcibly resisting them, to death. We are to see them in a state of general degradation and misery. The knowledge, which their oppressors have of their own crime in having violated the rights of nature, and of the disposition of the injured to seek all opportunities of revenge, produces a fear which dictates to them the necessity of a system of treatment by which they shall keep up a wide distinction between the two, and by which the noble feelings of the latter shall be kept down, and their spirits broken. We are to see them again subject to individual persecution, as anger, or malice, or any bad passion may suggest. Hence the whip; the chain; the iron-collar. Hence the various modes of private torture, of which so many accounts have been truly given. Nor can such horrible cruelties be discovered so as to be made punishable, while the testimony of any number of the oppressed is invalid against the oppressors, however they may be offences against the laws. And; lastly, we are to see their innocent offspring, against whose personal liberty the shadow of an argument cannot be advanced, inheriting all the miseries of their parents' lot.

* * * While the miseries endured by the unfortunate Africans excite our pity on the one hand, the vices, which are connected with them, provoke our indignation and abhorrence on the other. The Slave-trade, in this point of view, must strike us as an immense mass of evil on account of the criminality attached to it. * * * Is not that man made morally worse, who is induced to become a tyger to his species, or who, instigated by avarice, lies in wait in the thicket to get possession of his fellow-man? Is no injustice manifest in the land, where the prince, unfaithful to his duty, seizes his innocent subjects, and sells them for slaves? Are no moral evils produced among those communities, which make war upon other communities for the sake of plunder, and without any previous provocation or offence?

* * * The counterpart of the evil is to be seen in the conduct of those, who purchase the miserable natives in their own country, and convey them to distant lands. And here questions, similar to the former, may be asked. Do they experience no

2. Clarkson's analogy to cattle evokes "chattel," a synonym for "slave" that shares an etymology with "cattle" and "capital."

corruption of their nature, or become chargeable with no violation of right, who, when they go with their ships to this continent, know the enormities which their visits there will occasion, who buy their fellow-creature man, and this, knowing the way in which he comes into their hands, and who chain, and imprison, and scourge him? Do the moral feelings of those persons escape without injury, whose hearts are hardened? And can the hearts of those be otherwise than hardened, who are familiar with the tears and groans of innocent strangers forcibly torn away from every thing that is dear to them in life, who are accustomed to see them on board their vessels in a state of suffocation and in the agonies of despair, and who are themselves in the habits of the cruel use of arbitrary power?

The counterpart of the evil in its third branch is to be seen in the conduct of those, who, when these miserable people have been landed, purchase and carry them to their respective homes. And let us see whether a mass of wickedness is not generated also in the present case. Can those have nothing to answer for, who separate the faithful ties which nature and religion have created? Can their feelings be otherwise than corrupted, who consider their fellow-creatures as brutes, or treat those as cattle, who may become the temples of the Holy Spirit, and in whom the Divinity disdains not himself to dwell? Is there no injustice in forcing men to labour without wages? Is there no breach of duty, when we are commanded to clothe the naked, and feed the hungry, and visit the sick and in prison, in exposing them to want, in torturing them by cruel punishment, and in grinding them down by hard labour, so as to shorten their days? Is there no crime in adopting a system, which keeps down all the noble faculties of their souls, and which positively debases and corrupts their nature? Is there no crime in perpetuating these evils among their innocent offspring? And finally, besides all these crimes, is there not naturally in the familiar sight of the exercise, but more especially in the exercise itself, of uncontrolled power, that which vitiates the internal man? In seeing misery stalk daily over the land, do not all become insensibly hardened? By giving birth to that misery themselves, do they not become abandoned? In what state of society are the corrupt appetites so easily, so quickly, and so frequently indulged, and where else, by means of frequent indulgence, do these experience such a monstrous growth? Where else is the temper subject to such frequent irritation, or passion to such little controul? Yes; if the unhappy slave is in an unfortunate situation, so is the tyrant who holds him. * * *

If we were to take the vast extent of space occupied by these crimes and sufferings from the heart of Africa to its shores, and that which they filled on the continent of America and the islands adjacent, and were to join the crimes and sufferings in one to those in the other by the crimes and sufferings which took place in the track of the vessels successively crossing the Atlantic, we should behold a vast belt as it were of physical and moral evil, reaching through land and ocean to the length of nearly half the circle of the globe.

[The Recruitment of Seamen for the Slave-Ships]

The young mariner if a stranger to the port [Bristol] and unacquainted with the nature of the Slave-trade, was sure to be picked up. The novelty of the voyages, the superiority of the wages in this over any other trades, and the privileges of various kinds, were set before him. Gulled in this manner he was frequently enticed to the boat, which was waiting to carry him away. If these prospects did not attract him, he was plied with liquor till he became intoxicated, when a bargain was made over him between the landlord and the mate. After this his senses were kept in such a constant state of stupefaction by the liquor, that in time the former might do with him what he pleased. Seamen also were boarded in these houses, who, when the slave-ships were going out, but at no other time, were encouraged to spend more than they had money to pay for; and to these, when they had thus exceeded, but one alternative was given, namely, a slave-vessel, or a jail. These distressing scenes I found myself obliged frequently to witness, for I was no less than nineteen times occupied in making these hateful rounds. And I can say from my own experience, and all the information I could collect from Thompson and others, that no such practices were in use to obtain seamen for other trades.

The treatment of the seamen employed in the Slave-trade had so deeply interested me, and now the manner of procuring them, that I was determined to make myself acquainted with their whole history; for I found by report, that they were not only personally ill-treated, * * * but that they were robbed by artifice of those wages, which had been held up to them as so superior in this service. * * * On whatever branch of the system I turned my eyes, I found it equally barbarous. The trade was, in short, one mass of iniquity from the beginning to the end. * * *

In pursuing another object, which was that of going on board the slave-ships, and learning their construction and dimensions, I was greatly struck, and indeed affected, by the appearance of two little sloops, which were fitting out for Africa, the one of only twenty-five tons, which was said to be destined to carry seventy; and the other of only eleven, which was said to be destined to carry thirty slaves. I was told also that which was more affecting, namely, that these were not to act as tenders on the coast, by going up and down the rivers, and receiving three or four slaves at a time, and then carrying them to a large ship, which was to take them to the West Indies, but that it was actually intended, that they should transport their own slaves themselves. * * * In the vessel of twenty-five tons, the length of the upper part of the hold, or roof, of the room, where the seventy slaves were to be stowed, was but little better than ten yards, or thirty-one feet. The greatest breadth of the bottom, or floor, was ten feet four inches, and the least five. Hence, a grown person must sit down all the voyage, and contract his limbs within the narrow limits of three square feet. In the vessel of eleven tons, the length of the room for the thirty slaves was twenty-two feet. The greatest breadth of the floor was eight, and the least four. The whole height from the keel to the beam was but five feet eight inches, three feet of which were occupied by ballast, cargo, and provisions, so that two feet eight inches remained only as the height between the decks. Hence, each slave would have only four square feet to sit in, and, when in this posture, his head, if he were a full-grown person, would touch the ceiling, or upper deck.

[CLARKSON'S NIGHTMARES]

At Bristol my feelings had been harassed by the cruel treatment of the seamen, which had come to my knowledge there: but now I was doomed to see this treatment over again in many other melancholy instances; and additionally to take in the various sufferings of the unhappy slaves. These accounts I could seldom get time to read till late in the evening, and sometimes not till midnight, when the letters containing them were to be answered. The effect of these accounts was in some instances to overwhelm me for a time in tears, and in others to produce a vivid indignation, which affected my whole frame. Recovering from these, I walked up and down the room. I felt fresh vigour, and made new determinations of perpetual warfare against this impious trade. I implored strength that I might proceed. I then sat down, and continued my work as long as my wearied eyes would permit me to see. Having been agitated in this manner, I went to bed: but my rest was frequently broken by the visions which floated before me. When I awoke, these renewed themselves to me, and they flitted about with me for the remainder of the day. Thus I was kept continually harassed: my mind was confined to one gloomy and heart-breaking subject for months. It had no respite, and my health began now materially to suffer.

[THE DEFENSE OF THE TRADE IN PARLIAMENT]

The public papers began to be filled with such statements as were thought most likely to influence the members of the house of commons, previously to the discussion of the question [the bill for abolition].

The first impression attempted to be made upon them was with respect to the slaves themselves. It was contended, and attempted to be shown by the revival of the old argument of human sacrifices in Africa, that these were better off in the islands than in their own country. It was contended also, that they were people of very inferior capacities, and but little removed from the brute creation; whence an inference was drawn, that their treatment, against which so much clamour had arisen, was adapted to their intellect and feelings.

The next attempt was to degrade the abolitionists in the opinion of the house, by showing the wildness and absurdity of their schemes. It was again insisted upon that emancipation was the real object of the former; so that thousands of slaves would be let loose in the islands to rob or perish, and who could never be brought back again into habits of useful industry.

An attempt was then made to excite their pity in behalf of the planters. The abolition, it was said, would produce insurrections among the slaves. But insurrections would produce the massacre of their masters; and, if any of these should happily escape from butchery, they would be reserved only for ruin.

An appeal was then made to them on the ground of their own interest and of that of the people, whom they represented. It was stated that the ruin of the islands would be the ruin of themselves and of the country. Its revenue would be half annihilated. Its naval strength would decay. Merchants, manufacturers and others would come to beggary. But in this deplorable situation they would expect to be indemnified for their losses. Compensation indeed must follow. It could not be withheld. But what would be the amount of it? The country would have no less than from eighty to a hundred millions to pay the sufferers; and it would be driven to such distress in paying this sum as it had never before experienced.

The last attempt was to show them that a regulation of the trade was all that was now wanted. While this would remedy the evils complained of, it would prevent the mischief which would assuredly follow the abolition. The planters had already done their part. The assemblies of the different islands had most of them made wholesome laws upon the subject. The very bills passed for this purpose in Jamaica and Grenada had arrived in England, and might be seen by the public: the great grievances had been redressed: no slave could now be mutilated or wantonly killed by his owner; one man could not now maltreat, or bruise, or wound the slave of another; the aged could not now be turned off to perish by hunger. There were laws also relative to the better feeding and clothing of the slaves. It remained only that the trade to Africa should be put under as wise and humane regulations as the slavery in the islands had undergone.

[COUNTER-TESTIMONY FROM A SLAVE-SHIP INVESTIGATOR]

Having said thus much on the subject of procuring slaves in Africa, he would now go to that of the transportation of them. * * * This was the most wretched part of the whole subject. He was incapable of impressing the house with what he felt upon it. A description of their conveyance was impossible. So much misery condensed in so little room was more than the human imagination had ever before conceived. Think only of six hundred persons linked together, trying to get rid of each other, crammed in a close vessel with every object that was nauseous and disgusting, diseased, and struggling with all the varieties of wretchedness. It seemed impossible to add any thing more to human misery. Yet shocking as this description must be felt to be by every man, the transportation had been described by several witnesses from Liverpool to be a comfortable conveyance. Mr. Norris had painted the accommodations on board a slaveship in the most glowing colours. He had represented them in a manner which would have exceeded his attempts at praise of the most luxurious scenes. Their apartments, he said, were fitted up as advantageously for them as circumstances could possibly admit: they had several meals a day; some, of their own country provisions, with the best sauces of African cookery; and, by way of variety, another meal of pulse, according to the European taste. After breakfast they had water to wash themselves, while their apartments were perfumed with frankincense and lime-juice. Before dinner they were amused after the manner of their country: instruments of music were introduced: the song and the dance were promoted: games of chance were furnished them: the men played and sang, while the women and girls made fanciful ornaments from beads, with which they were plentifully supplied. They were indulged in all their little fancies, and kept in sprightly humour. Another of them had said, when the sailors were flogged, it was out of the hearing of the Africans, lest it should depress their spirits. He by no means wished to say that such descriptions were wilful misrepresentations. If they were not, it proved that interest or prejudice was capable of spreading a film over the eyes thick enough to occasion total blindness.

Others, however, and these men of the greatest veracity, had given a different account. What would the house think, when by the concurring testimony of these the true history was laid open? The slaves who had been described as rejoicing in their captivity, were so wrung with misery at leaving their country, that it was the constant practice to set sail in the night, lest they should know the moment of their departure. With respect to their accommodation, the right ancle of one was fastened to the left ancle of another by an iron fetter; and if they were turbulent, by another on the wrists. Instead of the apartments described, they were placed in niches, and along the decks, in such a manner, that it was impossible for any one to pass among them, however careful he might be, without treading upon them. Sir George Yonge had testified, that in a slave-ship, on board of which he went, and which had not completed her cargo by two hundred and fifty, instead of the scent of frankincense being perceptible to the nostrils, the stench was intolerable. The allowance of water was so deficient, that the slaves were frequently found gasping for life, and almost suffocated. The pulse with which they had been said to be favoured, were absolutely English horse-beans. The legislature of Jamaica had stated the scantiness both of water and provisions, as a subject which called for the interference of parliament. As Mr. Norris had said, the song and the dance were promoted, he could not pass over these expressions without telling the house what they meant. It would have been much more fair if he himself had explained the word *promoted*. The truth was,

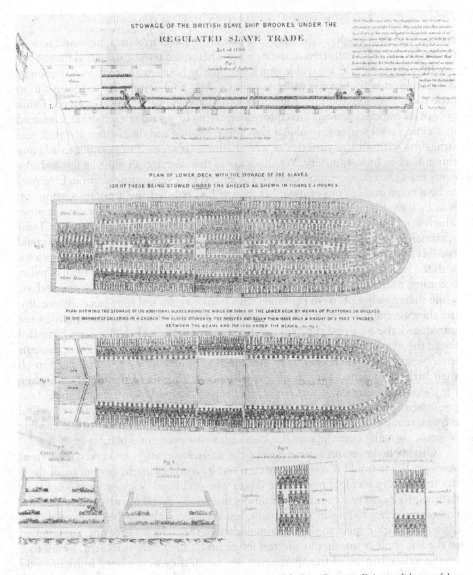

Packing methods on a slave ship. Illustration to *The History of the Rise, Progress, & Accomplishment of the Abolition of the African Slave-Trade by the British Parliament*, by Thomas Clarkson, 1808. The top image is "tight-packing"; the lower, a more "humane" arrangement.

that, for the sake of exercise, these miserable wretches, loaded with chains and oppressed with disease, were forced to dance by the terror of the lash, and sometimes by the actual use of it. "I," said one of the evidences, "was employed to dance the men, while another person danced the women." Such then was the meaning of the word *promoted*; and it might also be observed with respect to food, that instruments were sometimes carried out, in order to force them to eat; which was the same sort of proof, how much they enjoyed themselves in this instance also. With respect to their singing, it consisted of songs of lamentation for the loss of their country. While they sung they were in tears: so that one of the captains, more humane probably than the rest, threatened a woman with a flogging because the mournfulness of her song was too painful for his feelings. Perhaps he could not give a better proof of the sufferings of these injured people during their passage, than by stating the mortality which accompanied it. This was a species of evidence which was infallible on this occasion. Death was a witness which could not deceive them; and the proportion of deaths would not only confirm, but, if possible, even aggravate our suspicion of the misery of the transit. It would be found, upon an average of all the ships, upon which evidence had been given, that, exclusively of such as perished before they sailed from Africa, not less than twelve and a half per cent. died on their passage: besides these, the Jamaica report stated that four and a half per cent. died while in the harbours, or on shore before the day of sale, which was only about the space of twelve or fourteen days after their arrival there; and one third more died in the seasoning:[3] and this in a climate exactly similar to their own, and where, as some of the witnesses pretended, they were healthy and happy. Thus, out of every lot of one hundred, shipped from Africa, seventeen died in about nine weeks, and not more than fifty lived to become effective labourers in our islands.

["REFLECTIONS ON THIS GREAT EVENT"]

With respect to the end obtained by this contest, or the great measure of the abolition of the Slave-trade as it has now passed, I know not how to appreciate its importance. To our own country, indeed, it is invaluable. We have lived, in consequence of it, to see the day, when it has been recorded as a principle in our legislation, that commerce itself shall have its moral boundaries. We have lived to see the day, when we are likely to be delivered from the contagion of the most barbarous opinions. * * * though nature shrinks from pain, and compassion is engendered in us when we see it become the portion of others, yet what is physical suffering compared with moral guilt? The misery of the oppressed is, in the first place, not contagious like the crime of the oppressor. Nor is the mischief, which it generates, either so frightful or so pernicious. The body, though under affliction, may retain its shape; and, if it even perish, what is the loss of it but of worthless dust? But when the moral springs of the mind are poisoned, we lose the most excellent part of the constitution of our nature, and the divine image is no longer perceptible in us. Nor are the two evils of similar duration. By a decree of Providence, for which we cannot be too thankful, we are made mortal. Hence the torments of the oppressor are but temporary; whereas the immortal part of us, when once corrupted, may carry its pollutions with it into another world.

But independently of the quantity of physical suffering and the innumerable avenues to vice in more than a quarter of the globe, which this great measure will cut off, there are yet blessings, which we have reason to consider as likely to flow from it. Among these we cannot overlook the great probability, that Africa, now freed from the vicious and barbarous effects of this traffic, may be in a better state to comprehend and receive the sublime truths of the Christian religion. Nor can we overlook the probability, that, a new system of treatment necessarily springing up in our islands, the same bright sun of consolation may visit her children there. But here a

3. Breaking-in.

new hope rises to our view. Who knows but that emancipation, like a beautiful plant, may, in its due season, rise out of the ashes of the abolition of the Slave-trade, and that, when its own intrinsic value shall be known, the seed of it may be planted in other lands? And looking at the subject in this point of view, we cannot but be struck with the wonderful concurrence of events as previously necessary for this purpose, namely, that two nations, England and America, the mother and the child, should, in the same month of the same year, have abolished this impious traffic; nations, which at this moment have more than a million of subjects within their jurisdiction to partake of the blessing; and one of which, on account of her local situation and increasing power, is likely in time to give, if not law, at least a tone to the manners and customs of the great continent, on which she is situated.

Reader! Thou art now acquainted with the history of this contest! Rejoice in the manner of its termination! And, if thou feelest grateful for the event, retire within thy closet,[4] and pour out thy thanksgivings to the Almighty for this his unspeakable act of mercy to thy oppressed fellow-creatures.

William Wordsworth
1770–1850

When they were all living in the Lake District of England, the Wordsworths and Coleridge became close friends with Thomas Clarkson and his wife, and were inspired by Clarkson's intense commitment to abolition. William Wordsworth's sonnet *To Thomas Clarkson*, published in 1807, honors his heroic persistence in behalf of the Abolition Bill. *To Toussaint L'Ouverture* honors François Dominique Toussaint (1743?–1803), a self-educated slave freed shortly before the 1791 revolt in San Domingo, to become a leader of the revolutionaries (dubbed "L'Ouverture" for his skill in "opening" gaps in enemy ranks, he adopted this as a surname). In 1801, he conquered San Domingo and became governor of the whole island. When, in 1802, he resisted Napoleon's attempt to re-establish French rule and slavery, he was arrested and dungeoned in the French Alps, where he died in April 1803, after ten months of cold and hunger. Wordsworth published his sonnet in *The Morning Post*, 2 February 1803, and then in *Poems* of 1807 under "Sonnets Dedicated to Liberty." *Humanity*—written decades later, in 1829, before colonial emancipation, and published soon after, in 1835—demonstrates his unwavering moral revulsion at slavery and contempt for the economic justifications. But in a letter of 1833, he joined the now Tory Poet Laureate Southey in declining to contribute to a volume of antislavery poetry, arguing that the planters have been too one-sidedly villainized.

For more about Wordsworth, see his principal listing on page 410.

To Toussaint L'Ouverture

> Toussaint, the most unhappy man of men!
> Whether the rural Milk-maid by her Cow
> Sing in thy hearing, or thou liest now
> Alone in some deep dungeon's earless den,
> 5   O miserable Chieftain! where and when
> Wilt thou find patience? Yet die not; be thou

---

4. Private sitting room. This is the closing paragraph of the *History*.

Life to thyself in death; with chearful brow:
Live, loving death, nor let one thought in ten
Be painful to thee. Thou hast left behind
10   Powers that will work for thee; air, earth, and skies;
There's not a breathing of the common wind
That will forget thee; thou hast great allies;
Thy friends are exultations, agonies,
And love, and Man's unconquerable mind.

1802   2 February 1803
                                                 W.L.D.[1]

To Thomas Clarkson
On the final passing of the Bill for the Abolition of the Slave Trade, March, 1807

Clarkson! it was an obstinate Hill to climb;
How toilsome, nay how dire it was, by Thee
Is known,—by none, perhaps, so feelingly;
But Thou, who, starting in thy fervent prime,
5   Didst first lead forth this pilgrimage sublime,
Hast heard the constant Voice its charge repeat,
Which, out of thy young heart's oracular seat,
First roused thee.—O true yoke-fellow of Time
With unabating effort, see, the palm
10   Is won, and by all Nations shall be worn!
The bloody Writing is for ever torn,
And Thou henceforth shalt have a good Man's calm,
A great Man's happiness; thy zeal shall find
Repose at length, firm Friend of human kind!

1807   1807

from The Prelude[1]

When to my native Land,
(After a whole year's absence) I return'd
I found the air yet busy with the stir
Of a contention which had been rais'd up
205   Against the Traffickers in Negro blood,
An effort, which though baffled, nevertheless
Had call'd back old forgotten principles
Dismiss'd from service, had diffus'd some truths
And more of virtuous feeling through the heart

1. According to the poet's brother-in-law, the initials stand for "Wordsworthius Libertari Dedicavit" (dedicated to liberty); he signed seven sonnets this way in 1803.
1. From Book 10, written c. 1805; a revised text appears in the version of The Prelude published in 1850, a moment when it could address the abolition movement in the United States, where The Prelude was also published. For the verse immediately preceding, see page 523.

210   Of the English People.[2] And no few of those
    So numerous (little less in verity
    Than a whole Nation crying with one voice)
    Who had been cross'd in this their just intent
    And righteous hope, thereby were well prepared
215   To let that journey sleep a while and join
    Whatever other Caravan appear'd
    To travel forward towards Liberty
    With more success. For me that strife had ne'er
    Fasten'd on my affections, nor did now
220   Its unsuccessful issue much excite
    My sorrow, having laid this faith to heart,
    That if France prosper'd good Men would not long
    Pay fruitless worship to humanity,
    And this most rotten branch of human shame,
225   Object, as seem'd, of a superfluous pains,
    Would fall together with its parent tree.

1805   1926

from Humanity

    Though cold as winter, gloomy as the grave,
    Stone-walls a prisoner make, but not a slave.[1]
    Shall man assume a property in man?[2]
80   Lay on the moral will a withering ban?
    Shame that our laws at distance still protect
    Enormities, which they at home reject!
    "Slaves cannot breathe in England"[3]—yet that boast
    Is but a mockery! when from coast to coast,
85   Though *fettered* slave be none, her floors and soil
    Groan underneath a weight of slavish toil,
    For the poor Many, measured out by rules
    Fetched with cupidity from heartless schools,
    That to an Idol, falsely called "the Wealth
90   Of Nations,"[4] sacrifice a People's health,
    Body and mind and soul; a thirst so keen
    Is ever urging on the vast machine
    Of sleepless Labor, 'mid whose dizzy wheels
    The Power least prized is that which thinks and feels.

1829   1835

---

2. Wordsworth returned from revolutionary France late in 1792; the "effort" is Wilberforce's unsuccessful 1793 bill for abolition.

1. Revising Lovelace's famous declaration in *To Althea, from Prison* (1649): "Stone walls do not a prison make, / Nor iron bars a cage; / . . . I have freedom in my love, / And in my soul am free" (25ff).

2. A reference to Paine's statement in *The Rights of Man* that "Man has no property in man" (see page 132).

3. The Mansfield Decision of 1772 rejected the claims that "neither the air of England is too pure for a slave to breathe in, nor the laws of England have rejected servitude."

4. An influential argument for laissez-faire capitalism (self-interest, unrestricted by law, best serves the public welfare) put forth in Adam Smith's *Inquiry into the Nature and Causes of the Wealth of Nations* (1776).

Letter to Mary Ann Rawson[1]

[c. May 1833]

Dear Madam,

Your letter which I lose no time in replying to, has placed me under some embarrassment, as I happen to possess some Mss verses of my own[2] upon the subject to which you solicit my attention. But I frankly own to you, that neither with respect to this subject nor to the kindred one, the Slavery of the children in the Factories,[3] which is adverted to in the same Poem, am I prepared to add to the excitement already existing in the public mind upon these, and so many other points of legislation and government. Poetry, if good for any thing, must appeal forcibly to the Imagination and the feelings; but what at this period we want above every thing, is patient examination and sober judgement. It can scarcely be necessary to add that my mind revolts as strongly as any one's can, from the law that permits one human being to sell another. It is in principle monstrous, but it is not the worst thing in human nature. Let precipitate advocates for its destruction bear this in mind. But I will not enter farther into the question than to say, that there are three parties—the Slave—the Slave owner—and the imperial Parliament, or rather the people of the British Islands, acting through that Organ. Surely the course at present pursued is hasty, intemperate, and likely to lead to gross injustice. Who in fact are most to blame? the people—who, by their legislation, have sanctioned not to say encouraged, slavery. But now we are turning round at once upon the planters, and heaping upon them indignation without measure, as if we wished that the Slaves should believe that their Masters alone were culpable—and they alone fit objects of complaint and resentment.

Excuse haste and believe me Dear Madam
respectfully yours,
Wm Wordsworth

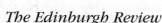

The Edinburgh Review

One of the most influential quarterlies of the day, the *Edinburgh Review* was edited by its cofounder Francis Jeffrey (1773–1850) from its inception in 1802 until 1829. Although Jeffrey tended to conservative literary judgment (famously attacking the Lake School for presenting peasants sympathetically), the *Edinburgh* was liberal in political opinion and supported the Whigs in their parliamentary campaign for reform. Among its other cofounders, Henry Brougham (1778–1868) was a leader in the abolitionist movement, and Sydney Smith (1771–1845) excoriated the slave trade as an "enormous wickedness." Although England had

---

1. An original member of the Sheffield Female Anti-Slavery Society (founded in 1825), Rawson began in 1826 to collect pieces for an anthology of antislavery prose and poetry, *The Bow in the Cloud*, which she published in 1834, after colonial Emancipation, in a small edition of 500.
2. *Humanity*, above.

3. A parliamentary commission issued a shocking report in 1832 about child labor in factories that led to the "Act of 1833," preventing those under nine from such labor and limited those under 13 to 48 hours a week, with no more than nine hours in any one day; it also required these children to receive at least two hours of schooling a day. It failed in its goal to secure a ten-hour day for teenagers.

abolished the trade in 1807, other countries, including France and the United States, had not, and slavery was still legal in England's colonies. Reports such as the one below (October 1821) kept public attention focused on the atrocities.

from **Abstract of the Information laid on the Table of the House of Commons, on the Subject of the Slave Trade**

The French ship Le Rodeur, of two hundred tons burden, sailed from the port of Havre for the river Calabar on the coast of Africa, where she arrived after a prosperous voyage, and anchored at Bonny on the fourteenth of March. Her crew, of twenty-two men, had enjoyed perfect health; and this continued during her stay of three weeks, while she received on board one hundred and sixty negroes, with whom she set sail for Guadaloupe[1] on the sixth of April. No traces of any epidemy had been perceived among the natives; the cargo (as it is called), no more than the crew, exhibited any symptoms of disease; and the first fortnight of the voyage to the West Indies promised a continuance of all the success which had seemed to attend the earlier stages of the expedition. The vessel had now approached the line,[2] when a frightful malady broke out. At first the symptoms were slight, little more than a redness of the eyes; and this being confined to the negroes, was ascribed to the want of air in the hold, and the narrow space between the decks, into which so large a number of those unhappy beings were crowded; something, too, was imagined to arise from the scarcity of water, which had thus early begun to be felt, and pressed chiefly upon the slaves; for they were allowed only eight ounces, which was soon reduced to half a wine glass per day. By the surgeon's advice, therefore, they were suffered, for the first time, to breathe the purer air upon the deck, where they were brought in succession; but many of these poor creatures being affected with that mighty desire of returning to their native country, which is so strong as to form a disease, termed *Nostalgia* by the physicians, no sooner found they were at liberty, than they threw themselves into the sea, locked in each other's arms, in the vain hope, known to prevail among them, of thus being swiftly transported again to their homes. With the view of counteracting this propensity, the Captain ordered several who were stopt in the attempt, to be shot or hanged in the sight of their companions; but this terrible example was unavailing to deter them; and it became necessary, once more, to confine them entirely to the hold.

    The disease proved to be a virulent ophthalmia, and it now spread with irresistible rapidity among the Africans, all of whom were seized; but it soon attacked the crew; and its ravages were attended, perhaps its violence exasperated, by a dysentery, which the use of rain-water was found to have produced. A sailor who slept near the hatch communicating with the hold, was the first who caught it; next day a landsman was taken ill; and in three days more, the Captain and almost all the rest of the crew were infected. The resources of medicine were tried in vain; the sufferings of the people, and the number of the blind, were daily increasing; and they were in constant expectation that the negroes, taking advantage of their numbers, would rise and destroy them. From this danger they were only saved by the mutual hatred of the

---

1. In the Caribbean.   2. Equator.

tribes to which these unfortunate beings belonged, and which was so fierce and inextinguishable, that, even under the load of chains and sickness, they were ready every instant, in their fury, to tear one another in pieces. * * *

The consternation now became general and horrid; but it did not preclude calculation; for, thirty-six of the negroes having become quite blind, were *thrown into the sea and drowned,* in order to save the expense of supporting slaves rendered unsaleable, and to obtain grounds for a claim against the under-writers.[3] * * *

The reader may think that we have been going back to the times when the slave-trade flourished under the protection of the law in England and France; and that we have been citing from the writings of some political author, some advocate for the abolition. Not so. All these horrors darken the history of the year 1819; and the tale is almost all told incidentally by the scientific compilers of a Medical Journal. Yes—in 1819 * * * twelve years after England had forbidden the traffic—eight years after she had declared it a crime—and four years after France, first by law, and then by solemn treaty, had become a party to its positive, unqualified, immediate abolition.

Dreadful as are the scenes disclosed in the case of the Rodeur, there are even worse horrors in the Parliamentary Papers of which the abstract lies before us. In March 1820, the Tartar, commanded by Sir George Collier, boarded a French vessel, called La Jeune Estelle of Martinique, after a long chase. The captain admitted that he had been engaged in the slave-trade, but denied that he had any slaves on board, declaring that he had been plundered of his cargo. The English officers, however, observed that all the French seamen appeared agitated and alarmed; and this led to an examination of the hold. Nothing, however, was found; and they would have departed with the belief that the captain's story was a true one, had not a sailor happened to strike a cask, and hear, or fancy he heard, a faint voice issue from within. The cask was opened, and two negro girls were found crammed into it, and in the last stage of suffocation. Being brought upon the deck of the Tartar, they were recognised by a person who had before seen them in the possession of an American who had died on the coast. An investigation now took place; and it was ascertained that they formed part of a cargo of fourteen slaves, whom the French captain had carried off by an attack which he and his crew made on the American's property after his decease. This led to a new search of the slave-ship for the other twelve, whom he was thus proved to have obtained by the robbery; when a platform was discovered, on which the negroes must have been laid in a space twenty-three inches in height, and beneath it a negro was found, not, however, one of the twelve, jammed into the crevice between two water casks. Still there were no traces of those twelve slaves; and the French captain persisted in his story, that he had been plundered by a Spanish pirate. But suddenly a most horrible idea darted across the minds of the English officers and men; they recollected that, when the chase began, they had seen several casks floating past them, which, at the time, they could not account for; but now, after the examination of the one which remained on board the Jeune Estelle, little doubt could be entertained that those casks contained the wretched slaves, whom

---

3. The notorious precedent was the case of the slave ship Zong (1781), whose captain ordered 133 weak and diseased slaves ejected into shark-infested waters in order to collect on a policy that held the insurer liable for cargo jettisoned in order to salvage the remainder. The insurance trial (not about the captain's criminal liability but the underwriter's financial liability) was presided over by Mansfield, who ruled in favor of the captain. See Color Plate 5.

the infernal monster had thus thrown overboard, to prevent the detection that would have ensued, either upon their being found in his ship, or by their bodies floating exposed on the sea. * * *

May we not then appeal to the body of our most enlightened European neighbours, and call upon them to stimulate their rulers not only to follow the example set by England and America in classing the slave-trade among heinous crimes, but to join them in that measure which, if those three great maritime powers adopt it, must speedily become the law of all nations? That the French people at large are prepared for such a step, there can be little reason to doubt. All their ablest statesmen have the most sound views upon this important question; and the remains of prejudice with respect to the means, when so generous an anxiety is entertained for the attainment of the object, must soon give way to the enlightened genius of the age; and certainly, what has passed in America, is calculated to assist in dispelling those prejudices beyond any thing we can conceive.

Our attention has, in this article, been confined to the portion of the Parliamentary Papers which treats of the French slave-trade, as out of all comparison the most important in every point of view. Much to lament and to amend is, however, contained in the correspondence with Spain, Portugal, and the Netherlands; and it is to be hoped that our Government, acting under the control of the almost unanimous opinion upon this subject entertained both by Parliament and the country, will be enabled, before long, to obtain some more satisfactory arrangements with those three powers. The late Revolutions, and the establishment of a popular constitution in Portugal and Spain, afford additional grounds for such expectations.

George Gordon, Lord Byron
1788–1824

from Detached Thoughts[1]

But there is no freedom—even for Masters—in the midst of slaves——it makes my blood boil to see the thing.—I sometimes wish that I was the Owner of Africa—to do at once—what Wilberforce will do in time—viz—sweep Slavery from her desarts—and look on upon the first dance of their Freedom.——As to political slavery—so general—it is men's own fault—if they will be slaves let them!——yet it is but "a word and a blow"—see how England formerly—France—Spain—Portugal—America—Switzerland—freed themselves!——there is no one instance of a long contest in which men did not triumph over Systems.—If Tyranny misses her first spring she is cowardly as the tiger and retires to be hunted.——

END OF PERSPECTIVES: THE ABOLITION OF SLAVERY AND THE SLAVE TRADE

---

1. Byron recorded these reflections in his journal in late 1821. He quotes *Romeo and Juliet* 3.1.41. For more about Byron, see his principal listing on page 708.

◆──◆ ◆ ◆──◆

Mary Robinson
1758–1800

As a child, Mary Darby attended a school run by Hannah More's sisters in Bristol. In her teens she married Thomas Robinson, a clerk who landed them and their daughter in debtor's prison. Her beauty and talent rescued her: under the patronage of Richard Brinsley Sheridan and David Garrick, she made her debut in 1776 as Juliet at Drury Lane Theatre, where she appeared with great success for four seasons. Her performance in Shakespeare's *The Winter's Tale* captivated the young Prince of Wales (afterward George IV), who in his letters assumed the role of Florizel to her Perdita, the name by which she was ever afterward known. She became his mistress, but the liaison ended within a year, and the Prince reneged on a promised financial settlement of £20,000. With the aid of the prominent Whig Charles James Fox, also a lover, she obtained an annuity of £500. A series of affairs with such fashionable figures as Colonel Banastre Tarleton, who had fought under Cornwallis in America and later became a Member of Parliament, kept her in the public eye even after her retirement from the stage. Witness this paragraph, under the head "Ship News," from the *Morning Post:*

> Yesterday, a messenger arrived in town, with the very interesting and pleasing intelligence of the Tarleton, armed ship, having, after a chace of some months, captured the Perdita frigate, and brought her safe into Egham port. The Perdita is a prodigious fine clean bottomed vessel, and had taken many prizes during her cruize, particularly the Florizel, a most valuable ship belonging to the Crown, but which was immediately released, after taking out the cargo. The Perdita was captured some time ago by the Fox, but was, afterwards, retaken by the Malden, and had a sumptuous suit of new rigging, when she fell in with the Tarleton. Her manoeuvering to escape was admirable; but the Tarleton, fully determined to take her, or perish, would not give up the chace; and at length, coming alongside the Perdita, fully determined to board her, sword in hand, she instantly surrendered at discretion.

At the height of her fame, Robinson was painted by Cosway, Reynolds, Gainsborough, and Romney. (See the Gainsborough portrait, Color Plate 2.) A miscarriage in 1783 paralyzed her legs, but the affair with Tarleton did not end until he married an heiress in 1798. Though Robinson's literary career was inseparable from her notoriety, it both predated and outlasted her life on the stage. Her first volume of poems appeared in 1775, and the two-volume *Poems* of 1791–1793 attracted 600 subscribers. Working in a variety of genres from the sentimental verse with which she began through ballads, tales, light occasional verse, and odes, producing plays and seven successful novels, Robinson confirmed her twofold status as celebrity and writer, and supported herself, her mother, and her daughter. *Sappho and Phaon* (1796) brought her the title of "the English Sappho" that to some degree overlaid her identity as "Perdita"; arguing in the preface for the "legitimate" Petrarchan sonnet, Robinson combined a poetry of passion (for which Sappho was an honorific female precursor) with formal control, and made a notable contribution to the revival of the sonnet upon which Wordsworth was to capitalize. Succeeding Southey as poetry editor of the *Morning Post,* she became an established figure on the London literary scene. Coleridge thought her "a woman of undoubted Genius . . . she overloads everything; but I never knew a human being with so full a mind—bad, good, and indifferent, I grant you—but full and overflowing." Her collection *Lyrical Tales* (1800), published in the last year of her life, acknowledges *Lyrical Ballads;* Coleridge thought the meter of *The Haunted Beach* "fascinating," and sent her *Kubla Khan* in manuscript, inspiring one of her last works, *To the Poet Coleridge* (see page 671), a record of response to the poem sixteen years before it was printed. Her career exemplifies the opportunities for self-fashioning the burgeoning literary marketplace offered a resourceful woman.

Ode to Beauty

EXULTING BEAUTY:—phantom of an hour,
   Whose magic spells enchain the heart,
Ah! what avails thy fascinating pow'r,
   Thy thrilling smile, thy witching art?
5   Thy lip, where balmy nectar glows;
        Thy cheek, where round the damask rose
        A thousand nameless Graces move,[1]
        Thy mildly speaking azure eyes,
        Thy golden hair, where cunning Love
10   In many a mazy ringlet lies?
        Soon as thy radiant form is seen,
        Thy native blush, thy timid mien,°   *appearance*
Thy hour is past! thy charms are vain!
ILL-NATURE haunts thee with her sallow train,
15   Mean JEALOUSY deceives thy list'ning ear,
And SLANDER stains thy cheek with many a bitter tear.

        In calm retirement form'd to dwell,
        NATURE, thy handmaid fair and kind,
        For thee a beauteous garland twin'd;
20   The vale-nurs'd Lily's downcast bell
          Thy modest mien display'd,
        The snow-drop, April's meekest child,
        With myrtle blossoms undefil'd.
          Thy mild and spotless mind pourtray'd;
25   Dear blushing maid, of cottage birth,
        'Twas thine, o'er dewy meads to stray,
        While sparkling health, and frolic mirth,
          Led on thy laughing Day.

        Lur'd by the babbling tongue of FAME,
30   Too soon, insidious FLATT'RY came;
        Flush'd VANITY her footsteps led,
        To charm thee from thy blest repose,
        While Fashion twin'd about thy head
          A wreath of wounding woes;
35   See Dissipation smoothly glide,
        Cold Apathy, and puny Pride,
        Capricious Fortune, dull, and blind,
          O'er splendid Folly throws her veil,

---

1. A paraphrase of Adam's enchantment with Eve, *Paradise Lost* 8.600–604.

While Envy's meagre tribe assail
40   Thy gentle form, and spotless mind.

Their spells prevail! no more those eyes
    Shoot undulating fires;
On thy wan cheek, the young rose dies,
    Thy lip's deep tint expires;
45   Dark Melancholy chills thy mind;
    Thy silent tear reveals thy woe;
TIME strews with thorns thy mazy way;
Where'er thy giddy footsteps stray,
    Thy thoughtless heart is doom'd to find
50   An unrelenting foe.

'Tis thus, the infant Forest flow'r,
    Bespangled o'er with glitt'ring dew,
At breezy morn's refreshing hour,
    Glows with pure tints of varying hue,
55   Beneath an aged oak's wide spreading shade,
Where no rude winds, or beating storms invade.
    Transplanted from its lonely bed,
    No more it scatters perfumes round,
No more it rears its gentle head,
60   Or brightly paints the mossy ground;
For ah! the beauteous bud, too soon,
    Scorch'd by the burning eye of day,
Shrinks from the sultry glare of noon,
Droops its enamell'd brow, and blushing, dies away.

1791

January, 1795

Pavement slippery, people sneezing
Lords in ermine, beggars freezing;
Titled gluttons dainties carving,
Genius in a garret starving.

5   Lofty mansions, warm and spacious;
Courtiers cringing and voracious;
Misers scarce the wretched heeding;
Gallant soldiers fighting, bleeding.

Wives who laugh at passive spouses;
10   Theatres, and meeting houses;
Balls, where simpering misses languish;
Hospitals, and groans of anguish.

Arts and sciences bewailing;
Commerce drooping, credit failing;
15   Placemen° mocking subjects loyal;   *political appointees*
Separations, weddings royal.

Authors who can't earn a dinner;
Many a subtle rogue a winner;
Fugitives for shelter seeking;
20   Misers hoarding, tradesmen breaking.°   *going bankrupt*

Taste and talents quite deserted;
All the laws of truth perverted;
Arrogance o'er merit soaring;
Merit silently deploring.

25   Ladies gambling night and morning;
Fools the works of genius scorning;
Ancient dames for girls mistaken;
Youthful damsels quite forsaken.

Some in luxury delighting;
30   More in talking than in fighting;
Lovers old, and beaux decrepid;
Lordlings empty and insipid.

Poets, painters, and musicians;
Lawyers, doctors, politicians;
35   Pamphlets, newspapers, and odes,
Seeking fame by different roads.

Gallant souls with empty purses;
Generals only fit for nurses;
School-boys, smit with martial spirit,
40   Taking places of veteran merit.

Honest men who can't get places,
Knaves who show unblushing faces;
Ruin hastened, peace retarded;
Candour spurn'd, and art° rewarded.   *hypocrisy*

1795   1795

from Sappho and Phaon, in a Series of Legitimate Sonnets[1]

Flendus amor meus est; elegeia flebile carmen;
Non facit ad lacrymas barbitos ulla meas.   OVID

Love taught my tears in sadder notes to flow,
And tuned my heart to elegies of woe.   POPE

---

1. Greek lyric poet Sappho of Lesbos (c. 600 B.C.E) was famous for love poems addressed to other women. Little is known of her. According to legend, she was banished from Lesbos, went to Sicily and fell in love with Phaon, a Lesbian boatman granted youth and beauty by Aphrodite. When her love was not returned, she threw herself from the Leucadian rock into the sea. Robinson narrates these events in a series of 44 sonnets, taking her epigraph from Epistle XV of the *Heroides*, by Ovid (43 B.C.E–18 C.E), which popularized the story; Alexander Pope's translation is from *Sappho to Phaon* (1712), lines 7–8.

III. The Bower of Pleasure

TURN to yon vale beneath, whose tangled shade
    Excludes the blazing torch of noon-day light,
    Where sportive Fawns, and dimpled Loves invite,[2]
The bow'r of Pleasure opens to the glade:
5 Lull'd by soft flutes, on leaves of violets laid,
    There witching beauty greets the ravish'd sight,
    More gentle than the arbitress of night
In all her silv'ry panoply° array'd![3]   *armor*
    The birds breathe bliss! light zephyrs kiss the ground,
10 Stealing the hyacinth's divine perfume;
    While from the pellucid fountains glitt'ring round,
Small tinkling rills° bid rival flow'rets bloom!   *streamlets*
    HERE, laughing Cupids bathe the bosom's wound;
THERE, tyrant passion finds a glorious tomb!

IV. Sappho discovers her Passion

Why, when I gaze on Phaon's beauteous eyes,
    Why does each thought in wild disorder stray?
    Why does each fainting faculty decay,
And my chill'd breast in throbbing tumults rise?
5 Mute on the ground my lyre neglected lies,
    The Muse forgot, and lost the melting lay;
    My down-cast looks, my faltering lips betray,
That stung by hopeless passion;—Sappho dies!
    Now on a bank of cypress° let me rest;   *emblem of death*
10 Come, tuneful maids, ye pupils of my care,
    Come, with your dulcet° numbers soothe my breast;   *sweet, melodious*
And, as the soft vibrations float on air,
    Let pity waft my spirit to the blest,
To mock the barbarous triumphs of despair!

VII. Invokes Reason

Come. Reason, come! each nerve rebellious bind,[4]
    Lull the fierce tempest of my fev'rish soul;
    Come, with the magic of thy meek controul,
And check the wayward wand'rings of my mind:
5 Estrang'd from thee, no solace can I find,
    O'er my rapt brain, where pensive visions stole,
    Now passion reigns and stormy tumults roll—
So the smooth Sea obeys the furious wind!
    In vain Philosophy unfolds his[5] store,
10 O'erwhelm'd is every source of pure delight;

2. Fawns: young deer, or mythological figures (fauns), half men half goats; Loves: cupids.
3. Moon goddess Diana, traditionally a virgin.
4. Compare to Wollstonecraft's *Rights of Woman*, which urges rational control of erotic passion.
5. Later revised to "her."

Dim is the golden page of wisdom's lore;
All nature fades before my sick'ning sight;
   For what bright scene can fancy's eye explore,
'Midst dreary labyrinths of mental night?

XI. Rejects the Influence of Reason

O Reason! vaunted Sov'reign of the mind!
   Thou pompous vision with a sounding name!
   Can'st thou the soul's rebellious passions tame?
Can'st thou in spells the vagrant fancy bind?
5   Ah, no! capricious as the wav'ring wind
   Are sighs of Love that dim thy boasted flame,
   While Folly's torch consumes the wreath of fame,
And Pleasure's hands the sheaves of Truth unbind.
   Press'd by the storms of fate, hope shrinks and dies,
10 Frenzy darts forth in mightiest ills array'd;
   Around thy throne destructive tumults rise,
And hell-fraught jealousies, thy rights invade!
   Then, what art thou? O Idol of the wise!
A visionary theme!—a gorgeous shade!°   *shadow; ghost*

XII. Previous to her Interview with Phaon

Now, o'er the tesselated° pavement strew   *mosaic*
   Fresh saffron, steep'd in essence of the rose,
   While down yon agate column gently flows
A glittering streamlet of ambrosial[6] dew!
5   My Phaon smiles! the rich carnation's hue,
   On his flush'd cheek in conscious lustre glows,
   While o'er his breast enamour'd Venus throws
Her starry mantle of celestial blue!
   Breathe soft, ye dulcet flutes, among the trees
10 Where clustering boughs with golden citron° twine;   *citrus fruit*
   While slow vibrations, dying on the breeze
Shall soothe his soul with harmony divine!
   Then let my form his yielding fancy seize,
And all his fondest wishes blend with mine.

XVIII. To Phaon

Why art thou changed? O Phaon! tell me why?
   Love flies reproach, when passion feels decay;
   Or, I would paint the raptures of that day,
When, in sweet converse, mingling sigh with sigh,
5   I mark'd the graceful languor of thine eye
   As on a shady bank entranced we lay:
   O! eyes! whose beamy radiance stole away,

---

6. In Greek mythology, ambrosia is the nectar of the gods; hence, divinely sweet.

As stars fade trembling from the burning sky!
    Why art thou changed, dear source of all my woes?
10 Though dark my bosom's tint, through every vein
    A ruby tide of purest lustre flows,
Warm'd by thy love, or chill'd by thy disdain;
    And yet no bliss this sensate being knows;
Ah! why is rapture so allied to pain?

XXX. Bids farewell to Lesbos

O'er the tall cliff that bounds the billowy main,
    Shadowing the surge that sweeps the lonely strand,
    While the thin vapours break along the sand,
Day's harbinger unfolds the liquid plain.
5 The rude sea murmurs, mournful as the strain
    That love-lorn minstrels strike with trembling hand,
    While from their green beds rise the Syren band[7]
With tongues aerial to repeat my pain!
    The vessel rocks beside the pebbly shore,
10 The foamy curls its gaudy trappings lave;
    Oh! bark propitious! bear me gently o'er;
Breathe soft, ye winds! rise slow, O swelling wave!
    Lesbos, these eyes shall meet thy sands no more:
I fly, to seek my lover, or my grave!

XXXVII. Foresees her Death

When, in the gloomy mansion of the dead,
    This withering heart, this faded form shall sleep:
    When these fond eyes at length shall cease to weep,
And earth's cold lap receive this feverish head;
5 Envy shall turn away, a tear to shed,
    And time's obliterating pinions sweep
    The spot, where poets shall their vigils keep,
To mourn and wander near my freezing bed!
    Then, my pale ghost, upon th' Elysian shore,
10 Shall smile, released from every mortal care;
    While, doom'd love's victim to repine no more,
My breast shall bathe in endless rapture there!
    Ah! no! my restless shade would still deplore,
Nor taste that bliss, which Phaon did not share.

1796

The Camp

Tents, *marquees*,° and baggage-waggons;   *military tents*
Suttling-houses,° beer in flagons;   *provision shops*
Drums and trumpets, singing, firing;

7. Mythical sea nymphs who lured men to destruction by their singing.

Girls seducing, beaux admiring;
5 Country lasses gay and smiling,
City lads their hearts beguiling;
Dusty roads, and horses frisky,
Many an *Eton Boy* in whisky;[1]
Tax'd carts full of farmers' daughters;
10 Brutes condemn'd, and man who slaughters!
Public-houses,° booths, and castles,   *pubs*
Belles of fashion, serving vassals;
Lordly gen'rals fiercely staring,
Weary soldiers, sighing, swearing!
15 *Petit-maitres*° always dressing,   *dandies*
In the glass themselves caressing;
Perfum'd, painted, patch'd, and blooming
Ladies—manly airs assuming!
Dowagers of fifty, simp'ring,
20 Misses for their lovers whimp'ring;
Husbands drill'd to household tameness;
Dames heart sick of wedded sameness.
Princes setting girls a-madding,
Wives for ever fond of gadding;
25 Princesses with lovely faces,
Beauteous children of the Graces!
Britain's pride and virtue's treasure,
Fair and gracious beyond measure!
Aid-de-camps° and youthful pages,   *officers' assistants*
30 Prudes and vestals° of all ages!   *virgins*
Old coquets and matrons surly,
Sounds of distant hurly-burly!
Mingled voices, uncouth singing,
Carts full laden, forage bringing;
35 Sociables° and horses weary,   *carriages*
Houses warm, and dresses airy;
Loads of fatten'd poultry; pleasure
Serv'd (to nobles) without measure;
Doxies,° who the waggons follow;   *prostitutes*
40 Beer, for thirsty hinds° to swallow;   *peasants*
Washerwomen, fruit-girls cheerful,
Ancient ladies—*chaste* and *fearful!!*
Tradesmen, leaving shops, and seeming
More of *war* than profit dreaming;
45 Martial sounds and braying asses,
Noise, that ev'ry noise surpasses!
All confusion, din, and riot,
Nothing clean—and nothing quiet.

1799   1802

---

1. Eton is an elite public (in American usage, private) school. Whisky is a light carriage, and perhaps also the liquor.

The Haunted Beach[1]

Upon a lonely desert Beach
   Where the white foam was scatter'd,
A little shed uprear'd its head
   Though lofty Barks° were shatter'd.   *sailing ships*
5   The Sea-weeds gath'ring near the door,
   A sombre path display'd;
And, all around, the deaf' ning roar,
Re-echo'd on the chalky shore,
   By the green billows made.

10 Above, a jutting cliff was seen
   Where Sea Birds hover'd, craving;
And all around, the craggs were bound
   With weeds—for ever waving.
And here and there, a cavern wide
15   Its shad'wy jaws display'd;
And near the sands, at ebb of tide,
A shiver'd mast was seen to ride
   Where the green billows stray'd.

And often, while the moaning wind
20   Stole o'er the Summer Ocean;
The moonlight scene, was all serene,
   The waters scarce in motion:
Then, while the smoothly slanting sand
   The tall cliff wrapp'd in shade,
25 The Fisherman beheld a band
Of Spectres, gliding hand in hand—
   Where the green billows play'd.

And pale their faces were, as snow,
   And sullenly they wander'd:
30 And to the skies with hollow eyes
   They look'd as though they ponder'd.
And sometimes, from their hammock shroud,
   They dismal howlings made,
And while the blast blew strong and loud
35 The clear moon mark'd the ghastly croud,
   Where the green billows play'd!

And then, above the haunted hut
   The Curlews° screaming hover'd;   *snipes; small birds*
And the low door with furious roar
40   The frothy breakers cover'd.
For, in the Fisherman's lone shed
   A MURDER'D MAN was laid,

---

1. From *Lyrical Tales*, 1800.

With ten wide gashes in his head
And deep was made his sandy bed
45   Where the green billows play'd.

A Shipwreck'd Mariner was he,
    Doom'd from his home to sever;
Who swore to be thro' wind and sea
    Firm and undaunted ever!
50   And when the wave resistless roll'd,
    About his arm he made
A packet rich of Spanish gold,
And, like a British sailor, bold,
    Plung'd, where the billows play'd!

55   The Spectre band, his messmates brave
    Sunk in the yawning ocean,
While to the mast he lash'd him fast
    And brav'd the storm's commotion.
The winter moon, upon the sand
60   A silv'ry carpet made,
And mark'd the Sailor reach the land,
And mark'd his murd'rer wash his hand
    Where the green billows play'd.

And since that hour the Fisherman
65   Has toil'd and toil'd in vain!
For all the night, the moony light
    Gleams on the specter'd main!
And when the skies are veil'd in gloom,
    The Murd'rer's liquid way
70   Bounds o'er the deeply yawning tomb,
And flashing fires the sands illume,
    Where the green billows play!

Full thirty years his task has been,
    Day after day more weary;
75   For Heav'n design'd, his guilty mind
    Should dwell on prospects dreary.
Bound by a strong and mystic chain,
    He has not pow'r to stray;
But, destin'd mis'ry to sustain,
80   He wastes, in Solitude and Pain—
    A loathsome life away.

1800

London's Summer Morning

Who has not wak'd to list° the busy sounds   *listen to; tally*
Of summer's morning, in the sultry smoke

Of noisy London? On the pavement hot
The sooty chimney-boy, with dingy face

5   And tatter'd covering, shrilly bawls his trade,
Rousing the sleepy housemaid. At the door
The milk-pail rattles, and the tinkling bell
Proclaims the dustman's office; while the street
Is lost in clouds impervious. Now begins

10   The din of hackney-coaches, waggons, carts;
While tinmen's shops, and noisy trunk-makers,
Knife-grinders, coopers, squeaking cork-cutters,
Fruit-barrows, and the hunger-giving cries
Of vegetable venders, fill the air.

15   Now ev'ry shop displays its varied trade,
And the fresh-sprinkled pavement cools the feet
Of early walkers. At the private door
The ruddy housemaid twirls the busy mop,[1]
Annoying the smart 'prentice,° or neat girl,   *apprentice*

20   Tripping with band-box° lightly. Now the sun   *hat box*
Darts burning splendour on the glitt'ring pane,
Save where the canvas awning throws a shade
On the gay merchandize. Now, spruce and trim,
In shops (where beauty smiles with industry,)

25   Sits the smart damsel; while the passenger
Peeps thro' the window, watching ev'ry charm.
Now pastry dainties catch the eye minute
Of humming insects, while the limy snare
Waits to enthral them. Now the lamp-lighter

30   Mounts the tall ladder, nimbly vent'rous,
To trim the half-fill'd lamp; while at his feet
The pot-boy° yells discordant! All along   *server of drinks*
The sultry pavement, the old-clothes-man cries
In tone monotonous, and side-long views

35   The area for his traffic: now the bag
Is slily open'd, and the half-worn suit
(Sometimes the pilfer'd treasure of the base
Domestic spoiler), for one half its worth,
Sinks in the green abyss. The porter now

40   Bears his huge load along the burning way;
And the poor poet wakes from busy dreams,
To paint the summer morning.

1800   1806

---

1. The detail recalls Jonathan Swift, *A Description of the Morning* (1709): "Now Moll had whirl'd her mop with dex'trous
Airs" (7).

The Old Beggar

Do you see the OLD BEGGAR who sits at yon gate,
    With his beard silver'd over like snow?
Tho' he smiles as he meets the keen arrows of fate,
    Still his bosom is wearied with woe.

5   Many years has he sat at the foot of the hill,
    Many days seen the summer sun rise;
And at evening the traveller passes him still,
    While the shadows steal over the skies.

In the bleak blast of winter he hobbles along
10   O'er the heath, at the dawning of day;
And the *dew-drops* that freeze the rude thistles among,
    Are the *stars* that illumine his way.

How mild is his aspect, how modest his eye,
    How meekly his soul bears each wrong!
15   How much does he speak by his eloquent sigh,
    Tho' no accent is heard from his tongue.

Time was, when this beggar, in martial trim dight,°   *dressed*
    Was as bold as the chief of his throng;
When he march'd thro' the storms of the day or the night,
20   And still smil'd as he journey'd along.

Then his form was athletic, his eyes' vivid glance
    Spoke the lustre of youth's glowing day!
And the village all mark'd, in the combat and dance,
    The brave younker° still valiant as gay.   *youth*

25   When the prize was propos'd, how his footsteps wou'd bound,
    While the MAID *of his heart* led the throng,
While the ribands that circled the May-pole around,
    Wav'd the trophies of garlands among!

But love o'er his bosom triumphantly reign'd,
30   Love taught him in secret to pine;
Love wasted his youth, yet he never complain'd,
    For the silence of love—is divine!

The dulcet° ton'd word, and the plaint° of despair,   *sweet / lament*
    Are no signs of the soul-wasting smart;
35   'Tis the pride of affection to cherish its care,
    And to count the quick throbs of the heart.

Amidst the loud din of the battle he stood,
    Like a lion, undaunted and strong;
But the tear of compassion was mingled with blood,
40   When his sword was the first in the throng.

When the bullet whizz'd by, and his arm bore away,
    Still he shrunk not, with anguish oppress'd;
And when victory shouted the fate of the day,
    Not a groan check'd the joy of his breast.

45   To his dear native shore the poor wand'rer hied;
    But he came to complete his despair:
For the maid of his soul was that morning *a bride!*
    And a gay *lordly rival* was there!

From that hour, o'er the world he has wander'd forlorn;
50   But still LOVE his companion would go;
And tho' deeply fond memory planted its thorn,
    Still he silently cherish'd his woe.

See him now, while with age and with sorrow oppress'd,
    He the gate opens slowly, and sighs!
55   See him drop the big tears on his woe-wither'd breast,
    The big tears that fall fast from his eyes!

See his habit all tatter'd, his shrivell'd cheek pale;
    See his locks, waving thin in the air;
See his lip is half froze with the sharp cutting gale,
60   And his head, o'er the temples, all bare!

His eye-beam no longer in lustre displays
    The warm sunshine that visits his breast;
For deep sunk is its orbit, and darken'd its rays,
    And he sighs for the grave's silent rest.

65   And his voice is grown feeble, his accent is slow,
    And he sees not the distant hill's side;
And he hears not the breezes of morn as they blow,
    Nor the streams that soft murmuring glide.

To him all is silent, and mournful, and dim,
70   E'en the seasons pass dreary and slow;
For affliction has plac'd its cold fetters on him,
    And his soul is enamour'd of woe.

See the TEAR, which, imploring, is fearful to roll,
    Tho' in silence he bows as you stray;
75   'Tis the eloquent silence which speaks to the soul,
    'Tis the *star* of his *slow-setting day!*

Perchance, ere the *May-blossoms* cheerfully wave,
    Ere the *zephyrs* of SUMMER soft sigh;
The sun-beams shall dance on the grass o'er his GRAVE,
80   And his *journey* be mark'd—TO THE SKY.

1799   1806

Mary Wollstonecraft
1759–1797

John Opie's famous portrait of Mary Wollstonecraft, probably painted in 1797 when she was pregnant with her and William Godwin's daughter Mary, was etched for this frontispiece of Godwin's posthumous *Memoirs of the Author of a Vindication of the Rights of Woman* (1798). The iconic image of an unadorned, wistful woman could not deflect the barrage of abuse provoked by the memoir's scandalous revelations.

It is hard to imagine how anyone advocating the education of young women, the virtues of sense over sensibility, chastity for men as well as women, school uniforms, and regular physical exercise, could be reviled as a radical revolutionary, an atheist, a slut, and a pathologically castrating threat to masculine authority. But Mary Wollstonecraft was thus abused. One provocation was her frequently caustic refutation in *A Vindication of the Rights of Men* of Edmund Burke's *Reflections on the Revolution in France*. She went further in her *Vindication of the Rights of Woman*, a trenchant critique of the ideologies of gender in such culturally revered works as Milton's *Paradise Lost* and the admired "conduct" literature of the day—advice to young women on how to be attractive to men and cultivate the Christian virtues of submission, obedience, and service. It was not only the publications; it was also her private life, taken to be the basis of her ideas. The indictments included helping a sister run away from an abusive husband (an assault on the social institution and religious sacrament of marriage); her financial independence and career as a professional writer (very unfeminine); her enamored pursuit of Swiss artist Henry Fuseli in the early 1790s (most immodest) and her affair with American adventurer Gilbert Imlay a few years later; her out-of-wedlock daughter by Imlay; the two attempts at suicide provoked by Imlay's infidelities; her affair with William Godwin and a premarital pregnancy. When she died from complications in childbirth, her detractors intuited divine judgment, and said so in print.

A brilliant thinker and conversationalist, a prolific polemical writer, a commanding social presence, Wollstonecraft led a life of passionate commitments, and was one of the most impressive figures of the radical circle in England in the 1790s. Born in 1759, she spent a childhood suffering the consequences of her father's failures at various enterprises, as he squandered a large inheritance and sought refuge in drink; more than once she defended her mother from his drunken rages. To escape, she became a lady's companion in Bath but returned after two years to nurse her mother. After her mother's death, she left home for good, supporting herself with eye-straining work as a seamstress and then as a schoolmistress in North London with a friend and another sister. When the school failed, Wollstonecraft wrote to pay off her debts, publishing *Thoughts on the Education of Daughters* in 1786; she worked for a year as a governess in an aristocratic Irish family, during which time she wrote her first novel, *Mary, A Fiction*.

Determined to make a living as a writer, she returned to London where she met Joseph Johnson, a radical bookseller who, in 1788, published *Mary* and her book for children, *Original Stories from Real Life*, and in 1789, her anthology, *The Female Reader* (under a male pen name). He also hired her to work for and write articles for *The Analytical Review* and to produce translations of German and French moral philosophers. In London Wollstonecraft became part of Johnson's lively circle of artists, writers, liberal political thinkers, progressive philosophers, and religious Dissenters—among them, Anna Letitia Barbauld, Tom Paine, William Blake, Joel Barlow, Joseph Priestley, Fuseli, and Godwin. Blake and Robert Southey were completely enamored of her, though Godwin was at first put off by her forwardness in conversation. In 1790 Johnson published her *A Vindication of the Rights of Men*, a rapid response to Edmund Burke's *Reflections on the Revolution in France*; it was anonymous, and when Wollstonecraft signed her name to the second edition, her fame was established.

She began *Rights of Woman* in 1791 and early in 1792 spent time with Talleyrand, the French minister of education, on his visit to London; she dedicated *Rights of Woman* to him when its second edition was published later that year. Her reasonable, modest proposals for the improved education and social development of young women were etched with acid comparisons of the state of women to that of plantation and harem slaves, equally oppressed, tyrannized, and brutalized by morally illegitimate masters. Wollstonecraft called for a "revolution in female manners," arguing that no agenda for "the rights of man" could claim moral authority if it entailed the unchanged degradation of women. At the end of 1792, she left on her own for Paris, partly to wean herself from her crush on Fuseli and partly to witness Revolutionary France. Here she met Helen Maria Williams, and within a few months, Imlay, dashing veteran of the American Revolution. Paris in 1793 was a dangerous world, still reeling from the September massacres of 1792 and the arrest and trial of Louis XVI, who was beheaded in January 1793. Over the course of this year, the Reign of Terror claimed thousands more, including Wollstonecraft's friend Madame Roland and Queen Marie Antoinette in October. Wollstonecraft left Paris to seek safety in the suburbs, but returned to register as Imlay's wife at the American embassy in order to gain protection as an American citizen, France being at war with England. Early in 1794, she and Imlay went to Le Havre, where their daughter Fanny was born. They all returned to Paris; then Imlay went to London, leaving wife and daughter behind.

Wollstonecraft's *Historical and Moral View of the Origin and Progress of the French Revolution* was published later that year. On returning to London, she was devastated to discover Imlay living with an actress. He prevented her attempted suicide, and to distance himself from her, sent her (with Fanny and a French nurse) on a dangerous business trip to Scandinavia during the summer of 1795. She returned in October to find him living with yet another actress and again attempted suicide, jumping off a bridge into the Thames. Imlay left for Paris with his new amour in November, and Wollstonecraft, ever resourceful, published her letters to him recording her experiences in Scandinavia. When *Letters Written during a Short Residence in Sweden, Norway, and Denmark* appeared the following year, Godwin exclaimed, "If ever there was a book calculated to make a man in love with its author, this appears to me to be the book." They renewed their friendship in January 1796 and by the summer, "friendship melting into love," they became lovers. When she became pregnant at the end of the year, they set aside principle and decided to marry. They wed in March, but insisted on keeping separate residences. Mary Wollstonecraft Godwin (later, Mary Shelley) was born in August; in ten days, her mother, having suffered agonizing pain from poisoning by an incompletely expelled placenta, was dead, at age thirty-seven.

When Godwin published his *Memoirs* and her unfinished novel, *The Wrongs of Woman, or Maria* in 1798, both works fed anti-Jacobin attacks on her ideas and moral character. His grief clouded his judgment about what he could recount without offending propriety, and the *Memoir* proved a scandal, embarrassing even those who had welcomed *Rights of Woman*. An anonymous *Defence of the Character and Conduct of the Late Mary Wollstonecraft Godwin* (often credited to Mary Hays, her friend and fellow feminist), appeared in 1803, but the defense could hardly rest. Hays did not feel safe including her in her *Female Biography, or Memoirs of Illustrious and Celebrated Women of all Ages and Countries* (also 1803), even though she found space for the Lesbian Sappho and Marat's assassin Charlotte Corday. Decades later, in 1869, John Stuart Mill forgot to mention *Rights of Woman* in his *Subjection of Women*. Attacks on Wollstonecraft's character and conduct persisted well into the 1970s, not only stigmatizing the arguments of her writing but providing antifeminists with fuel to impugn any advocacy of women's rights. Yet there always persisted a community of admiration for her courage and intelligence, including (for better or worse) Percy Shelley, and over ensuing decades, such women of intellect as George Eliot, Emma Goldman, and Virginia Woolf.

Selections from *A Vindication of the Rights of Men* are included in Perspectives: The Rights of Man and the Revolution Controversy, page 122.

A VINDICATION OF THE RIGHTS OF WOMAN   The French Revolutionary Assembly's Declaration of the Rights of Man granted participatory citizenship only to men. The vibrant declarations of the "Rights of Man" meant a *fraternity* of "liberty, fraternity, equality." Bluntly comparing marriage to slavery and tyrannical oppression, Wollstonecraft's "second" *Vindication* boldly challenges the thinking that sustains and frequently idealizes this subjection: the view of women's subordination as a universal fact of nature, human history, rational philosophy, and divine ordination. Identifying this view as a sociocultural text, a "prevailing opinion," she subjects it to a sharp critical reading. This critique is energized by the actual literary criticism that fills her pages, incisive and often sarcastic examinations of long-standing misogynist myths (Pandora) and their prestigious literary vehicles: John Milton's *Paradise Lost* (and its informing biblical stories); Alexander Pope's second *Moral Essay*, "Of the Characters of Women" (1735); Samuel Richardson's *Clarissa* (1747–1748); Jean-Jacques Rousseau's education novel *Émile* (1762) and his romance *Julie, ou la Nouvelle Héloïse* (1791); Dr. John Gregory's *A Father's Legacy to His Daughters* (1774); Dr. James Fordyce's *Sermons to Young Women* (1765). She turns an unforgiving focus on a set of interlocked key terms used to flatter women into subjection—*innocent, delicate, feminine, beautiful*—embellished with praise for their "fair defects" of character (an oxymoron she despises) and reverence for them as "angels" or "girls," rather than rationally capable, intelligent, mature adults.

Wollstonecraft's argument for gender-neutral "reason" undoes Milton's assignment of this capacity to men only. To Wollstonecraft, this is no divine arrangement but a social formation. She counters that God would not have created women without this capacity, the source of both virtuous conduct and spiritual salvation—a religious argument that invests her social polemic with unimpeachable moral foundation. Alongside this moral argument, *Vindication* wields the discourse of tyranny and revolution that already had currency with Wollstonecraft's male colleagues, allowing her to point out the reactionary attitudes about women that may be tolerated, even supported, by progressive political thinkers.

from **A Vindication of the Rights of Woman**
from *To M. Talleyrand-Périgord, Late Bishop of Autun*[1]

Contending for the rights of woman, my main argument is built on this simple principle, that if she be not prepared by education to become the companion of man, she will stop the progress of knowledge and virtue; for truth must be common to all, or it will be inefficacious with respect to its influence on general practice. * * *

In this work I have produced many arguments, which to me were conclusive, to prove that the prevailing notion respecting a sexual character was subversive of

---

1. Talleyrand (1754–1838) was Bishop of Autun (1788–1791) when he resigned to serve in the Constituent Assembly of the French Revolutionary government, where he recommended raising revenue by confiscating church properties. In 1791 he rendered a Report on Public Instruction, urging free education for both sexes but following the view of Rousseau's *Émile* (1762) that girls be trained for subservience to men. In the first sentence of her dedicatory letter, Wollstonecraft says she means "to induce [him] to reconsider the subject."

morality, and I have contended, that to render the human body and mind more perfect, chastity[2] must more universally prevail, and that chastity will never be respected in the male world till the person of a woman is not, as it were, idolized, when little virtue or sense embellish it with the grand traces of mental beauty, or the interesting simplicity of affection.

Consider, Sir, dispassionately, these observations—for a glimpse of this truth seemed to open before you when you observed, "that to see one half of the human race excluded by the other from all participation of government, was a political phænomenon that, according to abstract principles, it was impossible to explain."[3] If so, on what does your constitution rest? If the abstract rights of man will bear discussion and explanation, those of woman, by a parity of reasoning, will not shrink from the same test: though a different opinion prevails in this country, built on the very arguments which you use to justify the oppression of woman—prescription.

Consider, I address you as a legislator, whether, when men contend for their freedom, and to be allowed to judge for themselves respecting their own happiness, it be not inconsistent and unjust to subjugate women, even though you firmly believe that you are acting in the manner best calculated to promote their happiness? Who made man the exclusive judge, if woman partake with him the gift of reason?

In this style, argue tyrants of every denomination, from the weak king to the weak father of a family; they are all eager to crush reason; yet always assert that they usurp its throne only to be useful. Do you not act a similar part, when you *force* all women, by denying them civil and political rights, to remain immured in their families groping in the dark? for surely, Sir, you will not assert, that a duty can be binding which is not founded on reason? If indeed this be their destination, arguments may be drawn from reason: and thus augustly supported, the more understanding women acquire, the more they will be attached to their duty—comprehending it—for unless they comprehend it, unless their morals be fixed on the same immutable principle as those of man, no authority can make them discharge it in a virtuous manner. They may be convenient slaves, but slavery will have its constant effect, degrading the master and the abject dependent.

But, if women are to be excluded, without having a voice, from a participation of the natural rights of mankind, prove first, to ward off the charge of injustice and inconsistency, that they want reason—else this flaw in your NEW CONSTITUTION will ever shew that man must, in some shape, act like a tyrant, and tyranny, in whatever part of society it rears its brazen front, will ever undermine morality.

I have repeatedly asserted, and produced what appeared to me irrefragable arguments drawn from matters of fact, to prove my assertion, that women cannot, by force, be confined to domestic concerns; for they will, however ignorant, intermeddle with more weighty affairs, neglecting private duties only to disturb, by cunning tricks, the orderly plans of reason which rise above their comprehension.

Besides, whilst they are only made to acquire personal accomplishments,[4] men will seek for pleasure in variety, and faithless husbands will make faithless wives; such ignorant beings, indeed, will be very excusable when, not taught to respect public good, nor allowed any civil rights, they attempt to do themselves justice by retaliation.

2. Sexual self-control, including abstinence and fidelity to marriage.
3. Quoting Talleyrand's *Report*; the French Constitution of 1791 restricted citizenship to men over age 25; women did not gain the vote until 1944.
4. The 18th-century female curriculum for the leisure-class: basic literacy, embroidery, singing; playing a piano or harpsichord; dancing; sketching; conversational French or Italian.

The box of mischief thus opened in society,[5] what is to preserve private virtue, the only security of public freedom and universal happiness?

Let there be then no coercion *established* in society, and the common law of gravity prevailing, the sexes will fall into their proper places. And, now that more equitable laws are forming your citizens, marriage may become more sacred: your young men may choose wives from motives of affection, and your maidens allow love to root out vanity.

The father of a family will not then weaken his constitution and debase his sentiments, by visiting the harlot, nor forget, in obeying the call of appetite, the purpose for which it was implanted. And, the mother will not neglect her children to practise the arts of coquetry, when sense and modesty secure her the friendship of her husband.

But, till men become attentive to the duty of a father, it is vain to expect women to spend that time in their nursery which they, "wise in their generation,"[6] choose to spend at their glass;[7] for this exertion of cunning is only an instinct of nature to enable them to obtain indirectly a little of that power of which they are unjustly denied a share: for, if women are not permitted to enjoy legitimate rights, they will render both men and themselves vicious, to obtain illicit privileges.

I wish, Sir, to set some investigations of this kind afloat in France; and should they lead to a confirmation of my principles, when your constitution is revised the Rights of Woman may be respected, if it be fully proved that reason calls for this respect, and loudly demands Justice for one half of the human race.

I am, SIR,
Your's respectfully,
M. W.

Introduction

After considering the historic page, and viewing the living world with anxious solicitude, the most melancholy emotions of sorrowful indignation have depressed my spirits, and I have sighed when obliged to confess, that either nature has made a great difference between man and man, or that the civilization which has hitherto taken place in the world has been very partial. I have turned over various books written on the subject of education, and patiently observed the conduct of parents and the management of schools; but what has been the result?—a profound conviction that the neglected education of my fellow-creatures is the grand source of the misery I deplore; and that women, in particular, are rendered weak and wretched by a variety of concurring causes, originating from one hasty conclusion. The conduct and manners of women, in fact, evidently prove that their minds are not in a healthy state; for, like the flowers which are planted in too rich a soil, strength and usefulness are sacrificed to beauty; and the flaunting leaves, after having pleased a fastidious eye, fade, disregarded on the stalk, long before the season when they ought to have arrived at maturity.—One cause of this barren blooming I attribute to a false system of education, gathered from the books written on this subject by men who, considering females

---

5. In the Greek fable, Pandora, overcome by curiosity, opens a forbidden box, letting loose a host of evils on mankind but closing it before "hope" could escape. Wollstonecraft refuses the sexism of the myth by casting male politicians as the box-openers.
6. A sarcastic reference to Jesus's parable about rewarding a shrewd but dishonest steward (Luke 16.8).
7. Mirror.

rather as women than human creatures, have been more anxious to make them allur-ing mistresses than affectionate wives and rational mothers; and the understanding of the sex has been so bubbled[1] by this specious homage, that the civilized women of the present century, with a few exceptions, are only anxious to inspire love, when they ought to cherish a nobler ambition, and by their abilities and virtues exact respect.

In a treatise, therefore, on female rights and manners, the works which have been particularly written for their improvement must not be overlooked; especially when it is asserted, in direct terms, that the minds of women are enfeebled by false re-finement; that the books of instruction, written by men of genius, have had the same tendency as more frivolous productions; and that, in the true style of Mahometanism, they are treated as a kind of subordinate beings, and not as a part of the human spe-cies,[2] when improveable reason is allowed to be the dignified distinction which raises men above the brute creation, and puts a natural sceptre in a feeble hand.

Yet, because I am a woman, I would not lead my readers to suppose that I mean violently to agitate the contested question respecting the equality or inferiority of the sex; but as the subject lies in my way, and I cannot pass it over without subject-ing the main tendency of my reasoning to misconstruction, I shall stop a moment to deliver, in a few words, my opinion.—In the government of the physical world it is observable that the female in point of strength is, in general, inferior to the male. This is the law of nature; and it does not appear to be suspended or abrogated in favour of woman. A degree of physical superiority cannot, therefore, be denied—and it is a noble prerogative! But not content with this natural pre-eminence, men en-deavour to sink us still lower, merely to render us alluring objects for a moment; and women, intoxicated by the adoration which men, under the influence of their senses, pay them, do not seek to obtain a durable interest in their hearts, or to become the friends of the fellow creatures who find amusement in their society.

I am aware of an obvious inference:—from every quarter have I heard exclama-tions against masculine women; but where are they to be found? If by this appellation men mean to inveigh against their ardour in hunting, shooting, and gaming, I shall most cordially join in the cry; but if it be against the imitation of manly virtues, or, more properly speaking, the attainment of those talents and virtues, the exercise of which ennobles the human character, and which raise females in the scale of animal being, when they are comprehensively termed mankind;—all those who view them with a philosophic eye must, I should think, wish with me, that they may every day grow more and more masculine.

This discussion naturally divides the subject. I shall first consider women in the grand light of human creatures, who, in common with men, are placed on this earth to unfold their faculties; and afterwards I shall more particularly point out their pecu-liar designation.

I wish also to steer clear of an error which many respectable writers have fallen into; for the instruction which has hitherto been addressed to women, has rather been applicable to *ladies*, if the little indirect advice, that is scattered through Sandford and Merton, be excepted;[3] but, addressing my sex in a firmer tone, I pay particular attention to those in the middle class, because they appear to be in the

---

1. Gas-filled; deluded.
2. A misconception that the sacred texts of Islam stated that women lack souls and therefore have no afterlife in Heaven.

3. The tutor in Thomas Day's popular children's story, *The History of Sandford and Merton* (1786–1789), tells several moral tales.

most natural state.[4] Perhaps the seeds of false-refinement, immorality, and vanity, have ever been shed by the great. Weak, artificial beings, raised above the common wants and affections of their race, in a premature unnatural manner, undermine the very foundation of virtue, and spread corruption through the whole mass of society! As a class of mankind they have the strongest claim to pity; the education of the rich tends to render them vain and helpless, and the unfolding mind is not strengthened by the practice of those duties which dignify the human character.—They only live to amuse themselves, and by the same law which in nature invariably produces certain effects, they soon only afford barren amusement.

But as I purpose taking a separate view of the different ranks of society, and of the moral character of women, in each, this hint is, for the present, sufficient; and I have only alluded to the subject, because it appears to me to be the very essence of an introduction to give a cursory account of the contents of the work it introduces.

My own sex, I hope, will excuse me, if I treat them like rational creatures, instead of flattering their *fascinating* graces, and viewing them as if they were in a state of perpetual childhood, unable to stand alone. I earnestly wish to point out in what true dignity and human happiness consists—I wish to persuade women to endeavour to acquire strength, both of mind and body, and to convince them that the soft phrases, susceptibility of heart, delicacy of sentiment, and refinement of taste, are almost synonymous with epithets of weakness, and that those beings who are only the objects of pity and that kind of love, which has been termed its sister, will soon become objects of contempt.

Dismissing then those pretty feminine phrases, which the men condescendingly use to soften our slavish dependence, and despising that weak elegancy of mind, exquisite sensibility, and sweet docility of manners, supposed to be the sexual characteristics of the weaker vessel, I wish to shew that elegance is inferior to virtue, that the first object of laudable ambition is to obtain a character as a human being, regardless of the distinction of sex; and that secondary views should be brought to this simple touchstone.

This is a rough sketch of my plan; and should I express my conviction with the energetic emotions that I feel whenever I think of the subject, the dictates of experience and reflection will be felt by some of my readers. Animated by this important object, I shall disdain to cull my phrases or polish my style;—I aim at being useful, and sincerity will render me unaffected; for, wishing rather to persuade by the force of my arguments, than dazzle by the elegance of my language, I shall not waste my time in rounding periods,[5] or in fabricating the turgid bombast of artificial feelings, which, coming from the head, never reach the heart.—I shall be employed about things, not words!—and, anxious to render my sex more respectable members of society, I shall try to avoid that flowery diction which has slided from essays into novels, and from novels into familiar letters and conversation.

These pretty superlatives, dropping glibly from the tongue, vitiate the taste, and create a kind of sickly delicacy that turns away from simple unadorned truth; and a deluge of false sentiments and over-stretched feelings, stifling the natural emotions of the heart, render the domestic pleasures insipid, that ought to sweeten the exercise of those severe duties, which educate a rational and immortal being for a nobler field of action.

4. "Ladies" are upper class. The middle class is the most "natural" state because it has not been corrupted by extremes of wealth or poverty.

5. Crafting elaborate sentences—the oratorical style for which Burke was famous.

The education of women has, of late, been more attended to than formerly; yet they are still reckoned a frivolous sex, and ridiculed or pitied by the writers who endeavour by satire or instruction to improve them. It is acknowledged that they spend many of the first years of their lives in acquiring a smattering of accomplishments; meanwhile strength of body and mind are sacrificed to libertine notions of beauty, to the desire of establishing themselves,—the only way women can rise in the world,—by marriage. And this desire making mere animals of them, when they marry they act as such children may be expected to act:—they dress; they paint, and nickname God's creatures.[6]—Surely these weak beings are only fit for a seraglio![7]—Can they be expected to govern a family with judgment, or take care of the poor babes whom they bring into the world?

If then it can be fairly deduced from the present conduct of the sex, from the prevalent fondness for pleasure which takes place of ambition and those nobler passions that open and enlarge the soul; that the instruction which women have hitherto received has only tended, with the constitution of civil society, to render them insignificant objects of desire—mere propagators of fools!—if it can be proved that in aiming to accomplish them, without cultivating their understandings, they are taken out of their sphere of duties, and made ridiculous and useless when the short-lived bloom of beauty is over,[8] I presume that *rational* men will excuse me for endeavouring to persuade them to become more masculine and respectable.

Indeed the word masculine is only a bugbear: there is little reason to fear that women will acquire too much courage or fortitude; for their apparent inferiority with respect to bodily strength, must render them, in some degree, dependent on men in the various relations of life; but why should it be increased by prejudices that give a sex to virtue,[9] and confound simple truths with sensual reveries?

Women are, in fact, so much degraded by mistaken notions of female excellence, that I do not mean to add a paradox when I assert, that this artificial weakness produces a propensity to tyrannize, and gives birth to cunning, the natural opponent of strength, which leads them to play off those contemptible infantine airs that undermine esteem even whilst they excite desire. Let men become more chaste and modest, and if women do not grow wiser in the same ratio, it will be clear that they have weaker understandings. It seems scarcely necessary to say, that I now speak of the sex in general. Many individuals have more sense than their male relatives; and, as nothing preponderates where there is a constant struggle for an equilibrium, without it has naturally more gravity, some women govern their husbands without degrading themselves, because intellect will always govern.

from *Chapter 1. The Rights and Involved Duties of Mankind Considered*

In the present state of society it appears necessary to go back to first principles in search of the most simple truths, and to dispute with some prevailing prejudice every inch of ground. To clear my way, I must be allowed to ask some plain questions, and the answers will probably appear as unequivocal as the axioms on which reasoning is

6. Suspecting Ophelia of treachery, Hamlet rants about all women, "God hath given you one face, and you make yourselves another. You jig and amble, and you lisp; you nickname God's creatures and make your wantonness [seem] your ignorance" (3.1.145–48). Cf. *Rights of Men*, page 53, and Burke, page 41.

7. Harem.
8. A lively writer . . . asks what business women turned of forty have to do in the world? [Wollstonecraft's note.]
9. The prevailing opinion that only men have the rational and hence moral capacity for virtuous behavior.

built; though, when entangled with various motives of action, they are formally contradicted, either by the words or conduct of men.

In what does man's pre-eminence over the brute creation consist? The answer is as clear as that a half is less than the whole; in Reason.

What acquirement exalts one being above another? Virtue; we spontaneously reply.

For what purpose were the passions implanted? That man by struggling with them might attain a degree of knowledge denied to the brutes; whispers Experience.

Consequently the perfection of our nature and capability of happiness, must be estimated by the degree of reason, virtue, and knowledge, that distinguish the individual, and direct the laws which bind society: and that from the exercise of reason, knowledge and virtue naturally flow, is equally undeniable, if mankind be viewed collectively.

The rights and duties of man thus simplified, it seems almost impertinent to attempt to illustrate truths that appear so incontrovertible; yet such deeply rooted prejudices have clouded reason, and such spurious qualities have assumed the name of virtues, that it is necessary to pursue the course of reason as it has been perplexed and involved in error, by various adventitious circumstances, comparing the simple axiom with casual deviations.

* * * All power inebriates weak man; and its abuse proves that the more equality there is established among men, the more virtue and happiness will reign in society. But this and any similar maxim deduced from simple reason, raises an outcry—the church or the state is in danger, if faith in the wisdom of antiquity is not implicit; and they who, roused by the sight of human calamity, dare to attack human authority, are reviled as despisers of God, and enemies of man. These are bitter calumnies, yet they reached one of the best of men,[1] whose ashes still preach peace, and whose memory demands a respectful pause, when subjects are discussed that lay so near his heart.—

After attacking the sacred majesty of Kings, I shall scarcely excite surprise by adding my firm persuasion that every profession, in which great subordination of rank constitutes its power, is highly injurious to morality.

A standing army, for instance, is incompatible with freedom; because subordination and rigour are the very sinews of military discipline; and despotism is necessary to give vigour to enterprizes that one will directs. A spirit inspired by romantic notions of honour, a kind of morality founded on the fashion of the age, can only be felt by a few officers, whilst the main body must be moved by command, like the waves of the sea; for the strong wind of authority pushes the crowd of subalterns forward, they scarcely know or care why, with headlong fury.

Besides, nothing can be so prejudicial to the morals of the inhabitants of country towns as the occasional residence of a set of idle superficial young men, whose only occupation is gallantry, and whose polished manners render vice more dangerous, by concealing its deformity under gay ornamental drapery. An air of fashion, which is but a badge of slavery, and proves that the soul has not a strong individual character, awes simple country people into an imitation of the vices, when they cannot catch the slippery graces, of politeness. Every corps is a chain of despots, who, submitting and tyrannizing without exercising their reason, become dead weights of vice and folly on the community. A man of rank or fortune, sure of rising by interest, has

1. Dr. Price [Wollstonecraft's note]. "Calumnies" are maliciously false charges. Wollstonecraft's friend, dissenting minister Richard Price, championed the American and French Revolutions. His lecture to the Revolution Society in 1789, *A Discourse on the Love of our Country*, provoked sharp criticism in Burke's *Reflections on the Revolution in France* (see James Gillray's cartoon, *Smelling out a Rat*, page 114) and a spirited defense in Wollstonecraft's *Vindication of the Rights of Men*.

nothing to do but to pursue some extravagant freak; whilst the needy *gentleman*, who is to rise, as the phrase turns, by his merit, becomes a servile parasite or vile pander.

Sailors, the naval gentlemen, come under the same description, only their vices assume a different and a grosser cast. They are more positively indolent, when not discharging the ceremonials of their station; whilst the insignificant fluttering of soldiers may be termed active idleness. More confined to the society of men, the former acquire a fondness for humour and mischievous tricks; whilst the latter, mixing frequently with well-bred women, catch a sentimental cant.—But mind is equally out of the question, whether they indulge the horse-laugh, or polite simper.

May I be allowed to extend the comparison to a profession where more mind is certainly to be found; for the clergy have superior opportunities of improvement, though subordination almost equally cramps their faculties? The blind submission imposed at college to forms of belief serves as a novitiate to the curate, who must obsequiously respect the opinion of his rector or patron, if he mean to rise in his profession. Perhaps there cannot be a more forcible contrast than between the servile dependent gait of a poor curate and the courtly mien of a bishop. And the respect and contempt they inspire render the discharge of their separate functions equally useless.

It is of great importance to observe that the character of every man is, in some degree, formed by his profession. A man of sense may only have a cast of countenance that wears off as you trace his individuality, whilst the weak, common man has scarcely ever any character, but what belongs to the body; at least, all his opinions have been so steeped in the vat consecrated by authority, that the faint spirit which the grape of his own vine yields cannot be distinguished.

Society, therefore, as it becomes more enlightened, should be very careful not to establish bodies of men who must necessarily be made foolish or vicious by the very constitution of their profession.

from *Chapter 2. The Prevailing Opinion of a Sexual Character Discussed*

To account for, and excuse the tyranny of man, many ingenious arguments have been brought forward to prove, that the two sexes, in the acquirement of virtue, ought to aim at attaining a very different character: or, to speak explicitly, women are not allowed to have sufficient strength of mind to acquire what really deserves the name of virtue. Yet it should seem, allowing them to have souls, that there is but one way appointed by Providence to lead *mankind* to either virtue or happiness.

If then women are not a swarm of ephemeron[1] triflers, why should they be kept in ignorance under the specious name of innocence? Men complain, and with reason, of the follies and caprices of our sex, when they do not keenly satirize our headstrong passions and groveling vices.—Behold, I should answer, the natural effect of ignorance! The mind will ever be unstable that has only prejudices to rest on, and the current will run with destructive fury when there are no barriers to break its force. Women are told from their infancy, and taught by the example of their mothers, that a little knowledge of human weakness, justly termed cunning, softness of temper, *outward* obedience, and a scrupulous attention to a puerile kind of propriety, will obtain for them the protection of man; and should they be beautiful, every thing else is needless, for, at least, twenty years of their lives.

1. Winged insect that lives for only a day.

Thus Milton describes our first frail mother; though when he tells us that women are formed for softness and sweet attractive grace,[2] I cannot comprehend his meaning, unless, in the true Mahometan strain, he meant to deprive us of souls, and insinuate that we were beings only designed by sweet attractive grace, and docile blind obedience, to gratify the senses of man when he can no longer soar on the wing of contemplation.

How grossly do they insult us who thus advise us only to render ourselves gentle, domestic brutes! For instance, the winning softness so warmly, and frequently, recommended, that governs by obeying. What childish expressions, and how insignificant is the being—can it be an immortal one? who will condescend to govern by such sinister methods! "Certainly," says Lord Bacon, "man is of kin to the beasts by his body; and if he be not of kin to God by his spirit, he is a base and ignoble creature!"[3] Men, indeed, appear to me to act in a very unphilosophical manner when they try to secure the good conduct of women by attempting to keep them always in a state of childhood. Rousseau was more consistent when he wished to stop the progress of reason in both sexes, for if men eat of the tree of knowledge, women will come in for a taste; but, from the imperfect cultivation which their understandings now receive, they only attain a knowledge of evil.[4]

Children, I grant, should be innocent; but when the epithet is applied to men, or women, it is but a civil term for weakness. For if it be allowed that women were destined by Providence to acquire human virtues, and by the exercise of their understandings, that stability of character which is the firmest ground to rest our future hopes upon, they must be permitted to turn to the fountain of light, and not forced to shape their course by the twinkling of a mere satellite. Milton, I grant, was of a very different opinion; for he only bends to the indefeasible right of beauty, though it would be difficult to render two passages which I now mean to contrast, consistent. But into similar inconsistencies are great men often led by their senses.

> To whom thus Eve with *perfect beauty* adorn'd.
> "My Author and Disposer, what thou bidst
> *Unargued* I obey; So God ordains;
> God is *thy law, thou mine:* to know no more
> Is Woman's *happiest* knowledge and her *praise.*"[5]

These are exactly the arguments that I have used to children; but I have added, your reason is now gaining strength, and, till it arrives at some degree of maturity, you must look up to me for advice—then you ought to *think,* and only rely on God.

Yet in the following lines Milton seems to coincide with me; when he makes Adam thus expostulate with his Maker.

> Hast thou not made me here thy substitute,
> And these inferior far beneath me set?
> Among *unequals* what society
> Can sort, what harmony or true delight?
> Which must be mutual, in proportion due
> Giv'n and receiv'd; but in *disparity*
> The one intense, the other still remiss

---

2. Satan's first view of Adam and Eve in *Paradise Lost:* "Not equal, as thir sex not equal seem'd; / For contemplation hee and valor form'd, / For softness shee and sweet attractive Grace, / He for God only, shee for God in him" (4.296–99). Fordyce quotes these lines in *Sermons to* *Young Women,* ch. 13.

3. Francis Bacon, *Essay 16,* "Of Atheism" (1606).

4. See Rousseau's *Émile* (1.1): "Only reason teaches us good from evil."

5. *Paradise Lost* 4.634–38; Wollstonecraft's emphases.

> Cannot well suit with either, but soon prove
> Tedious alike: of *fellowship* I speak
> Such as I seek, fit to participate
> All rational delight[6]—

In treating, therefore, of the manners of women, let us, disregarding sensual arguments, trace what we should endeavour to make them in order to co-operate, if the expression be not too bold, with the supreme Being.

By individual education, I mean, for the sense of the word is not precisely defined, such an attention to a child as will slowly sharpen the senses, form the temper, regulate the passions as they begin to ferment, and set the understanding to work before the body arrives at maturity; so that the man may only have to proceed, not to begin, the important task of learning to think and reason. * * *

In fact, it is a farce to call any being virtuous whose virtues do not result from the exercise of its own reason. This was Rousseau's opinion respecting men: I extend it to women, and confidently assert that they have been drawn out of their sphere by false refinement, and not by an endeavour to acquire masculine qualities. Still the regal homage which they receive is so intoxicating, that till the manners of the times are changed, and formed on more reasonable principles, it may be impossible to convince them that the illegitimate power, which they obtain, by degrading themselves, is a curse, and that they must return to nature and equality, if they wish to secure the placid satisfaction that unsophisticated affections impart. * * *

In the education of women, the cultivation of the understanding is always subordinate to the acquirement of some corporeal accomplishment;[7] even while enervated by confinement and false notions of modesty, the body is prevented from attaining that grace and beauty which relaxed half-formed limbs never exhibit. Besides, in youth their faculties are not brought forward by emulation; and having no serious scientific study, if they have natural sagacity it is turned too soon on life and manners. They dwell on effects, and modifications, without tracing them back to causes; and complicated rules to adjust behaviour are a weak substitute for simple principles.

As a proof that education gives this appearance of weakness to females, we may instance the example of military men, who are, like them, sent into the world before their minds have been stored with knowledge or fortified by principles. The consequences are similar; soldiers acquire a little superficial knowledge, snatched from the muddy current of conversation, and, from continually mixing with society, they gain, what is termed a knowledge of the world; and this acquaintance with manners and customs has frequently been confounded with a knowledge of the human heart. But can the crude fruit of casual observation, never brought to the test of judgment, formed by comparing speculation and experience, deserve such a distinction? Soldiers, as well as women, practice the minor virtues with punctilious politeness. Where is then the sexual difference, when the education has been the same? All the difference that I can discern, arises from the superior advantage of liberty, which enables the former to see more of life.

* * *

Standing armies can never consist of resolute, robust men; they may be well disciplined machines, but they will seldom contain men under the influence of strong passions, or with very vigorous faculties. And as for any depth of understanding, I will

---

6. *Paradise Lost* 8.381–91; Wollstonecraft's emphases.   7. E.g., cosmetic adornment, dancing, singing.

venture to affirm, that it is as rarely to be found in the army as amongst women; and the cause, I maintain, is the same. It may be further observed, that officers are also particularly attentive to their persons, fond of dancing, crowded rooms, adventures, and ridicule.[8] Like the *fair* sex, the business of their lives is gallantry.—They were taught to please, and they only live to please. Yet they do not lose their rank in the distinction of sexes, for they are still reckoned superior to women, though in what their superiority consists, beyond what I have just mentioned, it is difficult to discover.

The great misfortune is this, that they both acquire manners before morals, and a knowledge of life before they have, from reflection, any acquaintance with the grand ideal outline of human nature. The consequence is natural; satisfied with common nature, they become a prey to prejudices, and taking all their opinions on credit, they blindly submit to authority. So that, if they have any sense, it is a kind of instinctive glance, that catches proportions, and decides with respect to manners; but fails when arguments are to be pursued below the surface, or opinions analyzed.

May not the same remark be applied to women? Nay, the argument may be carried still further, for they are both thrown out of a useful station by the unnatural distinctions established in civilized life. Riches and hereditary honours have made cyphers of women to give consequence to the numerical figure; and idleness has produced a mixture of gallantry and despotism into society, which leads the very men who are the slaves of their mistresses to tyrannize over their sisters, wives, and daughters. This is only keeping them in rank and file, it is true. Strengthen the female mind by enlarging it, and there will be an end to blind obedience; but, as blind obedience is ever sought for by power, tyrants and sensualists are in the right when they endeavour to keep women in the dark, because the former only want slaves, and the latter a play-thing. The sensualist, indeed, has been the most dangerous of tyrants, and women have been duped by their lovers, as princes by their ministers, whilst dreaming that they reigned over them. * * *

Probably the prevailing opinion, that woman was created for man, may have taken its rise from Moses's poetical story;[9] yet, as very few, it is presumed, who have bestowed any serious thought on the subject, ever supposed that Eve was, literally speaking, one of Adam's ribs, the deduction must be allowed to fall to the ground; or, only be so far admitted as it proves that man, from the remotest antiquity, found it convenient to exert his strength to subjugate his companion, and his invention to shew that she ought to have her neck bent under the yoke, because the whole creation was only created for his convenience or pleasure.

Let it not be concluded that I wish to invert the order of things; I have already granted, that, from the constitution of their bodies, men seem to be designed by Providence to attain a greater degree of virtue. I speak collectively of the whole sex; but I see not the shadow of a reason to conclude that their virtues should differ in respect to their nature. In fact, how can they, if virtue has only one eternal standard? I must therefore, if I reason consequentially, as strenuously maintain that they have the same simple direction, as that there is a God.

It follows then that cunning should not be opposed to wisdom, little cares to great exertions, or insipid softness, varnished over with the name of gentleness, to that fortitude which grand views alone can inspire.

8. Why should women be censured with petulant acrimony, because they seem to have a passion for a scarlet coat? Has not education placed them more on a level with soldiers than any other class of men?

[Wollstonecraft's note].
9. The first five books of the Old Testament are traditionally attributed to Moses; in Genesis 2.21–23, followed by Milton, God creates Eve out of Adam's rib.

I shall be told that woman would then lose many of her peculiar graces, and the opinion of a well known poet might be quoted to refute my unqualified assertion. For Pope has said, in the name of the whole male sex,

> Yet ne'er so sure our passion to create,
> As when she touch'd the brink of all we hate.

In what light this sally[1] places men and women, I shall leave to the judicious to determine; meanwhile I shall content myself with observing, that I cannot discover why, unless they are mortal, females should always be degraded by being made subservient to love or lust.

To speak disrespectfully of love is, I know, high treason against sentiment and fine feelings; but I wish to speak the simple language of truth, and rather to address the head than the heart. To endeavour to reason love out of the world, would be to out Quixote Cervantes, and equally offend against common sense;[2] but an endeavour to restrain this tumultuous passion, and to prove that it should not be allowed to dethrone superior powers, or to usurp the sceptre which the understanding should ever coolly wield, appears less wild.

Youth is the season for love in both sexes; but in those days of thoughtless enjoyment provision should be made for the more important years of life, when reflection takes place of sensation. But Rousseau, and most of the male writers who have followed his steps, have warmly inculcated that the whole tendency of female education ought to be directed to one point:—to render them pleasing.[3]

Let me reason with the supporters of this opinion who have any knowledge of human nature, do they imagine that marriage can eradicate the habitude of life? The woman who has only been taught to please will soon find that her charms are oblique sunbeams, and that they cannot have much effect on her husband's heart when they are seen every day, when the summer is passed and gone. Will she then have sufficient native energy to look into herself for comfort, and cultivate her dormant faculties? or, is it not more rational to expect that she will try to please other men; and, in the emotions raised by the expectation of new conquests, endeavour to forget the mortification her love or pride has received? When the husband ceases to be a lover—and the time will inevitably come, her desire of pleasing will then grow languid, or become a spring of bitterness; and love, perhaps, the most evanescent of all passions, gives place to jealousy or vanity.

I now speak of women who are restrained by principle or prejudice; such women, though they would shrink from an intrigue with real abhorrence, yet, nevertheless, wish to be convinced by the homage of gallantry that they are cruelly neglected by their husbands; or, days and weeks are spent in dreaming of the happiness enjoyed by congenial souls till their health is undermined and their spirits broken by discontent. How then can the great art of pleasing be such a necessary study? it is only useful to a mistress; the chaste wife, and serious mother, should only consider her power to please as the polish of her virtues, and the affection of her husband as one of the comforts that render her task less difficult and her life happier.—But, whether she be loved or neglected, her first wish should be to make herself respectable, and not to rely for all her happiness on a being subject to like infirmities with herself.

---

1. The "sally" (an attack by besieged troops; an outburst of wit) is from Pope's *Epistle II, To a Lady*, "Of the Characters of Women" (1735), 51–52.

2. To outdo Cervantes' comic hero Don Quixote in ineffectual idealism, including the ideals of courtly love.
3. *Émile*, ch. 5.

The worthy Dr. Gregory fell into a similar error. I respect his heart; but entirely disapprove of his celebrated Legacy to his Daughters.[4]

He advises them to cultivate a fondness for dress, because a fondness for dress, he asserts, is natural to them. I am unable to comprehend what either he or Rousseau mean, when they frequently use this indefinite term. If they told us that in a pre-existent state the soul was fond of dress, and brought this inclination with it into a new body, I should listen to them with a half smile, as I often do when I hear a rant about innate elegance.—But if he only meant to say that the exercise of the faculties will produce this fondness—I deny it.—It is not natural; but arises, like false ambition in men, from a love of power.

Dr. Gregory goes much further; he actually recommends dissimulation, and advises an innocent girl to give the lie to her feelings, and not dance with spirit, when gaiety of heart would make her feel eloquent without making her gestures immodest. In the name of truth and common sense, why should not one woman acknowledge that she can take more exercise than another? or, in other words, that she has a sound constitution; and why, to damp innocent vivacity, is she darkly to be told that men will draw conclusions which she little thinks of?—Let the libertine draw what inference he pleases; but, I hope, that no sensible mother will restrain the natural frankness of youth by instilling such indecent cautions. ***

Surely she has not an immortal soul who can loiter life away merely employed to adorn her person, that she may amuse the languid hours, and soften the cares of a fellow-creature who is willing to be enlivened by her smiles and tricks, when the serious business of life is over.

Besides, the woman who strengthens her body and exercises her mind will, by managing her family and practising various virtues, become the friend, and not the humble dependent of her husband; and if she, by possessing such substantial qualities, merit his regard, she will not find it necessary to conceal her affection, nor to pretend to an unnatural coldness of constitution to excite her husband's passions. In fact, if we revert to history, we shall find that the women who have distinguished themselves have neither been the most beautiful nor the most gentle of their sex. ***

Love, the common passion, in which chance and sensation take place of choice and reason, is, in some degree, felt by the mass of mankind; for it is not necessary to speak, at present, of the emotions that rise above or sink below love. This passion, naturally increased by suspense and difficulties, draws the mind out of its accustomed state, and exalts the affections; but the security of marriage, allowing the fever of love to subside, a healthy temperature is thought insipid, only by those who have not sufficient intellect to substitute the calm tenderness of friendship, the confidence of respect, instead of blind admiration, and the sensual emotions of fondness.

This is, must be, the course of nature.—Friendship or indifference inevitably succeeds love.—And this constitution seems perfectly to harmonize with the system of government which prevails in the normal world. Passions are spurs to action, and open the mind; but they sink into mere appetites, become a personal and momentary gratification, when the object is gained, and the satisfied mind rests in enjoyment. The man who had some virtue whilst he was struggling for a crown, often becomes a voluptuous tyrant when it graces his brow; and, when the lover is not lost in the husband, the dotard, a prey of childish caprices, and fond jealousies, neglects the serious

---

4. Dr. John Gregory's influential conduct manual, *A Father's Legacy to His Daughters* (1774).

duties of life, and the caresses which should excite confidence in his children are lavished on the overgrown child, his wife.

In order to fulfil the duties of life, and to be able to pursue with vigour the various employments which form the moral character, a master and mistress of a family ought not to continue to love each other with passion. I mean to say, that they ought not to indulge those emotions which disturb the order of society, and engross the thoughts that should be otherwise employed. The mind that has never been engrossed by one object wants vigour—if it can long be so, it is weak.

A mistaken education, a narrow, uncultivated mind, and many sexual prejudices, tend to make women more constant than men; but, for the present, I shall not touch on this branch of the subject. I will go still further, and advance, without dreaming of a paradox, that an unhappy marriage is often very advantageous to a family, and that the neglected wife is, in general, the best mother. ***

I own it frequently happens that women who have fostered a romantic unnatural delicacy of feeling,[5] waste their lives in *imagining* how happy they should have been with a husband who could love them with a fervid increasing affection every day, and all day. But they might as well pine married as single—and would not be a jot more unhappy with a bad husband than longing for a good one. That a proper education; or, to speak with more precision, a well stored mind, would enable a woman to support a single life with dignity, I grant; but that she should avoid cultivating her taste, lest her husband should occasionally shock it, is quitting a substance for a shadow. To say the truth, I do not know of what use is an improved taste, if the individual be not rendered more independent of the casualties of life; if new sources of enjoyment, only dependent on the solitary operations of the mind, are not opened. People of taste, married or single, without distinction, will ever be disgusted by various things that touch not less observing minds. On this conclusion the argument must not be allowed to hinge; but in the whole sum of enjoyment is taste to be denominated a blessing?

The question is, whether it procures most pain or pleasure? The answer will decide the propriety of Dr. Gregory's advice, and shew how absurd and tyrannic it is thus to lay down a system of slavery; or to attempt to educate moral beings by any other rules than those deduced from pure reason, which apply to the whole species.

Gentleness of manners, forbearance and long-suffering, are such amiable God-like qualities, that in sublime poetic strains the Deity has been invested with them; and, perhaps, no representation of his goodness so strongly fastens on the human affections as those that represent him abundant in mercy and willing to pardon.[6] Gentleness, considered in this point of view, bears on its front all the characteristics of grandeur, combined with the winning graces of condescension; but what a different aspect it assumes when it is the submissive demeanour of dependence, the support of weakness that loves, because it wants protection; and is forbearing, because it must silently endure injuries; smiling under the lash at which it dare not snarl. Abject as this picture appears, it is the portrait of an accomplished woman, according to the received opinion of female excellence, separated by specious reasoners from human

---

5. For example, the herd of novelists [Wollstonecraft's note, attacking popular sentimental fiction].
6. A repentant sinner will find that God "will have mercy upon him; and to our God, for he will abundantly pardon" (Isaiah 55.7).

excellence. Or, they[7] kindly restore the rib, and make one moral being of a man and woman; not forgetting to give her all the "submissive charms."[8]

How women are to exist in that state where there is to be neither marrying nor giving in marriage, we are not told.[9] For though moralists have agreed that the tenor of life seems to prove that *man* is prepared by various circumstances for a future state, they constantly concur in advising *woman* only to provide for the present. Gentleness, docility, and a spaniel-like affection are, on this ground, consistently recommended as the cardinal virtues of the sex; and, disregarding the arbitrary economy of nature, one writer has declared that it is masculine for a woman to be melancholy. She was created to be the toy of man, his rattle, and it must jingle in his ears whenever, dismissing reason, he chooses to be amused. * * *

As a philosopher, I read with indignation the plausible epithets which men use to soften their insults; and, as a moralist, I ask what is meant by such heterogeneous associations, as fair defects, amiable weaknesses, &c.?[1] If there be but one criterion of morals, but one archetype for man, women appear to be suspended by destiny, according to the vulgar tale of Mahomet's coffin;[2] they have neither the unerring instinct of brutes, nor are allowed to fix the eye of reason on a perfect model. They were made to be loved, and must not aim at respect, lest they should be hunted out of society as masculine.

But to view the subject in another point of view. Do passive indolent women make the best wives? Confining our discussion to the present moment of existence, let us see how such weak creatures perform their part? Do the women who, by the attainment of a few superficial accomplishments, have strengthened the prevailing prejudice, merely contribute to the happiness of their husbands? Do they display their charms merely to amuse them? And have women, who have early imbibed notions of passive obedience, sufficient character to manage a family or educate children? So far from it, that, after surveying the history of woman, I cannot help, agreeing with the severest satirist, considering the sex as the weakest as well as the most oppressed half of the species. What does history disclose but marks of inferiority, and how few women have emancipated themselves from the galling yoke of sovereign man?—So few, that the exceptions remind me of an ingenious conjecture respecting Newton: that he was probably a being of a superior order, accidentally caged in a human body.[3] Following the same train of thinking, I have been led to imagine that the few extraordinary women who have rushed in eccentric directions out of the orbit prescribed to their sex, were *male* spirits, confined by mistake in female frames. But if it be not philosophical to think of sex when the soul is mentioned, the inferiority

7. Vide [see] Rousseau and Swedenborg [Wollstonecraft's note]. In *Émile*, ch. 5, Rousseau argued that because man and wife were one ("one flesh"; Genesis 2.24), the wife could have no independent moral judgment. Emanuel Swedenborg (1688–1772), Swedish scientist, theologian, and mystic, argued that marriage persisted in the afterlife of heaven in the united form of a single angel.

8. In *Paradise Lost*, Adam smiles on Eve "with superior Love," delighted by her "Beauty and submissive Charms" (4.497–99).

9. Asked about the heavenly life of a woman who has married more than once ("whose wife shall she be?"), Jesus answers, "in the resurrection they neither marry, nor are given in marriage, but are as the angels of God in heaven" (Matthew 22.30). Wollstonecraft's *Mary, A Fiction* (1788)

closes with its ever frustrated, dying heroine cheered by the thought of "hastening to that world *where there is neither marrying*, nor giving in marriage"—where women are no longer controlled by fathers and husbands.

1. In *Paradise Lost*, after the Fall, Adam reviles Eve as a "fair defect / Of nature" (10.891–92) prone to Satanic temptation and tempting Adam from his better knowledge. Pope's "Of the Characters of Women" declares that "Ladies, like variegated tulips, show; . . . / Fine by defect, and delicately weak . . . " (41–43); the coloring of tulips is caused by a virus that renders them both beautiful and weak.

2. Muhammad's coffin was reputed to hang magically in the center of his tomb.

3. Isaac Newton (1642–1727), brilliant physicist and mathematician.

must depend on the organs; or the heavenly fire, which is to ferment the clay, is not given in equal portions.[4] * * *

Surely there can be but one rule of right, if morality has an eternal foundation, and whoever sacrifices virtue, strictly so called, to present convenience, or whose *duty* it is to act in such a manner, lives only for the passing day, and cannot be an accountable creature.

The poet then should have dropped his sneer when he says,

> If weak women go astray,
> The stars are more in fault than they.[5]

For that they are bound by the adamantine chain of destiny is most certain, if it be proved that they are never to exercise their own reason, never to be independent, never to rise above opinion, or to feel the dignity of a rational will that only bows to God, and often forgets that the universe contains any being but itself and the model of perfection to which its ardent gaze is turned, to adore attributes that, softened into virtues, may be imitated in kind, though the degree overwhelms the enraptured mind.

If, I say, for I would not impress by declamation when Reason offers her sober light,[6] if they be really capable of acting like rational creatures, let them not be treated like slaves; or, like the brutes who are dependent on the reason of man, when they associate with him; but cultivate their minds, give them the salutary, sublime curb of principle, and let them attain conscious dignity by feeling themselves only dependent on God. Teach them, in common with man, to submit to necessity, instead of giving, to render them more pleasing, a sex to morals.

Further, should experience prove that they cannot attain the same degree of strength of mind, perseverance, and fortitude, let their virtues be the same in kind, though they may vainly struggle for the same degree; and the superiority of man will be equally clear, if not clearer; and truth, as it is a simple principle, which admits of no modification, would be common to both. Nay, the order of society as it is at present regulated would not be inverted, for woman would then only have the rank that reason assigned her, and arts could not be practised to bring the balance even, much less to turn it.

These may be termed Utopian dreams.[7]—Thanks to that Being who impressed them on my soul, and gave me sufficient strength of mind to dare to exert my own reason, till, becoming dependent only on him for the support of my virtue, I view, with indignation, the mistaken notions that enslave my sex.

I love man as my fellow; but his scepter, real, or usurped, extends not to me, unless the reason of an individual demands my homage; and even then the submission is to reason, and not to man. In fact, the conduct of an accountable being must be regulated by the operations of its own reason; or on what foundation rests the throne of God? * * *

---

4. In the 18th century, the question whether the soul had a sex, like the body, was widely debated. "Clay" is a familiar term for the body.

5. "Hans Carvel" (11–12), a satire by Matthew Prior (1664–1721). These lines invert Cassius's remark in *Julius Caesar*: "The fault, dear Brutus, lies not in the stars, / But in ourselves, that we are underlings" (1.2.140–41).

6. This feminine gendering of "Reason" resists Milton's male assignment of Reason and evokes the deity of the French Revolution, "La Raison"—a feminine noun in French.

7. Impossible social ideals, derived from Sir Thomas More's 16th-century treatise, *Utopia*.

from *Chapter 3. The Same Subject Continued*

If it be granted that woman was not created merely to gratify the appetite of man, or to be the upper servant, who provides his meals and takes care of his linen, it must follow, that the first care of those mothers or fathers, who really attend to the education of females, should be, if not to strengthen the body, at least, not to destroy the constitution by mistaken notions of beauty and female excellence; nor should girls ever be allowed to imbibe the pernicious notion that a defect can, by any chemical process of reasoning, become an excellence. * * *

But should it be proved that woman is naturally weaker than man, whence does it follow that it is natural for her to labour to become still weaker than nature intended her to be? Arguments of this cast are an insult to common sense, and savour of passion. The *divine right* of husbands, like the divine right of kings, may, it is to be hoped, in this enlightened age, be contested without danger, and, though conviction may not silence many boisterous disputants, yet, when any prevailing prejudice is attacked, the wise will consider, and leave the narrow-minded to rail with thoughtless vehemence at innovation. * * *

Throughout the whole animal kingdom every young creature requires almost continual exercise, and the infancy of children, conformable to this intimation, should be passed in harmless gambols, that exercise the feet and hands, without requiring very minute direction from the head, or the constant attention of a nurse. In fact, the care necessary for self-preservation is the first natural exercise of the understanding, as little inventions to amuse the present moment unfold the imagination. But these wise designs of nature are counteracted by mistaken fondness or blind zeal. The child is not left a moment to its own direction, particularly a girl, and thus rendered dependent—dependence is called natural. * * *

I will venture to affirm, that a girl, whose spirits have not been damped by inactivity, or innocence tainted by false shame, will always be a romp, and the doll will never excite attention unless confinement allows her no alternative. Girls and boys, in short, would play harmlessly together, if the distinction of sex was not inculcated long before nature makes any difference.—I will go further, and affirm, as an indisputable fact, that most of the women, in the circle of my observation, who have acted like rational creatures, or shewn any vigour of intellect, have accidentally been allowed to run wild—as some of the elegant formers of the fair sex would insinuate.

The baneful consequences which flow from inattention to health during infancy, and youth, extend further than is supposed—dependence of body naturally produces dependence of mind; and how can she be a good wife or mother, the greater part of whose time is employed to guard against or endure sickness? Nor can it be expected that a woman will resolutely endeavour to strengthen her constitution and abstain from enervating indulgencies, if artificial notions of beauty, and false descriptions of sensibility, have been early entangled with her motives of action. Most men are sometimes obliged to bear with bodily inconveniencies, and to endure, occasionally, the inclemency of the elements; but genteel women are, literally speaking, slaves to their bodies, and glory in their subjection.

I once knew a weak woman of fashion, who was more than commonly proud of her delicacy and sensibility. She thought a distinguishing taste and puny appetite the height of all human perfection, and acted accordingly.—I have seen this weak sophisticated being neglect all the duties of life, yet recline with self-complacency on a sofa, and boast of her want of appetite as a proof of delicacy that extended to, or, perhaps, arose from, her exquisite sensibility: for it is difficult to render intelligible such ridiculous jargon.—Yet, at the moment, I have seen her insult a worthy old gentlewoman, whom unexpected misfortunes had made dependent on her ostentatious bounty, and who, in better days, had claims on her gratitude. Is it possible that a human creature could have become such a weak and depraved being, if, like the Sybarites,[1] dissolved in luxury, every thing like virtue had not been worn away, or never impressed by precept, a poor substitute, it is true, for cultivation of mind, though it serves as a fence against vice?

Such a woman is not a more irrational monster than some of the Roman emperors, who were depraved by lawless power. Yet, since kings have been more under the restraint of law, and the curb, however weak, of honour, the records of history are not filled with such unnatural instances of folly and cruelty, nor does the despotism that kills virtue and genius in the bud, hover over Europe with that destructive blast which desolates Turkey, and renders the men, as well as the soil, unfruitful.[2] ***

It is time to effect a revolution in female manners—time to restore to them their lost dignity—and make them, as a part of the human species, labour by reforming themselves to reform the world. It is time to separate unchangeable morals from local manners.—If men be demi-gods—why let us serve them! And if the dignity of the female soul be as disputable as that of animals—if their reason does not afford sufficient light to direct their conduct whilst unerring instinct is denied—they are surely of all creatures the most miserable! and, bent beneath the iron hand of destiny, must submit to be a *fair defect* in creation. But to justify the ways of Providence respecting them, by pointing out some irrefragable reason for thus making such a large portion of mankind accountable and not accountable, would puzzle the subtilest casuist.[3] * * *

If women be educated for dependence; that is, to act according to the will of another fallible being, and submit, right or wrong, to power, where are we to stop? Are they to be considered as viceregents allowed to reign over a small domain, and answerable for their conduct to a higher tribunal, liable to error?

It will not be difficult to prove that such delegates will act like men subjected by fear, and make their children and servants endure their tyrannical oppression. As they submit without reason, they will, having no fixed rules to square their conduct by, be kind, or cruel, just as the whim of the moment directs; and we ought not to wonder if sometimes, galled by their heavy yoke, they take a malignant pleasure in resting it on weaker shoulders.

But, supposing a woman, trained up to obedience, be married to a sensible man, who directs her judgment without making her feel the servility of her subjection, to act with as much propriety by this reflected light as can be expected when reason is taken at second hand, yet she cannot ensure the life of her protector; he may die and leave her with a large family.

A double duty devolves on her; to educate them in the character of both father and mother; to form their principles and secure their property. But, alas! she

---

1. The inhabitants of a 5th-century Greek colony in Italy famed for luxurious decadence.
2. Both the hot, dusty winds from the deserts to the south and the infamously despotic Ottoman Empire.

3. For "fair defect," see *Paradise Lost* 8.891–92; Milton begins his epic invoking divine inspiration to "justify the ways of God to men" (1.26); a casuist studies the relation of cases to principles (sometimes opportunistically).

has never thought, much less acted for herself. She has only learned to please[4] men, to depend gracefully on them; yet, encumbered with children, how is she to obtain another protector—a husband to supply the place of reason? A rational man, for we are not treading on romantic ground, though he may think her a pleasing docile creature, will not choose to marry a *family* for love, when the world contains many more pretty creatures. What is then to become of her? She either falls an easy prey to some mean fortune-hunter, who defrauds her children of their paternal inheritance,[5] and renders her miserable; or becomes the victim of discontent and blind indulgence. Unable to educate her sons, or impress them with respect; for it is not a play on words to assert, that people are never respected, though filling an important station, who are not respectable; she pines under the anguish of unavailing impotent regret. The serpent's tooth enters into her very soul,[6] and the vices of licentious youth bring her with sorrow, if not with poverty also, to the grave.

This is not an overcharged picture; on the contrary, it is a very possible case, and something similar must have fallen under every attentive eye.

I have, however, taken it for granted, that she was well-disposed, though experience shews, that the blind may as easily be led into a ditch as along the beaten road.[7] But supposing, no very improbable conjecture, that a being only taught to please must still find her happiness in pleasing;—what an example of folly, not to say vice, will she be to her innocent daughters! The mother will be lost in the coquette, and, instead of making friends of her daughters, view them with eyes askance, for they are rivals—rivals more cruel than any other, because they invite a comparison, and drive her from the throne of beauty, who has never thought of a seat on the bench of reason.

It does not require a lively pencil, or the discriminating outline of a caricature, to sketch the domestic miseries and petty vices which such a mistress of a family diffuses. Still she only acts as a woman ought to act, brought up according to Rousseau's system. She can never be reproached for being masculine, or turning out of her sphere; nay, she may observe another of his grand rules, and, cautiously preserving her reputation free from spot, be reckoned a good kind of woman. Yet in what respect can she be termed good? She abstains, it is true, without any great struggle, from committing gross crimes; but how does she fulfil her duties? Duties!—in truth she has enough to think of to adorn her body and nurse a weak constitution.

With respect to religion, she never presumed to judge for herself; but conformed, as a dependent creature should, to the ceremonies of the church which she was

---

4. "In the union of the sexes, both pursue one common object, but not in the same manner. From their diversity in this particular, arises the first determinate difference between the moral relations of each. The one should be active and strong, the other passive and weak: it is necessary the one should have both the power and the will, and that the other should make little resistance. This principle being established, it follows that woman is expressly formed to please the man . . . [who] pleases merely because he is strong. This, I must confess, is not one of the refined maxims of love; it is, however, one of the laws of nature, prior to love itself. . . . Hence arise the various modes of attack and defence between the sexes; the boldness of one sex and the timidity of the other; and, in a word, that bashfulness and modesty with which nature hath armed the weak, in order to subdue the strong." [From Wollstonecraft's longer quotation, in a footnote, of Rousseau's *Émile*, ch. 5, on which she remarks, "I shall make no other comment on this ingenious passage, than just to observe, that it is the philosophy of lasciviousness."]

5. The husband owned all property including the property a wife brought to a marriage.

6. Lear's lament over his daughters' inhospitality after he has ceded his kingdom to them and their husbands: "How sharper than a serpent's tooth it is / To have a thankless child" (*King Lear* 1.4.295–96).

7. See Jesus' admonition, "if the blind lead the blind, both shall fall into the ditch" (Matthew 15.14).

brought up in, piously believing that wiser heads than her own have settled that business:—and not to doubt is her point of perfection.[8] She therefore pays her tythe of mint and cummin[9]—and thanks her God that she is not as other women are. These are the blessed effects of a good education! These the virtues of man's help-mate![1]

I must relieve myself by drawing a different picture.

Let fancy now present a woman with a tolerable understanding, for I do not wish to leave the line of mediocrity, whose constitution, strengthened by exercise, has allowed her body to acquire its full vigour; her mind, at the same time, gradually expanding itself to comprehend the moral duties of life, and in what human virtue and dignity consist.

Formed thus by the discharge of the relative duties of her station, she marries from affection, without losing sight of prudence, and looking beyond matrimonial felicity, she secures her husband's respect before it is necessary to exert mean arts to please him and feed a dying flame, which nature doomed to expire when the object became familiar, when friendship and forbearance take place of a more ardent affection.—This is the natural death of love, and domestic peace is not destroyed by struggles to prevent its extinction. I also suppose the husband to be virtuous; or she is still more in want of independent principles.

Fate, however, breaks this tie.—She is left a widow, perhaps, without a sufficient provision; but she is not desolate! The pang of nature is felt; but after time has softened sorrow into melancholy resignation, her heart turns to her children with redoubled fondness, and anxious to provide for them, affection gives a sacred heroic cast to her maternal duties. She thinks that not only the eye sees her virtuous efforts from whom all her comfort now must flow, and whose approbation is life; but her imagination, a little abstracted and exalted by grief, dwells on the fond hope that the eyes which her trembling hand closed, may still see how she subdues every wayward passion to fulfil the double duty of being the father as well as the mother of her children. Raised to heroism by misfortunes, she represses the first faint dawning of a natural inclination, before it ripens into love, and in the bloom of life forgets her sex—forgets the pleasure of an awakening passion, which might again have been inspired and returned. She no longer thinks of pleasing, and conscious dignity prevents her from priding herself on account of the praise which her conduct demands. Her children have her love, and her brightest hopes are beyond the grave, where her imagination often strays.

I think I see her surrounded by her children, reaping the reward of her care. The intelligent eye meets hers, whilst health and innocence smile on their chubby cheeks, and as they grow up the cares of life are lessened by their grateful attention. She lives to see the virtues which she endeavoured to plant on principles, fixed into

---

8. In *Émile*, Rousseau advises, "The daughter should follow her mother's religion, the wife her husband's. Were that religion false, the docility which leads mother and daughter to submit to nature's laws would blot out the sin or error in the sight of God. Unable to judge for themselves they should accept the judgment of father and husband as that of the church" (ch. 5).

9. Minor obligation; Jesus admonishes, "Woe unto you, scribes and Pharisees, hypocrites! for ye pay tithe of mint and anise and cummin, and have omitted the weightier matters of the law, judgment, mercy, and faith" (Matthew 23.23).

Pharisees follow the letter rather than the spirit of the law.

1. "O how lovely," exclaims Rousseau of Sophia, "is her ignorance! Happy is he who is destined to instruct her! She will never pretend to be the tutor of her husband, but will be content to be his pupil. Far from attempting to subject him to her taste, she will accommodate herself to his. She will be more estimable to him, than if she was learned: he will have a pleasure in instructing her." I shall content myself with simply asking, how friendship can subsist, when love expires, between the master and his pupil? [Wollstonecraft's note, quoting from *Émile*, ch. 5].

habits, to see her children attain a strength of character sufficient to enable them to endure adversity without forgetting their mother's example.

The task of life thus fulfilled, she calmly waits for the sleep of death, and rising from the grave, may say—Behold, thou gavest me a talent—and here are five talents.[2]

from *Chapter 5. Animadversions on Some of the Writers Who Have Rendered Women Objects of Pity, Bordering on Contempt*
[PRAISE FOR CATHARINE MACAULAY]

The very word respect brings Mrs. Macaulay to my remembrance. The woman of the greatest abilities, undoubtedly, that this country has ever produced.—And yet this woman has been suffered to die without sufficient respect being paid to her memory.

Posterity, however, will be more just; and remember that Catharine Macaulay was an example of intellectual acquirements supposed to be incompatible with the weakness of her sex. In her style of writing, indeed, no sex appears, for it is like the sense it conveys, strong and clear.

I will not call hers a masculine understanding, because I admit not of such an arrogant assumption of reason; but I contend that it was a sound one, and that her judgment, the matured fruit of profound thinking, was a proof that a woman can acquire judgment, in the full extent of the word. Possessing more penetration than sagacity, more understanding than fancy, she writes with sober energy and argumentative closeness; yet sympathy and benevolence give an interest to her sentiments, and that vital heat to arguments, which forces the reader to weigh them.[1]

When I first thought of writing these strictures I anticipated Mrs. Macaulay's approbation, with a little of that sanguine ardour, which it has been the business of my life to depress; but soon heard with the sickly qualm of disappointed hope; and the still seriousness of regret—that she was no more![2]

from *Chapter 13. Some Instances of the Folly Which the Ignorance of Women Generates; with Concluding Reflections on the Moral Improvement That a Revolution in Female Manners Might Naturally Be Expected to Produce*
[CONCLUDING REFLECTIONS]

That women at present are by ignorance rendered foolish or vicious, is, I think, not to be disputed; and, that the most salutary effects tending to improve mankind might be expected from a REVOLUTION in female manners, appears, at least, with a face of probability, to rise out of the observation. For as marriage has been termed the parent of those endearing charities which draw man from the brutal herd, the corrupting intercourse that wealth, idleness, and folly, produce between the sexes, is more universally injurious to morality than all the other vices of mankind collectively considered. To adulterous lust the most sacred duties are sacrificed, because before marriage, men, by a promiscuous intimacy with women, learned to consider love as a selfish gratification—learned to separate it not only from esteem, but from the affection

2. An extravagant rewriting of Jesus's parable of the talents (Matthew 25.15–28), on the duty to make good use of God's gifts. A master, having given one servant five talents (a talent is a silver coin worth about $1,000 today), is pleased to learn that he doubled his money.
1. Coinciding in opinion with Mrs. Macaulay relative to

many branches of education, I refer to her valuable work, instead of quoting her sentiments to support my own. [Wollstonecraft's note, referring to *Letters on Education*, 1790; see selection from Macaulay, page 341].
2. Macaulay died in 1791; approbation: formal praise; sanguine: blushingly optimistic.

merely built on habit, which mixes a little humanity with it. Justice and friendship are also set at defiance, and that purity of taste is vitiated which would naturally lead a man to relish an artless display of affection rather than affected airs. But that noble simplicity of affection, which dares to appear unadorned, has few attractions for the libertine, though it be the charm, which by cementing the matrimonial tie, secures to the pledges of a warmer passion the necessary parental attention; for children will never be properly educated till friendship subsists between parents. Virtue flies from a house divided against itself—and a whole legion of devils take up their residence there.[1]

The affection of husbands and wives cannot be pure when they have so few sentiments in common, and when so little confidence is established at home, as must be the case when their pursuits are so different. That intimacy from which tenderness should flow, will not, cannot subsist between the vicious.

Contending, therefore, that the sexual distinction which men have so warmly insisted upon, is arbitrary, I have dwelt on an observation, that several sensible men, with whom I have conversed on the subject, allowed to be well founded; and it is simply this, that the little chastity to be found amongst men, and consequent disregard of modesty, tend to degrade both sexes; and further, that the modesty of women, characterized as such, will often be only the artful veil of wantonness instead of being the natural reflection of purity, till modesty be universally respected.[2]

From the tyranny of man, I firmly believe, the greater number of female follies proceed; and the cunning, which I allow makes at present a part of their character, I likewise have repeatedly endeavoured to prove, is produced by oppression.

Were not dissenters,[3] for instance, a class of people, with strict truth, characterized as cunning? And may I not lay some stress on this fact to prove, that when any power but reason curbs the free spirit of man, dissimulation is practised, and the various shifts of art are naturally called forth? Great attention to decorum, which was carried to a degree of scrupulosity, and all that puerile bustle about trifles and consequential solemnity, which Butler's caricature of a dissenter, brings before the imagination, shaped their persons as well as their minds in the mould of prim littleness.[4] I speak collectively, for I know how many ornaments to human nature have been enrolled amongst sectaries; yet, I assert, that the same narrow prejudice for their sect, which women have for their families, prevailed in the dissenting part of the community, however worthy in other respects; and also that the same timid prudence, or headstrong efforts, often disgraced the exertions of both. Oppression thus formed many of the features of their character perfectly to coincide with that of the oppressed half of mankind; or is it not notorious that dissenters were, like women, fond of deliberating together, and asking advice of each other, till by a complication of little contrivances, some little end was brought about? A similar attention to preserve their reputation was conspicuous in the dissenting and female world, and was produced by a similar cause.

Asserting the rights which women in common with men ought to contend for, I have not attempted to extenuate their faults; but to prove them to be the natural

---

1. Jesus advises, "if a house be divided against itself, that house cannot stand" (Mark 3.25).
2. Sexual self-control; male chastity refers to fidelity in marriage.
3. Those who left the established Church of England to form independent religious sects; many of Wollstonecraft's friends were dissenters.

4. Samuel Butler's mock-heroic, satirical poem *Hudibras* (1663–1678) takes aim at Puritans (dissenters who formed the commonwealth government after the execution of Charles I); Sir Hudibras, pedant and hypocrite, is a country justice who sets out to reform England of various popular entertainments.

consequence of their education and station in society. If so, it is reasonable to suppose that they will change their character, and correct their vices and follies, when they are allowed to be free in a physical, moral, and civil sense.[5]

Let woman share the rights and she will emulate the virtues of man; for she must grow more perfect when emancipated, or justify the authority that chains such a weak being to her duty.—If the latter, it will be expedient to open a fresh trade with Russia for whips; a present which a father should always make to his son-in-law on his wedding day, that a husband may keep his whole family in order by the same means; and without any violation of justice reign, wielding this sceptre, sole master of his house, because he is the only being in it who has reason:—the divine, indefeasible earthly sovereignty breathed into man by the Master of the universe. Allowing this position, women have not any inherent rights to claim; and, by the same rule, their duties vanish, for rights and duties are inseparable.

Be just then, O ye men of understanding! and mark not more severely what women do amiss, than the vicious tricks of the horse or the ass for whom ye provide provender—and allow her the privileges of ignorance, to whom ye deny the rights of reason, or ye will be worse than Egyptian task-masters, expecting virtue where nature has not given understanding!

⟨∞⟩

RESPONSES

Anna Letitia Barbauld: The Rights of Woman[1]

	Yes, injured Woman! rise, assert thy right!	
	Woman! too long degraded, scorned, opprest;	
	O born to rule in partial° Law's despite,	*one-sided*
	Resume thy native empire o'er the breast!	
5	Go forth arrayed in panoply° divine;	*armor*
	That angel pureness which admits no stain;	
	Go, bid proud Man his boasted rule resign,	
	And kiss the golden sceptre of thy reign.	
	Go, gird thyself with grace; collect thy store	
10	Of bright artillery glancing from afar;	
	Soft melting tones thy thundering cannon's roar,	
	Blushes and fears thy magazine° of war.	*storehouse*

5. I had further enlarged on the advantages which might reasonably be expected to result from an improvement in female manners, towards the general reformation of society; but it appeared to me that such reflections would more properly close the last volume. [Wollstonecraft's note; no further volumes were published.]
1. Barbauld wrote *The Rights of Woman* in 1795 in reaction to *A Vindication of the Rights of Woman* (it was not published until 1825). She was offended by the revolutionary rhetoric, and the seemingly un-Christian refutation of the "female" virtues of submission and obedience. In Chapter 4 ("Observations on the State of Degradation to Which Woman is Reduced by Various Causes"), moreover, Wollstonecraft cited her as a sorry example of how "even women of superiour sense" can voice sentiments that "rob the sex of its dignity": "How could Mrs. Barbauld write the following ignoble comparison?"

she exclaims, quoting "To a Lady, with some painted flowers" and pointedly italicizing several lines, among them: "Flowers SWEET, and gay, and DELICATE LIKE YOU; / Emblems of innocence, and beauty too . . . this soft family, to cares unknown, / Were born for pleasure and delight ALONE"; "Your BEST, your SWEETEST empire is—TO PLEASE." "So the men tell us," Wollstonecraft counters, "but virtue, says reason, must be acquired by . . . useful struggles with worldly *cares*." Barbauld's *Rights of Woman* retorts that women gain most from feminine influence of and on the heart. Yet her letters *On Female Studies* (1825) echo many of Wollstonecraft's values, including a lament on novel-reading and an insistence that the best wives, mothers, and family managers are educated in "the general character of a rational being."

For more about Barbauld, see her principal listing on page 65.

Thy rights are empire: urge no meaner° claim,—   *lower*
Felt, not defined, and if debated, lost;
15   Like sacred mysteries, which withheld from fame,
Shunning discussion, are revered the most.

Try all that wit and art suggest to bend
Of thy imperial foe the stubborn knee;
Make treacherous Man thy subject, not thy friend:
20   Thou mayst command, but never canst be free.[2]

Awe the licentious, and restrain the rude;
Soften the sullen, clear the cloudy brow:
Be, more than princes' gifts, thy favours sued;—
She hazards all, who will the least allow.

25   But hope not, courted idol of mankind,
On this proud eminence secure to stay;
Subduing and subdued, thou soon shalt find
Thy coldness soften, and thy pride give way.

Then, then, abandon each ambitious thought,
30   Conquest or rule thy heart shall feebly move,
In Nature's school, by her soft maxims taught,
That separate rights are lost in mutual love.

Ann Yearsley: The Indifferent Shepherdess to Colin[1]

Colin, why this mistake?
    Why plead thy foolish love?
My heart shall sooner break
    Than I a minion° prove;   *darling*
5   Nor care I half a rush,
    No snare I spread for thee:
Go home, my friend, and blush
    For love and liberty.

Remembrance is my own—
10   Dominion bright and clear,
Truth there was ever known
    To combat ev'ry care:
One image there imprest
    Thro' life shall ever be,
15   Whilst my innoxious° breast   *innocent, blameless*
    Owns love of liberty.

2. The tone of this address is perplexing: is Barbauld satirizing what she takes to be the power politics of Wollstonecraft's argument, or has she misread the argument?
1. Ann Yearsley (?1756–1806) adds a woman's poem to, and against, a famous late 16th-century dialogue volleyed by Christopher Marlowe's *The Passionate Shepherd to His Love* ("Come live with me, and be my love, / And we will all the pleasures prove . . . ") and Sir Walter Raleigh's wittily skeptical, *The Nymph's Reply to the Shepherd* ("If all the world and love were young, / And truth in every

shepherd's tongue . . . "). Her reply has a model in Cervantes' shepherdess Marcela, who defies all lovers to maintain her freedom (*Don Quixote*, pt. 1, chs. 12–14). Published in *The Rural Lyre* (1796), Yearsley's argument and key terms are also tuned to contemporary polemics on tyranny, slavery, and the oppression of women. For her abolition poetry, see page 251. Colin is a conventional name for a shepherd, deriving from Edmund Spenser's pastoral eclogues, *The Shepheardes Calender* (1579).

I ever taught thee how
    To prize the soul entire,
When on the mountain's brow
20   I tun'd my rural lyre:
Thou servile art and vain,
    Thy love unworthy me!
Away! nor hear my strain,°   *song*
    Of love or liberty.

25 What arts need I display
    To woo a soul like thine?
Thou ne'er canst know the way
    My mem'ry to confine;
For my eternal plan
30   Is to be calm and free.
Estrang'd from tyrant man
    I'll keep my liberty.

Yon woods their foliage wear,
    Be thou away or nigh;
35 The warblers of the year
    Instruct me not to sigh:
My tears ne'er roll the steep,
    Nor swell the restless sea,
Except for those who sleep
40   Bereft of liberty.

Slave to commanding eyes!
    Those eyes thou wouldst commend
My judgment must despise—
    My pity is thy friend:
45 If eyes alone can move
    A swain so dull as thee,
They mean but to reprove
    Thy loss of liberty.

I stray o'er rocks and fields
50   Where native beauties shine:
All fetter'd fancy yields
    Be, Colin, ever thine.
Complain no more! but rove—
    My cheek from crimson° free,   *shameful blush*
55 Within my native grove
    I'll guard my liberty.

Robert Southey: *To Mary Wollstonecraft*[1]

The lilly cheek, the "purple light of love,"[2]
The liquid lustre of the melting eye,—

1. This and a sonnet *To Edith Southey* (his wife), preface his long poem *The Triumph of Woman* (*Poems*, 1797). For more about Southey, see page 268. Southey had not yet met Wollstonecraft.

2. See Thomas Gray, *Progress of Poesy* (1751–1754): "O'er her warm cheek and rising bosom move / The bloom of young desire and purple light of love."

Mary! of these the Poet sung, for these
Did Woman triumph! with no angry frown
5   View this degrading conquest. At that age
No MAID OF ARC[3] had snatch'd from coward man
The heaven-blest sword of Liberty; thy sex
Could boast no female ROLAND's martyrdom;[4]
No CORDE's angel and avenging arm[5]
10   Had sanctified again the murderer's name
As erst when Caesar perish'd:[6] yet some strains
May even adorn this theme, befitting me
To offer, nor unworthy thy regard.

Bristol, 1795[7]   1797

William Blake: from *Mary*[1]

Some said she was proud some calld her a whore
And some when she passed by shut to the door
A damp cold came oer her her blushes all fled
20   Her lillies & roses are blighted & shed

"O why was I born with a different Face
Why was I not born like this Envious Race
Why did Heaven adorn me with bountiful hand
And then set me down in an envious Land

25   To be weak as a Lamb & smooth as a dove
And not to raise Envy is calld Christian Love
But if you raise Envy your Merits to blame
For planting such spite in the weak & the tame

I will humble my Beauty I will not dress fine
30   I will keep from the Ball & my Eyes shall not shine
And if any Girls Lover forsakes her for me
I'll refuse him my hand & from Envy be free."

She went out in Morning attird plain & neat
"Proud Mary's gone mad," said the Child in the Street
35   She went out in Morning in plain neat attire
And came home in Evening bespatterd with mire

She trembled & wept sitting on the Bed side
She forgot it was Night & she trembled & cried
She forgot it was Night she forgot it was Morn

3. Joan of Arc ("Maid of Orleans") led the Dauphin's army to victory over the British, only to be convicted of witchcraft by the French ecclesiastical court; she was handed over to the British, who burned her at the stake.
4. Mme. Roland, friend of Wollstonecraft, guillotined in 1793 during the Reign of Terror; her famous last words were "O Liberty, how many crimes are committed in thy name!" Southey fleetingly evokes the famous male "Roland," the courageous, self-sacrificing knight of medieval romance epics.

5. Charlotte Corday, French patriot allied with the moderate Girondists, repelled by the Reign of Terror, stabbed Jean Paul Marat to death in his bathtub in 1793; she was guillotined four days later.
6. Julius Caesar's assassination in the Senate (44 B.C.E.) was avenged by the Roman citizenry, led by Mark Antony and Augustus Caesar.
7. Added in Southey's 1837 Poems.
1. In the wake of the scandal of Godwin's *Memoir*, Blake casts "Mary" as a Blakean martyr and exile. For more about Blake, see his principal listing on page 169.

40   Her soft Memory imprinted with Faces of Scorn

With Faces of Scorn & with Eyes of disdain
Like foul Fiends inhabiting Marys mild Brain
She remembers no Face like the Human Divine
All Faces have Envy sweet Mary but thine

45   And thine is a Face of sweet Love in Despair
And thine is a Face of mild sorrow & care
And thine is a Face of wild terror & fear
That shall never be quiet till laid on its bier.

c. 1802–1803   1866

⟡

THE WRONGS OF WOMAN; OR MARIA   Taking a cue from the popular genres that
fueled the campaign for abolition in the 1790s, Wollstonecraft decided a novel could convey
the arguments of *Rights of Woman*. Even though *Rights* cited "stupid novelists" for corrupting
women into creatures of "sensation" and perpetuating damaging gender stereotypes, she was
aware of William Godwin's success in translating the themes of *Political Justice* (1793) into a
novel about legal tyranny, *Things As They Are; or, The Adventures of Caleb Williams* (1794). She
opens *Maria* with its heroine imprisoned in a madhouse by her husband, who has claimed her
property and her daughter. "Marriage has bastilled me for life," Maria says, with a historically
resonant verb; "the world is a vast prison" in which women are "born slaves." Of the several
stories of wronged women in *Maria*, one of the longest and most searing is told by Maria's warder
Jemima, hardened by life but pitying Maria and aiding her friendship with another prisoner,
Henry Darnford, soon to be her lover. Jemima's story conveys Wollstonecraft's concern not just
with middle-class women such as Maria but also with those from the margins of society. One
of the first "feminist" novels in English literature, *Maria* emphasizes the "wrongs" devolving
on "Woman," regardless of class. As in *Rights of Woman*, Wollstonecraft exposes a social and
political text that might be revised. Begun in 1796 and left unfinished, *Maria* was published
in 1798 by Joseph Johnson, in Godwin's *Posthumous Works of the Author of A Vindication of the
Rights of Woman*. Square brackets indicate Godwin's interpolations.

from The Wrongs of Woman; or Maria

"My father," said Jemima, "seduced my mother, a pretty girl, with whom he lived
fellow-servant; and she no sooner perceived the natural, the dreaded consequence,
than the terrible conviction flashed on her—that she was ruined.[1] Honesty, and a
regard for her reputation, had been the only principles inculcated by her mother; and
they had been so forcibly impressed, that she feared shame, more than the poverty to
which it would lead. Her incessant importunities to prevail upon my father to screen
her from reproach by marrying her, as he had promised in the fervour of seduction,
estranged him from her so completely, that her very person became distasteful to him;
and he began to hate, as well as despise me, before I was born.

"My mother, grieved to the soul by his neglect, and unkind treatment, actually
resolved to famish herself; and injured her health by the attempt; though she had not
sufficient resolution to adhere to her project, or renounce it entirely. Death came
not at her call; yet sorrow, and the methods she adopted to conceal her condition,
still doing the work of a house-maid, had such an effect on her constitution, that she

---

1. A sexual double standard strongly criticized in *Rights of Woman*.

died in the wretched garret, where her virtuous mistress had forced her to take refuge in the very pangs of labour, though my father, after a slight reproof, was allowed to remain in his place—allowed by the mother of six children, who, scarcely permitting a footstep to be heard, during her month's indulgence, felt no sympathy for the poor wretch, denied every comfort required by her situation.

"The day my mother died, the ninth after my birth,[2] I was consigned to the care of the cheapest nurse my father could find; who suckled her own child at the same time, and lodged as many more as she could get, in two cellar-like apartments.

"Poverty, and the habit of seeing children die off her hands, had so hardened her heart, that the office of a mother did not awaken the tenderness of a woman; nor were the feminine caresses which seem a part of the rearing of a child, ever bestowed on me. The chicken has a wing to shelter under; but I had no bosom to nestle in, no kindred warmth to foster me. Left in dirt, to cry with cold and hunger till I was weary, and sleep without ever being prepared by exercise, or lulled by kindness to rest; could I be expected to become any thing but a weak and rickety babe? Still, in spite of neglect, I continued to exist, to learn to curse existence, [her countenance grew ferocious as she spoke,] and the treatment that rendered me miserable, seemed to sharpen my wits. Confined then in a damp hovel, to rock the cradle of the succeeding tribe, I looked like a little old woman, or a hag shrivelling into nothing. The furrows of reflection and care contracted the youthful cheek, and gave a sort of supernatural wildness to the ever watchful eye. During this period, my father had married another fellow-servant, who loved him less, and knew better how to manage his passion, than my mother. She likewise proving with child, they agreed to keep a shop: my stepmother, if, being an illegitimate offspring, I may venture thus to characterize her, having obtained a sum of a rich relation, for that purpose.

"Soon after her lying-in,[3] she prevailed on my father to take me home, to save the expence of maintaining me, and of hiring a girl to assist her in the care of the child. I was young, it was true, but appeared a knowing little thing, and might be made handy. Accordingly I was brought to her house; but not to a home—for a home I never knew. Of this child, a daughter, she was extravagantly fond; and it was a part of my employment, to assist to spoil her, by humouring all her whims, and bearing all her caprices. Feeling her own consequence, before she could speak, she had learned the art of tormenting me, and if I ever dared to resist, I received blows, laid on with no compunctious hand, or was sent to bed dinnerless, as well as supperless.[4] I said that it was a part of my daily labour to attend this child, with the servility of a slave; still it was but a part. I was sent out in all seasons, and from place to place, to carry burdens far above my strength, without being allowed to draw near the fire, or ever being cheered by encouragement or kindness. No wonder then, treated like a creature of another species, that I began to envy, and at length to hate, the darling of the house. Yet, I perfectly remember, that it was the caresses, and kind expressions of my step-mother, which first excited my jealous discontent. Once, I cannot forget it, when she was calling in vain her wayward child to kiss her, I ran to her, saying, 'I will kiss you, ma'am!' and how did my heart, which was in my mouth, sink, what was my debasement of soul, when pushed away with—'I do not want you, pert thing!' Another day, when a new gown had excited the highest good humour, and she uttered the appropriate *dear*, addressed unexpectedly to me, I thought I could never do enough to please her; I was all alacrity, and rose proportionably in my own estimation.

---

2. Many women died in childbirth, often from infection. By the time *Maria* was published, Wollstonecraft herself had died thus, a little more than nine days after giving birth to daughter Mary.

3. Final weeks of pregnancy.

4. Dinner was a midday meal, supper an evening meal; consequence: importance; compunctious: remorseful.

"As her daughter grew up, she was pampered with cakes and fruit, while I was, literally speaking, fed with the refuse of the table, with her leavings. A liquorish tooth[5] is, I believe, common to children, and I used to steal any thing sweet, that I could catch up with a chance of concealment. When detected, she was not content to chastize me herself at the moment, but, on my father's return in the evening (he was a shopman), the principal discourse was to recount my faults, and attribute them to the wicked disposition which I had brought into the world with me, inherited from my mother. He did not fail to leave the marks of his resentment on my body, and then solaced himself by playing with my sister.—I could have murdered her at those moments. To save myself from these unmerciful corrections, I resorted to falsehood, and the untruths which I sturdily maintained, were brought in judgment against me, to support my tyrant's inhuman charge of my natural propensity to vice. Seeing me treated with contempt, and always being fed and dressed better, my sister conceived a contemptuous opinion of me, that proved an obstacle to all affection; and my father, hearing continually of my faults, began to consider me as a curse entailed on him for his sins: he was therefore easily prevailed on to bind me apprentice to one of my stepmother's friends, who kept a slop-shop in Wapping.[6] I was represented (as it was said) in my true colours; but she, 'warranted,' snapping her fingers, 'that she should break my spirit or heart.'

"My mother replied, with a whine, 'that if any body could make me better, it was such a clever woman as herself; though, for her own part, she had tried in vain; but good-nature was her fault.'

"I shudder with horror, when I recollect the treatment I had now to endure. Not only under the lash of my task-mistress, but the drudge of the maid, apprentices and children, I never had a taste of human kindness to soften the rigour of perpetual labour. I had been introduced as an object of abhorrence into the family; as a creature of whom my step-mother, though she had been kind enough to let me live in the house with her own child, could make nothing. I was described as a wretch, whose nose must be kept to the grinding stone—and it was held there with an iron grasp. It seemed indeed the privilege of their superior nature to kick me about, like the dog or cat. If I were attentive, I was called fawning, if refractory, an obstinate mule, and like a mule I received their censure on my loaded back. Often has my mistress, for some instance of forgetfulness, thrown me from one side of the kitchen to the other, knocked my head against the wall, spit in my face, with various refinements on barbarity that I forbear to enumerate, though they were all acted over again by the servant, with additional insults, to which the appellation of *bastard*,[7] was commonly added, with taunts or sneers. But I will not attempt to give you an adequate idea of my situation, lest you, who probably have never been drenched with the dregs of human misery, should think I exaggerate.

"I stole now, from absolute necessity,—bread; yet whatever else was taken, which I had it not in my power to take, was ascribed to me. I was the filching cat, the ravenous dog, the dumb brute, who must bear all; for if I endeavoured to exculpate myself,

---

5. Sweet tooth.

6. A shop selling cheap clothing; Wapping: the river-dock area of London. Lower-class children, usually boys, were apprenticed both to relieve their families and to learn a craft or trade. Typically beginning at age eight, apprenticeships bound a child for seven years of unpaid labor in exchange for training, shelter, food, and clothing. Apprentices were notoriously vulnerable to abuse,

often treated as slaves and sometimes quartered in the barn rather than the home.

7. Legal term for a child born out of wedlock. Common law denied bastards rights of inheritance, even of care, and left them to the poor-houses. The social and legal contempt is evident in the use of the term to signify inferiority and falseness.

I was silenced, without any enquiries being made, with 'Hold your tongue, you never tell truth.' Even the very air I breathed was tainted with scorn; for I was sent to the neighbouring shops with Glutton, Liar, or Thief, written on my forehead. This was, at first, the most bitter punishment; but sullen pride, or a kind of stupid desperation, made me, at length, almost regardless of the contempt, which had wrung from me so many solitary tears at the only moments when I was allowed to rest.

"Thus was I the mark of cruelty till my sixteenth year; and then I have only to point out a change of misery; for a period[8] I never knew. Allow me first to make one observation. Now I look back, I cannot help attributing the greater part of my misery, to the misfortune of having been thrown into the world without the grand support of life—a mother's affection. I had no one to love me; or to make me respected, to enable me to acquire respect. I was an egg dropped on the sand; a pauper by nature, hunted from family to family, who belonged to nobody—and nobody cared for me. I was despised from my birth, and denied the chance of obtaining a footing for myself in society. Yes; I had not even the chance of being considered as a fellow-creature—yet all the people with whom I lived, brutalized as they were by the low cunning of trade, and the despicable shifts of poverty,[9] were not without bowels, though they never yearned for me. I was, in fact, born a slave, and chained by infamy to slavery during the whole of existence, without having any companions to alleviate it by sympathy, or teach me how to rise above it by their example. But, to resume the thread of my tale—

"At sixteen, I suddenly grew tall, and something like comeliness appeared on a Sunday, when I had time to wash my face, and put on clean clothes. My master had once or twice caught hold of me in the passage; but I instinctively avoided his disgusting caresses. One day however, when the family were at a methodist meeting,[1] he contrived to be alone in the house with me, and by blows—yes; blows and menaces, compelled me to submit to his ferocious desire; and, to avoid my mistress's fury, I was obliged in future to comply, and skulk to my loft at his command, in spite of increasing loathing.

"The anguish which was now pent up in my bosom, seemed to open a new world to me: I began to extend my thoughts beyond myself, and grieve for human misery, till I discovered, with horror—ah! what horror!—that I was with child. I know not why I felt a mixed sensation of despair and tenderness, excepting that, ever called a bastard, a bastard appeared to me an object of the greatest compassion in creation.

"I communicated this dreadful circumstance to my master, who was almost equally alarmed at the intelligence; for he feared his wife, and public censure at the meeting. After some weeks of deliberation had elapsed, I in continual fear that my altered shape would be noticed, my master gave me a medicine in a phial, which he desired me to take, telling me, without any circumlocution, for what purpose it was designed.[2] I burst into tears, I thought it was killing myself—yet was such a self as I worth preserving? He cursed me for a fool, and left me to my own reflections. I could not resolve to take this infernal potion; but I wrapped it up in an old gown, and hid it in a corner of my box.

"Nobody yet suspected me, because they had been accustomed to view me as a creature of another species. But the threatening storm at last broke over my devoted[3] head—never shall I forget it! One Sunday evening when I was left, as usual, to take care of the house, my master came home intoxicated, and I became the prey of his

8. Termination.
9. Wollstonecraft's view that a life in trade, or worse, poverty, suppresses virtue in favor of pragmatic but dishonest practices; bowels: tenderness, pity.

1. Methodists (another Nonconformist sect) were popularly regarded as sexually licentious.
2. To induce miscarriage.
3. Doomed.

brutal appetite. His extreme intoxication made him forget his customary caution, and my mistress entered and found us in a situation that could not have been more hateful to her than me. Her husband was 'pot-valiant,' he feared her not at the moment, nor had he then much reason, for she instantly turned the whole force of her anger another way. She tore off my cap, scratched, kicked, and buffetted me, till she had exhausted her strength, declaring, as she rested her arm, 'that I had wheedled her husband from her.——But, could any thing better be expected from a wretch, whom she had taken into her house out of pure charity?' What a torrent of abuse rushed out? till, almost breathless, she concluded with saying, 'that I was born a strumpet; it ran in my blood, and nothing good could come to those who harboured me.'

"My situation was, of course, discovered, and she declared that I should not stay another night under the same roof with an honest family. I was therefore pushed out of doors, and my trumpery[4] thrown after me, when it had been contemptuously examined in the passage, lest I should have stolen any thing.

"Behold me then in the street, utterly destitute![5] Whither could I creep for shelter? To my father's roof I had no claim, when not pursued by shame—now I shrunk back as from death, from my mother's cruel reproaches, my father's execrations. I could not endure to hear him curse the day I was born, though life had been a curse to me. Of death I thought, but with a confused emotion of terror, as I stood leaning my head on a post, and starting at every footstep, lest it should be my mistress coming to tear my heart out. One of the boys of the shop passing by, heard my tale, and immediately repaired to his master, to give him a description of my situation; and he touched the right key—the scandal it would give rise to, if I were left to repeat my tale to every enquirer. This plea came home to his reason, who had been sobered by his wife's rage, the fury of which fell on him when I was out of her reach, and he sent the boy to me with half-a-guinea,[6] desiring him to conduct me to a house, where beggars, and other wretches, the refuse of society, nightly lodged.

"This night was spent in a state of stupefaction, or desperation. I detested mankind, and abhorred myself.

"In the morning I ventured out, to throw myself in my master's way, at his usual hour of going abroad. I approached him, he 'damned me for a——, declared I had disturbed the peace of the family, and that he had sworn to his wife, never to take any more notice of me.' He left me; but, instantly returning, he told me that he should speak to his friend, a parish-officer,[7] to get a nurse for the brat I laid to him; and advised me, if I wished to keep out of the house of correction, not to make free with his name.

"I hurried back to my hole, and, rage giving place to despair, sought for the potion that was to procure abortion, and swallowed it, with a wish that it might destroy me, at the same time that it stopped the sensations of new-born life, which I felt with indescribable emotion. My head turned round, my heart grew sick, and in the horrors of approaching dissolution, mental anguish was swallowed up. The effect of the medicine was violent, and I was confined to my bed several days; but, youth and a strong constitution prevailing, I once more crawled out, to ask myself the cruel question, 'Whither I should go?' I had but two shillings left in my pocket, the rest had been expended, by a poor woman who slept in the same room, to pay for my lodging, and purchase the necessaries of which she partook.

4. Worthless things.
5. In *Rights of Woman*, Wollstonecraft argued that a man should be legally required to support any woman he impregnated as well as any children produced.
6. Ten shillings, sixpence. The guinea was originally coined for use in slave-trading.
7. Parishes were responsible for providing for orphans, bastards, and other destitutes; house of correction: prison.

"With this wretch I went into the neighbouring streets to beg, and my disconsolate appearance drew a few pence from the idle, enabling me still to command a bed; till, recovering from my illness, and taught to put on my rags to the best advantage, I was accosted from different motives, and yielded to the desire of the brutes I met, with the same detestation that I had felt for my still more brutal master. I have since read in novels of the blandishments of seduction, but I had not even the pleasure of being enticed into vice."

"I shall not," interrupted Jemima, "lead your imagination into all the scenes of wretchedness and depravity, which I was condemned to view; or mark the different stages of my debasing misery. Fate dragged me through the very kennels of society: I was still a slave, a bastard, a common property. Become familiar with vice, for I wish to conceal nothing from you, I picked the pockets of the drunkards who abused me; and proved by my conduct, that I deserved the epithets, with which they loaded me at moments when distrust ought to cease.

"Detesting my nightly occupation, though valuing, if I may so use the word, my independence, which only consisted in choosing the street in which I should wander, or the roof, when I had money, in which I should hide my head, I was some time before I could prevail on myself to accept of a place in a house of ill fame,[8] to which a girl, with whom I had accidentally conversed in the street, had recommended me. I had been hunted almost into a fever, by the watchmen of the quarter of the town I frequented; one, whom I had unwittingly offended, giving the word to the whole pack. You can scarcely conceive the tyranny exercised by these wretches: considering themselves as the instruments of the very laws they violate, the pretext which steels their conscience, hardens their heart. Not content with receiving from us, outlaws of society (let other women talk of favours) a brutal gratification gratuitously as a privilege of office, they extort a tithe of prostitution, and harrass with threats the poor creatures whose occupation affords not the means to silence the growl of avarice. To escape from this persecution, I once more entered into servitude.

"A life of comparative regularity restored my health; and—do not start—my manners were improved, in a situation where vice sought to render itself alluring, and taste was cultivated to fashion the person, if not to refine the mind. Besides, the common civility of speech, contrasted with the gross vulgarity to which I had been accustomed, was something like the polish of civilization. I was not shut out from all intercourse of humanity. Still I was galled by the yoke of service, and my mistress often flying into violent fits of passion, made me dread a sudden dismission, which I understood was always the case. I was therefore prevailed on, though I felt a horror of men, to accept the offer of a gentleman, rather in the decline of years, to keep his house, pleasantly situated in a little village near Hampstead.[9]

"He was a man of great talents, and of brilliant wit; but, a worn-out votary of voluptuousness, his desires became fastidious in proportion as they grew weak, and the native tenderness of his heart was undermined by a vitiated imagination. A thoughtless career of libertinism and social enjoyment, had injured his health to such a degree, that, whatever pleasure his conversation afforded me (and my esteem was ensured by proofs of the generous humanity of his disposition), the being his mistress was purchasing it at a very dear rate. With such a keen perception of the delicacies of sentiment, with an imagination invigorated by the exercise of genius, how could he sink into the grossness of sensuality!

"But, to pass over a subject which I recollect with pain, I must remark to you, as an answer to your often-repeated question, 'Why my sentiments and language

8. Whorehouse.   9. Suburb north of London.

were superior to my station?' that I now began to read, to beguile the tediousness of solitude, and to gratify an inquisitive, active mind. I had often, in my childhood, followed a ballad-singer, to hear the sequel of a dismal story, though sure of being severely punished for delaying to return with whatever I was sent to purchase. I could just spell and put a sentence together, and I listened to the various arguments, though often mingled with obscenity, which occurred at the table where I was allowed to preside: for a literary friend or two frequently came home with my master, to dine and pass the night. Having lost the privileged respect of my sex, my presence, instead of restraining, perhaps gave the reins to their tongues; still I had the advantage of hearing discussions, from which, in the common course of life, women are excluded.

"You may easily imagine, that it was only by degrees that I could comprehend some of the subjects they investigated, or acquire from their reasoning what might be termed a moral sense. But my fondness of reading increasing, and my master occasionally shutting himself up in this retreat, for weeks together, to write, I had many opportunities of improvement. At first, considering money (I was right!" exclaimed Jemima, altering her tone of voice) "as the only means, after my loss of reputation, of obtaining respect, or even the toleration of humanity, I had not the least scruple to secrete a part of the sums intrusted to me, and to screen myself from detection by a system of falshood. But, acquiring new principles, I began to have the ambition of returning to the respectable part of society, and was weak enough to suppose it possible. The attention of my unassuming instructor, who, without being ignorant of his own powers, possessed great simplicity of manners, strengthened the illusion. Having sometimes caught up hints for thought, from my untutored remarks, he often led me to discuss the subjects he was treating, and would read to me his productions, previous to their publication, wishing to profit by the criticism of unsophisticated feeling. The aim of his writings was to touch the simple springs of the heart; for he despised the would-be oracles, the self-elected philosophers, who fright away fancy, while sifting each grain of thought to prove that slowness of comprehension is wisdom.

"I should have distinguished this as a moment of sunshine, a happy period in my life, had not the repugnance the disgusting libertinism of my protector inspired, daily become more painful.—And, indeed, I soon did recollect it as such with agony, when his sudden death (for he had recourse to the most exhilarating cordials to keep up the convivial tone of his spirits) again threw me into the desert of human society. Had he had any time for reflection, I am certain he would have left the little property in his power to me: but, attacked by the fatal apoplexy in town, his heir, a man of rigid morals, brought his wife with him to take possession of the house and effects, before I was even informed of his death,—'to prevent,' as she took care indirectly to tell me, 'such a creature as she supposed me to be, from purloining any of them, had I been apprized of the event in time.'

"The grief I felt at the sudden shock the information gave me, which at first had nothing selfish in it, was treated with contempt, and I was ordered to pack up my clothes; and a few trinkets and books, given me by the generous deceased, were contested, while they piously hoped, with a reprobating shake of the head, 'that God would have mercy on his sinful soul!' With some difficulty, I obtained my arrears of wages; but asking—such is the spirit-grinding consequence of poverty and infamy—for a character[1] for honesty and economy, which God knows I merited, I was told by this—why must I call her woman?—'that it would go against her conscience to

---

1. Letter of reference, necessary for respectable employment.

recommend a kept mistress.' Tears started in my eyes, burning tears; for there are situations in which a wretch is humbled by the contempt they are conscious they do not deserve.

"I returned to the metropolis; but the solitude of a poor lodging was inconceivably dreary, after the society I had enjoyed. To be cut off from human converse, now I had been taught to relish it, was to wander a ghost among the living. Besides, I foresaw, to aggravate the severity of my fate, that my little pittance would soon melt away. I endeavoured to obtain needlework; but, not having been taught early, and my hands being rendered clumsy by hard work, I did not sufficiently excel to be employed by the ready-made linen shops,[2] when so many women, better qualified, were suing for it. The want of a character prevented my getting a place; for, irksome as servitude would have been to me, I should have made another trial, had it been feasible. Not that I disliked employment, but the inequality of condition to which I must have submitted. I had acquired a taste for literature, during the five years I had lived with a literary man, occasionally conversing with men of the first abilities of the age; and now to descend to the lowest vulgarity, was a degree of wretchedness not to be imagined unfelt. I had not, it is true, tasted the charms of affection, but I had been familiar with the graces of humanity.

"One of the gentlemen, whom I had frequently dined in company with, while I was treated like a companion, met me in the street, and enquired after my health. I seized the occasion, and began to describe my situation; but he was in haste to join, at dinner, a select party of choice spirits; therefore, without waiting to hear me, he impatiently put a guinea into my hand, saying, 'It was a pity such a sensible woman should be in distress—he wished me well from his soul.'

"To another I wrote, stating my case, and requesting advice. He was an advocate for unequivocal sincerity; and had often, in my presence, descanted on the evils which arise in society from the despotism of rank and riches.

"In reply, I received a long essay on the energy of the human mind, with continual allusions to his own force of character. He added, 'That the woman who could write such a letter as I had sent him, could never be in want of resources, were she to look into herself, and exert her powers; misery was the consequence of indolence, and, as to my being shut out from society, it was the lot of man to submit to certain privations.'

"How often have I heard," said Jemima, interrupting her narrative, "in conversation, and read in books, that every person willing to work may find employment? It is the vague assertion, I believe, of insensible indolence, when it relates to men; but, with respect to women, I am sure of its fallacy, unless they will submit to the most menial bodily labour; and even to be employed at hard labour is out of the reach of many, whose reputation misfortune or folly has tainted.

"How writers, professing to be friends to freedom, and the improvement of morals, can assert that poverty is no evil, I cannot imagine."[3]

"No more can I," interrupted Maria, "yet they even expatiate on the peculiar happiness of indigence, though in what it can consist, excepting in brutal rest, when a man can barely earn a subsistence, I cannot imagine. The mind is necessarily imprisoned in its own little tenement; and, fully occupied by keeping it in repair, has not time to rove abroad for improvement. The book of knowledge is closely clasped, against those who must fulfil their daily task of severe manual labour or die; and curiosity, rarely excited by thought or information, seldom moves on the stagnate lake of ignorance."

---

2. Selling garments such as shirts, aprons, underwear.
3. This compassion usually cites scripture—e.g., "Blessed be ye poor: for yours is the kingdom of God," says Jesus in his Sermon on the Mount (Luke 6.20)—or more generally, inscrutable designs.

"As far as I have been able to observe," replied Jemima, "prejudices, caught up by chance, are obstinately maintained by the poor, to the exclusion of improvement; they have not time to reason or reflect to any extent, or minds sufficiently exercised to adopt the principles of action, which form perhaps the only basis of contentment in every station."[4]

"And independence," said Darnford, "they are necessarily strangers to, even the independence of despising their persecutors. If the poor are happy, or can be happy, *things are very well as they are*. And I cannot conceive on what principle those writers contend for a change of system, who support this opinion. The authors on the other side of the question are much more consistent, who grant the fact; yet, insisting that it is the lot of the majority to be oppressed in this life, kindly turn them over to another,[5] to rectify the false weights and measures of this, as the only way to justify the dispensations of Providence. I have not," continued Darnford, "an opinion more firmly fixed by observation in my mind, than that, though riches may fail to produce proportionate happiness, poverty most commonly excludes it, by shutting up all the avenues to improvement."[6]

"And as for the affections," added Maria, with a sigh, "how gross, and even tormenting do they become, unless regulated by an improving mind! The culture of the heart ever, I believe, keeps pace with that of the mind. But pray go on," addressing Jemima, "though your narrative gives rise to the most painful reflections on the present state of society."

"Not to trouble you," continued she, "with a detailed description of all the painful feelings of unavailing exertion, I have only to tell you, that at last I got recommended to wash in a few families, who did me the favour to admit me into their houses, without the most strict enquiry, to wash from one in the morning till eight at night, for eighteen or twenty-pence a day.[7] On the happiness to be enjoyed over a washing-tub I need not comment; yet you will allow me to observe, that this was a wretchedness of situation peculiar to my sex. A man with half my industry, and, I may say, abilities, could have procured a decent livelihood, and discharged some of the duties which knit mankind together; whilst I, who had acquired a taste for the rational, nay, in honest pride let me assert it, the virtuous enjoyments of life, was cast aside as the filth of society. Condemned to labour, like a machine, only to earn bread, and scarcely that, I became melancholy and desperate.

"I have now to mention a circumstance which fills me with remorse, and fear it will entirely deprive me of your esteem. A tradesman became attached to me, and visited me frequently,—and I at last obtained such a power over him, that he offered to take me home to his house.—Consider, dear madam, I was famishing: wonder not that I became a wolf!—The only reason for not taking me home immediately, was the having a girl in the house, with child by him—and this girl—I advised him—yes, I did! would I could forget it!—to turn out of doors: and one night he determined to follow my advice. Poor wretch! She fell upon her knees, reminded him that he had promised to marry her, that her parents were honest!—What did it avail?—She was turned out.

"She approached her father's door, in the skirts of London,—listened at the shutters,—but could not knock. A watchman had observed her go and return several times—Poor wretch!—[The remorse Jemima spoke of, seemed to be stinging her to the soul, as she proceeded.]

---

4. The copy which appears to have received the author's last corrections, ends at this place. [Godwin's note]
5. Heaven; Burke argues thus in *Reflections* as does Hannah More in *Cheap Repository Tracts.*
6. Such as a minimum wage, opposed by Prime Minister Pitt, who argued that the miseries of the poor were probably overstated, and that, in any event, they were remediable by charity alone.
7. This report of slightly more than penny-an-hour wage is historically accurate.

"She left it, and, approaching a tub where horses were watered, she sat down in it, and, with desperate resolution, remained in that attitude—till resolution was no longer necessary!

"I happened that morning to be going out to wash, anticipating the moment when I should escape from such hard labour. I passed by, just as some men, going to work, drew out the stiff, cold corpse—Let me not recall the horrid moment!— I recognized her pale visage; I listened to the tale told by the spectators, and my heart did not burst. I thought of my own state, and wondered how I could be such a monster!—I worked hard; and, returning home, I was attacked by a fever. I suffered both in body and mind. I determined not to live with the wretch. But he did not try me; he left the neighbourhood. I once more returned to the wash-tub.

"Still this state, miserable as it was, admitted of aggravation. Lifting one day a heavy load, a tub fell against my shin, and gave me great pain. I did not pay much attention to the hurt, till it became a serious wound; being obliged to work as usual, or starve. But, finding myself at length unable to stand for any time, I thought of getting into an hospital. Hospitals, it should seem (for they are comfortless abodes for the sick) were expressly endowed for the reception of the friendless; yet I, who had on that plea a right to assistance, wanted the recommendation of the rich and respectable, and was several weeks languishing for admittance; fees were demanded on entering; and, what was still more unreasonable, security for burying me, that expence not coming into the letter of the charity. A guinea was the stipulated sum—I could as soon have raised a million; and I was afraid to apply to the parish for an order, lest they should have passed me, I knew not whither.[8] The poor woman at whose house I lodged, compassionating my state, got me into the hospital; and the family where I received the hurt, sent me five shillings, three and six-pence of which I gave at my admittance—I know not for what.

"My leg grew quickly better; but I was dismissed before my cure was completed, because I could not afford to have my linen washed to appear decently, as the virago of a nurse said, when the gentlemen (the surgeons) came. I cannot give you an adequate idea of the wretchedness of an hospital; every thing is left to the care of people intent on gain. The attendants seem to have lost all feeling of compassion in the bustling discharge of their offices; death is so familiar to them, that they are not anxious to ward it off. Every thing appeared to be conducted for the accommodation of the medical men and their pupils, who came to make experiments on the poor, for the benefit of the rich. One of the physicians, I must not forget to mention, gave me half-a-crown, and ordered me some wine, when I was at the lowest ebb. I thought of making my case known to the lady-like matron; but her forbidding countenance prevented me. She condescended to look on the patients, and make general enquiries, two or three times a week; but the nurses knew the hour when the visit of ceremony would commence, and every thing was as it should be.

"After my dismission, I was more at a loss than ever for a subsistence, and, not to weary you with a repetition of the same unavailing attempts, unable to stand at the washing-tub, I began to consider the rich and poor as natural enemies, and became a thief from principle. I could not now cease to reason, but I hated mankind. I despised myself, yet I justified my conduct. I was taken, tried, and condemned to six months' imprisonment in a house of correction. My soul recoils with horror from the remembrance of the insults I had to endure, till, branded with shame, I was turned loose in the street, pennyless. I wandered from street to street, till, exhausted by hunger and fatigue, I sunk down senseless at a door, where I had vainly demanded a morsel of bread. I was sent by the inhabitant to the work-house, to which he had surlily bid me go, saying, he 'paid

8. Passed back to the last parish where the applicant was legally settled.

enough in conscience to the poor,' when, with parched tongue, I implored his charity.[9] If those well-meaning people who exclaim against beggars, were acquainted with the treatment the poor receive in many of these wretched asylums, they would not stifle so easily involuntary sympathy, by saying that they have all parishes to go to, or wonder that the poor dread to enter the gloomy walls. What are the common run of workhouses, but prisons, in which many respectable old people, worn out by immoderate labour, sink into the grave in sorrow, to which they are carried like dogs!"

Alarmed by some indistinct noise, Jemima rose hastily to listen, and Maria, turning to Darnford, said, "I have indeed been shocked beyond expression when I have met a pauper's funeral. A coffin carried on the shoulders of three or four ill-looking wretches, whom the imagination might easily convert into a band of assassins, hastening to conceal the corpse, and quarrelling about the prey on their way. I know it is of little consequence how we are consigned to the earth; but I am led by this brutal insensibility, to what even the animal creation appears forcibly to feel, to advert to the wretched, deserted manner in which they died."

"True," rejoined Darnford, "and, till the rich will give more than a part of their wealth, till they will give time and attention to the wants of the distressed, never let them boast of charity. Let them open their hearts, and not their purses, and employ their minds in the service, if they are really actuated by humanity; or charitable institutions will always be the prey of the lowest order of knaves."

Jemima returning, seemed in haste to finish her tale. "The overseer farmed the poor[1] of different parishes, and out of the bowels of poverty was wrung the money with which he purchased this dwelling, as a private receptacle for madness.[2] He had been a keeper at a house of the same description, and conceived that he could make money much more readily in his old occupation. He is a shrewd—shall I say it?—villain. He observed something resolute in my manner, and offered to take me with him, and instruct me how to treat the disturbed minds he meant to instruct to my care. The offer of forty pounds a year,[3] and to quit a workhouse, was not to be despised, though the condition of shutting my eyes and hardening my heart was annexed to it.

"I agreed to accompany him; and four years have I been attendant on many wretches, and"—she lowered her voice,—"the witness of many enormities. In solitude my mind seemed to recover its force, and many of the sentiments which I imbibed in the only tolerable period of my life, returned with their full force. Still what should induce me to be the champion for suffering humanity?—Who ever risked any thing for me?—Who ever acknowledged me to be a fellow-creature?"—

Maria took her hand, and Jemima, more overcome by kindness than she had ever been by cruelty, hastened out of the room to conceal her emotions.

Darnford soon after heard his summons, and, taking leave of him, Maria promised to gratify his curiosity, with respect to herself, the first opportunity.

Active as love was in the heart of Maria, the story she had just heard made her thoughts take a wider range. The opening buds of hope closed, as if they had put forth too early, and the happiest day of her life was overcast by the most melancholy reflections. Thinking of Jemima's peculiar fate and her own, she was led to consider the oppressed state of women, and to lament that she had given birth to a daughter.

---

9. The wealthier residents of a parish paid a "Poor tax" to support its dependents. By the late 1790s, on the theory that poverty stemmed from indolence, "poor laws" were being proposed in Parliament to prohibit almsgiving (charity) and to send the poor to workhouses, where the wages were appallingly low and families typically broken up.

1. Made money from them, as if they were a cash crop, by hiring them out as laborers, with part of their already meager wages taken in commission, as allowed by law.
2. The madhouse in which Maria and Darnford are imprisoned and where Jemima is a warder.
3. At the end of the 18th century, farm workers on a six-day week could expect £15–20 a year.

The Wollstonecraft Controversy and the Rights of Women

Mary Wollstonecraft's *Vindication of the Rights of Woman* challenged an age when women had no legal standing as daughters or wives, being under the coverture (legal identity) of fathers or husbands. They could not own property, form contracts, or conduct business. "Obedience" was expected behavior, sanctioned by religion, law, and custom; a rebellious daughter (one, for instance, refusing her father's choice of her husband) could be disowned; divorce was granted only by husbands, who retained custody of all property (including dowry) as well as the children (a prime reason many women remained in abusive marriages). Female suffrage was so remote that it could not be debated for another century or so. Women had no legal status, no representatives for their concerns in Parliament. It was not until 1870 that the Married Woman's Property Act was passed, allowing a wife to keep her earnings, and not until 1882 that it was amended to allow her to keep the property, including personal property, that she brought to the marriage (dowry) or acquired during it; this act also gave a woman the right to enter contracts and to sue in courts, as well as a legally distinct identity from her husband.

England was not alone in the 1790s in resisting change: even in Revolutionary France advocates for women's rights were sent to the guillotine. French women did not secure the vote until 1944, nearly a century after American feminists presented the Declaration of Sentiments and Resolutions at Seneca Falls. The way was paved for these changes by the debate from the 1790s onward over female education, women's rights, and social policy—a debate that even among women involved disparate, even opposed, commitments. When Maria Edgeworth proposed to Anna Barbauld that they coedit a periodical featuring "the literary ladies of the present day," Barbauld declined: "There is no bond of union among literary women, any more than among literary men; different sentiments and different connections separate them much more than the joint interest of their sex would unite them. Mrs. Hannah More would not write along with you or me, and we should probably hesitate at joining Miss Hays, or if she were living, Mrs. Godwin [Wollstonecraft]." Our selections suggest the wide range of concerns in this debate and the wide range of responses it involved, in particular to Wollstonecraft—a lightning rod in this charged atmosphere.

Catharine Macaulay
1731–1791

There was scarcely any woman Wollstonecraft esteemed more than Catharine Macaulay. Daughter of a wealthy landowner in Kent and an heiress of a London banker, young Catharine grew up in comfort, and was left well off at the death of her husband, an eminent London obstetrician, in 1776. Her major work is the controversial eight-volume *History of England from the Accession of James I to that of the Brunswick Line* (the current monarchy), published over twenty years (1763–1783). Its defense of Cromwell's regicidal government and its generally antimonarchal Whig sympathies endeared her to Wollstonecraft, poet Thomas Gray, and even Prime Minister William Pitt, while earning Edmund Burke's contempt of her as a "republican Virago." Not surprisingly, her political writings were more popular in France and America than in England. In 1785, she visited George and Martha Washington at Mount Vernon and later corresponded with them, as well as with John Adams and Benjamin Franklin. But as with Wollstonecraft, her politics produced enemies and vicious misogynist attacks on her private life, attacks gleefully sharpened by her marriage in 1779, at fifty-seven, to William Graham, age twenty-one.

Letters on Education (1790) deeply influenced Wollstonecraft, who deemed Macaulay "the woman of the greatest abilities, undoubtedly, that this country has ever produced." She did not live to see *Rights of Woman*, in which Wollstonecraft praised her "strong and clear" intellect and echoed many of her polemics: the attack on the gender ideologies proffered by Rousseau and Pope and on the cultural systems that educate women into "a state of slavery"; a disdain of "coquetry" (the female art of manipulating men through their passions); a scathing critique of the language of female compliments; and advocacy of coeducation and a gender-neutral standard of "rational" conduct.

Letters on Education
from *Letter 22: No Characteristic Difference in Sex*

The notion of a sexual difference in the human character has, with very few exceptions, universally prevailed from the earliest times, and the pride of one sex, and the ignorance and vanity of the other, have helped to support an opinion which a close observation of Nature, and a more accurate way of reasoning, would disprove.

It must be confessed, that the virtues of the males among the human species, though mixed and blended with a variety of vices and errors, have displayed a bolder and a more consistent picture of excellence than female nature has hitherto done. It is on these reasons that, when we compliment the appearance of a more than ordinary energy in the female mind, we call it masculine; and hence it is, that Pope has elegantly said *a perfect woman's but a softer man*.[1] And if we take in the consideration, that there can be but one rule of moral excellence for beings made of the same materials, organized after the same manner, and subjected to similar laws of Nature, we must either agree with Mr. Pope, or we must reverse the proposition, and say, that *a perfect man is a woman formed after a coarser mold*. The difference that actually does subsist between the sexes, is too flattering for men to be willingly imputed to accident; for what accident occasions, wisdom might correct; and it is better, says Pride, to give up the advantages we might derive from the perfection of our fellow associates, than to own that Nature has been just in the equal distribution of her favours. These are the sentiments of the men: but mark how readily they are yielded to by the women; not from humility I assure you, but merely to preserve with character those fond vanities on which they set their hearts. No; suffer them to idolize their persons, to throw away their life in the pursuit of trifles, and to indulge in the gratification of the meaner passions, and they will heartily join in the sentence of their degradation.

Among the most strenuous asserters of a sexual difference in character, Rousseau is the most conspicuous, both on account of that warmth of sentiment which distinguishes all his writings, and the eloquence of his compositions: but never did enthusiasm and the love of paradox, those enemies to philosophical disquisition, appear in more strong opposition to plain sense than in Rousseau's definition of this difference.[2] He sets out with a supposition, that Nature intended the subjection of the one sex to the other; that consequently there must be an inferiority of intellect in the subjected party; but as man is a very imperfect being, and apt to play the capricious tyrant, Nature, to bring things nearer to an equality, bestowed on the woman

---

1. *Epistle II*, "Of the Characters of Women": "Heaven, when it strives to polish all it can / Its last best work, but forms a softer man" (271–72).

2. The argument throughout *Émile*, especially ch. 5 ("Sophy").

such attractive graces, and such an insinuating address, as to turn the balance on the other scale. Thus Nature, in a giddy mood, recedes from her purposes, and subjects prerogative to an influence which must produce confusion and disorder in the system of human affairs. Rousseau saw this objection; and in order to obviate it, he has made up a moral person of the union of the two sexes, which, for contradiction and absurdity, outdoes every metaphysical riddle that was ever formed in the schools. In short, it is not reason, it is not wit; it is pride and sensuality that speak in Rousseau, and, in this instance, has lowered the man of genius to the licentious pedant. * * * for so little did a wise and just Providence intend to make the condition of slavery an unalterable law of female nature, that in the same proportion as the male sex have consulted the interest of their own happiness, they have relaxed in their tyranny over women; and such is their use in the system of mundane creation, and such their natural influence over the male mind, that were these advantages properly exerted, they might carry every point of any importance to their honour and happiness. However, till that period arrives in which women will act wisely, we will amuse ourselves in talking of their follies.

The situation and education of women, Hortensia,[3] is precisely that which must necessarily tend to corrupt and debilitate both the powers of mind and body. From a false notion of beauty and delicacy, their system of nerves is depraved before they come out of their nursery; and this kind of depravity has more influence over the mind, and consequently over morals, than is commonly apprehended. But it would be well if such causes only acted towards the debasement of the sex; their moral education is, if possible, more absurd than their physical. The principles and nature of virtue, which is never properly explained to boys, is kept quite a mystery to girls. They are told indeed, that they must abstain from those vices which are contrary to their personal happiness, or they will be regarded as criminals, both by God and man; but all the higher parts of rectitude, every thing that ennobles our being, and that renders us both innoxious and useful, is either not taught, or is taught in such a manner as to leave no proper impression on the mind. This is so obvious a truth, that the defects of female education have ever been a fruitful topic of declamation for the moralist; but not one of this class of writers have laid down any judicious rules for amendment. Whilst we still retain the absurd notion of a sexual excellence, it will mitigate against the perfecting a plan of education for either sex. The judicious Addison animadverts on the absurdity of bringing a young lady up with no higher idea of the end of education than to make her agreeable to a husband, and confining the necessary excellence for this happy acquisition to the mere graces of person.[4]

Every parent and tutor may not express himself in the same manner as is marked out by Addison; yet certain it is, that the admiration of the other sex is held out to women as the highest honour they can attain; and whilst this is considered as their *summum bonum* [highest good] and the beauty of their persons the chief *desideratum* [thing wanted] of men, Vanity, and its companion Envy, must taint, in their characters, every native and every acquired excellence. Nor can you, Hortensia, deny, that these qualities, when united to ignorance, are fully equal to the engendering and rivetting all those vices and foibles which are peculiar to the female sex; vices and foibles which have caused them to be considered, in ancient times, as beneath

---

3. Her fictitious addressee.
4. Joseph Addison (1672–1719), essayist and poet. The unsigned essay, published in *The Spectator*, was

actually by his collaborator, Richard Steele. Animadverts: criticizes.

cultivation, and in modern days have subjected them to the censure and ridicule of writers of all descriptions, from the deep thinking philosopher to the man of ton[5] and gallantry, who, by the bye, sometimes distinguishes himself by qualities which are not greatly superior to those he despises in women. Nor can I better illustrate the truth of this observation than by the following picture, to be found in the polite and gallant Chesterfield. "Women," says his Lordship, "are only children of a larger growth. They have an entertaining tattle, sometimes wit; but for solid reasoning, and good sense, I never in my life knew one that had it, or who acted or reasoned in consequence of it for four and twenty hours together. A man of sense only trifles with them, plays with them, humours and flatters them, as he does an engaging child; but he neither consults them, nor trusts them in serious matters."[6]

Richard Polwhele
1760–1838

Reverend Polwhele was educated at Oxford, first training for the law. He wrote poetry, histories, journalism, theological tracts, and translations of Greek literature, and was a frequent contributor to conservative journals, including the *Anti-Jacobin*. Among his mother's friends were two writers on the situation of women, Hannah More and Catharine Macaulay, whom he met in 1777. For an elaborate birthday celebration for Macaulay, he wrote an ode which he included in his first volume of poetry, 1777. *The Unsex'd Females* appeared in 1798, at the end of a decade of vigorous debate about women's rights inaugurated by Macaulay's *Letters on Education* (1790) and Wollstonecraft's *Rights of Woman* (1792).

By 1798, both Macaulay and Wollstonecraft were dead, and a reactionary political climate as well as the scandal of Godwin's *Memoirs* had dealt "rights of woman" a serious setback. The safest voices called for female education in modest, virtuous intelligence, trained to piety, obedience, and domestic duty, in order to become good Christian daughters, wives, and mothers. Fresh from reading Godwin's *Memoirs* of Wollstonecraft, Polwhele, with tones tipping from nasty to horrified, castigated its scandals in a review for the *European Magazine* and in *The Unsex'd Females*. The poem casts radicals such as Wollstonecraft as "unnatural," "licentious," anti-Christian revolutionaries, driven by godless "Reason." Yet its indictment, in addition to Wollstonecraft and allies Helen Maria Williams and Mary Hays, includes women of quite different views, having in common only a public voice: poet and novelist Charlotte Smith, initially a sympathizer with the French Revolution, but famous by 1793 for *The Emigrants* (see page 91) and by the decade's end, an outspoken reactionary; Anna Barbauld, an abolitionist, but no revolutionary, no fan of Wollstonecraft, and very qualified on women's rights; Mary Robinson, advocate of abolition but no political firebrand; Ann Yearsley, advocate for the poor, abolitionist, but also a voice of sympathy in *Reflections on the Death of Louis XVI* (1793) and *An Elegy on Marie Antoinette* (1795). So as not to seem categorically misogynist, Polwhele ends celebrating conservative eighteenth-century bluestocking women, a "kindred train" who "influence" through "modest virtue," and allied with such conservatives as Horace Walpole, Joshua Reynolds, Samuel Johnson, and Edmund Burke: the "Queen of the Blues" Elizabeth Montagu (1720–1800), scholar and poet Elizabeth Carter (1717–1806), poet and educational

---

5. Fashion.
6. *Letters to His Son* no. 294 (16 November 1752), also cited in *Rights of Woman*, ch. 4. Philip Chesterfield (1694–1773), statesman, author, and wit, wrote letters of advice to his illegitimate son from age five until his own death; published in 1774, these became famous (or infamous) for their comments on sexual behavior and rituals.

theorist Hester Chapone (1727–1801), poet Anna Seward (1743–1809), woman of letters Hester Thrale Piozzi (1741–1821), novelists Frances Burney (1752–1840) and Anne Radcliffe (1764–1823). He ventriloquizes his praise through the voice of their disciple Hannah More, whose views on the "natural" differences of the sexes and their separate spheres he warmly endorses. Polwhele's voluminous footnotes are an important part of his polemic. We include some, especially on the question of women's rights and on other writers in this volume.

from The Unsex'd Females[1]

Thou, who with all the poet's genuine rage,
Thy "fine eye rolling" o'er "this aweful age,"[2]
Where polish'd life unfolds its various views,
Hast mark'd the magic influence of the muse;
5   Sever'd, with nice precision, from her beam
Of genial power, her false and feeble gleam;
Expos'd the Sciolist's° vain-glorious claim,   *superficially learned*
And boldly thwarted Innovation's aim,
Where witlings wildly think, or madly dare,[3]
10   With Honor, Virtue, Truth, announcing war;
Survey with me, what ne'er our fathers saw,
A female band despising NATURE's law,[4]
As "proud defiance"[5] flashes from their arms,
And vengeance smothers all their softer charms.
15   *I* shudder at the new unpictur'd scene,
Where unsex'd woman vaunts the imperious mien;
Where girls, affecting to dismiss the heart,
Invoke the Proteus of petrific art;[6]
With equal ease, in body or in mind,
20   To Gallic freaks or Gallic faith[7] resign'd,
The crane-like neck, as Fashion bids, lay bare,

1. "Unsex'd" by a rejection of "feminine" decorum. "Come, unsex me here!" cries Shakespeare's Lady Macbeth to the spirits steeling her to regicide (1.5.42 ff).
2. The addressee is another Tory conservative scourge, Thomas James Mathias, whose long satirical poem *The Pursuits of Literature* (1794–1797), also encased in footnotes, inspired Polwhele's. In his Preface to the fourth dialogue of this popular poem (16 editions), Mathias lamented that "our *unsexed* female writers now instruct, or confuse, us and themselves, in the labyrinth of politics, or turn us wild with Gallic frenzy"—French-inspired ideas and fashions. He begins representing himself "not unconscious of this awful age" (1.7), echoing Milton's representation of himself and other visionary poets as chastisers of their own age, "fall'n on evil days" (*Paradise Lost* 7.25). Theseus in *A Midsummer Night's Dream* describes "the poet's eye, in a fine frenzy rolling" (5.1.12).
3. "Greatly think, or nobly die." Pope [Polwhele's note, slightly misquoting l.10 of *Elegy to the Memory of an Unfortunate Lady*, a suicide in despair of love].
4. Nature is the grand basis of all laws human and divine: and the woman, who has no regard to nature, either in the decoration of her person, or the culture of her mind, will soon "walk after the flesh, in the lust of uncleanness, and despise government" [Polwhele's note, quoting 2 Peter 2.10; Rousseau and other defenders of sexual inequality routinely invoke "Nature's" law].
5. "A troop came next, who crowns and armour wore, / And proud defiance in their looks they bore." Pope. The Amazonian band—the female Quixotes of the new philosophy, are, here, too justly characterised [Polwhele's note], quoting *The Temple of Fame* (1711, ll.342–343), the troop answering "the direful trump of Slander." The Amazons, legendary race of warrior women, were fabled to have burnt off the right breast (*a*, without; *mazos*, breast) to facilitate use of bow or javelin. Quixotes (from Cervantes' hero) are impractical idealists. The credulous heroine of Charlotte Lennox's popular novel, *The Female Quixote* (1752), expects her life to take shape as a French romance, only to be embarrassed by her folly.
6. Proteus: god able to change shapes at will; petrific: able to turn to stone, as if a Medusa, an unfeeling woman.
7. French fashions and the new (Godless) religion.

Or frizzle, bold in front, their borrow'd hair;°   *wigs*
Scarce by a gossamery film carest,
Sport, in full view, the meretricious breast;[8]
25   Loose the chaste cincture,[9] where the graces shone,
And languish'd all the Loves, the ambrosial zone;
As lordly domes inspire dramatic rage,
Court prurient Fancy to the private stage;
With bliss botanic[1] as their bosoms heave,
30   Still pluck forbidden fruit, with mother Eve,
For puberty in sighing florets pant,
Or point the prostitution of a plant;
Dissect[2] its organ of unhallow'd lust,
And fondly gaze the titillating[3] dust;
35   With liberty's sublimer views expand,
And o'er the wreck of kingdoms[4] sternly stand;
And, frantic, midst the democratic storm,
Pursue, Philosophy! thy phantom-form.
    Far other is the female shape and mind,
40   By modest luxury heighten'd and refin'd;
Those limbs, that figure, tho' by Fashion grac'd,
By Beauty polish'd, and adorn'd by Taste;

---

8. To "sport a face," is a cant phrase in one of our Universities, by which is meant an impudent obtrusion of a man's person in company. It is not inapplicable, perhaps, to the open bosom—a fashion which we have never invited or sanctioned. The fashions of France, which have been always imitated by the English, were, heretofore, unexceptionable in a moral point of view; since, however ridiculous or absurd, they were innocent. But they have now their source among prostitutes—among women of the most abandoned character [Polwhele's note]. Meretricious: whorish. An 18th-century French aristocratic fashion was a fancy-gown neckline plunged below the bosom, displaying it bare.

9. A wide belt around the waist and sometimes the bosom; it is "chaste" for concealing breasts and hips.

1. Botany has lately become a fashionable amusement with the ladies. But how the study of the sexual system of plants can accord with female modesty, I am not able to comprehend. I had first written: "More eager for illicit knowlege [sic] pant, / With lustful boys anatomize a plant; / The virtues of its dust prolific speak, / Or point its pistill with unblushing cheek." I have, several times, seen boys and girls botanizing together [Polwhele's note]. The immodesty of botanizing was broadcast by Erasmus Darwin's popular poem, *The Botanic Garden*, especially Part II, *The Loves of the Plants* (1789; 1791), explicit about sexual organs and activity.

2. Miss Wollstonecraft does not blush to say, in an introduction to a book designed for the use of young ladies, that, "in order to lay the axe at the root of corruption, it would be proper to familiarize the sexes to an unreserved discussion of those topics, which are generally avoided in conversation from a principle of false delicacy; and that it would be right to speak of the organs of generation as freely as we mention our eyes or our hands." To such language our botanizing girls are doubtless familiarized: and,

they are in a fair way of becoming worthy disciples of Miss W. If they do not take heed to their ways, they will soon exchange the blush of modesty for the bronze of impudence [Polwhele, alluding to Luke 3.9]. He misrepresents Wollstonecraft's statement in "Introductory Address to Parents," *Elements of Morality, For the Use of Children* (1792): concerned with masturbation and other "impure" practices, she contends that "the most efficacious method to root out this dreadful evil, which poisons the source of human happiness, would be to speak to children of the organs of generation as freely as we speak of the other parts of the body, and explain to them the noble use which they were designed for, and how they may be injured." In *Rights of Woman* (ch. 7: "Modesty") she refutes as "absurd" the "gross idea" that botany is inconsistent with female modesty, and lists it among the subjects that boys and girls might study together (ch. 12: "On National Education").

3. "Each pungent grain of titillating dust." Pope; "The prolific dust"—of the botanist [Polwhele's note, alluding to the "Charge of *Snuff*"—"The pungent Grains of titillating Dust"—Belinda hurls at her adversary in *The Rape of the Lock* (5.84)].

4. The female advocates of Democracy in this country, though they have had no opportunity of imitating the French ladies, in their atrocious acts of cruelty; have yet assumed a stern serenity in the contemplation of those savage excesses. "To express their abhorrence of royalty, they (the French ladies) threw away the character of their sex, and bit the amputated limbs of their murdered countrymen.—I say this on the authority of a young gentleman who saw it.—I am sorry to add, that the relation, accompanied with looks of horror and disgust, only provoked a contemptuous smile from an illuminated British fair-one." See Robinson [Polwhele's note, quoting *Proofs of a Conspiracy*].

That soul, whose harmony perennial flows,
In Music trembles, and in Color glows;
45   Which bids sweet Poesy reclaim the praise
With faery light to gild fastidious days,
From sullen clouds relieve domestic care,
And melt in smiles the withering frown of war.
Ah! once the female Muse, to NATURE true,
50   The unvalued store from FANCY, FEELING drew;
Won, from the grasp of woe, the roseate hours,
Cheer'd life's dim vale, and strew'd the grave with flowers.
    But lo! where, pale amidst the wild,[5] she draws
Each precept cold from sceptic Reason's[6] vase;
55   Pours with rash arm the turbid stream along,
And in the foaming torrent whelms the throng.[7]
    Alas! her pride sophistic° flings a gloom,   *specious*
To chase, sweet Innocence! thy vernal bloom,
Of each light joy to damp the genial glow,
60   And with new terrors clothe the groupe of woe,
Quench the pure daystar° in oblivion deep,   *sun*
And, Death! restore thy "long, unbroken sleep."[8]
    See Wollstonecraft, whom no decorum checks,
Arise, the intrepid champion of her sex;
65   O'er humbled man assert the sovereign claim,
And slight the timid blush[9] of virgin fame
    "Go, go (she cries) ye tribes of melting maids,
Go, screen your softness in sequester'd shades;
With plaintive whispers woo the unconscious grove,
70   And feebly perish, as depis'd ye love.
What tho' the fine Romances of Rousseau
Bid the frame flutter, and the bosom glow;
Tho' the rapt Bard, your empire fond to own,
Fall prostrate and adore your living throne,
75   The living throne his hands presum'd to rear,
Its seat a simper, and its base a tear;[1]
Soon shall the sex disdain the illusive sway,
And wield the sceptre in yon blaze of day;

---

5. "A wild, where flowers and weeds promiscuous shoot; / A garden tempting with forbidden fruit." Pope [Polwhele's note, quoting *Essay on Man* (1733): *Epistle I, 7–8*].
6. A troubled stream only, can proceed from the vase of scepticism [Polwhele's note, alluding to the Revolutionary goddess "Reason"].
7. "Raging waves, foaming out their own shame"—St. Jude. Such were those infamous publications of Paine and others, which, like the torrents of December, threatened to sweep all before them—to overwhelm the multitude [Polwhele's note].
8. "We, the great, the valiant and the wise, / When once the seal of death hath clos'd our eyes, / Shut in the hollow tomb obscure and deep, / Slumber, to wake no more, one long unbroken sleep." Moschus [Polwhele's note; Moschus: 2nd-century B.C.E. Greek pastoral poet, whom Polwhele translated in a well-received publication of 1786].
9. That Miss Wollstonecraft was a sworn enemy to blushes, I need not remark. But many of my readers, perhaps, will be astonished to hear, that at several of our boarding-schools for young ladies, a blush incurs a penalty [Polwhele's note]..
1. According to Rousseau, the empire of women is the empire of softness—of address: their commands, are caresses; their menaces, are tears [Polwhele's note, referring to *La Nouvelle Heloise* (1760) and *Émile* (1762), both criticized in *Rights of Woman*].

Ere long, each little artifice discard,
80   No more by weakness[2] winning fond regard;
Nor eyes, that sparkle from their blushes, roll,
Nor catch the languors of the sick'ning soul,
Nor the quick flutter, nor the coy reserve,
But nobly boast the firm gymnastic nerve;[3]
85   Nor more affect with Delicacy's fan
To hide the emotion from congenial man;
To the bold heights where glory beams, aspire,
Blend mental energy with Passion's fire,
Surpass their rivals in the powers of mind
90   And vindicate *the Rights of womankind."*

   She spoke: and veteran BARBAULD[4] caught the strain,
And deem'd her songs of Love, her Lyrics vain;
And ROBINSON[5] to Gaul her Fancy gave
And trac'd the picture of a Deist's grave!
95   And charming SMITH[6] resign'd her power to please,

2. "Like monarchs, we have been flattered into imbecility, by those who wish to take advantage of our weakness," says Mary Hays (*Essays and Letters*, p. 92). But, whether flattered or not, women were always weak: and female weakness hath accomplished, what the force of arms could not effect [Polwhele's note, quoting her passionate endorsement of Wollstonecraft's *Rights of Woman*]. Hays's feminist *Appeal to the Men of Great Britain on Behalf of Women* appeared anonymously in 1798.

3. Miss Wollstonecraft seriously laments the neglect of all muscular exercises, at our female Boarding-schools [Polwhele's note].

4. Here . . . I have formed a groupe of female Writers; whose productions have been appreciated by the public as works of learning or genius—though not praised with that extravagance of panegyric, which was once a customary tribute to the literary compositions of women. In this country, a female author was formerly esteemed a Phenomenon in Literature: and she was sure of a favourable reception among the critics, in consideration of her sex. This species of gallantry, however, conveyed no compliment to her understanding. It implied such an inferiority of woman in the scale of intellect as was justly humiliating: and critical forbearance was mortifying to female vanity. At the present day, indeed, our literary women are so numerous, that their judges, wa[i]ving all complimentary civilities, decide upon their merits with the same rigid impartiality as it seems right to exercise towards the men. The tribunal of criticism is no longer charmed into complacence by the blushes of modest apprehension. It no longer imagines the pleading eye of feminine diffidence that speaks a consciousness of comparative imbecillity, or a fearfulness of having offended by intrusion. Experience hath drawn aside the flimsy veil of affected timidity, that only served to hide the smile of complacency; the glow of self-gratulation. Yet, alas! the crimsoning blush of modesty, will be always more attractive, than the sparkle of confident intelligence.— Mrs. Barbauld stands the most conspicuous figure in the groupe. She is a veteran in Literature . . . Her poetry . . . is certainly, chaste and elegant. . . . I was sorry to find Mrs. B. . . . classed with such females as a Wollstonecraft. . . . But though Mrs. B. has lately published several political tracts, which if not discreditable to her talents and virtues, can by no means

add to her reputation, yet, I am sure, she must reprobate, with me, the alarming eccentricities of Miss Wollstonecraft [Polwhele's note].

5. In Mrs. Robinson's Poetry, there is a peculiar delicacy: but her Novels, as literary compositions, have no great claim to approbation—As containing the doctrines of Philosophism, they merit the severest censure. Would that, for the sake of herself and her beautiful daughter (whose personal charms are only equalled by the elegance of her mind) would, that, for the sake of the public morality, Mrs. Robinson were persuaded to dismiss the gloomy phantom of annihilation; to think seriously of a future retribution; and to communicate to the world, a recantation of errors that originated in levity, and have been nursed by pleasure! I have seen her, "glittering like the morning-star, full of life, and splendor and joy!" Such, and more glorious, may I meet her again, when the just "shall shine forth as the brightness of the firmament, and as the stars for ever and ever!" [Polwhele, quoting Burke's famous description of his first sight of princess Marie Antoinette; see *Reflections*, page 118.] "Philosophism" is the Enlightenment ideology of progress and human perfectibility through reason.

6. The Sonnets of Charlotte Smith, have a pensiveness peculiarly their own. It is not the monotonous plaintiveness of Shenstone, the gloomy melancholy of Gray, or the meek subdued spirit of Collins. It is a strain of wild, yet softened sorrow, that breathes a romantic air, without losing, for a moment, its mellowness. Her images, often original, are drawn from nature: the most familiar, have a new and charming aspect. Sweetly picturesque, she creates with the pencil of a Gilpin, and infuses her own soul into the landscape. There is so uncommon a variety in her expression, that I could read a thousand of such sonnets without lassitude. In general, a very few Sonnets fatigue attention, partly owing to the sameness of their construction. Petrarch, indeed, I can relish for a considerable time: but Spenser and Milton soon produce somnolence. . . . But why does she suffer her mind to be infected with the Gallic mania? [Polwhele's note. Other references are to the 18th-century poets William Shenstone, Thomas Gray, and William Collins, and to William Gilpin (1724–1804), author of illustrated picturesque tours of Britain, see page 47.]

Poetic feeling and poetic ease;
And HELEN,[7] fir'd by Freedom, bade adieu
To all the broken visions of Peru.
And YEARSELEY,[8] who had warbled, Nature's child,
100   Midst twilight dews, her minstrel ditties wild,
(Tho' soon a wanderer from her meads and milk,
She long'd to rustle, like her sex, in silk)
Now stole that modish grin, the sapient sneer,
And flippant HAYS[9] assum'd a cynic leer ***

1798

Priscilla Bell Wakefield
1751–1832

Of Quaker background, married to a prosperous London merchant, and devoted to philanthropy, Wakefield is best known for the instructional children's books she wrote in the 1790s,
with subjects ranging from travel in Europe and the British empire to botany and zoology.
Among her projects were "frugality banks" for the working classes and "lying-in" (childbirth)
hospitals for poor women. Prison reformer Elizabeth Fry (satirized by Byron) was her niece.
Wakefield's one work for adults, *Reflections on the Present Condition of the Female Sex* (1798),
vigorously argues for better education and more liberal employment opportunities for women
at a time when their vocations were limited to domestic situations as servants, nurses, govern-
esses, housekeepers, or slightly more independent enterprises as schoolmistresses, seamstresses,
and shopkeepers.

7. Miss Helen Williams is, doubtless, a true poet. But is
it not extraordinary, that such a genius, a female and so
young, should have become a politician—that the fair
Helen, whose notes of love have charmed the moonlight
vallies, should stand forward, an intemperate advocate for
Gallic licentiousness—that such a woman should import
with her, a blast more pestilential than that of Avernus,
though she has so often delighted us with melodies, soft
as the sighs of the Zephyr, delicious as the airs of Paradise? [Polwhele's note]. See Williams's *Letters from France*
(1792–1796), pages 109–110 and 138–43 her long political poem condemning imperial conquest, *Peru*, was published in 1784. Avernus is a lake in Italy thought to lead
to the underworld; zephyr is the spring breeze.
8. Mrs. Yearseley's [sic] Poems, as the product of an untutored milk-woman, certainly entitled her to patronage:
and patronage she received, from Miss H. More, liberal
beyond example. Yet, such is the depravity of the human heart, that this milk-woman had no sooner her hut
cheered by the warmth of benevolence, than she spurned
her benefactor from her door. . . . My business, however,
with Mrs. Y. is to recall her, if possible, from her Gallic wanderings—if an appeal to native ingenuousness be
not too late; if the fatal example of the Arch-priestess of
female Libertinism, have any influence on a mind once
stored with the finest moral sentiment [Polwhele's note].
For the falling out with More, see headnote to Yearsley,
page 251; the "fatal example" is Wollstonecraft.

9. Mary Hays from her "Letters and Essays" . . . is evidently a Wollstonecraftian. "I cannot mention (says
she) the admirable advocate for the rights of women,
without pausing to pay a tribute of grateful respect, in
the name of my sex, to the virtue and talents of a writer,
who with equal courage and ability, hath endeavoured
to rescue the female mind from those prejudices which
have been the canker of genuine virtue. . . . The rights
of woman and the name of Wollstonecraft, will go
down to posterity with reverence." Mary Hays ridicules
"the good lady who studied her Bible, and obliged her
children to say their prayers, and go statedly to church."
Her expressions respecting the European Governments
are, in a high degree, inflammatory [Polwhele's note].
The attacks on Wollstonecraft continue in the notes,
recounting her infatuation with the married Fuseli, her
affair with Imlay, her suicide attempts despite a young
daughter, her premarital affair with Godwin, and her
lack of church attendance or death-bed conversion.
"I cannot but think, that the Hand of Providence is
visible, in her life, her death and in [Godwin's] Memoirs. . . . As she was given up to her 'heart's lusts,' and
let 'to follow her own imaginations,' that the fallacy of
and the effects of an irreligious conduct, might be manifested to the world; and as she died a death that strongly
marked the distinction of the sexes, by pointing out the
destiny of women and the diseases to which they are
liable."

from Reflections on the Present Condition of the Female Sex;
with Suggestions for its Improvement

In civilized nations it has ever been the misfortune of the sex to be too highly elevated, or too deeply depressed; now raised above the condition of mortals, upon the score of their personal attractions; and now debased below that of reasonable creatures, with respect to their intellectual endowments. The result of this improper treatment has been a neglect of the mental powers, which women really possess, but know not how to exercise; and they have been contented to barter the dignity of reason, for the imaginary privilege of an empire, of the existence of which they can entertain no reasonable hope beyond the duration of youth and beauty. * * *

But notwithstanding these disadvantages, and others of less perceptible influence, the diffusion of christianity, and the progress of civilization, have raised the importance of the female character; and it has become a branch of philosophy, not a little interesting, to ascertain the offices which the different ranks of women are required to fulfil. Their rights and their duties have lately occupied the pens of writers of eminence; the employments which may properly exercise their faculties, and fill up their time in a useful manner, without encroaching upon those professions, which are appropriate to men, remain to be defined. There are many branches of science, as well as useful occupations, in which women may employ their time and their talents, beneficially to themselves and to the community, without destroying the peculiar characteristic of their sex, or exceeding the most exact limits of modesty and decorum. Whatever obliges them to mix in the public haunts of men, or places the young in too familiar a situation with the other sex; whatever is obnoxious to the delicacy and reserve of the female character, or destructive, in the smallest degree, to the strictest moral purity, is inadmissible. The sphere of feminine action is contracted by numberless difficulties, that are no impediments to masculine exertions. Domestic privacy is the only sure asylum for the juvenile part of the sex; nor can the grave matron step far beyond that boundary with propriety. Unfitted, by their relative situation in society, for many honourable and lucrative employments, those only are suitable for them, which can be pursued without endangering their virtue, or corrupting their manners.

But, under these restrictions, there may be found a multitude of objects adapted to the useful exertions of female talents, which it will be the principal design of these Reflections to point out, after making some remarks upon the present state of female education, and suggesting some improvements towards its reformation.

And here the author may perhaps be allowed to express her hope, that among the numbers of the female world, who appear to be satisfied with inferiority, many require only to be awakened to a true sense of their own real consequence, to be induced to support it by a rational improvement of those hours, which they have hitherto wasted in the most frivolous occupations. The promotion of so useful a design, is the only apology for intruding her opinions upon the subject; and it will be esteemed her highest recompence, should her observations contribute to its accomplishment. * * *

The difficulty of meeting with persons properly qualified to be the preceptors and guides of the uncorrupted minds of youth, is allowed to be great, and suggests the advantages which might arise, from the establishment of institutions for the express purpose of educating young women, of small expectations, for the office. These institutions should be sufficiently endowed, to provide masters in every useful science, and to furnish a well-chosen library, consisting of the most approved authors, with globes, and other suitable apparatus for instruction, and after a certain number of years, women only should be nominated to the charge of instruction. The effect of such seminaries would be a constant succession of female teachers properly prepared for their destination, not only by a regular course of study, but also by a thorough initiation into the philosophical principles of education, founded upon the opinions of the most eminent writers upon the subject. Another beneficial consequence would be, the affording a respectable subsistence to great numbers of young women, who are reduced to misery through want of employment, by enabling them to teach those sciences, which are exclusively taught by masters, an evil that calls loudly for redress. Surely it can never be denied, that the instruction of girls in every department of knowledge or art, is a fair field for the exertion of female talents. * * *

There is scarcely a more helpless object in the wide circle of misery which the vicissitudes of civilized society display, than a woman genteelly educated, whether single or married, who is deprived, by any unfortunate accident, of the protection and support of male relations; unaccustomed to struggle with difficulty, unacquainted with any resource to supply an independent maintenance, she is reduced to the depths of wretchedness, and not infrequently, if she be young and handsome, is driven by despair to those paths which lead to infamy. Is it not time to find a remedy for such evils, when the contention of nations has produced the most affecting transitions in private life, and transferred the affluent and the noble to the humiliating extremes of want and obscurity? When our streets teem with multitudes of unhappy women, many of whom might have been rescued from their present degradation, or who would perhaps never have fallen into it, had they been instructed in the exercise of some art or profession, which would have enabled them to procure for themselves a respectable support by their own industry. * * *

That which is moral excellence in one rational being, deserves the same estimation in another; therefore, if it be really honourable in a man, to exert the utmost of his abilities, whether mental or corporal, in the acquisition of a competent support for himself, and for those who have a natural claim upon his protection; it must be equally so in a woman, nay, perhaps still more incumbent, as in many cases, there is nothing so inimical to the preservation of her virtue as a state of poverty, which leaves her dependant upon the generosity of others, to supply those accommodations, which use has rendered necessary to her comfort.

There appears then no moral impediment to prevent women from the application of their talents to purposes of utility; on the contrary, an improvement in public manners must infallibly result from it; as their influence over the other sex is universally acknowledged, it may be boldly asserted, that a conversion of their time from trifling and unproductive employments, to those that are both useful and profitable, would operate as a check upon luxury, dissipation, and prodigality, and retard the progress of that general dissoluteness, the offspring of idleness, which is deprecated by all political writers, as the sure forerunner of national decay. * * *

Men monopolize not only the most advantageous employments, and such as exclude women from the exercise of them, by the publicity of their nature, or the extensive knowledge they require, but even many of those, which are consistent with the female character. Another heavy discouragement to the industry of women, is the inequality of the reward of their labour, compared with that of men, an injustice which pervades every species of employment performed by both sexes.[1]

---

1. This abuse is in no instance more conspicuous, than in the wages of domestic servants. A footman, especially of the higher kind, whose most laborious task is to wait at table, gains, including clothes, vails, and other perquisites, at least £50 per annum, whilst a cook-maid, who is mistress of her profession, does not obtain £20, though her office is laborious, unwholesome, and requires a much greater degree of skill than that of a valet. A similar disproportion is observable among the inferior servants of the establishment [Wakefield's note]. Vails: tips.

In employments which depend upon bodily strength the distinction is just; for it cannot be pretended that the generality of women can earn as much as men, where the produce of their labour is the result of corporeal exertion; but it is a subject of great regret, that this inequality should prevail, even where an equal share of skill and application are exerted. Male stay-makers, mantua-makers,[2] and hair-dressers are better paid than female artists of the same professions; but surely it will never be urged as an apology for this disproportion, that women are not as capable of making stays, gowns, dressing hair, and similar arts, as men; if they are not superior to them, it can only be accounted for upon this principle, that the prices they receive for their labour are not sufficient to repay them for the expence of qualifying themselves for their business, and that they sink under the mortification of being regarded as artizans of inferior estimation, whilst the men, who supplant them, receive all the encouragement of large profits and full employment, which is ensured to them by the folly of fashion. The occasion for this remark is a disgrace upon those who patronize such a brood of effeminate beings in the garb of men, when sympathy with their humblest sisters should direct them to act in a manner exactly opposite, by holding out every incitement to the industry of their own sex. This evil indeed calls loudly upon women of rank and fortune for redress: they should determine to employ women only, wherever they can be employed; they should procure female instructors for their children; they should frequent no shops that are not served by women; they should wear no clothes that are not made by them; they should reward them as liberally as they do the men who have hitherto supplanted them. Let it be considered a common cause to give them every possible advantage. For once let fashion be guided by reason, and let the mode sanction a preference to women in every profession, to which their pretensions are equal with those of the other sex. This is a patronage which the necessitous have a right to expect from the rich and powerful, whether they are poor by birth, or are unfortunately become so by that mutability of fortune to which every rank is liable. * * *

The serving of retail shops, which deal in articles of female consumption, should be exclusively appropriated to women. For were the multitudes of men, who are constantly employed in measuring linen, gauze, ribbons, and lace; selling perfumes and cosmetics; setting a value on feathers and trinkets; and displaying their talents in praising the elegance of bonnets and caps, to withdraw, they might benefit the community, by exchanging such frivolous avocations for something more worthy of the masculine character, and by this measure afford an opportunity of gaining a creditable livelihood to many destitute women, whom a dreadful necessity drives to the business of prostitution. * * * Every undertaker should employ women, for the express purpose of supplying the female dead, with those things which are requisite. How shocking is the idea of our persons being exposed, even after death, to the observation of a parcel of undertaker's men. * * * In the present state of things, if a poor frail unthinking girl yields to the ardent solicitations of the man who has won her affections, and he be so villainous as to abandon her, she is lost without resource, especially if she be qualified for no occupation but service; deprived of character, no person will take her into their family; the wants of nature must be satisfied, even at the price which produces utter destruction; and the forlorn deserted one is compelled to betake herself to that course, which presently terminates all hope of restoration to the esteem of others, or to her own approbation. * * *

2. Stay-makers: corsetmakers; mantua-makers: dressmakers.

There are some professions and trades customarily in the hands of men, which might be conveniently exercised by either sex.—Many parts of the business of a stationer, particularly ruling account books or making pens. The compounding of medicines in an apothecary's shop, requires no other talents than care and exactness; and if opening a vein[3] occasionally be an indispensible requisite, a woman may acquire the capacity of doing it for those of her own sex at least. * * * Pastry and confectionary appear particularly consonant to the habits of women, though generally performed by men: perhaps the heat of the ovens, and the strength requisite to fill and empty them, may render male assistants necessary; but certainly women are most eligible to mix up the ingredients, and prepare the various kinds of cake for baking.—Light turnery[4] and toy-making, depend more upon dexterity and invention than force, and are therefore suitable work for women and children.

There must be public houses for the reception of travellers, and labourers who are single, and have no homes: it were happy indeed for the community, that they were confined to such purposes, instead of being converted into receptacles for intemperance. * * * Without recommending it as an eligible employment for women, reasons may be urged for the widows of publicans, or even other women of a certain age, engaging in it; as houses of this description, which are under female management, are generally the most orderly, and the most successful.

━━ ❧ ━━

Mary Anne Radcliffe
c. 1746–after 1810

Born the only child to a mother of thirty and a father of seventy who was anxious for an heir, Radcliffe gained a fortune when he died two years later. In her teens, she eloped with a charming friend of her mother, some twenty years her senior, Joseph Radcliffe. He sired eight children but liking alcohol and not particularly good at "economy, method or industry" (Radcliffe wrote in her Memoir of 1810), what he didn't spend of her fortune on recreation he squandered on a series of ill-advised business ventures. Radcliffe realized that it was up to her to support herself and the children. She tried, variously, and without success, a shoe shop, a school, a coffeehouse, a cake-shop, selling patent medicines, taking lodgers—even as she was wracked with rheumatism. In desperation, she sent her sons to school and her daughters to her mother, while she worked as a lady's companion and housekeeper, then as a governess, a position that sexual harassment forced her to abandon. Bitter at finding men monopolizing respectable trades for women, shutting them out so that the most desperate became beggers and prostitutes, she began The Female Advocate in 1792, her full title announcing a debt to Wollstonecraft, and published it in 1799. Radcliffe's class politics are much more rigid than Wollstonecraft's: while she does assail the Vagrant Act's punishment of begging and defends many prostitutes as not morally culpable but economically desperate, she distinguishes these "innocents" from the "guilty," and discriminates in her proposed remedies "between the well-bred female, who is reduced by the unseen hand of fate, and the very poor and abject, whose birth has deprived them of the knowledge of refinement or delicacy."

---

3. Bleeding, for medical purposes.   4. Pottery.

The Female Advocate;
or An Attempt to Recover the Rights of Women
from Male Usurpation

from *"To the Reader"*

The subject of the following pages is an attempt to delineate the situation of those poor, helpless, females whose sufferings, from a variety of causes, are too grievous to be borne; the sources and dire consequences of which the exalted in life cannot form the least conception, unless they condescend to examine for themselves, when, it is to be hoped, their grievances will be sought into and redressed. The munificence of the people of Great Britain, which is ever ready and adequate to the support, aid, and comfort, of the afflicted, when their troubles are fully investigated; and the great number of unfortunate women, who, doubtless, would rejoice to become virtuous and useful members of society, in some lawful employment, have encouraged the author to offer this feeble representation. Nor can she despair of eventual success * * * if she is but so happy as to excite the attention of those whose souls are enlarged with the exalted ideas of Christian charity. * * *

The author, at the same time, wishes it to be understood, that she has not been stimulated, from vain and ambitious views, to appear in print, but rather from the pure philanthropic motive of throwing in her humble mite towards the much-wished-for relief of these most pitiable objects of distress.

from *Introduction*

I contend not with the lords of the creation, for any other privilege than that protection, which they themselves avow to be the *real rights of women*. * * * Advantages, in Britain, being monopolized by the male sex, permit me to ask, if it is not their duty, at least, to afford protection in their stead; for, surely, if they refuse to protect, they have no right whatever to govern. * * *

All women possess not the Amazonian spirit of a Wolstonecraft.[1] But, indeed, unremitted oppression is sometimes a sufficient apology for their throwing off the gentle garb of a female, and assuming some more masculine appearance; yet, when the curtain of misrepresentation is once withdrawn, it is to be hoped, (not doubted) that the cause of complaint will quickly be removed.

from *Part First. The Fatal Consequences of Men Traders Engrossing Women's Occupations*

When we look around us, nothing is more conspicuous in the eyes of the world, than the distresses of women. I do not say those whom a kind Providence hath placed under the immediate care of a tender father, or an affectionate and kind husband; or, *by chance*, a friend, or brother. But these, alas! comprise only one part of the community. Notwithstanding all are of the same nature, and were formed by the same Divine Power, yet their comforts differ very widely indeed. Still, as women seem formed by nature to seek protection from man, why, in the name of justice, refuse the boon?

---

1. Denoting fearlessness and forthrightness, this is a positive use, compared to Polwhele; see n. 5, page 345.

Does it not become highly worthy the attention of men in general, to consider in what manner to redress the grievances *already within their notice?*

Perhaps it may be said, and very justly, that, considering human frailty, there is amongst women, as well as men, a vast number of vicious and undeserving. Granted; still, is it not better to pass over a hundred guilty, than let punishment fall upon one innocent person?—Besides, IS THERE NOT A POSSIBILITY OF FORMING A PLAN OF DISCRIMINATION, FOR THE BENEFIT OF THOSE ONLY WHO MERIT SUCH HUMANE AND FRIENDLY INTERFERENCE? * * * Let us proceed to the ground-work of the design; and, before any further steps are taken, ask, What can be said in favour of men-milliners, men-mantua-makers, and men stay-makers? besides all the numerous train of other professions, such as hair-dressers, &c. &c.; all of which occupations are much more calculated for women than men. * * * "Look," says an observer, "to the shops of per-fumers, toymen, and others of a similar occupation; and, above all, look to the hab-erdashery magazines, where from ten to twenty fellows, six feet high, may be counted in each, to the utter exclusion of poor females, who could sell a tooth-pick, or a few ribbons, just as well." * * * A tax upon these fellows would be very salutary, so say I. * * * Men may be much better employed than in filling women's occupations. For, in the words of St. Luke, these poor females may very justly say, "to dig I cannot, to beg I am ashamed."[1] From this evil precedent, there is no other alternative for these poor women, but beggary or vice!

Let us then, if you please, select one of these distressed females, out of the pro-digious multitude, and pursue her through the humiliating scene of beggary. * * * Certain it must be, that after, perhaps, a life of ease and affluence, to be compelled to such a mortifying situation, requires more than a common share of fortitude to sup-port. Still this prevailing passion, with all its train of attendants, must be subdued, in the dreadful situation of beggary which cannot fail to bring down the spirits of these unhappy victims, with more oppressive force than it is in the power of words to express, or pen to paint, and can only be conceived, *in part,* by the silent sensations of those who can adopt another's woes, and trace the passions of the human mind. * * * See her trembling limbs, which are scarcely able to support her load of wretch-edness, whilst she asks an alms from the casual passenger. She who, perhaps, a short time since, charmed her acquaintance with her sprightly conversation and virtu-ous example, by one adverse stroke, is nevertheless so soon become the contempt, the scorn, and the outcast of mortals! Nor is this wretched doom confined to youth alone; but, by the cruel hand of fate, the poor, dejected mother, as well as daugh-ter, is condemned to share the same direful misfortunes, and be reduced to the same low state of wretchedness, from which their characters are stigmatized with infamy, and to which they unavoidably fall a sacrifice. In this miserable state they must for ever remain, until the spirit of oppression and mistaken prejudice is eradicated, and the heavy cloud of misrepresentation cleared away, through a proper investigation of the cause, which, doubtless, will lead to a conviction: that the distress and wretch-edness of these poor, abandoned creatures originate chiefly from the avaricious and mercenary views of that set of beings, who are "Eating the bread of the hungry, and drinking the drink of the thirsty." Nor are these poor women allowed "to pick up the crumbs," which will appear in the sequel.

1. From Jesus's parable of the unjust steward, Luke 16.3.

In the mean time, let us, if you please, take another view of this poor mother and her miserable daughter, in this forlorn and distressing state of beggary, and there see what relief they obtain, from their piercing accents and broken sighs—little more, it is to be feared, than contempt or insults. Even the hand of charity, accustomed to bestow on the needy, no sooner observes the appearance of youth, or a capability of industry, than it is instantly withdrawn, and kept in reserve (as it is thought) for some more proper object.

Good heavens, what a scene of woe! when the poor mother and her helpless daughter are turned adrift, to the mercy of an unfeeling world; which neither their genteel education, or delicate constitutions, broken down by poverty and hardships, can prevent. O! what distress, in a situation like this! * * * In vain do they supplicate their former friends, for the voice of censure has pointed them out as infamous! Good God! what grief can equal this? Abandoned by friends, and left to the reproach, contempt, and censure of a cruel world, without a provision, or any probable means of gaining a subsistence, or even the smallest glimpse of a distant hope.

And, though shocking to relate, yet such is the miserable situation of thousands of defenceless women. * * * What says the Vagrant Act?[2]—"Persons who beg in the streets are idle and disorderly; and any person who apprehends and carries such a beggar before a justice, shall receive five shillings, when the said justice may commit them to a house of correction."

However shocking the sentence, what numbers of these poor objects have been dragged away by the ruthless hand of the unfeeling savage, to some loathsome prison, without regard to the more refined or delicate sensations of one or another? Good heavens! there surely needs no Siddonian powers to heighten such a tragic scene.[3] She who, perhaps, was reared with all the gentle softness and maternal care of a fond parent; she, who so lately was looked upon as an ornament to her sex, until the pressure of misfortunes compelled her to seek for bread, to be at once confined in a dark prison, there to be obliged to hear all the opprobrious language of the very lowest set of beings, and that under a storm of oaths and imprecations, which, of itself, must pierce her very soul. There to have her ears grated with the rattling of bolts and bars, and all the adamantine fetters of misery. Good God! is it possible we can see our fellow creatures debased so low! * * *

What numbers of unguarded young men, even with hearts inclined to virtue, have unhappily been drawn on to vice, by the powerful insinuations of these poor abandoned females, who, like Eve in Paradise, is no sooner fallen herself, than, by deceitful artifice, she spreads the net of destruction to catch others. For example: need we go any farther than the theatres, the resort of all, both good and bad, and where abandoned females, of all ages and degrees of profligacy, attend to make their harvest, and gather in their unlawful plunder, to supply the ordinary wants of the ensuing day?[4] And what can better answer the purpose of decoy than the drama? for, should it be comedy, the obscenity which prevails in many of our modern plays, cannot fail to act as poison upon the young mind: or is it tragedy, what can have a greater influence upon the feelings of sensibility, or sooner awaken the tender passions, which these miserable women take special care to translate to their own evil purposes? * * *

---

2. Part of the Poor Laws prohibiting begging, these acts were also used to suppress loitering and prostitution.
3. Sarah Siddons (1755–1831), celebrated tragedian. See Burke's use of this trope, page 115.
4. Theaters were widely suspect as places of social mixing, disreputable characters, and prostitutes.

Nor does the dreadful calamity end here; for, notwithstanding so many unfortunate females have been obliged to seek bread in the paths of vice, and so many young men have fallen victims to their folly and wickedness, still the same devouring jaws of destruction are open for its future prey; nor can they ever possibly close, until the grievous precedent of men usurping females' occupations is entirely done away, *or some proper substitute provided,* so as to enable women to share the common necessaries along with their fellow-creatures: till then, we need not wonder at the vast number of pickpockets and housebreakers which, at all times, infest the streets, to the disturbance of civil society. * * *

It is said, the city of London alone pays upwards of twenty thousand pounds annually to patrols, beadles,[5] and watchmen; and it may be a much greater sum; yet, that of itself seems a vast sum indeed, to be raised by levy, in which the honest trader must unavoidably contribute a large share. Would not that contribution answer a much better purpose in providing for the necessitous poor, such as we have just been treating of, and who are judged unfit objects to be received into a parish workhouse;[6] being, *as it is termed,* able enough to earn their own bread out of the house?

Yet, so long as there continues a prohibition against women having an employment, it is to be feared, double the sum already raised by the inhabitants will be found inefficacious. * * * That political and private happiness are invariably connected, is beyond a doubt; and that the morals of this nation are very corrupt, is but too visible, from the vast numbers of disgraceful women who infest the face of the country. * * *

That great numbers would be happy in contributing to the aid and relief of those who appear to be objects of distress, is beyond a doubt: but, alas! for helpless, injured females! the heavy clouds of prejudice and misrepresentation have thrown so dark a veil between them and the pity of the world, that they are despised by all. Yet, when the curtain is once withdrawn, and the tragic scene exposed to open view, leading these poor creatures from obscurity into open light, then will be the crisis, when every good Christian may be impowered to soften the affliction of another's woes; and though it may not be in the power of every sympathising breast to contribute towards their temporal wants, they may still be impowered to sooth their sorrows, rather than drive the envenomed arrows of censure still deeper into their afflicted bosoms. * * *

The efficacy of these reflections to a feeling and generous mind, that can participate in another's woes, cannot be doubted; yet what will all that pity or all that sympathy avail, unless some exertions are used towards effecting a redress?

Suppose no lady would suffer herself to be served, in the shops of these effeminate traders, by any of the short-clothed gentry, would it not be a means of compelling all those who chuse to carry on the tragi-comic farce, to effect the business under the disguise of gown and petticoat?

But joking apart: believe me, ladies, it is past a joke, when poor, unfortunate females are compelled to go without clothing. * * *

Were a body of miserable women, be they really virtuous or not, to assemble with a petition to parliament, where is the person who would be persuaded to present it, particularly when they are all considered as worthless wretches.

---

5. Parish officers who kept order.
6. As Radcliffe makes clear, not everyone qualified for

this opportunity, and it was grim, at that. Recall Jemima's report, page 340.

But were a body of men artificers (be their conduct or morals as they may) to offer a representation of grievances, doubtless their case would be heard, and considered, in every sense of the word, both political and humane.

What statute is there, which grants that men alone shall live, and women scarcely exist?—Is it not an usurpation which every violator must blush at, when considered in the light it ought to be, as an act of the greatest injustice? Then, drive hence all such distress: let it not be said, that Britons can cherish a wish to oppress their sisters, wives, and mothers, but rather that they are merciful to the fatherless and the widow. * * *

The very poor, who are born in an abject state, are taught from their infancy to struggle through life in the same manner they see their needy connections: bread must be had, and all the instructions they can possibly get, is in what way to obtain it. Consequently, if by labour and industry, they can acquire a sufficiency to exist upon, they are perfectly at ease, without bestowing a single thought upon to-morrow.

But the poor, unfortunate woman, who has seen better days, and been reared and educated with tenderness and care, she it is that feels her broken slumbers can no longer give relief to her weary limbs. Her inability to wrestle with difficulties are great indeed; especially when she finds her whole endeavours fruitless: and, what is still as bad, by running to and fro, in pursuit of some means for bread, (which she is not able to obtain) the shrill voice of censure, or the destructive whisper of calumny, having breathed such a poisonous vapour over her character, she is despised by all. * * * O, cruel censure! what must be the sensations of oppressed innocence, * * * when they have tried every expedient to obtain employment, though to no effect?

from *Part Second. Which demonstrates that the Frailty of Female Virtue more frequently originates from embarrassed Circumstances, than from a depravity of Disposition.*
[ORPHAN GIRLS]

Pitiable object! thy fate seems hard indeed: yet so it but too frequently happens to hundreds. * * * Where wilt thou go, to secure thee from real want? A parish work-house is but a poor consolation for so great a loss, at a period when neither reason nor religion is ripened into maturity, to moderate the grievance. But, if, perhaps, a friend step forward, the Asylum for the protection of Orphan Girls may receive the poor fugitive; in which blessed and happy institution, through time, the memory of her woeful loss, in parents and provision, may, in some degree, be wiped away in the benevolence of her new protectors, who not only provide for her temporal, but also for her spiritual concerns, in instructing her as a good Christian and a useful member. But, alas! small is the number which this institution can admit, when compared with the vast numbers left in similar situations. And for those, who are more advanced in age, to what standard can they repair? It is true, necessity will teach people to exert themselves, who have nothing but their own industry to depend upon, and consequently they seek for a female occupation. But how great their surprise, and inexpressible their grief, to find, like the rest, that they are repulsed in every pursuit of industry, whereby they might expect a maintenance! * * * Were there a capacious establishment for industry, built upon such a basis as would form a discrimination between the well-bred female, who is reduced by the unseen hand of fate, and the very poor and abject, whose birth has deprived them of the knowledge of refinement or delicacy; what crouds of unprovided women would flock to the standard! * * *

Where do we see the father or mother of a family, with an independent fortune, be it ever so small, who would not be shocked at the bare idea of placing their daughter in the world in such situations as would enable them to rise, through their own industry and merit, or fit them for becoming wives to some honest and industrious tradesman?—No: that would be a degradation which must not take place. It is the etiquette of the times for the daughters to be bred fine ladies, although it be without a fortune, either dependent or independent, to support it. As for trade, that is out of the question. The sons indeed are differently provided: the eldest, in course, inherits the paternal estate, and the younger ones are placed in the church, the army, the navy, or at the bar; and others, again are genteelly situated in the mercantile world: the whole of which are fit professions for a gentleman, and by which, if they have merit and success, they may acquire a competency.

But for the female part of the family, what appears in their favour? what prospects have they in life?—The parents die, and leave them, without a provision, a burden upon their connections; which forms the first step to deprive them of friends as well as subsistence. A miserable inheritance, to be their best and only portion! What can be said in behalf of such parents? can their easy compliance with the fashion of the times form any apology for such a mistaken conduct?—This surely cannot be called true paternal affection, to entail upon these helpless young creatures such a succession of misery as must eventually ensue. * * *

Have we not had sufficient proofs, that the happiness and welfare of mortals have at all times been thought worthy the attention of a Briton. Witness the poor slaves; what exertions have not been used by the humane friends of liberty in their behalf? Yet less, much less, are their sufferings to be lamented than the poor females I speak of, who have been bred up and educated in the school of Christianity, and fostered by the tender hand of Care.

The slave is little acquainted with the severe pangs a virtuous mind labours under, when driven to the extreme necessity of forfeiting their virtue for bread. The slave cannot feel the pain at the loss of reputation, a term of which they never heard, and much less know the meaning. What are the untutored, wild imaginations of a slave, when put in the balance with the distressing sensations of a British female, who has received a refined, if not a classical, education, and is capable of the finest feelings the human heart is susceptible of. A slave, through want of education, has little more refinement than cattle in the field; nor can they know the want of what they never enjoyed, or were taught to expect; but a poor female, who has received the best instruction, and is endowed with a good understanding, what must not she feel in mind, independent of her corporeal wants, after the adversity of fate has set her up as a mark, for the ridicule, the censure, and contempt of the world? Her feelings cannot be described, nor her sufferings sufficiently lamented.

I recollect some observations, made some years ago, by a late honourable, humane, learned, and truly worthy member of the House of Commons,[1] respecting the business of the slave-trade, which doubly confirms my opinion of the great necessity there is for an investigation into the grievances I have been speaking of, since it leads to a clear demonstration, that the most judicious and benevolent may still remain in the dark, as to the sufferings of our Christian slaves at home.

---

1. Mr. Burke [Wakefield's note]; Edmund Burke opposed slavery.

"There is," said the honourable gentleman, "no state in human nature but had its compensations. What was a slave? a happy slave was a degraded man; his happiness consisted in having no thought of the past, or the future, and this deficiency of mind it was which lessened the dignity of man, and conferred happiness on the African."

A very striking and just observation, with regard to the African, it must be granted; yet I cannot but differ in opinion, when it is said, that all mankind are capable of a compensation. For, admitting the same mode of reasoning to stand good, if the oppressions of one part of the creation are moderated through their ignorance, how much must the other be heightened by their sensibility and the refinements of education. Nor can I see the smallest trait of compensation remaining for these miserable females, since the very education they have received in youth, redounds to their misfortunes in maturity.

Then, if an investigation into the business of the slave-trade has been founded on such humane and generous principles, how much greater pleasure must it give the feeling heart, to patronize the poor, unfortunate women of our own nation, who labour under the very worst kind of slavery, and must continue to languish under the fetters of a painful bondage, till death, or the kindly hand of interference, has severed the chain?

1795

—◆—

Hannah More
1745–1833

Hannah More came from a High Church–Tory family, and though she would turn Evangelical and become a vigorous abolitionist, her politics never swung left. In *Village Politics* (1792), she criticized the French Revolution and the "Rights of Man," hewing to the Evangelical line that the lot of the poor was to be improved by philanthropy and faith in salvation. "Rights of women! We shall be hearing of the Rights of Children next!" she scoffed on hearing of Wollstonecraft's *Rights of Woman*. Yet she shared many of its principles: rationality, modesty, chastity, and "practical education" over trivial "accomplishments." Her life, moreover, was not conducted in the "female sphere" of hearth and home. As a child, she learned Latin (a man's language) and mathematics from a father who wanted his daughters to be capable of self-sufficiency as teachers. She later learned French, Italian, and Spanish from her elder sisters. As a young woman, she came to London and entered a lively literary world, becoming friends with Samuel Johnson, actor David Garrick, and Horace Walpole, and frequented the salons celebrated in her long poem *The Bas Bleu* (1786). She was a successful writer even before she gained an annuity of £200 in compensation for a reneged marriage engagement; with this income she was able to live independently, never marrying, and devoting herself to philanthropy and writing, the latter with considerable financial success.

First published in 1799, *Strictures on Female Education* went through thirteen editions and was in demand for decades, selling 19,000 copies. Even more popular (eight editions in its first two months) was her "conduct" novel of 1809, *Coelebs in Search of a Wife*—an irresistible target for Byron (*Don Juan* 1.16). Like Wollstonecraft, More was willing to condescend to novel-writing for propaganda. In quest of an ideal wife, young Coelebs auditions several near and not so near Misses until he finds perfection in quiet, proper, prudent Lucilla, skilled in household management and given to visiting the poor to read to them from the Bible. *Strictures* sets the didactic curriculum, arguing for rational education, Christian virtue, the "separate spheres" of male and female life, and the subordination of women to men.

Works by More also appear in Perspectives: The Rights of Man and the Revolution Controversy, page 152, and Perspectives: The Abolition of Slavery and the Slave Trade, page 262.

Strictures on the Modern System of Female Education;
with a View of the Principles and Conduct Prevalent among Women of Rank and Fortune
from *Introduction*

It is a singular injustice which is often exercised towards women, first to give them a very defective education, and then to expect from them the most undeviating purity of conduct;—to train them in such a manner as shall lay them open to the most dangerous faults, and then to censure them for not proving faultless. Is it not unreasonable and unjust, to express disappointment if our daughters should, in their subsequent lives, turn out precisely that very kind of character for which it would be evident to an unprejudiced by-stander that the whole scope and tenour of their instruction had been systematically preparing them?

Some reflections on the present erroneous system are here with great deference submitted to public consideration. The author is apprehensive that she shall be accused of betraying the interests of her sex by laying open their defects; but surely an earnest wish to turn their attention to objects calculated to promote their true dignity, is not the office of an enemy. So to expose the weakness of the land, as to suggest the necessity of internal improvement, and to point out the means of effectual defence, is not treachery, but patriotism. * * *

Let it not be suspected that the author arrogantly conceives *herself* to be exempt from that natural corruption of the heart which it is one chief object of this slight work to exhibit; that she superciliously erects herself into the impeccable censor of her sex and of the world; as if from the critic's chair she were coldly pointing out the faults and errors of another order of beings, in whose welfare she had not that lively interest which can only flow from the tender and intimate participation of fellow-feeling.

Bath, March 14, 1799

from *Chapter 8. On Female Study*

Will it not be ascribed to a captious singularity, if I venture to remark that real knowledge and real piety, though they may have gained in many instances, have suffered in others from that profusion of little, amusing, sentimental books with which the youthful library overflows? Abundance has its dangers as well as scarcity. In the first place, may not the multiplicity of these alluring little works increase the natural reluctance to those more dry and uninteresting studies, of which, after all, the rudiments of every part of learning *must* consist? And, secondly, is there not some danger (though there are many honourable exceptions) that some of those engaging narratives may serve to infuse into the youthful heart a sort of spurious goodness, a confidence of virtue, a parade of charity? And that the benevolent actions with the recital of which they abound, when they are not made to flow from any source but *feeling*, may tend to inspire a self-complacency, a self-gratulation, a "stand by, for I am holier than thou?" May not the success with which the good deeds of the little heroes are uniformly crowned; the invariable reward which is made the instant concomitant of well-doing, furnish the young reader with false views of the condition of life, and the nature of the divine dealings with men? May they not help to suggest a false standard of morals, to infuse a love of popularity and an anxiety for praise, in the place of that simple and unostentatious rule of doing whatever good we do, *because it is the will of God?* The universal substitution of this principle would tend to purify the worldly morality of many a popular little story. And there are few dangers which good parents will more carefully guard against than that of giving their children a mere political piety; that sort of religion which just goes to make people more respectable, and to stand well with the world; a religion which is to save appearances without inculcating realities; a religion which affects to "preach peace and good will to men," but which forgets to give "glory to God in the highest."[1]

There is a certain precocity of mind which is much helped on by these superficial modes of instruction; for frivolous reading will produce its correspondent effect, in much less time than books of solid instruction; the imagination being liable to be worked upon, and the feelings to be set a going, much faster than the understanding can be opened and the judgment enlightened. A talent for conversation should be the result of instruction, not its precursor: it is a golden fruit when suffered to ripen gradually on the tree of knowledge; but if forced in the hot-bed of a circulating library,[2] it will turn out worthless and vapid in proportion as it was artificial and premature. Girls who have been accustomed to devour a multitude of frivolous books, will converse and write with a far greater appearance of skill, as to style and sentiment, at twelve or fourteen years old, than those of a more advanced age, who are under the discipline of severer studies; but the former having early attained to that low standard which had been held out to them, become stationary; while the latter, quietly progressive, are passing through just gradations to a higher strain of mind; and those who early begin with talking and writing like women, commonly end with thinking and acting like children.

I would not, however, prohibit such works of imagination as suit this early period. When moderately used, they serve to stretch the faculties and expand the mind; but I should prefer works of vigorous genius and pure unmixed fable to many of those tame and more affected moral stories, which are not grounded on Christian principle. I should suggest the use, on the one hand, of original and acknowledged fictions; and, on the other, of accurate and simple facts; so that truth and fable may ever be kept separate and distinct in the mind. * * *

This suggestion is, however, by no means intended to exclude works of taste and imagination, which must always make the ornamental part, and of course a very considerable part of female studies. It is only intimated, that they should not form them entirely and exclusively. For what is called dry tough reading, independent of the knowledge it conveys, is useful as a habit, and wholesome as an exercise. Serious study serves to harden the mind for more trying conflicts; it lifts the reader from sensation to intellect; it abstracts her from the world and its vanities; it fixes a wandering spirit and fortifies a weak one; it divorces her from matter; it corrects that spirit of trifling which she naturally contracts from the frivolous turn of female conversation and the petty nature of female employments. * * *

Far be it from me to desire to make scholastic ladies or female dialecticians; but there is little fear that the kind of books here recommended, if thoroughly studied, and not superficially skimmed, will make them pedants, or induce conceit; for by

---

1. An ingenious (and in many respects useful) French Treatise on Education has too much encouraged this political piety [More's note; quoting Luke 2.14].

2. Lending libraries carried stores of popular fiction, much of it written by and for women.

showing them the possible powers of the human mind, you will bring them to see the littleness of their own: and surely to get acquainted with the mind, to regulate, to inform it; to show it its own ignorance and its own weakness, does not seem the way to puff it up. But let her who is disposed to be elated with her literary acquisitions check the rising vanity by calling to mind the just remark of Swift, "that after all her boasted acquirements, a woman will, generally speaking, be found to possess less of what is called learning than a common school-boy."[3]

Neither is there any fear that this sort of reading will convert ladies into authors. The direct contrary effect will be likely to be produced by the perusal of writers who throw the generality of readers at such an unapproachable distance as to check presumption, instead of exciting it. Who are those ever-multiplying authors, that with unparalleled fecundity are overstocking the world with their quick-succeeding progeny? They are NOVEL-WRITERS: the easiness of whose productions is at once the cause of their own fruitfulness, and of the almost infinitely numerous race of imitators to whom they give birth. Such is the frightful facility of this species of composition, that every raw girl, while she reads, is tempted to fancy that she can also write. And as Alexander, on perusing the Iliad, found by congenial sympathy the image of Achilles stamped on his own ardent soul, and felt himself the hero he was studying; and as Corregio, on first beholding a picture which exhibited the perfection of the graphic art, prophetically felt all his own future greatness, and cried out in rapture, "And I, too, am a painter!" so a thorough-paced novel-reading Miss, at the close of every tissue of hackneyed adventures, feels within herself the stirring impulse of corresponding genius, and triumphantly exclaims, "And I, too, am an author!" The glutted imagination soon overflows with the redundance of cheap sentiment and plentiful incident, and by a sort of arithmetical proportion, is enabled by the perusal of any three novels, to produce a fourth; till every fresh production, like the prolific progeny of Banquo, is followed by "Another, and another, and another!"[4] Is a lady, however destitute of talents, education, or knowledge of the world, whose studies have been completed by a circulating library, in any distress of mind? the writing a novel suggests itself as the best soother of her sorrows! Does she labour under any depression of circumstances? writing a novel occurs as the readiest receipt for mending them! and she solaces her imagination with the conviction that the subscription which has been extorted by her importunity, or given to her necessities, has been offered as a homage to her genius; and this confidence instantly levies a fresh contribution for a succeeding work. Capacity and cultivation are so little taken into the account, that writing a book seems to be now considered as the only sure resource which the idle and the illiterate have always in their power.

May the Author be indulged in a short digression, while she remarks, though rather out of its place, that the corruption occasioned by these books has spread so wide, and descended so low, as to have become one of the most universal, as well as most pernicious, sources of corruption among us. Not only among milliners, mantua-makers, and other trades where numbers work together, the labour of one girl is frequently sacrificed that she may be spared to read those mischievous books to

---

3. From *Letter to a Young Lady* (1727) by Jonathan Swift: "Those who are commonly called Learned Women have lost all manner of Credit by their impertinent Talkativeness and Conceit of themselves; but there is an easy remedy for this, if you once consider, that after all the pains you may be at, you can never arrive in point of learning to the perfection of a School-boy."

4. References are to the famous anecdote of Alexander the Great's sympathy with the Greek hero Achilles in Homer's epic of the Trojan War; the Italian Renaissance painter; and to the vision of Banquo's royal heirs that frustrates childless Macbeth (4.1).

the others; but she has been assured by clergymen who have witnessed the fact, that they are procured and greedily read in the wards of our hospitals! an awful hint, that those who teach the poor to read, should not only take care to furnish them with principles which will lead them to abhor corrupt books, but that they should also furnish them with such books as shall strengthen and confirm their principles.[5]

from *Chapter 14. The Practical Use of Female Knowledge, with a Sketch of the Female Character, and a Comparative View of the Sexes*

The chief end to be proposed, in cultivating the understandings of women is to qualify them for the practical purposes of life. Their knowledge is not often, like the learning of men, to be reproduced in some literary composition, and never in any learned profession; but it is to come out in conduct: it is to be exhibited in life and manners. A lady studies, not that she may qualify herself to become an orator or a pleader; not that she may learn to debate, but to act. She is to read the best books, not so much to enable her to talk to them, as to bring the improvement which they furnish to the rectification of her principles and the formation of her habits. The great uses of study to a woman are to enable her to regulate her own mind, and to be instrumental to the good of others. * * *

But there is one *human* consideration which would perhaps more effectually tend to damp in an aspiring woman the ardours of literary vanity—I speak not of real genius, though there the remark often applies—than any which she will derive from motives of humility, or propriety, or religion; which is, that in the judgment passed on her performances, she will have to encounter the mortifying circumstance of having her sex always taken into account, and her highest exertions will probably be received with the qualified approbation *that it is really extraordinary for a woman*. Men of learning, who are naturally disposed to estimate works in proportion as they appear to be the result of art, study, and institution, are inclined to consider even the happier performances of the other sex as the spontaneous productions of a fruitful but shallow soil, and to give them the same kind of praise which we bestow on certain salads, which often draw from us a sort of wondering commendation, not, indeed, as being worth much in themselves, but because, by the lightness of the earth, and a happy knack of the gardener, these indifferent cresses spring up in a night, and therefore we are ready to wonder they are no worse.

As to men of sense, however, they need be the less hostile to the improvement of the other sex, as they themselves will be sure to be gainers by it; the enlargement of the female understanding being the most likely means to put an end to those petty and absurd contentions for equality which female smatterers so anxiously maintain. I say smatterers, for between the first class of both sexes the question is much more rarely and always more temperately agitated. Cooperation, and not competition, is, indeed, the clear principle we wish to see reciprocally adopted by those higher minds in each sex which really approximate the nearest to each other. The more a woman's understanding is improved, the more obviously she will discern that there can be no happiness in any society where there is a perpetual struggle for power; and the more

5. The above facts furnish no argument on the side of those who would keep the poor in ignorance. Those who cannot *read* can *hear*, and are likely to hear to worse purpose than those who have been better taught. And that ignorance furnishes no security for integrity either in morals or politics, the late revolts in more than one country, remarkable for the ignorance of the poor, fully illustrate. It is earnestly hoped that the above facts may tend to impress ladies with the importance of superintending the instruction of the poor, and of making it an indispensable part of their charity to give them moral and religious books [More's note].

her judgment is rectified, the more accurate views will she take of the station she was born to fill, and the more readily will she accommodate herself to it. * * *

There is this singular difference between a woman vain of her wit, and a woman vain of her beauty; * * * she who is vain of her genius, more liberal at least in her vanity, is jealous for the honour of her whole sex, and contends for the equality of their pretensions as a body, in which she feels that her own are involved as an individual. The beauty vindicates her own rights, the wit the rights of women; * * * and while the more selfish though more moderate beauty "would but be Queen for life," the public-spirited wit struggles to abrogate the Salique law of intellect, and to enthrone "a whole sex of Queens."[1]

At the revival of letters in the sixteenth and the following century, the controversy about this equality was agitated with more warmth than wisdom; and the process was instituted and carried on, on the part of the female complainant, with that sort of acrimony which always raises a suspicion of the justice of any cause; for violence commonly implies doubt, and invective indicates weakness rather than strength. * * * Among the innovations of this innovating period, the imposing term of *rights* has been produced to sanctify the claim of our female pretenders,[2] with a view not only to rekindle in the minds of women a presumptuous vanity, dishonourable to their sex, but produced with a view to excite in their hearts an impious discontent with the post which God has assigned them in this world.[3]

But *they* little understand the true interests of woman who would lift her from the important duties of her allotted station, to fill, with fantastic dignity, a loftier but less appropriate niche. Nor do they understand her true happiness, who seek to annihilate distinctions from which she derives advantages, and to attempt innovations which would depreciate her real value. Each sex has its proper excellences, which would be lost were they melted down into the common character by the fusion of the new philosophy. Why should we do away distinctions which increase the mutual benefits and enhance the satisfactions of life? Whence, but by carefully preserving the original marks of difference, stamped by the hand of the Creator, would be derived the superior advantage of mixed society? Is either sex so abounding in perfection, as to be independent on the other for improvement? Have men no need to have their rough angles filed off, and their harshnesses and asperities smoothed and polished by assimilating with beings of more softness and refinement? Are the ideas of women naturally so *very* judicious, are their principles so *invincibly* firm, are their views so *perfectly* correct, are their judgments so *completely* exact, that there is occasion for no additional weight, no superadded strength, no increased clearness, none of that enlargement of mind, none of that additional invigoration, which may be derived from the aids of the stronger sex? What identity could advantageously supersede such an enlivening opposition, such an interesting variety of character? * * *

Natural propensities best mark the designations of Providence as to their application. The fin was not more clearly bestowed on the fish that he should swim, nor the wing given to the bird that he should fly, than superior strength of body and a firmer texture of mind were given to man, that he might preside in the deep and

---

1. Pope's *Epistle II*, "of the Characters of Women," assumes that "ev'ry Lady would be Queen for life" and shudders at the thought of "a whole Sex of Queens! / Pow'r all their end" (218–20). Salique (Salic) law, deriving from old French law, excludes females from the line of royal succession.

2. False claimants, especially to a throne; More is also suggesting "fantasizers" and dissemblers.

3. This was written soon after the publication of a work intitled "The Rights of Woman" [More, referring to *Vindication*].

daring scenes of action and of council; in the complicated arts of government, in the contention of arms, in the intricacies and depths of science, in the bustle of commerce, and in those professions which demand a higher reach and a wider range of powers. The true value of woman is not diminished by the imputation of inferiority in those talents which do not belong to her, of those qualities in which her claim to excellence does not consist. She has other requisites, better adapted to answer the end and purposes of her being, from "Him who does all things well;" who suits the agent to the action; who accommodates the instrument to the work.

Let not, then, aspiring, because ill-judging, woman view with pining envy the keen satirist, hunting vice through all the doublings and windings of the heart; the sagacious politician, leading senates, and directing the fate of empires; the acute lawyer, detecting the obliquities of fraud; and the skilful dramatist, exposing the pretensions of folly; but let her ambition be consoled by reflecting, that those who thus excel, to all that Nature bestows and books can teach, must add besides that consummate knowledge of the world to which a delicate woman has no fair avenues, and which, even if she could attain, she would never be supposed to have come honestly by.

In almost all that comes under the description of polite letters, in all that captivates by vivid imagery or warms by just and affecting sentiment, women are excellent. They possess in a high degree that delicacy and quickness of perception, and that nice discernment between the beautiful and defective which comes under the denomination of taste. Both in composition and in action they excel in details; but they do not so much generalise their ideas as men, nor do their minds seize a great subject with so large a grasp. They are acute observers, and accurate judges of life and manners, as far as their own sphere of observation extends, but they describe a smaller circle. A woman sees the world, as it were, from a little elevation in her own garden, whence she makes an exact survey of home scenes, but takes not in that wider range of distant prospects which he who stands on a loftier eminence commands.

⊷ ⊱≬≲ ⊶

Mary Lamb
1764–1847

In a notebook of 1811, Samuel Taylor Coleridge recorded his desire to open "the eyes of the public to the real situation of Needle-workers, and women in general," adding, "Mary Lamb has promised me Facts in abundance." Needlework—an arduous, eye-straining, poorly paid, hand-labor before the invention of sewing machines—was no idle subject for Lamb. After her father lost his position as servant, she and her younger brother Charles supported their invalid mother and increasingly dotty father, he as a clerk at the East India Company and she with needlework. On one trying day in September 1796, her apprentice botched a job that had to be taken out and redone; overwrought, overworked, Mary exploded into a manic rage, chasing the girl with a knife. When her parents interceded, she wounded her father with a flying fork and fatally stabbed her mother in the heart. The intercession of her father's former employer, an attorney, spared her permanent sentencing to a lunatic asylum. She was remanded to the legal custody of Charles, then twenty-two, who lived with her for the rest of his life. Weathering this tragedy and several manic relapses, they remained very close. Mary's spirited intelligence and wit were cherished by Charles and their circle, which included Coleridge, the Wordsworth family, and just about everyone in London's literary world.

Charles and Mary collaborated on several books for children, with *Tales from Shakespear* their biggest success (see page 702). In a letter signed "Sempronia" to *The British Lady's Magazine* published 1 April 1815, Mary Lamb urged women of leisure not to do needlework as recreation: not only is it mind-numbing but it usurps women needing to earn a living thus. The argument reflects her own experience and the influence of Wollstonecraft, who had also made a living by needlework. *Rights of Woman* contains a scathing attack on this work as female recreation:

> When a woman in the lower ranks of life makes her husband's and children's clothes, she does her duty, this is her part in the family business; but when women work only to dress better than they could otherwise afford, it is worse than sheer loss of time. To render the poor virtuous they must be employed, and women in the middle rank of life, did they not ape the fashions of the nobility, . . . might employ them, whilst they themselves managed their families, instructed their children, and exercised their own minds.

Letter to *The British Lady's Magazine*
["THE STATE OF NEEDLEWORK IN THIS COUNTRY"]

Mr. Editor,—In early life I passed eleven years in the exercise of my needle for a livelihood. Will you allow me to address your readers, among whom might perhaps be found some of the kind patronesses of my former humble labours, on a subject widely connected with female life—the state of needlework in this country.

To lighten the heavy burthen which many ladies impose upon themselves is one object which I have in view: but, I confess, my strongest motive is to excite attention towards the industrious sisterhood to which I once belonged.

From books I have been informed of the fact, upon which "The British Lady's Magazine" chiefly founds its pretensions, namely, that women have of late been rapidly advancing in intellectual improvement. Much may have been gained in this way, indirectly, for that class of females for whom I wish to plead. Needlework and intellectual improvement are naturally in a state of warfare. But I am afraid the root of the evil has not as yet been struck at. Workwomen of every description were never in so much distress for want of employment.

Among the present circle of my acquaintance I am proud to rank many that may truly be called respectable; nor do the female part of them, in their mental attainments, at all disprove the prevailing opinion of that intellectual progression which you have taken as the basis of your work; yet I affirm that I know not a single family where there is not some essential drawback to its comfort which may be traced to needle-work *done at home*, as the phrase is for all needle-work performed in a family by some of its own members, and for which no remuneration in money is received or expected.

In money alone, did I say? I would appeal to all the fair votaries of voluntary housewifery, whether, in the matter of conscience, any one of them ever thought she had done as much needle-work as she ought to have done. Even fancy work,[1]

---

1. Embroidery.

the fairest of the tribe!—how delightful the arrangement of her materials! the fixing upon her happiest pattern, how pleasing an anxiety! how cheerful the commencement of the labour she enjoins! But that lady must be a true lover of the art, and so industrious a pursuer of a predetermined purpose, that it were pity her energy should not have been directed to some wiser end, who can affirm she neither feels weariness during the execution of a fancy piece, nor takes more time than she had calculated for the performance.

Is it too bold an attempt to persuade your readers that it would prove an incalculable addition to general happiness, and the domestic comfort of both sexes, if needle-work were never practised but for a remuneration in money? As nearly, however, as this desirable thing can be effected, so much more nearly will women be upon an equality with men, as far as respects the mere enjoyment of life. As far as that goes, I believe it is every woman's opinion that the condition of men is far superior to her own.

"They can do what they like," we say. Do not these words generally mean, they have time to seek out whatever amusements suit their tastes? We dare not tell them we have no time to do this; for, if they should ask in what manner we dispose of our time, we should blush to enter upon a detail of the minutiae which compose the sum of a woman's daily employment. Nay, many a lady who allows not herself one quarter of an hour's positive leisure during her waking hours, considers her own husband as the most industrious of men, if he steadily pursue his occupation till the hour of dinner, and will be perpetually lamenting her own idleness.

Real business and *real leisure* make up the portions of men's time—two sources of happiness which we certainly partake of in a very inferior degree. To the execution of employment, in which the faculties of the body or mind are called into busy action, there must be a consoling importance attached, which feminine duties (that generic term for all our business) cannot aspire to.

In the most meritorious discharges of those duties, the highest praise we can aim at is to be accounted the helpmates of *man*; who, in return for all he does for us, expects, and justly expects, us to do all in our power to soften and sweeten life.

In how many ways is a good woman employed, in thought or action, through the day, in order that her *good man* may be enabled to feel his leisure hours *real substantial holyday*, and perfect respite from the cares of business! Not the least part to be done to accomplish this end is to fit herself to become a conversational companion; that is to say, she has to study and understand the subjects on which he loves to talk. This part of our duty, if strictly performed, will be found by far our hardest part. The disadvantages we labour under from an education differing from a manly one make the hours in which we *sit and do nothing* in men's company too often any thing but a relaxation; although, as to pleasure and instruction, time so passed may be esteemed more or less delightful.

To make a man's home so desirable a place as to preclude his having a wish to pass his leisure hours at any fireside in preference to his own, I should humbly take to be the sum and substance of woman's domestic ambition. I would appeal to our *British ladies*, who are generally allowed to be the most zealous and successful of all women in the pursuit of this object,—I would appeal to them who have been most successful in the performance of this laudable service, in behalf of father, son, husband, or brother, whether an anxious desire to perform this duty well is not attended with enough of *mental* exertion, at least, to incline them to the opinion that women may be more properly ranked among the contributors to, than the partakers of, the undisturbed relaxation of man.

If a family be so well ordered that the master is never called in to its direction, and yet he perceives comfort and economy well attended to, the mistress of that family (especially if children form a part of it) has, I apprehend, as large a share of womanly employment as ought to satisfy her own sense of duty; even though the needle-book and thread-case were quite laid aside, and she cheerfully contributed her part to the slender gains of the corset-maker, the milliner, the dress-maker, the plain-worker, the embroidress, and all the numerous classifications of females supporting themselves by *needle-work*, that great staple commodity which is alone appropriated to the self-supporting part of our sex.[2]

Much has been said and written on the subject of men engrossing to themselves every occupation and calling. After many years of observation and reflection, I am obliged to acquiesce in the notion that it cannot well be ordered otherwise.

If at the birth of girls it were possible to foresee in what cases it would be their fortune to pass a single life, we should soon find trades wrested from their present occupiers, and transferred to the exclusive possession of our sex. The whole mechanical business of copying writings in the law department, for instance, might very soon be transferred with advantage to the poorer sort of women, who with very little teaching would soon beat their rivals of the other sex in facility and neatness. The parents of female children, who were known to be destined from their birth to maintain themselves through the whole course of their lives with like certainty as their sons are, would feel it a duty incumbent on themselves to strengthen the minds, and even the bodily constitutions, of their girls, so circumstanced, by an education which, without affronting the preconceived habits of society, might enable them to follow some occupation now considered above the capacity or too robust for the constitution of our sex. Plenty of resources would then lie open for single women to obtain an independent livelihood, when every parent would be upon the alert to encroach upon some employment, now engrossed by men, for such of their daughters as would then be exactly in the same predicament as their sons now are. Who, for instance, would lay by money to set up his sons in trade; give premiums, and in part maintain them through a long apprenticeship;[3] or, which men of moderate incomes frequently do, strain every nerve in order to bring them up to a learned profession; if it were in a very high degree probable that, by the time they were twenty years of age, they would be taken from this trade or profession, and maintained during the remainder of their lives by the *person whom they should marry*. Yet this is precisely the situation in which every parent, whose income does not very much exceed the moderate, is placed with respect to his daughters.

Even where boys have gone through a laborious education, superinducing habits of steady attention, accompanied with the entire conviction that the business which they learn is to be the source of their future distinction, may it not be affirmed that the persevering industry required to accomplish this desirable end causes many a hard

2. A milliner is a hat-maker; a plain-worker does simple, as opposed to "fancy," sewing.
3. A period of vocational training, usually seven years, commencing at age eight; middle-class families paid expenses for their children (usually sons) while they learned a trade or craft in exchange for labor. Situations for lower-class children could be considerably bleaker.

struggle in the minds of young men, even of the most hopeful disposition? What then must be the disadvantages under which a very young woman is placed who is required to learn a trade, from which she can never expect to reap any profit, but at the expence of losing that place in society, to the possession of which she may reasonably look forward, inasmuch as it is by far the most *common lot*, namely, the condition of a *happy* English wife?

As I desire to offer nothing to the consideration of your readers but what, at least as far as my own observation goes, I consider as truths confirmed by experience, I will only say that, were I to follow the bent of my own speculative opinion, I should be inclined to persuade every female over whom I hoped to have any influence to contribute all the assistance in her power to those of her own sex who may need it, in the employments they at present occupy, rather than to force them into situations now filled wholly by men. With the mere exception of the profits which they have a right to derive from their needle, I would take nothing from the industry of man which he already possesses.

"A penny saved is a penny earned," is a maxim not true, unless the penny be saved in the same time in which it might have been earned. I, who have known what it is to work for *money earned*, have since had much experience in working for *money saved;* and I consider, from the closest calculation I can make, that a *penny saved* in that way bears about a true proportion to a *farthing earned*. I am no advocate for women, who do not depend on themselves for a subsistence, proposing to themselves to *earn money*. My reasons for thinking it not advisable are too numerous to state— reasons deduced from authentic facts, and strict observations on domestic life in its various shades of comfort. But, if the females of a family, *nominally* supported by the other sex, find it necessary to add something to the common stock, why not endeavour to do something by which they may produce money *in its true shape?*

It would be an excellent plan, attended with very little trouble, to calculate every evening how much money has been saved by needle-work *done in the family*, and compare the result with the daily portion of the yearly income. Nor would it be amiss to make a memorandum of the time passed in this way, adding also a guess as to what share it has taken up in the thoughts and conversation. This would be an easy mode of forming a true notion, and getting at the exact worth of this species of *home* industry, and perhaps might place it in a different light from any in which it has hitherto been the fashion to consider it.

Needle-work, taken up as an amusement, may not be altogether unamusing. We are all pretty good judges of what entertains ourselves, but it is not so easy to pronounce upon what may contribute to the entertainment of others. At all events, let us not confuse the motives of economy with those of simple pastime. If *saving* be no object, and long habit have rendered needle-work so delightful an avocation that we cannot think of relinquishing it, there are the good old contrivances in which our grand-dames were used to beguile and lose their time—knitting, knotting, netting, carpet working, and the like ingenious pursuits—those so-often-praised but tedious works, which are so long in the operation, that purchasing the labour has seldom been thought good economy, yet, by a certain fascination, they have been found to chain down the great to a self-imposed slavery, from which they considerately, or haughtily, excuse the needy. These may be esteemed lawful and lady-like amusements. But, if those works, more usually denominated useful, yield greater satisfaction, it might be a laudable scruple of conscience, and no bad test to herself of her own motive, if a lady, who had no absolute need, were to give the money so saved to poor needle-women belonging to those branches of employment from which she has borrowed these shares of pleasurable labour.

SEMPRONIA[4]

━━┉≍◈≍┉━━

William Thompson and Anna Wheeler
1775–1833   1785–post-1848?

Karl Marx's *Manifesto of the Communist Party* (London, 1848) assured proletarians that they "have nothing to lose but their chains" and closed with the call, "Working Men of All Countries, Unite!" In these ringing phrases, English socialists heard a striking echo of the "Address to Women" that concluded William Thompson and Anna Wheeler's *Appeal:* "Women of England! women, in whatever country ye breathe—wherever ye breathe, degraded—awake! . . . O wretched slaves of such wretched masters! Awake, arise, shake off these fetters!" The work of two leading socialists of the 1820s, *Appeal* is the most important English feminist document between Wollstonecraft's *Rights of Woman* (1792) and John Stuart Mill's *Subjection of Women* (1869).

Born into Protestant Irish gentry, Thompson came of age during the era of the French Revolution. At his father's death in 1814, he inherited a thousand-acre estate and prosperous businesses, including a fleet of trading vessels. He did not fall into step with Protestant capitalism, however, but agitated for Catholic Emancipation, denounced the division between laborers and "idle classes," and experimented with socialist alternatives, including organizing the 700 vagrants on the family estate into a highly successful community. He then went to London, where he met leading social theorists John Stuart Mill, Jeremy Bentham, and Robert Owen. He published books on labor and wealth, including *An Inquiry into the Principles of the Distribution of Wealth Most Conducive to Human Happiness, Applied to the Newly Proposed System of Voluntary Equality of Wealth* (1824). Another London friend was Anna Wheeler, also from Irish gentry. A "reigning beauty" in her youth, she married a pampered Irish nobleman at age fifteen, bore six children (only two surviving infancy), and still found time to read widely, especially in philosophy and social theory. Wearying of her idle, drunkard husband, she left him in 1812, eventually heading for London and France, where she met leading socialists and feminists. A dynamic advocate for women's rights, she struck Benjamin Disraeli as "very clever, but awefully revolutionary."

Thompson and Wheeler were dismayed over the indifference of some of their socialist friends to women's rights. Some were even opposed—for instance, Bentham's disciple, James Mill, whose *Article on Government* for the 1824 *Encyclopaedia Britannica* (a pamphlet in 1825) argued against political representation for women, contending that their interests were "involved" and "included" with their fathers' or their husbands' and had no separate claim. Thompson and Wheeler's refutation appeared the same year, in 1825. Only Thompson was named on the title page of this *Appeal,* but his introduction credits Wheeler as co-author: he is the scribe of their "feelings, sentiments, and reasonings" and the work is their "joint property." Patently allied with Wollstonecraft, *Appeal* expands her social analysis into a critique of the underlying economic system. As the full title suggests, it also expands Wollstonecraft's discourse of female slavery. Blunt comparisons of English women to Turkish harem-slaves and new-world plantation slaves ally the polemic with the moral consensus fueling the expanding movement for the abolition of colonial slavery.

---

4. Lamb's pseudonym perhaps puns on "Sempstress" (seamstress).

Appeal of One Half the Human Race, Women, Against the Pretensions of the Other Half, Men, To Retain Them in Political, and Thence in Civil and Domestic Slavery

"'Tis all stern duty on the female side;
On man's, mere sensual gust and surly pride."[1]

from *Introductory Letter to Mrs. Wheeler*

The days of dedication and patronage are gone by. It is *not* with the view of obtaining the support of your name or your influence to the cause of truth and humanity that these lines are addressed to you. * * * I address you then simply to perform towards you a debt of justice. Anxious that you should take up the cause of your proscribed sex, and state to the world in writing, in your own name, what you have so often and so well stated in conversation, and under feigned names in such of the periodical publications of the day as would tolerate such a theme, I long hesitated to arrange our common ideas, even upon a branch of the subject like the present. Anxious that the hand of a woman should have the honor of raising from the dust that neglected banner which a woman's hand nearly thirty years ago unfolded boldly, in face of the prejudices of thousands of years, and for which a woman's heart bled, and her life was all but the sacrifice—I hesitated to write. Were courage the quality wanting, you would have shown, what every day's experience proves, that women have more fortitude in endurance than men. Were comprehensiveness of mind, above the narrow views which too often marred Mary Wolstonecroft's [sic] pages and narrowed their usefulness, the quality wanting,—above the timidity and impotence of conclusion accompanying the gentle eloquence of Mary Hays, addressed, about the same time that Mary Wolstonecroft wrote, in the shape of an *"Appeal"* to the then closed ears of unreasoning men;[2] yours was the eye which no prejudice obscured, open to the rays of truth from whatever quarter they might emanate. But leisure and resolution to undertake the drudgery of the task were wanting. A few only therefore of the following pages are the exclusive produce of your mind and pen, and written with your own hand. The remainder are our joint property, I being your interpreter and the scribe of your sentiments. * * *

You look forward, as I do, to a state of society very different from that which now exists, in which the effort of all is to out wit, supplant, and snatch from each other; where interest is systematically opposed to duty; where the so-called system of morals is little more than a mass of hypocrisy preached by knaves, unpractised by them, to keep their slaves, male as well as female, in blind uninquiring obedience; and where the whole motley fabric is kept together by fear and blood. You look forward to a better aspect of society, where the principle of benevolence shall supersede that of fear; where restless and anxious individual competition shall give place to

---

1. From Dryden's *Palamon and Arcite; or, The Knight's Tale, From Chaucer*, in *Fables Ancient and Modern; Translated into Verse* (1700). Virgin Emily begs the goddess Cynthia to accept her as a votress, pleading, "Like Death, thou know'st, I loath the Nuptial state, / And Man, the Tyrant of our Sex, I hate, / A lowly Servant, but a lofty Mate. / Where Love is Duty, on the Female side; / On theirs meer sensual Gust, and sought with surly Pride" (3.227–32); "Gust" is appetite. In *Rights of Woman*, ch. 6, Wollstonecraft uses lines 230–31 to gloss the lack of

"satisfaction" that any woman of delicate affections would find "in a union with such a man."
2. Disciple and friend of Wollstonecraft, Mary Hays published *Appeal to the Men of Great Britain in Behalf of Women* anonymously in 1798, by which time Wollstonecraft was a scandal and the political climate reactionary. Despite her numerous defenses of Wollstonecraft, Hays felt it unwise to include her in her *Female Biography, or Memoirs of Illustrious and Celebrated Women of All Ages and Countries* (1803).

mutual co-operation and joint possession; where individuals in large numbers, male and female, forming voluntary associations, shall become a mutual guarantee to each other for the supply of all useful wants, and form an unsalaried and uninsolvent insurance company against all insurable casualties; where perfect freedom of opinion and perfect equality will reign amongst the co-operators; and where the children of all will be equally educated and provided for by the whole, even these children longer the slaves of individual caprice.

In truth, under the present arrangements of society, the principle of individual competition remaining, as it is, the master-key and moving principle of the whole social organization, *individual* wealth the great object sought after by all, and the quantum of happiness of each individual (other things being equal) depending on the quantum of wealth, the means of happiness, possessed by each; it seems impossible—even were all unequal legal and unequal moral restraints removed, and were no secret current of force or influence exerted to baffle new regulations of equal justice—that women should attain to equal happiness with men. Two circumstances—permanent inferiority of strength, and occasional loss of time in gestation and rearing infants—must eternally render the average exertions of women in the race of the competition for wealth less successful than those of men. The pleasant compensation that men now affect to give for these two natural sources of inferior accumulation of wealth on the part of women (aggravated a thousand degrees by their exclusions from knowledge and almost all means of useful exertions, (the very lowest only excepted)), is the existing system of marriage; under which, for the mere faculty of eating, breathing and living, in whatever degree of comfort husbands may think fit, women are reduced to domestic slavery, without will of their own, or power of locomotion, otherwise than as permitted by their respective masters. * * *

With you I would equally elevate both sexes. Really enlightened women, disdaining equally the submissive tricks of the slave and the caprices of the despot, breathing freely only in the air of the esteem of equals, and of mutual, *unbought, uncommanded,* affection, would find it difficult to meet with associates worthy of them in men as now formed, full of ignorance and vanity, priding themselves on a *sexual* superiority, entirely independent of any merit, any superior qualities, or pretensions to them, claiming respect from the strength of their arm and the lordly faculty of producing beards attached by nature to their chins! No: unworthy of, as incapable of appreciating, the delight of the society of such women, are the great majority of the existing race of men. The pleasures of mere animal appetite, the pleasures of commanding (the prettier and more helpless the slave, the greater these pleasures of the brute), are the only pleasures which the majority of men seek for from women, are the only pleasures which their education and the hypocritical system of morals with which they have been necessarily imbued, permit them to expect. * * *

Even under the present arrangements of society, founded as they all are on the basis of individual competition, nothing could be more easy than to put the *rights* of women, political and civil, on a perfect equality with those of men. It is only to abolish all prohibitory and exclusive laws,—statute or what are called "common,"—the remnants of the barbarous customs of our ignorant ancestors; particularly the horrible and odious inequality and indissolubility of that disgrace of civilization, the present marriage code. Women then might exert in a free career with men their faculties of mind and body, to whatever degree developed, in pursuit of happiness by means of exertion, as men do. But this would not raise women to an equality of happiness with men: their rights might be equal, but not their happiness, because unequal powers under free competition must produce unequal effects.

In truth, the system of the most enlightened of the school of those reformers called political economists, is still founded on exclusions. Its basis is too narrow for human happiness. A more comprehensive system, founded on equal benevolence, on the true development of the principle of Utility, is wanting.[3] Let the *competitive* political economists be satisfied with the praise of causing the removal of some of the rubbish of ignorant restrictions, under the name of laws, impeding the development of human exertion in the production of wealth. To build up a new fabric of social happiness, comprehending equally the interests of all existing human beings, has never been contemplated by them, and is altogether beyond the scope of their little theories; aiming at the utmost at increasing the number of what they style the happy middling orders,[4] but leaving the great bulk of human beings to eternal ignorance and toil, requited by the mere means of prolonging from day to day an unhealthy and precarious existence. To a new science, the *social science*, or the science of promoting human happiness, that of political economy, or the mere science of producing wealth by individual competition, must give way.

from *Part 2*
[ON DAUGHTERS]

Business, professions, political concerns, local affairs, the whole field of sciences and arts, are open to the united and mutually sympathizing efforts of the males. To their mutual judgments and speculations, the disposal of the family income and capital are intrusted. From all these commanding sources of intellectual and muscular activity, the daughters, like the little children, are excluded, previous care having been taken, by shutting them out from all means of intellectual culture, and from the view of and participation in the real incidents of active life, to render them as unfit for, as unambitious of, such high occupations. Confined, like other domestic animals, to the house and its little details, their "sober wishes" are never permitted "to stray" into the enlarged plains of general speculation and action. The dull routine of domestic incidents is the world to them. * * *

So much more completely is the interest of the sons involved than that of the daughters in the interest of fathers, that as soon as the daughters become adult, they, necessarily operated upon by the system under which they live, look out of their artificial cages of restraint and imbecility, to catch glances at the world with the hope of freedom from parental control, by leaving behind them the very name of their fathers, and vainly hoping for happiness without independence, in the gratification of one passion, love, round which their absurd training for blind male sensuality, has caused all their little anxieties to centre. The adult sons go in and out of the father's house when they choose: they are frequently treated with liberality as visitors or equals. But the adult daughters are, for the most part, under as much restraint as little children: they must ask leave to open the door or take a walk: not one of their actions that does not depend on the will of another: they are never permitted, like

3. Utilitarianism, the philosophy of Jeremy Bentham and James Mill, rejected inherent right and wrong; the only issue is consequence, whether an action contributes to "the happiness of man."
4. Middle class.

the sons, to regulate their conduct by their own notions of propriety and prudence and to restrain them where necessary, like rational beings, from a regard to their consequences: every thing is prescribed to them: their reason and foresight are not cultivated like those of the sons; and the despotism which creates their imbecility, adduces its own work as a justification of its unrelenting pressure and of its eternal duration. To marriage therefore, as the only means allowed them of emerging from paternal control; as the only means of gratifying one passion, to which all their thoughts have been exclusively directed, but which they are at the same time told it is highly improper they should wish to enjoy; as the only means of obtaining, through cunning and blandishment, that direction of their own voluntary actions, which all rational beings ought to possess, and which is the sure and only basis of intelligence and morals; to marriage, as the fancied haven of pleasure and freedom—the freedom of the slave to-be-sure, to be acquired not by right but by coaxing, by the influence of passions inapplicable to the cold despotism of the fathers—daughters look forward. No sooner adult, than their home and their name are daughters anxious to get rid of, because the retaining of them is made incompatible with the only views of happiness presented to them.

[On Wives]

By way of distinguishing and honoring this class of the proscribed half of the human race, man condescends to enter into what he calls a *contract* with certain women, for certain purposes, the most important of which is, the producing and rearing of children to maturity. Each man yokes a woman to his establishment, and calls it a *contract*. Audacious falsehood! A contract! where are any of the attributes of contracts, of equal and just contracts, to be found in this transaction? A contract implies the voluntary assent of both the contracting parties. Can even both the parties, man and woman, by agreement alter the terms, as to *indissolubility* and *inequality*, of this pretended contract? No. Can any individual man divest himself, were he even so inclined, of his power of despotic control? He cannot. Have women been consulted as to the terms of this pretended contract? A contract, all of whose enjoyments—wherever nature has not imposed a physical bar on the depravity of selfishness—are on one side, while all of its pains and privations are on the other! A contract, giving all power, arbitrary will and unbridled enjoyment to the one side; to the other, unqualified obedience, and enjoyments meted out or withheld at the caprice of the ruling and enjoying party. Such a contract, as the owners of *slaves* in the West Indies and every other slave-polluted soil, enter into with their slaves—the law of the stronger imposed on the weaker, *in contempt* of the interests and wishes of the weaker. * * *

  As soon as adult daughters become wives, their civil rights disappear; they fall back again, and remain all their lives—should their owners and directors live so long—into the state of children or idiots, the passive property of their owners; protected by the law in some few respects only, like other slaves, from the excessive abuse of despotic power.

  Woman is then compelled, in marriage, by the possession of superior strength on the part of men, by the want of knowledge, skill and wealth, by the positive, cruel, partial, and cowardly enactments of law, by the terrors of superstition, by the mockery of a pretended vow of obedience, and to crown all, and as the result of all, by the force of an unrelenting, unreasoning, unfeeling, public opinion, to be the literal unequivocal *slave* of the man who may be styled her husband. I say emphatically the slave; for a slave is a person whose actions and earnings, instead of being, under his own control, liable only to equal laws, to public opinion, and to his own calculations, under these, of his own interest, are under the arbitrary control of any other human being, by whatever name called. This is the essence of slavery, and what distinguishes it from freedom. A domestic, a civil, a political slave, in the plain unsophisticated sense of the word—in no metaphorical sense—is every married woman. No matter with what wealth she may be surrounded, with what dainties she may be fed, with what splendor of trappings adorned, with what voluptuousness her corporeal, mental, or moral sweets may be gathered; that high prerogative of human nature, the faculty of self-government, the basis of intellectual development, without which no moral conduct can exist, is to her wanting. * * * Till laws afford married women the same protection against the restraints and violence of the men to whom they are married, that they affect to afford them against all other individuals; till they afford them the same protection against the restraints and violence of their husbands, that their husbands enjoy against their caprices and violence, the social condition of the civilized wife will remain more completely slavish than that of the female slave of the West Indies.

[EXHORTATION TO MEN]

Be consistent, men! Ye stronger half of the race, be at length rational! Three or four thousand years have worn threadbare your vile cloak of hypocrisy. Even women, your poor, weak, contented slaves, at whose impotence of penetration, the result of your vile exclusions, you have been accustomed to laugh, begin to see through it and to shudder at the loathsomeness beneath. Cast aside this tattered cloak before it leaves you naked and exposed. Clothe yourselves with the new garments of sincerity. Be rational human beings, not mere male sexual creatures. Cast aside the ferocious brute of your nature: give up the pleasures of the brute, those of mere lust and command, for the pleasures of the rational being. So shall you enjoy the love of your *equals*, enlightened, benevolent, graceful, like yourselves, founded on an appreciation of your real merits: so shall you be happy. For the intercourse of the *bought* prostitute, or of the *commanded* household slave, you shall have full and equal participation in the compounded and associated pleasures of sense, intellect and benevolence. To the highest enjoyments of which your nature is susceptible, there is no shorter road than the simple road of equal justice.

[WHAT DO WOMEN WANT?]

The simple and modest request is, that they may be permitted equal enjoyments with men, *provided they can by the free and equal development and exercise of their faculties procure for themselves such enjoyments.* They ask the same means that men possess of acquiring every species of knowledge, of unfolding every one of their faculties of mind and body that can be made tributary to their happiness. They ask every facility of access to every art, occupation, profession, from the highest to the lowest, without one exception, to which their inclination and talents may direct and may fit them to occupy. They ask the removal of *all* restraints and exclusions not applicable to men of equal capacities. They ask for perfectly equal political, civil and domestic rights. They ask for equal obligations and equal punishments from the law with men in case of infraction of the same law by either party. They ask for an equal system of morals, founded on utility instead of caprice and unreasoning despotism, in which the same action attended with the same consequences, whether done by man or woman, should be attended with the same portion of approbation or disapprobation; in which every pleasure, accompanied or followed by no preponderant evil, should be equally permitted to women and to men; in which every pleasure accompanied or followed by preponderant evil should be equally censured in women and in men.

* * *

Women of England! women, in whatever country ye breathe—wherever ye breathe, degraded—awake! Awake to the contemplation of the happiness that awaits you when all your faculties of mind and body shall be fully cultivated and developed; when every path in which ye can exercise those improved faculties shall be laid open and rendered delightful to you, even as to them who now ignorantly enslave and degrade you. If degradation from long habitude have lost its sting, if the iron have penetrated so deeply into your frame that it has been gradually taken up into the system and mingles unperceived amidst the fluids of your life; if the prostration of reason and the eradication of feeling have kept pace within you, so that you are insensible alike to what you suffer and to what you might enjoy,—your case were all but hopeless. Nothing less, then, than the sight presented before your eyes, of the superior happiness enjoyed by other women, under arrangements of perfect equality with men, could arouse you. Such a sight, even under such circumstances, would excite your envy and kindle up all your extinct desires. But you are not so degraded. The unvaried despotism of so many thousand years, has not so entirely degraded you, has not been able to extinguish within you the feelings of nature, the love of happiness and of equal justice. The united exertions of law, superstition, and pretended morals of past ages of ignorance, have not entirely succeeded. * * *

Nor will your fellow-creatures, men, long resist the change. They are too deeply concerned to continue long to oppose what palpably tends to their happiness: they are too deeply concerned not to be compelled to re-consider the barbarous systems of law and morals under which they have been brought up. In justice, in pity to them, submit no longer; no longer *willingly* submit to their caprices. Though your bodies may be a little longer kept in servitude, degrade not yourselves by the repetition of superfluous vows of obedience: cease to kiss the rod: let your *minds* be henceforth free. The morn of loosening your physical chains will not be far distant.

O woman, from your auspicious hands may the new destiny of your species proceed! The collective voices of your sex raised against oppression will ultimately make men themselves your advocates and debtors. Reflect then seriously on your miserable and degraded position—your youth, your beauty, your feelings, your opinions, your actions, your time, your few years' fever of meritricious life—all made tributary to the appetites and passions of men. Whatever pleasures you enjoy, are permitted you for man's sake. Nothing is your own; protection of person and of property are alike withheld from you. Nothing is yours, but secret pangs, the bitter burning tears of regret, the stifled sobs of outraged nature thrown back upon your own hearts, where the vital principle itself stands checked, or is agitated with malignant passions, until body and mind become the frequent prey to overwhelming disease; now finding vent in sudden phrensy, now plunged in pining melancholy, or bursting the weak tenement of reason, seeking relief in self-destruction.

How many thousand of your sex *daily* perish thus unpitied and unknown; often victims of pressing want, always of privation and the arbitrary laws of heartless custom; condemned to cheerless solitude, or an idiot round of idle fashionable pursuits; your morning of life perhaps passed by, and with it the lingering darling hope of sympathy expired—puppets once of doting ignorant parents, whose tenderness for you outlived not your first youth; who, careless of your future fate, "launched you into life without an oar," indigent and ignorant, to eat the tear-steeped bread of dependence as wives, sisters, hired mistresses or unpitied prostitutes! This is the fate of the many, nay, of all your sex, subject only to those shades of difference arising from very peculiar circumstances or the accident of independent fortune; though even here the general want of knowledge, withheld from your sex, keeps even those individuals who are favored by fortune bowed to the relentless yoke which man's laws, his superstitions, and hypocritical morality, have prepared for you.

For once then instruct man in what is good, wash out the foul stain, equally disgraceful to both sexes—that your sex has unbounded influence in making men to do evil, but cannot induce them to do good.

How many Thaises are there, who, vain of the empire they hold over the passions of men, exercise at all risks this contemptible and pernicious influence—the only influence permitted them—in stimulating these masters of the world to destroy cities; and, regardless of the whispers of conscience and humanity, often shake men's tardy resolutions to repair the evils they have caused![1]—Shall none be found with sufficient knowledge and elevation of mind to persuade men to do good, to make the most certain step towards the regeneration of degraded humanity, by opening a free course for justice and benevolence, for intellectual and social enjoyments, by no colour, by no sex to be restrained? As your bondage has chained down man to the ignorance and vices of despotism, so will your liberation reward him with knowledge, with freedom and with happiness.[2]

⇒ END OF PERSPECTIVES: THE WOLLSTONECRAFT CONTROVERSY AND ⇐
THE RIGHTS OF WOMAN

Joanna Baillie
1762–1851

In 1824, *Blackwood's Edinburgh Magazine* noted the influence of Joanna Baillie's plays on Lord Byron: "the dark shadows of his Lordship's imagination have received a deeper gloom from his early acquaintance with those wild and midnight forests, in which the passion of De Monfort [*De Monfort*, 1798] consummated its dreadful purpose, and the dim aisles in which it met its retribution." The influence was a nervous admiration. In 1813, Byron insisted that Baillie could not have "a more enthusiastic admirer than myself," and he was eager to meet her; in 1817, in the throes of rewriting his gothic closet drama *Manfred*, he mulled over Voltaire's reply to a question about "why no woman has ever written even a tolerable tragedy": "Ah (said the Patriarch) the composition of a tragedy requires *testicles*." "If this be true," Byron jested to his publisher, "Lord knows what Joanna Baillie does—I suppose she borrows them." Byron's

---

1. Thaïs, a 4th-century B.C.E. Athenian courtesan patronized by Alexander the Great and then by the King of Egypt; was said to have accompanied Alexander on his conquests. Another Thaïs was a 1st-century Alexandrian, famous for her beauty, wealth, and sexual indulgences, who repented and converted to Christianity and a life of piety.

2. The last paragraph of *Appeal*.

regard for Baillie's potency was shared (without a regendering) by many of her contemporaries, including William Wordsworth, who called her "the bold enchantress," Anna Letitia Barbauld, Maria Edgeworth, Robert Southey, Samuel Taylor Coleridge, Felicia Hemans (who dedicated *Records of Woman* to her), and Sir Walter Scott, who deemed her the finest English dramatist since Shakespeare.

Born in 1762 in Scotland, Baillie traced her ancestry to the famously brave-hearted patriot William Wallace. She never married and lived her adult life with her unmarried sister. Her first literary efforts were issued, unsigned, in 1790 as *Poems: Wherein it is Attempted to Describe Certain Views of Nature and Rustic Manners*. This was unsuccessful, and she turned to drama. *A Series of Plays in Which it is Attempted to Delineate the Stronger Passions of the Mind* appeared in three installments from 1798 to 1812. The first was anonymous, and a curious public speculated about the author, probably male. The "Introductory Discourse" could have been written only by a man, insisted Samuel Rogers in the *Monthly Review*, and he ascribed it to Baillie's brother. Baillie's project of "unveiling the human mind under the dominion of . . . strong and fixed passions" was matched two years later by Wordsworth in Preface to *Lyrical Ballads* (1800), presenting a poetry of "the essential passions of the heart" in states of excitement. *De Monfort* attracted the leading actors of the day, including Sarah Siddons, John Philip Kemble, and Edmund Kean, but the psychological emphases and philosophical introspectiveness of the plays were ill-suited to popular theater, however much other poets were impressed. Even without stage acclaim, Baillie continued to write and publish plays over the next three decades, conceiving them as dramas for "the mental theatre of the reader," in Byron's words, taking a cue from Charles Lamb's essay on the unsuitability of Shakespeare's tragedies for stage representation (1811). In 1821, she published *Metrical Legends of Exalted Characters*, including "chronicles" of her ancestors William Wallace and Lady Griselda Baillie, and she put out an expanded edition of her poems in 1840 titled *Fugitive Verses*. Some pieces show her skill at the poetry in Scots dialect that Robert Burns popularized, while others follow the program of her dramas, voicing passion, sometimes in stormy moods, but often in quieter and more domestic scenes.

from Introductory Discourse to Plays on the Passions

If man is an object of so much attention to man, engaged in the ordinary occurrences of life, how much more does he excite his curiosity and interest when placed in extraordinary situations of difficulty and distress? It cannot be any pleasure we receive from the sufferings of a fellow-creature which attracts such multitudes of people to a public execution, though it is the horror we conceive for such a spectacle that keeps so many more away. To see a human being bearing himself up under such circumstances, or struggling with the terrible apprehensions which such a situation impresses, must be the powerful incentive that makes us press forward to behold what we shrink from, and wait with trembling expectation for what we dread.[1] For though few at such a spectacle can get near enough to distinguish the expression of face, or the minuter parts of a criminal's behaviour, yet from a considerable distance will they eagerly mark whether he steps firmly; whether the motions of his body denote agitation or calmness; and if the wind does but ruffle his garment, they will, even from that change upon the outline of his distant figure, read some expression connected with his dreadful situation. Though there is a greater proportion of people in whom this strong curiosity will

---

1. In confirmation of this opinion I may venture to say that of the great numbers who go to see a public execution, there are but very few who would not run away from, and avoid it, if they happened to meet with it unexpectedly. We find people stopping to look at a procession, or any other common sight they may have fallen in with accidentally, but almost never an execution. No one goes there who has not made up his mind for the occasion; which would not be the case if any natural love of cruelty were the cause of such assemblies [Baillie's note].

be overcome by other dispositions and motives; though there are many more who will stay away from such a sight than will go to it; yet there are very few who will not be eager to converse with a person who has beheld it; and to learn, very minutely, every circumstance connected with it, except the very act itself of inflicting death. To lift up the roof of his dungeon, like the *Diable boiteux*,[2] and look upon a criminal the night before he suffers, in his still hours of privacy, when all that disguise is removed which is imposed by respect for the opinion of others, the strong motive by which even the lowest and wickedest of men still continue to be actuated, would present an object to the mind of every person, not withheld from it by great timidity of character, more powerfully attractive than almost any other.

Revenge, no doubt, first began among the savages of America that dreadful custom of sacrificing their prisoners of war. But the perpetration of such hideous cruelty could never have become a permanent national custom, but for this universal desire in the human mind to behold man in every situation, putting forth his strength against the current of adversity, scorning all bodily anguish, or struggling with those feelings of nature which, like a beating stream, will ofttimes burst through the artificial barriers of pride. Before they begin those terrible rites they treat their prisoners kindly; and it cannot be supposed that men, alternately enemies and friends to so many neighbouring tribes, in manners and appearance like themselves, should so strongly be actuated by a spirit of public revenge. This custom, therefore, must be considered as a grand and terrible game, which every tribe plays against another; where they try not the strength of the arm, the swiftness of the feet, nor the acuteness of the eye, but the fortitude of the soul. Considered in this light, the excess of cruelty exercised upon their miserable victim, in which every hand is described as ready to inflict its portion of pain, and every head ingenious in the contrivance of it, is no longer to be wondered at. To put into his measure of misery one agony less, would be, in some degree, betraying the honour of their nation, would be doing a species of injustice to every hero of their own tribe who had already sustained it, and to those who might be called upon to do so; among whom each of these savage tormenters has his chance of being one, and has prepared himself for it from his childhood. Nay, it would be a species of injustice to the haughty victim himself, who would scorn to purchase his place among the heroes of his nation at an easier price than his undaunted predecessors.

Amongst the many trials to which the human mind is subjected, that of holding intercourse,[3] real or imaginary, with the world of spirits: of finding itself alone with a being terrific and awful, whose nature and power are unknown, has been justly considered as one of the most severe. The workings of nature in this situation, we all know, have ever been the object of our most eager inquiry. No man wishes to see the Ghost himself, which would certainly procure him the best information on the subject, but every man wishes to see one who believes that he sees it, in all the agitation and wildness of that species of terror. To gratify this curiosity how many people have dressed up hideous apparitions to frighten the timid and superstitious! and have done it at the risk of destroying their happiness or understanding for ever. For the instances of intellect being destroyed by this kind of trial are more numerous, perhaps, in proportion to the few who have undergone it, than by any other.

How sensible are we of this strong propensity within us, when we behold any person under the pressure of great and uncommon calamity! Delicacy and respect for

---

2. A romance by LeSage (1707).   3. Communication.

the afflicted will, indeed, make us turn ourselves aside from observing him, and cast down our eyes in his presence; but the first glance we direct to him will involuntarily be one of the keenest observation, how hastily soever it may be checked; and often will a returning look of inquiry mix itself by stealth with our sympathy and reserve.

But it is not in situations of difficulty and distress alone, that man becomes the object of this sympathetic curiosity: he is no less so when the evil he contends with arises in his own breast, and no outward circumstance connected with him either awakens our attention or our pity. What human creature is there, who can behold a being like himself under the violent agitation of those passions which all have, in some degree, experienced, without feeling himself most powerfully excited by the sight? I say, all have experienced: for the bravest man on earth knows what fear is as well as the coward; and will not refuse to be interested for one under the dominion of this passion, provided there be nothing in the circumstances attending it to cre-ate contempt. Anger is a passion that attracts less sympathy than any other, yet the unpleasing and distorted features of an angry man will be more eagerly gazed upon by those who are no wise concerned with his fury, or the objects of it, than the most amiable placid countenance in the world. Every eye is directed to him; every voice hushed to silence in his presence: even children will leave off their gambols as he passes, and gaze after him more eagerly than the gaudiest equipage. The wild tossings of despair; the gnashing of hatred and revenge; the yearnings of affection, and the softened mien of love; all the language of the agitated soul, which every age and na-tion understand, is never addressed to the dull or inattentive.

It is not merely under the violent agitations of passion, that man so rouses and interests us; even the smallest indications of an unquiet mind, the restless eye, the muttering lip, the half-checked exclamation and the hasty start, will set our atten-tion as anxiously upon the watch, as the first distant flashes of a gathering storm. When some great explosion of passion bursts forth, and some consequent catastro-phe happens, if we are at all acquainted with the unhappy perpetrator, how mi-nutely shall we endeavour to remember every circumstance of his past behaviour! and with what avidity shall we seize upon every recollected word or gesture, that is in the smallest degree indicative of the supposed state of his mind, at the time when they took place. If we are not acquainted with him, how eagerly shall we listen to similar recollections from another! Let us understand, from observation or report, that any person harbours in his breast, concealed from the world's eye, some pow-erful rankling passion of what kind soever it may be, we shall observe every word, every motion, every look, even the distant gait of such a man, with a constancy and attention bestowed upon no other. Nay, should we meet him unexpectedly on our way, a feeling will pass across our minds as though we found ourselves in the neigh-bourhood of some secret and fearful thing. If invisible, would we not follow him into his lonely haunts, into his closet,[4] into the midnight silence of his chamber? There is, perhaps, no employment which the human mind will with so much avidity pur-sue, as the discovery of concealed passion, as the tracing the varieties and progress of a perturbed soul. * * *

The highest pleasures we receive from poetry, as well as from the real objects which surround us in the world, are derived from the sympathetic interest we all take in beings like ourselves; and I will even venture to say, that were the grandest

---

4. Private room.

scenes which can enter into the imagination of man, presented to our view, and all reference to man completely shut out from our thoughts, the objects that composed it would convey to our minds little better than dry ideas of magnitude, colour, and form; and the remembrance of them would rest upon our minds like the measurement and distances of the planets. * * *

[T]he last part of the task which I have mentioned as peculiarly belonging to Tragedy,—unveiling the human mind under the dominion of those strong and fixed passions, which, seemingly unprovoked by outward circumstances, will from small beginnings brood within the breast, till all the better dispositions, all the fair gifts of nature, are borne down before them,—her poets in general have entirely neglected, and even her first and greatest have but imperfectly attempted. They have made use of the passions to mark their several characters, and animate their scenes, rather than to open to our view the nature and portraitures of those great disturbers of the human breast, with whom we are all, more or less, called upon to contend. * * * To trace them in their rise and progress in the heart, seems but rarely to have been the object of any dramatist. We commonly find the characters of a tragedy affected by the passions in a transient, loose, unconnected manner; or if they are represented as under the permanent influence of the more powerful ones, they are generally introduced to our notice in the very height of their fury, when all that timidity, irresolution, distrust, and a thousand delicate traits, which make the infancy of every great passion more interesting, perhaps, than its full-blown strength, are fled. The impassioned character is generally brought into view under those irresistible attacks of their power, which it is impossible to repel; whilst those gradual steps that lead him into this state, in some of which a stand might have been made against the foe, are left entirely in the shade. Those passions that may be suddenly excited, and are of short duration, as anger, fear, and oftentimes jealousy, may in this manner be fully represented; but those great masters of the soul, ambition, hatred, love, every passion that is permanent in its nature, and varied in progress, if represented to us but in one stage of its course, is represented imperfectly. It is a characteristic of the more powerful passions, that they will increase and nourish themselves on very slender aliment; it is from within that they are chiefly supplied with what they feed on; and it is in contending with opposite passions and affections of the mind that we best discover their strength, not with events. But in Tragedy it is events, more frequently than opposite affections, which are opposed to them; and those often of such force and magnitude, that the passions themselves are almost obscured by the splendour and importance of the transactions to which they are attached. * * *

From this general view, which I have endeavoured to communicate to my reader of Tragedy, and those principles in the human mind upon which the success of her efforts depends, I have been led to believe, that an attempt to write a series of tragedies, of simpler construction, less embellished with poetical decorations, less constrained by that lofty seriousness which has so generally been considered as necessary for the support of tragic dignity, and in which the chief object should be to delineate the progress of the higher passions in the human breast, each play exhibiting a particular passion, might not be unacceptable to the public. * * *

It may, perhaps, be supposed, from my publishing these plays, that I have written them for the closet rather than the stage.[5] If, upon perusing them with attention,

---

5. Only for private reading (in one's private room); for a famous statement of the merits of this genre, see Charles Lamb, *On the Tragedies of Shakspeare,* page 703.

the reader is disposed to think they are better calculated for the first than the last, let him impute it to want of skill in the author, and not to any previous design. A play but of small poetical merit, that is suited to strike and interest the spectator, to catch the attention of him who will not, and of him who cannot read, is a more valuable and useful production than one whose elegant and harmonious pages are admired in the libraries of the tasteful and refined. To have received approbation from an audience of my countrymen, would have been more pleasing to me than any other praise. A few tears from the simple and young would have been, in my eyes, pearls of great price;[6] and the spontaneous, untutored plaudits of the rude and uncultivated would have come to my heart as offerings of no mean value. I should, therefore, have been better pleased to have introduced them to the world from the stage than from the press. I possess, however, no likely channel to the former mode of public introduction: and, upon further reflection, it appeared to me, that by publishing them in this way, I have an opportunity afforded me of explaining the design of my work, and enabling the public to judge, not only of each play by itself, but as making a part likewise of the whole; an advantage which, perhaps, does more than over-balance the splendour and effect of theatrical representation. * * *

Before I close this discourse, let me crave the forbearance of my reader, if he has discovered in the course of it any unacknowledged use of the thoughts of other authors, which he thinks ought to have been noticed; and let me beg the same favour, if in reading the following plays, any similar neglect seems to occur. There are few writers who have sufficient originality of thought to strike out for themselves new ideas upon every occasion. When a thought presents itself to me, as suited to the purpose I am aiming at, I would neither be thought proud enough to reject it, on finding that another has used it before me, nor mean enough to make use of it without acknowledging the obligation, when I can at all guess to whom such acknowledgments are due. But I am situated where I have no library to consult; my reading through the whole of my life has been of a loose, scattered, unmethodical kind, with no determined direction, and I have not been blessed by nature with the advantages of a retentive or accurate memory. * * * If this volume should appear, to any candid and liberal critic, to merit that he should take the trouble of pointing out to me in what parts of it I seem to have made that use of other authors' writings, which, according to the fair laws of literature, ought to have been acknowledged, I shall think myself obliged to him. I shall examine the sources he points out as having supplied my own lack of ideas; and if this book should have the good fortune to go through a second edition, I shall not fail to own my obligations to him, and the authors whom I may have borrowed.

How little credit soever, upon perusing these plays, the reader may think me entitled to in regard to the execution of the work, he will not, I flatter myself, deny me some credit in regard to the plan. I know of no series of plays, in any language, expressly descriptive of the different passions. * * * However, if I perform it ill, I am still confident that this (pardon me if I call it so) noble design will not be suffered to fall to the ground: some one will arise after me who will do it justice; and there is no poet possessing genius for such a work, who will not at the same time possess that spirit of justice and of candour, which will lead him to remember me with respect.

1798, 1853

6. From Jesus's parable: "The kingdom of heaven is like unto a merchant man, seeking goodly pearls: who, when he had found one pearl of great price, went and sold all that he had, and bought it" (Matthew 13.45–46).

London

It is a goodly sight through the clear air,
From Hampstead's heathy height[1] to see at once
England's vast capital in fair expanse,
Towers, belfries,° lengthen'd streets, and structures fair.   *bell-towers*
5   St. Paul's high dome[2] amidst the vassal bands
Of neighb'ring spires, a regal chieftain stands,
And over fields of ridgy roofs appear,
With distance softly tinted, side by side,
In kindred grace, like twain of sisters dear,
10   The Towers of Westminster, her Abbey's pride;[3]
While, far beyond, the hills of Surrey shine[4]
Through thin soft haze, and show their wavy line.
View'd thus, a goodly sight! but when survey'd
Through denser air when moisten'd winds prevail,
15   In her grand panoply° of smoke array'd,   *armor*
While clouds aloft in heavy volumes sail,
She is sublime.—She seems a curtain'd gloom
Connecting heaven and earth,—a threat'ning sign of doom.
With more than natural height, rear'd in the sky
20   'Tis then St. Paul's arrests the wondering eye;
The lower parts in swathing mist conceal'd,
The higher through some half spent shower reveal'd,
So far from earth removed, that well, I trow,°   *believe*
Did not its form man's artful structure show,
25   It might some lofty alpine peak be deem'd,
The eagle's haunt, with cave and crevice seam'd.
Stretch'd wide on either hand, a rugged screen,
In lurid dimness, nearer streets are seen
Like shoreward billows of a troubled main,°   *open sea*
30   Arrested in their rage. Through drizzly rain,
Cataracts of tawny sheen pour from the skies,
Of furnace smoke black curling columns rise,
And many tinted vapours, slowly pass
O'er the wide draping of that pictured mass.

35   So shows by day this grand imperial town,
And, when o'er all the night's black stole is thrown,
The distant traveller doth with wonder mark
Her luminous canopy athwart the dark,
Cast up, from myriads of lamps that shine
40   Along her streets in many a starry line:—
He wondering looks from his yet distant road,
And thinks the northern streamers° are abroad.   *northern lights*
"What hollow sound is that?" approaching near,

---

1. Hampstead heath, to the north, offers a view of London.
2. London's chief Anglican cathedral.
3. Westminster, a city within London, is the seat of government, the location of Westminster Palace (Parliament),
Buckingham Palace (the royal family home), and Westminster Abbey, an imposing gothic church.
4. County southwest of London.

The roar of many wheels breaks on his ear.
45   It is the flood of human life in motion!
It is the voice of a tempestuous ocean!
With sad but pleasing awe his soul is fill'd,
Scarce heaves his breast, and all within is still'd,
As many thoughts and feelings cross his mind,—
50   Thoughts, mingled, melancholy, undefined,
Of restless, reckless man, and years gone by,
And Time fast wending to Eternity.

                                        1790, 1840

A Mother to Her Waking Infant

Now in thy dazzling half-oped eye,
Thy curled nose, and lip awry,
Thy up-hoist arms, and noddling head,
And little chin with crystal spread,
5   Poor helpless thing! what do I see,
          That I should sing of thee?

From thy poor tongue no accents come,
Which can but rub thy toothless gum:
Small understanding boasts thy face,
10   Thy shapeless limbs nor step, nor grace:
A few short words thy feats may tell,
          And yet I love thee well.

When sudden wakes the bitter shriek,
And redder swells thy little cheek;
15   When rattled keys thy woes beguile,
And thro' the wet eye gleams the smile,
Still for thy weakly self is spent
          Thy little silly plaint.°   lament

But when thy friends are in distress,
20   Thou'lt laugh and chuckle ne'er the less;
Nor e'en with sympathy be smitten,
Tho' all are sad but thee and kitten;
Yet puny varlet that thou art,
          Thou twitchest at the heart.

25   Thy rosy round cheek so soft and warm;
Thy pinky hand, and dimpled arm;
Thy silken locks that scantly peep,
With gold-tip'd ends, where circle deep
Around thy neck in harmless grace
30   So soft and sleekly hold their place,
Might harder hearts with kindness fill,
          And gain our right good will.

Each passing clown bestows his blessing,
Thy mouth is worn with old wives' kissing;

35   E'en lighter looks the gloomy eye
     Of surly sense, when thou art by;
     And yet I think whoe'er they be,
          They love thee not like me.

     Perhaps when time shall add a few
40   Short years to thee, thou'lt love me too.
     Then wilt thou, thro' life's weary way
     Become my sure and cheering stay:
     Wilt care for me, and be my hold,
          When I am weak and old.

45   Thou'lt listen to my lengthen'd tale,
     And pity me when I am frail—
     But see, the sweepy spinning fly
     Upon the window takes thine eye.
     Go to thy little senseless play—
50   Thou dost not heed my lay.°   *lullaby*

                                                         1790

A Child to His Sick Grandfather

     Grand-dad, they say you're old and frail,
     Your stocked legs begin to fail:
     Your knobbed stick (that was my horse)
     Can scarce support your bended corse
5   While back to wall, you lean so sad,
          I'm vex'd to see you, dad.

     You us'd to smile, and stroke my head,
     And tell me how good children did;
     But now I wot° not how it be,   *know*
10   You take me seldom on your knee;
     Yet ne'ertheless I am right glad
          To sit beside you, dad.

     How lank and thin your beard hangs down!
     Scant are the white hairs on your crown:
15   How wan and hollow are your cheeks!
     Your brow is rough with crossing streaks
     But yet, for all his strength be fled,
          I love my own old dad.

     The housewives round their potions brew,
20   And gossips° come to ask for you;   *friends*
     And for your weal° each neighbour cares,   *well-being*
     And good men kneel, and say their prayers:
     And ev'ry body looks so sad,
          When you are ailing, dad.

25   You will not die, and leave us, then?
     Rouse up and be our dad again.

When you are quiet and laid in bed,
We'll doff° our shoes and softly tread;   *remove*
And when you wake we'll aye° be near,   *always*
30   To fill old dad his cheer.

When thro' the house you shift your stand,
I'll lead you kindly by the hand:
When dinner's set, I'll with you bide,
And aye be serving by your side:
35   And when the weary fire burns blue,
        I'll sit and talk with you.

I have a tale both long and good,
About a partlet° and her brood;   *hen*
And cunning greedy fox, that stole,
40   By dead of midnight thro' a hole,
Which slily to the hen-roost led,—
        You love a story, dad?

And then I have a wondrous tale
Of men all clad in coats of mail,
45   With glitt'ring swords—you nod,—I think?
Your fixed eyes begin to wink:
Down on your bosom sinks your head:
        You do not hear me, dad.

                                                    1790

Thunder

Spirit of strength! to whom in wrath 'tis given,
To mar the earth and shake its vasty dome,
Behold the sombre robes whose gathering folds,
Thy secret majesty conceal. Their skirts
5   Spread on mid air move slow and silently,
O'er noon-day's beam thy sultry shroud is cast,
Advancing clouds from every point of heaven,
Like hosts° of gathering foes in pitchy volumes,   *armies*
Grandly dilated, clothe the fields of air,
10   And brood° aloft o'er the empurpled earth.   *hover*
Spirit of strength! it is thy awful hour;
The wind of every hill is laid to rest,
And far o'er sea and land deep silence reigns.

        Wild creatures of the forest homeward hie,
15   And in their dens with fear unwonted° cower;   *unaccustomed*
Pride in the lordly palace is put down,
While in his humble cot° the poor man sits   *cottage*
With all his family round him hush'd and still,
In awful expectation. On his way
20   The traveller stands aghast and looks to heaven.
On the horizon's verge thy lightning gleams,

And the first utterance of thy deep voice
Is heard in reverence and holy fear.

    From nearer clouds bright burst more vivid gleams,
25   As instantly in closing darkness lost;
Pale sheeted flashes cross the wide expanse
While over boggy moor or swampy plain,
A streaming cataract of flame appears,
To meet a nether fire from earth cast up,
30   Commingling terribly; appalling gloom
Succeeds, and lo! the rifted° centre pours   *fissured*
A general blaze, and from the war of clouds,
Red, writhing falls the embodied bolt of heaven.
Then swells the rolling peal, full, deep'ning, grand,
35   And in its strength lifts the tremendous roar,
With mingled discord, rattling, hissing, growling;
Crashing like rocky fragments downward hurl'd,
Like the upbreaking of a ruined world,
In awful majesty the explosion bursts
40   Wide and astounding o'er the trembling land.
Mountain, and cliff, repeat the dread turmoil,
And all, to man's distinctive senses known,
Is lost in the immensity of sound.
Peal after peal succeeds with waning strength,
45   And hush'd and deep each solemn pause between.

      Upon the lofty mountain's side
The kindled forest blazes wide;
Huge fragments of the rugged steep
Are tumbled to the lashing deep;
50   Firm rooted in his cloven rock,
Crashing falls the stubborn oak.
The lightning keen in wasteful ire
Darts fiercely on the pointed spire,
Rending in twain the iron-knit stone,
55   And stately towers to earth are thrown.
No human strength may brave the storm,
Nor shelter screen the shrinking form,
Nor castle wall its fury stay,
Nor massy gate impede its way:
60   It visits those of low estate,°   *the poor*
It shakes the dwellings of the great,
It looks athwart the vaulted tomb,
And glares upon the prison's gloom.
Then dungeons black in unknown light,
65   Flash hideous on the wretches' sight,
And strangely groans the downward cell,
Where silence deep is wont to dwell.

      Now eyes, to heaven up-cast, adore,
Knees bend that never bent before,

70 The stoutest hearts begin to fail,
And many a manly face is pale;
Benumbing fear awhile up-binds,
The palsied action of their minds,
Till waked to dreadful sense they lift their eyes,
75 And round the stricken corse° shrill shrieks of horror rise.   *corpse*

Now rattling hailstones, bounding as they fall
To earth, spread motley winter o'er the plain;
Receding peals sound fainter on the ear,
And roll their distant grumbling far away:
80 The lightning doth in paler flashes gleam,
And through the rent cloud, silvered with his rays,
The sun on all this wild affray° looks down,   *tumult, quarrel*
As, high enthroned above all mortal ken,°   *understanding*
A higher Power beholds the strife of men.

1790; rev. 1840

Song: Woo'd and Married and A'
(Version taken from an old song of that name)

The bride she is winsome and bonny,
Her hair it is snooded° sae° sleek,   *tied up / so*
And faithfu' and kind is her Johnny,
Yet fast fa' the tears on her cheek.
5 New pearlins° are cause of her sorrow,   *fancy lacework*
New pearlins and plenishing° too,   *furnishings*
The bride that has a' to borrow,
Has e'en right mickle° ado,   *much*
Woo'd and married and a'!°   *all*
10 Woo'd and married and a'!
Is na' she very weel aff
To be woo'd and married at a'?

Her mither then hastily spak,
"The lassie is glaikit° wi' pride;   *foolish*
15 In my pouch I had never a plack°   *four-cent coin*
On the day when I was a bride.
E'en tak' to your wheel° and be clever,   *spinning-wheel*
And draw out your thread in the sun;
The gear° that is gifted° it never   *goods / given*
20 Will last like the gear that is won.°   *earned*
Woo'd and married and a'!
Wi' havins° and tocher° sae sma'!   *belongings / dowry*
I think ye are very weel aff,
To be woo'd and married at a'!"

25 "Toot, toot!" quo' her grey-headed faither,
"She's less o' a bride than a bairn,°   *child*
She's ta'en like a cout° frae the heather,   *colt*
Wi' sense and discretion to learn.

Half husband, I trow,° and half daddy,   *suppose*
30   As humour inconstantly leans,
The chiel maun° be patient and steady,   *fellow must*
        That yokes wi' a mate in her teens.
                A kerchief sae douce° and sae neat,   *proper*
                O'er her locks that the winds used to blaw!
35   I'm baith like to laugh and to greet,°   *weep*
                When I think o' her married at a'!"

Then out spak' the wily bridegroom,
        Weel waled° were his wordies, I ween,°   *well chosen / suppose*
"I'm rich, though my coffer be toom,°   *empty*
40   Wi' the blinks o' your bonny blue een.°   *eyes*
I'm prouder o' thee by my side,
        Though thy ruffles or ribbons be few,
Than if Kate o' the Croft were my bride,
        Wi' purfles° and pearlins enow.   *embroidery*
45   Dear and dearest of ony!°   *any*
                Ye're woo'd and buikit° and a'!"   *registered*
        And do ye think scorn o' your Johnny,
        And grieve to be married at a'?"

She turn'd, and she blush'd, and she smiled,
50   And she looket sae bashfully down;
The pride o' her heart was beguiled,
        And she played wi' the sleeves o' her gown;
She twirled the tag o' her lace,
        And she nippet her boddice sae blue,
55   Syne° blinket sae sweet in his face,   *then*
        And aff like a maukin° she flew.   *cat, slut*
                Woo'd and married and a'!
                Wi' Johnny to roose° her and a'!   *praise*
        She thinks hersel very weel aff,
60   To be woo'd and married at a'!

1822, 1840

LITERARY BALLADS

"I never heard the old song of Percy and Douglas," wrote Sir Philip Sidney in *Apology for Poetry* (1595), "that I found not my heart moved more than with a trumpet: and yet it is sung but by some blind crouder [fiddler], with no rougher voice than rude style: which being so evil apparelled in the dust and cobwebs of that uncivil age, what would it work trimmed in the gorgeous elegance of Pindar?" Sidney set the terms for the next three centuries: readers prized the directness of ballads, but could scarcely refrain from wishing to sophisticate them. In the eighteenth century, the numerous popular ballads composed between roughly 1200 and 1700 became a cherished alternative to norms of elegance and decorum. In *Spectator* 70 (1711), Joseph Addison devoted to *Chevy Chase* the kind of criticism previously limited to the classics, preferring its "essential and inherent perfection of simplicity of thought" to the "artificial taste" cultivated by "little fanciful authors and writers of epigram." Ballads appealed to readers of "plain common sense" across all classes and times. Yet no small part of the appeal was the evocation of a hazily indefinite Middle Ages. Thought to be the work of bards or minstrels in the employ of a chieftain, or anonymous folk songs, ballads signified a living oral tradition imperiled by the growing, standardizing print culture on which the eighteenth century prided itself. They harked back to an immediate contact between singer and audience lost in a culture of private reading and glamorized authors.

The basis of the ballads in music shaped their form—usually quatrains of four-beat lines— and permitted a number of haunting effects: repetitions, unexpected syncopations, and narrative compression. Even dilations, such as refrains or formulaic dialogue, made the expected end seem more inevitable. Often haunted by the supernatural that an age of reason dismissed as primitive, sometimes based on historical incidents, usually tragic, the ballads share an intense spareness that springs the reader's imagination. For a sample of Walter Scott's contribution to the genre of the literary ballad, see the spare lyricism of *Lord Randall* (page 1062).

Richard Hurd's *Letters on Chivalry and Romance* (1762) voiced the spirit of the ballad revival: the age of realism, reason, and "good sense" had sacrificed "a world of fine fabling." This revival generated fresh production. Thomas Chatterton (1752–1770) counterfeited a *mélange* of Elizabethan and medieval ballads that he attributed to a fifteenth-century monk, "Thomas Rowley." It was from Chatterton that Wordsworth derived the unusual stanza form of his *Resolution and Independence* (1807, see page 545), celebrating him there and pairing him with Burns. James Macpherson took Europe by storm with *Fingal* (1762) and other supposed versions of oral epics by the ancient Celtic bard Ossian. Bishop Lowth's Latin *Lectures on the Sacred Poetry of the Hebrews* (1753; English translation, 1793) defended the psalms against neo-classic norms by articulating a standard of impassioned sublimity, embodied in lyric. Scholars were suggesting that the Bible was not a unitary text but a composite, and German philologists were dissolving the *Iliad* and *Odyssey* into the stitched-together fragments of oral tradition. By the end of the century, divine scripture, epic, and ballad, high artistic monument and folk culture, had come together in a provocative upheaval of the long-established hierarchy of genres.

Reliques of Ancient English Poetry

Thomas Percy (1729–1811), a grocer's son who took a degree at Oxford in 1750, enjoyed a career in the Anglican church that culminated in his appointments as a chaplain to George III (1769), Dean of Carlisle (1778), and Bishop of Dromore, Ireland (1782). His celebrity derives from the *Reliques of Ancient Poetry* (1765), three volumes developed from a manuscript collection he had found at a friend's house "lying dirty on the floor under a Bureau in ye Parlour: being used by the Maids to light the fires." Fewer than fifty of the 175 poems in the first edition can be traced to this trove, however; for the rest Percy scoured manuscript archives and published collections. Traditional ballads were his object, but the *Reliques* mix them with sixteenth- and seventeenth-century poetry (by Shakespeare, Jonson, Carew, Crashaw, and others), works by contemporaries and himself, and substantial essays on "ancient English minstrels" and on the unrhymed alliterative verse of *Piers Plowman* and the Norse poets. A serious churchman, Percy apologized for bestowing "attention on a parcel of OLD BALLADS": his presentation dignified them, however, diminishing the strangeness of the medieval world, not least because (in a tactic excoriated by later scholars) he did not hesitate to "improve" his originals. Subsequent editions appeared across the century, exerting a wide influence on the Romantic period, visible in the meter of Coleridge's *Christabel* (page 652) and Scott's *The Lay of the Last Minstrel*. Wordsworth declared that British poetry had been "absolutely redeemed" by the *Reliques:* "I do not think that there is an able writer of verse of the present day who would not be proud to acknowledge his obligations to the Reliques; I know that it is so for my friends; and for myself, I am happy . . . to make a public avowal." Volume I of the *Reliques* printed such famous ballads as *Chevy Chase* and *Edward, Edward*, as well as *Sir Patrick Spence*, which provided Coleridge with the epigraph for his *Dejection: An Ode* (page 674).

Sir Patrick Spence[1]

The king sits in Dumferling[2] toune,
   Drinking the blude-reid wine:
O quhar° will I get guid sailòr,   *where*
   To sail this schip of mine?

5   Up and spak an eldern knicht,
   Sat at the kings richt kne:
Sir Patrick Spence is the best sailòr,
   That sails upon the se.

The king has written a braid° letter,   *open*
10   And signd it wi' his hand;
And sent it to Sir Patrick Spence,
   Was walking on the sand.

The first line that Sir Patrick red,
   Loud lauch° lauched he: *laugh*
15   The next line that Sir Patrick red,
   The teir blinded his ee.°   *eye*

O quha° is this has don this deid,   *who*
   This ill deid don to me;
To send me out this time o' the zeir,°   *year*
20   To sail upon the se?[3]

Mak hast, mak haste, my mirry men all,
   Our guid schip sails the morne,°   *on the morrow*
O say na sae, my master deir,
   For I feir a deadlie storme.

25   Late late yestreen I saw the new moone
   Wi' the auld moone in hir arme;
And I feir, I feir, my deir mastèr,
   That we will com to harme.

O our Scots nobles wer richt laith°   *loath*
30   To weet their cork-heild schoone;°   *shoes*
Bot lang owre° a' the play wer playd,   *long ere*
   Thair hats they swam aboone.°   *above (water)*

O lang, lang, may thair ladies sit
   Wi' thair fans into their hand,
35   Or eir they se Sir Patrick Spence
   Cum sailing to the land.

1. Percy confesses ignorance of the historical particulars of the events; Sir Walter Scott's version includes a stanza explaining that the Scots were bound for Norway to deliver their king's daughter for marriage to King Eric. The return voyage ended in shipwreck in 1281.

2. Dunfermline, site of Scottish royal palace.

3. "In the infancy of navigation, such [sailors] as used the northern seas were very liable to shipwreck in the wintry months: hence a law was enacted in the reign of James III," restricting winter ship travel [Percy's comment].

O lang, lang, may the ladies stand
   Wi' thair gold kems° in their hair,   *combs*
Waiting for thair ain deir lords,
40   For they'll se thame na mair.

Have owre,° have owre to Aberdour,[4]   *half over*
   It's fiftie fadom deip:
And thair lies guid Sir Patrick Spence,
   Wi' the Scots lords at his feit.

1765

━━ ≡✦≡ ━━

James Macpherson
1736–1796

James Macpherson, born in Ruthven in the Gaelic-speaking Highlands of Scotland, was educated at Aberdeen University, then the University of Edinburgh. His home district was involved in the uprising of 1745; in February 1746, the Jacobites set fire to the British Army barracks at Ruthven, but less than three months later they were crushed at the battle of Culloden, and the home of the Macpherson clan chief was burned. By 1759 young Macpherson was in touch with a circle of Edinburgh luminaries: philosopher and historian Adam Ferguson, playwright John Home, and rhetorician Hugh Blair. Blair fostered the publication of Macpherson's *Fragments of Ancient Poetry Collected in the Highlands of Scotland* (1760) and raised funds to return him to the north to collect more material. From his sources Macpherson claimed to have recovered the works of Ossian, a third-century blind Gaelic bard: *Fingal, An Ancient Epic Poem, in Six Books, Together with several other Poems, composed by Ossian the Son of Fingal* appeared in 1762, followed by *Temora* in 1763. The reception was overwhelming, though many doubted the existence of any ancient manuscripts. The poems, insisted Samuel Johnson, "never existed in any other form than that which we have seen. The editor, or author, never could shew the original"; he ascribed the credulity to Scots' "fondness for their supposed ancestors." Charges of fraud did not destroy the warm reception; the register just shifted to imaginative creation through the process of oral transmission and recreation. Thomas Gray exclaimed, "this Man is the very demon of Poetry, or he has lighted on a treasure hid for ages"; Thomas Jefferson declared, "I am not ashamed to own that I think this rude bard of the North the greatest Poet that has ever existed"; Napoleon carried a translation of Ossian on his campaigns; when Goethe has the protagonist of *The Sorrows of Young Werther* (1774) replace Homer with Ossian, he signals the suicidal end. The rhythmic, figurative, formulaic language, and the cloudy, emotion-laden descriptions pervaded by "the joy of grief" summoned a vanished world of warriors and bards, at once antique and responsive to the widespread eighteenth-century disruptions of traditional ways of life. William Hazlitt memorably epitomized the force: "Ossian is the decay and old age of poetry. He lives only in the recollection and regret of the past. There is one impression which he conveys more entirely than all other poets, namely, the sense of privation, the loss of all things, of friends, and good name, of country—he is even without God in the world. He converses only with the spirits of the departed; with the motionless and silent clouds." In Macpherson's specious character Hazlitt locates an origin of Romantic sensibility. Our text is from the two-volume *The Works of Ossian* (1765); Macpherson's notes are indicated in brackets.

4. A harbor in Fife, Scotland.

from **Carric-Thura: A Poem**[1]

HAST[2] thou left thy blue course in heaven, golden-haired son of the sky! The west has opened its gates; the bed of thy repose is there. The waves come to behold thy beauty: they lift their trembling heads they see thee lovely in thy sleep; but they shrink away with fear. Rest, in thy shadowy cave, O sun! And let thy return be in joy.————But let a thousand lights arise to the sound of harps of Selma: let the beam spread in the hall, the king of shells[3] is returned! The strife of Crona[4] is past, like sounds that are no more: raise the song, O bards, the king is returned with his fame!

SUCH was the song of Ullin, when Fingal returned from battle: when he returned in the fair blushing of youth; with all his heavy locks. His blue arms were on the hero; like a gray cloud on the sun, when he moves in his robes of mist, and shews but half his beams. His heroes follow the king: the feast of shells is spread. Fingal turns to his bards, and bids the song to rise.

VOICES of echoing Cona! He said, O bards of other times! Ye, on whose souls the blue hosts of our fathers rise! Strike the harp in my hall; and let Fingal hear the song. Pleasant is the joy of grief! It is like the shower of spring, when it softens the branch of the oak, and the young leaf lifts its green head. Sing on, O bards, tomorrow we lift the sail. My blue course is through the ocean, to Carric-thura's walls; the mossy walls of Sarno, where Comála dwelt. There the noble Cathulla spreads the feast of shells. The boars of his woods are many, and the sound of the chace shall arise.

CRONNAN,[5] son of song! Said Ullin, Minona, graceful at the harp! Raise the song of Shilric, to please the king of Morven. Let Vinvela come in her beauty, like the showery bow, when it shews its lovely head on the lake, and the setting sun is bright. And she comes, O Fingal! Her voice is soft but sad. * * *[6]

SUCH was the song of Cronnan, on the night of Selma's joy. But morning rose in the east; the blue waters rolled in light. Fingal bade his sails to rise, and the winds come rustling from their hills. Inis-tore rose to sight, and Carric-thura's mossy towers. But the sign of distress was on their top: the green flame edged with smoke. The king of Morven[7] struck his breast: he assumed, at once, his spear. His darkened brow bends

---

1. Fingal, returning from an expedition which he had made into the Roman province, resolved to visit Cathulla king of Inis-tore, and brother to Comála, whose story is related, at large in the dramatic poem, published in this collection. Upon his coming in sight of Carric-thura, the palace of Cathulla, he observed a flame on its top, which, in those days, was a signal of distress. The wind drove him into a bay, at some distance from Carric-thura, and he was obliged to pass the night on the shore. Next day he attacked the army of Frothal king of Sora [in Scandinavia] who had besieged Cathulla in his palace of Carric-thura, and took Frothal himself prisoner, after he had engaged him in single combat. The deliverance of Carric-thura is the subject of the poem, but several other episodes are interwoven with it. It appears from tradition, that this poem was addressed to a Culdee, or one of the first Christian missionaries, and that the story of the *Spirit of Loda*, supposed to be the ancient Odin of Scandinavia, was introduced by Ossian in opposition to the Culdee's doctrine. Be this as it will, it lets us into Ossian's notions of a superior being; and shews that he was not addicted to the superstition which prevailed all the world over, before the introduction of Christianity [Macpherson's note].
2. The song of Ullin, with which the poem opens, is in a lyric measure. It was usual with Fingal, when he returned from his expeditions, to send his bards singing before

him. This species of triumph is called, by Ossian, the *song of victory* [Macpherson's note].
3. Used as drinking cups: an emblem therefore of magnanimity.
4. Ossian has celebrated the *strife of Crona*, in a particular poem. This poem is connected with it, but it was impossible for the translator to procure that part which relates to Crona, with any degree of purity [Macpherson's note].
5. One should think that that the parts of Shilric and Vinvela were represented by Cronnan and Minona, whose very names denote that they were singers, who performed in public. Cronnan signifies a *mournful sound*; Minona, or *Mín-ónn, soft air*. All the dramatic poems of Ossian appear to have been presented before Fingal, upon solemn occasions [Macpherson's note].
6. The interlude recounts the fate of Shilric and his beloved Vinvela. Thinking him dead in the wars of Fingal, Vinvela expires with grief. Shilric returns to encounter her ghost—"she fleets, she sails away; as gray mist before the wind!"—and to remain fixed at her tomb: "By the mossy fountain I will sit; on the top of the hill of winds. When mid-day is silent around, converse, O my love with me!"
7. All the north-west coast of Scotland probably went of old under the name of Morven [Macpherson's note]; Selma is Fingal's palace.

forward to the coast: he looks back to the lagging winds. His hair is disordered on his back. The silence of the king is terrible. * * *[8]

THE flame was dim and distant; the moon hid her red face in the east. A blast came from the mountain, and bore, on its wings, the spirit of Loda. He came to the place in his terrors, and he shook his dusky spear.—His eyes appear like flames in his dark face; and his voice is like distant thunder. Fingal advanced with the spear of his strength, and raised his voice on high.

SON of night, retire: call thy winds and fly! Why dost thou come to my presence, with thy shadowy arms? Do I fear thy gloomy form, dismal spirit of Loda? Weak is thy shield of clouds: feeble is that meteor, thy sword. The blast rolls them together; and thou thyself dost vanish. Fly from my presence son of night! Call thy winds and fly!

DOST thou force me from my place, replied the hollow voice? The people bend before me. I turn the battle in the field of the valiant. I look on the nations and they vanish: my nostrils pour the blast of death. I come[9] abroad on the winds: the tempests are before my face. But my dwelling is calm, above the clouds, the fields of my rest are pleasant. * * *

HE lifted high his shadowy spear; and bent forward his terrible height. But the king, advancing, drew his sword; the blade of dark-brown Luno.[1] The gleaming path of the steel winds through the gloomy ghost. The form fell shapeless into air, like a column of smoke, which the staff of the boy disturbs, as it rises from the half-extinguished furnace.

THE spirit of Loda shrieked, as, rolled into himself, he rose on the wind. Inistore shook at the sound. The waves heard it on the deep; they stopped, in their course, with fear: the companions of Fingal started, at once; and took their heavy spears. They missed the king: they rose with rage; all their arms resound. * * *

MORNING rose on Inistore. Frothal struck his dark-brown shield. His chiefs started at the sound; they stood, but their eyes were turned to the sea. They saw Fingal coming in his strength. * * *

HE [Frothal] went forth with the stream of his people, but they met a rock: Fingal stood unmoved, broken they rolled back from his side. Nor did they roll in safety; the spear of the king pursued their flight. The field is covered with heroes. A rising hill preserved the flying host.

FROTHAL saw their flight. The rage of his bosom rose. He bent his eyes to the ground and called the noble Thubar.————Thubar! My people fled. My fame has ceased to rise. I will fight the king; I feel my burning soul. Send a bard to demand the combat. Speak not against Frothal's words.—But, Thubar! I love a maid; she dwells by Thano's stream, the white-bosomed daughter of Herman, Utha with the softly-rolling eyes. She feared the daughter[2] of Inistore, and her soft sighs rose, at my departure. Tell to Utha that I am low; but that my soul delighted in her.

SUCH were his words, resolved to fight. But the soft sigh of Utha was near. She had followed her hero over the sea, in the armour of a man. She rolled her eye on the youth, in secret, from beneath a glittering helmet. But now she saw the bard as he went, and the spear fell thrice from her hand. Her loose hair flew on the wind, her white breast rose, with sighs. She lifted up her eyes to the king; she would speak, but thrice she failed.

FINGAL heard the words of the bard; he came in the strength of steel. They mixed their deathful spears, and raised the gleam of their swords. But the steel of

---

8. The night before the battle Fingal is challenged by the spirit of Loda, who protects the invading Frothal.
9. There is a great resemblance between the terrors of this mock divinity, and those of the true God, as they are described in the 18th Psalm [Macpherson's note].
1. The famous sword of Fingal, made by Lun, or Luno, a smith of Lochlin [Scandinavia; Macpherson's note].
2. By the daughter of Inistore, Frothal means Comála, of whose death Utha probably had not heard; consequently she feared that the former passion of Frothal for Comála might return [Macpherson's note].

Fingal descended and cut Frothal's shield in twain. His fair side is exposed; half bent he foresees his death.

DARKNESS gathered on Utha's soul. The tear rolled down her cheek. She rushed to cover the chief with her shield; but a fallen oak met her steps. She fell on her arm of snow; her shield, her helmet flew wide. Her white bosom heaved to the sight; her dark-brown hair is spread on earth.

FINGAL pitied the white armed maid: he stayed the uplifted sword. The tear was in the eye of the king, as, bending forward, he spoke. King of streamy Sora! Fear not the sword of Fingal. It was never stained with the blood of the vanquished; it never pierced a fallen foe. Let thy people rejoice along the blue waters of Tora: let the maids of thy love be glad. Why shouldest thou fall in thy youth, king of streamy Sora?

DAUGHTER of Herman, said Frothal, didst thou come from Tora's streams; didst thou come, in thy beauty, to behold thy warrior low? But he was low before the mighty, maid of the slow-rolling eye! The feeble did not overcome the son of car-borne Annir. Terrible art thou, O king of Morven! in battles of the spear. But, in peace, thou art like the sun, when he looks through a silent shower: the flowers lift their fair heads before him; and the gales shake their rustling winds.[3] * * *

CRIMORA: Who cometh from the hill, like a cloud tinged with the beam of the west. Whose voice is that, loud as the wind, but pleasant as the harp of Carrill?[4] It is my love in the light of steel; but sad is his darkened brow. Live the mighty race of Fingal? Or what disturbs my Connal?[5]

CONNAL: They live, I saw them return from the chace, like a stream of light. The sun was on their shields. Like a ridge of fire they descended the hill. Loud is the voice of the youth; the war, my love, is near. To-morrow the terrible Dargo comes to try the force of our race. The race of Fingal he defies; the race of battle and wounds.

CRIMORA: Connal, I saw his sails like gray mist on the sable wave. They slowly came to land. Connal, many are the warriors of Dargo!

CONNAL: Bring me thy father's shield; the bossy, iron shield of Rinval; that shield like the full moon when it moves darkened through the heaven.

CRIMORA: That shield I bring, O Connal; but it did not defend my father. By the spear of Gormar he fell. Thou may'st fall, O Connal!

CONNAL: Fall indeed I may: But raise my tomb, Crimora. Gray stones, a mound of earth, shall keep my memory. Bend thy red eye over my tomb, and beat thy mournful heaving breast. Though fair thou art, my love, as the light; more pleas-ant than the gale of the hill; yet I will not stay. Raise my tomb, Crimora.

CRIMORA: Then give me those arms of light; that sword, and that spear of steel. I shall meet Dargo with thee, and aid my lovely Connal. Farewell, ye rocks of Ardven! Ye deer! And ye streams of the hill!—We shall return no more. Our tombs are distant far.

AND did they return no more? Said Utha's bursting sigh. Fell the mighty in battle, and did Crimora live?—Her steps were lonely, and her soul was sad for Connal. Was he not young and lovely; like the beam of the setting sun? Ullin saw the virgin's tear, and took the softly-trembling harp: the song was lovely, but sad, and silence was in Carric-thura.

---

3. Fingal, Frothal, and Utha enter the liberated castle. At the celebration, the bard Ullin performs the tale of Crimora and Connal: "the tale was long, but lovely; and pleased the blushing maid of Tora."
4. The name itself is proper to any bard, as it signifies *a sprightly and harmonious sound* [Macpherson's note].

5. Connal, the son of Diaran, was one of the most famous heroes of Fingal; he was slain in a battle against Dargo a Briton; but whether by the hand of the enemy, or that of his mistress, tradition does not determine [Macpherson's note].

AUTUMN is dark on the mountains; gray mist rests on the hills. The whirlwind is heard on the heath. Dark rolls the river through the narrow plain. A tree stands alone on the hill, and marks the slumbering Connal. The leaves whirl round with the wind, and strew the graves of the dead. At times are seen here the ghosts of the deceased, when the musing hunter alone stalks slowly over the heath. * * *

DARGO the mighty came on, like a cloud of thunder. His brows were contracted and dark. His eyes like two caves in a rock. Bright rose their swords on each side; dire was the clang of their steel.

THE daughter of Rinval was near; Crimora bright in the armour of man; her yellow hair is loose behind, her bow is in her hand. She followed the youth to the war, Connal her much-beloved. She drew the string on Dargo; but erring pierced her Connal. He falls like an oak on the plain; like a rock from the shaggy hill. What shall she do, hapless maid!—He bleeds; her Connal dies. All the night long she cries, and all the day, O Connal, my love, and my friend! With grief the sad mourner dies.

EARTH here incloses the loveliest pair on the hill. The grass grows between the stones of the tomb; I often sit in the mournful shade. The wind sighs through the grass; their memory rushes on my mind. Undisturbed you now sleep together; in the tomb of the mountain you rest alone.

AND soft be your rest, said Utha, children of streamy Lotha. I will remember you with tears, and my secret song shall rise; when the wind is in the groves of Tora, and the stream is roaring near. Then shall ye come on my soul, with all your lovely grief.

THREE days feasted the kings: on the fourth their white sails arose. The winds of the north carry the ship of Fingal to Morven's woody land.——But the spirit of Loda sat, in his cloud, behind the ships of Frothal. He hung forward with all his blast, and spread the white-bosomed sails.——The wounds of his form were not forgot; he still feared the hand of the king.[6]

1765

━━◄═◆═►━━

Robert Burns
1759–1796

A "striking example of native genius bursting through the obscurity of poverty and the obstructions of laborious life" exclaimed the *Edinburgh Magazine* when Robert Burns's *Poems, Chiefly in the Scottish Dialect* appeared from provincial Kilmarnock in 1786. Yet the reality of the "heaven-taught plow-man" was more complex. A tenant farmer like his father, Burns planned to accept a position on a Jamaican plantation until the success of his poetry provided an alternative. Though poor, Burns was well read; his poems, if "chiefly" in dialect, were never exclusively so: the accents and forms of folk culture play against a range of polite English genres. Fame brought Burns to Edinburgh, where he enlarged and reprinted his book. On the profits, he returned to farming and married Jean Armour, who had borne him children in 1786 and 1788.

The farm failed, as had its three predecessors, and Burns moved his family to Dumfries, where he obtained the post of exciseman, or tax-inspector. Government employment might

6. The story of Fingal and the spirit of Loda, supposed to be the famous Odin, is the most extravagant fiction in all Ossian's poems. It is not, however, without precedents in the best poets; and it must be said for Ossian, that he says nothing but what perfectly agreed with the notions of the times, concerning ghosts. They thought the souls of the dead were material, and consequently susceptible of pain. Whether a proof could be drawn from this passage, that Ossian had no notion of a divinity, I shall leave to others to determine: it appears, however, that he was of opinion, that superior beings ought to take no notice of what passed among men [Macpherson's note].

seem anomalous for one who championed the American and French Revolutions, who believed in the goodness of man against the tenets of the Scots church, which he repeatedly satirized, and flamboyantly defied in his many erotic escapades, but Burns fulfilled his duties responsibly. An invitation in 1787 to contribute to *The Scots Musical Museum* intensified his sense of his Scots identity: for the next six years he became "absolutely crazed," as he put it, with collecting and editing traditional songs for the successive volumes, and wrote more than two hundred himself, new or adapted. When the fourth volume was finished in 1792, Burns agreed to participate in a *Select Collection of Scottish Airs*, a far more genteelly refining version of Scottish poetry. The more earthy energies of Burns's poetry appear in the posthumously published *Merry Muses of Caledonia* (1799–1800), a collection printed at least partly from Burns's papers following his early death from heart disease at the age of thirty-seven. The second version of *Comin' Thro' the Rye* and *The Fornicator* appeared in this work.

To a Mouse
On Turning Her Up in Her Nest with the Plough, November, 1785

	Wee, sleekit,° cowrin, tim'rous beastie,	*sleek*
	O, what a panic's in thy breastie!	
	Thou need na start awa sac° hasty	*so*
	Wi' bickering brattle!°	*scurry*
5	I wad be laith° to rin an' chase thee,	*loath*
	Wi' murdering pattle!°	*plough-scraper*
	I'm truly sorry man's dominion	
	Has broken Nature's social union,	
	An' justifies that ill opinion	
10	Which makes thee startle	
	At me, thy poor, earth-born companion	
	An' fellow mortal!	
	I doubt na, whyles,° but thou may thieve;	*sometimes*
	What then? poor beastie, thou maun° live!	*must*
15	A daimen icker in a thrave°	*odd ear in 24 sheaves*
	'S a sma' request;	
	I'll get a blessin wi' the lave,°	*rest*
	An' never miss 't!	
	Thy wee-bit housie, too, in ruin!	
20	Its silly wa's° the win's are strewin!	*feeble walls*
	An' naething, now, to big° a new ane,	*build*
	O' foggage° green!	*coarse grass*
	An' bleak December's win's ensuin,	
	Baith snell° an' keen!	*bitter*
25	Thou saw the fields laid bare an' waste,	
	An' weary winter comin fast,	
	An' cozie here, beneath the blast,	
	Thou thought to dwell,	
	Till crash! the cruel coulter° past	*plow-blade*
30	Out thro' thy cell.	
	That wee bit heap o' leaves an' stibble,°	*stubble*
	Has cost thee monie a weary nibble!	

Now thou's turned out, for a' thy trouble,
    But° house or hald,°   *without / goods*
35 To thole° the winter's sleety dribble,   *endure*
    An' cranreuch° cauld!   *hoarfrost*

But Mousie, thou art no thy lane,°   *not alone*
In proving foresight may be vain:
The best-laid schemes o' mice an' men
40   Gang aft agley,°   *go oft awry*
An' lea'e us nought but grief an' pain,
    For promis'd joy!

Still thou art blest, compared wi' me!
The present only toucheth thee:
45 But och! I backward cast my e'e,
    On prospects drear!
An' forward, tho' I canna see,
    I guess an' fear!

1785   1786

To a Louse,
On Seeing one on a Lady's Bonnet at Church

Ha! Whare ye gaun,° ye crowlan ferlie!°   *going / creeping wonder*
Your impudence protects you sairly:°   *surely*
I canna say but ye strunt° rarely,   *strut*
    Owre *gawze* and *lace*;
5 Tho' faith, I fear ye dine but sparely,
    On sic a place.

Ye ugly, creepan, blastet° wonner,   *blasted, cursed*
Detested, shunn'd, by saunt an' sinner,
How daur ye set your fit upon her,
10   Sae fine a *Lady*!
Gae somewhere else and seek your dinner,
    On some poor body.

Swith,° in some beggar's haffet° squattle,°   *Away! / lock of hair / squat*
There ye may creep, and sprawl,° and sprattle,°   *struggle / scramble*
15 Wi'ither kindred, jumping cattle,°   *beasts*
    In shoals and nations;
Whare *horn* nor *bane*[1] ne'er daur unsettle,
    Your thick plantations.

Now haud° you there, ye're out o' sight,   *stay*
20 Below the fatt'rels,° snug and tight,   *ribbon ends*
Na faith ye° yet! Ye'll no be right,   *confound you*
    Till ye've got on it,
The vera tapmost, towrin height
    O' *Miss's* bonnet.

1. Combs were made of horn or bone.

25   My sooth! Right bauld ye set your nose,
  As plump an' gray as onie grozet°   *gooseberry*
   O for some rank, mercurial rozet,°   *rosin soap (used as insecticide)*
    Or fell,° red smeddum,°   *deadly / powder*
  I'd gie you sic a hearty dose o't,
30   Wad dress your droddum!°   *beat your backside*

  I wad na been surpriz'd to spy
  You on an auld wife's *flainen toy;*°   *flannel cap with flaps*
   Or aiblins° some bit duddie° boy,   *perhaps / ragged*
    On's *wylecoat;*°   *flannel vest*
35   But Miss's fine *Lunardi,*[2] fye!
   How daur ye do't?

  O *Jenny* dinna toss your head,
  An' set your beauties a' abroad!
   Ye little ken what cursed speed
40   The blastie's° makin!   *shrivelled dwarf*
  Thae *winks* and *finger-ends*, I dread,
   Are notice takin!

  O wad some Pow'r the giftie gie us
  To see oursels as others see us!
45   It wad frae monie a blunder free us
   An' foolish notion:
  What airs in dress an' gait wad lea'e us,
   And ev'n Devotion!

1785   1786

Flow gently, sweet Afton[1]

  Flow gently, sweet Afton, among thy green braes!°   *banks*
  Flow gently, I'll sing thee a song in thy praise!
  My Mary's asleep by thy murmuring stream—
  Flow gently, sweet Afton, disturb not her dream!

5   Thou stock-dove whose echo resounds thro' the glen,
  Ye wild whistling blackbirds in yon thorny den,
  Thou green-crested lapwing, thy screaming forbear—
  I charge you, disturb not my slumbering fair!

  How lofty, sweet Afton, thy neighbouring hills,
10   Far mark'd with the courses of clear, winding rills!°   *brooks*
  There daily I wander, as noon rises high,
  My flocks and my Mary's sweet cot° in my eye.   *cottage*

---

2. Vincenzo Lunardi (1759–1806) was an early balloon-
ist who made several ascents in Scotland in 1785. His
celebrity brought a bonnet shaped like a balloon into
fashion.

1. "There is a small river, Afton, that falls into [the river]
Nith, New Cumnock [in southwest Scotland]; which has
some charming wild, romantic scenery on its banks...."
[Burns's comment].

How pleasant thy banks and green vallies below,
Where wild in the woodlands the primroses blow;
15 There oft, as mild Ev'ning weeps over the lea,°   *meadow*
The sweet-scented birk° shades my Mary and me.   *birch*

Thy crystal stream, Afton, how lovely it glides,
And winds by the cot where my Mary resides!
How wanton thy waters her snowy feet lave,°   *wash*
20 As, gathering sweet flowerets, she stems thy clear wave.

Flow gently, sweet Afton, among thy green braes!
Flow gently, sweet river, the theme of my lays!
My Mary's asleep by thy murmuring stream—
Flow gently, sweet Afton, disturb not her dream!
1789   1792

Ae fond kiss[1]

Ae° fond kiss, and then we sever!   *one*
Ae farewell, and then forever!
Deep in heart-wrung tears I'll pledge thee,
Warring sighs and groans I'll wage° thee.   *pledge*
5 Who shall say that Fortune grieves him
While the star of hope she° leaves him   *Fortune*
Me, nae cheerfu' twinkle lights me,
Dark despair around benights me.

I'll ne'er blame my partial fancy:
10 Naething could resist my Nancy!
But to see her was to love her,
Love but her, and love for ever.
Had we never lov'd sae kindly,
Had we never lov'd sae blindly,
15 Never met—or never parted—
We had ne'er been broken-hearted.

Fare-the-weel, thou first and fairest!
Fare-the-weel, thou best and dearest!
Thine be ilka° joy and treasure,   *every*
20 Peace, Enjoyment, Love and Pleasure!
Ae fond kiss, and then we sever!
Ae farewell, alas, for ever!
Deep in heart-wrung tears I'll pledge thee,
Warring sighs and groans I'll wage thee.
1791   1792

---

1. Addressed to Agnes "Nancy" McLehose, leaving Edinburgh in 1792 to rejoin her husband in the West Indies.

Comin' Thro' the Rye (1)[1]

CHORUS

O, Jenny's a' weet, poor body,
　　Jenny's seldom dry:
　　She draigl't° a' her petticoatie,　　　　　　　*bedraggled*
　　Comin thro' the rye!

5　　Comin thro' the rye, poor body,
　　　　Comin thro' the rye,
　　She draigl't a' her petticoatie,
　　　　Comin thro' the rye!

　　Gin° a body meet a body　　　　　　　　　　*if*
10　　　Comin thro' the rye,
　　Gin a body kiss a body,
　　　　Need a body cry?

　　Gin a body meet a body
　　　　Comin thro' the glen,
15　　Gin a body kiss a body,
　　　　Need the warld ken?°　　　　　　　　　　*know*

CHORUS

　　　　　　　　　　　　　　　　　　　　　　1796

Comin' Thro' the Rye (2)

CHORUS

　　O gin a body meet a body,
　　　　Comin throu the rye;
　　Gin a body f—k a body,
　　　　Need a body cry.

5　　Comin' thro' the rye, my jo,°　　　　　　　*sweetheart*
　　　　An' comin' thro' the rye;
　　She fand a staun° o' staunin' graith,°　　　*stand / tools*
　　　　Comin' thro' the rye.

　　Gin a body meet a body,
10　　　Comin' thro' the glen;
　　Gin a body f—k a body,
　　　　Need the warld ken.

　　Gin a body meet a body,
　　　　Comin' thro' the grain;
15　　Gin a body f—k a body,
　　　　C—t's a body's ain.°　　　　　　　　　*own*

---

1. A revision and expansion of an old song, also popular in various bawdy versions, as in the second version which
follows, with obscenities tactfully hyphenated by the 1800 publisher.

Gin a body meet a body,
    By a body's sel,
What na body f—s a body,
20   Wad a body tell.

Mony a body meets a body,
    They dare na weel avow;
Mony a body f—s a body,
    Ye wadna think it true.

1799–1800

Scots, wha hae wi' Wallace bled[1]

Scots, wha hae° wi' Wallace bled,[2]   *who have*
Scots, wham° Bruce has aften led,   *whom*
Welcome to your gory bed
    Or to victorie!

5   Now's the day, and now's the hour:
See the front o' battle lour,°   *glare*
See approach proud Edward's° power—   *Edward II*
    Chains and slaverie!

Wha will be a traitor knave?
10   Wha can fill a coward's grave?
Wha sae base as be a slave?—
    Let him turn, and flee!

Wha for Scotland's King and Law
Freedom's sword will strongly draw,
15   Freeman stand or freeman fa',°   *fall*
    Let him follow me!

By Oppression's woes and pains,
By your sons in servile chains,
We will drain our dearest veins
20   But they shall be free!

Lay the proud usurpers low!
Tyrants fall in every foe!
Liberty's in every blow!
    Let us do, or die!

1793   1794

1. On 26 August 1787, Burns visited the field of Bannockburn, where Robert the Bruce vanquished the far larger English army in 1314. The victory gave Bruce the Scottish throne. Begged to make "soft verses" for the tune popularly believed to be Bruce's march at the battle, Burns said he "had no idea of giving myself any trouble on the subject, till the accidental recollection of that glorious struggle for Freedom . . . roused my rhyming mania." First published in the *Morning Chronicle*, May 1794, the poem spoke to current events—the French Revolution and the Edinburgh sedition trials—as much as to medieval history.
2. Sir William Wallace, famous Scots patriot, executed by the English King Edward I in 1305.

Is there for honest poverty[1]

Is there for honest poverty
    That hings° his head, an' a'° that?   *hangs / all*
The coward slave, we pass him by—
    We dare be poor for a' that!
5   For a' that, an' a' that,
    Our toils obscure, an' a' that,
The rank is but the guinea's stamp,°   *coin's marking*
    The man's the gowd° for a' that.   *gold*

What though on hamely fare we dine,
10   Wear hoddin grey,° an' a' that?   *coarse wool cloth*
Gie fools their silks, and knaves their wine—
    A man's a man for a' that.
For a' that, an' a' that,
    Their tinsel show, an' a' that,
15   The honest man, tho' e'er sae poor,
    Is king of men for a' that.

Ye see yon birkie ca'd° "a lord,"   *fellow called*
    Wha struts, an' stares, an' a' that!
Tho' hundreds worship at his word,
20   He's but a cuif° for a' that.   *fool*
For a' that, an' a' that,
    His ribband, star, and a' that,
The man o' independent mind,
    He looks and laughs at a' that.

25   A prince can mak a belted knight,
    A marquis, duke, an' a' that!
But an honest man's aboon° his might—   *above*
    Guid faith, he manna fa'° that!   *must not claim*
For a' that, an' a' that,
30   Their dignities, an' a' that,
The pith o' sense an' pride o' worth
    Are higher rank than a' that.

Then let us pray that come it may
    (As come it will for a' that)
35   That Sense and Worth o'er a' the earth
    Shall bear the gree° an' a' that!   *prize*
For a' that, an a' that,
    It's comin yet for a' that,
That man to man the world o'er
40   Shall brithers be for a' that.

1794   1795

---

1. In the month he composed this song, Burns remarked of the execution of Louis XVI and Marie Antoinette, "What is there in the delivering over a perjured Blockhead & an unprincipled Prostitute to the hands of the hangman, that it should arrest for a moment, attention, in an eventful hour, when . . . 'the welfare of millions is hung in the scale / And the balance yet trembles with fate!'" (quoting his friend William Roscoe).

RESPONSE

Charlotte Smith: To the shade of Burns[1]

Mute is thy wild harp, now, O Bard sublime!
    Who, amid Scotia's mountain solitude,
Great Nature taught to "build the lofty rhyme,"[2]
    And even beneath the daily pressure, rude,
5   Of labouring Poverty, thy generous blood,
    Fired with the love of freedom—Not subdued
Wert thou by thy low fortune: But a time
Like this we live in, when the abject chime
Of echoing Parasite is best approved,
10   Was not for thee—Indignantly is fled
Thy noble Spirit; and no longer moved
    By all the ills o'er which thine heart has bled,
    Associate, worthy of the illustrious dead,
Enjoys with them "the Liberty it loved."[3]

A Red, Red Rose[1]

O, my luve is like a red, red rose,
    That's newly sprung in June.
O, my luve is like the melodie,
    That's sweetly play'd in tune.

5 As fair art thou, my bonie lass,
    So deep in luve am I,
And I will luve thee still, my dear,
    Till a' the seas gang° dry.   *go*

Till a' the seas gang dry, my dear,
10   And the rocks melt wi' the sun!
And I will luve thee still, my dear,
    While the sands o' life shall run.

And fare thee weel, my only luve,
    And fare thee weel a while!

---

1. Whoever has tasted the charm of original genius so evident in the composition of this genuine Poet, a Poet "of nature's own creation," cannot surely fail to lament his unhappy life, (latterly passed, as I have understood, in an employment to which such a mind as his must have been averse,) nor his premature death. For one, herself made the object of *subscription*, it is proper to add, that whoever *has* thus been delighted with the wild notes of the Scottish bard, must have a melancholy pleasure in relieving by their benevolence the unfortunate family he has left? [Smith's note]. The quotation is from James Thomson's *Coriolanus* (3.3), where it is said that a peasant may be a nobleman "of nature's own creation." Smith wrote this sonnet in 1796, lamenting the death of poet Robert Burns; it appeared, with her note, in *Elegiac Sonnets* (1797), published by "subscription" (advanced purchase). For more about Charlotte Smith, see her principal listing on page 85.

2. Quoting Milton's famous elegy, *Lycidas* (line 11), whose eponym could do thus.

3. Pope [Smith's note]; quoting *Epitaph on Sir William Trumbull* (1716): "such this Man was, who now from earth remov'd, / At length enjoys that Liberty he lov'd" (11–12).

1. This poem incorporates elements of several old ballads and folk songs, a common practice of amalgamation at which Burns had great success.

15   And I will come again, my luve,
            Tho' it were ten thousand mile!

1794   1796

Auld Lang Syne

Should auld acquaintance be forgot,
    And never brought to mind?
Should auld acquaintance be forgot,
    And auld lang syne!°   *long ago times*

CHORUS

5   For auld lang syne, my dear,
                For auld lang syne,
            We'll tak a cup o' kindness yet
                For auld lang syne!

And surely ye'll be° your pint-stowp,°   *buy / pint-cup*
10   And surely I'll be mine,
And we'll tak a cup o' kindness yet
    For auld lang syne!

CHORUS

We twa hae run about the braes,°   *slopes*
    And pou'd° the gowans° fine,   *pulled / daisies*
15 But we've wander'd monie a weary fit°   *foot*
    Sin'° auld lang syne.   *since*

CHORUS

We twa hae paidl'd in the burn[1]
    Frae morning sun till dine,°   *dinner (noon)*
But seas between us braid° hae roar'd   *broad*
20   Sin' auld lang syne.

CHORUS

And there's a hand, my trusty fiere,°   *friend*
    And gie's a hand o' thine,
And we'll tak a right guid-willie waught°   *good-will swig*
    For auld lang syne!

CHORUS

25   For auld lang syne, my dear,
                For auld lang syne,
            We'll tak a cup o' kindness yet
                For auld lang syne!

1788   1796

The Fornicator. A New Song
Tune, Clout the Caldron

Ye jovial boys who love the joys
    The blissful joys of lovers;
Yet dare avow with dauntless brow,
    When the bony lass discovers:[1]

---

1. Stream; waters used for brewing. "Burns" would especially appreciate the double sense.

1. Reveals her pregnancy.

5 I pray draw near and lend an ear,
    And welcome in a Frater,°   *brother*
For I've lately been on quarantine,
    A proven Fornicator.

Before the Congregation wide
10   I pass'd the muster fairly,[2]
My handsome Betsey by my side,[3]
    We gat° our ditty° rarely;   *received / reproof*
But my downcast eye by chance did spy
    What made my lips to water,
15 Those limbs so clean where I, between
    Commenc'd a Fornicator.

With rueful face and signs of grace
    I pay'd the buttock-hire,[4]
The night was dark and thro the park
20   I could not but convoy her;
A parting kiss, what could I less,
    My vows began to scatter,
My Betsey fell—lal de dal lal lal,
    I am a Fornicator.

25 But for her sake this vow I make,
    And solemnly I swear it,
That while I own a single crown,
    She's welcome for to share it;
And my roguish boy his Mother's joy,
30   And the darling of his Pater,°   *father*
For him I boast my pains and cost,
    Although a Fornicator.

Ye wenching blades whose hireling jades[5]
    Have tipt you off blue-boram,[6]
35 I tell you plain, I do disdain
    To rank you in the Quorum;
But a bony lass upon the grass
    To teache her esse Mater,°   *to be a mother*
And no reward but for regard,
40   O that's a Fornicator.

Your warlike kings and heroes bold,
    Great Captains and Commanders;
Your mighty Cèsars fam'd of old,
    And Conquering Alexanders;
45 In fields they fought and laurels bought
    And bulwarks strong did batter,
But still they grac'd our noble list
    And ranked Fornicator!!!

1784–1785   1799

2. In the Scottish Church those found guilty of fornication were required to sit, clothed in black, for three successive Sundays on a raised "stool of repentance."
3. Usually taken as Elizabeth Paton, with whom Burns had an illegitimate child.
4. There was a six-pound fine for fornication.
5. Worn-out horses, a contemptuous term for women.
6. Infected you with syphilis. The term probably derives from the notorious Blue Boar Tavern in London.

———— ≍✦≍ ————

Thomas Moore
1779–1852

"Tommy loves a lord," Byron said of his friend and biographer. Thomas Moore was the Irish Catholic son of a grocer; he attended Trinity College, Dublin, and went to London in 1798 to study law. A translation of Anacreon, dedicated to the Prince of Wales, opened the doors of Whig society and fixed his career. His poetic success—lyrics and songs, seven volumes of satires, political lampoons in the newspapers—was inseparable from his genial presence as a wit and an accomplished singer. Appointed Admiralty Registrar at Bermuda in 1803, Moore soon transferred the work to a deputy and returned to the circles he loved; when the deputy embezzled and decamped in 1818, Moore was responsible for the debt and had to quit England for four years. His fame was by then secure, partly for *Lalla Rookh* (1817), an oriental romance for which his publisher paid £3,000, at the time the highest sum ever paid for a single work, and still more for his *Irish Melodies,* which began to appear in 1807. Set to traditional airs or to his own compositions, Moore's lyrics became a staple of nineteenth-century musical evenings and were enthusiastically recommended by James Joyce to his singer son. If Hazlitt thought Moore converted "the wild harp of Erin into a musical snuffbox," the Tory press was alert to the "rebel words" of a work such as *The harp that once through Tara's halls* and denounced the charm of the *Melodies* as "a vehicle of dangerous politics."

The harp that once through Tara's halls[1]

The harp that once through Tara's halls
    The soul of music shed,
Now hangs as mute on Tara's walls,
    As if that soul were fled.—
5   So sleeps the pride of former days,
        So glory's thrill is o'er,
And hearts, that once beat high for praise,
        Now feel that pulse no more.

No more to chiefs and ladies bright
10   The harp of Tara swells;
The chord alone, that breaks at night,
    Its tale of ruin tells.
Thus Freedom now so seldom wakes,
    The only throb she gives,
15   Is when some heart indignant breaks,
    To show that still she lives.

    1834

Believe me, if all those endearing young charms

Believe me, if all those endearing young charms,
    Which I gaze on so fondly to-day,
Were to change by to-morrow, and fleet in my arms,
    Like fairy-gifts fading away,

---

1. Tara was the ancient seat of the high kings of Ireland, northwest of Dublin.

5 Thou wouldst still be adored, as this moment thou art,
    Let thy loveliness fade as it will,
And around the dear ruin each wish of my heart
    Would entwine itself verdantly still.

It is not while beauty and youth are thine own,
10   And thy cheeks unprofaned by a tear
That the fervor and faith of a soul can be known,
    To which time will but make thee more dear;
No, the heart that has truly loved never forgets,
    But as truly loves on to the close,
15 As the sun-flower turns on her god, when he sets,
    The same look which she turn'd when he rose.[1]

1822

The time I've lost in wooing

The time I've lost in wooing,
In watching and pursuing
    The light, that lies
    In woman's eyes,
5 Has been my heart's undoing.
Though Wisdom oft has sought me,
I scorn'd the lore she brought me,
    My only books
    Were woman's looks,
10 And folly's all they've taught me.

Her smile when Beauty granted,
I hung with gaze enchanted,
    Like him the sprite,
    Whom maids by night
15 Oft meet in glen that's haunted.
Like him, too, Beauty won me,[1]
But while her eyes were on me,
    If once their ray
    Was turn'd away,
20 O! winds could not outrun me.

And are those follies going?
And is my proud heart growing
    Too cold or wise
    For brilliant eyes
25 Again to set it glowing?
No, vain, alas! th' endeavor
From bonds so sweet to sever;
    Poor Wisdom's chance
    Against a glance
30 Is now as weak as ever.

1834

[END OF LITERARY BALLADS]

1. The sunflower is a heliotrope.

1. According to legend, the Irish sprite (fairy) could be mastered by the fixed gaze of a mortal.

✦ ⟐ ✦

William Wordsworth
1770–1850

Meeting Wordsworth in 1815, Byron told his wife that he had "but one feeling . . . reverence!" The exemplar of "plain living and high thinking," Wordsworth provided an image of poetry and "the Poet" as at once humble and exalted, domestic and severely moral. By the end of his life he had become a cultural institution, respected even by those who opposed his politics. Admirers made pilgrimages to his home at Rydal Mount in the Lake District. His beginnings were less auspicious. Born in the beautiful, isolated Lake District, Wordsworth was the son of the steward of Lord Lonsdale (James Lowther), the dominant landowner. The death of Wordsworth's mother when he was eight years old broke a stable middle-class family life; William and his three brothers were sent to Hawkshead to school, and his sister Dorothy was sent to live with various distant relatives. His father died five years later, and Lord Lonsdale resisted paying monies owed; the children did not receive their due until 1802, when a new Lord Lonsdale, who became Wordsworth's patron, succeeded to the title. "The props of my affection were removed, / And yet the building stood," Wordsworth exclaimed in a passage of *The Prelude* that seems to refer to these early losses and separations; "taught to feel, perhaps too much, / The self-sufficing power of Solitude," Wordsworth developed a potent myth of himself as a "favoured being" shaped by the severe but mysteriously benevolent ministry of Nature.

In 1787 Wordsworth entered St. John's College, Cambridge, taking his degree in 1791 without distinction. As his autobiographical poem *The Prelude* testifies, his travels left deeper impressions than his studies: a summer walking tour in 1790 that brought him to France a year after the fall of the Bastille, a trip through North Wales in 1791, and a year-long stay in France (1791–1792). There he became an active partisan in the heady early phase of the Revolution. "Bliss was it in that dawn to be alive, / But to be young was very Heaven!" he wrote in *The Prelude*. The millenarian hopes of a new era were suffused with personal attachments: he had a love affair with Annette Vallon, who bore their daughter in December 1792. By then, lack of funds had forced him back to England, and the English declaration of war against France precluded his return until 1802. In him as in many of his generation, the war produced a crisis of loyalties, aggravated by the increasing violence of revolutionary France. "Sick, wearied out with contrarieties," Wordsworth recovered "a saving intercourse with [his] true self" only through the struggles that his poetry records.

A turning point came in 1795, when a small legacy of £900 from a friend enabled Wordsworth to devote himself to poetry. He reunited with Dorothy, and met Coleridge; in 1797 brother and sister moved to Alfoxden, to be near Coleridge at Nether Stowey. "[B]uoyant spirits / . . . were our daily portion when we first / Together wantoned in wild poesy," Wordsworth later wrote; comfortably housed, free to wander the countryside, Wordsworth and Coleridge collaborated on the poems that became *Lyrical Ballads*, published anonymously in 1798 to mixed reviews. The strangeness of *The Rime of the Ancyent Marinere* disconcerted some readers, and the audacious simplicity of Wordsworth's subjects and style offended more. But others felt the "power and pathos" of the poetry, even (in Hazlitt's words) "the sense of a new style and a new spirit." In 1800 Wordsworth published a second edition under his own name, adding a volume containing *Michael* and the "Lucy" poems and others written during the cold and lonely winter that he and Dorothy had passed in Germany between 1798 and 1799. A new Preface, defending his principles and repudiating the expectations of his readers, set the terms of his reception and continued to govern the charges against him by critics such as Francis Jeffrey for decades afterward.

In late 1799 William and Dorothy returned to the Lakes and settled in the beautiful Grasmere valley, where they remained together for the rest of their lives: first at Dove Cottage, then, after 1813, at the more spacious Rydal Mount. In 1802 their household had expanded when Wordsworth married a childhood friend, and the tenor of their life was steady thereafter, though the years were marred by grave losses—his brother John drowned in 1805, when the ship he captained went down in a storm, two of his five children died in 1812, and a rift with Coleridge was not patched up until the 1820s. Harsh reviews of *Poems, in Two Volumes* (1807) and *The Excursion* (1814) paradoxically attested to Wordsworth's emerging centrality, and the publication of his revised and reordered *Poems* in 1815 asserted his claim to enter the canon of English poetry. Wordsworth continued to write and publish almost to the end of his long life. Though his increasingly conservative politics led some of the next generation to regard him as having betrayed his republican youth, and put him in opposition to the democratic and commercializing spirit of post-Reform Bill England, his reputation grew steadily, and in 1843 he was appointed Poet Laureate.

The Prelude, the poem that has most compelled modern readers, was published posthumously. Wordsworth had held back the work ("Title not yet fixed upon") that he had referred to variously as "the poem to Coleridge," "the poem on the growth of my own mind," and "the poem on my own poetical education," in part because he thought it "unprecedented" that an author should talk so much about himself, in part so as to bequeath its copyright as a legacy to his family. Reserving his most intimate and ambitious poem while revising it across four decades must have affected his often touchy attitude to his critics; by the time *The Prelude* appeared in 1850, the same year as Tennyson's *In Memoriam*, not even the "jacobinical" strain that Thomas Macaulay detected could much alter the image of him. For the Victorians, Wordsworth was the poet of nature, whose writings made the Lake District a tourist spot (much to his disgruntlement) and provided a moral philosophy of life, of childhood and "joy in widest commonalty spread," and above all, of memory and consolation. It was chiefly Wordsworth's "healing power" that led Matthew Arnold to declare in 1879 that Wordsworth stood third only to Milton and Shakespeare in English poetry since the Renaissance. Twentieth-century readers have been captivated by the visionary power of his language, those transient moments when "forms and substances . . . through the turnings intricate of verse, / Present themselves as objects recognized, / In flashes, and with a glory scarce their own." In Wordsworth's sustained effort in *The Prelude* to trace the growth of his mind while attending to experiences lying beyond and beneath the rational mind's grasp— "Points have we all of us within our souls / Where all stand single; this I feel, and make / Breathings for incommunicable powers"—some critics have discerned the beginnings of modern subjectivity. For Geoffrey Hartman, Wordsworth is "the most isolated figure among the great English poets." Other readers, though, have found in the tensions and ambivalences of Wordsworth's project a particularly rich embodiment of the strains of the pivotal decades in which he wrote, and he remains a crucial focus for understanding the vivid and contradictory currents of his age.

Other writing by Wordsworth appears in Perspectives: The Abolition of Slavery and the Slave Trade, page 283, and in Felicia Hemans: Responses page 960.

LYRICAL BALLADS

In spring 1798 the young Wordsworth and Coleridge had been near neighbors in Somerset for almost a year. In the fall of 1797, they had decided to pay for a brief walking tour by collaborating on a poem to be sold to the *Monthly Magazine*. Uncompleted at the time, *The Rime of the Ancyent Marinere* became the opening poem of a more substantial enterprise: *Lyrical Ballads, with a few other poems*, the joint collection they published anonymously in October 1798. The exchange that nourished the project had been so close that Coleridge said that the two poets regarded the volume as "one work, in kind, though not in degree, as an ode is one work; and that our different poems are stanzas, good, relatively rather than absolutely," though of the twenty-three poems he wrote only four. A friend, Bristol bookseller Joseph Cottle, agreed to pay the poets £30 for the copyright; before the book appeared they had departed for Germany, Coleridge to study philosophy at Göttingen and Wordsworth to learn German at Goslar, in hopes of later earning money as a translator. Priced at five shillings, the volume sold steadily and earned favorable reviews, but the simplicity of style, the focus on rural life and language, and the obscurity of the *Ancyent Marinere* provoked memorably sharp criticism. The volume had been prefixed by an Advertisement describing the majority of the poems as "experiments" to "ascertain how far the language of conversation in the middle and lower classes of society is adapted to the purposes of poetic pleasure." Attacking "the gaudiness and inane phraseology of many modern writers," and anticipating that "readers of superior judgment" would find that many of the poems would not "suit their taste," the Advertisement deliberately positioned the volume as an affront to "pre-established codes of decision," and thereby claimed for its authors the status of innovators.

Returning from Germany in 1800 to live in the Lake District, Wordsworth planned a second edition, which he sold to Longman, an established London publisher. He now dominated the project: the collection was published under his name alone, and the Advertisement was replaced by a long Preface vindicating his principles. A new second volume was made up entirely of his poems; the *Ancyent Marinere* was retitled *The Ancient Mariner: A Poet's Reverie*, and moved from the head of the first volume to the twenty-third position, with a condescending note ("The Poem of my Friend has indeed great defects"). The collection sold quickly, and a revised edition appeared in 1802 with a significant addition to the Preface, "What is a poet?" The harsh critique by Francis Jeffrey in the newly founded *Edinburgh Review* (page 468) might have been welcome notoriety; it surely helped propel the final edition of *Lyrical Ballads* in 1805, after which the contents were dispersed among the author's separate publications. Years later, in 1843, Wordsworth dictated notes on the circumstances of the poems' composition to Isabella Fenwick, indicated here by "[I.F.]."

from Lyrical Ballads (1798)

Simon Lee[1]
The Old Huntsman, with an incident in which he was concerned.

In the sweet shire of Cardigan,
Not far from pleasant Ivor-hall,
An old man dwells, a little man,
I've heard he once was tall.
5   Of years he has upon his back,

---

1. "This old man had been huntsman to the squires of Alfoxden. . . . The old man's cottage stood upon the common, a little way from the entrance to Alfoxden Park. . . . I have, after an interval of 45 years, the image of the old man as fresh before my eyes as if I had seen him yesterday" [I.F.]. Wordsworth relocated the site from Somersetshire, where he and his sister Dorothy lived from 1797 to 1798, to Cardiganshire, a former county of southwest Wales. A huntsman manages the hunt and has charge of the hounds. In the Preface, Wordsworth said that he wrote the poem to place the reader "in the way of receiving from ordinary moral sensations another and more salutary impression than we are accustomed to receive from them."

No doubt, a burthen weighty;
He says he is three score and ten,°   *seventy years old*
But others say he's eighty.

A long blue livery-coat° has he,   *servant's uniform*
10 That's fair behind, and fair before;
Yet, meet him where you will, you see
At once that he is poor.
Full five and twenty years he lived
A running huntsman merry;
15 And, though he has but one eye left,
His cheek is like a cherry.

No man like him the horn could sound,
And no man was so full of glee;
To say the least, four counties round
20 Had heard of Simon Lee;
His master's dead, and no one now
Dwells in the hall of Ivor;
Men, dogs, and horses, all are dead;
He is the sole survivor.

25 His hunting feats have him bereft
Of his right eye, as you may see:
And then, what limbs those feats have left
To poor old Simon Lee!
He has no son, he has no child,
30 His wife, an aged woman,
Lives with him, near the waterfall,
Upon the village common.[2]

And he is lean and he is sick,
His little body's half awry
35 His ancles they are swoln and thick;
His legs are thin and dry.
When he was young he little knew
Of husbandry or tillage;
And now he's forced to work, though weak,
40 —The weakest in the village.

He all the country could outrun,
Could leave both man and horse behind;
And often, ere the race was done,
He reeled and was stone-blind.
45 And still there's something in the world
At which his heart rejoices;

---

2. Common lands were progressively being enclosed as private property. Wordsworth successfully fought the enclosure of Grasmere's commons.

For when the chiming hounds are out,
He dearly loves their voices![3]

Old Ruth works out of doors with him,
50   And does what Simon cannot do;
For she, not over stout° of limb,   *hardy*
Is stouter of the two.
And though you with your utmost skill
From labour could not wean them,
55   Alas! 'tis very little, all
Which they can do between them.

Beside their moss-grown hut of clay,
Not twenty paces from the door,
A scrap of land they have, but they
60   Are poorest of the poor.
This scrap of land he from the heath
Enclosed when he was stronger;
But what avails the land to them,
Which they can till no longer?

65   Few months of life has he in store,
As he to you will tell,
For still, the more he works, the more
His poor old ancles swell.
My gentle reader, I perceive
70   How patiently you've waited,
And I'm afraid that you expect
Some tale will be related.

O reader! had you in your mind
Such stores as silent thought can bring,
75   O gentle° reader! you would find   *kind, well-born*
A tale in every thing.
What more I have to say is short,
I hope you'll kindly take it;
It is no tale; but should you think,
80   Perhaps a tale you'll make it.

One summer-day I chanced to see
This old man doing all he could
About the root of an old tree,
A stump of rotten wood.
85   The mattock° totter'd in his hand;   *pick-ax*
So vain was his endeavour
That at the root of the old tree
He might have worked for ever.

"You're overtasked, good Simon Lee,
90   Give me your tool" to him I said;
And at the word right gladly he

---

3. "The expression when the hounds were out, 'I dearly love their voices,' was word for word from his own lips" [I.F.].

Received my proffer'd aid.
I struck, and with a single blow
The tangled root I sever'd,
95   At which the poor old man so long
And vainly had endeavour'd.

The tears into his eyes were brought,
And thanks and praises seemed to run
So fast out of his heart, I thought
100   They never would have done.
—I've heard of hearts unkind, kind deeds
With coldness still returning.
Alas! the gratitude of men
Has oftner left me mourning.

1798   1798

Anecdote for Fathers,
shewing how the art of lying may be taught

I have a boy of five years old,
His face is fair and fresh to see;
His limbs are cast in beauty's mould,
And dearly he loves me.

5   One morn we stroll'd on our dry walk,
Our quiet house all full in view,
And held such intermitted talk
As we are wont to do.

My thoughts on former pleasures ran;
10   I thought of Kilve's delightful shore,
My pleasant home, when spring began,
A long, long year before.

A day it was when I could bear
To think, and think, and think again;
15   With so much happiness to spare,
I could not feel a pain.

My boy was by my side, so slim
And graceful in his rustic dress!
And oftentimes I talked to him,
20   In very idleness.

The young lambs ran a pretty race;
The morning sun shone bright and warm;
"Kilve," said I, "was a pleasant place,
And so is Liswyn farm."

25   "My little boy, which like you more,"
I said and took him by the arm—
"Our home by Kilve's delightful shore,
Or here at Liswyn farm?"

"And tell me, had you rather be,"
30   I said and held him by the arm,
"At Kilve's smooth shore by the green sea,
Or here at Liswyn farm?"

In careless mood he looked at me,
While still I held him by the arm,
35   And said, "At Kilve I'd rather be
Than here at Liswyn farm."

"Now, little Edward, say why so;
My little Edward, tell me why";
"I cannot tell, I do not know."
40   "Why this is strange," said I.

"For, here are woods and green-hills warm;
There surely must some reason be
Why you would change sweet Liswyn farm
For Kilve by the green sea."

45   At this, my boy, so fair and slim,
Hung down his head, nor made reply;
And five times did I say to him,
"Why? Edward, tell me why?"

His head he raised—there was in sight,
50   It caught his eye, he saw it plain—
Upon the house-top, glittering bright,
A broad and gilded vane.

Then did the boy his tongue unlock,
And thus to me he made reply;
55   "At Kilve there was no weather-cock,
And that's the reason why."

Oh dearest, dearest boy! my heart
For better lore would seldom yearn,
Could I but teach the hundredth part
60   Of what from thee I learn.

We are seven[1]

A simple child, dear brother Jim,
That lightly draws its breath,
And feels its life in every limb,
What should it know of death?

---

1. "The little girl who is the heroine I met within the area of Goodrich Castle in the year 1793. . . . I composed it while walking in the grove at Alfoxden. My friends will not deem it too trifling to relate that while walking to and fro I composed the last stanza first having begun with the last line" [I.F.]. In the Preface Wordsworth pointed to this poem as "shewing . . . the perplexity and obscurity which in childhood attend our notion of death, or rather our utter inability to admit that notion." Wordsworth's mother died when he was turning eight, the age of the girl in the poem. Coleridge wrote the first stanza.

5   I met a little cottage girl,
She was eight years old, she said;
Her hair was thick with many a curl
That cluster'd round her head.

She had a rustic, woodland air,
10   And she was wildly clad;
Her eyes were fair, and very fair,
—Her beauty made me glad.

"Sisters and brothers, little maid,
How many may you be?"
15   "How many? seven in all," she said,
And wondering looked at me.

"And where are they, I pray you tell?"
She answered, "Seven are we,
And two of us at Conway° dwell,   *Welsh seaport*
20   And two are gone to sea.

"Two of us in the church-yard lie,
My sister and my brother,
And in the church-yard cottage, I
Dwell near them with my mother."

25   "You say that two at Conway dwell,
And two are gone to sea,
Yet you are seven; I pray you tell
Sweet Maid, how this may be?"

Then did the little Maid reply,
30   "Seven boys and girls are we;
Two of us in the church-yard lie,
Beneath the church-yard tree."

"You run about, my little Maid,
Your limbs they are alive;
35   If two are in the church-yard laid,
Then ye are only five."

"Their graves are green, they may be seen,"
The little Maid replied,
"Twelve steps or more from my mother's door,
40   And they are side by side.

"My stockings there I often knit,
My 'kerchief there I hem;
And there upon the ground I sit—
I sit and sing to them.

45   "And often after sunset, Sir,
When it is light and fair,
I take my little porringer,°   *porridge-bowl*
And eat my supper there.

"The first that died was little Jane;
50   In bed she moaning lay,
Till God released her of her pain,
And then she went away.

"So in the church-yard was she laid;
And all the summer dry,
55   Together round her grave we played,
My brother John and I.

"And when the ground was white with snow,
And I could run and slide,
My brother John was forced to go,
60   And he lies by her side."

"How many are you then," said I,
"If they two are in Heaven?"
The little Maiden did reply,
"O Master! we are seven."

65   "But they are dead; those two are dead!
Their spirits are in heaven!"
'Twas throwing words away; for still
The little Maid would have her will,
And said, "Nay, we are seven!"

1798   1798

Lines written in early spring

I heard a thousand blended notes,
While in a grove I sate reclined,
In that sweet mood when pleasant thoughts
Bring sad thoughts to the mind.

5   To her fair works did nature link
The human soul that through me ran;
And much it griev'd my heart to think
What man has made of man.

Through primrose-tufts, in that sweet bower,
10   The periwinkle trail'd its wreathes;
And 'tis my faith that every flower
Enjoys the air it breathes.

The birds around me hopp'd and play'd:
Their thoughts I cannot measure,°   assess; put in meters
15   But the least motion which they made,
It seem'd a thrill of pleasure.

The budding twigs spread out their fan,
To catch the breezy air;
And I must think, do all I can,
20   That there was pleasure there.

If I these thoughts may not prevent,
If such be of my creed the plan,
Have I not reason to lament
What man has made of man?

1798   1798

The Thorn[1]

I

There is a thorn; it looks so old,
In truth you'd find it hard to say,
How it could ever have been young,
It looks so old and grey.
5   Not higher than a two-years' child,
It stands erect this aged thorn;
No leaves it has, no thorny points;
It is a mass of knotted joints,
A wretched thing forlorn.
10   It stands erect, and like a stone
With lichens it is overgrown.

II

Like rock or stone, it is o'ergrown
With lichens to the very top,
And hung with heavy tufts of moss,
15   A melancholy crop:
Up from the earth these mosses creep,
And this poor thorn they clasp it round
So close, you'd say that they were bent
With plain and manifest intent,
20   To drag it to the ground;
And all had joined in one endeavour
To bury this poor thorn for ever.

III

High on a mountain's highest ridge,
Where oft the stormy winter gale
25   Cuts like a scythe, while through the clouds
It sweeps from vale to vale;
Not five yards from the mountain-path,
This thorn you on your left espy;
And to the left, three yards beyond,

---

1. "Arose out of my observing, on the ridge of Quantock Hill, on a Stormy day, a thorn [bush] which I had often passed in calm and bright weather without noticing it. I said to myself, 'Cannot I by some invention do as much to make this Thorn permanently an impressive object as the storm has made it to my eyes at this moment?' I began the poem accordingly, and composed it with great rapidity" [I.F.]. In the Advertisement (brief preface) of 1798, Wordsworth says that this poem "is not supposed to be spoken in the author's own person," but in "the character of a loquacious narrator"—a kind of dramatic monologue. Wordsworth was also influenced by a translation of a German ballad by Bürger that appeared in *The Monthly Magazine* in 1796, *The Lass of Fair Wone*. This is the only poem in the volume marked by roman-numbered stanzas.

30   You see a little muddy pond
        Of water, never dry;
        I've measured it from side to side:
        'Tis three feet long, and two feet wide.

                        IV
        And close beside this aged thorn,
35   There is a fresh and lovely sight,
        A beauteous heap, a hill of moss,
        Just half a foot in height.
        All lovely colours there you see,
        All colours that were ever seen,
40   And mossy network too is there,
        As if by hand of lady fair
        The work had woven been,
        And cups,° the darlings of the eye,   *blossoms*
        So deep is their vermilion dye.

                        V
45   Ah me! what lovely tints are there!
        Of olive-green and scarlet bright,
        In spikes, in branches, and in stars,
        Green, red, and pearly white.
        This heap of earth o'ergrown with moss,
50   Which close beside the thorn you see,
        So fresh in all its beauteous dyes,
        Is like an infant's grave in size
        As like as like can be:
        But never, never any where,
55   An infant's grave was half so fair.

                        VI
        Now would you see this aged thorn,
        This pond and beauteous hill of moss,
        You must take care and chuse your time
        The mountain when to cross.
60   For oft there sits, between the heap
        That's like an infant's grave in size,
        And that same pond of which I spoke,
        A woman in a scarlet cloak,
        And to herself she cries,
65   "Oh misery! oh misery!
        Oh woe is me! oh misery!"

                        VII
        At all times of the day and night
        This wretched woman thither goes,
        And she is known to every star,
70   And every wind that blows;
        And there beside the thorn she sits
        When the blue day-light's in the skies,

And when the whirlwind's on the hill,
Or frosty air is keen and still,
75   And to herself she cries,
"Oh misery! oh misery!
Oh woe is me! oh misery!"

VIII

"Now wherefore thus, by day and night,
In rain, in tempest, and in snow,
80   Thus to the dreary mountain-top
Does this poor woman go?
And why sits she beside the thorn
When the blue day-light's in the sky,
Or when the whirlwind's on the hill,
85   Or frosty air is keen and still,
And wherefore does she cry?
Oh wherefore? wherefore? tell me why
Does she repeat that doleful cry?"

IX

I cannot tell; I wish I could;
90   For the true reason no one knows,
But if you'd gladly view the spot,
The spot to which she goes;
The heap that's like an infant's grave,
The pond—and thorn, so old and grey,
95   Pass by her door—'tis seldom shut—
And if you see her in her hut,
Then to the spot away!—
I never heard of such as dare
Approach the spot when she is there.

X

100   "But wherefore to the mountain-top
Can this unhappy woman go,
Whatever star is in the skies,
Whatever wind may blow?"
Nay rack your brain—'tis all in vain,
105   I'll tell you every thing I know;
But to the thorn, and to the pond
Which is a little step beyond,
I wish that you would go:
Perhaps when you are at the place
110   You something of her tale may trace.

XI

I'll give you the best help I can:
Before you up the mountain go,
Up to the dreary mountain-top,
I'll tell you all I know.
115   'Tis now some two and twenty years,

Since she (her name is Martha Ray[2])
Gave with a maiden's true good will
Her company to Stephen Hill;
And she was blithe and gay,
120   And she was happy, happy still
Whene'er she thought of Stephen Hill.

XII
And they had fix'd the wedding-day,
The morning that must wed them both;
But Stephen to another maid
125   Had sworn another oath;
And with this other maid to church
Unthinking Stephen went—
Poor Martha! on that woful day
A cruel, cruel fire, they say,
130   Into her bones was sent:
It dried her body like a cinder,
And almost turn'd her brain to tinder.

XIII
They say, full six months after this,
While yet the summer-leaves were green,
135   She to the mountain-top would go,
And there was often seen.
'Tis said, a child was in her womb,
As now to any eye was plain;
She was with child, and she was mad,
140   Yet often she was sober sad
From her exceeding pain.
Oh me! ten thousand times I'd rather
That he had died, that cruel father!

XIV
Sad case for such a brain to hold
145   Communion with a stirring child!
Sad case, as you may think, for one
Who had a brain so wild!
Last Christmas when we talked of this,
Old Farmer Simpson did maintain,
150   That in her womb the infant wrought
About its mother's heart, and brought
Her senses back again:
And when at last her time drew near,
Her looks were calm, her senses clear.

2. The father of Basil Montagu, Wordsworth's companion on the stormy day he noticed the thorn, was the illegitimate son of Lord Sandwich and actress Martha Ray. She was shot by a rejected suitor while leaving Covent Garden Theatre in 1779; a sensational murder trial followed.

XV

155 No more I know, I wish I did,
And I would tell it all to you;
For what became of this poor child
There's none that ever knew:
And if a child was born or no,
160 There's no one that could ever tell;
And if 'twas born alive or dead,
There's no one knows, as I have said,
But some remember well,
That Martha Ray about this time
165 Would up the mountain often climb.

XVI

And all that winter, when at night
The wind blew from the mountain-peak,
'Twas worth your while, though in the dark,
The church-yard path to seek:
170 For many a time and oft were heard
Cries coming from the mountain-head,
Some plainly living voices were,
And others, I've heard many swear,
Were voices of the dead:
175 I cannot think, whate'er they say,
They had to do with Martha Ray.

XVII

But that she goes to this old thorn,
The thorn which I've described to you,
And there sits in a scarlet cloak,
180 I will be sworn is true.
For one day with my telescope,
To view the ocean wide and bright,
When to this country first I came,
Ere I had heard of Martha's name,
185 I climbed the mountain's height:
A storm came on, and I could see
No object higher than my knee.

XVIII

'Twas mist and rain, and storm and rain,
No screen, no fence could I discover,
190 And then the wind! in faith, it was
A wind full ten times over.
I looked around, I thought I saw
A jutting crag, and off I ran,
Head-foremost, through the driving rain,
195 The shelter of the crag to gain,
And, as I am a man,
Instead of jutting crag, I found
A woman seated on the ground.

XIX

I did not speak—I saw her face,
200 Her face it was enough for me;
I turned about and heard her cry,
"O misery! O misery!"
And there she sits, until the moon
Through half the clear blue sky will go,
205 And when the little breezes make
The waters of the pond to shake,
As all the country know,
She shudders and you hear her cry,
"Oh misery! oh misery!"

XX

210 "But what's the thorn? and what's the pond?
And what's the hill of moss to her?
And what's the creeping breeze that comes
The little pond to stir?"
I cannot tell; but some will say
215 She hanged her baby on the tree,
Some say she drowned it in the pond,
Which is a little step beyond,
But all and each agree,
The little babe was buried there,
220 Beneath that hill of moss so fair.

XXI

I've heard the scarlet moss is red
With drops of that poor infant's blood;
But kill a new-born infant thus!
I do not think she could.
225 Some say, if to the pond you go,
And fix on it a steady view,
The shadow of a babe you trace,
A baby and a baby's face,
And that it looks at you;
230 Whene'er you look on it, 'tis plain
The baby looks at you again.

XXII

And some had sworn an oath that she
Should be to public justice brought;
And for the little infant's bones
235 With spades they would have sought.
But then the beauteous hill of moss
Before their eyes began to stir;
And for full fifty yards around,
The grass it shook upon the ground;
240 But all do still aver
The little babe is buried there,
Beneath that hill of moss so fair.

XXIII

I cannot tell how this may be,
But plain it is, the thorn is bound
245 With heavy tufts of moss, that strive
To drag it to the ground.
And this I know, full many a time,
When she was on the mountain high,
By day, and in the silent night,
250 When all the stars shone clear and bright,
That I have heard her cry,
"Oh misery! oh misery!
O woe is me! oh misery!"

1798   1798

Note to *The Thorn*[1]

This Poem ought to have been preceded by an introductory Poem, which I have been prevented from writing by never having felt myself in a mood when it was probable that I should write it well.—The character which I have here introduced speaking is sufficiently common. The Reader will perhaps have a general notion of it, if he has ever known a man, a Captain of a small trading vessel for example, who being past the middle age of life, had retired upon an annuity or small independent income to some village or country town of which he was not a native, or in which he had not been accustomed to live. Such men having little to do become credulous and talkative from indolence; and from the same cause, and other predisposing causes by which it is probable that such men may have been affected, they are prone to superstition. On which account it appeared to me proper to select a character like this to exhibit some of the general laws by which superstition acts upon the mind. Superstitious men are almost always men of slow faculties and deep feelings; their minds are not loose, but adhesive; they have a reasonable share of imagination, by which word I mean the faculty which produces impressive effects out of simple elements; but they are utterly destitute of fancy, the power by which pleasure and surprise are excited by sudden varieties of situation and by accumulated imagery.

It was my wish in this poem to show the manner in which such men cleave to the same ideas; and to follow the turns of passion, always different, yet not palpably different, by which their conversation is swayed. I had two objects to attain; first, to represent a picture which should not be unimpressive yet consistent with the character that should describe it, secondly, while I adhered to the style in which such persons describe, to take care that words, which in their minds are impregnated with passion, should likewise convey passion to Readers who are not accustomed to sympathize with men feeling in that manner or using such language. It seemed to me that this might be done by calling in the assistance of Lyrical and rapid Metre.[2] It was necessary that the Poem, to be natural, should in reality move slowly; yet I hoped, that, by the aid of the metre, to those who should at all enter into the spirit of the Poem, it would appear to move quickly. The Reader will have the kindness to excuse this note as I am sensible that an introductory Poem is necessary to give this Poem its full effect.

---

1. To answer his critics, Wordsworth put this note in   2. Chiefly iambic tetrameter.
Lyrical Ballads (1800), and thereafter.

Upon this occasion I will request permission to add a few words closely connected with "The Thorn" and many other Poems in these volumes. There is a numerous class of readers who imagine that the same words cannot be repeated without tautology:[3] this is a great error: virtual tautology is much oftener produced by using different words when the meaning is exactly the same. Words, a Poet's words more particularly, ought to be weighed in the balance of feeling and not measured by the space which they occupy on paper. For the Reader cannot be too often reminded that Poetry is passion: it is the history or science of feelings; now every man must know that an attempt is rarely made to communicate impassioned feelings without something of an accompanying consciousness of the inadequateness of our own powers, or the deficiencies of language. During such efforts there will be a craving in the mind, and as long as it is unsatisfied the Speaker will cling to the same words, or words of the same character. There are also various other reasons why repetition and apparent tautology are frequently beauties of the highest kind. Among the chief of these reasons is the interest which the mind attaches to words, not only as symbols of the passion, but as *things*, active and efficient,[4] which are of themselves part of the passion. And further, from a spirit of fondness, exultation, and gratitude, the mind luxuriates in the repetition of words which appear successfully to communicate the feelings. The truth of these remarks might be shown by innumerable passages from the Bible and from the impassioned poetry of every nation.

"Awake, awake Deborah: awake, awake, utter a song: arise Barak, and lead thy captivity captive, thou son of Abinoam.

At her feet he bowed, he fell, he lay down: at her feet he bowed, he fell; where he bowed, there he fell down dead. Why is his chariot so long in coming? Why tarry the wheels of his chariot?"—*Judges*, chap. 5th, Verses 12th, 27th, and part of 28th.—[5] See also the whole of that tumultuous and wonderful Poem.

Expostulation and Reply[1]

"Why William, on that old grey stone,
Thus for the length of half a day,
Why William, sit you thus alone,
And dream your time away?

5   "Where are your books? that light bequeath'd
To beings else forlorn and blind!
Up! Up! and drink the spirit breath'd
From dead men to their kind.

You look round on your mother earth,
10   As if she for no purpose bore you;
As if you were her first-born birth,
And none had lived before you!"

---

3. Needless repetition.
4. Producing effects.
5. Jael has murdered an enemy general.
1. This and the next poem opened the 1800 *Lyrical Ballads*. The companion pieces, Wordsworth said, "arose out of a conversation with a friend who was somewhat unrea-

sonably attached to modern books of Moral Philosophy" ("Advertisement," 1798)—probably William Hazlitt, who visited in 1798 and argued about metaphysics; see Hazlitt's recollection, page 1111. Wordsworth later noted this poem's popularity with Quakers, whose worship is informal and spontaneous.

One morning thus, by Esthwaite lake,[2]
When life was sweet I knew not why,
15   To me my good friend Matthew spake,
And thus I made reply.

"The eye it cannot chuse but see,
We cannot bid the ear be still;
Our bodies feel, where'er they be,
20   Against, or with our will.

"Nor less I deem that there are powers,
Which of themselves our minds impress,
That we can feed this mind of ours,
In a wise passiveness.

25   "Think you, mid all this mighty sum
Of things for ever speaking,
That nothing of itself will come,
But we must still be seeking?

"—Then ask not wherefore, here, alone,
30   Conversing as I may,
I sit upon this old grey stone,
And dream my time away."

1798   1798

The Tables Turned
An Evening Scene, on the Same Subject

Up! up! my friend, and clear your looks,
Why all this toil and trouble?[1]
Up! up! my friend, and quit your books,
Or surely you'll grow double.°   *doubled over*

5   The sun above the mountain's head,
A freshening lustre mellow,
Through all the long green fields has spread,
His first sweet evening yellow.

Books! 'tis a dull and endless strife,
10   Come, hear the woodland linnet,°   *finch*
How sweet his music; on my life
There's more of wisdom in it.

And hark! how blithe the throstle° sings!   *thrush*
And he is no mean preacher;
15   Come forth into the light of things,
Let Nature be your teacher.

---

2. At Hawkshead, where Wordsworth went to school.   1. A joking reference to the witches' incantation in *Macbeth* (4.1.10).

She has a world of ready wealth,
Our minds and hearts to bless—
Spontaneous wisdom breathed by health,
20   Truth breathed by chearfulness.

One impulse from a vernal wood
May teach you more of man;
Of moral evil and of good,
Than all the sages can.

25   Sweet is the lore which nature brings;
Our meddling intellect
Misshapes the beauteous forms of things;
—We murder to dissect.

Enough of science and of art;°   *liberal arts*
30   Close up these barren leaves;°   *pages*
Come forth, and bring with you a heart
That watches and receives.

1798   1798

Old Man Travelling;

ANIMAL TRANQUILITY AND DECAY,[1]
A SKETCH

The little hedge-row birds,
That peck along the road, regard him not.
He travels on, and in his face, his step,
His gait, is one expression; every limb,
5   His look and bending figure, all bespeak
A man who does not move with pain, but moves
With thought—He is insensibly subdued
To settled quiet: he is one by whom
All effort seems forgotten, one to whom
10   Long patience has such mild composure given,
That patience now doth seem a thing, of which
He hath no need. He is by nature led
To peace so perfect, that the young behold
With envy, what the old man hardly feels.[2]
15   —I asked him whither he was bound, and what
The object of his journey; he replied
"Sir! I am going many miles to take
A last leave of my son, a mariner,

1. In 1800 the main title was discarded. "Animal" involves two nearly antithetical senses: mere physical existences; spiritually "animated" life. In the Preface Wordsworth includes the poem among those describing "characters under the influence of less impassioned feelings...characters of which the elements are simple, belonging rather to nature than to manners, such as exist now, and will probably always exist, and from which their constitution may be distinctly and profitably contemplated."
2. Lines 15–20 were dropped in 1815 and after. The subtitle "A Sketch" was dropped in 1845.

Who from a sea-fight has been brought to Falmouth,[3]
20   And there is dying in an hospital."

1798   1798

TINTERN ABBEY "No poem of mine was composed under circumstances more pleasant for me to remember than this. I began it upon leaving Tintern, after crossing the Wye, and concluded it just as I was entering Bristol in the evening, after a ramble of 4 or 5 days, with my sister. Not a line of it was altered, and not any part of it written down till I reached Bristol." So Wordsworth recalled in 1843, but he had been practicing the gestures of the poem for some time: a manuscript fragment of 1796–1797 underlies the seemingly spontaneous opening and one of its central formulations: "Yet once again do I behold the forms / Of these huge mountains, and yet once again, / Standing beneath these elms, I hear thy voice, / Beloved Derwent, that peculiar voice / Heard in the stillness of the evening air, / Half-heard and half-created." Wordsworth first visited the Wye valley in August 1793, on a solo walking tour; the return with his sister in July 1798 prompted this spacious meditation on time and memory, in which the ruined Abbey (see Girtin's water color, page 2), a famous picturesque destination, does not appear. It is replaced by the inward "fluxes and refluxes of the mind" that shape the poem, which concludes the 1798 *Lyrical Ballads*. In 1800 Wordsworth added a note on the elevated manner: "I have not ventured to call this Poem an Ode; but it was written with a hope that in the transitions, and the impassioned music of the versification, would be found the principal requisites of that species of composition."

Lines
written a few miles above Tintern Abbey,
On Revisiting the Banks of the Wye
during a Tour,
July 13, 1798

Five years have passed; five summers, with the length
Of five long winters! and again I hear
These waters, rolling from their mountain-springs
With a sweet inland murmur.[1]—Once again
5   Do I behold these steep and lofty cliffs,
Which on a wild secluded scene impress
Thoughts of more deep seclusion; and connect
The landscape with the quiet of the sky.
The day is come when I again repose
10   Here, under this dark sycamore, and view
These plots of cottage-ground, these orchard-tufts,
Which, at this season, with their unripe fruits,
Among the woods and copses lose themselves,
Nor, with their green and simple hue, disturb
15   The wild green landscape. Once again I see
These hedge-rows, hardly hedge-rows, little lines
Of sportive wood run wild; these pastoral farms
Green to the very door; and wreathes of smoke
Sent up, in silence, from among the trees,

---

3. On the south coast of Cornwall, a journey of more than 120 miles.

1. The river is not affected by the tides a few miles above Tintern [Wordsworth's note, 1798].

20   With some uncertain notice, as might seem,
      Of vagrant dwellers in the houseless woods,
      Or of some hermit's cave, where by his fire
      The hermit° sits alone.   *religious recluse*

                        Though absent long,
      These forms of beauty have not been to me,
25   As is a landscape to a blind man's eye:
      But oft, in lonely rooms, and mid the din
      Of towns and cities, I have owed to them,
      In hours of weariness, sensations sweet,
      Felt in the blood, and felt along the heart,
30   And passing even into my purer mind
      With tranquil restoration:—feelings too
      Of unremembered pleasure; such, perhaps,
      As may have had no trivial influence
      On that best portion of a good man's life;
35   His little, nameless, unremembered acts
      Of kindness and of love. Nor less, I trust,
      To them I may have owed another gift,
      Of aspect more sublime; that blessed mood,
      In which the burthen° of the mystery,[2]   *burden*
40   In which the heavy and the weary weight
      Of all this unintelligible world
      Is lighten'd:—that serene and blessed mood,
      In which the affections gently lead us on,
      Until, the breath of this corporeal frame,
45   And even the motion of our human blood
      Almost suspended, we are laid asleep
      In body, and become a living soul:
      While with an eye made quiet by the power
      Of harmony, and the deep power of joy,
50   We see into the life of things.

                        If this
      Be but a vain belief, yet, oh! how oft,
      In darkness, and amid the many shapes
      Of joyless day-light; when the fretful stir
      Unprofitable, and the fever of the world,
55   Have hung upon the beatings of my heart,[3]
      How oft, in spirit, have I turned to thee
      O sylvan Wye! Thou wanderer through the woods,
      How often has my spirit turned to thee!

      And now, with gleams of half-extinguish'd thought,
60   With many recognitions dim and faint,
      And somewhat of a sad perplexity,

---

2. Keats thought this phrase the core of Wordsworth's "genius." See his letter of 3 May 1818 (pages 1049–51).
3. Echoing Macbeth's sense of life's fitful fever (3.2.23) and Hamlet's view of life as "weary, stale, flat, and unprofitable" (1.2.133).

The picture of the mind revives again:
While here I stand, not only with the sense
Of present pleasure, but with pleasing thoughts
65 That in this moment there is life and food
For future years. And so I dare to hope
Though changed, no doubt, from what I was, when first
I came among these hills; when like a roe
I bounded o'er the mountains, by the sides
70 Of the deep rivers, and the lonely streams,
Wherever nature led; more like a man
Flying from something that he dreads, than one
Who sought the thing he loved. For nature then
(The coarser pleasures of my boyish days,
75 And their glad animal movements all gone by,)
To me was all in all.—I cannot paint
What then I was. The sounding cataract
Haunted me like a passion: the tall rock,
The mountain, and the deep and gloomy wood,
80 Their colours and their forms, were then to me
An appetite: a feeling and a love,
That had no need of a remoter charm,
By thought supplied, or any interest
Unborrowed from the eye.—That time is past,
85 And all its aching joys are now no more,
And all its dizzy raptures. Not for this
Faint° I, nor mourn nor murmur: other gifts   lose heart
Have followed, for such loss, I would believe,
Abundant recompence. For I have learned
90 To look on nature, not as in the hour
Of thoughtless youth, but hearing oftentimes
The still, sad music of humanity,
Not harsh nor grating, though of ample power
To chasten and subdue. And I have felt
95 A presence that disturbs me with the joy
Of elevated thoughts; a sense sublime
Of something far more deeply interfused,
Whose dwelling is the light of setting suns,
And the round ocean, and the living air,
100 And the blue sky, and in the mind of man,
A motion and a spirit, that impels
All thinking things, all objects of all thought,
And rolls through all things. Therefore am I still
A lover of the meadows and the woods,
105 And mountains; and of all that we behold
From this green earth; of all the mighty world
Of eye and ear, both what they half-create,[4]

4. This line has a close resemblance to an admirable line of Young, the exact expression of which I cannot recollect
[Wordsworth's note]. He is thinking of Edward Young's "half create the wondrous world they see" (*The Complaint or Night
Thoughts* [1744], 6.427).

And what perceive; well pleased to recognize
In nature and the language of the sense,
110 The anchor of my purest thoughts, the nurse,
The guide, the guardian of my heart, and soul
Of all my moral being.

                        Nor, perchance,
If I were not thus taught, should I the more
Suffer my genial° spirits to decay: *creative*
115 For thou art with me, here, upon the banks
Of this fair river; thou, my dearest Friend,[5]
My dear, dear Friend, and in thy voice I catch°   *sense, arrest*
The language of my former heart, and read
My former pleasures in the shooting lights
120 Of thy wild eyes. Oh! yet a little while
May I behold in thee what I was once,
My dear, dear Sister! And this prayer I make,
Knowing that Nature never did betray
The heart that loved her; 'tis her privilege,
125 Through all the years of this our life, to lead
From joy to joy: for she can so inform
The mind that is within us, so impress
With quietness and beauty, and so feed
With lofty thoughts, that neither evil tongues,[6]
130 Rash judgments, nor the sneers of selfish men,
Nor greetings where no kindness is, nor all
The dreary intercourse of daily life,
Shall e'er prevail against us, or disturb
Our chearful faith that all which we behold
135 Is full of blessings. Therefore let the moon
Shine on thee in thy solitary walk;
And let the misty mountain winds be free
To blow against thee: and in after years,
When these wild ecstasies shall be matured
140 Into a sober pleasure, when thy mind
Shall be a mansion for all lovely forms,
Thy memory be as a dwelling-place
For all sweet sounds and harmonies; Oh! then,
If solitude, or fear, or pain, or grief,
145 Should be thy portion,° with what healing thoughts   *dowry, bequest*
Of tender joy wilt thou remember me,
And these my exhortations! Nor, perchance,
If I should be, where I no more can hear
Thy voice, nor catch from thy wild eyes these gleams
150 Of past existence, wilt thou then forget

---

5. His sister Dorothy. The language echoes Psalm 23: "Yea, through I walk through the valley of the shadow of death, I will fear no evil: for thou art with me."

6. An echo of Milton's claim to "Sing with mortal voice, unchang'd / To hoarse or mute, though fall'n on evil days, / ...and evil tongues" (*Paradise Lost* 7.24–26).

That on the banks of this delightful stream
We stood together; and that I, so long
A worshipper of Nature, hither came,
Unwearied in that service: rather say
155   With warmer love, oh! with far deeper zeal
Of holier love. Nor wilt thou then forget,
That after many wanderings, many years
Of absence, these steep woods and lofty cliffs,
And this green pastoral landscape, were to me
160   More dear, both for themselves, and for thy sake.

1798   1798

from **Lyrical Ballads (1800, 1802)**

from **Preface**[1]

The first Volume of these Poems has already been submitted to general perusal. It was published, as an experiment, which, I hoped, might be of some use to ascertain, how far, by fitting to metrical arrangement a selection of the real language of men in a state of vivid sensation, that sort of pleasure and that quantity of pleasure may be imparted, which a Poet may rationally endeavour to impart.

    I had formed no very inaccurate estimate of the probable effect of those Poems: I flattered myself that they who should be pleased with them would read them with more than common pleasure: and, on the other hand, I was well aware, that by those who should dislike them they would be read with more than common dislike. The result has differed from my expectation in this only, that I have pleased a greater number, than I ventured to hope I should please. * * *

    Several of my Friends are anxious for the success of these Poems from a belief, that, if the views with which they were composed were indeed realized, a class of Poetry would be produced, well adapted to interest mankind permanently, and not unimportant in the multiplicity, and in the quality of its moral relations: and on this account they have advised me to prefix a systematic defence of the theory, upon which the poems were written. But I was unwilling to undertake the task, because I knew that on this occasion the Reader would look coldly upon my arguments, since I might be suspected of having been principally influenced by the selfish and foolish hope of reasoning him into an approbation of these particular Poems: and I was still more unwilling to undertake the task, because, adequately to display my opinions, and fully to enforce my arguments, would require a space wholly disproportionate to the nature of a preface. For to treat the subject with the clearness and coherence, of which I believe it susceptible, it would be necessary to give a full account of the present state of the public taste in this country, and to determine how far this taste is healthy or depraved; which, again, could not be determined, without pointing out, in what manner language and the human mind act and re-act on each other, and without retracing the revolutions, not of literature alone, but likewise of society itself. I have therefore altogether declined to enter regularly upon this defence; yet I am sensible, that there would be some impropriety in abruptly obtruding upon the Public,

---

1. In 1800 Wordsworth replaced the 1798 Advertisement with a substantial Preface, expanded for the 1802 edition (our text). The 1800 publication was in two volumes, the first comprised of poems published in the 1798 *Ballads*.

without a few words of introduction, Poems so materially different from those, upon which general approbation is at present bestowed.

It is supposed, that by the act of writing in verse an Author makes a formal engagement that he will gratify certain known habits of association; that he not only thus apprizes the Reader that certain classes of ideas and expressions will be found in his book, but that others will be carefully excluded. This exponent or symbol held forth by metrical language must in different eras of literature have excited very different expectations: for example, in the age of Catullus, Terence, and Lucretius and that of Statius or Claudian; and in our own country, in the age of Shakespeare and Beaumont and Fletcher, and that of Donne and Cowley, or Dryden, or Pope.[2] I will not take upon me to determine the exact import of the promise which by the act of writing in verse an Author, in the present day, makes to his Reader; but I am certain, it will appear to many persons that I have not fulfilled the terms of an engagement thus voluntarily contracted. They who have been accustomed to the gaudiness and inane phraseology of many modern writers, if they persist in reading this book to its conclusion, will, no doubt, frequently have to struggle with feelings of strangeness and aukwardness: they will look round for poetry, and will be induced to inquire by what species of courtesy these attempts can be permitted to assume that title. I hope therefore the Reader will not censure me, if I attempt to state what I have proposed to myself to perform; and also, (as far as the limits of a preface will permit) to explain some of the chief reasons which have determined me in the choice of my purpose: that at least he may be spared any unpleasant feeling of disappointment, and that I myself may be protected from the most dishonorable accusation which can be brought against an Author, namely, that of an indolence which prevents him from endeavouring to ascertain what is his duty, or, when his duty is ascertained, prevents him from performing it.

[THE PRINCIPAL OBJECT OF THE POEMS. HUMBLE AND RUSTIC LIFE]

The principal object, then, which I proposed to myself in these Poems was to chuse incidents and situations from common life, and to relate or describe them, throughout, as far as was possible, in a selection of language really used by men; and, at the same time, to throw over them a certain colouring of imagination, whereby ordinary things should be presented to the mind in an unusual way; and, further, and above all, to make these incidents and situations interesting by tracing in them, truly though not ostentatiously, the primary laws of our nature: chiefly, as far as regards the manner in which we associate ideas in a state of excitement. Low and rustic life was generally chosen, because in that condition, the essential passions of the heart find a better soil in which they can attain their maturity, are less under restraint, and speak a plainer and more emphatic language; because in that condition of life our elementary feelings co-exist in a state of greater simplicity, and, consequently, may be more accurately contemplated, and more forcibly communicated; because the manners of rural life germinate from those elementary feelings; and, from the necessary character of rural occupations, are more easily comprehended; and are more durable; and lastly, because in that condition the passions of men are incorporated with the beautiful and permanent forms of nature.[3] The language, too, of these men is adopted (purified

---

2. Wordsworth contrasts the Silver Age Latin rhetoric of Statius (45–96 B.C.E.) and the still more elaborate verse of Claudian (c. 370–404) to the earlier less artificial styles of Catullus (84–54 B.C.E.), Terence (c. 195–159 B.C.E.), and Lucretius (c. 94–54 B.C.E.).

3. Compare Coleridge's account of the genesis of *Lyrical Ballads* in *Biographia Literaria*, Ch. 14 (page 690).

indeed from what appear to be its real defects, from all lasting and rational causes of dislike or disgust) because such men hourly communicate with the best objects from which the best part of language is originally derived; and because, from their rank in society and the sameness and narrow circle of their intercourse, being less under the influence of social vanity they convey their feelings and notions in simple and unelaborated expressions. Accordingly, such a language, arising out of repeated experience and regular feelings, is a more permanent, and a far more philosophical language, than that which is frequently substituted for it by Poets, who think that they are conferring honour upon themselves and their art, in proportion as they separate themselves from the sympathies of men, and indulge in arbitrary and capricious habits of expression, in order to furnish food for fickle tastes, and fickle appetites, of their own creation.[4]

["The Spontaneous Overflow of Powerful Feelings"]

I cannot, however, be insensible of the present outcry against the triviality and meanness both of thought and language, which some of my contemporaries have occasionally introduced into their metrical compositions; and I acknowledge, that this defect, where it exists, is more dishonorable to the Writer's own character than false refinement or arbitrary innovation, though I should contend at the same time that it is far less pernicious in the sum of its consequences. From such verses the Poems in these volumes will be found distinguished at least by one mark of difference, that each of them has a worthy *purpose*. Not that I mean to say, that I always began to write with a distinct purpose formally conceived; but I believe that my habits of meditation have so formed my feelings, as that my descriptions of such objects as strongly excite those feelings, will be found to carry along with them a purpose. If in this opinion I am mistaken, I can have little right to the name of a Poet. For all good poetry is the spontaneous overflow of powerful feelings: but though this be true, Poems to which any value can be attached, were never produced on any variety of subjects but by a man, who being possessed of more than usual organic sensibility, had also thought long and deeply. For our continued influxes of feeling are modified and directed by our thoughts, which are indeed the representatives of all our past feelings; and, as by contemplating the relation of these general representatives to each other we discover what is really important to men, so, by the repetition and continuance of this act, our feelings will be connected with important subjects, till at length, if we be originally possessed of much sensibility, such habits of mind will be produced, that, by obeying blindly and mechanically the impulses of those habits, we shall describe objects, and utter sentiments, of such a nature and in such connection with each other, that the understanding of the being to whom we address ourselves, if he be in a healthful state of association, must necessarily be in some degree enlightened, and his affections ameliorated.

I have said that each of these poems has a purpose. I have also informed my Reader what this purpose will be found principally to be: namely to illustrate the manner in which our feelings and ideas are associated in a state of excitement. But, speaking in language somewhat more appropriate, it is to follow the fluxes and refluxes of the mind when agitated by the great and simple affections of our

---

4. It is worth while here to observe that the affecting parts of Chaucer are almost always expressed in language pure and universally intelligible even to this day [Wordsworth's note].

nature. * * * I should mention one other circumstance which distinguishes these Poems from the popular Poetry of the day; it is this, that the feeling therein developed gives importance to the action and situation, and not the action and situation to the feeling. * * *

I will not suffer a sense of false modesty to prevent me from asserting, that I point my Reader's attention to this mark of distinction, far less for the sake of these particular Poems than from the general importance of the subject. The subject is indeed important! For the human mind is capable of being excited without the application of gross and violent stimulants; and he must have a very faint perception of its beauty and dignity who does not know this, and who does not further know, that one being is elevated above another, in proportion as he possesses this capability. It has therefore appeared to me, that to endeavour to produce or enlarge this capability is one of the best services in which, at any period, a Writer can be engaged; but this service, excellent at all times, is especially so at the present day. For a multitude of causes, unknown to former times, are now acting with a combined force to blunt the discriminating powers of the mind, and unfitting it for all voluntary exertion to reduce it to a state of almost savage torpor. The most effective of these causes are the great national events which are daily taking place, and the increasing accumulation of men in cities, where the uniformity of their occupations produces a craving for extraordinary incident, which the rapid communication of intelligence hourly gratifies.[5] To this tendency of life and manners the literature and theatrical exhibitions of the country have conformed themselves. The invaluable works of our elder writers, I had almost said the works of Shakespear and Milton, are driven into neglect by frantic novels, sickly and stupid German Tragedies, and deluges of idle and extravagant stories in verse.[6]—When I think upon this degrading thirst after outrageous stimulation, I am almost ashamed to have spoken of the feeble effort with which I have endeavoured to counteract it; and, reflecting upon the magnitude of the general evil, I should be oppressed with no dishonorable melancholy, had I not a deep impression of certain inherent and indestructible qualities of the human mind, and likewise of certain powers in the great and permanent objects that act upon it which are equally inherent and indestructible; and did I not further add to this impression a belief, that the time is approaching when the evil will be systematically opposed, by men of greater powers, and with far more distinguished success.

[THE LANGUAGE OF POETRY]

Having dwelt thus long on the subjects and aim of these Poems, I shall request the Reader's permission to apprize him of a few circumstances relating to their style, in order, among other reasons, that I may not be censured for not having performed what I never attempted. The Reader will find that personifications of abstract ideas rarely occur in these volumes; and, I hope, are utterly rejected as an ordinary device to elevate the style, and raise it above prose. I have proposed to myself to imitate, and, as far as is possible, to adopt the very language of men; and assuredly such personifications do not make any natural or regular part of that language. They are, indeed, a

---

5. That is, the rapid increase in daily newspaper production at this time. The "events" include the war with France, the Irish rebellion, and the sedition trials at home.

6. For example, sentimental melodramas, the popular Gothic novels of Ann Radcliffe and "Monk" Lewis, and the poetry of sensibility.

figure of speech occasionally prompted by passion, and I have made use of them as such; but I have endeavoured utterly to reject them as a mechanical device of style, or as a family language which Writers in metre seem to lay claim to by prescription. I have wished to keep my Reader in the company of flesh and blood, persuaded that by so doing I shall interest him. I am, however, well aware that others who pursue a different track may interest him likewise; I do not interfere with their claim, I only wish to prefer a different claim of my own. There will also be found in these volumes little of what is usually called poetic diction; I have taken as much pains to avoid it as others ordinarily take to produce it; this I have done for the reason already alleged, to bring my language near to the language of men, and further, because the pleasure which I have proposed to myself to impart is of a kind very different from that which is supposed by many persons to be the proper object of poetry. I do not know how without being culpably particular I can give my Reader a more exact notion of the style in which I wished these poems to be written than by informing him that I have at all times endeavoured to look steadily at my subject, consequently, I hope that there is in these Poems little falsehood of description, and that my ideas are expressed in language fitted to their respective importance. Something I must have gained by this practice, as it is friendly to one property of all good poetry, namely, good sense; but it has necessarily cut me off from a large portion of phrases and figures of speech which from father to son have long been regarded as the common inheritance of Poets. I have also thought it expedient to restrict myself still further, having abstained from the use of many expressions, in themselves proper and beautiful, but which have been foolishly repeated by bad Poets, till such feelings of disgust are connected with them as it is scarcely possible by any art of association to overpower.

If in a Poem there should be found a series of lines, or even a single line, in which the language, though naturally arranged and according to the strict laws of metre, does not differ from that of prose, there is a numerous class of critics, who, when they stumble upon these prosaisms as they call them, imagine that they have made a notable discovery, and exult over the Poet as over a man ignorant of his own profession. Now these men would establish a canon of criticism which the Reader will conclude he must utterly reject, if he wishes to be pleased with these volumes. And it would be a most easy task to prove to him, that not only the language of a large portion of every good poem, even of the most elevated character, must necessarily, except with reference to the metre, in no respect differ from that of good prose, but likewise that some of the most interesting parts of the best poems will be found to be strictly the language of prose, when prose is well written. The truth of this assertion might be demonstrated by innumerable passages from almost all the poetical writings, even of Milton himself. * * * [T]o illustrate the subject in a general manner, I will here adduce a short composition of Gray,[7] who was at the head of those who by their reasonings have attempted to widen the space of separation betwixt Prose and Metrical composition, and was more than any other man curiously elaborate in the structure of his own poetic diction.

---

7. Thomas Gray (1716–1771) is best known for *Elegy Written in a Country Churchyard* (1751). The inset poem, with Wordsworth's italics, is *Sonnet on the Death of Richard West* (1775). Gray had said to West that "the language of the age is never the language of poetry."

In vain to me the smiling mornings shine,
And reddening Phœbus° lifts his golden fire: [sun god]
The birds in vain their amorous descant° join,   [song]
Or chearful fields resume their green attire:
These ears alas! for other notes repine;°   [languish]
A different object do these eyes require;
My lonely anguish melts no heart but mine;
And in my breast the imperfect joys expire;
Yet Morning smiles the busy race to cheer,
And new-born pleasure brings to happier men;
The fields to all their wonted tribute bear;
To warm their little loves the birds complain.
I fruitless mourn to him that cannot hear
And weep the more because I weep in vain.

It will easily be perceived that the only part of this Sonnet which is of any value is the lines printed in Italics: it is equally obvious, that, except in the rhyme, and in the use of the single word "fruitless" for fruitlessly, which is so far a defect, the language of these lines does in no respect differ from that of prose.

By the foregoing quotation I have shewn that the language of Prose may yet be well adapted to Poetry; and I have previously asserted that a large portion of the language of every good poem can in no respect differ from that of good Prose. I will go further. I do not doubt that it may be safely affirmed, that there neither is, nor can be, any essential difference between the language of prose and metrical composition. We are fond of tracing the resemblance between Poetry and Painting, and, accordingly, we call them Sisters: but where shall we find bonds of connection sufficiently strict to typify the affinity betwixt metrical and prose composition? They both speak by and to the same organs; the bodies in which both of them are clothed may be said to be of the same substance, their affections are kindred and almost identical, not necessarily differing even in degree; Poetry[8] sheds no tears "such as Angels weep," but natural and human tears; she can boast of no celestial Ichor that distinguishes her vital juices from those of prose; the same human blood circulates through the veins of them both.

If it be affirmed that rhyme and metrical arrangement of themselves constitute a distinction which overturns what I have been saying on the strict affinity of metrical language with that of prose, and paves the way for other artificial distinctions which the mind voluntarily admits, I answer that the language of such Poetry as I am recommending is, as far as is possible, a selection of the language really spoken by men; that this selection, wherever it is made with true taste and feeling, will of itself form a distinction far greater than would at first be imagined, and will entirely separate the composition from the vulgarity and meanness of ordinary life; and, if metre be superadded thereto, I believe that a dissimilitude will be produced altogether sufficient for the gratification of a rational mind. What other distinction would we have? Whence is it to come? And where is it to exist? Not, surely, where the Poet speaks through the mouths of his characters: it cannot be necessary here, either for elevation of style,

8. I here use the word "Poetry" (though against my own judgment) as opposed to the word Prose, and synonomous with metrical composition. But much confusion has been introduced into criticism by this contradistinction of Poetry and Prose, instead of the more philosophical one of Poetry and Matter of fact, or Science. The only strict antithesis to Prose is Metre; nor is this, in truth, a strict antithesis; because lines and passages of metre so naturally occur in writing prose, that it would be scarcely possible to avoid them, even were it desirable [Wordsworth's note]. The ensuing quotation is from *Paradise Lost*, 1.620 (Satan's tears, as he attempts to address his fallen comrades, now in Hell).

or any of its supposed ornaments: for, if the Poet's subject be judiciously chosen, it will naturally, and upon fit occasion, lead him to passions the language of which, if selected truly and judiciously, must necessarily be dignified and variegated, and alive with metaphors and figures. * * *

[WHAT IS A POET?]

Taking up the subject, then, upon general grounds, I ask what is meant by the word Poet? What is a Poet? To whom does he address himself? And what language is to be expected from him? He is a man speaking to men: a man, it is true, endued with more lively sensibility, more enthusiasm and tenderness, who has a greater knowledge of human nature, and a more comprehensive soul, than are supposed to be common among mankind; a man pleased with his own passions and volitions, and who rejoices more than other men in the spirit of life that is in him; delighting to contemplate similar volitions and passions as manifested in the goings-on of the Universe, and habitually impelled to create them where he does not find them. To these qualities he has added a disposition to be affected more than other men by absent things as if they were present; an ability of conjuring up in himself passions, which are indeed far from being the same as those produced by real events, yet (especially in those parts of the general sympathy which are pleasing and delightful) do more nearly resemble the passions produced by real events, than any thing which, from the motions of their own minds merely, other men are accustomed to feel in themselves; whence, and from practice, he has acquired a greater readiness and power in expressing what he thinks and feels, and especially those thoughts and feelings which, by his own choice, or from the structure of his own mind, arise in him without immediate external excitement.

But, whatever portion of this faculty we may suppose even the greatest Poet to possess, there cannot be a doubt but that the language which it will suggest to him, must, in liveliness and truth, fall far short of that which is uttered by men in real life, under the actual pressure of those passions, certain shadows of which the Poet thus produces, or feels to be produced, in himself. However exalted a notion we would wish to cherish of the character of a Poet, it is obvious, that, while he describes and imitates passions, his situation is altogether slavish and mechanical, compared with the freedom and power of real and substantial action and suffering. So that it will be the wish of the Poet to bring his feelings near to those of the persons whose feelings he describes, nay, for short spaces of time perhaps, to let himself slip into an entire delusion, and even confound and identify his own feelings with theirs; modifying only the language which is thus suggested to him, by a consideration that he describes for a particular purpose, that of giving pleasure. Here, then, he will apply the principle on which I have so much insisted, namely, that of selection * * *

But it may be said by those who do not object to the general spirit of these remarks, that, as it is impossible for the Poet to produce upon all occasions language as exquisitely fitted for the passion as that which the real passion itself suggests, it is proper that he should consider himself as in the situation of a translator, who deems himself justified when he substitutes excellences of another kind for those which are unattainable by him; and endeavours occasionally to surpass his original, in order to make some amends for the general inferiority to which he feels that he must submit. But this would be to encourage idleness and unmanly despair. Further, it is the language of men who speak of what they do not understand; who talk of poetry as a matter of amusement and idle pleasure; who will converse with us as gravely about a taste for Poetry, as they express it, as if it were a thing as indifferent as a taste for Rope-dancing, or Frontiniac[9] or Sherry. Aristotle, I have been told, hath said, that Poetry is the most philosophic of all writing:[1] it is so: its object is truth, not individual and local, but general, and operative; not standing upon external testimony, but carried alive into the heart by passion; truth which is its own testimony, which gives strength and divinity to the tribunal to which it appeals, and receives them from the same tribunal. Poetry is the image of man and nature. The obstacles which stand in the way of the fidelity of the Biographer and Historian, and of their consequent utility, are incalculably greater than those which are to be encountered by the Poet who has an adequate notion of the dignity of his art. The Poet writes under one restriction only, namely, that of the necessity of giving immediate pleasure to a human Being possessed of that information which may be expected from him, not as a lawyer, a physician, a mariner, an astronomer or a natural philosopher, but as a Man. Except this one restriction, there is no object standing between the Poet and the image of things; between this, and the Biographer and Historian there are a thousand.

Nor let this necessity of producing immediate pleasure be considered as a degradation of the Poet's art. It is far otherwise. It is an acknowledgment of the beauty of the universe, an acknowledgment the more sincere because it is not formal, but indirect; it is a task light and easy to him who looks at the world in the spirit of love: further, it is a homage paid to the native and naked dignity of man, to the grand elementary principle of pleasure, by which he knows, and feels, and lives, and moves.[2] We have no sympathy but what is propagated by pleasure: I would not be misunderstood; but wherever we sympathize with pain it will be found that the sympathy is produced and carried on by subtle combinations with pleasure. We have no knowledge, that is, no general principles drawn from the contemplation of particular facts, but what has been built up by pleasure, and exists in us by pleasure alone. The Man of Science, the Chemist and Mathematician, whatever difficulties and disgusts they may have had to struggle with, know and feel this. However painful may be the objects with which the Anatomist's knowledge is connected, he feels that his knowledge is pleasure; and where he has no pleasure he has no knowledge. What then does the Poet? He considers man and the objects that surround him as acting and re-acting upon each other, so as to produce an infinite complexity of pain and pleasure; he considers man in his own nature and in his ordinary life as contemplating this with a certain quantity of immediate knowledge, with certain convictions, intuitions, and deductions which by habit become of the nature of intuitions; he considers him as looking upon this complex scene of ideas and sensations, and finding every where objects that immediately excite in him sympathies which, from the necessities of his nature, are accompanied by an overbalance of enjoyment.

To this knowledge which all men carry about with them, and to these sympathies in which without any other discipline than that of our daily life we are fitted to take delight, the Poet principally directs his attention. He considers man and nature as essentially adapted to each other, and the mind of man as naturally the mirror of the fairest and most interesting qualities of nature. And thus the Poet, prompted

---

9. A much-prized sweet French wine.
1. "[T]he historian speaks of what has happened, the poet of the kind of thing that *can* happen. Hence poetry is a more philosophical and serious business than history; for

poetry speaks more of universals, history of particulars" (Aristotle, *Poetics*, 1451b, Else translation).
2. Echoing St. Paul's declaration that in God "we live, and move, and have our being" (Acts 17.28).

by this feeling of pleasure which accompanies him through the whole course of his studies, converses with general nature with affections akin to those, which, through labour and length of time, the Man of Science has raised up in himself, by conversing with those particular parts of nature which are the objects of his studies. The knowledge both of the Poet and the Man of Science is pleasure; but the knowledge of the one cleaves to us as a necessary part of our existence, our natural and unalienable inheritance; the other is a personal and individual acquisition, slow to come to us, and by no habitual and direct sympathy connecting us with our fellow-beings. The Man of Science seeks truth as a remote and unknown benefactor; he cherishes and loves it in his solitude: the Poet, singing a song in which all human beings join with him, rejoices in the presence of truth as our visible friend and hourly companion. Poetry is the breath and finer spirit of all knowledge; it is the impassioned expression which is in the countenance of all Science. Emphatically may it be said of the Poet, as Shakespeare hath said of man, "that he looks before and after."[3] He is the rock of defence of human nature; an upholder and preserver, carrying every where with him relationship and love. In spite of difference of soil and climate, of language and manners, of laws and customs, in spite of things silently gone out of mind and things violently destroyed, the Poet binds together by passion and knowledge the vast empire of human society, as it is spread over the whole earth, and over all time. The objects of the Poet's thoughts are every where; though the eyes and senses of man are, it is true, his favorite guides, yet he will follow wheresoever he can find an atmosphere of sensation in which to move his wings. Poetry is the first and last of all knowledge—it is as immortal as the heart of man. If the labours of men of Science should ever create any material revolution, direct or indirect, in our condition, and in the impressions which we habitually receive, the Poet will sleep then no more than at present, but he will be ready to follow the steps of the man of Science, not only in those general indirect effects, but he will be at his side, carrying sensation into the midst of the objects of the Science itself. The remotest discoveries of the Chemist, the Botanist, or Mineralogist, will be as proper objects of the Poet's art as any upon which it can be employed, if the time should ever come when these things shall be familiar to us, and the relations under which they are contemplated by the followers of these respective Sciences shall be manifestly and palpably material to us as enjoying and suffering beings. If the time should ever come when what is now called Science, thus familiarized to men, shall be ready to put on, as it were, a form of flesh and blood, the Poet will lend his divine spirit to aid the transfiguration, and will welcome the Being thus produced, as a dear and genuine inmate of the household of man. * * *

What I have thus far said applies to Poetry in general; but especially to those parts of composition where the Poet speaks through the mouths of his characters; and upon this point it appears to have such weight that I will conclude, there are few persons, of good sense, who would not allow that the dramatic parts of composition are defective, in proportion as they deviate from the real language of nature, and are coloured by a diction of the Poet's own, either peculiar to him as an individual Poet, or belonging simply to Poets in general, to a body of men who, from the circumstance of their compositions being in metre, it is expected will employ a particular language.

It is not, then, in the dramatic parts of composition that we look for this distinction of language; but still it may be proper and necessary where the Poet speaks to

---

3. From Hamlet's last soliloquy, contemplating the cognition that distinguishes humans from animals (*Hamlet* 4.4.37).

us in his own person and character. To this I answer by referring my Reader to the description which I have before given of a Poet. Among the qualities which I have enumerated as principally conducting to form a Poet, is implied nothing differing in kind from other men, but only in degree. The sum of what I have there said is, that the Poet is chiefly distinguished from other men by a greater promptness to think and feel without immediate external excitement, and a greater power in expressing such thoughts and feelings as are produced in him in that manner. But these passions and thoughts and feelings are the general passions and thoughts and feelings of men. And with what are they connected? Undoubtedly with our moral sentiments and animal sensations, and with the causes which excite these; with the operations of the elements and the appearances of the visible universe; with storm and sunshine, with the revolutions of the seasons, with cold and heat, with loss of friends and kindred, with injuries and resentments, gratitude and hope, with fear and sorrow. These, and the like, are the sensations and objects which the Poet describes, as they are the sensations of other men, and the objects which interest them. The Poet thinks and feels in the spirit of the passions of men. How, then, can his language differ in any material degree from that of all other men who feel vividly and see clearly? It might be proved that it is impossible. But supposing that this were not the case, the Poet might then be allowed to use a peculiar language, when expressing his feelings for his own gratification, or that of men like himself. But Poets do not write for Poets alone, but for men. Unless therefore we are advocates for that admiration which depends upon ignorance, and that pleasure which arises from hearing what we do not understand, the Poet must descend from this supposed height, and, in order to excite rational sympathy, he must express himself as other men express themselves. * * *

[THE FUNCTION OF METRE]

It will now be proper to answer an obvious question, namely, why, professing these opinions, have I written in verse? To this, in addition to such answer as is included in what I have already said, I reply in the first place, because, however I may have restricted myself, there is still left open to me what confessedly constitutes the most valuable object of all writing whether in prose or verse, the great and universal passions of men, the most general and interesting of their occupations, and the entire world of nature, from which I am at liberty to supply myself with endless combinations of forms and imagery. Now, supposing for a moment that whatever is interesting in these objects may be as vividly described in prose, why am I to be condemned, if to such description I have endeavoured to superadd the charm which, by the consent of all nations, is acknowledged to exist in metrical language? To this, by such as are unconvinced by what I have already said, it may be answered, that a very small part of the pleasure given by Poetry depends upon the metre, and that it is injudicious to write in metre, unless it be accompanied with the other artificial distinctions of style with which metre is usually accompanied, and that by such deviation more will be lost from the shock which will be thereby given to the Reader's associations, than will be counterbalanced by any pleasure which he can derive from the general power of numbers. In answer to those who still contend for the necessity of accompanying metre with certain appropriate colours of style in order to the accomplishment of its appropriate end, and who also, in my opinion, greatly under-rate the power of metre in itself, it might perhaps, as far as relates to these Poems, have been almost sufficient to observe, that poems are extant, written upon more humble subjects, and in a more naked and simple style than I have aimed at, which poems have continued to give pleasure from generation to generation. * * *

The end of Poetry is to produce excitement in co-existence with an over-balance of pleasure. Now, by the supposition, excitement is an unusual and irregular state of the mind; ideas and feelings do not in that state succeed each other in accustomed order. But, if the words by which this excitement is produced are in themselves pow-erful, or the images and feelings have an undue proportion of pain connected with them, there is some danger that the excitement may be carried beyond its proper bounds. Now the co-presence of something regular, something to which the mind has been accustomed in various moods and in a less excited state, cannot but have great efficacy in tempering and restraining the passion by an intertexture of ordinary feeling, and of feeling not strictly and necessarily connected with the passion. This is unquestionably true, and hence, though the opinion will at first appear paradoxical, from the tendency of metre to divest language in a certain degree of its reality, and thus to throw a sort of half consciousness of unsubstantial existence over the whole composition, there can be little doubt but that more pathetic situations and senti-ments, that is, those which have a greater proportion of pain connected with them, may be endured in metrical composition, especially in rhyme, than in prose. The metre of the old Ballads is very artless; yet they contain many passages which would illustrate this opinion, and, I hope, if the following Poems be attentively perused, similar instances will be found in them. This opinion may be further illustrated by appealing to the Reader's own experience of the reluctance with which he comes to the re-perusal of the distressful parts of Clarissa Harlowe, or the Gamester.[4] While Shakespeare's writings, in the most pathetic scenes, never act upon us as pathetic be-yond the bounds of pleasure—an effect which, in a much greater degree than might at first be imagined, is to be ascribed to small, but continual and regular impulses of pleasurable surprise from the metrical arrangement. * * *

["EMOTION RECOLLECTED IN TRANQUILLITY"]

I have said that Poetry is the spontaneous overflow of powerful feelings: it takes its origin from emotion recollected in tranquillity: the emotion is contemplated till by a species of reaction the tranquillity gradually disappears, and an emotion, kindred to that which was before the subject of contemplation, is gradually produced, and does itself actually exist in the mind. In this mood successful composition generally begins, and in a mood similar to this it is carried on; but the emotion, of whatever kind and in whatever degree, from various causes is qualified by various pleasures, so that in de-scribing any passions whatsoever, which are voluntarily described, the mind will upon the whole be in a state of enjoyment. Now, if Nature be thus cautious in preserving in a state of enjoyment a being thus employed, the Poet ought to profit by the lesson thus held forth to him, and ought especially to take care, that whatever passions he communicates to his Reader, those passions, if his Reader's mind be sound and vigor-ous, should always be accompanied with an overbalance of pleasure. Now the music of harmonious metrical language, the sense of difficulty overcome, and the blind asso-ciation of pleasure which has been previously received from works of rhyme or metre of the same or similar construction, an indistinct perception perpetually renewed of

4. Wordsworth adduces Samuel Richardson's moving novel Clarissa (1747–48) and Edward Moore's prose tragedy The Gamester (1753).

language closely resembling that of real life, and yet, in the circumstance of metre, differing from it so widely, all these imperceptibly make up a complex feeling of delight, which is of the most important use in tempering the painful feeling which will always be found intermingled with powerful descriptions of the deeper passions. This effect is always produced in pathetic and impassioned poetry; while, in lighter compositions, the case and gracefulness with which the Poet manages his numbers are themselves confessedly a principal source of the gratification of the Reader. I might perhaps include all which it is necessary to say upon this subject by affirming, what few persons will deny, that, of two descriptions, either of passions, manners, or characters, each of them equally well executed, the one in prose and the other in verse, the verse will be read a hundred times where the prose is read once. * * *

Having thus explained a few of the reasons why I have written in verse, and why I have chosen subjects from common life, and endeavoured to bring my language near to the real language of men, if I have been too minute in pleading my own cause, I have at the same time been treating a subject of general interest; and it is for this reason that I request the Reader's permission to add a few words with reference solely to these particular poems, and to some defects which will probably be found in them. I am sensible that my associations must have sometimes been particular instead of general, and that, consequently, giving to things a false importance, sometimes from diseased impulses I may have written upon unworthy subjects; but I am less apprehensive on this account, than that my language may frequently have suffered from those arbitrary connections of feelings and ideas with particular words and phrases, from which no man can altogether protect himself. Hence I have no doubt, that, in some instances, feelings even of the ludicrous may be given to my Readers by expressions which appeared to me tender and pathetic. Such faulty expressions, were I convinced they were faulty at present, and that they must necessarily continue to be so, I would willingly take all reasonable pains to correct. But it is dangerous to make these alterations on the simple authority of a few individuals, or even of certain classes of men; for where the understanding of an Author is not convinced, or his feelings altered, this cannot be done without great injury to himself: for his own feelings are his stay and support, and, if he sets them aside in one instance, he may be induced to repeat this act till his mind loses all confidence in itself, and becomes utterly debilitated. To this it may be added, that the Reader ought never to forget that he is himself exposed to the same errors as the Poet, and perhaps in a much greater degree: for there can be no presumption in saying, that it is not probable he will be so well acquainted with the various stages of meaning through which words have passed, or with the fickleness or stability of the relations of particular ideas to each other; and above all, since he is so much less interested in the subject, he may decide lightly and carelessly. * * *

I have one request to make of my Reader, which is, that in judging these Poems he would decide by his own feelings genuinely, and not by reflection upon what will probably be the judgment of others. * * *

If an Author by any single composition has impressed us with respect for his talents, it is useful to consider this as affording a presumption, that, on other occasions where we have been displeased, he nevertheless may not have written ill or absurdly; and, further, to give him so much credit for this one composition as may induce us to review what has displeased us with more care than we should otherwise have bestowed upon it. This is not only an act of justice, but in our decisions upon poetry especially, may conduce in a high degree to the improvement of our own taste: for an accurate taste in poetry, and in all the other arts, as Sir Joshua Reynolds has observed, is an acquired talent, which can only be produced by thought and a long continued intercourse with the best models of composition.[5] This is mentioned, not with so ridiculous a purpose as to prevent the most inexperienced Reader from judging for himself, (I have already said that I wish him to judge for himself;) but merely to temper the rashness of decision, and to suggest, that, if Poetry be a subject on which much time has not been bestowed, the judgment may be erroneous; and that in many cases it necessarily will be so.

I know that nothing would have so effectually contributed to further the end which I have in view as to have shown of what kind the pleasure is, and how the pleasure is produced, which is confessedly produced by metrical composition essentially different from that which I have here endeavoured to recommend: for the Reader will say that he has been pleased by such composition; and what can I do more for him? The power of any art is limited; and he will suspect, that, if I propose to furnish him with new friends, it is only upon condition of his abandoning his old friends. Besides, as I have said, the Reader is himself conscious of the pleasure which he has received from such composition, composition to which he has peculiarly attached the endearing name of Poetry; and all men feel an habitual gratitude, and something of an honorable bigotry for the objects which have long continued to please them: we not only wish to be pleased, but to be pleased in that particular way in which we have been accustomed to be pleased. There is a host of arguments in these feelings; and I should be the less able to combat them successfully, as I am willing to allow, that, in order entirely to enjoy the Poetry which I am recommending, it would be necessary to give up much of what is ordinarily enjoyed. But, would my limits have permitted me to point out how this pleasure is produced, I might have removed many obstacles, and assisted my Reader in perceiving that the powers of language are not so limited as he may suppose; and that it is possible that poetry may give other enjoyments, of a purer, more lasting, and more exquisite nature. This part of my subject I have not altogether neglected; but it has been less my present aim to prove, that the interest excited by some other kinds of poetry is less vivid, and less worthy of the nobler powers of the mind, than to offer reasons for presuming, that, if the object which I have proposed to myself were adequately attained, a species of poetry would be produced, which is genuine poetry; in its nature well adapted to interest mankind permanently, and likewise important in the multiplicity and quality of its moral relations.

From what has been said, and from a perusal of the Poems, the Reader will be able clearly to perceive the object which I have proposed to myself: he will determine how far I have attained this object; and, what is a much more important question, whether it be worth attaining; and upon the decision of these two questions will rest my claim to the approbation of the public.

1802

5. See Sir Joshua Reynolds, "The reality of a standard of Taste," (Discourse 7, delivered 1776): "He therefore who is acquainted with the works which have pleased different ages and different countries, and has formed his opinion on them, has more materials, and more means of knowing what is analogous to the mind of man, than he who is conversant only with the works of his own age or country. What has pleased, and continues to please, is likely to please again: hence are derived the rules of art, and on this immovable foundation they must ever stand" (quoted from *Discourses*, collected 1797; rpt. 1798).

"There was a Boy"[1]

There was a Boy; ye knew him well, ye Cliffs
And Islands of Winander![2] many a time,
At evening, when the earliest stars had just begun
To move along the edges of the hills,
5 Rising or setting, would he stand alone,
Beneath the trees, or by the glimmering lake,
And there, with fingers interwoven, both hands
Press'd closely palm to palm and to his mouth
Uplifted, he, as through an instrument,
10 Blew mimic hootings to the silent owls
That they might answer him. And they would shout
Across the wat'ry vale and shout again
Responsive to his call, with quivering peals,
And long halloos, and screams, and echoes loud
15 Redoubled and redoubled, a wild scene
Of mirth and jocund din! And, when it chanced
That pauses of deep silence mock'd his skill,
Then, sometimes, in that silence, while he hung
Listening, a gentle shock of mild surprize
20 Has carried far into his heart the voice
Of mountain-torrents; or the visible scene
Would enter unawares into his mind
With all its solemn imagery, its rocks,
Its woods, and that uncertain heaven receiv'd
25 Into the bosom of the steady lake.
  Fair are the woods, and beauteous is the spot,
The vale where he was born: the Church-yard hangs
Upon a slope above the village school;[3]
And there along that bank where I have pass'd
30 At evening, I believe, that near his grave
A full half-hour together I have stood,
Mute—for he died when he was ten years old.

1797–1798   1800

"Strange fits of passion have I known"[1]

Strange fits of passion have I known,
And I will dare to tell,

1. First drafted in Germany in 1798 in the first person, these lines were later assimilated to *The Prelude* Book 5 as an example of education by "Nature." In his collection of 1815, Wordsworth placed this poem first in the subsection "Poems of the Imagination," commenting in his Preface that it displayed "one of the earliest processes of Nature in the development of this faculty. Guided by one of my own primary consciousnesses, I have presented a commutation and transfer of internal feelings, co-operating with external accidents, to plant, for immortality, images of sound and sight, in the celestial soil of the Imagination."

2. Windermere, in the Lake District.
3. Hawkshead Grammar School, which Wordsworth attended in the Lake District village of Esthwaite.
1. This and the two following lyrics written during a lonely winter that William and Dorothy spent in Germany comprise three of five lyrics traditionally called the "Lucy Poems." *Three years she grew* appears later in the volume. *I travell'd among unknown Men* was published in 1807 (see page 545). "Lucy" has not been identified. The name comes from the Latin "lux" (light); "Lucina" is an old name for the goddess of the moon.

But in the lover's ear alone,
What once to me befel.

5   When she I lov'd, was strong and gay
And like a rose in June,
I to her cottage bent my way,
Beneath the evening moon.

Upon the moon I fix'd my eye,
10   All over the wide lea;
My horse trudg'd on, and we drew nigh
Those paths so dear to me.

And now we reach'd the orchard plot,
And, as we climb'd the hill,
15   Towards the roof of Lucy's cot°   *cottage*
The moon descended still.

In one of those sweet dreams I slept,
Kind Nature's gentlest boon!
And, all the while, my eyes I kept
20   On the descending moon.

My horse mov'd on; hoof after hoof
He rais'd, and never stopp'd:
When down behind the cottage roof
At once the planet dropp'd.

25   What fond and wayward thoughts will slide
Into a Lover's head—
"O mercy!" to myself I cried,
"If Lucy should be dead!"[2]

1798–1799   1800

Song ("She dwelt among th' untrodden ways")

She dwelt among th' untrodden ways
    Beside the springs of Dove,[1]
A Maid whom there were none to praise
    And very few to love:

5   A Violet by a mossy stone
    Half-hidden from the Eye![2]
—Fair, as a star when only one
    Is shining in the sky!

She liv'd unknown, and few could know
10   When Lucy ceas'd to be;

---

2. A manuscript from 1799 shows a final stanza: "I told her this: her laughter light / Is ringing in my ears: / And when I think upon that night / My eyes are dim with tears."

1. A river in England.
2. See Gray's *Elegy Written in a Country Churchyard:* "Full many a flower is born to blush unseen" (55).

But she is in her Grave, and Oh!
   The difference to me!

1798   1800

"A slumber did my spirit seal"[1]

A slumber did my spirit seal,
   I had no human fears:
She seem'd a thing that could not feel
   The touch of earthly years.

5   No motion has she now, no force
   She neither hears nor sees
Roll'd round in earth's diurnal° course   *daily*
   With rocks, and stones, and trees!

1798–1799   1800

Lucy Gray[1]

Oft I had heard of Lucy Gray,
   And when I cross'd the Wild,
I chanc'd to see at break of day
   The solitary Child.

5   No Mate, no comrade Lucy knew;
   She dwelt on a wild Moor,
The sweetest Thing that ever grew
   Beside a human door!

You yet may spy the Fawn at play,
10   The Hare upon the Green;
But the sweet face of Lucy Gray
   Will never more be seen.

"To-night will be a stormy night,
   You to the Town must go,
15   And take a lantern, Child, to light
   Your Mother thro' the snow."

"That, Father! will I gladly do;
   'Tis scarcely afternoon—

1. Wordsworth published this poem without a title. Coleridge thought that this "most sublime Epitaph" exposed Wordsworth's fear that "his Sister might die."
1. "Founded on a circumstance told me by my Sister, of a little girl who, not far from Halifax in Yorkshire, was bewildered in a snow-storm.... Her footsteps were traced by her parents to the middle of the lock of a canal, and no other vestige of her, backward or forward, could be traced. The body, however, was found in the canal. The way in which the incident was treated & the spiritualizing of the character might furnish hints for contrasting the imaginative influences which I have endeavoured to throw over common life with Crabbe's matter of fact style of treating subjects of the same kind" [I.F., referring to poet George Crabbe]. In 1815, Wordsworth changed the title to *Lucy Gray*, or *Solitude*.

The Minster°-clock has struck two,   *church*
20   And yonder is the Moon." [2]

At this the Father rais'd his hook
And snapp'd a faggot-band;°   *bundle of firewood*
He plied his work; and Lucy took
The lantern in her hand.

25   Not blither is the mountain roe,
With many a wanton° stroke   *frolicsome*
Her feet disperse the powd'ry snow
That rises up like smoke.

The storm came on before its time,
30   She wander'd up and down,
And many a hill did Lucy climb
But never reach'd the Town.

The wretched Parents all that night
Went shouting far and wide;
35   But there was neither sound nor sight
To serve them for a guide.

At day-break on a hill they stood
That overlook'd the Moor;
And thence they saw the Bridge of Wood,
40   A furlong° from their door.   *one-eight of a mile*

And now they homeward turn'd, and cry'd
"In Heaven we all shall meet!"
When in the snow the Mother spied
The print of Lucy's feet.

45   Then downward from the steep hill's edge
They track'd the footmarks small;
And through the broken hawthorn-hedge,
And by the long stone-wall;

And then an open field they cross'd,
50   The marks were still the same;
They track'd them on, nor ever lost,
And to the Bridge they came.

They follow'd from the snowy bank
Those footmarks, one by one,
55   Into the middle of the plank,
And further there were none.

Yet some maintain that to this day
She is a living Child,
That you may see sweet Lucy Gray
60   Upon the lonesome Wild.

2. Wordsworth remarked that "the day-moon" is something "no town or village girl would ever notice" (1816).

O'er rough and smooth she trips along,
And never looks behind;
And sings a solitary song
That whistles in the wind.

1798–1799   1800

Poor Susan[1]

At the corner of Wood-Street, when day-light appears,
There's a Thrush that sings loud, it has sung for three years:
Poor Susan has pass'd by the spot, and has heard
In the silence of morning the song of the bird.

5   'Tis a note of enchantment; what ails her? She sees
A mountain ascending, a vision of trees;
Bright volumes of vapour through Lothbury glide,
And a river flows on through the vale of Cheapside.

Green pastures she views in the midst of the dale,
10   Down which she so often has tripp'd with her pail,
And a single small cottage, a nest like a dove's,
The one only dwelling on earth that she loves.

She looks, and her heart is in Heaven, but they fade,
The mist and the river, the hill and the shade;
15   The stream will not flow, and the hill will not rise,
And the colours have all pass'd away from her eyes.

Poor Outcast! return—to receive thee once more
The house of thy Father will open its door,
And thou once again, in thy plain russet gown,
20   May'st hear the thrush sing from a tree of its own.[2]

1798   1800

Nutting[1]

It seems a day,
(I speak of one from many singled out)
One of those heavenly days which cannot die,
When forth I sallied from our cottage-door,[2]
5   And with a wallet o'er my shoulder slung,
A nutting crook in hand, and turn'd my steps
Towards the distant wood, a Figure quaint,

1. The title was changed to *The Reverie of Poor Susan* in 1815. The poem is set in London's mercantile district. In the Preface Wordsworth instances *Poor Susan* as exemplifying poetry in which "the feeling therein developed gives importance to the action and situation, and not the action and situation to the feeling."
2. Charles Lamb felt this last stanza "threw a kind of dubiety upon Susan's moral conduct"; it was dropped after 1800.
1. "Intended as part of a poem on my own life, but

struck out as not being wanted there. Like most of my schoolfellows I was an impassioned nutter. For this pleasure, the vale of Esthwaite, abounding in coppice-wood, furnished a very wide range. The verses arose out of the remembrance of feelings I had when a boy" [I.F.].
2. The house at which I boarded during the time I was at School [Wordsworth's note]; it was supervised by Ann Tyson, the Dame of line 10.

Trick'd out in proud disguise of Beggar's weeds°   *clothing*
Put on for the occasion, by advice
10 And exhortation of my frugal Dame.
Motley accoutrement! of power to smile
At thorns, and brakes, and brambles, and, in truth,
More ragged than need was. Among the woods,
And o'er the pathless rocks, I forc'd my way
15 Until, at length, I came to one dear nook
Unvisited, where not a broken bough
Droop'd with its wither'd leaves, ungracious sign
Of devastation, but the hazels rose
Tall and erect, with milk-white clusters hung,
20 A virgin scene!³ —A little while I stood,
Breathing with such suppression of the heart
As joy delights in; and with wise restraint
Voluptuous, fearless of a rival, eyed
The banquet; or beneath the trees I sate
25 Among the flowers, and with the flowers I play'd;
A temper known to those, who, after long
And weary expectation, have been bless'd
With sudden happiness beyond all hope.—
—Perhaps it was a bower beneath whose leaves
30 The violets of five seasons re-appear
And fade, unseen by any human eye,
Where fairy water-breaks⁴ do murmur on
For ever, and I saw the sparkling foam,
And with my cheek on one of those green stones
35 That, fleec'd with moss, beneath the shady trees,
Lay round me, scatter'd like a flock of sheep,
I heard the murmur and the murmuring sound,
In that sweet mood when pleasure loves to pay
Tribute to ease, and, of its joy secure
40 The heart luxuriates with indifferent things,
Wasting its kindliness on stocks° and stones,   *tree stumps*
And on the vacant air. Then up I rose,
And dragg'd to earth both branch and bough, with crash
And merciless ravage; and the shady nook
45 Of hazels, and the green and mossy bower
Deform'd and sullied, patiently gave up
Their quiet being: and unless I now
Confound my present feelings with the past,
Even then, when from⁵ the bower I turn'd away,
50 Exulting, rich beyond the wealth of kings
I felt a sense of pain when I beheld
The silent trees, and saw the intruding sky.—

3. The moral terrain evokes Spenser's "Bower of Blisse"
in *The Faerie Queene*, a dangerously seductive pleasure
garden, and the Garden of Eden in Milton's *Paradise Lost*,
which Satan invades to ravage Eve.

4. Wordsworth's coinage: "little rapids."
5. Later revised to "ere from," making the "sense of pain"
precede rather than coincide with "exulting."

Then, dearest Maiden!⁶ move along these shades°   *shadows, spirits*
In gentleness of heart with gentle hand
55   Touch,—for there is a Spirit in the woods.

1798–1799   1800

"Three years she grew in sun and shower"¹

Three years she grew in sun and shower,
Then Nature said, "A lovelier flower
On earth was never sown;
This Child I to myself will take
5   She shall be mine, and I will make
A Lady of my own.

"Myself will to my darling be
Both law and impulse, and with me
The Girl in rock and plain,
10   In earth and heaven, in glade and bower,
Shall feel an overseeing power
To kindle or restrain.

"She shall be sportive as the fawn
That wild with glee across the lawn
15   Or up the mountain springs,
And hers shall be the breathing balm,
And hers the silence and the calm
Of mute insensate things.

"The floating clouds their state shall lend
20   To her; for her the willow bend,
Nor shall she fail to see
Even in the motions of the storm
Grace that shall mould the Maiden's form
By silent sympathy.

25   "The stars of midnight shall be dear
To her, and she shall lean her ear
In many a secret place
Where rivulets dance their wayward round,
And beauty born of murmuring sound
30   Shall pass into her face.

"And vital feelings of delight
Shall rear her form to stately height,
Her virgin bosom swell,
Such thoughts to Lucy I will give
35   While she and I together live
Here in this happy dell."

6. In a much longer manuscript draft, Wordsworth preceded this poem with the story of a "Lucy" who had been
ravaging a bower—her ungentle, unmaidenly action

provoking her companion to recount this episode from
his past, seemingly to admonish her with his remorse.
1. Not titled by Wordsworth.

Thus Nature spake—The work was done—
How soon my Lucy's race was run!
She died, and left to me
40 This heath, this calm and quiet scene,
The memory of what has been,
And never more will be.

1798–1799   1800

The Old Cumberland Beggar
A DESCRIPTION

The class of Beggars, to which the old man here described belongs, will probably soon be extinct. It consisted of poor, and, mostly, old and infirm persons, who confined themselves to a stated round in their neighbourhood, and had certain fixed days, on which, at different houses, they regularly received charity, sometimes in money, but mostly in provisions.

I saw an aged Beggar in my walk,
And he was seated, by the highway side
On a low structure of rude masonry
Built at the foot of a huge hill, that they
5   Who lead their horses down the steep rough road
May thence remount at ease. The aged man
Had placed his staff across the broad smooth stone
That overlays the pile, and from a bag
All white with flour, the dole of village dames,
10 He drew his scraps and fragments, one by one;
And scann'd them with a fix'd and serious look
Of idle computation. In the sun,
Upon the second step of that small pile,
Surrounded by those wild unpeopled hills,
15 He sate, and eat° his food in solitude: *past tense*
And ever, scatter'd from his palsied hand,
That still attempting to prevent the waste,
Was baffled still, the crumbs in little showers
Fell on the ground; and the small mountain birds,
20 Not venturing yet to peck their destin'd meal,
Approached within the length of half his staff.

Him from my childhood have I known, and then
He was so old, he seems not older now;
He travels on, a solitary man,
25 So helpless in appearance, that for him
The sauntering horseman-traveller does not throw
With careless hand his alms upon the ground,
But stops, that he may safely lodge the coin
Within the old Man's hat; nor quits him so,
30 But still, when he has given his horse the rein,
Towards the aged Beggar turns a look

Sidelong, and half-reverted. She who tends
The toll-gate, when in summer at her door
She turns her wheel,° if on the road she sees   *spinning wheel*
35   The aged Beggar coming, quits her work,
And lifts the latch for him that he may pass.
The Post-boy, when his rattling wheels o'ertake
The aged Beggar, in the woody lane,
Shouts to him from behind; and, if perchance
40   The old Man does not change his course, the Boy
Turns with less noisy wheels to the road-side,
And passes gently by, without a curse
Upon his lips, or anger at his heart.
He travels on, a solitary Man,
45   His age has no companion. On the ground
His eyes are turn'd, and, as he moves along,
They move along the ground; and evermore,
Instead of common and habitual sight
Of fields with rural works, of hill and dale,
50   And the blue sky, one little span of earth
Is all his prospect. Thus, from day to day,
Bowbent, his eyes for ever on the ground,
He plies his weary journey; seeing still,
And never knowing that he sees, some straw,
55   Some scatter'd leaf, or marks which, in one track,
The nails of cart or chariot-wheel have left
Impress'd on the white road, in the same line,
At distance still the same. Poor Traveller!
His staff trails with him; scarcely do his feet
60   Disturb the summer dust, he is so still
In look and motion, that the cottage curs,
Ere he has pass'd the door, will turn away,
Weary of barking at him. Boys and girls,
The vacant and the busy, maids and youths,
65   And urchins newly breech'd[1]—all pass him by:
Him even the slow-pac'd waggon leaves behind.

But deem not this man useless.—Statesmen![2] ye
Who are so restless in your wisdom, ye
Who have a broom still ready in your hands
70   To rid the world of nuisances; ye proud,
Heart-swoln, while in your pride ye contemplate
Your talents, power, or wisdom, deem him not
A burthen of the earth! 'Tis Nature's law
That none, the meanest° of created things,   *lowest, humblest*
75   Of forms created the most vile and brute,

---

1. Boys got to wear pants (breeches) at age five or so, before which they and girls wore frocks.   2. The legislators who would write Poor Laws to force beggars off public roads and into the misery of workhouses.

The dullest or most noxious, should exist
Divorced from good, a spirit and pulse of good,
A life and soul to every mode of being
Inseparably link'd. While thus he creeps
80 From door to door, the Villagers in him
Behold a record which together binds
Past deeds and offices of charity
Else unremember'd, and so keeps alive
The kindly mood in hearts which lapse of years,
85 And that half-wisdom half-experience gives,
Make slow to feel, and by sure steps resign
To selfishness and cold oblivious cares.
Among the farms and solitary huts
Hamlets, and thinly-scattered villages,
90 Where'er the aged Beggar takes his rounds,
The mild necessity of use compels
To acts of love; and habit does the work
Of reason; yet prepares that after joy
Which reason cherishes. And thus the soul,
95 By that sweet taste of pleasure unpursu'd
Doth find herself insensibly dispos'd
To virtue and true goodness. Some there are,
By their good works exalted, lofty minds
And meditative, authors of delight
100 And happiness, which to the end of time
Will live, and spread, and kindle; minds like these,
In childhood, from this solitary being,
The helpless wanderer, have perchance receiv'd,
(A thing more precious far than all that books
105 Or the solicitudes of love can do!)
That first mild touch of sympathy and thought,
In which they found their kindred with a world
Where want and sorrow were. The easy man
Who sits at his own door, and, like the pear
110 That overhangs his head from the green wall,
Feeds in the sunshine; the robust and young,
The prosperous and unthinking, they who live
Shelter'd, and flourish in a little grove
Of their own kindred; all behold in him
115 A silent monitor, which on their minds
Must needs impress a transitory thought
Of self-congratulation, to the heart
Of each recalling his peculiar boons,
His charters° and exemptions; and, perchance,   *privileges*
120 Though he to no one give the fortitude
And circumspection needful to preserve
His present blessings, and to husband up
The respite of the season, he, at least,
And 'tis no vulgar service, makes them felt.

125   Yet further.—Many, I believe, there are
Who live a life of virtuous decency,
Men who can hear the Decalogue° and feel   *Ten Commandments*
No self-reproach; who of the moral law
Establish'd in the land where they abide
130   Are strict observers, and not negligent,
Meanwhile, in any tenderness of heart
Or act of love to those with whom they dwell,
Their kindred, and the children of their blood.
Praise be to such, and to their slumbers peace!
135   —But of the poor man ask, the abject poor,
Go and demand of him, if there be here,
In this cold abstinence from evil deeds,
And these inevitable charities,
Wherewith to satisfy the human soul.
140   No—man is dear to man: the poorest poor
Long for some moments in a weary life
When they can know and feel that they have been
Themselves the fathers and the dealers out
Of some small blessings, have been kind to such
145   As needed kindness, for this single cause,
That we have all of us one human heart.[3]
—Such pleasure is to one kind Being known,
My Neighbour, when with punctual care, each week
Duly as Friday comes, though press'd herself
150   By her own wants, she from her chest of meal
Takes one unsparing handful for the scrip°   *small bag*
Of this old Mendicant, and, from her door
Returning with exhilarated heart,
Sits by her fire, and builds her hope in heav'n.

155   Then let him pass, a blessing on his head!
And while in that vast solitude to which
The tide of things has led him, he appears
To breathe and live but for himself alone,
Unblamed, uninjured, let him bear about
160   The good which the benignant law of Heaven
Has hung around him, and, while life is his,
Still let him prompt the unletter'd° Villagers   *illiterate, unlearned*
To tender offices and pensive thoughts.
Then let him pass, a blessing on his head!
165   And, long as he can wander, let him breathe
The freshness of the vallies; let his blood
Struggle with frosty air and winter snows,
And let the charter'd wind that sweeps the heath
Beat his grey locks against his wither'd face.

---

3. Keats admired this line; see his letter, page 1056.

170 Reverence the hope whose vital anxiousness
    Gives the last human interest to his heart.
    May never House, misnamed of industry,°   *workhouse*
    Make him a captive; for that pent-up din,
    Those life-consuming sounds that clog the air,
175 Be his the natural silence of old age.
    Let him be free of mountain solitudes;
    And have around him, whether heard or not,
    The pleasant melody of woodland birds.[4]
    Few are his pleasures; if his eyes, which now
180 Have been so long familiar with the earth,
    No more behold the horizontal sun
    Rising or setting, let the light at least
    Find a free entrance to their languid orbs.
    And let him, *where* and *when* he will, sit down
185 Beneath the trees, or by the grassy bank
    Of high-way side, and with the little birds
    Share his chance-gather'd meal, and, finally,
    As in the eye of Nature he has liv'd,
    So in the eye of Nature let him die!

1798   1800

MICHAEL   Sending the 1800 *Lyrical Ballads* to Charles James Fox, leader of the Whig opposition in Parliament, Wordsworth drew attention to *Michael*:

> I have attempted to draw a picture of the domestic affections as I know they exist amongst a class of men who are now almost confined to the North of England. They are small independent *proprietors* of land here called statesmen, men of respectable education who daily labour on their own little properties. The domestic affections will always be strong amongst men who live in a country not crowded with population, if these men are placed above poverty. But if they are proprietors of small estates, which have descended to them from their ancestors, the power which these affections will acquire amongst such men is inconceivable by those who have only had an opportunity of observing hired labourers, farmers, and the manufacturing Poor. Their little tract of land serves as a kind of permanent rallying point for their domestic feelings, as a tablet upon which they are written which makes them objects of memory in a thousand instances when they would otherwise be forgotten . . . men who do not wear fine cloaths can feel deeply. (14 January 1801)

On 9 April 1801 Wordsworth wrote to a friend, "I have attempted to give a picture of a man, of strong mind and lively sensibility, agitated by two of the most powerful affections of the human heart; the parental affection, and the love of property, *landed* property, including the feelings of inheritance, home, and personal and family independence." In 1836 Wordsworth recalled the poem's foundation "on the son of an old couple having become dissolute and run away from his parents" (who once owned Dove Cottage, Wordsworth's home at the time) "and on an old shepherd having been seven years in building up a sheepfold in a solitary valley." The austere biblical aura of the "covenant" between Michael and his son evokes Old Testament prototypes, and Luke is the Gospel that contains the parable of the Prodigal Son (15.11–32). In focusing on contemporary conditions and refusing to provide any relief except in Michael's "comfort in the strength of love," Wordsworth significantly revises the genre of pastoral.

---

4. See Charles Lamb's letter to Wordsworth about the strangeness of this spectacle, as well as his impatience with the lecture-like parts of the verse (page 472).

Michael
A Pastoral Poem

  If from the public way you turn your steps
  Up the tumultuous brook of Green-head Gill,[1]
  You will suppose that with an upright path
  Your feet must struggle; in such bold ascent
5 The pastoral Mountains front you, face to face.
  But, courage! for around that boisterous Brook
  The mountains have all open'd out themselves,
  And made a hidden valley of their own.
  No habitation can be seen; but such
10 As journey thither find themselves alone
  With a few sheep, with rocks and stones, and kites°   *hawks*
  That overhead are sailing in the sky.

  It is in truth an utter solitude;
  Nor should I have made mention of this Dell
15 But for one object which you might pass by,
  Might see and notice not. Beside the brook
  There is a straggling heap of unhewn stones!
  And to that place a story appertains,
  Which, though it be ungarnish'd with events,
20 Is not unfit, I deem, for the fire-side,
  Or for the summer shade. It was the first,
  The earliest of those tales that spake to me
  Of Shepherds, dwellers in the valleys, men
  Whom I already lov'd; not verily
25 For their own sakes, but for the fields and hills
  Where was their occupation and abode.
  And hence this Tale, while I was yet a boy
  Careless of books, yet having felt the power
  Of Nature, by the gentle agency
30 Of natural objects, led me on to feel
  For passions that were not my own, and think
  At random and imperfectly indeed
  On man; the heart of man, and human life.
  Therefore, although it be a history
35 Homely and rude, I will relate the same
  For the delight of a few natural hearts,
  And with yet fonder feeling, for the sake
  Of youthful Poets, who among these Hills
  Will be my second self when I am gone.

40 Upon the Forest-side in Grasmere Vale
  There dwelt a Shepherd, Michael was his name,
  An old man, stout of heart, and strong of limb.
  His bodily frame had been from youth to age

---

1. Green-head Gill (valley) and the poem's other settings are near Wordsworth's cottage at Grasmere.

Of an unusual strength; his mind was keen
Intense and frugal, apt for all affairs,
And in his Shepherd's calling he was prompt
And watchful more than ordinary men.
Hence had he learn'd the meaning of all winds,
Of blasts of every tone, and often-times,
When others heeded not, He heard the South°   *south wind*
Make subterraneous music, like the noise
Of Bagpipers on distant Highland hills;
The Shepherd, at such warning, of his flock
Bethought him, and he to himself would say
The winds are now devising work for me!
And truly at all times the storm, that drives
The Traveller to a shelter, summon'd him
Up to the mountains: he had been alone
Amid the heart of many thousand mists
That came to him, and left him, on the heights.
So liv'd he till his eightieth year was pass'd.

And grossly that man errs, who should suppose
That the green Valleys, and the Streams and Rocks
Were things indifferent to the Shepherd's thoughts.
Fields, where with chearful spirits he had breath'd
The common air; the hills, which he so oft
Had climb'd, with vigorous steps; which had impress'd
So many incidents upon his mind
Of hardship, skill or courage, joy or fear;
Which, like a book, preserv'd the memory
Of the dumb animals, whom he had sav'd,
Had fed or shelter'd, linking to such acts,
So grateful in themselves, the certainty
Of honourable gains; these fields, these hills
Which were his living Being, even more
Than his own Blood—what could they less? had laid
Strong hold on his affections, were to him
A pleasurable feeling of blind love,
The pleasure which there is in life itself.

He had not passed his days in singleness.
He had a Wife, a comely Matron, old
Though younger than himself full twenty years.
She was a woman of a stirring life
Whose heart was in her house: two wheels she had
Of antique form; this large, for spinning wool,
That small for flax; and if one wheel had rest,
It was because the other was at work.
The Pair had but one Inmate° in their house,   *resident*
An only Child, who had been born to them
When Michael telling° o'er his years began   *counting*
To deem that he was old, in Shepherd's phrase,

45
50
55
60
65
70
75
80
85
90

With one foot in the grave. This only son,
With two brave sheep dogs tried° in many a storm,   *tested*
The one of an inestimable worth,
95   Made all their Household. I may truly say,
That they were as a proverb in the vale
For endless industry. When day was gone,
And from their occupations out of doors
The Son and Father were come home, even then
100   Their labour did not cease, unless when all
Turn'd to the cleanly supper-board, and there
Each with a mess of pottage° and skimm'd milk,   *stew*
Sate round the basket pil'd with oaten cakes,
And their plain home-made cheese. Yet when their meal
105   Was ended, LUKE (for so the Son was nam'd)
And his old Father, both betook themselves
To such convenient work as might employ
Their hands by the fire-side; perhaps to card°   *comb out*
Wool for the House-wife's spindle, or repair
110   Some injury done to sickle, flail, or scythe,
Or other implement of house or field.

Down from the ceiling, by the chimney's edge,
That in our ancient uncouth country style
Did with a huge projection overbrow
115   Large space beneath, as duly as the light
Of day grew dim, the House-wife hung a lamp;
An aged utensil, which had perform'd
Service beyond all others of its kind.
Early at evening did it burn and late,
120   Surviving Comrade of uncounted Hours
Which going by from year to year had found
And left the Couple neither gay perhaps
Nor chearful, yet with objects and with hopes
Living a life of eager industry.
125   And now, when LUKE was in his eighteenth year,
There by the light of this old lamp they sate,
Father and Son, while late into the night
The House-wife plied her own peculiar work,
Making the cottage thro' the silent hours
130   Murmur as with the sound of summer flies.
Not with a waste of words, but for the sake
Of pleasure, which I know that I shall give
To many living now, I of this Lamp
Speak thus minutely: for there are no few
135   Whose memories will bear witness to my tale.
This Light was famous in its neighbourhood,
And was a public Symbol of the life,
That thrifty Pair had liv'd. For, as it chanc'd,
Their Cottage on a plot of rising ground
140   Stood single, with large prospect North and South,

High into Easedale, up to Dunmal-Raise,
And Westward to the village near the Lake;
And from this constant light so regular
And so far seen, the House itself by all
145   Who dwelt within the limits of the vale,
Both old and young, was nam'd The Evening Star.

Thus living on through such a length of years,
The Shepherd, if he lov'd himself, must needs
Have lov'd his Help-mate; but to Michael's heart
150   This Son of his old age was yet more dear—
Effect which might perhaps have been produc'd
By that instinctive tenderness, the same
Blind Spirit, which is in the blood of all,
Or that a child, more than all other gifts,
155   Brings hope with it, and forward-looking thoughts,
And stirrings of inquietude, when they
By tendency of nature needs must fail.
From such, and other causes, to the thoughts
Of the old Man his only Son was now
160   The dearest object that he knew on earth.
Exceeding was the love he bare to him,
His Heart and his Heart's joy! For oftentimes
Old Michael, while he was a babe in arms,
Had done him female service, not alone
165   For dalliance and delight, as is the use
Of Fathers, but with patient mind enforc'd
To acts of tenderness; and he had rock'd
His cradle, as with a woman's gentle hand.

And in a later time, ere yet the Boy
170   Had put on Boy's attire, did Michael love,
Albeit of a stern unbending mind,
To have the young one in his sight, when he
Had work by his own door, or when he sate
With sheep before him on his Shepherd's stool,
175   Beneath that large old Oak, which near their door
Stood, and from its enormous breadth of shade
Chosen for the Shearer's covert from the sun,
Thence in our rustic dialect was call'd
The CLIPPING TREE,[2] a name which yet it bears.
180   There, while they two were sitting in the shade,
With others round them, earnest all and blithe,
Would Michael exercise his heart with looks
Of fond correction and reproof bestow'd
Upon the child, if he disturb'd the sheep
185   By catching at their legs, or with his shouts
Scar'd them, while they lay still beneath the shears.

2. Clipping is the word used in the North of England for shearing [Wordsworth's note].

And when by Heaven's good grace the Boy grew up
A healthy Lad, and carried in his cheek
Two steady roses that were five years old,
190   Then Michael from a winter coppice° cut   *grove of small trees*
With his own hand a sapling, which he hoop'd
With iron, making it throughout in all
Due requisites a perfect Shepherd's Staff,
And gave it to the Boy; wherewith equipp'd
195   He as a Watchman oftentimes was plac'd
At gate or gap, to stem or turn the flock,
And to his office prematurely call'd
There stood the urchin, as you will divine,
Something between a hindrance and a help,
200   And for this cause not always, I believe,
Receiving from his Father hire of praise.
Though nought was left undone which staff or voice,
Or looks, or threatening gestures, could perform.
But soon as Luke, full ten years old, could stand
205   Against the mountain blasts, and to the heights,
Not fearing toil, nor length of weary ways,
He with his Father daily went, and they
Were as companions, why should I relate
That objects which the Shepherd loved before
210   Were dearer now? that from the Boy there came
Feelings and emanations, things which were
Light to the sun and music to the wind;
And that the Old Man's heart seemed born again.
Thus in his Father's sight the Boy grew up:
215   And now, when he had reached his eighteenth year,
He was his comfort and his daily hope.

While this good household thus were living on
From day to day, to Michael's ear there came
Distressful tidings. Long before the time
220   Of which I speak, the Shepherd had been bound
In surety° for his Brother's Son, a man   *guaranteed a loan*
Of an industrious life, and ample means;
But unforeseen misfortunes suddenly
Had press'd upon him, and old Michael now
225   Was summon'd to discharge the forfeiture,°   *collateral*
A grievous penalty, but little less
Than half his substance. This un-look'd for claim,
At the first hearing, for a moment took
More hope out of his life than he supposed
230   That any old man ever could have lost.
As soon as he had gather'd so much strength
That he could look his trouble in the face,
It seem'd that his sole refuge was to sell
A portion of his patrimonial fields.

235 Such was his first resolve; he thought again,
     And his heart fail'd him. "Isabel," said he,
     Two evenings after he had heard the news,
     "I have been toiling more than seventy years,
     And in the open sun-shine of God's love
240 Have we all liv'd; yet if these fields of ours
     Should pass into a Stranger's hand, I think
     That I could not lie quiet in my grave.
     Our lot is a hard lot; the Sun itself
     Has scarcely been more diligent than I,
245 And I have liv'd to be a fool at last
     To my own family. An evil Man
     That was, and made an evil choice, if he
     Were false to us; and if he were not false,
     There are ten thousand to whom loss like this
250 Had been no sorrow. I forgive him—but
     'Twere better to be dumb than to talk thus.
     When I began, my purpose was to speak
     Of remedies and of a chearful hope.
     Our Luke shall leave us, Isabel; the land
255 Shall not go from us, and it shall be free;°   not mortgaged
     He° shall possess it, free as is the wind   (Luke)
     That passes over it. We have, thou knowest,
     Another Kinsman, he will be our friend
     In this distress. He is a prosperous man,
260 Thriving in trade, and Luke to him shall go,
     And with his Kinsman's help and his own thrift,
     He quickly will repair this loss, and then
     May come again to us. If here he stay,
     What can be done? Where every one is poor
265 What can be gained?" At this the old Man paus'd,
     And Isabel sate silent, for her mind
     Was busy, looking back into past times.
     There's Richard Bateman, thought she to herself,[3]
     He was a parish-boy° at the church-door   on welfare
270 They made a gathering for him, shillings, pence,
     And halfpennies, wherewith the Neighbours bought
     A Basket, which they fill'd with Pedlar's wares,
     And with this Basket on his arm, the Lad
     Went up to London, found a Master° there,   employer
275 Who out of many chose the trusty Boy
     To go and overlook his merchandise
     Beyond the seas, where he grew wond'rous rich,
     And left estates and monies to the poor,
     And at his birth-place, built a Chapel, floor'd
280 With Marble, which he sent from foreign lands.

3. The story alluded to here is well known in the country [Wordsworth's note, 1802].

These thoughts, and many others of like sort,
Pass'd quickly thro' the mind of Isabel,
And her face brighten'd. The old Man was glad,
And thus resum'd. "Well! Isabel, this scheme
285   These two days, has been meat and drink to me.
Far more than we have lost is left us yet.
—We have enough—I wish indeed that I
Were younger, but this hope is a good hope.
—Make ready Luke's best garments, of the best
290   Buy for him more, and let us send him forth
To-morrow, or the next day, or to-night:
—If he could go, the Boy should go to-night."

Here Michael ceas'd, and to the fields went forth
With a light heart. The House-wife for five days
295   Was restless° morn and night, and all day long   *without rest*
Wrought on with her best fingers to prepare
Things needful for the journey of her Son.
But Isabel was glad when Sunday came
To stop her in her work; for, when she lay
300   By Michael's side, she through the last two nights
Heard him, how he was troubled in his sleep:
And when they rose at morning she could see
That all his hopes were gone. That day at noon
She said to Luke, while they two by themselves
305   Were sitting at the door, "Thou must not go,
We have no other Child but thee to lose,
None to remember—do not go away,
For if thou leave thy Father he will die."[4]
The Lad made answer with a jocund voice,
310   And Isabel, when she had told her fears,
Recover'd heart. That evening her best fare
Did she bring forth, and all together sate
Like happy people round a Christmas fire.

Next morning Isabel resum'd her work,
315   And all the ensuing week the house appear'd
As chearful as a grove in Spring: at length
The expected letter from their Kinsman came,
With kind assurances that he would do
His utmost for the welfare of the Boy,
320   To which requests were added, that forthwith
He might be sent to him. Ten times or more
The letter was read over; Isabel
Went forth to shew it to the neighbours round:
Nor was there at that time on English Land
325   A prouder heart than Luke's. When Isabel

---

4. Echoing the story of Joseph in Genesis 44.22: "The lad cannot leave his father: for if he should leave his father, his father would die."

Had to her house return'd, the Old Man said,
"He shall depart to-morrow." To this word
The House-wife answered, talking much of things
Which, if at such short notice he should go,
330 Would surely be forgotten. But at length
She gave consent, and Michael was at ease.

Near the tumultuous brook of Green-head Gill,
In that deep Valley, Michael had design'd
To build a Sheep-fold;[5] and, before he heard
335 The tidings of his melancholy loss,
For this same purpose he had gathered up
A heap of stones, which close to the brook side
Lay thrown together, ready for the work.
With Luke that evening thitherward he walk'd;
340 And soon as they had reach'd the place he stopp'd,
And thus the Old Man spake to him. "My Son,
To-morrow thou wilt leave me; with full heart
I look upon thee, for thou art the same
That wert a promise to me ere thy birth,
345 And all thy life hast been my daily joy.
I will relate to thee some little part
Of our two histories; 'twill do thee good
When thou art from me, even if I should speak
On things thou canst not know of.—After thou
350 First cam'st into the world—as oft befalls
To new-born infants, thou didst sleep away
Two days, and blessings from thy Father's tongue
Then fell upon thee. Day by day pass'd on,
And still I lov'd thee with encreasing love.
355 Never to living ear came sweeter sounds
Than when I heard thee by our own fire-side
First uttering without words a natural tune,
While thou, a feeding babe, didst in thy joy
Sing at thy Mother's breast. Month followed month,
360 And in the open fields my life was pass'd
And on the mountains, else I think that thou
Hadst been brought up upon thy father's knees.
—But we were playmates, Luke; among these hills,
As well thou know'st, in us the old and young
365 Have play'd together, nor with me didst thou
Lack any pleasure which a boy can know."

Luke had a manly heart; but at these words
He sobb'd aloud. The Old Man grasp'd his hand,
And said, "Nay do not take it so—I see

5. A sheepfold in these mountains is an unroofed building of stone walls, with different divisions. It is generally placed by the side of a brook [Wordsworth's note, 1802]. "The Sheepfold...remains, or rather ruins of it," Wordsworth remarked in 1843.

370 That these are things of which I need not speak.
     —Even to the utmost I have been to thee
     A kind and a good Father: and herein
     I but repay a gift which I myself
     Receiv'd at others' hands, for, though now old
375 Beyond the common life of man, I still
     Remember them who lov'd me in my youth.
     Both of them sleep together: here they liv'd,
     As all their Forefathers had done, and when
     At length their time was come, they were not loth
380 To give their bodies to the family mold.
     I wish'd that thou should'st live the life they liv'd.
     But 'tis a long time to look back, my Son,
     And see so little gain from sixty years.
     These fields were burthen'd° when they came to me;   mortgaged
385 'Till I was forty years of age, not more
     Than half of my inheritance was mine.
     I toil'd and toil'd; God bless'd me in my work,
     And 'till these three weeks past the land was free.
     —It looks as if it never could endure
390 Another Master. Heaven forgive me, Luke,
     If I judge ill for thee, but it seems good
     That thou should'st go." At this the Old Man paus'd;
     Then, pointing to the Stones near which they stood,
     Thus, after a short silence, he resum'd:
395 "This was a work for us, and now, my Son,
     It is a work for me. But, lay one Stone—
     Here, lay it for me, Luke, with thine own hands.
     I for the purpose brought thee to this place.
     Nay, Boy, be of good hope:—we both may live
400 To see a better day. At eighty-four
     I still am strong and stout;°—do thou thy part;   hardy
     I will do mine[6]—I will begin again
     With many tasks that were resign'd to thee;
     Up to the heights, and in among the storms,
405 Will I without thee go again, and do
     All works which I was wont to do alone,
     Before I knew thy face.—Heaven bless thee, Boy!
     Thy heart these two weeks has been beating fast
     With many hopes—it should be so—yes—yes—
410 I knew that thou could'st never have a wish
     To leave me, Luke, thou hast been bound to me
     Only by links of love, when thou art gone
     What will be left to us!—But, I forget
     My purposes. Lay now the corner-stone,

6. "Nature...hath done her part; / Do thou but thine," Raphael instructs Adam about his responsibility for Eve (*Paradise Lost* 8.561–62); "God toward thee hath done his part, do thine," Adam cautions Eve, before she goes off alone in Eden, the prelude to her Fall (9.375).

415 As I requested, and hereafter, Luke,
When thou art gone away, should evil men
Be thy companions, let this sheep-fold be
Thy anchor and thy shield; amid all fear
And all temptation, let it be to thee
420 An emblem of the life thy Fathers liv'd,
Who, being innocent, did for that cause
Bestir them in good deeds. Now, fare thee well—
When thou return'st, thou in this place wilt see
A work which is not here, a covenant
425 'Twill be between us—but, whatever fate
Befall thee, I shall love thee to the last,
And bear thy memory with me to the grave."

The Shepherd ended here; and Luke stoop'd down,
And as his Father had requested, laid
430 The first stone of the Sheep-fold; at the sight
The Old Man's grief broke from him, to his heart
He press'd his Son, he kissed him and wept;
And to the House together they return'd.

Next morning, as had been resolv'd, the Boy
435 Began his journey, and when he had reach'd
The public Way, he put on a bold face;
And all the Neighbours, as he pass'd their doors
Came forth with wishes and with farewell pray'rs,
That follow'd him 'till he was out of sight.

440 A good report did from their Kinsman come,
Of Luke and his well-doing; and the Boy
Wrote loving letters, full of wond'rous news,
Which, as the House-wife phrased it, were throughout
The prettiest letters that were ever seen.
445 Both parents read them with rejoicing hearts.
So, many months pass'd on: and once again
The Shepherd went about his daily work
With confident and chearful thoughts; and now
Sometimes when he could find a leisure hour
450 He to that valley took his way, and there
Wrought at the Sheep-fold. Meantime Luke began
To slacken in his duty; and, at length
He in the dissolute city gave himself
To evil courses: ignominy and shame
455 Fell on him, so that he was driven at last
To seek a hiding-place beyond the seas.

There is a comfort in the strength of love;
'Twill make a thing endurable, which else
Would break the heart:—Old Michael found it so.
460 I have convers'd with more than one who well
Remember the Old Man, and what he was

Years after he had heard this heavy news.
His bodily frame had been from youth to age
Of an unusual strength. Among the rocks
465   He went, and still look'd up upon the sun,
And listen'd to the wind; and as before
Perform'd all kinds of labour for his Sheep,
And for the land, his small inheritance.
And to that hollow Dell from time to time
470   Did he repair, to build the Fold of which
His flock had need. 'Tis not forgotten yet
The pity which was then in every heart
For the Old Man—and 'tis believed by all
That many and many a day he thither went,
475   And never lifted up a single stone.

There, by the Sheep-fold, sometimes was he seen
Sitting alone, with that his faithful Dog,
Then old, beside him, lying at his feet.
The length of full seven years from time to time
480   He at the building of this Sheep-fold wrought,
And left the work unfinished when he died.

Three years, or little more, did Isabel,
Survive her Husband: at her death the estate
Was sold, and went into a Stranger's hand.
485   The Cottage which was nam'd The Evening Star
Is gone, the ploughshare has been through the ground
On which it stood;[7] great changes have been wrought
In all the neighbourhood, yet the Oak is left
That grew beside their Door; and the remains
490   Of the unfinished Sheep-fold may be seen
Beside the boisterous brook of Green-head Gill.

1800   1800

<hr/>

RESPONSES

Francis Jeffrey: ["the new poetry"][1]

Poetry has this much, at least, in common with religion, that its standards were fixed
long ago, by certain inspired writers, whose authority it is no longer lawful to call
in question; and that many profess to be entirely devoted to it, who have no *good*

<hr/>

7. The grazing fields have been enclosed for agriculture;
also evoking the strife between the shepherd Abel and
his farming brother Cain.
1. By 1802, when this essay appeared in the *Edinburgh
Review* (its occasion was Robert Southey's exotic verse
romance, *Thalaba, the Destroyer*), the second edition of
Lyrical Ballads, with the Preface, had appeared. Southey,
like fellow "Lake Poet" Wordsworth, advocated politi-

cal reform in the 1790s (see his abolition poetry, pages
268–72). Francis Jeffrey (1773–1850) was the editor and
chief literary critic for the *Edinburgh*, soon to be one of
the most influential reviews of the age. His tastes were
more neoclassical than modern, and his attacks on
Wordsworth's poetic principles persisted for decades.
For another of his *Edinburgh* essays, see the Responses for
Felicia Hemans (page 957).

works to produce in support of their pretensions. * * * The author who is now before us, belongs to a *sect* of poets, that has established itself in this country within these ten or twelve years, and is looked upon, we believe, as one of its chief champions and apostles. The peculiar doctrines of this sect, it would not, perhaps, be very easy to explain; but, that they are *dissenters* from the established systems in poetry and criticism, is admitted, and proved indeed, by the whole tenor of their compositions. Though they lay claim, we believe, to a creed and a revelation of their own, there can be little doubt, that their doctrines are of *German* origin, and have been derived from some of the great modern reformers in that country. Some of their leading principles, indeed, are probably of an earlier date, and seem to have been borrowed from the great apostle of Geneva.[2] * * *

The disciples of this school boast much of its originality, and seem to value themselves very highly, for having broken loose from the bondage of ancient authority, and re-asserted the independence of genius. Originality, however, we are persuaded, is rarer than mere alteration; and a man may change a good master for a bad one, without finding himself at all nearer to independence. * * * The productions of this school, we conceive, are so far from being entitled to the praise of originality, that they cannot be better characterised, than by an enumeration of the sources from which their materials have been derived. The greater part of them, we apprehend, will be found to be composed of the following elements: 1. The antisocial principles, and distempered sensibility of Rousseau—his discontent with the present constitution of society—his paradoxical morality, and his perpetual hankerings after some unattainable state of voluptuous virtue and perfection. 2. The simplicity and energy (*horresco referens* [I dread to say it]) of Kotzebue and Schiller. 3. The homeliness and harshness of some of Cowper's language and versification, interchanged occasionally with the *innocence* of Ambrose Philips, or the quaintness of Quarles and Dr Donne.[3] * * *

The authors, of whom we are now speaking [Southey, Wordsworth, and Coleridge], have, among them, unquestionably, a very considerable portion of poetical talent, and have, consequently, been enabled to seduce many into an admiration of the false taste (as it appears to us) in which most of their productions are composed. They constitute, at present, the most formidable conspiracy that has lately been formed against sound judgment in matters poetical; and are entitled to a larger share of our censorial notice, than could be spared for an individual delinquent. * * *

Their most distinguishing symbol, is undoubtedly an affection of great simplicity and familiarity of language. They disdain to make use of the common poetical phraseology, or to ennoble their diction by a selection of fine or dignified expressions. There would be too much *art* in this, for that great love of nature with which they are all of them inspired; and their sentiments, they are determined shall be indebted, for their effect, to nothing but their intrinsic tenderness or elevation. There is something very noble and conscientious, we will confess, in this plan of composition; but the misfortune is, that there are passages in all poems, that can neither be pathetic nor sublime; and that, on these occasions, a neglect of the embellishments

2. J. J. Rousseau (1712–1778). The Germans are J. W. von Goethe (1749–1832) and poets of sensational verse narratives.
3. August von Kotzebue (1761–1819) was famed for his sentimental plays. Ambrose Phillips (1675–1749) was admired and ridiculed for his sweet verses; Frances Quarles (1592–1644) was best known for *Emblems* (1635), a book of devotional poems with quaint illustrations. John Donne (1572–1631) wrote boldly experimental poetry famed for its passion, its rough meters, and extravagant wit.

of language is very apt to produce absolute meanness and insipidity. * * * It is in such passages, accordingly, that we are most frequently offended with low and inelegant expressions; and that the language, which was intended to be simple and natural, is found oftenest to degenerate into mere slovenliness and vulgarity. * * *

One of their own authors, indeed, has very ingeniously set forth, (in a kind of manifesto that preceded one of their most flagrant acts of hostility), that it was their capital object "to adapt to the uses of poetry, the ordinary language of conversation among the middling and lower orders of the people." What advantages are to be gained by the success of this project, we confess ourselves unable to conjecture. The language of the higher and more cultivated orders may fairly be presumed to be better than that of their inferiors: at any rate, it has all those associations in its favour, by means of which, a style can ever appear beautiful or exalted, and is adapted to the purposes of poetry, by having been long consecrated to its use. The language of the vulgar, on the other hand, has all the opposite associations to contend with; and must seem unfit for poetry, (if there were no other reason), merely because it has scarcely ever been employed in it. A great genius may indeed overcome these disadvantages; but we can scarcely conceive that he should court them. We may excuse a certain homeliness of language in the productions of a ploughman or a milkwoman;[4] but we cannot bring ourselves to admire it in an author, who has had occasion to indite odes to his college bell, and inscribe hymns to the Penates.[5]

But the mischief of this new system is not confined to the depravation of language only; it extends to the sentiments and emotions, and leads to the debasement of all those feelings which poetry is designed to communicate. It is absurd to suppose, that an author should make use of the language of the vulgar, to express the sentiments of the refined. His professed object, in employing that language, is to bring his compositions nearer to the true standard of nature; and his intention to copy the sentiments of the lower orders, is implied in his resolution to make use of their style. Now, the different classes of society have each of them a distinct character, as well as a separate idiom; and the names of the various passions to which they are subject respectively, have a signification that varies essentially, according to the condition of the persons to whom they are applied. The love, or grief, or indignation of an enlightened and refined character, is not only expressed in a different language, but is in itself a different emotion from the love, or grief, or anger, of a clown,[6] a tradesman, or a market-wench. The things themselves are radically and obviously distinct; and the representation of them is calculated to convey a very different train of sympathies and sensations to the mind. The question, therefore, comes simply to be—which of them is the most proper object for poetical imitation? It is needless for us to answer a question, which the practice of all the world has long ago decided irrevocably. The poor and vulgar may interest us, in poetry, by their *situation;* but never, we apprehend, by any sentiments that are peculiar to their condition, and still less by any language that is characteristic of it. The truth is, that it is impossible to copy their diction or their sentiments correctly, in a serious composition; and this, not merely because poverty makes men ridiculous, but because just taste and refined sentiment are rarely

4. Robert Burns (Scots farmer poet) and Ann Yearsley, "the poetical milkwoman." See pages 397 and 251, 327.
5. A sarcastic reference to Southey's mock ode

The Chapel-Bell (1793) and his long *Hymn to the Penates* (1796); penates were Roman household deities.
6. A peasant.

to be met with among the uncultivated part of mankind; and a language, fitted for their expression, can still more rarely form any part of their "ordinary conversation."

* * * It has been argued, indeed, (for men will argue in support of what they do not venture to practice), that as the middling and lower orders of society constitute by far the greater part of mankind, so, their feelings and expressions should interest more extensively, and may be taken, more fairly than any other, for the standards of what is natural and true. To this, it seems obvious to answer, that the arts that aim at exciting admiration and delight, do not take their models from what is ordinary, but from what is excellent; and that our interest in the representation of any event, does not depend upon our familiarity with the original, but on its intrinsic importance, and the celebrity of the parties it concerns. The sculptor employs his art in delineating the graces of Antinous or Apollo, and not in the representation of those ordinary forms that belong to the crowd of his admirers. When a chieftain perishes in battle, his followers mourn more for him, than for thousands of their equals that may have fallen around him. * * *

The qualities of style and imagery, however, form but a small part of the characteristics by which a literary faction is to be distinguished. The subject and object of their compositions, and the principles and opinions they are calculated to support, constitute a far more important criterion, and one to which it is usually altogether easy to refer. Some poets are sufficiently described as the flatterers of greatness and power, and others as the champions of independence. One set of writers is known by its antipathy to decency and religion; another, by its methodistical cant and intolerance. Our new school of poetry has a moral character also; though it may not be possible, perhaps, to delineate it quite so concisely.

A splenetic and idle discontent with the existing institutions of society, seems to be at the bottom of all their serious and peculiar sentiments. Instead of contemplating the wonders and the pleasures which civilization has created for mankind, they are perpetually brooding over the disorders by which its progress has been attended. They are filled with horror and compassion at the sight of poor men spending their blood in the quarrels of princes, and brutifying their sublime capabilities in the drudgery of unremitting labour. For all sorts of vice and profligacy in the lower orders of society, they have the same virtuous horror, and the same tender compassion. While the existence of these offences overpowers them with grief and confusion, they never permit themselves to feel the smallest indignation or dislike towards the offenders. The present vicious constitution of society alone is responsible for all these enormities: the poor sinners are but the helpless victims or instruments of its disorders, and could not possibly have avoided the errors into which they have been betrayed. Though they can bear with crimes, therefore, they cannot reconcile themselves to punishments; and have an unconquerable antipathy to prisons, gibbets, and houses of correction, as engines of oppression, and instruments of atrocious injustice. While the plea of moral necessity is thus artfully brought forward to convert all the excesses of the poor into innocent misfortunes, no sort of indulgence is shown to the offences of the powerful and rich. Their oppressions, and seductions, and debaucheries, are the theme of many an angry verse; and the indignation and abhorrence of the reader is relentlessly conjured up against those perturbators of society, and scourges of mankind.

It is not easy to say, whether the fundamental absurdity of this doctrine, or the partiality of its application, be entitled to the severest reprehension.

1802

Charles Lamb: from *A letter to William Wordsworth*[1]

[Jan. 30, 1801]

Thanks for your Letter and Present. I had already borrowed your second volume.[2] What most please me are, the Song of Lucy.[3] ...I will mention one more: the delicate and curious feeling in the wish for the Cumberland Beggar, that he may have about him the melody of Birds, altho' he hear them not. Here the mind knowingly passes a fiction upon herself, first substituting her own feelings for the Beggar's, and, in the same breath detecting the fallacy, will not part with the wish.—* * * I will just add that it appears to me a fault in the Beggar, that the instructions conveyed in it are too direct and like a lecture:[4] they don't slide into the mind of the reader, while he is imagining no such matter. An intelligent reader finds a sort of insult in being told, I will teach you how to think upon this subject. * * * There is implied an unwritten compact between Author and reader; I will tell you a story, and I suppose you will understand it. * * *—I am sorry that Coleridge has christened his Ancient Marinere "a poet's Reverie"—it is as bad as Bottom the Weaver's declaration that he is not a Lion but only the scenical representation of a Lion.[5] What new idea is gained by this Title, but one subversive of all credit, which the tale should force upon us, of its truth? For me, I was never so affected with any human Tale. After first reading it, I was totally possessed with it for many days.—I dislike all the miraculous part of it, but the feelings of the man under the operation of such scenery dragged me along like Tom Piper's magic whistle. I totally differ from your idea that the Marinere should have had a character and profession. This is a Beauty in Gulliver's Travels, where the mind is kept in a placid state of little wonderments; but the Ancient Marinere undergoes such Trials, as overwhelm and bury all individuality or memory of what he was, like the state of a man in a Bad dream, one terrible peculiarity of which is: that all consciousness of personality is gone. Your other observation is I think as well a little unfounded: the Marinere from being conversant in supernatural events *has* acquired a supernatural and strange cast of *phrase*, eye, appearance, &c. which frighten the wedding guest. You will excuse my remarks, because I am hurt and vexed that you should think it necessary, with a prose apology,[6] to open the eyes of dead men that cannot see. To sum up a general opinion of the second vol.—I do not feel any one poem in it so forcibly as the Ancient Marinere, the Mad Mother, and the Lines at Tintern Abbey in the first.—I could, too, have wished the Critical preface had appeared in a separate treatise. All its dogmas are true and just, and most of them new, *as* criticism. But they associate a *diminishing* idea with the Poems which follow, as having been written for *Experiment* on the public taste, more than having sprung (as they must have done) from living and daily circumstances.—I am prolix, because I am gratifyed in the opportunity of writing to you, and I don't well know when to leave off. I ought before this to have reply'd to your very kind invitation into Cumberland.[7] With you and your Sister I could gang any where. But I am

1. For more about Lamb, see principal listing on page 1087. At the time of these letters, Lamb was an old friend of Coleridge and a newer acquaintance of the Wordsworths; he had published a novel and some verses, but his major career as an essayist was still to come.
2. Wordsworth had sent *Lyrical Ballads* (1800) to Lamb, who knew the poems in the first volume from the 1798 edition. The poems he discusses are newly published in Volume 2.

3. *Song* ("She dwelt among th'untrodden ways").
4. See lines 177–78.
5. In 1800, the subtitle was "A Poet's Reverie." In Shakespeare's *Midsummer Night's Dream* (5.1), Snug the Joiner says this, to allay Bottom's fear that the ladies in the audience will take him for a real lion (5.1.220 ff; cf. Bottom, 3.1.35–45).
6. The Preface of 1800.
7. In the Lake District.

afraid whether I shall ever be able to afford so desperate a Journey. Separate from the pleasure of your company, I don't much care if I never see a mountain in my life. I have passed all my days in London, until I have formed as many and intense local attachments, as any of you mountaineers can have done with dead nature. The Lighted shops of the Strand and Fleet Street, the innumerable trades, tradesmen and customers, coaches, waggons, playhouses, all the bustle and wickedness round about Covent Garden, the very women of the Town, the Watchmen, drunken scenes, rattles,[8]—life awake, if you awake, at all hours of the night, the impossibility of being dull in Fleet Street, the crowds, the very dirt & mud, the Sun shining upon houses and pavements, the print shops, the old book stalls, parsons cheap'ning books, coffee houses, steams of soups from kitchens, the pantomimes, London itself a pantomime and a masquerade,—all these things work themselves into my mind and feed me, without a power of satiating me. The wonder of these sights impells me into night-walks about her crowded streets, and I often shed tears in the motley Strand from fulness of joy at so much Life.—All these emotions must be strange to you. So are your rural emotions to me. But consider, what must I have been doing all my life, not to have lent great portions of my heart with usury to such scenes?—

Charles Lamb: from *A letter to Thomas Manning*[1]
[Feb. 15, 1801]

I had need be cautious henceforward what opinion I give of the "Lyrical Ballads." All the North of England are in a turmoil. Cumberland and Westmoreland have already declared a state of war.[2] I lately received from Wordsworth a copy of the second volume, accompanied by an acknowledgement of having received from me many months since a copy of a certain Tragedy,[3] with excuses for not having made any acknowledgement sooner, it being owing to an "almost insurmountable aversion from Letter-writing." This letter I answered in due form and time, and enumerated several of the passages which had most affected me, adding, unfortunately, that no single piece had moved me so forcibly as the "Ancient Mariner," "The Mad Mother," or the "Lines at Tintern Abbey." The Post did not sleep a moment. I received almost instantaneously a long letter of four sweating pages from my Reluctant Letter-Writer, the purport of which was, that he was sorry his 2d vol. had not given me more pleasure (Devil a hint did I give that it had *not pleased me*), and "was compelled to wish that my range of sensibility was more extended, being obliged to believe that I should receive large influxes of happiness and happy Thoughts" (I suppose from the L. B.)—With a deal of stuff about a certain Union of Tenderness and Imagination, which in the sense he used Imagination was not the characteristic of Shakspeare, but which Milton possessed in a degree far exceeding other Poets: which Union, as the highest species of Poetry, and chiefly deserving that name "He was most proud to aspire to;" then illustrating the said Union by two quotations from his own 2d vol. (which I had been so unfortunate as to miss) [quotes *Michael* 349–53]. These lines [352–53] were thus undermarked, and then followed "This Passage, as combining in an extraordinary

8. Watchmen's alarms.
1. One of Lamb's closest friends, Manning (1772–1840), mathematician and traveler, was considered the first scholar of Chinese literature in Europe; he was the first and, for many years, only Englishman to enter the holy

city of Lhasa, Tibet.
2. Coleridge was living in Cumberland county, the Wordsworths in Westmorelan.
3. By Lamb.

degree that Union of Imagination and Tenderness which I am speaking of, I consider as one of the Best I ever wrote!" * * * good Poetry: but after one has been reading Shakspeare twenty of the best years of one's life, to have a fellow start up, and prate about some unknown quality, which Shakspeare possessed in a degree inferior to Milton and *somebody else!!* This was not to be *all* my castigation. Coleridge, who had not written to me some months before, starts up from his bed of sickness to reprove me for my hardy presumption: four long pages, equally sweaty and more tedious, came from him; assuring me that, when the works of a man of true genius such as W. undoubtedly was, do not please me at first sight, I should suspect the fault to lie "in me and not in them," etc. etc. etc. etc. etc. What am I to do with such people? I certainly shall write them a very merry Letter. Writing to *you*, I may say that the 2d vol. has no such pieces. * * * It is full of original thinking and an observing mind, but it does not often make you laugh or cry.—It too artfully aims at simplicity of expression. And you sometimes doubt if Simplicity be not a cover for Poverty. The best Piece in it I will send you, being *short*. I have grievously offended my friends in the North by declaring my undue preference; but I need not fear you:—[quotes *Song (She dwelt among th'untrodden ways)*]. This is choice and genuine, and so are many, many more. But one does not like to have 'em rammed down one's throat. "Pray, take it—it's very good—let me help you—eat faster."

⌘

SONNETS, 1802–1807[1]

Prefatory Sonnet

Nuns fret not at their Convent's narrow room;[2]
And Hermits are contented with their Cells;
And Students with their pensive Citadels;
Maids at the Wheel, the Weaver at his Loom,
5 Sit blithe and happy; Bees that soar for bloom,
High as the highest Peak of Furness fells,°   *mountains*
Will murmur by the hour in Foxglove bells:
In truth, the prison, into which we doom
Ourselves, no prison is: and hence for me,
10 In sundry moods, 'twas pastime to be bound
Within the Sonnet's scanty plot of ground:
Pleas'd if some Souls (for such there needs must be)
Who have felt the weight of too much liberty,
Should find brief solace there, as I have found.

1802   1807

1. Wordsworth's first publication was his sonnet On seeing *Miss Helen Maria Williams Weep at a Tale of Distress* (1787), and he was encouraged by the revival of sonnet-writing at the end of the 18th century as well as by Milton's political sonnets. He wrote a number of sonnets in 1802, when he briefly visited France during the Peace of Amiens to settle affairs with Annette Vallon, prior to his marriage. For other sonnets from this period, see pages 282–83.

2. In 1802 Wordsworth praised Milton's sonnets for the "energetic and varied flow of sound crowding into narrow room more of the combined effect of rhyme and blank verse than can be done by any other kind of verse that I know of." He particularly liked Milton's stanzaic and linear enjambments (see his own wit about this device in line 10 where *bound* is unbound). For other sonnets on sonnet writing, see his "Scorn not the Sonnet" (page 591) and Keats's *Incipit altera Sonneta* (page 1003).

COMPOSED UPON
Westminster Bridge,
Sept. 3, 1802[1]

Earth has not any thing to shew more fair:
Dull would he be of soul who could pass by
A sight so touching in it's majesty:
This City now doth like a garment wear
5   The beauty of the morning; silent, bare,
Ships, towers, domes, theatres, and temples lie
Open unto the fields, and to the sky;
All bright and glittering in the smokeless air.
Never did sun more beautifully steep
10 In his first splendor, valley, rock, or hill;
Ne'er saw I, never felt, a calm so deep!
The river glideth at his own sweet will:
Dear God! the very houses seem asleep;
And all that mighty heart is lying still!

1802   1807

"The world is too much with us"

The world is too much with us; late and soon,
Getting and spending, we lay waste our powers:
Little we see in nature that is ours;
We have given our hearts away, a sordid boon!
5   The Sea that bares her bosom to the moon;
The Winds that will be howling at all hours
And are up-gathered now like sleeping flowers;
For this, for every thing, we are out of tune;
It moves us not. Great God! I'd rather be
10 A Pagan° suckled in a creed outworn;   *pre-Christian*
So might I, standing on this pleasant lea,
Have glimpses that would make me less forlorn;
Have sight of Proteus rising from the sea;
Or hear old Triton blow his wreathed horn.[1]

1802–1804   1807

"It is a beauteous Evening"[1]

It is a beauteous Evening, calm and free;
The holy time is quiet as a Nun
Breathless with adoration; the broad sun
Is sinking down in its tranquillity;

---

1. "Composed on the roof of a coach, on my way to
France" [I.F., 1843]. For the circumstances, see Dorothy
Wordsworth's *Grasmere Journals*, July 1802, page 610.
Wordsworth perhaps finished it in September (on his
return), and he did give the year as 1803 (corrected to
1802 in 1838). His confusion may have had to do with
his anxiety about his reunion with—and final departure
from—Annette Vallon and daughter Caroline.

1. Proteus is the shape-changing herdsman of the sea;
Triton, usually depicted blowing a conch shell, is a sea
deity. Cf. the personified "Sea" in line 5. See Dorothy
Wordsworth, page 610.
1. This was composed on the beach near Calais, in the
autumn of 1802 [Wordsworth's note, 1843]. Actually,
late August. See Dorothy Wordsworth, page 610.

5   The gentleness of heaven is on[2] the Sea:
Listen! the mighty Being is awake
And doth with his eternal motion make
A sound like thunder—everlastingly.
Dear Child! dear Girl! that walkest with me here,[3]
10 If thou appear'st untouch'd by solemn thought,
Thy nature is not therefore less divine:
Thou liest in Abraham's bosom[4] all the year;
And worshipp'st at the Temple's inner shrine,
God being with thee when we know it not.

1802   1807

"I griev'd for Buonaparte"[1]

I griev'd for Buonaparte, with a vain
And an unthinking grief! the vital blood
Of that Man's mind what can it be? What food
Fed his first hopes? What knowledge could *He* gain?
5   'Tis not in battles that from youth we train
The Governor who must be wise and good,
And temper with the sternness of the brain
Thoughts motherly, and meek as womanhood.
Wisdom doth live with children round her knees:
10 Books, leisure, perfect freedom, and the talk
Man holds with week-day man in the hourly walk
Of the mind's business: these are the degrees
By which true Sway° doth mount; this is the stalk   authority
True Power doth grow on; and her rights are these.

1802   1802/1803/1807

London, 1802[1]

Milton! thou should'st be living at this hour:
England hath need of thee: she is a fen
Of stagnant waters: altar, sword, and pen,

---

2. 1836] broods o'er.
3. Daughter Caroline.
4. Christ's description of the resting place for heaven-bound souls (Luke 16.22).
1. One afternoon in 1801, my sister read to me the Sonnets of Milton. I had long been well acquainted with them, but I was particularly struck on that occasion with the dignified simplicity and majestic harmony that runs through most of them,—in character so totally different from the Italian, and still more so from Shakspeare's fine sonnets. I took fire, if I may be allowed to say so, and produced three Sonnets the same afternoon, the first I ever wrote except an irregular one at school. Of these three, the only one I distinctly remember is, "I grieved for Buonaparté" [I.F., 1843]. Dorothy Wordsworth records the date as 21 May 1802. Buonaparte named himself

First Consul of France for life in 1802, taking the name Napoleon. His forces invaded Switzerland in October. Wordsworth's sonnet was first published in *The Morning Post* in September 1802. In the *Poems* of 1807, this sonnet and the next, as well as To *Toussaint L'Ouverture* (page 282) appear in a unit titled "Sonnets Dedicated to Liberty."
1. Written immediately after my return from France to London, when I could not but be struck...with the vanity and parade of our own country, especially in great towns and cities as contrasted with the quiet, and I may say desolation, that the revolution had produced in France. This must be borne in mind, or else the reader may think...I have exaggerated the mischief engendered and fostered among us by undisturbed wealth [Wordsworth's note, 1843].

Fireside, the heroic wealth of hall and bower,
5   Have forfeited their ancient English dower
Of inward happiness. We are selfish men;
Oh! raise us up, return to us again;
And give us manners, virtue, freedom, power.
Thy soul was like a Star and dwelt apart:
10   Thou hadst a voice whose sound was like the sea;.
Pure as the naked heavens, majestic, free,
So didst thou travel on life's common way,
In chearful godliness; and yet thy heart
The lowliest duties on itself did lay.

1802   1807

THE PRELUDE   Now regarded as Wordsworth's major work, The Prelude was unknown in his lifetime except to a small circle of family and friends. Though the poem was largely complete by 1805, Wordsworth continued to rework and polish it for the remaining forty-five years of his life, in an ongoing and intense self-inquiry into his childhood and youth. Published post-humously in 1850, The Prelude incorporates passages first written in the late 1790s. On a first reading, The Prelude appears to be a paean to the recovery of the past; on closer acquaintance it emerges as a great, self-conscious testimony to the construction of the past out of the urgent needs of the present. To compose the poem was also to compose the poet, to create Words-worth as The Poet, a meditative and resolute figure who had struggled through years of family disruption and revolutionary turmoil to a position of authority.

The Prelude evolved in three principal versions. Isolated in Germany in the coldest winter of the century, 1798–1799, Wordsworth wrote several passages about his childhood experiences in nature—sketches meant for The Recluse, a philosophic poem that Coleridge had urged him to write. By the time he and his sister Dorothy had settled in Grasmere in 1799, he had com-pleted a two-part poem of almost a thousand lines of blank verse, narrating his life from boy-hood through the age of seventeen. In 1801 he began to revise, though it was not until 1804 that he set to work in earnest. An initial plan for five books quickly became thirteen books, in-volving experiences in France and the crisis that followed the failure of his hopes for the French Revolution. The full version finished in 1805 combines earlier and later material, not always in chronological order, suggesting that the sequence of Wordsworth's life is less important than the imperatives shaping its argument. Further revised over the years, the poem was published by Wordsworth's widow in 1850. This was the only known text until 1926, when Ernest de Selin-court published that of 1805, the version we use.

Part confession, a crisis-autobiography descended from Saint Augustine's exemplary Confessions, The Prelude is also consciously English. Exceptionally personal, it is also a representa-tive story of youthful radicalism and a return to native heritage to become a national poet. To this degree, The Prelude stands as a rejoinder to Rousseau's notorious Confessions, but its chief, self-conscious parallel is Milton's Paradise Lost. The Prelude turns epic inward, claiming the growth of the poet's mind as an exalted subject. But it is not everywhere epic and prophetic: it is also an epistle to Coleridge, intimate and domestic, a record of friendship. The result is a shifting interplay between high genre and familiar conversation, between the adult poet looking back and trying to explain and the boy from whose sense of the mysterious the poem derives its originating power. Writing his story, Wordsworth sometimes felt possessed by "Two consciousnesses, conscious of myself / And of some other Being" (2.32–33). As he tries to close the gap in the act of writing, the ungraspable, elusive vacancies generate a structure that circles back in its large patterns, animated throughout by countermovements that uncannily create the effect of authenticity:

As oftentimes a River, it might seem,
Yielding in part to old remembrances,
Part sway'd by fear to tread an onward road
That leads direct to the devouring sea,
Turns and will measure back his course, far back
Towards the very regions which he cross'd
In his first outset; so have we long time
Made motions retrograde, in like pursuit
Detain'd.   (9.1–9)

The simile, in suggesting the "fear" of concluding as well as the pull of "old remembrances,"
lays open to view the conflicting dynamics of Wordsworth's autobiographical enterprise.

from The Prelude, or Growth of a Poet's Mind

Book First. Introduction, Childhood, and School time

Oh there is blessing in this gentle breeze[1]
That blows from the green fields and from the clouds
And from the sky: it beats against my cheek
And seems half conscious of the joy it gives.
5   O welcome Messenger! O welcome Friend!
A Captive greets thee, coming from a house
Of bondage,[2] from yon City's walls set free,
A prison where he hath been long immured.
Now I am free, enfranchis'd and at large,
10   May fix my habitation where I will.
What dwelling shall receive me? In what Vale
Shall be my harbour? Underneath what grove
Shall I take up my home, and what sweet stream
Shall with its murmurs lull me to my rest?
15   The earth is all before me:[3] with a heart
Joyous, nor scar'd at its own liberty
I look about, and should the guide I chuse
Be nothing better than a wandering cloud
I cannot miss my way. I breathe again;
20   Trances of thought and mountings of the mind
Come fast upon me: it is shaken off,
As by miraculous gift 'tis shaken off,
That burthen of my own unnatural self,
The heavy weight of many a weary day
25   Not mine, and such as were not made for me.
Long months of peace (if such bold word accord
With any promises of human life)
Long months of ease and undisturb'd delight
Are mine in prospect: whither shall I turn

---

1. Lines 1–54, which Wordsworth later called his "glad
preamble" (7.4), were composed in late 1799 or 1800.
Nature is his inspiring Muse or spirit ("spiritus" in Latin
means both "spirit" and "breeze").

2. Evoking Exodus 13.14: "the Lord brought us out from
Egypt, from the house of bondage."

3. At the end of *Paradise Lost*, Adam and Eve leave Eden:
"the world was all before them" (12.646ff.).

30   By road or pathway or through open field,
        Or shall a twig or any floating thing
        Upon the river, point me out my course?
            Enough that I am free; for months to come
        May dedicate myself to chosen tasks;
35   May quit the tiresome sea, and dwell on shore,
        If not a settler on the soil, at least
        To drink wild water, and to pluck green herbs,
        And gather fruits fresh from their native bough.
        Nay more, if I may trust myself, this hour
40   Hath brought a gift that consecrates my joy;
        For I, methought, while the sweet breath of Heaven
        Was blowing on my body, felt within
        A corresponding mild creative breeze,
        A vital breeze which travell'd gently on
45   O'er things which it had made, and is become
        A tempest, a redundant° energy   *abounding*
        Vexing its own creation. 'Tis a power
        That does not come unrecognis'd, a storm,
        Which, breaking up a long continued frost
50   Brings with it vernal° promises, the hope   *springtime*
        Of active days, of dignity and thought,
        Of prowess in an honorable field,
        Pure passions, virtue, knowledge, and delight,
        The holy life of music and of verse.
55   Thus far, O Friend! did I, not used to make
        A present joy the matter of my Song,[4]
        Pour out, that day, my soul in measur'd strains,
        Even in the very words which I have here
        Recorded: to the open fields I told
60   A prophecy: poetic numbers° came   *verses*
        Spontaneously, and cloth'd in priestly robe
        My spirit, thus singled out, as it might seem,
        For holy services: great hopes were mine;
        My own voice chear'd me, and, far more, the mind's
65   Internal echo of the imperfect sound:
        To both I listen'd, drawing from them both
        A chearful confidence in things to come.
            Whereat, being not unwilling now to give
        A respite to this passion, I paced on
70   Gently, with careless steps, and came erelong
        To a green shady place where down I sate
        Beneath a tree, slackening my thoughts by choice
        And settling into gentler happiness.
        'Twas Autumn, and a calm and placid day,
75   With warmth as much as needed from a sun

4. Coleridge is this Friend. In Preface to *Lyrical Ballads*, Wordsworth calls poetry "emotion recollected in tranquillity."

Two hours declin'd towards the west, a day
With silver clouds, and sunshine on the grass
And, in the shelter'd grove where I was couch'd,
A perfect stillness. On the ground I lay
80   Passing through many thoughts, yet mainly such
As to myself pertain'd. I made a choice
Of one sweet Vale° whither my steps should turn   *Grasmere*
And saw, methought, the very house and fields
Present before my eyes: nor did I fail
85   To add, meanwhile, assurance of some work
Of glory, there forthwith to be begun,[5]
Perhaps, too, there perform'd. Thus, long I lay
Chear'd by the genial pillow of the earth
Beneath my head, sooth'd by a sense of touch
90   From the warm ground, that balanced me, though lost
Entirely, seeing nought, nought hearing, save
When here and there, about the grove of Oaks
Where was my bed, an acorn from the trees
Fell audibly, and with a startling sound.
95   Thus occupied in mind, I linger'd here
Contented, nor rose up until the sun
Had almost touch'd the horizon; bidding then
A farewell to the City left behind,
Even on the strong temptation of that hour
100   And with its chance equipment, I resolved
To journey towards the Vale which I had chosen.
It was a splendid evening: and my soul
Did once again make trial of her strength
Restored to her afresh; nor did she want
105   Eolian visitations; but the harp[6]
Was soon defrauded, and the banded host
Of harmony dispers'd in straggling sounds
And, lastly, utter silence. "Be it so,
It is an injury," said I, "to this day
110   To think of any thing but present joy."
So like a Peasant I pursued my road
Beneath the evening sun; nor had one wish
Again to bend the sabbath of that time
To a servile yoke. What need of many words?
115   A pleasant loitering journey, through two days
Continued, brought me to my hermitage.°   *secluded dwelling*
    I spare to speak, my Friend, of what ensued,
The admiration and the love, the life
In common things; the endless store of things
120   Rare, or at least so seeming, every day
Found all about me in one neighbourhood,

---

5. *The Recluse* (never finished).   6. The Aeolian harp, named for Aeolus, mythic god of
                                                  the winds, resounds at the wind's touch.

The self-congratulation,° the complete   *rejoicing*
Composure, and the happiness entire.
But speedily a longing in me rose
125   To brace myself to some determin'd aim,
Reading or thinking, either to lay up
New stores, or rescue from decay the old
By timely interference, I had hopes
Still higher, that with a frame of outward life,
130   I might endue,° might fix in a visible home   *endow*
Some portion of those phantoms of conceit°   *mental images*
That had been floating loose about so long,
And to such Beings temperately deal forth
The many feelings that oppress'd my heart.
135   But I have been discouraged: gleams of light
Flash often from the East, then disappear
And mock me with a sky that ripens not
Into a steady morning: if my mind,
Remembering the sweet promise of the past,
140   Would gladly grapple with some noble theme,
Vain is her wish; where'er she turns she finds
Impediments from day to day renew'd.
        And now it would content me to yield up
Those lofty hopes a while for present gifts
145   Of humbler industry. But, O dear Friend!
The Poet, gentle creature as he is,
Hath, like the Lover, his unruly times;
His fits when he is neither sick nor well,
Though no distress be near him but his own
150   Unmanageable thoughts. The mind itself,
The meditative mind, best pleased, perhaps,
While she, as duteous as the Mother Dove,
Sits brooding,[7] lives not always to that end
But hath less quiet instincts, goadings-on
155   That drive her, as in trouble, through the groves.
With me is now such passion, which I blame
No otherwise than as it lasts too long.
        When, as becomes a man who would prepare
For such a glorious work, I through myself
160   Make rigorous inquisition, the report
Is often chearing; for I neither seem
To lack, that first great gift! the vital soul,
Nor general truths which are themselves a sort
Of Elements and Agents, Under-Powers,
165   Subordinate helpers of the living mind.
Nor am I naked in external things,
Forms, images; nor numerous other aids

---

7. Incubating; but with a pun on mental work.

Of less regard, though won perhaps with toil,
And needful to build up a Poet's praise.

170 Time, place, and manners;° these I seek, and these   *customs*
I find in plenteous store; but nowhere such
As may be singled out with steady choice;
No little Band of yet remember'd names
Whom I, in perfect confidence, might hope

175 To summon back from lonesome banishment
And make them inmates in the hearts of men
Now living, or to live in times to come.
Sometimes, mistaking vainly, as I fear,
Proud spring-tide swellings for a regular sea

180 I settle on some British theme, some old
Romantic tale, by Milton left unsung:[8]
More often, resting at some gentle place
Within the groves of Chivalry, I pipe
Among the Shepherds, with reposing Knights

185 Sit by a Fountain-side, and hear their tales.
Sometimes, more sternly mov'd, I would relate
How vanquish'd Mithridates northward pass'd,
And, hidden in the cloud of years, became
That Odin, Father of a Race by whom

190 Perish'd the Roman Empire:[9] how the Friends
And Followers of Sertorius, out of Spain
Flying, found shelter in the Fortunate Isles;[1]
And left their usages, their arts, and laws
To disappear by a slow gradual death;

195 To dwindle and to perish one by one
Starved in those narrow bounds: but not the Soul
Of Liberty, which fifteen hundred years
Surviv'd, and when the European° came   *(Spanish conquerors)*
With skill and power that could not be withstood,

200 Did like a pestilence maintain its hold,
And wasted down by glorious death that Race
Of natural Heroes: or I would record
How in tyrannic times some unknown Man,
Unheard of in the Chronicles of Kings,

205 Suffer'd in silence for the love of truth:
How that one Frenchman,[2] through continued force
Of meditation on the inhuman deeds
Of the first Conquerors of the Indian Isles,
Went single in his ministry across

---

8. Milton considered writing tales of "Heroic Martyrdom" or a "Romantic" epic about Arthurian knights before settling on his biblical theme.
9. In *Decline and Fall of the Roman Empire* (1776–1788), Edward Gibbon had proposed that the Norse god Odin was originally a tribal chieftain who had attacked Rome, perhaps historical King Mithridates of Asia Minor,

defeated by the Romans in the 1st century B.C.E.
1. Canary Islands. Roman general Sertorius, ally of Mithridates, was assassinated in 72 B.C.E.
2. In 1568 Dominique de Gourges "went to Florida to avenge the massacre of the French by the Spaniards there" [Wordsworth's note, 1850].

210   The Ocean, not to comfort the Oppress'd,
      But, like a thirsty wind, to roam about,
      Withering the Oppressor: how Gustavus found
      Help at his need in Dalecarlia's Mines;³
      How Wallace fought for Scotland,⁴ left the name
215   Of Wallace to be found like a wild flower,
      All over his dear Country, left the deeds
      Of Wallace, like a Family of Ghosts,
      To people the steep rocks and river banks,
      Her natural sanctuaries, with a local soul
220   Of independence and stern liberty.
      Sometimes it suits me better to shape out
      Some Tale from my own heart, more near akin
      To my own passions and habitual thoughts,
      Some variegated story, in the main
225   Lofty, with interchange of gentler things;
      But deadening admonitions will succeed,
      And the whole beauteous Fabric seems to lack
      Foundation, and, withal, appears throughout
      Shadowy and unsubstantial. Then, last wish,
230   My last and favorite aspiration! then
      I yearn towards some philosophic Song
      Of Truth that cherishes° our daily life;   holds dear
      With meditations passionate from deep
      Recesses in man's heart, immortal verse
235   Thoughtfully fitted to the Orphean lyre;⁵
      But from this awful° burthen I full soon   solemn
      Take refuge, and beguile myself with trust
      That mellower years will bring a riper mind
      And clearer insight. Thus from day to day
240   I live, a mockery of the brotherhood
      Of vice and virtue, with no skill to part
      Vague longing that is bred by want of power
      From paramount impulse not to be withstood,
      A timorous capacity from prudence;
245   From circumspection infinite delay.
      Humility and modest awe themselves
      Betray me, serving often for a cloak
      To a more subtle selfishness, that now
      Doth lock my functions up in blank reserve,°   inertia
250   Now dupes me by an over anxious eye
      That with a false activity beats off
      Simplicity and self-presented truth.
      —Ah! better far than this, to stray about

3. Where, in hiding, Gustavus I of Sweden (1496–1530) planned his country's revolt from Danish rule.
4. William Wallace fought for the liberty of Scotland; he was executed by the British in 1305. See Robert Burns, *Scots wha' hae*, page 403.
5. In Greek myth, musician Orpheus could enthrall all creation. Coleridge praised *The Prelude* as "an Orphic Tale indeed."

Voluptuously° through fields and rural walks,   *luxuriantly*
255 And ask no record of the hours, given up
      To vacant musing, unreprov'd neglect
      Of all things, and deliberate holiday:
      Far better never to have heard the name
      Of zeal and just ambition, than to live
260 Thus baffled by a mind that every hour
      Turns recreant to her task, takes heart again
      Then feels immediately some hollow thought
      Hang like an interdict° upon her hopes.   *prohibition*
      This is my lot; for either still I find
265 Some imperfection in the chosen theme;
      Or see of absolute accomplishment
      Much wanting, so much wanting in myself,
      That I recoil and droop, and seek repose
      In indolence from vain perplexity,
270 Unprofitably travelling towards the grave,
      Like a false Steward who hath much receiv'd
      And renders nothing back.⁶—Was it for this
      That one, the fairest of all Rivers,⁷ lov'd
      To blend his murmurs with my Nurse's song
275 And from his alder shades and rocky falls,
      And from his fords and shallows sent a voice
      That flow'd along my dreams? For this didst Thou,
      O Derwent! travelling over the green Plains
      Near my sweet birth-place,⁸ didst thou, beauteous Stream,
280 Make ceaseless music through the night and day
      Which with its steady cadence tempering
      Our human waywardness, composed my thoughts
      To more than infant softness, giving me,
      Among the fretful dwellings of mankind,
285 A knowledge, a dim earnest of the calm
      Which Nature breathes among the hills and groves.
          When, having left his Mountains, to the Towers
      Of Cockermouth that beauteous River came,
      Behind my Father's House he pass'd, close by,
290 Along the margin of our Terrace Walk.
      He was a Playmate whom we dearly lov'd.
      Oh! many a time have I, a five years' Child,
      A naked Boy, in one delightful Rill,
      A little Mill-race sever'd from his stream,
295 Made one long bathing of a summer's day,
      Bask'd in the sun, and plunged, and bask'd again,
      Alternate all a summer's day, or cours'd

---

6. Jesus's parable of the steward who fails to use his talents (literally a coin; metaphorically, God's gifts), in Matthew 25.14–30, also the referent of Milton's famous sonnet, *On His Blindness*.

7. The Derwent flows behind Wordsworth's childhood home in Cockermouth, Cumberland.
8. Quoting Coleridge's *Frost at Midnight* (line 28).

Over the sandy fields, leaping through groves
Of yellow grunsel,° or when crag and hill,   *ragweed*
300   The woods, and distant Skiddaw's[9] lofty height,
Were bronz'd with a deep radiance, stood alone
Beneath the sky, as if I had been born
On Indian Plains,° and from my Mother's hut   *in America*
Had run abroad in wantonness, to sport,
305   A naked Savage, in the thunder shower.
     Fair seed-time had my soul, and I grew up
Foster'd alike by beauty and by fear;
Much favor'd in my birth-place, and no less
In that beloved Vale[1] to which, erelong,
310   I was transplanted. Well I call to mind,
('Twas at an early age, ere I had seen
Nine summers) when upon the mountain slope
The frost, and breath of frosty wind had snapp'd
The last autumnal crocus, 'twas my joy
315   To wander half the night among the Cliffs
And the smooth Hollows, where the woodcocks ran
Along the open turf. In thought and wish,
That time, my shoulder all with springes° hung,   *bird-traps*
I was a fell destroyer. On the heights
320   Scudding away from snare to snare, I plied
My anxious visitation, hurrying on,
Still hurrying, hurrying onward: moon and stars
Were shining o'er my head; I was alone
And seem'd to be a trouble to the peace
325   That was among them. Sometimes it befel
In these night-wanderings, that a strong desire
O'erpower'd my better reason, and the bird
Which was the captive of another's toils°   *labors, snares*
Became my prey; and, when the deed was done,
330   I heard among the solitary hills
Low breathings coming after me, and sounds
Of undistinguishable motion, steps
Almost as silent as the turf they trod.
     Nor less in spring-time when on southern banks
335   The shining sun had from her knot of leaves
Decoy'd the primrose flower, and when the Vales
And woods were warm, was I a plunderer then
In the high places, on the lonesome peaks
Where'er, among the mountains and the winds,
340   The Mother Bird had built her lodge. Though mean
My object, and inglorious, yet the end
Was not ignoble. Oh! when I have hung
Above the raven's nest, by knots of grass,

---

9. At 3,053 feet, one of the highest peaks of the Lake District, nine miles east of Cockermouth.

1. Esthwaite, where Wordsworth went to school, 35 miles
from Cockermouth.

And half-inch fissures in the slippery rock
345   But ill sustain'd, and almost, as it seem'd,
Suspended by the blast which blew amain,
Shouldering the naked crag; Oh! at that time,
While on the perilous ridge I hung alone,
With what strange utterance did the loud dry wind
350   Blow through my ears! the sky seem'd not a sky
Of earth, and with what motion mov'd the clouds!
        The mind of man is framed even like the breath
And harmony of music. There is a dark
Invisible workmanship that reconciles
355   Discordant elements, and makes them move
In one society. Ah me! that all
The terrors, all the early miseries,
Regrets, vexations, lassitudes, that all
The thoughts and feelings which have been infus'd
360   Into my mind should ever have made up
The calm existence that is mine when I
Am worthy of myself. Praise to the end!
Thanks likewise for the means! But I believe
That Nature, oftentimes, when she would frame
365   A favor'd Being, from his earliest dawn
Of infancy doth open out the clouds,
As at the touch of lightning, seeking him
With gentlest visitation: not the less,
Though haply° aiming at the self-same end,   *perhaps*
370   Does it delight her sometimes to employ
Severer interventions, ministry
More palpable, and so she dealt with me.
        One evening (surely I was led by her)
I went alone into a Shepherd's Boat,
375   A Skiff that to a Willow tree was tied
Within a rocky Cave, its usual home.
'Twas by the Shores of Patterdale, a Vale
Wherein I was a Stranger, thither come,
A School-boy Traveller, at the Holidays.
380   Forth rambled from the Village Inn alone
No sooner had I sight of this small Skiff,
Discover'd thus by unexpected chance,
Than I unloos'd her tether and embark'd.
The moon was up, the Lake was shining clear
385   Among the hoary mountains: from the Shore
I push'd, and struck the oars and struck again
In cadence, and my little Boat mov'd on
Even like a Man who walks with stately step
Though bent on speed. It was an act of stealth
390   And troubled pleasure: nor without the voice
Of mountain echoes did my Boat move on,
Leaving behind her still on either side

Small circles glittering idly in the moon
Until they melted all into one track
395   Of sparkling light. A rocky steep uprose
Above the Cavern of the Willow tree
And now, as suited one who proudly row'd
With his best skill, I fix'd a steady view
Upon the top of that same craggy ridge,[2]
400   The bound of the horizon, for behind
Was nothing but the stars and the grey sky.
She was an elfin Pinnace;° lustily   *small boat*
I dipp'd my oars into the silent Lake,
And, as I rose upon the stroke, my Boat
405   Went heaving through the water, like a Swan,
When from behind that craggy Steep, till then
The bound of the horizon, a huge Cliff,
As if with voluntary power instinct,°   *endowed*
Uprear'd its head: I struck, and struck again,
410   And, growing still in stature, the huge Cliff
Rose up between me and the stars, and still,
With measur'd motion, like a living thing,
Strode after me. With trembling hands I turn'd,
And through the silent water stole my way
415   Back to the Cavern of the Willow tree.
There, in her mooring-place, I left my Bark
And, through the meadows homeward went with grave
And serious thoughts: and after I had seen
That spectacle, for many days my brain
420   Work'd with a dim and undetermin'd sense
Of unknown modes of being: in my thoughts
There was a darkness, call it solitude,
Or blank desertion, no familiar shapes
Of hourly objects, images of trees,
425   Of sea, or sky, no colours of green fields;
But huge and mighty Forms that do not live
Like living men mov'd slowly through my mind
By day and were the trouble of my dreams.
          Wisdom and Spirit of the Universe![3]
430   Thou Soul that art the Eternity of Thought!
And giv'st to forms and images a breath
And everlasting motion! not in vain,
By day or starlight thus from my first dawn
Of Childhood didst Thou intertwine for me
435   The passions that build up our human Soul,
Not with the mean and vulgar° works of Man,   *lowly and ordinary*
But with high objects, with enduring things,

2. The rower faces the stern and fixes his sight on a shore-
point, in order to move the boat in a straight line.
3. Coleridge published 429–90 in *The Friend* (28

December 1809), under the title "Growth of Genius from
the Influence of Natural Objects, on the Imagination in
Boyhood, and Early Youth."

With life and nature, purifying thus
The elements of feeling and of thought,
440   And sanctifying by such discipline
Both pain and fear until we recognise
A grandeur in the beatings of the heart.
        Nor was this fellowship vouchsaf'd to me
With stinted kindness. In November days
445   When vapours, rolling down the valleys, made
A lonely scene more lonesome; among woods
At noon, and 'mid the calm of summer nights,
When by the margin of the trembling Lake
Beneath the gloomy hills I homeward went
450   In solitude, such intercourse was mine;
'Twas mine among the fields both day and night,
And by the waters all the summer long.
—And in the frosty season, when the sun
Was set, and, visible for many a mile,
455   The cottage windows through the twilight blaz'd,
I heeded not the summons:—happy time
It was indeed for all of us; to me
It was a time of rapture: clear and loud
The village clock toll'd six; I wheel'd about,
460   Proud and exulting, like an untired horse,
That cares not for its home.—All shod with steel
We hiss'd along the polish'd ice, in games
Confederate, imitative of the chace,
And woodland pleasures, the resounding horn,
465   The Pack, loud bellowing, and the hunted hare.
So through the darkness and the cold we flew,
And not a voice was idle: with the din,
Meanwhile, the precipices rang aloud,
The leafless trees, and every icy crag
470   Tinkled like iron, while the distant hills
Into the tumult sent an alien sound
Of melancholy, not unnoticed, while the stars,
Eastward, were sparkling clear, and in the west,
The orange sky of evening died away.
475   Not seldom from the uproar I retired
Into a silent bay, or sportively
Glanced sideway, leaving the tumultuous throng,
To cut across the image of a star
That gleam'd upon the ice: and oftentimes,
480   When we had given our bodies to the wind,
And all the shadowy banks, on either side,
Came sweeping through the darkness, spinning still
The rapid line of motion; then at once
Have I, reclining back upon my heels,
485   Stopp'd short, yet still the solitary Cliffs
Wheel'd by me, even as if the earth had roll'd

With visible motion her diurnal° round;   *daily*
Behind me did they stretch in solemn train
Feebler and feebler, and I stood and watch'd
490   Till all was tranquil as [   ]⁴
    Ye Presences of Nature, in the sky
Or on the earth! Ye Visions of the hills!
And Souls of lonely places! can I think
A vulgar hope was yours when Ye employ'd
495   Such ministry, when Ye through many a year
Haunting me thus among my boyish sports,
On caves and trees, upon the woods and hills,
Impress'd upon all forms the characters°   *marks, signs*
Of danger or desire, and thus did make
500   The surface of the universal earth
With triumph, and delight, and hope, and fear
Work° like a sea.   *seethe*
        Not uselessly employ'd,
I might pursue this theme through every change
Of exercise and play, to which the year
505   Did summon us in its delightful round.
—We were a noisy crew; the sun in heaven
Beheld not vales more beautiful than ours
Nor saw a race, in happiness and joy
More worthy of the fields where they were sown.
510   I would record with no reluctant voice
The woods of autumn and their hazel bowers⁵
With milk-white clusters hung; the rod and line,
True symbol of the foolishness of hope,
Which with its strong enchantment led us on
515   By rocks and pools, shut out from every star
All the green summer, to forlorn cascades
Among the windings of the mountain-brooks.
—Unfading recollections! at this hour
The heart is almost mine with which I felt
520   From some hill-top, on sunny afternoons,
The Kite high up among the fleecy clouds
Pull at its rein, like an impatient Courser,°   *racehorse*
Or, from the meadows sent on gusty days
Beheld her breast the wind, then suddenly
525   Dash'd headlong; and rejected by the storm.
    Ye lowly Cottages in which we dwelt,
A ministration of your own was yours,
A sanctity, a safeguard, and a love!
Can I forget you, being as ye were
530   So beautiful among the pleasant fields
In which ye stood? Or can I here forget

---

4. Wordsworth left the end of this line blank in 1805. In   5. *Nutting* (page 450) was originally part of this poem.
1809, it was completed as "a dreamless sleep."

The plain and seemly countenance with which
Ye dealt out your plain comforts? Yet had ye
Delights and exultations of your own.
535   Eager and never weary we pursued
Our home amusements by the warm peat fire
At evening; when with pencil and with slate,
In square divisions parcell'd out, and all
With crosses and with cyphers scribbled o'er,°   *tic-tac-toe*
540   We schemed and puzzled, head opposed to head,
In strife too humble to be named in Verse;
Or round the naked Table, snow-white deal,°   *pine*
Cherry, or maple, sate in close array,
And to the combat, Lu or Whist,° led on   *(card games)*
545   A thick-ribb'd Army, not as in the world
Neglected and ungratefully thrown by
Even for the very service they had wrought,
But husbanded through many a long campaign.
Uncouth assemblage was it, where no few
550   Had changed their functions, some, plebean cards,
Which Fate beyond the promise of their birth
Had glorified, and call'd to represent
The persons of departed Potentates.
Oh! with what echoes on the Board they fell!
555   Ironic Diamonds; Clubs, Hearts, Diamonds, Spades,
A congregation piteously akin;
Cheap matter did they give to boyish wit,
Those sooty Knaves, precipitated down
With scoffs and taunts, like Vulcan out of Heaven,
560   The paramount Ace, a moon in her eclipse,
Queens, gleaming through their splendour's last decay,
And Monarchs, surly at the wrongs sustain'd
By royal visages. Meanwhile, abroad
The heavy rain was falling, or the frost
565   Raged bitterly, with keen and silent tooth,
And, interrupting the impassion'd game,
From Esthwaite's neighbouring Lake the splitting ice,
While it sank down towards the water, sent,
Among the meadows and the hills, its long
570   And dismal yellings, like the noise of wolves
When they are howling round the Bothnic Main.°   *Baltic Sea*
     Nor, sedulous[6] as I have been to trace
How Nature by extrinsic passion first
Peopled my mind with beauteous forms or grand,
575   And made me love them, may I well forget
How other pleasures have been mine, and joys
Of subtler origin; how I have felt
Not seldom, even in that tempestuous time,

6. Diligent; revising Milton's claim that he is "Not sedulous by Nature" to treat epic themes (*Paradise Lost* 9.27).

Those hallow'd and pure motions of the sense
580 Which seem, in their simplicity, to own
An intellectual charm, that calm delight
Which, if I err not, surely must belong
To those first-born affinities that fit
Our new existence to existing things
585 And, in our dawn of being, constitute
The bond of union betwixt life and joy.
　　　Yes, I remember, when the changeful earth,
And twice five seasons on my mind had stamp'd
The faces of the moving year, even then,
590 A Child, I held unconscious intercourse
With the eternal Beauty, drinking in
A pure organic pleasure from the lines
Of curling mist, or from the level plain
Of waters colour'd by the steady clouds.
595 　　　The Sands of Westmoreland, the Creeks and Bays
Of Cumbria's rocky limits, they can tell
How when the Sea threw off his evening shade
And to the Shepherd's hut beneath the crags
Did send sweet notice of the rising moon,
600 How I have stood to fancies such as these,
Engrafted in the tenderness of thought,
A stranger, linking with the spectacle
No conscious memory of a kindred sight,
And bringing with me no peculiar sense
605 Of quietness or peace, yet have I stood,
Even while mine eye has mov'd o'er three long leagues°　　　*about nine miles*
Of shining water, gathering, as it seem'd,
Through every hair-breadth of that field of light,
New pleasure, like a bee among the flowers.
610 　　　Thus, often in those fits of vulgar° joy　　　*ordinary*
Which through all seasons, on a child's pursuits
Are prompt attendants, 'mid that giddy bliss
Which, like a tempest, works along the blood
And is forgotten; even then I felt
615 Gleams like the flashing of a shield: the earth
And common face of Nature spake to me
Remembrable things: sometimes, 'tis true,
By chance collisions, and quaint accidents
Like those ill-sorted unions, work suppos'd
620 Of evil-minded fairies, yet not vain,
Nor profitless, if haply they impress'd
Collateral° objects and appearances,　　　*secondary*
Albeit lifeless then, and doom'd to sleep
Until maturer seasons call'd them forth
625 To impregnate and to elevate the mind.
And if the vulgar joy by its own weight
Wearied itself out of the memory

The scenes which were a witness of that joy
Remained, in their substantial lineaments
630 Depicted on the brain, and to the eye
Were visible, a daily sight: and thus,
By the impressive discipline of fear,
By pleasure, and repeated happiness,
So frequently repeated, and by force
635 Of obscure feelings representative
Of joys that were forgotten, these same scenes,
So beauteous and majestic in themselves,
Though yet the day was distant, did at length
Become habitually dear; and all
640 Their hues and forms were by invisible links
Allied to the affections.
                                      I began
My Story early, feeling as I fear,
The weakness of a human love, for days
Disown'd by memory, ere the birth of spring
645 Planting my snow-drops among winter snows.
Nor will it seem to thee, my Friend! so prompt
In sympathy, that I have lengthen'd out,
With fond and feeble tongue, a tedious tale.
Meanwhile, my hope has been that I might fetch
650 Invigorating thoughts from former years,
Might fix the wavering balance of my mind,
And haply meet reproaches, too, whose power
May spur me on, in manhood now mature,
To honorable toil. Yet should these hopes
655 Be vain, and thus should neither I be taught
To understand myself, nor thou to know
With better knowledge how the heart was fram'd
Of him thou lovest, need I dread from thee
Harsh judgments, if I am so loth to quit
660 Those recollected hours that have the charm
Of visionary things, and lovely forms,
And sweet sensations that throw back our life
And almost make our Infancy itself
A visible scene on which the sun is shining.
665   One end hereby, at least, hath been attain'd—
My mind hath been reviv'd, and if this mood
Desert me not, I will forthwith bring down,
Through later years, the story of my life.
The road lies plain before me; 'tis a theme
670 Single, and of determin'd bounds; and hence
I chuse it rather, at this time, than work
Of ampler or more varied argument.[7]

7. Wordsworth wrote this last paragraph in 1804, addressing Coleridge's desire for a major philosophical epic.

from **Book Second. School time continued**

[TWO CONSCIOUSNESSES]

Thus far, O Friend! have we, though leaving much
Unvisited, endeavour'd to retrace
My life through its first years, and measur'd back[1]
The way I travell'd when I first began
5   To love the woods and fields: the passion yet
Was in its birth, sustain'd, as might befal,
By nourishment that came unsought; for still,
From week to week, from month to month we liv'd
A round of tumult: duly were our games
10   Prolong'd in summer till the daylight fail'd;
No chair remain'd before the doors, the bench
And threshold steps were empty; fast asleep
The Labourer, and the Old Man who had sate,
A later lingerer, yet the revelry
15   Continued, and the loud uproar: at last,
When all the ground was dark, and the huge clouds
Were edged with twinkling stars, to bed we went
With weary joints, and with a beating mind.
Ah! is there one who ever has been young,
20   And needs a monitory voice to tame
The pride of virtue, and of intellect?
And is there one, the wisest and the best
Of all mankind, who does not sometimes wish
For things which cannot be, who would not give,
25   If so he might, to duty and to truth
The eagerness of infantine desire?
A tranquillizing spirit presses now
On my corporeal frame: so wide appears
The vacancy between me and those days,
30   Which yet have such self-presence in my mind
That, sometimes, when I think of them, I seem
Two consciousnesses, conscious of myself
And of some other Being.

[BLESSED INFANT BABE]

Bless'd the infant Babe,[2]
(For with my best conjectures I would trace
The progress of our being) blest the Babe,
240   Nurs'd in his Mother's arms, the Babe who sleeps
Upon his Mother's breast, who, when his soul
Claims manifest kindred with an earthly soul,

---

1. A pun on poetic measures (meters). See "measur'd strains" (1.57).
2. Just before this speculation on psychobiography, Words-

worth had been musing on how hard it is "to analyse a soul" when no certain origin can be known for one's habits and desires, or any "obvious and particular thought."

Doth gather passion from his Mother's eye!
Such feelings pass into his torpid life
245   Like an awakening breeze, and hence his mind
Even [in the first trial of its powers,][3]
Is prompt and watchful, eager to combine
In one appearance, all the elements
And parts of the same object, else detach'd
250   And loth to coalesce. Thus, day by day,
Subjected to the discipline of love,
His organs and recipient faculties
Are quicken'd, are more vigorous, his mind spreads,
Tenacious of the forms which it receives.
255   In one beloved presence, nay and more,
In that most apprehensive habitude°   *capacity to assimilate*
And those sensations which have been deriv'd
From this beloved Presence, there exists
A virtue which irradiates and exalts
260   All objects through all intercourse of sense.
No outcast he, bewilder'd and depress'd:
Along his infant veins are interfus'd
The gravitation and the filial bond
Of nature, that connect him with the world.
265   Emphatically such a Being lives,
An inmate of this *active* universe;
From nature largely he receives; nor so
Is satisfied, but largely gives again,
For feeling has to him imparted strength,
270   And powerful in all sentiments of grief,
Of exultation, fear, and joy, his mind,
Even as an agent of the one great mind,
Creates, creator and receiver both,
Working but in alliance with the works
275   Which it beholds.—Such, verily, is the first
Poetic spirit of our human life;
By uniform controul of after years
In most abated and suppress'd, in some,
Through every change of growth or of decay,
280   Pre-eminent till death.
                              From early days,
Beginning not long after that first time
In which, a Babe, by intercourse of touch,
I held mute dialogues with my Mother's heart,
I have endeavour'd to display the means
285   Whereby the infant sensibility,
Great birth-right of our Being, was in me
Augmented and sustain'd. Yet is a path

---

3. This line was completed decades later.

More difficult before me, and I fear
That in its broken windings we shall need
290   The chamois'° sinews, and the eagle's wing: *mountain antelope*
For now a trouble came into my mind
From unknown causes. I was left alone,
Seeking the visible world, nor knowing why.
The props of my affections were remov'd,
295   And yet the building stood, as if sustain'd
By its own spirit![4] All that I beheld
Was dear to me, and from this cause it came,
That now to Nature's finer influxes°   *influences, impressions*
My mind lay open, to that more exact
300   And intimate communion which our hearts
Maintain with the minuter properties
Of objects which already are belov'd,
And of those only.

from Book Fourth. Summer Vacation

[A SIMILE FOR AUTOBIOGRAPHY]

As one who hangs, down-bending from the side
Of a slow-moving Boat, upon the breast
Of a still water, solacing himself
250   With such discoveries as his eye can make,
Beneath him, in the bottom of the deeps,
Sees many beauteous sights, weeds, fishes, flowers,
Grots, pebbles, roots of trees, and fancies[1] more;
Yet often is perplex'd, and cannot part
255   The shadow from the substance, rocks and sky,
Mountains and clouds, from that which is indeed
The region, and the things which there abide
In their true dwelling; now is cross'd by gleam
Of his own image, by a sun-beam now
260   And motions that are sent he knows not whence,
Impediments that make his task more sweet.
—Such pleasant office have we long pursued,
Incumbent o'er the surface of past time
With like success: nor have we often look'd
265   On more alluring shows (to me at least)
More soft, or less ambiguously descried,
Than those which now we have been passing by,
And where we still are lingering. Yet, in spite
Of all these new employments of the mind
270   There was an inner falling-off.

4. Perhaps an oblique reference to the death of his   1. The syntax allows *fancies* to be a noun or a verb.
mother when he was almost eight years old.

[Encounter with a "Dismissed" Soldier]²

360   From many wanderings that have left behind
         Remembrances not lifeless, I will here
         Single out one, then pass to other themes.
         ————A favorite pleasure hath it been with me,
         From time of earliest youth, to walk alone,
365   Along the public Way, when, for the night
         Deserted, in its silence it assumes
         A character of deeper quietness
         Than pathless solitudes. At such an hour
         Once, ere those summer months were pass'd away
370   I slowly mounted up a steep ascent
         Where the road's watry surface, to the ridge
         Of that sharp rising, glitter'd in the moon,
         And seem'd before my eyes another stream
         Creeping with silent lapse° to join the brook   *downward flow*
375   That murmur'd in the Valley. On I went
         Tranquil, receiving in my own despite
         Amusement, as I slowly pass'd along,
         From such near objects as from time to time
         Perforce intruded on the listless sense
380   Quiescent, and dispos'd to sympathy
         With an exhausted mind, worn out by toil,
         And all unworthy of the deeper joy
         Which waits on distant prospect, cliff, or sea,
         The dark blue vault, and universe of stars.
385   Thus did I steal along that silent road,
         My body from the stillness drinking in
         A restoration like the calm of sleep
         But sweeter far. Above, before, behind,
         Around me, all was peace and solitude;
390   I look'd not round, nor did the solitude
         Speak to my eye; but it was heard and felt.
         O happy state! what beauteous pictures now
         Rose in harmonious imagery—they rose
         As from some distant region of my soul
395   And came along like dreams; yet such as left
         Obscurely mingled with their passing forms
         A consciousness of animal delight,
         A self-possession felt in every pause
         And every gentle movement of my frame.
400   While thus I wander'd, step by step led on,
         It chanced a sudden turning of the road
         Presented to my view an uncouth° shape   *unfamiliar, strange*

---

2. Wordsworth is home on vacation from Cambridge University. This episode, which closes Book 4, was originally an independent poem, written in early 1798.

So near, that, slipping back into the shade
Of a thick hawthorn, I could mark him well,
405 Myself unseen. He was of stature tall,
A foot above man's common measure tall,
Stiff in his form, and upright, lank and lean,
A man more meagre,° as it seem'd to me,   *gaunt*
Was never seen abroad by night or day.
410 His arms were long, and bare his hands; his mouth
Shew'd ghastly in the moonlight: from behind
A mile-stone propp'd him, and his figure seem'd
Half-sitting, and half-standing. I could mark
That he was clad in military garb,
415 Though faded yet entire. He was alone,
Had no attendant, neither Dog, nor Staff,
Nor knapsack; in his very dress appear'd
A desolation, a simplicity
That seem'd akin to solitude. Long time
420 Did I peruse him with a mingled sense
Of fear and sorrow. From his lips, meanwhile,
There issued murmuring sounds, as if of pain
Or of uneasy thought; yet still his form
Kept the same steadiness, and at his feet
425 His shadow lay and mov'd not. In a Glen
Hard by, a Village stood, whose roofs and doors
Were visible among the scatter'd trees,
Scarce distant from the spot an arrow's flight;
I wish'd to see him move; but he remain'd
430 Fix'd to his place, and still from time to time
Sent forth a murmuring voice of dead complaint,
Groans scarcely audible. Without self-blame
I had not thus prolong'd my watch; and now,
Subduing my heart's specious cowardice,
435 I left the shady nook where I had stood,
And hail'd him. Slowly from his resting-place
He rose, and, with a lean and wasted arm
In measur'd gesture lifted to his head,
Return'd my salutation; then resum'd
440 His station as before: and when, erelong,
I ask'd his history, he in reply
Was neither slow nor eager; but unmov'd,
And with a quiet, uncomplaining voice,
A stately air of mild indifference
445 He told, in simple words, a Soldier's Tale,
That in the Tropic Islands he had serv'd,[3]
Whence he had landed, scarcely ten days past,
That on his landing he had been dismiss'd,

---

3. In the West Indies, Britain had more than 80,000 troops in the 1790s to regulate the slave trade, recapture runaways, and put down slave revolts. Many soldiers fell sick or deserted; the troops were withdrawn in 1797.

And now was travelling to his native home.
450 At this, I turn'd and look'd towards the Village
But all were gone to rest, the fires all out;
And every silent window to the moon
Shone with a yellow glitter. "No one there,"
Said I, "is waking; we must measure back
455 The way which we have come: behind yon wood
A Labourer dwells; and, take it on my word
He will not murmur should we break his rest;
And with a ready heart will give you food
And lodging for the night." At this he stoop'd,
460 And from the ground took up an oaken Staff,
By me yet unobserv'd, a Traveller's Staff;
Which I suppose from his slack hand had dropp'd,
And lain till now neglected in the grass.
     Towards the Cottage without more delay
465 We shaped our course; as it appear'd to me,
He travell'd without pain, and I beheld
With ill-suppress'd astonishment his tall
And ghastly figure moving at my side;
Nor, while we journey'd thus could I forbear
470 To question him of what he had endured
From hardship, battle, or the pestilence.
He, all the while, was in demeanor calm,
Concise in answer: solemn and sublime
He might have seem'd but that in all he said
475 There was a strange half-absence, and a tone
Of weakness and indifference, as of one
Remembering the importance of his theme
But feeling it no longer. We advanced
Slowly, and, ere we to the wood were come,
480 Discourse had ceas'd. Together on we pass'd,
In silence, through the shades gloomy and dark;
Then turning up along an open field
We gain'd the Cottage. At the door I knock'd,
Calling aloud, "My Friend, here is a Man
485 By sickness overcome; beneath your roof
This night let him find rest, and give him food,
If food he need, for he is faint and tired."
Assured that now my Comrade would repose
In comfort, I entreated that henceforth
490 He would not linger in the public ways
But ask for timely furtherance and help
Such as his state requir'd.—At this reproof,
With the same ghastly mildness in his look,
He said, "My trust is in the God of Heaven
495 And in the eye of him that passes me."
     The Cottage door was speedily unlock'd,
And now the Soldier touch'd his hat again

With his lean hand; and, in a voice that seem'd
To speak with a reviving interest,
500 Till then unfelt, he thank'd me; I return'd
The blessing of the poor unhappy Man,[4]
And so we parted. Back I cast a look,
And linger'd near the door a little space;
Then sought with quiet heart my distant home.

from **Book Fifth. Books**

[MEDITATION ON BOOKS. THE DREAM OF THE ARAB]

10   Hitherto,
In progress through this Verse, my mind hath look'd
Upon the speaking face of earth and heaven
As her prime Teacher, intercourse with man
Establish'd by the sovereign Intellect,°   *God*
15 Who through that bodily Image° hath diffus'd   *nature*
A soul divine which we participate,
A deathless spirit. Thou also, Man, hast wrought,
For commerce of thy nature with itself,
Things worthy of unconquerable life;
20 And yet we feel, we cannot chuse but feel
That these must perish. Tremblings of the heart
It gives, to think that the immortal being
No more shall need such garments;[1] and yet Man,
As long as he shall be the Child of Earth,
25 Might almost "weep to have" what he may lose,[2]
Nor be himself extinguish'd; but survive
Abject, depress'd, forlorn, disconsolate.
A thought is with me sometimes, and I say,
Should earth by inward throes be wrench'd throughout,
30 Or fire be sent from far to wither all
Her pleasant habitations, and dry up
Old Ocean in his bed left sing'd and bare,
Yet would the living Presence still subsist
Victorious: and composure would ensue,
35 And kindlings like the morning; presage sure,
Though slow perhaps, of a returning day!
But all the meditations of mankind,
Yea, all the adamantine holds° of truth,   *fortresses*
By reason built, or passion, which itself
40 Is highest reason in a soul sublime;
The consecrated works of Bard and Sage,
Sensuous or intellectual, wrought by men,
Twin labourers and heirs of the same hopes,

---

4. In 1850 the phrase became "patient Man" (4.465).
1. In the traditional imagery, the body is the garment of the soul, discarded at death.

2. Shakespeare, Sonnet 64, on the destructiveness of time: "This thought is as a death, which cannot choose / But weep to have that which it fears to lose" (13–14).

Where would they be? Oh! why hath not the mind
45   Some element to stamp her image on
In nature somewhat nearer to her own?
Why, gifted with such powers to send abroad
Her spirit, must it lodge in shrines so frail?
    One day, when, in the hearing of a Friend,
50   I had given utterance to thoughts like these,
He answer'd with a smile, that, in plain truth
'Twas going far to seek disquietude;
But, on the front of his reproof, confess'd
That he, at sundry seasons, had himself
55   Yielded to kindred hauntings. And forthwith
Added, that, once, upon a summer's noon,
While he was sitting in a rocky cave
By the sea-side, perusing, as it chanced,
The famous History of the Errant Knight,°   *Don Quixote*
60   Recorded by Cervantes, these same thoughts
Came to him; and to height unusual rose
While listlessly he sate, and having closed
The Book, had turn'd his eyes towards the Sea.
On Poetry, and geometric Truth,
65   The knowledge that endures, upon these two,
And their high privilege of lasting life,
Exempt from all internal injury,
He mused; upon these chiefly: and at length
His senses yielding to the sultry air,
70   Sleep seiz'd him, and he pass'd into a dream.[3]
He saw before him an Arabian Waste,
A Desart; and he fancied that himself
Was sitting there in the wide wilderness,
Alone, upon the Sands. Distress of mind
75   Was growing in him when, behold! at once
To his great joy a Man was at his side,
Upon a Dromedary mounted high.
He seem'd an Arab of the Bedouin Tribes,°   *desert nomads*
A Lance he bore, and underneath one arm
80   A Stone; and, in the opposite hand, a Shell
Of a surpassing brightness. Much rejoic'd
The dreaming Man, that he should have a Guide
To lead him through the Desart; and he thought,
While questioning himself what this strange freight
85   Which the New-comer carried through the Waste
Could mean, the Arab told him that the Stone,
To give it in the language of the Dream,
Was Euclid's Elements;[4] "And this," said he,

---

3. In the 1850 *Prelude* this dream is the poet's own; it is based on a dream of French philosopher and mathematician René Descartes in 1619 (published 1691).
4. Treatise on geometry by the Greek mathematician Euclid (3rd century B.C.E.), still a basic text in Wordsworth's day. Mathematics flourished in Arabic cultures, which preserved much Greek learning in the centuries following the collapse of the Roman Empire.

"This other," pointing to the Shell, "this book
90   Is something of more worth." And, at the word,
The Stranger, said my Friend continuing,
Stretch'd forth the Shell towards me, with command
That I should hold it to my ear: I did so;
And heard that instant in an unknown Tongue,
95   Which yet I understood, articulate sounds,
A loud, prophetic blast of harmony,
An Ode, in passion utter'd, which foretold
Destruction to the Children of the Earth,
By deluge now at hand. No sooner ceas'd
100   The song, but with calm look, the Arab said
That all was true; that it was even so
As had been spoken; and that he himself
Was going then to bury those two Books,
The one that held acquaintance with the stars,
105   And wedded man to man by purest bond
Of nature undisturb'd by space or time;
Th'other that was a God, yea many Gods,
Had voices more than all the winds, and was
A joy, a consolation and a hope.
110   My Friend continued, "Strange as it may seem,
I wonder'd not, although I plainly saw
The one to be a Stone, th'other a Shell,
Nor doubted once but that they both were Books,
Having a perfect faith in all that pass'd.
115   A wish was now engender'd in my fear
To cleave unto this Man, and I begg'd leave
To share his errand with him. On he pass'd,
Not heeding me; I follow'd, and took note
That he look'd often backward with wild look,
120   Grasping his twofold treasure to his side.
—Upon a Dromedary, Lance in rest,
He rode, I keeping pace with him; and now
I fancied that he was the very Knight
Whose tale Cervantes tells, yet not the Knight,
125   But, was an Arab of the Desart, too;
Of these was neither, and was both at once.
His countenance, meanwhile, grew more disturb'd,
And, looking backwards when he look'd, I saw
A glittering light, and ask'd him whence it came;
130   'It is,' said he, 'the waters of the deep
Gathering upon us'; quickening then his pace,
He left me; I call'd after him aloud,
He heeded not; but with his twofold charge
Beneath his arm, before me full in view
135   I saw him riding o'er the Desart Sands,
With the fleet waters of the drowning world
In chace of him, whereat I wak'd in terror,

And saw the Sea before me; and the Book,
In which I had been reading, at my side."
140   Full often, taking from the world of sleep
This Arab Phantom, which my Friend beheld,
This Semi-Quixote, I to him have given
A substance, fancied him a living man,
A gentle Dweller in the Desart, craz'd
145   By love and feeling and internal thought,
Protracted among endless solitudes;
Have shap'd him, in the oppression of his brain,
Wandering upon this quest, and thus equipp'd.
And I have scarcely pitied him; have felt
150   A reverence for a Being thus employ'd;
And thought that in the blind and awful lair
Of such a madness reason did lie couch'd.
Enow° there are on earth to take in charge   *enough*
Their Wives, their Children, and their virgin Loves,
155   Or whatsoever else the heart holds dear;
Enow to think of these; yea, will I say,
In sober contemplation of the approach
Of such great overthrow, made manifest
By certain evidence, that I, methinks,
160   Could share that Maniac's anxiousness, could go
Upon like errand. Oftentimes, at least,
Me hath such deep entrancement half-possess'd,
When I have held a volume in my hand,
Poor earthly casket of immortal Verse!
165   Shakespeare, or Milton, Labourers divine.

[A DROWNING IN ESTHWAITE'S LAKE][5]

450   Well do I call to mind the very week,
When I was first entrusted to the care
Of that sweet Valley; when its paths, its shores,
And brooks, were like a dream of novelty
To my half infant thoughts; that very week
455   While I was roving up and down alone,
Seeking I knew not what, I chanced to cross
One of those open fields, which, shaped like ears,
Make green peninsulas on Esthwaite's Lake.
Twilight was coming on; yet through the gloom,
460   I saw distinctly on the opposite Shore
A heap of garments; left, as I suppos'd,
By one who there was bathing: long I watch'd,
But no one own'd° them: meanwhile, the calm Lake   *claimed*
Grew dark, with all the shadows on its breast,
465   And, now and then, a fish, upleaping, snapp'd

5. At age nine, Wordsworth was sent away to Hawkshead Grammar School in Esthwaite valley.

The breathless stillness. The succeeding day,
(Those unclaim'd garments telling a plain Tale)
Went there a Company, and, in their Boat,
Sounded with grappling-irons, and long poles.
470 At length, the dead Man, 'mid that beauteous scene
Of trees, and hills, and water, bolt upright
Rose with his ghastly face; a spectre-shape
Of terror even! and yet no vulgar fear,
Young as I was, a Child not nine years old,
475 Possess'd me; for my inner eye had seen
Such sights before, among the shining streams
Of Fairy Land, the Forests of Romance:°   *a literary genre*
Thence came a spirit, hallowing what I saw
With decoration and ideal grace;
480 A dignity, a smoothness, like the works
Of Grecian Art, and purest Poesy.

["The Mystery of Words"]

610   he, who, in his youth
A wanderer among the woods and fields,
With living Nature hath been intimate,
Not only in that raw unpractis'd time
Is stirr'd to ecstasy, as others are,
615 By glittering verse; but he doth furthermore,
In measure only dealt out to himself,
Receive enduring touches of deep joy
From the great Nature that exists in works
Of mighty Poets. Visionary Power
620 Attends upon the motions of the winds
Embodied in the mystery of words.
There darkness makes abode, and all the host
Of shadowy things do work their changes there,
As in a mansion like their proper home:—
625 Even forms and substances are circumfus'd
By that transparent veil with light divine;
And through the turnings intricate of Verse[6]
Present themselves as objects recognis'd,
In flashes, and with a glory scarce their own.

from Book Sixth. Cambridge, and the Alps

[The Pleasure of Geometric Science][1]

140   there I found
Enough to exalt, to chear me, and compose.
With Indian° awe and wonder, ignorance   *Native American*

---

6. "Verse" derives from the Latin word for "turning."   1. Wordsworth is back at Cambridge.

Which even was cherish'd, did I meditate
Upon the alliance of those simple, pure
145   Proportions and relations with the frame
And laws of Nature, how they could become
Herein a leader to the human mind,
And made endeavours frequent to detect
The process by dark guesses of my own,
150   Yet from this source more frequently I drew
A pleasure calm and deeper, a still sense
Of permanent and universal sway
And paramount endowment in the mind,
An image not unworthy of the one
155   Surpassing Life, which out of space and time,
Nor touch'd by welterings of passions, is
And hath the name of God. Transcendant peace
And silence did await upon these thoughts
That were a frequent comfort to my youth.
160   And as I have read of one by shipwreck thrown,[2]
With Fellow-sufferers whom the waves had spared,
Upon a region uninhabited,
An island of the deep, who having brought
To land a single Volume and no more,
165   A Treatise of Geometry, was used,
Although of food and clothing destitute,
And beyond common wretchedness depress'd,
To part from company and take this book
(Then first a self-taught pupil in those truths)
170   To spots remote and corners of the Isle
By the sea-side, and draw his diagrams
With a long stick upon the sand, and thus
Did oft beguile his sorrow, and almost
Forget his feeling; even so, (if things
175   Producing like effect from outward cause,
So different may rightly be compared)
So was it with me then, and so will be
With Poets ever. Mighty is the charm
Of those abstractions to a mind beset
180   With images, and haunted by itself;
And specially delightful unto me
Was that clear Synthesis, built up aloft
So gracefully! even then when it appear'd
No more than as a plaything or a toy
185   Embodied to the sense; not what it is
In verity, an independent world
Created out of pure Intelligence.

---

2. Abolitionist John Newton (see page 250). Dorothy Wordsworth copied the passage referred to here in a notebook in 1798–1799.

[ARRIVAL IN FRANCE]³

340
A Fellow Student and myself, he, too,
A Mountaineer, together sallied forth
And, Staff in hand, on foot pursu'd our way
Towards the distant Alps. An open slight
Of College cares and study was the scheme,
Nor entertain'd without concern for those

345
To whom my worldly interests were dear:⁴
But Nature then was sovereign in my heart,
And mighty forms seizing a youthful Fancy
Had given a charter to irregular hopes.
In any age, without an impulse sent

350
From work of Nations, and their goings-on,
I should have been possess'd by like desire:
But 'twas a time when Europe was rejoiced,
France standing on the top of golden hours,⁵
And human nature seeming born again.

355
Bound, as I said, to the Alps, it was our lot
To land at Calais on the very Eve
Of that great federal Day;⁶ and there we saw
In a mean City, and among a few,
How bright a face is worn when joy of one

360
Is joy of tens of millions. Southward thence
We took our way direct, through Hamlets, Towns,
Gaudy with reliques of that Festival,
Flowers left to wither on triumphal Arcs,
And window-garlands. On the public roads,

365
And once, three days successively, through paths
By which our toilsome journey was abridg'd,
Among sequester'd villages we walked,
And found benevolence and blessedness
Spread like a fragrance every where, like Spring

370
That leaves no corner of the Land untouch'd.
Where Elms, for many and many a league, in files,
With their thin umbrage,° on the stately roads   *foliage*
Of that great Kingdom rustled o'er our heads,
For ever near us as we paced along,

375
'Twas sweet, at such a time, with such delights
On every side, in prime of youthful strength,
To feed a Poet's tender melancholy
And fond conceit of sadness to the noise

---

3. In summer 1790, a year after the French Revolution, Wordsworth and a friend toured France, the Swiss Alps, and Italy. France was still in the "golden hours" (353) of Revolutionary optimism.
4. Undergraduates usually spent the third summer studying for impending final examinations, which would determine their rank on graduation and shape their future prospects.

5. Shakespeare, Sonnet 16: "Now stand you on the top of happy hours," he says to a young man.
6. On the Festival of the Federation, 14 July 1790, the first anniversary of the fall of the Bastille, Louis XVI swore fidelity to the new constitution. Calais is a seaport in northern France.

And gentle undulation which they made.
380   Unhous'd, beneath the Evening Star we saw
      Dances of Liberty, and in late hours
      Of darkness, dances in the open air.
      Among the vine-clad Hills of Burgundy,
      Upon the bosom of the gentle Soane
385   We glided forward with the flowing stream:
      Swift Rhone, thou wert the wings on which we cut
      Between thy lofty rocks! Enchanting show
      Those woods, and farms, and orchards did present,
      And single Cottages, and lurking Towns,
390   Reach after reach, procession without end
      Of deep and stately Vales. A lonely Pair
      Of Englishmen we were, and sail'd along
      Cluster'd together with a merry crowd
      Of those emancipated, with a host
395   Of Travellers, chiefly Delegates, returning
      From the great Spousals newly solemniz'd
      At their chief City in the sight of Heaven.[7]
      Like bees they swarm'd, gaudy and gay as bees;
      Some vapour'd° in the unruliness of joy   blustered
400   And flourish'd with their swords, as if to fight
      The saucy air. In this blithe Company
      We landed, took with them our evening meal,
      Guests welcome almost as the Angels were
      To Abraham of old.[8] The Supper done,
405   With flowing cups elate, and happy thoughts,
      We rose at signal given, and form'd a ring
      And, hand in hand, danced round and round the Board:
      All hearts were open, every tongue was loud
      With amity and glee: we bore a name
410   Honour'd in France, the name of Englishmen,
      And hospitably did they give us Hail
      As their forerunners in a glorious course,[9]
      And round and round the Board they danced again.
      With this same Throng our voyage we pursued
415   At early dawn; the Monastery Bells
      Made a sweet jingling in our youthful ears;
      The rapid River, flowing without noise,
      And every Spire we saw among the rocks
      Spake with a sense of peace, at intervals
420   Touching the heart amid the boisterous Crew
      With which we were environ'd.

---

7. Louis XVI's oath of fidelity was described as a marriage between monarch and nation.
8. Abraham lavishes hospitality on three disguised angels, who inform him his aged wife will bear a son (Genesis 18).
9. Referring to England's "Glorious Revolution" of 1688, which deposed the autocratic James II.

[Travelling in the Alps. Simplon Pass]

	Yet still in me, mingling with these delights°	*of travel*

Yet still in me, mingling with these delights°   *of travel*
Was something of stern mood, an under thirst
490 Of vigour, never utterly asleep.
Far different dejection once was mine,
A deep and genuine sadness then I felt:
The circumstances I will here relate
Even as they were. Upturning with a Band
495 Of Travellers, from the Valais we had clomb
Along the road that leads to Italy;°   *Simplon Pass*
A length of hours, making of these our guides
Did we advance, and having reach'd an Inn
Among the mountains, we together ate
500 Our noon's repast, from which the Travellers rose,
Leaving us at the Board. Erelong we follow'd,
Descending by the beaten road that led
Right to a rivulet's edge, and there broke off.
The only track now visible was one
505 Upon the further side, right opposite,
And up a lofty Mountain. This we took
After a little scruple,° and short pause,   *hesitation*
And climb'd with eagerness, though not, at length,
Without surprize and some anxiety
510 On finding that we did not overtake
Our Comrades gone before. By fortunate chance,
While every moment now encreas'd our doubts,
A Peasant met us and from him we learn'd
That to the place which had perplex'd us first
515 We must descend, and there should find the road
Which in the stony channel of the Stream
Lay a few steps, and then along its Banks,
And, further, that thenceforward all our course
Was downwards, with the current of that Stream.
520 Hard of belief we questioned him again,
And all the answers which the Man return'd
To our inquiries, in their sense and substance,
Translated by the feelings which we had,
Ended in this, that we had cross'd the Alps.
525 Imagination! lifting up itself
Before the eye and progress of my Song°   *this poem*
Like an unfather'd vapour; here that Power,
In all the might of its endowments, came
Athwart me; I was lost as in a cloud,
530 Halted without a struggle to break through,
And now[1] recovering to my Soul I say
I recognize thy glory; in such strength

---

1. This apostrophe was written in 1804, 14 years after the disappointment of the missed climax.

Of usurpation, in such visitings
Of awful° promise, when the light of sense   *awe-filled*
535   Goes out in flashes that have shewn to us
The invisible world, doth Greatness make abode,
There harbours whether we be young or old.
Our destiny, our nature, and our home
Is with infinitude, and only there;
540   With hope it is, hope that can never die,
Effort, and expectation, and desire,
And something evermore about to be.
The mind beneath such banners militant
Thinks not of spoils, trophies nor of aught
545   That may attest its prowess, blest in thoughts
That are their own perfection and reward,
Strong in itself, and in the access of joy
Which hides it like the overflowing Nile.
        The dull and heavy slackening which ensu'd
550   Upon those tidings by the Peasant given
Was soon dislodg'd; downwards we hurried fast,
And enter'd with the road which we had miss'd
Into a narrow chasm: the brook and road[2]
Were fellow-travellers in this gloomy Pass,
555   And with them did we journey several hours
At a slow step. The immeasurable height
Of woods decaying, never to be decay'd,
The stationary blasts of waterfalls,
And every where along the hollow rent
560   Winds thwarting winds, bewilder'd and forlorn,[3]
The torrents shooting from the clear blue sky,
The rocks that mutter'd close upon our ears,
Black drizzling crags that spake by the way-side
As if a voice were in them, the sick sight
565   And giddy prospect of the raving stream,
The unfetter'd clouds, and region of the heavens,
Tumult and peace, the darkness and the light
Were all like workings of one mind, the features
Of the same face, blossoms upon one tree,
570   Character° of the great Apocalyps,   *signs, letters*
The types and symbols of Eternity,
Of first and last, and midst, and without end.[4]
        That night our lodging was an Alpine House,
An Inn or Hospital, as they are named,
575   Standing in that same valley by itself

2. Lines 553 (from "the") through 572 were published
as *The Simplon Pass* in Wordsworth's 1845 *Poems*, under
"Poems of the Imagination."
3. A contrasting echo of 2.261.
4. Milton's terms for God (*Paradise Lost* 5.165), echoing

God's self-description in Revelation (the Apocalypse) as
"Alpha and Omega, the beginning and the ending"—the
first and last letters of the Greek alphabet. "Types" are
foreshadowings and prefigurations of God's plans.

And close upon the confluence of two streams,
A dreary Mansion, large beyond all need,
With high and spacious rooms, deafen'd and stunn'd
By noise of waters, making innocent Sleep
580 Lie melancholy among weary bones.[5]
    Uprisen betimes, our journey we renew'd
Led by the Stream, ere noon-day magnified
Into a lordly River, broad and deep,
Dimpling along in silent majesty,
585 With mountains for its neighbours, and in view
Of distant mountains and their snowy tops,
And thus proceeding to Locarno's Lake,
Fit resting-place for such a Visitant.
—Locarno, spreading out in width like Heaven,
590 And Como, thou a treasure by the earth
Kept to itself, a darling bosom'd up
In Abyssinian[6] privacy, I spake
Of thee, thy chesnut woods, and garden plots
Of Indian corn tended by dark-eyed Maids,
595 Thy lofty steeps, and path-ways roof'd with vines
Winding from house to house, from town to town,
Sole link that binds them to each other, walks
League after league, and cloistral avenues
Where silence is, if music be not there:
600 While yet a Youth, undisciplined in Verse,
Through fond ambition of my heart, I told
Your praises; nor can I approach you now,
Ungreeted by a more melodious Song,
Where tones of learned Art and Nature mix'd
605 May frame enduring language. Like a breeze
Or sunbeam over your domain I pass'd
In motion without pause; but Ye have left
Your beauty with me, an impassion'd sight
Of colours and of forms, whose power is sweet
610 And gracious, almost might I dare to say,
As virtue is, or goodness, sweet as love
Or the remembrance of a noble deed,
Or gentlest visitations of pure thought
When God, the Giver of all joy, is thank'd
615 Religiously, in silent blessedness,
Sweet as this last itself, for such it is.
    Through those delightful pathways we advanced
Two days, and still in presence of the Lake,
Which, winding up among the Alps, now changed
620 Slowly its lovely countenance, and put on
A sterner character. The second night,

---

5. King-killer Macbeth laments the loss of "innocent sleep" (2.2.35).   6. Abyssinia was a legendary location of Paradise.

In eagerness, and by report misled
Of those Italian Clocks that speak the time
In fashion different from ours, we rose
625   By moonshine, doubting not that day was near,
And that, meanwhile, coasting the Water's edge,
As hitherto, and with as plain a track
To be our guide, we might behold the scene
In its most deep repose.—We left the Town
630   Of Gravedona with this hope; but soon
Were lost, bewilder'd among woods immense,
Where, having wander'd for a while, we stopp'd
And on a rock sate down, to wait for day.
An open place it was, and overlook'd
635   From high the sullen water underneath,
On which a dull red image of the moon
Lay bedded, changing oftentimes its form
Like an uneasy snake: long time we sate,
For scarcely more than one hour of the night,
640   Such was our error, had been gone, when we
Renew'd our journey. On the rock we lay,
And wish'd to sleep but could not for the stings
Of insects, which with noise like that of noon
Fill'd all the woods: the cry of unknown birds,
645   The mountains, more by darkness visible[7]
And their own size than any outward light,
The breathless wilderness of clouds, the clock
That told with unintelligible voice
The widely-parted hours, the noise of streams
650   And sometimes rustling motions nigh at hand
Which did not leave us free from personal fear,
And lastly the withdrawing Moon, that set
Before us while she yet was high in heaven,
These were our food; and such a summer night
655   Did to that pair of golden days succeed,
With now and then a doze and snatch of sleep,
On Como's Banks, the same delicious Lake.

from Book Seventh. Residence in London
[A Blind Beggar. Bartholomew Fair][1]

O Friend! one feeling was there which belong'd
To this great City by exclusive right:
595   How often in the overflowing Streets
Have I gone forwards with the Crowd, and said
Unto myself, the face of every one

---

7. Milton's description of Hell (*Paradise Lost* 1.61ff.) reso-
nates throughout this passage.
1. Wordsworth has been half-seriously comparing Lon-

don to Milton's Hell and its infernal city, Pandemonium
("all the devils"). He had spent a few unhappy months in
London in 1791.

That passes by me is a mystery!
Thus have I look'd, nor ceas'd to look, oppress'd
600   By thoughts of what, and whither, when and how,
Until the shapes before my eyes became
A second-sight procession, such as glides
Over still mountains, or appears in dreams;
And all the ballast of familiar life,
605   The present, and the past; hope, fear; all stays,
All laws of acting, thinking, speaking man
Went from me, neither knowing me nor known.
And once, far travell'd in such mood, beyond
The reach of common indications, lost
610   Amid the moving pageant, 'twas my chance
Abruptly to be smitten with the view
Of a blind Beggar, who, with upright face,
Stood propp'd against a Wall;[2] upon his Chest
Wearing a written paper, to explain
615   The Story of the Man and who he was;
My mind did at this spectacle turn round
As with the might of waters, and it seem'd
To me that in this Label was a type,
Or emblem, of the utmost that we know,
620   Both of ourselves and of the universe;
And on the shape of this unmoving Man,
His fixed face, and sightless eyes, I look'd
As if admonish'd from another world.
　　　Though rear'd upon the base of outward things,
625   These, chiefly, are such structures as the mind
Builds for itself. Scenes different there are,
Full-form'd, which take with small internal help
Possession of the faculties; the peace
Of night, for instance, the solemnity
630   Of nature's intermediate hours of rest,
When the great tide of human life stands still,
The business of the day to come unborn,
Of that gone by, lock'd up as in the grave:
The calmness, beauty of the spectacle;
635   Sky, stillness, moonshine, empty streets, and sounds
Unfrequent as in desarts: at late hours
Of winter evenings when unwholesome rains
Are falling hard, with people yet astir,
The feeble salutation from the voice
640   Of some unhappy Woman, now and then
Heard as we pass, when no one looks about,
Nothing is listen'd to. But these I fear
Are falsly catalogu'd, things that are, are not,

---

2. Compare to the old veteran (4.412).

Even as we give them welcome, or assist,
645   Are prompt, or are remiss. What say you then
To times when half the City shall break out
Full of one passion, vengeance, rage, or fear,
To executions, to a Street on fire,
Mobs, riots, or rejoicings? From those sights
650   Take one, an annual Festival, the Fair
Holden where Martyrs suffer'd in past time,
And named of Saint Bartholomew;[3] there see
A work that's finish'd to our hands, that lays,
If any spectacle on earth can do,
655   The whole creative powers of man asleep!
For once the Muse's help will we implore,
And she shall lodge us, wafted on her wings,
Above the press and danger of the Crowd
Upon some Show-man's Platform: what a hell
660   For eyes and ears! what anarchy and din
Barbarian and infernal! 'tis a dream
Monstrous in colour, motion, shape, sight, sound.
Below, the open space, through every nook
Of the wide area, twinkles, is alive
665   With heads; the midway region and above
Is throng'd with staring pictures, and huge scrolls,
Dumb proclamations of the prodigies!
And chattering monkeys dangling from their poles,
And children whirling in their roundabouts;°   merry-go-rounds
670   With those that stretch the neck, and strain the eyes,
And crack the voice in rivalship, the crowd
Inviting; with buffoons against buffoons
Grimacing, writhing, screaming; him who grinds
The hurdy-gurdy;° at the fiddle weaves;   stringed instrument
675   Rattles the salt-box; thumps the kettle-drum;
And him who at the trumpet puffs his cheeks;
The silver-collar'd Negro with his timbrel,°   tambourine
Equestrians, Tumblers, Women, Girls and Boys,
Blue-breech'd, pink-vested, and with towering plumes.
680   —All moveables of wonder from all parts
Are here, Albinos, painted Indians, Dwarfs,
The Horse of Knowledge, and the learned Pig,[4]
The Stone-eater, the Man that swallows fire,
Giants, Ventriloquists, the Invisible Girl,
685   The Bust that speaks, and moves its goggling eyes,
The Wax-work,[5] Clock-work,° all the marvellous craft   robot

---

3. A four-day fair in September, commemorating Protestant martyrs burnt in nearby Smithfield during the reign
of Catholic Queen Mary (1553–1558). William and Dorothy Wordsworth attended the fair in 1802, with Charles
and Mary Lamb.

4. Both supposed to be able to count and identify playing
cards; the pig was better at it.
5. In 1802 Madame Tussaud displayed her gallery of wax
figures of leaders and victims of the French Revolution.
The gallery still thrives.

Of modern Merlins,° wild Beasts, Puppet-shows,   *magicians*
All out-o'th'-way, far-fetch'd, perverted things,
All freaks of Nature, all Promethean thoughts[6]
690 Of man; his dullness, madness, and their feats,
All jumbled up together, to make up
This Parliament of Monsters: Tents and Booths,
Meanwhile, as if the whole were one vast Mill,°   *factory*
Are vomiting, receiving, on all sides,
695 Men, Women, three years Children, Babes in arms.
    O blank confusion! and a type° not false   *image*
Of what the mighty City is itself
To all except a Straggler here and there,
To the whole swarm of its inhabitants;
700 An undistinguishable world to men,
The slaves unrespited of° low pursuits,   *devoted to*
Living amid the same perpetual flow
Of trivial objects, melted and reduced
To one identity, by differences
705 That have no law, no meaning, and no end;[7]
Oppression under which even highest minds
Must labour, whence the strongest are not free!
But though the picture weary out the eye,
By nature an unmanageable sight,
710 It is not wholly so to him who looks
In steadiness, who hath among least things
An under sense of greatest; sees the parts
As parts, but with a feeling of the whole.
This, of all acquisitions first, awaits
715 On sundry and most widely-different modes
Of education; nor with least delight
On that through which I pass'd. Attention comes,
And comprehensiveness, and memory,
From early converse with the works of God,
720 Among all regions; chiefly where appear
Most obviously simplicity and power.
By influence habitual to the mind
The mountain's outline and its steady form
Gives a pure grandeur; and its presence shapes
725 The measure and the prospect of the soul
To majesty; such virtue have the forms
Perennial of the ancient hills; nor less,
The changeful language of their countenances
Gives movement to the thoughts, and multitude,
730 With order and relation. This, if still,
As hitherto, with freedom I may speak,

---

6. Milton's Hell contains "Perverse, all monstrous, all prodigious things" (*Paradise Lost* 2.625); "Promethean thoughts" are daringly inventive, potentially transgressive.
7. A contrasting echo of 6.571–72 (the Alpine ravine).

And the same perfect openness of mind,
Not violating any just restraint,
As I would hope, of real modesty,
735   This did I feel in that vast receptacle:
The Spirit of Nature was upon me here:
The Soul of Beauty and enduring life
Was present as a habit; and diffused,
Through meagre lines and colours, and the press
740   Of self-destroying, transitory things,
Composure and ennobling harmony.

from **Book Ninth. Residence in France**[1]
[PARIS]

40   Through Paris lay my readiest path, and there
I sojourn'd a few days, and visited
In haste each spot of old and recent fame,[2]
The latter chiefly, from the Field of Mars
Down to the Suburbs of St Anthony,
45   And from Mont Martyr southward, to the Dome
Of Genevieve.[3] In both her clamorous Halls,
The National Synod and the Jacobins,[4]
I saw the revolutionary Power
Toss like a Ship at anchor, rock'd by storms;
50   The Arcades I traversed in the Palace huge
Of Orleans,° coasted round and round the line   *the Royal Palace*
Of Tavern, Brothel, Gaming-house, and Shop,
Great rendezvous of worst and best, the walk
Of all who had a purpose, or had not:
55   I stared and listen'd with a stranger's ears
To Hawkers and Haranguers, hubbub wild![5]
And hissing Factionists with ardent eyes,
In knots, or pairs, or single, ant-like swarms
Of Builders and Subverters,° every face   *political theorists*
60   That hope or apprehension could put on,
Joy, anger, and vexation in the midst
Of gaiety and dissolute idleness.
Where silent Zephyrs° sported with the dust   *breezes*
Of the Bastile,[6] I sate in the open sun,
65   And from the rubbish gather'd up a stone

---

1. After four months in London in 1791, Wordsworth returned to France. He had an affair with Annette Vallon, whom he left pregnant when he returned to England in December 1792, sensing the peril for an Englishman as the Reign of Terror spread.
2. An echo of Archangel Michael's preview of urban civilization (*Paradise Lost* 11.386).
3. Champ de Mars was the site of the Festival of the Federation on 14 July 1790. St-Antoine was a militant working-class suburb, near Bastille prison. Montmartre (Mount Martyr) was the site of revolutionary meetings.

The Dome of Genevieve is the Pantheon, the tomb of Rousseau, Voltaire, and other Republican heroes.
4. The National Assembly and the radical Jacobin Club, places of vigorous policy debates.
5. As he leaves Hell to seek Eden, Satan is assaulted by "a universal hubbub wild / Of stunning sounds and voices all confus'd" (*Paradise Lost* 2.951–52). Wordsworth echoes this passage to describe London (7.227).
6. The Revolution began on 14 July 1789 with the storming of the Bastille, which was later demolished.

And pocketed the relick in the guise
Of an Enthusiast,° yet, in honest truth   *devotee*
Though not without some strong incumbences;
And glad (could living man be otherwise?)
70   I look'd for something which I could not find,
Affecting more emotion than I felt,
For 'tis most certain that the utmost force
Of all these various objects, which may shew
The temper of my mind as then it was,
75   Seem'd less to recompense the Traveller's pains,
Less mov'd me, gave me less delight than did
A single picture merely, hunted out
Among other sights, the Magdalene of le Brun,[7]
A Beauty exquisitely wrought, fair face
80   And rueful with it's ever flowing tears.
          But hence to my more permanent residence°   *in Orléans*
I hasten: there by novelties in speech,
Domestic manners, customs, gestures, looks,
And all the attire of ordinary life,
85   Attention was at first engross'd, and thus,
Amused and satisfied, I scarcely felt
The shock of these concussions, unconcern'd,
Tranquil, almost, and careless as a flower
Glass'd in a Green-house, or a Parlour shrub
90   When every bush and tree, the country through,
Is shaking to the roots; indifference this
Which may seem strange; but I was unprepared
With needful knowledge, had abruptly pass'd
Into a theatre, of which the stage
95   Was busy with an action far advanced.
Like others I had read, and eagerly
Sometimes, the master Pamphlets of the day;[8]
Nor wanted° such half-insight as grew wild   *lacked*
Upon that meagre soil, help'd out by Talk
100   And public News; but having never chanced
To see a regular Chronicle which might shew,
If any such indeed existed then,
Whence the main organs° of the public Power   *institutions*
Had sprung, their transmigrations when and how
105   Accomplish'd, giving thus unto events
A form and body, all things were to me
Loose and disjointed, and the affections left
Without a vital interest. At that time,
Moreover, the first storm was overblown,
110   And the strong hand of outward violence

---

7. A greatly admired painting of a penitent Mary Magdalene by Charles Le Brun (1616–1690) was a tourist
attraction.

8. Burke's *Reflections*, Wollstonecraft's *Rights of Men*,
Paine's *Rights of Man*, among them.

Lock'd up in quiet.[9] For myself, I fear
Now in connection with so great a Theme
To speak (as I must be compell'd to do)
Of one so unimportant: a short time
115   I loiter'd, and frequented night by night
Routs,° card-tables, the formal haunts of men,   *social events*
Whom in the City privilege of birth
Sequester'd from the rest, societies
Where through punctilios° of elegance   *refinements*
120   And deeper causes, all discourse, alike
Of good and evil in the time, was shunn'd
With studious care: but 'twas not long ere this
Proved tedious, and I gradually withdrew
Into a noisier world; and thus did soon
125   Become a Patriot,° and my heart was all   *Revolutionary partisan*
Given to the People, and my love was theirs.
    A Knot of military Officers
That to a Regiment appertain'd which then
Was station'd in the City were the chief
130   Of my associates: some of these wore Swords
Which had been season'd in the Wars, and all
Were men well born, at least laid claim to such
Distinction, as the Chivalry of France.°   *the old nobility*
In age and temper differing, they had yet
135   One spirit ruling in them all, alike
(Save only one, hereafter to be named)
Were bent upon undoing what was done:°   *the new Republic*
This was their rest and only hope, therewith
No fear had they of bad becoming worse,
140   For worst to them was come, nor would have stirr'd,
Or deem'd it worth a moment's while to stir
In any thing, save only as the act
Look'd thitherward. One, reckoning by years,
Was in the prime of manhood, and erewhile
145   He had sate Lord in many tender hearts,
Though heedless of such honours now, and changed:
His temper was quite master'd by the times,
And they had blighted him, had eat away
The beauty of his person, doing wrong
150   Alike to body and to mind: his port,°   *bearing*
Which once had been erect and open, now
Was stooping and contracted, and a face
By nature lovely in itself, express'd
As much as any that was ever seen,
155   A ravage out of season, made by thoughts
Unhealthy and vexatious. At the hour,

9. The new Republic turned scandalously violent with the September Massacres of 1792.

The most important of each day, in which
The public News was read, the fever came,
A punctual visitant, to shake this Man,
160   Disarm'd his voice, and fann'd his yellow cheek
Into a thousand colours; while he read,
Or mused, his sword was haunted by his touch
Continually, like an uneasy place
In his own body. 'Twas in truth an hour
165   Of universal ferment; mildest men
Were agitated, and commotions, strife
Of passion and opinion fill'd the walls
Of peaceful houses with unquiet sounds.
The soil of common life was at that time
170   Too hot to tread upon: oft said I then,
And not then only, "What a mockery this
Of history, the past, and that to come!
Now do I feel how I have been deceived,
Reading of Nations and their works, in faith,
175   Faith given to vanity and emptiness;
Oh! laughter for the Page that would reflect
To future times the face of what now is!"
The Land all swarm'd with passion, like a Plain
Devour'd by locusts, Carra, Gorsas,[1] add
180   A hundred other names, forgotten now,
Nor to be heard of more, yet were they Powers
Like earthquakes, shocks repeated day by day,
And felt through every nook of town and field.
        The Men already spoken of as chief
185   Of my Associates were prepared for flight
To augment the Band of Emigrants in Arms
Upon the Borders of the Loire,[2] and leagued
With foreign Foes muster'd for instant war.
This was their undisguised intent, and they
190   Were waiting with the whole of their desires
The moment to depart.
                            An Englishman,
Born in a Land, the name of which appear'd
To licence some unruliness of mind,
A Stranger, with Youth's further privilege,
195   And that indulgence which a half-learn'd speech
Wins from the courteous, I who had been else
Shunn'd and not tolerated freely lived
With these Defenders of the Crown, and talk'd

---

1. Influential journalists of the moderate faction executed
by the radical Robespierre in October 1793. In 1840
Wordsworth told Thomas Carlyle that he had witnessed
the execution of Gorsas, having undertaken a dangerous
return to France to see Annette Vallon and their infant
daughter. In Exodus, Moses calls down a plague of locusts
on the Egyptians (10.12–15).
2. An error for Rhine. Royalists, backed by Austria and
Prussia, were preparing to invade France.

And heard their notions, nor did they disdain
200   The wish to bring me over to their cause.
      But though untaught by thinking or by books
To reason well of polity or law
And nice° distinctions, then on every tongue,   *subtle*
Of natural rights and civil, and to acts
205   Of Nations, and their passing interests,
(I speak comparing these with other things)
Almost indifferent, even the Historian's Tale
Prizing but little otherwise than I prized
Tales of the Poets, as it made my heart
210   Beat high and fill'd my fancy with fair forms,
Old Heroes and their sufferings and their deeds;
Yet in the regal Sceptre and the pomp
Of Orders and Degrees° I nothing found   *aristocratic ranks*
Then, or had ever, even in crudest youth,
215   That dazzled me; but rather what my soul
Mourn'd for, or loath'd, beholding that the best
Ruled not, and feeling that they ought to rule.

[REVOLUTION, ROYALISTS, AND PATRIOTS]

                day by day the roads,
(While I consorted with these Royalists)
Were crowded with the bravest Youth of France
270   And all the promptest of her Spirits, link'd
In gallant Soldiership, and posting on
To meet the War, upon her Frontier Bounds.[3]
Yet at this very moment do tears start
Into mine eyes; I do not say I weep,
275   I wept not then, but tears have dimm'd my sight
In memory of the farewells of that time,
Domestic severings, female fortitude
At dearest separation, patriot love[4]
And self-devotion,° and terrestrial hope   *self-devoting, self-dooming*
280   Encouraged with a martyr's confidence;
Even files of Strangers merely, seen but once,
And for a moment, men from far with sound
Of music, martial tunes, and banners spread
Entering the City, here and there a face
285   Or person singled out among the rest,
Yet still a stranger and beloved as such,
Even by these passing spectacles my heart
Was oftentimes uplifted, and they seem'd
Like arguments from Heaven that 'twas a cause
290   Good, and which no one could stand up against

---

3. France declared war on Austria in April 1792.   4. Royalists as well as Republicans regarded themselves as patriots.

Who was not lost, abandon'd, selfish, proud,
Mean, miserable, wilfully depraved,
Hater perverse of equity and truth.
    Among that Band of Officers was one
295 Already hinted at,[5] of other mold,
A Patriot, thence rejected by the rest
And with an oriental loathing spurn'd,
As of a different Cast.° A meeker Man   *caste*
Than this lived never, or a more benign,
300 Meek though enthusiastic to the height
Of highest expectation. Injuries
Made him more gracious, and his nature then
Did breathe its sweetness out most sensibly°   *perceptibly*
As aromatic flowers on Alpine turf
305 When foot hath crush'd them. He thro' the events
Of that great change wander'd in perfect faith,
As through a Book, an old Romance or Tale
Of Fairy, or some dream of actions wrought
Behind the summer clouds. By birth he rank'd
310 With the most noble, but unto the poor
Among mankind he was in service bound
As by some tie invisible, oaths profess'd
To a religious Order. Man he lov'd
As man; and to the mean° and the obscure   *humble*
315 And all the homely in their homely works
Transferr'd a courtesy which had no air
Of condescension; but did rather seem
A passion and a gallantry, like that
Which he, a Soldier, in his idler day
320 Had payed to Woman; somewhat vain he was,
Or seem'd so, yet it was not vanity
But fondness, and a kind of radiant joy
That cover'd him about when he was bent
On works of love or freedom, or revolved
325 Complacently° the progress of a cause   *with pleasure*
Whereof he was a part; yet this was meek
And placid, and took nothing from the Man
That was delightful: oft in solitude
With him did I discourse about the end°   *aims*
330 Of civil government, and its wisest forms,
Of ancient prejudice, and charter'd rights,
Allegiance, faith, and laws by time matured,
Custom and habit, novelty and change,
Of self-respect and virtue in the Few
335 For patrimonial honour set apart,
And ignorance in the labouring Multitude.

5. Michel Beaupuy (1755–1796), born into the nobility but devoted to the ideals of the new Republic, was a powerful influence on young Wordsworth.

> * * * And when we chanced[6]
> One day to meet a hunger-bitten Girl
> Who crept along, fitting her languid self
> Unto a Heifer's motion, by a cord

515 Tied to her arm, and picking thus from the lane
> Its sustenance, while the Girl with her two hands
> Was busy knitting, in a heartless° mood   *disheartened*
> Of solitude, and at the sight my Friend
> In agitation said, "'Tis against that

520 Which we are fighting," I with him believed
> Devoutly that a spirit was abroad
> Which could not be withstood, that poverty,
> At least like this, would in a little time
> Be found no more, that we should see the earth

525 Unthwarted in her wish to recompense
> The industrious and the lowly Child of Toil,
> All institutes for ever blotted out
> That legalized exclusion, empty pomp
> Abolish'd, sensual state and cruel power

530 Whether by edict of the one or few,
> And finally, as sum and crown of all,
> Should see the People having a strong hand
> In making their own Laws, whence better days
> To all mankind. * * *

from **Book Tenth. Residence in France and French Revolution**

[THE REIGN OF TERROR. CONFUSION. RETURN TO ENGLAND]

> It was a beautiful and silent day
> That overspread the countenance of earth,
> Then fading, with unusual quietness
> When from the Loire I parted, and through scenes

5 Of vineyard, orchard, meadow-ground and tilth,°   *tilled land*
> Calm waters, gleams of sun, and breathless trees
> Towards the fierce Metropolis turn'd my steps
> Their homeward way to England. From his Throne
> The King had fallen;[1] the congregated Host,

10 Dire cloud upon the front of which was written
> The tender mercies of the dismal wind
> That bore it, on the Plains of Liberty
> Had burst innocuously:—say more, the swarm
> That came elate and jocund, like a Band

15 Of Eastern Hunters, to enfold in ring
> Narrowing itself by moments and reduce
> To the last punctual spot of their despair

---

6. By this time, Beaupuy had become an officer in the army of the Republic. He died in battle in 1796.
1. Louis XVI was imprisoned in August 1792, and the invading armies of Austria and Prussia were defeated by the French at Valmy on 20 September 1792, a month before Wordsworth returned from Orleans to Paris.

A race of victims, so they deem'd, themselves
Had shrunk from sight of their own task, and fled
20   In terror; desolation and dismay
Remain'd for them whose fancies had grown rank
With evil expectations, confidence
And perfect triumph to the better cause.
The State, as if to stamp the final seal
25   On her security, and to the world
Shew what she was, a high and fearless soul,
Or rather in a spirit of thanks to those
Who had stirr'd up her slackening faculties
To new transition, had assumed with joy
30   The body and the venerable name
Of a Republic:² lamentable crimes
'Tis true had gone before this hour, the work
Of massacre in which the senseless sword
Was pray'd to as a judge; but these were past,
35   Earth free from them for ever, as was thought,
Ephemeral monsters, to be seen but once,
Things that could only shew themselves and die.
        This was the time in which enflam'd with hope,
To Paris I return'd. Again I rang'd,
40   More eagerly than I had done before,
Through the wide City and in progress pass'd
The Prison where the unhappy Monarch lay
Associate with his Children and his Wife
In bondage; and the Palace lately storm'd
45   With roar of canon, and a numerous Host.
I cross'd, (a blank and empty area then)
The Square of the Carousel, few weeks back
Heap'd up with dead and dying,³ upon these
And other sights looking as doth a man
50   Upon a volume whose contents he knows
Are memorable, but from him lock'd up,
Being written in a tongue he cannot read;
So that he questions the mute leaves with pain
And half upbraids their silence. But that night
55   When on my bed I lay I was most mov'd
And felt most deeply in what world I was;
My room was high and lonely, near the roof
Of a large Mansion° or Hotel, a spot   townhouse
That would have pleas'd me in more quiet times
60   Nor was it wholly without pleasure then.
With unextinguish'd taper I kept watch,
Reading at intervals; the fear gone by
Press'd on me almost like a fear to come;

2. On 22 September 1792.
3. The royal palace had been stormed by a mob in
August, with over a thousand lives lost; their bodies were
cremated in the square in front of the palace.

I thought of those September Massacres,
65	Divided from me by a little month,[4]
And felt and touch'd them, a substantial dread;
The rest was conjured up from tragic fictions
And mournful Calendars° of true history,	records
Remembrances and dim admonishments.
70	"The horse is taught his manage° and the wind	paces
Of heaven wheels round and treads in his own steps,[5]
Year follows year, the tide returns again,
Day follows day, all things have second birth;
The earthquake is not satisfied at once."
75	And in such way I wrought upon myself
Until I seem'd to hear a voice that cried
To the whole City, "Sleep no more."[6] To this
Add comments of a calmer mind, from which
I could not gather full security,
80	But at the best it seemed a place of fear,
Unfit for the repose of night,
Defenceless as a wood where tigers roam.
　　Betimes next morning to the Palace Walk
Of Orleans I repair'd and entering there
85	Was greeted, among divers° other notes,	various
By voices of the Hawkers in the crowd
Bawling, *Denunciation of the crimes
Of Maximilian Robespierre:* the speech
Which in their hands they carried was the same
90	Which had been recently pronounced the day
When Robespierre, well-knowing for what mark
Some words of indirect reproof had been
Intended, rose in hardihood and dared
The Man who had an ill surmise of him
95	To bring his charge in openness: whereat
When a dead pause ensued and no one stirr'd,
In silence of all present, from his seat
Louvet walked singly through the avenue
And took his station in the Tribune,° saying	rostrum
100	"I, Robespierre, accuse thee"! 'Tis well known
What was the issue of that charge, and how
Louvet was left alone without support
Of his irresolute Friends:[7] but these are things
Of which I speak only as they were storm

---

4. Between September 2 and 7, Robespierre's newly powerful radical faction organized the massacres of 3,000 prisoners. Wordsworth echoes Hamlet's anger at his mother's
betrayal of his recently deceased father (1.2.147).
5. The National Convention of France now met at a
former riding school near the Tuileries. The first six
words of the quotation echo Shakespeare's *As You Like
It* (1.1.11–12).

6. Macbeth's guilty fantasy after he has murdered his
king: "Methought I heard a voice cry 'Sleep no more!'"
(*Macbeth* 2.2.35).
7. In the National Convention, on 29 October 1792, moderate Girondist J. B. Louvet de Couvray accused Robespierre
of tyranny. The phrase "walked singly" in line 98 evokes
the solitary resistance of archangel Abdiel to Satan's revolt
against God (*Paradise Lost* 5.877ff.).

105   Or sunshine to my individual mind,
      No further. * * *

         Well might my wishes be intense, my thoughts
      Strong and perturb'd, not doubting at that time,
      Creed which ten shameful years[8] have not annull'd,
      But that the virtue of one paramount mind
180   Would have abash'd those impious crests, have quell'd
      Outrage and bloody power, and in despite
      Of what the People were through ignorance
      And immaturity, and, in the teeth
      Of desperate opposition from without,
185   Have clear'd a passage for just government,
      And left a solid birth-right to the State,
      Redeem'd according to example given
      By ancient Lawgivers.
                              In this frame of mind
      Reluctantly to England I return'd,[9]
190   Compell'd by nothing less than absolute want
      Of funds for my support, else, well assured
      That I both was and must be of small worth,
      No better than an alien in the Land,
      I doubtless should have made a common cause
195   With some who perish'd, haply° perish'd too.[1]   *perhaps*
      A poor mistaken and bewilder'd offering,
      Should to the breast of Nature have gone back
      With all my resolutions, all my hopes,
      A Poet only to myself, to Men
200   Useless, and even, beloved Friend, a soul
      To thee unknown.[2]

                  [FURTHER EVENTS IN FRANCE]

      In France, the Men who for their desperate ends
      Had pluck'd up mercy by the roots were glad
      Of this new enemy. Tyrants, strong before
310   In devilish pleas were ten times stronger now,[3]
      And thus beset with Foes on every side
      The goaded Land wax'd mad; the crimes of few
      Spread into madness of the many, blasts
      From hell came sanctified like airs from heaven;[4]
315   The sternness of the Just,[5] the faith of those

---

8. Since 1793.
9. Late in 1792.
1. Wordsworth's sympathies were with the moderate Girondins, almost all of whom were executed or committed suicide following Robespierre's rise to power.
2. Wordsworth met Coleridge in 1795. See page 283 for the next 25 lines.
3. After France declared war on England in February

1793, England joined the coalition against France led by Austria and Prussia. Except for a brief peace in 1802, England would be at war with France until 1815.
4. Hamlet wonders if the ghost of his murdered father brings "airs from heaven or blasts from hell" (*Hamlet* 1.4.41).
5. Perhaps a glance at Robespierre's associate Louis St. Just.

Who doubted not that Providence had times
Of anger and vengeance, theirs who throned
The human understanding paramount
And made of that their God,[6] the hopes of those
320 Who were content to barter short-lived pangs
For a paradise of ages,[7] the blind rage
Of insolent tempers, the light vanity
Of intermeddlers, steady purposes
Of the suspicious, slips of the indiscreet,
325 And all the accidents of life were press'd
Into one service, busy with one work;
The Senate was heart-stricken, not a voice
Uplifted, none to oppose or mitigate:
Domestic carnage now fill'd all the year
330 With Feast-days; the Old Man from the chimney-nook,
The Maiden from the bosom of her Love,
The Mother from the Cradle of her Babe,
The Warrior from the Field, all perish'd,
Friends, enemies, of all parties, ages, ranks,
335 Head after head, and never heads enough
For those who bade them fall: they found their joy,
They made it, ever thirsty.[8]—As a Child,
(If light desires of innocent little Ones
May with such heinous appetites be match'd)
340 Having a toy, a windmill, though the air
Do of itself blow fresh, and makes the vane
Spin in his eyesight, he is not content,
But with the play-thing at arm's length, he sets
His front against the blast, and runs amain°   *full force*
345 To make it whirl the faster.
                                        In the depth
Of these enormities, even thinking minds
Forgot at seasons whence they had their being,
Forgot that such a sound was ever heard
As Liberty, upon earth; yet all beneath
350 Her innocent authority was wrought,
Nor could have been without her blessed name.
The illustrious Wife of Roland, in the hour
Of her composure, felt that agony
And gave it vent in her last words.[9] O Friend!
355 It was a lamentable time for man
Whether a hope had e'er been his or not,
A woful time for them whose hopes did still

6. "La Raison" (Reason) was a goddess of the Republic, and churches were turned into Temples of Reason.
7. Radicals regarded the terror as a necessary purge to secure the safety of the Republic.
8. At the height of the Terror in 1793, 1,376 people were guillotined in Paris in 49 days, and in the city of Nantes 15,000 by the end of the year.
9. Madame Roland, Wollstonecraft's friend and an important supporter of the Girondins, was guillotined in November 1793. Her famous last words were: "O Liberté, que des crimes l'on commet en ton nom!" ("O Liberty, what crimes are committed in thy name!").

Outlast the shock, most woful for those few—
They had the deepest feeling of the grief—
360   Who still were flatter'd,° and had trust in man.   *deluded*
Meanwhile, the Invaders fared as they deserv'd;
The Herculean Commonwealth had put forth her arms
And throttled with an infant Godhead's might
The snakes about her cradle:[1] that was well
365   And as it should be, yet no cure for those
Whose souls were sick with pain of what would be
Hereafter brought in charge against mankind;
Most melancholy at that time, O Friend!
Were my day thoughts, my dreams were miserable;
370   Through months, through years, long after the last beat
Of those atrocities (I speak bare truth,
As if to thee alone in private talk)
I scarcely had one night of quiet sleep,
Such ghastly visions had I of despair
375   And tyranny and implements of death,
And long orations which in dreams I pleaded
Before unjust Tribunals, with a voice
Labouring, a brain confounded, and a sense
Of treachery and desertion in the place
380   The holiest that I knew of, my own soul.

[THE DEATH OF ROBESPIERRE AND RENEWED OPTIMISM][2]

                    when a Traveller
Chancing to pass, I carelessly inquired
If any news were stirring: he replied
In the familiar language of the day
535   That "*Robespierre was dead.*" Nor was a doubt,
On further question, left within my mind
But that the tidings were substantial truth,
That he and his supporters all were fallen.
      Great was my glee of spirit, great my joy
540   In vengeance, and eternal justice, thus
Made manifest. "Come now ye golden times,"
Said I, forth-breathing on those open Sands
A Hymn of triumph, "as the morning comes
Out of the bosom of the night, come Ye:
545   Thus far our trust is verified; behold!
They who with clumsy desperation brought
A river of blood, and preach'd that nothing else
Could cleanse the Augean Stable,[3] by the might

1. Cradled infant Hercules strangled the two serpents
sent by Hera to destroy him, just as the infant Republic
had repelled foreign invasions.
2. Wordsworth is back in England, spending the summer
on the coast near Peele Castle. On 28 July 1794, Robespierre and 21 associates were guillotined. Wordsworth was
walking near the shore when he heard the news.
3. In one of his 12 labors, Hercules cleaned the filthy stables
of King Augeus, by diverting two rivers through them. See
Tom Paine, page 131, Wordsworth's likely reference.

Of their own helper have been swept away;
550   Their madness is declared and visible,
Elsewhere will safety now be sought,[4] and Earth
March firmly towards righteousness and peace."
Then schemes I framed more calmly, when and how
The madding Factions might be tranquillised,
555   And though through hardships manifold and long,
The mighty renovation would proceed:
Thus, interrupted by uneasy bursts
Of exultation, I pursued my way
Along that very Shore which I had skimm'd
560   In former times, when, spurring from the Vale
Of Nightshade and St Mary's mouldering Fane°   *shrine*
And the Stone Abbot, after circuit made
In wantonness of heart, a joyous Crew
Of School-boys, hastening to their distant home,
565   Along the margin of the moonlight Sea,
We beat with thundering hoofs the level Sand.

                              * * *

O pleasant exercise of hope and joy![5]
690   For great were the auxiliars° which then stood   *allies*
Upon our side, we who were strong in love;
Bliss was it in that dawn to be alive,
But to be young was very heaven: O times,
In which the meagre, stale, forbidding ways
695   Of custom, law and statute took at once
The attraction of a Country in Romance;
When Reason seem'd the most to assert her rights
When most intent on making of herself
A prime Enchanter to assist the work
700   Which then was going forwards in her name:
Not favor'd spots alone, but the whole earth
The beauty wore of promise, that which sets,
To take an image which was felt, no doubt,
Among the bowers of paradise itself,
705   The budding rose above the rose full blown.
What temper° at the prospect did not wake   *temperament*
To happiness unthought-of? The inert
Were rouz'd, and lively natures rapt° away.   *carried, enraptured*
They who had fed their childhood upon dreams,
710   The Play-fellows of Fancy, who had made
All powers of swiftness, subtlety, and strength
Their ministers, used to stir in lordly wise
Among the grandest objects of the sense
And deal with whatsoever they found there

---

4. A dig at Robespierre's Committee of Public Safety, which had instigated the Terror.
5. Wordsworth's renewed faith in the French Republic extended to hope for peaceful reforms in England. He published this passage in Coleridge's journal *The Friend* in 1809 and in his own *Poems* of 1815, as *French Revolution as It Appeared to Enthusiasts at Its Commencement*, classing it with "Poems of the Imagination."

715 As if they had within some lurking right
    To wield it:—they too, who, of gentle mood,
    Had watch'd all gentle motions, and to these
    Had fitted their own thoughts, schemers more mild,
    And in the region of their peaceful selves—
720 Did now find helpers to their heart's desire,
    And stuff at hand, plastic° as they could wish,   *malleable*
    Were call'd upon to exercise their skill,
    Not in Utopia, subterraneous fields,
    Or some secreted Island Heaven knows where;
725 But in the very world which is the world
    Of all of us, the place on which in the end
    We find our happiness, or not at all.

[BRITAIN DECLARES WAR ON FRANCE.[6]
THE RISE OF NAPOLEON AND IMPERIALIST FRANCE]

    In the main outline, such, it might be said
    Was my condition, till with open war
    Britain opposed the Liberties of France:
760 This threw me first out of the pale° of love,   *boundary*
    Sour'd, and corrupted upwards to the source
    My sentiments, was° not, as hitherto,   *this was*
    A swallowing up of lesser things in great;
    But change of them into their opposites,
765 And thus a way was open'd for mistakes
    And false conclusions of the intellect
    As gross in their degree and in their kind
    Far, far more dangerous. What had been a pride
    Was now a shame; my likings and my loves
770 Ran in new channels, leaving old ones dry,
    And thus a blow which in maturer age
    Would but have touch'd the judgement struck more deep
    Into sensations near the heart. * * *

    And now, become Oppressors in their turn,
    Frenchmen had changed a war of self-defense
    For one of conquest,[7] losing sight of all
    Which they had struggled for; and mounted up
795 Openly in the view of earth and heaven
    The scale of Liberty. I read her doom,
    Vex'd inly somewhat, it is true, and sore,
    But not dismay'd, nor taking to the shame
    Of a false Prophet; but, rouz'd up, I stuck
800 More firmly to old tenets, and to prove
    Their temper,° strain'd them more, and thus in heat   *test their strength*
    Of contest did opinions every day

6. France declared war on 1 February 1793. Ten days   7. By late 1794.
later, England reciprocated.

Grow into consequence till round my mind
They clung, as if they were the life of it.

*** After what hath been
Already said of patriotic love,
865 And hinted at in other sentiments
We need not linger long upon this theme.
This only may be said, that from the first
Having two natures in me, joy the one
The other melancholy, and withal
870 A happy man, and therefore bold to look
On painful things, slow somewhat too and stern
In temperament, I took the knife in hand
And stopping not at parts less sensitive,
Endeavour'd with my best of skill to probe
875 The living body of society
Even to the heart: I push'd without remorse
My speculations forward; yea, set foot
On Nature's holiest places. Time may come
When some dramatic Story may afford
880 Shapes livelier to convey to thee, my Friend,
What then I learn'd, or think I learn'd of truth
And the errors into which I was betray'd
By present objects, and by reasonings false
From the beginning, inasmuch as drawn
885 Out of a heart which had been turn'd aside
From nature by external accidents,
And which was thus confounded more and more,
Misguiding and misguided. Thus I fared,
Dragging all passions, notions, shapes of faith
890 Like culprits to the bar,° suspiciously   *courtroom*
Calling the mind to establish in plain day
Her titles and her honours, now believing,
Now disbelieving, endlessly perplex'd
With impulse, motive, right and wrong, the ground
895 Of moral obligation, what the rule
And what the sanction, till, demanding proof
And seeking it in every thing, I lost
All feeling of conviction, and in fine°   *in the end*
Sick, wearied out with contrarieties,
900 Yielded up moral questions in despair,
And for my future studies, as the sole
Employment of the inquiring faculty,
Turn'd towards mathematics, and their clear
And solid evidence.—Ah! then it was
905 That Thou, most precious Friend! about this time
First known to me, didst lend a living help
To regulate my soul, and then it was,
That the beloved Woman,[8] in whose sight

---

8. After a long separation, in September 1795, Dorothy and William were able to realize their dream of sharing a household; Coleridge lived nearby.

Those days were pass'd, now speaking in a voice
910   Of sudden admonition like a brook
That does but cross a lonely road, and now
Seen, heard, and felt, and caught at every turn,
Companion never lost through many a league,
Maintain'd for me a saving intercourse°   communion
915   With my true self: for, though impair'd and changed,
Much, as it seem'd, I was no further changed
Than as a clouded, not a waning moon.
She in the midst of all preserv'd me still
A Poet, made me seek beneath that name
920   My office upon earth, and nowhere else,
And lastly, Nature's self, by human love
Assisted, through the weary labyrinth
Conducted me again to open day,
Revived the feelings of my earlier life,
925   Gave me that strength, and knowledge full of peace,
Enlarged, and never more to be disturb'd,
Which through the steps of our degeneracy,
All degradation of this age, hath still
Upheld me, and upholds me at this day°   1804
930   In the catastrophe (for so they dream,
And nothing less) when finally, to close
And rivet up the gains of France, a Pope
Is summon'd in, to crown an Emperor;
This last opprobrium° when we see the dog   disgrace
935   Returning to his vomit,[9] when the sun
That rose in splendour, was alive, and moved
In exultation among living clouds
Hath put his function and his glory off,
And, turn'd into a gewgaw, a machine,°   stage machine
940   Sets like an opera phantom. * * *

from The Prelude 1850

[APOSTROPHE TO EDMUND BURKE][1]

Genius of Burke! forgive the pen seduced
By specious wonders, and too slow to tell
Of what the ingenuous, what bewildered men,
515   Beginning to mistrust their boastful guides,
And wise men, willing to grow wiser, caught,
Rapt auditors! from thy most eloquent tongue—
Now mute, for ever mute in the cold grave.
I see him,—old, but vigorous in age,—
520   Stand like an oak whose stag-horn branches start

9. In November 1804 Pope Pius VII attended Napoleon's coronation as Emperor; as Pius was about to place the crown on his head, Napoleon snatched it and did the honors himself. The persistently evil man is like a dog "turned to his own vomit again" (2 Peter 2.22).

1. Composed in 1832, this verse appears in Book 7, as Wordsworth pauses before Parliament to remember Burke's parliamentary career and his *Reflections on the Revolution in France*.

Out of its leafy brow, the more to awe
The younger brethren of the grove. But some—
While he forewarns, denounces, launches forth,
Against all systems built on abstract rights,

525   Keen ridicule; the majesty proclaims
Of Institutes and Laws, hallowed by time;
Declares the vital power of social ties
Endeared by Custom; and with high disdain,
Exploding upstart Theory, insists

530   Upon the allegiance to which men are born—
Some—say at once a froward° multitude—   *willful*
Murmur (for truth is hated, where not loved)
As the winds fret within the Aeolian cave,
Gall'd by their monarch's chain.[2] The times were big

535   With ominous change, which, night by night, provoked
Keen struggles, and black clouds of passion raised;
But memorable moments intervened,
When Wisdom, like the Goddess° from Jove's brain,   *Athena*
Broke forth in armour of resplendent words,

540   Startling the Synod.° Could a youth, and one   *Parliament*
In ancient story versed, whose breast had heaved
Under the weight of classic eloquence,
Sit, see, and hear, unthankful, uninspired?

from Book Eleventh. Imagination, How Impaired and Restored

[IMAGINATION RESTORED BY NATURE]

Long time hath Man's unhappiness and guilt
Detain'd us; with what dismal sights beset
For the outward view, and inwardly oppress'd
With sorrow, disappointment, vexing thoughts,

5   Confusion of the judgement, zeal decay'd
And lastly, utter loss of hope itself,
And things to hope for. Not with these began
Our Song; and not with these our Song must end:
Ye motions of delight that through the fields

10   Stir gently, breezes and soft airs that breathe
The breath of paradise, and find your way
To the recesses of the soul! Ye Brooks
Muttering along the stones, a busy noise
By day, a quiet one in silent night,

15   And you, Ye Groves, whose ministry it is
To interpose the covert of your shades,
Even as a sleep, betwixt the heart of man
And the uneasy world, 'twixt man himself,
Not seldom, and his own unquiet heart,

20   Oh! that I had a music and a voice,

2. The god Aeolus kept his winds chained in a cave.

Harmonious as your own, that I might tell
What ye have done for me. The morning shines,
Nor heedeth Man's perverseness; Spring returns,
I saw the Spring return when I was dead
25 To deeper hope, yet had I joy for her,
And welcomed her benevolence, rejoiced
In common with the Children of her Love,
Plants, insects, beast in field, and bird in bower.
So neither were complacency° nor peace   *satisfaction*
30 Nor tender yearnings wanting° for my good   *lacking*
Through those distracted times; in Nature still
Glorying, I found a counterpoise in her,
Which, when the spirit of evil was at height
Maintain'd for me a secret happiness;
35 Her I resorted to, and lov'd so much
I seem'd to love as much as heretofore;
And yet this passion, fervent as it was,
Had suffer'd change; how could there fail to be
Some change, if merely hence, that years of life
40 Were going on, and with them loss or gain
Inevitable, sure alternative.
        This History, my Friend, hath chiefly told
Of intellectual° power, from stage to stage   *mental nad spiritual*
Advancing, hand in hand with love and joy,
45 And of imagination teaching truth
Until that natural graciousness of mind
Gave way to over-pressure of the times
And their disastrous issues. * * *

["SPOTS OF TIME." TWO MEMORIES FROM CHILDHOOD AND LATER REFLECTIONS][1]

In truth, this degradation, howsoe'er
Induced, effect in whatsoe'er degree
245 Of custom, that prepares such wantonness
As makes the greatest things give way to least,
Of any other cause which hath been named,
Or, lastly, aggravated by the times,
Which with their passionate sounds might often make
250 The milder minstrelsies of rural scenes
Inaudible, was transient; I had felt
Too forcibly, too early in my life
Visitings of imaginative power,
For this to last: I shook the habit off
255 Entirely and for ever, and again
In Nature's presence stood, as I stand now,

1. This passage, which concludes Book 11, was drafted in 1799. Originally set early in part 1 of the *Two-Part Prelude* with other boyhood memories (boat-stealing, ice-skating, the drowned man), it argues that memory can restore power to the imagination. Transferring early memories to this late point in his autobiography, Wordsworth empowers them to enact what they describe—poetic power revivified through recollection.

A sensitive and a creative Soul.
  There are in our existence spots of time,
Which with distinct preeminence retain

260 A renovating Virtue,° whence, depress'd   *power*
By false opinion and contentious thought,
Or aught of heavier or more deadly weight
In trivial occupations, and the round
Of ordinary intercourse, our minds

265 Are nourish'd, and invisibly repair'd,
A virtue by which pleasure is enhanced
That penetrates, enables us to mount
When high, more high, and lifts us up when fallen.
This efficacious spirit chiefly lurks

270 Among those passages of life in which
We have had deepest feeling that the mind
Is lord and master, and that outward sense
Is but the obedient servant of her will.
Such moments, worthy of all gratitude,

275 Are scatter'd every where, taking their date
From our first childhood; in our childhood even
Perhaps are most conspicuous. Life with me
As far as memory can look back, is full
Of this beneficent influence. At a time

280 When scarcely (I was then not six years old)
My hand could hold a bridle, with proud hopes
I mounted, and we rode towards the hills:
We were a pair of Horsemen; honest James[2]
Was with me, my encourager and guide.

285 We had not travell'd long ere some mischance
Disjoin'd me from my Comrade, and through fear
Dismounting, down the rough and stony Moor
I led my Horse, and, stumbling on, at length
Came to a bottom,° where in former times   *dell*

290 A Murderer had been hung in iron chains.
The Gibbet mast was moulder'd down, the bones
And iron case were gone; but on the turf
Hard by, soon after that fell deed was wrought
Some unknown hand had carved the Murderer's name.

295 The monumental writing was engraven
In times long past, and still, from year to year,
By superstition of the neighbourhood
The grass is clear'd away; and to this hour
The letters are all fresh and visible.

300 Faltering, and ignorant where I was, at length
I chanced to espy those characters inscribed
On the green sod: forthwith I left the spot
And, reascending the bare Common,° saw   *field*
A naked Pool that lay beneath the hills,

2. 1850] "an ancient servant of my father's house."

305   The Beacon on the summit, and more near
      A Girl who bore a Pitcher on her head
      And seem'd with difficult steps to force her way
      Against the blowing wind. It was, in truth,
      An ordinary sight; but I should need
310   Colours and words that are unknown to man
      To paint the visionary dreariness
      Which, while I look'd all round for my lost Guide,
      Did at that time invest the naked Pool,
      The Beacon on the lonely Eminence,
315   The Woman, and her garments vex'd and toss'd
      By the strong wind. When in a blessed season[3]
      With those two dear Ones,[4] to my heart so dear,
      When in the blessed time of early love,
      Long afterwards, I roam'd about
320   In daily presence of this very scene;
      Upon the naked pool and dreary crags,
      And on the melancholy Beacon, fell
      The spirit of pleasure, and youth's golden gleam;
      And think ye not with radiance more divine
325   From these remembrances, and from the power
      They left behind? So feeling comes in aid
      Of feeling, and diversity of strength
      Attends us, if but once we have been strong.
      Oh! mystery of Man, from what a depth
330   Proceed thy honours! I am lost, but see
      In simple childhood something of the base
      On which thy greatness stands, but this I feel,
      That from thyself it is that thou must give,
      Else never canst receive. The days gone by
335   Come back upon me from the dawn almost
      Of life: the hiding-places of my power
      Seem open; I approach, and then they close;[5]
      I see by glimpses now; when age comes on
      May scarcely see at all, and I would give,
340   While yet we may, as far as words can give,
      A substance and a life to what I feel:
      I would enshrine the spirit of the past
      For future restoration. Yet another
      Of these to me affecting incidents
345   With which we will conclude.
                            One Christmas-time,
      The day before the Holidays began,
      Feverish, and tired, and restless, I went forth
      Into the fields, impatient for the sight
      Of those two Horses which should bear us home,
350   My Brothers and myself.[6] There was a Crag,

---

3. Before he left for France in 1802. The verse from here to the end of the paragraph was drafted in 1804, just after he completed the "Intimations" Ode.
4. His sister and fiancée Mary Hutchinson.

5. 1850] "I would approach them, but they close" (12.280).
6. December 1783; they were away from home at Hawkshead Grammar School.

An Eminence, which from the meeting point
Of two high-ways ascending, overlook'd
At least a long half-mile of those two roads,
By each of which the expected Steeds might come,
355   The choice uncertain. Thither I repair'd,
Up to the highest summit: 'twas a day
Stormy, and rough and wild, and on the grass
I sate, half shelter'd by a naked wall:
Upon my right hand was a single sheep,
360   A whistling hawthorn on my left, and there
With those Companions at my side, I watch'd,
Straining my eyes intensely, as the mist
Gave intermitting prospect of the wood
And plain beneath. Ere I to School return'd
365   That dreary time, ere I had been ten days
A Dweller in my Father's House, he died
And I and my two Brothers, Orphans then,
Followed his Body to the Grave.[7] The event
With all the sorrow which it brought appear'd
370   A chastisement; and when I call'd to mind
That day so lately pass'd, when from the crag
I look'd in such anxiety of hope,
With trite reflections of morality,
Yet in the deepest passion, I bow'd low
375   To God, who thus corrected my desires;
And afterwards, the wind and sleety rain
And all the business of the elements,
The single sheep, and the one blasted tree,
And the bleak music of that old stone wall,
380   The noise of wood and water, and the mist
Which on the line of each of those two Roads
Advanced in such indisputable shapes,[8]
All these were spectacles and sounds to which
I often would repair, and thence would drink
385   As at a fountain: and I do not doubt
That in this later time, when storm and rain
Beat on my roof at midnight, or by day
When I am in the woods, unknown to me
The workings of my spirit thence are brought.
390   Thou wilt not languish here, O Friend! for whom
I travel in these dim uncertain ways;
Thou wilt assist me as a pilgrim gone
In quest of highest truth. Behold me then
Once more in Nature's presence, thus restored
395   Or otherwise, and strengthen'd once again
(With memory left of what had been escaped)
To habits of devoutest sympathy.

7. Wordsworth's father died on 30 December 1783; his
mother had died five years earlier.
8. Hamlet cries to his father's ghost: "Thou com'st in such
a questionable shape / That I will speak to thee" (*Hamlet*
1.4.43–44).

from **Book Thirteenth. Conclusion**

[CLIMBING MOUNT SNOWDON. MOONLIT VISTA.
MEDITATION ON "MIND," "SELF," "IMAGINATION," "FEAR," AND "LOVE"]

In one of these excursions, travelling then
Through Wales, on foot, and with a youthful Friend,[1]
I left Bethkelet's huts at couching-time,°   bedtime
And westward took my way to see the sun
5   Rise from the top of Snowdon. Having reach'd
The Cottage at the Mountain's foot, we there
Rouz'd up the Shepherd, who by ancient right
Of office is the Stranger's usual Guide,
And after short refreshment sallied forth.
10   —It was a Summer's night, a close warm night,
Wan, dull and glaring,° with a dripping mist   clammy
Low-hung and thick that cover'd all the sky,
Half-threatening storm and rain: but on we went
Uncheck'd, being full of heart and having faith
15   In our tried Pilot. Little could we see,
Hemm'd round on every side with fog and damp,
And, after ordinary Traveller's chat
With our Conductor, silently we sunk
Each into commerce with his private thoughts:
20   Thus did we breast the ascent, and by myself
Was nothing either seen or heard the while
Which took me from my musings, save that once
The Shepherd's Cur did to his own great joy
Unearth a hedge-hog in the mountain crags
25   Round which he made a barking turbulent.
This small adventure, (for even such it seem'd
In that wild place and at the dead of night)
Being over and forgotten, on we wound
In silence as before. With forehead bent
30   Earthward, as if in opposition set
Against an enemy, I panted up
With eager pace, and no less eager thoughts.
Thus might we wear perhaps an hour away,
Ascending at loose distance each from each,
35   And I, as chanced, the foremost of the Band,
When at my feet the ground appear'd to brighten,
And with a step or two seem'd brighter still,
Nor had I time to ask the cause of this,
For instantly a Light upon the turf
40   Fell like a flash: I look'd about, and lo!

---

1. Robert Jones, with whom Wordsworth toured Europe in 1790. During a walking tour of North Wales in the summer of 1791, they climbed Snowdon, at nearly 3,600 feet the highest peak in Wales. The party set out from the village of Beddgelert, four miles away.

The Moon stood naked in the Heavens, at height
Immense above my head, and on the shore
I found myself of a huge sea of mist,
Which meek and silent, rested at my feet:

45   A hundred hills their dusky backs upheaved
All over this still Ocean,[2] and beyond,
Far, far beyond, the vapours shot themselves,
In headlands, tongues, and promontory shapes
Into the Sea, the real Sea,° that seem'd   *Irish Sea*

50   To dwindle and give up its majesty,
Usurp'd upon as far as sight could reach.
Meanwhile the Moon look'd down upon this shew
In single glory, and we stood, the mist
Touching our very feet: and from the shore

55   At distance not the third part of a mile
Was a blue chasm, a fracture in the vapour,
A deep and gloomy breathing-place thro' which
Mounted the roar of waters, torrents, streams
Innumerable, roaring with one voice.[3]

60   The universal spectacle throughout
Was shaped for admiration and delight,
Grand in itself alone, but in that breach
Through which the homeless voice of waters rose,
That dark deep thorough-fare had Nature lodg'd

65   The Soul, the Imagination of the whole.
      A meditation rose in me that night
Upon the lonely Mountain when the scene
Had pass'd away, and it appear'd to me
The perfect image of a mighty Mind,

70   Of one that feeds upon infinity,
That is exalted by an underpresence,
The sense of God, or whatsoe'er is dim
Or vast in its own being; above all
One function of such mind had Nature there

75   Exhibited by putting forth, in midst
Of circumstance most awful° and sublime,[4]   *awe-inspiring*
That domination which she oftentimes
Exerts upon the outward face of things,
So molds them and endues, abstracts, combines

80   Or by abrupt and unhabitual influence
Doth make one object so impress itself
Upon all others, and pervade them so
That even the grossest minds must see and hear

---

2. Echoing Milton's description of God's creation of land
from the sea (*Paradise Lost* 7.285–877).
3. Compare 6.566–69.

4. Lines 66–76 were written one year after the rest of this
passage.

And cannot chuse but feel. The Power which these
85 Acknowledge when thus moved, which Nature thus
Thrusts forth upon the senses, is the express
Resemblance, in the fullness of its strength
Made visible, a genuine Counterpart
And Brother of the glorious faculty
90 Which higher minds bear with them as their own;
This is the very spirit in which they deal
With all the objects of the universe.
They from their native selves can send abroad
Like transformation, for themselves create
95 A like existence, and whene'er it is
Created for them catch it by an instinct;
Them the enduring and the transient both
Serve to exalt; they build up greatest things
From least suggestions; ever on the watch,
100 Willing to work and to be wrought upon,
They need not extraordinary calls
To rouze them, in a world of life they live
By sensible impressions not enthrall'd,
But quicken'd, rouz'd, and made thereby more fit
105 To hold communion with the invisible world.
Such minds are truly from the Deity;
For they are Powers; and hence the highest bliss
That can be known is theirs, the consciousness
Of whom they are habitually infused
110 Through every image, and through every thought,
And all impressions: hence religion, faith,
And endless occupation for the soul
Whether discursive or intuitive,[5]
Hence sovereignty within and peace at will,
115 Emotion which best foresight need not fear,
Most worthy then of trust when most intense:
Hence chearfulness in every act of life,
Hence truth in moral judgements and delight
That fails not in the external universe.
120   Oh! who is he that hath his whole life long
Preserved, enlarged this freedom in himself!
For this alone is genuine Liberty.
Witness, ye Solitudes! where I received
My earliest visitations, careless then
125 Of what was given me, and which now I roam
A meditative, oft a suffering Man,

---

5. Archangel Raphael tells Adam that the soul has powers of Reason "Discursive or Intuitive" (*Paradise Lost* 5.485–88);
discursive: learned.

And yet, I trust, with undiminish'd powers,
Witness, whatever falls my better mind,
Revolving with the accidents of life,
130   May have sustain'd, that, howsoe'er misled,
I never, in the quest of right and wrong,
Did tamper with myself° from private aims;   *my conscience*
Nor was in any of my hopes the dupe
Of selfish passions; nor did wilfully
135   Yield ever to mean cares and low pursuits;
But rather did with jealousy° shrink back   *vigilance*
From every combination that might aid
The tendency, too potent in itself,
Of habit to enslave the mind, I mean
140   Oppress it by the laws of vulgar° sense,   *mere*
And substitute a universe of death,[6]
The falsest of all worlds, in place of that
Which is divine and true. To fear and love,
To love, as first and chief, for there fear ends,
145   Be this ascribed; to early intercourse,
In presence of sublime and lovely Forms,
With the adverse principles of pain and joy,
Evil, as one° is rashly named by those   *i.e., pain*
Who know not what they say.[7] From love, for here
150   Do we begin and end, all grandeur comes,
All truth and beauty, from pervading love,
That gone, we are as dust. Behold the fields
In balmy spring-time, full of rising flowers
And blissful Creatures: see that Pair, the Lamb
155   And the Lamb's Mother, and their tender ways
Shall touch thee to the heart: in some green bower
Rest, and be not alone, but have thou there
The One who is thy choice of all the world;
There linger, lull'd, and lost, and rapt away,
160   Be happy to thy fill: thou call'st this love,
And so it is; but there is higher love
Than this, a love that comes into the heart
With awe and a diffusive° sentiment;   *bountiful*
Thy love is human merely; this proceeds
165   More from the brooding Soul, and is divine.
    This love more intellectual° cannot be   *spiritual*
Without Imagination, which in truth
Is but another name for absolute strength
And clearest insight, amplitude of mind,

---

6. Milton's description of Hell (*Paradise Lost* 2.622).   7. Jesus's description of his executioners (Luke 23.34).

170 And reason in her most exalted mood.
This faculty hath been the moving soul
Of our long labour: we have traced the stream
From darkness, and the very place of birth
In its blind cavern, whence is faintly heard
175 The sound of waters, follow'd it to light
And open day, accompanied its course
Among the ways of Nature; afterwards
Lost sight of it, bewilder'd and engulph'd,
Then given it greeting, as it rose once more
180 With strength, reflecting in its solemn breast
The works of man and face of human life,
And lastly, from its progress have we drawn
The feeling of life endless, the one thought
By which we live, Infinity and God.
185 Imagination having been our theme,
So also hath that intellectual love,
For they are each in each, and cannot stand
Dividually.°—Here must thou be, O Man!   *separately*
Strength to thyself; no Helper hast thou here;
190 Here keepest thou thy individual state:
No other can divide with thee this work,
No secondary hand can intervene
To fashion this ability; 'tis thine,
The prime and vital principle is thine
195 In the recesses of thy nature, far
From any reach of outward fellowship,
Else 'tis not thine at all.—But joy to him,
O joy to him who here hath sown, hath laid
Here the foundations of his future years!
200 For all that friendship, all that love can do,
All that a darling countenance can look
Or dear voice utter to complete the man,
Perfect him, made imperfect in himself,
All shall be his: and he whose soul hath risen
205 Up to the height of feeling intellect
Shall want no humbler tenderness, his heart
Be tender as a nursing Mother's heart,
Of female softness shall his life be full,
Of little loves and delicate desires,
210 Mild interests and gentlest sympathies.

[CONCLUDING RETROSPECT AND PROPHECY]

Having now
Told what best merits mention, further pains
Our present labour seems not to require

370 And I have other tasks. Call back to mind
The mood in which this Poem was begun,
O Friend! the termination of my course
Is nearer now, much nearer; yet even then
In that distraction and intense desire

375 I said unto the life which I had lived,
Where art thou? Hear I not a voice from thee
Which 'tis reproach to hear?[8] Anon I rose
As if on wings, and saw beneath me stretch'd
Vast prospect of the world which I had been

380 And was;[9] and hence this Song which like a lark
I have protracted, in the unwearied Heavens
Singing,[1] and often with more plaintive voice
Attemper'd to the sorrows of the earth;
Yet centring all in love, and in the end

385 All gratulant° if rightly understood.   *expressing joy*
    Whether to me shall be allotted life,
And with life power to accomplish aught of worth
Sufficient to excuse me in men's sight
For having given this Record of myself

390 Is all uncertain: but, beloved Friend,
When, looking back, thou seest in clearer view
Than any sweetest sight of yesterday
That summer when on Quantock's grassy Hills[2]
Far ranging, and among the sylvan Coombs°   *small valleys*

395 Thou in delicious words with happy heart
Didst speak the Vision of that Ancient Man,
The bright-eyed Mariner, and rueful woes
Didst utter of the Lady Christabel
And I, associate in such labour, walk'd

400 Murmuring of him who, joyous hap! was found,
After the perils of his moonlight ride
Near the loud Waterfall; or her who sate
In misery near the miserable Thorn;[3]
When thou dost to that summer turn thy thoughts,

405 And hast before thee all which then we were,
To thee, in memory of that happiness
It will be known, by thee at least, my Friend,
Felt, that the history of a Poet's mind
Is labour not unworthy of regard.

410 To thee the work shall justify itself.

8. See Book 1.625–72.
9. Echoing Eve's dream (*Paradise Lost* 5.86–88).
1. Echoing Shakespeare, Sonnet 29 (9–12).
2. Above Alfoxden, in Somerset, where the Wordsworths

lived, near Coleridge, from 1797 to 1798.
3. Lyrical ballads by Wordsworth (*The Idiot Boy* and *The Thorn*), and Coleridge's *Rime of the Ancyent Marinere* and *Christabel*.

The last, and later portions of this Gift
Which I for Thee design have been prepared
In times which have from those wherein we first
Together wanton'd in wild Poesy,
415 Differ'd thus far, that they have been, O Friend,
Times of much sorrow, of a private grief
Keen and enduring,[4] which the frame of mind
That in this meditative History
Hath been described, more deeply makes me feel;
420 Yet likewise hath enabled me to bear
More firmly; and a comfort now, a hope,
One of the dearest which this life can give,
Is mine; that Thou art near and wilt be soon
Restored to us in renovated health:[5]
425 When, after the first mingling of our tears,
'Mong other consolations we may find
Some pleasure from this Offering of my love.
      Oh! yet a few short years of useful life,
And all will be complete, thy race be run,
430 Thy monument of glory will be raised;
Then, though, too weak to tread the ways of truth,
This Age fall back to old idolatry,
Though men return to servitude as fast
As the tide ebbs, to ignominy and shame
435 By Nations° sink together, we shall still   *nation by nation*
Find solace in the knowledge which we have,
Bless'd with true happiness if we may be
United helpers forward of a day
Of firmer trust, joint-labourers in the work,
440 (Should Providence such grace to us vouchsafe)
Of their redemption, surely yet to come.
Prophets of Nature, we to them will speak
A lasting inspiration, sanctified
By reason and by truth: what we have loved
445 Others will love; and we may teach them how,
Instruct them how the mind of man becomes
A thousand times more beautiful than the earth
On which he dwells, above this Frame of things
(Which 'mid all revolutions in the hopes
450 And fears of men doth still remain unchanged)
In beauty exalted, as it is itself
Of substance and of fabric more divine.

---

4. Wordsworth's younger brother John drowned in a ship-wreck, 5 February 1805; see *Elegiac Stanzas*, page 559.

5. Coleridge had gone to the Mediterranean island of Malta for his health.

RESPONSE

Samuel Taylor Coleridge:
TO A GENTLEMAN.[1]

Composed on the night after his recitation of Poem on the Growth of an Individual Mind.

FRIEND of the Wise! and Teacher of the Good!
Into my heart have I received that Lay°   *song*
More than historic, that prophetic Lay
Wherein (high theme by thee first sung aright)
5   Of the foundations and the building up
Of the Human Spirit, thou hast dared to tell
What may be told, to th' understanding mind
Revealable; and what within the mind
By vital Breathings, like the secret soul
10   Of vernal growth, oft quickens in the Heart
Thoughts all too deep for words![2]—

                  Theme hard as high![3]
Of smiles spontaneous, and mysterious fears
(The first-born they of Reason and twin-birth)
Of tides obedient to external force,
15   And currents self-determined, as might seem,
Or by some inner Power; of moments awful,°   *awe-filled*
Now in thy inner life, and now abroad,
When Power streamed from thee, and thy soul received
The light reflected, as a light bestow'd—
20   Of Fancies fair, and milder hours of youth,
Hyblean murmurs[4] of Poetic Thought
Industrious in its Joy, in Vales and Glens
Native or outland,° Lakes and famous Hills!   *foreign*
Or on the lonely High-road, when the Stars
25   Were rising; or by secret Mountain-streams,
The Guides and the Companions of thy way!

    Of more than Fancy, of the Social Sense
Distending wide, and Man belov'd as Man,
Where France in all her Towns lay vibrating

---

1. In October 1806, Wordsworth's "Friend" and collaborator Coleridge returned to the Lake District of England from Malta, where he had gone in the spring of 1804 for his health. Although he had managed two ascents of Mount Etna on a visit to Sicily later that year, and over the next year and a half returned to Sicily and went to Naples, Florence, Rome, and Pisa, his health was worsening, his marriage was in shambles, and his friendship with Wordsworth and beloved Sarah Hutchinson ever more distant. At the end of 1806, Wordsworth began, across the evenings of two weeks, to read him his "Poem, Title not yet fixed upon, by William Wordsworth, Addressed to S. T. Coleridge." At the conclusion, 7 January 1807, Coleridge was inspired to this response, first published, ten years later, in a collection titled *Sibylline Leaves*. This is the version of Coleridge's lifetime editions, and our text here. The manuscript published at the end of the 19th century has the main title by which it has become better known: *To William Wordsworth. Composed for the greater part on the same night after the finishing of his recitation of the Poem in thirteen Books, on the Growth of his own Mind.* Although "Gentleman" might be decoded by those who had heard of this Poem, that its publication was decades off advertised Coleridge as a highly privileged, intimately addressed audience, and its first public interpreter.
2. Echoing the last line of the "Intimations" Ode, with "words" rather than "tears." See page 558.
3. Echoing Milton's description of his task in *Paradise Lost.*
4. Hybla, in Sicily, is famed for its honeybees.

30 Even as a Bark becalm'd beneath the Burst
     Of Heaven's immediate Thunder, when no cloud
     Is visible, or shadow on the Main.°   *open sea*
     For thou wert there, thine own brows garlanded,
     Amid the tremor of a realm aglow,
35   Amid a mighty nation jubilant,
     When from the general Heart of Human kind
     Hope sprang forth like a full-born Deity![5]
     —— Of that dear Hope afflicted and struck down,
     So summon'd homeward, thenceforth calm and sure
40   From the dread Watch-Tower of man's absolute Self,
     With light unwaning on her eyes, to look
     Far on—herself a glory to behold,
     The Angel of the vision! Then (last strain)
     Of Duty, chosen Laws controlling choice,
45   Action and Joy!—An orphic song[6] indeed,
     A song divine of high and passionate thoughts,
     To their own Music chaunted!

                    O great Bard!
     Ere yet that last strain dying awed the air,
     With stedfast eye I view'd thee in the choir
50   Of ever-enduring men. The truly Great
     Have all one age, and from one visible space
     Shed influence! They, both in power and act,
     Are permanent, and Time is not with *them*,
     Save as it worketh *for* them, they *in* it.
55   Nor less a sacred Roll, than those of old,
     And to be placed, as they, with gradual fame
     Among the Archives of Mankind, thy work
     Makes audible a linked lay of Truth,
     Of Truth profound a sweet continuous lay,
60   Not learnt, but native, her own natural notes!
     Ah! as I listen'd with a heart forlorn
     The pulses of my Being beat anew:
     And even as Life returns upon the Drown'd,
     Life's joy rekindling rous'd a throng of Pains—
65   Keen Pangs of Love, awakening as a babe
     Turbulent, with an outcry in the heart;
     And Fears self-will'd, that shunn'd the eye of Hope;
     And Hope that scarce would know itself from Fear;
     Sense of past Youth, and Manhood come in vain,
70   And Genius given, and Knowledge won in vain;
     And all which I had cull'd in Wood-walks wild,
     And all which patient toil had rear'd, and all,
     Commune with *thee* had open'd out—but Flowers

---

5. Goddess of wisdom and war, Minerva was born fully formed from the brow (brain) of Jupiter, king of the gods.
6. In ancient myth, Orpheus's music enchanted all nature, and even convinced the gods to let him redeem his beloved Euridyce from Hell. Wordsworth used this allusion in Book 1 (line 235).

Strew'd on my corse,° and borne upon my Bier,[7]   *corpse*
75   In the same Coffin, for the self-same Grave!

That way no more! and ill beseems it me,
Who came a welcomer in Herald's Guise,
Singing of Glory, and Futurity,
To wander back on such unhealthful road,
80   Plucking the poisons of self-harm! And ill
Such Intertwine beseems triumphal wreaths
Strew'd before *thy* advancing!

Nor do thou,
Sage Bard! impair the memory of that hour
Of thy communion with my nobler mind
85   By Pity or Grief, already felt too long!
Nor let my words import more blame than needs.
The tumult rose and ceas'd: for Peace is nigh
Where wisdom's voice has found a listening heart.
Amid the howl of more than wintry storms,
90   The Halcyon hears the voice of vernal° Hours   *spring*
Already on the wing.[8]

Eve following Eve,
Dear tranquil time, when the sweet sense of Home
Is sweetest! moments for their own sake hail'd
And more desired, more precious for thy song,
95   In silence listening, like a devout child,
My soul lay passive, by thy various strain
Driven, as in surges now beneath the stars,
With momentary Stars of my own birth,
Fair constellated Foam,[9] still darting off
100   Into the darkness; now a tranquil sea,
Outspread and bright, yet swelling to the Moon.

And when—O Friend! my comforter and guide!
Strong in thy self, and powerful to give strength!—
Thy long sustained Song finally closed,
105   And thy deep voice had ceased—yet thou thyself
Wert still before my eyes, and round us both
That happy vision of beloved Faces—
Scarce conscious, and yet conscious of its close
I sate, my being blended in one thought
110   (Thought was it? or Aspiration? or Resolve?)

7. Echoing Shakespeare, Sonnet 12: "And summer's green, all girded up in sheaves, / Borne on the bier with white and bristly beard" (7–8); bier: platform for a coffin.
8. In the story of Ovid's *Metamorphoses*, Halcyone, forlorn at the drowning of her husband, drowned herself. In pity the gods changed the pair into seabirds, and calmed the seas for two weeks before the winter solstice so that they could mate. Hence, an interval of unusual calm.
9. "A beautiful white cloud of Foam at momentary intervals coursed by the side of the Vessel with a Roar, and little stars of flame danced and sparkled and went out in it: and every now and then light detachments of this white cloud-like foam darted off from the vessel's side, each with its own small constellation, over the Sea, and scoured out of sight like a Tartar Troop over a Wilderness."—THE FRIEND, p. 220 [Coleridge's note]. From a travelogue letter published in issue 14 of this periodical, 23 November 1809, published again as "Letter I" of *Satyrane's Letters*, in *Biographia Literaria* (1817).

Absorb'd, yet hanging still[1] upon the sound—
And when I rose, I found myself in prayer.

January 1807   1817

"I travell'd among unknown Men"[1]

I travell'd among unknown Men,
    In Lands beyond the Sea;
Nor England! did I know till then
    What love I bore to thee.

5   'Tis past, that melancholy dream!
    Nor will I quit thy shore
A second time; for still I seem
    To love thee more and more.

Among thy mountains did I feel
10   The joy of my desire;
And She I cherish'd turn'd her wheel°   *spinning wheel*
    Beside an English fire.

Thy mornings shew'd—thy nights conceal'd
    The bowers where Lucy play'd;
15 And thine is, too, the last green field
    Which Lucy's eyes survey'd!

1801   1807

Resolution and Independence[1]

There was a roaring in the wind all night;
The rain came heavily and fell in floods;
But now the sun is rising calm and bright;
The birds are singing in the distant woods;
5 Over his own sweet voice the Stock-dove broods;[2]
The Jay makes answer as the Magpie chatters;
And all the air is fill'd with pleasant noise of waters.

All things that love the sun are out of doors;
The sky rejoices in the morning's birth;
10 The grass is bright with rain-drops; on the moors
The Hare is running races in her mirth;

---

1. Blending senses of *unmoving, in duration*, and *quiet.*
1. A kin of the "Lucy" poems of *Lyrical Ballads* (1800), this was intended for the 1802 edition.
1. The working title was *The Leech-gatherer.* Leeches were used for blood-letting, the sucking out of supposedly bad blood. In 1843 Wordsworth recalled, "This old Man I met a few hundred yards from my cottage [in Grasmere]; and the account of him is taken from his own mouth. I was in the state of feeling described in the beginning of the poem" [I.F.]. See Dorothy Wordsworth's journal, 3 October 1800 (page 606).

2. The stock-dove is said to *coo*, a sound well imitating the note of the bird; but by the intervention of the metaphor *broods*, the affections are called in by the imagination to assist in marking the manner in which the bird reiterates and prolongs her soft note, as if herself delighting to listen to it, and participating of a still and quiet satisfaction, like that which may be supposed inseparable from the continuous process of incubation [Wordsworth, Preface to 1815 *Poems*].

And with her feet she from the plashy earth
Raises a mist, which, glittering in the sun,
Runs with her all the way, wherever she doth run.

15 I was a Traveller then upon the moor;
I saw the Hare that rac'd about with joy;
I heard the woods, and distant waters roar;
Or heard them not, as happy as a Boy:
The pleasant season did my heart employ:
20 My old remembrances went from me wholly;
And all the ways of men, so vain and melancholy.

But, as it sometimes chanceth, from the might
Of joy in minds that can no farther go,
As high as we have mounted in delight
25 In our dejection do we sink as low;
To me that morning did it happen so;
And fears, and fancies, thick upon me came;
Dim sadness, and blind thoughts I knew not nor could name.

I heard the Sky-lark singing in the sky;
30 And I bethought me of the playful Hare:
Even such a happy Child of earth am I;
Even as these blissful Creatures do I fare;
Far from the world I walk, and from all care;
But there may come another day to me,
35 Solitude, pain of heart, distress, and poverty.

My whole life I have liv'd in pleasant thought,
As if life's business were a summer mood;
As if all needful things would come unsought
To genial faith, still rich in genial good;
40 But how can He expect that others should
Build for him, sow for him, and at his call
Love him, who for himself will take no heed at all?

I thought of Chatterton, the marvellous Boy,
The sleepless Soul that perish'd in his pride;
45 Of Him who walk'd in glory and in joy
Behind his plough, along the mountain-side:[3]
By our own spirits are we deified:
We Poets in our youth begin in gladness;
But thereof comes in the end despondency and madness.

50 Now, whether it were by peculiar grace,
A leading from above, a something given,

---

3. In 1770, the year Wordsworth was born, Thomas Chatterton (famed for pseudo-archaic poetry he attributed to a 15th-century monk) committed suicide by arsenic, amid dire poverty in a London garret; dead at 17, he became an icon of youthful suffering and neglected genius (see Shelley's *Adonais*, 894; Keats dedicated his longest poem, *Endymion*, to him). Robert Burns, the "plowman" poet, also died young, poor, and under-appreciated.

Yet it befel, that, in this lonely place,
When up and down my fancy thus was driven,
And I with these untoward thoughts had striven,[4]
55   I saw a Man before me unawares:
The oldest man he seem'd that ever wore grey hairs.

My course I stopped as soon as I espied
The Old Man in that naked wilderness:
Close by a Pond, upon the further side,
60   He stood alone: a minute's space I guess
I watch'd him, he continuing motionless:
To the Pool's further margin then I drew;
He being all the while before me full in view.[5]

As a huge stone is sometimes seen to lie
65   Couch'd on the bald top of an eminence;
Wonder to all who do the same espy,
By what means it could thither come, and whence;
So that it seems a thing endued with sense:
Like a Sea-beast crawl'd forth, which on a shelf
70   Of rock or sand reposeth, there to sun itself;[6]

Such seem'd this Man, not all alive nor dead,
Nor all asleep; in his extreme old age:
His body was bent double, feet and head
Coming together in their pilgrimage;
75   As if some dire constraint of pain, or rage
Of sickness felt by him in times long past,
A more than human weight upon his frame had cast.

Himself he propp'd, limbs, body, and pale face,
Upon a long grey Staff of shaven wood:
80   And, still as I drew near with gentle pace,
Beside the little pond or moorish flood
Motionless as a Cloud the Old Man stood,
That heareth not the loud winds when they call;
And moveth altogether, if it move at all.

85   At length, himself unsettling, he the Pond
Stirred with his Staff, and fixedly did look
Upon the muddy water, which he conn'd,°   *studied*
As if he had been reading in a book:
And now such freedom as I could I took;
90   And, drawing to his side, to him did say,
"This morning gives us promise of a glorious day."

A gentle answer did the old Man make,
In courteous speech which forth he slowly drew:

---

4. 1820] line 53 is deleted; new line 54: "Beside a Pool bare to the eye of Heaven."
5. This stanza was omitted after 1820.
6. In these images, the conferring, the abstracting, and the modifying powers of the Imagination, immediately and mediately acting, are all brought into conjunction [Wordsworth, 1815 Preface].

And him with further words I thus bespake,
95   "What kind of work is that which you pursue?
This is a lonesome place for one like you."
He answer'd me with pleasure and surprize;
And there was, while he spake, a fire about his eyes.[7]

His words came feebly, from a feeble chest,
100   But each in solemn order follow'd each,
With something of a lofty utterance drest;
Choice word, and measured phrase; above the reach
Of ordinary men; a stately speech!
Such as grave Livers do in Scotland use,
105   Religious men, who give to God and man their dues.

He told me that he to this Pond had come
To gather Leeches, being old and poor:
Employment hazardous and wearisome![8]
And he had many hardships to endure:
110   From Pond to Pond he roam'd, from moor to moor;
Housing, with God's good help, by choice or chance:
And in this way he gain'd an honest maintenance.

The Old Man still stood talking by my side;
But now his voice to me was like a stream
115   Scarce heard; nor word from word could I divide;
And the whole Body of the man did seem
Like one whom I had met with in a dream;
Or like a Man from some far region sent,
To give me human strength, and strong admonishment.

120   My former thoughts return'd: the fear that kills;
And hope that is unwilling to be fed;
Cold, pain, and labour, and all fleshly ills;
And mighty Poets in their misery dead.
And now, not knowing what the Old Man had said,[9]
125   My question eagerly did I renew,
"How is it that you live, and what is it you do?"

He with a smile did then his words repeat;
And said, that, gathering Leeches, far and wide
He travelled; stirring thus above his feet
130   The waters of the Ponds where they abide.
"Once I could meet with them on every side;
But they have dwindled long by slow decay;
Yet still I persevere, and find them where I may."

While he was talking thus, the lonely place,
135   The Old Man's shape, and speech, all troubled me:

---

7. 1820] "He answered, while a flash of mild surprise /
Broke from the sable orbs of his yet-vivid eyes."
8. Leech-gathering required wading bare-legged into shallow water, stirring the surface to attract them, and then
plucking them off one's legs.
9. 1815]—Perplexed, and longing to be comforted.

In my mind's eye I seem'd to see him pace[1]
    About the weary moors continually,
    Wandering about alone and silently.
    While I these thoughts within myself pursued,
140   He, having made a pause, the same discourse renewed.

And soon with this he other matter blended,
    Chearfully uttered, with demeanour kind,
    But stately in the main; and when he ended,
    I could have laugh'd myself to scorn, to find
145   In that decrepit Man so firm a mind.
    "God," said I, "be my help and stay secure;
    I'll think of the Leech-gatherer on the lonely moor!"[2]

1802   1807

RESPONSE

Lewis Carroll: Upon the Lonely Moor[1]

[It is always interesting to ascertain the sources from which our great poets obtained their ideas: this motive has dictated the publication of the following: painful as its appearance must be to the admirers of Wordsworth and his poem of "Resolution and Independence."]

I met an aged, aged man
    Upon the lonely moor:
I knew I was a gentleman,
    And he was but a boor.
5   So I stopped and roughly questioned him,
    "Come, tell me how you live!"
But his words impressed my ear no more
    Than if it were a sieve.

He said, "I look for soap-bubbles,
10   That lie among the wheat,
And bake them into mutton-pies,
    And sell them in the street.
I sell them unto men," he said,
    "Who sail on stormy seas;
15   And that's the way I get my bread.
    A trifle, if you please."

1. Hamlet sees his recently deceased father "in my mind's eye" (1.2.184–85).
2. Writing to a friend who was "displeased" by this "tedious" poem, Wordsworth exclaims, "I can *confidently* affirm, that, though I believe God has given me a strong imagination, I cannot conceive a figure more impressive than that of an old Man like this... travelling alone among the mountains and all lonely places, carrying with him his own fortitude, and the necessities which an unjust state of society has entailed upon him.... Everything is tedious when one does not read with the feelings of the

Author.... It is in the character of the old man to tell his story in a manner in which an *impatient* reader must necessarily feel as tedious" (14 June 1802).
1. With a mock-scholarly headnote and jaunty ballad meters conspicuously refusing Wordsworth's stately rime royal, Lewis Carroll (Charles Lutwidge Dodson, 1832–1898) published this poem in the short-lived comic periodical *The Train: a first-class magazine* in October 1856. A revision appeared as *The White Knight's Song* in his *Through the Looking Glass* (1871). For more on Carroll, see the main entry in The Victorian Period, this anthology.

But I was thinking of a way
    To multiply by ten,
And always, in the answer, get
20   The question back again.
I did not hear a word he said,
    But kicked that old man calm,
And said, "Come, tell me how you live!"
    And pinched him in the arm.

25 His accents mild took up the tale:
    He said, "I go my ways,
And when I find a mountain-rill,
    I set it in a blaze.
And thence they make a stuff they call
30   Rowland's Macassar Oil;[2]
But fourpence-halfpenny is all
    They give me for my toil."

But I was thinking of a plan
    To paint one's gaiters green,
35 So much the colour of the grass
    That they could not be seen.
I gave his ear a sudden box,
    And questioned him again,
And tweaked his grey and reverend locks,
40   And put him into pain.

He said, "I hunt for haddocks' eyes
    Among the heather bright,
And work them into waistcoat-buttons
    In the silent night.
45 And these I do not sell for gold,
    Or coin from silver-mine,
But for a copper-halfpenny,
    And that will purchase nine.

I sometimes dig for buttered rolls,
50   Or set limed twigs for crabs;
I sometimes search the flowery knolls
    For wheels of Hansom-cabs.[3]
And that's the way" (he gave a wink)
    "I get my living here,
55 And very gladly will I drink
    Your honour's health in beer."

I heard him then, for I had just
    Completed my design
To keep the Menai bridge[4] from rust

---

2. This hair oil manufactured by A. Rowland and Son sold widely; Byron's *Don Juan*, Canto I, line 136 (page 790).
3. This two-wheeled carriage, seating two, patented in 1834, became the most popular cab in London.

4. The 580-foot span of the iron suspension bridge over the Menai Strait between Bangor and the island of Anglesey in Wales, completed in 1826, was the longest in the world.

60   By boiling it in wine.
  I duly thanked him, ere I went,
    For all his stories queer,
  But chiefly for his kind intent
    To drink my health in beer.

65 And now if e'er by chance I put
    My fingers into glue,
  Or madly squeeze a right-hand foot
    Into a left-hand shoe;
  Or if a statement I aver
70   Of which I am not sure,
  I think of that strange wanderer
    Upon the lonely moor.

"I wandered lonely as a Cloud"[1]

I wandered lonely as a Cloud
That floats on high o'er Vales and Hills,
When all at once I saw a crowd,
A host, of dancing[2] Daffodils;
5 Along the Lake, beneath the trees,
Ten thousand dancing in the breeze.[3]

Continuous as the stars that shine
And twinkle on the milky way,
They stretched in never-ending line
10 Along the margin of a bay:
Ten thousand saw I at a glance,
Tossing their heads in sprightly dance.

The waves beside them danced; but they
Outdid the sparkling waves in glee:—
15 A Poet could not but be gay,
In such a laughing company:
I gaz'd—and gaz'd—but little thought
What wealth the show to me had brought:

For oft when on my couch I lie
20 In vacant or in pensive mood,
They flash upon that inward eye
Which is the bliss of solitude;[4]
And then my heart with pleasure fills,
And dances with the Daffodils.

1804/1815   1807/1815

---

1. See Dorothy Wordsworth's *Grasmere Journal*, 15 April 1802, page 609.
2. Revised to "golden" in 1815.
3. In 1815, Wordsworth changed "Ten thousand" to "Fluttering" and added the next stanza. He also changed "laughing" (16) to "jocund."
4. Lines 21–22 were composed by Wordsworth's wife. He thought them the "two best lines," though Coleridge called them "mental bombast" (*Biographia Literaria*, ch. 22).

"My heart leaps up"

My heart leaps up when I behold
   A Rainbow in the sky:
So was it when my life began;
So is it now I am a Man;
So be it when I shall grow old,
   . Or let me die!
The Child is Father of the Man;
And I could wish my days to be
Bound each to each by natural piety.

5

1802   1807

ODE: INTIMATIONS OF IMMORTALITY FROM RECOLLECTIONS OF EARLY CHILD-
HOOD   In a letter from 1814, Wordsworth remarks, "The poem rests entirely on two recollections of childhood, one that of a splendour in the objects of sense which is passed away,
and the other an indisposition to bend to the law of death as applying to our particular case.
A Reader who has not a vivid recollection of these feelings having existed in his mind cannot
understand that Poem." In 1843 he recalled, "Two years at least passed between the writing of
the four first stanzas and the remaining part. To the attentive and competent reader the whole
sufficiently explains itself; but there may be no harm in adverting here to particular feelings or
experiences of my own mind on which the structure of the poem partly rests. Nothing was more
difficult for me in childhood than to admit the notion of death as a state applicable to my own
being. I have said elsewhere—

> A simple child,
> That lightly draws its breath,
> And feels its life in every limb,
> What should it know of death!— [*We Are Seven*, 1–4]

But it was not so much from feelings of animal vivacity that my difficulty came as from a
sense of the indomitableness of the Spirit within me. I used to brood over the stories of Enoch
and Elijah, and almost to persuade myself that, whatever might become of others, I should be
translated, in something of the same way, to heaven.[1] With a feeling congenial to this, I was
often unable to think of external things as having external existence, and I communed with
all that I saw as something not apart from, but inherent in, my own immaterial nature. Many
times while going to school have I grasped at a wall or tree to recall myself from this abyss of
idealism to the reality. At that time I was afraid of such processes. In later periods of life I have
deplored, as we have all reason to do, a subjugation of an opposite character, and have rejoiced
over the remembrances, as is expressed in the lines—

> Obstinate questionings
> Of sense and outward things,
> Fallings from us, vanishings; etc. [141–43]

To that dream-like vividness and splendour which invest objects of sight in childhood, every
one, I believe, if he would look back, could bear testimony, and I need not dwell upon it here:
but having in the poem regarded it as presumptive evidence of a prior state of existence, I
think it right to protest against a conclusion, which has given pain to some good and pious persons, that I meant to inculcate such a belief. It is far too shadowy a notion to be recommended

---

1. Old Testament prophets: Enoch did not die, but was taken directly to heaven (Genesis 5.24) and Elijah was carried to
heaven in a chariot of fire (2 Kings 2.11).

to faith, as more than an element in our instincts of immortality. But let us bear in mind that, though the idea is not advanced in revelation, there is nothing there to contradict it, and the fall of Man presents an analogy in its favour. Accordingly, a pre-existent state has entered into the popular creeds of many nations; and, among all persons acquainted with classic literature, is known as an ingredient in Platonic philosophy. Archimedes said that he could move the world if he had a point whereon to rest his machine. Who has not felt the same aspirations as regards the world of his own mind? Having to wield some of its elements when I was impelled to write this poem on the 'Immortality of the Soul,' I took hold of the notion of pre-existence as having sufficient foundation in humanity for authorising me to make for my purpose the best use of it I could as a Poet." [I.F.]

Ode
Intimations of Immortality from Recollections of Early Childhood[1]

The Child is Father of the Man;
And I could wish my days to be
Bound each to each by natural piety.

1

There was a time when meadow, grove, and stream,
The earth, and every common sight,
  To me did seem
  Apparelled in celestial light,
5 The glory and the freshness of a dream.
It is not now as it hath been of yore;—
  Turn wheresoe'er I may,
   By night or day,
The things which I have seen I now can see no more.

2

10 The Rainbow comes and goes,
  And lovely is the Rose,
  The Moon doth with delight
Look round her when the heavens are bare,
  Waters on a starry night
15 Are beautiful and fair;
  The sunshine is a glorious birth;
  But yet I know, where'er I go,
That there hath past away a glory from the earth.

3

Now, while the birds thus sing a joyous song,
20 And while the young lambs bound
  As to the tabor's° sound,   *small drum*
To me alone there came a thought of grief:
A timely utterance gave that thought relief,
  And I again am strong:

---

1. The ode published in 1807 was titled simply *Ode*, with an epigraph from Virgil's *Fourth (Messianic) Eclogue: Paulò majora canamus* (Let us sing of somewhat higher things). The long title and epigraph from *My heart leaps up* were added in 1815, and the Latin motto was dropped.

25   The cataracts blow their trumpets from the steep;
      No more shall grief of mine the season wrong;
      I hear the Echoes through the mountains throng,
      The Winds come to me from the fields of sleep,
          And all the earth is gay;
30   Land and sea
          Give themselves up to jollity,
            And with the heart of May
          Doth every Beast keep holiday;—
            Thou Child of Joy,
35   Shout round me, let me hear thy shouts, thou happy Shepherd-boy!

                              4

      Ye blessèd Creatures, I have heard the call
          Ye to each other make; I see
      The heavens laugh with you in your jubilee;
          My heart is at your festival,
40   My head hath its coronal,°   *flower wreath*
      The fulness of your bliss, I feel—I feel it all.
          Oh evil day! if I were sullen
          While Earth herself is adorning,
            This sweet May-morning,
45   And the Children are culling
            On every side,
      In a thousand valleys far and wide,
      Fresh flowers; while the sun shines warm,
      And the Babe leaps up on his Mother's arm:—
50   I hear, I hear, with joy I hear!
          —But there's a Tree, of many, one,
      A single Field which I have looked upon,
      Both of them speak of something that is gone:
          The Pansy[2] at my feet
55   Doth the same tale repeat:
      Whither is fled the visionary gleam?
      Where is it now, the glory and the dream?[3]

                              5

      Our birth is but a sleep and a forgetting:
      The Soul that rises with us, our life's Star,°   *the sun*
60   Hath had elsewhere its setting,
            And cometh from afar:
          Not in entire forgetfulness,
          And not in utter nakedness,
      But trailing clouds of glory do we come[4]
65   From God, who is our home:

---

2. From the French *pensée*, "thought," this flower is its emblem.
3. The "Ubi sunt" trope of elegiac literary tradition. In 1802, Wordsworth stopped writing the ode at this point

and did not resume for two years.
4. Revising a famous line in Thomas Gray's *Elegy Written in a Country Churchyard* (1751): "The paths of glory lead but to the grave."

Heaven lies about us in our infancy!
Shades of the prison-house begin to close
    Upon the growing Boy,
But He beholds the light, and whence it flows,
70   He sees it in his joy;
The Youth, who daily farther from the east
    Must travel, still is Nature's Priest,
    And by the vision splendid
    Is on his way attended;
75 At length the Man perceives it die away,
And fade into the light of common day.

6

Earth fills her lap with pleasures of her own;
Yearnings she hath in her own natural kind,
And, even with something of a Mother's mind,
80   And no unworthy aim,
    The homely° Nurse doth all she can   *simple*
To make her Foster-child, her Inmate° Man,   *resident*
    Forget the glories he hath known,
And that imperial palace whence he came.

7

85 Behold the Child among his new-born blisses,
A six years' Darling of a pigmy size!
See, where 'mid work of his own hand he lies,
Fretted by sallies of his mother's kisses,
With light upon him from his father's eyes!
90 See, at his feet, some little plan or chart,
Some fragment from his dream of human life,
Shaped by himself with newly-learned art;
    A wedding or a festival,
    A mourning or a funeral;
95   And this hath now his heart,
    And unto this he frames his song:
      Then will he fit his tongue
To dialogues of business, love, or strife;
    But it will not be long
100   Ere this be thrown aside,
    And with new joy and pride
The little Actor cons another part;
Filling from time to time his "humorous stage"[5]
With all the Persons, down to palsied Age,
105 That Life brings with her in her equipage;
    As if his whole vocation
    Were endless imitation.

---

5. A phrase from the dedicatory sonnet for Samuel Daniel's *Musophilus* (1599), referring to the different character types of Renaissance drama, defined by their "humors" (natural temperaments).

8

Thou, whose exterior semblance doth belie
   Thy Soul's immensity;
110 Thou best Philosopher, who yet dost keep[6]
Thy heritage, thou Eye among the blind,
That, deaf and silent, read'st the eternal deep,
Haunted for ever by the eternal mind,—
   Mighty Prophet! Seer blest!
115   On whom those truths do rest,
Which we are toiling all our lives to find,
In darkness lost, the darkness of the grave;
Thou, over whom thy Immortality
Broods like the Day, a Master o'er a Slave,
120 A Presence which is not to be put by;
Thou little Child, yet glorious in the might
Of heaven-born freedom on thy being's height,
Why with such earnest pains dost thou provoke
The years to bring the inevitable yoke,
125 Thus blindly with thy blessedness at strife?
Full soon thy Soul shall have her earthly freight,
And custom lie upon thee with a weight,
Heavy as frost, and deep almost as life!

9

   O joy! that in our embers
130   Is something that doth live,
   That nature yet remembers
   What was so fugitive!
The thought of our past years in me doth breed
Perpetual benediction: not indeed
135 For that which is most worthy to be blest;
Delight and liberty, the simple creed
Of Childhood, whether busy or at rest,
With new-fledged hope still fluttering in his breast:—
   Not for these I raise
140   The song of thanks and praise;
   But for those obstinate questionings
   Of sense and outward things,
   Fallings from us, vanishings;
   Blank misgivings of a Creature
145 Moving about in worlds not realised,°   *seeming unreal*
High instincts before which our mortal Nature
Did tremble like a guilty Thing surprised:[7]
   But for those first affections,
   Those shadowy recollections,
150   Which, be they what they may,

6. For Coleridge's comment on this mythology, see page 696.
7. At dawn, the ghost of Hamlet's father "started, like a guilty thing / Upon a fearful summons" and vanished (*Hamlet* 1.1.148-49).

Are yet the fountain light of all our day,
Are yet a master light of all our seeing;
    Uphold us, cherish, and have power to make
Our noisy years seem moments in the being
155 Of the eternal Silence: truths that wake,
        To perish never;
Which neither listlessness, nor mad endeavour,
        Nor Man nor Boy,
Nor all that is at enmity with joy,
160 Can utterly abolish or destroy!
        Hence in a season of calm weather
        Though inland far we be,
Our Souls have sight of that immortal sea
        Which brought us hither,
165   Can in a moment travel thither,
And see the Children sport upon the shore,
And hear the mighty waters rolling evermore.

                    10
Then sing, ye Birds, sing, sing a joyous song!
    And let the young Lambs bound
170   As to the tabor's sound!
We in thought will join your throng,
    Ye that pipe and ye that play,
    Ye that through your hearts to-day
    Feel the gladness of the May!
175 What though the radiance which was once so bright
Be now for ever taken from my sight,
    Though nothing can bring back the hour
Of splendour in the grass, of glory in the flower;
    We will grieve not, rather find
180   Strength in what remains behind;
    In the primal sympathy
    Which having been must ever be;
    In the soothing thoughts that spring
    Out of human suffering;
185   In the faith that looks through death,
In years that bring the philosophic mind.

                    11
And O, ye Fountains, Meadows, Hills, and Groves,
Forebode not any severing of our loves!
Yet in my heart of hearts I feel your might;
190 I only have relinquished one delight
To live beneath your more habitual sway.
I love the Brooks which down their channels fret,
Even more than when I tripped lightly as they;
The innocent brightness of a new-born Day
195   Is lovely yet;

The Clouds that gather round the setting sun
Do take a sober colouring from an eye
That hath kept watch o'er man's mortality;
Another race hath been, and other palms° are won.   *prizes*
200   Thanks to the human heart by which we live,
Thanks to its tenderness, its joys, and fears,
To me the meanest° flower that blows can give   *humblest*
Thoughts that do often lie too deep for tears.

1802–1804/1815   1807/1815

The Solitary Reaper[1]

Behold her, single in the field,
Yon solitary Highland Lass!
Reaping and singing by herself;
Stop here, or gently pass!
5   Alone she cuts, and binds the grain,
And sings a melancholy strain;
O listen! for the Vale profound
Is overflowing with the sound.

No Nightingale did ever chaunt
10   More welcome notes to weary bands
Of Travellers in some shady haunt,
Among Arabian Sands:
No sweeter voice was ever heard[2]
In spring-time from the Cuckoo-bird,
15   Breaking the silence of the seas
Among the farthest Hebrides.°   *Scottish islands*

Will no one tell me what she sings?—
Perhaps the plaintive numbers flow
For old, unhappy, far-off things,
20   And battles long ago:
Or is it some more humble lay,
Familiar matter of today?
Some natural sorrow, loss, or pain,
That has been, and may be again!

25   Whate'er the theme, the Maiden sang
As if her song could have no ending;
I saw her singing at her work,
And o'er the sickle bending;
I listen'd till I had my fill.[3]
30   And, as I mounted up the hill,

---

1. Suggested by Wordsworth's reading in manuscript "a beautiful sentence" in Thomas Wilkinson's *Tours to the British Mountains* (1824): "Passed a female who was reaping alone: she sung in Erse [Scottish Gaelic] as she bended over her sickle; the sweetest human voice I ever heard: her strains were tenderly melancholy, and felt delicious, long after they were heard no more."
2. 1836] "A voice so thrilling ne'er was heard".
3. 1820] "I listened, motionless and still."

The music in my heart I bore,
Long after it was heard no more.

1805   1807

ELEGIAC STANZAS,
Suggested by a Picture of PEELE CASTLE, in a Storm
painted BY SIR GEORGE BEAUMONT[1]

I was thy Neighbour once, thou rugged Pile!°   *building*
Four summer weeks I dwelt in sight of thee:
I saw thee every day; and all the while
Thy Form was sleeping on a glassy sea.

5   So pure the sky, so quiet was the air!
So like, so very like, was day to day!
Whene'er I looked, thy Image still was there;
It trembled, but it never pass'd away.

How perfect was the calm! it seem'd no sleep;
10   No mood, which season takes away, or brings:
I could have fancied that the mighty Deep°   *Ocean*
Was even the gentlest of all gentle Things.

Ah! THEN, if mine had been the Painter's hand,
To express what then I saw; and add the gleam,
15   The light that never was, on sea or land,
The consecration, and the Poet's dream;[2]

I would have planted thee, thou hoary Pile!
Amid a world how different from this!
Beside a sea that could not cease to smile;
20   On tranquil land, beneath a sky of bliss.

Thou shouldst have seem'd a treasure-house divine
Of peaceful years; a chronicle of heaven;—
Of all the sunbeams that did ever shine
The very sweetest had to thee been given.

25   A Picture had it been of lasting ease,
Elysian[3] quiet, without toil or strife
No motion but the moving tide, a breeze,
Or merely silent Nature's breathing life.

Such, in the fond illusion of my heart,
30   Such Picture would I at that time have made:

1. In 1806 Wordsworth's wealthy friend and patron, Sir
George Beaumont, painted two pictures of the ruined Peele
Castle on the Furness Peninsula in the genre of dark gothic.
Wordsworth had visited the area in 1794. An "elegiac"
stanza is a verse form named for its signature site, Thomas
Gray's famous *Elegy Written in a Country Churchyard*.

2. Compare "Intimations" Ode 56–57. In the Poems of
1807, *Elegiac Stanzas* came just before the "Intimations"
Ode, the work that closed the collection.
3. In classical mythology, Elysium is the abode of the
blessed after death.

And seen the soul of truth in every part;
A faith, a trust, that could not be betray'd.[4]

So once it would have been,—'tis so no more;
I have submitted to a new controul:
35 A power is gone, which nothing can restore;
A deep distress hath humaniz'd my Soul.[5]

Not for a moment could I now behold
A smiling sea and be what I have been:
The feeling of my loss will ne'er be old;
40 This, which I know, I speak with mind serene.

Then, Beaumont, Friend! who would have been the Friend,
If he had lived, of Him whom I deplore,°   lament
This Work of thine I blame not, but commend;
This sea in anger, and that dismal shore.

45 Oh 'tis a passionate Work!—yet wise and well;
Well chosen is the spirit that is here;
That Hulk° which labours in the deadly swell,   ship
This rueful sky, this pageantry of fear!

And this huge Castle, standing here sublime,
50 I love to see the look with which it braves,
Cased in the unfeeling armour of old time,
The light'ning, the fierce wind, and trampling waves.

Farewell, farewell the Heart that lives alone,
Hous'd in a dream, at distance from the Kind!°   humankind, nature
55 Such happiness, wherever it be known,
Is to be pitied; for 'tis surely blind.

But welcome fortitude, and patient cheer,
And frequent sights of what is to be borne!
Such sights, or worse, as are before me here.—
60 Not without hope we suffer and we mourn.

1805–1806   1807

⌘

RESPONSE

Mary Shelley: On Reading Wordsworth's Lines on Peele Castle[1]

It is with me, as erst with you,
    Oh poet, nature's chronicler,
The summer seas have lost their hue
    And storm sits brooding everywhere.

---

4. 1815] A stedfast peace that might not be betrayed.
5. The Wordsworths' brother John drowned in a shipwreck on 5 February 1805.

1. Percy Bysshe Shelley, Mary's husband, drowned in a
storm at sea in July 1822.

⁵ The gentlest rustling of the deep
    Is but the dirge of him I lost,
And when waves raise their furrows steep,
    And bring foam in which is tossed

A voice I hear upon the wind
10   Which bids me haste to join him there,
And woo the tempest's breath unkind
    Which gives to me a kindred bier.

And when all smooth are ocean's plains
    And sails afar are glittering,
15 The fairest skiff his form contains
    To my poor heart's fond picturing.

Then wildly to the beach I rush,
    And fain would seize the frailest boat,
And from dull earth the slight hull push,
20   On dancing waves towards him to float.

"Nor may I e'er again behold
    The sea, and be as I have been;
My bitter grief will ne'er grow old,
    Nor say I this with mind serene."[2]

25 For oft I weep in solitude
    And shed so many bitter tears,
While on past joys I vainly brood
    And shrink in fear from coming years.

8 December 1825

THE EXCURSION   Francis Jeffrey's blast at *The Excursion* in the *Edinburgh Review*, excerpted on page 588, remains one of the most devastating in the history of British literature. Though the poor reception of the poem, published in an expensive quarto, embittered Wordsworth, time brought other assessments. The second, cheaper edition of 1820 fared better, and as successive editions appeared across the poet's lifetime its reputation climbed. Reading *The Excursion* led the Victorian clergyman, Christian Socialist, and novelist Charles Kingsley to declare Wordsworth the "preacher and prophet of God's new philosophy." Although Matthew Arnold declared that to endure, Wordsworth would have to be saved from those who praised him as a systematic philosopher, he predicted that Wordsworth would by 1900 stand first among the national "poetic glories" of the century. Other writers were less pontifical: Lamb called *The Excursion* "a day in heaven," and to poets from Keats and Byron through the Victorians the mythological richness of our excerpt from Book IV, radically different from the plain language of *Lyrical Ballads*, proved seminal.

2. Echoing Wordsworth's *Elegiac Stanzas*, 37–40.

from THE EXCURSION (1814)

from Preface

Several years ago, when the Author retired to his native Mountains, with the hope of being enabled to construct a literary Work that might live, it was a reasonable thing that he should take a review of his own Mind, and examine how far Nature and Education had qualified him for such employment. As subsidiary to this preparation, he undertook to record, in Verse, the origin and progress of his own powers, as far as he was acquainted with them. That Work, addressed to a dear Friend,[1] most distinguished for his knowledge and genius, and to whom the Author's Intellect is deeply indebted, has been long finished; and the result of the investigation which gave rise to it was a determination to compose a philosophical Poem, containing views of Man, Nature, and Society; and to be entitled, The Recluse; as having for its principal subject the sensations and opinions of a Poet living in retirement.—The preparatory Poem is biographical, and conducts the history of the Author's mind to the point when he was emboldened to hope that his faculties were sufficiently matured for entering upon the arduous labour which he had proposed to himself; and the two Works have the same kind of relation to each other, if he may so express himself, as the Ante-chapel has to the body of a gothic Church. Continuing this allusion, he may be permitted to add, that his minor Pieces, which have been long before the Public, when they shall be properly arranged, will be found by the attentive Reader to have such connection with the main Work as may give them claim to be likened to the little Cells, Oratories, and sepulchral Recesses, ordinarily included in those Edifices. * * *

It is not the Author's intention formally to announce a system: it was more animating to him to proceed in a different course; and if he shall succeed in conveying to the mind clear thoughts, lively images, and strong feelings, the Reader will have no difficulty in extracting the system for himself. And in the mean time the following passage, taken from the conclusion of the first Book of the Recluse, may be acceptable as a kind of Prospectus of the design and scope of the whole Poem.[2]

> "On Man, on Nature, and on Human Life
> Musing in Solitude, I oft perceive
> Fair trains of imagery before me rise,
> Accompanied by feelings of delight
> 5   Pure, or with no unpleasing sadness mixed;
> And I am conscious of affecting thoughts
> And dear remembrances, whose presence soothes
> Or elevates the Mind, intent to weigh
> The good and evil of our mortal state.[3]
> 10   —To these emotions, whencesoe'er they come,
> Whether from breath of outward circumstance,

---

1. Wordsworth referred to The Prelude as the "Poem Addressed to Coleridge."
2. This excerpt from Home at Grasmere, the only completed section of Part One of The Recluse, is self-consciously infused with the rhythms, style, and language of Milton's Paradise Lost.
3. Recalling Milton's intent to "assert Eternal Providence, / And justify the ways of God to men" (Paradise Lost 1.25–26).

Or from the Soul—an impulse to herself,
I would give utterance in numerous Verse.[4]
—Of Truth, of Grandeur, Beauty, Love, and Hope—
15 And melancholy Fear subdued by Faith;
Of blessed consolations in distress;
Of moral strength, and intellectual power;
Of joy in widest commonalty spread;
Of the individual Mind that keeps her own
20 Inviolate retirement, subject there
To Conscience only, and the law supreme
Of that Intelligence which governs all;
I sing:—"fit audience let me find though few!"[5]

So prayed, more gaining than he asked, the Bard,
25 Holiest of Men.—Urania, I shall need
Thy guidance, or a greater Muse, if such
Descend to earth or dwell in highest heaven!
For I must tread on shadowy ground, must sink
Deep—and, aloft ascending, breathe in worlds
30 To which the heaven of heavens is but a veil.[6]
All strength—all terror, single or in bands,
That ever was put forth in personal form;
Jehovah°—with his thunder, and the choir   God
Of shouting Angels, and the empyreal thrones,°   a rank of angels
35 I pass them, unalarmed.[7] Not Chaos, not
The darkest pit of lowest Erebus,[8]
Nor aught of blinder vacancy—scooped out
By help of dreams, can breed such fear and awe
As fall upon us often when we look
40 Into our Minds, into the Mind of Man,
My haunt, and the main region of my Song.
—Beauty—a living Presence of the earth,
Surpassing the most fair ideal Forms
Which craft of delicate Spirits hath composed
45 From earth's materials—waits upon my steps;
Pitches her tents before me as I move,
An hourly neighbour. Paradise, and groves
Elysian, Fortunate Fields—like those of old
Sought in the Atlantic Main,[1] why should they be
50 A history only of departed things,
Or a mere fiction of what never was?
For the discerning intellect of Man,
When wedded to this goodly universe

---

4. Metrical blank verse; in *Paradise Lost* 5.150, Adam and Eve praise God in "numerous Verse."
5. "Still govern thou my Song," Milton implores his heavenly muse Urania, "and fit audience find, though few" (*Paradise Lost* 7.30–31).
6. The inner, invisible Heaven of God and his angels in *Paradise Lost*.

7. Blake thought this claim blasphemous; one of Wordsworth's friends thought it revealed him to be a "pagan."
8. In *Paradise Lost*, Satan journeys through Chaos, the unformed universe. Erebus is the classical underworld.
1. The Elysian fields where blessed souls dwelled in classical mythology were sometimes thought to be located on islands in the Atlantic.

In love and holy passion, shall find these
55   A simple produce of the common day.
        —I, long before the blissful hour arrives,
        Would chaunt, in lonely peace, the spousal verse°   *marriage hymn*
        Of this great consummation:—and, by words
        Which speak of nothing more than what we are,
60   Would I arouse the sensual° from their sleep   *sense-bound*
        Of Death,[2] and win the vacant and the vain
        To noble raptures; while my voice proclaims
        How exquisitely the individual Mind
        (And the progressive powers perhaps no less
65   Of the whole species) to the external World
        Is fitted:—and how exquisitely, too,
        Theme this but little heard of among Men,
        The external World is fitted to the Mind;
        And the creation (by no lower name
70   Can it be called) which they with blended might
        Accomplish:—this is our high argument.[3]
        —Such grateful haunts foregoing, if I oft
        Must turn elsewhere—to travel near the tribes
        And fellowships of men, and see ill sights
75   Of madding passions mutually inflamed;
        Must hear Humanity in fields and groves
        Pipe solitary anguish; or must hang
        Brooding above the fierce confederate storm
        Of sorrow, barricadoed evermore
80   Within the walls of Cities; may these sounds
        Have their authentic comment,—that, even these
        Hearing, I be not downcast or forlorn!
        —Come thou prophetic Spirit, that inspir'st
        The human Soul of universal earth,
85   Dreaming on things to come;[4] and dost possess
        A metropolitan Temple in the hearts
        Of mighty Poets; upon me bestow
        A gift of genuine insight; that my Song
        With star-like virtue in its place may shine;
90   Shedding benignant influence,—and secure,
        Itself, from all malevolent effect
        Of those mutations that extend their sway°   *influence*
        Throughout the nether sphere![5] —And if with this
        I mix more lowly matter; with the thing
95   Contemplated, describe the Mind and Man

---

2. In Psalm 13, the psalmist David asks for divine guidance to keep him from "the sleep of death."
3. Milton speaks of "the highth of [his] great Argument" (*Paradise Lost* 1.24). The "argument" is the poem's subject or theme.
4. In a note, Wordsworth cites Shakespeare's Sonnet 107: "the prophetic soul / Of the wide world dreaming on things to come."
5. According to Ptolemy, the concentric spheres of the universe were fixed, except for "the nether sphere" below the moon, the place of Earth.

Contemplating; and who, and what he was,
The transitory Being that beheld
This Vision,—when and where, and how he lived;—
Be not this labour useless. If such theme
100 May sort with highest objects, then, dread Power,
Whose gracious favour is the primal source
Of all illumination, may my life
Express the image of a better time,
More wise desires, and simpler manners;—nurse
105 My Heart in genuine freedom:—all pure thoughts
Be with me;—so shall thy unfailing love
Guide, and support, and cheer me to the end!

Book First. The Wanderer.

'TWAS summer, and the sun had mounted high:
Southward the landscape indistinctly glared
Through a pale steam; but all the northern downs,
In clearest air ascending, shew'd far off
5 A surface dappled o'er with shadows, flung
From many a brooding cloud; far as the sight
Could reach, these many shadows lay in spots
Determined and unmoved, with steady beams
Of bright and pleasant sunshine interposed.
10 Pleasant to him who on the soft cool moss
Extends his careless limbs along the front
Of some huge cave, whose rocky ceiling casts
A twilight of its own, an ample shade,
Where the wren warbles; while the dreaming Man,
15 Half conscious of the soothing melody,
With side-long eye looks out upon the scene,
By that impending covert made more soft,
More low and distant! Other lot was mine;
Yet with good hope that soon I should obtain
20 As grateful resting-place, and livelier joy.
Across a bare wide Common I was toiling
With languid feet, which by the slippery ground
Were baffled; nor could my weak arm disperse
The host of insects gathering round my face,
25 And ever with me as I paced along.

Upon that open level stood a Grove,
The wished-for port to which my steps were bound.
Thither I came, and there—amid the gloom
Spread by a brotherhood of lofty elms—
30 Appeared a roofless Hut; four naked walls
That stared upon each other! I looked round,

And to my wish and to my hope espied
Him whom I sought; a Man of reverend age,
But stout and hale, for travel unimpaired.
35 There was he seen upon the Cottage bench,
Recumbent in the shade, as if asleep;
An iron-pointed staff lay at his side.

Him had I marked the day before—alone
And in the middle of the public way
40 Stationed, as if to rest himself, with face
Turned tow'rds the sun then setting, while that staff
Afforded to his Figure, as he stood,
Detained for contemplation or repose,
Graceful support; the countenance of the Man
45 Was hidden from my view, and he himself
Unrecognized; but, stricken by the sight,
With slacken'd footsteps I advanced, and soon
A glad congratulation we exchanged
At such unthought-of meeting.—For the night
50 We parted, nothing willingly; and now
He by appointment waited for me here,
Beneath the shelter of these clustering elms.

We were tried Friends: I from my Childhood up
Had known him.—In a little Town obscure,
55 A market-village, seated in a tract
Of mountains, where my school-day time was pass'd,
One room he owned, the fifth part of a house
A place to which he drew, from time to time,
And found a kind of home or harbour there.

60 He loved me; from a swarm of rosy Boys
Singled out me, as he in sport would say,
For my grave looks—too thoughtful for my years.
As I grew up it was my best delight
To be his chosen Comrade. Many a time,
65 On holidays, we wandered through the woods,
A pair of random travellers; we sate—
We walked; he pleas'd me with his sweet discourse
Of things which he had seen; and often touch'd
Abstrusest matter, reasonings of the mind
70 Turned inward; or at my request he sang
Old songs—the product of his native hills;
A skilful distribution of sweet sounds,
Feeding the soul, and eagerly imbibed
As cool refreshing Water, by the care
75 Of the industrious husbandman, diffused
Through a parched meadow-ground, in time of drought.
Still deeper welcome found his pure discourse;

How precious when in riper days I learned
To weigh with care his words, and to rejoice
80   In the plain presence of his dignity!

Oh! many are the Poets that are sown
By Nature; Men endowed with highest gifts,
The vision and the faculty divine;
Yet wanting the accomplishment of Verse,
85   (Which, in the docile season of their youth
It was denied them to acquire, through lack
Of culture and the inspiring aid of books,
Or haply by a temper too severe,
Or a nice backwardness afraid of shame),
90   Nor having e'er, as life advanced, been led
By circumstance to take unto the height
The measure of themselves, these favored Beings,
All but a scattered few, live out their time,
Husbanding that which they possess within,
95   And go to the grave, unthought of. Strongest minds
Are often those of whom the noisy world
Hears least; else surely this Man had not left
His graces unrevealed and unproclaimed.
But, as the mind was filled with inward light,
100   So not without distinction had he lived,
Beloved and honoured—far as he was known.
And some small portion of his eloquent speech,
And something that may serve to set in view
The feeling pleasures of his loneliness,
105   The doings, observations, which his mind
Had dealt with—I will here record in verse;
Which, if with truth it correspond, and sink
Or rise, as venerable Nature leads,
The high and tender Muses shall accept
110   With gracious smile, deliberately pleased,
And listening Time reward with sacred praise.

Among the hills of Athol° he was born;   *in Perthshire*
There, on a small hereditary Farm,
An unproductive slip of rugged ground,
115   His Father dwelt; and died in poverty;
While He, whose lowly fortune I retrace,
The youngest of three sons, was yet a babe,
A little One—unconscious of their loss.
But ere he had outgrown his infant days
120   His widowed Mother, for a second Mate,
Espoused the Teacher of the Village School;
Who on her offspring zealously bestowed
Needful instruction; not alone in arts
Which to his humble duties appertained,

125 But in the lore of right and wrong, the rule
Of human kindness, in the peaceful ways
Of honesty, and holiness severe.
A virtuous Household though exceeding poor!
Pure Livers were they all, austere and grave,
130 And fearing God; the very Children taught
Stern self-respect, a reverence for God's word,
And an habitual piety, maintained
With strictness scarcely known on English ground.

From his sixth year, the Boy of whom I speak,
135 In summer, tended cattle on the hills;
But, through the inclement and the perilous days
Of long-continuing winter, he repaired
To his Step-father's School, that stood alone,
Sole Building on a mountain's dreary edge,
140 Far from the sight of City spire, or sound
Of Minster° clock! From that bleak Tenement   *cathedral*
He, many an evening, to his distant home
In solitude returning, saw the Hills
Grow larger in the darkness, all alone
145 Beheld the stars come out above his head,
And travelled through the wood, with no one near
To whom he might confess the things he saw.
So the foundations of his mind were laid.
In such communion, not from terror free,
150 While yet a Child, and long before his time,
He had perceived the presence and the power
Of greatness; and deep feelings had impress'd
Great objects on his mind, with portraiture
And colour so distinct, that on his mind
155 They lay like substances, and almost seemed
To haunt the bodily sense. He had received
(Vigorous in native genius as he was)
A precious gift; for, as he grew in years,
With these impressions would he still compare
160 All his remembrances, thoughts, shapes, and forms;
And, being still unsatisfied with aught
Of dimmer character, he thence attained
An active power to fasten images
Upon his brain; and on their pictured lines
165 Intensely brooded, even till they acquired
The liveliness of dreams. Nor did he fail,
While yet a Child, with a Child's eagerness
Incessantly to turn his ear and eye
On all things which the moving seasons brought
170 To feed such appetite: nor this alone

Appeased his yearning:—in the after day
Of Boyhood, many an hour in caves forlorn,

And 'mid the hollow depths of naked crags
He sate, and even in their fix'd lineaments,
175 Or from the power of a peculiar eye,
Or by creative feeling overborne,
Or by predominance of thought oppress'd,
Even in their fix'd and steady lineaments
He traced an ebbing and a flowing mind,
180 Expression ever varying!
              Thus informed,
He had small need of books; for many a Tale
Traditionary, round the mountains hung,
And many a Legend, peopling the dark woods,
Nourished Imagination in her growth,
185 And gave the Mind that apprehensive power
By which she is made quick to recognize
The moral properties and scope of things.
But eagerly he read, and read again,
Whate'er the Minister's old Shelf supplied;
190 The life and death of martyrs, who sustained,
With will inflexible, those fearful pangs
Triumphantly displayed in records left
Of Persecution, and the Covenant—Times
Whose echo rings through Scotland to this hour!
195 And there, by lucky hap, had been preserved
A straggling volume, torn and incomplete,
That left half-told the preternatural tale,
Romance of Giants, chronicle of Fiends,
Profuse in garniture of wooden cuts
200 Strange and uncouth; dire faces, figures dire,
Sharp-knee'd, sharp-elbowed, and lean-ankled too,
With long and ghostly shanks—forms which once seen
Could never be forgotten!
             In his heart,
Where Fear sate thus, a cherished visitant,
205 Was wanting yet the pure delight of love
By sound diffused, or by the breathing air,
Or by the silent looks of happy things,
Or flowing from the universal face
Of earth and sky. But he had felt the power
210 Of Nature, and already was prepared,
By his intense conceptions, to receive
Deeply the lesson deep of love which he,
Whom Nature, by whatever means, has taught
To feel intensely, cannot but receive.

215   From early childhood, even, as hath been said,
From his sixth year, he had been sent abroad
In summer to tend herds: such was his task
Thenceforward 'till the later day of youth.
O then what soul was his, when, on the tops

220   Of the high mountains, he beheld the sun
Rise up, and bathe the world in light! He looked—
Ocean and earth, the solid frame of earth
And ocean's liquid mass, beneath him lay
In gladness and deep joy. The clouds were touch'd,
225   And in their silent faces did he read
Unutterable love. Sound needed none,
Nor any voice of joy; his spirit drank
The spectacle; sensation, soul, and form
All melted into him; they swallowed up
230   His animal being; in them did he live,
And by them did he live; they were his life.
In such access of mind, in such high hour
Of visitation from the living God,
Thought was not; in enjoyment it expired.
235   No thanks he breathed, he proffered no request;
Rapt into still communion that transcends
The imperfect offices of prayer and praise,
His mind was a thanksgiving to the power
That made him; it was blessedness and love!

240   A Herdsman on the lonely mountain tops,
Such intercourse was his, and in this sort
Was his existence oftentimes *possessed*.
O then how beautiful, how bright, appeared
The written Promise! He had early learned
245   To reverence the Volume which displays
The mystery, the life which cannot die;
But in the mountains did he *feel* his faith;
There did he see the writing;—all things there
Breathed immortality, revolving life
250   And greatness still revolving; infinite:
There littleness was not; the least of things
Seemed infinite; and there his spirit shaped
Her prospects, nor did he believe,—he *saw*.
What wonder if his being thus became
255   Sublime and comprehensive! Low desires,
Low thoughts had there no place; yet was his heart
Lowly; for he was meek in gratitude,
Oft as he called those extacies to mind,
And whence they flowed; and from them he acquired
260   Wisdom, which works through patience; thence he learned
In many a calmer hour of sober thought
To look on Nature with a humble heart,
Self-questioned where it did not understand,
And with a superstitious eye of love.

265   So passed the time; yet to a neighbouring town
He duly went with what small overplus

His earnings might supply, and brought away
The Book that most had tempted his desires
While at the Stall he read. Among the hills
270 He gazed upon that mighty Orb of Song,
The divine Milton. Lore of different kind,
The annual savings of a toilsome life,
His Step-father supplied; books that explain
The purer elements of truth involved
275 In lines and numbers, and, by charm severe,
(Especially perceived where nature droops
And feeling is suppressed,) preserve the mind
Busy in solitude and poverty.
These occupations oftentimes deceived
280 The listless hours, while in the hollow vale,
Hollow and green, he lay on the green turf
In pensive idleness. What could he do
With blind endeavours, in that lonesome life,
Thus thirsting daily? Yet still uppermost,
285 Nature was at his heart as if he felt,
Though yet he knew not how, a wasting power
In all things that from her sweet influence
Might tend to wean him. Therefore with her hues,
Her forms, and with the spirit of her forms,
290 He clothed the nakedness of austere truth.
While yet he lingered in the rudiments
Of science, and among her simplest laws,
His triangles—they were the stars of heaven,
The silent stars! Oft did he take delight
295 To measure th' altitude of some tall crag
Which is the eagle's birth-place, or some peak
Familiar with forgotten years, that shews
Inscribed, as with the silence of the thought,
Upon it's bleak and visionary sides,
300 The history of many a winter storm,
Or obscure records of the path of fire.

And thus, before his eighteenth year was told,
Accumulated feelings pressed his heart
With still increasing weight; he was o'er-powered
305 By Nature; by the turbulence subdued
Of his own mind; by mystery and hope,
And the first virgin passion of a soul
Communing with the glorious Universe.
Full often wished he that the winds might rage
310 When they were silent: far more fondly now
Than in his earlier season did he love
Tempestuous nights—the conflict and the sounds
That live in darkness:—from his intellect
And from the stillness of abstracted thought

315 He asked repose; and I have heard him say
That often, failing at this time to gain
The peace required, he scanned the laws of light
Amid the roar of torrents, where they send
From hollow clefts up to the clearer air
320 A cloud of mist, which in the sunshine frames
A lasting tablet—for the observer's eye
Varying its rainbow hues. But vainly thus,
And vainly by all other means, he strove
To mitigate the fever of his heart.

325 In dreams, in study, and in ardent thought,
Thus, even from Childhood upward, was he reared;
For intellectual progress wanting much,
Doubtless, of needful help—yet gaining more;
And every moral feeling of his soul
330 Strengthened and braced, by breathing in content
The keen, the wholesome air of poverty,
And drinking from the well of homely life.
—But, from past liberty, and tried restraints,
He now was summoned to select the course
335 Of humble industry that promised best
To yield him no unworthy maintenance.
The Mother strove to make her Son perceive
With what advantage he might teach a School
In the adjoining Village; but the Youth,
340 Who of this service made a short essay,
Found that the wanderings of his thought were then
A misery to him: that he must resign
A task he was unable to perform.

That stern yet kindly spirit, Who constrains
345 The Savoyard to quit his naked rocks,
The free-born Swiss to leave his narrow vales,
(Spirit attached to regions mountainous
Like their own stedfast clouds)—did now impel
His restless Mind to look abroad with hope.
350 —An irksome drudgery seems it to plod on,
Through dusty ways, in storm, from door to door
A vagrant Merchant bent beneath his load!
Yet do such Travellers find their own delight;
And their hard service, deemed debasing now,
355 Gained merited respect in simpler times;
When Squire, and Priest, and they who round them dwelt
In rustic sequestration, all, dependant
Upon the PEDLAR's toil—supplied their wants,
Or pleased their fancies, with the wares he brought.
360 Not ignorant was the Youth that still no few
Of his adventurous Countrymen were led

By perseverance in this Track of life
To competence and ease;—for him it bore
Attractions manifold;—and this he chose.
365 He asked his Mother's blessing; and, with tears
Thanking his second father, asked from him
Paternal blessings. The good Pair bestowed
Their farewell benediction, but with hearts
Foreboding evil. From his native hills
370 He wandered far; much did he see of Men,
Their manners, their enjoyments, and pursuits,
Their passions, and their feelings; chiefly those
Essential and eternal in the heart,
Which, mid the simpler forms of rural life,
375 Exist more simple in their elements,
And speak a plainer language. In the woods,
A lone Enthusiast, and among the fields,
Itinerant in this labour, he had passed
The better portion of his time; and there
380 Spontaneously had his affections thriven
Upon the bounties of the year, and felt
The liberty of Nature; there he kept
In solitude and solitary thought
His mind in a just equipoise of love.
385 Serene it was, unclouded by the cares
Of ordinary life; unvexed, unwarped
By partial bondage. In his steady course,
No piteous revolutions had he felt,
No wild varieties of joy and grief.
390 Unoccupied by sorrow of it's own,
His heart lay open; and, by Nature tuned
And constant disposition of his thoughts
To sympathy with Man, he was alive
To all that was enjoyed where'er he went,
395 And all that was endured; for, in himself
Happy, and quiet in his cheerfulness,
He had no painful pressure from without
That made him turn aside from wretchedness
With coward fears. He could *afford* to suffer
400 With those whom he saw suffer. Hence it came
That in our best experience he was rich,
And in the wisdom of our daily life.
For hence, minutely, in his various rounds,
He had observed the progress and decay
405 Of many minds, of minds and bodies too;
The History of many Families;
How they had prospered; how they were o'erthrown
By passion or mischance, or such misrule
Among the unthinking masters of the earth
410 As makes the nations groan.—This active course,

Chosen in youth, through manhood he pursued,
Till due provision for his modest wants
Had been obtained;—and, thereupon, resolved
To pass the remnant of his days—untasked
415   With needless services,—from hardship free.
His Calling laid aside, he lived at ease:
But still he loved to pace the public roads
And the wild paths; and, when the summer's warmth
Invited him, would often leave his home
420   And journey far, revisiting those scenes
Which to his memory were most endeared.
—Vigorous in health, of hopeful spirits, untouched
By worldly-mindedness or anxious care;
Observant, studious, thoughtful, and refreshed
425   By knowledge gathered up from day to day;—
Thus had he lived a long and innocent life.

　　　The Scottish Church, both on himself and those
With whom from childhood he grew up, had held
The strong hand of her purity; and still
430   Had watched him with an unrelenting eye.
This he remembered in his riper age
With gratitude, and reverential thoughts.
But by the native vigour of his mind,
By his habitual wanderings out of doors,
435   By loneliness, and goodness, and kind works,
Whate'er, in docile childhood or in youth,
He had imbibed of fear or darker thought
Was melted all away: so true was this,
That sometimes his religion seemed to me
440   Self-taught, as of a dreamer in the woods;
Who to the model of his own pure heart
Framed his belief, as grace divine inspired,
And human reason dictated with awe.
—And surely never did there live on earth
445   A Man of kindlier nature. The rough sports
And teazing ways of Children vexed not him,
Nor could he bid them from his presence, tired
With questions and importunate demands:
Indulgent listener was he to the tongue
450   Of garrulous age; nor did the sick man's tale,
To his fraternal sympathy addressed,
Obtain reluctant hearing.
　　　　　　　　　　Plain his garb;
Such as might suit a rustic sire, prepared
For sabbath duties; yet he was a Man
455   Whom no one could have passed without remark.
Active and nervous was his gait; his limbs
And his whole figure breathed intelligence.

Time had compressed the freshness of his cheek
Into a narrower circle of deep red
460   But had not tamed his eye; that, under brows
Shaggy and grey, had meanings which it brought
From years of youth; which, like a Being made
Of many Beings, he had wondrous skill
To blend with knowledge of the years to come,
465   Human, or such as lie beyond the grave.

——————————————

So was He framed; and such his course of life
Who now, with no Appendage but a Staff,
The prized memorial of relinquish'd toils,
Upon that Cottage bench reposed his limbs,
470   Screened from the sun. Supine the Wanderer lay,
His eyes as if in drowsiness half shut,
The shadows of the breezy elms above
Dappling his face. He had not heard my steps
As I approached; and near him did I stand
475   Unnotic'd in the shade, some minutes' space.
At length I hailed him, seeing that his hat
Was moist with water-drops, as if the brim
Had newly scooped a running stream. He rose,
And ere the pleasant greeting that ensued
480   Was ended, "'Tis," said I, "a burning day:
My lips are parched with thirst, but you, I guess,
Have somewhere found relief." He, at the word,
Pointing towards a sweet-briar, bade me climb
The fence hard by, where that aspiring shrub
485   Looked out upon the road. It was a plot
Of garden-ground run wild, it's matted weeds
Marked with the steps of those, whom, as they pass'd,
The gooseberry trees that shot in long lank slips,
Or currants hanging from their leafless stems
490   In scanty strings, had tempted to o'erleap
The broken wall. I looked around, and there,
Where two tall hedge-rows of thick alder boughs
Joined in a cold damp nook, espied a Well
Shrouded with willow-flowers and plumy fern.
495   My thirst I slaked, and, from the chearless spot
Withdrawing, straightway to the shade returned
Where sate the old Man on the Cottage bench;
And, while, beside him, with uncovered head,
I yet was standing, freely to respire,
500   And cool my temples in the fanning air,
Thus did he speak. "I see around me here
Things which you cannot see: we die, my Friend,
Nor we alone, but that which each man loved
And prized in his peculiar nook of earth
505   Dies with him, or is changed; and very soon

Even of the good is no memorial left.
—The Poets, in their elegies and songs
Lamenting the departed, call the groves,
They call upon the hills and streams, to mourn,
510   And senseless rocks; nor idly; for they speak,
In these their invocations, with a voice
Obedient to the strong creative power
Of human passion. Sympathies there are
More tranquil, yet perhaps of kindred birth,
515   That steal upon the meditative mind,
And grow with thought. Beside yon Spring I stood,
And eyed its waters till we seemed to feel
One sadness, they and I. For them a bond
Of brotherhood is broken: time has been
520   When, every day, the touch of human hand
Dislodged the natural sleep that binds them up
In mortal stillness; and they minister'd
To human comfort. As I stooped to drink,
Upon the slimy foot-stone I espied
525   The useless fragment of a wooden bowl,
Green with the moss of years, a pensive sight
That moved my heart!—recalling former days
When I could never pass that road but She
Who lived within these walls, at my approach,
530   A daughter's welcome gave me; and I loved her
As my own child. O Sir! the good die first,
And they whose hearts are dry as summer dust
Burn to the socket. Many a Passenger
Hath blessed poor Margaret for her gentle looks,
535   When she upheld the cool refreshment drawn
From that forsaken Spring; and no one came
But he was welcome; no one went away
But that it seemed she loved him. She is dead,
The light extinguished of her lonely Hut,
540   The Hut itself abandoned to decay,
And She forgotten in the quiet grave!

    "I speak," continued he, "of One whose stock
Of virtues bloom'd beneath this lowly roof.
She was a Woman of a steady mind,
545   Tender and deep in her excess of love,
Not speaking much, pleased rather with the joy
Of her own thoughts: by some especial care
Her temper had been framed, as if to make
A Being—who by adding love to peace
550   Might live on earth a life of happiness.
Her wedded Partner lacked not on his side
The humble worth that satisfied her heart:
Frugal, affectionate, sober, and withal

Keenly industrious. She with pride would tell
555 That he was often seated at his loom,
In summer, ere the Mower was abroad
Among the dewy grass,—in early spring,
Ere the last Star had vanished.—They who passed
At evening, from behind the garden fence
560 Might hear his busy spade, which he would ply,
After his daily work, until the light
Had failed, and every leaf and flower were lost
In the dark hedges. So their days were spent
In peace and comfort; and a pretty Boy
565 Was their best hope,—next to the God in heaven.

Not twenty years ago, but you I think
Can scarcely bear it now in mind, there came
Two blighting seasons when the fields were left
With half a harvest. It pleased heaven to add
570 A worse affliction in the plague of war:
This happy Land was stricken to the heart!
A Wanderer then among the Cottages
I, with my freight of winter raiment, saw
The hardships of that season; many rich
575 Sank down, as in a dream, among the poor;
And of the poor did many cease to be
And their place knew them not. Meanwhile abridg'd
Of daily comforts, gladly reconciled
To numerous self-denials, Margaret
580 Went struggling on through those calamitous years
With chearful hope: but ere the second autumn,
Her life's true Help-mate on a sick-bed lay,
Smitten with perilous fever. In disease
He lingered long; and when his strength return'd,
585 He found the little he had stored, to meet
The hour of accident or crippling age,
Was all consumed. Two children had they now,
One newly born. As I have said, it was
A time of trouble; shoals of Artisans
590 Were from their daily labour turn'd adrift
To seek their bread from public charity,
They, and their wives and children—happier far
Could they have lived as do the little birds
That peck along the hedges, or the Kite
That makes his dwelling on the mountain Rocks!

595 A sad reverse it was for Him who long
Had filled with plenty, and possess'd in peace,
This lonely Cottage. At the door he stood,
And whistled many a snatch of merry tunes
600 That had no mirth in them; or with his knife

Carved uncouth figures on the heads of sticks—
Then, not less idly, sought, through every nook
In house or garden, any casual work
Of use or ornament; and with a strange,
605 Amusing, yet uneasy, novelty,
He blended, where he might, the various tasks
Of summer, autumn, winter, and of spring.
But this endured not; his good humour soon
Became a weight in which no pleasure was:
610 And poverty brought on a petted mood
And a sore temper: day by day he drooped,
And he would leave his work—and to the Town
Without an errand, would direct his steps,
Or wander here and there among the fields.
615 One while he would speak lightly of his Babes,
And with a cruel tongue: at other times
He toss'd them with a false unnatural joy:
And 'twas a rueful thing to see the looks
Of the poor innocent children. "Every smile,"
620 Said Margaret to me, here beneath these trees,
"Made my heart bleed."
                              At this the Wanderer paused;
And, looking up to those enormous elms,
He said, "'Tis now the hour of deepest noon.—
At this still season of repose and peace,
625 This hour, when all things which are not at rest
Are chearful; while this multitude of flies
Is filling all the air with melody;
Why should a tear be in an Old Man's eye?
Why should we thus, with an untoward mind,
630 And in the weakness of humanity,
From natural wisdom turn our hearts away;
To natural comfort shut our eyes and ears,
And, feeding on disquiet, thus disturb
The calm of nature with our restless thoughts?"
                      _____

635 HE spake with somewhat of a solemn tone:
But, when he ended, there was in his face
Such easy chearfulness, a look so mild,
That for a little time it stole away
All recollection, and that simple Tale
640 Passed from my mind like a forgotten sound.
A while on trivial things we held discourse,
To me soon tasteless. In my own despite
I thought of that poor Woman as of one
Whom I had known and loved. He had rehearsed
645 Her homely tale with such familiar power,
With such an active countenance, an eye
So busy, that the things of which he spake

Seemed present; and, attention now relax'd,
There was a heart-felt chillness in my veins.—
650   I rose; and, turning from the breezy shade,
Went forth into the open air, and stood
To drink the comfort of the warmer sun.
Long time I had not staid, ere, looking round
Upon that tranquil Ruin, I return'd,
655   And begged of the Old Man that, for my sake,
He would resume his story.—
                     He replied,
"It were a wantonness, and would demand
Severe reproof, if we were Men whose hearts
Could hold vain dalliance with the misery
660   Even of the dead; contented thence to draw
A momentary pleasure, never marked
By reason, barren of all future good.
But we have known that there is often found
In mournful thoughts, and always might be found,
665   A power to virtue friendly; were't not so,
I am a Dreamer among men, indeed
An idle Dreamer! 'Tis a common Tale,
An ordinary sorrow of Man's life,
A tale of silent suffering, hardly clothed
670   In bodily form.—But, without further bidding

I will proceed.—
               While thus it fared with them,
To whom this Cottage, till those hapless years,
Had been a blessed home, it was my chance
To travel in a Country far remote;
675   And glad I was, when, halting by yon gate
That leads from the green lane, once more I saw
These lofty elm-trees. Long I did not rest:
With many pleasant thoughts I chear'd my way
O'er the flat Common.—Having reached the door
680   I knock'd,–and when I entered with the hope
Of usual greeting, Margaret looked at me
A little while; then turn'd her head away
Speechless,—and, sitting down upon a chair,
Wept bitterly. I wist not what to do,
685   Or how to speak to her. Poor Wretch! at last
She rose from off her seat, and then,—O Sir!
I cannot *tell* how she pronounced my name:—
With fervent love, and with a face of grief
Unutterably helpless, and a look
690   That seemed to cling upon me, she enquired
If I had seen her Husband. As she spake
A strange surprize and fear came to my heart,
Nor had I power to answer ere she told

That he had disappear'd—not two months gone.
695   He left his House: two wretched days had pass'd,
And on the third, as wistfully she rais'd
Her head from off her pillow, to look forth,
Like one in trouble, for returning light,
Within her chamber-casement she espied
700   A folded paper, lying as if placed
To meet her waking eyes. This tremblingly
She open'd—found no writing, but therein
Pieces of money carefully enclosed,
Silver and gold.° "I shuddered at the sight,"   *his recruitment bonus*
705   Said Margaret, "for I knew it was his hand
Which placed it there: and ere that day was ended,
That long and anxious day! I learned from One
Sent hither by my Husband to impart
The heavy news,— that he had joined a Troop
710   Of Soldiers, going to a distant Land.
—He left me thus—he could not gather heart
To take a farewell of me; for he fear'd
That I should follow with my Babes, and sink
Beneath the misery of that wandering Life."

715   This Tale did Margaret tell with many tears:
And when she ended I had little power
To give her comfort, and was glad to take
Such words of hope from her own mouth as served
To chear us both:—but long we had not talked
720   Ere we built up a pile of better thoughts,
And with a brighter eye she look'd around
As if she had been shedding tears of joy.
We parted.—'Twas the time of early spring;
I left her busy with her garden tools;
725   And well remember, o'er that fence she looked,
And, while I paced along the foot-way path,
Called out, and sent a blessing after me,
With tender chearfulness, and with a voice
That seem'd the very sound of happy thoughts.

730   I roved o'er many a hill and many a dale,
With my accustomed load; in heat and cold,
Through many a wood, and many an open ground,
In sunshine and in shade, in wet and fair,
Drooping, or blithe of heart, as might befal;
735   My best companions now the driving winds,
And now the "trotting brooks" and whispering trees,
And now the music of my own sad steps,
With many a short-lived thought that passed between,
And disappeared.—I journey'd back this way
740   Towards the wane of Summer; when the wheat

Was yellow; and the soft and bladed grass
Springing afresh had o'er the hay-field spread
Its tender verdure. At the door arrived,
I found that she was absent. In the shade,
745   Where now we sit, I waited her return.
Her Cottage, then a chearful Object, wore
Its customary look,—only, I thought,
The honeysuckle, crowding round the porch,
Hung down in heavier tufts; and that bright weed,
750   The yellow stone-crop, suffered to take root
Along the window's edge, profusely grew,
Blinding the lower panes. I turned aside,
And strolled into her garden. It appeared
To lag behind the season, and had lost
755   Its pride of neatness. From the border lines
Composed of daisy and resplendent thrift,
Flowers straggling forth on those paths encroached
Which they were used to deck:—Carnations, once
Prized for surpassing beauty, and no less
760   For the peculiar pains they had required,
Declined their languid heads—without support.
The cumbrous bind-weed, with its wreaths and bells,
Had twined about her two small rows of pease,
And dragged them to the earth.—Ere this an hour
765   Was wasted.—Back I turned my restless steps,
And, as I walked before the door, it chanced
A Stranger passed; and, guessing whom I sought,
He said that she was used to ramble far.—
The sun was sinking in the west; and now
770   I sate with sad impatience. From within
Her solitary Infant cried aloud;
Then, like a blast that dies away self-stilled,
The voice was silent. From the bench I rose;
But neither could divert nor soothe my thoughts.
775   The spot, though fair, was very desolate—
The longer I remained more desolate—
And, looking round, I saw the corner stones,
Till then unnotic'd, on either side the door
With dull red stains discolour'd, and stuck o'er
780   With tufts and hairs of wool, as if the Sheep,
That fed upon the Common, thither came
Familiarly, and found a couching-place
Even at her threshold. Deeper shadows fell
From these tall elms;—the Cottage-clock struck eight;—
785   I turned, and saw her distant a few steps.
Her face was pale and thin, her figure too
Was changed. As she unlocked the door, she said,
"It grieves me you have waited here so long,
But, in good truth, I've wandered much of late;

790 And sometimes—to my shame I speak, have need
Of my best prayers to bring me back again."
While on the board she spread our evening meal,
She told me,—interrupting not the work
Which gave employment to her listless hands,
795 That she had parted with her elder Child;
To a kind Master on a distant farm
Now happily apprenticed—"I perceive
You look at me, and you have cause; to-day
I have been travelling far; and many days
800 About the fields I wander, knowing this
Only, that what I seek I cannot find;
And so I waste my time: for I am changed;
And to myself, said she, have done much wrong
And to this helpless Infant. I have slept
805 Weeping, and weeping I have waked; my tears
Have flowed as if my body were not such
As others are; and I could never die.
But I am now in mind and in my heart
More easy; and I hope," said she, "that heaven
810 Will give me patience to endure the things
Which I behold at home." It would have grieved
Your very soul to see her; Sir, I feel
The story linger in my heart; I fear
'Tis long and tedious; but my spirit clings
815 To that poor Woman:—so familiarly
Do I perceive her manner, and her look,
And presence; and so deeply do I feel
Her goodness, that, not seldom, in my walks
A momentary trance comes over me;
820 And to myself I seem to muse on One
    By sorrow laid asleep;—or borne away,
A human being destined to awake
To human life, or something very near
To human life, when he shall come again
825 For whom she suffered. Yes, it would have grieved
Your very soul to see her: evermore
Her eyelids drooped, her eyes were downward cast;
And, when she at her table gave me food,
She did not look at me. Her voice was low,
830 Her body was subdued. In every act
Pertaining to her house-affairs, appeared
The careless stillness of a thinking mind
Self-occupied; to which all outward things
Are like an idle matter. Still she sighed,
835 But yet no motion of the breast was seen,
No heaving of the heart. While by the fire
We sate together, sighs came on my ear,
I knew not how, and hardly whence they came.

Ere my departure to her care I gave,
840   For her Son's use, some tokens of regard,
Which with a look of welcome She received;
And I exhorted her to have her trust
In God's good love, and seek his help by prayer.
I took my staff, and when I kissed her babe,
845   The tears stood in her eyes. I left her then
With the best hope and comfort I could give;
She thanked me for my wish;—but for my hope
Methought she did not thank me.
                          I returned,
And took my rounds along this road again
850   When on its sunny bank the primrose flower
Peeped forth, to give an earnest of the Spring.
I found her sad and drooping: she had learned
No tidings of her Husband; if he lived
She knew not that he lived; if he were dead,
855   She knew not he was dead. She seem'd the same
In person and appearance; but her House
Bespake a sleepy hand of negligence.
The floor was neither dry nor neat, the hearth
Was comfortless, and her small lot of books,
860   Which, in the Cottage window, heretofore
Had been piled up against the corner panes
In seemly order, now, with straggling leaves
Lay scattered here and there, open or shut,
As they had chanced to fall. Her Infant Babe
865   Had from its Mother caught the trick of grief,
And sighed among its playthings. Once again
I turned towards the garden gate, and saw,
More plainly still, that poverty and grief
Were now come nearer to her: weeds defaced
870   The harden'd soil, and knots of wither'd grass;
No ridges there appeared of clear black mold,
No winter greenness; of her herbs and flowers,
It seemed the better part were gnawed away
Or trampled into earth; a chain of straw,
875   Which had been twined about the slender stem
Of a young apple-tree, lay at its root;
The bark was nibbled round by truant Sheep.
—Margaret stood near, her Infant in her arms,
And, noting that my eye was on the tree,
880   She said, "I fear it will be dead and gone
Ere Robert come again." Towards the House
Together we returned; and she enquired
If I had any hope:—but for her babe
And for her little orphan Boy, she said,
885   She had no wish to live, that she must die
Of sorrow. Yet I saw the idle loom

Still in its place; his Sunday garments hung
Upon the self-same nail; his very staff
Stood undisturbed behind the door. And when,
890   In bleak December, I retraced this way,
She told me that her little Babe was dead,
And she was left alone. She now, released
From her maternal cares, had taken up
The employment common through these Wilds, and gain'd,
895   By spinning hemp a pittance for herself;
And for this end had hired a neighbour's Boy
To give her needful help. That very time
Most willingly she put her work aside,
And walked with me along the miry road,
900   Heedless how far; and, in such piteous sort
That any heart had ached to hear her, begged
That, wheresoe'er I went, I still would ask
For him whom she had lost. We parted then—
Our final parting; for from that time forth
905   Did many seasons pass ere I returned
Into this tract again.
                        Nine tedious years;
From their first separation, nine long years,
She lingered in unquiet widowhood;
A Wife and Widow. Needs must it have been
910   A sore heart-wasting! I have heard, my Friend,
That in yon arbour oftentimes she sate
Alone, through half the vacant Sabbath day,
And if a dog passed by she still would quit
The shade, and look abroad. On this old Bench
915   For hours she sate; and evermore her eye
Was busy in the distance, shaping things
That made her heart beat quick. You see that path,
Now faint,—the grass has crept o'er its grey line;
There, to and fro, she paced through many a day
920   Of the warm summer, from a belt of hemp
That girt her waist, spinning the long-drawn thread
With backward steps. Yet ever as there passed
A man whose garments shewed the Soldiers red,
Or crippled Mendicant in Sailor's garb,
925   The little Child who sate to turn the wheel
Ceas'd from his task; and she with faultering voice
Made many a fond enquiry; and when they,
Whose presence gave no comfort, were gone by,
Her heart was still more sad. And by yon gate,
930   That bars the Traveller's road, she often stood,
And when a stranger Horseman came, the latch
Would lift, and in his face look wistfully;
Most happy, if, from aught discovered there
Of tender feeling, she might dare repeat

935 The same sad question. Meanwhile her poor Hut
Sank to decay; for he was gone—whose hand,
At the first nipping of October frost,
Closed up each chink, and with fresh bands of straw
Chequered the green-grown thatch. And so she lived
940 Through the long winter, reckless and alone;
Until her House by frost, and thaw, and rain,
Was sapped; and while she slept the nightly damps
Did chill her breast; and in the stormy day
Her tattered clothes were ruffled by the wind,
Even at the side of her own fire. Yet still
945 She loved this wretched spot, nor would for worlds
Have parted hence; and still that length of road,
And this rude bench, one torturing hope endeared,
Fast rooted at her heart: and here, my Friend,—
950 In sickness she remained; and here she died;
Last human Tenant of these ruined Walls!"

    The Old Man ceased: he saw that I was moved;
From that low Bench, rising instinctively
I turn'd aside in weakness, nor had power
955 To thank him for the Tale which he had told.
I stood, and leaning o'er the Garden wall
Reviewed that Woman's sufferings; and it seemed
To comfort me while with a Brother's love
I bless'd her—in the impotence of grief.
960 At length towards the Cottage I returned
Fondly,—and traced, with interest more mild,
That secret spirit of humanity
Which, mid the calm oblivious tendencies
Of Nature, mid her plants, and weeds, and flowers,
965 And silent overgrowings, still survived.
The old Man, noting this, resumed, and said,
"My Friend! enough to sorrow you have given,
The purposes of wisdom ask no more;
Be wise and chearful; and no longer read
970 The forms of things with an unworthy eye.
She sleeps in the calm earth, and peace is here.
I well remember that those very plumes,
Those weeds, and the high spear-grass on that wall,
By mist and silent rain-drops silver'd o'er,
975 As once I passed, did to my heart convey
So still an image of tranquillity,
So calm and still, and looked so beautiful
Amid the uneasy thoughts which filled my mind,
That what we feel of sorrow and despair
980 From ruin and from change, and all the grief
That passing shews of Being leave behind,
Appeared an idle dream, that could not live

Where meditation was. I turned away
And walked along my road in happiness."

985   He ceased. Ere long the sun declining shot
A slant and mellow radiance, which began
To fall upon us, while beneath the trees,
We sate on that low Bench: and now we felt,
Admonished thus, the sweet hour coming on.
990   A linnet warbled from those lofty elms,
A thrush sang loud, and other melodies,
At distance heard, peopled the milder air.
The Old Man rose, and, with a sprightly mien
Of hopeful preparation, grasped his Staff:
995   Together casting then a farewell look
Upon those silent walls, we left the Shade;
And, ere the Stars were visible, had reached
A Village Inn,—our Evening resting-place.

from Book Fourth. Despondency Corrected.[1]

Once more to distant Ages of the world
865   Let us revert, and place before our thoughts
The face which rural Solitude might wear
To the unenlightened Swains of pagan° Greece.   *pre-Christian era*
In that fair Clime, the lonely Herdsman, stretched
On the soft grass through half a summer's day,
870   With music lulled his indolent repose:
And, in some fit of weariness, if he,
When his own breath was silent, chanced to hear
A distant strain, far sweeter than the sounds
Which his poor skill could make, his Fancy fetched,
875   Even from the blazing Chariot of the Sun,
A beardless Youth, who touched a golden lute,
And filled the illumined groves with ravishment.
The nightly Hunter, lifting up his eyes
Towards the crescent Moon, with grateful heart
880   Called on the lovely wanderer who bestowed
That timely light, to share his joyous sport:
And hence, a beaming Goddess with her Nymphs,
Across the lawn and through the darksome grove,
(Not unaccompanied with tuneful notes
885   By echo multiplied from rock or cave)
Swept in the storm of chase; as Moon and Stars

---

1. One of the "things to rejoice at in this Age," poet John Keats told artist Benjamin Robert Haydon (10 Jan. 1818), was *The Excursion*. Wordsworth recited Book IV to Haydon while he was sitting for his portrait in 1815, and Haydon may have encouraged Keats's attention, marking this passage in his copy as one Keats admired.

Glance rapidly along the clouded heavens,
When winds are blowing strong. The Traveller slaked
His thirst from Rill or gushing Fount, and thanked
890 The Naiad,°—Sunbeams, upon distant Hills   *water-nymph*
Gliding apace, with Shadows in their train,
Might, with small help from fancy, be transformed
Into fleet Oreads° sporting visibly.   *mountain-nymphs*
The Zephyrs, fanning as they passed, their wings,
895 Lacked not, for love, fair Objects whom they wooed
With gentle whisper. Withered Boughs grotesque,
Stripped of their leaves and twigs by hoary age,
From depth of shaggy covert peeping forth
In the low vale, or on steep mountain side;
900 And, sometimes, intermixed with stirring horns
Of the live Deer, or Goat's depending beard,—
These were the lurking Satyrs, a wild brood
Of gamesome Deities! or Pan himself,
The simple Shepherd's awe-inspiring God!

1814

❧

RESPONSES

William Hazlitt: from *The Character of Mr. Wordsworth's New Poem,*
The Excursion[1]

The *Excursion* may be considered as a philosophical pastoral poem—as a scholastic romance. It is less a poem on the country, than on the love of the country. It is not so much a description of natural objects, as of the feelings associated with them, not an account of the manners of rural life, but the result of the Poet's reflections on it. He does not present the reader with a distinct succession of images or incidents, but paints the outgoings of his own heart, the shapings of his own fancy. He may be said to create his own materials: his thoughts are his real subject. His imagination broods over that which is "without form and void," and "makes it pregnant."[2] He sees all things in his own mind; he contemplates effects in their causes, and passions in their principles. He hardly ever avails himself of striking subjects, or remarkable combinations of events, but in general rejects them as interfering with the workings of his own mind, as disturbing the smooth, deep, majestic current of his own feelings. Thus his descriptions of pastoral scenery are not brought home distinctly to the naked eye by forms and circumstances, but every object is seen through the medium of innumerable recollections, is clothed with the haze of imagination like a glittering vapour, is

---

1. For more about Hazlitt, see Perspectives: Popular Prose (page 1098). Hazlitt praised the "beauty, . . . originality and pathos" of many of Wordsworth's odes and lyrics, but loathed his "egotism" and his elevation of rural life and speech. He was also a liberal, and the publication of this review in 1814 in Leigh Hunt's liberal weekly, *The Examiner,*

tacitly emphasized Wordsworth's shift into political conservatism, a development evident in several passages of *The Excursion.*
2. Alluding to Milton's description of Creation, when the Holy Spirit "Dove-like satst brooding on the vast Abyss / And mad'st it pregnant" (*Paradise Lost* 1.21–22).

obscured with the excess of glory, has the shadowy brightness of a waking dream. The object is lost in the sentiment, as sound in the multiplication of echoes—

> And visions, as prophetic eyes avow,
> Hang on each leaf, and cling to every bough.[3]

In describing human nature, Mr. Wordsworth equally shuns the common vantage-grounds of popular story, of striking incident, or fatal catastrophe, as illegitimate or vulgar modes of producing an effect. He scans the human race as the naturalist measures the earth's zone, without attending to the picturesque points of view, the inequalities of surface. He contemplates the passions and habits of men, not in their extremes, but in their first elements, their follies and vices, not at their height, with all their embossed evils and putrid sores, but as lurking in embryo, the seeds of the disorder inwoven with our very constitution. He only sympathises with those simple forms of feeling, which mingle at once with his own identity, or the stream of general humanity. To him the great and the small are the same; the near and the remote; what appears, and what only is. The common and the permanent, like the Platonic ideas, are his only realities. All accidental varieties and individual contrasts are lost in an endless continuity of feeling; like drops of water in the ocean-stream! An intense intellectual egotism swallows up every thing. Even the dialogues introduced in the present volume are soliloquies of the same character, taking different views of the subject. The recluse, the pastor, and the pedlar, are three persons in one poet. We ourselves disapprove of these interlocutions between Lucius and Caius[4] as impertinent babbling, where there is no dramatic distinction of character. But the evident scope and tendency of Mr. Wordsworth's mind is the reverse of dramatic. It resists all change of character, all variety of scenery, all the bustle, machinery, and pantomime of the stage, or of real life,—whatever might relieve or relieve or relax or change the direction of its own activity, jealous of all competition. The power of his mind preys upon itself. It is as if there were nothing but himself and the universe. He lives in the busy solitude of his own heart; in the deep silence of thought. His imagination lends life and feeling only to "the bare trees and mountains bare;"[5] peoples the viewless tracts of air, and converses with the silent clouds! * * * There is, in fact, in Mr. Wordsworth's mind (if we may hazard the conjecture) a repugnance to admit any thing that tells for itself, without the interpretation of the poet,—a fastidious antipathy to immediate effect,—a systematic unwillingness to share the palm with his subject.

Francis Jeffrey: from *A Review of William Wordsworth's* Excursion[1]

This will never do. It bears no doubt the stamp of the author's heart and fancy; but unfortunately not half so visibly as that of his peculiar system. * * * It is longer, weaker, and tamer, than any of Mr Wordsworth's other productions; with less boldness of originality, and less even of that extreme simplicity and lowliness of tone which wavered so prettily, in the Lyrical Ballads, between silliness and pathos. * * * The case of Mr Wordsworth, we perceive, is now manifestly hopeless; and we give him up as altogether incurable, and beyond the power of criticism. We cannot indeed altogether

---

3. *Lines on Beech Trees*, by Thomas Gray (pub. 1775).
4. Stereotypes of rural speakers in Roman poetry.
5. Quoting Wordsworth's *Lines* ("It is the first mild day of March") line 7 (*Lyrical Ballads*).

1. For additional works by Jeffrey, see the review of 1802 in Companion Readings, page 468. This unsigned article appeared in *The Edinburgh Review* in November 1814.

omit taking precautions now and then against the spreading of the malady;—but for himself, though we shall watch the progress of his symptoms as a matter of professional curiosity and instruction, we really think it right not to harass him any longer with nauseous remedies,—but rather to throw in cordials and lenitives, and wait in patience for the natural termination of the disorder. In order to justify this desertion of our patient, however, it is proper to state why we despair of the success of a more active practice.

* * * Long habits of seclusion, and an excessive ambition of originality, can alone account for the disproportion which seems to exist between this author's taste and his genius; or for the devotion with which he has sacrificed so many precious gifts at the shrine of those paltry idols which he has set up for himself among his lakes and his mountains. Solitary musings, amidst such scenes, might no doubt be expected to nurse up the mind to the majesty of poetical conception,—(though it is remarkable, that all the greater poets lived, or had lived, in the full current of society):—But the collision of equal minds,—the admonition of prevailing impressions—seems necessary to reduce its redundancies, and repress that tendency to extravagance or puerility, into which the self-indulgence and self-admiration of genius is so apt to be betrayed, when it is allowed to wanton, without awe or restraint, in the triumph and delight of its own intoxication. That its flights should be graceful and glorious in the eyes of men, it seems almost to be necessary that they should be made in the consciousness that men's eyes are to behold them,—and that the inward transport and vigour by which they are inspired, should be tempered by an occasional reference to what will be thought of them by those ultimate dispensers of glory. An habitual and general knowledge of the few settled and permanent maxims, which form the canon of general taste in all large and polished societies—a certain tact, which informs us at once that many things, which we still love and are moved by in secret, must necessarily be despised as childish, or derided as absurd, in all such societies—though it will not stand in the place of genius, seems necessary to the success of its exertions; and though it will never enable any one to produce the higher beauties of art, can alone secure the talent which does produce them, from errors that must render it useless. Those who have most of the talent, however, commonly acquire this knowledge with the greatest facility;—and if Mr Wordsworth, instead of confining himself almost entirely to the society of the dalesmen and cottagers, and little children, who form the subjects of his book, had condescended to mingle a little more with the people that were to read and judge of it, we cannot help thinking, that its texture would have been considerably improved: At least it appears to us to be absolutely impossible, that any one who had lived or mixed familiarly with men of literature and ordinary judgment in poetry, (of course we exclude the coadjutors and disciples of his own school), could ever have fallen into such gross faults, or so long mistaken them for beauties. His first essays we looked upon in a good degree as political paradoxes,—maintained experimentally, in order to display talent, and court notoriety;—and so maintained, with no more serious belief in their truth, than is usually generated by an ingenious and animated defence of other paradoxes. But when we find, that he has been for twenty years exclusively employed upon articles of this very fabric, and that he has still enough of raw material on hand to keep him so employed for twenty years to come, we cannot refuse him the justice of believing that he is a sincere convert to his own system, and must ascribe the peculiarities of his composition, not to any transient affectation, or accidental caprice of imagination, but to a settled perversity of taste or understanding, which has been fostered, if not altogether created, by the circumstances to which we have already alluded.

The volume before us, if we were to describe it very shortly, we should characterize as a tissue of moral and devotional ravings, in which innumerable changes are rung upon a few very simple and familiar ideas:—but with such an accompaniment of long words, long sentences, and unwieldy phrases—and such a hubbub of strained raptures and fantastical sublimities, that it is often extremely difficult for the most skilful and attentive student to obtain a glimpse of the author's meaning—and altogether impossible for an ordinary reader to conjecture what he is about. * * *

Nobody can be more disposed to do justice to the great powers of Mr Wordsworth than we are; and, from the first time that he came before us, down to the present moment, we have uniformly testified in their favour, and assigned indeed our high sense of their value as the chief ground of the bitterness with which we resented their perversion. That perversion, however, is now far more visible than their original dignity; and while we collect the fragments, it is impossible not to lament the ruins from which we are condemned to pick them.

✎

"Surprized by joy"

Surprized by joy—impatient as the Wind
I turned to share the transport—Oh! with whom
But thee, long buried in the silent Tomb,
That spot which no vicissitude can find?[1]
5   Love, faithful love, recalled thee to my mind—
But how could I forget thee? Through what power,
Even for the least division of an hour,
Have I been so beguiled as to be blind
To my most grievous loss!—That thought's return
10 Was the worst pang that sorrow ever bore,
Save one, one only, when I stood forlorn,
Knowing my heart's best treasure was no more;
That neither present time, nor years unborn
Could to my sight that heavenly face restore.

1812–1815   1815

Mutability[1]

From low to high doth dissolution climb,
And sink from high to low, along a scale
Of awful° notes, whose concord shall not fail;   awe-filled
A musical but melancholy chime,
5   Which they can hear who meddle not with crime,
Nor avarice, nor over-anxious care.
Truth fails not; but her outward forms that bear
The longest date do melt like frosty rime,

1. Daughter Catherine died in 1812 at age three.
1. From *Ecclesiastical Sonnets*, a sequence tracing the history of the Church of England. The poem begins by evoking the dissolution of the monastic orders (and the ruining of their Abbeys, including Tintern Abbey) with Henry VIII's break from the Church of Rome.

That in the morning whitened hill and plain
10   And is no more; drop like the tower sublime
Of yesterday, which royally did wear
His crown of weeds, but could not even sustain
Some casual shout that broke the silent air,
Or the unimaginable touch of Time.

1821   1822

"Scorn not the Sonnet"[1]

Scorn not the Sonnet; Critic, you have frowned,
Mindless of its just honors; with this key
Shakspeare unlocked his heart; the melody
Of this small lute gave ease to Petrarch's wound;
5   A thousand times this pipe did Tasso sound;
With it Camoëns soothed an exile's grief;
The Sonnet glittered a gay myrtle leaf
Amid the cypress with which Dante crowned
His visionary brow: a glow-worm lamp,
10   It cheered mild Spenser, called from Faëryland
To struggle through dark ways; and, when a damp
Fell round the path of Milton, in his hand
The Thing became a trumpet; when he blew
Soul-animating strains—alas, too few!

1827   1827

Extempore Effusion upon the Death of James Hogg[1]

When first, descending from the moorlands,
I saw the Stream of Yarrow[2] glide
Along a bare and open valley,
The Ettrick Shepherd was my guide.

5   When last along its banks I wandered,
Through groves that had begun to shed
Their golden leaves upon the pathways,
My steps the Border-minstrel[3] led

The mighty Minstrel breathes no longer,
10   'Mid mouldering ruins low he lies;
And death upon the braes° of Yarrow,   *banks, meadows*
Has closed the Shepherd-poet's eyes:

1. In this record of devotion to the form and its tradition, Wordsworth combats the regard of sonnet-writing as less mature than epic poetry or tragic drama. Because many women poets were writing sonnets, sonnet-writing could seem "feminine," as opposed to "masculine" epic. The sonnet cites a range of major Renaissance sonnet-writers.
1. First published in the *Newcastle Journal* December 1835; the penultimate stanza on Hemans was added the next year. James Hogg, known as "The Ettrick Shepherd," after his forest birthplace and occupation, died

in November 1835. Discovered by Sir Walter Scott, he became the friend of many writers, and himself wrote poems, essays, and novels. "Extempore" means "immediate and spontaneous"; the occasion was Hogg's death, but in wider scope, a sense of an era come to an end.
2. River in Scotland, and the subject of several poems by Wordsworth.
3. Scott, who died in September 1832, was buried at Dryburgh Abbey, the "mouldering ruins."

Nor has the rolling year twice measured,
From sign to sign, its stedfast course,
15　Since every mortal power of Coleridge
Was frozen at its marvellous source;

The rapt One, of the godlike forehead,
The heaven-eyed creature sleeps in earth:
And Lamb, the frolic and the gentle,
20　Has vanished from his lonely hearth.[4]

Like clouds that rake the mountain-summits,
Or waves that own no curbing hand,
How fast has brother followed brother
From sunshine to the sunless land!

25　Yet I, whose lids from infant slumber
Were earlier raised, remain to hear
A timid voice, that asks in whispers,
"Who next will drop and disappear?"

Our haughty life is crowned with darkness,
30　Like London with its own black wreath,
On which with thee, O Crabbe! forth-looking,
I gazed from Hampstead's breezy heath.[5]

As if but yesterday departed,
Thou too art gone before; but why,
35　O'er ripe fruit, seasonably gathered,
Should frail survivors heave a sigh?

Mourn rather for that holy Spirit,[6]
Sweet as the spring, as ocean deep;
For Her, who, ere her summer faded,
40　Has sunk into a breathless sleep.

No more of old romantic sorrows,
For slaughtered Youth or love-lorn Maid!
With sharper grief is Yarrow smitten,
And Ettrick mourns with her their Poet dead.

1835–1836　　　　　　　　　　　　　　　　　　　　　　1836

⊷⊷⊱◈⊰⊷

Dorothy Wordsworth
1771–1855

Dorothy Wordsworth would probably be surprised to see herself in our pages, for unlike just about everyone else here, she did not think of herself primarily as a writer, and she did not aspire to publication. Her brother William did put a few of her poems in his volumes (including *Address to*

---

4. Coleridge and Lamb had died in 1834.
5. Poet George Crabbe died in 1832; Hampstead heath is
north of London.
6. Felicia Hemans, who died in 1836; see page 930.

a Child and *Floating Island*), identified as "By my Sister"—an apt credit, for this was Dorothy's own chief self-identification. When friends urged her to publish her remarkable account of her community's response to a local tragedy (*George and Sarah Green*, 1808), she protested that she had written it only at her brother's urging and only as a local record; "I should detest the idea of setting myself as an Author," she said. Similar encouragement for her journals of her tours of Scotland and Europe was similarly rebuffed, Dorothy insisting that she had written only for family and friends. When she began her Grasmere journal, she told herself that she was writing to give William "pleasure."

Born in the Lake District of England in 1771, Dorothy Wordsworth lived happily there with her four brothers until 1778, when their mother died. Their father, often absent on business, felt unable to sustain the household and sent the boys away to school and Dorothy to live with a series of distant relatives, in situations ranging from happy to bleak. She saw her brothers rarely and especially missed William, with whom she was closest, less than two years his junior. Reunited in 1787, they longed to have a home together, and in 1795, with the advantage of William's legacy from a college friend, they realized this dream. They first lived in southwest England, in Dorset, as a quasi-family with a friend's young son as their ward. Moving to Alfoxden in 1797 to be near Samuel Taylor Coleridge, they became acquainted with Charles and Mary Lamb and Robert Southey. During their summer tour of the Wye valley in 1798, William wrote *Tintern Abbey* with its homage to Dorothy's companionship. They spent the next winter miserably in Goslar, Germany (following Coleridge there on a scheme to learn the language), and settled at the end of 1799 in Grasmere, in their beloved native Lake District, where they remained together for the rest of their lives.

Dorothy began her Grasmere journal in May 1800, just as William was beginning to court their childhood friend, Mary Hutchinson, and she left off at the beginning of 1803, a few months after Mary joined their household. There was never any question about her remaining there: Mary married *them*. A beloved aunt to her nieces and nephews, Dorothy was really more a third parent. She not only shared the domestic labors but remained William's companion, encourager, sounding-board, secretary, and (along with Mary) perpetual transcriber of his drafts into fair-copy. In 1829 she was stricken by the first in a series of devastating illnesses, with relapses and new afflictions occurring over the next six years, each event wracking her with pain and leaving her further debilitated. By 1835 her temperament and mental acuity were also afflicted in a pre-senile dementia akin to Alzheimer's. Cared for with affection by her family, she lived a kind of invalid half-life, with lucid intervals, for the next twenty years, surviving her brother by five.

This demise is especially poignant, given the intelligence, sensitivity, and physical vitality with which she had impressed everyone. It was not until the end of the nineteenth century that her poems and journals were collected and published, and for a long time the journals were read chiefly for information about Coleridge, William, and the circumstances of the poems he wrote between 1798 and 1802. Placed alongside these poems, however, some of Dorothy's passages suggest that William may have been inspired as much by her language as by events and appearances in the external world; and recently Dorothy Wordsworth has been taken seriously as a writer in her own right. Her Grasmere journal is a fascinating chronicle of early nineteenth-century life in the Lake District—full of brilliantly detailed descriptions of nature (admired by Virginia Woolf), accounts of domestic life and household labors, precise observations of the people, the social textures and economic distresses of rural England. In the cast of characters that cross her pages—children, neighbors, local laborers, tinkers and itinerants, beggars and vagrants, abandoned wives and mothers, a leech-gatherer, discharged and often injured soldiers, sailors, and veterans—Dorothy Wordsworth captures, as much as her brother hoped his poetry would, the "language really used by men" (and women). In addition to journals, records of tours, numerous letters, and ceaseless secretarial work and manuscript transcription for William, Dorothy wrote about thirty poems. Composed sporadically from 1805 to 1840, these often allude to or converse with her brother's poetry, sometimes marking different investments of imagination, alternative views of the world they share, or a different sensibility—one less solitary and more sociable, less visionary than domestic, and more self-effacing, especially about the vocation and practice of writing poetry.

A selection from Dorothy Wordsworth's journal appears in Perspectives: The Abolition of Slavery and the Slave Trade, page 273.

Grasmere—A Fragment

Peaceful our valley, fair and green,
And beautiful her cottages,
Each in its nook, its sheltered hold,
Or underneath its tuft of trees

5   Many and beautiful they are;
But there is *one* that I love best,
A lowly shed, in truth, it is,
A brother of the rest.

Yet when I sit on rock or hill,
10   Down looking on the valley fair,
That Cottage with its clustering trees
Summons my heart; it settles there.

Others there are whose small domain
Of fertile fields and hedgerows green
15   Might more seduce a wanderer's mind
To wish that *there* his home had been.

Such wish be his! I blame him not,
My fancies they perchance are wild
—I love that house because it is
20   The very Mountains' child.

Fields hath it of its own, green fields,
But they are rocky steep and bare;
Their fence is of the mountain stone,
And moss and lichen flourish there.

25   And when the storm comes from the North
It lingers near that pastoral spot,
And, piping through the mossy walls,
It seems delighted with its lot.

And let it take its own delight;
30   And let it range the pastures bare;
Until it reach that group of trees,
—It may not enter there!

A green unfading grove it is,
Skirted with many a lesser tree,
35   Hazel & holly, beech and oak,
A bright and flourishing company.

Precious the shelter of those trees;
They screen the cottage that I love;
The sunshine pierces to the roof,
40   And the tall pine-trees tower above.

When first I saw that dear abode,
It was a lovely winter's day:[1]
After a night of perilous storm
The west wind ruled with gentle sway;

45   A day so mild, it might have been
The first day of the gladsome spring;
The robins warbled, and I heard
One solitary throstle sing.

A Stranger, Grasmere, in thy Vale,
50   All faces then to me unknown,
I left my sole companion-friend
To wander out alone.

Lured by a little winding path,
I quitted soon the public road,
55   A smooth and tempting path it was,
By sheep and shepherds trod.[2]

Eastward, towards the lofty hills,
This pathway led me on
Until I reached a stately Rock,
60   With velvet moss o'ergrown.

With russet oak and tufts of fern
Its top was richly garlanded;
Its sides adorned with eglantine
Bedropp'd with hips of glossy red.

65   There, too, in many a sheltered chink
The foxglove's broad leaves flourished fair,
And silver birch whose purple twigs
Bend to the softest breathing air.

Beneath that Rock my course I stayed,
70   And, looking to its summit high,
"Thou wear'st," said I, "a splendid garb,
Here winter keeps his revelry."

"Full long a dweller on the Plains,
I griev'd when summer days were gone;
75   No more I'll grieve; for Winter here
Hath pleasure gardens of his own.

1. Dorothy and William, her "sole companion-friend"   2. Compare the opening of William's *Michael*, page 458.
(51), moved to Grasmere just before Christmas 1799.

What need of flowers? The splendid moss
Is gayer than an April mead;
More rich its hues of various green,
80   Orange, and gold, & glittering red."

—Beside that gay and lovely Rock
There came with merry voice
A foaming streamlet glancing by;
It seemed to say "Rejoice!"

85   My youthful wishes all fulfill'd,
Wishes matured by thoughtful choice,
I stood an Inmate° of this vale   *dweller*
How *could* I but rejoice?

late 1805

Address to a Child
During a boisterous Winter Evening in a high wind [1]

What way does the wind come? what way does he go?
He rides over the water and over the snow,
Through wood, and through vale; and o'er rocky height
Which the goat cannot climb takes his sounding flight.[2]
5   He tosses about in every bare tree,
As, if you look up you plainly may see
But how he will come, and whither he goes
There's never a Scholar in England knows.

He will suddenly stop in a cunning nook
10   And rings a sharp larum:°—but if you should look   *call to arms*
There's nothing to see but a cushion of snow,
Round as a pillow and whiter than milk
And softer than if it were cover'd with silk.

Sometimes he'll hide in the cave of a rock;
15   Then whistle as shrill as the buzzard cock;
—Yet seek him and what shall you find in his place
Nothing but silence and empty space
Save in a corner a heap of dry leaves
That he's left for a bed for beggars or thieves.

20   As soon as 'tis daylight tomorrow with me
You shall go to the orchard & then you will see
That he has been there, & made a great rout,°   *debacle*
And cracked the branches, & strew'd them about:

---

1. Written 1806 for nephew Johnny (see letter to Lady Beaumont, page 612); see also her comment in late 1805: "what a fearful thing a windy night is now at our house! I am too often haunted with dreadful images of Shipwrecks and the Sea when I am in bed and hear a stormy wind" (page 613)—evoking the loss of her beloved brother John in a shipwreck in 1805. Published unsigned in William's *Poems*, 1815; our text follows this version, with significant variants from the ms. ("An address to a Child in a high wind") indicated.
2. Manuscript: "Through the valley, and over the hill / And roars as loud as a thundering Mill" (waterfall where a mill is located).

25 Heaven grant that he spare but that one upright twig
That look'd up at the sky so proud & so big
All last summer, as well you know
Studded with apples, a beautiful shew!

Hark! over the roof he makes a pause
And growls as if he would fix his claws
30 Right in the slates, and with a huge rattle
Drive them down like men in a battle.
—But let him range round; he does us no harm
We build up the fire; we're snug and warm,
Untouch'd by his breath see the candle shines bright,
35 And burns with a clear and steady light;
Books have we to read,—hush! that half-stifled knell,
Methinks 'tis the sound of the eight o'clock bell.[3]

Come, now we'll to bed, and when we are there
He may work his own will, & what shall we care.
40 He may knock at the door—we'll not let him in
May drive at the windows—we'll laugh at his din
Let him seek his own home wherever it be
Here's a cozy warm house for Edward and me.[4]

1806   1815

Irregular Verses[1]

Ah Julia! ask a Christmas rhyme
Of *me* who in the golden time
Of careless, hopeful, happy youth
Ne'er strove to decorate the truth,
5 Contented to lay bare my heart
To one dear Friend, who had her part
In all the love and all the care
And every joy that harboured there.
—To her I told in simple prose
10 Each girlish vision, as it rose
Before an active busy brain
That needed neither spur nor rein,
That still enjoyed the present hour
Yet for the *future* raised a tower
15 Of bliss more exquisite and pure
Bliss that (so deemed we) should endure
Maxims of caution, prudent fears
Vexed not the projects of those years
Simplicity our steadfast theme,

---

3. Manuscript lines: "Old Madam has brought us plenty of coals / And the Glazier has closed up all the holes / In every window that Johnny broke / And the walls are tighter than Molly's new cloak."
4. In the manuscript, the synonym *canny* is used instead of *cozy*; Edward is a pseudonym to protect Johnny's privacy.
1. Written in 1829 as Christmas-verses to her 20-year-old goddaughter, daughter of childhood friend Jane Pollard, later Mrs. Marshall. Dorothy encouraged Julia's efforts to write poetry. "Irregular" means not metrically regular.

20   No works of Art adorned our scheme.—
        A cottage in a verdant dell,
        A foaming stream, a crystall Well,
        A garden stored with fruit and flowers
        And sunny seats and shady bowers,
25   A file of hives for humming bees
        Under a row of stately trees
        And, sheltering all this faery ground,
        A belt of hills must wrap it round,
        Not stern or mountainous, or bare,
30   Nor lacking herbs to scent the air;
        Nor ancient trees, nor scattered rocks,
        And pastured by the blameless flocks
        That print their green tracks to invite
        Our wanderings to the topmost height.
35   Such was the spot I fondly framed
        When life was new, and hope untamed:[2]
        There with my one dear Friend would dwell,
        Nor wish for aught beyond the dell.
         Alas! the cottage fled in air,
40   The streamlet never flowed:
        —Yet did those visions pass away[3]
        So gently that they seemed to stay,
        Though in our riper years we each pursued a different way.

        —We parted, sorrowful; by duty led;
45   My Friend, ere long a happy Wife
        Was seen with dignity to tread
        The paths of usefulness, in active life;
        And such her course through later days;
        The same her honour and her praise;
50   As thou canst witness, thou dear Maid,
        One of the Darlings of her care;[4]
        Thy *Mother* was that Friend who still repaid
        Frank confidence with unshaken truth:
        This was the glory of her youth,
55   A brighter gem than shines in prince's diadem.

         You ask why in that jocund time
        Why did I not in jingling rhyme
        Display those pleasant guileless dreams
        That furnished still exhaustless themes?
60   —I *reverenced* the Poet's skill,
        And *might have* nursed a mounting Will
        To imitate the tender Lays°   *songs*

---

2. Cf. W. Wordsworth's, *Elegiac Stanzas*: "Such, in the fond illusion of my heart, / Such Picture would I at that time have made" (29–30).
3. Cf. W. Wordsworth's, *The Reverie of Poor Susan*: "The stream will not flow, and the hill will not rise, / And the colours will all passed away from her eyes!" (15–16).
4. Jane Marshall bore 11 children.

Of them who sang in Nature's praise;
But bashfulness, a struggling shame
65   A fear that elder heads might blame
—Or something worse—a lurking pride
Whispering my playmates would deride
Stifled ambition, checked the aim
If e'er by chance "the numbers came"[5]
70   —Nay even the mild maternal smile,
That oft-times would repress, beguile
The over-confidence of youth,
Even that dear smile, to own the truth,
Was dreaded by a fond self-love;
75   "'Twill glance on me—and to reprove
Or," (sorest wrong in childhood's school)
"Will *point* the sting of ridicule."[6]

And now, dear Girl, I hear you ask
Is this your lightsome, chearful task?
80   You tell us tales of forty years,
Of hopes extinct, of childish fears,
Why cast among us thoughts of sadness
When we are seeking mirth and gladness?[7]
Nay, ill those words befit the Maid
85   Who pleaded for my Christmas rhyme
Mirthful she is; but placid—staid—
Her heart beats to no giddy chime
Though it with Chearfulness keep time
For Chearfulness, a willing guest,
90   Finds ever in her tranquil breast
A fostering home, a welcome rest.
And well she knows that, casting *thought* away,
We lose the best part of our day;
That joys of youth remembered when our youth is past
95   Are joys that to the end of life will last;[8]

And if this poor memorial strain,
Breathed from the depth of years gone by,
Should touch her Mother's heart with tender pain,
Or call a tear into her loving eye,
100   She will not check the tear or still the rising sigh.
—The happiest heart is given to sadness;
The saddest heart feels deepest gladness.

5. From Pope's *Epistle To Dr. Arbuthnot* (1735): "Why did
I write? what sin to me unknown / Dipt me in Ink, my
Parents', or my own? / As yet a Child, nor yet a Fool to
Fame, / I lisp'd in Numbers, for the Numbers came" (125–
28). Also involved is W. Wordsworth's beginning of *The
Prelude*: "To the open fields I told / A prophecy; poetic
numbers came / Spontaneously, and clothed in priestly
robe / My spirit, thus singled out, as it might seem, / For
holy services" (59–63).

6. An imaginary reproof; her mother died when she was
seven, before the era recounted here.
7. Along with lines 101–102, compare to W. Wordsworth's *Resolution and Independence* "We Poets in our
youth begin in gladness; / But thereof come in the end
despondency and madness" (48–49).
8. A hope frequently voiced in W. Wordsworth's poetry,
e.g., *Tintern Abbey*, 64–65: "in this moment there is life
and food / For future years".

Thou dost not ask, thou dost not need
A verse from me; nor wilt thou heed
105   A greeting masked in laboured rhyme
From one whose heart has still kept time
With every pulse of thine

1829

Floating Island[1]

Harmonious Powers with Nature work
On sky, earth, river, lake, and sea:
Sunshine and storm, whirlwind and breeze
All in one duteous task agree.

5   Once did I see a slip of earth,
By throbbing waves long undermined,
Loosed from its hold;—*how* no one knew
But all might see it float, obedient to the wind.

Might see it, from the verdant shore
10   Dissevered float upon the Lake,
Float, with its crest of trees adorned
On which the warbling birds their pastime take.

Food, shelter, safety there they find
There berries ripen, flowerets bloom;
15   There insects live their lives—and die:
A peopled *world* it is;—in size a tiny room.

And thus through many seasons' space
This little Island may survive
But Nature, though we mark her not,
20   Will take away—may cease to give.

Perchance when you are wandering forth
Upon some vacant sunny day
Without an object, hope, or fear,
Thither your eyes may turn—the Isle is passed away.

25   Buried beneath the glittering Lake!
Its place no longer to be found,
Yet the lost fragments shall remain,
To fertilize some other ground.

Late 1820s   1842

1. Published by W. Wordsworth in *Poems, Chiefly of Early and Late Years* (1842) with the attribution "by the author of the Address to the Wind, & c. published heretofore along with my Poems." Text follows this version; the ms. title is *Floating Island at Hawkshead, An Incident in the Schemes of Nature*. The brothers went to school at Hawkshead, a village in the Lakes rather far from home in Cockermouth. There was an actual floating island at the southern end of Derwent Water, which William uses in *The Prelude* as a figure of indolence: "my life became / A floating island, an amphibious thing, / Unsound, of spungy texture, yet withal, / Not wanting a fair face of water weeds / And pleasant flowers" (1805: 13.339–43); and as an element of a revelation: "Emerging from the silvery vapours, lo! / A Shepherd and his Dog! in open day: / Girt round with mists they stood, and look'd about / From that enclosure small, inhabitants / Of an aerial Island floating" (8.94–98).

Lines Intended for My Niece's Album[1]

Dear Maiden did thy youthful mind
Dally with emblems sad? or gay?
When thou gavest the word—and it was done,—
"My Book shall appear in green array."

5   Well didst thou speak, and well devise;
'Tis Nature's choice, her favored hue,
The badge she carries on her front,
And Nature faithful is, and true.

She, careful Warder, duly guards
10   The works of God's Almighty power,
Sustains with her diffusive breath
All moving things & tree & herb & flower

Like office hath this tiny Book;
Memorials of the Good and Wise,
15   Kind counsels, mild reproofs that bind
The Dead to the Living by holy ties,

Parental blessings, Friendship's vows,
Hope, love, and Brother's truth
Here, all preserved with duteous care,
20   Retain their dower of endless youth.

Perennial green enfolds these leaves;
They lie enclosed in glossy sheath
As spotless as the lily flower,
Till touched by a quickening breath

25   And it *has* touched them: Yes dear Girl,
In reverence of thy "gifted Sire"[2]
A wreath for thee is here entwined
By his true Brothers of the Lyre[3]

The Farewell of the laurelled Knight
30   Traced by a brave but tremulous hand,
Pledge of his truth and loyalty,
Through changeful years unchanged shall stand.

Confiding hopes of youthful hearts
And each bright visionary scheme
35   Shall here remain in vivid hues,
The hues of a celestial dream.

But why should *I* inscribe my name,
No poet I—no longer young?

---

1. Dora Wordsworth, niece and namesake, kept an album
to which her father's friends (among them, Scott, Lamb,
Coleridge, Hemans, and Jewsbury) contributed poems.
Her father's contribution was a sonnet on sonnet-writing,
"Nuns fret not" (see page 474). After Dora's death in
1847, poets, including Arnold and Tennyson, continued
the practice in her memory.
2. A phrase in many poems, from the celebratory to the
satiric.
3. Instrument of Apollo, Greek god of poetry.

40 The ambition of a loving heart
Makes garrulous the tongue.

Memorials of thy aged Friend,
Dora! thou dost not need,
And when the cold earth covers her
No praises shall she heed.

45 Yet still a lurking wish prevails
That, when from Life we all have passed
The Friends who love thy Parents' name
On her's a thought may cast.

1832

Thoughts on My Sick-bed[1]

And has the remnant of my life
Been pilfered of this sunny Spring?
And have its own prelusive sounds
Touched in my heart no echoing string?

5 Ah! say not so—the hidden life
Couchant° within this feeble frame   *lying down*
Hath been enriched by kindred gifts,
That, undesired, unsought-for, came

With joyful heart in youthful days
10 When fresh each season in its Round
I welcomed the earliest Celandine[2]
Glittering upon the mossy ground;

With busy eyes I pierced the lane
In quest of known and *un*known things,
15 —The primrose a lamp on its fortress rock,
The silent butterfly spreading its wings,

The violet betrayed by its noiseless breath,
The daffodil dancing in the breeze,
The carolling thrush, on his naked perch,
20 Towering above the budding trees.[3]

Our cottage-hearth no longer our home,
Companions of Nature were we,
The Stirring, the Still, the Loquacious, the Mute—
To all we gave our sympathy.

1. Written in spring 1832, by which time Dorothy was stricken with a series of debilitating illnesses.
2. A resilient flower, treated by William in *The Small Celandine* (1804; 1807) as an emblem of inevitable old age.
3. A bouquet of references to William's poems: *The Primrose of the Rock* (c. 1831, a flower on the Grasmere-Rydal road); *To a Butterfly* ("Stay near me") and *To a Butterfly* ("I've watched you") (both 1802; 1807); *Song* ("She dwelt among th'untrodden ways") ("a violet by a mossy stone, half hidden from the eye"); *I wandered lonely as a cloud* ("golden daffodils...dancing in the breeze").

25   Yet never in those careless days
    When spring-time in rock, field, or bower
    Was but a fountain of earthly hope
    A promise of fruits & the *splendid* flower.[4]

    No! then I never felt a bliss
30   That might with *that* compare
    Which, piercing to my couch of rest,
    Came on the vernal air.

    When loving Friends an offering brought,
    The first flowers of the year,
35   Culled from the precincts of our home,
    From nooks to Memory dear.[5]

    With some sad thoughts the work was done,[6]
    Unprompted and unbidden,
    But joy it brought to my *hidden* life,
40   To consciousness no longer hidden.

    I felt a Power unfelt before,
    Controlling weakness, languor, pain;
    It bore me to the Terrace walk
    I trod the Hills again;—

45   No prisoner in this lonely room,
    I *saw* the green Banks of the Wye,
    Recalling thy prophetic words,
    Bard, Brother, Friend from infancy![7]

    No need of motion, or of strength,[8]
50   Or even the breathing air:
    —I thought of Nature's loveliest scenes;
    And with Memory I was there.

1832

When Shall I Tread Your Garden Path?[1]

    When shall I tread your garden path?
    Or climb your sheltering hill?
    When shall I wander, free as air,
    And track the foaming rill?

4. W. Wordsworth's "Intimations" Ode: "Though nothing can bring back the hour / Of splendour in the grass, of glory in the flower; / We will grieve not, rather find / Strength in what remains behind" (177–80).
5. "Intimations" Ode: "The fulness of your bliss, I feel— I feel it all. / O evil day! if I were sullen / While Earth herself is adorning, / This sweet May-morning, / And the Children are culling / On every side, / In a thousand valleys far and wide, / Fresh flowers" (41–48).
6. W. Wordsworth's *Lines Written in Early Spring* ("I sate

reclined, / In that sweet mood when pleasant thoughts / Bring sad thoughts to the mind") and *Three Years She Grew* ("Thus nature spake—The work was done—/ How soon my Lucy's race was run! / She died").
7. See *Tintern Abbey*, especially 111ff.
8. W. Wordsworth's *A slumber did my spirit seal* ("No motion has she now, no force").
1. Addressed to John Carter, William's assistant in the stamp office and Wordsworths handyman for more than 40 years.

5   A prisoner on my pillowed couch
       Five years in feebleness I've lain,
       Oh! shall I e'er with vigorous step
       Travel the hills again?

To Mr Carter DW
Novr 11—1835

Lines Written (Rather Say *Begun*) on the Morning of Sunday April 6th
The Third Approach of Spring-Time Since My Illness Began.
It Was a Morning of Surpassing Beauty.

       The worship of this sabbath morn,
       How sweetly it begins!
       With the full choral hymn of birds
       Mingles no[1] sad lament for sins.

5   The air is clear, the sunshine bright.
       The dew-drops glitter on the trees;
       My eye beholds a perfect Rest,
       I hardly hear a stirring breeze.

       A robe of quiet overspreads
10   The living lake and verdant field;
       The very earth seems sanctified,
       Protected by a holy shield.

       The steed, now vagrant on the hill,
       Rejoices in this sacred day,
15   Forgetful of the plough—the goad—
       And, though subdued, is happy as the gay.

       A chastened call of bleating lambs
       Drops steadily from that lofty Steep;
       —I could believe this sabbath peace
20   Was felt even by the mother sheep.[2]

       Conscious that they are safe from man
       On this glad day of punctual rest,
       By God himself—his work being done—
       Pronounced the holiest and the best

25   'Tis but a fancy, a fond thought,
       To which a waking dream gave birth,
       Yet heavenly, in this brilliant Calm,
       —Yea *heavenly* is the spirit of earth—

       Nature attunes the pious heart
30   To gratitude and fervent love

---

1. One manuscript has "so"—an opposite meaning. This same manuscript lacks the next eleven stanzas, resuming at line 48, here.
2. In another copy, Dorothy ends the poem here, adding this last stanza: "Thus have ye passed one gladsome hour / But [earnest?] youth exhausts its power / The weary limbs, the panting breast / The throbbing head / Plead piteously for rest."

By visible stillne[ss] the chearful voice
Of living things in budding trees & in the air above.

Fit prelude are these lingering hours
To man's appointed, holy task
35   Of prayer and social gratitude:
They prompt our hearts in faith to ask,

Ask humbly for the precious boon
Of pious hope and fixed content
And pardon, sought through trust in Him
40   Who died to save the Penitent.

And now the chapel bell invites
The Old, the Middle-aged, and Young
To meet beneath those sacred walls,
And give to pious thought a tongue

45   That simple bell of jingling tone
To careless ears unmusical,
Speaks to the Serious in a strain
That might their wisest hours recal.

Alas! my feet no more may join
50   The chearful sabbath train;
But if I inwardly lament
Soon may a will subdued[3] all grief restrain.

No prisoner am I on this couch
My mind is free to roam,
55   And leisure, peace, and loving Friends
Are the best treasures of an[4] earthly home

Such gifts are mine: then why deplore
The body's gentle slow decay,
A warning mercifully sent
60   To fix my hopes upon a surer stay?[5]

from The Grasmere Journals

[HOME ALONE]

May 14 1800 [Wednesday]. Wm and John set off into Yorkshire[1] after dinner at 1/2 past 2 o'clock—cold pork in their pockets. I left them at the turning of the Low-wood bay under the trees. My heart was so full that I could hardly speak to W when I gave him a farewell kiss. I sate a long time upon a stone at the margin of the lake, & after a flood of tears my heart was easier. The lake looked to me I knew not why dull and melancholy, the weltering on the shores seemed a heavy sound. I walked as long as I could amongst the stones of the shore. The wood rich in flowers. A beautiful yellow,

3. In another copy, this verb is *resigned*.
4. short ms] our.
5. short ms] a dash instead of a question mark.
1. William and younger brother John, who lived

with them at Dove Cottage in 1800; the trip through Yorkshire was to visit childhood friend Mary Hutchinson, whom William would marry in October 1802.

palish yellow flower, that looked thick round & double, and smelt very sweet—I supposed it was a ranunculus—Crowfoot, the grassy-leaved Rabbit-toothed white flower, strawberries, Geranium—scentless violet, anemones two kinds, orchises, primroses. The heckberry very beautiful. * * * Met a blind man, driving a very large beautiful Bull & a cow—he walked with two sticks. Came home by Clappersgate. The valley very green, many sweet views up to Rydale head when I could juggle away the fine houses, but they disturbed me even more than when I have been happier—one beautiful view of the Bridge, without Sir Michaels.[2] Sate down very often, tho' it was cold. I resolved to write a journal of the time till W & J return, and I set about keeping my resolve because I will not quarrel with myself, & because I shall give Wm Pleasure by it when he comes home again. At Rydale a woman of the village, stout & well dressed, begged a halfpenny—she had never she said done it before, but these hard times— Arrived at home with a bad head-ach, set some slips of privett. The evening cold had a fire—my face now flame-coloured. It is nine o'clock. I shall soon go to bed. A young woman begged at the door—she had come from Manchester on Sunday morn with two shillings & a slip of paper which she supposed a Bank note—it was a cheat. She had buried her husband & three children within a year & a half—all in one grave— burying very dear—paupers all put in one place—20 shillings paid for as much ground as will bury a man—a stone to be put over it or the right will be lost—11/6 each time the ground is opened.[3] Oh! that I had a letter from William!

Sunday [*18th*.] Went to church, slight showers, a cold air. The mountains from this window look much greener & I think the valley is more green than ever. The corn begins to shew itself. The ashes are still bare. * * * A little girl from Coniston came to beg. She had lain out all night—her step-mother had turned her out of doors.

[A LEECH GATHERER]

3 October 1800. * * * Wm and I * * * met an old man almost double, he had on a coat thrown over his shoulders above his waistcoat & coat. Under this he carried a bundle and had an apron on and a night cap. His face was interesting. He had dark eyes & a long nose. John who afterwards met him at Wythburn took him for a Jew. He was of Scotch parents but had been born in the army. He had had a wife "& a good woman & it pleased God to bless us with ten children"—all these were dead but one of whom he had not heard for many years, a sailor—his trade was to gather leeches,[4] but now leeches are scarce & he had not strength for it—he lived by begging and was making his way to Carlisle where he should buy a few godly books to sell. He said leeches were very scarce partly owing to this dry season, but many years they have been scarce—he supposed it owing to their being much sought after, that they did not breed fast, & were of slow growth. Leeches were formerly 2/6 [per] 100; they are now 30/.[5] He had been hurt in driving a cart, his leg broke his body driven over his skull fractured—he felt no pain till he recovered from his first insensibility. It was then "late in the evening—when the light was just going away."

---

2. Rydal Hall, the home of Sir Michael le Fleming; in 1813, the Wordsworth household would move to Rydal Mount, the substantial residence next door, where they lived the rest of their lives.
3. Eleven shillings, 6 pence; dear: expensive. William and Dorothy lived modestly but comfortably on 130–40 a year.

4. Cf. the poem William wrote 18 months later, first titled *The Leech Gatherer*, then published as *Resolution and Independence* in 1807. Leeches were used medicinally, to suck out supposedly "bad blood."
5. Two shillings, 6 pence per 100 leeches; their value had now risen twelvefold to 30 shillings.

[A Woman Beggar]

Friday 27th [November 1801] Snow upon the ground thinly scattered. It snowed after we got up & then the sun shone & it was very warm though frosty—now the sun shines sweetly. A woman came who was travelling with her husband—he had been wounded & was going with her to live at Whitehaven. She had been at Ambleside[6] the night before, offered 4d[7] at the Cock for a bed—they sent her to one Harrison's where she and her husband had slept upon the hearth & bought a penny-worth of chips for a fire. Her husband was gone before very lame—"Aye" says she "I was once an officers wife I, as you see me now. My first husband married me at Appleby. I had 18£ a year for teaching a school & because I had no fortune his father turned him out of doors. I have been in the West Indies[8]—I lost the use of this Finger just before he died he came to me and said he must bid farewell to his dear children and me. I had a muslin gown on like yours—I seized hold of his coat as he went from me & slipped the joint of my finger. He was shot directly.[9] I came to London & married this man. He was clerk to Judge Chambray, *that man*, that man that's going on the Road now. If he, Judge Chambray, had been at Kendal he would [have] given us a guinea or two & made nought of it, for he is very generous."[1]

[An Old Sailor]

Tuesday 22nd [December 1801] * * * Wm & I went to Rydale for letters, the road was covered with dirty snow, rough & rather slippery. * * * As we came up the White Moss[2] we met an old man, who I saw was a beggar by his two bags hanging over his shoulder, but from a half laziness, half indifference & a wanting to *try* him if he would speak I let him pass. He said nothing, & my heart smote me. I turned back and said You are begging? "Ay," says he—I gave him a halfpenny. William, judging from his appearance joined in, "I suppose you were a sailor?" "Ay," he replied, "I have been 57 years at sea, 12 of them on board a man-of-war under Sir Hugh Palmer." "Why have you not a pension?" "I have no pension, but I could have got into Greenwich hospital[3] but all my officers are dead." He was 75 years of age, had a freshish colour in his cheeks, grey hair, a decent hat with a binding round the edge, the hat worn brown & glossy, his shoes were small thin shoes low in the quarters, pretty good—they had belonged to a gentleman. His coat was blue, frock shaped coming over his thighs, it had been joined up at the seams behind with paler blue to let it out, & there were three Bell-shaped patches of darker blue behind where the Buttons had been. His breeches were either of fustian[4] or grey cloth, with strings hanging down, whole & tight; he had a checked shirt on, & a small coloured handkerchief tyed round his neck. His bags were hung over each shoulder & lay on each side of him, below his breast. One was brownish & of coarse stuff, the other was white with meal on the outside, & his blue waistcoat was whitened with meal.[5] In the coarse bag I guessed he put his scraps of meat &c. He walked with a slender stick decently stout, but his legs bowed outwards.

6. A village three miles from Grasmere; the Cock is a small inn.
7. Four pence.
8. Where the plantation economy involved slave labor; her husband may have been assigned with the army there to keep order after numerous slave uprisings and revolts.
9. Perhaps for desertion.

1. At the time, Judge Chambré resided at his home, Abbot Hall, in Kendal, a city about 20 miles away. A guinea is £1, 1 shilling.
2. White Moss Common, a field near Grasmere Lake.
3. For seamen.
4. Sturdy cotton or linen.
5. Flour, part of his provisions.

We overtook old Fleming at Rydale,[6] leading his little Dutchman-like grandchild along the slippery road. The same pace seemed to be natural to them both, the old man & the little child, and they went hand in hand, the grandfather cautious, yet looking proud of his charge. He had two patches of new cloth at the shoulder blades of his faded claret coloured coat, like eyes at each shoulder, not worn elsewhere. * * * We stopped to look at the Stone seat at the top of the Hill. There was a white cushion upon it round at the edge like a cushion & the Rock behind looked soft as velvet, of a vivid green & so tempting! The snow too looked as soft as a down cushion. A young Foxglove, like a Star in the Centre. There were a few green lichens about it & a few withered Brackens of Fern here & there & upon the ground near. All else was a thick snow—no foot mark to it, not the foot of a sheep.—

[THE GRASMERE MAILMAN]

Monday Morning 8th February 1802. It was very windy & rained very hard all the morning. William worked at his poem & I read a little in Lessing and the Grammar.[7] A chaise came past to fetch Ellis the Carrier who had hurt his head. After dinner (i.e. we set off at about 1/2 past 4) we went towards Rydale[8] for letters. It was a cold "*Cauld Clash*"—the Rain had been so cold that it hardly melted the snow. We stopped at Park's to get some straw in William's shoes. The young mother was sitting by a bright wood fire with her youngest child upon her lap & the other two sate on each side of the chimney. The light of the fire made them a beautiful sight, with their innocent countenances, their rosy cheeks & glossy curling hair. We sate & talked about poor Ellis, and our journey over the Hawes. It had been reported that we came over in the night. Willy told us of 3 men who were once lost in crossing that way in the night, they had carried a lantern with them—the lantern went out at the Tarn[9] & they all perished. Willy had seen their cloaks drying at the public house in Patterdale[1] the day before their funeral. We walked on very wet through the clashy cold roads in bad spirits at the idea of having to go as far as Rydale, but before we had come again to the shore of the Lake, we met our patient, bow-bent Friend with his little wooden box at his Back. "Where are you going?" said he. "To Rydale for letters.—I have two for you in my Box." We lifted up the lid & there they lay. Poor Fellow, he straddled & pushed on with all his might but we soon out-stripped him far away when we had turned back with our letters. We were very thankful that we had not to go on, for we should have been sadly tired. In thinking of this I could not help comparing lots with him! He goes at that slow pace every morning, & after having wrought a hard days work returns at night, however weary he may be, takes it all quietly, & though perhaps he neither feels thankfulness, nor pleasure when he eats his supper, & has no luxury to look forward to but falling asleep in bed, yet I daresay he neither murmurs nor thinks it hard. He seems mechanized to labour.

[A VISION OF THE MOON]

[18 March 1802] * * * As we came along Ambleside vale in the twilight—it was a grave evening—there was something in the air that compelled me to serious

6. Sir Michael le Fleming of Rydal Hall.
7. William's poem is *The Pedlar*, abandoned as an independent piece and later incorporated into the first part of Book 1 of his long poem, *The Excursion* (1814). Lessing (1729–1781) is a German dramatist, art theorist, and critic; "the Grammar" is most likely a German grammar

(Dorothy had learned German in Germany).
8. About a mile away.
9. Mountain lake.
1. An inn in the village several miles away, reached by a treacherous pass over the high mountains.

thought—the hills were large, closed in by the sky. It was nearly dark * * * night was come on & the moon was overcast. But as I climbed Moss the moon came out from behind a Mountain Mass of Black clouds—O the unutterable darkness of the sky & the Earth below the Moon! & the glorious brightness of the moon itself! There was a vivid sparkling streak of light at this end of Rydale water but the rest was very dark & Loughrigg fell and Silver How were white & bright as if they were covered with hoar frost.[2] The moon retired again & appeared & disappeared several times before I reached home. Once there was no moonlight to be seen but upon the Island house & the promontory of the Island where it stands, "That needs must be a holy place" &c—&c.[3] I had many many exquisite feelings and when I saw this lowly Building in the waters among the dark & lofty hills, with that bright soft light upon it—it made me more than half a poet. I was tired when I reached home. I could not sit down to reading & tried to write verses but alas! I gave up expecting William & went soon to bed. Fletcher's carts came home late.[4]

[A FIELD OF DAFFODILS]

Thursday 15th. [April 1802] * * * When we were in the woods beyond Gowbarrow[5] park we saw a few daffodils close to the water side, we fancied that the lake had floated the seeds ashore & that the little colony had so sprung up—But as we went along there were more & yet more & at last under the boughs of the trees, we saw that there was a long belt of them along the shore, about the breadth of a country turnpike road.[6] I never saw daffodils so beautiful they grew among the mossy stones about & about them, some rested their heads upon these stones as on a pillow for weariness & the rest tossed & reeled & danced & seemed as if they verily laughed with the wind that blew upon them over the Lake, they looked so gay ever glancing ever changing. This wind blew directly over the lake to them. There was here & there a little knot & a few stragglers a few yards higher up but they were so few as not to disturb the simplicity & unity & life of that one busy highway. We rested again & again. The Bays were stormy, & we heard the waves at different distances and in the middle of the water like the Sea.

[A BEGGAR WOMAN FROM COCKERMOUTH[7]]

Tuesday 4th May [1802]. William had slept pretty well & though he went to bed nervous & jaded in the extreme he rose refreshed. I wrote the Leech Gatherer[8] for him which he had begun the night before & of which he wrote several stanzas in bed this Monday morning. It was very hot, we called at Mr Simpson's door as we passed but did not go in. We rested several times by the way, read & repeated the Leech Gatherer. We were almost melted before we were at the top of the hill. * * * William & I ate a Luncheon, then went on towards the Waterfall. It is a glorious wild solitude under that lofty purple crag. It stood upright by itself. Its own self and its shadow below, one mass—all else was sunshine. We went on further. A Bird at the top of the crags was

---

2. White Moss Common, Rydale water (a lake nearby Grasmere Lake and the Common), and two peaks to the south of these lakes, Loughrigg and Silver How.
3. Perhaps recalling an early draft of Coleridge's *Kubla Khan*, line 14, or William's feeling in *Home at Grasmere* that "dwellers in this holy place / Must need themselves be hallow'd" (366–67).
4. William's ride, via the mail carrier.

5. Several miles away near Patterdale on Ullswater.
6. Dorothy erased the next words, "the end we did not see." Cf. W. Wordsworth's poem, *I wandered lonely as a cloud:* "They stretched in never-ending line."
7. The small town where Dorothy and her brothers were born and lived until the break-up of the household.
8. The early title for *Resolution and Independence*.

flying round & round & looked in thinness & transparency, shape & motion, like a moth. We climbed the hill but looked in vain for a shade except at the foot of the great waterfall, & there we did not like to stay on account of the loose stones above our heads. We came down & rested upon a moss covered Rock, rising out of the bed of the River. There we lay ate our dinner & stayed there till about 4 o clock or later. Wm & C[9] repeated & read verses. I drank a little Brandy & water & was in Heaven. The Stags horn is very beautiful & fresh springing upon the fells. Mountain ashes, green. * * * On the Rays we met a woman with 2 little girls one in her arms the other about 4 years old walking by her side, a pretty little thing, but half starved. She had on a pair of slippers that had belonged to some gentlemans child, down at the heels it was not easy to keep them on but, poor thing! young as she was, she walked carefully with them. Alas too young for such cares & such travels. The Mother when we accosted her told us that her husband had left her & gone off with another woman & how she "pursued" them. Then her fury kindled & her eyes rolled about. She changed again to tears. She was a Cockermouth woman 30 years of age— a child at Cockermouth when I was. I was moved & gave her a shilling—I believe 6[d] more than I ought to have given.[1] We had the crescent moon with the "auld moon in her arms."[2] We rested often—always upon the Bridges. Reached home at about 10 o clock.

[THE CIRCUMSTANCES OF "COMPOSED UPON WESTMINISTER BRIDGE"[3]]

[27 July 1802] * * * After various troubles & disasters we left London on Saturday morning at 1/2 past 5 or 6. * * * we mounted the Dover Coach at Charing Cross. It was a beautiful morning. The City, St Pauls, with the River & a multitude of little Boats, made a most beautiful sight as we crossed Westminster Bridge. The houses were not overhung by their cloud of smoke & they were spread out endlessly, yet the sun shone so brightly with such a pure light that there was even something like the purity of one of nature's own grand Spectacles.

[THE CIRCUMSTANCES OF "IT IS A BEAUTEOUS EVENING"[4]]

[1 August 1802] * * * We walked by the sea-shore almost every Evening with Annette & Caroline or Wm & I alone.[5] * * * there was always light, & life, & joy upon the Sea.—One night, though, I shall never forget. The day had been very hot, & William & I walked alone together upon the pier—the sea was gloomy for there was a blackness over all the sky except when it was overspread with lightning which often revealed to us a distant vessel. Near us the waves roared & broke against the pier, & as they broke & as they travelled towards us, they were interfused with greenish fiery light. The more distant sea always black & gloomy. It was also beautiful on the calm hot night to see the little Boats row out of harbour with wings of fire & the sail boats with the fiery track which they cut as they went along & which closed up after

9. Coleridge, whom they met up with on their excursion.

1. Six pence; Dorothy inserted "30 years of age—a child at Cockermouth when I was" to explain the generosity.

2. A line from *Sir Patrick Spence* (see page 392, also quoted by Coleridge in his epigraph for *Dejection: An Ode*.

3. See page 475; they are on their way to Calais, France, sailing from Dover, to settle affairs with Annette Vallon

and her daughter by William, Caroline, prior to William's marriage to Mary Hutchinson in October. The City is Westminster, a district of London where Parliament, Westminster Abbey, and Buckingham Palace are located; St. Paul's is the chief Anglican church. Westminster Bridge crosses the Thames river.

4. See William's sonnet, page 475.

5. Without Annette, that is.

them with a hundred thousand sparkles balls shootings, & streams of glowworm light. Caroline was delighted.

[THE HOUSEHOLD IN WINTER, WITH WILLIAM'S NEW WIFE. GINGERBREAD]

[25 December 1802] * * * It is today Christmas-day Saturday 25th December 1802. I am 31 years of age.—It is a dull frosty day. * * *

   Tuesday January 11th [1803] A very cold day. Wm promised me he would rise as soon as I had carried him his Breakfast but he lay in bed till between 12 & one. We talked of walking, but the blackness of the Cold made us slow to put forward & we did not walk at all. Mary read the Prologue to Chaucer's tales to me, in the morning William was working at his poem to C.[6] Letter from Keswick & from Taylor on Wm's marriage. C poorly, in bad spirits. Canaries.[7] Before tea I sate 2 hours in the parlour— read part of The Knight's Tale with exquisite delight. Since Tea Mary has been down stairs copying out Italian poems for Stuart. Wm has been working beside me, & here ends this imperfect summary. I will take a nice Calais Book[8] & will for the future write regularly &, if I can legibly, so much for this my resolution on Tuesday night, January 11th 1803. Now I am going to take Tapioca for my supper, & Mary an Egg. William some cold mutton—his poor chest is tired.

   Wednesday 12th. Very cold, & cold all the week.

   Sunday the 16th. Intensely cold. Wm had a fancy for some ginger-bread I put on Molly's Cloak & my Spenser,[9] and we walked towards Matthew Newtons.[1] I went into the house. The blind Man & his Wife & Sister were sitting by the fire, all dressed very clean in their Sunday's Clothes, the sister reading. They took their little stock of gingerbread out of the cubboard & I bought 6 pennyworth. They were so grateful when I paid them for it that I could not find it in my heart to tell them we were going to make Gingerbread ourselves. I had asked them if they had no thick "No" answered Matthew "there was none on Friday but we'll endeavour to get some." The next Day the woman came just when we were baking & we bought 2 pennyworth.

LETTERS

To Jane Pollard[1]
[A SCHEME OF HAPPINESS]

16 Feb. 1793

* * * [William] is steady and sincere in his attachments, has both these Virtues in an eminent degree; and a sort of violence of Affection if I may so Term it which demon-strates itself every moment of the Day when the Objects of his affection are present with him, in a thousand almost imperceptible attentions to their wishes, in a sort of restless watchfulness which I know not how to describe, a Tenderness that never sleeps, and at the same Time such a Delicacy of Manners as I have observed in few Men. I hope you will one day be much better acquainted with him than you are at

6. *The Prelude*, known during William's lifetime as *Poem to Coleridge*, his addressee.
7. Canary Islands, where Coleridge hoped to go for his health. *The Knight's Tale* is one of Chaucer's *Canterbury Tales*.
8. A blank notebook purchased in Calais; Dorothy did

not continue her journal.
9. Close-fitting jacket.
1. A gingerbread shop in Grasmere.
1. Close childhood friend. Jane Pollard (1771–1847), later Mrs. John Marshall.

present, much as I have talked to you about him. I look forward with full confidence to the Happiness of receiving you in my little Parsonage,[2] I hope you will spend at least a year with me. I have laid the particular scheme of happiness for each Season. When I think of Winter I hasten to furnish our little Parlour, I close the Shutters, set out the Tea-table, brighten the Fire. When our Refreshment is ended I produce our Work, and William brings his book to our Table and contributes at once to our Instruction and amusement, and at Intervals we lay aside the Book and each hazard our observations upon what has been read without the fear of Ridicule or Censure. We talk over past days, we do not sigh for any Pleasures beyond our humble Habitation "The central point of all our joys."[3] Oh Jane! with such romantic dreams as these I amuse my fancy during many an hour which would otherwise pass heavily along, for kind as are my Uncle and Aunt,[4] much as I love my sweet little Cousins, I cannot help heaving many a Sigh at the Reflection that I have passed one and twenty years of my Life, and that the first six years only of this Time was spent in the Enjoyment of the same Pleasures that were enjoyed by my Brothers, and that I was then too young to be sensible of the Blessing. We have been endeared to each other by early misfortune. We in the same moment lost a father, a mother, a home, we have been equally deprived of our patrimony by the cruel Hand of lordly Tyranny.[5] These afflictions have all contributed to unite us closer by the Bonds of affection notwithstanding we have been compelled to spend our youth far asunder. "We drag at each remove a lengthening Chain"[6] this Idea often strikes me very forcibly. Neither absence nor Distance nor Time can ever break the Chain that links me to my Brothers. * * *

To Lady Beaumont[1]
[A GLOOMY CHRISTMAS]

Grasmere—Christmas day—[and 26 Dec.] 1805

* * * I began this letter yesterday, on Christmas-day, but was interrupted. It is a day of dear and interesting remembrances, and to me peculiarly, therefore I was unwilling to take another sheet of paper for the Date's sake. I yesterday completed my thirty fourth year—a birthday is to every body a time of serious thought, but more so, I should think, when it happens to be upon a day of general festivity, and especially on Christmas-day, when all persons, however widely scattered, are in their thoughts gathered together at home. I can almost tell where every Birthday of my life was spent, many of them even *how* from a very early time. The Day was always kept by my Brothers with rejoicing in my Father's house, but for six years (the interval between my Mother's Death and his) I was never once at home, never was for a single moment under my Father's Roof after her Death, which I cannot think of without regret for many causes, and particularly, that I have been thereby put out of the way of many recollections in common with my Brothers of that period of life, which,

2. Dorothy planned to keep house for William, who intended a career in the Church, before the bequest in 1795 that enabled a career as a poet.
3. William's *Descriptive Sketches* (1793), line 571.
4. She had been living with her uncle William Cookson and his wife in Norfolk, in northeast England, since 1788.
5. Their mother died in 1778, their father in 1783; she had been separated from her brothers since 1778. Their inheritance was tied up in legal wrangling for several years, complicated by a debt owed by Lord Lowther,

whose family did not settle it until 1803.
6. Oliver Goldsmith, *The Traveller, or A Prospect of Society* (1755–1764): "Where'er I roam, whatever realms to see, / My heart untravelled fondly returns to thee; / Still to my brother turns with ceaseless pain, / And drags at each remove a lengthening chain" (7–10).
1. Lady Beaumont (1756–1829), close friend, wife of Sir George Beaumont (1753–1827), who was a painter, patron of the arts, and William's benefactor. Christmas day is Dorothy's birthday.

whatever it may be actually as it goes along, generally appears more delightful than any other when it is over. Poor Coleridge was with us two years ago at this time. He came over with Derwent on his way to London, and was detained week after week by sickness. We hear no further tidings of him, and I cannot help being very uneasy and anxious; though without any evil, many causes might delay him; yet it is a long time since he left Malta.[2] The weather is dreadful for a sea voyage. Oh my dear Friend, what a fearful thing a windy night is now at our house! I am too often haunted with dreadful images of Shipwrecks and the Sea when I am in bed and hear a stormy wind, and now that we are thinking so much about Coleridge it is worse than ever.[3] My Sister[4] is not yet returned, we expect her at home tomorrow if the day be tolerable, but wind rain and snow are driving down the vale, and the chimney every now and then roars as if it were going to come down upon us. I am very anxious that this bois-terous day should be followed by a gentle one (as often happens). I should be exceed-ingly disappointed if My Sister should not come home,—she has stayed much longer than she intended, and is anxious to be with us again, and to see the Children. John[5] is grown very much during her absence, and Dorothy,[6] till within these three days, has been advancing rapidly, but she is now very poorly, having caught cold, and will be quite thrown back again, when her Mother sees her, which is mortifying to me. You are very good in taking so much thought about us. It is true that Miss Hutchin-son[7] will be of great use in assisting us in the care of the Children; not that when we are both well we are over-fatigued with them but, even at a[ll] times it would be better if we had more time for the cultivation of our minds by reading. I do not read much—very little, indeed; but in this house it would be exceedingly unpleasant to have two Servants, not to speak of an *insurmountable* objection, the want of room for another person;[8] but as soon as we can meet with a suitable house in a situation that we like, we are resolved to remove, and by keeping a couple of cows (even if my Sister should have no more children) we shall have sufficient employment for two Servants, and she and I might have much more leisure. I have been summoned into the kitchen to dance with Johnny and have danced till I am out of Breath. Accord-ing to annual custom, our Grasmere Fidler is going his rounds, and all the children of the neighbouring houses are assembled in the kitchen to dance. Johnny has long talked of the time when the Fiddler was to come; but he was too shy to dance with any Body but me, and though he exhibited very boldly when I was down stairs, I find they cannot persuade him to stir again. It is a pleasant sound they make with their little pattering feet upon the stone floor, half a dozen of them, Boys and Girls; Doro-thy is in ecstasy, and John looks as grave as an old Man. I am very glad that you hear so frequently from your Sister. If the Lyrical Ballads do but give her half the plea-sure which you have received from them it will be very gratifying to me. I have no thoughts more soothing than those connected with the hope that my dear Brother and Coleridge may be the means of ministering consolation to the unhappy, or el-evating and worthy thoughts to many who live in solitude or retirement; or have too

2. Derwent is Coleridge's son; Coleridge was spending a year in Malta for his health.

3. Sailor brother John died in a stormy shipwreck the pre-vious February.

4. Sister-in-law, Mary, William's wife since 1802; they all lived together.

5. Johnny, William and Mary's son, born 1803, named for their brother.

6. William and Mary's daughter, born 1804.

7. Sarah, Mary's sister, beloved by Coleridge. See his *Dejection Ode*.

8. Dove Cottage was proving cramped quarters for three adults, two small children, and frequent guests.

much of the bustle of the world without unhappiness. I have transcribed two thirds of the Poem addressed to Coleridge,[9] and am far more than pleased with it as I go along. I often think of the time when William shall have the pleasure of reading it to you and Sir George. He is very anxious to get forward with The Recluse, and is reading for the nourishment of his mind, preparatory to beginning.[1]

To Lady Beaumont

[HER POETRY, WILLIAM'S POETRY]

Grasmere. Saturday afternoon 4 o'clock. April 20th [1806]

* * * I am truly glad that my Brother's manuscript poems give you so much pleasure— I was sure that you would be deeply impressed by the Ode.[1] The last time I read it over, I said: "Lady Beaumont will like this." I long to know your opinion and Sir George's of Benjamin, the Waggoner;[2] I *think* you will be pleased with it, but cannot be so sure of this—And you would persuade *me* that I am capable of writing poems that might give pleasure to others besides my own particular friends!! indeed, indeed you do not know me thoroughly; you think far better of me than I deserve—I must tell you the history of those two little things which William in his fondness read to you.[3] I happened to be writing a letter one evening when he and my Sister were last at Park house,[4] I laid down the pen and thinking of little Johnny (then in bed in the next room) I muttered a few lines of that address to him about the Wind, and having paper before me, wrote them down, and went on till I had finished. The other lines I wrote in the same way, and as William knows every thing that I do, I shewed them to him when he came home, and he was very much pleased; but this I attributed to his partiality; yet because they gave him pleasure and for the sake of the children I ventured to hope that I might do something more at some time or other. Do not think that I was ever bold enough to hope to compose verses for the pleasure of grown persons. Descriptions, Sentiments, or little stories for children was all I could be ambitious of doing, and I did try one story,[5] but failed so sadly that I was completely discouraged. Believe me, since I received your letter I have made several attempts (could I do less as you requested that I would *for your sake?*) and have been obliged to give it up in despair; and looking into my mind I find nothing there, even if I had the gift of language and numbers,[6] that I could have the vanity to suppose could be of any use beyond our own fireside, or to please, as in your case, a few partial friends; but I have no command of language, no power of expressing my ideas, and no one was ever more inapt at molding words into regular metre. I have often tried when I have been walking alone (muttering to myself as is my Brother's custom) to express my feelings in verse; feelings, and *ideas* such as they were, I have never wanted at those times; but prose and rhyme and blank verse were jumbled together and nothing ever came of it. As to those two little things which I did write, I was very unwilling to place them beside my Brother's poems, but he insisted upon it, and I was obliged to submit; and though you have been pleased with them I cannot but think that it was chiefly owing

---

9. The working title of *The Prelude*.
1. A projected long poem on "Man, Nature, and Society," of which only *Home at Grasmere* (unpub.) and *The Excursion* (pub. 1814) were completed.
1. Eventually titled *Ode: Intimations of Immortality.*
2. Published in 1819.

3. *An Address to a Child* and *To My Niece Dorothy, a Sleepless Baby.*
4. The Hutchinsons' home, near Penrith.
5. *Mary Jones and Her Pet Lamb.*
6. Metrical verse.

to the spirit which William gave them in the reading and to your kindness for me. I have said far more than enough on this subject * * *

Believe me affectionately yours, D. Wordsworth.

My Brother has a copy of my Journal of our Scotch Tour[7] which I have desired him to leave with you when it comes from the Bookbinders, but perhaps you may be too much engaged to find time to read it. My Sister begs her kind remembrances. Excuse blunders and scrawling and this torn paper. I have a very inconvenient desk to write upon * * *

To Mrs Thomas Clarkson[1]
[HOUSEHOLD LABORS]

Thursday Evening December 8 [1808]

* * * I will not attempt to detail the height and depth and number of our sorrows in connection with the smoky chimneys. They are in short so very bad that if they cannot be mended we must leave the house,[2] beautiful as everything will soon be out of doors, dear as is the vale where we have so long lived. The labour of the house is literally doubled. Dishes are washed, and no sooner set into the pantry than they are covered with smoke.—Chairs—carpets—the painted ledges of the rooms, all are ready for the reception of soot and smoke, requiring endless cleaning, and are never clean. This is not certainly the worst part of the business, but the smarting of the eyes etc. etc. you may guess at, and I speak of these other discomforts as more immediately connected with myself. In fact we have seldom an hour's leisure (either Mary or I) till after 7 o'clock (when the children go to bed), for all the time that we have for sitting still in the course of the day we are obliged to employ in scouring (and many of our evenings also). We are regularly thirteen in family, and on Saturdays and Sundays 15 (for when Saturday morning is not very stormy Hartley and Derwent[3] come). I include the servants in the number, but as you may judge, in the most convenient house there would be work enough for two maids and a little Girl. In ours there is far too much. We keep a cow—the stable is two short field lengths from the house, and the cook has both to fodder, and clean after the cow. We have also two pigs, bake all our bread at home and though we do not *wash all* our clothes, yet we wash a part every week, and mangle or iron the whole. This is a tedious tale and I should not have troubled you with it but to let you see plainly that idleness has nothing to do with my putting off to write to you. * * * William and Mary (alas! all involved in smoke) in William's study, where she is writing for him (he dictating). He is engaged in a work which occupies all his thoughts. It will be a pamphlet of considerable length, entitled The Convention of Cintra brought to the Test of Principles and the People of England justified from the Charge of Prejudging, or something to that effect.[4] I believe it will first appear in the *Courier* in different sections. Mr De Quincey,[5] whom you would love dearly, as I am sure I do, is beside me, quietly turning over the leaves of a

---

7. With William and Coleridge in late summer 1803.
1. Catherine Clarkson (1772–1856), wife of Thomas Clarkson, the famous abolitionist.
2. Allan Bank, the new residence in Grasmere.
3. Coleridge's sons, both at school nearby.
4. One of many criticisms of the British agreement of August 1808, by which Napoleon's imperialist army, halted by

Spanish resistance and British forces, was given safe passage home from Spain with their booty, in British ships. Many Britons sympathized with the "noble Spaniards."
5. Thomas De Quincey was helping William with the Cintra pamphlet, which appeared in installments in the *Courier*, a daily newspaper, in late 1808 and early 1809, and then as a separate pamphlet later in 1809.

Greek book—and God be praised *we* are breathing a clear air, for the night is calm, and this room (the Dining-room) only smokes very much in a high wind. Mr De Q. will stay with us, we hope, at least till the Spring. We feel often as if he were one of the Family—he is loving, gentle, and happy—a very good scholar, and an acute Logician—so much for his mind and manners. His person is *unfortunately* diminutive, but there is a sweetness in his looks, especially about the eyes, which soon overcomes the oddness of your first feeling at the sight of so very little a Man. John[6] sleeps with him and is passionately fond of him. * * *

Believe me evermore your affectionate D. W.

To Mrs Thomas Clarkson
[A PROSPECT OF PUBLISHING]

Kendal,[1] Sunday 9 Dec. 1810

My dear Friend, * * * I cannot express what pain I feel in refusing to grant any request of yours, and above all one in which dear Mr Clarkson joins so earnestly, but indeed I cannot have that narrative[2] published. My reasons are entirely disconnected with myself, much as I should detest the idea of setting myself up as an Author. I should not object on that score as if it had been an invention of my own it might have been published without a name, and nobody would have thought of me. But on account of the Family of the Greens I cannot consent. Their story was only represented to the world in that narrative which was drawn up for the collecting of the subscription, so far as might tend to produce the end desired, but by publishing this narrative of mine I should bring the children forward to notice as Individuals, and we know not what injurious effect this might have upon them. Besides it appears to me that the events are too recent to be published in delicacy to others as well as to the children. I should be the more hurt at having to return such an answer to your request, if I could believe that the story would be of that service to the work which Mr Clarkson imagines. I cannot believe that it would do much for it. Thirty or forty years hence when the Characters of the children are formed and they can be no longer objects of curiosity, if it should be thought that any service would be done, it is my present wish that it should then be published whether I am alive or dead. * * *

yours affectionately D. W.
I am called to dinner.

To William Johnson[1]
[MOUNTAIN-CLIMBING WITH A WOMAN]

October 21st, 1818.

* * * we all dined together in the romantic Vale of Borrowdale, at the house of a female friend, an unmarried Lady, who, bewitched with the charms of the rocks, and streams, and mountains of that secluded spot, has there built herself a house,

---

6. Nephew Johnny.
1. A town about 20 miles from Grasmere.
2. *A Narrative concerning George and Sarah Green of the Parish of Grasmere* (1808). The Greens perished in a snowstorm, leaving behind six children. The *Narrative* was written to raise funds for the orphans beyond the minimal parish allotment; the hope was to place them with local families and secure them an education. The

narrative circulated to several prominent people, including Scott, Southey, Baillie, De Quincey, and several of the aristocracy. William did publish a poem on the death of the couple, and De Quincey gave his version of the events some decades later in a magazine article and again in *Recollections of the Lakes*.
1. Rev. William Johnson (1784–1864), schoolmaster in Grasmere and later London.

and though she is admirably fitted for society, and has as much enjoyment when surrounded by her friends as any one *can* have, her chearfulness has never flagged, though she has lived more than the year round alone in Borrowdale, at six miles distance from Keswick, with bad roads between.[2] You will guess that she has resources within herself; such indeed she has. She is a painter and labours hard in depicting the beauties of her favorite Vale; she is also fond of music and of reading, and has a reflecting mind; besides (though before she lived in Borrowdale she was no great walker) she is become an active climber of the hills, and I must tell you of a feat that she and I performed on Wednesday the 7th of this month. * * * Miss Barker proposed that * * * she and I should go to Seathwaite beyond the Black lead mines at the head of Borrowdale, and thence up a mountain called at the top *Ash Course* * * * At the top of Ash Course Miss Barker had promised that I should see a magnificent prospect; but we had some miles to travel to the foot of the mountain, and accordingly went thither in a cart—Miss Barker, her maid, and myself. We departed before nine o' clock, the sun shone; the sky was clear and blue; and light and shade fell in masses upon the mountains; the fields below *glittered* with the dew, where the beams of the sun could reach them; and every little stream tumbling down the hills seemed to add to the chearfulness of the scene.

    We left our cart at Seathwaite and proceeded, with a man to carry our provisions, and a kind neighbour of Miss Barker's, a statesman shepherd of the vale, as our companion and guide. We found ourselves at the top of Ash Course without a weary limb, having had the fresh air of autumn to help us up by its invigorating power, and the sweet warmth of the unclouded sun to tempt us to sit and rest by the way. From the top of Ash Course we beheld a prospect which would indeed have amply repaid us for a *toilsome* journey, if such it had been; and a sense of thankfulness for the continuance of that vigour of body, which enabled me to climb the high mountain, as in the days of my youth, inspiring me with fresh chearfulness, added a delight, a charm to the contemplation of the magnificent scenes before me, which I cannot describe.

    * * * We had attained the object of our journey; but our ambition mounted higher. We saw the summit of Scaw Fell, as it seemed, very near to us; we were indeed, three parts up that mountain, and thither we determined to go. We found the distance greater than it had appeared to us, but our courage did not fail; however, when we came nearer we perceived that in order to attain that summit we must make a great dip, and that the ascent afterwards would be exceedingly steep and difficult, so that we might have been benighted if we had attempted it; therefore, unwillingly, we gave it up, and resolved, instead, to ascend another point of the same mountain, called *the Pikes*, and which, I have since found, the measurers of the mountains estimate as higher than the larger summit which bears the name of Scaw Fell, and where the Stone Man is built which we, at the time, considered as the point of highest honour. The sun had never once been overshadowed by a cloud during the whole of our progress from the centre of Borrowdale; at the summit of the Pike there was not a breath of air to stir even the papers which we spread out containing our food. There we ate our dinner in summer warmth; and the stillness seemed to be not of this world. We paused, and kept silence to listen, and not a sound of any kind was

2. Borrowdale and Keswick are at opposite ends of Derwentwater in the Lake District.

to be heard. We were far above the reach of the cataracts of Scaw Fell; and not an insect was there to hum in the air. The Vales before described lay in view, and side by side with Eskdale, we now saw the sister Vale of Donnerdale terminated by the Duddon Sands. But the majesty of the mountains below and close to us, is not to be conceived. We now beheld the whole mass of Great Gavel from its base, the Den of Wasdale at our feet, the gulph immeasurable, Grasmere and the other mountains of Crummock, Ennerdale and *its* mountains, and the sea beyond.

While we were looking round after dinner our Guide said that we must not linger long, for we should have a storm. We looked in vain to espy the traces of it; for mountains, vales, and the sea were all touched with the clear light of the sun. "It is there," he said, pointing to the sea beyond Whitehaven, and, sure enough, we there perceived a light cloud, or mist, unnoticeable but by a shepherd, accustomed to watch all mountain bodings. We gazed around again and yet again, fearful to lose the remembrance of what lay before us in that lofty solitude; and then prepared to depart. Meanwhile the air changed to cold, and we saw the tiny vapour swelled into mighty masses of cloud which came boiling over the mountains. Great Gavel, Helvellyn, and Skiddaw were wrapped in storm; yet Langdale and the mountains in that quarter were all bright with sunshine. Soon the storm reached us; we sheltered under a crag, and almost as rapidly as it had come, it passed away, and left us free to observe the goings-on of storm and sunshine in other quarters—Langdale had now its share, and the Pikes were decorated by two splendid rainbows; Skiddaw also had its own rainbows, but we were glad to see them and the clouds disappear from that mountain. ∗∗∗ we, indeed, were hardly at all wetted; and before we found ourselves again upon that part of the mountain called Ash Course every cloud had vanished from every summit.

Do not think we here gave up our spirit of enterprise. No! I had heard much of the grandeur of the view of Wasdale from Stye Head, the point from which Wasdale is first seen in coming by the road from Borrowdale; but though I had been in Wasdale I had never entered the dale by that road, and had often lamented that I had not seen what was so much talked of by travellers. Down to that Pass (for we were yet far above it) we bent our course by the side of Ruddle Gill, a very deep red chasm in the mountains which begins at a spring—that spring forms a stream, which must, at times, be a mighty torrent, as is evident from the channel which it has wrought out—thence by Sprinkling Tarn to Stye Head; and there we sate and looked down into Wasdale. We were now upon Great Gavel which rose high above us. Opposite was Scaw Fell and we heard the roaring of the stream from one of the ravines of that mountain, which, though the bending of Wasdale Head lay between us and Scaw Fell, we could look into, as it were, and the depth of the ravine appeared tremendous; it was black and the crags were awful.

We now proceeded homewards by Stye head Tarn along the road into Borrowdale. Before we reached Stonethwaite a few stars had appeared, and we travelled home in our cart by moonlight.

I ought to have described the last part of our ascent to Scaw Fell Pike. There, not a blade of grass was to be seen—hardly a cushion of moss, and that was parched and brown; and only growing rarely between the huge blocks and stones which cover the summit and lie in heaps all round to a great distance, like skeletons or bones of the earth not wanted at the creation, and there left to be covered with never-dying lichens, which the clouds and dews nourish; and adorn with colours of the most vivid and exquisite beauty, and endless in variety. No gems or flowers can surpass in colouring the beauty of some of these masses of stone which no human eye beholds except the shepherd led thither by chance or traveller by curiosity; and how seldom must this happen! The other eminence is that which is visited by the adventurous traveller, and the shepherd has no temptation to go thither in quest of his sheep; for on the Pike there is no food to tempt them. We certainly were singularly fortunate in the day; for when we were seated on the summit our Guide, turning his eyes thoughtfully round, said to us, "I do not know that in my whole life I was ever at any season of the year so high up on the mountains on so calm a day." Afterwards, you know, we had the storm which exhibited to us the grandeur of earth and heaven commingled, yet without terror; for we knew that the storm would pass away; for so our prophetic guide assured us. I forget to tell you that I espied a ship upon the glittering sea while we were looking over Eskdale. "Is it a ship?" replied the Guide. "A ship, yes, it can be nothing else, don't you see the shape of it?" Miss Barker interposed, "It is a ship, of that I am certain. I cannot be mistaken, I am so accustomed to the appearance of ships at sea." The Guide dropped the argument; but a moment was scarce gone when he quietly said, "Now look at your ship, it is now a horse." So indeed it was—a horse with a gallant neck and head. We laughed heartily, and, I hope when again inclined to positiveness, I may remember the ship and the horse upon the glittering sea; and the calm confidence, yet submissiveness, of our wise Man of the Mountains, who certainly had more knowledge of clouds than we, whatever might be our knowledge of ships. To add to our uncommon performance on that day Miss Barker and I each wrote a letter from the top of the Pike to our far distant friend in S. Wales, Miss Hutchinson. I believe that you are not much acquainted with the Scenery of this Country, except in the Neighbourhood of Grasmere, your duties when you were a resident here, having confined you so much to that one Vale; I hope, however, that my long story will not be very dull; and even I am not without a further hope, that it may awaken in you a desire to spend a long holiday among the mountains, and explore their recesses.

RESPONSES

Samuel Taylor Coleridge: from *A letter to Joseph Cottle,*[1]

c. 3 July 1797

Wordsworth & his exquisite Sister are with me—She is a woman indeed!—in mind, I mean, & heart—for her person is such, that if you expected to see a pretty woman, you would think her ordinary—if you expected to find an ordinary woman, you would think her pretty!—But her manners are simple, ardent, impressive—.

1. Friend and patron of William Wordsworth and Coleridge, this Bristol bookseller published Coleridge's poems in 1796 and *Lyrical Ballads* in 1798.

> In every motion her most innocent soul
> Outbeams so brightly, that who saw would say,
> Guilt was a thing impossible in her.[2]

Her information various—her eye watchful in minutest observation of nature—and her taste a perfect electrometer—it bends, protrudes, and draws in, at subtlest beauties & most recondite faults.

Thomas De Quincey: from Recollections of the Lake Poets[1]

Immediately behind [William's wife] moved a lady, shorter, slighter, and perhaps, in all other respects, as different from her in personal characteristics as could have been wished for the most effective contrast. "Her face was of Egyptian brown";[2] rarely, in a woman of English birth, had I seen a more determinate gipsy tan. Her eyes were not soft, as Mrs. Wordsworth's, nor were they fierce or bold; but they were wild and startling,[3] and hurried in their motion. Her manner was warm and even ardent; her sensibility seemed constitutionally deep; and some subtle fire of impassioned intellect apparently burned within her, which, being alternately pushed forward into a conspicuous expression by the irrepressible instincts of her temperament, and then immediately checked, in obedience to the decorum of her sex and age, and her maidenly condition (for she had rejected all offers of marriage, out of pure sisterly regard to her brother and his children,) gave to her whole demeanour, and to her conversation, an air of embarrassment, and even of self-conflict, that was almost distressing to witness. Even her very utterance and enunciation often suffered, in point of clearness and steadiness, from the agitation of her excessive organic sensibility. At times, the self-counteraction and self-baffling of her feelings caused her even to stammer, and so determinately to stammer that a stranger who should have seen her and quitted her in that state of feeling would have certainly set her down for one plagued with that infirmity of speech as distressingly as Charles Lamb himself. This was Miss Wordsworth, the only sister of the poet—his "Dorothy"; who naturally owed so much to the life-long intercourse[4] with her great brother in his most solitary and sequestered years; but, on the other hand, to whom he has acknowledged obligations of the profoundest nature; and, in particular, this mighty one, through which we also, the admirers and the worshippers of this great poet, are become equally her debtors—that, whereas the intellect of Wordsworth was, by its original tendency, too stern, too austere, too much enamoured of an ascetic harsh sublimity, she it was—the lady who paced by his side continually through sylvan and mountain tracks, in Highland glens, and in the dim recesses of German charcoal-burners—that first *couched* his eye to the sense of beauty, humanized him by the gentler charities, and engrafted, with her delicate female touch, those graces upon the ruder growths of his nature which have since clothed the forest of his genius with a foliage corresponding in loveliness and beauty to the strength of its boughs and the massiness of its trunks. The greatest deductions from Miss

---

2. A description of Joan of Arc, eventually published as lines 173–75 of *The Destiny of Nations* (1817).
1. Originally, an essay in *Tait's Edinburgh Magazine* in 1839.

2. A description of a beggar-woman in William Wordsworth's *The Beggars* (1807).
3. Cf. *Tintern Abbey*, lines 119–20.
4. Domestic and social interaction.

Wordsworth's attractions, and from the exceeding interest which surrounded her in right of her character, of her history, and of the relation which she fulfilled towards her brother, were the glancing quickness of her motions, and other circumstances in her deportment (such as her stooping attitude when walking), which gave an ungraceful, and even an unsexual character to her appearance when out-of-doors. She did not cultivate the graces which preside over the person and its carriage. But, on the other hand, she was a person of very remarkable endowments intellectually; and, in addition to the other great services which she rendered to her brother, this I may mention, as greater than all the rest, and it was one which equally operated to the benefit of every casual companion in a walk—viz. the exceeding sympathy, always ready and always profound, by which she made all that one could tell her, all that one could describe, all that one could quote from a foreign author, reverberate, as it were, *à plusieurs reprises* [in several returns], to one's own feelings, by the manifest impression it made upon *hers*. The pulses of light are not more quick or more inevitable in their flow and undulation, than were the answering and echoing movements of her sympathizing attention. Her knowledge of literature was irregular, and thoroughly unsystematic. She was content to be ignorant of many things; but what she knew and had really mastered lay where it could not be disturbed—in the temple of her own most fervid heart. * * *

    A much larger number of voices would proclaim her to have been unfortunate in life because she made no marriage connexion; and certainly, the insipid as well as unfeeling ridicule which descends so plentifully upon those women who, perhaps from strength of character, have refused to make such a connexion where it promised little of elevated happiness, *does* make the state of singleness somewhat of a trial to the patience of many; and to many the vexation of this trial has proved a snare for beguiling them of their honourable resolutions. Meantime, as the opportunities are rare in which all the conditions concur for happy marriage connexions, how important it is that the dignity of high-minded women should be upheld by society in the honourable election they make of a self-dependent virgin seclusion, by preference to a heartless marriage! Such women, as Mrs Trollope[5] justly remarks, fill a place in society which in their default would *not* be filled, and are available for duties requiring a tenderness and a punctuality that could not be looked for from women preoccupied with household or maternal claims. If there were no regular fund (so to speak) of women free from conjugal and maternal duties, upon what body could we draw for our "sisters of mercy," &c.? In another point Mrs Trollope is probably right: few women live unmarried from necessity. Miss Wordsworth had several offers; amongst them, to my knowledge, one from Hazlitt;[6] all of them she rejected decisively. And she did right. A happier life, by far, was hers in youth. * * * Miss Wordsworth was too ardent and fiery a creature to maintain the reserve essential to dignity; and dignity was the last thing one thought of in the presence of one so natural, so fervent in her feelings, and so embarrassed in their utterance—sometimes, also, in the attempt to check them. It

5. Novelist Anthony Trollope's mother Frances (1780–1863), also a well-known writer.
6. William Hazlitt; the proposal is probably a fantasy. De

Quincey himself had been regarded as a possible match for Dorothy Wordsworth when he first became part of their circle, in 1807.

must not, however, be supposed that there was any silliness or weakness of enthusiasm about her. She was under the continual restraint of severe good sense, though liberated from that false shame which, in so many persons, accompanies all expressions of natural emotion; and she had too long enjoyed the ennobling conversation of her brother, and his admirable comments on the poets, which they read in common, to fail in any essential point of logic or propriety of thought. Accordingly, her letters, though the most careless and unelaborate—nay, the most hurried that can be imagined—are models of good sense and just feeling. In short, beyond any person I have known in this world, Miss Wordsworth was the creature of impulse; but, as a woman most thoroughly virtuous and well-principled, as one who could not fail to be kept right by her own excellent heart, and as an intellectual creature from her cradle, with much of her illustrious brother's peculiarity of mind— finally, as one who had been, in effect, educated and trained by that very brother— she won the sympathy and the respectful regard of every man worthy to approach her. * * * Properly, and in a spirit of prophecy, was she named *Dorothy*; in its Greek meaning, *gift of God*, well did this name prefigure the relation in which she stood to Wordsworth, the mission with which she was charged—to wait upon him as the tenderest and most faithful of domestics; to love him as a sister; to sympathize with him as a confidante; to counsel him; to cheer him and sustain him by the natural expression of her feelings—so quick, so ardent, so unaffected—upon the probable effect of whatever thoughts or images he might conceive; finally, and above all other ministrations, to ingraft, by her sexual[7] sense of beauty, upon his masculine austerity that delicacy and those graces which else (according to the grateful acknowledgments of his own maturest retrospect) it never could have. * * * I may sum up in one brief abstract the amount of Miss Wordsworth's character, as a companion, by saying, that she was the very wildest (in the sense of the most natural) person I have ever known; and also the truest, most inevitable, and at the same time the quickest and readiest in her sympathy with either joy or sorrow, with laughter or with tears, with the realities of life or the larger realities of the poets!

Meantime, amidst all this fascinating furniture of her mind, won from nature, from solitude, from enlightened companionship, Miss Wordsworth was as thoroughly deficient (some would say painfully deficient—I say charmingly deficient) in ordinary female accomplishments.[8] * * * But the case in which the irregularity of Miss Wordsworth's education *did* astonish one was in that part which respected her literary knowledge. In whatever she read, or neglected to read, she had obeyed the single impulse of her own heart; where that led her, *there* she followed: where that was mute or indifferent, not a thought had she to bestow upon a writer's high reputation, or the call for some acquaintance with his works to meet the demands of society. And thus the strange anomaly arose, of a woman deeply acquainted with some great authors, whose works lie pretty much out of the fashionable beat; able, moreover, in her own person, to produce brilliant effects; able on some subjects to write delightfully, and

---

7. Essentially feminine.

8. Singing, sketching, dancing, piano-playing, flower-arranging. Recall Wollstonecraft's critique (page 302).

with the impress of originality upon all she uttered; and yet ignorant of great classical works in her own mother tongue, and careless of literary history in a degree which at once exiled her from the rank and privileges of *bluestockingism*.[9] * * *

But the point in which Miss Wordsworth made the most ample amends for all that she wanted of more customary accomplishments, was this very originality and native freshness of intellect, which settled with so bewitching an effect upon some of her writings, and upon many a sudden remark or ejaculation, extorted by something or other that struck her eye, in the clouds, or in colouring, or in accidents of light and shade, of form or combination of form. To talk of her "writings" is too pompous an expression, or at least far beyond any pretensions that she ever made for herself. Of poetry she has written little indeed; and that little not, in my opinion, of much merit. The verses published by her brother, and beginning, "Which way does the wind come?"[1] meant only as nursery lines, are certainly wild and pretty; but the other specimen is likely to strike most readers as feeble and trivial in the sentiment. Meantime, the book which is in very deed a monument to her power of catching and expressing all the hidden beauties of natural scenery, with a felicity of diction, a truth and strength, that far transcend Gilpin, or professional writers on those subjects, is her record of a *first* tour in Scotland, made about the year 1802.[2] * * * I here notice a defect in Miss Wordsworth's self-education of something that might have mitigated the sort of suffering which, more or less, ever since the period of her too genial, too radiant youth, I suppose her to have struggled with. I have mentioned the narrow basis on which her literary interests had been made to rest—the exclusive character of her reading, and the utter want of pretension, and of all that looks like *bluestockingism*, in the style of her habitual conversation and mode of dealing with literature. Now, to me it appears, upon reflection, that it would have been far better had Miss Wordsworth condescended a little to the ordinary mode of pursuing literature; better for her own happiness if she *had* been a bluestocking; or, at least, if she had been, in good earnest, a writer for the press, with the pleasant cares and solicitudes of one who has some little ventures, as it were, on that vast ocean.

We all know with how womanly and serene a temper literature has been pursued by Joanna Baillie, by Miss Mitford,[3] and other women of admirable genius—with how absolutely no sacrifice or loss of feminine dignity they have cultivated the profession of authorship * * * Had that been opened for Miss Wordsworth, I am satisfied that she would have passed a more cheerful middle-age, and would not, at any period, have yielded to that nervous depression (or is it, perhaps, nervous irritation?) which, I grieve to hear, has clouded her latter days.

9. By the mid-19th century, a disparaging term for learned and literary women, who, unlike De Quincey and William Wordsworth, had no access to university education.
1. *Address to a Child*.
2. In 1803, with Coleridge and her brother; see the post-

script to Lady Beaumont, 20 April 1806 (page 615). Dorothy's "Recollections" of this tour were shared with family and friends, but despite their encouragement, she would not publish her notebook. For Gilpin, see page 47.
3. Mary Russell Mitford (1787–1855), poet, playwright, essayist, friend of Joanna Baillie and Felicia Hemans.

Samuel Taylor Coleridge
1772–1834

"Come back into memory, like as thou wert in the dayspring of thy fancies, with hope like a fiery column before thee—the dark pillar not yet turned—Samuel Taylor Coleridge—Logician, Metaphysician, Bard!—How have I seen the casual passer through the cloisters stand still, entranced with admiration . . . while the walls of the old Grey Friars re-echoed to the accents of the *inspired charity-boy!*" When Charles Lamb thus memorialized his former schoolfellow, Coleridge had more than a decade yet to live, but he had already made himself into the mythic Romantic figure of promise and failure whom Lamb salutes.

Born in 1772, the last child of the vicar of Ottery St. Mary's in Devon, Coleridge developed a reputation for precocity even before the death of his father led to his enrollment at Christ's Hospital, a London boarding school for the sons of distressed families, where Lamb met him. A brilliant career at Jesus College, Cambridge, ended in an unhappy attempt to enlist in the army under an assumed name, and he left without a degree in 1794. With Robert Southey, a fellow Oxford enthusiast for poetry and radical politics, he planned an ideal democratic community on the banks of the Susquehanna in Pennsylvania, to be named "Pantisocracy," or equal rule by all. The project collapsed over a dispute whether they would have servants, but not before Coleridge had cemented the social bonds by becoming engaged to Sara Fricker, the sister of Southey's fiancee; the marriage proved unhappy. Coleridge later minimized his youthful "squeaking baby-trumpet of sedition," but he founded a short-lived antigovernment periodical, *The Watchman* (1796); to earn a living, he was pointing in the unorthodox direction of the Unitarian ministry until he was relieved by a moderate annuity of £150 from the Wedgwoods, of the famous pottery firm. In 1796 he published *Poems on Various Subjects,* containing the poem later titled *The Eolian Harp,* and in 1797 he began the collaboration with Wordsworth that produced *Lyrical Ballads* (1798), headed by *The Rime of the Ancyent Marinere,* as the poem was called in its archaizing first version. Before the volume was published, Coleridge and the Wordsworths departed for Germany, where Coleridge studied philosophy at Göttingen. Charges of plagiarism have swirled ever since around the readings of Kant, Schiller, Schelling, and Fichte that animated his lifelong effort to combat what he regarded as the spiritless mechanical world of eighteenth-century British empiricism.

In 1800 Coleridge followed the Wordsworths to the Lake District, where his love for Sara Hutchinson, sister of Wordsworth's future wife, sharpened his estrangement from his own wife. He became addicted to laudanum (opium dissolved in alcohol), a standard medical remedy for the rheumatic pains he suffered, but the stomach disorders it produced increased his dependency. The physiology of addiction was not understood in his day, and what was a widespread social phenomenon Coleridge regarded as a personal moral flaw. His inability to break the habit produced a spiral of depression: guilt, a paralytic doubt of his strength of will, the fear that he was unworthy of love. By 1802, in *Dejection: An Ode,* he declared the failure of his "genial spirits" and "shaping spirit of Imagination," but he carried on an active public career. An important political commentator in the newspapers, he also undertook another periodical, *The Friend* (1809–1810), saw his play *Remorse* succeed at Drury Lane (1813), and gave a series of brilliant lectures on Shakespeare, Milton, poetry, drama, and philosophy (1808–1818). That these enterprises often fell short of the triumphant fullness he forecast for them fixed the myth of promise unfulfilled, even as his accomplishments won increasing influence. From 1816 on, he lived in a London suburb under the care of a young doctor, James Gillman, and he flourished in this stable environment. The fabled talk of the "Sage of Highgate," as Carlyle called him, "had a charm much more than literary, a charm almost religious and prophetic." If the "practical intellects of the world did not much heed him," Carlyle continued, "to the rising spirits of the young generation he had this dusky sublime character; and sat there as a kind of *Magus*." Coleridge became, in the judgment of John Stuart Mill, one of the two seminal minds of the nineteenth century, the idealist, Christian, philosopher of organic unity around whose work the opposition to Benthamite utilitarianism crystalized.

In his final decades, Coleridge joined new work and old into a substantial body of publication. *Christabel*, long known by reputation, appeared with Byron's enthusiastic sponsorship, in 1816, together with *Kubla Khan*. 1817 brought *Sibylline Leaves* (Coleridge's collected poems, including the marginal-gloss version of the lyrical ballad now titled *The Rime of the Ancient Mariner*) and *Biographia Literaria*, the account of his "literary life and opinions" that has provided the starting-point for much twentieth-century literary criticism. In a series of works, Coleridge explicated conservative principles continuous with but far evolved from the Jacobin associations that had led him to urge anonymous publication of the *Lyrical Ballads* because "Wordsworth's name is nothing, and mine stinks": two *Lay Sermons* (1816–1817), articulating his views in the debate over reform; *The Friend*, expanded in 1818 into a three-volume collection of essays on "politics, morals, and religion"; *Aids to Reflection* (1825), emphasizing Christianity as "personal revelation"; and *On the Constitution of Church and State* (1830), outlining conceptions of national culture (and the "clerisy" responsible for preserving it) that resonate throughout the Victorian period. *Table Talk* (1836) posthumously captured the echoes of his voice, and Coleridge has enjoyed a resurrection in our own day. As new scholarly editions bring more writings to light, they deepen the fascination of a man who was the author of some of the most suggestive poems in the language and an erudite philosopher, a poet who in the *Biographia Literaria* transformed the role of the critic, a theorist of the unifying imagination whose works and life are marked by fragments and discontinuities, a believer in the unity of all whose own method has been aptly described as marginal glosses on the works of others, and an idealist engaged with the daily politics of a turbulent era.

For Coleridge's ode to Wordsworth, *To a Gentleman*, see page 542.

SONNET TO THE RIVER OTTER[1]

Dear native Brook! wild Streamlet of the West!
  How many various-fated years have past,
    What happy, and what mournful hours, since last
I skimm'd the smooth thin stone along thy breast,
5   Numbering its light leaps! yet so deep impresst
Sink the sweet scenes of childhood, that mine eyes
  I never shut amid the sunny ray,
But strait with all their tints their waters rise,
  Thy crossing plank, thy marge with willows grey,
10 And bedded sand that vein'd with various dyes
Gleam'd through thy bright transparence! On my way,
    Visions of childhood! oft have ye beguiled
Lone manhood's cares, yet waking fondest sighs.
    Ah! that I were once more a careless child!

c. 1796   1797/1817

---

1. In Devon, where Coleridge grew up. His father was the vicar of nearby Ottery St. Mary's.

∽∾

COMPANION READING

William Lisle Bowles: *To the River Itchin, Near Winton*[1]

Itchin, when I behold thy banks again,
    Thy crumbling margin, and thy silver breast
    On which the self-same tints still seem to rest,
Why feels my heart the shiv'ring sense of pain?
5   Is it that many a summer's day has passed
Since in life's morn I carolled on thy side?
Is it that oft since then my heart has sighed
    As youth, and hope's delusive gleams, flew fast?
Is it that those who circled on thy shore,
10 Companions of my youth, now meet no more?
    Whate'er the cause, upon thy banks I bend
Sorrowing, yet feel such solace at my heart,
    As at the meeting of some long-lost friend
    From whom, in happier hours, we wept to part.

c. 1789   1789

∽∾

The Eolian Harp[1]

Composed at Clevedon, Somersetshire

My pensive Sara![2] thy soft cheek reclined
Thus on mine arm, most soothing sweet it is
To sit beside our cot,° our cot o'ergrown   *cottage*
With white-flower'd Jasmin, and the broad-leave'd Myrtle,
5 (Meet° emblems they of Innocence and Love!)   *fit*
And watch the clouds, that late were rich with light,
Slow sad'ning round, and mark the star of eve°   *Venus*
Serenely brilliant (such should wisdom be)
Shine opposite! How exquisite the scents
10 Snatch'd from yon bean-field! and the world so hush'd!
The stilly murmur of the distant Sea
Tells us of Silence.
                 And that simplest Lute,
Placed length-ways in the clasping casement, hark!
How by the desultory breeze caress'd,

---

1. Bowles (1762–1850), most famous for his *Fourteen Sonnets* (1789), was greatly admired by Coleridge, Lamb, and Southey, but not by Byron, who once called him "the Maudlin prince of mournful sonneteers." Coleridge read Bowles's sonnet in school, and wrote his sonnet in imitation. But where for Bowles, the visit to the river is just a stimulus to memory and sorrow, for Coleridge the river becomes the source of metaphors for memory informed by manhood's cares.

1. Named for Aeolus, god of winds, the harp consisted of a guitarlike box, set in an open window where the breeze would cause its strings to sound. Originally titled *Effusion.xxxv. / Composed August 20th, 1795, at Clevedon, Somersetshire.* This poem was first published in 1796; we print the text of 1817.
2. Formerly Sara Fricker; the poem was composed on their honeymoon.

15   Like some coy maid half yielding to her lover,
    It pours such sweet upbraidings,° as must needs   *reproaches*
    Tempt to repeat the wrong! And now, its strings
    Boldlier swept, the long sequacious notes
    Over delicious surges sink and rise,
20   Such a soft floating witchery of sound
    As twilight Elfins make, when they at eve
    Voyage on gentle gales from Fairy-Land,
    Where Melodies round honey-dropping flowers,
    Footless and wild, like birds of Paradise,[3]
25   Nor pause, nor perch, hovering on untamed wing!
    O! the one Life, within us and abroad,
    Which meets all Motion, and becomes its soul,
    A Light in Sound, a sound-like power in Light,
    Rhythm in all Thought, and Joyance every where—
30   Methinks, it should have been impossible
    Not to love all things in a world so fill'd,
    Where the breeze warbles and the mute still Air
    Is Music slumbering on its instrument.[4]

       And thus, my love! as on the midway slope
35   Of yonder hill I stretch my limbs at noon,
    Whilst thro' my half-closed eye-lids I behold
    The sunbeams dance, like diamonds, on the main,
    And tranquil muse upon tranquillity;
    Full many a thought uncall'd and undetain'd,
40   And many idle flitting phantasies,
    Traverse my indolent and passive brain,
    As wild and various as the random gales
    That swell and flutter on this subject lute!

       And what if all of animated nature
45   Be but organic harps diversely fram'd,
    That tremble into thought, as o'er them sweeps
    Plastic° and vast, one intellectual breeze,   *creatively shaping*
    At once the Soul of each, and God of All?

       But thy more serious eye a mild reproof
50   Darts, O beloved woman! nor such thoughts
    Dim and unhallow'd dost thou not reject,
    And biddest me walk humbly with my God.
    Meek daughter in the family of Christ!
    Well hast thou said and holily disprais'd
55   These shapings of the unregenerate° mind,   *sinful*
    Bubbles that glitter as they rise and break
    On vain Philosophy's aye°-babbling spring.   *ever*

---

3. Tropical birds famed for colorful plumage.
4. Lines 26–34 were added in 1817, on a corrections page

at the front of the volume, marked for insertion here;
"Its" (33) was later revised to "her."

For never guiltless may I speak of him,
Th' Incomprehensible! save when with awe
60   I praise him, and with Faith that inly feels;
Who with his saving mercies healed me,
A sinful and most miserable Man,
Wilder'd and dark, and gave me to possess
Peace, and this Cot, and Thee, heart-honour'd Maid!

1795–1817   1817

THIS LIME-TREE BOWER MY PRISON[1]

ADVERTISEMENT

In the June of 1797, some long-expected Friends paid a visit
to the Author's Cottage; and on the morning of their arrival, he met
with an accident, which disabled him from walking during the whole
time of their stay. One Evening, when they had left him for a few
hours, he composed the following lines in the Garden-Bower.

Well, they are gone, and here must I remain,
This Lime-Tree Bower my Prison! I have lost
Such beauties and such feelings, as had been
Most sweet to my remembrance even when age
5   Had dimmed mine eyes to blindness! They, meanwhile,
My Friends, whom I may never meet again,
On springy heath, along the hill-top edge,
Wander in gladness, and wind down, perchance,
To that still roaring dell, of which I told;
10   The roaring dell, o'erwooded, narrow, deep,
And only speckled by the mid-day Sun;
Where its slim trunk the Ash from rock to rock
Flings arching like a Bridge;—that branchless Ash,
Unsunn'd and damp, whose few poor yellow leaves
15   Ne'er tremble in the gale, yet tremble still,
Fann'd by the water-fall! and there my friends
Behold the dark green file of long lank Weeds,
That all at once (a most fantastic sight!)
Still nod and drip beneath the dripping edge
20   Of the blue clay-stone.

            Now, my Friends emerge
Beneath the wide wide Heaven—and view again
The many-steepled track magnificent
Of hilly fields and meadows, and the sea,

---

1. The title of the first publication (*Annual Anthology*, 1800) added "A Poem Addressed to Charles Lamb, of the India-House, London." Lamb was a clerk in the East India Company's London office. The headnote was added in 1834.

With some fair bark,° perhaps, whose Sails light up   *small boat*
25   The slip of smooth clear blue betwixt two Isles
Of purple shadow! Yes! they wander on
In gladness all; but thou, methinks, most glad,
My gentle-hearted Charles! for thou hast pined
And hunger'd after Nature, many a year,
30   In the great City pent,[2] winning thy way
With sad yet patient soul, through evil and pain
And strange calamity![3] Ah! slowly sink
Behind the western ridge, thou glorious Sun!
Shine in the slant beams of the sinking orb
35   Ye purple heath-flowers! richlier burn, ye clouds!
Live in the yellow light, ye distant groves!
And kindle, thou blue Ocean! So my Friend
Struck with deep joy may stand, as I have stood,[4]
Silent with swimming sense; yea, gazing round
40   On the wide landscape, gaze till all doth seem
Less gross than bodily;° and of such hues   *less than bodied*
As cloath[5] the Almighty Spirit, when yet he makes
Spirits perceive his presence.
                    A delight
Comes sudden on my heart, and I am glad
45   As I myself were there! Nor in this bower,
This little lime-tree bower, have I not mark'd
Much that has sooth'd me. Pale beneath the blaze
Hung the transparent foliage; and I watch'd
Some broad and sunny leaf, and lov'd to see
50   The shadow of the leaf and stem above
Dappling its sunshine! And that Walnut-tree
Was richly ting'd, and a deep radiance lay
Full on the ancient Ivy, which usurps
Those fronting elms, and now, with blackest mass
55   Makes their dark branches gleam a lighter hue
Through the late twilight: and though now the Bat
Wheels silent by, and not a Swallow twitters,
Yet still the solitary humble Bee
Sings in the bean-flower! Henceforth I shall know
60   That Nature ne'er deserts the wise and pure,
No Plot so narrow, be but Nature there,
No waste so vacant, but may well employ
Each faculty of sense, and keep the heart
Awake to Love and Beauty! and sometimes
65   'Tis well to be bereft of promised good,
That we may lift the Soul, and contemplate

---

2. "City pent" alludes to Milton's analogy for Hell's city in *Paradise Lost* (9.445).
3. The fit of insanity in which Mary Lamb, Charles's sister, killed their mother the year before.

4. Coleridge signed this poem "ESTESSI"—an English transliteration, pronounced "S-T-C," of the Greek letters spelling "He hath stood."
5. Later, "veil."

With lively joy the joys we can not share.
My gentle-hearted Charles! when the last Rook
Beat its straight path along the dusky air
70   Homewards, I blest it! deeming, its black wing
(Now a dim speck, now vanishing in light)
Had cross'd the mighty Orb's dilated glory,
While thou stood'st gazing; or when all was still,
Flew creeking o'er thy head, and had a charm
75   For thee, my gentle-hearted Charles, to whom
No Sound is dissonant which tells of Life.

1797/1800   1800/1817

Frost at Midnight

The frost performs its secret ministry,
Unhelped by any wind. The owlet's cry
Came loud—and hark, again! loud as before.
The inmates of my cottage, all at rest,
5   Have left me to that solitude, which suits
Abstruser musings: save that at my side
My cradled infant° slumbers peacefully.   *son Hartley*
'Tis calm indeed! so calm, that it disturbs
And vexes meditation with its strange
10   And extreme silentness. Sea, hill, and wood,
This populous village!° Sea, and hill, and wood,   *Nether Stowey*
With all the numberless goings on of life,
Inaudible as dreams! the thin blue flame
Lies on my low burnt fire, and quivers not;
15   Only that film,[1] which fluttered on the grate,
Still flutters there, the sole unquiet thing.
Methinks, its motion in this hush of nature
Gives it dim sympathies with me who live,
Making it a companionable form,
20   Whose puny flaps and freaks the idling Spirit
By its own moods interprets, everywhere
Echo or mirror seeking of itself,
And makes a toy of Thought.

                                        But O! how oft,
How oft, at school, with most believing mind,
25   Presageful, have I gazed upon the bars,
To watch that fluttering stranger! and as oft
With unclosed lids, already had I dreamt
Of my sweet birth-place, and the old church-tower,
Whose bells, the poor man's only music, rang
30   From morn to evening, all the hot Fair-day,

---

1. A piece of soot. "In all parts of the kingdom these films are called *strangers* and supposed to portend the arrival of some absent friend" [Coleridge's note, 1798].

So sweetly, that they stirred and haunted me
With a wild pleasure, falling on mine ear
Most like articulate sounds of things to come!
So gazed I, till the soothing things I dreamt
35 Lulled me to sleep, and sleep prolonged my dreams!
And so I brooded all the following morn,
Awed by the stern preceptor's° face, mine eye   *teacher's*
Fixed with mock study on my swimming book:
Save if the door half opened, and I snatched
40 A hasty glance, and still my heart leaped up,
For still I hoped to see the stranger's face,
Townsman, or aunt, or sister more beloved,
My play-mate when we both were clothed alike![2]

Dear Babe, that sleepest cradled by my side,
45 Whose gentle breathings, heard in this deep calm,
Fill up the interspersed vacancies
And momentary pauses of the thought!
My babe so beautiful! it thrills my heart
With tender gladness, thus to look at thee,
50 And think that thou shalt learn far other lore
And in far other scenes! For I was reared
In the great city, pent 'mid cloisters dim,
And saw naught lovely but the sky and stars.
But *thou*, my babe! shalt wander like a breeze
55 By lakes and sandy shores, beneath the crags
Of ancient mountain, and beneath the clouds,
Which image in their bulk both lakes and shores
And mountain crags: so shalt thou see and hear
The lovely shapes and sounds intelligible
60 Of that eternal language, which thy God
Utters, who from eternity doth teach
Himself in all, and all things in himself.
Great universal Teacher! he shall mould
Thy spirit, and by giving make it ask.

65 Therefore all seasons shall be sweet to thee,
Whether the summer clothe the general earth
With greenness, or the redbreast sit and sing
Betwixt the tufts of snow on the bare branch
Of mossy apple-tree, while the nigh thatch
70 Smokes in the sun-thaw; whether the eave-drops fall
Heard only in the trances of the blast,
Or if the secret ministry of frost
Shall hang them up in silent icicles,
Quietly shining to the quiet Moon.

[February] 1798   1798–1834[3]

---

2. Boys and girls were dressed alike until age 5.   3. Published in several various forms across these years;
the text here is 1834.

from The Rime of the Ancyent Marinere

IN SEVEN PARTS[1]

ARGUMENT

How a Ship having passed the Line[2] was driven by Storms to the cold Country towards the South Pole; and how from thence she made her course to the tropical Latitude of the Great Pacific Ocean; and of the strange things that befell; and in what manner the Ancyent Marinere came back to his own Country.

Part 1

It is an ancient Marinere,
And he stoppeth one of three:
"By thy long grey beard and thy glittering eye
Now wherefore stoppest me?

5   The Bridegroom's doors are open'd wide
And I am next of kin;
The Guests are met, the Feast is set,—
May'st hear the merry din."

But still he holds the wedding-guest—
10   There was a Ship, quoth he—
"Nay, if thou'st got a laughsome tale,
Marinere! come with me."

He holds him with his skinny hand,
Quoth he, there was a Ship—
15   "Now get thee hence, thou grey-beard Loon!
Or my Staff shall make thee skip.

He holds him with his glittering eye—
The wedding guest stood still
And listens like a three year's child;
20   The Marinere hath his will.

The wedding-guest sate on a stone,
He cannot chuse but hear:
And thus spake on that ancient man,
The bright-eyed Marinere.

25   The Ship was cheer'd, the Harbour clear'd—
Merrily did we drop
Below the Kirk,° below the Hill,   *church*
Below the Light-house top.

1. The opening poem of *Lyrical Ballads*, 1798. "Rime" puns poetry into rime-frost. Coleridge later described the genesis in Chapter 14 of the *Biographia Literaria* (see pages 688–89). The immediate motive was to fund a trip the friends had planned by selling the poem to a periodical, but it grew too long for the purpose. The skeleton ship derived from a dream of a friend of Coleridge; Wordsworth contributed the idea of shooting the albatross, the stanza beginning "He holds him with his glittering eye" and a few other verses, but "soon found that the style of Coleridge and myself would not assimilate." As the sample here suggests, the ballad was rife with archaisms. Wordsworth was convinced that "the old words and the strangeness" hurt sales. For the 1800 *Ballads*, Coleridge trimmed the archaisms and the poem was relocated to the back of the volume.
2. Equator.

The Sun came up upon the left,
30 Out of the Sea came he:
And he shone bright, and on the right
Went down into the Sea.

Higher and higher every day,
Till over the mast at noon—
35 The wedding-guest here beat his breast,
For he heard the loud bassoon.

The Bride hath pac'd into the Hall,
Red as a rose is she;
Nodding their heads before her goes
40 The merry Minstralsy.

The wedding-guest he beat his breast,
Yet he cannot chuse but hear:
And thus spake on that ancyent Man,
The bright-eyed Marinere.

45 Listen, Stranger! Storm and Wind,
A Wind and Tempest strong!
For days and weeks it play'd us freaks—
Like Chaff° we drove along.   *husks of grain*

Listen, Stranger! Mist and Snow,
50 And it grew wond'rous cauld:
And Ice mast-high came floating by
As green as Emerauld.

And thro' the drifts the snowy clifts
Did send a dismal sheen;
55 Ne shapes of men ne beasts we ken—
The Ice was all between.

The Ice was here, the Ice was there,
The Ice was all around;
It crack'd and growl'd, and roar'd and howl'd—
60 Like noises of a swound.

At length did cross an Albatross,
Thorough the Fog it came;
And an° it were a Christian Soul,   *as if*
We hail'd it in God's name.

65 The Marineres gave it biscuit-worms,
And round and round it flew:
The Ice did split with a Thunder-fit;
The Helmsman steer'd us thro'.

And a good south wind sprung up behind,
70 The Albatross did follow:
And every day for food or play
Came to the Marinere's hollo!

In mist or cloud on mast or shroud
It perch'd for vespers nine,
75   Whiles all the night thro' fog smoke-white
Glimmer'd the white moon shine.

"God save thee, ancyent Marinere!
From the fiends that plague thee thus—
Why look'st thou so?"—with my cross bow
80   I shot the Albatross.

1797   1798

The Rime
of the
Ancient Mariner[1]

IN SEVEN PARTS

Facile credo, plures esse Naturas invisibiles quam visi-
biles in rerum universitate. Sed horum omnium familiam quis
nobis enarrabit? et gradus et cognationes et discrimina et sin-
gulorum munera? Quid agunt? quæ loca habitant? Harum rerum notitiam semper ambivit ingenium humanum, nunquam
attigit. Juvat, interea, non diffiteor, quandoque in animo,
tanquam in Tabulâ, majoris et melioris mundi imaginem
contemplari: ne mens assuefacta hodiernæ vitæ minutiis se
contrahat nimis, & tota subsidat in pusillas cogitationes. Sed
veritati interea invigilandum est, modusque servandus, ut
certa ab incertis, diem a nocte, distinguamus.[2]

T. BURNET. Archaeol. Phil. p. 68.

An ancient Mariner meeteth three Gallants bidden to a wedding-feast, and detaineth one.	IT is an ancient Mariner, And he stoppeth one of three. "By thy long grey beard and glittering eye, Now wherefore stopp'st thou me?

"The Bridegroom's doors are open'd wide,   5
And I am next of kin;
The guests are met, the feast is set:
May'st hear the merry din."

---

1. A somewhat revised Rime appeared in the 1800 Lyrical
Ballads, and each publication thereafter reflected further
revisions. It was the first poem proper in Sibylline Leaves
"By S. T. Coleridge, Esq." (1817), in which the Latin
epigraph replaced the "Argument" and the marginal commentary first appeared. This gloss surrounded the verse,
printed on the left margin of the left-hand pages, and
the right margin of the right-hand pages, and sometimes
underneath the verse.
2. From English theologian Thomas Burnet's Archaeolo-
giae Philosophicae (1692): "I can easily believe that there
are more invisible creatures in the universe than visible
ones. But who will tell us to what family each belongs,

their ranks and relationships, and what their distinguishing characteristics may be? What do they do? Where do
they live? The human mind has always circled around
these matters without finding satisfaction. But I do not
doubt that it is beneficial sometimes to contemplate in
the mind, as in a picture, the image of a grander and
better world; for if the mind becomes used to the trivial
things of everyday life, it may limit itself too much and
decline completely into worthless thinking. Meanwhile,
however, we must be on the lookout for the truth, keeping a sense of proportion so that we can distinguish what
is sure from what is uncertain, and day from night."

10

immediately

He holds him with his skinny hand,
"There was a ship," quoth he.
"Hold off! unhand me, grey-beard loon!"
Eftsoons° his hand dropt he.

He holds him with his glittering eye—
The wedding-guest stood still,
And listens like a three years child:
The Mariner hath his will.

15

The wedding-guest is spellbound by the eye of the old sea-faring man, and constrained to hear his tale.

The wedding-guest sat on a stone:
He can not chuse but hear;
And thus spake on that ancient man,
The bright-eyed mariner.

20

The ship was cheer'd, the harbour clear'd,
Merrily did we drop
Below the kirk, below the hill.
Below the light-house top.

The Sun came up upon the left,
Out of the sea came he;
And he shone bright, and on the right
Went down into the sea.

25

The Mariner tells how the ship sailed southward with a good wind and fair weather, till it reached the line.

Higher and higher every day,
Till over the mast at noon—
The Wedding-Guest here beat his breast,
For he heard the loud bassoon.

30

The bride hath paced into the hall,
Red as a rose is she;
Nodding their heads before her goes
The merry minstrelsy.

35

The wedding-guest heareth the bridal music; but the mariner continueth his tale.

The Wedding-Guest he beat his breast,
Yet he can not chuse but hear;
And thus spake on that ancient man,
The bright-eyed Mariner.

40

And now the STORM-BLAST came, and he
Was tyrannous and strong:
He struck with his o'ertaking wings,
And chased us south along.

The ship drawn by a storm toward the south pole.

With sloping masts and dipping prow,
As who pursued with yell and blow
Still treads the shadow of his foe
And forward bends his head,
The ship drove fast, loud roar'd the blast,
And southward aye° we fled.

45

ever

And now there came both mist and snow,
And it grew wondrous cold:
And ice, mast-high, came floating by,
As green as emerald.

The land of ice, and of fearful sounds, where no living thing was to be seen.	And through the drifts the snowy clift Did send a dismal sheen: Nor shapes of men nor beast we ken°— The ice was all between.	55 *knew*

The ice was here, the ice was there,
The ice was all around:
It cracked and growled, and roar'd and howl'd,
Like noises in a swound!   60

Till a great sea-bird, called the Albatross came through the snow-fog, and was received with great joy and hospitality.

At length did cross an Albatross:
Thorough the fog it came;
As if it had been a Christian soul,
We hailed it in God's name.   65

It ate the food it ne'er had eat,
And round and round it flew.
The ice did split with a thunder-fit;
The helmsman steer'd us through!   70

And lo! the Albatross proveth a bird of good omen, and followeth the ship as it returned northward, through fog and floating ice.

And a good south wind sprung up behind;
The Albatross did follow,
And every day, for food or play,
Came to the Mariner's hollo!

In mist or cloud, on mast or shroud,   75
It perch'd for vespers° nine;   *evening prayers*
Whiles all the night, through fog-smoke white,
Glimmered the white Moon-shine.

The ancient Mariner inhospitably killeth the pious bird of good omen.

"God save thee, ancient Mariner!
From the fiends, that plague thee thus!—   80
Why look'st thou so?"—With my cross-bow
I shot the ALBATROSS!.

PART THE SECOND

THE Sun now rose upon the right:
Out of the sea came he,
Still hid in mist, and on the left   85
Went down into the sea.

And the good south wind still blew behind,
But no sweet bird did follow,
Nor any day for food or play
Came to the mariners' hollo!   90

His shipmates cry out against the ancient Mariner, for killing the bird of good luck.

And I had done a hellish thing,
And it would work 'em woe:
For all averred, I had killed the bird
That made the breeze to blow.
Ah wretch! said they, the bird to slay,   95
That made the breeze to blow!

Nor dim nor red, like God's own head,
The glorious Sun uprist:
Then all averred, I had killed the bird
That brought the fog and mist.
'Twas right, said they, such birds to slay,
That bring the fog and mist.

> But when the fog cleared off, they justify the same—and thus make themselves accomplices in the crime.

The fair breeze blew, the white foam flew,
The furrow stream'd off free;[3]
We were the first that ever burst
Into that silent sea.

> The fair breeze continues; the ship enters the Pacific Ocean, and sails northward, even till it reaches the Line.

Down dropt the breeze, the sails dropt down,
'Twas sad as sad could be;
And we did speak only to break
The silence of the sea!

> The ship hath been suddenly becalmed.

All in a hot and copper sky,
The bloody Sun, at noon,
Right up above the mast did stand,
No bigger than the Moon.

Day after day, day after day,
We stuck, nor breath nor motion;
As idle as a painted ship
Upon a painted ocean.

Water, water, every where,
And all the boards did shrink;
Water, water, every where,
Nor any drop to drink.

> And the Albatross begins to be avenged.

The very deep did rot: O Christ!
That ever this should be!
Yea, slimy things did crawl with legs
Upon the slimy sea.

About, about, in reel and rout
The death-fires danced at night;
The water, like a witch's oils,
Burnt green, and blue and white.

And some in dreams assured were
Of the spirit that plagued us so:
Nine fathom deep he had followed us
From the land of mist and snow.

> A spirit had followed them; one of the invisible inhabitants of this planet, neither departed souls nor

Line numbers in left margin: 100, 105, 110, 115, 120, 125, 130

3. In the former edition the line was,

the furrow follow'd free

but I had not been long on board a ship, before I perceived that this was the image as seen by a spectator from the shore, or from another vessel. From the ship itself the *Wake* appears like a brook flowing off from the stern [Coleridge's note, 1817]; subsequent editions restore "follow'd.'

angels; concerning whom the learned Jew, Josephus, and the Platonic Constantinopolitan, Michael Psellus, may be consulted. They are very numerous, and there is no climate or element without one or more.

And every tongue, through utter drought,   135
Was wither'd at the root;
We could not speak, no more than if
We had been choak'd with soot.

The shipmates, in their sore distress, would fain throw the whole guilt on the ancient Mariner: in sign whereof they hang the dead sea-bird round his neck.

Ah! well a-day! what evil looks
Had I from old and young!   140
Instead of the cross, the Albatross
About my neck was hung.

PART THE THIRD

THERE passed a weary time. Each throat
Was parched, and glazed each eye.
A weary time! a weary time!   145
How glazed each weary eye!

The ancient Mariner beholdeth a sign in the element afar off.

When looking westward, I beheld
A something in the sky.

At first it seem'd a little speck,
And then it seem'd a mist!   150
It moved and moved, and took at last
A certain shape, I wist.°   knew

A speck, a mist, a shape, I wist!
And still it near'd and near'd:
And as if it dodged a water-sprite,   155
It plunged and tack'd and veer'd.

At its nearer approach, it seemeth him to be a ship; and at a dear ransom he freeth his speech from the bonds of thirst.

With throat unslack'd, with black lips baked,
We could nor laugh nor wail;
Through utter drought all dumb we stood!
I bit my arm, I sucked the blood,   160
And cried, A sail! a sail!

With throat unslacked,[4] with black lips baked,
Agape they heard me call:
A flash of joy.
Gramercy! they for joy did grin,
And all at once their breath drew in,   165
As they were drinking all.

And horror follows. For can it be a *ship* that comes onward without wind or tide?

See! see! (I cried) she tacks no more!
Hither to work us weal;°   benefit
Without a breeze, without a tide,
She steddies with upright keel!   170

4. 1834] throats unslaked.

The western wave was all a-flame.
The day was well nigh done!
Almost upon the western wave
Rested the broad bright Sun;
175 When that strange shape drove suddenly
Betwixt us and the Sun.

And straight the Sun was flecked with bars,   *It seemeth him but the*
(Heaven's Mother send us grace!)   *skeleton of a ship.*
As if through a dungeon-grate he peer'd
180 With broad and burning face.

Alas! (thought I, and my heart beat loud)
How fast she nears and nears!
Are those *her* sails that glance in the Sun,
cobwebs Like restless gossameres?°

185 Are those *her* ribs through which the Sun   *And its ribs are seen as*
Did peer, as through a grate?   *bars on the face of the*
And is that Woman all her crew?   *setting Sun. The spectre-*
Is that a* DEATH? *and are there two?   *woman and her death-*
Is* DEATH *that woman's mate?   *mate, and no other on*
                                                 board the skeleton-ship.

190 *Her* lips were red, *her* looks were free,
Her locks were yellow as gold:
Her skin was as white as leprosy,   *Like vessel, like crew!*
The Night-Mair LIFE-IN-DEATH was she,
Who thicks man's blood with cold.

195 The naked hulk alongside came,   DEATH, *and* LIFE-IN-
And the twain were casting dice;   DEATH *have diced for*
"The game is done! I've, I've won!"   *the ship's crew, and she*
Quoth she, and whistles thrice.[5]   *(the latter) winneth the*
                                                 ancient Mariner.

The Sun's rim dips; the stars rush out: *No twilight within the*
200 At one stride comes the dark;   *courts of the Sun.*
With far-heard whisper, o'er the sea,
Off shot the spectre-bark.

We listen'd and look'd sideways up!
Fear at my heart, as at a cup,
205 My life-blood seem'd to sip!
The stars were dim, and thick the night,
The steersman's face by his lamp gleam'd white;

From the sails the dew did drip—
Till clombe above the eastern bar   *At the rising of the*
210 The horned Moon, with one bright star   *Moon,*
Within the nether tip.

---

5. In 1817 only, this stanza followed: "A gust of wind sterte up behind / And whistled through the bones, / Through the holes of his eyes and the hole of his mouth, / Half whistles and half groans." Coleridge had wanted to "erase" this stanza.

One after another,

One after one, by the star-dogg'd Moon,
Too quick for groan or sigh,
Each turn'd his face with a ghastly pang,
And curs'd me with his eye.   215

His ship-mates drop
down dead;

Four times fifty living men,
(And I heard nor sigh nor groan)
With heavy thump, a lifeless lump,
They dropped down one by one.

But LIFE-IN-DEATH
begins her work on the
ancient Mariner.

The souls did from their bodies fly,—   220
They fled to bliss or woe!
And every soul, it passed me by,
Like the whizz of my CROSS-BOW!

PART THE FOURTH

The wedding-guest
feareth that a spirit is
talking to him;

"I FEAR thee, ancient Mariner!
I fear thy skinny hand!   225
And thou art long, and lank, and brown,
As is the ribbed sea-sand.[6]

I fear thee and thy glittering eye,
And thy skinny hand, so brown."—

But the ancient
Mariner assureth him
of his bodily life, and
proceedeth to relate his
horrible penance.

Fear not, fear not, thou Wedding-Guest!   230
This body dropt not down.

Alone, alone, all, all alone,
Alone on a wide wide sea!
And never a saint took pity on
My soul in agony   235

He despiseth the
creatures of the calm,

The many men, so beautiful!
And they all dead did lie:
And a thousand thousand slimy things
Liv'd on; and so did I.

And envieth that *they*
should live, and so many
lie dead.

I looked upon the rotting sea,   240
And drew my eyes away;
I looked upon the rotting deck,
And there the dead men lay.

I looked to Heaven, and tried to pray;
But or ever a prayer had gusht,   245
A wicked whisper came, and made
My heart as dry as dust.

I closed my lids, and kept them close,
And the balls like pulses beat;
For the sky and the sea, and the sea and the sky   250
Lay, like a load, on my weary eye,
And the dead were at my feet.

6. For the last two lines of this stanza, I am indebted to Mr. Wordsworth. It was on a delightful walk from Nether Stowey to Dulverton, with him and his sister, in the Autumn of 1797, that this poem was planned, and in part composed [Coleridge's note].

The cold sweat melted from their limbs,
Not rot nor reek did they:
255 The look with which they looked on me
Had never passed away.

An orphan's curse would drag to Hell
A spirit from on high;
But oh! more horrible than that
260 Is the curse in a dead man's eye!
Seven days, seven nights, I saw that curse,
And yet I could not die.

The moving Moon went up the sky,
And nowhere did abide:
265 Softly she was going up,
And a star or two beside—

Her beams bemock'd the sultry main,
Like April hoar-frost spread;
But where the ship's huge shadow lay,
270 The charmed water burnt alway
A still and awful red.

But the curse liveth for him in the eye of the dead men.

In his loneliness and fixedness he yearneth towards the journeying Moon, and the stars that still sojourn, yet still move onward; and every where the blue sky belongs to them, and is their appointed rest, and their native country, and their own natural homes, which they enter unannounced, as lords that are certainly expected, and yet there is a silent joy at their arrival.

Beyond the shadow of the ship,
I watch'd the water-snakes:
They moved in tracks of shining white,
275 And when they reared, the elfish light
Fell off in hoary flakes.

Within the shadow of the ship
I watched their rich attire:
Blue, glossy green, and velvet black,
280 They coiled and swam; and every track
Was a flash of golden fire.

By the light of the Moon he beholdeth God's creatures of the great calm.

O happy living things! no tongue
Their beauty might declare:
A spring of love gusht from my heart,
285 And I blessed them unaware!
Sure my kind saint took pity on me,
And I blessed them unaware.

Their beauty and their happiness.

He blesseth them in his heart.

The self same moment I could pray;
And from my neck so free
290 The Albatross fell off, and sank
Like lead into the sea.

The spell begins to break.

PART THE FIFTH

Oh SLEEP! it is a gentle thing,
Belov'd from pole to pole!
To Mary Queen the praise be given!

She sent the gentle sleep from Heaven,   295
That slid into my soul.

By grace of the holy
Mother, the ancient
Mariner is refreshed
with rain.

The silly° buckets on the deck,   *helpless*
That had so long remained,
I dreamt that they were filled with dew;
And when I awoke, it rained.   300

My lips were wet, my throat was cold,
My garments all were dank;
Sure I had drunken in my dreams,
And still my body drank.

I moved, and could not feel my limbs: 305
I was so light—almost
I thought that I had died in sleep,
And was a blessed ghost.

He heareth sounds, and
seeth strange sights and
commotions in the sky
and the element.

And soon I heard a roaring wind:
It did not come anear;   310
But with its sound it shook the sails,
That were so thin and sere.

The upper air burst into life!
And a hundred fire-flags° sheen,   *meteors*
To and fro they were hurried about;   315
And to and fro, and in and out,
The wan stars danced between.

And the coming wind did roar more loud,
And the sails did sigh like sedge;°   *marsh grass*
And the rain pour'd down from one black cloud;   320
The Moon was at its edge.

The thick black cloud was cleft, and still
The Moon was at its side:
Like waters shot from some high crag,
The lightning fell with never a jag,   325
A river steep and wide.

The bodies of the ship's
crew are inspirited, and
the ship moves on;

The loud wind never reached the ship,
Yet now the ship moved on!
Beneath the lightning and the Moon
The dead men gave a groan.   330

They groan'd, they stirr'd, they all uprose,
Nor spake, nor moved their eyes;
It had been strange, even in a dream,
To have seen those dead men rise.

The helmsman steered, the ship moved on;   335
Yet never a breeze up blew;
The mariners all 'gan work the ropes,
Where they were wont to do:

They raised their limbs like lifeless tools—
340   We were a ghastly crew.

The body of my brother's son
Stood by me, knee to knee:
The body and I pulled at one rope,
But he said nought to me.

345   "I fear thee, ancient Mariner!"
Be calm, thou Wedding-Guest!
'Twas not those souls that fled in pain,
corpses   Which to their corses° came again,
But a troop of spirits blest:

But not by the souls of
the men, nor by dæmons
of earth or middle air,
but by a blessed troop of
angelic spirits, sent down
by the invocation of the
guardian saint.

350   For when it dawned—they dropped their arms,
And clustered round the mast;
Sweet sounds rose slowly through their mouths,
And from their bodies passed.

Around, around, flew each sweet sound,
355   Then darted to the Sun;
Slowly the sounds came back again,
Now mixed, now one by one.

Sometimes a-dropping from the sky
I heard the sky-lark sing;
360   Sometimes all little birds that are,
How they seem'd to fill the sea and air
warbling   With their sweet jargoning!°

And now 'twas like all instruments,
Now like a lonely flute;
365   And now it is an angel's song,
That makes the Heavens be mute.

It ceased; yet still the sails made on
A pleasant noise till noon,
A noise like of a hidden brook
370   In the leafy month of June,
That to the sleeping woods all night
Singeth a quiet tune.

Till noon we quietly sailed on,
Yet never a breeze did breathe:
375   Slowly and smoothly went the ship,
Moved onward from beneath.

Under the keel nine fathom deep,
From the land of mist and snow,
The spirit slid: and it was he
380   That made the ship to go.
The sails at noon left off their tune,
And the ship stood still also.

The lonesome spirit from
the south-pole carries
on the ship as far as the
line, in obedience to the
angelic troop, but still
requireth vengeance.

The Sun, right up above the mast,
Had fixt her to the ocean;
But in a minute she 'gan stir,   385
With a short uneasy motion—
Backwards and forwards half her length,
With a short uneasy motion.

Then like a pawing horse let go,
She made a sudden bound: 390
It flung the blood into my head,
And I fell down in a swound.

How long in that same fit I lay,
I have not to declare;
But ere my living life returned,   395
I heard and in my soul discerned
Two VOICES in the air.

"Is it he?" quoth one, "Is this the man?
By him who died on cross,
With his cruel bow he laid full low,   400
The harmless Albatross.

The spirit who bideth by himself
In the land of mist and snow,
He loved the bird that loved the man
Who shot him with his bow."   405

The other was a softer voice,
As soft as honey-dew.
Quoth he, "The man hath penance done,
And penance more will do."

The Polar Spirit's fellow-dæmons, the invisible inhabitants of the element, take part in his wrong; and two of them relate, one to the other, that penance long and heavy for the ancient Mariner hath been accorded to the Polar Spirit, who returneth southward.

PART THE SIXTH

FIRST VOICE.

But tell me, tell me! speak again,   410
Thy soft response renewing—
What makes that ship drive on so fast?
What is the OCEAN doing?

SECOND VOICE.

Still as a slave before his lord,
The OCEAN hath no blast;   415
His great bright eye most silently
Up to the Moon is cast—

If he may know which way to go;
For she guides him smooth or grim.
See, brother, see! how graciously   420
She looketh down on him.

FIRST VOICE.

But why drives on that ship so fast,
Without or wave or wind?

The Mariner hath been
cast into a trance; for the
angelic power causeth
the vessel to drive
northward, faster than
human life could endure.

SECOND VOICE.

The air is cut away before,
425   And closes from behind.

Fly, brother, fly! more high, more high!
Or we shall be belated:
For slow and slow that ship will go,
When the Mariner's trance is abated."

430   I woke, and we were sailing on
As in a gentle weather:
'Twas night, calm night, the Moon was high;
The dead men stood together.

The supernatural motion
is retarded; the Mariner
awakes, and his penance
begins anew.

All stood together on the deck,
tomb   For a charnel-dungeon° fitter:
All fixed on me their stony eyes,
That in the Moon did glitter.

The pang, the curse, with which they died,
Had never passed away:
440   I could not draw my eyes from theirs,
Nor turn them up to pray.

And now this spell was snapt: once more
I viewed the ocean green,
And looked far forth, yet little saw
445   Of what had else been seen—

The curse is finally
expiated.

Like one, that on a lonesome road
Doth walk in fear and dread,
And having once turn'd round, walks on,
And turns no more his head;
450   Because he knows, a frightful fiend
Doth close behind him tread.

But soon there breathed a wind on me,
Nor sound nor motion made:
Its path was not upon the sea,
455   In ripple or in shade.

It raised my hair, it fanned my cheek
Like a meadow-gale of spring—
It mingled strangely with my fears,
Yet it felt like a welcoming.

460   Swiftly, swiftly flew the ship,
Yet she sailed softly too:

Sweetly, sweetly blew the breeze—
On me alone it blew.

And the ancient
Mariner beholdeth his
native country.

Oh! dream of joy! is this indeed
The light-house top I see?   465
Is this the hill? is this the kirk?
Is this mine own countree?

We drifted o'er the harbour-bar,
And I with sobs did pray—
O let me be awake, my God!   470
Or let me sleep alway.

The harbour-bay was clear as glass,
So smoothly it was strewn!
And on the bay the moonlight lay,
And the shadow of the moon.   475

The rock shone bright, the kirk no less,
That stands above the rock:
The moonlight steeped in silentness
The steady weathercock.

The angelic spirits
leave the dead bodies,

And the bay was white with silent light,   480
Till rising from the same,
Full many shapes, that shadows were,
In crimson colours came.

And appear in their
own forms of light.

A little distance from the prow
Those crimson shadows were: 485
I turned my eyes upon the deck—
Oh, Christ! what saw I there!

Each corse lay flat, lifeless and flat,
And, by the holy rood!°   *cross*
A man all light, a seraph-man,   490
On every corse there stood.

This seraph-band, each waved his hand:
It was a heavenly sight!
They stood as signals to the land,
Each one a lovely light: 495

This seraph-band, each waved his hand,
No voice did they impart—
No voice; but oh! the silence sank
Like music on my heart.

But soon I heard the dash of oars,   500
I heard the Pilot's cheer;
My head was turn'd perforce away,
And I saw a boat appear.

505 The Pilot, and the Pilot's boy,
I heard them coming fast:
Dear Lord in Heaven! it was a joy
The dead men could not blast.

I saw a third—I heard his voice:
510 It is the Hermit good!
He singeth loud his godly hymns
That he makes in the wood.

absolve He'll shrieve° my soul, he'll wash away
The Albatross's blood.

PART THE SEVENTH

This Hermit good lives in that wood   The Hermit of the
515 Which slopes down to the sea.   Wood,
How loudly his sweet voice he rears!
He loves to talk with marineres
That come from a far countree.

He kneels at morn, and noon, and eve—
520 He hath a cushion plump:
It is the moss that wholly hides
The rotted old oak-stump.

The Skiff-boat near'd: I heard them talk,
"Why, this is strange, I trow!
525 Where are those lights so many and fair,
That signal made but now?"

"Strange, by my faith!" the Hermit said—   Approacheth the ship
"And they answered not our cheer!   with wonder.
The planks looked warped! and see those sails,
530 How thin they are and sere!
I never saw aught like to them,
Unless perchance it were

Brown skeletons of leaves that lag
My forest-brook along;
clump When the ivy-tod° is heavy with snow,
And the owlet whoops to the wolf below,
That eats the she-wolf's young."

Dear Lord! it hath a fiendish look—
(The Pilot made reply)
540 I am a-feared—Push on, push on!
Said the Hermit cheerily.

The boat came closer to the ship,
But I nor spake nor stirred;

The boat came close beneath the ship,
And straight a sound was heard.   545

The ship suddenly
sinketh.

Under the water it rumbled on,
Still louder and more dread:
It reach'd the ship, it split the bay;
The ship went down like lead.

The ancient Mariner is
saved in the Pilot's
boat.

Stunned by that loud and dreadful sound,   550
Which sky and ocean smote,
Like one that hath been seven days drown'd,
My body lay afloat;
But swift as dreams, myself I found
Within the Pilot's boat.   555

Upon the whirl, where sank the ship,
The boat spun round and round;
And all was still, save that the hill
Was telling of the sound.

I moved my lips—the Pilot shrieked   560
And fell down in a fit;
The holy Hermit raised his eyes,
And prayed where he did sit.

I took the oars: the Pilot's boy,
Who now doth crazy go,   565
Laughed loud and long, and all the while
His eyes went to and fro.
"Ha! ha!" quoth he, "full plain I see,
The Devil knows how to row."

And now, all in my own countree,   570
I stood on the firm land!
The Hermit stepped forth from the boat,
And scarcely he could stand.

The ancient Mariner
earnestly entreateth the
Hermit to shrieve him;
and the penance of
life falls on him.

"O shrieve me, shrieve me, holy man!"
The Hermit cross'd his brow.   575
"Say quick," quoth he, "I bid thee say—
What manner of man art thou?"

Forthwith this frame of mine was wrench'd
With a woeful agony,
Which forced me to begin my tale;   580
And then it left me free.

And ever and anon
throughout his future life
an agony constraineth
him to travel from land
to land,

Since then, at an uncertain hour,
That agony returns;
And till my ghastly tale is told,
This heart within me burns.   585

I pass, like night, from land to land;
I have strange power of speech;
That moment that his face I see,
I know the man that must hear me:
590   To him my tale I teach.

What loud uproar bursts from that door!
The wedding-guests are there;
But in the garden-bower the bride
And bride-maids singing are;
595   And hark the little vesper bell,
Which biddeth me to prayer!

O Wedding-Guest! this soul hath been
Alone on a wide wide sea:
So lonely 'twas, that God himself
600   Scarce seemed there to be.

O sweeter than the marriage-feast,
'Tis sweeter far to me,
To walk together to the kirk
With a goodly company!—

605   To walk together to the kirk,
And all together pray,
While each to his great Father bends,
Old men, and babes, and loving friends,
And youths and maidens gay!

And to teach by his own example, love and reverence to all things that God made and loveth.

610   Farewell, farewell! but this I tell
To thee, thou Wedding-Guest!
He prayeth well, who loveth well
Both man and bird and beast.

He prayeth best, who loveth best
615   All things both great and small;
For the dear God who loveth us,
He made and loveth all."

The Mariner, whose eye is bright,
Whose beard with age is hoar,
620   Is gone: and now the Wedding-Guest
Turned from the bridegroom's door.

He went like one that hath been stunned,
And is of sense forlorn:
A sadder and a wiser man,
625   He rose the morrow morn.

1817   1798–1817

COMPANION READINGS

William Cowper: *The Castaway* [1]

Obscurest night involv'd the sky;
    Th' Atlantic billows roar'd,
When such a destin'd wretch as I,
    Wash'd headlong from on board,
5   Of friends, of hope, of all bereft,
His floating home for ever left.

No braver chief could Albion° boast,   *England*
    Than he, with whom he went,
Nor ever ship left Albion's coast,
10   With warmer wishes sent.
He lov'd them both, but both in vain,
Nor him beheld, nor her again.

Not long beneath the whelming brine,
    Expert to swim, he lay:
15 Nor soon he felt his strength decline,
    Or courage die away;
But wag'd with Death a lasting strife,
Supported by despair of life.

He shouted; nor his friends had fail'd
20   To check the vessel's course,
But so the furious blast prevail'd,
    That, pitiless, perforce,
They left their outcast mate behind,
And scudded still before the wind.

25 Some succour° yet they could afford   *aid*
    And, such as storms allow,
The cask, the coop, the floated cord.
    Delay'd not to bestow.
But he (they knew) nor ship nor shore,
30 Whate'er they gave, should visit more.

Nor, cruel as it seem'd, could he
    Their haste himself condemn,
Aware that flight, in such a sea,
    Alone could rescue them;
35 Yet bitter felt it still to die
Deserted, and his friends so nigh.

---

1. William Cowper (1731–1800) influenced Wordsworth and Burns with subjects drawn from ordinary life and simple, direct language. *The Castaway* is based on an incident recorded in *Voyage Around the World* (1748) by George Anson, commander of the fleet: a man lost overboard during a violent storm off Cape Horn struggled to stay afloat, but Anson's ship was unable to rescue him. This is the last poem Cowper ever wrote, left in manuscript at his death. For more about Cowper, see page 256.

He long survives, who lives an hour
    In ocean, self-upheld:
And so long he, with unspent pow'r
40   His destiny repell'd:
And ever as the minutes flew,
Entreated help, or cried—"Adieu!"

At length, his transient respite past,
    His comrades, who before
45 Had heard his voice in ev'ry blast,
    Could catch the sound no more.
For then, by toil subdu'd, he drank
The stifling wave, and then he sank.

No poet wept him: but the page
50   Of narrative sincere,°   *the ship's log*
That tells his name, his worth,° his age   *rank*
    Is wet with Anson's tear.
And tears by bards or heroes shed
Alike immortalize the dead.

55 I therefore purpose not, or dream,
    Descanting° on his fate,   *singing*
To give the melancholy theme
    A more enduring date:
But misery still delights to trace
60 Its semblance in another's case.

No voice divine the storm allay'd,
    No light propitious shone;
When, snatch'd from all effectual aid,
    We perish'd, each alone:
65 But I beneath a rougher sea,
And whelm'd in deeper gulfs than he.

1799   1803

Samuel Taylor Coleridge: from *Table Talk, May 31, 1830.*

Mrs. Barbauld[1] once told me that she admired the Ancient Mariner very much, but
that there were two faults in it, it was improbable, and had no moral. As for the probability, I owned that that might admit some question; but as to the want of a moral,
I told her that in my own judgment the poem had too much; and that the only, or
chief fault, if I might say so, was the obtrusion of the moral sentiment so openly on the
reader as a principle or cause of action in a work of such pure imagination. It ought to
have had no more moral than the Arabian Nights' tale of the merchant's sitting down
to eat dates by the side of a well, and throwing the shells aside, and lo! a genie starts
up, and says he *must* kill the aforesaid merchant, *because* one of the date shells had, it
seems, put out the eye of the genie's son.

                                      ⌒∽⌒

---

1. Anna Letitia Barbauld; see page 65.

Christabel[1]
Preface

The first part of the following poem was written in the year one thousand seven hundred and ninety seven,[2] at Stowey, in the county of Somerset. The second part, after my return from Germany, in the year one thousand eight hundred, at Keswick, Cumberland. Since the latter date, my poetic powers have been, till very lately, in a state of suspended animation. But as, in my very first conception of the tale, I had the whole present to my mind, with the wholeness, no less than with the liveliness of a vision; I trust that I shall be able to embody in verse the three parts yet to come, in the course of the present year.

It is probable, that if the poem had been finished at either of the former periods, or if even the first and second part had been published in the year 1800, the impression of its originality would have been much greater than I dare at present expect. But for this, I have only my own indolence to blame. The dates are mentioned for the exclusive purpose of precluding charges of plagiarism or servile imitation from myself. For there is among us a set of critics, who seem to hold, that every possible thought and image is traditional; who have no notion that there are such things as fountains in the world, small as well as great; and who would therefore charitably derive every rill they behold flowing, from a perforation made in some other man's tank. I am confident, however, that as far as the present poem is concerned, the celebrated poets whose writings I might be suspected of having imitated,[3] either in particular passages, or in the tone and the spirit of the whole, would be among the first to vindicate me from the charge, and who, on any striking coincidence, would permit me to address them in this doggerel version of two monkish Latin hexameters:

> 'Tis mine and it is likewise yours,
> But an if this will not do;
> Let it be mine, good friend! for I
> Am the poorer of the two.

I have only to add, that the metre of the Christabel is not, properly speaking, irregular, though it may seem so from its being founded on a new principle: namely, that of counting in each line the accents, not the syllables. Though the latter may vary from seven to twelve, yet in each line the accents will be found to be only four. Nevertheless this occasional variation in number of syllables is not introduced wantonly, or for the mere ends of convenience, but in correspondence with some transition, in the nature of the imagery or passion.

PART I

> 'Tis the middle of night by the castle clock,
> And the owls have awakened the crowing cock;

---

1. *Christabel* circulated in manuscript and recitation long before it was published in 1816, along with *Kubla Khan* and *The Pains of Sleep*, by Byron's publisher John Murray, and advertised with Byron's praise: "That wild and singularly original and beautiful Poem." But it proved controversial, some reviewers finding the heroine's encounter with Geraldine confusing, or worse: "disgusting" said one; "obscene" said another. Even so, the volume was popular enough to see two more editions in 1816. In 1824 Coleridge wrote nine notes on the margins of his copy of the 1816 volume (which we include with a caution: as with the 1817 gloss to *The Ancient Mariner*, these might satirize rather than satisfy desire for clarification). There is no other record of further work on the poem.

2. Actually, spring 1798; it was to be the closing poem of *Lyrical Ballads* 1800 (see Coleridge's account of the project, pages 689–90), but Wordsworth thought it unsuitable and replaced it with *Michael*.

3. He is thinking of Scott's metrical tales, Byron's Eastern tales, and even Wordsworth's *White Doe of Rylstone*.

Tu—whit!——Tu—whoo!
And hark, again! the crowing cock,
5   How drowsily it crew.

Sir Leoline, the Baron rich,
Hath a toothless mastiff bitch;
From her kennel beneath the rock
She maketh answer to the clock,
10   Four for the quarters, and twelve for the hour;
Ever and aye,° by shine or shower,   *always*
Sixteen short howls, not over loud;
Some say, she sees my lady's shroud.

Is the night chilly and dark?
15   The night is chilly, but not dark.
The thin gray cloud is spread on high,
It covers but not hides the sky.
The moon is behind, and at the full;
And yet she looks both small and dull.
20   The night is chill, the cloud is gray:
'Tis a month before the month of May,
And the Spring comes slowly up this way.

The lovely lady, Christabel,
Whom her father loves so well,
25   What makes her in the wood so late,
A furlong° from the castle gate?   *220 yards*
She had dreams all yesternight
Of her own betrothed knight;
Dreams that made her moan and leap,
30   As on her bed she lay in sleep;[4]
And she in the midnight wood will pray
For the weal° of her lover that's far away.   *well-being*

She stole along, she nothing spoke,
The sighs she heaved were still also;
35   And nought was green upon the oak,
But moss and rarest mistletoe:[5]
She kneels beneath the huge oak tree,
And in silence prayeth she.

The lady leaps up suddenly,
40   The lovely lady, Christabel!
It moan'd as near, as near can be,
But what it is, she can not tell,—
On the other side it seems to be,
Of the huge, broad-breasted, old oak tree.

45   The night is chill; the forest bare;
Is it the wind that moaneth bleak?

---

4. Lines 29–30 were deleted in 1824.   5. Ancient Druids held such a sight in veneration, because the parasite mistletoe is rare on oak.

There is not wind enough in the air
To move away the ringlet curl
From the lovely lady's cheek—
50   There is not wind enough to twirl
The one red leaf, the last of its clan,
That dances as often as dance it can,
Hanging so light, and hanging so high,
On the topmost twig that looks up at the sky.
55   Hush! beating heart of Christabel!
Jesu, Maria, shield her well!

She folded her arms beneath her cloak,
And stole to the other side of the oak.
    What sees she there?

60   There she sees a damsel bright,
Drest in a silken robe of white;
Her neck, her feet, her arms were bare;
And the jewels disorder'd in her hair.[6]
I guess, 'twas frightful there to see
65   A lady so richly clad as she—
Beautiful exceedingly!

Mary mother, save me now!
(Said Christabel,) And who art thou?

The lady strange made answer meet,
70   And her voice was faint and sweet:—
Have pity on my sore distress,
I scarce can speak for weariness.
Stretch forth thy hand, and have no fear!
Said Christabel, How cam'st thou here?
75   And the lady, whose voice was faint and sweet,
Did thus pursue her answer meet:—

My sire is of a noble line,
And my name is Geraldine.
Five warriors seiz'd me yestermorn,
80   Me, even me, a maid forlorn:
They chok'd my cries with force and fright,
And tied me on a palfrey° white.   *horse*
The palfrey was as fleet as wind,
And they rode furiously behind.
85   They spurrd amain,° their steeds were white;   *with full force*
And once we cross'd the shade of night.
As sure as Heaven shall rescue me,
I have no thought what men they be;

---

6. 62–63, revised 1824] That shadowy in the moonlight shone: / The Neck, that made her white robe wan, / Her stately Neck, and Arms were bare; / Her blue-vein'd Feet unsandal'd were; / And wildly glitter'd here and there / The Gems entangled in her hair!

Nor do I know how long it is
90   (For I have lain in fits I wis°)   *believe*
Since one, the tallest of the five,
Took me from the palfrey's back,
A weary woman, scarce alive.
Some mutter'd words his comrades spoke:
95   He plac'd me underneath this oak,
He swore they would return with haste;
Whither they went I cannot tell—
I thought I heard, some minutes past,
Sounds as of a castle bell.
100   Stretch forth thy hand (thus ended she),
And help a wretched maid to flee.

Then Christabel stretch'd forth her hand
And comforted fair Geraldine,
Saying, that she should command
105   The service of Sir Leoline;
And straight be convoy'd, free from thrall,
Back to her noble father's hall.

So up she rose, and forth they pass'd
With hurrying steps, yet nothing fast.
110   Her lucky stars the lady blest,
And Christabel she sweetly said—
All our household are at rest,
Each one sleeping in his bed;
Sir Leoline is weak in health,
115   And may not well awaken'd be;
So to my room we'll creep in stealth,
And you tonight must sleep with me.[7]

They cross'd the moat, and Christabel
Took the key that fitted well;
120   A little door she opened straight,
All in the middle of the gate;
The gate that was iron'd within and without,
Where an army in battle array had march'd out.

The lady sank, belike thro' pain,
125   And Christabel with might and main
Lifted her up, a weary weight,
Over the threshold of the gate:
Then the lady rose again,
And mov'd, as she were not in pain.[8]

130   So free from danger, free from fear,
They cross'd the court: right glad they were.

---

7. marginal note, 1824] The Strange Lady cannot rise, without the touch of Christabel's Hand: and now she blesses her <u>Stars</u>. She will not praise the <u>Creator</u> of the Heavens, or name the saints.

8. marginal note, 1824] The strange lady may not pass the threshold without Christabel's help and will.

And Christabel devoutly cried,
To the lady by her side,
Praise we the Virgin all divine
135   Who hath rescued thee from thy distress!
Alas, alas! said Geraldine,
I can not speak for weariness.[9]
So free from danger, free from fear,
They cross'd the court: right glad they were.

140   Outside her kennel, the mastiff old
Lay fast asleep, in moonshine cold.
The mastiff old did not awake,
Yet she an angry moan did make!
And what can ail the mastiff bitch?
145   Never till now she utter'd yell
Beneath the eye of Christabel.
Perhaps it is the owlet's scritch:
For what can ail the mastiff bitch?

They pass'd the hall, that echoes still,
150   Pass as lightly as you will!
The brands° were flat, the brands were dying,   *fireplace logs*
Amid their own white ashes lying;
But when the lady pass'd, there came
A tongue of light, a fit of flame;
155   And Christabel saw the lady's eye,
And nothing else saw she thereby,
Save the boss of the shield of Sir Leoline tall,
Which hung in a murky old nitch in the wall.
O softly tread, said Christabel,
160   My father seldom sleepeth well.

Sweet Christabel her feet she bares,
And they are creeping up the stairs;
Now in glimmer, and now in gloom,
And now they pass the Baron's room,
165   As still as death with stifled breath!
And now have reach'd her chamber door;
And now doth Geraldine press down
The rushes of the chamber floor.

The moon shines dim in the open air,
170   And not a moonbeam enters here:
But they without its light can see
The chamber carv'd so curiously,
Carv'd with figures strange and sweet,
All made out of the carver's brain,
175   For a lady's chamber meet:

---

9. marginal note, 1824] The strange Lady makes an excuse, not to praise the Holy Virgin.

The lamp with twofold silver chain
Is fasten'd to an angel's feet.

The silver lamp burns dead and dim;
But Christabel the lamp will trim.
180 She trimm'd the lamp, and made it bright,
And left it swinging to and fro,
While Geraldine, in wretched plight,
Sank down upon the floor below.

O weary lady, Geraldine,
185 I pray you, drink this cordial wine!
It is a wine of virtuous powers;
My mother made it of wild flowers.

And will your mother pity me,
Who am a maiden most forlorn?

190 Christabel answer'd—Woe is me!
She died the hour that I was born.
I have heard the gray-hair'd friar tell,
How on her death-bed she did say,
That she should hear the castle-bell
195 Strike twelve upon my wedding-day.
O mother dear! that thou wert here!
I would, said Geraldine, she were!

But soon with alter'd voice, said she—
"Off, wandering mother![1] Peak and pine!
200 I have power to bid thee flee."
Alas! what ails poor Geraldine?
Why stares she with unsettled eye?
Can she the bodiless dead espy?[2]
And why with hollow voice cries she,
205 "Off, woman, off! this hour is mine—
Though thou her guardian spirit be,
Off, woman, off! 'tis given to me."

Then Christabel knelt by the lady's side,
And raised to heaven her eyes so blue—
210 Alas! said she, this ghastly ride—
Dear lady! it hath wilder'd you!
The lady wip'd her moist cold brow,
And faintly said, "'Tis over now!"

Again the wild-flower wine she drank:
215 Her fair large eyes 'gan glitter bright,
And from the floor whereon she sank,
The lofty lady stood upright:

1. Literally, "hysteria," one symptom being an altered voice.
2. marginal note, 1824] The Mother of Christabel, who is now her Guardian Spirit, appears to Geraldine, as in answer to her wish. Geraldine fears the Spirit, but yet has power over it for a time.

She was most beautiful to see,
Like a lady of a far countrée.

220 And thus the lofty lady spake—
All they, who live in the upper sky,
Do love you, holy Christabel!
And you love them, and for their sake
And for the good which me befel,
225 Even I in my degree will try,
Fair maiden, to requite you well.
But now unrobe yourself; for I
Must pray, ere yet in bed I lie.

Quoth Christabel, so let it be!
230 And as the lady bade, did she.
Her gentle limbs did she undress,
And lay down in her loveliness.

But thro' her brain of weal and woe
So many thoughts mov'd to and fro,
235 That vain it were her lids to close;
So half-way from the bed she rose,
And on her elbow did recline
To look at the lady Geraldine.

Beneath the lamp the lady bow'd,
240 And slowly roll'd her eyes around;
Then drawing in her breath aloud,
Like one that shudder'd, she unbound
The cincture° from beneath her breast: *belt*
Her silken robe, and inner vest,
245 Dropt to her feet, and full in view,
Behold! her bosom and half her side—
A sight to dream of, not to tell!
And she is to sleep by Christabel!

She took two Paces, and a Stride,[3]
250 And lay down by the maiden's side!:[4]
And in her arms the maid she took,
    Ah wel-a-day!
And with low voice and doleful look
These words did say:
255 In the touch of this bosom there worketh a spell,
Which is lord of thy utterance, Christabel!
Thou knowest to-night, and wilt know to-morrow
This mark of my shame, this seal of my sorrow;

---

3. 248–49 revised 1817–1824] O shield her! shield sweet
Christabel / But Geraldine nor moves nor stirs; / Ah!
what a stricken Look was her's! / Deep from within she
seems half-way / To lift some weight, with Faint assay, /
And eyes the Maid, and seeks delay: / Then suddenly as
one defied / Collects herself in scorn and pride . . .
4. marginal note, 1824] As soon as the wicked Bosom,
with the mysterious sign of Evil stamped thereby, touches
Christabel, she is deprived of the power of disclosing
what has occurred.

But vainly thou warrest,
260   For this is alone in
Thy power to declare,
      That in the dim forest
      Thou heard'st a low moaning,
And found'st a bright lady, surpassingly fair:
265   And didst bring her home with thee in love and in charity,
To shield her and shelter her from the damp air.

THE CONCLUSION TO PART THE FIRST

It was a lovely sight to see
The lady Christabel, when she
Was praying at the old oak tree.
270   Amid the jagged shadows
      Of mossy leafless boughs,
      Kneeling in the moonlight,
      To make her gentle vows;
Her slender palms together prest,
275   Heaving sometimes on her breast;
Her face resigned to bliss or bale°—   *woe, evil*
Her face, oh call it fair not pale;
And both blue eyes more bright than clear,
Each about to have a tear.

280   With open eyes (ah woe is me!)
Asleep, and dreaming fearfully,
Fearfully dreaming, yet I wis,°   *believe*
Dreaming that alone, which is—
O sorrow and shame! Can this be she,
285   The lady, who knelt at the old oak tree?
And lo! the worker of these harms,
That holds the maiden in her arms,
Seems to slumber still and mild,
As a mother with her child.

290   A star hath set, a star hath risen,
O Geraldine! since arms of thine
Have been the lovely lady's prison.
O Geraldine! one hour was thine—
Thou'st had thy will! By tairn° and rill,   *mountain pool*
295   The night-birds all that hour were still.
But now they are jubilant anew,
From cliff and tower, tu—whoo! tu—whoo!
Tu—whoo! tu—whoo! from wood and fell!°   *highland*

And see! the lady Christabel
300   Gathers herself from out her trance;
Her limbs relax, her countenance
Grows sad and soft; the smooth thin lids
Close o'er her eyes; and tears she sheds—

Large tears that leave the lashes bright!
305   And oft the while she seems to smile
As infants at a sudden light!

Yea, she doth smile, and she doth weep,
Like a youthful hermitess,
Beauteous in a wilderness,
310   Who, praying always, prays in sleep.
And, if she move unquietly,
Perchance, 'tis but the blood so free,
Comes back and tingles in her feet.
No doubt, she hath a vision sweet.
315   What if her guardian spirit 'twere?
What if she knew her mother near?
But this she knows, in joys and woes,
That saints will aid if men will call:
For the blue sky bends over all!

PART II

320   Each matin bell, the Baron saith,
Knells us back to a world of death.
These words Sir Leoline first said,
When he rose and found his lady dead:
These words Sir Leoline will say,
325   Many a morn to his dying day.

And hence the custom and law began,
That still at dawn the sacristan,°   *sexton*
Who duly pulls the heavy bell,
Five and forty beads° must tell   *the rosary*
330   Between each stroke—a warning knell,
Which not a soul can choose but hear
From Bratha Head to Wyn'dermere.[5]

Saith Bracy the bard, So let it knell!
And let the drowsy sacristan
335   Still count as slowly as he can!
There is no lack of such, I ween,°   *believe*
As well fill up the space between.
In Langdale Pike and Witch's Lair,
And Dungeon-ghyll° so foully rent,   *ravine*
340   With ropes of rock and bells of air
Three sinful sextons' ghosts are pent,
Who all give back, one after t'other,
The death-note to their living brother;
And oft too, by the knell offended,
345   Just as their one! two! three! is ended,

---

5. These and the following names refer to places in the Lake District.

The devil mocks the doleful tale
With a merry peal from Borrowdale.

The air is still! thro' mist and cloud
That merry peal comes ringing loud;
350   And Geraldine shakes off her dread,
And rises lightly from the bed;
Puts on her silken vestments white,
And tricks her hair in lovely plight,°   *plait*
And nothing doubting of her spell
355   Awakens the lady Christabel.
"Sleep you, sweet lady Christabel?
I trust that you have rested well."

And Christabel awoke and spied
The same who lay down by her side—
360   O rather say, the same whom she
Rais'd up beneath the old oak-tree!
Nay, fairer yet! and yet more fair!
For she belike hath drunken deep
Of all the blessedness of sleep!
365   And while she spake, her looks, her air
Such gentle thankfulness declare,
That (so it seem'd) her girded vests
Grew tight beneath her heaving breasts.
"Sure I have sinn'd!" said Christabel,
370   "Now heaven be prais'd if all be well!"
And in low faltering tones, yet sweet,[6]
Did she the lofty lady greet
With such perplexity of mind
As dreams too lively leave behind.

375   So quickly she rose, and quickly array'd
Her maiden limbs, and having pray'd
That He, who on the cross did groan,
Might wash away her sins unknown,
She forthwith led fair Geraldine
380   To meet her sire, Sir Leoline.

The lovely maid and the lady tall
Are pacing both into the hall,
And pacing on thro' page and groom
Enter the Baron's presence-room.

385   The Baron rose, and while he prest
His gentle daughter to his breast,
With cheerful wonder in his eyes
The lady Geraldine espies,
And gave such welcome to the same,
390   As might beseem so bright a dame!

---

6. marginal note, 1824] Christabel is made to believe, that the fearful Sight had taken place only in a dream.

But when he heard the lady's tale,
And when she told her father's name,
Why wax'd Sir Leoline so pale,
Murmuring o'er the name again,
395   Lord Roland de Vaux of Tryermaine?

Alas! they had been friends in youth;
But whispering tongues can poison truth;
And constancy lives in realms above;
And life is thorny; and youth is vain;
400   And to be wroth with one we love,
Doth work like madness in the brain.
And thus it chanc'd, as I divine,
With Roland and Sir Leoline.
Each spake words of high disdain
405   And insult to his heart's best brother:
They parted—ne'er to meet again!
But never either found another
To free the hollow heart from paining—
They stood aloof, the scars remaining,
410   Like cliffs which had been rent asunder;
A dreary sea now flows between,
But neither heat, nor frost, nor thunder,
Shall wholly do away, I ween,
The marks of that which once hath been.[7]

415   Sir Leoline, a moment's space,
Stood gazing on the damsel's face;
And the youthful Lord of Tryermaine
Came back upon his heart again.

O then the Baron forgot his age,
420   His noble heart swell'd high with rage;
He swore by the wounds in Jesu's side,
He would proclaim it far and wide
With trump and solemn heraldry,
That they, who thus had wronged the dame,
425   Were base as spotted infamy!
"And if they dare deny the same,
   My herald shall appoint a week,
   And let the recreant traitors seek
   My tourney court°—that there and then   *jousting arena*
430   I may dislodge their reptile souls
From the bodies and forms of men!"
He spake: his eye in lightning rolls!
For the lady was ruthlessly seiz'd; and he kenn'd
In the beautiful lady the child of his friend!

7. Lord Byron and Victorian essayist Walter Pater admired this passage on male friendship.

435   And now the tears were on his face,
And fondly in his arms he took
Fair Geraldine, who met th' embrace,
Prolonging it with joyous look.
Which when she view'd, a vision fell
440   Upon the soul of Christabel,
The vision of fear, the touch and pain!
She shrunk and shudder'd, and saw again
(Ah, woe is me! Was it for thee,
Thou gentle maid! such sights to see?)[8]
445   Again she saw that bosom old,
Again she felt that bosom cold,
And drew in her breath with a hissing sound:
Whereat the Knight turned wildly round,
And nothing saw, but his own sweet maid
450   With eyes upraised, as one that pray'd.

The touch, the sight, had pass'd away,[9]
And in its stead that vision blest,
Which comforted her after-rest,
While in the lady's arms she lay,
455   Had put a rapture in her breast,
And on her lips and o'er her eyes
Spread smiles like light!
                With new surprise,
"What ails then my beloved child?"
The Baron said—His daughter mild
460   Made answer, "All will yet be well!"
I ween, she had no power to tell
Aught else: so mighty was the spell.
Yet he, who saw this Geraldine,
Had deem'd her sure a thing divine,
465   Such sorrow with such grace she blended,
As if she fear'd, she had offended
Sweet Christabel, that gentle maid!
And with such lowly tones she prayed,
She might be sent without delay
470   Home to her father's mansion.
                      "Nay!
Nay, by my soul!" said Leoline.
"Ho! Bracy, the bard, the charge be thine!
Go thou, with music sweet and loud,
And take two steeds with trappings proud,
475   And take the youth whom thou lov'st best
To bear thy harp, and learn thy song,

---

8. marginal note, 1824] Christabel then recollects the whole, and knows that it was not a Dream: but yet cannot disclose the fact, that the strange Lady is a supernatural Being with the stamp of the Evil Ones on her.
9. marginal note, 1824] Christabel for a moment sees her Mother's Spirit.

And clothe you both in solemn vest,
And over the mountains haste along,
Lest wand'ring folk, that are abroad,
480   Detain you on the valley road.

And when he has cross'd the Irthing flood,
My merry bard! he hastes, he hastes
Up Knorren Moor, thro' Halegarth Wood,
And reaches soon that castle good
485   Which stands and threatens Scotland's wastes.

Bard Bracy! bard Bracy! your horses are fleet,[1]
Ye must ride up the hall, your music so sweet,
More loud than your horses' echoing feet!
And loud and loud to Lord Roland call,
490   Thy daughter is safe in Langdale hall!
Thy beautiful daughter is safe and free—
Sir Leoline greets thee thus thro' me.
He bids thee come without delay
With all thy numerous array;
495   And take thy lovely daughter home,
And he will meet thee on the way
With all his numerous array
White with their panting palfreys' foam:
And by mine honour! I will say,
500   That I repent me of the day
When I spake words of fierce disdain
To Roland de Vaux of Tryermaine!—
—For since that evil hour hath flown,
Many a summer's sun have shone;
505   Yet ne'er found I a friend again
Like Roland de Vaux of Tryermaine."

The lady fell, and clasped his knees,
Her face uprais'd, her eyes o'erflowing;
And Bracy replied, with faltering voice,
510   His gracious hail on all bestowing:—
Thy words, thou sire of Christabel,
Are sweeter than my harp can tell;
Yet might I gain a boon° of thee,   favor
This day my journey should not be,
515   So strange a dream hath come to me:
That I had vow'd with music loud
To clear yon wood from thing unblest,
Warn'd by a vision in my rest!
For in my sleep I saw that dove,
520   That gentle bird, whom thou dost love,

---

1. marginal note, 1824] How gladly Sir Leoline repeats the names and shows, how familiarly he had once been acquainted with all the spots & paths in the neighborhood of his former Friend's Castle & Residence.

And call'st by thy own daughter's name—
Sir Leoline! I saw the same,
Fluttering, and uttering fearful moan,
Among the green herbs in the forest alone.
525 Which when I saw and when I heard,
I wonder'd what might ail the bird:
For nothing near it could I see,
Save the grass and green herbs underneath the old tree.

And in my dream, methought, I went
530 To search out what might there be found;
And what the sweet bird's trouble meant,
That thus lay fluttering on the ground.
I went and peer'd, and could descry
No cause for her distressful cry;
535 But yet for her dear lady's sake
I stoop'd, methought the dove to take,
When lo! I saw a bright green snake
Coil'd around its wings and neck
Green as the herbs on which it couch'd,
540 Close by the dove's its head it crouch'd;
And with the dove it heaves and stirs,
Swelling its neck as she swell'd hers!
I woke; it was the midnight hour,
The clock was echoing in the tower;
545 But tho' my slumber was gone by,
This dream it would not pass away—
It seems to live upon my eye!
And thence I vow'd this self-same day,
With music strong and saintly song
550 To wander through the forest bare,
Lest aught unholy loiter there.

Thus Bracy said: the Baron, the while,
Half-listening heard him with a smile;
Then turn'd to Lady Geraldine,
555 His eyes made up of wonder and love;
And said in courtly accents fine,
Sweet maid, Lord Roland's beauteous dove,
With arms more strong than harp or song,
Thy sire and I will crush the snake!
560 He kiss'd her forehead as he spake,
And Geraldine in maiden wise
Casting down her large bright eyes,
With blushing cheek and courtesy fine
She turn'd her from Sir Leoline;
565 Softly gathering up her train,
That o'er her right arm fell again;
And folded her arms across her chest,
And couch'd her head upon her breast,

And look'd askance at Christabel——
570 Jesu Maria, shield her well!

A snake's small eye blinks dull and shy,
And the lady's eyes they shrunk in her head,
Each shrunk up to a serpent's eye,
And with somewhat of malice, and more of dread,
575 At Christabel she look'd askance!——
One moment—and the sight was fled!
But Christabel in dizzy trance,
Stumbling on the unsteady ground——
Shudder'd aloud, with a hissing sound;
580 And Geraldine again turn'd round,
And like a thing, that sought relief,
Full of wonder and full of grief,
She roll'd her large bright eyes divine
Wildly on Sir Leoline.

585 The maid, alas! her thoughts are gone,
She nothing sees—no sight but one!
The maid, devoid of guile and sin,
I know not how, in fearful wise
So deeply had she drunken in
590 That look, those shrunken serpent eyes,
That all her features were resign'd
To this sole image in her mind:
And passively did imitate
That look of dull and treacherous hate.
595 And thus she stood, in dizzy trance,
Still picturing that look askance
With forc'd unconscious sympathy
Full before her father's view——
As far as such a look could be,
600 In eyes so innocent and blue!

But when the trance was o'er, the maid
Paus'd awhile, and inly pray'd:
Then falling at her father's feet,
"By my mother's soul do I entreat
605   That thou this woman send away!"
She said: and more she could not say,
For what she knew she could not tell,
O'er-master'd by the mighty spell.

Why is thy cheek so wan and wild,
610 Sir Leoline? Thy only child
Lies at thy feet, thy joy, thy pride,
So fair, so innocent, so mild;
The same, for whom thy lady died!
O by the pangs of her dear mother
615 Think thou no evil of thy child!

For her, and thee, and for no other,
She pray'd the moment, ere she died:
Pray'd that the babe for whom she died,
Might prove her dear lord's joy and pride!
620   That prayer her deadly pangs beguil'd,
      Sir Leoline!
    And wouldst thou wrong thy only child,
      Her child and thine?
Within the Baron's heart and brain
625 If thoughts, like these, had any share,
They only swell'd his rage and pain,
And did but work confusion there.
His heart was cleft with pain and rage,
His cheeks they quiver'd, his eyes were wild.
630 Dishonour'd thus in his old age;
Dishonour'd by his only child,
And all his hospitality
To th'insulted daughter of his friend
By more than woman's jealousy,
635 Brought thus to a disgraceful end—
He roll'd his eye with stern regard
Upon the gentle minstrel bard,
And said in tones abrupt, austere—
Why, Bracy! dost thou loiter here?
640 I bade thee hence! The bard obey'd;
And turning from his own sweet maid,
The aged knight, Sir Leoline,
Led forth the lady Geraldine!

THE CONCLUSION TO PART THE SECOND[2]

A little child, a limber elf,
645 Singing, dancing to itself,
A fairy thing with red round cheeks
That always finds, and never seeks,
Makes such a vision to the sight
As fills a father's eyes with light;
650 And pleasures flow in so thick and fast
Upon his heart, that he at last
Must needs express his love's excess
With words of unmeant bitterness.
Perhaps 'tis pretty to force together
655 Thoughts so all unlike each other;

---

2. This conclusion, not in any known manuscript of this poem, was drafted in a letter to Robert Southey, May 1801.

To mutter and mock a broken charm,
To dally with wrong that does no harm.
Perhaps 'tis tender too and pretty
At each wild word to feel within,
660   A sweet recoil of love and pity.
And what, if in a world of sin
(O sorrow and shame should this be true!)
Such giddiness of heart and brain
Comes seldom save from rage and pain,
665   So talks as it's most used to do.

1797–1801   1816

COMPANION READING

Mary Elizabeth Coleridge, *The Witch*[1]

I have walked a great while over the snow,
And I am not tall nor strong.
My clothes are wet, and my teeth are set,
And the way was hard and long.
5   I have wandered over the fruitful earth,
But I never came here before.
Oh, lift me over the threshold, and let me in at the door!

The cutting wind is a cruel foe.
I dare not stand in the blast.
10   My hands are stone, and my voice a groan,
And the worst of death is past.
I am but a little maiden still,
My little white feet are sore.
Oh, lift me over the threshold, and let me in at the door!

15   Her voice was the voice that women have,
Who plead for their heart's desire.
She came—she came—and the quivering flame
Sunk and died in the fire.
It never was lit again on my hearth
20   Since I hurried across the floor,
To lift her over the threshold, and let her in at the door.

1892   *Poems*, 1908

---

1. Mary Elizabeth Coleridge (1861–1907) was a novelist, poet, essayist, and reviewer. Samuel Taylor Coleridge was her great grand-uncle.

Kubla Khan:
or
A Vision in a Dream[1]

Of the Fragment of Kubla Khan

The following fragment is here published at the request of a poet of great and deserved celebrity,[2] and, as far as the Author's own opinions are concerned, rather as a psychological curiosity, than on the ground of any supposed *poetic* merits.

In the summer of the year 1797, the Author, then in ill health, had retired to a lonely farm house between Porlock and Linton, on the Exmoor confines of Somerset and Devonshire. In consequence of a slight indisposition, an anodyne[3] had been prescribed, from the effects of which he fell asleep in his chair at the moment that he was reading the following sentence, or words of the same substance, in "Purchas's Pilgrimage":[4] "Here the Khan Kubla commanded a palace to be built, and a stately garden thereunto: and thus ten miles of fertile ground were inclosed with a wall." The Author continued for about three hours in a profound sleep, at least of the external senses, during which time he has the most vivid confidence, that he could not have composed less than from two to three hundred lines; if that indeed can be called composition in which all the images rose up before him as *things*, with a parallel production of the correspondent expressions, without any sensation or consciousness of effort. On awaking he appeared to himself to have a distinct recollection of the whole, and taking his pen, ink, and paper, instantly and eagerly wrote down the lines that are here preserved. At this moment he was unfortunately called out by a person on business from Porlock, and detained by him above an hour, and on his return to his room, found, to his no small surprise and mortification, that though he still retained some vague and dim recollection of the general purpose of the vision, yet, with the exception of some eight or ten scattered lines and images, all the rest had passed away like the images on the surface of a stream into which a stone has been cast, but, alas! without the after restoration of the latter:

> Then all the charm
> Is broken—all that phantom-world so fair
> Vanishes, and a thousand circlets spread,
> And each mis-shape the other. Stay awhile,
> Poor youth! who scarcely dar'st lift up thine eyes—
> The stream will soon renew its smoothness, soon
> The visions will return! And lo, he stays,
> And soon the fragments dim of lovely forms
> Come trembling back, unite, and now once more
> The pool becomes a mirror.[5]

---

1. Grandson of Genghis Khan and Emperor of China in the 13th century.
2. Byron convinced his own publisher to issue the poem, together with *Christabel* and *The Pains of Sleep*.
3. A painkiller, probably laudanum (tincture of opium).

4. A collection of often fantastical accounts of foreign lands compiled by Samuel Purchas (1613). As a boy, Coleridge was an avid reader of such literature.
5. Coleridge, *The Picture* (91–100), also in *Sibylline Leaves* (1817).

Yet from the still surviving recollections in his mind, the Author has frequently purposed to finish for himself what had been originally, as it were, given to him. Σαμερον αδιον ασω:[6] but the to-morrow is yet to come.

As a contrast to this vision, I have annexed a fragment of a very different character, describing with equal fidelity the dream of pain and disease.[7]

(1816)

In Xanadu did KUBLA KHAN
A stately pleasure-dome decree
Where ALPH, the sacred river, ran
Through caverns measureless to man
5   Down to a sunless sea.
So twice five miles of fertile ground
With walls and towers were girdled round;
And here were gardens bright with sinuous rills
Where blossomed many an incense-bearing tree;
10   And here were forests ancient as the hills,
Enfolding[8] sunny spots of greenery.

But oh that deep romantic chasm which slanted
Down the green hill athwart a cedarn cover!
A savage place! as holy and inchanted
15   As e'er beneath a waning moon was haunted
By woman wailing for her demon-lover!
And from this chasm, with ceaseless turmoil seething,
As if this earth in fast thick pants were breathing,
A mighty fountain momently was forced:
20   Amid whose swift half-intermitted Burst
Huge fragments vaulted like rebounding hail,
Or chaffy grain beneath the thresher's flail:
And mid these dancing rocks at once and ever
It flung up momently the sacred river.
25   Five miles meandering with a mazy motion
Through wood and dale the sacred river ran,
Then reached the caverns measureless to man,
And sank in tumult to a lifeless ocean:
And 'mid this tumult Kubla heard from far
30   Ancestral voices prophesying war!

The shadow of the dome of pleasure
Floated midway on the waves;
Where was heard the mingled measure
From the fountain and the caves.
35   It was a miracle of rare device,
A sunny pleasure-dome with caves of ice!

---

6. From Theocritus, *Idyls*, 1.145: "I'll sing a sweeter song tomorrow."
7. *The Pains of Sleep.*

8. Revised from a likely printer's error, this was "And folding" in 1816.

A damsel with a dulcimer
In a vision once I saw:
It was an Abyssinian maid
40   And on her dulcimer she played,
Singing of Mount Abora.[9]
Could I revive within me
Her symphony and song,
To such a deep delight 'twould win me
45   That with music loud and long,
I would build that dome in air,
That sunny dome! those caves of ice!
And all who heard should see them there,
And all should cry, Beware! Beware!
50   His flashing eyes, his floating hair!
Weave a circle round him thrice,
And close your eyes with holy dread:
For he on honey-dew hath fed,
And drank[1] the milk of Paradise.

1797   1816

⁂

RESPONSE

Mary Robinson: To the Poet Coleridge[1]

Rapt in the visionary theme!
   Spirit Divine! with thee I'll wander!
Where the blue, wavy, lucid stream
   Mid forest glooms shall slow meander!
5   With thee I'll trace the circling bounds
   Of thy new paradise, extended;
And listen to the varying sounds
   Of winds, and foamy torrents blended!

Now by the source, which lab'ring heaves
10   The mystic fountain, bubbling, panting,[2]
While gossamer° its network weaves   *fine cobwebs*
   Adown the blue lawn, slanting—
I'll mark thy "sunny dome," and view
   Thy "caves of ice," thy fields of dew,[3]
15   Thy ever-blooming mead, whose flow'r
Waves to the cold breath of the moonlight hour!
Or when the day-star,° peering bright   *sun*
On the grey wing of parting night;
While more than vegetating pow'r
20   Throbs, grateful to the burning hour,

9. A fabled Paradise in equatorial Abyssinia, thought to be the head of the Nile River, mentioned by Purchas, and by Milton in *Paradise Lost* (4.280–85).
1. Changed to "drunk" in 1832.
1. A response to *Kubla Khan*, written between 1797 and 1798, and recited to friends for many years prior to its publication in 1816. For more about Robinson, see her principal listing on page 289.
2. Cf. *Kubla Khan*, 18–19.
3. Cf. *Kubla Khan*, 35–36.

As summer's whispered sighs unfold
Her million million buds of gold!—

Then will I climb the breezy bounds
   Of thy new paradise, extended,
25 And listen to the distant sounds
   Of winds, and foamy torrents blended!

   Spirit Divine! with thee I'll trace
   Imagination's boundless space!
With thee, beneath thy "sunny dome,"
30   I'll listen to the minstrel's lay
   Hymning the gradual close of day;
In "caves of ice" enchanted roam,
Where on the glitt'ring entrance plays
The moon's beam with its silv'ry rays;
35 Or, when the glassy stream
That through the deep dell flows,
Flashes the noon's hot beam
   The noon's hot beam, that midway shows
Thy flaming temple, studded o'er
40 With all Peruvia's lustrous store![4]
There will I trace the circling bounds
   Of thy new paradise, extended!
And listen to the awful° sounds   *awe-inspiring*
   Of winds, and foamy torrents blended!

45 And now I'll pause to catch the moan
   Of distant breezes, cavern-pent;
Now, ere the twilight tints are flown,
   Purpling the landscape far and wide,
   On the dark promontory's side
50   I'll gather wild flowers, dew besprent,°   *sprinkled over*
And weave a crown for thee,
Genius of heav'n-taught poesy!
While, opening to my wond'ring eyes,
Thou bid'st a new creation rise,
55 I'll raptured trace the circling bounds
   Of thy rich paradise, extended,
And listen to the varying sounds
   Of winds, and foamy torrents blended.
And now, with lofty tones inviting,
60 Thy nymph, her dulcimer swift-smiting,
Shall wake me in ecstatic measures
Far, far removed from mortal pleasures;[5]
In cadence rich, in cadence strong,
Proving the wondrous witcheries of song!
65 I hear her voice—thy "sunny dome,"
   Thy "caves of ice," aloud repeat—
   Vibrations, madd'ning sweet,
Calling the visionary wand'rer home.
She sings of thee, oh favoured child

4. Peru was famed for mineral and gem mines.   5. Cf. *Kubla Khan*, 37.

70   Of minstrelsy, sublimely wild!—
      Of thee whose soul can feel the tone
      Which gives to airy dreams a magic all thy own!

                                        SAPPHO

1800   1801

The Pains of Sleep

In September 1803, on his return, alone, from a walking tour of Scotland begun with the Wordsworths, Coleridge sent this poem to brother-in-law Robert Southey, in a letter about his struggle to break a dependency on opium: "I have walked 263 miles in eight Days—so I must have strength somewhere but my spirits are dreadful, owing entirely to the Horrors of every night—I truly dread to sleep it is no shadow with me, but substantial Misery foot-thick, that makes me sit by my bedside of a morning, & cry—. I have abandoned all opiates except Ether be one; & that only in fits—& that is a blessed medicine!—& when you see me drink a glass of Spirit & Water, except by prescription of a physician, you shall despise me—but still I can not get quiet rest. . . . I do not know how I came to scribble down these verses to you—my heart was aching, my head all confused—but they are, doggrels as they may be, a true portrait of my nights.—What to do, I am at a loss, for it is hard thus to be withered, having the faculty & attainments, which I have." In 1806, Coleridge drafted *A Child's Evening Prayer*, which begins, "Ere on my bed my limbs I lay, / God grant me grace my prayers to say."

      Ere on my bed my limbs I lay,
      It hath not been my use to pray
      With moving lips or bended knees;
      But silently, by slow degrees,
5   My spirit I to Love compose,
      In humble trust mine eye-lids close,
      With reverential resignation,
      No wish conceived, no thought exprest,
      Only a *sense* of supplication;
10   A sense o'er all my soul imprest
      That I am weak, yet not unblest,
      Since in me, round me, every where
      Eternal Strength and Wisdom are.

      But yester-night I prayed aloud
15   In anguish and in agony,
      Up-starting from the fiendish crowd
      Of shapes and thoughts that tortured me:
      A lurid light, a trampling throng,
      Sense of intolerable wrong,
20   And whom I scorned, those only strong!
      Thirst of revenge, the powerless will
      Still baffled, and yet burning still!
      Desire with loathing strangely mixed
      On wild or hateful objects fixed.
25   Fantastic passions! maddening brawl!

And shame and terror over all!
Deeds to be hid which were not hid,
Which all confused I could not know
Whether I suffered, or I did:
30   For all seemed guilt, remorse or woe,
My own or others still the same
Life-stifling fear, soul-stifling shame.

So two nights passed: the night's dismay
Saddened and stunned the coming day.
35   Sleep, the wide blessing, seemed to me
Distemper's worst calamity.
The third night, when my own loud scream
Had waked me from the fiendish dream,
O'ercome with sufferings strange and wild,
40   I wept as I had been a child;
And having thus by tears subdued
My anguish to a milder mood,
Such punishments, I said, were due
To natures deepliest stained with sin,—
45   For aye entempesting anew
The unfathomable hell within,[1]
The horror of their deeds to view,
To know and loathe, yet wish and do!
Such griefs with such men well agree,
50   But wherefore, wherefore fall on me?
To be beloved is all I need,
And whom I love, I love indeed.

1803   1816

DEJECTION:
An Ode[1]

Late, late yestreen I saw the new Moon,
With the old Moon in her arms;
And I fear, I fear, my Master dear!
We shall have a deadly storm.

Ballad of Sir PATRICK SPENCE[2]

I

WELL! If the Bard was weather-wise, who made
The grand old ballad of Sir Patrick Spence,

---

1. A painful affiliation with Milton's Satan: "the hot Hell that always in him burns" (9.467).
1. Originally a long verse-letter addressed to Sarah Hutchinson (beloved sister of William Wordsworth's wife) in April 1802, after hearing the first four stanzas of Wordsworth's "Intimations" Ode. When Coleridge put it in the Morning Post on 4 October 1802, Wordsworth's wedding day and the seventh anniversary of his own unhappy marriage, he cut it by half and made the addressee a generic "Edmund." Our text is from Sibylline Leaves (1817).
2. See page 392.

This night, so tranquil now, will not go hence
Unrous'd by winds, that ply a busier trade
5 Than those which mould yon cloud in lazy flakes,
Or the dull sobbing draft, that moans and rakes
  Upon the strings of this Æolian lute,[3]
  Which better far were mute.
 For lo! the New-moon winter-bright!
10 And overspread with phantom-light,
 (With swimming phantom light o'erspread
 But rimm'd and circled by a silver thread)
I see the old Moon in her lap, foretelling
 The coming on of rain and squally blast.
15 And oh! that even now the gust were swelling,
 And the slant night-shower driving loud and fast!
Those sounds which oft have raised me, whilst they awed,
  And sent my soul abroad,
Might now perhaps their wonted impulse give,
20 Might startle this dull pain, and make it move and live!

II

A grief without a pang, void, dark, and drear,
 A stifled, drowsy, unimpassion'd grief,
 Which finds no natural outlet, no relief,
  In word, or sigh, or tear—
25 O Lady! in this wan and heartless mood,
To other thoughts by yonder throstle° woo'd,   *thrush*
 All this long eve, so balmy and serene,
Have I been gazing on the western sky,
 And it's peculiar tint of yellow green:
30 And still I gaze—and with how blank an eye!
And those thin clouds above, in flakes and bars,
That give away their motion to the stars;
Those stars, that glide behind them or between,
Now sparkling, now bedimm'd, but always seen;
35 Yon crescent Moon, as fix'd as if it grew
In its own cloudless, starless lake of blue;
I see them all so excellently fair,
I see, not feel how beautiful they are![4]

III

 My genial° spirits fail;[5]   *creative*
40 And what can these avail,
To lift the smothering weight from off my breast?
 It were a vain endeavor,
 Though I should gaze for ever

3. See *The Eolian Harp.*
4. Compare Wordsworth's *Ode,* 36–50.

5. Compare *Tintern Abbey,* lines 114ff.

On that green light that lingers in the west:
45   I may not hope from outward forms to win
The passion and the life, whose fountains are within.

IV

O Lady! we receive but what we give,
And in our life alone does nature live:
Ours is her wedding-garment, ours her shroud!
50   And would we aught behold, of higher worth,
Than that inanimate° cold world allow'd   *soulless*
To the poor loveless ever-anxious crowd,
    Ah! from the soul itself must issue forth,
A light, a glory, a fair luminous cloud
55   Enveloping the Earth—
And from the soul itself must there be sent
    A sweet and potent voice, of its own birth,
Of all sweet sounds the life and element!

V

O pure of heart! thou need'st not ask of me
60   What this strong music in the soul may be!
What, and wherein it doth exist,
This light, this glory, this fair luminous mist,
This beautiful and beauty-making power.
      Joy, virtuous Lady! Joy that ne'er was given,
65   Save to the pure, and in their purest hour,
Life, and life's effluence, cloud at once and shower.
Joy, Lady! is the spirit and the power,
Which wedding Nature to us gives in dow'r,
    A new Earth and new Heaven,[6]
70   Undreamt of by the sensual and the proud—
Joy is the sweet voice, Joy the luminous cloud—
      We in ourselves rejoice!
And thence flows all that charms or ear or sight,
    All melodies the echoes of that voice,
75   All colours a suffusion from that light.

VI

There was a time when, though my path was rough,
    This joy within me dallied with distress,
And all misfortunes were but as the stuff
    Whence Fancy made me dreams of happiness:[7]
80   For hope grew round me, like the twining vine,
And fruits, and foliage, not my own, seem'd mine.
But now afflictions bow me down to earth:
Nor care I that they rob me of my mirth,

---

6. "And I saw a new heaven and a new earth: for the first heaven and the first earth were passed away" (Revelation 21.1).

7. Compare the opening of Wordsworth's *Ode*.

But oh! each visitation
85   Suspends what nature gave me at my birth,
      My shaping spirit of Imagination.
For not to think of what I needs must feel,
      But to be still and patient, all I can;
And haply° by abstruse research to steal   *perhaps*
90   From my own nature all the natural Man—
    This was my sole resource, my only plan:
Till that which suits a part infects the whole,
And now is almost grown the habit of my Soul.

VII

Hence, viper thoughts, that coil around my mind,
95   Reality's dark dream!
I turn from you, and listen to the wind,
      Which long has rav'd unnotic'd. What a scream
Of agony by torture lengthen'd out
That lute sent forth! Thou Wind, that rav'st without,
100   Bare craig, or mountain-tairn,[8] or blasted tree,
Or pine-grove whither woodman never clomb,
Or lonely house, long held the witches' home,
      Methinks were fitter instruments for thee,
Mad Lutanist! who in this month of show'rs,
105   Of dark brown gardens, and of peeping flow'rs,
Mak'st Devils' yule,° with worse than wint'ry song,   *Christmas*
The blossoms, buds, and tim'rous leaves among.
    Thou Actor, perfect in all tragic sounds!
Thou mighty Poet, e'en to Frenzy bold!
110   What tell'st thou now about?
    'Tis of the Rushing of an Host in rout,
      With groans of trampled men, with smarting wounds—
At once they groan with pain, and shudder with the cold!
But hush! there is a pause of deepest silence![9]
115   And all that noise, as of a rushing crowd,
With groans, and tremulous shudderings—all is over—
      It tells another tale, with sounds less deep and loud!
      A tale of less affright,
      And temper'd with delight,
120   As Otway's self had fram'd the tender lay[1]—
      'Tis of a little child,
      Upon a lonesome wild,
Not far from home, but she hath lost her way:
And now moans low in bitter grief and fear,
125   And now screams loud, and hopes to make her mother hear.

---

8. This address to the wind will not appear extravagant to those who have heard it at night, and in a mountainous country [Coleridge's note]. A tairn is a small mountain lake.
9. Echoing Wordsworth's "There was a Boy," 17ff (page 446).

1. Thomas Otway, author of *The Orphan* (1680) and other tragedies noted for pathos. In a letter draft, "William's" appears instead of "Otway's"; the next five lines allude to Wordsworth's *Lucy Gray*, sounding its keynote rhymes (see pages 448–50).

VIII

'Tis midnight, but small thoughts have I of sleep;
Full seldom may my friend such vigils keep!
Visit her, gentle Sleep! with wings of healing,
   And may this storm be but a mountain-birth,°   *short-lived*
130   May all the stars hang bright above her dwelling,
   Silent as though they watch'd the sleeping Earth!
      With light heart may she rise,
      Gay fancy, cheerful eyes,
   Joy lift her spirit, joy attune her voice:
135   To her may all things live, from Pole to Pole,
Their life the eddying of her living soul!
     O simple spirit, guided from above,
Dear Lady! friend devoutest of my choice,
Thus may'st thou ever, evermore rejoice.[2]

1802–1817   1817

LETTERS

To William Godwin[1]

Greta Hall, Keswick Wednesday, March 25, 1801

Dear Godwin

   * * * In my long Illness I had compelled into hours of Delight many a sleepless, painful hour of Darkness by chasing down metaphysical Game—and since then I have continued the Hunt, till I found myself unaware at the Root of Pure Mathematics—and up that tall smooth Tree, whose few poor Branches are all at it's very summit, am I climbing by pure adhesive strength of arms and thighs—still slipping down, still renewing my ascent.—You would not know me—! all sounds of similitude keep at such a distance from each other in my mind, that I have <u>forgotten</u> how to make a rhyme—I look at the Mountains (that visible God Almighty that looks in at all my windows) I look at the Mountains only for the Curves of their outlines; the Stars, as I behold them, form themselves into Triangles—and my hands are scarred with scratches from a Cat, whose back I was rubbing in the Dark in order to see whether the sparks from it were refrangible by a Prism. The Poet is dead in me—my imagination (or rather the Somewhat that had been imaginative) lies, like a Cold Snuff on the circular Rim of a Brass Candle-stick, without even a stink of Tallow to remind you that it was once cloathed & mitred with Flame. That is past by!—I was once a Volume of Gold Leaf, rising & riding on every breath of Fancy—but I have beaten myself back into weight & density, & now I sink in quicksilver, yea, remain squat and square on the earth amid the hurricane, that makes Oaks and Straws join in one Dance, fifty yards high in the Element. * * *

   Have you seen the second Volume of the Lyrical Ballads, & the Preface prefixed to the First?——I should judge of a man's Heart, and Intellect precisely according to the degree & intensity of the admiration, with which he read those poems——Perhaps, instead of Heart I should have said Taste, but when I think of The Brothers,

---

2. The *Morning Post* version is signed ΕΣ ΤΗ ΣΕ, Greek phonics for STC.

1. For more about Godwin, see his principal listing on page 144.

of Ruth, and of Michael, I recur to the expression, & am enforced to say <u>Heart</u>. If I die, and the Booksellers will give you any thing for my Life, be sure to say— 'Wordsworth descended on him, like the Γνῶθι σεαυτόν² from Heaven; by shewing to him what true Poetry was, he made him know, that he himself was no Poet.' * * *

God bless you
& S. T. Coleridge

To Thomas Poole¹

Friday, Oct. 14, 1803. Greta Hall, Keswick

My dearest Poole

I received your letter this evening, thank you for your kindness in answering it immediately, and will prove my thankfulness by doing the same. In answer to your Question respecting Leslie & T. Wedgwood,² I say—to the best of my Knowledge, <u>Not a word, at any time</u>. I have examined & cross-examined my recollective Faculty with no common earnestness; and I cannot produce in myself even the dimmest <u>Feeling</u> of any such conversation. Yet I talk so much & so variously, that doubtless I say a thousand Things that exist in the minds of others, when to my own consciousness they are as if they have never been. I lay too many Eggs in the hot Sands with Ostrich Carelessness & Ostrich oblivion—And tho' many are luckily trod on & smashed; as many crawl forth into Life, some to Furnish Feathers for the Caps of others, and more alas! to plume the Shafts in the Quivers of my Enemies and of them "that lie in wait against my Soul."³ * * *

Wordsworth is in good health, & all his family. He has one LARGE Boy, christened John. He has made a Beginning to his Recluse.⁴ * * * I now see very little of Wordsworth: my own Health makes it inconvenient & unfit for me to go thither one third as often, as I used to do—and Wordsworth's Indolence, &c keeps him at home. Indeed, were I an irritable man, and an unthinking one, I should probably have considered myself as having been very unkindly used by him in this respect—for I was at one time confined for two months, & he never came in to see me / me, who had ever payed such unremitting attentions to him. But we must take the good & the ill together; & by seriously & habitually reflecting on our own faults & endeavouring to amend them we shall then find little difficulty in confining our attention as far as it acts on our Friends' characters, to their good Qualities.—Indeed, I owe it to Truth & Justice as well as to myself to say, that the concern, which I have felt in this instance, and one or two other more <u>crying</u> instances, of Self-involution in Wordsworth, has been almost wholly a Feeling of friendly Regret, & disinterested Apprehension— I saw him more & more benetted in hypochondriachal Fancies, living wholly among <u>Devotees</u>—having every the minutest Thing, almost his very Eating & Drinking, done for him by his Sister, or Wife—& I trembled, lest a Film should rise, and thicken on his moral Eye.—The habit too of writing such a multitude of small Poems was in this instance hurtful to him—such Things as that Sonnet of his in Monday's Morning Post, about Simonides & the Ghost—I rejoice therefore with a deep & true Joy, that

---

2. Know thyself (Greek), the instruction of Socrates.
1. A neighbor in Nether Stowey, fan, friend, and sometimes patron.
2. The Wedgewood family, of pottery fame, were Coleridge's patrons. Everyone was fascinated by Tom. Poole was worried that Coleridge had blabbed his dislike of Leslie to Tom.
3. "Deliver me from mine enemies . . . they lie in wait against my soul" (Psalm 59).
4. The long philosophical poem Coleridge was urging, never completed.

he has at length yielded to my urgent & repeated—almost unremitting—requests & remonstrances—& will go on with the Recluse exclusively.—A Great Work, in which he will sail; on an open Ocean, & a steady wind; unfretted by short tacks, reefing, & hawling & disentangling the ropes——great work necessarily comprehending his attention & Feelings within the circle of great objects & elevated Conceptions—this is his natural Element—the having been out of it has been his Disease—to return into it is the specific Remedy, both Remedy & Health. It is what Food is to Famine. I have seen enough, positively to give me feelings of hostility towards the plan of several of the Poems in the L. Ballads: & I really consider it as a misfortune, that Wordsworth ever deserted his former mountain Track to wander in the Lanes & allies; tho' in the event it may prove to have been a great Benefit to him. He will steer, I trust, the middle course.—But he found himself to be, or rather to be called, the Head & founder of a <u>Sect</u> in Poetry.[5] & assuredly he has written—& published in the M. Post, as W. L. D.[6] & sometimes with no signature—poems written with a <u>sectarian</u> spirit, & in a sort of Bravado.—I know, my dear Poole, that you are in the habit of keeping my Letters; but I must request of you, & do rely on it—that you will be so good as to destroy this Letter— * * *

S. T. Coleridge

On Donne's Poetry[1]

With Donne, whose muse on dromedary trots,
Wreathe iron pokers into true-love knots;
Rhyme's sturdy cripple, fancy's maze and clue,
Wit's forge and fire-blast, meaning's press and screw.

1818   1836

Work Without Hope[1]
Lines composed 21st February 1825

All Nature seems at work. Slugs leave their lair—
The bees are stirring—birds are on the wing—
And Winter slumbering in the open air,
Wears on his smiling face a dream of Spring!
5   And I the while, the sole unbusy thing,[2]
Nor honey make, nor pair, nor build, nor sing.

     Yet well I ken° the banks where amaranths blow,[3]   know
Have traced the fount whence streams of nectar flow.
Bloom, O ye amaranths! bloom for whom ye may,
10   For me ye bloom not! Glide, rich streams, away!

---

5. See Francis Jeffrey's recent review, page 468.
6. In 1803 Wordsworth signed seven sonnets in the liberal *Morning Post* W. L. D.—standing for Wordsworthius Libertati Dedicavit (Dedicated to Liberty), said his brother-in-law. See one such, page 283. This one (pub. 10 October 1803) recounts the tale of poet Simonides, who finds an exposed corpse and pays for its proper burial. Its ghost warns him not to board a ship on which he was

planning to travel. He heeds the warning, and the ship is wrecked and everyone on board dies.
1. Early modern poet John Donne was little read in the 18th century.
1. First published in *The Bijou*, a gift-book annual 1828.
2. Cf. *Frost at Midnight*, line 16.
3. Blow: bloom. Milton places this unfading flower "in paradise, fast by the Tree of Life" (*Paradise Lost* 4.354).

With lips unbrightened, wreathless brow,[4] I stroll:
And would you learn the spells that drowse my soul?
Work without Hope draws nectar in a sieve,
And Hope without an object cannot live.

1825–27   1828

Constancy to an Ideal Object

Since all that beat about in Nature's range,
Or veer or vanish; why should'st thou remain
The only constant in a world of change,
O yearning Thought! that liv'st but in the brain?
5 Call to the Hours, that in the distance play,
The faery people of the future day————
Fond Thought! not one of all that shining swarm
Will breathe on *thee* with life-enkindling breath,
Till when, like strangers shelt'ring from a storm,
10 Hope and Despair meet in the porch of Death!
Yet still thou haunt'st me; and though well I see,
She is not thou, and only thou art she,
Still, still as though some dear *embodied* Good,
Some *living* Love before my eyes there stood
15 With answering look a ready ear to lend,
I mourn to thee and say—"Ah! loveliest friend!
That this the meed of all my toils might be,
To have a home, an English home, and thee!"
Vain repetition! Home and Thou are one.
20 The peacefull'st cot,° the moon shall shine upon,   cottage
Lulled by the thrush, and wakened by the lark,
Without thee were but a becalméd bark,°   boat
Whose Helmsman on an ocean waste and wide
Sits mute and pale his mouldering helm beside.

25 And art thou nothing? Such thou art, as when
The woodman winding westward up the glen
At wintry dawn, where o'er the sheep-track's maze
The viewless° snow-mist weaves a glist'ning haze,   invisible
Sees full before him, gliding without tread,
30 An image with a glory round its head;[1]
The enamored rustic worships its fair hues,
Nor knows he *makes* the shadow, he pursues!

1804–1826?   1828

Epitaph

Stop, Christian Passer-by—Stop, child of God,
And read with gentle breast. Beneath this sod

---

4. Without the poet's prize, the wreath of laurel.
1. A walker in the mountains, the sun behind him, casts
a magnified vertical shadow on the crystalized mists
before him.

A poet lies, or that which once seem'd he—
O, lift one thought in prayer for S. T. C.;[1]
5 That he who many a year with toil of breath
Found death in life, may here find life in death!
Mercy for° praise—to be forgiven for° fame   *instead of*
He ask'd, and hoped, through Christ. Do thou the same!

9th November, 1833   1834

from The Statesman's Manual[1]
[SYMBOL AND ALLEGORY]

A hunger-bitten and idea-less philosophy naturally produces a starveling and comfortless religion. It is among the miseries of the present age that it recognizes no *medium* between literal and metaphorical. Faith is either to be buried in the dead letter, or its name and honors usurped by a counterfeit product of the mechanical understanding, which in the blindness of self-complacency confounds symbols with allegories. Now an allegory is but a translation of abstract notions into a picture-language, which is itself nothing but an abstraction from objects of the senses; the principal being more worthless even than its phantom proxy, both alike unsubstantial, and the former shapeless to boot. On the other hand a symbol (ὁ ἔστιν ἀεὶ ταυτηγόρικον)[2] is characterized by a translucence of the special in the individual, or of the general in the special, or of the universal in the general; above all by the translucence of the eternal through and in the temporal. It always partakes of the reality which it renders intelligible; and while it enunciates the whole, abides itself as a living part in that unity of which it is the representative. The other are but empty echoes which the fancy arbitrarily associates with apparitions of matter, less beautiful but not less shadowy than the sloping orchard or hill-side pasture-field seen in the transparent lake below. Alas, for the flocks that are to be led forth to such pastures! *It shall even be as when a hungry man dreameth, and behold, he eateth; but he awaketh and his soul is empty: or as when a thirsty man dreameth, and behold he drinketh; but he awaketh and behold, he is faint!*[3] O! that we would seek for the bread which was given from heaven, that we should eat thereof and be strengthened! O that we would draw at the well at which the flocks of our forefathers had living water drawn for them, even that water which, instead of mocking the thirst of him to whom it is given, becomes a well within himself *springing up to life everlasting!*

1816

from The Friend[1]
["MY GHOST-THEORY"]

I will endeavour to make my Ghost-Theory more clear to those of my readers, who are fortunate enough to find it obscure in consequence of their own good health and unshattered nerves. The window of my Library at Keswick is opposite to the fire-place, and looks out on the very large garden that occupies the whole slope of the hill on

1. Coleridge commented that he was "more commonly known by the Initials of his name than by the Name Itself." He signed one copy of this verse (to J. G. Lockhart) ΕΣ ΤΗ ΣΕ. He died 25 July 1834.
1. *The Statesman's Manual* is one of a pair of "lay sermons" addressed to the governing classes, arguing that Scripture provides moral principles in social and economic crises.

2. To express the same idea but with a difference (Greek). Coleridge's word for this is "tautegorical."
3. Isaiah 29.8.
1. *The Friend* was published in weekly intervals between 1809 and 1810. This passage is from an essay published on 5 October 1809. Our text is from the edition of 1818.

which the house stands. Consequently, the rays of light transmitted *through* the glass, (i.e. the rays from the garden, the opposite mountains, and the bridge, river, lake, and vale interjacent) and the rays reflected *from* it, (of the fire-place, &c.) enter the eye at the same moment. At the coming on of evening, it was my frequent amusement to watch the image or reflection of the fire, that seemed burning in the bushes or between the trees in different parts of the garden or the fields beyond it, according as there was more or less light; and which still arranged itself among the real objects of vision, with a distance and magnitude proportioned to its greater or lesser faintness. For still as the darkness encreased, the image of the fire lessened and grew nearer and more distinct, till the twilight had deepened into perfect night, when all outward objects being excluded, the window became a perfect looking-glass: save only that my books on the side shelves of the room were lettered, as it were, on their backs with stars, more or fewer as the sky was more or less clouded, (the rays of the stars being at that time the only ones transmitted.) Now substitute the Phantom from [the] brain for the images of *reflected* light (the fire for instance) and the forms of [the] room and its furniture for the *transmitted* rays, and you have a fair resemblance of an apparition, and a just conception of the manner in which it is seen together with real objects. I have long wished to devote an entire work to the subject of Dreams, Visions, Ghosts, Witchcraft, &c. in which I might first give, and then endeavour to explain the most interesting and best attested fact of each, which has come within my knowledge, either from books or from personal testimony, I might then explain in a more satisfactory way the mode in which our thoughts, in states of morbid slumber, become at times perfectly *dramatic* (for in certain sorts of dreams the dullest Wight becomes a Shakespeare) and by what law the *Form* of the vision appears to talk to us its own thoughts in a voice as audible as the shape is visible; and this too oftentimes in connected trains, and not seldom even with a concentration of power which may easily impose on the soundest judgements, uninstructed in the *Optics* and *Acoustics* of the inner sense, for Revelations and gifts of Prescience. In aid of the present case, I will only remark, that it would appear incredible to persons not accustomed to these subtle notices of self observation, what small and remote resemblances, what mere *hints* of likeness from some real external object, especially if the shape be aided by colour, will suffice to make a vivid thought consubstantiate with the real object, and derive from it an outward perceptibility.

1818

BIOGRAPHIA LITERARIA   In 1803 Coleridge contemplated writing "my metaphysical works *as my life, & in* my life—intermixed with all the other events of history of the mind and fortunes of S.T. Coleridge." Nothing came of this Romantic interfusion of personal experience and philosophical generalization until 1815, when Coleridge decided to prefix *Sibylline Leaves* with "a general preface...on the principles" of criticism. Wordsworth's *Poems* (1815), with an extensive prefatory essay, further prompted Coleridge to clarify his theoretical divergences from his former collaborator. The resulting *Biographia Literaria,* grown from preface to two independent volumes, is an extraordinary work: a revisionary autobiography, minimizing the youthful radicalism; a philosophical argument to establish the freedom of the will, yet so enmeshed in the material exigencies of book production that publication was delayed for two years; a meditation on original genius heavily indebted to recent German thought; and, in Chapter 13, a comic masquerade that has proved a seminal passage for literary studies. In his sustained, probing commentary on Wordsworth, unprecedented in discussions of modern literature, Coleridge confirmed Wordsworth's stature and, at the same time, by claiming to understand Wordsworth better than he did himself, institutionalized the role of the critic as the reader who completes the poet's task. *Lyrical Ballads* (1798) had been a joint project of Wordsworth and Coleridge; Coleridge said in 1800 that the new Preface "contains our joint opinions on Poetry," but by 1802 he had begun "to suspect, that there is, somewhere or other, a *radical* difference in our opinions."

Biographia Literaria or, Biographical Sketches of My Literary Life and Opinions

from *Chapter* 4
[WORDSWORTH'S EARLIER POETRY]

I was in my twenty-fourth year, when I had the happiness of knowing Mr. Wordsworth personally, and while memory lasts, I shall hardly forget the sudden effect produced on my mind, by his recitation of a manuscript poem, which still remains unpublished.[1] * * * There was here, no mark of strained thought, or forced diction, no crowd or turbulence of imagery, and, as the poet hath himself well described in his lines "on revisiting the Wye," manly reflection, and human associations had given both variety, and an additional interest to natural objects, which in the passion and appetite of the first love they had seemed to him neither to need or permit. The occasional obscurities, which had risen from an imperfect controul over the resources of his native language, had almost wholly disappeared, together with that worse defect of arbitary and illogical phrases, at once hackneyed, and fantastic, which hold so distinguished a place in the *technique* of ordinary poetry, and will, more or less, alloy the earlier poems of the truest genius, unless the attention has been specifically directed to their worthlessness and incongruity.[2] * * * It was not however the freedom from false taste, whether as to common defects, or to those more properly his own, which made so unusual an impression on my feelings immediately, and subsequently on my judgement. It was the union of deep feeling with profound thought; the fine balance of truth in observing with the imaginative faculty in modifying the objects observed; and above all the original gift of spreading the tone, the *atmosphere,* and with it the depth and height of the ideal world around forms, incidents, and situations, of which, for the common view, custom had bedimmed all the lustre, had dried up the sparkle and the dew drops. To find no contradiction in the union of old and new; to contemplate the ANCIENT of days and all his works with feelings as fresh, as if all had then sprang forth at the first creative fiat;[3] characterizes the mind that feels the riddle of the world, and may help to unravel it. To carry on the feelings of childhood into the powers of manhood; to combine the child's sense of wonder and novelty with the appearances, which every day for perhaps forty years had rendered familiar;

> With sun and moon and stars throughout the year,
> And man and woman;[4]

this is the character and privilege of genius, and one of the marks which distinguish genius from talents. And therefore is it the prime merit of genius and its most unequivocal mode of manifestation, so to represent familiar objects as to awaken in the minds of others a kindred feeling concerning them and that freshness of sensation

---

1. *Guilt and Sorrow; or, Incidents upon Salisbury Plain,* written in 1793–1794, not published until 1842.
2. Coleridge described Wordsworth's *Descriptive Sketches* (1793) as work of "genius" but "knotty and contorted."
3. Divine command. The Ancient of Days is God the Creator. See the cover of this volume.
4. What Milton can no longer see (*To Mr. Cyriack Skinner upon his Blindness,* 5–6).

which is the constant accompaniment of mental, no less than of bodily, convalescence. Who has not a thousand times seen snow fall on water? Who has not watched it with a new feeling, from the time that he has read Burns' comparison of sensual pleasure

> To snow that falls upon a river
> A moment white—then gone for ever![5]

from *Chapter 11*
[THE PROFESSION OF LITERATURE]

With no other privilege than that of sympathy and sincere good wishes, I would address an affectionate exhortation to the youthful literati, grounded on my own experience. It will be but short; for the beginning, middle, and end converge to one charge: NEVER PURSUE LITERATURE AS A TRADE. With the exception of one extraordinary man, I have never known an individual, least of all an individual of genius, healthy or happy without a *profession*, i.e. some *regular* employment, which does not depend on the will of the moment, and which can be carried on so far *mechanically* that an average quantum only of health, spirits, and intellectual exertion are requisite to its faithful discharge. Three hours of leisure, unannoyed by any alien anxiety, and looked forward to with delight as a change and recreation, will suffice to realize in literature a larger product of what is truly *genial*, than weeks of compulsion. Money, and immediate reputation form only an arbitrary and accidental end of literary labor. The *hope* of increasing them by any given exertion will often prove a stimulant to industry; but the *necessity* of acquiring them will in all works of genius convert the stimulant into a *narcotic*. Motives by excess reverse their very nature, and instead of exciting, stun and stupify the mind. For it is one contradistinction of genius from talent, that its predominant end is always comprized in the means; and this is one of the many points, which establish an analogy between genius and virtue. Now though talents may exist without genius, yet as genius cannot exist, certainly not manifest itself, without talents, I would advise every scholar, who feels the genial power working within him, so far to make a division between the two, as that he should devote his *talents* to the acquirement of competence in some known trade or profession, and his genius to objects of his tranquil and unbiassed choice; while the consciousness of being actuated in both alike by the sincere desire to perform his duty, will alike ennoble both. My dear young friend (I would say) suppose yourself established in any honourable occupation. From the manufactory or counting-house, from the law-court, or from having visited your last patient, you return at evening,

> Dear tranquil time, when the sweet sense of home
> Is sweetest[1]———

to your family, prepared for its social enjoyments, with the very countenances of your wife and children brightened, and their voice of welcome made doubly welcome, by the knowledge that, as far as they are concerned, you have satisfied the demands of the day by the labor of the day. Then, when you retire into your study, in the books on your shelves you revisit so many venerable friends with whom you can converse. Your own spirit scarcely less free from personal anxieties than the great minds, that in those books are still living for you! Even your writing desk with its blank paper and all its other implements will appear as a chain of flowers, capable of linking your feelings

---

5. Robert Burns, *Tam O'Shanter* (lines 61–62).   1. Coleridge's *To a Gentleman* (92–93).

as well as thoughts to events and characters past or to come; not a chain of iron which binds you down to think of the future and the remote by recalling the claims and feelings of the peremptory present. But why should I say *retire?* The habits of active life and daily intercourse with the stir of the world will tend to give you such self-command, that the presence of your family will be no interruption. Nay, the social silence, or undisturbing voices of a wife or sister will be like a restorative atmosphere, or soft music which moulds a dream without becoming its object. If facts are required to prove the possibility of combining weighty performances in literature with full and independent employment, the works of Cicero and Xenophon among the ancients; of Sir Thomas Moore, Bacon, Baxter, or to refer at once to later and contemporary instances, DARWIN and ROSCOE,[2] are at once decisive of the question.

＊ ＊ ＊ It would be a sort of irreligion, and scarcely less than a libel on human nature to believe, that there is any established and reputable profession or employment, in which a man may not continue to act with honesty and honor; and doubtless there is likewise none, which may not at times present temptations to the contrary. But woefully will that man find himself mistaken, who imagines that the profession of literature, or (to speak more plainly) the *trade* of authorship, besets its members with fewer or with less insidious temptations, than the church, the law, or the different branches of commerce. But I have treated sufficiently on this unpleasant subject in an early chapter of this volume. I will conclude the present therefore with a short extract from HERDER,[3] whose name I might have added to the illustrious list of those, who have combined the successful pursuit of the muses, not only with the faithful discharge, but with the highest honors and honorable emoluments, of an established profession. [Coleridge prints the German passage and translates] "With the greatest possible solicitude avoid authorship. Too early or immoderately employed, it makes the head *waste* and the heart empty; even were there no other worse consequences. A person, who reads only to print, in all probability reads amiss; and he, who sends away through the pen and the press every thought, the moment it occurs to him, will in a short time have sent all away, and will become a mere journeyman of the printing-office, a *compositor*."

To which I may add from myself, that what medical physiologists affirm of certain secretions, applies equally to our thoughts; they too must be taken up again into the circulation, and be again and again re-secreted in order to ensure a healthful vigor, both to the mind and to its intellectual offspring.

from *Chapter 13*
[IMAGINATION AND FANCY]
On the imagination, or esemplastic power

Thus far had the work been transcribed for the press, when I received the following letter from a friend,[1] whose practical judgement I have had ample reason to estimate and revere, and whose taste and sensibility preclude all the excuses which my self-love might possibly have prompted me to set up in plea against the decision of advisers of equal good sense, but with less tact and feeling.

---

2. Cicero and Xenophon were illustrious statesmen. More (1478–1535) and Bacon (1561–1626) both served as Lord Chancellor in their public careers. Erasmus Darwin, a physician and a poet, and William Roscoe, a lawyer and abolitionist, were contemporaries and friends of Coleridge.
3. J. G. Herder (1744–1803), German poet, critic, and

philosopher of history, was superintendent of religious and educational affairs at Weimar. Coleridge quotes from his *Letters on the Study of Theology*.
1. Coleridge wrote the letter himself, and coined the word "esemplastic" (molding into unity).

Dear C.

You ask my opinion concerning your Chapter on the Imagination, both as to the impressions it made on myself, and as to those which I think it will make on the PUBLIC, *i.e. that part of the public, who from the title of the work and from its forming a sort of introduction to a volume of poems, are likely to constitute the great majority of your readers.*

As to myself, and stating in the first place the effect on my understanding, your opinions and method of argument were not only so new to me, but so directly the reverse of all I had ever been accustomed to consider as truth, that even if I had comprehended your premises sufficiently to have admitted them, and had seen the necessity of your conclusions, I should still have been in that state of mind, which in your note, p. 75, 76, you have so ingeniously evolved, as the antithesis to that in which a man is, when he makes a bull.[2] *In your own words, I should have felt as if I had been standing on my head.*

The effect on my feelings, on the other hand, I cannot better represent, than by supposing myself to have known only our light airy modern chapels of ease, and then for the first time to have been placed, and left alone, in one of our largest Gothic cathedrals in a gusty moonlight night of autumn. "Now in glimmer, and now in gloom;"[3] *often in palpable darkness not without a chilly sensation of terror; then suddenly emerging into broad yet visionary lights with coloured shadows, of fantastic shapes yet all decked with holy insignia and mystic symbols; and ever and anon coming out full upon pictures and stone-work images of great men, with whose names I was familiar, but which looked upon me with countenances and an expression, the most dissimilar to all I had been in the habit of connecting with those names. Those whom I had been taught to venerate as almost super-human in magnitude of intellect, I found perched in little fret-work niches, as grotesque dwarfs; while the grotesques, in my hitherto belief, stood guarding the high altar with all the characters of Apotheosis.*[4] *In short, what I had supposed substances were thinned away into shadows, while every where shadows were deepened into substances:*

> If substance may be call'd what shadow seem'd,
> For each seem'd either!   Milton[5]

Yet after all, I could not but repeat the lines which you had quoted from a MS. poem of your own in the FRIEND[6] *and applied to a work of Mr. Wordsworth's though with a few of the words altered:*

> ____An orphic tale indeed,
> A tale obscure of high and passionate thoughts
> To a strange music chaunted!*[7]

Be assured, however, that I look forward anxiously to your great book on the CONSTRUCTIVE PHILOSOPHY,[8] *which you have promised and announced: and that I will do my best to understand it. Only I will not promise to descend into the dark cave of Trophonius*[9] *with you, there to rub my own eyes, in order to make the sparks and figured flashes, which I am required to see.*

---

2. Contradicts himself, inviting ridicule.
3. *Christabel*, line 163.
4. Divinity.
5. A famous description of Death; *Paradise Lost*, 2.669–70. Cf. Burke, page 39 and Coleridge, page 699.
6. The journal produced by Coleridge in 1809–1810.
7. *To a Gentleman*, 45–47 (variant).

8. Perhaps the *Logic* or *Opus Maximum*, or Coleridge's Kantian model of philosophy.
9. Legendary architect of the temple of Apollo at Delphi. After his death an oracle was consecrated to him; visitors were dragged into a cave filled with strange sounds and glaring lights, where they received the oracle's messages.

So much for myself. But as for the PUBLIC, *I do not hesitate a moment in advising and urging you to withdraw the Chapter from the present work, and to reserve it for your announced treatises on the Logos or communicative intellect in Man and Deity.[1] First, because imperfectly as I understand the present Chapter, I see clearly that you have done too much, and yet not enough. You have been obliged to omit so many links, from the necessity of compression, that what remains, looks (if I may recur to my former illustration) like the fragments of the winding steps of an old ruined tower. Secondly, a still stronger argument (at least one that I am sure will be more forcible with you) is, that your readers will have both right and reason to complain of you. This Chapter, which cannot, when it is printed, amount to so little as an hundred pages, will of necessity greatly increase the expense of the work; and every reader who, like myself, is neither prepared or perhaps calculated for the study of so abstruse a subject so abstrusely treated, will, as I have before hinted, be almost entitled to accuse you of a sort of imposition on him. For who, he might truly observe, could from your title-page, viz. "*𝔐𝔶 𝔏𝔦𝔱𝔢𝔯𝔞𝔯𝔶 𝔏𝔦𝔣𝔢 𝔞𝔫𝔡 𝔒𝔭𝔦𝔫𝔦𝔬𝔫𝔰,*" *published too as introductory to a volume of miscellaneous poems, have anticipated, or even conjectured, a long treatise on ideal Realism, which holds the same relation in abstruseness to Plotinus, as Plotinus does to Plato.[2] It will be well, if already you have not too much of metaphysical disquisition in your work, though as the larger part of the disquisition is historical, it will doubtless be both interesting and instructive to many to whose unprepared minds your speculations on the esemplastic power would be utterly unintelligible. Be assured, if you do publish this Chapter in the present work, you will be reminded of Bishop Berkley's Siris,[3] announced as an Essay on Tar-water, which beginning with Tar ends with the Trinity, the omne scibile [everything knowable] forming the interspace. I say in the present work. In that greater work to which you have devoted so many years, and study so intense and various, it will be in its proper place. Your prospectus will have described and announced both its contents and their nature; and if any persons purchase it, who feel no interest in the subjects of which it treats, they will have themselves only to blame.*

I could add to these arguments one derived from pecuniary[4] motives, and particularly from the probable effects on the sale of your present publication; but they would weigh little with you compared with the preceding. Besides, I have long observed, that arguments drawn from your own personal interests more often act on you as narcotics than as stimulants, and that in money concerns you have some small portion of pig nature in your moral idiosyncracy, and like these amiable creatures, must occasionally be pulled backward from the boat in order to make you enter it. All success attend you, for if hard thinking and hard reading are merits, you have deserved it.

Your affectionate, & c.

In consequence of this very judicious letter, which produced complete conviction on my mind, I shall content myself for the present with stating the main result of the Chapter, which I have reserved for that future publication, a detailed prospectus of which the reader will find at the close of the second volume.

---

1. The Word of God, incarnated in Jesus Christ. Coleridge announced a study of the Gospel of John as part of a work that never appeared, the *Logosophia*.
2. An "ideal realist," Coleridge rejected the Platonic distinction between the essence and appearance of things for an idea of the world and the mind infused by one spirit, a position derived from Plato's inheritor Plotinus.

3. George Berkeley (1685–1753), Irish bishop and philosopher. *Siris* (1744) begins with a chemical description of the medicinal advantages of tar and proceeds to reflections on theology. Coleridge admired philosophy tied to the empirical truths of the natural sciences.
4. Financial.

The IMAGINATION then I consider either as primary, or secondary. The primary IMAGINATION I hold to be the living Power and prime Agent of all human Perception, and as a repetition in the finite mind of the eternal act of creation in the infinite I AM. The secondary I consider as an echo of the former, co-existing with the conscious will, yet still as identical with the primary in the *kind* of its agency, and differing only in *degree*, and in the *mode* of its operation. It dissolves, diffuses, dissipates, in order to re-create; or where this process is rendered impossible, yet still at all events it struggles to idealize and to unify. It is essentially *vital*, even as all objects (*as* objects) are essentially fixed and dead.

FANCY, on the contrary, has no other counters to play with, but fixities and definites. The Fancy is indeed no other than a mode of Memory emancipated from the order of time and space; and blended with, and modified by that empirical phenomenon of the will, which we express by the word CHOICE. But equally with the ordinary memory it must receive all its materials ready made from the law of association.

Whatever more than this, I shall think it fit to declare concerning the powers and privileges of the imagination in the present work, will be found in the critical essay on the uses of the Supernatural in poetry and the principles that regulate its introduction: which the reader will find prefixed to the poem of 𝔗𝔥𝔢 𝔄𝔫𝔠𝔦𝔢𝔫𝔱 𝔐𝔞𝔯𝔦𝔫𝔢𝔯.[5]

from *Chapter 14*
[OCCASION OF THE *LYRICAL BALLADS*—PREFACE TO THE SECOND EDITION— THE ENSUING CONTROVERSY]

During the first year that Mr. Wordsworth and I were neighbours, our conversations turned frequently on the two cardinal points of poetry, the power of exciting the sympathy of the reader by a faithful adherence to the truth of nature, and the power of giving the interest of novelty by the modifying colours of imagination. The sudden charm, which accidents of light and shade, which moon-light or sun-set diffused over a known and familiar landscape, appeared to represent the practicability of combining both. These are the poetry of nature. The thought suggested itself (to which of us I do not recollect) that a series of poems might be composed of two sorts. In the one, the incidents and agents were to be, in part at least, supernatural; and the excellence aimed at was to consist in the interesting of the affections by the dramatic truth of such emotions, as would naturally accompany such situations, supposing them real. And real in *this* sense they have been to every human being who, from whatever source of delusion, has at any time believed himself under supernatural agency. For the second class, subjects were to be chosen from ordinary life; the characters and incidents were to be such, as will be found in every village and its vicinity, where there is a meditative and feeling mind to seek after them, or to notice them, when they present themselves.

In this idea originated the plan of the *Lyrical Ballads*; in which it was agreed, that my endeavours should be directed to persons and characters supernatural, or at least romantic; yet so as to transfer from our inward nature a human interest and a semblance of truth sufficient to procure for these shadows of imagination that willing suspension of disbelief for the moment, which constitutes poetic faith. Mr. Wordsworth, on the other hand, was to propose to himself as his object, to give the charm of novelty to things of every day, and to excite a feeling analogous to the supernatural,

5. The essay did not appear, but the subject is addressed in Chapter 14.

by awakening the mind's attention from the lethargy of custom, and directing it to the loveliness and the wonders of the world before us; an inexhaustible treasure, but for which in consequence of the film of familiarity and selfish solicitude we have eyes, yet see not, ears that hear not, and hearts that neither feel nor understand.[1]

With this view I wrote the "Ancient Mariner," and was preparing among other poems, the "Dark Ladie," and the "Christabel," in which I should have more nearly realized my ideal, than I had done in my first attempt. But Mr. Wordsworth's industry had proved so much more successful, and the number of his poems so much greater, that my compositions, instead of forming a balance, appeared rather an interpolation of heterogeneous matter. Mr. Wordsworth added two or three poems written in his own character, in the impassioned, lofty, and sustained diction, which is characteristic of his genius. In this form the *Lyrical Ballads* were published; and were presented by him, as an *experiment*,[2] whether subjects, which from their nature rejected the usual ornaments and extra-colloquial style of poems in general, might not be so managed in the language of ordinary life as to produce the pleasurable interest, which it is the peculiar business of poetry to impart. To the second edition he added a preface of considerable length; in which notwithstanding some passages of apparently a contrary import, he was understood to contend for the extension of this style to poetry of all kinds, and to reject as vicious and indefensible all phrases and forms of style that were not included in what he (unfortunately, I think, adopting an equivocal expression) called the language of *real life*. From this preface, prefixed to poems in which it was impossible to deny the presence of original genius, however mistaken its direction might be deemed, arose the whole long continued controversy. For from the conjunction of perceived power with supposed heresy I explain the inveteracy[3] and in some instances, I grieve to say, the acrimonious passions, with which the controversy has been conducted by the assailants.

Had Mr. Wordsworth's poems been the silly, the childish things, which they were for a long time described as being; had they been really distinguished from the compositions of other poets merely by meanness of language and inanity of thought; had they indeed contained nothing more than what is found in the parodies and pretended imitations of them; they must have sunk at once, a dead weight, into the slough of oblivion, and have dragged the preface along with them. But year after year increased the number of Mr. Wordsworth's admirers. They were found too not in the lower classes of the reading public, but chiefly among young men of strong sensibility and meditative minds; and their admiration (inflamed perhaps in some degree by opposition) was distinguished by its intensity, I might almost say, by its *religious* fervour. These facts, and the intellectual energy of the author, which was more or less consciously felt, where it was outwardly and even boisterously denied, meeting with sentiments of aversion to his opinions, and of alarm at their consequences, produced an eddy of criticism, which would of itself have borne up the poems by the violence, with which it whirled them round and round. With many parts of this preface in the sense attributed to them and which the words undoubtedly seem to authorise, I never concurred; but on the contrary objected to them as erroneous in principle, and as contradictory (in appearance at least) both to other parts of the same preface, and to the author's own practice in the greater number of the poems themselves.

---

1. Echoing Jeremiah 5.21 and Isaiah 6.10.
2. "Experiments" is Wordsworth's term in the Advertisement
to the 1798 *Lyrical Ballads*.
3. Deep-seated prejudice.

Mr. Wordsworth in his recent collection[4] has, I find, degraded this prefatory disquisition to the end of his second volume, to be read or not at the reader's choice. But he has not, as far as I can discover, announced any change in his poetic creed. [At] all events, considering it as the source of a controversy, in which I have been honored more, than I deserve, by the frequent conjunction of my name with his, I think it expedient to declare once for all, in what points I coincide with his opinions, and in what points I altogether differ. But in order to render myself intelligible I must previously, in as few words as possible, explain my ideas, first, of a POEM; and secondly, of POETRY itself, in *kind*, and in *essence*.

[PHILOSOPHIC DEFINITIONS OF A POEM AND POETRY]

A poem is that species of composition, which is opposed to works of science, by proposing for its *immediate* object pleasure, not truth; and from all other species (having *this* object in common with it) it is discriminated by proposing to itself such delight from the *whole*, as is compatible with a distinct gratification from each component part. * * *

But if this should be admitted as a satisfactory character of a poem, we have still to seek for a definition of poetry. The writings of PLATO, and Bishop TAYLOR, and the *Theoria Sacra* of BURNET,[5] furnish undeniable proofs that poetry of the highest kind may exist without metre, and even without the contra-distinguishing objects of a poem. The first chapter of Isaiah (indeed a very large proportion of the whole book) is poetry in the most emphatic sense; yet it would be not less irrational than strange to assert, that pleasure, and not truth, was the immediate object of the prophet. In short, whatever *specific* import we attach to the word, poetry, there will be found involved in it, as a necessary consequence, that a poem of any length neither can be, or ought to be, all poetry. * * *

What is poetry? is so nearly the same question with, what is a poet? that the answer to the one is involved in the solution of the other. For it is a distinction resulting from the poetic genius itself, which sustains and modifies the images, thoughts, and emotions of the poet's own mind. The poet, described in ideal perfection, brings the whole soul of man into activity, with the subordination of its faculties to each other, according to their relative worth and dignity. He diffuses a tone, and spirit of unity, that blends, and (as it were) *fuses*, each into each, by that synthetic and magical power, to which we have exclusively appropriated the name of imagination. This power, first put in action by the will and understanding, and retained under their irremissive, though gentle and unnoticed, controul (*laxis effertur habenis* [guided by loose reins]) reveals itself in the balance or reconciliation of opposite or discordant qualities: of sameness, with difference; of the general, with the concrete; the idea, with the image; the individual, with the representative; the sense of novelty and freshness, with old and familiar objects; a more than usual state of emotion, with more than usual order; judgement ever awake and steady self-possession, with enthusiasm and feeling profound or vehement; and while it blends and harmonizes the natural and the artificial, still subordinates art to nature; the manner to the matter; and our admiration of the poet to our sympathy with the poetry. * * *

---

4. *Poems* (1815).
5. Jeremy Taylor, author of *Holy Living* and *Holy Dying* (1650–1651); and 17th-century theologian Thomas

Burnet (who supplies the epigraph for the 1817 *Ancient Mariner*).

Finally, GOOD SENSE is the BODY of poetic genius, FANCY its DRAPERY, MOTION its LIFE, and IMAGINATION the SOUL that is every where, and in each; and forms all into one graceful and intelligent whole.

from *Chapter 17*
[EXAMINATION OF THE TENETS PECULIAR TO MR. WORDSWORTH.
RUSTIC LIFE AND POETIC LANGUAGE]

As far then as Mr. Wordsworth in his preface contended, and most ably contended, for a reformation in our poetic diction, as far as he has evinced the truth of passion, and the *dramatic* propriety of those figures and metaphors in the original poets, which stript of their justifying reasons, and converted into mere artifices of connection or ornament, constitute the characteristic falsity in the poetic style of the moderns; and as far as he has, with equal acuteness and clearness, pointed out the process in which this change was effected, and the resemblances between that state into which the reader's mind is thrown by the pleasureable confusion of thought from an unaccustomed train of words and images; and that state which is induced by the natural language of empassioned feeling; he undertook a useful task, and deserves all praise, both for the attempt and for the execution. * * *

My own differences from certain supposed parts of Mr. Wordsworth's theory ground themselves on the assumption, that his words had been rightly interpreted, as purporting that the proper diction for poetry in general consists altogether in a language taken, with due exceptions, from the mouths of men in real life, a language which actually constitutes the natural conversation of men under the influence of natural feelings. * * * The poet informs his reader, that he had generally chosen *low and rustic* life; but not *as* low and rustic, or in order to repeat that pleasure of doubtful moral effect, which persons of elevated rank and of superior refinement oftentimes derive from a happy *imitation* of the rude unpolished manners and discourse of their inferiors. * * * He chose low and rustic life, "because in that condition the essential passions of the heart find a better soil, in which they can attain their maturity, are less under restraint, and speak a plainer and more emphatic language; because in that condition of life our elementary feelings coexist in a state of greater simplicity, and consequently may be more accurately contemplated, and more forcibly communicated; because the manners of rural life germinate from those elementary feelings; and from the necessary character of rural occupations are more easily comprehended, and are more durable; and lastly, because in that condition the passions of men are incorporated with the beautiful and permanent forms of nature."

Now it is clear to me, that in the most interesting of the poems, in which the author is more or less dramatic, as the "Brothers," "Michael," "Ruth," the "Mad Mother," &c. the persons introduced are by no means taken *from low* or *rustic life* in the common acceptation of those words; and it is not less clear, that the sentiments and language, as far as they can be conceived to have been really transferred from the minds and conversation of such persons, are attributable to causes and circumstances not necessarily connected with "their occupations and abode." The thoughts, feelings, language, and manners of the shepherd-farmers in the vales of Cumberland and Westmoreland,[1] as far as they are actually adopted in those poems, may be accounted for from causes, which will and do produce the same results in *every* state of life,

1. The Lake District.

whether in town or country. As the two principal I rank that INDEPENDENCE, which raises a man above servitude, or daily toil for the profit of others, yet not above the necessity of industry and a frugal simplicity of domestic life; and the accompanying unambitious, but solid and religious EDUCATION, which has rendered few books familiar, but the bible, and the liturgy or hymn book. * * *

I am convinced, that for the human soul to prosper in rustic life, a certain vantage-ground is pre-requisite. It is not every man, that is likely to be improved by a country life or by country labours. Education, or original sensibility, or both, must pre-exist, if the changes, forms, and incidents of nature are to prove a sufficient stimulant. And where these are not sufficient, the mind contracts and hardens by want of stimulants; and the man becomes selfish, sensual, gross, and hard-hearted. * * *

I adopt with full faith the principle of Aristotle,[2] that poetry as poetry is essentially *ideal*, that it avoids and excludes all *accident*; that its apparent individualities of rank, character, or occupation must be *representative* of a class; and that the *persons* of poetry must be clothed with *generic* attributes, with the *common* attributes of the class; not with such as one gifted individual might *possibly* possess, but such as from his situation it is most probable before-hand, that he *would* possess. If my premises are right, and my deductions legitimate, it follows that there can be no *poetic* medium between the swains of Theocritus[3] and those of an imaginary golden age.

The characters of the vicar and the shepherd-mariner in the poem of the BROTHERS, those of the shepherd of Green-head Gill in the "MICHAEL," have all the verisimilitude and representative quality, that the purposes of poetry can require. They are persons of a known and abiding class, and their manners and sentiments the natural product of circumstances common to the class. * * *

On the other hand, in the poems which are pitched at a lower note, as the "Harry Gill," "Idiot Boy," &c. the *feelings* are those of human nature in general; though the poet has judiciously laid the *scene* in the country, in order to place *himself* in the vicinity of interesting images, without the necessity of ascribing a sentimental perception of their beauty to the persons of his drama. * * *

In the "Thorn," the poet himself acknowledges in a note the necessity of an introductory poem, in which he should have pourtrayed the character of the person from whom the words of the poem are supposed to proceed: a superstitious man moderately imaginative, of slow faculties and deep feelings, "a captain of a small trading vessel, for example, who being past the middle age of life, had retired upon an annuity, or small independent income, to some village or country town of which he was not a native, or in which he had not been accustomed to live. Such men having nothing to do become credulous and talkative from indolence." But in a poem, still more in a lyric poem (and the NURSE in Shakspeare's Romeo and Juliet alone prevents me from extending the remark even to dramatic *poetry*, if indeed the Nurse itself can be deemed altogether a case in point) it is not possible to imitate truly a dull and garrulous discourser, without repeating the effects of dulness and garrulity. * * *

Still more must I hesitate in my assent to the sentence which immediately follows the former citation[:] * * * "The language too of these men is adopted (purified indeed from what appears to be its real defects, from all lasting and rational causes of dislike or disgust) because such men hourly communicate with the best objects from which the best part of language is originally derived; and because, from their rank

---

2. Author of the earliest known treatise on the theory of poetry (5th century B.C.E.), the *Poetics*.

3. Greek poet, 3rd century B.C.E. His *Idylls* are the origin of the Western pastoral tradition.

in society, and the sameness and narrow circle of their intercourse, being less un-der the action of social vanity, they convey their feelings and notions in simple and unelaborated expressions." To this I reply; that a rustic's language, purified from all provincialism and grossness, and so far re-constructed as to be made consistent with the rules of grammar (which are in essence no other than the laws of universal logic, applied to Psychological materials) will not differ from the language of any other man of common-sense, however learned or refined he may be, except as far as the notions, which the rustic has to convey, are fewer and more indiscriminate. This will become still clearer, if we add the consideration (equally important though less obvious) that the rustic, from the more imperfect development of his faculties, and from the lower state of their cultivation, aims almost solely to convey *insulated facts*, either those of his scanty experience or his traditional belief; while the educated man chiefly seeks to discover and express those *connections* of things, or those relative *bearings* of fact to fact, from which some more or less general law is deducible. For *facts* are valuable to a wise man, chiefly as they lead to the discovery of the in-dwelling *law*, which is the true *being* of things, the sole solution of their modes of existence, and in the knowl-edge of which consists our dignity and our power.

As little can I agree with the assertion, that from the objects with which the rustic hourly communicates, the best part of language is formed. For first, if to com-municate with an object implies such an acquaintance with it, as renders it capable of being discriminately reflected on; the distinct knowledge of an uneducated rustic would furnish a very scanty vocabulary. The few things, and modes of action, requi-site for his bodily conveniences, would alone be individualized; while all the rest of nature would be expressed by a small number of confused, general terms. Secondly, I deny that the words and combinations of words derived from the objects, with which the rustic is familiar, whether with distinct or confused knowledge, can be justly said to form the best part of language. It is more than probable, that many classes of the brute creation possess discriminating sounds, by which they can convey to each other notices of such objects as concern their food, shelter, or safety. Yet we hesitate to call the aggregate of such sounds a language, otherwise than metaphorically. The best part of human language, properly so called, is derived from reflection on the acts of the mind itself. It is formed by a voluntary appropriation of fixed symbols to internal acts, to processes and results of imagination, the greater part of which have no place in the consciousness of uneducated man; though in civilized society, by imitation and passive remembrance of what they hear from their religious instructors and other superiors, the most uneducated share in the harvest which they neither sowed or reaped. * * *

The positions, which I controvert, are contained in the sentences—"*a selection of the* REAL *language of men;*"—"*the language of these men* (i.e. men in low and rustic life) *I propose to myself to imitate, and as far as possible, to adopt the very language of men.*" "*Between the language of prose and that of metrical composition, there neither is, nor can be any essential difference.*" It is against these exclusively, that my opposition is directed.

I object, in the very first instance, to an equivocation in the use of the word "real." Every man's language varies, according to the extent of his knowledge, the ac-tivity of his faculties, and the depth or quickness of his feelings. Every man's language has, first, its *individualities;* secondly, the common properties of the *class* to which he belongs; and thirdly, words and phrases of *universal* use. The language of Hooker, Ba-con, Bishop Taylor, and Burke, differ from the common language of the learned class only by the superior number and novelty of the thoughts and relations which they had to convey. The language of Algernon Sidney[4] differs not at all from that, which every well educated gentleman would wish to write, and (with due allowances for the undeliberateness, and less connected train, of thinking natural and proper to conversation) such as he would wish to talk. Neither one or the other differ half as much from the general language of cultivated society, as the language of Mr. Wordsworth's homeliest composition differs from that of a common peasant. For "real" therefore, we must substitute *ordinary*, or *lingua communis* [common language]. And this, we have proved, is no more to be found in the phraseology of low and rustic life, than in that of any other class. Omit the peculiarities of each, and the result of course must be common to all. * * *

    Neither is the case rendered at all more tenable by the addition of the words, "*in a state of excitement*." For the nature of a man's words, when he is strongly affected by joy, grief, or anger, must necessarily depend on the number and quality of the general truths, conceptions and images, and of the words expressing them, with which his mind had been previously stored. For the property of passion is not to *create*; but to set in increased activity. At least, whatever new connections of thoughts or images, or (which is equally, if not more than equally, the appropriate effect of strong excitement) whatever generalizations of truth or experience, the heat of passion may produce; yet the terms of their conveyance must have pre-existed in his former conversations, and are only collected and crowded together by the unusual stimulation. It is indeed very possible to adopt in a poem the unmeaning repetitions, habitual phrases, and other blank counters, which an unfurnished or confused understanding interposes at short intervals, in order to keep hold of his subject which is still slipping from him, and to give him time for recollection; or in mere aid of vacancy, as in the scanty companies of a country stage the same player pops backwards and forwards, in order to prevent the appearance of empty spaces, in the procession of Macbeth, or Henry VIIIth. But what assistance to the poet, or ornament to the poem, these can supply, I am at a loss to conjecture. Nothing assuredly can differ either in origin or in mode more widely from the *apparent* tautologies of intense and turbulent feeling, in which the passion is greater and of longer endurance, than to be exhausted or satisfied by a single representation of the image or incident exciting it. Such repetitions I admit to be a beauty of the highest kind; as illustrated by Mr. Wordsworth himself from the song of Deborah [Judges 5.27]. "*At her feet he bowed, he fell, he lay down; at her feet he bowed, he fell; where he bowed, there he fell down dead.*"[5]

from *Chapter 22*
[THE CHARACTERISTIC DEFECTS OF WORDSWORTH'S POETRY, WITH THE PRINCIPLES FROM WHICH THE JUDGEMENT, THAT THEY ARE DEFECTS, IS DEDUCED][1]

This is an approximation to what might be called *mental* bombast, as distinguished from verbal: for, as in the latter there is a disproportion of the expression to the thoughts, so in this there is a disproportion of thought to the circumstance and

4. Richard Hooker (1554–1600) wrote *The Laws of Ecclesiastical Polity*; he and Taylor were known for style as well as ideas, as were Bacon and Burke. The republican Algernon Sidney, executed for his supposed complicity in a plot to assassinate Charles II in 1683, wrote *Discourses*

on Government (1698).
5. Cited in the Note to *The Thorn* (see page 425).
1. One such defect, "thoughts and images too great for the subject," Coleridge instances with stanza 8 of "Intimations" Ode, page 556.

occasion. This, by the bye, is a fault of which none but a man of genius is capable. It is the awkwardness and strength of Hercules with the distaff of Omphale.[2]

* * * speaking of a child, "a six year's darling of a pigmy size," he thus addresses him [quotes lines 110–119: "Thou best philosopher..."]. * * * we will merely ask, what does all this mean? In what sense is a child of that age a *philosopher*? In what sense does he *read* "the eternal deep"? In what sense is he declared to be "*for ever haunted* by a Supreme Being? or so inspired as to deserve the splendid titles of a *mighty prophet*, a *blessed seer*? By reflection? by knowledge" by conscious intuition? or by *any* form or modification of consciousness?" These would be tidings indeed; but such as would pre-suppose an immediate revelation to the inspired communicator, and require miracles to authenticate his inspiration. Children at this age give us no such information of themselves; and at what time were we dipt in Lethe, which has produced such utter oblivion of a state so godlike?[3] There are many of us that still possess some remembrances, more or less distinct, respecting themselves at six years old; pity that the worthless straws only should float, while treasures, compared with which all the mines of Golconda and Mexico were but straws, should be absorbed by some unknown gulf into some unknown abyss.

But if this be too wild and exorbitant to be suspected as having been the poet's meaning; if these mysterious gifts, faculties, and operations, and *not* accompanied with consciousness; who *else* is conscious of them? or how can it be called the child, if it be no part of the child's conscious being? * * * In what sense can the magnificent attributes, above quoted, be appropriate to a *child*, which would not make them equally suitable to a *bee*, or a *dog*, or a *field of corn*; or even to a ship, or to the wind and waves that propel it? The omnipresent Spirit works equally in *them*, as in the child; and the child is equally unconscious of it as they.

from Lectures on Shakespeare[1]

[MECHANIC VS. ORGANIC FORM]

—Imagine not that I am about to oppose genius to rules. No! the comparative value of these rules is the very cause to be tried. The spirit of poetry, like all other living powers, must of necessity circumscribe itself by rules, were it only to unite power with beauty. It must embody in order to reveal itself; but a living body is of necessity an organized one; and what is organization but the connection of parts in and for a whole, so that each part is at once end and means?—This is no discovery of criticism;—it is a necessity of the human mind; and all nations have felt and obeyed it, in the invention of metre, and measured sounds, as the vehicle and *involucrum* [covering] of poetry—itself a fellow-growth from the same life—even as the bark is to the tree!

No work of true genius dares want its appropriate form, neither indeed is there any danger of this. As it must not, so genius can not, be lawless; for it is even this that constitutes it genius—the power of acting creatively under laws of its own

2. As slave to Queen Omphale of Lydia, Hercules plied such woman's tasks as weaving and spinning, while she wore his lion's skin and wielded his club.
3. In Wordsworth's theory of the soul's pre-existence, "Our birth is but a sleep and a forgetting" (stanza 5). In classical mythology, the souls of the dead cross Lethe, the river of forgertfulness, on the way to an afterlife in the underworld.
1. Coleridge gave these lectures in 1811–1812, speaking from notes. The texts were assembled from notes by attendees, which scholars later developed.

origination. How then comes it that not only single *Zoili*,[2] but whole nations have combined in unhesitating condemnation of our great dramatist, as a sort of African nature, rich in beautiful monsters—as a wild heath where islands of fertility look the greener from the surrounding waste, where the loveliest plants now shine out among unsightly weeds, and now are choked by their parasitic growth, so intertwined that we can not disentangle the weed without snapping the flower? * * * The true ground of the mistake lies in the confounding mechanical regularity with organic form. The form is mechanic, when on any given material we impress a pre-determined form, not necessarily arising out of the properties of the material;—as when to a mass of wet clay we give whatever shape we wish it to retain when hardened. The organic form, on the other hand, is innate; it shapes, as it develops itself from within, and the fulness of its development is one and the same with the perfection of its outward form. Such as the life is, such is the form. Nature, the prime genial artist, inexhaustible in diverse powers, is equally inexhaustible in forms;—each exterior is the physiognomy of the being within—its true image reflected and thrown out from the concave mirror;—and even such is the appropriate excellence of her chosen poet, of our own Shakespeare—himself a nature humanized, a genial understanding directing self-consciously a power and an implicit wisdom deeper even than our consciousness.

[THE CHARACTER OF HAMLET]

The seeming inconsistencies in the conduct and character of Hamlet have long exercised the conjectural ingenuity of critics; and, as we are always loth to suppose that the cause of defective apprehension is in ourselves, the mystery has been too commonly explained by the very easy process of setting it down as in fact inexplicable, and by resolving the phenomenon into a misgrowth or *lusus* [trick] of the capricious and irregular genius of Shakspeare. The shallow and stupid arrogance of these vulgar and indolent decisions I would fain do my best to expose. I believe the character of Hamlet may be traced to Shakspeare's deep and accurate science in mental philosophy. Indeed, that this character must have some connection with the common fundamental laws of our nature may be assumed from the fact, that Hamlet has been the darling of every country in which the literature of England has been fostered. In order to understand him, it is essential that we should reflect on the constitution of our own minds. Man is distinguished from the brute animals in proportion as thought prevails over sense: but in the healthy processes of the mind, a balance is constantly maintained between the impressions from outward objects and the inward operations of the intellect:—for if there be an overbalance in the contemplative faculty, man thereby becomes the creature of mere meditation, and loses his natural power of action. Now one of Shakespeare's modes of creating characters is, to conceive any one intellectual or moral faculty in morbid excess, and then to place himself, Shakespeare, thus mutilated or diseased, under given circumstances. In Hamlet he seems to have wished to exemplify the moral necessity of a due balance between our attention to the objects of our senses, and our meditation on the workings of our minds,—an *equilibrium* between the real and the imaginary worlds. In Hamlet this balance is disturbed: his thoughts, and the images of his fancy, are far more vivid than his actual perceptions, and his very perceptions, instantly passing through the

---

2. Malicious or pedantic critics. Greek grammarian Zoilus (4th century B.C.E.) was known for unforgiving criticism of Homer.

medium of his contemplations, acquire, as they pass, a form and a color not naturally their own. Hence we see a great, an almost enormous, intellectual activity, and a proportionate aversion to real action, consequent upon it, with all its symptoms and accompanying qualities. This character Shakespeare places in circumstances, under which it is obliged to act on the spur of the moment:—Hamlet is brave and careless of death; but he vacillates from sensibility, and procrastinates from thought, and loses the power of action in the energy of resolve. Thus it is that this tragedy presents a direct contrast to that of Macbeth; the one proceeds with the utmost slowness, the other with a crowded and breathless rapidity.

The effect of this overbalance of the imaginative power is beautifully illustrated in the everlasting broodings and superfluous activities of Hamlet's mind, which, unseated from its healthy relation, is constantly occupied with the world within, and abstracted from the world without,—giving substance to shadows, and throwing a mist over all common-place actualities. It is the nature of thought to be indefinite;—definiteness belongs to external imagery alone.

[STAGE ILLUSION AND THE WILLING SUSPENSION OF DISBELIEF]

[T]here is one preliminary point to be first settled, as the indispensable condition not only of just and genial criticism, but of all consistency in our opinions.—This point is contained in the words, probable, natural. We are all in the habit of praising Shakespeare or of hearing him extolled for his fidelity to Nature. Now what are we to understand by these words, in their application to the Drama? Assuredly, not the ordinary meaning of them * * * the Drama is an *imitation* of reality, not a Copy—and that Imitation is contra-distinguished from Copy by this: that a certain quantum of Difference is essential to the former, and an indispensable condition and cause of the pleasure we derive from it; while in a Copy it is a defect, contravening its name and purpose. If illustration were needed, it would be sufficient to ask—why we prefer a Fruit Piece of van Huysum's to a marble Peach on a mantel-piece, or why we prefer an historical picture of West to Mrs Salmon's Wax-figure Gallery.[3] Not that we ought, but that we actually do, all of us judge of the Drama under this impression, we need no other proof than the impassive slumber of our sense of Probability when we hear an Actor announce himself a Greek, Roman, Venetian or Persian in good Mother English. * * *

[W]e must first ascertain what the immediate End of object of the Drama is—Here I find two extremes in critical decision—The French, which evidently presupposes that a perfect Delusion is to be aimed at—an Opinion which now needs no fresh confutation—The opposite, supported by Dr Johnson, supposes the auditors throughout as in the full and positive reflective knowledge of the contrary.[4] In evincing the impossibility of Delusion he makes no sufficient allowance for an intermediate State, which we distinguish by the term, Illusion. In what this consists, I cannot better explain, than by referring you to the highest degree of it, namely, dreaming. It is laxly said, that during Sleep we take our dreams for Realities; but this is irreconcilable

3. Dutch artist Jan van Huysum (1682–1749) was known for his paintings of flowers and fruits; American artist Benjamin West was famed for epic-scale historical subjects; Mrs. Salmon's gallery of wax figures was a popular site in London.
4. In his Preface to Shakespeare, Samuel Johnson refuted the French neoclassical standard of verisimilar unities of time, place, and action (by which Shakespeare was condemned) by asserting that an audience is never deluded, but always knows "from the first act to the last, that the stage is only a stage, and the players are only players."

with the nature of Sleep, which consists in a suspension of the voluntary and therefore of the comparative power. The fact is, that we pass no judgement either way—
we simply do *not* judge them to be unreal—in consequence of which the Images act
on our minds, as far as they act at all, by their own force as images. Our state while
we are dreaming differs from that in which we are in the perusal of a deeply interesting Novel, in the degree rather than in the Kind. * * * in sleep we pass at once by a
sudden collapse into this suspension of Will and the Comparative power: whereas in
an interesting Play, read or represented, we are brought up to this point, as far as it is
requisite or desirable gradually, by the Art of the Poet and the Actors, and with the
consent and positive Aidance of our own Will.[5] We *chuse* to be deceived. * * * this
chief end, that of producing and supporting this willing Illusion.

[SHAKESPEARE'S IMAGES]

In my mind, what have often been censured as Shakespeare's conceits are completely
justifiable, as belonging to the state, age, or feeling of the individual. Sometimes,
when they cannot be vindicated on these grounds, they may well be excused by the
taste of his own and of the preceding age; as for instance, in Romeo's speech,

> Here's much to do with hate, but more with love:—
> Why then, O brawling love! O loving hate!
> O anything, of nothing first created!
> O heavy lightness! serious vanity!
> Misshapen chaos of well-seeming forms!
> Feather of lead, bright smoke, cold fire, sick health!
> Still-waking sleep, that is not what it is!   [*Romeo and Juliet* 1.1.182–88][6]

I dare not pronounce such passages as these to be absolutely unnatural, not merely
because I consider the author a much better judge than I can be, but because I can
understand and allow for an effort of the mind, when it would describe what it cannot satisfy itself with the description of, to reconcile opposites and qualify contradictions, leaving a middle state of mind more strictly appropriate to the imagination
than any other, when it is, as it were, hovering between images. As soon as it is fixed
on one image, it becomes understanding; but while it is unfixed and wavering between them, attaching itself permanently to none, it is imagination. Such is the fine
description of Death in Milton:—

> The other shape,
> If shape it might be call'd, that shape had none
> Distinguishable in member, joint, or limb,
> Or substance might be call'd, that shadow seem'd,
> For each seem'd either: black it stood as night;
> Fierce as ten furies, terrible as hell,
> And shook a dreadful dart: what seem'd his head
> The likeness of a kingly crown had on.   [*Paradise Lost* 2.666–73][7]

---

5. Coleridge applied this principle to his contributions to
Lyrical Ballads; see *Biographia Literaria*, ch 14, page 689.
6. Romeo is describing being in love in a world of feuds.

7. This passage was a famous example of "the sublime" in
18th-century aesthetic theory. See page 39.

The grandest efforts of poetry are where the imagination is called forth, not to produce a distinct form, but a strong working of the mind, still offering what is still repelled, and again creating what is again rejected; the result being what the poet wishes to impress, namely, the substitution of a sublime feeling of the unimaginable for a mere image. I have sometimes thought that the passage just read might be quoted as exhibiting the narrow limit of painting, as compared with the boundless power of poetry: painting cannot go beyond a certain point; poetry rejects all control, all confinement. Yet we know that sundry painters have attempted pictures of the meeting between Satan and Death at the gates of Hell; and how was Death represented? Not as Milton has described him, but by the most defined thing that can be imagined—a skeleton, the dryest and hardest image that it is possible to discover; which, instead of keeping the mind in a state of activity, reduces it to the merest passivity—an image, compared with which a square, a triangle, or any other mathematical figure, is a luxuriant fancy.

[OTHELLO]

RODERIGO: What a full fortune does the *thick-lips* owe,
           If he can carry't thus   [1.1.63–64][8]

Roderigo turns off to Othello; and here comes one, if not the only, seeming justification of our blackamoor or negro Othello. Even if we supposed this an uninterrupted tradition of the theatre, and that Shakespeare himself, from want of scenes, and the experience that nothing could be made too marked for the senses of his audience, had practically sanctioned it,—would this prove aught concerning his own intention as a poet for all ages? Can we imagine him so utterly ignorant as to make a barbarous negro plead royal birth [2.1.21–22]—at a time, too, when negroes were not known except as slaves?—As for Iago's language to Brabantio, it implies merely that Othello was a Moor, that is, black. Though I think the rivalry of Roderigo sufficient to account for his wilful confusion of Moor and Negro,—yet, even if compelled to give this up, I should think it only adapted for the acting of the day, and should complain of an enormity built on a single word, in direct contradiction to Iago's "Barbary horse."[9] Besides, if we could in good earnest believe Shakspeare ignorant of the distinction, still why should we adopt one disagreeable possibility instead of a ten times greater and more pleasing probability? It is a common error to mistake the epithets applied by the *dramatis personae* to each other, as truly descriptive of what the audience ought to see or know. No doubt Desdemona saw Othello's visage in his mind;[1] yet, as we are constituted, and most surely as an English audience was disposed in the beginning of the seventeenth century, it would be something monstrous to conceive this beautiful Venetian girl falling in love with a veritable negro. It would argue a disproportionateness, a want of balance, in Desdemona, which Shakspeare does not appear to have in the least contemplated. * * *

Iago's speech:—

Virtue! a fig! 'tis in ourselves, that we are thus, or thus, & c. [1.3.314ff][2]

---

8. Roderigo has just learned that Othello has married Desdemona, whom he desires; owe: own.
9. "You'll have your daughter covered with a Barbary horse," he taunts Desdemona's father (1.1.108).

1. So she pleads to her father and the Senate (1.3.247). See also Lamb on this phrase (page 706).
2. Iago is duping Roderigo into giving him all his money, to woo Desdemona for him.

This speech comprises the passionless character of Iago. It is all will in intellect; and therefore he is here a bold partisan of a truth, but yet of a truth converted into a falsehood by the absence of all the necessary modifications caused by the frail nature of man. And then comes the last sentiment:—

> Our raging motions, our carnal stings, our unbitted lusts, whereof I take this, that
> you call—love, to be a sect or scion! [1.3.324–26][3]

Here is the true Iagoism of, alas! how many! Note Iago's pride of mastery in the repetition of "Go, make money!" [1.3.357] to his anticipated dupe, even stronger than his love of lucre: and when Roderigo is completely won—

> I am chang'd. I'll go sell all my land—[1.3.371]

when the effect has been fully produced, the repetition of triumph—

> Go to; farewell; put money enough in your purse! [1.3.334]

The remainder—Iago's soliloquy [1.3.372–93]—the motive-hunting of a motiveless malignity—how awful it is! Yea, whilst he is still allowed to bear the divine image, it is too fiendish for his own steady view,—for the lonely gaze of a being next to devil—and only not quite devil, and yet a character which Shakspeare has attempted and executed, without disgust and without scandal!

1811–1817   1854

❧ COLERIDGE'S "LECTURES" AND THEIR TIME ❧
Shakespeare in the Nineteenth Century

By Coleridge's day, Shakespeare was England's celebrated poet, surpassed only by the Bible in common reference. As with the Bible, any number of cultural issues were reflected, along with paradigms of aesthetic practice and examples of the suppleness and subtlety of the English language. His language was so familiar that it could be alluded to with conversational ease, played with, parodied, and echoed at will; to write on Shakespeare was to indulge in a national pastime in which all readers were invested and interested.

Coleridge formulated many of his most influential critical views in lecturing on Shakespeare. So did Keats (see letters, pages 1048 and 1057). The poets were also inspired by Shakespeare's sonnets, often neglected in the previous century; "with this key," Wordsworth said, "Shakespeare unlocked his heart." Our selections show some of the wealth of ways Shakespeare mattered in the Romantic era. Hazlitt and De Quincey were most interested in the characters, and the "mental theater" (as Byron called it) of complex psychology. For De Quincey, this psychology is not only in Shakespeare's characterization, but in the reader and spectator, too, especially under the power of villainous actions. See De Quincey's gorgeous essay on this effect, "On the Knocking at the Gate in *Macbeth*" (page 1142). Others reveled in the gorgeous language. At the same time, Shakespeare's very prominence caused problems. With many readers fascinated from an early age by such strong and problematic figures as Hamlet and Cleopatra, parents and teachers faced a dilemma: Shakespeare could be profane, even blasphemous, and his themes could be immoral. Shakespeare could not be denied; he had to be managed, as in the artful retellings of *Tales from*

---

3. Unbitted: wanton (without a bit); scion: offshoot.

Shakespear. The preface shows the difficulties that society continued to have in assimilating its most revered poet.

Charles Lamb [and Mary Lamb]
Preface to *Tales From Shakespear*[1]

The following Tales are meant to be submitted to the young reader as an introduction to the study of Shakspeare, for which purpose his words are used whenever it seemed possible to bring them in; and in whatever has been added to give them the regular form of a connected story, diligent care has been taken to select such words as might least interrupt the effect of the beautiful English tongue in which he wrote: therefore, words introduced into our language since his time have been as far as possible avoided.

In those tales which have been taken from the Tragedies, my young readers will perceive, when they come to see the source from which these stories are derived, that Shakspear's own words, with little alteration, recur very frequently in the narrative as well as in the dialogue; but in those made from the Comedies I found myself scarcely ever able to turn his words into the narrative form: therefore I fear that, in them, I have made use of dialogue too frequently for young people not accustomed to the dramatic form of writing. But this fault, if it be as I fear a fault, has been caused by an earnest wish to give as much of Shakspear's own words as possible: and if the "*He said*," and "*She said*," the question and the reply, should sometimes seem tedious to their young ears, they must pardon it, because it was the only way I knew of, in which I could give them a few hints and little foretastes of the great pleasure which awaits them in their elder years, when they come to the rich treasures from which these small and valueless coins are extracted; pretending to no other merit than as faint and imperfect stamps of Shakspear's matchless image. Faint and imperfect images they must be called, because the beauty of his language is too frequently destroyed by the necessity of changing many of his excellent words into words far less expressive of his true sense, to make it read something like prose; and even in some few places, where his blank verse is given unaltered, as hoping from its simple plainness to cheat the young readers into the belief that they are reading prose, yet still his language being transplanted from its own natural soil and wild poetic garden, it must want much of its native beauty.

I have wished to make these Tales easy reading for very young children. To the utmost of my ability I have constantly kept this in mind; but the subjects of most of them made this a very difficult task. It was no easy matter to give the histories of men and women in terms familiar to the apprehension of a very young mind. For young ladies too, it has been my intention chiefly to write; because boys being generally permitted the use of their fathers' libraries at a much earlier age than girls are, they frequently have the best scenes of Shakspear by heart, before their sisters are permitted to look into this manly book; and, therefore, instead of recommending these Tales to the perusal of young gentlemen who can read them so much better in the originals, I must rather beg their kind assistance in explaining to their sisters such parts as are

---

1. *Tales from Shakespear* has never been out of print since it appeared in 1807, and has been widely translated. The chief audience is "young ladies," often forbidden to read Shakespeare, whose plays were regarded as too obscene, vulgar, and blasphemous. (A sanitized *Family Shakspeare* by brother and sister Thomas and Henrietta Bowdler—whence "bowdlerized"—also appeared in 1807.) Mary retold 14 comedies and romances, and Charles six tragedies. His *King Lear* is notable for adhering to the deaths of Lear and Cordelia in an age when Nahum Tate's "happy ending" revision (1681) held the stage. The Lambs also divided the Preface, Mary stopping at "imperfect abridgments—" (about two-thirds into paragraph three). Only Charles's name appeared on the title page; Mary's participation was not publicly credited during their lifetime.

hardest for them to understand: and when they have helped them to get over the difficulties, then perhaps they will read to them (carefully selecting what is proper for a young sister's ear) some passage which has pleased them in one of these stories, in the very words of the scene from which it is taken; and I trust they will find that the beautiful extracts, the select passages, they may chuse to give their sisters in this way, will be much better relished and understood from their having some notion of the general story from one of these imperfect abridgments:—which if they be fortunately so done as to prove delightful to any of you, my young readers, I hope will have no worse effect upon you, than to make you wish yourselves a little older, that you may be allowed to read the Plays at full length (such a wish will be neither peevish nor irrational). When time and leave of judicious friends shall put them into your hands, you will discover in such of them as are here abridged (not to mention almost as many more, which are left untouched) many surprising events and turns of fortune, which for their infinite variety could not be contained in this little book, besides a world of sprightly and cheerful characters, both men and women, the humour of which I was fearful of losing if I attempted to reduce the length of them.

What these Tales shall have been to you in childhood, that and much more it is the writers' wish that the true Plays of Shakspear may prove to you in older years—enrichers of the fancy, strengtheners of virtue, a withdrawing from all selfish and mercenary thoughts, a lesson of all sweet and honourable thoughts and actions, to teach you courtesy, benignity, generosity, humanity: for of examples, teaching these virtues, his pages are full.

Charles Lamb
from On the Tragedies of Shakspeare
CONSIDERED WITH REFERENCE TO THEIR FITNESS FOR STAGE REPRESENTATION[1]

Such is the instantaneous nature of the impressions which we take in at the eye and ear at a playhouse, compared with the slow apprehension oftentimes of the understanding in reading, that we are apt not only to sink the play-writer in the consideration which we pay to the actor, but even to identify in our minds, in a perverse manner, the actor with the character which he represents. It is difficult for a frequent play-goer to disembarrass the idea of Hamlet from the person and voice of Mr. K——. We speak of Lady Macbeth, while we are in reality thinking of Mrs. S——.[2] * * *

Never let me be so ungrateful as to forget the very high degree of satisfaction which I received some years back from seeing for the first time a tragedy of Shakspeare's performed, in which those two great performers sustained the principal parts. It seemed to embody and realise conceptions which had hitherto assumed no distinct shape. But dearly do we pay all our life after for this juvenile pleasure, this sense of distinctness. When the novelty is past, we find to our cost that instead of realising an idea, we have only materialised and brought down a fine vision to the standard of flesh and blood. We have let go a dream, in quest of an unattainable substance.

1. Published in Leigh Hunt's *Reflector* in 1811. The hostility to representation exemplifies Romantic inwardness, but it should be remembered that contemporary theaters were vast—Drury Lane and Covent Garden, the only venues for legitimate spoken drama, each held over 3,000. This site fostered declamatory acting and spectacle. Lamb's farce, Mr. H., failed at Drury Lane in 1806: "like a congregation of mad geese . . . with roaring sometimes like bears, mows and mops [grimaces] like apes, sometimes snakes, [they] hiss'd me into madness."
2. Celebrated actors John Philip Kemble (1757–1823) and his sister Sarah Siddons (1755–1831).

How cruelly this operates upon the mind, to have its free conceptions thus cramped and pressed down to the measure of a strait-lacing actuality, may be judged from that delightful sensation of freshness, with which we turn to those plays of Shakspeare which have escaped being performed, and to those passages in the acting plays of the same writer which have happily been left out in the performance. * * * I confess myself utterly unable to appreciate that celebrated soliloquy in Hamlet, beginning "To be, or not to be," or to tell whether it be good, bad, or indifferent, it has been so handled and pawed about by declamatory boys and men, and torn so inhumanly from its living place and principle of continuity in the play, till it is become to me a perfect dead member.

It may seem a paradox, but I cannot help being of opinion that the plays of Shakspeare are less calculated for performance on a stage than those of almost any other dramatist whatever. Their distinguishing excellence is a reason that they should be so; there is so much in them, which comes not under the province of acting, with which eye, and tone, and gesture, have nothing to do.

The glory of the scenic art is to personate passion, and the turns of passion. * * * in all the best dramas, and in Shakspeare's above all, how obvious it is, that the form of *speaking,* whether it be in soliloquy or dialogue, is only a medium, and often a highly artificial one, for putting the reader or spectator into possession of that knowledge of the inner structure and workings of mind in a character. * * * But the practice of stage representation reduces every thing to a controversy of elocution. * * *

The character of Hamlet is perhaps that by which, since the days of Betterton,[3] a succession of popular performers have had the greatest ambition to distinguish themselves. The length of the part may be one of their reasons. But for the character itself, we find it in a play, and therefore we judge it a fit subject of dramatic representation. The play itself abounds in maxims and reflections beyond any other, and therefore we consider it as a proper vehicle for conveying moral instruction. But Hamlet himself— what does he suffer meanwhile by being dragged forth as a public schoolmaster, to give lectures to the crowd! Why, nine parts in ten of what Hamlet does, are transactions between himself and his moral sense; they are the effusions of his solitary musings, which he retires to holes and corners and the most sequestered parts of the palace to pour forth; or rather, they are the silent meditations with which his bosom is bursting, reduced to *words* for the sake of the reader, who must else remain ignorant of what is passing there. These profound sorrows, these light-and-noise-abhorring ruminations, which the tongue scarce dares utter to deaf walls and chambers, how can they be represented by a gesticulating actor, who comes and mouths them out before an audience, making four hundred people his confidants at once! I say not that it is the fault of the actor so to do; he must pronounce them *ore rotundo* [in full voice]; he must accompany them with his eye; he must insinuate them into his auditory by some trick of eye, tone, or gesture,—or he fails. *He must be thinking all the while of his appearance, because he knows that all the while the spectators are judging of it.* And this is the way to represent the shy, negligent, retiring Hamlet!

It is true that there is no other mode of conveying a vast quantity of thought and feeling to a great portion of the audience, who otherwise would never earn it for themselves by reading; and the intellectual acquisition gained this way may, for aught I know, be inestimable; but I am not arguing that Hamlet should not be acted,

---

3. Thomas Bettetton (1635?–1710), a leading Restoration actor and dramatist.

but how much Hamlet is made another thing by being acted. I have heard much of the wonders which Garrick[4] performed in this part; but as I never saw him, I must have leave to doubt whether the representation of such a character came within the province of his art. Those who tell me of him, speak of his eye, of the magic of his eye, and of his commanding voice;—physical properties, vastly desirable in an actor, and without which he can never insinuate meaning into an auditory: but what have they to do with Hamlet; what have they to do with intellect? In fact, the things aimed at in theatrical representation are to arrest the spectator's eye upon the form and the gesture, and so to gain a more favourable hearing to what is spoken: it is not what the character is, but how he looks; not what he says, but how he speaks it. * * *

So to see Lear acted,—to see an old man tottering about the stage with a walking-stick, turned out of doors by his daughters in a rainy night, has nothing in it but what is painful and disgusting. We want to take him into shelter and relieve him. That is all the feeling which the acting of Lear ever produced in me. But the Lear of Shakspeare cannot be acted. The contemptible machinery by which they mimic the storm which he goes out in, is not more inadequate to represent the horrors of the real elements, than any actor can be to represent Lear: they might more easily propose to personate the Satan of Milton upon a stage, or one of Michael Angelo's terrible figures. The greatness of Lear is not in corporal dimension, but in intellectual: the explosions of his passion are terrible as a volcano; they are storms turning up and disclosing to the bottom that sea, his mind, with all its vast riches. It is his mind which is laid bare. This case of flesh and blood seems too insignificant to be thought on; even as he himself neglects it. On the stage we see nothing but corporal infirmities and weakness, the impotence of rage. While we read it, we see not Lear, but we are Lear: we are in his mind, we are sustained by a grandeur which baffles the malice of daughters and storms. In the aberrations of his reason, we discover a mighty irregular power of reasoning, immethodized from the ordinary purposes of life, but exerting its powers, as "the wind bloweth where it listeth,"[5] at will upon the corruptions and abuses of mankind. What have looks, or tones, to do with that sublime identification of his age with that of the *heavens themselves*, when, in his reproaches to them for conniving at the injustice of his children, he reminds them that "they themselves are old" [2.4.188]? What gesture shall we appropriate to this? What has the voice or the eye to do with such things? But the play is beyond all art, as the tamperings with it show: it is too hard and stony; it must have love-scenes, and a happy ending.[6] * * * A happy ending!—as if the living martyrdom that Lear had gone through,—the flaying of his feelings alive, did not make a fair dismissal from the stage of life the only decorous thing for him. If he is to live and be happy after, if he could sustain this world's burden after, why all this pudder and preparation,—why torment us with all this unnecessary sympathy? As if the childish pleasure of getting his gilt robes and sceptre again could tempt him to act over again his misused station!—as if, at his years and with his experience, any thing was left but to die!

Lear is essentially impossible to be represented on a stage. But how many dramatic personages are there in Shakspeare, which though more tractable and feasible (if I may so speak) than Lear, yet from some circumstance, some adjunct to their

---

4. David Garrick (1717–1779), the most celebrated actor and producer of his day.
5. Christ's instruction in John 3.8.
6. Nahum Tate's adaptation of *King Lear*, in which Lear regains his throne and Cordelia survives to marry Edgar, supplanted Shakespeare's original on the stage from 1681 until 1838.

character, are improper to be shown to our bodily eye! Othello for instance. Nothing can be more soothing, more flattering to the nobler parts of our natures, than to read of a young Venetian lady of the highest extraction, through the force of love and from a sense of merit in him whom she loved, laying aside every consideration of kindred, and country, and colour, and wedding with a *coal-black Moor*—(for such he is represented, in the imperfect state of knowledge respecting foreign countries in those days, compared with our own, or in compliance with popular notions, though the Moors are now well enough known to be by many shades less unworthy of a white woman's fancy)—it is the perfect triumph of virtue over accidents, of the imagination over the senses. She sees Othello's colour in his mind [1.3.247]. But upon the stage, when the imagination is no longer the ruling faculty, but we are left to our poor unassisted senses, I appeal to every one that has seen Othello played, whether he did not, on the contrary, sink Othello's mind in his colour; whether he did not find something extremely revolting in the courtship and wedded caresses of Othello and Desdemona; and whether the actual sight of the thing did not over-weigh all that beautiful compromise which we make in reading. And the reason it should do so is obvious, because there is just so much reality presented to our senses as to give a perception of disagreement, with not enough of belief in the internal motives,—all that which is unseen,—to overpower and reconcile the first and obvious prejudices. What we see upon a stage is body and bodily action; what we are conscious of in reading is almost exclusively the mind, and its movements; and this I think may sufficiently account for the very different sort of delight with which the same play so often affects us in the reading and the seeing.

William Hazlitt
Lectures on the English Poets[1]
from LECTURE 3. ON SHAKESPEARE AND MILTON

The striking peculiarity of Shakspeare's mind was its generic quality, its power of communication with all other minds, so that it contained a universe of thought and feeling within itself, and had no one peculiar bias or exclusive excellence more than another. He was just like any other man, but that he was like all other men. He was the least of an egotist that it was possible to be. He was nothing in himself; but he was all that others were, or that they could become.[2] He not only had in himself the germs of every faculty and feeling, but he could follow them by anticipation, intuitively, into all their conceivable ramifications, through every change of fortune or conflict of passion, or turn of thought. He had "a mind reflecting ages past"[3] and present: all the people that ever lived are there. There was no respect of persons with him. His genius shone equally on the evil and on the good, on the wise and the foolish, the monarch and the beggar. * * * He had only to think of anything in order to become that thing, with all the circumstances belonging to it. * * * The poet may be

---

1. Hazlitt delivered these lectures, ranging from Chaucer to contemporary poets, January to March 1818, and published them the same year. Keats attended all but one, and was deeply struck by what he praised as "Hazlitt's depth of Taste."
2. Cf. Keats's letters on "Negative Capability" and the

Shakespearean "camelion" poet (pages 1047 and 1053).
3. The first line of a praising poem on Shakespeare, by "I.M.S." prefixed to the Second Folio (1632). Hazlitt extended such praise to Coleridge in *The Spirit of the Age* (1825).

said, for the time, to identify himself with the character he wishes to represent, and to pass from one to another, like the same soul successively animating different bodies. By an art like that of the ventriloquist, he throws his imagination out of himself, and makes every word appear to proceed from the mouth of the person in whose name it is given. * * *

In Shakspeare there is a continual composition and decomposition of its elements,[4] a fermentation of every particle in the whole mass, by its alternate affinity or antipathy to other principles which are brought in contact with it. * * *

Shakspeare's language and versification are like the rest of him. He has a magic power over words; they come winged at his bidding, and seem to know their places. They are struck out at a heat on the spur of the occasion, and have all the truth and vividness which arise from an actual impression of the objects. His epithets and single phrases are like sparkles, thrown off from an imagination fired by the whirling rapidity of its own motion. His language is hieroglyphical. It translates thoughts into visible images. It abounds in sudden transitions and elliptical expressions. This is the source of his mixed metaphors, which are only abbreviated forms of speech. These, however, give no pain from long custom. They have, in fact, become idioms in the language. They are the building, and not the scaffolding to thought.

The Characters of Shakespeare's Plays[1]
from HAMLET

Hamlet is a name: his speeches and sayings but the idle coinage of the poet's brain. What then, are they not real? They are as real as our own thoughts. Their reality is in the reader's mind. It is we who are Hamlet. This play has a prophetic truth, which is above that of history. Whoever has become thoughtful and melancholy through his own mishaps or those of others; whoever has borne about with him the clouded brow of reflection, and thought himself "too much i' th' sun" [1.2.67]; whoever has seen the golden lamp of day dimmed by envious mists rising in his own breast, and could find in the world before him only a dull blank with nothing left remarkable in it; whoever has known "the pangs of despised love, the insolence of office, or the spurns which patient merit of the unworthy takes" [3.1.72–74]; he who has felt his mind sink within him, and sadness cling to his heart like a malady, who has had his hopes blighted and his youth staggered by the apparitions of strange things; who cannot be well at ease, while he sees evil hovering near him like a spectre; whose powers of action have been eaten up by thought [3.1.82–88]; he to whom the universe seems infinite, and himself nothing [2.2.252–64]; whose bitterness of soul makes him careless of consequences, and who goes to a play as his best resource to drive off, to a second remove, the evils of life by a mock-representation of them— this is the true Hamlet.

END OF COLERIDGE'S "LECTURES" AND THEIR TIME

---

4. Comparing the "fixed essence" of Chaucer's characters.
1. Hazlitt dedicated *Characters* (181.7) to Charles Lamb, with whom he shared an interest in the psychological bases of action and inaction, and, like many male contemporaries, an identification with Hamlet.

George Gordon, Lord Byron
1788–1824

"Mad, bad, and dangerous to know," pronounced Lady Caroline Lamb, before becoming his lover; a "splendid and imperishable excellence of sincerity and strength," declared Matthew Arnold: the fascination that made Byron the archetypal Romantic, in Europe even more than in Britain, grew from both judgments. He was born in London in 1788, the son of Captain John "Mad Jack" Byron and his second wife, Catherine Gordon, a Scots heiress. The Captain quickly ran through her fortune and departed; Byron and his mother withdrew to Aberdeen in 1789. He passed the next ten years in straitened circumstances, sensitive to the clubfoot with which he had been born, left with a mother who displaced resentment against her absconded husband onto him, and tended by a Calvinist nurse whom he later said had early awakened his sexuality. In 1798 his great-uncle the fifth Baron Byron, "the wicked Lord," died childless, and just after his tenth birthday Byron unexpectedly inherited his title. He asked his mother "whether she perceived any difference in him since he had been made a lord, as he perceived none himself," but the difference shaped the poet.

Byron and his mother returned to England and moved into Newstead Abbey, near Nottingham, the now debt-ridden estate presented to the Byrons by Henry VIII; to the lonely boy, the Gothic hall embodied his tempestuous family heritage. In 1801 Byron was sent to school at Harrow; in the same year he probably met his half-sister Augusta. He entered Trinity College, Cambridge, in 1805, living extravagantly and entangling himself with moneylenders, but also making enduring friendships. His first published volume, *Hours of Idleness*, appeared in 1807, when he was nineteen; the lofty pose he struck as "Lord Byron: A Minor" provoked a savage notice from the *Edinburgh Review*, to which he retaliated in 1809 with a satire in Popean couplets, *English Bards and Scotch Reviewers*. "Written when I was very young and very angry," Byron later confessed to Coleridge, the poem "has been a thorn in my side ever since; more particularly as almost all the Persons animadverted upon became subsequently my acquaintances, and some of them my friends." He suppressed the fifth edition, but so memorable were its attacks on Coleridge, Southey, Wordsworth, Scott, and others that pirated editions continued to appear. Byron took his seat in the House of Lords the same year, then departed on a grand tour shaped by the Napoleonic wars, which barred much of Europe. He sailed to Lisbon, crossed Spain, and proceeded to Greece and Albania, through country little known to Western Europeans. There he began *Childe Harold's Pilgrimage*. In March 1810 he sailed for Constantinople, visited the site of Troy and swam the Hellespont in imitation of mythical Greek lover, Leander. In the East, Byron not only found a world in which the love of an older aristocrat for a beautiful boy was accepted, but also developed a political identity as the Western hero who would liberate Greece from the Turks.

Byron returned to London in July 1811, but too late to see his mother before she died. In February 1812 he made his first speech in the House of Lords, denouncing the death penalty proposed for weavers who had smashed the machines they blamed for their loss of work. Byron's parliamentary activity was superseded the next month when the first two cantos of *Childe Harold's Pilgrimage* appeared and he "woke to find himself famous." The poem joined the immediacy of a travelogue to the disillusionment of a speaker who voiced the melancholy of a generation wearied by prolonged war. Despite Byron's claim that Harold was a fiction designed merely to connect a picaresque narrative, readers heard his author speaking passionately of his own concerns. The magnetism of this personality offset the cynicism the poem displayed: the handsome, aristocratic poet, returned from exotic travels, himself became a figure of force. Byron followed this success with a series of "Eastern" tales that added to his aura: one,

The Corsair (1814), written in ten days, sold ten thousand copies on the day of publication. *Hebrew Melodies* (1815) contains some of Byron's most famous lyrics (*She walks in beauty*) and accorded with the vogue for nationalist themes. Byron was both a sensational commercial success and a noble who gave away his copyrights because aristocrats do not write for money. Like all myths, "Byron" embodied contradictions more than he resolved them.

This literary celebrity was enhanced by Byron's lionizing in Whig society. Liaisons with Lady Caroline Lamb and the "autumnal" Lady Oxford magnified his notoriety, but it was his relationship with his half-sister Augusta, now married, that most gave rise to scandal; her daughter Medora, born in 1814 and given the name of the heroine of *The Corsair*, was widely thought to be Byron's, and probably was. Seeking to escape these agitating affairs, and also to repair his debts, Byron proposed to wealthy heiress Annabella Milbanke. They married in January 1815; their daughter Augusta Ada was born at the end of the year, but a few weeks later Annabella left Byron to live with her parents, amid rumors of insanity, incest, and sodomy. Pirated editions of Byron's poems on the separation made marital discord into public scandal.

In April 1816 Byron quit England, bearing the pageant of his bleeding heart, in Matthew Arnold's famous phrase, across Europe. He settled in Geneva, near Percy Bysshe Shelley and Mary Godwin, who had eloped two years before. They were joined by Mary's stepsister, Claire Clairmont, with whom Byron resumed an affair he had begun in England. Poetry was as much in the air as romance: Byron reported that Shelley "dosed him with Wordsworth physic even to nausea"; the influence and resistance the phrase shows are both evident in the third canto of *Childe Harold* (1816). He wrote *The Prisoner of Chillon* at this time and began the closet-drama *Manfred* (1817). At the end of the summer the Shelley party left for England, where Claire gave birth to daughter Allegra; in October Byron departed for Venice, where he rented a palazzo on the Grand Canal.

Byron described his Venetian life in brilliant letters, some of which were meant for circulation in the circle of his publisher John Murray. To a ceaseless round of sexual activity, he joined substantial literary productivity. He studied Armenian, completed *Manfred,* and visited Rome, gathering materials for a fourth canto of *Childe Harold* (1818). The canto was his longest and most sublime, and its invocation of Freedom's torn banner streaming "*against the wind*" fixed his revolutionary reputation. Yet Byron began to feel trapped by the modes that had won him popularity; determining to "repel charges of monotony and mannerism," he wrote *Beppo,* a comic verse tale of a Venetian *ménage-à-trois* (1818). In its colloquial, digressive ease, Byron was testing the form of his greatest poem, *Don Juan,* at once fictional autobiography, picaresque narrative, literary burlesque, and exposure of social, sexual, and religious hypocrisies. The first two cantos were published in 1819 in an expensive edition meant to forestall charges of blasphemy and bearing neither the author's nor the publisher's name. The authorship was nonetheless known: *Blackwood's Magazine* criticized Byron for "a filthy and impious" attack on his wife (the model for Juan's mother), and the second canto, which turns to shipwreck and cannibalism, redoubled charges of nihilism. Shocking the proprieties of one audience, Byron moved toward another; the poem sold well in increasingly cheap editions.

In April 1819 Byron met his "last attachment," Countess Teresa Gamba Guiccioli, nineteen years old and married to a man nearly three times her age. Through her family, Byron was initiated into the Carbonari, a clandestine revolutionary organization devoted to Italian independence from Austria. While continuing *Don Juan,* he wrote *Marino Faliero, Sardanapalus,* and *The Two Foscari* (all 1821), historical dramas exploring the relationship between the powerful individual and the post-revolutionary state. To the same year belongs *Cain,* a "mystery" drama refused copyright for its unorthodoxy and immediately pirated by radicals. When Teresa's father and brother were exiled for their part in an abortive uprising, she followed them, and Byron reluctantly went with her to Pisa. There he reunited with Percy Shelley, with whom he planned a radical journal, *The Liberal*. The first number contained *The Vision of*

Judgment, a devastating rebuttal to a eulogy of George III by Robert Southey, in the preface to which the Poet Laureate had alluded to Byron as the head of a "Satanic School."

Restive in domestic life with Teresa, Byron agreed to act as agent of a London committee aiding the Greek struggle for independence. In July 1823 he left for Cephalonia, an island in western Greece. Clear of debt and now attentive to his literary income, Byron devoted his fortune to the cause. Philhellenic idealism was soon confronted by motley reality, but Byron founded, paid, and trained a brigade of soldiers. A serious illness in February 1824, followed by the usual remedy of bleeding, weakened him; in April he contracted a fever, treated by further bleeding, from which he died on April 19 at age thirty-six. Deeply mourned, he became a Greek national hero, and throughout Europe his name became synonymous with Romanticism. In England, the stunned reaction of young Tennyson spoke for many: hearing the news, he sadly wrote on a rock "Byron is dead." As Arnold later recalled, in placing Byron with Wordsworth as the great English poets of the century, he had "subjugated" his readers, and his influence was immense and lasting.

Additional selections by Byron appear on pages 288 and 909.

She walks in beauty[1]

1

    She walks in beauty, like the night
       Of cloudless climes and starry skies;
    And all that's best of dark and bright
       Meet in her aspect and her eyes:
5   Thus mellow'd to that tender light
       Which heaven to gaudy day denies.

2

    One shade the more, one ray the less,
       Had half impair'd the nameless grace
    Which waves in every raven tress,
10   Or softly lightens o'er her face;
    Where thoughts serenely sweet express
       How pure, how dear their dwelling-place.

3

    And on that cheek, and o'er that brow,
       So soft, so calm, yet eloquent,
15   The smiles that win, the tints that glow,
       But tell of days in goodness spent,
    A mind at peace with all below,
       A heart whose love is innocent!

1814   1815

---

1. The first poem in *Hebrew Melodies*, a collection initiated by Jewish composer Isaac Nathan, with his music. The subject is Anne Wilmot, the wife of Byron's cousin, whom he had seen at a party wearing "mourning, with dark spangles on her dress."

So, we'll go no more a-roving

1
So, we'll go no more a-roving[1]
   So late into the night,
Though the heart be still as loving,
   And the moon be still as bright.

2
5   For the sword outwears its sheath,
   And the soul wears out the breast.
And the heart must pause to breathe,
   And love itself have rest.

3
Though the night was made for loving,
10   And the day returns too soon,
Yet we'll go no more a-roving
   By the light of the moon.

1817   1830

MANFRED, A DRAMATIC POEM In summer 1816 English tourists in Switzerland had grist for gossip: Byron and Shelley had settled in neighboring houses near Geneva. With Shelley were Mary Wollstonecraft Godwin, with whom he had eloped, their infant son William, and Mary's stepsister, Claire Clairmont, who had introduced the poets and was pregnant with Byron's daughter (Allegra, born 1817). Rumors swirled about "a league of Incest," which Byron indignantly denied. Into this hothouse in August came a visiting M. G. Lewis, author of the sensational Gothic novel *The Monk* (1796) and the hugely successful Drury Lane melodrama *Castle Spectre* (1797). Lewis translated most of Goethe's *Faust* (Part 1, 1808) *viva voce* to Byron. "I was naturally much struck with it," Byron told John Murray, "but it was the *Staubach* & the *Jungfrau*—and something else—much more than Faustus that made me write Manfred." The effect of the surrounding mountains is corroborated by the many echoes in the play of the journal Byron kept for Augusta of his Alpine tour in September. And before this encounter with *Faust* were the Gothic melodramas that Byron met on the Drury Lane Committee of Management in 1815, the success in 1813 of Coleridge's drama *Remorse* (a title which might serve for an entire heritage), and Byron's general knowledge of the Gothic: William Beckford's Oriental tale *Vathek* (1786) supplied the details of Manfred's underworld journey, and Horace Walpole's seminal *Castle of Otranto* (1764) is the probable source of his name. Subtitling the play "a dramatic poem," Byron signaled that it wasn't for performance—he insisted that he had rendered it "*quite impossible* for the stage"—but he was probably tempted: despite the disavowals, *Manfred* was the first of several of his plays to enjoy theatrical success in the nineteenth century.

    The momentous "something else" Byron hinted to Murray was his bitterness over the separation from Annabella, from which Augusta was inextricable. By naming Manfred's beloved Astarte (an incestuous pagan goddess) Byron refueled the scandal, and in interrupting the dialogue between Manuel and Herman just as the former is about to name "The lady Astarte, his—" (3.3.47), Byron tantalized prurient or literal-minded readers looking for autobiographical confession.

---

1. The poem first appeared in a letter Byron wrote from Venice to Thomas Moore: "The Carnival—that is, the latter part of it—and sitting up late o'nights, had knocked me up a little. But it is over—and it is now Lent...though I did not dissipate much upon the whole, yet I find 'the sword wearing out the scabbard,' though I have but just turned the corner of twenty-nine." Carnival, literally "farewell to flesh," is the period of festival before Lent.

Byron's deepest confrontation was with his own image. Manfred is the epitome of the titanic, gloomy Byronic Hero who dominates *Childe Harold's Pilgrimage* and the popular "Eastern" tales, a figure whose notoriety Byron exploited but by which he was beginning to feel constrained. *Manfred* was "too much in my old style," he told Murray; "I certainly am a devil of a mannerist—and must leave off—but what could I do? without exertion of some kind—I should have sunk under my imagination and reality." The autonomy that Manfred claims—"The mind which is immortal makes itself / Requital for its good or evil thoughts— / Is its own origin of ill and end— / And its own place and time" (3.4.129–32)—is the sign of an independence of all authority that Nietzsche recognized as a precursor of his own Superman, but which in its extremism tips into the self-parody Byron acknowledged to Murray. The rhythm of repeated rejections that constitutes the dramatic action produces an intensifying isolation that tends only toward death.

Manfred
A Dramatic Poem

"There are more things in heaven and earth, Horatio,
Than are dreamt of in your philosophy."[1]

Dramatis Personae

MANFRED	WITCH OF THE ALPS
CHAMOIS HUNTER	ARIMANES
ABBOT OF ST MAURICE	NEMESIS
MANUEL	THE DESTINIES
HERMAN	SPIRITS, & C.

The Scene of the Drama is amongst the Higher Alps—partly in the Castle of Manfred, and partly in the Mountains.

ACT 1

Scene 1

Manfred alone.—Scene, a Gothic Gallery.—Time, Midnight.

MANFRED: The lamp must be replenish'd, but even then
    It will not burn so long as I must watch:
    My slumbers—if I slumber—are not sleep,
    But a continuance of enduring thought,
5   Which then I can resist not: in my heart
    There is a vigil, and these eyes but close
    To look within; and yet I live, and bear
    The aspect and the form of breathing men.
    (But grief should be the instructor of the wise;)
10   Sorrow is knowledge: they who know the most
    Must mourn the deepest o'er the fatal truth,
    The Tree of Knowledge is not that of Life.[2]
    Philosophy and science, and the springs

---

1. Hamlet's reminder to his friend after having seen his father's ghost (*Hamlet* 1.5.66–67).

2. See Genesis chs. 2–3; Milton, *Paradise Lost*, 4.194–222.

Of wonder, and the wisdom of the world,
15   I have essay'd, and in my mind there is
A power to make these subject to itself—
But they avail not: I have done men good,
And I have met with good even among men—
But this avail'd not: I have had my foes,
20   And none have baffled, many fallen before me—
But this avail'd not:—Good, or evil, life,
Powers, passions, all I see in other beings,
Have been to me as rain unto the sands,
Since that all-nameless hour. I have no dread,
25   And feel the curse to have no natural fear,
Nor fluttering throb, that beats with hopes or wishes,
Or lurking love of something on the earth.—
Now to my task.—
                    Mysterious Agency!
Ye spirits of the unbounded Universe!
30   Whom I have sought in darkness and in light—
Ye, who do compass earth about, and dwell
In subtler essence—ye, to whom the tops
Of mountains inaccessible are haunts,
And earth's and ocean's caves familiar things—
35   I call upon ye by the written charm
Which gives me power upon you—Rise! appear!
[A pause.]
They come not yet.—Now by the voice of him
Who is the first among you—by this sign,
Which makes you tremble—by the claims of him
40   Who is undying,—Rise! appear!—Appear!
[A pause.]
If it be so.—Spirits of earth and air,
Ye shall not thus elude me: by a power,
Deeper than all yet urged, a tyrant-spell,
Which had its birthplace in a star condemn'd,
45   The burning wreck of a demolish'd world,
A wandering hell in the eternal space;
By the strong curse which is upon my soul,
The thought which is within me and around me,
I do compel ye to my will.—Appear!

[A star is seen at the darker end of the gallery: it is stationary; and a voice is heard singing.]

FIRST SPIRIT
50   Mortal! to thy bidding bow'd,
                    From my mansion in the cloud,
                    Which the breath of twilight builds,
                    And the summer's sunset gilds
                    With the azure and vermilion,
55   Which is mix'd for my pavilion;
                    Though thy quest may be forbidden,

On a star-beam I have ridden;
   To thine adjuration bow'd,
Mortal—be thy wish avow'd!

Voice of the SECOND SPIRIT

60   Mont Blanc is the monarch of mountains;[3]
    They crown'd him long ago
On a throne of rocks, in a robe of clouds,
    With a diadem of snow.
Around his waist are forests braced,
65   The Avalanche in his hand;
But ere it fall, that thundering ball
    Must pause for my command.
The Glacier's cold and restless mass
    Moves onward day by day;
70   But I am he who bids it pass,
    Or with its ice delay.
I am the spirit of the place,
    Could make the mountain bow
And quiver to his cavern'd base—
75   And what with me wouldst *Thou?*

Voice of the THIRD SPIRIT

In the blue depth of the waters,
    Where the wave hath no strife,
Where the wind is a stranger,
    And the sea-snake hath life,
80   Where the Mermaid is decking
    Her green hair with shells;
Like the storm on the surface
    Came the sound of thy spells;
O'er my calm Hall of Coral
85   The deep echo roll'd—
To the Spirit of Ocean
    Thy wishes unfold!

FOURTH SPIRIT

Where the slumbering earthquake
    Lies pillow'd on fire,
90   And the lakes of bitumen[4]
    Rise boilingly higher;
Where the roots of the Andes
    Strike deep in the earth,
As their summits to heaven

---

3. See P. B. Shelley's *Mont Blanc,* page 871.
4. Cf. the "bituminous lake where Sodom flared" to which

Milton compares Hell (*Paradise Lost* 10.562). Bitumen:
mineral pitch.

95 Shoot soaringly forth;
I have quitted my birthplace,
Thy bidding to bide—
Thy spell hath subdued me,
Thy will be my guide!

FIFTH SPIRIT

100 I am the Rider of the wind,
The Stirrer of the storm;
The hurricane I left behind
Is yet with lightning warm;
To speed to thee, o'er shore and sea
105 I swept upon the blast:
The fleet I met sail'd well, and yet
'Twill sink ere night be past.

SIXTH SPIRIT

My dwelling is the shadow of the night,
Why doth thy magic torture me with light?

SEVENTH SPIRIT

110 The star which rules thy destiny
Was ruled, ere earth began, by me:
It was a world as fresh and fair
As e'er revolved round sun in air;
Its course was free and regular,
115 Space bosom'd not a lovelier star.
The hour arrived—and it became
A wandering mass of shapeless flame,
A pathless comet, and a curse,
The menace of the universe;
120 Still rolling on with innate force,
Without a sphere, without a course,
A bright deformity on high,
The monster of the upper sky!
And thou! beneath its influence born—
125 Thou worm! whom I obey and scorn—
Forced by a power (which is not thine,
And lent thee but to make thee mine)
For this brief moment to descend,
Where these weak spirits round thee bend
130 And parley with a thing like thee—
What wouldst thou, Child of Clay! with me?

THE SEVEN SPIRITS

Earth, ocean, air, night, mountains, winds, thy star,
Are at thy beck and bidding, Child of Clay!
Before thee at thy quest their spirits are—
135 What wouldst thou with us, son of mortals—say?

MANFRED: Forgetfulness—
FIRST SPIRIT: Of what—of whom—and why?
MANFRED: Of that which is within me; read it there—
          Ye know it, and I cannot utter it.
SPIRIT: We can but give thee that which we possess:
140   Ask of us subjects, sovereignty, the power
          O'er earth, the whole, or portion, or a sign
          Which shall control the elements, whereof
          We are the dominators, each and all,
          These shall be thine.
MANFRED: Oblivion, self-oblivion—
145   Can ye not wring from out the hidden realms
          Ye offer so profusely what I ask?
SPIRIT: It is not in our essence, in our skill;
          But—thou mayst die.
MANFRED: Will death bestow it on me?
SPIRIT: We are immortal, and do not forget;
150   We are eternal; and to us the past
          Is, as the future, present. Art thou answer'd?
MANFRED: Ye mock me—but the power which brought ye here
          Hath made you mine. Slaves, scoff not at my will!
          The mind, the spirit, the Promethean spark,[5]
155   The lightning of my being, is as bright,
          Pervading, and far darting as your own,
          And shall not yield to yours, though coop'd in clay!
          Answer, or I will teach you what I am.
SPIRIT: We answer as we answer'd; our reply
160   Is even in thine own words.
MANFRED: Why say ye so?
SPIRIT: If, as thou say'st, thine essence be as ours,
          We have replied in telling thee, the thing
          Mortals call death hath nought to do with us.
MANFRED: I then have call'd ye from your realms in vain;
165   Ye cannot, or ye will not, aid me.
SPIRIT: Say;
          What we possess we offer; it is thine:
          Bethink ere thou dismiss us, ask again—
          Kingdom, and sway, and strength, and length of days—
MANFRED: Accursed! what have I to do with days?
170   They are too long already.—Hence—begone!
SPIRIT: Yet pause: being here, our will would do thee service;
          Bethink thee, is there then no other gift
          Which we can make not worthless in thine eyes?
MANFRED: No, none: yet stay—one moment, ere we part—

5. Greek myths relate that Prometheus stole fire from the gods to give to humankind. "Of the Prometheus of Aeschylus [*Prometheus Bound*] I was passionately fond as a boy," Byron recalled; "[it] has always been so much in my head—that I can easily conceive its influence over all or anything that I have written." Mary Shelley subtitled *Frankenstein* "The Modern Prometheus"—a novel conceived and begun in summer 1816 at Byron's villa.

175   I would behold ye face to face. I hear
       Your voices, sweet and melancholy sounds,
       As music on the waters; and I see
       The steady aspect of a clear large star;
       But nothing more. Approach me as ye are,
180   Or one, or all, in your accustom'd forms.
SPIRIT: We have no forms, beyond the elements
       Of which we are the mind and principle:
       But choose a form—in that we will appear.
MANFRED: I have no choice; there is no form on earth
185   Hideous or beautiful to me. Let him,
       Who is most powerful of ye, take such aspect
       As unto him may seem most fitting—Come!
SEVENTH SPIRIT [*Appearing in the shape of a beautiful female figure*]:
       Behold!
MANFRED: Oh God! if it be thus, and *thou*
       Art not a madness and a mockery,
190   I yet might be most happy. I will clasp thee,
       And we again will be— [*The figure vanishes.*]
                My heart is crush'd! [*Manfred falls senseless.*]
    [*A Voice is heard in the Incantation which follows.*][6]

           When the moon is on the wave,
              And the glow-worm in the grass,
           And the meteor on the grave,
195   And the wisp on the morass;
           When the falling stars are shooting,
              And the answer'd owls are hooting,
           And the silent leaves are still
              In the shadow of the hill,
200   Shall my soul be upon thine,
              With a power and with a sign.

           Though thy slumber may be deep,
              Yet thy spirit shall not sleep;
           There are shades which will not vanish,
205   There are thoughts thou canst not banish;
           By a power to thee unknown,
              Thou canst never be alone;
           Thou art wrapt as with a shroud,
              Thou art gather'd in a cloud;
210   And for ever shalt thou dwell
              In the spirit of this spell.

---

6. The "Incantation" was published some months before *Manfred*, with *The Prisoner of Chillon* (1816), where it is headed by a note: "The following poem was a Chorus in an unfinished Witch drama, which was begun some years ago." The time aligns the Incantation with Byron's first encounter with excerpts of Goethe's *Faust* in a "sorry French translation" in de Staël's *Corinne* and with the success of Coleridge's *Remorse*. Stanzas 5 and 6, inserted later, were recognized as pointing toward Lady Byron, from whom Byron had separated early in 1816.

Though thou seest me not pass by,
   Thou shalt feel me with thine eye
As a thing that, though unseen,
215   Must be near thee, and hath been;
And when in that secret dread
   Thou hast turn'd around thy head,
Thou shalt marvel I am not
   As thy shadow on the spot,
220   And the power which thou dost feel
   Shall be what thou must conceal.

And a magic voice and verse
   Hath baptized thee with a curse;
And a spirit of the air
225   Hath begirt thee with a snare;
In the wind there is a voice
   Shall forbid thee to rejoice;
And to thee shall Night deny
   All the quiet of her sky;
230   And the day shall have a sun,
   Which shall make thee wish it done.

From thy false tears I did distil
   An essence which hath strength to kill;
From thy own heart I then did wring
235   The black blood in its blackest spring;
From thy own smile I snatch'd the snake,
   For there it coil'd as in a brake;
From thy own lip I drew the charm
   Which gave all these their chiefest harm;
240   In proving every poison known,
   I found the strongest was thine own.

By thy cold breast and serpent smile,
   By thy unfathom'd gulfs of guile,
By that most seeming virtuous eye,
245   By thy shut soul's hypocrisy;
By the perfection of thine art
   Which pass'd for human thine own heart;
By thy delight in others' pain,
   And by thy brotherhood of Cain,[7]
250   I call upon thee! and compel
   Thyself to be thy proper Hell![8]

And on thy head I pour the vial
   Which doth devote thee to this trial;
Nor to slumber, nor to die,
255   Shall be in thy destiny;
Though thy death shall still seem near
   To thy wish, but as a fear;

---

7. Kinship with the brother-murderer (Genesis Ch. 4).   8. "Myself am Hell," says Milton's Satan (*Paradise Lost* 4.75).

Ford Madox Brown, *Manfred on the Jungfrau*, 1840. Byron's flamboyant protagonist inspired many later works. Robert Schumann set the play to music (1848–1849) and Peter Ilyich Tchaikovsky composed a Manfred symphony (1885). Famous representations include two watercolors by John Martin (1837) and this painting by Ford Madox Brown, imagining the moment in Act I, Scene 2, when Manfred, about to indulge a suicidal leap, is interrupted by a chamois hunter. Standing on the brink of a precipice crowned with thick snow, Manfred clutches his hands to his head in a gesture of despair; his dress is intended to be in the style of the tenth or eleventh century.

> Lo! the spell now works around thee,
> And the clankless chain hath bound thee;
> O'er thy heart and brain together
> Hath the word been pass'd—now wither!

260

Scene 2

The Mountain of the Jungfrau.[9]*—Time, Morning.—Manfred alone upon the Cliffs.*

MANFRED: The spirits I have raised abandon me—
The spells which I have studied baffle me—
The remedy I reck'd of tortured me;
I lean no more on super-human aid,
It hath no power upon the past, and for
The future, till the past be gulf'd in darkness,
It is not of my search.—My mother Earth!
And thou fresh breaking Day, and you, ye Mountains,
Why are ye beautiful? I cannot love ye.
And thou, the bright eye of the universe,
That openest over all, and unto all
Art a delight—thou shin'st not on my heart.
And you, ye crags, upon whose extreme edge
I stand, and on the torrent's brink beneath
Behold the tall pines dwindled as to shrubs
In dizziness of distance; when a leap,
A stir, a motion, even a breath, would bring
My breast upon its rocky bosom's bed

5

10

15

9. A peak in the Swiss Alps.

To rest for ever—wherefore do I pause?
20   I feel the impulse—yet I do not plunge;
        I see the peril—yet do not recede;
        And my brain reels—and yet my foot is firm:
        There is a power upon me which withholds,
        And makes it my fatality to live;
25   If it be life to wear within myself
        This barrenness of spirit, and to be
        My own soul's sepulchre, for I have ceased
        To justify my deeds unto myself—
        The last infirmity of evil.[1] Ay,
30   Thou winged and cloud-cleaving minister,
    [*An eagle passes.*]
        Whose happy flight is highest into heaven,
        Well may'st thou swoop so near me—I should be
        Thy prey, and gorge thine eaglets; thou art gone
        Where the eye cannot follow thee; but thine
35   Yet pierces downward, onward, or above,
        With a pervading vision.—Beautiful!
        How beautiful is all this visible world!
        How glorious in its action and itself!
        But we, who name ourselves its sovereigns, we,
40   Half dust, half deity, alike unfit
        To sink or soar, with our mix'd essence make
        A conflict of its elements, and breathe
        The breath of degradation and of pride,
        Contending with low wants and lofty will,
45   Till our mortality predominates,
        And men are—what they name not to themselves,
        And trust not to each other.[2] Hark! the note,
    [*The Shepherd's pipe in the distance is heard.*]
        The natural music of the mountain reed—
        For here the patriarchal days[3] are not
50   A pastoral fable—pipes in the liberal air,
        Mix'd with the sweet bells of the sauntering herd;
        My soul would drink those echoes.—Oh, that I were
        The viewless° spirit of a lovely sound,   *invisible*
        A living voice, a breathing harmony,
55   A bodiless enjoyment—born and dying
        With the blest tone which made me!
    [*Enter from below a Chamois° Hunter.*]   *native antelope*
CHAMOIS HUNTER: Even so
        This way the chamois leapt: her nimble feet
        Have baffled me; my gains to-day will scarce
        Repay my break-neck travail.—What is here?

---

1. An echo of Milton's *Lycidas*, on the love of fame as the last infirmity of noble mind (71).
2. Echoing Hamlet's confession of his lost responsiveness to "this goodly frame, the earth" and the despair that to him renders "man, how noble in reason, how infinite in faculties . . . in action how like an angel" the "quintessence of dust" (2.2.301–19).
3. The days of the Old Testament elders, the shepherds Abraham, Isaac, and Jacob.

60 Who seems not of my trade, and yet hath reach'd
 A height which none even of our mountaineers,
 Save our best hunters, may attain: his garb
 Is goodly, his mien manly, and his air
 Proud as a free-born peasant's, at this distance—
65 I will approach him nearer.
MANFRED [*not perceiving the other*]: To be thus—
 Grey-hair'd with anguish, like these blasted pines,
 Wrecks of a single winter, barkless, branchless,
 A blighted trunk upon a cursed root,
 Which but supplies a feeling to decay—
70 And to be thus, eternally but thus,
 Having been otherwise! Now furrow'd o'er
 With wrinkles, plough'd by moments, not by years
 And hours—all tortured into ages—hours
 Which I outlive!—Ye toppling crags of ice!
75 Ye avalanches, whom a breath draws down
 In mountainous o'erwhelming, come and crush me!
 I hear ye momently above, beneath,
 Crash with a frequent conflict; but ye pass,
 And only fall on things that still would live;
80 On the young flourishing forest, or the hut
 And hamlet of the harmless villager.
CHAMOIS HUNTER: The mists begin to rise from up the valley;
 I'll warn him to descend, or he may chance
 To lose at once his way and life together.
MANFRED: The mists boil up around the glaciers; clouds
86 Rise curling fast beneath me, white and sulphury,
 Like foam from the roused ocean of deep Hell,
 Whose every wave breaks on a living shore,
 Heap'd with the damn'd like pebbles.—I am giddy.
CHAMOIS HUNTER: I must approach him cautiously; if near,
91 A sudden step will startle him, and he
 Seems tottering already.
MANFRED: Mountains have fallen,
 Leaving a gap in the clouds, and with the shock
 Rocking their Alpine brethren; filling up
95 The ripe green valleys with destruction's splinters;
 Damming the rivers with a sudden dash,
 Which crush'd the waters into mist, and made
 Their fountains find another channel—thus,
 Thus, in its old age, did Mount Rosenberg[4]—
100 Why stood I not beneath it?
CHAMOIS HUNTER: Friend! have a care,
 Your next step may be fatal!—for the love
 Of him who made you, stand not on that brink!
MANFRED [*not hearing him*]: Such would have been for me a fitting tomb;
 My bones had then been quiet in their depth;

4. In 1806 an avalanche on Mt. Rossberg had crushed several villages.

105   They had not then been strewn upon the rocks
        For the wind's pastime—as thus—thus they shall be—
        In this one plunge.—Farewell, ye opening heavens!
        Look not upon me thus reproachfully—
        Ye were not meant for me—Earth! take these atoms!
        [*As Manfred is in act to spring from the cliff, the Chamois Hunter seizes and retains
        him with a sudden grasp.*]
CHAMOIS HUNTER: Hold, madman!—though aweary of thy life,
111   Stain not our pure vales with thy guilty blood—
        Away with me—I will not quit my hold.
MANFRED: I am most sick at heart—nay, grasp me not—
        I am all feebleness—the mountains whirl
115   Spinning around me—I grow blind—What art thou?
CHAMOIS HUNTER: I'll answer that anon.—Away with me—
        The clouds grow thicker—there—now lean on me—
        Place your foot here—here, take this staff, and cling
        A moment to that shrub—now give me your hand,
120   And hold fast by my girdle—softly—well—
        The Chalet will be gain'd within an hour—
        Come on, we'll quickly find a surer footing,
        And something like a pathway, which the torrent
        Hath wash'd since winter.—Come, 'tis bravely done—
125   You should have been a hunter.—Follow me.
        [*As they descend the rocks with difficulty, the scene closes.*]

ACT 2

Scene 1

A Cottage amongst the Bernese Alps. [*Manfred and the Chamois Hunter.*]

CHAMOIS HUNTER: No, no—yet pause—thou must not yet go forth:
        Thy mind and body are alike unfit
        To trust each other; for some hours, at least;
        When thou art better, I will be thy guide—
5   But whither?
MANFRED: It imports not: I do know
        My route full well, and need no further guidance.
CHAMOIS HUNTER: Thy garb and gait bespeak thee of high lineage—
        One of the many chiefs, whose castled crags
        Look o'er the lower valleys—which of these
10   May call thee lord? I only know their portals;
        My way of life leads me but rarely down
        To bask by the huge hearths of those old halls,
        Carousing with the vassals; but the paths,
        Which step from out our mountains to their doors,
15   I know from childhood—which of these is thine?
MANFRED: No matter.
CHAMOIS HUNTER: Well, sir, pardon me the question,
        And be of better cheer. Come, taste my wine;

'Tis of an ancient vintage; many a day
'T has thawed my veins among our glaciers, now
20   Let it do thus for thine—Come, pledge me fairly.
MANFRED: Away, away! there's blood upon the brim!
    Will it then never—never sink in the earth?
CHAMOIS HUNTER: What dost thou mean? thy senses wander from thee.
MANFRED: I say 'tis blood—my blood! the pure warm stream
25   Which ran in the veins of my fathers, and in ours
    When we were in our youth, and had one heart,
    And loved each other as we should not love,
    And this was shed: but still it rises up,
    Colouring the clouds, that shut me out from heaven,
30   Where thou art not—and I shall never be.
CHAMOIS HUNTER: Man of strange words, and some half-maddening sin,
    Which makes thee people vacancy, whate'er
    Thy dread and sufferance be, there's comfort yet—
    The aid of holy men, and heavenly patience—
MANFRED: Patience and patience! Hence—that word was made
    For brutes of burthen, not for birds of prey;
    Preach it to mortals of a dust like thine,—
    I am not of thine order.
CHAMOIS HUNTER: Thanks to heaven!
    I would not be of thine for the free fame
40   Of William Tell;[1] but whatsoe'er thine ill,
    It must be borne, and these wild starts are useless.
MANFRED: Do I not bear it?—Look on me—I live.
CHAMOIS HUNTER: This is convulsion, and no healthful life.
MANFRED: I tell thee, man! I have lived many years,
45   Many long years, but they are nothing now
    To those which I must number: ages—ages—
    Space and eternity—and consciousness,
    With the fierce thirst of death—and still unslaked!
CHAMOIS HUNTER: Why, on thy brow the seal of middle age
50   Hath scarce been set; I am thine elder far.
MANFRED: Think'st thou existence doth depend on time?
    It doth; but actions are our epochs: mine
    Have made my days and nights imperishable,
    Endless, and all alike, as sands on the shore,
55   Innumerable atoms; and one desert,
    Barren and cold, on which the wild waves break,
    But nothing rests, save carcasses and wrecks,
    Rocks, and the salt-surf weeds of bitterness.
CHAMOIS HUNTER: Alas! he's mad—but yet I must not leave him.
MANFRED: I would I were—for then the things I see
    Would be but a distemper'd dream.

1. The legendary 14th-century liberator of Switzerland from Austrian domination.

CHAMOIS HUNTER: What is it
          That thou dost see, or think thou look'st upon?
MANFRED: Myself, and thee—a peasant of the Alps—
          Thy humble virtues, hospitable home,
65   And spirit patient, pious, proud, and free;
          Thy self-respect, grafted on innocent thoughts;
          Thy days of health, and nights of sleep; thy toils,
          By danger dignified, yet guiltless; hopes
          Of cheerful old age and a quiet grave,
70   With cross and garland over its green turf,
          And thy grandchildren's love for epitaph;
          This do I see—and then I look within—
          It matters not—my soul was scorch'd already!
CHAMOIS HUNTER: And would'st thou then exchange thy lot for mine?
MANFRED: No, friend! I would not wrong thee, nor exchange
          My lot with living being: I can bear—
          However wretchedly, 'tis still to bear—
          In life what others could not brook to dream,
          But perish in their slumber.
CHAMOIS HUNTER: And with this—
80   This cautious feeling for another's pain,
          Canst thou be black with evil?—say not so.
          Can one of gentle thoughts have wreak'd revenge
          Upon his enemies?
MANFRED: Oh! no, no, no!
          My injuries came down on those who loved me—
85   On those whom I best loved: I never quell'd
          An enemy, save in my just defence—
          My wrongs were all on those I should have cherished
          But my embrace was fatal.
CHAMOIS HUNTER: Heaven give thee rest!
          And penitence restore thee to thyself;
90   My prayers shall be for thee.
MANFRED: I need them not,
          But can endure thy pity. I depart—
          'Tis time—farewell!—Here's gold, and thanks for thee—
          No words—it is thy due.—Follow me not—
          I know my path—the mountain peril's past:
95   And once again, I charge thee, follow not!
          [Exit Manfred.]

                          Scene 2

A lower Valley in the Alps.—A Cataract. [Enter Manfred.]

MANFRED: It is not noon—the sunbow's rays[2] still arch
          The torrent with the many hues of heaven,

---

2. This iris is formed by the rays of the sun over the lower part of the Alpine torrents: it is exactly like a rainbow come to pay a visit, and so close that you may walk into it: this effect lasts until noon [Byron's note].

And roll the sheeted silver's waving column
O'er the crag's headlong perpendicular,
5   And fling its lines of foaming light along,
And to and fro, like the pale courser's tail,
The Giant steed, to be bestrode by Death,
As told in the Apocalypse.[3] No eyes
But mine now drink this sight of loveliness;
10   I should be sole in this sweet solitude,
And with the Spirit of the place divide
The homage of these waters.—I will call her.

[*Manfred takes some of the water into the palm of his hand, and flings it into the air, muttering the adjuration. After a pause, the Witch of the Alps rises beneath the arch of the sunbow of the torrent.*]

Beautiful Spirit! with thy hair of light,
And dazzling eyes of glory, in whose form
15   The charms of earth's least mortal daughters grow
To an unearthly stature, in an essence
Of purer elements; while the hues of youth,—
Carnation'd like a sleeping infant's cheek,
Rock'd by the beating of her mother's heart,
20   Or the rose tints, which summer's twilight leaves
Upon the lofty glacier's virgin snow,
The blush of earth embracing with her heaven,—
Tinge thy celestial aspect, and make tame
The beauties of the sunbow which bends o'er thee.
25   Beautiful Spirit! in thy calm clear brow,
Wherein is glass'd serenity of soul,
Which of itself shows immortality,
I read that thou wilt pardon to a Son
Of Earth, whom the abstruser powers permit
30   At times to commune with them—if that he
Avail him of his spells—to call thee thus,
And gaze on thee a moment.

WITCH: Son of Earth!
I know thee, and the powers which give thee power;
I know thee for a man of many thoughts,
35   And deeds of good and ill, extreme in both,
Fatal and fated in thy sufferings.
I have expected this—what would'st thou with me?

MANFRED: To look upon thy beauty—nothing further.
The face of the earth hath madden'd me, and I
40   Take refuge in her mysteries, and pierce
To the abodes of those who govern her—
But they can nothing aid me. I have sought
From them what they could not bestow, and now
I search no further.

---

3. Revelation 6.8: "And I looked, and behold a pale horse: and his name that sat on him was Death, and Hell followed with him."

WITCH: What could be the quest
45   Which is not in the power of the most powerful,
      The rulers of the invisible?
MANFRED: A boon;
      But why should I repeat it? 'twere in vain.
WITCH: I know not that; let thy lips utter it.
MANFRED: Well, though it torture me, 'tis but the same;
50   My pang shall find a voice. From my youth upwards
      My spirit walk'd not with the souls of men,
      Nor look'd upon the earth with human eyes;
      The thirst of their ambition was not mine,
      The aim of their existence was not mine;
55   My joys, my griefs, my passions, and my powers,
      Made me a stranger; though I wore the form,
      I had no sympathy with breathing flesh,
      Nor midst the creatures of clay that girded me
      Was there but one who—but of her anon.
60   I said with men, and with the thoughts of men,
      I held but slight communion; but instead,
      My joy was in the Wilderness, to breathe
      The difficult air of the iced mountain's top,
      Where the birds dare not build, nor insect's wing
65   Flit o'er the herbless granite; or to plunge
      Into the torrent, and to roll along
      On the swift whirl of the new breaking wave
      Of river-stream, or ocean, in their flow.
      In these my early strength exulted; or
70   To follow through the night the moving moon,
      The stars and their development; or catch
      The dazzling lightnings till my eyes grew dim;
      Or to look, list'ning, on the scatter'd leaves,
      While Autumn winds were at their evening song.
75   These were my pastimes, and to be alone;
      For if the beings, of whom I was one,—
      Hating to be so,—cross'd me in my path,
      I felt myself degraded back to them,
      And was all clay again. And then I dived,
80   In my lone wanderings, to the caves of death,
      Searching its cause in its effect; and drew
      From wither'd bones, and skulls, and heap'd up dust,
      Conclusions most forbidden. Then I pass'd
      The nights of years in sciences untaught,
85   Save in the old time; and with time and toil,
      And terrible ordeal, and such penance
      As in itself hath power upon the air,
      And spirits that do compass air and earth,
      Space, and the peopled infinite, I made
90   Mine eyes familiar with Eternity,

Such as, before me, did the Magi, and
He who from out their fountain dwellings raised
Eros and Anteros, at Gadara,[4]
As I do thee;—and with my knowledge grew
95   The thirst of knowledge, and the power and joy
Of this most bright intelligence, until—
WITCH: Proceed.
MANFRED: Oh! I but thus prolong'd my words,
Boasting these idle attributes, because
As I approach the core of my heart's grief—
100   But to my task. I have not named to thee
Father or mother, mistress, friend, or being,
With whom I wore the chain of human ties;
If I had such, they seem'd not such to me—
Yet there was one—
WITCH: Spare not thyself—proceed.
MANFRED: She was like me in lineaments—her eyes,
Her hair, her features, all, to the very tone
Even of her voice, they said were like to mine;
But soften'd all, and temper'd into beauty;
She had the same lone thoughts and wanderings,
110   The quest of hidden knowledge, and a mind
To comprehend the universe: nor these
Alone, but with them gentler powers than mine,
Pity, and smiles, and tears—which I had not;
And tenderness—but that I had for her;
115   Humility—and that I never had.
Her faults were mine—her virtues were her own—
I loved her, and destroy'd her!
WITCH: With thy hand?
MANFRED: Not with my hand, but heart—which broke her heart—
It gazed on mine, and wither'd. I have shed
120   Blood, but not hers—and yet her blood was shed—
I saw—and could not stanch it.
WITCH: And for this—
A being of the race thou dost despise,
The order which thine own would rise above,
Mingling with us and ours, thou dost forego
125   The gifts of our great knowledge, and shrink'st back
To recreant mortality—Away!
MANFRED: Daughter of Air! I tell thee, since that hour—
But words are breath—look on me in my sleep,
Or watch my watchings—Come and sit by me!

4. The philosopher Jamblicus. The story of the raising of Eros and Anteros may be found in his life by Eunapius. It is well told [Byron's note]. Jamblicus, a 4th-century Neo-Platonist, called up Eros, the god of love, and Anteros, the god of unrequited love, from the springs named after them in Syria.

130   My solitude is solitude no more,
        But peopled with the Furies;[5] —I have gnash'd
        My teeth in darkness till returning morn,
        Then cursed myself till sunset;—I have pray'd
        For madness as a blessing— 'tis denied me.
135   I have affronted death—but in the war
        Of elements the waters shrunk from me,
        And fatal things pass'd harmless—the cold hand
        Of an all-pitiless demon held me back,
        Back by a single hair, which would not break.
140   In fantasy, imagination, all
        The affluence of my soul—which one day was
        A Croesus[6] in creation—I plunged deep,
        But, like an ebbing wave, it dash'd me back
        Into the gulf of my unfathom'd thought.
145   I plunged amidst mankind—Forgetfulness
        I sought in all, save where 'tis to be found,
        And that I have to learn—my sciences,
        My long pursued and super-human art,
149   Is mortal here—I dwell in my despair—
        And live—and live for ever.[7]
WITCH: It may be
        That I can aid thee.
MANFRED: To do this thy power
        Must wake the dead, or lay me low with them.
        Do so—in any shape—in any hour—
154   With any torture—so it be the last.
WITCH: That is not in my province; but if thou
        Wilt swear obedience to my will, and do
        My bidding, it may help thee to thy wishes.
MANFRED: I will not swear—Obey! and whom? the spirits
159   Whose presence I command, and be the slave
        Of those who served me—Never!
WITCH: Is this all?
        Hast thou no gentler answer?—Yet bethink thee,
        And pause ere thou rejectest.
MANFRED: I have said it.
WITCH: Enough!—I may retire then—say!
MANFRED: Retire!
        [The Witch disappears.]
MANFRED [alone]: We are the fools of time and terror: Days
165   Steal on us and steal from us; yet we live,
        Loathing our life, and dreading still to die.

---

5. Greek goddesses of revenge.
6. The legendary wealthy monarch.
7. Byron evokes the legend of the Wandering Jew, who is
punished for his cruelty to Jesus by the eternal refusal of
the death for which he yearns.

In all the days of this detested yoke—
This heaving burthen, this accursed breath—
This vital weight upon the struggling heart,
170   Which sinks with sorrow, or beats quick with pain,
Or joy that ends in agony or faintness—
In all the days of past and future, for
In life there is no present, we can number
How few—how less than few—wherein the soul
175   Forbears to pant for death, and yet draws back
As from a stream in winter, though the chill
Be but a moment's. I have one resource
Still in my science—I can call the dead,
And ask them what it is we dread to be:
180   The sternest answer can but be the Grave,
And that is nothing—if they answer not—
The buried Prophet answered to the Hag
Of Endor; and the Spartan Monarch drew
From the Byzantine maid's unsleeping spirit
185   An answer and his destiny—he slew
That which he loved, unknowing what he slew,
And died unpardon'd—though he call'd in aid
The Phyxian Jove, and in Phigalia roused
The Arcadian Evocators to compel
190   The indignant shadow to depose her wrath,
Or fix her term of vengeance—she replied
In words of dubious import, but fulfill'd.[8]
If I had never lived, that which I love
Had still been living; had I never loved,
195   That which I love would still be beautiful—
Happy and giving happiness. What is she?
What is she now?—a sufferer for my sins—
A thing I dare not think upon—or nothing.
Within few hours I shall not call in vain—
200   Yet in this hour I dread the thing I dare:
Until this hour I never shrunk to gaze
On spirit, good or evil—now I tremble,
And feel a strange cold thaw upon my heart.
But I can act even what I most abhor,
205   And champion human fears.—The night approaches.[9]

                                     [*Exit.*]

8. A pair of grim prophecies, biblical and classical: at the request of Saul, the woman of Endor summons the spirit of the prophet Samuel, who foretells that the Philistines will defeat Saul and kill him and his sons (1 Samuel 28.7–19); King Pausanias, according to Plutarch and a later Pausanias, author of the *Description of Greece*, learns from the ghost of the beloved whom he had inadvertently slain that he will die, despite his calling Jupiter Phyxius for aid and his enlistment of the priests at Phygalia to get her to lay aside ("depose") her anger.

9. Macbeth says, as Scots forces close on his castle: "I have almost forgot the taste of fears" (5.5.9).

Scene 3

The Summit of the Jungfrau Mountain.

[*Enter First Destiny.*]

The moon is rising broad, and round, and bright;
And here on snows, where never human foot
Of common mortal trod, we nightly tread,
And leave no traces; o'er the savage sea,
5   The glassy ocean of the mountain ice,
We skim its rugged breakers, which put on
The aspect of a tumbling tempest's foam,
Frozen in a moment—a dead whirlpool's image:
And this most steep fantastic pinnacle,
10   The fretwork of some earthquake—where the clouds
Pause to repose themselves in passing by—
Is sacred to our revels, or our vigils;
Here do I wait my sisters, on our way
To the Hall of Arimanes,[1] for to-night
15   Is our great festival—'tis strange they come not.

A Voice without, singing.

> The Captive Usurper,[2]
>   Hurl'd down from the throne,
> Lay buried in torpor,
>   Forgotten and lone;
20 I broke through his slumbers,
>   I shiver'd his chain,
> I leagued him with numbers—
>   He's Tyrant again!

With the blood of a million he'll answer my care,
25 With a nation's destruction—his flight and despair.

Second Voice, without.

The ship sail'd on, the ship sail'd fast,
But I left not a sail, and I left not a mast;
There is not a plank of the hull or the deck,
And there is not a wretch to lament o'er his wreck;
30   Save one, whom I held, as he swam, by the hair,
And he was a subject well worthy my care;
A traitor on land, and a pirate at sea—
But I saved him to wreak further havoc for me!

FIRST DESTINY, *answering.*

> The city lies sleeping;
35 >   The morn, to deplore it,

---

1. Arimanes is derived from Ahriman, the principle of
evil in Zoroastrianism.
2. Napoleon escaped from captivity on Elba in March

1815, returned triumphantly to France; his recovered
power ended at Waterloo, followed by exile to St. Helena. See Byron's *Childe Harold* 3 (page 765).

May dawn on it weeping:
  Sullenly, slowly,
The black plague flew o'er it—
  Thousands lie lowly;

40   Tens of thousands shall perish—
  The living shall fly from
The sick they should cherish;
  But nothing can vanquish
The touch that they die from.

45   Sorrow and anguish,
And evil and dread,
  Envelope a nation—
The blest are the dead,
  Who see not the sight

50 Of their own desolation—
  This work of a night—

This wreck of a realm—this deed of my doing—
For ages I've done, and shall still be renewing!
[*Enter the Second and Third Destinies.*]

THE THREE:

Our hands contain the hearts of men,
55   Our footsteps are their graves;
We only give to take again
  The spirits of our slaves!

FIRST DESTINY: Welcome!—Where's Nemesis?
SECOND DESTINY: At some great work;
But what I know not, for my hands were full.
THIRD DESTINY: Behold she cometh.
  [*Enter Nemesis.*]
FIRST DESTINY: Say, where hast thou been?
My sisters and thyself are slow to-night.
NEMESIS: I was detain'd repairing shatter'd thrones,
Marrying fools, restoring dynasties,
Avenging men upon their enemies,
65 And making them repent their own revenge;
Goading the wise to madness; from the dull
Shaping out oracles to rule the world
Afresh, for they were waxing out of date,
And mortals dared to ponder for themselves,
70 To weigh kings in the balance, and to speak
Of freedom, the forbidden fruit.—Away!
We have outstay'd the hour—mount we our clouds![3]

                           [*Exeunt.*]

---

3. The scene blends the Three Witches of *Macbeth* with Byron's review of the restored monarchies of post-Napoleonic Europe.

Scene 4

The Hall of Arimanes—Arimanes on his Throne, a Globe of Fire, surrounded by the Spirits.

HYMN OF THE SPIRITS

   Hail to our Master!—Prince of Earth and Air!
    Who walks the clouds and waters—in his hand
   The sceptre of the elements, which tear
    Themselves to chaos at his high command!
5   He breatheth—and a tempest shakes the sea;
    He speaketh—and the clouds reply in thunder;
   He gazeth—from his glance the sunbeams flee;
    He moveth—earthquakes rend the world asunder.
   Beneath his footsteps the volcanoes rise;
10   His shadow is the Pestilence; his path
   The comets herald through the crackling skies;
    And planets turn to ashes at his wrath.
   To him War offers daily sacrifice;
    To him Death pays his tribute; Life is his,
15   With all its infinite of agonies—
    And his the spirit of whatever is!
  [*Enter the Destinies and Nemesis.*]
FIRST DESTINY: Glory to Arimanes! on the earth
   His power increaseth—both my sisters did
   His bidding, nor did I neglect my duty!
SECOND DESTINY: Glory to Arimanes! we who bow
   The necks of men, bow down before his throne!
THIRD DESTINY: Glory to Arimanes! we await His nod!
NEMESIS: Sovereign of Sovereigns! we are thine,
   And all that liveth, more or less, is ours,
25   And most things wholly so; still to increase
   Our power, increasing thine, demands our care,
   And we are vigilant—Thy late commands
   Have been fulfill'd to the utmost.
  [*Enter Manfred*]
A SPIRIT: What is here?
   A mortal!—Thou most rash and fatal wretch,
30   Bow down and worship!
SECOND SPIRIT: I do know the man—
   A Magian° of great power, and fearful skill!   *magus*
THIRD SPIRIT: Bow down and worship, slave!—What, know'st thou not
   Thine and our Sovereign?—Tremble, and obey!
ALL THE SPIRITS: Prostrate thyself, and thy condemned clay,
35   Child of the Earth! or dread the worst.
MANFRED: I know it;
   And yet ye see I kneel not.
FOURTH SPIRIT: 'Twill be taught thee.
MANFRED: 'Tis taught already;—many a night on the earth,
   On the bare ground, have I bow'd down my face,

And strew'd my head with ashes; I have known
40   The fulness of humiliation, for
    I sunk before my vain despair, and knelt
    To my own desolation.

FIFTH SPIRIT: Dost thou dare
    Refuse to Arimanes on his throne
    What the whole earth accords, beholding not
45   The terror of his Glory?—Crouch! I say.

MANFRED: Bid *him* bow down to that which is above him,
    The overruling Infinite—the Maker
    Who made him not for worship—let him kneel,
    And we will kneel together.

THE SPIRITS: Crush the worm!
50   Tear him in pieces!—

FIRST DESTINY: Hence! Avaunt!—he's mine.
    Prince of the Powers invisible! This man
    Is of no common order, as his port°   *bearing*
    And presence here denote; his sufferings
    Have been of an immortal nature, like
55   Our own; his knowledge, and his powers and will,
    As far as is compatible with clay,
    Which clogs the ethereal essence, have been such
    As clay hath seldom borne; his aspirations
    Have been beyond the dwellers of the earth,
60   And they have only taught him what we know—
    That knowledge is not happiness, and science
    But an exchange of ignorance for that
    Which is another kind of ignorance.
    This is not all—the passions, attributes
65   Of earth and heaven, from which no power, nor being,
    Nor breath from the worm upwards is exempt,
    Have pierced his heart; and in their consequence
    Made him a thing, which I, who pity not,
    Yet pardon those who pity. He is mine,
70   And thine, it may be—be it so, or not,
    No other Spirit in this region hath
    A soul like his—or power upon his soul.

NEMESIS: What doth he here then?

FIRST DESTINY: Let him answer that.

MANFRED: Ye know what I have known; and without power
75   I could not be amongst ye: but there are
    Powers deeper still beyond—I come in quest
    Of such, to answer unto what I seek.

NEMESIS: What would'st thou?

MANFRED: Thou canst not reply to me.
    Call up the dead—my question is for them.

NEMESIS: Great Arimanes, doth thy will avouch°   *support, confirm*
    The wishes of this mortal?

ARIMANES: Yea.
NEMESIS: Whom would'st thou
        Uncharnel?
MANFRED: One without a tomb—call up
        Astarte.[4]
NEMESIS:
                        Shadow! or Spirit!
85   Whatever thou art,
                    Which still doth inherit
                        The whole or a part
                    Of the form of thy birth,
                        Of the mould of thy clay,
90   Which return'd to the earth,
                        Re-appear to the day!
                    Bear what thou borest,
                        The heart and the form,
                    And the aspect thou worest
95   Redeem from the worm.

            Appear!—Appear!—Appear!
            Who sent thee there requires thee here!
        [*The Phantom of Astarte rises and stands in the midst.*]
MANFRED: Can this be death? there's bloom upon her cheek;
            But now I see it is no living hue,
100   But a strange hectic—like the unnatural red
            Which Autumn plants upon the perish'd leaf.
            It is the same! Oh, God! that I should dread
            To look upon the same—Astarte!—No,
            I cannot speak to her—but bid her speak—
105   Forgive me or condemn me.

NEMESIS:
                    By the power which hath broken
                        The grace which enthrall'd thee,
                    Speak to him who hath spoken,
                        Or those who have call'd thee!

MANFRED: She is silent,
            And in that silence I am more than answer'd.
NEMESIS: My power extends no further. Prince of air!
            It rests with thee alone—command her voice.
ARIMANES: Spirit—obey this sceptre!
NEMESIS: Silent still!
115   She is not of our order, but belongs
            To the other powers. Mortal! thy quest is vain,
            And we are baffled also.

---

4. Astarte is a variant of Ashtareth ("*Astoreth*, whom the *Phoenicians* call'd / *Astarte*, Queen of Heav'n," *Paradise Lost*
1.438–39), the Near Eastern equivalent of the Greek Aphrodite, goddess of love and fertility.

MANFRED: Hear me, hear me—
    Astarte! my beloved! speak to me:
    I have so much endured—so much endure—
120   Look on me! the grave hath not changed thee more
    Than I am changed for thee. Thou lovedst me
    Too much, as I loved thee: we were not made
    To torture thus each other, though it were
    The deadliest sin to love as we have loved.
125   Say that thou loath'st me not—that I do bear
    This punishment for both—that thou wilt be
    One of the blessed—and that I shall die;
    For hitherto all hateful things conspire
    To bind me in existence—in a life
130   Which makes me shrink from immortality—
    A future like the past. I cannot rest.
    I know not what I ask, nor what I seek:
    I feel but what thou art—and what I am;
    And I would hear yet once before I perish
135   The voice which was my music—Speak to me!
    For I have call'd on thee in the still night,
    Startled the slumbering birds from the hush'd boughs,
    And woke the mountain wolves, and made the caves
    Acquainted with thy vainly echoed name,
140   Which answer'd me—many things answer'd me—
    Spirits and men—but thou wert silent all.
    Yet speak to me! I have outwatch'd the stars,
    And gazed o'er heaven in vain in search of thee.
    Speak to me! I have wander'd o'er the earth,
145   And never found thy likeness—Speak to me!
    Look on the fiends around—they feel for me!
    I fear them not, and feel for thee alone—
    Speak to me! though it be in wrath;—but say—
    I reck not what—but let me hear thee once—
150   This once—once more!
PHANTOM OF ASTARTE: Manfred!
MANFRED: Say on, say on—
    I live but in the sound—it is thy voice!
PHANTOM: Manfred! To-morrow ends thine earthly ills. Farewell!
MANFRED: Yet one word more—am I forgiven?
PHANTOM: Farewell!
MANFRED: Say, shall we meet again?
PHANTOM: Farewell!
MANFRED: One word for mercy! Say, thou lovest me.
PHANTOM: Manfred!
    [*The Spirit of Astarte disappears.*]
NEMESIS: She's gone, and will not be recall'd;
    Her words will be fulfill'd. Return to the earth.
A SPIRIT: He is convulsed—This is to be a mortal
159   And seek the things beyond mortality.

ANOTHER SPIRIT: Yet, see, he mastereth himself, and makes
    His torture tributary to his will.
    Had he been one of us, he would have made
    An awful[5] spirit.
NEMESIS: Hast thou further question
164   Of our great sovereign, or his worshippers?
MANFRED: None.
NEMESIS: Then for a time farewell.
MANFRED: We meet then—
    Where? On the earth?
NEMESIS: That will be seen hereafter.
MANFRED: Even as thou wilt: and for the grace accorded
    I now depart a debtor. Fare ye well!   [Exit Manfred.]
          [Scene closes]

ACT 3[1]

Scene 1

A Hall in the Castle of Manfred.

[Manfred and Herman.]
MANFRED: What is the hour?
HERMAN: It wants but one till sunset,
    And promises a lovely twilight.
MANFRED: Say,
    Are all things so disposed of in the tower
    As I directed?
HERMAN: All, my lord, are ready:
5   Here is the key and casket.
MANFRED: It is well:
    Thou may'st retire.

                        [Exit Herman.]

        There is a calm upon me—
    Inexplicable stillness! which till now
    Did not belong to what I knew of life.
    If that I did not know philosophy
10   To be of all our vanities the motliest,
    The merest word that ever fool'd the ear
    From out the schoolman's jargon, I should deem
    The golden secret, the sought "Kalon,"[2] found,
    And seated in my soul. It will not last,

---

5. The sense wavers between "awe-inspiring" and "despicable."

1. In March 1817 Byron sent Murray from Venice a fair copy of his "very wild—metaphysical—and inexplicable play," and commented "I have really & truly no notion whether it is good or bad." When Murray's literary advisor William Gifford criticized the third act, Byron

conceded that "it was certainly d—d bad" and agreed to rewrite it. In the original (see vol. 4 of Complete Poetical Works) the Abbot crudely threatens Manfred, and is carried off by a demon named Ashtaroth; in the revision, the "Abbot is become a good man."

2. The "Supreme Good" (Greek).

15   But it is well to have known it, though but once:
      It hath enlarged my thoughts with a new sense,
      And I within my tablets would note down
      That there is such a feeling. Who is there?
      [*Re-enter Herman.*]
HERMAN: My lord, the abbot of St Maurice craves
20   To greet your presence.
      [*Enter the Abbot of St Maurice.*]
ABBOT: Peace be with Count Manfred!
MANFRED: Thanks, holy father! welcome to these walls;
      Thy presence honours them, and blesseth those
      Who dwell within them.
ABBOT: Would it were so, Count!—
      But I would fain confer with thee alone.
MANFRED: Herman, retire.—What would my reverend guest?
ABBOT: Thus, without prelude:—Age and zeal, my office,
      And good intent, must plead my privilege;
      Our near, though not acquainted neighbourhood,
      May also be my herald. Rumours strange,
30   And of unholy nature, are abroad,
      And busy with thy name; a noble name
      For centuries: may he who bears it now
      Transmit it unimpair'd!
MANFRED: Proceed,—I listen.
ABBOT: 'Tis said thou holdest converse with the things
35   Which are forbidden to the search of man;
      That with the dwellers of the dark abodes,
      The many evil and unheavenly spirits
      Which walk the valley of the shade of death,
      Thou communest. I know that with mankind,
40   Thy fellows in creation, thou dost rarely
      Exchange thy thoughts, and that thy solitude
      Is as an anchorite's,° were it but holy.   *ascetic, religious hermit*
MANFRED: And what are they who do avouch these things?
ABBOT: My pious brethren—the scared peasantry—
45   Even thy own vassals—who do look on thee
      With most unquiet eyes. Thy life's in peril.
MANFRED: Take it.
ABBOT: I come to save, and not destroy—
      I would not pry into thy secret soul;
      But if these things be sooth, there still is time
50   For penitence and pity: reconcile thee
      With the true church, and through the church to heaven.
MANFRED: I hear thee. This is my reply: whate'er
      I may have been, or am, doth rest between
      Heaven and myself.—I shall not choose a mortal
55   To be my mediator. Have I sinn'd
      Against your ordinances? prove and punish!

ABBOT: My son! I did not speak of punishment,
    But penitence and pardon;—with thyself
    The choice of such remains—and for the last,
60   Our institutions and our strong belief
    Have given me power to smooth the path from sin—
    To higher hope and better thoughts; the first
    I leave to heaven,—"Vengeance is mine alone!"
    So saith the Lord,[3] and with all humbleness
65   His servant echoes back the awful word.
MANFRED: Old man! there is no power in holy men,
    Nor charm in prayer—nor purifying form
    Of penitence—nor outward look—nor fast—
    Nor agony—nor, greater than all these,
70   The innate tortures of that deep despair,
    Which is remorse without the fear of hell,
    But all in all sufficient to itself
    Would make a hell of heaven—can exorcise
    From out the unbounded spirit the quick sense
75   Of its own sins, wrongs, sufferance, and revenge
    Upon itself; there is no future pang
    Can deal that justice on the self-condemn'd
    He deals on his own soul.[4]
ABBOT: All this is well;
    For this will pass away, and be succeeded
80   By an auspicious hope, which shall look up
    With calm assurance to that blessed place,
    Which all who seek may win, whatever be
    Their earthly errors, so they be atoned:
    And the commencement of atonement is
85   The sense of its necessity.—Say on—
    And all our church can teach thee shall be taught;
    And all we can absolve thee shall be pardon'd.
MANFRED: When Rome's sixth emperor was near his last,
    The victim of a self-inflicted wound,
90   To shun the torments of a public death
    From senates once his slaves, a certain soldier,
    With show of loyal pity, would have stanch'd
    The gushing throat with his officious robe;
    The dying Roman thrust him back, and said—
95   Some empire still in his expiring glance,
    "It is too late—is this fidelity?"[5]
ABBOT: And what of this?

---

3. Romans 12.19: "Dearly beloved, avenge not yourselves, but *rather* give place unto wrath; for it is written,
Vengeance *is* mine; I will repay, saith the Lord" (said
with reference to Cain).
4. Compare the boast of Milton's Satan: "The mind is its

own place, and in itself / Can make a Heav'n of Hell, a
Hell of Heav'n" (*Paradise Lost*, 1.254–55). Cf. 1.1.251.
5. Byron transposes to Otho a story Suetonius relates of
Nero in his *Lives of the Emperors*.

MANFRED: I answer with the Roman—
       "It is too late!"
ABBOT: It never can be so,
       To reconcile thyself with thy own soul,
100   And thy own soul with heaven. Hast thou no hope?
       'Tis strange—even those who do despair above,
       Yet shape themselves some fantasy on earth,
       To which frail twig they cling, like drowning men.
MANFRED: Ay—father! I have had those earthly visions
105   And noble aspirations in my youth,
       To make my own the mind of other men;
       The enlightener of nations; and to rise
       I knew not whither—it might be to fall;
       But fall, even as the mountain-cataract,
110   Which having leapt from its more dazzling height,
       Even in the foaming strength of its abyss,
       (Which casts up misty columns that become
       Clouds raining from the re-ascended skies,)
       Lies low but mighty still.—But this is past,
115   My thoughts mistook themselves.
ABBOT: And wherefore so?
MANFRED: I could not tame my nature down; for he
       Must serve who fain would sway—and soothe—and sue—
       And watch all time—and pry into all place—
       And be a living lie—who would become
120   A mighty thing amongst the mean, and such
       The mass are; I disdain'd to mingle with
       A herd, though to be leader—and of wolves.
       The lion is alone, and so am I.
ABBOT: And why not live and act with other men?
MANFRED: Because my nature was averse from life;
       And yet not cruel; for I would not make,
       But find a desolation:—like the wind,
       The red-hot breath of the most lone Simoom,[6]
       Which dwells but in the desert, and sweeps o'er
130   The barren sands which bear no shrubs to blast,
       And revels o'er their wild and arid waves,
       And seeketh not, so that it is not sought,
       But being met is deadly; such hath been
       The course of my existence; but there came
135   Things in my path which are no more.
ABBOT: Alas!
       I 'gin to fear that thou art past all aid
       From me and from my calling; yet so young,
       I still would—

---

6. The Simoom, or Simoon, is a seasonal hot sandy wind of the African and Arabian deserts.

MANFRED: Look on me! there is an order
                Of mortals on the earth, who do become
140   Old in their youth, and die ere middle age,
                Without the violence of warlike death:
                Some perishing of pleasure—some of study—
                Some worn with toil—some of mere weariness—
                Some of disease—and some insanity—
145   And some of wither'd, or of broken hearts;
                For this last is a malady which slays
                More than are number'd in the lists of Fate,
                Taking all shapes, and bearing many names.
                Look upon me! for even of all these things
150   Have I partaken; and of all these things,
                One were enough; then wonder not that I
                Am what I am, but that I ever was,
                Or having been, that I am still on earth.
ABBOT: Yet, hear me still—
MANFRED: Old man! I do respect
155   Thine order, and revere thine years; I deem
                Thy purpose pious, but it is in vain:
                Think me not churlish; I would spare thyself,
                Far more than me, in shunning at this time
                All further colloquy—and so—farewell.   [Exit Manfred.]
ABBOT: This should have been a noble creature: he
                Hath all the energy which would have made
                A goodly frame of glorious elements,[7]
                Had they been wisely mingled; as it is,
                It is an awful chaos—light and darkness—
165   And mind and dust—and passions and pure thoughts
                Mix'd, and contending without end or order,
                All dormant or destructive: he will perish,
                And yet he must not; I will try once more,
                For such are worth redemption; and my duty
170   Is to dare all things for a righteous end.
                I'll follow him—but cautiously, though surely.   [Exit Abbot.]

                            Scene 2

Another Chamber.
    [Manfred and Herman.]
HERMAN: My lord, you bade me wait on you at sunset:
                He sinks behind the mountain.
MANFRED: Doth he so?
        I will look on him.
    [Manfred advances to the Window of the Hall.]
                            Glorious Orb! the idol
        Of early nature, and the vigorous race

7. See n. 2, page 720.

5   Of undiseased mankind, the giant sons
        Of the embrace of angels, with a sex
        More beautiful than they, which did draw down
        The erring spirits who can ne'er return.[8]—
        Most glorious orb! that wert a worship, ere
10   The mystery of thy making was reveal'd!
        Thou earliest minister of the Almighty,
        Which gladden'd, on their mountain tops, the hearts
        Of the Chaldean shepherds, till they pour'd
        Themselves in orisons! Thou material God!
15   And representative of the Unknown—
        Who chose thee for his shadow! Thou chief star!
        Centre of many stars! which mak'st our earth
        Endurable, and temperest the hues
        And hearts of all who walk within thy rays!
20   Sire of the seasons! Monarch of the climes,
        And those who dwell in them! for near or far,
        Our inborn spirits have a tint of thee
        Even as our outward aspects;—thou dost rise,
        And shine, and set in glory. Fare thee well!
25   I ne'er shall see thee more. As my first glance
        Of love and wonder was for thee, then take
        My latest look: thou wilt not beam on one
        To whom the gifts of life and warmth have been
        Of a more fatal nature. He is gone:
30   I follow.   *[Exit Manfred.]*

Scene 3

*The Mountains—The Castle of Manfred at some distance—A Terrace before a Tower.—
Time, Twilight. [Herman, Manuel, and other Dependants of Manfred.]*

HERMAN: 'Tis strange enough; night after night, for years,
        He hath pursued long vigils in this tower,
        Without a witness. I have been within it,—
        So have we all been oft-times; but from it,
5   Or its contents, it were impossible
        To draw conclusions absolute, of aught
        His studies tend to. To be sure, there is
        One chamber where none enter: I would give
        The fee of what I have to come these three years,
10   To pore upon its mysteries.
MANUEL: 'Twere dangerous;
        Content thyself with what thou know'st already.
HERMAN: Ah! Manuel! thou art elderly and wise,
        And couldst say much; thou hast dwelt within the castle—
        How many years is't?

---

8. "There were giants in the earth in those days, and also after that, when the sons of God came in unto the daughters of men, and they bare *children* to them, the same *became* mighty men which *were* of old, men of renown" (Genesis 6.4).

MANUEL: Ere Count Manfred's birth,
15   I served his father, whom he nought resembles.
HERMAN: There be more sons in like predicament.
       But wherein do they differ?
MANUEL: I speak not
       Of features or of form, but mind and habits;
       Count Sigismund was proud,—but gay and free,—
20   A warrior and a reveller; he dwelt not
       With books and solitude, nor made the night
       A gloomy vigil, but a festal time,
       Merrier than day; he did not walk the rocks
       And forests like a wolf, nor turn aside
25   From men and their delights.
HERMAN: Beshrew° the hour,   *curse*
       But those were jocund times! I would that such
       Would visit the old walls again; they look
       As if they had forgotten them.
MANUEL: These walls
       Must change their chieftain first. Oh! I have seen
30   Some strange things in them, Herman.
HERMAN: Come, be friendly;
       Relate me some to while away our watch:
       I've heard thee darkly speak of an event
       Which happen'd hereabouts, by this same tower.
MANUEL: That was a night indeed! I do remember
35   'Twas twilight, as it may be now, and such
       Another evening;—yon red cloud, which rests
       On Eigher's pinnacle,[9] so rested then,—
       So like that it might be the same; the wind
       Was faint and gusty, and the mountain snows
40   Began to glitter with the climbing moon;
       Count Manfred was, as now, within his tower,—
       How occupied, we knew not, but with him
       The sole companion of his wanderings
       And watchings—her, whom of all earthly things
45   That lived, the only thing he seem'd to love,—
       As he, indeed, by blood was bound to do,
       The lady Astarte, his—
                          Hush! who comes here?
       [*Enter the Abbot.*]
ABBOT: Where is your master?
HERMAN: Yonder in the tower.
ABBOT: I must speak with him.
MANUEL: 'Tis impossible;
50   He is most private, and must not be thus
       Intruded on.

---

9. The Eigher is an Alpine peak north of the Jungfrau.

ABBOT: Upon myself I take
   The forfeit of my fault, if fault there be—
   But I must see him.
HERMAN: Thou hast seen him once
   This eve already.
ABBOT: Herman! I command thee,
55 Knock, and apprize the Count of my approach.
HERMAN: We dare not.
ABBOT: Then it seems I must be herald
   Of my own purpose.
MANUEL: Reverend father, stop—
   I pray you pause.
ABBOT: Why so?
MANUEL: But step this way,
   And I will tell you further.

                 [Exeunt.]

        Scene 4

Interior of the Tower.
 [Manfred alone.]

   The stars are forth, the moon above the tops
   Of the snow-shining mountains.—Beautiful!
   I linger yet with Nature, for the night
   Hath been to me a more familiar face
5 Than that of man; and in her starry shade
   Of dim and solitary loveliness,
   I learn'd the language of another world.
   I do remember me, that in my youth,
   When I was wandering,—upon such a night
10 I stood within the Coliseum's wall,
   Midst the chief relics of almighty Rome;
   The trees which grew along the broken arches
   Waved dark in the blue midnight, and the stars
   Shone through the rents of ruin; from afar
15 The watchdog bay'd beyond the Tiber; and
   More near from out the Cæsars' palace came
   The owl's long cry, and, interruptedly,
   Of distant sentinels the fitful song
   Begun and died upon the gentle wind.
20 Some cypresses beyond the time-worn breach
   Appear'd to skirt the horizon, yet they stood
   Within a bowshot—Where the Cæsars dwelt,
   And dwell the tuneless birds of night, amidst
   A grove which springs through levell'd battlements,
25 And twines its roots with the imperial hearths,
   Ivy usurps the laurel's place of growth;—
   But the gladiators' bloody Circus stands,
   A noble wreck in ruinous perfection!
   While Cæsar's chambers, and the Augustan halls,

30 Grovel on earth in indistinct decay.—
And thou didst shine, thou rolling moon, upon
All this, and cast a wide and tender light,
Which soften'd down the hoar austerity
Of rugged desolation, and fill'd up,
35 As 'twere anew, the gaps of centuries;
Leaving that beautiful which still was so,
And making that which was not, till the place
Became religion, and the heart ran o'er
With silent worship of the great of old!
40 The dead, but sceptred sovereigns, who still rule
Our spirits from their urns.[1]—
                      'Twas such a night!
'Tis strange that I recall it at this time;
But I have found our thoughts take wildest flight
Even at the moment when they should array
45 Themselves in pensive order.
  [Enter the Abbot.]
ABBOT: My good lord!
I crave a second grace for this approach;
But yet let not my humble zeal offend
By its abruptness—all it hath of ill
Recoils on me; its good in the effect
50 May light upon your head—could I say *heart*—
Could I touch *that,* with words or prayers, I should
Recall a noble spirit which hath wander'd;
But is not yet all lost.
MANFRED: Thou know'st me not;
My days are number'd, and my deeds recorded:
55 Retire, or 'twill be dangerous—Away!
ABBOT: Thou dost not mean to menace me?
MANFRED: Not I;
I simply tell thee peril is at hand,
And would preserve thee.
ABBOT: What dost thou mean?
MANFRED: Look there!
What dost thou see?
ABBOT: Nothing.
MANFRED: Look there, I say,
60 And steadfastly;—now tell me what thou seest?
ABBOT: That which should shake me,—but I fear it not—
I see a dusk and awful figure rise,
Like an infernal god, from out the earth;
His face wrapt in a mantle, and his form
65 Robed as with angry clouds: he stands between
Thyself and me—but I do fear him not.

1. Compare *Childe Harold's Pilgrimage,* canto 4, stanzas 139–45 (pages 775–77).

MANFRED: Thou hast no cause—he shall not harm thee—but
　　　His sight may shock thine old limbs into palsy.
　　　I say to thee—Retire!
ABBOT:　　　　　　　　　And I reply—
70　　Never—till I have battled with this fiend:—
　　　What doth he here?
MANFRED:　　　　　　Why—ay—what doth he here?—
　　　I did not send for him,—he is unbidden.
ABBOT: Alas! lost mortal! what with guests like these
　　　Hast thou to do? I tremble for thy sake:
75　　Why doth he gaze on thee, and thou on him?
　　　Ah! he unveils his aspect: on his brow
　　　The thunder-scars are graven; from his eye
　　　Glares forth the immortality of hell[2]—
　　　Avaunt!°—　　　　　　　　　　　　　　　　　　　　　*Away, be gone*
MANFRED:　　　Pronounce—what is thy mission?
SPIRIT:　　　　　　　　　　　　　　　　Come!
ABBOT: What art thou, unknown being? answer!—speak!
SPIRIT: The genius° of this mortal.—Come! 'tis time.　　　*presiding spirit*
MANFRED: I am prepared for all things, but deny
　　　The power which summons me. Who sent thee here?
SPIRIT: Thou'lt know anon—Come! come!
MANFRED:　　　　　　　　　　　　I have commanded
85　　Things of an essence greater far than thine,
　　　And striven with thy masters. Get thee hence!
SPIRIT: Mortal! thine hour is come—Away! I say.
MANFRED: I knew, and know my hour is come, but not
　　　To render up my soul to such as thee:
90　　Away! I'll die as I have lived—alone.
SPIRIT: Then I must summon up my brethren.—Rise!
　　　[*Other Spirits rise up.*]
ABBOT: Avaunt! ye evil ones!—Avaunt! I say,—
　　　Ye have no power where piety hath power,
　　　And I do charge ye in the name—
SPIRIT:　　　　　　　　　　　　　Old man!
95　　We know ourselves, our mission, and thine order;
　　　Waste not thy holy words on idle uses,
　　　It were in vain: this man is forfeited.
　　　Once more I summon him—Away! away!
MANFRED: I do defy ye,—though I feel my soul
100　　Is ebbing from me, yet I do defy ye;
　　　Nor will I hence, while I have earthly breath
　　　To breathe my scorn upon ye—earthly strength
　　　To wrestle, though with spirits; what ye take
　　　Shall be ta'en limb by limb.

---

2. See Milton's description of the fallen Satan: "his face / Deep scars of thunder had intrenched" (*Paradise Lost* 1.600–601).

SPIRIT: Reluctant mortal!
105   Is this the Magian who would so pervade
        The world invisible, and make himself
        Almost our equal?—Can it be that thou
        Art thus in love with life? the very life
        Which made thee wretched!
MANFRED: Thou false fiend, thou liest!
110   My life is in its last hour,—*that* I know,
        Nor would redeem a moment of that hour;
        I do not combat against death, but thee
        And thy surrounding angels; my past power
        Was purchased by no compact with thy crew,
115   But by superior science—penance—daring—
        And length of watching—strength of mind—and skill
        In knowledge of our fathers—when the earth
        Saw men and spirits walking side by side,
        And gave ye no supremacy: I stand
120   Upon my strength—I do defy—deny—
        Spurn back, and scorn ye!—
SPIRIT: But thy many crimes
        Have made thee—
MANFRED: What are they to such as thee?
        Must crimes be punish'd but by other crimes,
        And greater criminals?[3]—Back to thy hell!
125   Thou hast no power upon me, *that* I feel;
        Thou never shalt possess me, *that* I know:
        What I have done is done; I bear within
        A torture which could nothing gain from thine:
        The mind which is immortal makes itself
130   Requital for its good or evil thoughts—
        Is its own origin of ill and end—
        And its own place and time[4]—its innate sense,
        When stripp'd of this mortality, derives
        No colour from the fleeting things without;
135   But is absorb'd in sufferance or in joy,
        Born from the knowledge of its own desert.
        Thou didst not tempt me, and thou couldst not tempt me;
        I have not been thy dupe, nor am thy prey—
        But was my own destroyer, and will be
140   My own hereafter.—Back, ye baffled fiends!
        The hand of death is on me—but not yours!
        [*The Demons disappear.*]
ABBOT: Alas! how pale thou art—thy lips are white—
        And thy breast heaves—and in thy gasping throat
        The accents rattle—Give thy prayers to Heaven—

---

3. Compare *Childe Harold's Pilgrimage*, "Can tyrants but   4. See n. 4, page 738.
by tyrants conquer'd be" (4.96; page 774).

145   Pray—albeit but in thought,—but die not thus.
MANFRED: 'Tis over—my dull eyes can fix thee not;
      But all things swim around me, and the earth
      Heaves as it were beneath me. Fare thee well—
      Give me thy hand.
ABBOT: Cold—cold—even to the heart—
150   But yet one prayer—Alas! how fares it with thee?
MANFRED: Old man! 'tis not so difficult to die.[5]
      [*Manfred expires.*]
ABBOT: He's gone—his soul hath ta'en its earthless flight—
      Whither? I dread to think—but he is gone.

August 1815–February 1817

❂ "MANFRED" AND ITS TIME ❂
The Byronic Hero

In *Manfred,* Byron trades on and pushes to an unstable extreme an established character type, the Byronic Hero. To some, Manfred seems a tragic figure of modern existential angst, with a taint of mysterious crime, possibly of an incestuous nature. To others, he is a case study in narcissism, psychological disease, and antisocial pride. And to still others, he seems a gothic parody of this character type, Byron's strategic exhaustion of a figure who was to give way within a year to an altogether different type, the boyish hero of *Don Juan,* perpetually resilient, unburdened by memory or remorse. Whatever the view, the focus is the Byronic Hero, "mad, bad, and dangerous to know," so said Byron's onetime lover, Caroline Lamb, of the author himself. The defining traits are a contempt of conventional morality, alienation, burning inward torment, and a heroic defiance of fate. A "strange union of opposite extremes," Thomas Macaulay wrote in the *Edinburgh Review* in 1831; "proud, moody, cynical,—with defiance on his brow, and misery in his heart; a scorner of his kind, implacable in revenge, yet capable of deep and strong affection."

    The contours draw on Shakespeare's tormented heroes—Hamlet, Othello, Macbeth, and Coriolanus—and their descendant, Milton's Satan, the antihero of *Paradise Lost,* a figure who in the Romantic era focused interest as a complex psychology, even a potential political hero. In *The Marriage of Heaven and Hell,* William Blake, one of the earliest voices of this "Romantic Satanism," argued that the magnificent poetry Milton wrote for Satan showed Milton to be of "the devil's party," and that Satan was the true hero of *Paradise Lost,* the caustic antagonist of a vengeful oppressor called God (see page 172). Percy Shelley (in *A Defence of Poetry,* written 1820; published 1840) argued that Satan's "magnificence" called into question the "superiority of moral virtue" in Milton's God, and in so doing confirmed "the supremacy of Milton's own genius" (for this discussion, see p. 925). The Byronic Hero frequently evokes the Romantic Satan, emulating his oppositional energy, sharing a torment by unredeemable sin, and bearing an anguished heart. Byron's modern articulation is psychological and dramatic, rather than judgmental and moralistic, the very quality of the Byronic Hero confounding easy determinations. This hero debuted in the sensationally successful *Childe Harold's Pilgrimage* (1812), at once defining the type and implying an authorial investment. Across the next decade, Byron produced a series of dashing,

---

5. When this line was dropped in the first edition, Byron told Murray, "You have destroyed the whole effect & moral of the poem by omitting the last line of Manfred's speaking."

transgressive heroes, and was not above performing the role himself, as seen in his famous portrait in exotic Eastern garb (Color Plate 3).

Byron was not the only producer of the Byronic Hero. Its magnetic popularity guaranteed its attraction to other writers. Caroline Lamb's roman à clef, *Glenarvon*, published in 1816, combined moral evil, devastating seductiveness, and political courage in its Satanic/Byronic Hero. Mary Shelley's *Frankenstein*, begun the same year at Byron's villa on Lake Geneva, links both Frankenstein and his Creature to the Byronic type, and ultimately to Milton's Satan. Felicia Hemans, wondering if women could play the part, presents a cross-dressed Byronic Heroine in *The Widow of Crescentius*. Even as Byron was casting Napoleon as a Byronic Hero, a mixture of antitheses, extreme in all things, Samuel Taylor Coleridge was linking Napoleon to an un-Byronic Satan, all pride and aggression. And conservative monitors, such as Tory Poet Laureate Robert Southey, feeling a danger to the nation in the vogue of Byronism, sounded the alarm, dubbing the whole literary culture "the Satanic School" and holding Byron responsible. Byron replied in *The Vision of Judgment* by bringing Satan himself on stage as the latest version of the Byronic Hero: wry, urbane, not particularly damnable, and with a polite disdain of Southey, another character in this poem. The Byronic Hero outlasted Byron, enduring in cultural imagination, in such figures as Charlotte Brontë's Rochester (*Jane Eyre*), Emily Brontë's Heathcliff (*Wuthering Heights*), Herman Melville's Captain Ahab, Robert Louis Stevenson's Dr. Jekyll, Oscar Wilde's Dorian Gray, and every hard-boiled detective of Hollywood *film noir*.

Byron's Earlier Heroes

from *The Giaour*[1]

> The Mind, that broods o'er guilty woes,
>   Is like the Scorpion girt by fire,
> In circle narrowing as it glows,
425 The flames around their captive close,
> Till inly search'd by thousand throes,
>   And maddening in her ire,
> One sad and sole relief she knows,
> The sting she nourish'd for her foes,
430 Whose venom never yet was vain,
> Gives but one pang, and cures all pain,
> And darts into her desperate brain;
> So do the dark in soul expire,
> Or live like Scorpion girt by fire;[2]
435 So writhes the mind Remorse hath riven,
> Unfit for earth, undoom'd for heaven,
> Darkness above, despair beneath,
> Around it flame, within it death!

1812–1813   1813

---

1. The tormented hero of this tale is an aristocratic Venetian, a "giaour," or infidel, by Arabic/Muslim lights. This famous passage impressed Percy Shelley and Felicia Hemans.
2. Alluding to the dubious suicide of the scorpion, so placed for experiment by gentle philosophers. Some maintain that the position of the sting, when turned toward the head, is merely a convulsive movement; but others have actually brought in the verdict "Felo de se." The scorpions are surely interested in a speedy decision of the question; as, if once fairly established as insect Catos, they will probably be allowed to live as long as they think proper, without being martyred for the sake of an hypothesis [Byron's note]. Cato the Republican committed suicide ("Felo de se") rather than surrender to Julius Caesar.

from *The Corsair*[1]

II

His soul was changed, before his deeds had driven
Him forth to war with man and forfeit heaven.
Warp'd by the world in Disappointment's school,
In words too wise, in conduct *there* a fool;
255   Too firm to yield, and far too proud to stoop,
Doom'd by his very virtues for a dupe,
He cursed those virtues as the cause of ill,
And not the traitors who betray'd him still;
Nor deem'd that gifts bestow'd on better men
260   Had left him joy, and means to give again.
Fear'd—shunn'd—belied—ere youth had lost her force,
He hated man too much to feel remorse,
And thought the voice of wrath a sacred call,
To pay the injuries of some on all.
265   He knew himself a villain—but he deem'd
The rest no better than the thing he seem'd;
And scorn'd the best as hypocrites who hid
Those deeds the bolder spirit plainly did.
He knew himself detested, but he knew
270   The hearts that loath'd him, crouch'd and dreaded too.
Lone, wild, and strange, he stood alike exempt
From all affection and from all contempt:
His name could sadden, and his acts surprise;
But they that fear'd him dared not to despise:
275   Man spurns the worm, but pauses ere he wake
The slumbering venom of the folded snake;
The first may turn—but not avenge the blow;
The last expires—but leaves no living foe;
Fast to the doom'd offender's form it clings,
280   And he may crush—not conquer—still it stings!

1813

1814

from *Lara*[1]

Whate'er he be, 'twas not what he had been:
That brow in furrow'd lines had fix'd at last,
And spake of passions, but of passion past:
The pride, but not the fire, of early days,
70   Coldness of mien, and carelessness of praise;
A high demeanour, and a glance that took
Their thoughts from others by a single look;
And that sarcastic levity of tongue,

1. This immensely popular tale sold 10,000 copies on the day of publication, and burned through several editions over the next few years. Its hero is a pirate, described in this stanza from Canto 1.

1. Byron followed the success of *The Corsair* with *Lara*, whose hero has a mysterious, possibly criminal past. This passage from Canto 1 became a set piece of the character type.

The stinging of a heart the world hath stung,
75   That darts in seeming playfulness around,
And makes those feel that will not own the wound;
All these seem'd his, and something more beneath
Than glance could well reveal, or accent breathe.
Ambition, glory, love, the common aim,
80   That some can conquer, and that all would claim,
Within his breast appear'd no more to strive,
Yet seem'd as lately they had been alive;
And some deep feeling it were vain to trace
At moments lighten'd o'er his livid face.

1814   1814

Prometheus[1]

Titan! to whose immortal eyes
    The sufferings of mortality,
    Seen in their sad reality,
Were not as things that gods despise;
5   What was thy pity's recompense?
A silent suffering, and intense;
The rock, the vulture, and the chain,
All that the proud can feel of pain,
The agony they do not show,
10   The suffocating sense of woe,
    Which speaks but in its loneliness,
And then is jealous lest the sky
Should have a listener, nor will sigh
    Until its voice is echoless.

15   Titan! to thee the strife was given
    Between the suffering and the will,
    Which torture where they cannot kill;
And the inexorable Heaven,
And the deaf tyranny of Fate,
20   The ruling principle of Hate,
Which for its pleasure doth create
The things it may annihilate,
Refused thee even the boon to die:
The wretched gift eternity
25   Was thine—and thou hast borne it well.
All that the Thunderer[2] wrung from thee
Was but the menace which flung back
On him the torments of thy rack;[3]

1. The Greek god punished by Jupiter for stealing fire from heaven and bestowing it, in compassion, on humankind. Jupiter has Prometheus chained to a mountain, where a vulture gnaws eternally at his liver.

2. Jupiter is also the god of thunder; "Thunderer" is aptly Satan's name for God (*Paradise Lost* 1.258).
3. An instrument of bone-breaking torture; heroically defiant, Prometheus was eventually liberated by Hercules.

The fate thou didst so well foresee,[4]

30   But would not to appease him tell;
And in thy Silence was his Sentence,
And in his Soul a vain repentance,
And evil dread so ill dissembled
That in his hand the lightnings trembled.

35   Thy Godlike crime was to be kind,
To render with thy precepts less
The sum of human wretchedness,
And strengthen Man with his own mind;
But baffled as thou wert from high,
40   Still in thy patient energy,
In the endurance, and repulse
Of thine impenetrable Spirit,
Which Earth and Heaven could not convulse,
A mighty lesson we inherit:
45   Thou art a symbol and a sign
To Mortals of their fate and force;
Like thee, Man is in part divine,
A troubled stream from a pure source;
And Man in portions can foresee
50   His own funereal destiny;
His wretchedness, and his resistance,
And his sad unallied existence:
To which his Spirit may oppose
Itself—and equal to all woes,
55   And a firm will, and a deep sense,
Which even in torture can descry
Its own concenter'd recompense,
Triumphant where it dares defy,
And making Death a Victory.

Diodati, July 1816   1816

from *Childe Harold's Pilgrimage, Canto the Third*

[NAPOLEON BUONAPARTE][1]

36

There sunk the greatest, nor the worst of men,
Whose spirit antithetically mixt
One moment of the mightiest, and again
On little objects with like firmness fixt,
320   Extreme in all things! hadst thou been betwixt,

---

4. Prometheus, whose name means "foreseeing," prophesied the downfall not only of his fellow Titans but also of their conqueror, Jupiter. Jupiter offered to end Prometheus's torture if he would tell him the secret of averting his downfall—a crisis that shapes Percy Shelley's *Prometheus Unbound* (written 1818–1819).
1. Napoleon was defeated at Waterloo in June 1815 by the allied forces of Britain and Prussia, then exiled for the rest of his life to St. Helena, a small island in the Atlantic Ocean. Amid British triumphalism, Byron visited Waterloo in May 1816. He reflected on the fate of this extraordinary figure. For the stanzas on Waterloo that precede these, see pages 765–71.

Thy throne had still been thine, or never been;
For daring made thy rise as fall: thou seek'st
Even now to re-assume the imperial mien,
And shake again the world, the Thunderer[2] of the scene!

37

325   Conqueror and captive of the earth art thou!
She trembles at thee still, and thy wild name
Was ne'er more bruited° in men's minds than now   *reported*
That thou art nothing, save the jest of Fame,
Who woo'd thee once, thy vassal, and became
330   The flatterer of thy fierceness, till thou wert
A god unto thyself; nor less the same
To the astounded kingdoms all inert,
Who deem'd thee for a time whate'er thou didst assert.

38

Oh, more or less than man—in high or low,
335   Battling with nations, flying from the field;
Now making monarchs' necks thy footstool, now
More than thy meanest° soldier taught to yield;   *lowest*
An empire thou couldst crush, command, rebuild,
But govern not thy pettiest passion, nor,
340   However deeply in men's spirits skill'd,
Look through thine own, nor curb the lust of war,
Nor learn that tempted Fate will leave the loftiest star.

39

Yet well thy soul hath brook'd the turning tide
With that untaught innate philosophy,
345   Which, be it wisdom, coldness, or deep pride,
Is gall and wormwood to an enemy.
When the whole host of hatred stood hard by,
To watch and mock thee shrinking, thou hast smiled
With a sedate and all-enduring eye;—
350   When Fortune fled her spoil'd and favourite child,
He stood unbow'd beneath the ills upon him piled.

40

Sager than in thy fortunes; for in them
Ambition steel'd thee on too far to show
That just habitual scorn, which could contemn
355   Men and their thoughts; 'twas wise to feel, not so
To wear it ever on thy lip and brow,
And spurn the instruments thou wert to use
Till they were turn'd unto thine overthrow;
'Tis but a worthless world to win or lose;
360   So hath it proved to thee, and all such lot who choose.

---

2. "Thunder" is Satan's term for God's surprising potency against his rebel forces (*Paradise Lost* 1.93, 174).

41

If, like a tower upon a headlong rock,
Thou hadst been made to stand or fall alone,
Such scorn of man had help'd to brave the shock;
But men's thoughts were the steps which paved thy throne,
365   *Their* admiration thy best weapon shone;
The part of Philip's son[3] was thine, not then
(Unless aside thy purple had been thrown)
Like stern Diogenes to mock at men;
For sceptred cynics earth were far too wide a den.[4]

42

370   But quiet to quick bosoms is a hell,
And *there* hath been thy bane; there is a fire
And motion of the soul which will not dwell
In its own narrow being, but aspire
Beyond the fitting medium of desire;
375   And, but once kindled, quenchless evermore,
Preys upon high adventure, nor can tire
Of aught but rest; a fever at the core,
Fatal to him who bears, to all who ever bore.

1816   1816

Samuel Taylor Coleridge

from *The Statesman's Manual*[1]

["Satanic Pride and Rebellious Self-Idolatry"]

[I]n its utmost abstraction and consequent state of reprobation, the Will becomes Satanic pride and rebellious self-idolatry in the relations of the spirit to itself, and remorseless despotism relatively to others; the more hopeless as the more obdurate by its subjugation of sensual impulses, by its superiority to toil and pain and pleasure; in short, by the fearful resolve to find in itself alone the one absolute motive of action, under which all other motives from within and from without must be either subordinated or crushed.

This is the character which Milton has so philosophically as well as sublimely embodied in the Satan of his Paradise Lost. Alas! too often has it been embodied in *real* life! Too often has it given a dark and savage grandeur to the historic page! And wherever it has appeared, under whatever circumstances of time and country, the same ingredients have gone to its composition; and it has been identified by the same attributes. Hope in which there is no Chearfulness; Stedfastness within and immovable Resolve,

3. Alexander the Great, son of Philip II of Macedon, famed for his conquest of the eastern Mediterranean world in the 4th century B.C.E. Purple is the color of royalty.
4. The great error of Napoleon, . . . was a continued obtrusion on mankind of his want of all community of feeling for, or with them; perhaps more offensive to human vanity than the active cruelty of more trembling and suspicious tyranny. Such were his speeches to public assemblies as well as individuals; and the single expression which he is said to have used on returning to Paris after the Russian winter had destroyed his army, rubbing his hands over a fire, "This is pleasanter than Moscow,"

would probably alienate more favour from his cause than the destruction and reverses which led to the remark [Byron's note]. Greek philosopher Diogenes the Cynic (4th century B.C.E.) impressed Alexander with his resolute independence.
1. The defeat of Napoleon in 1815 ended nearly 25 years of war, but peacetime brought new crises: unemployment, inflation, food shortages, and agitations for political and social reform. Coleridge joined the debates with a set of pamphlets, of which *The Statesman's Manual*, "Addressed to the higher classes of society," was the first, published in 1816.

with outward Restlessness and whirling Activity; Violence with Guile; Temerity with Cunning; and, as the result of all, Interminableness of Object with perfect Indifference of Means; these are the qualities that have constituted the Commanding GENIUS! these are the Marks, that have characterized the Masters of Mischief, the Liberticides,[2] and mighty Hunters of Mankind, from NIMROD[3] to NAPOLEON. And from inattention to the possibility of such a character as well as from ignorance of its elements, even men of honest intentions too frequently become fascinated. Nay, whole nations have been so far duped by this want of insight and reflection as to regard with palliative admiration, instead of wonder and abhorrence, the Molocks[4] of human nature, who are indebted for the larger portion of their meteoric success, to their total want of principle, and who surpass the generality of their fellow creatures in one act of courage only, that of daring to say with their whole heart, "Evil, be thou my good!"[5]—All *system* so far is power; and a *systematic* criminal, self-consistent and entire in wickedness, who entrenches villainy within villainy and barricadoes crime by crime, has removed a world of obstacles by the mere decision, that he will have no obstacles, but those of force and brute matter.

1816

Caroline Lamb[1]
from Glenarvon

Those who have given way to the violence of any uncontrouled passion know that during its influence, all other considerations vanish. It is of little use to upbraid or admonish the victim who pursues his course: the fires that goad him on to his ruin, prevent his return. A kind word, an endearing smile, may excite one contrite tear; but he never pauses to reflect, or turns his eyes from the object of his pursuit. In vain the cold looks of an offended world, the heavy censures, and the pointed, bitter sarcasms of friends and dependants. Misfortunes, poverty, pain, even to the rack, are nothing if he obtain his view. It is a madness that falls upon the brain and heart. All is at stake for that one throw; and he who dares all, is desperate, and cannot fear. It was phrenzy, not love, that raged in Calantha's bosom.

To the prayers of a heart-broken parent, Lady Avondale opposed the agonizing threats of a distempered mind. "I will leave you all, if you take him from me. On earth there is nothing left me but Glenarvon.—Oh name not virtue and religion to me.— What are its hopes, its promises, if I lose him." The fever of her mind was such, that she could not for one hour rest: he saw the dreadful power he had gained, and he lost no opportunity of encreasing it. Ah did he share it? In language the sweetest, and the most persuasive, he worked upon her passions, till he inflamed them beyond endurance.

"This, this is sin," he cried, as he held her to his bosom, and breathed vows of ardent, burning love. "This is what moralists rail at, and account degrading. Now tell them, Calantha, thou who didst affect to be so pure—so chaste, whether the human heart can resist it? Religion bids thee fly me," he cried: "every hope of heaven and hereafter warns thee from my bosom. Glenarvon is the hell thou art to shun:—this is the hour of trial. Christians must resist. Calantha arise, and fly me; leave me alone, as before I found thee.

---

2. "Killers of liberty."
3. "The mighty hunter" (Genesis 10.8–9).
4. The idol to whom children were sacrificed in the Old Testament world (Leviticus 18.21), and in *Paradise Lost*, Satan's compatriot in Hell (1.392–96).
5. Satan's oath (*Paradise Lost* 4.110).
1. Caroline Lamb (1785–1828) had a tempestuous affair with Byron across 1812. When an exasperated Byron

bluntly ditched her, she collapsed in hysterics, but by 1816, after Byron's marriage to her cousin Annabella Milbanke had collapsed, she avenged herself with a *roman à clef*, whose evil hero, the Earl of Glenarvon, is not only Byronic, but transparently Byron. The heroine, Calantha, Lady Avondale, has fallen under his spell, even though she is married to a good man, has children, and her course is opposed by her family.

Desert me, and thy father and relations shall bless thee for the sacrifice: and thy God, who redeemed thee, shall mark thee for his own." With bitter taunts he smiled as he thus spoke: then clasping her nearer to his heart, "Tell both priests and parents," he said exultingly, "that one kiss from the lips of those we love, is dearer than every future hope."

All day,—every hour in the day,—every instant of passing time Glenarvon thought but of Calantha. It was not love, it was distraction. When near him, she felt ecstacy; but if separated, though but for one moment, she was sullen and desponding. At night she seldom slept; a burning fever quickened every pulse: the heart beat as if with approaching dissolution,—delirium fell upon her brain. No longer innocent, her fancy painted but visions of love; and to be his alone, was all she now wished for, or desired on earth. He felt, he saw, that the peace of her mind, her life itself were gone for ever, and he rejoiced in the thought.

* * *

[Calantha dies after being jilted by Glenarvon; Glenarvon, in the disguise of "Viviani," has murdered a child and the sister of the duke to whom he is talking in the following passage, describing himself. In another character, Glenarvon is the leader of Irish patriots plotting a rebellion—they are the multitude to whom the passage refers.]

The duke started, and looked full in the face of Glenarvon. "Who is this Viviani?" he said, in a tone of voice loud and terrible. "An idol," replied Glenarvon, "whom the multitude have set up for themselves, and worshipped, forsaking their true faith, to follow after a false light—a man who is in love with crime and baseness—one, of whom it has been said, that he hath an imagination of fire playing around a heart of ice—one whom the never-dying worm feeds on by night and day—a hypocrite," continued Glenarvon, with a smile of bitterness, "who wears a mask to his friends, and defeats his enemies by his unexpected sincerity—a coward, with more of bravery than some who fear nothing; for, even in his utmost terror, he defies that which he fears." "And where is this wretch?" said the duke: "what dungeon is black enough to hold him? What rack has been prepared to punish him for his crimes?" "He is as I have said," replied Glenarvon triumphantly, "the idol of the fair, and the great. Is it virtue that women prize? Is it honour and renown they worship? Throw but the dazzling light of genius upon baseness, and corruption, and every crime will be to them but an additional charm."

* * *

[Glenarvon goes on to ruin several women, fatally wounds Calantha's husband in a duel, and abandons the Irish patriots, whose rebellion is crushed; having confessed all to the duke, he flees Ireland for England. At the novel's end, he has become captain of a ship in the navy. Commanding his ship in an engagement against the French, he fights bravely, but is then seized with a vision of a ghost-ship, which he is determined to pursue.]

Madness to phrenzy came upon him. In vain his friends, and many of the brave companions in his ship, held him struggling in their arms. He seized his opportunity. "Bear on," he cried: "pursue, till death and vengeance—" and throwing himself from the helm, plunged headlong into the waters. They rescued him; but it was too late. In the struggles of ebbing life, even as the spirit of flame rushed from the bands of mortality, visions of punishment and hell pursued him. Down, down, he seemed to sink with horrid precipitance from gulf to gulf, till immured in darkness; and as he closed his eyes in death, a voice, loud and terrible, from beneath, thus seemed to address him:

"Hardened and impenitent sinner! the measure of your iniquity is full: the price of crime has been paid: here shall your spirit dwell for ever, and for ever. You have dreamed away life's joyous hour, nor made atonement for error, nor denied yourself aught that the fair earth presented you. You did not controul the fiend in your bosom, or stifle him in his first growth: he now has mastered you, and brought you here: and you did not bow the knee for mercy whilst time was given you: now mercy shall not be shewn. O, cry upwards from these lower pits, to the friends and companions you have left, to the sinner who hardens himself against his Creator—who basks in the ray of prosperous guilt, nor dreams that his hour like your's is at hand. Tell him how terrible a thing is death; how fearful at such an hour is remembrance of the past. Bid him repent, but he shall not hear you. Bid him amend, but like you he shall delay till it is too late. Then, neither his arts, nor talents, nor his possessions, shall save him, nor friends, though leagued together more than ten thousand strong; for the axe of justice must fall. God is just; and the spirit of evil infatuates before he destroys."

1816   1816

William Hazlitt
from *Lectures on the English Poets*
ON SHAKESPEARE AND MILTON[1]

I am ready to give up the dialogues in Heaven where, as Pope justly observes, "God the Father turns a school divine."[2] * * * The interest of the poem arises from the daring ambition and fierce passions of Satan, and from the account of the paradisaical happiness, and the loss of it by our first parents. Three-fourths of the work are taken up with these characters, and nearly all that relates to them is unmixed sublimity and beauty. The two first books alone are like two massy pillars of solid gold.

Satan is the most heroic subject that ever was chosen for a poem; and the execution is as perfect as the design is lofty. He was the first of created beings who, for endeavouring to be equal with the highest, and to divide the empire of heaven with the Almighty, was hurled down to hell. His aim was no less than the throne of the universe; his means, myriads of angelic armies bright, the third part of the heavens, whom he lured after him with his countenance, and who durst defy the, Omnipotent in arms.[3] His ambition was the greatest, and his punishment was the greatest; but not so his despair: for his fortitude was as great as his sufferings. His strength of mind was matchless as his strength of body; the vastness of his designs did not surpass the firm, inflexible determination with which he submitted to his irreversible doom and final loss of all good. His power of action and of suffering was equal. He was the greatest power that was ever overthrown, with the strongest will left to resist or to endure. He was baffled, not confounded. * * * The sense of his punishment seems lost in the magnitude of it; the fierceness of tormenting flames is qualified and made innoxious by the greater fierceness of his pride; the loss of infinite happiness to himself is compensated in thought by the power of inflicting infinite misery on others. Yet Satan is not the principle of malignity, or of the abstract love of evil, but of the abstract love of power, of pride, of self-will personified, to which last principle all other good and evil, and even his own, are subordinate. From this principle he never once flinches. His love of power and contempt for suffering are never once relaxed from the highest pitch of intensity. His thoughts burn like a hell within him; but the power of thought holds dominion in his mind over

---

1. See p. 706 for another excerpt from this lecture.
2. Referring to the discussion in *Paradise Lost* 3 between the "Almighty Father" and his "only begotten Son" about Adam and Eve's revolt, and quoting Pope's *First Epistle of*

the *Second Book of Horace* (1737) 102; a school-divine is a scholastic theologian.
3. Paraphrasing *Paradise Lost* 1.49 (see page 1036); Hazlitt uses Satan's voice to shape his praise.

every other consideration. The consciousness of a determined purpose, of "that intellectual being, those thoughts that wander through eternity," though accompanied with endless pain, he prefers to nonentity, to "being swallowed up and lost in the wide womb of uncreated night."[4] He expresses the sum and substance of all ambition in one line: "Fallen cherub, to be weak is miserable, doing or suffering!" [l.157–158]. After such a conflict as his and such a defeat, to retreat in order, to rally, to make terms, to exist at all, is something; but he does more than this: he founds a new empire in hell, and from it conquers this new world, whither he bends his undaunted flight, forcing his way through nether and surrounding fires. * * * Prometheus chained to his rock was not a more terrific example of suffering and of crime. * * * The deformity of Satan is only in the depravity of his will; he has no bodily deformity to excite our loathing or disgust. The horns and tail are not there, poor emblems of the unbending, unconquered spirit, of the writhing agonies within. Milton was too magnanimous and open an antagonist to support his argument by the by-tricks of a hump and cloven foot. * * * He relied on the justice of his cause, and did not scruple to give the devil his due.

Mary Wollstonecraft Shelley
from *Frankenstein; or The Modern Prometheus*[1]
[VICTOR FRANKENSTEIN IN THE LABORATORY]

No one can conceive the variety of feelings which bore me onwards, like a hurricane, in the first enthusiasm of success. Life and death appeared to me ideal bounds, which I should first break through, and pour a torrent of light into our dark world. A new species would bless me as its creator and source; many happy and excellent natures would owe their being to me. No father could claim the gratitude of his child so completely as I should deserve their's. Pursuing these reflections, I thought, that if I could bestow animation upon lifeless matter, I might in process of time (although I now found it impossible) renew life where death had apparently devoted the body to corruption.

These thoughts supported my spirits, while I pursued my undertaking with unremitting ardour. My cheek had grown pale with study, and my person had become emaciated with confinement. Sometimes, on the very brink of certainty, I failed; yet still I clung to the hope which the next day or the next hour might realize. One secret which I alone possessed was the hope to which I had dedicated myself; and the moon gazed on my midnight labours, while, with unrelaxed and breathless eagerness, I pursued nature to her hiding places. Who shall conceive the horrors of my secret toil, as I dabbled among the unhallowed damps of the grave, or tortured the living animal to animate the lifeless clay?[2] My limbs now tremble, and my eyes swim with

4. Belial, a rebel who is intellectual, worries that to persist against God is to risk total annihilation; and "who would lose, / Though full of pain, this intellectual being, / Those thoughts that wander through Eternity, / To perish rather, swallow'd up and lost / In the wide womb of uncreated night, / Devoid of sense and motion?" (*Paradise Lost* 2.146–51).

1. Shelley began this novel at Byron's villa in 1816 and it was published in 1818. The subtitle, "the Modern Prometheus," may describe both Frankenstein and his Creature, the former as a transgressor of divine law, stealing power from heaven, the latter as a compassionate firebringer to suffering humanity, punished for his deed. In this excerpt from vol. 1, ch. 3, Frankenstein recounts his project to create life, a daring idealism betrayed and tormented

by horrific consequences: a malformed creature, whom he calls "Monster" and "Demon." In the excerpt from vol. 2, ch. 7, the Creature, having finally caught up with the creator who abandoned him at birth, tells his story, a narrative in which he is the victim, alienated and tormented by his physical difference from humanity, anguished in his loneliness. Having learned to read, the Creature studies *Paradise Lost* (found by chance in a satchel in the woods) and what amounts to his prenatal biography, Victor's laboratory notes on his science project.

2. In the Greek myth, Prometheus fashions man out of clay, and breathes life into him, later giving him fire to raise him above the level of the beasts. In the story of Genesis (2.7), God creates man out of clay and breathes life into him.

the remembrance; but then a resistless, and almost frantic impulse, urged me forward; I seemed to have lost all soul or sensation but for this one pursuit. It was indeed but a passing trance, that only made me feel with renewed acuteness so soon as, the unnatural stimulus ceasing to operate, I had returned to my old habits. I collected bones from charnel houses; and disturbed, with profane fingers, the tremendous secrets of the human frame. In a solitary chamber, or rather cell, at the top of the house, and separated from all the other apartments by a gallery and staircase, I kept my workshop of filthy creation; my eyeballs were starting from their sockets in attending to the details of my employment. The dissecting room and the slaughter-house furnished many of my materials; and often did my human nature turn with loathing from my occupation, whilst, still urged on by an eagerness which perpetually increased, I brought my work near to a conclusion.

[The Creature, Now Literate, Reads *Paradise Lost*]

But *Paradise Lost* excited different and far deeper emotions. I read it, as I had read the other volumes which had fallen into my hands, as a true history. It moved every feeling of wonder and awe, that the picture of an omnipotent God warring with his creatures was capable of exciting. I often referred the several situations, as their similarity struck me, to my own. Like Adam, I was created apparently united by no link to any other being in existence; but his state was far different from mine in every other respect. He had come forth from the hands of God a perfect creature, happy and prosperous, guarded by the especial care of his Creator; he was allowed to converse with, and acquire knowledge from beings of a superior nature:[3] but I was wretched, helpless, and alone. Many times I considered Satan as the fitter emblem of my condition; for often, like him, when I viewed the bliss of my protectors, the bitter gall of envy rose within me.[4]

Another circumstance strengthened and confirmed these feelings. Soon after my arrival in the hovel, I discovered some papers in the pocket of the dress[5] which I had taken from your laboratory. At first I had neglected them; but now that I was able to decypher the characters in which they were written, I began to study them with diligence. It was your journal of the four months that preceded my creation. You minutely described in these papers every step you took in the progress of your work; this history was mingled with accounts of domestic occurrences. You, doubtless, recollect these papers. Here they are. Every thing is related in them which bears reference to my accursed origin; the whole detail of that series of disgusting circumstances which produced it is set in view; the minutest description of my odious and loathsome person is given, in language which painted your own horrors, and rendered mine ineffaceable. I sickened as I read. "Hateful day when I received life!" I exclaimed in agony. "Cursed creator! Why did you form a monster so hideous that even you turned from me in disgust? God in pity made man beautiful and alluring, after his own image;[6] but my form is a filthy type of your's, more horrid from its very resemblance. Satan had his companions, fellow-devils, to admire and encourage him; but I am solitary and detested."[7]

1816   1818

3. *Paradise Lost* 8.250–559; Adam recounts several conversations with his Creator, and he is tutored in Eden by the "affable" Archangel Raphael.
4. *Paradise Lost* 4.358–69.

5. Lab coat.
6. "God created man in his own image" (Genesis 1.27).
7. *Frankenstein* may be read in full in the Longman Cultural Edition, edited by Susan Wolfson.

Felicia Hemans

from *The Widow of Crescentius*[1]

So wildly sweet, its° notes might seem   *Guido's song*
Th' ethereal music of a dream,
125   A spirit's voice from worlds unknown,
Deep thrilling power in every tone!
Sweet is that lay, and yet its flow
Hath language only given to woe;
And if at times its wakening swell
130   Some tale of glory seems to tell,
Soon the proud notes of triumph die,
Lost in a dirge's harmony:
Oh! many a pang the heart hath proved,
Hath deeply suffer'd, fondly loved,
135   Ere the sad strain could catch from thence
Such deep impassion'd eloquence!—
Yes! gaze on him, that minstrel boy—
He is no child of hope and joy;
Though few his years, yet have they been
140   Such as leave traces on the mien,
And o'er the roses of our prime
Breathe other blights than those of time.

    Yet, seems his spirit wild and proud,
By grief unsoften'd and unbow'd.
145   Oh! there are sorrows which impart
A sternness foreign to the heart,
And rushing with an earthquake's power,
That makes a desert in an hour;
Rouse the dread passions in their course,
150   As tempests wake the billows' force!—
'Tis sad, on youthful Guido's face,
The stamp of woes like these to trace.
Oh! where can ruins awe mankind,
Dark as the ruins of the mind?

155   His mien is lofty, but his gaze
Too well a wandering soul betrays:
His full dark eye at times is bright
With strange and momentary light,
Whose quick uncertain flashes throw
160   O'er his pale cheek a hectic glow:
And oft his features and his air

---

1. For more about Hemans, see her principal listing on page 930. This poem is in *Tales, and Historic Scenes*, published in 1819 by John Murray, also Byron's publisher. Hemans was one of many female poets inspired by Byron's poetry. In this historically based poem, Stephania's husband, a Republican opponent of papal rule in late 10th-century Rome, has been tortured and executed by the Holy Roman Emperor, Otto III of Germany. Stephania takes revenge by disguising herself as the minstrel-boy Guido and insinuating herself into Otto's court, where she eventually poisons him, gloating in her triumph before she is led off to execution. This excerpt from Part 2 describes the mysteriously sad "Guido," before "his" true identity is disclosed.

A shade of troubled mystery wear,
A glance of hurried wildness, fraught
With some unfathomable thought.[2]
165   Whate'er that thought, still, unexpress'd,
Dwells the sad secret in his breast;
The pride his haughty brow reveals,
All other passion well conceals.[3]
He breathes each wounded feeling's tone,
170   In music's eloquence alone;
His soul's deep voice is only pour'd
Through his full song and swelling chord.

Percy Bysshe Shelley
from *Preface to Prometheus Unbound*[1]

The only imaginary being resembling in any degree Prometheus, is Satan; and Prometheus is, in my judgement, a more poetical character than Satan, because, in addition to courage, and majesty, and firm and patient opposition to omnipotent force, he is susceptible of being described as exempt from the taints of ambition, envy, revenge, and a desire for personal aggrandisement, which, in the Hero of Paradise Lost, interfere with the interest. The character of Satan engenders in the mind a pernicious casuistry[2] which leads us to weigh his faults and his wrongs,[3] and to excuse the former because the latter exceed all measure. In the minds of those who consider that magnificent fiction with a religious feeling it engenders something worse. But Prometheus is, as it were, the type of the highest perfection of moral and intellectual nature, impelled by the purest and the truest motives to the best and noblest ends.

from *Prometheus Unbound, Act 1*[4]

Monarch of Gods and Dæmons,[5] and all Spirits
But One,° who throng those bright and rolling worlds   *i.e., himself*
Which Thou and I alone of living things
Behold with sleepless eyes! regard this Earth
5   Made multitudinous with thy slaves, whom thou
Requitest for knee-worship, prayer, and praise,
And toil, and hecatombs[6] of broken hearts,
With fear and self-contempt and barren hope;
Whilst me, who am thy foe, eyeless° in hate,   *blind*
10   Hast thou made reign and triumph, to thy scorn,
O'er mine own misery and thy vain revenge.
Three thousand years of sleep-unsheltered hours,
And moments aye° divided by keen pangs   *forever*
Till they seemed years, torture and solitude,

---

2. Readers of *The Giaour* and *Lara* would grasp the allusion to a Byronic heroine in page's guise, and recognize the iconography of the Byronic hero.
3. In Byron's portrait of the charismatic, mysterious hero of *The Corsair* (1814) this rhyme is a keynote: "And oft perforce his rising lip reveals / The haughtier thought it curbs, but scarce conceals" (1.205–6).
1. Shelley's epic verse drama, written in 1818–1819 and published in 1820, concerns Prometheus's struggle

against and eventual liberation from Jupiter's tyranny, an emblem of modern tyrannies as well.
2. Specious moral reasoning.
3. Oppression and suffering.
4. Prometheus, bound to a precipice in a ravine of icy rocks, invokes Jupiter.
5. Beings between mortals and gods able to communicate with both.
6. Massive public sacrifices (heca: 100).

15   Scorn and despair,—these are mine empire:—
More glorious far than that which thou surveyest
From thine unenvied throne, O Mighty God!
Almighty, had I deigned to share the shame
Of thine ill tyranny, and hung not here
20   Nailed to this wall of eagle-baffling mountain,
Black, wintry, dead, unmeasured; without herb,
Insect, or beast, or shape or sound of life.
Ah me! alas, pain, pain ever, for ever!

No change, no pause, no hope! Yet I endure.
25   I ask the Earth, have not the mountains felt?
I ask yon Heaven, the all-beholding Sun,
Has it not seen? The Sea, in storm or calm
Heaven's ever-changing Shadow, spread below,
Have its deaf waves not heard my agony?
30   Ah me! alas, pain, pain ever, for ever!

The crawling glaciers pierce me with the spears
Of their moon-freezing crystals; the bright chains
Eat with their burning cold into my bones.
Heaven's winged hound, polluting from thy lips
35   His beak in poison not his own, tears up
My heart;[7] and shapeless sights come wandering by,
The ghastly people of the realm of dream,
Mocking me: and the Earthquake-fiends are charged
To wrench the rivets from my quivering wounds
40   When the rocks split and close again behind;
While from their loud abysses howling throng
The genii of the storm, urging the rage
Of whirlwind, and afflict me with keen hail.
And yet to me welcome is day and night,
45   Whether one breaks the hoar frost of the morn,
Or starry, dim, and slow, the other climbs
The leaden-coloured east; for then they lead
The wingless, crawling hours, one among whom
  —As some dark Priest hales° the reluctant victim—   *hauls*
50   Shall drag thee, cruel King, to kiss the blood
From these pale feet, which then might trample thee
If they disdained not such a prostrate slave.
Disdain! Ah no! I pity thee. What ruin
Will hunt thee undefended through the wide Heaven!
55   How will thy soul, cloven to its depth with terror,
Gape like a Hell within! I speak in grief,
Not exultation, for I hate no more,
As then ere misery made me wise. The curse
Once breathed on thee I would recall.

1818–1819   1820

7. See page 750, n. 1. Jupiter kisses the vulture on his return.

Robert Southey
from Preface to *A Vision of Judgement* [1]
[THE "SATANIC SCHOOL"]

Would that [the public's "literary intolerance"] were directed against those monstrous combinations of horrors and mockery, lewdness and impiety, with which English poetry has, in our days, first been polluted! For more than half a century English literature had been distinguished by its moral purity, the effect, and in its turn, the cause of an improvement in national manners. A father might, without apprehension of evil, have put into the hands of his children any book which issued from the press, if it did not bear, either in its title-page or frontispiece, manifest signs that it was intended as furniture for the brothel. There was no danger in any work which bore the name of a respectable publisher, or was to be procured at any respectable bookseller's. This was particularly the case with regard to our poetry. It is now no longer so; and woe to those by whom the offence cometh! The greater the talents of the offender, the greater is his guilt, and the more enduring will be his shame. Whether it be that the laws are in themselves unable to abate an evil of this magnitude, or whether it be that they are remissly administered, and with such injustice that the celebrity of an offender serves as a privilege whereby he obtains impunity, individuals are bound to consider that such pernicious works would neither be published nor written, if they were discouraged as they might, and ought to be, by public feeling; every person, therefore, who purchases such books, or admits them into his house, promotes the mischief, and thereby, as far as in him lies, becomes an aider and abettor of the crime.

The publication of a lascivious book is one of the worst offences that can be committed against the well-being of society. It is a sin, to the consequences of which no limits can be assigned, and those consequences no after repentance in the writer can counteract. Whatever remorse of conscience he may feel when his hour comes (and come it must!) will be of no avail. The poignancy of a death-bed repentance cannot cancel one copy of the thousands which are sent abroad; and as long as it continues to be read, so long is he the pandar of posterity, and so long is he heaping up guilt upon his soul in perpetual accumulation.

These remarks are not more severe than the offence deserves, even when applied to those immoral writers who have not been conscious of any evil intention in their writings, who would acknowledge a little levity, a little warmth of colouring, and so forth, in that sort of language with which men gloss over their favourite vices, and deceive themselves. What then should be said of those for whom the thoughtlessness and inebriety of wanton youth can no longer be pleaded, but who have written in sober manhood and with deliberate purpose? . . Men of diseased hearts and depraved imaginations, who, forming a system of opinions to suit their own unhappy course of conduct, have rebelled against the holiest ordinances of human society, and hating that revealed religion which, with all their efforts and bravadoes, they are unable entirely to disbelieve, labour to make others as miserable as themselves, by infecting them with a moral virus that eats into the soul! The school which they have set up may properly be called the Satanic school; for though their productions breathe the spirit of Belial in their lascivious parts, and the spirit of Moloch in those loathsome

---

1. When Poet Laureate Southey published *A Vision of Judgement* in 1821, on the occasion of the death of George III, he took the opportunity to settle scores with his detractors, chiefly Byron. In *A Vision* Satan arrives at the gates of heaven, where the king's spirit is to be admitted amid beatification, to carry the monarch's political antagonists off to hell. In his preface Southey wished the same for Byron and his compeers, in punishment for polluting the "moral purity" of English literature with the works of a "Satanic school."

images of atrocities and horrors which they delight to represent, they are more especially characterised by a Satanic spirit of pride and audacious impiety, which still betrays the wretched feeling of hopelessness wherewith it is allied.

This evil is political as well as moral for indeed moral and political evils are inseparably connected. * * * Let rulers of the state look to this, in time!

George Gordon, Lord Byron
from *The Vision of Judgment*[1]

24

185   But bringing up the rear of this bright host
        A Spirit of a different aspect waved
     His wings, like thunder-clouds above some coast
        Whose barren beach with frequent wrecks is paved;
     His brow was like the deep when tempest-tost;
190   Fierce and unfathomable thoughts engraved
     Eternal wrath on his immortal face,
     And *where* he gazed a gloom pervaded space.

25

     As he drew near, he gazed upon the gate
        Ne'er to be enter'd more by him or sin,
195   With such a glance of supernatural hate,
        As made Saint Peter wish himself within;
     He potter'd with his keys at a great rate,
        And sweated through his apostolic skin:
     Of course his perspiration was but ichor,
200   Or some such other spiritual liquor.

26

     The very cherubs huddled altogether,
        Like birds when soars the falcon; and they felt
     A tingling to the tip of every feather,
        And form'd a circle like Orion's belt
205   Around their poor old charge; who scarce knew whither
        His guards had led him, though they gently dealt
     With royal manes (for by many stories,
     And true, we learn the angels all are Tories.)

27

     As things were in this posture, the gate flew
210   Asunder, and the flashing of its hinges
     Flung over space an universal hue
        Of many-coloured flame, until its tinges

---

1. Outraged by Southey's politics of Heaven, whereby a reactionary king was canonized and his political opponents damned, Byron began a counter-*Vision* immediately, in the spring of 1821, but his longtime publisher John Murray, tied in with the Tory establishment, demurred and delayed publication. Testing other London publishers, even the radical press, without success, Byron put the poem in the first issue of *The Liberal*, October 1822. Its publisher John Hunt was prosecuted for "calumniating the late king, and wounding the feelings of his present majesty," and was fined £100. In this excerpt, Satan arrives at the gates of heaven to make his claim for the king's soul and is greeted by Archangel Michael.

Reach'd even our speck of earth, and made a new
    Aurora borealis spread its fringes
215   O'er the North Pole; the same seen, when ice-bound,
By Captain Parry's crews, in "Melville's Sound."

         * * *

33

But here they were in neutral space: we know
    From Job, that Satan hath the power to pay
A heavenly visit thrice a year or so;[2]
260   And that "the sons of God," like those of clay,°   *mortals*
Must keep him company; and we might show
    From the same book, in how polite a way
The dialogue is held between the Powers
Of Good and Evil—but 'twould take up hours.

         * * *

35

The spirits were in neutral space, before
    The gate of heaven; like eastern thresholds is
275   The place where Death's grand cause is argued o'er,
    And souls despatch'd to that world or to this;
And therefore Michael and the other wore
    A civil aspect: though they did not kiss,
Yet still between his Darkness and his Brightness
280   There pass'd a mutual glance of great politeness.

36

The Archangel bowd, not like a modern beau,
    But with a graceful Oriental bend,
Pressing one radiant arm just where below
    The heart in good men is supposed to tend.
285   He turn'd as to an equal, not too low,
    But kindly; Satan met his ancient friend
With more hauteur, as might an old Castilian[3]
Poor noble meet a mushroom rich civilian.

37

He merely bent his diabolic brow
290   An instant; and then raising it, he stood
In act to assert his right or wrong, and show
    Cause why King George by no means could or should
Make out a case to be exempt from woe
    Eternal, more than other kings endued
295   With better sense and hearts, whom history mentions,
Who long have "paved hell with their good intentions."

END OF "MANFRED" AND ITS TIME

2. Job 1.2

3. Old nobility, descended from the medieval Spanish kingdom of Castile.

from CHILDE HAROLD'S PILGRIMAGE
Canto the Third[1]

[WATERLOO FIELDS][2]

17

145   Stop!—for thy tread is on an Empire's dust!
              An Earthquake's spoil is sepulchred below!
              Is the spot mark'd with no colossal bust?
              Nor column trophied for triumphal show?[3]
150   None; but the moral's truth tells simpler so,
              As the ground was before, thus let it be;—
              How that red rain hath made the harvest grow!
              And is this all the world has gain'd by thee,
     Thou first and last of fields! king-making Victory?[4]

18

              And Harold stands upon this place of skulls,
155   The grave of France, the deadly Waterloo;
              How in an hour the power which gave annuls
              Its gifts, transferring fame as fleeting too!
              In "pride of place"[5] here last the eagle flew,
              Then tore with bloody talon the rent plain,
160   Pierced by the shaft of banded nations through;
              Ambition's life and labours all were vain;
     He wears the shatter'd links of the world's broken chain.[6]

19

              Fit retribution! Gaul° may champ the bit   *France*
              And foam in fetters;—but is Earth more free?
165   Did nations combat to make *One* submit;
              Or league to teach all kings true sovereignty?
              What! shall reviving Thraldom again be
              The patched-up idol of enlighten'd days?

1. The first two cantos appeared in 1812. As the subtitle "A Romaunt" indicated, Byron had adopted the genre of romance for his unnervingly contemporary poem. The Spenserian stanzas and mock-archaisms—a "childe" is a youth of noble birth—played discordantly against the account of his travels in 1809–1811 through Spain (and his acerbic commentary on the Peninsular War; see Introduction, pages 16–17) and then on into parts of Greece unfrequented by Westerners. The overwhelming success of the poem ensured that Byron would be identified with Childe Harold. Byron protested, but the connection is reinforced by the manuscripts, which disclose that Childe Harold was once Childe Burun, an ancient form of his family name. Although Canto 3 was published independently in 1816, protagonist and poet had come to figure each other. Byron left England on 25 April 1816, and wrote the opening stanzas while crossing the Channel. For a counterpoint to the poem's melancholy sublimity see Byron's letter of 28 January 1817 to Thomas Moore, page 863.

2. Napoleon was vanquished by a British-Prussian alliance on 4 May 1815, at Waterloo, near Brussels, with a loss of over 50,000 lives, about half on each side. The site drew British tourists and pilgrims. Byron visited it in June 1815, and these stanzas, including an account of the Duchess of Richmond's ball in Brussels the night before the battle of Quatre-Bras (two days before Waterloo), memorialized the events for a generation, their drama making them favorite recitation pieces.

3. Military victors in ancient Rome erected decorative columns or triumphal arches to commemorate their successes, a tradition Napoleon emulated with the Arc de Triomphe in Paris.

4. King-making, because the European monarchies were now restored, with renewed repressive powers.

5. [This] is a term of falconry, and means the highest pitch of flight [Byron's note]. Napoleon's symbol was the eagle.

6. Napoleon was now a prisoner.

Shall we, who struck the Lion down, shall we
170 Pay the Wolf homage? proffering lowly gaze
And servile knees to thrones? No; *prove*° before ye praise!   get proof

20

If not, o'er one fallen despot boast no more!
In vain fair cheeks were furrow'd with hot tears
For Europe's flowers long rooted up before
175 The trampler of her vineyards; in vain years
Of death, depopulation, bondage, fears,
Have all been borne, and broken by the accord
Of roused-up millions: all that most endears
Glory, is when the myrtle wreathes a sword
180 Such as Harmodius drew on Athens' tyrant lord.[7]

21

There was a sound of revelry by night,
And Belgium's capital had gathered then
Her Beauty and her Chivalry, and bright
The lamps shone o'er fair women and brave men;
185 A thousand hearts beat happily; and when
Music arose with its voluptuous swell,
Soft eyes look'd love to eyes which spake again,
And all went merry as a marriage-bell;
But hush! hark! a deep sound strikes like a rising knell!

22

190 Did ye not hear it?—No; 'twas but the wind,
Or the car rattling o'er the stony street;
On with the dance! let joy be unconfined;
No sleep till morn, when Youth and Pleasure meet
To chase the glowing Hours with flying feet—
195 But, hark!—that heavy sound breaks in once more,
As if the clouds its echo would repeat;
And nearer, clearer, deadlier than before!
Arm! Arm! it is—it is—the cannon's opening roar!

23

Within a windowed niche of that high hall
200 Sate Brunswick's fated chieftain;[8] he did hear
That sound the first amidst the festival,
And caught its tone with Death's prophetic ear;
And when they smiled because he deem'd it near,
His heart more truly knew that peal too well
205 Which stretch'd his father on a bloody bier,[9]
And roused the vengeance blood alone could quell:
He rush'd into the field, and, foremost fighting, fell.

7. In 514 B.C.E. Harmodius killed the Athenian tyrant Hipparchus with a dagger hidden in a branch of myrtle. Although it was a private vengeance, he came to be honored as a patriot and liberator.

8. The Duke of Brunswick was killed at Quatre-Bras.
9. Killed in Napoleon's rout of the Prussian forces at a battle in 1806.

24

Ah! then and there was hurrying to and fro,
And gathering tears, and tremblings of distress,
210 And cheeks all pale, which but an hour ago
Blush'd at the praise of their own loveliness;
And there were sudden partings, such as press
The life from out young hearts, and choking sighs
Which ne'er might be repeated; who could guess
215 If ever more should meet those mutual eyes,
Since upon night so sweet such awful morn could rise?

25

And there was mounting in hot haste: the steed,
The mustering squadron, and the clattering car,°   *carriage*
Went pouring forward with impetuous speed,
220 And swiftly forming in the ranks of war;
And the deep thunder peal on peal afar;
And near, the beat of the alarming drum
Roused up the soldier ere the morning star;
While throng'd the citizens with terror dumb,
225 Or whispering, with white lips—"The foe! they come! they come!"

26

And wild and high the "Cameron's gathering"[1] rose!
The war-note of Lochiel, which Albyn's° hills   *Scotland's*
Have heard, and heard, too, have her Saxon° foes:—   *English*
How in the noon of night that pibroch[2] thrills,
230 Savage and shrill! But with the breath which fills
Their mountain-pipe, so fill the mountaineers
With the fierce native daring which instils
The stirring memory of a thousand years,
And Evan's, Donald's[3] fame rings in each clansman's ears!

27

235 And Ardennes[4] waves above them her green leaves,
Dewy with nature's tear-drops, as they pass,
Grieving, if aught inanimate e'er grieves,
Over the unreturning brave,—alas!
Ere evening to be trodden like the grass
240 Which now beneath them, but above shall grow
In its next verdure, when this fiery mass
Of living valour, rolling on the foe
And burning with high hope, shall moulder cold and low.

---

1. The war song of the clan, headed by Lochiel.
2. War song played on bagpipes.
3. Sir Evan Cameron, and his descendant Donald. [Byron's note]; Evan fought for James II, and Donald for the Young Pretender, "bonny Prince Charlie."
4. A remnant of the forest of Ardennes, famous in Boiardo's *Orlando*, and immortal in Shakespeare's *As You Like It*. It is celebrated in Tacitus as being the spot of successful defence by the Germans against the Roman encroachments. I have ventured to adopt the name connected with nobler associations than those of mere slaughter [Byron's note]. The chief work of Boiardo, a 15th-century Italian poet, is *Orlando Innamorato*, an epic of knightly adventure and love, lightly alluded to in Shakespeare's comedy. Ardennes would be a battlefield in both world wars of the 20th century.

28

Last noon beheld them full of lusty life,
245   Last eve in Beauty's circle proudly gay,
The midnight brought the signal-sound of strife,
The morn the marshalling in arms,—the day
Battle's magnificently-stern array!
The thunder-clouds close o'er it, which when rent
250   The earth is cover'd thick with other clay,°   *human flesh*
Which her own clay shall cover, heap'd and pent,
Rider and horse,—friend, foe,—in one red burial blent!

29

Their praise is hymn'd by loftier harps than mine;
Yet one I would select from that proud throng,
255   Partly because they blend me with his line,
And partly that I did his sire some wrong,
And partly that bright names will hallow song;
And his was of the bravest, and when shower'd
The death-bolts deadliest the thinn'd files along,
260   Even where the thickest of War's tempest lower'd,
They reach'd no nobler breast than thine, young, gallant Howard![5]

30

There have been tears and breaking hearts for thee,
And mine were nothing, had I such to give;
But when I stood beneath the fresh green tree,
265   Which living waves where thou didst cease to live,
And saw around me the wide field revive
With fruits and fertile promise, and the Spring
Come forth her work of gladness to contrive,
With all her reckless birds upon the wing,
270   I turn'd from all she brought to those she could not bring.[6]

31

I turn'd to thee, to thousands, of whom each
And one as all a ghastly gap did make
In his own kind and kindred, whom to teach

---

5. Frederick Howard, son of the Earl of Carlisle, whom Byron had satirized in *English Bards and Scotch Reviewers.*
6. My guide from Mount St. Jean over the field seemed intelligent and accurate. The place where Major Howard fell was not far from two tall and solitary trees (there was a third cut down, or shivered in the battle), which stand a few yards from each other at a pathway's side. Beneath these he died and was buried. The body has since been removed to England. A small hollow for the present marks where it lay, but will probably soon be effaced; the plough has been upon it, and the grain is. After pointing out the different spots where Picton and other gallant men had perished; the guide said, "Here Major Howard lay: I was near him when wounded." I told him my relationship, and he seemed then still more anxious to point out the particular spot and circumstances. The place is one of the most marked in the field, from the peculiarity of the two trees above mentioned. I went on horseback twice over the field, comparing it with my recollection of similar scenes. As a plain, Waterloo seems marked out for the scene of some great action, though this may be mere imagination: I have viewed with attention those of Platea, Troy, Mantinea, Leuctra, Chaeronea, and Marathon; and the field around Mount St. Jean and Hougoumont appears to want little but a better cause, and that undefinable but impressive halo which the lapse of ages throws around a celebrated spot, to vie in interest with any or all of these, except, perhaps, the last mentioned [Byron's note].

Forgetfulness were mercy for their sake;
275   The Archangel's trump,[7] not Glory's, must awake
Those whom they thirst for; though the sound of Fame
May for a moment soothe, it cannot slake
The fever of vain longing, and the name
So honoured but assumes a stronger, bitterer claim.

32

280   They mourn, but smile at length; and, smiling, mourn:
The tree will wither long before it fall;
The hull drives on, though mast and sail be torn;
The roof-tree sinks, but moulders on the hall
In massy hoariness; the ruined wall
285   Stands when its wind-worn battlements are gone;
The bars survive the captive they enthral;
The day drags through though storms keep out the sun;
And thus the heart will break, yet brokenly live on:

33

Even as a broken mirror, which the glass
290   In every fragment multiplies; and makes
A thousand images of one that was,
The same, and still the more, the more it breaks;
And thus the heart will do which not forsakes,
Living in shattered guise; and still, and cold,
295   And bloodless, with its sleepless sorrow aches,
Yet withers on till all without is old,
Showing no visible sign, for such things are untold.

34

There is a very life in our despair,
Vitality of poison,—a quick root
300   Which feeds these deadly branches; for it were
As nothing did we die; but Life will suit
Itself to Sorrow's most detested fruit,
Like to the apples on the Dead Sea's shore,[8]
All ashes to the taste: Did man compute
305   Existence by enjoyment, and count o'er
Such hours 'gainst years of life,—say, would he name threescore?°   *sixty*

35

The Psalmist[9] numbered out the years of man:
They are enough; and if thy tale° be *true*,   *tally; story*

---

7. The trumpet (in *Revelation*) heralding the end of the world and the resurrection of the dead.
8. The (fabled) apples on the brink of the lake Asphaltites were said to be fair without, and, within, ashes [Byron's note].
9. David; the reference is to Psalm 90 ("The days of our years are threescore years and ten").

Thou, who didst grudge him even that fleeting span,
310   More than enough, thou fatal Waterloo!
Millions of tongues record thee, and anew
Their children's lips shall echo them, and say—
"Here, where the sword united nations drew,
Our countrymen were warring on that day!"[1]
315   And this is much—and all—which will not pass away.[2]

[THUNDERSTORM IN THE ALPS][3]

92

860   Thy sky is changed!—and such a change! Oh night,
And storm, and darkness, ye are wondrous strong,
Yet lovely in your strength, as is the light
Of a dark eye in woman! Far along,
From peak to peak, the rattling crags among
865   Leaps the live thunder! Not from one lone cloud,
But every mountain now hath found a tongue,
And Jura answers, through her misty shroud,
Back to the joyous Alps, who call to her aloud![4]

93

And this is in the night:—Most glorious night!
870   Thou wert not sent for slumber! let me be
A sharer in thy fierce and far delight,—
A portion of the tempest and of thee!
How the lit lake shines, a phosphoric sea,
And the big rain comes dancing to the earth!
875   And now again 'tis black,—and now, the glee
Of the loud hills shakes with its mountain-mirth,
As if they did rejoice o'er a young earthquake's birth.

94

Now, where the swift Rhone cleaves his way between
Heights which appear as lovers who have parted
880   In hate, whose mining depths so intervene,
That they can meet no more, though broken-hearted!
Though in their souls, which thus each other thwarted,
Love was the very root of the fond rage
Which blighted their life's bloom, and then departed:—
885   Itself expired, but leaving them an age
Of years all winters,—war within themselves to wage.[5]

1. In November 1942, Winston Churchill read this passage at the conclusion of a stirring speech rallying the Allies in the wartime struggle against the Nazis.
2. For ensuing stanzas 36–42, on the extremes in the career and character of Napoleon, see pages 751–53.
3. The thunder-storms to which these lines refer occurred on the thirteenth of June, 1816, at midnight. I have seen among the Acroceraunian mountains of Chimari several more terrible, but none more beautiful [Byron's note].

Byron moved into Villa Diodati on 10 June, near the Shelley party; a few days after these storms Mary Shelley began Frankenstein at Byron's villa.
4. The Jura Mountains, north and west of Geneva, form the boundary between Switzerland and France; the Alps run to the east and south.
5. The simile, obliquely recalling Byron's separation from his wife, illustrates his tendency to turn nature into sublime self-projection.

95

Now, where the quick Rhone thus hath cleft his way,
The mightiest of the storms hath ta'en his stand:
For here, not one, but many, make their play,
890 And fling their thunder-bolts from hand to hand,
Flashing and cast around: of all the band,
The brightest through these parted hills hath fork'd
His lightnings,—as if he did understand,
That in such gaps as desolation work'd,
895 There the hot shaft should blast whatever therein lurk'd.

96

Sky, mountains, river, winds, lake, lightnings! ye!
With night, and clouds, and thunder, and a soul
To make these felt and feeling, well may be
Things that have made me watchful; the far roll
900 Of your departing voices, is the knoll
Of what in me is sleepless,—if I rest.
But where of ye, oh tempests! is the goal?
Are ye like those within the human breast?
Or do ye find, at length, like eagles, some high nest?

97

905 Could I embody and unbosom now
That which is most within me,—could I wreak
My thoughts upon expression, and thus throw
Soul, heart, mind, passions, feelings, strong or weak,
All that I would have sought, and all I seek,
910 Bear, know, feel, and yet breathe—into *one* word,
And that one word were Lightning, I would speak;
But as it is, I live and die unheard,
With a most voiceless thought, sheathing it as a sword.

[BYRON'S STRAINED IDEALISM. APOSTROPHE TO HIS DAUGHTER]

111

Thus far have I proceeded in a theme
Renew'd with no kind auspices:°—to feel   *hopeful signs*
We are not what we have been, and to deem
We are not what we should be,—and to steel
1035 The heart against itself; and to conceal,
With a proud caution, love, or hate, or aught,—
Passion or feeling, purpose, grief, or zeal,—
Which is the tyrant spirit of our thought,
Is a stern task of soul:—No matter,—it is taught.

112

1040 And for these words, thus woven into song,
It may be that they are a harmless wile,—

The colouring of the scenes which fleet along,
Which I would seize, in passing, to beguile
My breast, or that of others, for a while.
1045   Fame is the thirst of youth,—but I am not
So young as to regard men's frown or smile,
As loss or guerdon° of a glorious lot;   prize
I stood and stand alone,—remember'd or forgot.

113
I have not loved the world, nor the world me;
1050   I have not flatter'd its rank breath,[6] nor bow'd
To it's idolatries a patient knee,—
Nor coin'd my cheek to smiles,—nor cried aloud
In worship of an echo; in the crowd
They could not deem me one of such; I stood
1055   Among them, but not of them; in a shroud
Of thoughts which were not their thoughts, and still could,
Had I not filed° my mind, which thus itself subdued.[7]   defiled

114
I have not loved the world, nor the world me,—
But let us part fair foes; I do believe,
1060   Though I have found them not, that there may be
Words which are things,—hopes which will not deceive,
And virtues which are merciful, nor weave
Snares for the failing: I would also deem
O'er others' griefs that some sincerely grieve;[8]
1065   That two, or one, are almost what they seem,—
That goodness is no name, and happiness no dream.

115
My daughter![9] with thy name this song begun
My daughter! with thy name thus much shall end—
I see thee not,—I hear thee not,—but none
1070   Can be so wrapt in thee; thou art the friend
To whom the shadows of far years extend:
Albeit my brow thou never should'st behold,
My voice shall with thy future visions blend
And reach into thy heart,—when mine is cold,—
1075   A token and a tone, even from thy father's mould.

116
To aid thy mind's developement,—to watch
Thy dawn of little joys,—to sit and see

---

6. Echoing Shakespeare's *Coriolanus*, 3.1.66–67. Byron frequently voices himself through this willful Roman general, who retorts to the plebeians who banish him: "I banish you" (3.3.124).
7. Byron adds a note citing *Macbeth*, 3.1.65.

8. It is said by Rochefoucault that "there is *always* something in the misfortunes of men's best friends not displeasing to them" [Byron's note].
9. Ada, whom Byron never saw again, after leaving England in her infancy. These stanzas close the canto.

Almost thy very growth,—to view thee catch
Knowledge of objects,—wonders yet to thee!
1080   To hold thee lightly on a gentle knee,
And print on thy soft cheek a parent's kiss,—
This, it should seem, was not reserved for me;
Yet this was in my nature:—as it is,
  I know not what is there, yet something like to this.

117

1085   Yet, though dull Hate as duty should be taught,
I know that thou wilt love me; though my name
Should be shut from thee, as a spell still fraught
With desolation,—and a broken claim:
Though the grave closed between us,—'twere the same,
1090   I know that thou wilt love me; though to drain
My blood from out thy being were an aim,
And an attainment,—all would be in vain,—
  Still thou would'st love me, still that more than life retain.

118

The child of love,—though born in bitterness
1095   And nurtured in convulsion. Of thy sire
These were the elements,—and thine no less.
As yet such are around thee,—but thy fire
Shall be more temper'd, and thy hope far higher.
Sweet be thy cradled slumbers! O'er the sea,
1100   And from the mountains where I now respire,
Fain would I waft such blessing upon thee,
  As, with a sigh, I deem thou might'st have been to me!

from Canto the Fourth[1]

[ROME. POLITICAL HOPES]

93

What from this barren being do we reap?
830   Our senses narrow, and our reason frail,
Life short, and truth a gem which loves the deep,
And all things weigh'd in custom's falsest scale;
Opinion an omnipotence,—whose veil
Mantles the earth with darkness, until right
835   And wrong are accidents, and men grow pale
Lest their own judgments should become too bright,
  And their free thoughts be crimes, and earth have too much light.

---

1. Begun in June 1817, published April 1818. In the dedication Byron announced that the reader would find "less of the pilgrim" than in preceding cantos: "I had become weary," he declared of the fiction, "of drawing a line which every one seemed determined not to perceive." Canto 4 is spoken in his own person and carries the account of his travels into Italy.

94

And thus they plod in sluggish misery,
Rotting from sire to son, and age to age,
840   Proud of their trampled nature, and so die,
Bequeathing their hereditary rage
To the new race of inborn slaves, who wage
War for their chains, and rather than be free,
Bleed gladiator-like, and still engage
845   Within the same arena where they see
Their fellows fall before, like leaves of the same tree.

95

I speak not of men's creeds—they rest between
Man and his Maker—but of things allowed,
Averr'd,° and known,—and daily, hourly seen—   *affirmed*
850   The yoke that is upon us doubly bowed,
And the intent of tyranny avowed,
The edict of Earth's rulers, who are grown
The apes of him who humbled once the proud,
And shook them from their slumbers on the throne;
855   Too glorious, were this all his mighty arm had done.[2]

96

Can tyrants but by tyrants conquered be,
And Freedom find no champion and no child
Such as Columbia saw arise when she
Sprung forth a Pallas, armed and undefiled?[3]
860   Or must such minds be nourished in the wild,
Deep in the unpruned forest, 'midst the roar
Of cataracts, where nursing Nature smiled
On infant Washington?[4] Has Earth no more
Such seeds within her breast, or Europe no such shore?

97

865   But France got drunk with blood to vomit crime,
And fatal have her Saturnalia[5] been
To Freedom's cause, in every age and clime;
Because the deadly days which we have seen,
And vile Ambition, that built up between
870   Man and his hopes an adamantine° wall,   *impregnable*

2. At the Congress of Vienna in 1815, the nations that defeated Napoleon implemented a system of alliances to check the power of France. Reactionary regimes were installed throughout Europe; in France, the pre-Revolutionary Bourbon monarchy was restored.
3. The Greek goddess of wisdom and counsel in war, Pallas Athena, sprang fully formed from the head of Zeus, as Columbia, the figure of America, sprang from Britain.
4. Byron's admiration for George Washington was constant. He ended *Ode to Napoleon Buonaparte* (1814)

declaring him "the first—the last—the best / The Cincinnatus of the West, / Whom envy dared not hate, / Bequeath'd the name of Washington, / To make man blush there was but one!" Cincinnatus, a model of Republican virtue, left his plough in 458 B.C.E. to defend Rome; having succeeded, he resigned his command and returned to his farm.
5. The Roman festival of the god Saturn was a time of general license.

And the base pageant last upon the scene,
Are grown the pretext for the eternal thrall
Which nips life's tree, and dooms man's worst—his second fall.[6]

98

875   Yet, Freedom! yet thy banner, torn, but flying,
Streams like the thunder-storm *against* the wind;
Thy trumpet voice, though broken now and dying,
The loudest still the tempest leaves behind;
Thy tree hath lost its blossoms, and the rind,°   *bark*
Chopp'd by the axe, looks rough and little worth,
880   But the sap lasts, and still the seed we find
Sown deep, even in the bosom of the North;
So shall a better spring less bitter fruit bring forth.

[THE COLISEUM. THE DYING GLADIATOR]

139

And here the buzz of eager nations ran,
In murmured pity, or loud-roar'd applause,
1245   As man was slaughtered by his fellow man.[7]
And wherefore slaughtered? wherefore, but because
Such were the bloody Circus' genial laws,
And the imperial pleasure.—Wherefore not?
What matters where we fall to fill the maws°   *stomachs*
1250   Of worms—on battle-plains or listed spot?
Both are but theatres where the chief actors rot.

140

I see before me the Gladiator lie:
He leans upon his hand—his manly brow
Consents to death, but conquers agony,
1255   And his drooped head sinks gradually low—
And through his side the last drops, ebbing slow
From the red gash, fall heavy, one by one,
Like the first of a thunder-shower; and now
The arena swims around him—he is gone,
1260   Ere ceased the inhuman shout which hail'd the wretch who won.

141

He heard it, but he heeded not—his eyes
Were with his heart, and that was far away:

---

6. The "base pageant" is the Congress of Vienna; the concept of a second fall, repeating the eating of the apple by Adam and Eve, originates in St. Augustine.
7. This famous ruin was a vast amphitheater completed about 80 C.E., the site of gladiatorial combats in which prisoners of war or slaves fought to the death. Spectators could signal mercy to the defeated by waving handkerchiefs; turning thumbs down doomed the loser.

He reck'd not of the life he lost nor prize,
But where his rude° hut by the Danube lay,   *lowly*
1265   *There* were his young barbarians all at play,
    There was their Dacian mother[8]—he, their sire,
    Butcher'd to make a Roman holiday—
    All this rush'd with his blood—Shall he expire
And unavenged?—Arise! ye Goths,[9] and glut your ire!

142

1270   But here, where Murder breathed her bloody steam;
    And here, where buzzing nations choked the ways,
    And roar'd or murmur'd like a mountain stream
    Dashing or winding as its torrent strays;
    Here, where the Roman millions' blame or praise
1275   Was death or life, the playthings of a crowd,
    My voice sounds much—and fall the stars' faint rays
    On the arena void—seats crush'd—walls bow'd—
And galleries, where my steps seem echoes strangely loud.

143

    A ruin—yet what ruin! from its mass
1280   Walls, palaces, half-cities, have been rear'd;
    Yet oft the enormous skeleton ye pass
    And marvel where the spoil could have appeared.
    Hath it indeed been plundered, or but cleared?
    Alas! developed,° opens the decay,   *disclosed*
1285   When the colossal fabric's form is neared:
    It will not bear the brightness of the day,
Which streams too much on all years, man, have reft° away.   *ravaged*

144

    But when the rising moon begins to climb
    Its topmost arch, and gently pauses there;
1290   When the stars twinkle through the loops of time,
    And the low night-breeze waves along the air
    The garland forest, which the gray walls wear,
    Like laurels on the bald first Caesar's head;[1]
    When the light shines serene but doth not glare,
1295   Then in this magic circle raise the dead:
Heroes have trod this spot—'tis on their dust ye tread.

---

8. The Dacians, a people north of the Danube River in what is now Romania, harried the Romans until their defeat by the Emperor Trajan (101–107).
9. Germanic tribes who overran the Roman Empire in the 5th century. The stanza was inspired by the statue of a dying Gaul in the Capitoline Museum, in Byron's day thought to be a gladiator.
1. Roman historian Suetonius records that Julius Caesar was gratified by a decree of the Roman Senate that permitted him to wear a laurel wreath (an emblem of victory) at all times, because it hid his baldness.

145

"While stands the Coliseum, Rome shall stand;
When falls the Coliseum, Rome shall fall;
And when Rome falls—the World."[2] From our own land
Thus spake the pilgrims o'er this mighty wall
In Saxon times, which we are wont to call
Ancient;[3] and these three mortal things are still
On their foundations, and unaltered all;
Rome and her Ruin past Redemption's skill,
The World, the same wide den—of thieves, or what ye will.

[APOSTROPHE TO THE OCEAN. CONCLUSION]

178

There is a pleasure in the pathless woods,
There is a rapture on the lonely shore,
There is society, where none intrudes,
By the deep Sea, and music in its roar:
I love not Man the less, but Nature more,
From these our interviews, in which I steal
From all I may be, or have been before,
To mingle with the Universe, and feel
What I can ne'er express, yet can not all conceal.

179

Roll on, thou deep and dark blue ocean—roll!
Ten thousand fleets sweep over thee in vain;
Man marks the earth with ruin—his control
Stops with the shore;—upon the watery plain
The wrecks are all thy deed, nor doth remain
A shadow of man's ravage, save his own,
When, for a moment, like a drop of rain,
He sinks into thy depths with bubbling groan,
Without a grave, unknell'd, uncoffin'd, and unknown.

180

His steps are not upon thy paths,—thy fields
Are not a spoil for him,—thou dost arise
And shake him from thee; the vile strength he wields
For earth's destruction thou dost all despise,
Spurning him from thy bosom to the skies,
And send'st him, shivering in thy playful spray
And howling, to his Gods, where haply lies

---

2. A note by Byron cites Chapter 71 of *The Decline and Fall of the Roman Empire*, by Edward Gibbon (1737–1794), a work he had known since adolescence: "Reduced to its naked majesty, the Flavian amphitheatre was contemplated with awe and admiration by the pilgrims of the North: and their rude enthusiasm broke forth in a sublime proverbial expression, which is recorded in the eighth century in the fragments of the venerable Bede."

3. The Anglo-Saxon kingdoms in Britain, established following the withdrawal of the Romans in the 4th century, consolidated into one Saxon kingdom that lasted until the Norman Conquest of 1066.

His petty hope in some near port or bay,
1620   And dashest him again to earth:—there let him lay.[4]

181

The armaments which thunderstrike the walls
Of rock-built cities, bidding nations quake,
And monarchs tremble in their capitals,
The oak leviathans, whose huge ribs make
1625   Their clay creator the vain title take
Of lord of thee, and arbiter of war;[5]
These are thy toys, and, as the snowy flake,
They melt into thy yeast of waves, which mar
Alike the Armada's pride, or spoils of Trafalgar.[6]

182

1630   Thy shores are empires, changed in all save thee—
Assyria, Greece, Rome, Carthage, what are they?
Thy waters wasted them while they were free,
And many a tyrant since; their shores obey
The stranger, slave, or savage; their decay
1635   Has dried up realms to desarts:—not so thou,
Unchangeable save to thy wild waves' play—
Time writes no wrinkle on thine azure brow—
Such as creation's dawn beheld, thou rollest now.

183

Thou glorious mirror, where the Almighty's form
1640   Glasses itself in tempests; in all time,
Calm or convuls'd—in breeze, or gale, or storm,
Icing the pole, or in the torrid clime
Dark-heaving;—boundless, endless, and sublime—
The image of Eternity—the throne
1645   Of the Invisible; even from out thy slime
The monsters of the deep are made; each zone
Obeys thee; thou goest forth, dread, fathomless, alone.

184

And I have loved thee, Ocean! and my joy
Of youthful sports was on thy breast to be
1650   Borne, like thy bubbles, onward: from a boy
I wantoned with thy breakers—they to me
Were a delight; and if the freshening sea
Made them a terror—'twas a pleasing fear,

---

4. When his publisher's reader queried, "I have a doubt about *lay*" (instead of *lie*, perhaps the most famous solecism in English poetry), Byron replied: "So have I—but the *post* and *indolence* and *illness!*" He "manages his pen with the careless and negligent ease of a man of quality," Scott wrote of Byron; the nonchalant manner marked his aristocratic status.
5. The imagery is from the Book of Job: bemoaning his condition, Job acknowledges that God has made him "as the clay" (Job 10.9); God, showing his power, asks: "Canst thou draw out leviathan with a hook?" (41.1). The comparison of ships to this sea beast was familiar.
6. Storms severely damaged the Spanish fleet sent against England in 1588; a subsequent storm destroyed many of the ships taken as prizes in Admiral Nelson's victory over the French fleet at Trafalgar (1805).

For I was as it were a child of thee,
1655   And trusted to thy billows far and near,
And laid my hand upon thy mane—as I do here.

185

My task is done—my song hath ceased—my theme
Has died into an echo; it is fit
The spell should break of this protracted dream.
1660   The torch shall be extinguish'd which hath lit
My midnight lamp—and what is writ, is writ,—
Would it were worthier! but I am not now
That which I have been—and my visions flit
Less palpably before me—and the glow
1665 Which in my spirit dwelt is fluttering, faint, and low.

186

Farewell! a word that must be, and hath been—
A sound which makes us linger;—yet—farewell!
Ye! who have traced the Pilgrim to the scene
Which is his last, if in your memories dwell
1670   A thought which once was his, if on ye swell
A single recollection, not in vain
He wore his sandal-shoon, and scallop-shell;[7]
Farewell! with *him* alone may rest the pain,
If such there were—with *you*, the moral of his strain!

⁓

RESPONSES

John Wilson: from A review of *Childe Harold's Pilgrimage*[1]

It might, on a hasty consideration, seem to us, that such undisguised revelation of feelings and passions, which the becoming pride of human nature, jealous of its own dignity, would, in general, desire to hold in unviolated silence, could produce in the public mind only pity, sorrow, or repugnance. But, in the case of men of real genius, like Rousseau or Byron, it is otherwise. Each of us must have been aware in himself of a singular illusion, by which these disclosures, when read with that tender or high interest which attaches to poetry, seem to have something of the nature of private and confidential communications. They are not felt, while we read, as declarations published to the world,—but almost as secrets whispered to chosen ears. Who is there

---

7. The shell of a scallop found on the Mediterranean coast was formerly worn by pilgrims returned from the Holy Land.
1. Scotsman John Wilson (1785–1844), a staunch Tory, became Professor of Moral Philosophy at Edinburgh University in 1820, a position for which he had been recommended by Wordsworth, whose reputation Wilson had helped to establish. His fame rests on his irreverent contributions to *Blackwood's Magazine*, which he joined in 1817, under the pseudonym "Christopher North." "He is a perverse mortal—not to say worse of him," Wordsworth later declared. This unsigned review of *Childe Harold's Pilgrimage* appeared in *Edinburgh Review* in 1818. Of it Byron remarked, "Wilson's [is] the review of a poet, too, on another—his *idol*; for he likes me better than he chooses to avow to the public, with all his eulogy. I speak, judging only from the article, for I don't know him personally."

that feels, for a moment, that the voice which reaches the inmost recesses of his heart is speaking to the careless multitudes around him? Or, if we do so remember, the words seem to pass by others like air, and to find their way to the hearts for whom they were intended,—kindred and sympathizing spirits, who discern and own that secret language, of which the privacy is not violated, though spoken in hearing of the uninitiated,—because it is not understood. There is an unobserved beauty that smiles on us alone; and the more beautiful to us, because we feel as if chosen out from a crowd of lovers. * * *

But there are other reasons why we read with complacency writings which, by the most public declaration of most secret feelings, ought, it might seem, to shock and revolt our sympathy. A great poet may address the whole world in the language of intensest passion, concerning objects of which, rather than speak, face to face, with any one human being on earth, he would perish in his misery. For it is in solitude that he utters what is to be wafted by all the winds of heaven. There are, during his inspiration, present with him only the shadows of men. He is not daunted, or perplexed, or disturbed, or repelled by real living breathing features. He can updraw just as much as he chuses of the curtain that hangs between his own solitude and the world of life. He thus pours his soul out, partly to himself alone,—partly to the ideal abstractions, and impersonated images that float round him at his own conjuration,—and partly to human beings like himself, moving in the dark distance of the every-day world. He confesses himself, not before men, but before the Spirit of Humanity. And he thus fearlessly lays open his heart,—assured that nature never prompted unto genius that which will not triumphantly force its wide way into the human heart. We can thus easily imagine the poet whom, in real life, the countenances and voices of his fellow men might silence into shame, or fastidiousness, or timidity, or aversion or disdain,— yet kindling in his solitude into irrepressible passion and enthusiasm towards human nature and all its transitory concerns,—anxiously moulding himself into the object of men's most engrossing and vehement love or aversion,—identifying his own existence with all their strongest and profoundest passions,—claiming kindred with them, not in their virtues alone, but in their darkest vices and most fatal errors; yet, in the midst of all this, proudly guarding his own prevailing character, so that it shall not merge in the waves of a common nature, but stand "in shape and gesture proudly eminent,"[2] contemplated with still-increasing interest by the millions that, in spite of themselves, feel and acknowledge its strange and unaccountable ascendency.

John Scott:[1] from An article on Byron

Lord Byron's creations * * * are addressed to the poetical sympathies of his readers while their main interest is derived from awakening a recollection of some fact of the author's life, or a conviction of an analogy to the author's own character. A confusion is thus occasioned, in the breast of him whose attention is captivated by the productions in question, unfavourable altogether to right and pure feeling. The impression left on the mind, is neither strictly that of a work of art, to be pronounced upon according to the rules applicable to art,—nor of a matter-of-fact, appealing to

2. Milton's description of Satan (*Paradise Lost* 1.590).
1. John Scott, author of the lively travelogues *A Visit to Paris* (1814) and *Paris Revisited* (1815), edited *The London Magazine* in its most brilliant days. His attack on the irresponsibilities of the rival *Blackwood's* led

J. G. Lockhart, Walter Scott's son-in-law, to challenge him to a duel; the clumsy resolution of the quarrel prompted a counter-challenge from John Scott, who was then killed by a friend of Lockhart. This critique of Byron appeared in *The London Magazine* in 1821.

the principles of sound judgment in such cases;—but what is striking in poetry is made a set-off against what is objectionable in morals,—while that which would be condemned as false, theatrical, or inconsistent, according to laws of poetical criticism, is often rendered the most taking part of the whole composition by its evident connection with real and private circumstances, that are of a nature to tickle the idle, impertinent, and most unpoetical curiosity of the public.

DON JUAN   "Give me a poem," Byron's publisher John Murray wrote him in January 1817, "a good Venetian tale describing manners formerly from the story itself, and now from your own observations." The response was *Beppo*, which Byron based on an anecdote heard from the husband of his mistress, turning it into a seemingly effortless comparison of Italian and British manners. Its success led Murray to ask in July 1818: "Have you not another lively tale like *Beppo*? Or will you not give me some prose in three volumes?—all the adventures that you have undergone, seen, heard of, or imagined, with your reflections on life and manners." In the same week Byron had begun *Don Juan*; his own inclination consorted with the publisher's sketch of a suitable "work to open [his] campaign" for fall sales.

For a work of which he remarked "I *have* no plan—I *had* no plan—but I had or have materials," Byron found an ideal model in the seriocomic Italian romances of the fifteenth and sixteenth centuries by Pulci, Berni, and Ariosto. Their episodic, digressive mode, flexible enough to incorporate a wide range of moods and stylistic levels, enabled Byron to stage aspects of himself that had not appeared in the titanism of his Eastern tales and the loftiness of *Childe Harold's Pilgrimage*. He could treat public issues with the conversational fluency of a skeptical intelligence engaged with the ordinary materiality of the world: brand names and ship's pumps, indigestion and thinning hair, literary rivalries and reviewers. The story was a "hinge" on which to mount his reflections, and as the poem proceeds its title character retreats before the ceaseless inventions of the narrator, who both is and is not Byron. "If people contradict themselves," he wrote, "can I / Help contradicting them, and everybody, / Even my veracious self?" Truth's streams, he continued, "cut through such canals of contradiction, / That she must often navigate o'er fiction" (15.88). Such teasing of the borders between fiction and fact intrigued readers, and enhanced the allure of "Byron." *Don Juan* is a seemingly inexhaustible improvisatory monologue—sixteen cantos were published between 1819 and 1824, with a fragmentary seventeenth left uncompleted at Byron's death. Through a range of voices, by allusion and quotation, and in the number of perspectives entertained or denounced, the poem generates a sense of dialogue and exchange. As critic Jerome McGann has argued, the poem superimposes three historical levels: Juan's own late eighteenth century career; to Byron's years of fame in Regency London (1812–1816); and the post-Napoleonic moment of the actual writing (1818–1823). As it proceeds, *Don Juan* depicts Greek pirates and Turkish harems, Russian armies and Spanish families, British highwaymen and British aristocrats, story and commentary together building a critical portrait of the Europe of Byron's era, torn by revolution and now subsiding into the conservative restoration the poet condemns. Though he might have begun the poem intending only "to giggle and make giggle," Byron's purposes deepened as he advanced, often in opposition to his friends and publisher.

Byron intensifies the sense that he is speaking in *Don Juan*—forms of the first-person pronoun occur almost two thousand times—and he repeatedly reminds the reader of his capricious playing with form. The poem is personal in a more specific way as well. Readers familiar with Byron's life—and his celebrity had assured that many were—could perceive in Juan's mother, Donna Inez, a caricature of Byron's estranged wife Lady Byron. The account of Juan's youth with Inez also draws on Byron's childhood, "an only son left with an only mother" (1.37). Like Wordsworth's *Prelude*, *Don Juan* is autobiography—but in the form of oblique and theatricalized fiction. It is also picaresque adventure, satire, and mock-Homeric epic, whose hero belies the legacy of his name, seduced more often than seducing, kindhearted rather than ruthless and conniving. As Byron's rhymes make clear (*Juan* rhymes with *new one*), this half-Englished modern hero is not the legendary Don Juan. Byron's genre-crossing revision of literary tradition made "something wholly new & relative to the age," as Shelley recognized.

Much of the poem's power arises from Byron's fluent handling of the ottava rima stanza, rhyming *abababcc*. He credited *The Monks and the Giants* (1817) by his friend John Hookham Frere for the inspiration, but Frere's work shows little of Byron's deftness. Byron employed a fantastic wealth of rhymes ("Plato" with "potato," "intellectual" with "hen-peck'd you all"), often emphasizing the snap of the concluding couplet for comic surprise; he could also downplay the rhymes and enjamb lines to yield a rhythm like blank verse. "The most readable poem of its length ever written," Virginia Woolf marveled, because its "method is a discovery by itself...an elastic shape which will hold whatever you choose to put in it." "Like all free and easy things," she added, "only the skilled and mature really bring them off successfully. But Byron was full of ideas—a quality that gives his verse a toughness." The rare combination of ease and power to which both Shelley and Woolf point keeps *Don Juan* subversively fresh today.

from DON JUAN

Dedication[1]

1

Bob Southey! You're a poet, Poet-laureate,[2]
    And representative of all the race,
Although 'tis true that you turn'd out a Tory at
    Last,—yours has lately been a common case,—
5   And now, my Epic Renegade! what are ye at?
    With all the Lakers,[3] in and out of place?
A nest of tuneful persons, to my eye
Like "four and twenty Blackbirds in a pye;[4]

2

"Which pye being open'd they began to sing"
10   (This old song and new simile holds good),
"A dainty dish to set before the King,"
    Or Regent, who admires such kind of food;—
And Coleridge, too, has lately taken wing,
    But like a hawk encumber'd with his hood,—
15   Explaining metaphysics to the nation—
I wish he would explain his Explanation.[5]

1. Byron sent the dedication to his publisher in November 1818 with Canto 1. When Cantos 1 and 2 were published together, anonymously, in 1819, Byron removed the dedication because he did not want "to attack the dog [Southey] so fiercely without putting my name." It appeared for the first time in the 1832–1833 edition of Byron's works. Southey was still Poet Laureate.
2. Southey became Poet Laureate in 1813, and earned Byron's contempt, not only for abandoning the republican principles of his youth but also for his malicious gossip in 1816 about Byron, Shelley, Claire Clairmont, and Mary Shelley: "The Son of a Bitch...said that Shelley and I 'had formed a League of Incest and practiced

our precepts with &c'." The phrase "Epic Renegade" (5) glances both at Southey's political reversal and his series of epic poems such as *Thalaba* (1801) and *The Curse of Kehama* (1810). For Southey's attack on "the Satanic School" see page 762.
3. Applied by the *Edinburgh Review* to Coleridge, Southey, and Wordsworth, from their common residence in the Lake District.
4. Henry James Pye (1745–1813), Poet Laureate before Southey; his first official ode had provoked the nursery-rhyme parody Byron repeats here.
5. *The Statesman's Manual* (1816) and *Biographia Literaria* (1817).

3

You, Bob! are rather insolent, you know,
    At being disappointed in your wish
To supersede all warblers here below,
      And be the only Blackbird in the dish;
And then you overstrain yourself, or so,
    And tumble downward like the flying fish
Gasping on deck, because you soar too high, Bob,
And fall, for lack of moisture quite a-dry, Bob![6]

4

And Wordsworth, in a rather long "Excursion"[7]
    (I think the quarto holds five hundred pages),
Has given a sample from the vasty version
    Of his new system to perplex the sages;
'Tis poetry—at least by his assertion,
      And may appear so when the dog-star rages—
And he who understands it would be able
To add a story to the Tower of Babel.[8]

5

You—Gentlemen! by dint of long seclusion
    From better company, have kept your own
At Keswick,[9] and, through still continued fusion
    Of one another's minds, at last have grown
To deem as a most logical conclusion,
    That Poesy has wreaths for you alone:
There is a narrowness in such a notion,
Which makes me wish you'd change your lakes for ocean.

6

I would not imitate the petty thought,
    Nor coin my self-love to so base a vice,
For all the glory your conversion brought,
    Since gold alone should not have been its price.
You have your salary; was't for that you wrought?
    And Wordsworth has his place in the Excise.[1]
You're shabby fellows—true—but poets still,
And duly seated on the immortal hill.°   *Parnassus*

7

Your bays° may hide the baldness of your brows[2]—   *laurel wreaths*
    Perhaps some virtuous blushes;—let them go—
To you I envy neither fruit nor boughs—
    And for the fame you would engross below,

---

6. A "dry bob" was slang for sex without ejaculation.
7. This nine-book poem appeared in 1814.
8. To punish human presumption, God destroys the Tower of Babel and institutes the multiplicity of languages (Genesis 11.1–9); note the pun on "story."
9. Southey's home, where the Coleridges moved in 1800;

Wordsworth lived nearby in Grasmere.
1. In March 1813 Wordsworth obtained a sinecure as distributor of tax stamps for Westmoreland through the aid of his patron, the Earl of Lonsdale, to whom he dedicated *The Excursion*.
2. See *Childe Harold* 4.144 (page 776).

The field is universal, and allows
    Scope to all such as feel the inherent glow:
55 Scott, Rogers, Campbell, Moore, and Crabbe,[3] will try
    'Gainst you the question with posterity.

8

For me, who, wandering with pedestrian Muses,
    Contend not with you on the winged steed,[4]
I wish your fate may yield ye, when she chooses,
60   The fame you envy, and the skill you need;
And recollect a poet nothing loses
    In giving to his brethren their full meed°   *reward*
Of merit, and complaint of present days
Is not the certain path to future praise.

9

65 He that reserves his laurels for posterity
    (Who does not often claim the bright reversion)
Has generally no great crop to spare it, he
    Being only injured by his own assertion;
And although here and there some glorious rarity
70   Arise like Titan from the sea's immersion,
The major part of such appellants go
To—God knows where—for no one else can know.

10

If, fallen in evil days on evil tongues,
    Milton appeal'd to the Avenger, Time,[5]
75 If Time, the Avenger, execrates his wrongs,
    And makes the word "Miltonic" mean "*sublime*,"
He deign'd not to belie his soul in songs,
    Nor turn his very talent to a crime;
He did not loathe the Sire to laud the Son,
80 But closed the tyrant-hater he begun.[6]

11

Think'st thou, could he—the blind Old Man—arise
    Like Samuel from the grave, to freeze once more
The blood of monarchs with his prophecies,[7]
    Or be alive again—again all hoar
85   With time and trials, and those helpless eyes,

3. In ranking the living poets in an 1813 journal, Byron declared Walter Scott the "Monarch of Parnassus," Samuel Rogers (1763–1855) next, Thomas Moore (1779–1852) and Thomas Campbell (1777–1844) third, "Southey-Wordsworth-Coleridge" below these. George Crabbe (1754–1832) he elsewhere praised for being "free" of the "wrong revolutionary poetical system" that he and his contemporaries exemplified: "and if I had to begin again—I would model myself accordingly—Crabbe's the man."
4. The "musa pedestris" of Latin poet Horace (65–8 B.C.E.) signals a humble, as opposed to exalted or epic,

style (*Satires* 2.6.17). The winged horse Pegasus is an old symbol of poetic imagination.
5. Milton's self-description in Book 7 of *Paradise Lost*: "On evil days though fall'n, and evil tongues" (26).
6. A supporter of the Commonwealth party that overthrew Charles I in 1649, Milton held to principle and did not praise Charles II after the Restoration in 1660.
7. King Saul, attacked by the Philistines, raises the ghost of the prophet Samuel to ask advice, only to learn that he has disobeyed the Lord and will be delivered to the enemy (1 Samuel 28).

And heartless daughters[8]—worn—and pale—and poor;
    Would *he* adore a sultan? *he* obey
The intellectual eunuch Castlereagh?[9]

12

Cold-blooded, smooth-faced, placid miscreant!
    Dabbling its sleek young hands in Erin's° gore,   *Ireland's*
And thus for wider carnage taught to pant,
    Transferr'd to gorge upon a sister shore,
The vulgarest tool that Tyranny could want,
    With just enough of talent, and no more,
To lengthen fetters by another fix'd,
And offer poison long already mix'd.[1]

13

An orator of such set trash of phrase
    Ineffably—legitimately vile,[2]
That even its grossest flatterers dare not praise,
    Nor foes—all nations—condescend to smile,—
Not even a sprightly blunder's spark can blaze
    From that Ixion grindstone's ceaseless toil,[3]
That turns and turns to give the world a notion
Of endless torments and perpetual motion.

14

A bungler even in its disgusting trade,
    And botching, patching, leaving still behind
Something of which its masters are afraid,
    States to be curb'd, and thoughts to be confined,
Conspiracy or Congress to be made[4]—
    Cobbling at manacles for all mankind—
A tinkering slave-maker, who mends old chains,
With God and man's abhorrence for its gains.

15

If we may judge of matter by the mind,
    Emasculated to the marrow *It*
Hath but two objects, how to serve, and bind,
    Deeming the chain it wears even men may fit,

---

8. Milton's two elder daughters are said to have robbed him of his books, besides cheating and plaguing him in the economy of his house [Byron's note].

9. Irish nobleman Robert Stewart, Viscount Castlereagh, as chief secretary for Ireland (1799–1801), suppressed the Irish rebellion and secured the Act of Union with England that ended the Irish Parliament. As British Foreign Secretary (1812–1822), he was instrumental in arranging the balance of power in post-Napoleonic Europe, for which he was detested by Byron and the liberals.

1. His opponents regarded Castlereagh as the pawn of the Austrian foreign minister, Prince Metternich.

2. Castlereagh's poor speaking was notorious: "It is the first time indeed since the Normans," Byron wrote in the preface to Cantos 6–8, "that England has been insulted by a *Minister* (at least) who could not speak English, and that Parliament permitted itself to be dictated to in the language of Mrs. Malaprop" [the character from R. B. Sheridan's *The Rivals* (1773) who has given her name to verbal slips].

3. In Greek mythology Ixion is punished in Hades by being chained to a perpetually rolling wheel.

4. In 1814 Austria, Russia, Prussia, and England formed the Quadruple Alliance; after the fall of Napoleon, Castlereagh and Metternich reestablished the "legitimate" governments of Europe at the Congress of Vienna (1815), restoring the Bourbons in France and acknowledging Ferdinand VII in Spain.

Eutropius[5] of its many masters,—blind
     To worth as freedom, wisdom as to wit,
Fearless—because *no* feeling dwells in ice,
120   Its very courage stagnates to a vice.

16

Where shall I turn me not to *view* its bonds,
     For I will never *feel* them;—Italy!
Thy late reviving Roman soul desponds
     Beneath the lie this State-thing breathed o'er thee—
125   Thy clanking chain, and Erin's yet green wounds,
     Have voices—tongues to cry aloud for me.
Europe has slaves—allies—kings—armies still,
And Southey lives to sing them very ill.

17

Meantime—Sir Laureate—I proceed to dedicate,
130   In honest simple verse, this song to you.
And, if in flattering strains I do not predicate,
     'Tis that I still retain my "buff and blue";[6]
My politics as yet are all to educate:
     Apostasy's so fashionable, too,
135   To keep *one* creed's a task grown quite Herculean;
Is it not so, my Tory, ultra-Julian?[7]

Canto 1

1

I want a hero: an uncommon want,
     When every year and month sends forth a new one,
Till, after cloying the gazettes with cant,
     The age discovers he is not the true one;
5   Of such as these I should not care to vaunt,
     I'll therefore take our ancient friend Don Juan—
We all have seen him, in the pantomime,
Sent to the devil somewhat ere his time.[1]

2

Vernon, the butcher Cumberland, Wolfe, Hawke,
10   Prince Ferdinand, Granby, Burgoyne, Keppel, Howe,[2]

---

5. The career of Eutropius, a eunuch who became a
magistrate and general in the Eastern Roman Empire
(395–408), is narrated by Gibbon, *Decline and Fall* (ch.
32). Byron's denunciation of Castlereagh as a "eunuch"
and an "It" may hint at private knowledge. Castlereagh's
suicide in 1822, officially attributed to overwork, was preceded by an attempt to blackmail him on the grounds of
homosexuality: sodomy was a capital crime.
6. Colors adopted by the Whigs and by the *Edinburgh
Review*.
7. Julian was raised as a Christian, but on becoming
Roman emperor in 361 he revived the worship of the

pagan gods. He was killed in battle in 363. See Gibbon,
Decline and Fall, ch. 23.
1. Popular melodrama portrayed Don Juan as a seducer
who ends in hell; Byron plays against his own reputation
as notorious lover by presenting Juan as an innocent boy
overwhelmed by women. "Juan" is Anglicized into two syllables, as the rhymes with "true one" and "new one" indicate. "Inez" rhymes with "fine as" and "Jóse" with "nosey."
2. Recent military heroes. The Duke of Cumberland
defeated the Stuart army in 1745; he earned the title
"Butcher" for his subsequent suppression of Jacobitism in
Scotland.

Evil and good, have had their tithe of talk,
  And fill'd their sign-posts then, like Wellesley now;[3]
Each in their turn like Banquo's monarchs stalk,
  Followers of fame, "nine farrow" of that sow:[4]
15 France, too, had Buonaparté and Dumourier
  Recorded in the Moniteur and Courier.[5]

3

Barnave, Brissot, Condorcet, Mirabeau,
  Petion, Clootz, Danton, Marat, La Fayette,[6]
Were French, and famous people, as we know;
20 And there were others, scarce forgotten yet,
Joubert, Hoche, Marceau, Lannes, Desaix, Moreau,
  With many of the military set,
Exceedingly remarkable at times,
But not at all adapted to my rhymes.

4

25 Nelson was once Britannia's god of war,
  And still should be so, but the tide is turn'd;
There's no more to be said of Trafalgar
  'Tis with our hero quietly inurn'd;[7]
Because the army's grown more popular,
30 At which the naval people are concern'd;
Besides, the prince is all for the land-service,
Forgetting Duncan, Nelson, Howe, and Jervis.[8]

5

Brave men were living before Agamemnon[9]
  And since, exceeding valorous and sage,
35 A good deal like him too, though quite the same none;
  But then they shone not on the poet's page,
And so have been forgotten:—I condemn none,
  But can't find any in the present age
Fit for my poem (that is, for my new one);
40 So, as I said, I'll take my friend Don Juan.

---

3. Arthur Wellesley, Duke of Wellington, born in Ireland, the most celebrated British general of his time. Granted a peerage for his victory over the French at Talavera (1808), he led the British forces at Waterloo.
4. In Shakespeare's *Macbeth* (4.1), the witches show Macbeth a vision of future Scots kings descended from the murdered Banquo, establishing the triumph of his line and the frustration of Macbeth's ambitions.
5. Charles Dumouriez was a French general and Girondist (moderate); suspected by the Jacobins in 1793, he fled to the Austrians whom he had defeated the year before. He settled in England in 1804, and advised the British in their war against Buonaparte. The *Moniteur* and *Courier* were French newspapers.

6. All figures of the French Revolution. Jean Baptiste, Baron von Cloots, a zealot, dropped his title and took the pseudonym Anacharsis; elected to the Convention in 1792, he voted for the King's death and was himself executed in 1794. Byron wrote that he meant Juan "to finish as *Anacharsis Cloots*—in the French Revolution."
7. Admiral Horatio Nelson died in the Battle of Trafalgar (1805) at which he defeated the French fleet.
8. Byron plays the four distinguished British admirals against the Regent's support of the army.
9. An adaptation of Horace (*Odes* 4.9.25–28): "Many heroes lived before Agamemnon; but all are overwhelmed in unending night, unwept, unknown, because they lacked a sacred bard" (trans. by C. E. Bennett).

6

Most epic poets plunge "in medias res"
   (Horace makes this the heroic turnpike road),[1]
And then your hero tells, whene'er you please,
   What went before—by way of episode,
45   While seated after dinner at his ease,
     Beside his mistress in some soft abode,
Palace, or garden, paradise, or cavern,
Which serves the happy couple for a tavern.

7

That is the usual method, but not mine—
50   —My way is to begin with the beginning;
The regularity of my design
   Forbids all wandering as the worst of sinning,[2]
And therefore I shall open with a line
   (Although it cost me half an hour in spinning)
55 Narrating somewhat of Don Juan's father,
And also of his mother, if you'd rather.

8

In Seville was he born, a pleasant city,
   Famous for oranges and women—he
Who has not seen it will be much to pity,
60   So says the proverb—and I quite agree;
Of all the Spanish towns is none more pretty,
   Cadiz perhaps—but that you soon may see:—
Don Juan's parents lived beside the river,
A noble stream, and call'd the Guadalquivir.

9

65 His father's name was Jóse—*Don*, of course,
   A true Hidalgo,° free from every stain   *nobleman*
Of Moor or Hebrew blood, he traced his source
   Through the most Gothic gentlemen of Spain;
A better cavalier ne'er mounted horse,
70   Or, being mounted, e'er got down again,
Than Jóse, who begot our hero, who
Begot—but that's to come————Well, to renew:

10

His mother was a learned lady, famed
   For every branch of every science known—
75 In every Christian language ever named,
     With virtues equall'd by her wit alone,
She made the cleverest people quite ashamed,
     And even the good with inward envy groan,
Finding themselves so very much exceeded
80   In their own way by all the things that she did.

---

1. In *Ars Poetica* Horace recommends that the epic poet begin dramatically, like Homer, by taking the audience directly "into the midst of things."

2. That is, digression, literally "off the path." The Latin word for "wandering," *erratus*, also means "sinning."

11

Her memory was a mine: she knew by heart
  All Calderon and greater part of Lopé,[3]
So that if any actor miss'd his part
  She could have served him for the prompter's copy;
85 For her Feinagle's were an useless art,[4]
  And he himself obliged to shut up shop—he
Could never make a memory so fine as
That which adorn'd the brain of Donna Inez.

12

Her favourite science was the mathematical,
90 Her noblest virtue was her magnanimity,
Her wit (she sometimes tried at wit) was Attic° all,   *refined*
  Her serious sayings darken'd to sublimity;
In short, in all things she was fairly what I call
  A prodigy—her morning dress was dimity,°   *plain cotton*
95 Her evening silk, or, in the summer, muslin,
And other stuffs, with which I won't stay puzzling.

13

She knew the Latin—that is, "the Lord's prayer,"
  And Greek—the alphabet—I'm nearly sure;
She read some French romances here and there,
100 Although her mode of speaking was not pure;
For native Spanish she had no great care,
  At least her conversation was obscure;
Her thoughts were theorems, her words a problem,
As if she deem'd that mystery would ennoble 'em.

14

105 She liked the English and the Hebrew tongue,
  And said there was analogy between 'em;
She proved it somehow out of sacred song,
  But I must leave the proofs to those who've seen 'em,
But this I heard her say, and can't be wrong,
110 And all may think which way their judgments lean 'em,
"'Tis strange—the Hebrew noun which means 'I am,'[5]
The English always use to govern d—n."

15

Some women use their tongues—she *look'd* a lecture,
  Each eye a sermon, and her brow a homily,
115 An all-in-all-sufficient self-director,
  Like the lamented late Sir Samuel Romilly,
The Law's expounder, and the State's corrector,
  Whose suicide was almost an anomaly—

3. Pedro Calderón de la Barca (1600–1681) and Lope de Vega (1562–1635), Spanish dramatists.
4. In 1812 Gregor von Feinagle lectured on mnemonics,

under bluestocking patronage.
5. "God," *Yahweh* in Hebrew, which God renders to Moses as "I AM THAT I AM" (Exodus 3.14).

One sad example more, that "All is vanity,"—
120   (The jury brought their verdict in "Insanity.")[6]

16

In short, she was a walking calculation,
    Miss Edgeworth's novels stepping from their covers,
Or Mrs. Trimmer's books on education,
    Or "Cœlebs' Wife" set out in quest of lovers,[7]
125   Morality's prim personification,
    In which not Envy's self a flaw discovers;
To others' share let "female errors fall,"[8]
For she had not even one—the worst of all.

17

Oh! she was perfect past all parallel—
130   Of any modern female saint's comparison;
So far above the cunning powers of hell,
    Her guardian angel had given up his garrison;
Even her minutest motions went as well
    As those of the best time-piece made by Harrison:[9]
135   In virtues nothing earthly could surpass her,
Save thine "incomparable oil," Macassar![1]

18

Perfect she was, but as perfection is
    Insipid in this naughty world of ours,
Where our first parents never learn'd to kiss
140   Till they were exiled from their earlier bowers,
Where all was peace, and innocence, and bliss
    (I wonder how they got through the twelve hours)
Don Jóse, like a lineal son of Eve,
Went plucking various fruit without her leave.

19

145   He was a mortal of the careless kind,
    With no great love for learning, or the learn'd,
Who chose to go where'er he had a mind,
    And never dream'd his lady was concern'd;
The world, as usual, wickedly inclined
150   To see a kingdom or a house o'erturn'd,
Whisper'd he had a mistress, some said *two*,
But for domestic quarrels *one* will do.

6. Romilly (1757–1818), a liberal member of Parliament, accepted a retainer to represent Byron in the separation proceedings but then switched to Lady Byron. Even his suicide did not soften Byron's resentment; Murray refused to print this stanza in the first edition. It was not printed until after 1822. "All is vanity" (emptiness) is the Preacher's refrain in Ecclesiastes.
7. Maria Edgeworth was a popular Irish novelist and educational writer; Sarah Trimmer (1741–1810) was a popular writer on education and of children's books. Cœlebs

in Search of a Wife (1809)—its title deliberately distorted by Byron—was the only, but quite successful novel of Hannah More, for whom see page 152.
8. Alexander Pope, *The Rape of the Lock* (1714), 2.17.
9. In 1762 English clockmaker John Harrison claimed the government prize of £20,000 for a chronometer able to determine longitude. In 1812 Byron satirized Miss Milbanke (his wife to be) as "my Princess of Parallelograms."
1. Byron cites the advertisements of the firm A. Rowland and Son for their widely used hair oil.

20

Now Donna Inez had, with all her merit,
    A great opinion of her own good qualities;
155   Neglect, indeed, requires a saint to bear it,
    And such, indeed, she was in her moralities;
But then she had a devil of a spirit,
    And sometimes mix'd up fancies with realities,
And let few opportunities escape
160   Of getting her liege lord into a scrape.

21

This was an easy matter with a man
    Oft in the wrong, and never on his guard;
And even the wisest, do the best they can,
    Have moments, hours, and days, so unprepared,
165   That you might "brain them with their lady's fan";[2]
    And sometimes ladies hit exceeding hard,
And fans turn into falchions° in fair hands,   *swords*
And why and wherefore no one understands.

22

'Tis pity learned virgins ever wed
170   With persons of no sort of education,
Or gentlemen, who, though well born and bred,
    Grow tired of scientific conversation:
I don't choose to say much upon this head,
    I'm a plain man, and in a single station,
175   But—Oh! ye lords of ladies intellectual,
Inform us truly, have they not hen-peck'd you all?

23

Don Jóse and his lady quarrell'd—*why*,
    Not any of the many could divine,
Though several thousand people chose to try,
180   'Twas surely no concern of theirs nor mine;
I loathe that low vice—curiosity;
    But if there's any thing in which I shine,
'Tis in arranging all my friends' affairs,
Not having, of my own, domestic cares.

24

185   And so I interfered, and with the best
    Intentions, but their treatment was not kind;
I think the foolish people were possess'd,
    For neither of them could I ever find,
Although their porter afterwards confess'd—
190   But that's no matter, and the worst's behind,
For little Juan o'er me threw, down stairs,
A pail of housemaid's water unawares.

2. Shakespeare, *1 Henry IV*, 2.3.23.

25

A little curly-headed, good-for-nothing,
    And mischief-making monkey from his birth;
195 His parents ne'er agreed except in doting
    Upon the most unquiet imp on earth;
Instead of quarrelling, had they been but both in
    Their senses, they'd have sent young master forth
To school, or had him soundly whipp'd at home,
200 To teach him manners for the time to come.

26

Don Jóse and the Donna Inez led
    For some time an unhappy sort of life,
Wishing each other, not divorced, but dead;
    They lived respectably as man and wife,
205 Their conduct was exceedingly well-bred,
    And gave no outward signs of inward strife,
Until at length the smother'd fire broke out,
And put the business past all kind of doubt.

27

For Inez call'd some druggists, and physicians,
210   And tried to prove her loving lord was *mad*,[3]
But as he had some lucid intermissions,
    She next decided he was only *bad*;
Yet when they ask'd her for her depositions,
    No sort of explanation could be had,
215 Save that her duty both to man and God
Required this conduct—which seem'd very odd.

28

She kept a journal, where his faults were noted,
    And open'd certain trunks of books and letters,
All which might, if occasion served, be quoted;
220   And then she had all Seville for abettors,
Besides her good old grandmother (who doted);
    The hearers of her case became repeaters,
Then advocates, inquisitors, and judges,
Some for amusement, others for old grudges.

29

225 And then this best and meekest woman bore
    With such serenity her husband's woes,
Just as the Spartan ladies did of yore,
    Who saw their spouses kill'd, and nobly chose
Never to say a word about them more—
230   Calmly she heard each calumny that rose,
And saw *his* agonies with such sublimity,
That all the world exclaim'd, "What magnanimity!"

---

3. As Byron believed Lady Byron had tried to do; stanzas 27 and 28 replay details of their separation.

30

No doubt this patience, when the world is damning us,
    Is philosophic in our former friends;
235 'Tis also pleasant to be deem'd magnanimous,
    The more so in obtaining our own ends;
And what the lawyers call a *"malus animus"*°   *ill will*
    Conduct like this by no means comprehends:
Revenge in person's certainly no virtue,
240 But then 'tis not *my* fault, if *others* hurt you.

31

And if our quarrels should rip up old stories,
    And help them with a lie or two additional,
I'm not to blame, as you well know—no more is
    Any one else—they were become traditional;
245 Besides, their resurrection aids our glories
    By contrast, which is what we just were wishing all:
And science profits by this resurrection—
Dead scandals form good subjects for dissection.

32

Their friends had tried at reconciliation,
250   Then their relations, who made matters worse.
('Twere hard to tell upon a like occasion
    To whom it may be best to have recourse—
I can't say much for friend or yet relation):
    The lawyers did their utmost for divorce,
255 But scarce a fee was paid on either side
Before, unluckily, Don Jóse died.

33

He died: and most unluckily, because,
    According to all hints I could collect
From counsel learned in those kinds of laws,
260   (Although their talk's obscure and circumspect)
His death contrived to spoil a charming cause;
    A thousand pities also with respect
To public feeling, which on this occasion
Was manifested in a great sensation.

34

265 But ah! he died; and buried with him lay
    The public feeling and the lawyers' fees:
His house was sold, his servants sent away,
    A Jew took one of his two mistresses,
A priest the other—at least so they say:
270   I ask'd the doctors after his disease—
He died of the slow fever call'd the tertian,°   *malaria*
And left his widow to her own aversion.

35

Yet Jóse was an honourable man,[4]
   That I must say, who knew him very well;
275 Therefore his frailties I'll no further scan,
   Indeed there were not many more to tell:
And if his passions now and then outran
   Discretion, and were not so peaceable
   As Numa's (who was also named Pompilius),[5]
280 He had been ill brought up, and was born bilious.

36

Whate'er might be his worthlessness or worth,
   Poor fellow! he had many things to wound him.
Let's own—since it can do no good on earth—
   It was a trying moment that which found him
285 Standing alone beside his desolate hearth,
   Where all his household gods lay shiver'd round him
No choice was left his feelings or his pride,
   Save death or Doctors' Commons[6]—so he died.

37

Dying intestate,° Juan was sole heir   *without a will*
290 To a chancery suit, and messuages,° and lands,   *houses*
Which, with a long minority and care,
   Promised to turn out well in proper hands:
Inez became sole guardian, which was fair,
   And answer'd but to nature's just demands;
295 An only son left with an only mother
Is brought up much more wisely than another.

38

Sagest of women, even of widows, she
   Resolved that Juan should be quite a paragon,
And worthy of the noblest pedigree:
300   (His sire was of Castile, his dam from Aragon.)
Then for accomplishments of chivalry,
   In case our lord the king should go to war again,
He learn'd the arts of riding, fencing, gunnery,
   And how to scale a fortress—or a nunnery.

39

305 But that which Donna Inez most desired,
   And saw into herself each day before all
The learned tutors whom for him she hired,
   Was, that his breeding should be strictly moral:
Much into all his studies she enquired,
310   And so they were submitted first to her, all,

---

4. Parodying Marc Antony's ironic praise of assassin Brutus at Caesar's funeral (*Julius Caesar* 3.2.84).
5. The second king of Rome, renowned for his piety.

6. The court that presided over divorces; Chancery presided over inheritance.

Arts, sciences, no branch was made a mystery
To Juan's eyes, excepting natural history.

40

The languages, especially the dead,
    The sciences, and most of all the abstruse,
315 The arts, at least all such as could be said
    To be the most remote from common use,
In all these he was much and deeply read;
    But not a page of any thing that's loose,
    Or hints continuation of the species,
320 Was ever suffer'd, lest he should grow vicious.

41

His classic studies made a little puzzle,
    Because of filthy loves of gods and goddesses,
Who in the earlier ages raised a bustle,
    But never put on pantaloons or bodices;
325 His reverend tutors had at times a tussle,
    And for their Aeneids, Iliads, and Odysseys,
Were forced to make an odd sort of apology,
For Donna Inez dreaded the Mythology.

42

Ovid's a rake, as half his verses show him,
330   Anacreon's morals are a still worse sample,
Catullus scarcely has a decent poem,
    I don't think Sappho's Ode a good example,
Although Longinus tells us there is no hymn
    Where the sublime soars forth on wings more ample;
335 But Virgil's songs are pure, except that horrid one
Beginning with "Formosum Pastor Corydon."[7]

43

Lucretius' irreligion is too strong
    For early stomachs, to prove wholesome food;
I can't help thinking Juvenal was wrong,
340   Although no doubt his real intent was good,
For speaking out so plainly in his song,
    So much indeed as to be downright rude;
And then what proper person can be partial
To all those nauseous epigrams of Martial?[8]

---

7. All erotic poets: the Roman Ovid (43 B.C.E.–18 C.E.), author of the *Amores* and *The Art of Love*; Anacreon, 6th-century B.C.E.; Catullus (c. 84–54 B.C.E.); Sappho, 7th-century B.C.E. Greek poet; her ode beginning "To me he seems like a god / as he sits facing you" (trans. by Willis Barnstone) was praised by Longinus in his essay *On the Sublime* (1st century B.C.E.). The second Eclogue of Virgil (70–19 B.C.E.), is homoerotic: "Corydon the shepherd burned for lovely Alexis, / His master's beloved."
8. *De Rerum Natura* ("On the Nature of Things"), by 1st-century B.C.E. Roman poet Lucretius, argues a materialistic view of the world; the 16 satires of Juvenal (60–130 C.E.) sternly denounce Roman society; the epigrams of Martial (40–104 C.E.) are witty but often blunt.

44

345 Juan was taught from out the best edition,
       Expurgated by learned men, who place,
     Judiciously, from out the schoolboy's vision,
       The grosser parts; but fearful to deface
     Too much their modest bard by this omission,
350   And pitying sore his mutilated case,
     They only add them all in an appendix,
     Which saves, in fact, the trouble of an index;[9]

45

     For there we have them all "at one fell swoop,"
       Instead of being scatter'd through the pages;
355 They stand forth marshall'd in a handsome troop,
       To meet the ingenuous youth of future ages,
     Till some less rigid editor shall stoop
       To call them back into their separate cages,
     Instead of standing staring altogether,
360 Like garden gods—and not so decent either.

46

     The Missal too (it was the family Missal)
       Was ornamented in a sort of way
     Which ancient mass-books often are, and this all
       Kinds of grotesques illumined; and how they,
365 Who saw those figures on the margin kiss all,
       Could turn their optics to the text and pray,
     Is more than I know—but Don Juan's mother
     Kept this herself, and gave her son another.

47

     Sermons he read, and lectures he endured,
370   And homilies, and lives of all the saints;
     To Jerome and to Chrysostom inured,[1]
       He did not take such studies for restraints;
     But how faith is acquired, and then ensured,
       So well not one of the aforesaid paints
375 As Saint Augustine in his fine Confessions,
     Which make the reader envy his transgressions.[2]

48

     This, too, was a seal'd book to little Juan—
       I can't but say that his mamma was right,
     If such an education was the true one.
380   She scarcely trusted him from out her sight;
     Her maids were old, and if she took a new one,

9. Fact. There is, or was, such an edition, with all the obnoxious epigrams of Martial placed by themselves at the end [Byron's note].
1. St. Jerome (340–420), translator of the Vulgate, and St. John Chrysostom (c. 345–407) were famous ascetics.
2. Augustine's Confessions (397–398) describes his life in Carthage, "a hissing cauldron of lust," before his conversion to Christianity.

You might be sure she was a perfect fright,
She did this during even her husband's life—
I recommend as much to every wife.

49

385 Young Juan wax'd in goodliness and grace;
    At six a charming child, and at eleven
With all the promise of as fine a face
    As e'er to man's maturer growth was given:
He studied steadily, and grew apace,
390   And seem'd, at least, in the right road to heaven,
For half his days were pass'd at church, the other
Between his tutors, confessor, and mother.

50

    At six, I said, he was a charming child,
    At twelve he was a fine, but quiet boy;
395 Although in infancy a little wild,
    They tamed him down amongst them: to destroy
His natural spirit not in vain they toil'd.
    At least it seem'd so; and his mother's joy
Was to declare how sage, and still, and steady,
400 Her young philosopher was grown already.

51

I had my doubts, perhaps I have them still,
    But what I say is neither here nor there:
I knew his father well, and have some skill
    In character—but it would not be fair
405 From sire to son to augur good or ill:
    He and his wife were an ill-sorted pair—
But scandal's my aversion—I protest
Against all evil speaking, even in jest.

52

For my part I say nothing—nothing—but
410   *This* I will say—my reasons are my own—
That if I had an only son to put
    To school (as God be praised that I have none),
'Tis not with Donna Inez I would shut
    Him up to learn his catechism alone,
415 No—no—I'd send him out betimes to college,
For there it was I pick'd up my own knowledge.

53

For there one learns—'tis not for me to boast,
    Though I acquired—but I pass over *that*,
As well as all the Greek I since have lost:
420   I say that there's the place—but "*Verbum sat*,"[3]

---

3. Proverbial: "A word to the wise suffices."

I think I pick'd up too, as well as most,
　　Knowledge of matters—but no matter *what*—
I never married—but, I think, I know
That sons should not be educated so.

54

425　Young Juan now was sixteen years of age,
　　Tall, handsome, slender, but well knit: he seem'd
Active, though not so sprightly, as a page;
　　And every body but his mother deem'd
Him almost man; but she flew in a rage
430　　And bit her lips (for else she might have scream'd)
If any said so, for to be precocious
Was in her eyes a thing the most atrocious.

55

Amongst her numerous acquaintance, all
　　Selected for discretion and devotion,
435　There was the Donna Julia, whom to call
　　Pretty were but to give a feeble notion
Of many charms in her as natural
　　As sweetness to the flower, or salt to ocean,
Her zone to Venus,[4] or his bow to Cupid,
440　(But this last simile is trite and stupid.)

56

The darkness of her Oriental eye
　　Accorded with her Moorish origin;
(Her blood was not all Spanish, by the by;
　　In Spain, you know, this is a sort of sin.)
445　When proud Granada fell, and, forced to fly,
　　Boabdil[5] wept, of Donna Julia's kin
Some went to Africa, some stay'd in Spain,
Her great great grandmamma chose to remain.

57

She married (I forget the pedigree)
450　　With an Hidalgo, who transmitted down
His blood less noble than such blood should be;
　　At such alliances his sires would frown,
In that point so precise in each degree
　　That they bred *in and in*, as might be shown,
455　Marrying their cousins—nay, their aunts, and nieces,
Which always spoils the breed, if it increases.

58

This heathenish cross restored the breed again,
　　Ruin'd its blood, but much improved its flesh;

---

4. The belt ("zone") of Venus was sexy.

5. Mohammed XI, the last Moorish king of Granada, expelled by Ferdinand and Isabella in 1492.

For from a root the ugliest in Old Spain
460 Sprung up a branch as beautiful as fresh;
The sons no more were short, the daughters plain:
  But there's a rumour which I fain would hush,
'Tis said that Donna Julia's grandmamma
Produced her Don more heirs at love than law.

59

465 However this might be, the race went on
  Improving still through every generation,
Until it centred in an only son,
  Who left an only daughter; my narration
May have suggested that this single one
470 Could be but Julia (whom on this occasion
I shall have much to speak about), and she
Was married, charming, chaste, and twenty-three.

60

Her eye (I'm very fond of handsome eyes)
  Was large and dark, suppressing half its fire
475 Until she spoke, then through its soft disguise
  Flash'd an expression more of pride than ire,
And love than either; and there would arise
  A something in them which was not desire,
But would have been, perhaps, but for the soul
480 Which struggled through and chasten'd down the whole.

61

Her glossy hair was cluster'd o'er a brow
  Bright with intelligence, and fair, and smooth;
Her eyebrow's shape was like th' aërial bow,
  Her cheek all purple with the beam of youth,
485 Mounting, at times, to a transparent glow,
  As if her veins ran lightning; she, in sooth,
Possess'd an air and grace by no means common:
Her stature tall—I hate a dumpy woman.

62

Wedded she was some years, and to a man
490 Of fifty, and such husbands are in plenty;
And yet, I think, instead of such a ONE
  'Twere better to have TWO of five-and-twenty,
Especially in countries near the sun:
  And now I think on't, "mi vien in mente,"°   *it comes to mind*
495 Ladies even of the most uneasy virtue
Prefer a spouse whose age is short of thirty.

63

'Tis a sad thing, I cannot choose but say,
  And all the fault of that indecent sun,
Who cannot leave alone our helpless clay,

500   But will keep baking, broiling, burning on,
            That howsoever people fast and pray,
                The flesh is frail, and so the soul undone:
            What men call gallantry, and gods adultery,
            Is much more common where the climate's sultry.

                                    64

505   Happy the nations of the moral North!
                Where all is virtue, and the winter season
            Sends sin, without a rag on, shivering forth
                ('Twas snow that brought St. Anthony to reason);[6]
            Where juries cast up what a wife is worth,
510   By laying whate'er sum, in mulct,° they please on   penalty
            The lover, who must pay a handsome price,
            Because it is a marketable vice.

                                    65

        Alfonso was the name of Julia's lord,
                A man well looking for his years, and who
515   Was neither much beloved nor yet abhorr'd:
                They lived together, as most people do,
            Suffering each other's foibles by accord,
                And not exactly either *one* or *two*;
            Yet he was jealous, though he did not show it,
520   For jealousy dislikes the world to know it.

                                    66

        Julia was—yet I never could see why—
                With Donna Inez quite a favourite friend;
            Between their tastes there was small sympathy,
                For not a line had Julia ever penn'd:
525   Some people whisper (but, no doubt, they lie,
                For malice still imputes some private end)
            That Inez had, ere Don Alfonso's marriage,
            Forgot with him her very prudent carriage;

                                    67

        And that still keeping up the old connection,
530   Which time had lately render'd much more chaste,
            She took his lady also in affection,
                And certainly this course was much the best:
            She flatter'd Julia with her sage protection,
                And complimented Don Alfonso's taste;
535   And if she could not (who can?) silence scandal,
            At least she left it a more slender handle.

                                    68

        I can't tell whether Julia saw the affair
                With other people's eyes, or if her own

---

6. Byron later realized it was St. Francis of Assisi (1181?–1226) who cast himself on the snow to quell his desires.

Discoveries made, but none could be aware
540   Of this, at least no symptom e'er was shown;
Perhaps she did not know, or did not care,
    Indifferent from the first, or callous grown:
I'm really puzzled what to think or say,
She kept her counsel in so close a way.

69

545 Juan she saw, and, as a pretty child,
    Caress'd him often—such a thing might be
Quite innocently done, and harmless styled,
    When she had twenty years, and thirteen he;
But I am not so sure I should have smiled
550   When he was sixteen, Julia twenty-three;
These few short years make wondrous alterations,
Particularly amongst sun-burnt nations.

70

Whate'er the cause might be, they had become
    Changed; for the dame grew distant, the youth shy,
555 Their looks cast down, their greetings almost dumb,
    And much embarrassment in either eye;
There surely will be little doubt with some
    That Donna Julia knew the reason why,
But as for Juan, he had no more notion
560 Than he who never saw the sea of ocean.

71

Yet Julia's very coldness still was kind,
    And tremulously gentle her small hand
Withdrew itself from his, but left behind
    A little pressure, thrilling, and so bland
565 And slight, so very slight, that to the mind
    'Twas but a doubt; but ne'er magician's wand
Wrought change with all Armida's fairy art[7]
Like what this light touch left on Juan's heart.

72

And if she met him, though she smiled no more,
570   She look'd a sadness sweeter than her smile,
As if her heart had deeper thoughts in store
    She must not own, but cherish'd more the while
For that compression in its burning core;
    Even innocence itself has many a wile,
575 And will not dare to trust itself with truth,
And love is taught hypocrisy from youth.

---

7. Armida, sorceress in *Jerusalem Delivered* by Torquato Tasso (1544–1595), causes the crusader hero to forget his vows.

73

But passion most dissembles, yet betrays
   Even by its darkness; as the blackest sky
Foretells the heaviest tempest, it displays
580   Its workings through the vainly guarded eye,
And in whatever aspect it arrays
   Itself, 'tis still the same hypocrisy;
Coldness or anger, even disdain or hate,
Are masks it often wears, and still too late.

74

585 Then there were sighs, the deeper for suppression,
   And stolen glances, sweeter for the theft,
And burning blushes, though for no transgression,
   Tremblings when met, and restlessness when left;
All these are little preludes to possession,
590   Of which young passion cannot be bereft,
And merely tend to show how greatly love is
Embarrass'd at first starting with a novice.

75

Poor Julia's heart was in an awkward state;
   She felt it going, and resolved to make
595 The noblest efforts for herself and mate,
   For honour's, pride's, religion's, virtue's sake;
Her resolutions were most truly great,
   And almost might have made a Tarquin quake:[8]
She pray'd the Virgin Mary for her grace,
600 As being the best judge of a lady's case.

76

She vow'd she never would see Juan more,
   And next day paid a visit to his mother,
And look'd extremely at the opening door,
   Which, by the Virgin's grace, let in another;
605 Grateful she was, and yet a little sore—
   Again it opens, it can be no other,
'Tis surely Juan now—No! I'm afraid
That night the Virgin was no further pray'd.

77

She now determined that a virtuous woman
610   Should rather face and overcome temptation,
That flight was base and dastardly, and no man
   Should ever give her heart the least sensation;
That is to say, a thought beyond the common
   Preference, that we must feel upon occasion,

---

8. The Tarquins were noted for arrogance and cruelty; after his son Sextus raped Lucretia, Tarquinius Superbus, the last king of Rome, was exiled in a revolt led by Brutus. See Shakespeare, *The Rape of Lucrece* (1594).

615 For people who are pleasanter than others,
    But then they only seem so many brothers.

                    78

    And even if by chance—and who can tell?
        The devil's so very sly—she should discover
    That all within was not so very well,
620   And, if still free, that such or such a lover
    Might please perhaps, a virtuous wife can quell
        Such thoughts, and be the better when they're over;
    And if the man should ask, 'tis but denial:
    I recommend young ladies to make trial.

                    79

625 And then there are such things as love divine,
        Bright and immaculate, unmix'd and pure,
    Such as the angels think so very fine,
        And matrons, who would be no less secure,
    Platonic, perfect, "just such love as mine":
630   Thus Julia said—and thought so, to be sure;
    And so I'd have her think, were I the man
    On whom her reveries celestial ran.

                    80

    Such love is innocent, and may exist
        Between young persons without any danger.
635 A hand may first, and then a lip be kist;
        For my part, to such doings I'm a stranger,
    But *hear* these freedoms form the utmost list
        Of all o'er which such love may be a ranger:
    If people go beyond, 'tis quite a crime,
640 But not my fault—I tell them all in time.

                    81

    Love, then, but love within its proper limits,
        Was Julia's innocent determination
    In young Don Juan's favour, and to him its
        Exertion might be useful on occasion;
645 And, lighted at too pure a shrine to dim its
        Ethereal lustre, with what sweet persuasion
    He might be taught, by love and her together—
    I really don't know what, nor Julia either.

                    82

    Fraught with this fine intention, and well fenced
650   In mail of proof—her purity of soul,
    She, for the future of her strength convinced,
        And that her honour was a rock, or mole,°   breakwater
    Exceeding sagely from that hour dispensed
        With any kind of troublesome control;
655 But whether Julia to the task was equal
    Is that which must be mention'd in the sequel.

83

Her plan she deem'd both innocent and feasible,
    And, surely, with a stripling of sixteen
Not scandal's fangs could fix on much that's seizable,
660   Or if they did so, satisfied to mean
Nothing but what was good, her breast was peaceable—
    A quiet conscience makes one so serene!
Christians have burnt each other, quite persuaded
That all the Apostles would have done as they did.

84

665 And if in the mean time her husband died,
    But Heaven forbid that such a thought should cross
Her brain, though in a dream! (and then she sigh'd)
    Never could she survive that common loss;
But just suppose that moment should betide,
670   I only say suppose it—*inter nos.*°   *between us (Latin)*
(This should be *entre nous*, for Julia thought
In French, but then the rhyme would go for nought.)

85

I only say suppose this supposition:
    Juan being then grown up to man's estate
675 Would fully suit a widow of condition,
    Even seven years hence it would not be too late
And in the interim (to pursue this vision)
    The mischief, after all, could not be great,
For he would learn the rudiments of love,
680 I mean the seraph° way of those above.   *angelic*

86

So much for Julia. Now we'll turn to Juan,
    Poor little fellow! he had no idea
Of his own case, and never hit the true one;
    In feelings quick as Ovid's Miss Medea,[9]
685 He puzzled over what he found a new one,
    But not as yet imagined it could be a
Thing quite in course, and not at all alarming,
Which, with a little patience, might grow charming.

87

Silent and pensive, idle, restless, slow,
690   His home deserted for the lonely wood,
Tormented with a wound he could not know,
    His, like all deep grief, plunged in solitude:
I'm fond myself of solitude or so,
    But then, I beg it may be understood,

---

9. Ovid's *Metamorphoses* 7 tells of how Medea was overcome by passion for Jason; though she struggled, her reason could not defeat her desire.

695   By solitude I mean a sultan's, not
       A hermit's, with a haram for a grot.

                          88

       "Oh Love! in such a wilderness as this,
          Where transport and security entwine,
       Here is the empire of thy perfect bliss,
700   And here thou art a god indeed divine."[1]
       The bard I quote from does not sing amiss,
          With the exception of the second line,
       For that same twining "transport and security"
       Are twisted to a phrase of some obscurity.

                          89

705   The poet meant, no doubt, and thus appeals
          To the good sense and senses of mankind,
       The very thing which every body feels,
          As all have found on trial, or may find,
       That no one likes to be disturb'd at meals
710   Or love.—I won't say more about "entwined"
       Or "transport," as we knew all that before,
       But beg "Security" will bolt the door.

                          90

       Young Juan wander'd by the glassy brooks
          Thinking unutterable things; he threw
715   Himself at length within the leafy nooks
          Where the wild branch of the cork forest grew:
       There poets find materials for their books,
          And every now and then we read them through,
       So that their plan and prosody are eligible,
720   Unless, like Wordsworth, they prove unintelligible.

                          91

       He, Juan, (and not Wordsworth) so pursued
          His self-communion with his own high soul,
       Until his mighty heart, in its great mood,
          Had mitigated part, though not the whole
725   Of its disease; he did the best he could
          With things not very subject to control,
       And turn'd, without perceiving his condition,
       Like Coleridge, into a metaphysician.

                          92

       He thought about himself, and the whole earth,
730   Of man the wonderful, and of the stars,
       And how the deuce they ever could have birth;

---

1. Campbell's Gertrude of Wyoming, (I think) the opening of Canto II; but quote from memory [Byron's note; see Thomas Campbell's *Gertrude of Wyoming* (1809), Canto III, 1–4].

And then he thought of earthquakes, and of wars,
   How many miles the moon might have in girth,
Of air-balloons, and of the many bars
735   To perfect knowledge of the boundless skies;—
And then he thought of Donna Julia's eyes.

93

In thoughts like these true wisdom may discern
   Longings sublime, and aspirations high,
Which some are born with, but the most part learn
740   To plague themselves withal, they know not why:
'Twas strange that one so young should thus concern
   His brain about the action of the sky;
If *you* think 'twas philosophy that this did,
I can't help thinking puberty assisted.

94

745 He pored upon the leaves, and on the flowers,
   And heard a voice in all the winds; and then
He thought of wood-nymphs and immortal bowers,
   And how the goddesses came down to men:
He miss'd the pathway, he forgot the hours,
750   And when he look'd upon his watch again,
He found how much old Time had been a winner—
He also found that he had lost his dinner.

95

Sometimes he turn'd to gaze upon his book,
   Boscan, or Garcilasso;[2]—by the wind
755 Even as the page is rustled while we look,
   So by the poesy of his own mind
Over the mystic leaf his soul was shook,
   As if 'twere one whereon magicians bind
Their spells, and give them to the passing gale,
760 According to some good old woman's tale.

96

Thus would he while his lonely hours away
   Dissatisfied, nor knowing what he wanted;
Nor glowing reverie, nor poet's lay,
   Could yield his spirit that for which it panted,
765 A bosom whereon he his head might lay,
   And hear the heart beat with the love it granted,
With——several other things, which I forget,
Or which, at least, I need not mention yet.

---

2. Juan Boscán Almogáver and Garcilaso de la Vega, 16th-century poets who introduced the Petrarchan style in Castilian poetry.

97

Those lonely walks, and lengthening reveries,
770   Could not escape the gentle Julia's eyes;
She saw that Juan was not at his ease;
      But that which chiefly may, and must surprise,
Is, that the Donna Inez did not tease
      Her only son with question or surmise;
775   Whether it was she did not see, or would not,
Or, like all very clever people, could not.

98

This may seem strange, but yet 'tis very common;
      For instance—gentlemen, whose ladies take
Leave to o'erstep the written rights of woman,
780   And break the——Which commandment is't they break?
(I have forgot the number, and think no man
      Should rashly quote, for fear of a mistake.)
I say, when these same gentlemen are jealous,
They make some blunder, which their ladies tell us.

99

785   A real husband always is suspicious,
      But still no less suspects in the wrong place,
Jealous of some one who had no such wishes,
      Or pandering blindly to his own disgrace,
By harbouring some dear friend extremely vicious;
790   The last indeed's infallibly the case:
And when the spouse and friend are gone off wholly,
He wonders at their vice, and not his folly.

100

Thus parents also are at times short-sighted;
      Though watchful as the lynx, they ne'er discover,
795   The while the wicked world beholds delighted,
      Young Hopeful's mistress, or Miss Fanny's lover,
Till some confounded escapade has blighted
      The plan of twenty years, and all is over;
And then the mother cries, the father swears,
800   And wonders why the devil he got heirs.

101

But Inez was so anxious, and so clear
      Of sight, that I must think, on this occasion,
She had some other motive much more near
      For leaving Juan to this new temptation;
805   But what that motive was, I sha'n't say here;
      Perhaps to finish Juan's education,
Perhaps to open Don Alfonso's eyes,
In case he thought his wife too great a prize.

102

It was upon a day, a summer's day;—
    Summer's indeed a very dangerous season,
And so is spring about the end of May;
    The sun, no doubt, is the prevailing reason;
But whatsoe'er the cause is, one may say,
    And stand convicted of more truth than treason,
That there are months which nature grows more merry in,—
March has its hares,[3] and May must have its heroine.

103

'Twas on a summer's day—the sixth of June:—
    I like to be particular in dates,
Not only of the age, and year, but moon;
    They are a sort of post-house, where the Fates
Change horses, making history change its tune,
    Then spur away o'er empires and o'er states,
Leaving at last not much besides chronology,
Excepting the post-obits of theology.

104

'Twas on the sixth of June, about the hour
    Of half-past six—perhaps still nearer seven—
When Julia sate within as pretty a bower
    As e'er held houri in that heathenish heaven
Described by Mahomet, and Anacreon Moore,[4]
    To whom the lyre and laurels have been given,
With all the trophies of triumphant song—
He won them well, and may he wear them long!

105

She sate, but not alone; I know not well
    How this same interview had taken place,
And even if I knew, I should not tell—
    People should hold their tongues in any case;
No matter how or why the thing befell,
    But there were she and Juan, face to face—
When two such faces are so, 'twould be wise,
But very difficult, to shut their eyes.

106

How beautiful she look'd! her conscious heart
    Glow'd in her cheek, and yet she felt no wrong.
Oh Love! how perfect is thy mystic art,
    Strengthening the weak, and trampling on the strong,
How self-deceitful is the sagest part

---

3. Proverbial: "Mad as a March hare" (the mating season).
4. The houris are the maidens who await heroes in the Muslim paradise; Thomas Moore translated the erotic odes of Anacreon in 1800 and described the "heathenish heaven" in his popular poem *Lalla Rookh* (1817).

Of mortals whom thy lure hath led along—
The precipice she stood on was immense,
So was her creed in her own innocence.

107

She thought of her own strength, and Juan's youth,
850   And of the folly of all prudish fears,
Victorious virtue, and domestic truth,
    And then of Don Alfonso's fifty years:
I wish these last had not occurr'd, in sooth,
    Because that number rarely much endears,
855 And through all climes, the snowy and the sunny,
Sounds ill in love, whate'er it may in money.

108

When people say, "I've told you *fifty* times,"
    They mean to scold, and very often do;
When poets say, "I've written *fifty* rhymes,"
860   They make you dread that they'll recite them too;
In gangs of *fifty*, thieves commit their crimes;
    At *fifty* love for love is rare, 'tis true,
But then, no doubt, it equally as true is,
A good deal may be bought for *fifty* Louis.°   *gold coins*

109

865 Julia had honour, virtue, truth, and love,
    For Don Alfonso; and she inly swore,
By all the vows below to powers above,
    She never would disgrace the ring she wore,
Nor leave a wish which wisdom might reprove;
870   And while she ponder'd this, besides much more,
One hand on Juan's carelessly was thrown,
Quite by mistake—she thought it was her own;

110

Unconsciously she lean'd upon the other,
    Which play'd within the tangles of her hair;
875 And to contend with thoughts she could not smother
    She seem'd, by the distraction of her air.
'Twas surely very wrong in Juan's mother
    To leave together this imprudent pair,
She who for many years had watch'd her son so—
880 I'm very certain *mine* would not have done so.

111

The hand which still held Juan's, by degrees
    Gently, but palpably confirm'd its grasp,
As if it said, "Detain me, if you please";
    Yet there's no doubt she only meant to clasp
885 His fingers with a pure Platonic squeeze;
    She would have shrunk as from a toad, or asp,

Had she imagined such a thing could rouse
A feeling dangerous to a prudent spouse.

112

I cannot know what Juan thought of this,
890   But what he did, is much what you would do;
His young lip thank'd it with a grateful kiss,
    And then, abash'd at its own joy, withdrew
In deep despair, lest he had done amiss,
    Love is so very timid when 'tis new:
895 She blush'd, and frown'd not, but she strove to speak,
And held her tongue, her voice was grown so weak.

113

The sun set, and up rose the yellow moon:
    The devil's in the moon for mischief; they
Who call'd her chaste, methinks, began too soon
900   Their nomenclature; there is not a day,
The longest, not the twenty-first of June,
    Sees half the business in a wicked way
On which three single hours of moonshine smile—
And then she looks so modest all the while.

114

905 There is a dangerous silence in that hour,
    A stillness, which leaves room for the full soul
To open all itself, without the power
    Of calling wholly back its self-control;
The silver light which, hallowing tree and tower,
910   Sheds beauty and deep softness o'er the whole,
Breathes also to the heart, and o'er it throws
A loving languor, which is not repose.

115

And Julia sate with Juan, half embraced
    And half retiring from the glowing arm,
915 Which trembled like the bosom where 'twas placed;
    Yet still she must have thought there was no harm,
Or else 'twere easy to withdraw her waist;
    But then the situation had its charm,
And then——God knows what next—I can't go on;
920 I'm almost sorry that I e'er begun.

116

Oh Plato! Plato! you have paved the way,
    With your confounded fantasies, to more
Immoral conduct by the fancied sway
    Your system feigns o'er the controulless core
925 Of human hearts, than all the long array
    Of poets and romancers:—You're a bore,
A charlatan, a coxcomb—and have been,
At best, no better than a go-between.

117

And Julia's voice was lost, except in sighs,
930   Until too late for useful conversation;
The tears were gushing from her gentle eyes,
      I wish, indeed, they had not had occasion,
But who, alas! can love, and then be wise?
      Not that remorse did not oppose temptation,
935   A little still she strove, and much repented,
And whispering "I will ne'er consent"—consented.

118

'Tis said that Xerxes⁵ offer'd a reward
      To those who could invent him a new pleasure:
Methinks, the requisition's rather hard,
940   And must have cost his majesty a treasure:
For my part, I'm a moderate-minded bard,
      Fond of a little love (which I call leisure);
I care not for new pleasures, as the old
Are quite enough for me, so they but hold.

119

945   Oh Pleasure! you are indeed a pleasant thing,
      Although one must be damn'd for you, no doubt:
I make a resolution every spring
      Of reformation, ere the year run out,
But somehow, this my vestal vow takes wing,
950   Yet still, I trust, it may be kept throughout:
I'm very sorry, very much ashamed,
And mean, next winter, to be quite reclaim'd.

120

Here my chaste Muse a liberty must take—
      Start not! still chaster reader—she'll be nice hence-
955   Forward, and there is no great cause to quake;
      This liberty is a poetic licence,
Which some irregularity may make
      In the design, and as I have a high sense
Of Aristotle and the Rules, 'tis fit
960   To beg his pardon when I err a bit.

121

This licence is to hope the reader will
      Suppose from June the sixth (the fatal day,
Without whose epoch my poetic skill
      For want of facts would all be thrown away),
965   But keeping Julia and Don Juan still
      In sight, that several months have pass'd; we'll say
'Twas in November, but I'm not so sure
About the day—the era's more obscure.

---

5. An anecdote drawn from Cicero and Montaigne (*Of Experience*).

122

970

We'll talk of that anon.—'Tis sweet to hear
    At midnight on the blue and moonlit deep
The song and oar of Adria's gondolier,[6]
    By distance mellow'd, o'er the waters sweep;
'Tis sweet to see the evening star° appear;   *Venus*
    'Tis sweet to listen as the night-winds creep

975

From leaf to leaf; 'tis sweet to view on high
The rainbow, based on ocean, span the sky.

123

'Tis sweet to hear the watch-dog's honest bark
    Bay deep-mouth'd welcome as we draw near home;
'Tis sweet to know there is an eye will mark

980

    Our coming, and look brighter when we come;
'Tis sweet to be awaken'd by the lark,
    Or lull'd by falling waters; sweet the hum
Of bees, the voice of girls, the song of birds,
The lisp of children, and their earliest words.

124

985

Sweet is the vintage, when the showering grapes
    In Bacchanal[7] profusion reel to earth
Purple and gushing: sweet are our escapes
    From civic revelry to rural mirth;
Sweet to the miser are his glittering heaps,

990

    Sweet to the father is his first-born's birth,
Sweet is revenge—especially to women,
Pillage to soldiers, prize-money to seamen.

125

Sweet is a legacy, and passing sweet
    The unexpected death of some old lady

995

Or gentleman of seventy years complete,
    Who've made "us youth" wait too—too long already
For an estate, or cash, or country-seat,
    Still breaking, but with stamina so steady,[8]
That all the Israelites are fit to mob its

1000

Next owner for their double-damn'd post-obits.[9]

126

'Tis sweet to win, no matter how, one's laurels,
    By blood or ink; 'tis sweet to put an end
To strife; 'tis sometimes sweet to have our quarrels,
    Particularly with a tiresome friend:

---

6. The famous singing of the boatmen of Venice, on the Adriatic Sea.
7. Bacchus is the Greek god of wine.
8. "us youth" is fat, aging Falstaff's self-reference (Shakespeare, 1 Henry IV 2.2.85); Byron glances at his estranged wife's mother, who did not die until the age of 70 in 1822, when Byron received the inheritance.
9. At college Byron had borrowed from Jewish money lenders on the prospects of his inheritance; "post-obit," after death (i.e., the death of the current heir).

1005   Sweet is old wine in bottles, ale in barrels;
       Dear is the helpless creature we defend
    Against the world; and dear the schoolboy spot
    We ne'er forget, though there we are forgot.

127

    But sweeter still than this, than these, than all,
1010   Is first and passionate love—it stands alone,
    Like Adam's recollection of his fall;
       The tree of knowledge has been pluck'd—all's known—
    And life yields nothing further to recall
       Worthy of this ambrosial sin, so shown,
1015   No doubt in fable, as the unforgiven
    Fire which Prometheus filch'd for us from heaven.[1]

128

    Man's a strange animal, and makes strange use
       Of his own nature, and the various arts,
    And likes particularly to produce
1020   Some new experiment to show his parts;
    This is the age of oddities let loose,
       Where different talents find their different marts;
    You'd best begin with truth, and when you've lost your
    Labour, there's a sure market for imposture.

129

1025   What opposite discoveries we have seen!
       (Signs of true genius, and of empty pockets.)
    One makes new noses, one a guillotine,
       One breaks your bones, one sets them in their sockets;
    But vaccination certainly has been
1030   A kind antithesis to Congreve's rockets,[2]
    With which the Doctor paid off an old pox,
    By borrowing a new one from an ox.[3]

130

    Bread has been made (indifferent) from potatoes;
       And galvanism has set some corpses grinning,[4]
1035   But has not answer'd like the apparatus
       Of the Humane Society's beginning
    By which men are unsuffocated gratis:[5]
       What wondrous new machines have late been spinning!

---

1. See *Prometheus*, page 750.
2. Sir William Congreve invented the rockets used against the French at the Battle of Leipzig in 1813.
3. Edward Jenner first vaccinated against smallpox in 1796 with a serum made from cowpox. In the first edition the references to syphilis (the "great pox" and "lues") caused this couplet and several ensuing lines to be omitted.

4. Theories that electricity might be the vital force of life led to a number of experiments, on both living and dead bodies, with galvanism, or electricity generated by chemical reaction. Shelley's *Frankenstein* (1818) reflects these experiments.
5. The Humane Society rescued drowned persons and sought means to revive them.

I said the small-pox has gone out of late;
1040   Perhaps it may be follow'd by the great.

131

'Tis said the great came from America;
    Perhaps it may set out on its return,—
The population there so spreads, they say
    'Tis grown high time to thin it in its turn,
1045   With war, or plague, or famine, any way,
    So that civilisation they may learn;
And which in ravage the more loathsome evil is—
Their real lues, or our pseudo-syphilis?

132

This is the patent-age of new inventions
1050   For killing bodies, and for saving souls,
All propagated with the best intentions;
    Sir Humphry Davy's lantern, by which coals
Are safely mined for in the mode he mentions,[6]
    Timbuctoo travels, voyages to the Poles,
1055   Are ways to benefit mankind, as true,
Perhaps, as shooting them at Waterloo.

133

Man's a phenomenon, one knows not what,
    And wonderful beyond all wondrous measure;
'Tis pity though, in this sublime world, that
1060   Pleasure's a sin, and sometimes sin's a pleasure;
Few mortals know what end they would be at,
    But whether glory, power, or love, or treasure,
The path is through perplexing ways, and when
The goal is gain'd, we die, you know—and then—

134

1065   What then?—I do not know, no more do you—
    And so good night.—Return we to our story:
'Twas in November, when fine days are few,
    And the far mountains wax a little hoary,
And clap a white cape on their mantles blue[7]
1070   And the sea dashes round the promontory,
And the loud breaker boils against the rock,
And sober suns must set at five o'clock.

135

'Twas, as the watchmen say, a cloudy night;
    No moon, no stars, the wind was low or loud
1075   By gusts, and many a sparkling hearth was bright
    With the piled wood, round which the family crowd;
There's something cheerful in that sort of light,
    Even as a summer sky's without a cloud:

---

6. Sir Humphry Davy in 1815 invented the safety lamp   7. A comic echo of the end of Milton's elegy, *Lycidas*.
that protected miners from explosions of gas.

I'm fond of fire, and crickets, and all that,
1080 A lobster salad, and champagne, and chat.

136

'Twas midnight—Donna Julia was in bed,
　　Sleeping, most probably,—when at her door
Arose a clatter might awake the dead,
　　If they had never been awoke before,
1085 And that they have been so we all have read,
　　And are to be so, at the least, once more;
The door was fasten'd, but with voice and fist
First knocks were heard, then "Madam—Madam—hist!

137

"For God's sake, Madam—Madam—here's my master,
1090 　　With more than half the city at his back—
Was ever heard of such a curst disaster!
　　'Tis not my fault—I kept good watch—Alack!
Do pray undo the bolt a little faster—
　　They're on the stair just now, and in a crack
1095 Will all be here; perhaps he yet may fly—
Surely the window's not so *very* high!"

138

By this time Don Alfonso was arrived,
　　With torches, friends, and servants in great number;
The major part of them had long been wived,
1100 　　And therefore paused not to disturb the slumber
Of any wicked woman, who contrived
　　By stealth her husband's temples to encumber:[8]
Examples of this kind are so contagious,
Were *one* not punish'd, *all* would be outrageous.

139

1105 I can't tell how, or why, or what suspicion
　　Could enter into Don Alfonso's head;
But for a cavalier of his condition
　　It surely was exceedingly ill-bred,
Without a word of previous admonition,
1110 　　To hold a levee[9] round his lady's bed,
And summon lackeys, arm'd with fire and sword,
To prove himself the thing he most abhorr'd.

140

Poor Donna Julia! starting as from sleep,
　　(Mind—that I do not say—she had not slept)
1115 Began at once to scream, and yawn, and weep;
　　Her maid Antonia, who was an adept,
Contrived to fling the bed-clothes in a heap,
　　As if she had just now from out them crept:

8. With horns, traditional sign of a cuckold.　　9. A formal morning reception.

I can't tell why she should take all this trouble
1120   To prove her mistress had been sleeping double.

141

But Julia mistress, and Antonia maid,
 Appear'd like two poor harmless women, who
Of goblins, but still more of men afraid,
 Had thought one man might be deterr'd by two,
1125   And therefore side by side were gently laid,
 Until the hours of absence should run through,
And truant husband should return, and say,
"My dear, I was the first who came away."

142

Now Julia found at length a voice, and cried,
1130   "In heaven's name, Don Alfonso, what d' ye mean?
Has madness seized you? would that I had died
 Ere such a monster's victim I had been!
What may this midnight violence betide,
 A sudden fit of drunkenness or spleen?
1135   Dare you suspect me, whom the thought would kill?
Search, then, the room!"—Alfonso said, "I will."

143

He search'd, *they* search'd, and rummaged every where,
 Closet and clothes' press, chest and window-seat,
And found much linen, lace, and several pair
1140   Of stockings, slippers, brushes, combs, complete,
With other articles of ladies fair,
 To keep them beautiful, or leave them neat:
Arras° they prick'd and curtains with their swords,   *tapestry*
And wounded several shutters, and some boards.

144

1145   Under the bed they search'd, and there they found—
 No matter what—it° was not that they sought;   *a chamber pot*
They open'd windows, gazing if the ground
 Had signs or footmarks, but the earth said nought;
And then they stared each others' faces round:
1150   'Tis odd, not one of all these seekers thought,
And seems to me almost a sort of blunder,
Of looking *in* the bed as well as under.

145

During this inquisition, Julia's tongue
 Was not asleep—"Yes, search and search," she cried,
1155   "Insult on insult heap, and wrong on wrong!
 It was for this that I became a bride!
For this in silence I have suffer'd long
 A husband like Alfonso at my side;
But now I'll bear no more, nor here remain.
1160   If there be law, or lawyers, in all Spain.

146

"Yes, Don Alfonso! husband now no more,
 If ever you indeed deserved the name,
Is't worthy of your years?—you have threescore—
 Fifty, or sixty, it is all the same—
1165 Is't wise or fitting, causeless to explore
  For facts against a virtuous woman's fame?
Ungrateful, perjured, barbarous Don Alfonso,
How dare you think your lady would go on so?

147

"Is it for this I have disdain'd to hold
1170 The common privileges of my sex?
That I have chosen a confessor so old
 And deaf, that any other it would vex,
And never once he has had cause to scold,
 But found my very innocence perplex
1175 So much, he always doubted I was married—
How sorry you will be when I've miscarried!

148

"Was it for this that no Cortejo[1] e'er
 I yet have chosen from out the youth of Seville?
Is it for this I scarce went anywhere,
1180 Except to bull-fights, mass, play, rout, and revel?
Is it for this, whate'er my suitors were,
 I favour'd none—nay, was almost uncivil?
Is it for this that General Count O'Reilly,
Who took Algiers, declares I used him vilely?[2]

149

1185 "Did not the Italian Musico° Cazzani   *musician*
 Sing at my heart six months at least in vain?
Did not his countryman, Count Corniani,
 Call me the only virtuous wife in Spain?[3]
Were there not also Russians, English, many?
1190 The Count Strongstroganoff I put in pain,
And Lord Mount Coffeehouse, the Irish peer,
Who kill'd himself for love (with wine) last year.

150

"Have I not had two bishops at my feet?
 The Duke of Ichar, and Don Fernan Nunez,
1195 And is it thus a faithful wife you treat?
 I wonder in what quarter now the moon is:
I praise your vast forbearance not to beat
 Me also, since the time so opportune is—

---

1. The socially accepted "escort" (lover) of a married
woman.
2. Donna Julia here made a mistake. Count O'Reilly
did not take Algiers—but Algiers very nearly took him

[Byron's note]. Irish-born Spanish general O'Reilly led an
unsuccessful expedition to Algiers in 1775.
3. "Cazzano" is slang for a penis, by extension a dunce
or a rogue; "Cornuto" means horned, that is, cuckolded.

Oh, valiant man! with sword drawn and cock'd trigger,
1200   Now, tell me, don't you cut a pretty figure?

151

"Was it for this you took your sudden journey,
    Under pretence of business indispensable
With that sublime of rascals your attorney,
    Whom I see standing there, and looking sensible
1205 Of having play'd the fool? though both I spurn, he
    Deserves the worst, his conduct's less defensible,
Because, no doubt, 'twas for his dirty fee,
And not from any love to you nor me.

152

"If he comes here to take a deposition,
1210   By all means let the gentleman proceed;
You've made the apartment in a fit condition:—
    There's pen and ink for you, sir, when you need—
Let every thing be noted with precision,
    I would not you for nothing should be fee'd—
1215 But, as my maid's undrest, pray turn your spies out."
"Oh!" sobb'd Antonia, "I could tear their eyes out."

153

"There is the closet, there the toilet,° there   *dressing table*
    The antechamber—search them under, over;
There is the sofa, there the great arm-chair,
1220   The chimney—which would really hold a lover.
I wish to sleep, and beg you will take care
    And make no further noise, till you discover
The secret cavern of this lurking treasure—
And when 'tis found, let me, too, have that pleasure.

154

1225 "And now, Hidalgo! now that you have thrown
    Doubt upon me, confusion over all,
Pray have the courtesy to make it known
    Who is the man you search for? how d'ye call
Him? what's his lineage? let him but be shown—
1230   I hope he's young and handsome—is he tall?
Tell me—and be assured, that since you stain
My honour thus, it shall not be in vain.

155

"At least, perhaps, he has not sixty years,
    At that age he would be too old for slaughter,
1235 Or for so young a husband's jealous fears—
    (Antonia! let me have a glass of water.)
I am ashamed of having shed these tears,
    They are unworthy of my father's daughter;
My mother dream'd not in my natal hour
1240 That I should fall into a monster's power.

156

"Perhaps 'tis of Antonia you are jealous,
    You saw that she was sleeping by my side
When you broke in upon us with your fellows:
    Look where you please—we've nothing, sir, to hide;
1245   Only another time, I trust, you'll tell us,
    Or for the sake of decency abide
A moment at the door, that we may be
Drest to receive so much good company.

157

"And now, sir, I have done, and say no more;
1250   The little I have said may serve to show
The guileless heart in silence may grieve o'er
    The wrongs to whose exposure it is slow:—
I leave you to your conscience as before,
    'Twill one day ask you *why* you used me so?
1255   God grant you feel not then the bitterest grief!—
Antonia! where's my pocket-handkerchief?"

158

She ceased, and turn'd upon her pillow; pale
    She lay, her dark eyes flashing through their tears,
Like skies that rain and lighten; as a veil,
1260   Waved and o'ershading her wan cheek, appears
Her streaming hair; the black curls strive, but fail,
    To hide the glossy shoulder, which uprears
Its snow through all;—her soft lips lie apart,
And louder than her breathing beats her heart.

159

1265 The Senhor Don Alfonso stood confused;
    Antonia bustled round the ransack'd room,
And, turning up her nose, with looks abused
    Her master, and his myrmidons, of whom
Not one, except the attorney, was amused;
1270   He, like Achates, faithful to the tomb,[4]
So there were quarrels, cared not for the cause,
Knowing they must be settled by the laws.

160

With prying snub-nose, and small eyes, he stood,
    Following Antonia's motions here and there,
1275 With much suspicion in his attitude;
    For reputations he had little care;
So that a suit or action were made good,
    Small pity had he for the young and fair,
And ne'er believed in negatives, till these
1280 Were proved by competent false witnesses.

---

4. Aeneas's loyal companion, a synonym for fidelity. The Myrmidons are the private army of Greek hero Achilles.

161

But Don Alfonso stood with downcast looks,
 And, truth to say, he made a foolish figure;
When, after searching in five hundred nooks,
 And treating a young wife with so much rigour,
1285 He gain'd no point, except some self-rebukes,
 Added to those his lady with such vigour
Had pour'd upon him for the last half-hour,
Quick, thick, and heavy—as a thunder-shower.

162

At first he tried to hammer an excuse,
1290 To which the sole reply was tears, and sobs,
And indications of hysterics, whose
 Prologue is always certain throes, and throbs,
Gasps, and whatever else the owners choose:
 Alfonso saw his wife, and thought of Job's;[5]
1295 He saw too, in perspective, her relations,
And then he tried to muster all his patience.

163

He stood in act to speak, or rather stammer,
 But sage Antonia cut him short before
The anvil of his speech received the hammer,
1300 With "Pray, sir, leave the room, and say no more,
Or madam dies."—Alfonso mutter'd, "D—n her,"
 But nothing else, the time of words was o'er;
He cast a rueful look or two, and did,
He knew not wherefore, that which he was bid.

164

1305 With him retired his "*posse comitatus*,"[6]
 The attorney last, who linger'd near the door,
Reluctantly, still tarrying there as late as
 Antonia let him—not a little sore
At this most strange and unexplain'd "*hiatus*"
1310 In Don Alfonso's facts, which just now wore
An awkward look; as he revolved the case,
The door was fasten'd in his legal face.

165

No sooner was it bolted, than—Oh shame!
 Oh sin! Oh sorrow! and Oh womankind!
1315 How can you do such things and keep your fame,
 Unless this world, and t' other too, be blind?
Nothing so dear as an unfilch'd good name![7]
 But to proceed—for there is more behind:
With much heartfelt reluctance be it said,
1320 Young Juan slipp'd, half-smother'd, from the bed.

---

5. Job's wife advises him to "curse God, and die" (2.9).
6. The "power of the country," a group deputized to maintain order.

7. Thus Iago says, leading Othello to believe that his new bride has been unfaithful and so a scandal to his good name (*Othello*, 3.3.159).

166

He had been hid—I don't pretend to say
　　How, nor can I indeed describe the where—
Young, slender, and pack'd easily, he lay,
　　No doubt, in little compass, round or square;
1325　But pity him I neither must nor may
　　His suffocation by that pretty pair;
'Twere better, sure, to die so, than be shut
With maudlin Clarence in his Malmsey butt.[8]

167

And, secondly, I pity not, because
1330　He had no business to commit a sin,
Forbid by heavenly, fined by human laws,
　　At least 'twas rather early to begin;
But at sixteen the conscience rarely gnaws
　　So much as when we call our old debts in
1335　At sixty years, and draw the accompts of evil,
And find a deuced balance with the devil.

168

Of his position I can give no notion:
　　'Tis written in the Hebrew Chronicle,
How the physicians, leaving pill and potion,
1340　Prescribed, by way of blister, a young belle,
When old King David's blood grew dull in motion,
　　And that the medicine answer'd very well;[9]
Perhaps 'twas in a different way applied,
For David lived, but Juan nearly died.

169

1345　What's to be done? Alfonso will be back
　　The moment he has sent his fools away.
Antonia's skill was put upon the rack,
　　But no device could be brought into play—
And how to parry the renew'd attack?
1350　Besides, it wanted but few hours of day:
Antonia puzzled; Julia did not speak,
But press'd her bloodless lip to Juan's cheek.

170

He turn'd his lip to hers, and with his hand
　　Call'd back the tangles of her wandering hair;
1355　Even then their love they could not all command,
　　And half forgot their danger and despair:
Antonia's patience now was at a stand—
　　"Come, come, 'tis no time now for fooling there,"
She whisper'd, in great wrath—"I must deposit
1360　This pretty gentleman within the closet:

8. In Shakespeare's *Richard III* (1.4), the Duke of Clarence is murdered by being drowned in a cask of sweet wine.

9. When the aged King David was afflicted with chills, a beautiful maiden was found to warm him at night (1 Kings 1).

171

"Pray, keep your nonsense for some luckier night—
    Who can have put my master in this mood?
What will become on 't—I'm in such a fright,
    The devil's in the urchin, and no good—
1365   Is this a time for giggling? this a plight?
    Why, don't you know that it may end in blood?
You'll lose your life, and I shall lose my place,
My mistress all, for that half-girlish face.

172

"Had it but been for a stout cavalier
1370   Of twenty-five or thirty—(Come, make haste)
But for a child, what piece of work is here!
    I really, madam, wonder at your taste—
(Come, sir, get in)—my master must be near:
    There, for the present, at the least, he's fast,
1375   And if we can but till the morning keep
Our counsel—(Juan, mind, you must not sleep.)"

173

Now, Don Alfonso entering, but alone,
    Closed the oration of the trusty maid:
She loiter'd, and he told her to be gone,
1380   An order somewhat sullenly obey'd;
However, present remedy was none,
    And no great good seem'd answer'd if she staid:
Regarding both with slow and sidelong view,
She snuff'd the candle, curtsied, and withdrew.

174

1385   Alfonso paused a minute—then begun
    Some strange excuses for his late proceeding;
He would not justify what he had done,
    To say the best, it was extreme ill-breeding;
But there were ample reasons for it, none
1390   Of which he specified in this his pleading:
His speech was a fine sample, on the whole,
Of rhetoric, which the learn'd call "*rigmarole*."

175

Julia said nought; though all the while there rose
    A ready answer, which at once enables
1395   A matron, who her husband's foible knows,
    By a few timely words to turn the tables,
Which, if it does not silence, still must pose,—
    Even if it should comprise a pack of fables;
'Tis to retort with firmness, and when he
1400   Suspects with *one*, do you reproach with *three*.

176

Julia, in fact, had tolerable grounds,—
    Alfonso's loves with Inez were well known;
But whether 'twas that one's own guilt confounds—
    But that can't be, as has been often shown,
1405 A lady with apologies° abounds;—   *defenses*
    It might be that her silence sprang alone
From delicacy to Don Juan's ear,
To whom she knew his mother's fame° was dear.   *good reputation*

177

There might be one more motive, which makes two;
1410   Alfonso ne'er to Juan had alluded,—
Mention'd his jealousy, but never who
    Had been the happy lover, he concluded,
Conceal'd amongst his premises; 'tis true,
    His mind the more o'er this its mystery brooded;
1415 To speak of Inez now were, one may say,
Like throwing Juan in Alfonso's way.

178

A hint, in tender cases, is enough;
    Silence is best, besides there is a *tact*—
(That modern phrase appears to me sad stuff,
1420   But it will serve to keep my verse compact)—
Which keeps, when push'd by questions rather rough,
    A lady always distant from the fact:
The charming creatures lie with such a grace,
There's nothing so becoming to the face.

179

1425 They blush, and we believe them; at least I
    Have always done so; 'tis of no great use,
In any case, attempting a reply,
    For then their eloquence grows quite profuse;
And when at length they're out of breath, they sigh,
1430   And cast their languid eyes down, and let loose
A tear or two, and then we make it up;
And then—and then—and then—sit down and sup.

180

Alfonso closed his speech, and begg'd her pardon,
    Which Julia half withheld, and then half granted,
1435 And laid conditions, he thought, very hard on,
    Denying several little things he wanted:
He stood like Adam lingering near his garden,[1]

---

1. After his expulsion from Eden (Milton, *Paradise Lost*, 12.637–39).

With useless penitence perplex'd and haunted,
Beseeching she no further would refuse,
1440   When, lo! he stumbled o'er a pair of shoes.

181

A pair of shoes!—what then? not much, if they
    Are such as fit with ladies' feet, but these
(No one can tell how much I grieve to say)
    Were masculine; to see them, and to seize,
1445   Was but a moment's act.—Ah! well-a-day!
    My teeth begin to chatter, my veins freeze—
Alfonso first examined well their fashion,
And then flew out into another passion.

182

He left the room for his relinquish'd sword,
1450   And Julia instant to the closet flew.
"Fly, Juan, fly! for heaven's sake—not a word—
    The door is open—you may yet slip through
The passage you so often have explored—
    Here is the garden-key—Fly—fly—Adieu!
1455   Haste—haste! I hear Alfonso's hurrying feet—
Day has not broke—there's no one in the street."

183

None can say that this was not good advice,
    The only mischief was, it came too late;
Of all experience 'tis the usual price,
1460   A sort of income-tax laid on by fate:
Juan had reach'd the room-door in a trice,
    And might have done so by the garden-gate,
But met Alfonso in his dressing-gown,
Who threaten'd death—so Juan knock'd him down.

184

1465   Dire was the scuffle, and out went the light;
    Antonia cried out "Rape!" and Julia "Fire!"
But not a servant stirr'd to aid the fight.
    Alfonso, pommell'd to his heart's desire,
Swore lustily he'd be revenged this night;
1470   And Juan, too, blasphemed an octave higher;
His blood was up: though young, he was a Tartar,°   *fierce warrior*
And not at all disposed to prove a martyr.

185

Alfonso's sword had dropp'd ere he could draw it,
    And they continued battling hand to hand,
1475   For Juan very luckily ne'er saw it;
    His temper not being under great command,
If at that moment he had chanced to claw it,
Alfonso's days had not been in the land

Much longer.—Think of husbands', lovers' lives!
1480 And how ye may be doubly widows—wives!

186

Alfonso grappled to detain the foe,
    And Juan throttled him to get away,
And blood ('twas from the nose) began to flow;
    At last, as they more faintly wrestling lay,
1485 Juan contrived to give an awkward blow,
    And then his only garment quite gave way;
He fled, like Joseph, leaving it; but there,
I doubt, all likeness ends between the pair.[2]

187

Lights came at length, and men, and maids, who found
1490   An awkward spectacle their eyes before;
Antonia in hysterics, Julia swoon'd,
    Alfonso leaning, breathless, by the door;
Some half-torn drapery scatter'd on the ground,
    Some blood, and several footsteps, but no more:
1495 Juan the gate gain'd, turn'd the key about,
And liking not the inside, lock'd the out.

188

Here ends this canto.—Need I sing, or say,
    How Juan, naked, favour'd by the night,
Who favours what she should not, found his way,
1500   And reach'd his home in an unseemly plight?
The pleasant scandal which arose next day,
    The nine days' wonder which was brought to light,
And how Alfonso sued for a divorce,
Were in the English newspapers, of course.

189

1505 If you would like to see the whole proceedings,
    The depositions, and the cause at full,
The names of all the witnesses, the pleadings
    Of counsel to nonsuit, or to annul,
There's more than one edition, and the readings
1510   Are various, but they none of them are dull;
The best is that in short-hand ta'en by Gurney,
Who to Madrid on purpose made a journey.[3]

190

But Donna Inez, to divert the train
    Of one of the most circulating scandals
1515 That had for centuries been known in Spain,
    At least since the retirement of the Vandals,

---

2. The chaste Joseph fled Potiphar's seductive wife, leaving "his garment in her hand" (Genesis 39).

3. William Brodie Gurney (1777–1855) was the official shorthand writer to Parliament and a noted trial reporter.

First vow'd (and never had she vow'd in vain)
　　To Virgin Mary several pounds of candles;
And then, by the advice of some old ladies,
1520　　She sent her son to be shipp'd off from Cadiz.

191

She had resolved that he should travel through
　　All European climes, by land or sea,
To mend his former morals, and get new,
　　Especially in France and Italy,
1525　(At least this is the thing most people do.)
　　Julia was sent into a convent: she
Grieved, but, perhaps, her feelings may be better
Shown in the following copy of her Letter:—

192

"They tell me 'tis decided; you depart:
1530　　'Tis wise, 'tis well, but not the less a pain;
I have no further claim on your young heart,
　　Mine was the victim, and would be again;
To love too much has been the only art
　　I used;—I write in haste, and if a stain
1535　Be on this sheet, 'tis not what it appears;
My eyeballs burn and throb, but have no tears.

193

"I loved, I love you, for this love have lost
　　State, station, heaven, mankind's, my own esteem,
And yet can not regret what it hath cost,
1540　　So dear is still the memory of that dream;
Yet, if I name my guilt, 'tis not to boast,
　　None can deem harshlier of me than I deem:
I trace this scrawl because I cannot rest—
I've nothing to reproach, or to request.

194

1545　"Man's love is of man's life a thing apart,
　　'Tis woman's whole existence; man may range
The court, camp, church, the vessel, and the mart,
　　Sword, gown, gain, glory, offer in exchange
Pride, fame, ambition, to fill up his heart,
1550　　And few there are whom these can not estrange;
Men have all these resources, we but one,
To love again, and be again undone.

195

"You will proceed in pleasure, and in pride,
　　Beloved and loving many; all is o'er
1555　For me on earth, except some years to hide
　　My shame and sorrow deep in my heart's core;
These I could bear, but cannot cast aside
　　The passion which still rages as before,—

And so farewell—forgive me, love me—No,
1560   That word is idle now—but let it go.

196

"My breast has been all weakness, is so yet;
    But still I think I can collect my mind;
My blood still rushes where my spirit's set,
    As roll the waves before the settled wind;
1565   My heart is feminine, nor can forget—
    To all, except one image, madly blind;
So shakes the needle, and so stands the pole,
As vibrates my fond heart to my fix'd soul.

197

"I have no more to say, but linger still,
1570   And dare not set my seal upon this sheet,
And yet I may as well the task fulfil,
    My misery can scarce be more complete:
I had not lived till now, could sorrow kill;
    Death shuns the wretch who fain the blow would meet,
1575   And I must even survive this last adieu,
And bear with life, to love and pray for you!"

198

This note was written upon gilt-edged paper
    With a neat little crow-quill, slight and new;
Her small white hand could hardly reach the taper,
1580   It trembled as magnetic needles do,
And yet she did not let one tear escape her;
    The seal a sun-flower; *Elle vous suit partout*,"[4]
The motto, cut upon a white cornelian;
The wax was superfine, its hue vermilion.

199

1585   This was Don Juan's earliest scrape; but whether
    I shall proceed with his adventures is
Dependent on the public altogether;
    We'll see, however, what they say to this,
Their favour in an author's cap's a feather,
1590   And no great mischief's done by their caprice;
And if their approbation we experience,
Perhaps they'll have some more about a year hence.

200

My poem's epic, and is meant to be
    Divided in twelve books; each book containing,
1595   With love, and war, a heavy gale at sea,
    A list of ships, and captains, and kings reigning,
New characters; the episodes are three:

---

4. "She follows you everywhere," the motto of one of Byron's own seals, also inscribed on a jewel he received from John Edleston, his beloved at Cambridge.

A panoramic view of hell's in training,
After the style of Virgil and of Homer,
1600   So that my name of Epic's no misnomer.

201

All these things will be specified in time,
    With strict regard to Aristotle's rules,
The *Vade Mecum*° of the true sublime,   *handbook*
    Which makes so many poets, and some fools:
1605 Prose poets like blank-verse, I'm fond of rhyme,
    Good workmen never quarrel with their tools;
I've got new mythological machinery,
And very handsome supernatural scenery.

202

There's only one slight difference between
1610   Me and my epic brethren gone before,
And here the advantage is my own, I ween;
    (Not that I have not several merits more,
But this will more peculiarly be seen);
    They so embellish, that 'tis quite a bore;
1615 Their labyrinth of fables to thread through,
Whereas this story's actually true.

203

If any person doubt it, I appeal
    To history, tradition, and to facts,
To newspapers, whose truth all know and feel,
1620   To plays in five, and operas in three acts;
All these confirm my statement a good deal,
    But that which more completely faith exacts
Is, that myself, and several now in Seville,
Saw Juan's last elopement with the devil.

204

1625 If ever I should condescend to prose,
    I'll write poetical commandments, which
Shall supersede beyond all doubt all those
    That went before; in these I shall enrich
My text with many things that no one knows,
1630   And carry precept to the highest pitch:
I'll call the work "Longinus o'er a Bottle,
Or, Every Poet his *own* Aristotle."[5]

205

Thou shalt believe in Milton, Dryden, Pope;[6]
    Thou shalt not set up Wordsworth, Coleridge, Southey;

5. Two famous ancient literary treatises: the *Poetics* of Aristotle, and Longinus, *On the Sublime*.
6. This parody of the Ten Commandments provoked cries of blasphemy. Byron feared that if Murray put his name on the poem "in these canting days—any lawyer might oppose my Guardian right of my daughter in Chancery—on the plea of it's containing the parody—such are the perils of a foolish jest." Percy Shelley lost custody of children by his first wife on such charges.

1635   Because the first is crazed beyond all hope,
      The second drunk, the third so quaint and mouthy:
   With Crabbe it may be difficult to cope,
      And Campbell's Hippocrene[7] is somewhat drouthy:
   Thou shalt not steal from Samuel Rogers, nor
1640   Commit—flirtation with the muse of Moore.

              206

   Thou shalt not covet Mr. Sotheby's Muse,
      His Pegasus, nor any thing that's his;[8]
   Thou shalt not bear false witness like "the Blues"—
      (There's one, at least, is very fond of this);[9]
1645   Thou shalt not write, in short, but what I choose:
      This is true criticism, and you may kiss—
   Exactly as you please, or not,—the rod;
   But if you don't, I'll lay it on, by G—d!

              207

   If any person should presume to assert
1650   This story is not moral, first, I pray,
   That they will not cry out before they're hurt,
      Then that they'll read it o'er again, and say,
   (But, doubtless, nobody will be so pert,)
      That this is not a moral tale, though gay;
1655   Besides, in Canto Twelfth, I mean to show
   The very place where wicked people go.

              208

   If, after all, there should be some so blind
      To their own good this warning to despise,
   Led by some tortuosity of mind,
1660   Not to believe my verse and their own eyes,
   And cry that they "the moral cannot find,"
      I tell him, if a clergyman, he lies;
   Should captains the remark, or critics, make,
   They also lie too—under a mistake.

              209

1665   The public approbation I expect,
      And beg they'll take my word about the moral,
   Which I with their amusement will connect
      (So children cutting teeth receive a coral);
   Meantime, they'll doubtless please to recollect
1670   My epical pretensions to the laurel:
   For fear some prudish readers should grow skittish.
   I've bribed my grandmother's review—the British.[1]

---

7. Fountain on Mount Helicon, sacred to the Muses.
8. William Sotheby (1757–1833), minor poet, man of letters, and translator of Wieland's *Oberon*, is satirized in Byron's *Beppo*. Samuel Rogers, a popular poet, published his *Jacqueline* with Byron's *Lara* in 1814.

9. Probably Lady Byron; "Blue Stockings" is a derogatory term for intellectual women.
1. William Roberts, editor of the *British Review*, missed this joke and printed a solemn denial.

210

I sent it in a letter to the Editor,
   Who thank'd me duly by return of post—
1675   I'm for a handsome article his creditor;
   Yet, if my gentle Muse he please to roast,
And break a promise after having made it her,
   Denying the receipt of what it cost,
And smear his page with gall instead of honey,
1680   All I can say is—that he had the money.

211

I think that with this holy new alliance[2]
   I may ensure the public, and defy
All other magazines of art or science,
   Daily, or monthly, or three monthly; I
1685   Have not essay'd to multiply their clients,
   Because they tell me 'twere in vain to try,
And that the Edinburgh Review and Quarterly
Treat a dissenting author very martyrly.

212

"*Non ego hoc ferrem calida juventâ*
1690   *Consule Planco,*" Horace said,[3] and so
Say I; by which quotation there is meant a
   Hint that some six or seven good years ago
(Long ere I dreamt of dating from the Brenta)[4]
   I was most ready to return a blow,
1695   And would not brook at all this sort of thing
In my hot youth—when George the Third was King.

213

But now at thirty years my hair is grey—
   (I wonder what it will be like at forty?
I thought of a peruke° the other day—)   *wig*
1700   My heart is not much greener; and, in short, I
Have squander'd my whole summer while 'twas May,
   And feel no more the spirit to retort; I
Have spent my life, both interest and principal,
And deem not, what I deem'd, my soul invincible.

---

2. Glancing at the Holy Alliance formed in 1815 between Russia, Austria, and Prussia to join their countries in Christian brotherhood.
3. Horace, *Odes* 3.14.27: "I had not brooked such insult when hot with youth in Plancus's consulship" (trans. by C. E. Bennett). The joke, clinched in the last two lines of the stanza, is that George III was still king.
4. In the summer of 1817 Byron rented a villa on the river Brenta, near Venice.

214

1705   No more—no more—Oh! never more on me
      The freshness of the heart can fall like dew,
  Which out of all the lovely things we see
      Extracts emotions beautiful and new,
  Hived in our bosoms like the bag o' the bee:
1710   Think'st thou the honey with those objects grew?
  Alas! 'twas not in them, but in thy power
  To double even the sweetness of a flower.

215

  No more—no more—Oh! never more, my heart.
      Canst thou be my sole world, my universe!
1715   Once all in all, but now a thing apart,
      Thou canst not be my blessing or my curse:
  The illusion's gone for ever, and thou art
      Insensible, I trust, but none the worse,
  And in thy stead I've got a deal of judgment,
1720   Though heaven knows how it ever found a lodgement.

216

  My days of love are over; me no more
      The charms of maid, wife, and still less of widow,
  Can make the fool of which they made before,[5]
      In short, I must not lead the life I did do;
1725   The credulous hope of mutual minds is o'er,
      The copious use of claret is forbid too,
  So for a good old-gentlemanly vice,
  I think I must take up with avarice.

217

  Ambition was my idol, which was broken
1730   Before the shrines of Sorrow, and of Pleasure;
  And the two last have left me many a token
      O'er which reflection may be made at leisure:
  Now, like Friar Bacon's brazen head, I've spoken,
      "Time is, Time was, Time's past:"[6]—a chymic° treasure   *alchemic*
1735   Is glittering youth, which I have spent betimes—
  My heart in passion, and my head on rhymes.

218

  What is the end of Fame? 'tis but to fill
      A certain portion of uncertain paper:

---

5. Horace, *Odes* 4.1.29–32: "Neither boy nor woman can please me any more...nor drinking bouts and brows with garlands bound."
6. Quoting *Friar Bacon and Friar Bungay* (1594), a comedy based on the legend of Roger Bacon, a 13th-century Oxford philosopher regarded as a necromancer and said to have constructed a brazen head capable of speech.

Some liken it to climbing up a hill,
1740   Whose summit, like all hills, is lost in vapour;
For this men write, speak, preach, and heroes kill,
    And bards burn what they call their "midnight taper,"
To have, when the original is dust,
A name, a wretched picture, and worse bust.

219

1745   What are the hopes of man? Old Egypt's King
    Cheops erected the first pyramid
And largest, thinking it was just the thing
    To keep his memory whole, and mummy hid;
But somebody or other rummaging,
1750   Burglariously broke his coffin's lid:
Let not a monument give you or me hopes,
Since not a pinch of dust remains of Cheops.

220

But I being fond of true philosophy,
    Say very often to myself, "Alas!
1755   All things that have been born were born to die,
    And flesh (which Death mows down to hay) is grass;
You've pass'd your youth not so unpleasantly,
    And if you had it o'er again—'twould pass—
So thank your stars that matters are no worse,
1760   And read your Bible, sir, and mind your purse."

221

But for the present, gentle reader! and
    Still gentler purchaser! the bard—that's I—
Must, with permission, shake you by the hand,
    And so your humble servant, and good-b'ye!
1765   We meet again, if we should understand
    Each other; and if not, I shall not try
Your patience further than by this short sample—
'Twere well if others follow'd my example.

222

"Go, little book, from this my solitude!
1770   I cast thee on the waters—go thy ways!
And if, as I believe, thy vein be good,
    The world will find thee after many days."[7]
When Southey's read, and Wordsworth understood,
    I can't help putting in my claim to praise—
1775   The four first rhymes are Southey's every line:
For God's sake, reader! take them not for mine.

---

7. Byron quotes from the final stanza of Southey's *Carmen Nuptiale: The Lay of the Laureate* (1816).

from **Canto 2**

[SHIPWRECK. JUAN AND HAIDÉE][1]

27

At one o'clock the wind with sudden shift
210   Threw the ship right into the trough of the sea,
Which struck her aft,° and made an awkward rift,   *astern*
      Started the stern-post, also shatter'd the
Whole of her stern-frame, and, ere she could lift
      Herself from out her present jeopardy,
215 The rudder tore away: 'twas time to sound
The pumps, and there were four feet water found.

28

One gang of people instantly was put
      Upon the pumps, and the remainder set
To get up part of the cargo, and what not;
220   But they could not come at the leak as yet;
At last they did get at it really, but
      Still their salvation was an even bet:
The water rush'd through in a way quite puzzling,
While they thrust sheets, shirts, jackets, bales of muslin,

29

225 Into the opening; but all such ingredients
      Would have been vain, and they must have gone down.
Despite of all their efforts and expedients,
      But for the pumps: I'm glad to make them known
To all the brother tars° who may have need hence,   *sailors*
230   For fifty tons of water were upthrown
By them per hour, and they had all been undone,
But for the maker, Mr. Mann, of London.[2]

30

As day advanced the weather seem'd to abate,
      And then the leak they reckon'd to reduce,
235 And keep the ship afloat, though three feet yet
      Kept two hand and one chain-pump still in use.
The wind blew fresh again: as it grew late
      A squall came on, and while some guns broke loose,
A gust—which all descriptive power transcends—
240 Laid with one blast the ship on her beam ends.°   *overturned*

31

There she lay, motionless, and seem'd upset;
      The water left the hold, and wash'd the decks,
And made a scene men do not soon forget;

---

1. Juan has begun his voyage away from Spain, bound for Leghorn (Livorno) in northern Italy, where he has relatives. He is suffering equally from sorrow for Julia and from seasickness, when his ship is overtaken by a violent storm.

2. Byron wrote that there was "not a *single circumstance* of [the shipwreck] not taken from *fact*—not indeed from any *single* shipwreck—but all from *actual* facts of different wrecks." His chief source was J. G. Dalyell's *Shipwrecks and Disasters at Sea* (1812).

For they remember battles, fires, and wrecks,
245   Or any other thing that brings regret,
    Or breaks their hopes, or hearts, or heads, or necks:
Thus drownings are much talk'd of by the divers,
And swimmers, who may chance to be survivors.

32

Immediately the masts were cut away,
250   Both main and mizen;° first the mizen went,   *rear mast*
The main-mast follow'd: but the ship still lay
    Like a mere log, and baffled our intent.
Foremast and bowsprit were cut down, and they
    Eased her at last (although we never meant
255 To part with all till every hope was blighted),
And then with violence the old ship righted.

* * *

45

Some lash'd them in their hammocks; some put on
    Their best clothes, as if going to a fair;
355 Some cursed the day on which they saw the sun,
    And gnash'd their teeth, and, howling, tore their hair;
And others went on as they had begun,
    Getting the boats° out, being well aware   *lifeboats*
That a tight boat will live in a rough sea,
360 Unless with breakers close beneath her lee.[3]

46

The worst of all was, that in their condition,
    Having been several days in great distress,
'Twas difficult to get out such provision
    As now might render their long suffering less:
365 Men, even when dying, dislike inanition;
    Their stock was damaged by the weather's stress:
Two casks of biscuit, and a keg of butter,
Were all that could be thrown into the cutter.°   *small boat*

47

But in the long-boat they contrived to stow
370   Some pounds of bread, though injured by the wet:
Water, a twenty-gallon cask or so;
    Six flasks of wine; and they contrived to get
A portion of their beef up from below,
    And with a piece of pork, moreover, met
375 But scarce enough to serve them for a luncheon—
Then there was rum, eight gallons in a puncheon.°   *cask*

48

The other boats, the yawl and pinnace, had
    Been stove° in the beginning of the gale;   *broken*

3. The side sheltered from the wind.

And the long-boat's condition was but bad,
380   As there were but two blankets for a sail,
And one oar for a mast, which a young lad
    Threw in by good luck over the ship's rail;
And two boats could not hold, far less be stored,
To save one half the people then on board.

49

385 'Twas twilight, and the sunless day went down
    Over the waste of waters; like a veil,
Which, if withdrawn, would but disclose the frown
    Of one whose hate is mask'd but to assail,
Thus to their hopeless eyes the night was shown,
390   And grimly darkled o'er the faces pale,
And the dim desolate deep: twelve days had Fear
Been their familiar, and now Death was here.

50

Some trial had been making at a raft,
    With little hope in such a rolling sea,
395 A sort of thing at which one would have laugh'd,
    If any laughter at such times could be,
Unless with people who too much have quaff'd,
    And have a kind of wild and horrid glee,
Half epileptical, and half hysterical:—
400 Their preservation would have been a miracle.

51

At half-past eight o'clock, booms, hencoops, spars,
    And all things, for a chance, had been cast loose,
That still could keep afloat the struggling tars,
    For yet they strove, although of no great use:
405 There was no light in heaven but a few stars,
    The boats put off o'ercrowded with their crews;
She gave a heel, and then a lurch to port,
And, going down head foremost—sunk, in short.

52

Then rose from sea to sky the wild farewell—
410   Then shriek'd the timid, and stood still the brave,—
Then some leap'd overboard with dreadful yell,
    As eager to anticipate their grave;
And the sea yawn'd around her like a hell,
    And down she suck'd with her the whirling wave,
415 Like one who grapples with his enemy,
And strives to strangle him before he die.

53

And first one universal shriek there rush'd,
    Louder than the loud ocean, like a crash
Of echoing thunder; and then all was hush'd,
420   Save the wild wind and the remorseless dash

Of billows; but at intervals there gush'd,
    Accompanied with a convulsive splash,
A solitary shriek, the bubbling cry
Of some strong swimmer in his agony.

54

425   The boats, as stated, had got off before,
    And in them crowded several of the crew;
And yet their present hope was hardly more
    Than what it had been, for so strong it blew
There was slight chance of reaching any shore;
430   And then they were too many, though so few—
Nine in the cutter, thirty in the boat,
Were counted in them when they got afloat.

55

All the rest perish'd; near two hundred souls
    Had left their bodies; and what's worse, alas!
435   When over Catholics the ocean rolls,
    They must wait several weeks before a mass
Takes off one peck of purgatorial coals,
    Because, till people know what's come to pass,
They won't lay out their money on the dead—
440   It costs three francs for every mass that's said.

56

Juan got into the long-boat, and there
    Contrived to help Pedrillo° to a place;   *Juan's tutor*
It seem'd as if they had exchanged their care,
    For Juan wore the magisterial face
445   Which courage gives, while poor Pedrillo's pair
    Of eyes were crying for their owner's case:
Battista, though, (a name call'd shortly Tita)
Was lost by getting at some aqua-vita.[4]

57

Pedro, his valet, too, he tried to save,
450   But the same cause, conducive to his loss,
Left him so drunk, he jump'd into the wave
    As o'er the cutter's edge he tried to cross,
And so he found a wine-and-watery grave;
    They could not rescue him although so close,
455   Because the sea ran higher every minute,
And for the boat—the crew kept crowding in it.

58

A small old spaniel,—which had been Don Jóse's,
    His father's, whom he loved, as ye may think,
For on such things the memory reposes

---

4. Ironically, "water of life": liquor. Juan's servant Battista has the name of Byron's own gondolier.

460
With tenderness—stood howling on the brink,
Knowing, (dogs have such intellectual noses!)
    No doubt, the vessel was about to sink;
And Juan caught him up, and ere he stepp'd
Off, threw him in, then after him he leap'd.

59

465
He also stuff d his money where he could
    About his person, and Pedrillo's too,
Who let him do, in fact, whate'er he would,
    Not knowing what himself to say, or do,
As every rising wave his dread renew'd;
470
    But Juan, trusting they might still get through,
And deeming there were remedies for any ill,
Thus re-embark'd his tutor and his spaniel.

60

'Twas a rough night, and blew so stiffly yet,
    That the sail was becalm'd between the seas,
475
Though on the wave's high top too much to set,
    They dared not take it in for all the breeze:
Each sea curl'd o'er the stern, and kept them wet,
    And made them bale without a moment's ease,
So that themselves as well as hopes were damp'd,
480
And the poor little cutter quickly swamp'd.

61

Nine souls more went in her: the long-boat still
    Kept above water, with an oar for mast,
Two blankets stitch'd together, answering ill
    Instead of sail, were to the oar made fast:
485
Though every wave roll'd menacing to fill,
    And present peril all before surpass'd,
They grieved for those who perish'd with the cutter,
And also for the biscuit-casks and butter.

62

The sun rose red and fiery, a sure sign
490
    Of the continuance of the gale: to run
Before the sea until it should grow fine,
    Was all that for the present could be done:
A few tea-spoonfuls of their rum and wine
    Were served out to the people, who begun
495
To faint, and damaged bread wet through the bags,
And most of them had little clothes but rags.

63

They counted thirty, crowded in a space
    Which left scarce room for motion or exertion;
They did their best to modify their case,
500
    One half sate up, though numb'd with the immersion
While t' other half were laid down in their place,

At watch and watch; thus, shivering like the tertian
Ague° in its cold fit, they fill'd their boat,   *fever*
With nothing but the sky for a great coat.

64

505   'Tis very certain the desire of life
      Prolongs it: this is obvious to physicians,
   When patients, neither plagued with friends nor wife,
      Survive through very desperate conditions,
   Because they still can hope, nor shines the knife
510   Nor shears of Atropos[5] before their visions:
   Despair of all recovery spoils longevity,
   And makes men's miseries of alarming brevity.

65

   'Tis said that persons living on annuities
      Are longer lived than others,—God knows why,
515   Unless to plague the grantors,—yet so true it is,
      That some, I really think, *do* never die;
   Of any creditors the worst a Jew it is,
      And *that's* their mode of furnishing supply:
   In my young days they lent me cash that way,
520   Which I found very troublesome to pay.

66

   'Tis thus with people in an open boat,
      They live upon the love of life, and bear
   More than can be believed, or even thought,
      And stand like rocks the tempest's wear and tear:
525   And hardship still has been the sailor's lot,
      Since Noah's ark went cruising here and there;
   She had a curious crew as well as cargo,
   Like the first old Greek privateer, the Argo.[6]

67

   But man is a carnivorous production,
530   And must have meals, at least one meal a day;
   He cannot live, like woodcocks, upon suction,[7]
      But, like the shark and tiger, must have prey;
   Although his anatomical construction
      Bears vegetables, in a grumbling way,
535   Your labouring people think beyond all question,
   Beef, veal, and mutton, better for digestion.

68

   And thus it was with this our hapless crew;
      For on the third day there came on a calm,

---

5. One of the three mythologic Fates, she cuts the thread of life.
6. In Greek legend, the ship in which Jason sailed in search of the Golden Fleece.
7. By sucking up its food; Byron probably recalled this image from Pliny's *Natural History*.

And though at first their strength it might renew,
540   And lying on their weariness like balm,
Lull'd them like turtles sleeping on the blue
    Of ocean, when they woke they felt a qualm,
And fell all ravenously on their provision,
Instead of hoarding it with due precision.

69

545 The consequence was easily foreseen—
    They ate up all they had, and drank their wine,
In spite of all remonstrances, and then
    On what, in fact, next day were they to dine?
They hoped the wind would rise, these foolish men!
550   And carry them to shore; these hopes were fine,
But as they had but one oar, and that brittle,
It would have been more wise to save their victual.

70

The fourth day came, but not a breath of air,
    And Ocean slumber'd like an unwean'd child:
555 The fifth day, and their boat lay floating there,
    The sea and sky were blue, and clear, and mild—
With their one oar (I wish they had had a pair)
    What could they do? and hunger's rage grew wild:
So Juan's spaniel, spite of his entreating,
560 Was kill'd, and portion'd out for present eating.

71

On the sixth day they fed upon his hide,
    And Juan, who had still refused, because
The creature was his father's dog that died,
    Now feeling all the vulture in his jaws,
565 With some remorse received (though first denied)
    As a great favour one of the fore-paws,
Which he divided with Pedrillo, who
Devour'd it, longing for the other too.

72

The seventh day, and no wind—the burning sun
570   Blister'd and scorch'd, and, stagnant on the sea,
They lay like carcasses; and hope was none,
    Save in the breeze that came not; savagely
They glared upon each other—all was done,
    Water, and wine, and food,—and you might see
575 The longings of the cannibal arise
(Although they spoke not) in their wolfish eyes.

73

At length one whisper'd his companion, who
    Whisper'd another, and thus it went round,
And then into a hoarser murmur grew,
580   An ominous, and wild, and desperate sound;

And when his comrade's thought each sufferer knew,
    'Twas but his own, suppress'd till now, he found:
And out they spoke of lots for flesh and blood,
And who should die to be his fellow's food.

74

585   But ere they came to this, they that day shared
        Some leathern caps, and what remain'd of shoes;
And then they look'd around them, and despair'd,
        And none to be the sacrifice would choose;
At length the lots were torn up, and prepared,
590   But of materials that much shook the Muse—
Having no paper, for the want of better,
They took by force from Juan Julia's letter.

75

The lots were made, and mark'd, and mix'd, and handed,
    In silent horror, and their distribution
595   Lull'd even the savage hunger which demanded,
        Like the Promethean vulture,[8] this pollution;
None in particular had sought or plann'd it,
        'Twas nature gnaw'd them to this resolution,
By which none were permitted to be neuter—
600   And the lot fell on Juan's luckless tutor.

76

He but requested to be bled to death:
    The surgeon had his instruments, and bled
Pedrillo, and so gently ebb'd his breath,
    You hardly could perceive when he was dead.
605   He died as born, a Catholic in faith,
        Like most in the belief in which they're bred,
And first a little crucifix he kiss'd,
And then held out his jugular and wrist.

77

The surgeon, as there was no other fee,
610   Had his first choice of morsels for his pains;
But being thirstiest at the moment, he
    Preferr'd a draught from the fast-flowing veins:
Part was divided, part thrown in the sea,
    And such things as the entrails and the brains
615   Regaled two sharks, who follow'd o'er the billow—
The sailors ate the rest of poor Pedrillo.

78

The sailors ate him, all save three or four,
    Who were not quite so fond of animal food;

8. To punish Prometheus for his theft of fire, Zeus chained him to a mountain where every day an eagle gnawed his liver. See Byron's *Prometheus*, page 750.

To these was added Juan, who, before
620   Refusing his own spaniel, hardly could
Feel now his appetite increased much more;
        'Twas not to be expected that he should,
Even in extremity of their disaster,
Dine with them on his pastor and his master.

79

625   'Twas better that he did not; for, in fact,
        The consequence was awful in the extreme;
For they, who were most ravenous in the act,
        Went raging mad—Lord! how they did blaspheme!
And foam and roll, with strange convulsions rack'd,
630   Drinking salt-water like a mountain-stream,
Tearing, and grinning, howling, screeching, swearing,
And, with hyaena-laughter, died despairing.

80

Their numbers were much thinn'd by this infliction,
        And all the rest were thin enough, Heaven knows;
635   And some of them had lost their recollection,
        Happier than they who still perceived their woes;
But others ponder'd on a new dissection,
        As if not warn'd sufficiently by those
Who had already perish'd, suffering madly,
640   For having used their appetites so sadly.

81

And next they thought upon the master's mate,
        As fattest; but he saved himself, because,
Besides being much averse from such a fate,
        There were some other reasons: the first was,
645   He had been rather indisposed of late;
        And that which chiefly proved his saving clause,
Was a small present° made to him at Cadiz,   *syphilis*
By general subscription of the ladies.

82

Of poor Pedrillo something still remain'd,
650   But was used sparingly,—some were afraid,
And others still their appetites constrain'd,
        Or but at times a little supper made;
All except Juan, who throughout abstain'd,
        Chewing a piece of bamboo, and some lead:
655   At length they caught two boobies, and a noddy,°   *sea-birds*
And then they left off eating the dead body.

83

And if Pedrillo's fate should shocking be,
        Remember Ugolino condescends
To eat the head of his arch-enemy
660   The moment after he politely ends

His tale:[9] if foes be food in hell, at sea
   'Tis surely fair to dine upon our friends,
When shipwreck's short allowance grows too scanty,
Without being much more horrible than Dante.

84

665   And the same night there fell a shower of rain,
   For which their mouths gaped, like the cracks of earth
When dried to summer dust; till taught by pain,
   Men really know not what good water's worth;
If you had been in Turkey or in Spain,
670   Or with a famish'd boat's-crew had your berth,
Or in the desert heard the camel's bell,
You'd wish yourself where Truth is—in a well.

85

It pour'd down torrents, but they were no richer
   Until they found a ragged piece of sheet,
675   Which served them as a sort of spongy pitcher,
   And when they deem'd its moisture was complete,
They wrung it out, and though a thirsty ditcher
   Might not have thought the scanty draught so sweet
As a full pot of porter, to their thinking
680   They ne'er till now had known the joys of drinking.

86

And their baked lips, with many a bloody crack,
   Suck'd in the moisture, which like nectar stream'd:
Their throats were ovens, their swoln tongues were black,
   As the rich man's in hell, who vainly scream'd
685   To beg the beggar, who could not rain back
   A drop of dew, when every drop had seem'd
To taste of heaven—If this be true, indeed,
Some Christians have a comfortable creed.[1]

* * *

102

Famine, despair, cold, thirst, and heat, had done
810   Their work on them by turns, and thinn'd them to
Such things a mother had not known her son
   Amidst the skeletons of that gaunt crew;
By night chill'd, by day scorch'd, thus one by one
   They perish'd, until wither'd to these few,

---

9. In the *Inferno* Ugolino tells Dante of his imprisonment and the death of his children, and then "with eyes
askance he took hold of [his enemy's] wretched skull
again with his teeth, which were strong on the bone like
a dog's" (33.76–78; trans. by J. D. Sinclair).

1. In Jesus's parable, a rich man refuses to feed the beggar
Lazarus; after they die, the rich man, now in hell, begs
Abraham to send Lazarus down from heaven to bring
him a drop of water; Abraham replies that it is too late to
show him mercy (Luke 16.19–26).

815　But chiefly by a species of self-slaughter,
　　In washing down Pedrillo with salt water.

103

As they drew nigh the land, which now was seen
　　Unequal in its aspect here and there,
They felt the freshness of its growing green,
820　　That waved in forest-tops, and smooth'd the air,
And fell upon their glazed eyes like a screen
　　From glistening waves, and skies so hot and bare—
Lovely seem'd any object that should sweep
Away the vast, salt, dread, eternal deep.

104

825　The shore look'd wild, without a trace of man,
　　And girt by formidable waves; but they
Were mad for land, and thus their course they ran,
　　Though right ahead the roaring breakers lay:
A reef between them also now began
830　　To show its boiling surf and bounding spray,
But finding no place for their landing better,
They ran the boat for shore,—and overset her.

105

But in his native stream, the Guadalquivir,
　　Juan to lave° his youthful limbs was wont;　　　　*bathe*
835　And having learnt to swim in that sweet river,
　　Had often turn'd the art to some account:
A better swimmer you could scarce see ever,
　　He could, perhaps, have pass'd the Hellespont,
As once (a feat on which ourselves we prided)
840　Leander, Mr. Ekenhead, and I did.[2]

106

So here, though faint, emaciated, and stark,
　　He buoy'd his boyish limbs, and strove to ply
With the quick wave, and gain, ere it was dark,
　　The beach which lay before him, high and dry:
845　The greatest danger here was from a shark,
　　That carried off his neighbour by the thigh;
As for the other two, they could not swim,
So nobody arrived on shore but him.

107

Nor yet had he arrived but for the oar,
850　　Which, providentially for him, was wash'd
Just as his feeble arms could strike no more,

---

2. In May 1810 Byron and Lieutenant Ekenhead repeated Leander's exploit of swimming to his beloved Hero, first made famous by Ovid; Byron commemorated the event in a poem, *Written after Swimming from Sestos to Abydos.*

And the hard wave o'erwhelm'd him as 'twas dash'd
Within his grasp; he clung to it, and sore
   The waters beat while he thereto was lash'd;
855   At last, with swimming, wading, scrambling, he
Roll'd on the beach, half senseless, from the sea:

108

There, breathless, with his digging nails he clung
   Fast to the sand, lest the returning wave,
From whose reluctant roar his life he wrung,
860   Should suck him back to her insatiate grave:
And there he lay, full length, where he was flung,
   Before the entrance of a cliff-worn cave,
With just enough of life to feel its pain,
And deem that it was saved, perhaps, in vain.[3]

109

865   With slow and staggering effort he arose,
   But sunk again upon his bleeding knee
And quivering hand; and then he look'd for those
   Who long had been his mates upon the sea;
But none of them appear'd to share his woes,
870   Save one, a corpse from out the famish'd three,
Who died two days before, and now had found
An unknown barren beach for burial ground.

110

And as he gazed, his dizzy brain spun fast,
   And down he sunk; and as he sunk, the sand
875   Swam round and round, and all his senses pass'd:
   He fell upon his side, and his stretch'd hand
Droop'd dripping on the oar (their jury-mast),
   And, like a wither'd lily, on the land
His slender frame and pallid aspect lay,
880   As fair a thing as e'er was form'd of clay.

111

How long in his damp trance young Juan lay
   He knew not, for the earth was gone for him,
And Time had nothing more of night nor day
   For his congealing blood, and senses dim;
885   And how this heavy faintness pass'd away
   He knew not, till each painful pulse and limb,
And tingling vein, seem'd throbbing back to life,
For Death, though vanquish'd, still retired with strife.

112

His eyes he open'd, shut, again unclosed,
890   For all was doubt and dizziness; he thought

---

3. This and the next two stanzas are modeled on shipwrecked Ulysses's staggering to land in Homer's *Odyssey*, bk. 5. See pages 978–79 for two English translations.

He still was in the boat, and had but dozed,
  And felt again with his despair o'erwrought,
And wish'd it death in which he had reposed,
  And then once more his feelings back were brought,
895 And slowly by his swimming eyes was seen
  A lovely female face of seventeen.

113

'Twas bending close o'er his, and the small mouth
  Seem'd almost prying into his for breath;
And chafing him, the soft warm hand of youth
900   Recall'd his answering spirits back from death;
And, bathing his chill temples, tried to soothe
  Each pulse to animation, till beneath
Its gentle touch and trembling care, a sigh
To these kind efforts made a low reply.

114

905 Then was the cordial pour'd, and mantle flung
  Around his scarce-clad limbs; and the fair arm
Raised higher the faint head which o'er it hung;
  And her transparent cheek, all pure and warm,
Pillow'd his death-like forehead; then she wrung
910   His dewy curls, long drench'd by every storm;
And watch'd with eagerness each throb that drew
A sigh from his heaved bosom—and hers, too.

115

And lifting him with care into the cave,
  The gentle girl, and her attendant,—one
915 Young, yet her elder, and of brow less grave,
  And more robust of figure,—then begun
To kindle fire, and as the new flames gave
  Light to the rocks that roof'd them, which the sun
Had never seen, the maid, or whatsoe'er
920 She was, appear'd distinct, and tall, and fair.

116

Her brow was overhung with coins of gold,
  That sparkled o'er the auburn of her hair,
Her clustering hair, whose longer locks were roll'd
  In braids behind; and though her stature were
925 Even of the highest for a female mould,
  They nearly reach'd her heel; and in her air
There was a something which bespoke command,
As one who was a lady in the land.[4]

---

4. Juan has landed on a Greek island, and is found by Haidée, daughter of absent wealthy pirate Lambro. Fearful that Lambro will sell Juan, Haidée hides him in a cave and brings him breakfast and fresh clothes the next morning. The episode plays against the welcome of shipwrecked Odysseus by the young princess Nausicaa.

117

Her hair, I said, was auburn; but her eyes
930   Were black as death, their lashes the same hue,
Of downcast length, in whose silk shadow lies
    Deepest attraction; for when to the view
Forth from its raven fringe the full glance flies,
    Ne'er with such force the swiftest arrow flew;
935 'Tis as the snake late coil'd, who pours his length,
And hurls at once his venom and his strength.

* * *

161

And then fair Haidée tried her tongue at speaking,
    But not a word could Juan comprehend,
Although he listen'd so that the young Greek in
    Her earnestness would ne'er have made an end;
1285 And, as he interrupted not, went eking
    Her speech out to her protégé and friend,
Till pausing at the last her breath to take,
She saw he did not understand Romaic.

162

And then she had recourse to nods, and signs,
1290   And smiles, and sparkles of the speaking eye,
And read (the only book she could) the lines
    Of his fair face, and found, by sympathy,
The answer eloquent, where the soul shines
    And darts in one quick glance a long reply;
1295 And thus in every look she saw exprest
A world of words, and things at which she guess'd.

163

And now, by dint of fingers and of eyes,
    And words repeated after her, he took
A lesson in her tongue; but by surmise,
1300   No doubt, less of her language than her look:
As he who studies fervently the skies
    Turns oftener to the stars than to his book,
Thus Juan learn'd his alpha beta better
From Haidée's glance than any graven letter.

* * *

182

And forth they wander'd, her sire being gone,
1450   As I have said, upon an expedition;
And mother, brother, guardian, she had none,
    Save Zoe,° who, although with due precision   *Haidée's maid*
She waited on her lady with the sun,
    Thought daily service was her only mission,
1455 Bringing warm water, wreathing her long tresses,
And asking now and then for cast-off dresses.

183

It was the cooling hour, just when the rounded
　　Red sun sinks down behind the azure hill,
Which then seems as if the whole earth it bounded,
1460　　　Circling all nature, hush'd, and dim, and still,
With the far mountain-crescent half surrounded
　　On one side, and the deep sea calm and chill
Upon the other, and the rosy sky,
With one star sparkling through it like an eye.

184

1465 And thus they wander'd forth, and hand in hand,[5]
　　Over the shining pebbles and the shells,
Glided along the smooth and harden'd sand,
　　And in the worn and wild receptacles
Work'd by the storms, yet work'd as it were plann'd,
1470　　In hollow halls, with sparry roofs and cells,
They turn'd to rest; and, each clasp'd by an arm,
Yielded to the deep twilight's purple charm.

185

They look'd up to the sky, whose floating glow
　　Spread like a rosy ocean, vast and bright;
1475 They gazed upon the glittering sea below,
　　Whence the broad moon rose circling into sight;
They heard the wave's splash, and the wind so low,
　　And saw each other's dark eyes darting light
Into each other—and, beholding this,
1480 Their lips drew near, and clung into a kiss;

186

A long, long kiss, a kiss of youth, and love,
　　And beauty, all concentrating like rays
Into one focus, kindled from above;
　　Such kisses as belong to early days,
1485 Where heart, and soul, and sense, in concert move,
　　And the blood's lava, and the pulse a blaze,
Each kiss a heart-quake,—for a kiss's strength,
I think, it must be reckon'd by its length.

187

By length I mean duration; theirs endured
1490　　Heaven knows how long—no doubt they never reckon'd;
And if they had, they could not have secured
　　The sum of their sensations to a second:
They had not spoken; but they felt allured,
　　As if their souls and lips each other beckon'd,
1495 Which, being join'd, like swarming bees they clung—
Their hearts the flowers from whence the honey sprung.

5. The echo of the end of *Paradise Lost* is softly ominous: "They hand in hand with wandering steps and slow, / Through Eden took their solitary way" (12.648–49).

188

They were alone, but not alone as they
    Who shut in chambers think it loneliness;
The silent ocean, and the starlight bay,
1500   The twilight glow, which momently grew less,
The voiceless sands, and dropping caves, that lay
    Around them, made them to each other press,
As if there were no life beneath the sky
Save theirs, and that their life could never die.

189

1505 They fear'd no eyes nor ears on that lone beach,
    They felt no terrors from the night, they were
All in all to each other: though their speech
    Was broken words, they *thought* a language there,—
And all the burning tongues the passions teach
1510   Found in one sigh the best interpreter
Of nature's oracle—first love,—that all
Which Eve has left her daughters since her fall.

190

Haidée spoke not of scruples, ask'd no vows,
    Nor offer'd any; she had never heard
1515 Of plight and promises to be a spouse,
    Or perils by a loving maid incurr'd;
She was all which pure ignorance allows,
    And flew to her young mate like a young bird;
And, never having dreamt of falsehood, she
1520 Had not one word to say of constancy.

191

She loved, and was beloved—she adored,
    And she was worshipp'd; after nature's fashion,
Their intense souls, into each other pour'd,
    If souls could die, had perish'd in that passion,—
1525 But by degrees their senses were restored,
    Again to be o'ercome, again to dash on;
And, beating 'gainst *his* bosom, Haidée's heart
Felt as if never more to beat apart.

192

Alas! they were so young, so beautiful,
1530   So lonely, loving, helpless, and the hour
Was that in which the heart is always full,
    And, having o'er itself no further power,
Prompts deeds eternity can not annul,
    But pays off moments in an endless shower
1535 Of hell-fire—all prepared for people giving
Pleasure or pain to one another living.

193

Alas! for Juan and Haidée! they were
    So loving and so lovely—till then never,

Excepting our first parents, such a pair
    Had run the risk of being damn'd for ever;
1540 And Haidée, being devout as well as fair,
    Had, doubtless, heard about the Stygian river,[6]
And hell and purgatory—but forgot
Just in the very crisis she should not.

from Canto 3[1]

[JUAN AND HAIDÉE. THE POET FOR HIRE]

1

Hail, Muse! *et cetera.*—We left Juan sleeping,
    Pillow'd upon a fair and happy breast,
And watch'd by eyes that never yet knew weeping,
    And loved by a young heart, too deeply blest
5 To feel the poison through her spirit creeping,
    Or know who rested there; a foe to rest,
Had soil'd the current of her sinless years,
And turn'd her pure heart's purest blood to tears!

2

Oh, Love! what is it in this world of ours
10   Which makes it fatal to be loved? Ah why
With cypress branches[2] hast thou wreathed thy bowers,
    And made thy best interpreter a sigh?
As those who dote on odours pluck the flowers,
    And place them on their breast—but place to die—
15 Thus the frail beings we would fondly cherish
Are laid within our bosoms but to perish.

3

In her first passion woman loves her lover,
    In all the others all she loves is love,
Which grows a habit she can ne'er get over,
20   And fits her loosely—like an easy glove,
As you may find, whene'er you like to prove her:
    One man alone at first her heart can move;
She then prefers him in the plural number,
Not finding that the additions much encumber.

4

25 I know not if the fault be men's or theirs;
    But one thing's pretty sure; a woman planted°—   *abandoned*
(Unless at once she plunge for life in prayers)—
    After a decent time must be gallanted;
Although, no doubt, her first of love affairs
30   Is that to which her heart is wholly granted;

---

6. The river Styx encircles Hades.
1. Composed between September and November 1819. Cantos 3–5 were published together in 1821, still anonymously. The outcry over Cantos 1 and 2, Byron

confessed, had "*hurt*" him and made Murray reluctant to publish more, but 3–5 sold extremely well.
2. Symbol of mourning.

Yet there are some, they say, who have had *none*,
But those who have ne'er end with only *one*.

5

'Tis melancholy, and a fearful sign
    Of human frailty, folly, also crime,
35 That love and marriage rarely can combine,
    Although they both are born in the same clime;
Marriage from love, like vinegar from wine—
    A sad, sour, sober beverage—by time
Is sharpen'd from its high celestial flavour
40 Down to a very homely household savour.

6

There's something of antipathy, as 'twere,
    Between their present and their future state;
A kind of flattery that's hardly fair
    Is used until the truth arrives too late—
45 Yet what can people do, except despair?
    The same things change their names at such a rate;
For instance—passion in a lover's glorious,
But in a husband is pronounced uxorious.°   *wife-dominated*

7

Men grow ashamed of being so very fond;
50   They sometimes also get a little tired
(But that, of course, is rare), and then despond:
    The same things cannot always be admired,
Yet 'tis "so nominated in the bond,"[3]
    That both are tied till one shall have expired.
55 Sad thought! to lose the spouse that was adorning
Our days, and put one's servants into mourning.

8

There's doubtless something in domestic doings
    Which forms, in fact, true love's antithesis;
Romances paint at full length people's wooings,
60   But only give a bust of marriages;
For no one cares for matrimonial cooings,
    There's nothing wrong in a connubial kiss:
Think you, if Laura had been Petrarch's wife,
He would have written sonnets all his life?[4]

9

65 All tragedies are finish'd by a death,
    All comedies are ended by a marriage;
The future states of both are left to faith,
    For authors fear description might disparage
The worlds to come of both, or fall beneath,

---

3. "Specified in the contract"; Shakespeare, *The Merchant of Venice*, 4.1.258. (Shylock's legalism).

4. Laura was the famous subject of the poems of Italian poet Petrarch (1304–1374), who loved her from afar.

70 And then both worlds would punish their miscarriage;
 So leaving each their priest and prayer-book ready,
 They say no more of Death or of the Lady.[5]

* * *

70[6]

 Of all the dresses I select Haidée's:
  She wore two jelicks°—one was of pale yellow;   *Turkish vests*
555 Of azure, pink, and white was her chemise—
  'Neath which her breast heaved like a little billow;
 With buttons form'd of pearls as large as peas,
  All gold and crimson shone her jelick's fellow,
 And the striped white gauze baracan° that bound her,   *robe*
560 Like fleecy clouds about the moon, flow'd round her.

71

 One large gold bracelet clasp'd each lovely arm,
  Lockless—so pliable from the pure gold
 That the hand stretch'd and shut it without harm,
  The limb which it adorn'd its only mould;
565 So beautiful—its very shape would charm,
  And clinging as if loath to lose its hold,
 The purest ore enclosed the whitest skin
 That e'er by precious metal was held in.

72

 Around, as princess of her father's land,
570 A like gold bar above her instep roll'd
 Announced her rank;[7] twelve rings were on her hand;
  Her hair was starr'd with gems; her veil's fine fold
 Below her breast was fasten'd with a band
  Of lavish pearls, whose worth could scarce be told;
575 Her orange silk full Turkish trousers furl'd
 About the prettiest ankle in the world.

73

 Her hair's long auburn waves down to her heel
  Flow'd like an Alpine torrent which the sun
 Dyes with his morning light,—and would conceal
580 Her person if allow'd at large to run,[8]
 And still they seem resentfully to feel
  The silken fillet's° curb, and sought to shun   *hairband's*
 Their bonds whene'er some Zephyr° caught began   *breeze*
 To offer his young pinion° as her fan.   *wing*

---

5. An allusion to the ballad *Death and the Lady*.
6. Hearing that Lambro has died, Haidée and Juan have made the island a place of pleasure.
7. The bar of gold above the instep is a mark of sovereign rank in the women of the families of the deys, and is worn as such by their female relatives [Byron's note]. Deys are rulers.

8. This is no exaggeration; there were four women whom I remember to have seen, who possessed their hair in this profusion; of these, three were English, the other a Levantine. . . . when let down, it almost entirely shaded the person, so as nearly to render dress a superfluity [Byron's note].

74

585   Round her she made an atmosphere of life,
           The very air seem'd lighter from her eyes,
       They were so soft and beautiful, and rife
           With all we can imagine of the skies,
       And pure as Psyche ere she grew a wife[9]—
590   Too pure even for the purest human ties;
       Her overpowering presence made you feel
       It would not be idolatry to kneel.

75

       Her eyelashes, though dark as night, were tinged
           (It is the country's custom), but in vain;
595   For those large black eyes were so blackly fringed,
           The glossy rebels mock'd the jetty stain,
       And in their native beauty stood avenged:
           Her nails were touch'd with henna; but again
       The power of art was turn'd to nothing, for
600   They could not look more rosy than before.

76

       The henna should be deeply dyed to make
           The skin relieved appear more fairly fair;
       She had no need of this, day ne'er will break
           On mountain tops more heavenly white than her:
605   The eye might doubt if it were well awake,
           She was so like a vision; I might err,
       But Shakspeare also says 'tis very silly
       "To gild refined gold, or paint the lily."[1]

77

       Juan had on a shawl of black and gold,
610   But a white baracan, and so transparent
       The sparkling gems beneath you might behold,
           Like small stars through the milky way apparent;
       His turban, furl'd in many a graceful fold,
           An emerald aigrette[2] with Haidée's hair in't
615   Surmounted, as its clasp, a glowing crescent,
       Whose rays shone ever trembling, but incessant.

78

       And now they were diverted by their suite,
           Dwarfs, dancing girls, black eunuchs, and a poet,
       Which made their new establishment complete;
620   The last was of great fame, and liked to show it:
       His verses rarely wanted their due feet—

---

9. Beloved of Cupid, Psyche was separated from him by
the jealousy of his mother Venus, but after many trials
was reunited with him and immortalized.

1. *King John*, 4.2.11; needless ornamentation.
2. A decorative spray of egret feathers, often bejeweled.

And for his theme—he seldom sung below it,
He being paid to satirise or flatter,
As the psalm says, "inditing a good matter."[3]

79

625   He praised the present, and abused the past,
        Reversing the good custom of old days,
An Eastern anti-jacobin[4] at last
        He turn'd, preferring pudding to *no* praise—
For some few years his lot had been o'ercast
630   By his seeming independent in his lays,
But now he sung the Sultan and the Pacha
With truth like Southey, and with verse like Crashaw.[5]

80

He was a man who had seen many changes,
        And always changed as true as any needle;
635   His polar star being one which rather ranges,
        And not the fix'd—he knew the way to wheedle:
So vile he 'scaped the doom which oft avenges;
        And being fluent (save indeed when fee'd ill),
He lied with such a fervour of intention—
640   There was no doubt he earn'd his laureate pension.

81

But he had genius,—when a turncoat has it,
        The "Vates irritabilis" takes care[6]
That without notice few full moons shall pass it;
        Even good men like to make the public stare:—
645   But to my subject—let me see—what was it?—
        Oh!—the third canto—and the pretty pair—
Their loves, and feasts, and house, and dress, and mode
Of living in their insular abode.

82

Their poet, a sad trimmer,° but no less   *opportunist*
650   In company a very pleasant fellow,
Had been the favourite of full many a mess
        Of men, and made them speeches when half mellow;
And though his meaning they could rarely guess,
        Yet still they deign'd to hiccup or to bellow
655   The glorious meed of popular applause,
Of which the first ne'er knows the second cause.

---

3. Psalm 45.1, in praise of the King.
4. An opponent of the French Jacobins, hence of radicalism generally, and thus suited to be a court poet.
5. For Southey as venal poet, see the Dedication to *Don*

Juan. Poet Richard Crashaw (1612?–1649) was known for his extravagant style.
6. "Irritable race" (Horace on poets, *Epistles* 2.2.102).

83

But now being lifted into high society,
      And having pick'd up several odds and ends
Of free thoughts in his travels for variety,
660   He deem'd, being in a lone isle, among friends,
That without any danger of a riot, he
      Might for long lying make himself amends;
And singing as he sung in his warm youth,
Agree to a short armistice with truth.

84

665 He had travell'd 'mongst the Arabs, Turks, and Franks,[7]
      And knew the self-loves of the different nations;
And having lived with people of all ranks,
      Had something ready upon most occasions—
Which got him a few presents and some thanks.
670   He varied with some skill his adulations;
To "do at Rome as Romans do," a piece
Of conduct was which he observed in Greece.

85

Thus, usually, when he was ask'd to sing,
      He gave the different nations something national;
675 'Twas all the same to him—"God save the king,"
      Or "Ça ira," according to the fashion all:[8]
His muse made increment of any thing,
      From the high lyric down to the low rational:
If Pindar sang horse-races, what should hinder
680 Himself from being as pliable as Pindar?[9]

86

In France, for instance, he would write a chanson;
      In England a six canto quarto tale;
In Spain, he'd make a ballad or romance on
      The last war—much the same in Portugal;
685 In Germany, the Pegasus he'd prance on
      Would be old Goethe's—(see what says De Staël)[1]
In Italy he'd ape the "Trecentisti";[2]
In Greece, he'd sing some sort of hymn like this t'ye:

1

The isles of Greece, the isles of Greece![3]
690   Where burning Sappho loved and sung,
Where grew the arts of war and peace,—

---

7. Eastern Mediterranean term for Western Europeans.
8. "God save the king" is the British national anthem; "Ça ira" (It will go on) is a French revolutionary chant.
9. Pindar (c. 522–442 B.C.) wrote odes celebrating the victors in the Olympic Games.
1. In *On Germany* (1810–1813), Mme de Staël suggested that Goethe (whom she and Byron admired) could repre-

sent the whole of German literature.
2. The writers of the 1300s (Dante, Petrarch, Boccaccio).
3. This song, frequently anthologized, became one of Byron's most famous. In the 1820s it spoke to the current War for Greek Independence. See Percy Shelley's *Hellas*, page 913.

Where Delos rose, and Phoebus sprung![4]
Eternal summer gilds them yet,
But all, except their sun, is set.

2

695   The Scian and the Teian muse,[5]
The hero's harp, the lover's lute,
Have found the fame your shores refuse;
Their place of birth alone is mute
700   To sounds which echo further west
Than your sires' "Islands of the Blest."[6]

3

The mountains look on Marathon—
And Marathon looks on the sea;
And musing there an hour alone,
I dream'd that Greece might still be free;
705   For standing on the Persians' grave,
I could not deem myself a slave.[7]

4

A king sate on the rocky brow
Which looks o'er sea-born Salamis;[8]
And ships, by thousands, lay below,
710   And men in nations;—all were his!
He counted them at break of day—
And when the sun set where were they?

5

And where are they? and where art thou,
My country? On thy voiceless shore
715   The heroic lay is tuneless now—
The heroic bosom beats no more!
And must thy lyre, so long divine,
Degenerate into hands like mine?

6

'Tis something, in the dearth of fame,
720   Though link'd among a fetter'd race,
To feel at least a patriot's shame,
Even as I sing, suffuse my face;
For what is left the poet here?
For Greeks a blush—for Greece a tear.

7

725   Must we but weep o'er days more blest?
Must *we* but blush?—Our fathers bled.

---

4. Delos, the birthplace of Phoebus Apollo, was said to
have been raised from the sea by Poseidon. Sappho lived
on Lesbos.
5. Scio (Chios) was the birthplace of Homer, Teos of the
erotic lyricist Anacreon.

6. Described by Hesiod (8th century B.C.) in *Works and Days*.
7. At Marathon in 490 B.C. the Greeks defeated the far
larger invading Persian army.
8. In 480 B.C. Xerxes watched the Greeks defeat of the
Persian fleet at Salamis.

Earth! render back from out thy breast
   A remnant of our Spartan dead!
Of the three hundred grant but three,
730   To make a new Thermopylae![9]

        8

What, silent still? and silent all?
   Ah! no;—the voices of the dead
Sound like a distant torrent's fall,
   And answer, "Let one living head,
735   But one arise,—we come, we come!"
'Tis but the living who are dumb.

        9

In vain—in vain: strike other chords;
   Fill high the cup with Samian wine!
Leave battles to the Turkish hordes,
740   And shed the blood of Scio's vine!
Hark! rising to the ignoble call—
How answers each bold Bacchanal!

       10

You have the Pyrrhic dance as yet
   Where is the Pyrrhic phalanx° gone?   *military formation*
745   Of two such lessons, why forget
     The nobler and the manlier one?
You have the letters Cadmus gave—
Think ye he meant them for a slave?[1]

       11

Fill high the bowl with Samian wine!
750   We will not think of themes like these!
It made Anacreon's song divine:
   He served—but served Polycrates[2]—
A tyrant; but our masters then
Were still, at least, our countrymen.

       12

755   The tyrant of the Chersonese
   Was freedom's best and bravest friend;
That tyrant was Miltiades![3]
   Oh! that the present hour would lend
Another despot of the kind!
760   Such chains as his were sure to bind.

---

9. In 480 B.C. Leonidas and 300 Spartans held off the Persian army at Thermopylae until they were betrayed and overwhelmed.
1. The introduction of the alphabet was ascribed to Cadmus, founder of Thebes.
2. The tyrant of Samos, Anacreon's adopted home.
3. Commander of the Greek forces at Marathon.

13

Fill high the bowl with Samian wine!
   On Suli's rock, and Parga's shore,
Exists the remnant of a line°   *lineage*
   Such as the Doric mothers bore;
765   And there, perhaps, some seed is sown,
The Heracleidan blood might own.[4]

14

Trust not for freedom to the Franks—
   They have a king who buys and sells:
In native swords, and native ranks,
770   The only hope of courage dwells;
But Turkish force, and Latin fraud,
Would break your shield, however broad.

15

Fill high the bowl with Samian wine!
   Our virgins dance beneath the shade—
775   I see their glorious black eyes shine;
   But gazing on each glowing maid,
My own the burning tear-drop laves,
To think such breasts must suckle slaves.

16

Place me on Sunium's marbled steep,°   *Cape Colonna*
780   Where nothing, save the waves and I,
May hear our mutual murmurs sweep;
   There, swan-like, let me sing and die:
A land of slaves shall ne'er be mine—
Dash down yon cup of Samian wine!

87

785   Thus sung, or would, or could, or should have sung,
   The modern Greek, in tolerable verse;
If not like Orpheus quite, when Greece was young,
   Yet in these times he might have done much worse:
His strain display'd some feeling—right or wrong;
790   And feeling, in a poet, is the source
Of others' feeling; but they are such liars,
And take all colours—like the hands of dyers.[5]

88

But words are things, and a small drop of ink,
   Falling like dew, upon a thought, produces
795   That which makes thousands, perhaps millions, think;

---

4. Suli, in northwest Greece, where Byron traveled in 1809; Parga is on the Ionian coast. The warlike Suliotes are seen as descendants of the Spartans, themselves descended from the Dorians and, mythically, from Hercules.

5. In Sonnet 111, Shakespeare laments that writing for the public subdues one's nature to "what it works in, like the dyer's hand."

'Tis strange, the shortest letter which man uses
   Instead of speech, may form a lasting link
     Of ages; to what straits old Time reduces
      Frail man, when paper—even a rag° like this,   *cheap paper*
800   Survives himself, his tomb, and all that's his.

from Canto 7[1]
[Critique of Military "Glory"][2]

78

—The work of glory still went on
   In preparations for a cannonade
     As terrible as that of Ilion,[3]
620   If Homer had found mortars ready made;
   But now, instead of slaying Priam's son,[4]
     We only can but talk of escalade,°   *scaling walls by ladder*
Bombs, drums, guns, bastions, batteries, bayonets, bullets;
Hard words, which stick in the soft Muses' gullets.

79

625   Oh, thou eternal Homer! who couldst charm
     All ears, though long; all ages, though so short,
   By merely wielding with poetic arm
     Arms to which men will never more resort,
Unless gunpowder should be found to harm
630   Much less than is the hope of every court,
Which now is leagued young Freedom to annoy;
But they will not find Liberty a Troy:—

80

Oh, thou eternal Homer! I have now
   To paint a siege, wherein more men were slain,
635   With deadlier engines and a speedier blow,
     Than in thy Greek gazette of that campaign;
And yet, like all men else, I must allow,
   To vie with thee would be about as vain

1. Byron composed Cantos 6–8 between January and July 1822. He intended to publish as usual with John Murray, but increasing controversy—his drama *Cain* had caused an outcry in 1821—and the violent critique in the new cantos caused Murray to delay. In a preface, Byron denounced Castlereagh, a recent suicide, as a Minister "the most despotic in intention and weakest in intellect that ever tyrannized over a country," and he attacked "the degraded and hypocritical mass" of "this double-dealing and false-speaking time of selfish Spoilers." See also the Dedication, pages 782–86. Byron moved from his respectable Tory publisher to John Hunt, brother of Leigh Hunt, with whom he was engaged on *The Liberal;* in 1813 both Hunts had been sentenced to two years' imprisonment for libeling the Prince Regent. Hunt published Cantos 6–8 in July 1823, still anonymously, though Byron's authorship had never been doubted. A motto from Shakespeare

on the title page marked Byron's repudiation of English censoriousness: "Dost thou think, because thou art virtuous, there shall be no more Cakes and Ale?"—"Yes, by St. Anne; and Ginger shall be hot i' the mouth too!" (*Twelfth Night* 2.3.104–106).
2. The idyll of Haidée and Juan is ended by the unexpected return of her father, who sells him as a slave in Constantinople. Juan is bought by the Sultan's wife, who disguises him as "Juanna" and hides him in her husband's harem. There his adventures with a harem girl arouse the Sultana's wrath. He escapes a death sentence and joins the Russian army, then besieging Ismail, a Turkish town on the north shore of the Danube, during November–December 1790.
3. Troy; the Siege of Ismail corresponds both to the *Iliad* and, in its hellish quality, to the underworld journey of epic.
4. Hector, the Trojan hero.

640   As for a brook to cope with ocean's flood;
     But still we moderns equal you in blood;

81

     If not in poetry, at least in fact;
       And fact is truth, the grand desideratum!
     Of which, howe'er the Muse describes each act,
       There should be ne'ertheless a slight substratum.
645   But now the town is going to be attack'd;
       Great deeds are doing—how shall I relate 'em?
     Souls of immortal generals! Phoebus° watches   *the sun god*
     To colour up his rays from your despatches.

1822   1823

from Canto 11[1]
[JUAN IN ENGLAND][2]

21

     Through Groves, so call'd as being void of trees,
       (Like *lucus* from *no* light);[3] through prospects named
     Mount Pleasant, as containing nought to please,
       Nor much to climb; through little boxes framed
165   Of bricks, to let the dust in at your ease,
       With "To be let,"° upon their doors proclaim'd;   *rented*
     Through "Rows" most modestly call'd "Paradise,"
     Which Eve might quit without much sacrifice;—

22

     Through coaches, drays, choked turnpikes, and a whirl
170   Of wheels, and roar of voices, and confusion;
     Here taverns wooing to a pint of "purl,"°   *gin and beer*
       There mails° fast flying off like a delusion;   *mail-coaches*
     There barbers' blocks with periwigs in curl
       In windows; here the lamplighter's infusion
175   Slowly distill'd into the glimmering glass
     (For in those days we had not got to gas—);[4]

23

     Through this, and much, and more, is the approach
       Of travellers to mighty Babylon:
     Whether they come by horse, or chaise, or coach,
180   With slight exceptions, all the ways seem one.
     I could say more, but do not choose to encroach
       Upon the Guide-book's privilege. The sun

1. Composed October 1822. John Hunt published Cantos 9–11 in August 1823, again anonymously.
2. Having distinguished himself at Ismail, Juan is sent to St. Petersburg, where he becomes the favorite of Empress Catherine the Great, whose sexual appetite was notorious. Amply rewarded but exhausted, Juan is sent on a diplomatic mission to England to restore his declining health. His journey across Europe enabled Byron lightly

to revisit the materials of *Childe Harold's Pilgrimage*, and the arrival in England returns *Don Juan*, in a vivid act of memory, to the Regency England in which Byron had shined. Here Juan is approaching London.
3. A famous ancient false etymology derived the Latin word for "grove," *lucus*, from the lack of light (*lux*) under the trees.
4. Gas came into use in London in 1812.

Had set some time, and night was on the ridge
Of twilight, as the party cross'd the bridge.

24

185   That's rather fine, the gentle sound of Thamis°—   *river Thames*
    Who vindicates a moment, too, his stream—
      Though hardly heard through multifarious "damme's."
      The lamps of Westminster's more regular gleam,
    The breadth of pavement, and yon shrine[5] where fame is
190   A spectral resident—whose pallid beam
In shape of moonshine hovers o'er the pile—
Make this a sacred part of Albion's isle.

25

The Druids' groves are gone—so much the better:
    Stone-Henge[6] is not—but what the devil is it?—
195   But Bedlam still exists with its sage fetter,
    That madmen may not bite you on a visit;
The Bench too seats or suits full many a debtor;
    The Mansion House too (though some people quiz it)
To me appears a stiff yet grand erection;
200   But then the Abbey's worth the whole collection.[7]

26

The line of lights too up to Charing Cross,
    Pall Mall,[8] and so forth, have a coruscation°   *sparkle*
Like gold as in comparison to dross,
    Match'd with the Continent's illumination,
205   Whose cities Night by no means deigns to gloss.
    The French were not yet a lamp-lighting nation,
And when they grew so—on their new-found lantern,
Instead of wicks, they made a wicked man turn.[9]

27

A row of gentlemen along the streets
210   Suspended, may illuminate mankind,
As also bonfires made of country seats;
    But the old way is best for the purblind:
The other looks like phosphorus on sheets,
    A sort of ignis fatuus° to the mind,   *will-o'-the-wisp*
215   Which, though 'tis certain to perplex and frighten,
Must burn more mildly ere it can enlighten.

28

But London's so well lit, that if Diogenes
    Could recommence to hunt his *honest man*,[1]

---

5. Westminster Abbey, filled with shrines.
6. Interest in the ancient Celtic Druids, to whom the oak was sacred, and Stonehenge, the Druid stone circle on Salisbury Plain, had grown in the 18th century.
7. Bedlam, a corruption of Bethlehem Hospital for the insane; the Bench, the Court of Common Pleas; the Mansion House, the residence of the Lord Mayor.

8. Juan is proceeding to the fashionable West End.
9. A punning capsule history, from the rationalism of the Enlightenment to the hanging of offending persons from lampposts during the French Revolution.
1. Greek philosopher Diogenes the Cynic (c. 423–323 B.C.) took a lantern in broad daylight to search for an honest man.

And found him not amidst the various progenies
220   Of this enormous city's spreading spawn,
'Twere not for want of lamps to aid his dodging his
    Yet undiscover'd treasure. What *I* can,
I've done to find the same throughout life's journey,
But see the world is only one attorney.

* * *

65[2]

His morns he pass'd in business—which dissected,
    Was like all business, a laborious nothing,
515   That leads to lassitude, the most infected
    And Centaur Nessus garb of mortal clothing,[3]
And on our sofas makes us lie dejected,
    And talk in tender horrors of our loathing
All kinds of toil, save for our country's good—.
520   Which grows no better, though 'tis time it should.

66

His afternoons he pass'd in visits, luncheons,
    Lounging, and boxing; and the twilight hour
In riding round those vegetable puncheons
    Call'd "Parks," where there is neither fruit nor flower
525   Enough to gratify a bee's slight munchings;
    But after all it is the only "bower,"
(In Moore's phrase) where the fashionable fair
Can form a slight acquaintance with fresh air.

67

Then dress, then dinner, then awakes the world!
530   Then glare the lamps, then whirl the wheels, then roar
Through street and square fast flashing chariots hurl'd
    Like harness'd meteors; then along the floor
Chalk mimics painting; then festoons are twirl'd;
    Then roll the brazen thunders of the door,
535   Which opens to the thousand happy few
An earthly Paradise of "Or Molu."[4]

* * *

74

585   Our hero, as a hero, young and handsome,
    Noble, rich, celebrated, and a stranger,
Like other slaves of course must pay his ransom
    Before he can escape from so much danger
As will environ a conspicuous man.[5] Some
590   Talk about poetry, and "rack and manger,"°   *rack and ruin*

---

2. The intervening stanzas record Juan's enthusiastic reception by high society.
3. When her husband Hercules was unfaithful, Deianira sent him the tunic of the Centaur Nessus, whom he had killed. Believing it to be a love charm, Hercules died in agony.
4. Gilded bronze, a popular ornamental material.
5. Echoing Samuel Butler's satiric poem, *Hudibras* (1663–1678), "Ah me! what perils do environ / The man who meddles with cold iron" (pt. 1, ch. 3).

And ugliness, disease, as toil and trouble;—
I wish they knew the life of a young noble.

75

They are young, but know not youth—it is anticipated;
    Handsome but wasted, rich without a sou;
595   Their vigour in a thousand arms is dissipated;
    Their cash comes *from,* their wealth goes to a Jew;
Both senates see their nightly votes participated
    Between the tyrant's and the tribunes' crew;[6]
And having voted, dined, drank, gamed, and whored,
600   The family vault receives another lord.

1822   1823

Stanzas[1]

When a man hath no freedom to fight for at home,
    Let him combat for that of his neighbours;
Let him think of the glories of Greece and of Rome,
    And get knock'd on the head for his labours.

5   To do good to mankind is the chivalrous plan,
    And is always as nobly requited;
Then battle for freedom wherever you can,
    And, if not shot or hang'd, you'll get knighted.

1820   1830

Messolonghi, Jan 22. 1824[1]
On this day I complete my thirty sixth year

'Tis time this heart should be unmoved
    Since others it hath ceased to move,
Yet, though I cannot be beloved
    Still let me love.

5   My days are in the yellow leaf[2]
    The flowers and fruits of love are gone—
The worm, the canker, and the grief
    Are mine alone.

The fire that on my bosom preys
10   Is lone as some Volcanic Isle,
No torch is kindled at its blaze
    A funeral pile!

---

6. The tyrants are the Tories, in power; the tribunes, representatives of the people, are the opposition Whigs and radicals. The Jews are moneylenders.
1. Sent to Thomas Moore in a letter of 5 November 1820, and published posthumously, the poem reflects—with his usual irony—Byron's involvement with the Carbonari, rebels against the Austrian domination of Italy.

1. Two weeks earlier, Byron had arrived in Missolonghi, a marshy town in western Greece, to support the Greek war against Turkish rule. The poem is the final entry in his journal; he died from a fever and ignorant medical practice on 19 April. The poem reflects Byron's feelings for his 15-year-old page, Loukas Chalandritsanos.
2. Echoing Shakespeare, *Macbeth,* 5.3.22, on old age.

The hope, the fear, the jealous care
    The exalted portion of the pain
15 And power of Love I cannot share
    But wear the chain.

But 't is not *thus*—and 't is not *here*
    Such thoughts should shake my soul nor *now*
Where glory decks the hero's bier
20   Or binds his brow.[3]

The Sword the Banner and the Field
    Glory and Greece, around me see!
The Spartan borne upon his shield[4]
    Was not more free!

25 Awake! (*not* Greece—She *is* awake!)
    Awake, my spirit—think through *whom*
Thy Life blood tracks its parent lake
    And then strike home!

Tread those reviving passions down
30   Unworthy Manhood; unto thee
Indifferent should the smile or frown
    Of Beauty be.

If thou regret'st thy youth, *why live?*
    The Land of honourable death
35 Is here—up to the Field! and give
    Away thy Breath.

Seek out—less often sought than found,
    A Soldier's Grave—for thee the best,
Then look around, and choose thy ground
40   And take thy Rest.

1824   1824[5]

LETTERS

To Thomas Moore[1]
[ON *CHILDE HAROLD* CANTO III]

Venice, January 28th, 1817

* * * I think of being in England in the spring. If there is a row, by the sceptre of King Ludd,[2] but I'll be one; and if there is none, and only a continuance of "this meek, piping time of peace,"[3] I will take a cottage a hundred yards to the south of your abode, and become your neighbour; and we will compose such canticles, and hold such

3. (With the victor's laurel wreath).
4. Spartan warriors were exhorted not to drop their shields and flee battle but to return either with their shields or carried, dead, upon them.
5. Published immediately in the *Morning Chronicle*, and much republished, this poem was influential in establishing Byron's fame as a martyr to "Liberty" and as a national hero in Greece.

1. For Moore, a lifelong friend from the moment Byron met him in 1811, see page 408.
2. Ned Ludd, hero of the "Luddites," the workers who destroyed the machinery they feared would displace them. In his maiden speech in Parliament in 1812 Byron had defended the frame-breaking weavers of Nottingham, near Newstead Abbey.
3. Quoting Shakespeare, *Richard III*, 1.1.24.

dialogues, as shall be the terror of the *Times* (including the newspaper of that name), and the wonder, and honour, and praise, of the Morning Chronicle[4] and posterity.

I rejoice to hear of your forthcoming[5] in February—though I tremble for the "magnificence," which you attribute to the new Childe Harold. I am glad you like it; it is a fine indistinct piece of poetical desolation, and my favourite. I was half mad during the time of its composition, between metaphysics, mountains, lakes, love unex-tinguishable, thoughts unutterable, and the nightmare of my own delinquen-cies. I should, many a good day, have blown my brains out, but for the recollection that it would have given pleasure to my mother-in-law; and, even *then,* if I could have been certain to haunt her—but I won't dwell upon these trifling family matters. * * *

To John Murray[1]
[ON DON JUAN]

Venice April 6 1819

Dear Sir—The Second Canto of Don Juan was sent on Saturday last by post in 4 packets—two of 4—& two of three sheets each—containing in all two hundred & seventeen stanzas octave measure.—But I will permit no curtailments except those mentioned about Castlereagh & the two "*Bobs*" in the introduction.[2]—You sha'n't make *Canticles* of my Cantos. The poem will please if it is lively—if it is stupid it will fail—but I will have none of your damned cutting & slashing.—If you please you may publish *anonymously[;]* it will perhaps be better;—but I will battle my way against them all—like a Porcupine.—So you and Mr. Foscolo &c.[3] want me to undertake what you call a "great work" an Epic poem I suppose or some such pyramid.—I'll try no such thing—I hate tasks—and then "seven or eight years!" God send us all well this day three months—let alone years—if one's years can't be better employed than in sweating poesy—a man had better be a ditcher.—And works too!—is Childe Harold nothing? you have so many "*divine*" poems, is it nothing to have written a *Human* one? without any of your worn out machinery.—Why—man—I could have spun the thought of the four cantos of that poem into twenty—had I wanted to book-make—& it's passion into as many modern tragedies—since you want *length* you shall have enough of *Juan* for I'll make 50 cantos.—And Foscolo too! why does *he* not do some-thing more than the letters of Ortis—and a tragedy—and pamphlets—he has good fifteen years more at his command than I have—what has he done all that time?— proved his Genius doubtless—but not fixed it's fame—nor done his utmost.—Besides I mean to write my best work in *Italian*—& it will take me nine years more thoroughly to master the *language*—& then if my fancy exists & I exist too—I will try what I *can*

4. The *Morning Chronicle,* a Whig London newspaper; both Thomas Moore and Charles Lamb contributed.
5. *Lalla Rookh,* Moore's immensely successful poem.
1. John Murray II was the most important publisher of his day, "the Anax [lord] of stationers," in Byron's phrase. Sir Walter Scott, Felicia Hemans, Jane Austen, and many other leading writers appeared under his imprint, and cookbooks and guidebooks enhanced his commercial success. He was also the official publisher to the Admiralty, and the founder of the *Quarterly Review* (1809). Since the publication of *Childe Harold's Pilgrimage* Byron had been Murray's star, and his popularity owed much to Murray's management. Murray made a fortune from

their relationship, but *Don Juan* was highly controversial, and "the most timid of God's booksellers" (as Byron also called him) declined the later cantos. After Byron's death, Murray purchased the copyrights of the works he had not published, and in 1832–1834 he consolidated Byron's reputation with a 17-volume edition, including a biography by Thomas Moore.
2. Dedication to *Don Juan,* stanzas 11–16.
3. Italian writer Ugo Foscolo, author of *Letters of Jacopo Ortis* (1798) and the tragedies *Aiace* and *Ricciarda,* had fled from the Austrians to London where he joined the Murray circle.

do *really*.—As to the Estimation of the English which you talk of, let them calculate what it is worth—before they insult me with their insolent condescension.—I have not written for their pleasure;—if they are pleased—it is that they chose to be so,—I have never flattered their opinions—nor their pride—nor will I.—Neither will I make "Ladies books" "al dilettar le femine e la plebe"[4]—I have written from the fullness of my mind, from passion—from impulse—from many motives—but not for their "sweet voices."[5]—I know the precise worth of popular applause—for few Scribblers have had more of it—and if I chose to swerve into their paths—I could retain it or resume it—or increase it—but I neither love ye—nor fear ye—and though I buy with ye—and sell with ye—and talk with ye—I will neither eat with ye—drink with ye—nor pray with ye.[6]—They made me without my search a species of popular Idol—they—without reason or judgement beyond the caprice of their Good pleasure—threw down the Image from it's pedestal—it was not broken with the fall—and they would it seems again replace it—but they shall not. You ask about my health—about the beginning of the year—I was in a state of great exhaustion—attended by such debility of Stomach—that nothing remained upon it—and I was obliged to reform my "way of life" which was conducting me from the "yellow leaf"[7] to the Ground with all deliberate speed.—I am better in health and morals—and very much yrs. ever,

P.S.—Tell Mrs. Leigh I never had "my Sashes" and I want some tooth-powder—the red—by all or any means.—

To John Murray
[ON DON JUAN]

Bologna. August 12th. 1819

* * * But to return to your letter of the 23d. of July.—You are right—Gifford is right—Crabbe is right—Hobhouse is right—you are all right—and I am all wrong—but do pray let me have that pleasure.[1] Cut me up root and branch—quarter me in the Quarterly—send round my "disjecti membra poetae"[2] like those of the Levite's Concubine—make—if you will—a spectacle to men and angels—but don't ask me to alter for I can't—I am obstinate and lazy—and there's the truth.—But nevertheless—I will answer your friend C. V.[3] who objects to the quick succession of fun and gravity—as if in that case the gravity did not (in intention at least) heighten the fun.—His metaphor is that "we are never scorched and drenched at the same time!"—Blessings on his experience!—Ask him these questions about "scorching and drenching".—Did he never play at Cricket or walk a mile in hot weather?—did he never spill a dish of tea over his testicles in handing the cup to his charmer to the great shame of his nankeen breeches?[4]—did he never swim in the sea at Noonday

4. "To please the women and the common people."
5. Citing Coriolanus's rejection of mere popularity (Shakespeare, *Coriolanus*, Act 2, Scene 3).
6. Echoing Shylock's social rejection of the Gentiles (Shakespeare, *Merchant of Venice*, 1.3.32–34) with whom he still does business.
7. Echoing Macbeth (5.3.22); see page 862, n. 2.
1. Murray's advisors, William Gifford, editor of the *Quarterly Review*, poet George Crabbe, and Byron's friend John Cam Hobhouse, all warned that *Don Juan* was scandalous.

2. Alluding to the dismemberment of poet Orpheus by his adorers, the phrase became a term for poetic remains or scattered quotations. Byron combines this with a reference to Judges 19, in which a Levite's concubine is raped and murdered; he cuts up her body and sends the pieces around to the other tribes of Israel, to rouse them to aid him in attacking the city of the wrongdoers.
3. Historian Sir Francis Cohen, later Palgrave (1788–1861).
4. Brown cotton trousers (originally from Nanking, China).

with the Sun in his eyes and on his head—which all the foam of ocean could not cool? did he never draw his foot out of a tub of too hot water damning his eyes & his valet's? did he never inject for a Gonorrhea?[5]—or make water through an ulcerated Urethra?—was he ever in a Turkish bath—that marble paradise of sherbet and sodomy?—was he ever in a cauldron of boiling oil like St. John?[6]—or in the sulphureous waves of hell? (where he ought to be for his "scorching and drenching at the same time") did he never tumble into a river or lake fishing—and sit in his wet cloathes in the boat—or on the bank afterwards "scorched and drenched" like a true sportsman?—"Oh for breath to utter"[7]—but make him my compliments—he is a clever fellow for all that—a very clever fellow.—You ask me for the plan of Donny Johnny—I *have* no plan—I *had* no plan—but I had or have materials—though if like Tony Lumpkin—I am "to be snubbed so when I am in spirits"[8] the poem will be naught—and the poet turn serious again.—If it don't take I will leave it off where it is with all due respect to the Public—but if continued it must be in my own way—you might as well make Hamlet (or Diggory)[9] "act mad" in a strait waistcoat—as trammel my buffoonery—if I am to be a buffoon—their gestures and my thoughts would only be pitiably absurd—and ludicrously constrained.—Why Man the Soul of such writing is it's licence?—at least the *liberty* of that *licence* if one likes—*not* that one should abuse it—it is like trial by Jury and Peerage—and the Habeas Corpus[1]—a very fine thing—but chiefly in the *reversion*—because no one wishes to be tried for the mere pleasure of proving his possession of the privilege.—But a truce with these reflections;—you are too earnest and eager about a work never intended to be serious;—do you suppose that I could have any intention but to giggle and make giggle?—a playful satire with as little poetry as could be helped—was what I meant—and as to the indecency—do pray read in Boswell—what *Johnson* the sullen moralist—says of *Prior* and *Paulo Purgante*[2]— * * *

To Douglas Kinnaird[1]
[ON *DON JUAN*]

Venice. Octr. 26th. 1818 [1819]

My dear Douglas—My late expenditure has arisen from living at a distance from Venice and being obliged to keep up two establishments, from frequent journeys—and buying some furniture and books as well as a horse or two—and not from any renewal of the epicurean system as you suspect. I have been faithful to my honest liaison with Countess Guiccioli—and I can assure you that *She* has never cost me directly or indirectly a sixpence—indeed the circumstances of herself and family render this no merit.—I never offered her but one present—a broach of brilliants—and she sent it back to me with her *own hair* in it (I shall *not* say of *what part* but *that* is an Italian custom) and a note to say that she was not in the habit of receiving presents of

5. Gonorrhea was treated by injections of mercury.
6. St. John the Apostle was said by Tertullian miraculously to have survived immersion in boiling oil.
7. Falstaff's cry in Shakespeare, *1 Henry IV*, 2.4.244.
8. Quoting Tony Lumpkin, the bumpkin character in Oliver Goldsmith's *She Stoops to Conquer* (1773).
9. Diggory, from Isaac Jackman's farce *All the World's a Stage* (1777), is a servant who proposes to play a madman.
1. A writ inquiring into the legality of imprisonment; hence a safeguard against unjust imprisonment. Habeas

corpus had been suspended in Britain.
2. James Boswell records that Samuel Johnson defended his tale *Paulo Purganti and his Wife* against charges of lewdness by declaring "There is nothing in [Matthew] Prior that will excite to lewdness" (*Life*, 22 Sept. 1777).
1. This liberal, and Member of Parliament in 1819, met Byron at Cambridge. By 1814 they were close friends, and when Byron left England in 1816 Kinnaird became his banker and agent.

that value—but hoped that I would not consider her sending it back as an affront—nor the value diminished by the enclosure.—I have not had a whore this half-year—confining myself to the strictest adultery.—Why should you prevent Hanson[2] from making *a. peer* if he likes it—I think the *"Garret-ting"* would be by far the best parliamentary privilege—I know of.—Damn your delicacy.—It is a low commercial quality—and very unworthy a man who prefixes "honourable" to his nomenclature. If you say that I must sign the bonds—I suppose that I must—but it is very iniquitous to make me pay my debts—you have no idea of the pain it gives one.—Pray do three things—get my property out of the *funds*—get Rochdale[3] sold—get me some information from Perry about *South America*[4]—and 4thly. ask Lady Noel[5] not to live so very long.—As to Subscribing to Manchester—if I do that—I will write a letter to Burdett[6]—for publication—to accompany the Subscription—which shall be more radical than anything yet rooted—but I feel lazy.—I have thought of this for some time—but alas! the air of this cursed Italy enervates—and disfranchises the thoughts of a man after nearly four years of respiration—to say nothing of emission.—As to "Don Juan"—confess—confess—you dog—and be candid—that it is the sublime of *that there* sort of writing—it may be bawdy—but is it not good English?—it may be profligate—but is it not *life*, is it not *the thing*?—Could any man have written it—who has not lived in the world?—and tooled in a post-chaise? in a hackney coach? in a Gondola? against a wall? in a court carriage? in a vis a vis?[7]—on a table?—and under it?—I have written about a hundred stanzas of a third Canto—but it is damned modest—the outcry has frightened me.—I had such projects for the Don—but the *Cant* is so much stronger than *Cunt*—now a days,—that the benefit of experience in a man who had well weighed the worth of both monosyllables—must be lost to despairing posterity.—After all what stuff this outcry is—Lalla Rookh and Little[8]—are more dangerous than my burlesque poem can be—Moore has been here—we got tipsy together—and were very amicable—he is gone on to Rome—I put my life (in M.S.) into his hands—(*not for publication*)[9] you—or any body else may see it—at his return.—It only comes up to 1816.—He is a noble fellow—and looks quite fresh and poetical—nine years (the age of a poem's education) my Senior—he looks younger—this comes of marriage and being settled in the Country. I want to go to South America—I have written to Hobhouse[1] all about it.—I wrote to my wife—three months ago—under care to Murray—has she got the letter—or is the letter got into Blackwood's magazine?—You ask after my Christmas pye—Remit it any how—*Circulars*[2] is the best—you are right about *income*—I must have it all—how the devil do I know that I may live a year or a month?—I wish I knew that I might regulate my spending in more ways than one.—As it is one always thinks that there is but a span.—A man may as well break or be damned for a large sum as a small one—I should be loth to pay the devil or any other creditor more than sixpence in the pound.—

---

2. John Hanson had become Byron's solicitor when he came into his title at the age of ten. Byron eventually felt this to be "a great disadvantage" and transferred most of his business to Kinnaird.

3. A Lancashire estate Byron had inherited.

4. Byron was contemplating emigration.

5. To Byron's regret, his mother-in-law Lady Noel lived until 1822. See *Don Juan* 1.125.

6. Sir Francis Burdett, Member of Parliament for Westminster, was a leader in the reform movement. The subscription was for relief of the victims of the "Peterloo massacre" the previous August. See Shelley's *The Mask of Anarchy*, p. 878.

7. A small carriage in which the passengers sit face-to-face. A hackney is a hired carriage.

8. Thomas Little was the early pseudonym of Thomas Moore, author of *Lalla Rookh* (1817).

9. Byron's *Memoirs*, given to Moore with the intention that he might profit from them, were sold to Murray but, after Byron's death, burnt in the publisher's office.

1. John Cam Hobhouse, Member of Parliament and Byron's friend, with whom he had traveled on the journeys memorialized in *Childe Harold's Pilgrimage*.

2. Letters of credit.

To John Murray

[ON *DON JUAN*]

Ravenna—Feb[brai]o 16 1821

I agree to your request of leaving in abeyance the terms for the three D. J.s till you can ascertain the effect of publication.—If I refuse to alter—you have a claim to so much courtesy in return.—I had let you off your proposal about the price of the Cantos, last year (the 3d. & 4th. always to reckon as *one* only—which they originally were) and I do not call upon you to renew it.—You have therefore no occasion to fight so shy of such subjects as I am not conscious of having given you occasion.—The 5th. is so far from being the last of D. J. that it is hardly the beginning.—I meant to take him the tour of Europe—with a proper mixture of siege—battle—and adventure—and to make him finish as *Anacharsis Cloots*—in the French revolution.[1] To how many cantos this may extend—I know not—nor whether (even if I live) I shall complete it—but this was my notion.—I meant to have made him a Cavalier Servente[2] in Italy and a cause for a divorce in England—and a Sentimental "Werther-faced man"[3] in Germany—so as to show the different ridicules of the society in each of those countries—and to have displayed him gradually gate and blase as he grew older—as is natural.—But I had not quite fixed whether to make him end in Hell—or in an unhappy marriage,—not knowing which would be the severest.—The Spanish tradition says Hell—but it is probably only an Allegory of the other state.—You are now in possession of my notions on the subject.— * * *

━━◆◈◆━━

Percy Bysshe Shelley

1792–1822

One of the most radically visionary of the Romantics, Percy Bysshe Shelley has always had countercultural prestige. In the nineteenth century, Karl Marx and Friedrich Engels praised his "prophetic genius," and in the twentieth century, Paul Foot, head of England's Socialist Workers Party, edited an inexpensive volume of his political writing both to answer "the enthusiasm of the members of the SWP for Shelley's revolutionary writings" and to give socialists a means to disseminate their views not "with dogmatic propaganda but with the poetry which carries revolutionary ideas through the centuries."

Shelley's esteem in these countercultures emerges from a selective reading of his work and life, the full range of which complicates and challenges partisan evaluation. Variously described as a selflessly devoted, often misunderstood idealist and as appallingly selfish, Shelley was always a risk-taker, and could be careless of the consequences. As an Oxford undergraduate, he collaborated with a friend on *The Necessity of Atheism*, a pamphlet that got them promptly expelled after they sent it to every university professor and administrative official, as well as every bishop in the United Kingdom. His first long poem *Queen Mab* included a vitriolic attack on "Priestcraft" and "Kingcraft" that earned him celebrity in the radical press

---

1. For Cloots, see *Don Juan* 1.3.
2. The socially accepted "escort" (lover) of a married woman, as Byron was to Teresa Guiccioli, a role he anxiously mocked in poems and letters.
3. Goethe's novel, *The Sorrows of Young Werther* (1784),

recounts the hero's love for a married woman and his despairing suicide. "Werther" became synonymous with melancholy youth, as the quoted phrase, from Moore's *Fudge Family in Paris* (1818) suggests.

and infamy in the conservative press; well into the nineteenth century, these atheist and revolutionary passages were expurgated. This censorship was part of the refashioning of Shelley in the Victorian period. In a well-orchestrated campaign by his grieving widow and devoted disciples of his poetry, he was made safe for parlors, refurbished from a dangerous thinker into an impossibly delicate visionary given to chanting at skylarks, "Hail to thee, blithe Spirit!"

Shelley's life is marked by idealism, scandal, and passionate but shifting emotional commitments, especially to women. Grandson of a wealthy landowner and son of a member of Parliament, he was born into conservative aristocracy. Expected to continue in this world, he was sent to the best schools. But he began to rebel early. At Eton (1804–1810), he challenged the tyrannical system of "fagging," whereby upperclassmen had the privilege of abusing their juniors. He no sooner enrolled in Oxford, in 1810, than he got himself expelled for that pamphlet on atheism, an event that at once surprised him and enraged his father. He took off for London, where he met Harriet Westbrook and, believing her oppressed by her father, convinced her to elope with him in August 1811 (he was eighteen, she sixteen). The next year, he was in Ireland irritating its Protestant aristocracy by distributing pamphlets urging Catholic emancipation and improved conditions for its large population of the poor. Eager to meet William Godwin, author of *Political Justice*, he returned to London, and began *Queen Mab*, a Godwinian dream vision. In 1813 Harriet bore a daughter, and he published *Mab* at his own expense. At once celebrated (and pirated) by the radical press and denounced by the Tory press, this poem would be linked to Shelley for the rest of his life, its infamy persisting even into his obituaries.

In the heat of his Godwinian enthusiasms and mindful of Godwin's disdain of the institution of marriage, Shelley allowed himself to tire of Harriet and become enamored of Godwin and Wollstonecraft's beautiful, intelligent daughter Mary. In July 1814, he and Mary eloped to France, accompanied by her stepsister Claire Clairmont. After a six-week tour of Europe, marveling at the Alps and dismayed by the ravages of the Napoleonic wars, they returned to England and the scandal of their elopement. In December Harriet bore her second child by Percy but declined his invitation to join their menage as a platonic sister. When Shelley's grandfather died at the beginning of 1815, he gained a modest fortune of £1000 per year, one-fifth of which was paid directly to Harriet and a good portion of which he would always spend on philanthropy and loans to friends. Mary's first child, a daughter, was born prematurely in February, and died within a few weeks, an event that devastated her. During this year, they experimented with an "open" relationship, in which Percy had a romance with Claire and Mary with his college friend T. J. Hogg (collaborator on the pamphlet on atheism). Still at odds with their fathers, Mary and Percy were further strained by debts and a constant shift of residences to avoid creditors and bailiffs. Percy wrote *Alastor*, a somewhat equivocally framed story of a young visionary poet alienated by life in the world who seeks visionary fulfillment, finding this ultimately in death. Their second child, William, was born early in 1816.

They left for Switzerland in May 1816 with Claire, to meet Lord Byron, now Claire's lover. During this summer, Mary wrote *Frankenstein*, and Percy wrote *Hymn to Intellectual Beauty* and *Mont Blanc*, and toured the lakes with Byron. At the summer's end, the Shelley party returned to England and several catastrophes. Mary's half-sister Fanny Imlay committed suicide in October on discovering that Godwin was not her father, and in November, Harriet, pregnant by a new lover and in despair over rejection by him, drowned herself. Percy and Mary were now able to marry, but the scandal of his life and political writings cost him custody of his children by Harriet—an extraordinary ruling in an age when fathers automatically had custody. He was shocked by this judgment, which deepened his self-mythology as an idealist persecuted by social and political injustice and despised by a world unable to appreciate his "beautiful idealisms of moral excellence" (as he would phrase it in the Preface to *Prometheus Unbound*).

Over the course of 1817, Shelley consoled himself with new political writing and his friendship with Leigh Hunt, man of letters and editor of the radical newspaper *The Examiner*; through Hunt he met John Keats. Mary was pregnant again, and Clara was born in September.

In 1818 they moved to Europe. Eager to spend as much time as possible with Byron, now in Italy, Percy subjected his family to much arduous travel during an oppressively hot summer. Clara did not fare well and died in September. The year 1819 was a productive one for Shelley's writing. He finished *Prometheus Unbound*, an epic "closet-drama" begun the year before about the Titan's war with his oppressor; he wrote *The Cenci*, a gothic political tragedy of incestuous rape, parricide, and persecution; several other political poems, including *The Mask of Anarchy*, in reaction to the infamous "Peterloo Massacre" of a peaceful workers' rally; a long proto-Marxist political pamphlet, *A Philosophical View of Reform*; and a witty satire of Wordsworth (*Peter Bell the Third*), energized by dismay at the middle-aged poet's didacticism and swing to the political right. He also composed one of his most famous poems, *Ode to the West Wind*, an impassioned cry for spiritual transformation rendered in the astonishingly intricate, overflowing verse of terza-rima sonnet-stanzas. The death of William in June, at age three and a half, wrenched the Shelleys with a grief only partly allayed by the birth, five months later, of a second son, Percy Florence—the only of their children to survive into adulthood.

Shelley continued to write poetry over the next two years, including *To a Sky-Lark*, and *Adonais*, an elegy for Keats, representing him as a martyr to vicious, politically motivated reviews. Increasingly identifying with this myth himself, and despairing of his bid for poetic fame, in 1821 he began his *Defence of Poetry* (published posthumously by Mary in 1840), in which he set forth his views on the relation of poets both to their immediate social and historical circumstances and to the "Eternity" that authorized their visions and would vindicate their merits. He was also becoming infatuated with Jane Williams, who with her common-law husband Edward had joined their circle in Pisa, Italy. The Williamses and the Shelleys decided to live together on the Bay of Spezia in the summer of 1822. More and more alienated from Mary, who was understandably moody (pregnant for the fifth time in six years and still grieving for her first three children), Percy frequently left her behind to enjoy excursions with the Williamses or Jane alone. He was charmed by their company, jealous of their relationship, and in love with Jane, to whom he addressed a set of beautiful lyrics interwoven with his affection for her, his resentment of Edward, and his withdrawal from Mary. Mary suffered a nearly fatal miscarriage in June. In July, Percy and Edward sailed to Leghorn to greet Leigh Hunt, who was joining Shelley and Byron in Italy to establish *The Liberal*, a journal of opinion and the arts. On the sail back, Percy and Edward were caught in a sudden storm, and both drowned. Byron wrote to his publisher, sponsor of the most influential Tory periodical of the day, *The Quarterly Review* (which had savaged Shelley): "You are all brutally mistaken about Shelley who was without exception—the *best* and least selfish man I ever knew.—I never knew one who was not a beast in comparison." Whether or not one shares this judgment of the man, Shelley's accomplishment as an artist has always compelled admiration. Wordsworth, who thought him too fantastic by half and who was famously sparing in praise of other poets, judged Shelley "one of the best *artists* of us all . . . in workmanship of style."

For the opening of *Prometheus Unbound* see "*Manfred* and Its Time," pages 760–61.

To Wordsworth[1]

Poet of Nature, thou hast wept to know
That things depart which never may return:
Childhood and youth, friendship, and love's first glow,
Have fled like sweet dreams, leaving thee to mourn.

---

1. By 1816 Wordsworth had abandoned the radicalism of his youth and was inclined to spiritual rather than political remedies, a view frequently voiced in his long poem, *The Excursion* (1814). Now in a government patronage position, he was supporting conservative (Tory) politics. Deploying a form dear to Wordsworth, Shelley's sonnet interweaves several critical allusions to his early poetry, including his "Intimations" Ode (lines 9, 56–57) and his sonnet *London, 1802*.

5 These common woes I feel. One loss is mine,
Which thou too feel'st, yet I alone deplore.[2]
Thou wert as a lone star whose light did shine
On some frail bark in winter's midnight roar:
Thou hast like to a rock-built refuge stood
10 Above the blind and battling multitude:
In honoured poverty thy voice did weave
Songs consecrate to truth and liberty.[3]
Deserting these, thou leavest me to grieve,
Thus having been, that thou shouldst cease to be.[4]

1816

Mont Blanc
Lines Written in the Vale of Chamouni[1]

1

The everlasting universe of things
Flows through the mind, and rolls its rapid waves,
Now dark—now glittering—now reflecting gloom—
Now lending splendour, where from secret springs
5 The source of human thought its tribute brings
Of waters,—with a sound but half its own,
Such as a feeble brook will oft assume
In the wild woods, among the mountains lone,
Where waterfalls around it leap for ever,
10 Where woods and winds contend, and a vast river
Over its rocks ceaselessly bursts and raves.[2]

2

Thus thou, Ravine of Arve—dark, deep Ravine—
Thou many-coloured, many-voiced vale,
Over whose pines and crags and caverns sail
15 Fast cloud-shadows and sunbeams: awful° scene,   *awesome*
Where Power in likeness of the Arve comes down
From the ice gulphs that gird his secret throne,

2. Lament, disparage
3. *Sonnets Dedicated to Liberty* (including *London, 1802*) was a subsection of Wordsworth's *Poems* of 1807.
4. A potentially satiric echo of *Song* ("She dwelt among th'untrodden ways"), "Lucy ceased to be" (10).
1. At nearly 16,000 ft. Mont Blanc, in the French Alps, is the highest peak in Europe, a must-see on everyone's Grand Tour as the epitome of "the sublime"; its summit had been attained only a few times by 1816. In Mary's *History of a Six Weeks' Tour*, Percy said the poem "was composed under the immediate impression of the deep and powerful feelings excited by the objects which it attempts to describe; and, as an undisciplined overflowing of the soul, rests its claim to approbation on an attempt to imitate the untamable wildness and inaccessible solemnity from which those feelings sprang." The "imitation" involves a dizzying play of imagery and language:

wildly dilated and piled-up syntaxes, dazzling verbal transformations and a welter of sublime negatives (*unknown, infinite, unearthly, unfathomable, viewless*). Amid this drama, Shelley poses questions of the mind's ability to perceive and comprehend transcendent power, and ultimately its existence. He portrays the perceiving "mind" with metaphors drawn from the scene before him, as he stands on a bridge over the River Arve, a deep ravine, and the valley below, the mountain and glacier above. Echoing with a difference Wordsworth's love for "all the mighty world / Of eye, and ear,—both what they half create, / And what perceive; well pleased to recognise / In nature and the language of the sense / The anchor of my purest thoughts" (*Tintern Abbey* 105–109), Shelley alludes to and contests this philosophy of "Nature."
2. Echoing Coleridge's *Kubla Khan* (1816) 17–21; the landscape of this poem also appears at 122.

Bursting thro' these dark mountains like the flame
Of lightning through the tempest;—thou dost lie,—
20   Thy giant brood of pines around thee clinging,
Children of elder° time, in whose devotion   *older and earlier*
The chainless winds still come and ever came
To drink their odours, and their mighty swinging
To hear, an old and solemn harmony;
25   Thine earthly rainbows stretched across the sweep
Of the ethereal waterfall, whose veil
Robes some unsculptured image;³ the strange sleep
Which, when the voices of the desert fail,
Wraps all in its own deep eternity;—
30   Thy caverns echoing to the Arve's commotion,
A loud, lone sound no other sound can tame;
Thou art pervaded with that ceaseless motion
Thou art the path of that unresting sound—
Dizzy Ravine! and when I gaze on thee
35   I seem as in a trance sublime and strange
To muse on my own separate phantasy,°   *fantasy, delusion*
My own, my human mind, which passively
Now renders and receives fast influencings,
Holding an unremitting interchange
40   With the clear universe of things around;
One legion of wild thoughts, whose wandering wings
Now float above thy darkness, and now rest
Where that° or thou° art no unbidden guest,   *thy darkness / ravine*
In the still cave of the witch Poesy,
45   Seeking among the shadows that pass by,
Ghosts of all things that are, some shade of thee,
Some phantom, some faint image; till the breast
From which they fled recalls them, thou art there!⁴

3

Some say that gleams of a remoter world
50   Visit the soul in sleep,⁵—that death is slumber,
And that its shapes the busy thoughts outnumber
Of those who wake and live.—I look on high;
Has some unknown omnipotence unfurled
The veil of life and death?⁶ or do I lie
55   In dream, and does the mightier world of sleep
Spread far around and inaccessibly
Its circles? For the very spirit fails,
Driven like a homeless cloud from steep to steep

3. Rocks behind the waterfall.
4. Plato's allegory in *Republic* 7 compares the mind to a cave in which our sense of reality consists of the shadows cast by firelight on its walls, ignorant of the light of "Reality" outside. Shelley's difficult syntax blurs the distinction of inner and outer, human mind and Ravine.
5. Revising Wordsworth's philosophy of Platonic amnesia in stanza 5 of the "Intimations" Ode, Shelley offers the idea that this spiritual reality is not forgotten but visits the soul in sleep.
6. The screen of phenomena separating physical from spiritual reality (lifted in sleep, in daydreams and visions); see "Lift not the painted veil," page 877.

	That vanishes among the viewless° gales!	*unseeing, invisible*
60	Far, far above, piercing the infinite sky,	
	Mont Blanc appears,—still, snowy, and serene—	
	Its subject mountains their unearthly forms	
	Pile around it, ice and rock; broad vales between	
	Of frozen floods, unfathomable deeps,	
65	Blue as the overhanging heaven, that spread	
	And wind among the accumulated steeps;	
	A desert peopled by the storms alone,	
	Save° when the eagle brings some hunter's bone,	*except*
	And the wolf tracts° her there—how hideously	*tracks, traces*
70	Its shapes are heaped around! rude, bare, and high,	
	Ghastly, and scarred, and riven.°—Is this the scene	*split*
	Where the old Earthquake-dæmon[7] taught her young	
	Ruin? Were these their toys? or did a sea	
	Of fire, envelope once this silent snow?	
75	None can reply—all seems eternal now.	
	The wilderness has a mysterious tongue	
	Which teaches awful doubt,° or faith so mild,	*awe-filled*
	So solemn, so serene, that man may be	*questioning*
	But for such faith, with nature reconciled.[8]	
80	Thou hast a voice, great Mountain, to repeal	
	Large codes of fraud and woe; not understood	
	By all, but which the wise and great and good	
	Interpret, or make felt, or deeply feel.	

4

	The fields, the lakes, the forests, and the streams,
85	Ocean, and all the living things that dwell
	Within the daedal[9] earth, lightning, and rain,
	Earthquake, and fiery flood, and hurricane,
	The torpor of the year when feeble dreams
	Visit the hidden buds, or dreamless sleep
90	Holds every future leaf and flower;—the bound
	With which from that detested trance they leap;
	The works and ways of man, their death and birth,
	And that of him, and all that his may be;
	All things that move and breathe with toil and sound
95	Are born and die; revolve, subside, and swell.
	Power dwells apart in its tranquillity
	Remote, serene, and inaccessible:
	And *this,* the naked countenance of earth,
	On which I gaze, even these primaeval mountains

7. In Greek mythology daemons are (often playful) spirits, usually personifications of natural forces.
8. Shelley first wrote "In such wise faith with Nature reconciled," then revised to "But for such faith" and lowercased "nature." The sense is ambiguous: "But for" may indicate "Only by means of" faith in Nature, over the "Large codes of fraud and woe" promulgated by institutional religions (81). Or it may mean "Except for": a bland faith in a nature that is unknowable and perhaps indifferent to human needs and values, is paradoxically, no faith.
9. From Daedalus, architect of the famous labyrinth in Crete, and of wings for flight crafted with feathers and wax; hence, a wonderfully wrought, inspired creation.

100 Teach the adverting mind. The glaciers creep
Like snakes that watch their prey, from their far fountains,
Slow rolling on; there, many a precipice,
Frost and the Sun in scorn of mortal power
Have piled: dome, pyramid, and pinnacle,
105 A city of death, distinct with many a tower
And wall impregnable of beaming ice.
Yet not a city, but a flood of ruin
Is there, that from the boundary of the sky
Rolls its perpetual stream; vast pines are strewing
110 Its destined path, or in the mangled soil
Branchless and shattered stand: the rocks, drawn down
From yon remotest waste, have overthrown
The limits of the dead and living world,
Never to be reclaimed. The dwelling-place
115 Of insects, beasts, and birds, becomes its spoil;
Their food and their retreat for ever gone,
So much of life and joy is lost. The race
Of man, flies far in dread; his work and dwelling
Vanish, like smoke before the tempest's stream,
120 And their place is not known.[1] Below, vast caves
Shine in the rushing torrent's restless gleam,
Which from those secret chasms in tumult welling
Meet in the vale, and one majestic River,
The breath and blood of distant lands, for ever
125 Rolls its loud waters to the ocean waves,
Breathes its swift vapours to the circling air.

5

Mont Blanc yet gleams on high:—the power is there,
The still and solemn power, of many sights,
And many sounds, and much of life and death.
130 In the calm darkness of the moonless nights,
In the lone glare of day, the snows descend
Upon that Mountain; none beholds them there,
Nor when the flakes burn in the sinking sun,
Or the star-beams dart through them:—Winds contend
135 Silently there, and heap the snow with breath
Rapid and strong, but silently! Its home
The voiceless lightning in these solitudes
Keeps innocently, and like vapour broods
Over the snow. The secret strength of things
140 Which governs thought, and to the infinite dome
Of heaven is as a law, inhabits thee!
And what were thou,° and earth, and stars, and sea,   *Mont Blanc*

---

1. Echoing Psalm 103: "As for man, his days are as grass . . . For the wind passeth over it, and it is gone; and the place thereof shall know it no more" (15–16)..

If to the human mind's imaginings
Silence and solitude were vacancy?

23 July 1816   1817

Hymn to Intellectual Beauty[1]

1

The awful° shadow of some unseen Power   *awe-inspiring*
   Floats, though unseen, amongst us, visiting
   This various world with as inconstant wing
As summer winds that creep from flower to flower.—
5   Like moonbeams that behind some piny mountain shower,°   *(verb)*
     It visits with inconstant glance
     Each human heart and countenance;
Like hues and harmonies of evening,—
     Like clouds in starlight widely spread,—
10   Like memory of music fled,—
     Like aught that for its grace may be
Dear, and yet dearer for its mystery.

2

Spirit of BEAUTY, that dost consecrate
   With thine own hues all thou dost shine upon
   Of human thought or form,—where art thou gone?
15 Why dost thou pass away, and leave our state,
This dim vast vale of tears, vacant and desolate?—
     Ask why the sunlight not for ever
     Weaves rainbows o'er yon mountain river;
20 Why aught should fail and fade that once is shown;
     Why fear and dream and death and birth
     Cast on the daylight of this earth
     Such gloom,—why man has such a scope
For love and hate, despondency and hope?

3

25 No voice from some sublimer world hath ever
   To sage or poet these responses given—
   Therefore the names of God and ghost and Heaven,
Remain the records of their° vain endeavour,   *sages and poets*
Frail spells[2]—whose uttered charm might not avail to sever
30   From all we hear and all we see,
     Doubt, chance, and mutability.
Thy light alone like mist o'er mountains driven,
   Or music by the night wind sent

---

1. Composed the same summer as *Mont Blanc* (1816), *Hymn* shares its metaphysics. "Intellectual" refers to the ideal Spirit apprehended by the mind, over the faint and fleeting information of the senses; Shelley may have taken this term from Wollstonecraft's lament in *Rights of Woman* over the low cultural esteem of women's "intellectual beauty" (ch. 3). As in *Mont Blanc*, "unseen Power" is evoked by a language of negation, questions, and merely proximate similes.
2. The languages of institutional religion.

Through strings of some still instrument,[3]
35   Or moonlight on a midnight stream,
Gives grace and truth to life's unquiet dream.

4

Love, Hope, and Self-esteem, like clouds depart
    And come, for some uncertain moments lent.
    Man were° immortal, and omnipotent,   *would be*
40 Didst thou,° unknown and awful as thou art,   *if thou didst*
Keep with thy glorious train firm state within his heart.
        Thou messenger of sympathies
        That wax and wane in lovers' eyes—
Thou, that to human thought art nourishment,
45   Like darkness to a dying flame![4]
        Depart not—as thy shadow came:
        Depart not, lest the grave should be,
Like life and fear, a dark reality!

5

While yet a boy, I sought for ghosts, and sped
50   Through many a listening chamber, cave and ruin,
        And starlight wood, with fearful steps pursuing
Hopes of high talk with the departed dead.[5]
I called on poisonous names with which our youth is fed.[6]
        I was not heard—I saw them not—
55   When musing deeply on the lot
Of life at that sweet time when winds are wooing
        All vital things that wake to bring
        News of birds and blossoming,—
        Sudden, thy shadow fell on me;
60 I shrieked, and clasped my hands in exstasy!

6

I vowed that I would dedicate my powers
    To thee and thine—have I not kept the vow?
    With beating heart and streaming eyes, even now
I call the phantoms of a thousand hours
65 Each from his voiceless grave: they have in visioned bowers
        Of studious zeal or love's delight
        Outwatched with me the envious night—
They know that never joy illumed my brow
        Unlinked with hope that thou wouldst free
70   This world from its dark slavery,
        That thou, O awful LOVELINESS,
Wouldst give whate'er these words cannot express.

---

3. An aeolian or "wind" harp; see Coleridge's *The Eolian Harp*.
4. Darkness offsets its glow, even as the flame ultimately dies into darkness.
5. Evoking Wordsworth's shadowy recollection in the "Intimations" Ode of a boyhood sense of a spiritual reality

behind the veil of phenomena; see lines 141–147 (page 556). Shelley is referring to boyhood experiments in conjuration.
6. The vocabulary for divinity in institutional religions.

7

The day becomes more solemn and serene
    When noon is past—there is a harmony
75   In autumn, and a lustre in its sky,
Which through the summer is not heard or seen,
As if it could not be, as if it had not been!
    Thus let thy power, which like the truth
    Of Nature on my passive youth
80 Descended, to my onward life supply
    Its calm—to one who worships thee,
    And every form containing thee,
    Whom, SPIRIT fair, thy spells did bind
To fear° himself, and love all humankind.   *revere, fear for*

1816   1817

Ozymandias[1]

I MET a Traveller from an antique land,
Who said, "Two vast and trunkless legs of stone
Stand in the desert. Near them on the sand,
Half sunk, a shattered visage lies, whose frown,
5 And wrinkled lip, and sneer of cold command,
Tell that its sculptor well those passions read,
Which yet survive, stamped on these lifeless things,
The hand that mocked them, and the heart that fed.[2]
And on the pedestal these words appear:
10 'My name is OZYMANDIAS, King of Kings:[3]
Look on my works, ye Mighty, and despair!'[4]
No thing beside remains. Round the decay
Of that Colossal[5] Wreck, boundless and bare,
The lone and level sands stretch far away."

The Examiner January 11, 1818

Sonnet ("Lift not the painted veil")[1]

Lift not the painted veil which those who live
Call Life: though unreal shapes be pictured there,
And it but mimic all we would believe
With colours idly spread,—behind, lurk Fear

1. Ozymandias (the Greek name for Ramses II) reigned 1292–1225 B.C.E.; he is thought to be the pharaoh of Exodus whom Moses challenged. The story of the statue and its inscription is taken from the Greek historian Diodorus Siculus, 1st century B.C.E.
2. The sculptor read well those passions that survive his hand and the tyrant's heart; "mocked": "imitated," with a sense of caricature or derision. The passions survive in modern tyrants. Shelley published this sonnet in 1818 in Leigh Hunt's radical paper, *The Examiner.*
3. By Shelley's time "King of Kings" referred to Christ, though it was a common boast of many ancient-world kings.
4. According to Diodorus, this is the actual boast. Shelley is also mindful of William Cowper's famous poem. *Verses*

supposed to have been written by Alexander Selkirk, during his solitary abode on the Island of Juan Fernandez (1782), which begins, "I am the Monarch of all I survey."
5. An adjective derived from "colossus," the term in antiquity for any large statue; there were several such of 50 to 60 feet in height in ancient Egypt. Shelley is also recalling the depiction of Julius Caesar by one of the conspirators in his assassination: "he doth bestride the narrow world / Like a Colossus" (*Julius Caesar* 1.2.135–36). The ruin of the Coliseum in Rome was a famous tourist site in Shelley's day. See Byron, pages 775–77.
1. The veil is all the visual (and all sensory) phenomena normally called "Life."

5   And Hope, twin Destinies; who ever weave
    Their shadows, o'er the chasm, sightless and drear.
    I knew one who had lifted it—he sought,
    For his lost heart was tender, things to love,
    But found them not, alas! nor was there aught
10 The world contains, the which he could approve.
    Through the unheeding many he did move,
    A splendour among shadows, a bright blot
    Upon this gloomy scene, a Spirit that strove
    For truth, and like the Preacher found it not.[2]

1818   1824

Sonnet: England in 1819[1]

    An old, mad, blind, despised, and dying King,—
    Princes, the dregs of their dull race, who flow
    Through public scorn,—mud from a muddy spring,—
    Rulers who neither see nor feel nor know,
5   But leechlike to their fainting country cling,
    Till they drop, blind in blood, without a blow,—
    A people starved and stabbed in the untilled field,[2]—
    An army, which liberticide[3] and prey
    Make as a two-edged sword to all who wield;—
10 Golden and sanguine laws which tempt and slay;[4]
    Religion Christless, Godless, a book sealed;
    A Senate,—Time's worst statute unrepealed,[5]—
    Are graves from which a glorious Phantom may
    Burst, to illumine our tempestuous day.

1819   1839

THE MASK OF ANARCHY   On 16 August 1819, nearly 100,000 millworkers and their families gathered at Saint Peter's Field outside Manchester for a peaceful demonstration, capped by an address by radical Henry "Orator" Hunt calling for parliamentary reform, especially greater representation for the working classes. Alarmed by the spectacle, the local ruling class sent a drunken, sabre-wielding militia to charge the rally and arrest Hunt; they brutally wounded hundreds, a dozen fatally. It is unclear whether the London Home Office (internal security) collaborated in advance against the reform movement, or whether, along with the Prince Regent (later George IV), it merely offered congratulations after the fact. The opposition press, notably *The Examiner* (published by Shelley's friends Leigh and John Hunt, no relation to Henry), fueled public outrage with a flow of reports, beginning with eyewitness accounts of

2. The refrain of the Preacher of Ecclesiastes, "all is vanity and vexation of spirit." Shelley's first draft read, "I should be happier had I ne'er known / This mournful man—he was himself alone."
1. Unpublishable in 1819 for its probable libel; first-printed in Mary Shelley's edition of 1839 (when George III was long dead). George III, king since 1760, had been declared insane in 1811, when his son became Prince Regent. The first line echoes Lear's self-description on the heath: "a poor, infirm, weak, and despised old man" (3.3.20); *King Lear* was kept out of production by the Examiner of Plays because of its suggestion of George III.

George III's sons were notoriously dissolute, given to sexual scandal, gluttony, gambling, outrageous expenditure, and taking bribes for army commissions.
2. The "Peterloo Massacre," 16 August 1819.
3. Liberty-killing; normally a term for a tyrant (*Adonais* 32), this is the first use in this sense noted by OED.
4. Laws procured with gold and enacted with bloodshed; see also *Mask of Anarchy*, 65, 298.
5. Perhaps referring to the exclusion of most citizens, including Catholics, Dissenters, women, and workers, from representation in Parliament.

what came to be dubbed the "Peterloo Massacre" in sardonic parody of the celebrated English victory at Waterloo, and continuing through Hunt's triumphant entry and subsequent trial in London (he was convicted and sent to prison for two years).

An expatriate in Italy at the time, Shelley was inspired by a self-described "torrent of indignation" to write *The Mask of Anarchy*, which he sent to Leigh Hunt on 23 September 1819, hoping for publication in *The Examiner*. Hunt was already immersed in a series of articles defending Shelley from defamations in the Tory press provoked by *The Revolt of Islam* (another political poem); he backed off from *The Mask* as too risky. Despite its politics of nonviolent resistance, to print a popular ballad advocating the rights of the poor and envisioning the overthrow of a corrupt and tyrannical government would guarantee prosecution, fines, imprisonment, perhaps even exile to Australia; the Hunts had already been jailed and heavily fined for prior "libels," and here was Shelley likening "Murder" to the Tory Foreign Secretary Castlereagh (also reviled by Byron in the unpublishable Dedication of *Don Juan*), "Hypocrisy" to Sidmouth the Home Secretary, and "Fraud" to Lord Chancellor Eldon (who had deprived Shelley of his children by Harriet). Leigh Hunt waited to print the poem until 1832, ten years after Shelley's death and just after the passage of the Reform Bill, when Shelley's hotter rhetoric could be set at historical distance and its cooler advice admired as prophetic of the nonviolent persuasion by which reform had been won. By this time, too, the notoriety of "Peterloo" was undisputed as a breach of the right of peaceful assembly. Even so, Hunt felt it best to cancel the names Eldon and Sidmouth, as well as the subtitle. Shelley's main title tweaks Eldon's condemnation of the rally as "an overt act of treason" posing a "shocking choice between military government and anarchy"; he turns the word back on the government itself, to name its tyranny. "Mask" builds on *The Examiner*'s reference to the government's "Brazen Masks of power" (22 August) and also puns on the literary-theatrical genre of the "masque" (Shelley called the poem *Masque of Anarchy* in a letter to Hunt, who used this title in 1832). Thus he describes government officials as parading in a "ghastly masquerade" (27), a spectacle that travesties the court-masques of the early seventeenth century, performances for the court and the aristocracy that typically celebrated the structures of order and authority that defined their power.

The Mask of Anarchy
Written on the Occasion of the Massacre at Manchester

As I lay asleep in Italy
There came a voice from over the Sea
And with great power it forth led me
To walk in the visions of Poesy.

5   I met Murder on the way—
He had a mask like Castlereagh—
Very smooth he looked, yet grim;
Seven bloodhounds followed him.[1]

All were fat; and well they might
10   Be in admirable plight,
For one by one, and two by two,
He tossed them human hearts to chew
Which from his wide cloak he drew.

1. Castlereagh, Tory Foreign Secretary and leader in the House of the Commons, was known for his violent suppression of political unrest in Ireland and his support of the reactionary Holy Alliance in Europe and of Austria's domination of Italy. In 1815 he secured England's support for the postponement of the abolition of the slave trade by seven European nations; the pro-war faction in Parliament was known as "bloodhounds" (cf. "hawks").

Next came Fraud, and he had on,
15   Like Eldon, an ermined gown;
His big tears, for he wept well,
Turned to mill-stones as they fell:[2]

And the little children, who
Round his feet played to and fro,
20   Thinking every tear a gem,
Had their brains knocked out by them.

Clothed with the Bible, as with light,
And the shadows of the night,
Like Sidmouth, next, Hypocrisy
25   On a crocodile rode by.[3]

And many more Destructions played
In this ghastly masquerade,
All disguised, even to the eyes,
Like Bishops, lawyers, peers, or spies.

30   Last came Anarchy: he rode
On a white horse splashed with blood;
He was pale even to the lips,
Like Death in the Apocalypse.[4]

And he wore a kingly crown,
35   And in his grasp a sceptre° shone;   *royal staff*
On his brow this mark I saw—
"I AM GOD, AND KING, AND LAW!"

With a pace stately and fast
Over English land he passed,
40   Trampling to a mire of blood
The adoring multitude.

And a mighty troop around
With their trampling shook the ground,
Waving each a bloody sword,
45   For the service of their Lord.

And with glorious triumph, they
Rode through England proud and gay

---

2. Eldon was Lord Chancellor (an office identified by its ermine gown) and famous for his public shedding of tears.
3. Sidmouth was Home Secretary (officer of internal security). The crocodile, fabled to weep as it devours its prey, symbolizes hypocrisy; Sidmouth had used provocateurs to incite illegal action among discontented workers (who were then arrested, jailed, deported, or executed); he also spent millions to build churches to teach spiritual patience to the starving poor rather than improve their material conditions.

4. St. John the Divine's vision of the fourth horseman of the Apocalypse: "behold a pale horse: and his name that sat on him was Death" (Revelation 6.8). Benjamin West's famous painting, *Death on a Pale Horse* (which Shelley may have seen in London in late 1817 or read about in the press), depicts a crowd trampled by crowned Death and his sword-wielding army. See Keats, page 1047.

Drunk as with intoxication
Of the wine of desolation.

50   O'er fields and towns, from sea to sea,
Passed the Pageant swift and free,
Tearing up and trampling down,
Till they came to London town.

And each dweller, panic-stricken,
55   Felt his heart with terror sicken,
Hearing the tempestuous cry
Of the triumph of Anarchy.

For with pomp to meet him came,
Clothed in arms like blood and flame,
60   The hired Murderers who did sing
"Thou art God, and Law, and King!

We have waited, weak and lone,
For thy coming, Mighty One!
Our purses are empty, our swords are cold,
65   Give us glory, and blood, and gold."

Lawyers and priests, a motley° crowd,   *ragtag*
To the earth their pale brows bowed;
Like a bad prayer not over loud,
Whispering—"Thou art Law and God!"

70   Then all cried with one accord,
"Thou art King, and God, and Lord;
Anarchy, to Thee we bow,
Be thy name made holy now!"

And Anarchy the Skeleton
75   Bowed and grinned to every one,
As well as if his education
Had cost ten millions to the Nation.

For he knew the Palaces
Of our Kings were rightly his;
80   His the sceptre, crown, and globe,°   *royal emblems*
And the gold-inwoven robe.

So he sent his slaves before
To seize upon the Bank and Tower,[5]
And was proceeding with intent
85   To meet his pensioned Parliament,

When one fled past, a maniac maid,
And her name was Hope, she said,

5. The Bank of England is the national treasury; the Tower of London houses the crown jewels. Parliament had been bought off with bribes and other lucrative corruption.

But she looked more like Despair,
And she cried out in the air:

90 "My father Time is weak and grey
With waiting for a better day;
See how idiot-like he stands,
Fumbling with his palsied hands![6]

He has had child after child
95 And the dust of death is piled
Over every one but me—
Misery! oh Misery!"

Then she lay down in the street,
Right before the horses' feet,
100 Expecting, with a patient eye,
Murder, Fraud, and Anarchy—

When between her and her foes
A mist, a light, an image rose,
Small at first, and weak, and frail
105 Like the vapour of a vale:

Till as clouds grow on the blast,
Like tower-crowned giants striding fast,
And glare with lightnings as they fly,
And speak in thunder to the sky,

110 It grew—a Shape arrayed in mail°   suit of armor
Brighter than the Viper's scale,
And upborne on wings whose grain°   pattern
Was as the light of sunny rain.

On its helm, seen far away,
115 A planet, like the Morning's,° lay;   Venus as morning
And those plumes its light rained through,   star
Like a shower of crimson dew.

With step as soft as wind it passed
O'er the heads of men—so fast
120 That they knew the presence there,
And looked,—but all was empty air.

As flowers beneath May's footstep waken
As stars from Night's loose hair are shaken
As waves arise when loud winds call
125 Thoughts sprung where'er that step did fall.

And the prostrate multitude
Looked—and ankle-deep in blood,
Hope, that maiden most serene,
Was walking with a quiet mien;°   appearance

6. A gibe at George III; see *England in 1819*.

130   And Anarchy, the ghastly birth,
Lay dead earth upon the earth
The Horse of Death tameless as wind
Fled, and with his hoofs did grind
To dust the murderers thronged behind.

135   A rushing light of clouds and splendour,
A sense awakening and yet tender,
Was heard and felt—and at its close
These words of joy and fear arose

As if their Own indignant Earth,
140   Which gave the sons of England birth,
Had felt their blood upon her brow,
And shuddering with a mother's throe

Had turned every drop of blood
By which her face had been bedewed
145   To an accent unwithstood,—
As if her heart had cried aloud:

"Men of England, heirs of Glory,
Heroes of unwritten story,
Nurslings of one mighty Mother,
150   Hopes of her and one another!

Rise, like Lions after slumber
In unvanquishable number!
Shake your chains to Earth, like dew
Which in sleep had fallen on you—
155   Ye are many, they are few.

What is Freedom? ye can tell
That which Slavery is, too well—
For its very name has grown
To an echo of your own.

160   'Tis to work and have such pay
As just keeps life from day to day
In your limbs, as in a cell
For the tyrants' use to dwell:

So that ye for them are made
165   Loom and plough and sword and spade;
With or without your own will, bent
To their defence and nourishment.

'Tis to see your children weak
With their mothers pine° and peak°   *long / waste away*
170   When the winter winds are bleak,—
They are dying whilst I speak.

'Tis to hunger for such diet
As the rich man in his riot

Casts to the fat dogs that lie
175   Surfeiting beneath his eye.

'Tis to let the Ghost of Gold[7]
Take from Toil a thousand fold
More than e'er its substance could
In the tyrannies of old.

180   Paper coin—that forgery
Of the title deeds which ye
Hold to something of the worth
Of the inheritance of Earth.

'Tis to be a slave in soul,
185   And to hold no strong control
Over your own wills, but be
All that others make of ye.

And, at length when ye complain
With a murmur weak and vain,
190   'Tis to see the Tyrant's crew
Ride over your wives and you—
Blood is on the grass like dew!

Then it is to feel revenge,
Fiercely thirsting to exchange
195   Blood for blood—and wrong for wrong—
Do not thus when ye are strong!

Birds find rest in narrow nest,
When weary of their winged quest;
Beasts find fare in woody lair
200   When storm and snow are in the air;

Horses, oxen, have a home
When from daily toil they come;
Household dogs, when the wind roars,
Find a home within warm doors;[8]

205   Asses, swine, have litter spread,
And with fitting food are fed;
All things have a home but one—
Thou, O Englishman, hast none![9]

This is Slavery!—savage men,
210   Or wild beasts within a den,
Would endure not as ye do—
But such ills they never knew.

---

7. Debased paper money; though legal tender today, in Shelley's day its use as wages was controversial and devastating. Paper could be issued without adequate backing and thus was subject to inflation. The doubly evil effect was to depress the cost of labor to employers and the purchasing worth of the wages.

8. This stanza is only in *The Masque of Anarchy* (1832).
9. Jesus cautions a scribe who wants to join his ministry: "The foxes have holes, and the birds of the air have nests; but the Son of man hath no where to lay his head" (Matthew 8.20).

What art thou, Freedom? O! could slaves
Answer from their living graves
215 This demand, tyrants would flee
Like a dream's dim imagery;

Thou art not, as impostors say,
A shadow soon to pass away,
A superstition, and a name
220 Echoing from the cave of Fame.°   *Rumor*

For the labourer, thou art bread
And a comely table spread,
From his daily labour come
To a neat and happy home.

225 Thou art clothes, and fire, and food
For the trampled multitude—
No—in countries that are free
Such starvation cannot be
As in England now we see!

230 To the rich thou art a check;
When his foot is on the neck
Of his victim, thou dost make
That he treads upon a snake.[1]

Thou art Justice—ne'er for gold
235 May thy righteous laws be sold
As laws are in England—thou
Shield'st alike the high and low.

Thou art Wisdom: Freemen never
Dream that God will damn for ever
240 All who think those things untrue
Of which Priests make such ado.

Thou art Peace—never by thee
Would blood and treasure wasted be
As tyrants wasted them, when all
245 Leagued to quench thy flame in Gaul.°   *Revolutionary France*

What if English toil and blood
Was poured forth, even as a flood?
It availed, Oh, Liberty!
To dim but not extinguish thee.

250 Thou art Love—the rich have kissed
Thy feet, and, like him following Christ,
Give their substance to the free
And through the rough world follow thee,[2]

---

1. A famous image from the American Revolutionary
flag, whose motto was "Don't Tread on Me!"
2. Jesus counsels a rich young man, "If thou wilt be perfect go and sell that thou hast, and give to the poor, and
thou shalt have treasure in heaven: and come and follow
me" (Matthew 19.21). He ignores him.

Or turn their wealth to arms, and make
255   War for thy beloved sake
On wealth and war and fraud—whence they
Drew the power which is their prey.

Science, Poetry, and Thought,
Are thy lamps; they make the lot
260   Of the dwellers in a cot°   cottage
So serene, they curse it not.

Spirit, Patience, gentleness,
All that can adorn and bless
Art thou—let deeds, not words, express
265   Thine exceeding loveliness.

Let a great Assembly be
Of the fearless and the free
On some spot of English ground
Where the plains stretch wide around.

270   Let the blue sky overhead,
The green earth on which ye tread,
All that must eternal be,
Witness the solemnity.

From the corners uttermost
275   Of the bounds of English coast,
From every hut, village, and town
Where those who live and suffer moan
For others' misery or their own;

From the workhouse[3] and the prison
280   Where, pale as corpses newly risen,
Women, children, young and old,
Groan for pain, and weep for cold—

From the haunts of daily life
Where is waged the daily strife
285   With common wants and common cares
Which sows the human heart with tares[4]

Lastly, from the palaces
Where the murmur of distress
Echoes, like the distant sound
290   Of a wind alive around

3. In a system to replace begging and alms-giving, the poor were forced into workhouses where they labored for meager wages in miserable conditions, often with families separated. See Wordsworth's *Old Cumberland Beggar*.
4. Jesus's parable of the tares (weeds) in the wheat field, Matthew 13.24–30.

Those prison halls of wealth and fashion,
Where some few feel such compassion
For those who groan and toil and wail
As must make their brethren pale—

295 Ye who suffer woes untold
Or° to feel, or to behold   *either*
Your lost country bought and sold
With a price of blood and gold—

Let a vast assembly be,
300 And with great solemnity
Declare with measured words that ye
Are, as God has made ye, free!

Be your strong and simple words
Keen to wound as sharpened swords,
305 And wide as targes° let them be,   *shields*
With their shade to cover ye.

Let the tyrants pour around
With a quick and startling sound,
Like the loosening of a sea
310 Troops of armed emblazonry.

Let the charged artillery drive
Till the dead air seems alive
With the clash of clanging wheels,
And the tramp of horses' heels.

315 Let the fixed bayonet
Gleam with sharp desire to wet
Its bright point in English blood,
Looking keen as one for food.

Let the horsemen's scimitars°   *curved Turkish swords*
320 Wheel and flash, like sphereless stars°   *lacking an orbit*
Thirsting to eclipse their burning
In a sea of death and mourning.

Stand ye calm and resolute,
Like a forest close and mute,
325 With folded arms, and looks which are
Weapons of an unvanquished war,

And let Panic, who outspeeds
The career of armed steeds
Pass, a disregarded shade
330 Through your phalanx° undismayed.   *arrayed troops*

Let the Laws of your own land,
Good or ill, between ye stand,
Hand to hand, and foot to foot,
Arbiters of the dispute,

335   The old laws of England—they
Whose reverend heads with age are grey,
Children of a wiser day;
And whose solemn voice must be
Thine own echo—Liberty!

340   On those who first should violate
Such sacred heralds in their state
Rest the blood that must ensue,
And it will not rest on you.

    And, if then the tyrants dare,
345   Let them ride among you there,
Slash and stab and maim and hew,—
What they like, that let them do.

With folded arms and steady eyes,
And little fear and less surprise,
350   Look upon them as they slay
Till their rage has died away.

Then they will return with shame
To the place from which they came,
And the blood thus shed will speak
355   In hot blushes on their cheek.

Every woman in the land
Will point at them as they stand—
They will hardly dare to greet
Their acquaintance in the street.

360   And the bold, true warriors
Who have hugged Danger in wars
Will turn to those who would be free,
Ashamed of such base company.

And that slaughter to the Nation
365   Shall steam up like inspiration,
Eloquent, oracular,
A volcano heard afar;

And these words shall then become
Like Oppression's thundered doom
370   Ringing through each heart and brain
Heard again—again—again!

Rise like lions after slumber,
In unvanquishable number!
Shake your chains to earth like dew
375   Which in sleep had fallen on you—
Ye are many—they are few."

1819   1832

Ode to the West Wind[1]

1

O wild West Wind, thou breath of Autumn's being,
Thou from whose unseen presence the leaves dead
Are driven like ghosts from an enchanter fleeing,

Yellow, and black, and pale, and hectic° red,   *feverish*
5 Pestilence-stricken multitudes![2] O Thou
Who chariotest to their dark wintry bed

The winged seeds, where they lie cold and low,
Each like a corpse within its grave, until
Thine azure sister of the Spring° shall blow   *spring wind*

10 Her clarion° o'er the dreaming earth, and fill   *shrill trumpet*
(Driving sweet buds like flocks to feed in air)
With living hues and odours plain and hill:

Wild Spirit, which art moving everywhere;
Destroyer and Preserver;[3] hear, O hear!

2

15 Thou on whose stream, mid the steep sky's commotion,
Loose clouds like earth's decaying leaves are shed,
Shook from the tangled boughs of heaven and ocean,

Angels° of rain and lightning! there are spread   *messengers*
On the blue surface of thine airy surge,
20 Like the bright hair uplifted from the head

Of some fierce Maenad, even from the dim verge
Of the horizon to the zenith's height,
The locks of the approaching storm.[4] Thou dirge°   *funeral chant*

Of the dying year, to which this closing night
25 Will be the dome of a vast sepulchre,
Vaulted with all thy congregated might

Of vapours, from whose solid atmosphere
Black rain, and fire, and hail, will burst: Oh hear!

3

Thou who didst waken from his summer dreams
30 The blue Mediterranean, where he lay,
Lulled by the coil of his crystalline streams,

1. There is a tradition, as old as the Bible, of wind as meta-phor of life and inspiration—particularly the West Wind as harbinger of future seasons, events, and transformations, not only in weather, but by symbolic extension, in emotional, spiritual, and political life. The Latin for "wind," *spiritus*, also means "breath" (1) and soul or spirit (13, 61–62), as well as being the root-word for "inspiration" (a taking-in of energy). The ode is in terza rima sonnet stanzas.
2. A traditional epic simile (Milton, Dante, Virgil) com-pares the dead to wind-driven fallen leaves.
3. Titles for major Hindu gods, Siva the Destroyer and Vishnu the Preserver.

4. The god of wine Bacchus was attended by Maenads, female votaries who danced in wild worship. Viewing a sculpture of them in Florence, Shelley commented: "The tremendous spirit of superstition aided by drunkenness... seems to have caught them in its whirlwinds, and to bear them over the earth as the rapid volutions of a tempest have the ever-changing trunk of a water-spout.... Their hair, loose and floating, seems caught in tempest of their own tumultuous motion." Associated with vegetation, Bacchus was fabled to die in the autumn and be reborn in the spring.

Beside a pumice° isle in Baiae's bay,   *volcanic*
And saw in sleep old palaces and towers
Quivering within the wave's intenser day,

35   All overgrown with azure moss, and flowers
So sweet, the sense faints picturing them![5] Thou
For whose path the Atlantic's level powers

Cleave themselves into chasms, while far below
The sea-blooms and the oozy woods which wear

40   The sapless foliage of the ocean, know

Thy voice, and suddenly grow grey with fear,
And tremble and despoil themselves:[6] O hear!

4

If I were a dead leaf thou mightest bear;
If I were a swift cloud to fly with thee;

45   A wave to pant beneath thy power, and share

The impulse of thy strength, only less free
Than thou, O uncontrollable! if even
I were as in my boyhood, and could be

The comrade of thy wanderings over heaven,

50   As then, when to outstrip thy skiey speed
Scarce seemed a vision,—I would ne'er have striven

As thus with thee in prayer in my sore need.
Oh lift me as a wave, a leaf, a cloud!
I fall upon the thorns of life![7] I bleed!

55   A heavy weight of hours has chained and bowed
One too like thee—tameless, and swift, and proud.

5

Make me thy lyre,[8] even as the forest is:
What if my leaves are falling like its own?
The tumult of thy mighty harmonies

60   Will take from both a deep autumnal tone,
Sweet though in sadness. Be thou, Spirit fierce,
My spirit! Be thou me, impetuous one![9]

Drive my dead thoughts over the universe,
Like withered leaves, to quicken a new birth;

65   And, by the incantation of this verse,

---

5. Ruins of imperial Roman villas in the Bay of Baiae, west of Naples.

6. In a note, Shelley says he is alluding to the seasonal change (despoiling) of seaweed, a process he imagines as instigated by the autumn wind.

7. A risky self-comparison to Jesus's torture by a crown of thorns; see also *Adonais* 305–306, page 904.

8. A wind-harp, an image used again in *A Defence* (page 921), and in Coleridge's *The Eolian Harp*.

9. Shelley hazards the ungrammatical objective case ("me" instead of "I") not only to chime with "Be" but also to represent himself as an object.

Scatter, as from an unextinguished hearth
Ashes and sparks, my words among mankind!
Be through my lips to unawakened earth

The trumpet of a prophecy! O Wind,
70   If Winter comes, can Spring be far behind?

1819   1820

To a Sky-Lark

    Hail to thee, blithe Spirit!
      Bird thou never wert—
    That from Heaven or near it
      Pourest thy full heart
5   In profuse strains of unpremeditated art.[1]

    Higher still and higher
      From the earth thou springest,
    Like a cloud of fire;
      The blue deep thou wingest,
10   And singing still dost soar, and soaring ever singest.

    In the golden lightning
      Of the sunken sun,
    O'er which clouds are bright'ning,
      Thou dost float and run,
15   Like an unbodied joy whose race is just begun.

    The pale purple even°   *evening*
      Melts around thy flight;
    Like a star of Heaven,
      In the broad daylight
20   Thou art unseen, but yet I hear thy shrill delight—

    Keen as are the arrows
      Of that silver sphere°   *morning star*
    Whose intense lamp narrows
      In the white dawn clear
25   Until we hardly see—we feel, that it is there.

    All the earth and air
      With thy voice is loud,
    As, when night is bare,
      From one lonely cloud
30   The moon rains out her beams, and Heaven is overflowed.

    What thou art we know not;
      What is most like thee?
    From rainbow clouds there flow not

1. The skylark sings only in flight; Shelley evokes Milton's thanks to his "Celestial patroness," who "inspires / Easy [his] unpremeditated Verse" (*Paradise Lost* 9.21–24).

Drops so bright to see
35 As from thy presence showers a rain of melody:—

Like a Poet hidden
    In the light of thought,
Singing hymns unbidden,
    Till the world is wrought
40 To sympathy with hopes and fears it heeded not:

Like a high-born maiden
    In a palace tower,
Soothing her love-laden
    Soul in secret hour
45 With music sweet as love which overflows her bower:

Like a glow-worm golden
    In a dell of dew,
Scattering unbeholden
    Its aerial hue
50 Among the flowers and grass which screen it from the view:

Like a rose embowered
    In its own green leaves,
By warm winds deflowered,
    Till the scent it gives
55 Makes faint with too much sweet these heavy-winged thieves:

Sound of vernal° showers   *springtime*
    On the twinkling grass,
Rain-awakened flowers,
    All that ever was,
60 Joyous and clear and fresh,—thy music doth surpass.

Teach us, Sprite° or Bird,   *spirit, fairy*
    What sweet thoughts are thine:
I have never heard
    Praise of love or wine
65 That panted forth a flood of rapture so divine.

Chorus Hymeneal°   *wedding song*
    Or triumphal° chaunt,   *military*
Matched with thine, would be all
    But an empty vaunt—
70 A thing wherein we feel there is some hidden want.

What objects are the fountains
    Of thy happy strain?
What fields, or waves, or mountains?
    What shapes of sky or plain?
75 What love of thine own kind? what ignorance of pain?

With thy clear keen joyance
    Languor cannot be:

<pre>
            Shadow of annoyance
              Never came near thee:
80   Thou lovest—but ne'er knew love's sad satiety.°   (over)fullness

            Waking or asleep,
              Thou of death must deem
            Things more true and deep
              Than we mortals dream,
85   Or how could thy notes flow in such a crystal stream?

            We look before and after,²
              And pine for what is not:
            Our sincerest laughter
              With some pain is fraught;
90   Our sweetest songs are those that tell of saddest thought.

            Yet if we could scorn
              Hate and pride and fear,
            If we were things born
              Not to shed a tear,
95   I know not how thy joy we ever should come near.

            Better than all measures
              Of delightful sound,
            Better than all treasures
              That in books are found,
100   Thy skill to poet were, thou scorner of the ground!

            Teach me half the gladness
              That thy brain must know,
            Such harmonious madness³
              From my lips would flow
105   The world should listen then—as I am listening now.
</pre>

1820   1820

To ——

<pre>
        Music, when soft voices die,
        Vibrates in the memory;
        Odours, when sweet violets sicken,
        Live within the sense they quicken;°   enliven

5   Rose-leaves, when the rose is dead,
        Are heaped for the beloved's bed;
        And so thy thoughts, when thou art gone,
        Love itself shall slumber on.
</pre>

1821   1824

2. Echoing Hamlet's comment on the human capability of "looking before and after" (4.4.36), as well as alluding to Wordsworth's use of this phrase in Preface to *Lyrical Ballads* (see page 441).

3. Echoing Wordsworth's rhyme in *Resolution and Independence*: "We Poets in our youth begin in gladness; / But thereof come in the end despondency and madness" (48–49). See also the last lines of Coleridge's *Kubla Khan*.

ADONAIS   Although Shelley knew Keats only casually, he was impressed by his poetry and pained by his abuse in the Tory press for his political sentiments. When he and Mary Shelley learned of Keats's failing health, they invited him to Italy as their guest; Keats went first to Rome for treatment, and he died there after a few months, in February 1821. Shelley had heard that his demise was brought on by the vicious reviews that began to appear in 1818, capped by ridicule of *Endymion* in the Tory *Quarterly Review*, which had also cut into Shelley. Shelley's intent in *Adonais* is both to honor the dead poet (the protocol of elegy) and to wage his own polemic against the reviews. Deploying Spenserian stanzas (Keats's form in *The Eve of St. Agnes*) and classical allusions, he fashioned a self-advertising, "highly wrought piece of art." Characteristically, Shelley took risks, notably in stanza 34, a daring self-portrait in the combined figure of tormented Christ and branded Cain. Though he had expected a drubbing from the Tory press, he was crushed when hostile reviews discouraged publication in England. Enough of the poem was quoted in the first reviews, however, to launch the legend of Keats's death, which proved durable: until the late 1840s, Keats was known more widely by *Adonais* than by his own poetry. Using the pattern of "pastoral elegy" (a call to mourning; a grieving accusation in the invocation of the muse; sympathy of nature with the death; the procession of mourners; the turn from grief to consolation), Shelley develops a master-myth: a "beautiful," "frail," "defenceless" poet fatally savaged, and vindicated in "Eternity"—a judgment Shelley means for himself as well. So disdainful is he of a world where "*We* decay / Like corpses in a charnel," that *Adonais* strains the obligation of elegy to reconcile mourners to death, all but recommending "Die, / If thou wouldst be with that which thou dost seek!" In an elegiac tribute to a friend and former band member (Brian Jones) at a huge concert in Hyde Park, London, Mick Jagger read part of this famous stanza in a tone of celebration.

Shelley's twinning with Keats received fresh credit when he drowned in a storm at sea a little over a year after publishing *Adonais*. "Who but will regard as a prophecy the last stanza?" Mary Shelley wrote in a note in her 1839 edition; the poem now seemed "more applicable to Shelley, than to the young and gifted poet whom he mourned. The poetic view he takes of death, and the lofty scorn he displays towards his calumniators, are as a prophecy on his own destiny, when received among immortal names, and the poisonous breath of critics has vanished into emptiness before the fame he inherits." There are some weirdly textual doublings. When Shelley's corpse washed ashore, a friend identified it by a copy of Keats's 1820 volume in the coat pocket, which he knew Shelley had taken with him. Then, after a cremation in which Shelley's heart, hardened by calcium, did not burn, this same friend snatched it from the embers and presented it to Mary Shelley, who kept it thereafter in her desk, wrapped in a copy of *Adonais*.

Adonais
An Elegy on the Death of John Keats, Author of Endymion, Hyperion, Etc.

Ἀστὴρ πρὶν μὲν ἔλαμπες ἐνὶ ζωοῖσιν Ἑῷος·
νῦν δὲ θανὼν λάμπεις Ἕσπερος ἐν φθιμένοις.

Plato[1]

Preface

Φάρμακον ἦλθε, Βίων, ποτὶ σὸν στόμα, φάρμακον εἶδες.
πῶς τεν τοῖς χείλεσσι ποτέδραμε, κοὐκ ἐγλυκάνθη;

---

1. "Thou wert the morning star among the living, / Ere thy fair light had fled; / Now, having died, thou art as Hesperus, giving / New splendour to the dead"; Shelley's translation of *Epigram on Aster* by Plato; Aster (Star) was a young man whom he loved. Hesperus is the evening star; it and the morning star are both the planet Venus. Shelley's Greek texts for both epigraphs designate an elite audience.

τὶς δὲ βροτὸς τοσσοῦτον ἀνάμερος ἢ κεράσαι τοι,
ἢ δοῦναι λαλέοντι τὸ φάρμακον; ἔκφυγεν ὠδάν.

Moschus, Epitaph. Bion[2]

It is my intention to subjoin to the London edition[3] of this poem a criticism upon the claims of its lamented object to be classed among the writers of the highest genius who have adorned our age. My known repugnance to the narrow principles of taste on which several of his earlier compositions were modelled proves at least that I am an impartial judge. I consider the fragment of *Hyperion* as second to nothing that was ever produced by a writer of the same years.[4]

John Keats died at Rome of a consumption, in his twenty-fourth year, on the [23rd] of [February] 1821; and was buried in the romantic and lonely cemetery of the protestants in that city, under the pyramid which is the tomb of Cestius, and the massy walls and towers, now mouldering and desolate, which formed the circuit of ancient Rome. The cemetery is an open space among the ruins, covered in winter with violets and daisies. It might make one in love with death to think that one should be buried in so sweet a place.[5]

The genius of the lamented person to whose memory I have dedicated these unworthy verses was not less delicate and fragile than it was beautiful; and, where canker-worms abound, what wonder if its young flower was blighted in the bud? The savage criticism on his *Endymion* which appeared in the *Quarterly Review* produced the most violent effect on his susceptible mind.[6] The agitation thus originated ended in the rupture of a blood-vessel in the lungs; a rapid consumption ensued; and the succeeding acknowledgements, from more candid critics,[7] of the true greatness of his powers, were ineffectual to heal the wound thus wantonly inflicted.

It may be well said that these wretched men know not what they do.[8] They scatter their insults and their slanders without heed as to whether the poisoned shaft lights on a heart made callous by many blows, or one, like Keats's, composed of more penetrable stuff.[9] One of their associates is, to my knowledge, a most base and unprincipled calumniator. As to *Endymion*, was it a poem, whatever might be its defects, to be treated contemptuously by those who had celebrated with various degrees of complacency and panegyric *Paris*, and *Woman*, and *A Syrian Tale*, and Mrs. Lefanu, and Mr. Barret, and Mr. Howard Payne, and a long list of the illustrious

2. From *Lament for Bion*: "Poison came, Bion, to thy mouth; thou didst know poison. To such lips as thine did it come, and was not sweetened? What mortal was so cruel that could mix poison for thee, or give thee venom, who heard thy voice? Surely he had no music in his soul." The next line, which Shelley does not quote, is "Yet justice overtakes all." As this Preface makes clear, Bion is Keats, and his poison, the reviews. Moschus (2nd century B.C.E.) also wrote a *Lament for Adonis*.
3. *Adonais* was printed in Pisa, Italy, in 1821; although the London reviews quoted it extensively, its first English edition did not appear until 1829.
4. The fragment of *Hyperion* published in Keats's 1820 volume was written in late 1819, around his twenty-fourth birthday. The "narrow principles of taste" were voiced chiefly in *Sleep and Poetry*, the final poem in his harshly reviewed debut volume of 1817; see page 981.
5. The Shelleys' son William, who died in Rome in 1819 at age three, is buried there, as would be Shelley himself in 1822. Shelley is echoing Keats's *Ode to a Nightingale*:

"I have been half in love with easeful Death" (line 52).
6. Shelley believed the reviewer of *Endymion* for *The Quarterly Review* (April 1818) to have been Poet Laureate Robert Southey (now a Tory); it was actually John Wilson Croker (the savager of Barbauld's *Eighteen Hundred and Eleven*; see page 80). Croker was less unkind than others (e.g., *Blackwood's*; see page 982), but *The Quarterly*'s wide circulation, influence, and establishment credentials made its voice the most damaging—to Shelley and others, as well as to Keats.
7. Francis Jeffrey, for example, gave a favorable review to Keats's 1820 volume in the *Edinburgh Review*.
8. Jesus's exculpation of his crucifiers, "Father, forgive them; for they know not what they do" (Luke 23.34).
9. An allusion both to Hamlet's sneer at his remarried mother—whether her heart is insensitive, or "made of penetrable stuff" (*Hamlet* 3.4.36–40)—and to Byron's use of this phrase in *English Bards and Scotch Reviewers*, when he warns his hostile reviewers that "they too are 'penetrable stuff'"; Shelley refers to this poem in stanza 28.

obscure? Are these the men who, in their venal good-nature, presumed to draw a parallel between the Rev. Mr. Milman and Lord Byron?[1] What gnat did they strain at here, after having swallowed all those camels? Against what woman taken in adultery dares the foremost of these literary prostitutes to cast his opprobrious stone? Miserable man: you, one of the meanest, have wantonly defaced one of the noblest, specimens of the workmanship of God. Nor shall it be your excuse that, murderer as you are, you have spoken daggers, but used none.[2]

The circumstances of the closing scene of poor Keats's life were not made known to me until the Elegy was ready for the press. I am given to understand that the wound which his sensitive spirit had received from the criticism of Endymion was exasperated by the bitter sense of unrequited benefits; the poor fellow seems to have been hooted from the stage of life, no less by those on whom he had wasted the promise of his genius than those on whom he had lavished his fortune and his care. He was accompanied to Rome, and attended in his last illness, by Mr. Severn, a young artist of the highest promise, who, I have been informed, "almost risked his own life, and sacrificed every prospect to unwearied attendance upon his dying friend." Had I known these circumstances before the completion of my poem, I should have been tempted to add my feeble tribute of applause to the more solid recompense which the virtuous man finds in the recollection of his own motives. Mr. Severn can dispense with a reward from "such stuff as dreams are made of."[3] His conduct is a golden augury of the success of his future career. May the unextinguished spirit of his illustrious friend animate the creations of his pencil, and plead against oblivion for his name!

Adonais[4]

I

I weep for Adonais—he is dead!
Oh weep for Adonais, though our tears
Thaw not the frost which binds so dear a head!
And thou, sad Hour° selected from all years   *goddess of the season*
5   To mourn our loss, rouse thy obscure compeers,
And teach them thine own sorrow! Say: "With me
Died Adonais! Till the Future dares
Forget the Past, his fate and fame shall be
An echo and a light unto eternity!"

---

1. Now forgotten writers: *Paris in 1815* (1817) by Rev. George Croly was favorably reviewed in *The Quarterly* (he would go on to write a nasty review of *Adonais*); *The Quarterly* also reviewed *Woman* (1810) by Eaton Stannard Barrett, a Tory wit, and H. Galley Knight's *Ilderim: A Syrian Tale* (1816), and gave favorable reviews to Rev. Henry Hart Milman's *Saviour, Lord of the Bright City* and *Fall of Jerusalem* but drubbed *Brutus* by American dramatist John Howard Payne (who would court the widowed Mary Shelley). Alicia Lefanu wrote *The Flowers* (1809).
2. Shelley's pile of allusions are to Jesus's upbraiding of the "blind guides, which strain at a gnat, and swallow a camel" (Matthew 23.24), his challenge to the would-be executioners of the woman taken in adultery (John 8.3–11), and to Hamlet's barely restrained anger at his mother, his intent to "speak daggers to her, but use none"

(3.2.404). Opprobrious: punitive, bearing public disgrace.
3. Prospero's elegy for his art: "We are such stuff / As dreams are made on, and our little life / Is rounded with a sleep" (*Tempest* 4.1.156–58). Joseph Severn, a painter and friend of Keats, accompanied him to Rome and nursed him in his final months, holding him in his arms as he died.
4. "Adonais" is derived from Adonis, a beautiful youth in classical mythology fatally gored while hunting a boar. To settle the contention between Venus and Persephone over who should possess him in the afterlife, Zeus decreed that he would spend half the year in the underworld with Persephone and half the year above ground with Venus— a perpetual death and rebirth reflecting the seasonal cycles of vegetation. Keats treated Venus's love for Adonis in Book 2 of *Endymion*.

II

10 Where wert thou, mighty Mother, when he lay,
    When thy Son lay, pierced by the shaft which flies
    In darkness? Where was lorn° Urania   *forlorn*
    When Adonais died?[5] With veilèd eyes,
    Mid listening Echoes,° in her Paradise   *personified echoes*
15 She sate, while one,° with soft enamoured breath,   *an Echo*
    Rekindled all the fading melodies°   *Keats's poetry*
    With which, like flowers that mock the corse beneath,
He had adorned and hid the coming bulk of Death.

III

    Oh weep for Adonais—he is dead!
20 Wake, melancholy Mother, wake and weep!—
    Yet wherefore? Quench within their burning bed
    Thy fiery tears, and let thy loud heart keep
    Like his, a mute and uncomplaining sleep;
    For he is gone where all things wise and fair
25 Descend. Oh dream not that the amorous Deep°   *abyss*
    Will yet restore him to the vital air;
Death feeds on his mute voice, and laughs at our despair.

IV

    Most musical of mourners, weep again!
    Lament anew, Urania!—He° died   *Milton*
30 Who was the Sire of an immortal strain,
    Blind, old, and lonely, when his country's pride,
    The priest, the slave, and the liberticide,°   *liberty-killer*
    Trampled and mocked with many a loathèd rite
    Of lust and blood; he went unterrified
35 Into the gulf of death; but his clear Sprite°   *spirit*
Yet reigns o'er earth, the third among the sons of light.[6]

V

    Most musical of mourners, weep anew!
    Not all to that bright station dared to climb:
    And happier they their happiness who knew,
40 Whose tapers yet burn through that night of time
    In which suns perished. Others more sublime,
    Struck by the envious wrath of man or god,
    Have sunk, extinct in their refulgent° prime;   *radiant*
    And some yet live, treading the thorny road
45 Which leads, through toil and hate, to Fame's serene abode.

---

5. Urania, the mighty Mother, is the "Heav'nly Muse" of astronomy whom Milton invokes at the opening of *Paradise Lost* (1.6) and in the first line of Book 7. The name is also an epithet of Aphrodite (Venus, the goddess who loved Adonis), "Aphrodite Urania," the heavenly goddess of pure or spiritual love. The fatal shaft images *The Quarterly's* supposedly fatal review of Keats; "in darkness" refers to its lack of signature.
6. The other two are Homer and Dante. Milton served Cromwell's parliamentary government, which had executed Charles I. After the monarchy was restored in 1660, Milton was imprisoned, heavily fined, and only narrowly escaped the execution suffered by others of Cromwell's party.

VI

But now thy youngest, dearest one has perished,
The nursling of thy widowhood, who grew,
Like a pale flower by some sad maiden cherished,
And fed with true-love tears instead of dew.
50 Most musical of mourners, weep anew!
Thy extreme° hope, the loveliest and the last,   *final, highest*
The bloom whose petals, nipped before they blew,°   *blossomed*
Died on the promise of the fruit, is waste;
The broken lily lies—the storm is overpast.

VII

55 To that high Capital° where kingly Death   *Rome*
Keeps his pale court° in beauty and decay   *the cemetery*
He came; and bought, with price of purest breath,
A grave among the eternal.—Come away!
Haste, while the vault of blue Italian day
60 Is yet his fitting charnel-roof, while still
He lies, as if in dewy sleep he lay.
Awake him not! surely he takes his fill
Of deep and liquid rest, forgetful of all ill.

VIII

He will awake no more, oh never more!
65 Within the twilight chamber spreads apace
The shadow of white Death, and at the door
Invisible Corruption waits to trace
His extreme way to her dim dwelling-place;
The eternal Hunger sits, but pity and awe
70 Soothe her pale rage, nor dares she to deface
So fair a prey, till darkness and the law
Of change shall o'er his sleep the mortal curtain draw.

IX

Oh weep for Adonais!—The quick Dreams,°   *living poetry*
The passion-winged Ministers of thought,
75 Who were his flocks, whom near the living streams
Of his young spirit he fed, and whom he taught
The love which was its music, wander not—
Wander no more from kindling brain to brain,
But droop there whence they sprung; and mourn their lot
80 Round the cold heart where, after their sweet pain,
They ne'er will gather strength or find a home again.

X

And one° with trembling hands clasps his cold head,   *of the Dreams*
And fans him with her moonlight wings, and cries,
"Our love, our hope, our sorrow, is not dead!
85 See, on the silken fringe of his faint eyes,
Like dew upon a sleeping flower, there lies
A tear some Dream has loosened from his brain."
Lost Angel of a ruined Paradise!

She knew not 'twas her own,—as with no stain
90   She faded, like a cloud which had outwept its rain.

XI

One from a lucid urn of starry dew
Washed his light limbs, as if embalming them;
Another clipped her profuse locks, and threw
The wreath upon him, like an anadem°   *head-garland*
95   Which frozen tears instead of pearls begem;
Another in her wilful grief would break
Her bow and winged reeds,° as if to stem   *arrows*
A greater loss with one which was more weak,—
And dull the barbed fire against his frozen cheek.

XII

100   Another Splendour on his mouth alit,
That mouth whence it was wont° to draw the breath   *used*
Which gave it strength to pierce the guarded wit,°   *mind*
And pass into the panting heart beneath
With lightning and with music: the damp death
105   Quenched its caress upon his icy lips;
And, as a dying meteor stains a wreath
Of moonlight vapour which the cold night clips,°   *clasps, cuts off*
It flushed through his pale limbs, and passed to its eclipse.

XIII

And others came. Desires and Adorations;
110   Wingèd Persuasions, and veiled Destinies;
Splendours, and Glooms, and glimmering incarnations
Of Hopes and Fears, and twilight Phantasies;
And Sorrow, with her family of Sighs;
And Pleasure, blind with tears, led by the gleam
115   Of her own dying smile instead of eyes,
Came in slow pomp;—the moving pomp might seem
Like pageantry of mist on an autumnal stream.

XIV

All he had loved, and moulded into thought
From shape and hue and odour and sweet sound,
120   Lamented Adonais. Morning sought
Her eastern watch-tower, and her hair unbound,
Wet with the tears which should adorn the ground,
Dimmed the aerial eyes that kindle day;
Afar the melancholy Thunder moaned,
125   Pale Ocean in unquiet slumber lay,
And the wild Winds flew round, sobbing in their dismay.

XV

Lost Echo sits amid the voiceless mountains,
And feeds her grief with his remembered lay,°   *song*
And will no more reply to winds or fountains,
130   Or amorous birds perched on the young green spray,

Or herdsman's horn, or bell° at closing day;   *church bell*
Since she can mimic not his lips, more dear
Than those for whose disdain she pined away
Into a shadow of all sounds:[7]—a drear
135   Murmur, between their songs, is all the woodmen hear.

XVI

Grief made the young Spring wild, and she threw down
Her kindling buds, as if she Autumn were,
Or they dead leaves; since her delight is flown,
For whom should she have waked the sullen Year?
140   To Phoebus was not Hyacinth so dear,
Nor to himself Narcissus,[8] as to both°   *as dear to both are*
Thou, Adonais; wan they stand and sere°   *withered*
Amid the faint companions of their youth,
With dew all turned to tears,—odour, to sighing ruth.°   *pity*

XVII

145   Thy spirit's sister, the lorn nightingale,
Mourns not her mate with such melodious pain;[9]
Not so the eagle, who like thee could scale
Heaven, and could nourish in the sun's domain
Her mighty youth with morning, doth complain,°   *lament*
150   Soaring and screaming round her empty nest,[1]
As Albion° wails for thee: the curse of Cain[2]   *mythical England*
Light on his° head who pierced thy innocent breast,   *the reviewer's*
And scared the angel soul that was its earthly guest!

XVIII

Ah woe is me! Winter is come and gone,
155   But grief returns with the revolving year.
The airs and streams renew their joyous tone;
The ants, the bees, the swallows, re-appear;
Fresh leaves and flowers deck the dead Seasons' bier;°   *coffin platform*
The amorous birds now pair in every brake,°   *thicket*
160   And build their mossy homes in field and brere;°   *briar*
And the green lizard and the golden snake,
Like unimprisoned flames, out of their trance° awake.   *hibernation*

XIX

Through wood and stream and field and hill and Ocean,
A quickening life from the Earth's heart has burst,
165   As it has ever done, with change and motion,
From the great morning of the world when first

7. Narcissus rejected the nymph Echo who, lovelorn, faded into an echo.
8. In punishment for his scorn of love from others, Narcissus was cursed to fall in love with his reflection in a pool of water; he pined away until he turned into a narcissus flower. The beautiful youth Hyacinthus was loved by Phoebus (Apollo, god of poetry); when Hyacinthus rebuffed the advances of Zephyr (Keats's reviewer), Zephyr caused him to be slain, but Apollo engendered the hyacinth flower from his blood.
9. Shelley returns the happy nightingale of Keats's *Ode* to its tradition of sorrowful, lovelorn song.
1. Although the eagle bewails the death of her brood (the empty nest), she may (as legend has it) soar toward the sun, which restores her to youth.
2. For murdering Abel, Cain is "cursed from the earth," (Genesis 4.10–15).

God dawned on Chaos.[3] In its steam immersed,
The lamps° of heaven flash with a softer light;   *lights, stars*
All baser things pant with life's sacred thirst,
170 Diffuse themselves, and spend in love's delight
The beauty and the joy of their renewed might.

     XX

The leprous corpse, touched by this spirit tender,
Exhales itself in flowers of gentle breath;
Like incarnations° of the stars, when splendour   *embodiments*
175 Is changed to fragrance, they illumine death,
And mock the merry worm that wakes beneath.
Nought we know dies: shall that alone which knows° *the mind*
Be as a sword consumed before the sheath
By sightless° lightning? The intense atom glows *invisible, morally*
180 A moment, then is quenched in a most cold repose.   *blind*

     XXI

Alas that all we loved of him should be,
But for our grief, as if it had not been,
And grief itself be mortal! Woe is me!
Whence are we, and why are we? of what scene
185 The actors or spectators? Great and mean
Meet massed in death, who lends what life must borrow.
As long as skies are blue and fields are green,
Evening must usher night, night urge the morrow,
Month follow month with woe, and year wake year to sorrow.

     XXII

190 *He* will awake no more, oh never more!
"Wake thou," cried Misery, "childless Mother! Rise
Out of thy sleep, and slake in thy heart's core
A wound more fierce than his, with tears and sighs."
And all the Dreams that watched Urania's eyes,
195 And all the Echoes whom their Sister's° song   *Echo's*
Had held in holy silence, cried "Arise";
Swift as a Thought by the snake Memory stung,
From her ambrosial[4] rest the fading Splendour° sprung. *Urania*

     XXIII

She rose like an autumnal Night that springs
200 Out of the East, and follows wild and drear
The golden Day, which, on eternal wings,
Even as a ghost abandoning a bier,
Had left the Earth a corpse. Sorrow and fear
So struck, so roused, so rapt, Urania;
205 So saddened round her like an atmosphere
Of stormy mist; so swept her on her way,
Even to the mournful place where Adonais lay.

---

3. Alluding to Genesis 1.3–5 and evoking the myth of
Adonis's seasonal rebirth.

4. Delightful; ambrosia (from Greek for "immortal, immune to murder") is the food of the gods in classical myth.

XXIV

Out of her secret Paradise she sped,
Through camps and cities rough with stone and steel
210   And human hearts, which, to her aery tread
Yielding not, wounded the invisible
Palms of her tender feet where'er they fell.
And barbed tongues, and thoughts more sharp than they,
Rent° the soft form they never could repel,   *tore*
215   Whose sacred blood, like the young tears of May,
Paved with eternal flowers that undeserving way.

XXV

In the death-chamber for a moment Death,
Shamed by the presence of that living Might,
Blushed to annihilation, and the breath
220   Revisited those° lips, and life's pale light   *Adonais's*
Flashed through those limbs so late° her dear delight.   *recently*
"Leave me not wild and drear and comfortless,
As silent lightning leaves the starless night!
Leave me not!" cried Urania. Her distress
225   Roused Death: Death rose and smiled, and met her vain caress.

XXVI

"Stay yet awhile! speak to me once again!
Kiss me, so long but as a kiss may live!
And in my heartless° breast and burning brain   *love-lorn*
That word, that kiss, shall all thoughts else survive,
230   With food of saddest memory kept alive,
Now thou art dead, as if it were a part
Of thee, my Adonais! I would give
All that I am, to be as thou now art!
But I am chained to Time, and cannot thence depart.

XXVII

235   O gentle child, beautiful as thou wert,
Why didst thou leave the trodden paths of men
Too soon, and with weak hands though mighty heart
Dare° the unpastured dragon° in his den?   *provoke / the reviewer*
Defenceless as thou wert, oh where was then
240   Wisdom the mirrored shield,[5] or scorn° the spear?—   *(Keats's)*
Or, hadst thou waited the full cycle when
Thy spirit should have filled its crescent sphere,[6]
The monsters of life's waste had fled from thee like deer.

XXVIII

The herded wolves bold only to pursue,
245   The obscene ravens clamorous o'er the dead,
The vultures to the conqueror's banner true,

---

5. Because the stare of gorgon Medusa turned its beholders to stone, shields often bore her image, including the shield of warrior Athena, goddess of Wisdom. In the fable, Perseus manages to decapitate Medusa by viewing her reflection in his shield.
6. Reached maturity, like the full moon.

Who feed where Desolation first has fed,
And whose wings rain contagion,—how they° fled,   *these reviewers*
When, like Apollo from his golden bow,
250 The Pythian of the age one arrow sped,
And smiled!—The spoilers tempt no second blow,
They fawn on the proud feet that spurn them lying low.[7]

XXIX

The sun comes forth, and many reptiles spawn;
He sets, and each ephemeral° insect then   *living for one day*
255 Is gathered into death without a dawn,
And the immortal stars awake again.
So is it in the world of living men:
A godlike mind soars forth, in its delight
Making earth bare and veiling heaven; and, when
260 It sinks, the swarms that dimmed or shared its light
Leave to its kindred lamps° the spirit's awful° night."   *stars / awesome*

XXX

Thus ceased she:° and the mountain shepherds° came,   *Urania / fellow poets*
Their garlands sere, their magic mantles° rent.   *capes*
The Pilgrim of Eternity,° whose fame   *Byron*
265 Over his living head like heaven is bent,
An early but enduring monument,
Came, veiling all the lightnings of his song
In sorrow. From her wilds Ierne° sent   *Ireland*
The sweetest lyrist of her saddest wrong,
270 And love taught grief to fall like music from his tongue.[8]

XXXI

Midst others of less note came one frail Form,°   *(Shelley)*
A phantom among men, companionless
As the last cloud of an expiring storm
Whose thunder is its knell.° He, as I guess,   *funeral bell*
275 Had gazed on Nature's naked loveliness
Actaeon-like; and now he fled astray
With feeble steps o'er the world's wilderness,
And his own thoughts along that rugged way
Pursued like raging hounds their father and their prey.[9]

XXXII

280 A pard-like° Spirit beautiful and swift—   *leopard like*
A Love in desolation masked—a Power
Girt round with weakness; it can scarce uplift
The weight of the superincumbent hour.[1]
It is a dying lamp, a falling shower,

---

7. Byron skewered his harsh reviewers in *English Bards and Scotch Reviewers;* by 1821, many had been converted to praise. Apollo earns the title "Pythian" from slaying the dragon Python.
8. Thomas Moore's *Irish Melodies* voiced the "wrongs" Ire-

land suffered from Britain.
9. Hunter Actaeon angered the goddess Diana by accidentally beholding her bathing naked; she turned him into a stag, and his own hounds tore him apart.
1. The overhanging hour of Adonais-Keats's death.

285   A breaking billow;—even whilst we speak
        Is it not broken? On the withering flower
        The killing sun smiles brightly: on a cheek
    The life can burn in blood even while the heart may break.

XXXIII

        His head was bound with pansies overblown,°   *past blooming*
290   And faded violets, white and pied and blue;
        And a light spear topped with a cypress-cone,
        Round whose rude shaft dark ivy-tresses grew[2]
        Yet dripping with the forest's noonday dew,
        Vibrated, as the ever-beating heart
295   Shook the weak hand that grasped it. Of that crew
        He came the last, neglected and apart;
    A herd-abandoned deer struck by the hunter's dart.

XXXIV

        All stood aloof, and at his partial° moan   *compassionate, partisan*
        Smiled through their tears. Well knew that gentle band
300   Who in another's fate now wept his own.
        As in the accents of an unknown land
        He sang new sorrow, sad Urania scanned
        The Stranger's mien, and murmured "Who art thou?"
        He answered not, but with a sudden hand
305   Made bare his branded and ensanguined° brow,   *bloody*
    Which was like Cain's or Christ's—oh that it should be so![3]

XXXV

        What softer voice is hushed over the dead?
        Athwart what brow is that dark mantle thrown?
        What form leans sadly o'er the white death-bed,
310   In mockery° of monumental stone,   *imitation*
        The heavy heart heaving without a moan?
        If it be He who, gentlest of the wise,
        Taught, soothed, loved, honoured, the departed one,[4]
        Let me not vex with inharmonious sighs
315   The silence of that heart's accepted sacrifice.

XXXVI

        Our Adonais has drunk poison—oh
        What deaf and viperous murderer could crown
        Life's early cup with such a draught of woe?
        The nameless worm° would now itself disown;   *anonymous reviewer*
320   It felt, yet could escape, the magic tone
        Whose prelude held all envy, hate, and wrong,
        But what was howling in one breast alone,

---

2. Among these emblems of sorrow, death, and mourning, some signify potential rebirth: the spear decorated with evergreen cypress and ivy evokes the thyrsus staff of Dionysus, Greek god of fertility.
3. A stanza deemed blasphemous in the first reviews, not only for the comparison of Shelley's suffering to Christ's

torture by the crown of thorns, but also for his refusal to distinguish Christ's agony from Cain's.
4. Leigh Hunt, radical journalist, poet, and close friend of Shelley and Keats; grateful for his encouragement, Keats dedicated his first volume to him.

Silent with expectation of the song
Whose master's hand is cold, whose silver lyre unstrung.[5]

XXXVII

325 Live thou, whose infamy is not thy fame!
Live! fear no heavier chastisement from me,
Thou noteless[6] blot on a remembered name!
But be thyself, and know thyself to be!
And ever at thy season be thou free
330 To spill the venom when thy fangs o'erflow:
Remorse and Self-contempt shall cling to thee,
Hot Shame shall burn upon thy secret brow,
And like a beaten hound tremble thou shalt—as now.

XXXVIII

Nor let us weep that our delight is fled
335 Far from these carrion kites° that scream below.   *corpse-eating hawks*
He wakes or sleeps with the enduring dead;
Thou canst not soar where he is sitting now.[7]
Dust to the dust[8] but the pure spirit shall flow
Back to the burning fountain whence it came,
340 A portion of the Eternal,[9] which must glow
Through time and change, unquenchably the same,
Whilst thy cold embers choke the sordid hearth of shame.

XXXIX

Peace, peace! he is not dead, he doth not sleep!
He hath awakened from the dream of life.
345 'Tis we who, lost in stormy visions, keep
With phantoms an unprofitable strife,
And in mad trance strike with our spirit's knife
Invulnerable nothings. *We* decay
Like corpses in a charnel; fear and grief
350 Convulse us and consume us day by day,
And cold hopes swarm like worms within our living clay.

XL

He has outsoared the shadow of our night.
Envy and calumny° and hate and pain,   *slander*
And that unrest which men miscall delight,
355 Can touch him not and torture not again.
From the contagion of the world's slow stain
He is secure; and now can never mourn

---

5. Keats's tomb bears an image of a Greek lyre with half its strings broken, signifying, in Severn's words, "his Classical Genius cut off by death before its maturity."
6. "Noteless" for several reasons: its anonymity, its insignificance and forgettability against Keats's assured fame, and its own lack of poetic music (notes).
7. A sympathetic echo of Satan's reminder of his former glory to the Angelic Squadron who eject him from Eden (where he had been corrupting Eve's dreams): "said Satan, fill'd with scorn, / Know ye not mee? ye knew me once no mate / For you, there sitting where ye durst not soar" (4.827–829); see also *Defence*, page 927.
8. Body to the earth; see the Lord's chastisement of fallen Adam, "dust thou art, and unto dust shalt thou return" (Genesis 3.19).
9. Eternal Spirit and Eternity.

A heart grown cold, a head grown grey, in vain—
Nor, when the spirit's self has ceased to burn,
360 With sparkless ashes load an unlamented urn.°   *burial urn*

XLI

He lives, he wakes—'tis Death is dead, not he;[1]
Mourn not for Adonais.—Thou young Dawn,
Turn all thy dew to splendour, for from thee
The spirit thou lamentest is not gone!
365 Ye caverns and ye forests, cease to moan!
Cease, ye faint flowers and fountains! and, thou Air,
Which like a mourning-veil thy scarf hadst thrown
O'er the abandoned Earth, now leave it bare
Even to the joyous stars which smile on its despair!

XLII

370 He is made one with Nature. There is heard
His voice in all her music, from the moan
Of thunder to the song of night's sweet bird.[2]
He is a presence to be felt and known
In darkness and in light, from herb and stone,—
375 Spreading itself where'er that Power may move
Which has withdrawn his being to its own,
Which wields the world with never-wearied love,
Sustains it from beneath, and kindles it above.

XLIII

He is a portion of the loveliness
380 Which once he made more lovely. He doth bear
His part, while the one Spirit's plastic° stress   *shaping, formative*
Sweeps through the dull dense world; compelling there
All new successions to the forms they wear;
Torturing th'unwilling dross, that checks its flight
385 To its° own likeness, as each mass may bear;   *the Spirit's*
And bursting in its beauty and its might
From trees and beasts and men into the Heaven's light.

XLIV

The splendours of the firmament of time
May be eclipsed, but are extinguished not;
390 Like stars to their appointed height they climb,
And death is a low mist which cannot blot
The brightness it may veil. When lofty thought
Lifts a young heart above its mortal lair,
And love and life contend in it for what
395 Shall be its earthly doom, the dead live there
And move like winds of light on dark and stormy air.

---

1. The consolation of Donne's famous sonnet (1633), *Death be not proud.*

2. From the Titans of Keats's *Hyperion* fragment to *Ode to a Nightingale.*

XLV

The inheritors of unfulfilled renown
Rose from their thrones, built beyond mortal thought
Far in the Unapparent. Chatterton
400 Rose pale, his solemn agony had not
Yet faded from him; Sidney, as he fought,
And as he fell, and as he lived and loved,
Sublimely mild, a Spirit without spot,
Arose; and Lucan, by his death approved;°—   *honored*
405 Oblivion as they rose shrank like a thing reproved.[3]

XLVI

And many more, whose names on earth are dark,
But whose transmitted effluence° cannot die   *radiance, influence*
So long as fire outlives the parent spark,
Rose, robed in dazzling immortality.
410 "Thou art become as one of us," they cry;
"It was for thee yon kingless° sphere has long   *awaiting its king*
Swung blind in unascended majesty,
Silent alone amid an Heaven of song.
Assume thy winged throne, thou Vesper° of our throng!"   *evening star*

XLVII

415 Who mourns for Adonais? Oh come forth,
Fond wretch, and know thyself and him aright.
Clasp with thy panting soul the pendulous earth;
As from a centre, dart thy spirit's light
Beyond all worlds, until its spacious might°   *power*
420 Satiate the void circumference: then shrink
Even to a point within our day and night;°   *ordinary time*
And keep thy heart light, lest it make thee sink,
When hope has kindled hope, and lured thee to the brink.

XLVIII

Or go to Rome, which is the sepulchre,
425 Oh not of him, but of our joy. 'Tis nought
That ages, empires, and religions, there
Lie buried in the ravage they have wrought;
For such as he° can lend°—they borrow not   *Keats / bestow (glory)*
Glory from those° who made the world their prey;   *Romans*
430 And he is gathered to the kings of thought
Who waged contention with their time's° decay,   *own life's or age's*
And of the past are all that cannot pass away.

---

3. Poets who, dying young, did not achieve their full potential for fame ("renown"). Thomas Chatterton (1752–1770), in despair of success, killed himself with arsenic at age 17; Keats addressed one of his *Poems* of 1817 to him, and dedicated his longest work, *Endymion* (1818), to his memory. Sir Philip Sidney (1554–1586) died heroically in battle at age 32. Roman poet Lucan (39–65 C.E.), in preference to execution for conspiring against the tyrant Nero, committed suicide at age 26; he recited his poetry to his friends while he bled to death.

XLIX

Go thou to Rome,—at once the Paradise,
The grave, the city, and the wilderness;
435 And where its wrecks° like shattered mountains rise,   *ruins*
And flowering weeds and fragrant copses° dress   *thickets*
The bones of Desolation's nakedness,
Pass, till the Spirit of the spot shall lead
Thy footsteps to a slope of green access,
440 Where, like an infant's smile, over the dead
A light of laughing flowers along the grass is spread.[4]

L

And grey walls moulder round, on which dull Time
Feeds, like slow fire upon a hoary brand;°   *ash-covered log*
And one keen pyramid with wedge sublime,
445 Pavilioning the dust of him who planned
This refuge for his memory, doth stand
Like flame transformed to marble; and beneath
A field is spread, on which a newer band
Have pitched in Heaven's smile their camp of death,[5]
450 Welcoming him we lose with scarce-extinguished breath.

LI

Here pause. These graves are all too young as yet
To have outgrown the sorrow which consigned
Its charge to each; and, if the seal is set
Here on one fountain of a mourning mind,
455 Break it not thou! too surely shalt thou find
Thine own well full, if thou returnest home,
Of tears and gall. From the world's bitter wind[6]
Seek shelter in the shadow of the tomb.
What Adonais is why fear we to become?

LII

460 The One remains, the many change and pass;
Heaven's light for ever shines, earth's shadows fly;
Life, like a dome of many-coloured glass,
Stains the white radiance of eternity,[7]
Until Death tramples it to fragments.—Die,
465 If thou wouldst be with that which thou dost seek!
Follow where all is fled!—Rome's azure sky,
Flowers, ruins, statues, music, words, are weak
The glory they transfuse with fitting truth to speak.

---

4. The Protestant Cemetery in Rome, where Keats is
buried; one of its walls incorporates the pyramid-tomb of
Caius Cestius, a Roman tribune. The image of "the infant's
smile" evokes the grave of the Shelleys' son William
(see Preface).

5. Military imagery with a pun on *campo* (field); *cam-
posanto* ("sacred field") is Italian for cemetery.
6. A hint of the malaria ("bad air" or "bitter wind") that
was fatal to William Shelley.
7. "Stain" can mean color, refract, discolor, or degrade.

LIII

Why linger, why turn back, why shrink, my Heart?
470 Thy hopes are gone before: from all things here
They have departed;[8] thou shouldst now depart.
A light is past from the revolving year,
And man and woman; and what still is dear
Attracts to crush, repels to make thee wither.
475 The soft sky smiles, the low wind whispers near:
'Tis Adonais calls! Oh hasten thither!
No more let Life divide what Death can join together.

LIV

That Light whose smile kindles the Universe,
That Beauty in which all things work and move,
480 That Benediction which the eclipsing Curse
Of birth can quench not, that sustaining Love
Which through the web of being blindly wove
By man and beast and earth and air and sea,
Burns bright or dim, as° each are mirrors of   ° to the extent that
485 The fire for which all thirst, now beams on me,
Consuming the last clouds of cold mortality.

LV

The breath whose might I have invoked in song[9]
Descends on me; my spirit's bark is driven
Far from the shore, far from the trembling throng
490 Whose sails were never to the tempest given.
The massy earth and sphered skies are riven!
I am borne darkly, fearfully, afar!
Whilst, burning through the inmost veil of Heaven,
The soul of Adonais, like a star,
495 Beacons from the abode where the Eternal are.

1821   1821

RESPONSES

George Gordon, Lord Byron: from *Don Juan* (11.59)

John Keats, who was kill'd off by one critique,
    Just as he really promised something great,
If not intelligible, without Greek
    Contrived to talk about the gods of late,

---

8. Multiple possible allusions to lost hopes: the death of two children and the lost custody of two others, exile from England, estrangement from Mary, tensions with Byron, neglect by his publisher, hostile reviews, failure to find a broad audience and fame, despair over his health, loss of hope for his political ideals.
9. Other poems expressing such ideal thirsting, e.g., *Ode to the West Wind.*

5   Much as they might have been supposed to speak.[1]
           Poor fellow! His was an untoward fate;
        'Tis strange the mind, that very fiery particle,
        Should let itself be snuff'd out by an article.

1822–1823   1823

George Gordon, Lord Byron: Letter to Percy Bysshe Shelley

Ravenna, April 26th, 1821

* * * I am very sorry to hear what you say of Keats—is it *actually* true? I did not think criticism had been so killing. Though I differ from you essentially in your estimate of his performances, I so much abhor all unnecessary pain, that I would rather he had been seated on the highest peak of Parnassus[1] than have perished in such a manner. Poor fellow! though with such inordinate self-love he would probably have not been very happy. I read the review of "Endymion" in the Quarterly.[2] It was severe,—but surely not so severe as many reviews in that and other journals upon others.

I recollect the effect on me of the Edinburgh[3] on my first poem; it was rage, and resistance, and redress—but not despondency nor despair. I grant that those are not amiable feelings; but, in this world of bustle and broil, and especially in the career of writing, a man should calculate upon his powers of *resistance* before he goes into the arena.

      "Expect not life from pain nor danger free,
      Nor deem the doom of man reversed for thee."[4]

George Gordon, Lord Byron: Letter to John Murray

R[avenn]a July 30th. 1821

* * * Are you aware that Shelley has written an elegy on Keats—and accuses the Quarterly of killing him?—

      Who killed John Keats?
      I, says the Quarterly
      So savage & Tartarly
      ~~Martyrly~~
      'Twas one of my feats—
      Who ~~drew the [pen?]~~ shot the arrow?
      The poet-priest Milman
      (So ready to kill man)
      Or Southey or Barrow.[1]—

---

1. The *Hyperion* fragment (1820).
1. A mountain in Greece, sacred to the Muses.
2. See n. 6 to Shelley's Preface, page 895.
3. The nasty, unsigned review of *Hours of Idleness* (1807) in the *Edinburgh Review* in 1808 was a target of Byron's satire in *English Bards and Scotch Reviewers*.
4. Echoing Samuel Johnson's *The Vanity of Human Wishes* (1749): "Yet hope not life from grief or danger free, / Nor

think the doom of man revers'd for thee" (155–156).
1. Byron had already used the "Quarterly / Martyrly" rhyme in *Don Juan* 1.211. The likely assassins are Henry Hart Milman (see Shelley's Preface) an ecclesiastical scholar and vicar as well as poet; Robert Southey (see Preface) and John Barrow, a travel writer who published frequently in *The Quarterly*.

You know very well that I did not approve of Keats's poetry or principles of poetry—or of his abuse of Pope—but as he is dead—omit *all* that is said *about him* in any M.S.S. of mine—or publication.—His Hyperion is a fine monument & will keep his name—I do not envy the man—who wrote the article—your review people have no more right to kill than any other foot pads.—However—he who would die of an article in a review—would probably have died of something else equally trivial—the same thing nearly happened to Kirke White[2]—who afterwards died of consumption.

The Cloud[1]

1

I bring fresh showers for the thirsting flowers,
    From the seas and streams;
I bear light shade for the leaves when laid
    In their noon-day dreams.
5   From my wings are shaken the dews that waken
    The sweet buds every one,
When rocked to rest on their mother's breast,
    As she dances about the sun.
I wield the flail of the lashing hail,
10   And whiten the green plains under,
And then again I dissolve it in rain,
    And laugh as I pass in thunder.

2

I sift the snow on the mountains below,
    And their great pines groan aghast;
15   And all the night 'tis my pillow white,
    While I sleep in the arms of the blast.
Sublime on the towers of my skiey bowers,
    Lightning my pilot sits,
In a cavern under is fettered the thunder,
20   It struggles and howls at fits;°   *fitfully*
Over earth and ocean, with gentle motion,
    This pilot is guiding me,
Lured by the love of the genii that move
    In the depths of the purple sea;
25   Over the rills, and the crags, and the hills,
    Over the lakes and the plains,
Wherever he dream, under mountain or stream,
    The Spirit he loves remains;
And I all the while bask in heaven's blue smile,
30   Whilst he is dissolving in rains.

---

2. Henry Kirke White, working-class poet who suffered bad reviews and died of tuberculosis (Keats's disease) in 1806 at age 21, famously eulogized by Byron in *English Bards*: "Oh! what a noble heart was here undone!"
1. This poem is a rare representation, for Shelley, of ceaseless transformation without agony.

3

The sanguine sunrise, with his meteor eyes,
    And his burning plumes outspread,
Leaps on the back of my sailing rack,[2]
    When the morning star shines dead.
35 As on the jag of a mountain crag,
    Which an earthquake rocks and swings,
An eagle alit one moment may sit
    In the light of its golden wings.
And when sunset may breathe, from the lit sea beneath,
40   Its ardours of rest and of love,
And the crimson pall of eve may fall
    From the depth of heaven above,
With wings folded I rest, on mine aëry nest,
    As still as a brooding dove.[3]

4

45 That orbèd maiden, with white fire laden,
    Whom mortals call the moon,
Glides glimmering o'er my fleece-like floor,
    By the midnight breezes strewn;
And wherever the beat of her unseen feet,
50   Which only the angels hear,
May have broken the woof° of my tent's thin roof,   *fabric*
    The stars peep behind her, and peer;
And I laugh to see them whirl and flee,
    Like a swarm of golden bees,
55 When I widen the rent in my wind-built tent,
    Till the calm rivers, lakes, and seas,
Like strips of the sky fallen through me on high,
    Are each paved with the moon and these.°   *stars*

5

I bind the sun's throne with a burning zone,°   *sash*
60   And the moon's with a girdle of pearl;
The volcanos are dim, and the stars reel and swim,
    When the whirlwinds my banner unfurl.
From cape to cape, with a bridge-like shape,
    Over a torrent sea,
65 Sunbeam-proof, I hang like a roof,
    The mountains its columns be,
The triumphal arch through which I march
    With hurricane, fire, and snow,
When the powers of the air are chained to my chair,
70   Is the million-coloured bow;°   *rainbow*

---

2. A mass of wind-blown clouds scattered in the upper air.
3. An echo of Milton's description of his muse at the outset of *Paradise Lost* as an original agent of creation:

"Thou . . . with mighty wings outspread / Dove-like satst brooding on the vast Abyss / And mad'st it pregnant" (1.19–22); brooding: incubating.

The sphere-fire° above its soft colours wove,   *sunlight*
   While the moist earth was laughing below.

6

I am the daughter of earth and water,
   And the nursling of the sky:
75   I pass through the pores of the ocean and shores;
   I change, but I cannot die.
For after the rain when with never a stain,
   The pavilion of heaven is bare,
And the winds and sunbeams with their convex gleams,
80   Build up the blue dome of air,
I silently laugh at my own cenotaph,[4]
   And out of the caverns of rain,
Like a child from the womb, like a ghost from the tomb,
   I arise and unbuild it again.

1820   1820/1839

from **Hellas**[1]

195   MAHMUD:…Kings are like stars: they rise and set, they have
   The worship of the world, but no repose. [*exeunt severally*]

Chorus[2]

Worlds on worlds are rolling ever
   From creation to decay,
Like the bubbles on a river,
200   Sparkling, bursting, borne away.
   But *they*[3] are still immortal
   Who, through birth's orient° portal   *eastern, dawning*
And death's dark chasm hurrying to and fro,
   Clothe their unceasing flight

4. A monument honoring someone interred elsewhere.
1. Shelley wrote *Hellas* (classical name for Greece) in October 1821, inspired by a Greek revolt against centuries of Turkish domination, initiating the war won in 1832. In his Preface, he says he gives "a series of lyric pictures," its "figures of indistinct and visionary delineation" meant to "suggest the final triumph of the Greek cause as a portion of the cause of civilization and social improvement"; a later sentence, censored by his publisher, went on to declare, "This is the age of the war of the oppressed against the oppressors." His enthusiasm derives from his conviction that "we are all Greeks—our laws, our literature, our religion, our arts have their root in Greece," a widely shared sympathy that has been named "Romantic Hellenism." He modeled *Hellas* on Aeschylus's *Persians* (472 B.C.E.), which records the defeat of the invading Persians under Xerxes at the naval battle of Salamis eight years before. As in the Greek tragedy, Shelley uses a chorus for communal comment, reflection, hope, and sometimes prophecy. His Chorus is the "Greek Captive Women" in Constantinople, the city in Turkey founded 330 C.E. by the first Christian Emperor of Rome (Constantine the

Great), who made it the capital of the Roman Empire; it was conquered by the Ottoman Empire in 1453. In the first excerpt, Sultan Mahmud (Mahmud II, named for the prophet Muhammed, founder of Islam) has woken from a dream of the destruction of his empire so disturbing that he has asked a mystical Jew to interpret it; he has ordered the silencing of drunken sailors (one by decapitation) who are vexing his "need of rest."
2. The popular notions of Christianity are represented in this chorus as true in their relation to the worship they superseded . . . . The first stanza contrasts the immortality of the living and thinking beings which inhabit the planets . . . with the transience of the noblest manifestations of the external world . . . . [T]he concluding verses indicate a progressive state of more or less exalted existence, according to the degree of perfection which every distinct intelligence may have attained . . . the condition of that futurity towards which we are all impelled by an inextinguishable thirst for immortality . . . the strongest and the only presumption that eternity is the inheritance of every thinking being [Shelley's note].
3. "The living and thinking beings" of the previous note.

205 　　　　In the brief dust and light
　　Gathered around their chariots as they go:
　　　　　New shapes they still may weave,
　　　　　New gods, new laws, receive:
　　Bright or dim are they, as the robes they last
210 　　　　　On Death's bare ribs had cast.

　　　　　A Power from the unknown God,
　　　　　A Promethean Conqueror, came;[4]
　　　　Like a triumphal path he trod
　　　　The thorns of death and shame.
215 　　　　　A mortal shape to him
　　　　　Was like the vapour dim
　　Which the orient planet animates with light.[5]
　　　　　Hell, sin, and Slavery, came,
　　　　　Like bloodhounds mild and tame,
220 　　Nor preyed until their Lord had taken flight.
　　　　　The moon of Mahomet[6]
　　　　　Arose, and it shall set:
　　While blazoned as on heaven's immortal noon,
　　　　The cross leads generations on.[7]

225 　　　　Swift as the radiant shapes of sleep
　　　　From one whose dreams are Paradise
　　Fly, when the fond wretch wakes to weep,
　　　　And Day peers forth with her blank eyes;
　　　　　So fleet, so faint, so fair,
230 　　　　　The Powers of Earth and Air

　　Fled from the folding-star[8] of Bethlehem:
　　　　　Apollo, Pan, and Love,
　　　　　And even Olympian Jove,
　　Grew weak, for killing Truth had glared on them.[9]
235 　　　　　Our hills and seas and streams,
　　　　　Dispeopled of their dreams,
　　Their waters turned to blood, their dew to tears,
　　　　Wailed for the golden years.[1]

　　Enter Mahmud [and associates]

---

4. The identity of God was "unknown" in ancient Greece and Rome (Acts 17.23) before Jesus Christ, whom Shelley compares to Prometheus, the god of classical myth who stole fire from heaven and gave it to humanity; tortured for this transgression by Jupiter, he was often compared to Christ, the bearer of God's light into the mortal world. See Byron's *Prometheus*, page 750.
5. Venus appears as the morning star in the eastern, or orient, sky.
6. The emblem of Islam; these lines echo 195–96 (see n. 1).
7. Before a battle with rivals for the rule of Rome in 312, Constantine I is said to have beheld a flaming cross in front of the noonday sun, inscribed "In this sign, thou shalt conquer." He converted to Christianity and was

victorious; the Roman empire was henceforth safe for Christians. *Hellas* is set in Constantinople.
8. Called thus because it appeared in the sky at evening, when shepherds return their grazing flocks to the fold (pen).
9. Shelley follows Milton's *Ode on the Morning of Christ's Nativity* (165–236) in portraying the classical gods fleeing from and even annihilated by Christian "Truth."
1. Nature is "dispeopled" of classical river- and sea-gods, mountain-nymphs, etc.; blood and tears report their "killing" by Christian "Truth"; "the golden years" are the Golden Age of Saturn's rule, an era of perfect peace and plenty, analogous to the Judaeo-Christian Eden before the Fall.

MAHMUD: More gold? Our ancestors bought gold with victory,
And shall I sell it for defeat?

240 DAOD: The Janizars[2]
Clamour for pay.

MAHMUD: Go bid them pay themselves
With Christian blood! Are there no Grecian virgins
Whose shrieks and spasms and tears they may enjoy?
No infidel° children to impale on spears?   *non-Islamic*
245 No hoary priests after that Patriarch
Who bent to curse against his country's heart,
Which clove his own at last?[3] Go bid them kill:
Blood is the seed of gold.

* * *

Chorus[1]

1060 The world's great age begins anew,
        The golden years° return,   *the Golden Age*
The earth doth like a snake renew
        Her winter weeds[2] outworn:
Heaven smiles, and faiths and empires gleam
1065 Like wrecks of a dissolving dream.

A brighter Hellas rears its mountains
        From waves serener far;
A new Peneus[3] rolls his fountains°   *waters*
        Against the morning star;°   *eastward*
1070 Where fairer Tempes[4] bloom, there sleep
Young Cyclads[5] on a sunnier deep.°   *sea*

A loftier Argo[6] cleaves the main,
        Fraught with a later prize;
Another Orpheus sings again,
1075   And loves, and weeps, and dies;[7]

2. The chief standing army of the Turkish Empire.
3. After the Greek rebels killed Turks in Greece, the Turks massacred the Greeks in Asia Minor; on 22 April 1821, they hanged Gregorios, the Orthodox Patriarch of Constantinople.
1. After the Turks have vanquished the Greek rebels, the Chorus is comforted by the thought that "Greece which was dead is arisen!" (1059), and concludes the play with this song. "The final chorus is indistinct and obscure, as the event of the living drama whose arrival it foretells. Prophecies of wars . . . may safely be made by poet or prophet in any age, but to anticipate however darkly a period of regeneration and happiness is a more hazardous exercise which bards possess or fain. It will remind the reader . . . of Isaiah and Virgil, whose ardent spirits overleaping the actual reign of evil which we endure and bewail, already saw the possible and perhaps approaching state of society in which the '*lion shall lie down with the lamb*' and '*omnis feret omnia tellus* [each land will produce all things].' Let these great names be my authority

and excuse" [Shelley's note, paraphrasing Isaiah (11.6, 35.9, 65.25) and Virgil's *Eclogue* IV ("The Golden Age Returns")].
2. Dead grass; also mourning clothes to be shed.
3. River in northeast Greece.
4. Tempe is the valley reputed to be a playground of the gods.
5. Cyclades, an island chain in the Aegean.
6. The ship in which Jason and his crew (Argonauts) sailed in quest of the Golden Fleece.
7. In Greek legend, Orpheus played the lyre so beautifully that he charmed even the rocks and stones. When his beloved Eurydice was killed by a snake while fleeing a ravisher, he descended to the underworld to find her, and so moved its ruler, Hades, with his music that he was allowed to reclaim her—provided he did not look back at her until they reached the upper world. He anxiously looked back, and lost her forever. In grief, he refused all women, so enraging the Thracian women that they tore him to pieces at a Bacchanalian revel.

A new Ulysses leaves once more
Calypso for his native shore.[8]

Oh write no more the tale of Troy,
    If earth Death's scroll must be—
1080   Nor mix with Laian rage the joy
        Which dawns upon the free,
Although a subtler Sphinx renew
Riddles of death Thebes never knew.[9]

Another Athens shall arise,
1085   And to remoter time
Bequeath, like sunset to the skies,
        The splendour of its prime;
And leave, if nought so bright may live,
All earth can take or heaven can give.

1090   Saturn and Love their long repose
        Shall burst, more bright and good
Than all who fell, than one who rose,
        Than many unsubdued:[1]
Not gold, not blood, their altar dowers,°   gifts, dowries
1095   But votive tears and symbol flowers.

Oh cease! must hate and death return?
        Cease! must men kill and die?
Cease! drain not to its dregs the urn
        Of bitter prophecy!
1100   The world is weary of the past,—
Oh might it die or rest at last!

With a Guitar, to Jane[1]

Ariel to Miranda.[2]—Take
This slave of Music,° for the sake   *the guitar*

8. Sailing home to Greece from the Trojan War, Ulysses was shipwrecked on the island of the nymph Calypso, where he dallied for seven years before returning to his wife.

9. A reference to the story of the riddle-solver Oedipus, whose father Laius, alarmed by a prophecy that he would be killed by his son, ordered the newborn's death by exposure. Oedipus was rescued, and as a young man got into an argument with Laius (not knowing him), and killed him in rage. He later married Laius's widow, not knowing she was his mother. When his parentage was revealed, she committed suicide and he blinded himself.

1. Saturn and Love were among the deities of a real or imaginary state of innocence and happiness. *All those who fell* [are] the Gods of Greece, Asia, and Egypt; the *One who rose* [is] Jesus Christ, at whose appearance the idols of the Pagan World were amerced [deprived] of their worship; and *the many unsubdued* [are] the monstrous objects of the idolatry of China, India, the Antarctic islands, and the native tribes of America. [Shelley's note, which goes on to lament the lack of "temperance

and chastity" in otherwise "innocent" Grecian gods, to praise "the sublime human character of Jesus Christ," to honor true Christian martyrs, and to denigrate the "horrors of the Mexican, the Peruvian, and the Indian superstitions"].

1. Jane Williams was the common-law wife of Edward Williams, the Shelleys' housemates in the spring of 1822. Percy Shelley bought her an Italian guitar, and presented it with this poem (not published in full until 1839/1840). He, Jane, and Edward often went sailing together, and Jane enraptured Shelley with her guitar-music and singing. Edward drowned with him in the storm at sea in July 1822. In the first publishings (1832, 1839) of this and the next poem, the texts were truncated or revised to delete the name "Jane" to protect her privacy.

2. Shelley speaks as Ariel, the magician-sprite of Shakespeare's *Tempest*, enslaved as servant to Prospero, father of Miranda ("to be admired")—i.e., Jane; Prince Ferdinand of Naples is her suitor, coded as Edward. In the play, Prospero thwarts their romance before finally giving his blessing and releasing Ariel from slavery.

Of him° who is the slave of thee,
And teach it all the harmony
5   In which thou canst, and only thou,
Make the delighted spirit glow,
Till joy denies itself again,
And, too intense, is turned to pain;
For by permission and command
10   Of thine own Prince Ferdinand,
Poor Ariel sends this silent token
Of more than ever can be spoken;
Your guardian spirit, Ariel, who,
From life to life must still pursue
15   Your happiness;—for thus alone
Can Ariel ever find his own.
From Prospero's inchanted cell,
As the mighty verses tell,
To the throne of Naples, he
20   Lit you o'er the trackless sea,
Flitting on, your prow before,
Like a living meteor.[3]
When you die, the silent Moon
In her interlunar swoon[4]
25   Is not sadder in her cell
Than deserted Ariel.
When you live again on earth,
Like an unseen star of birth,
Ariel guides you o'er the sea
30   Of life from your nativity.
Many changes have been run,
Since Ferdinand and you begun
Your course of love, and Ariel still
Has tracked your steps and served your will;
35   Now, in humbler happier lot,
This is all remembered not;
And now, alas! the poor sprite[5] is
Imprisoned, for some fault of his,
In a body like a grave;—
40   From you he only dares to crave,
For his service and his sorrow,
A smile to-day, a song to-morrow.

3. An imaginative addition to the end of *The Tempest*, where Prospero promises the King of Naples (whose party has been shipwrecked on his island), "I'll bring you to your ship, and so to Naples, / Where I have hope to see the nuptial / Of these our dear beloved" (5.1.308–10).
4. An imagined extension of Miranda's history into her death and later reincarnation; "interlunar" darkness intervenes between the old and the new moons, the lines echoing the lament of Milton's blinded Samson: "dark / And silent as the Moon, / When she deserts the night, / Hid in her vacant interlunar cave" (*Samson Agonistes*, 86–89).
5. Fairy spirit (Ariel) and, in general, the soul or spirit-self.

The artist who this idol° wrought,   *the guitar*
To echo all harmonious thought,
45   Felled a tree while on the steep
The woods were in their winter-sleep,
Rocked in that repose divine
On the wind-swept Apennine;[6]
And dreaming, some of Autumn past,
50   And some of Spring approaching fast,
And some of April buds and showers,
And some of songs in July bowers,
And all of love; and so this tree,—
O that such our death may be!—
55   Died in sleep, and felt no pain,
To live in happier form again:
From which, beneath Heaven's fairest star,[7]
The artist wrought this loved Guitar,
And taught it justly to reply,
60   To all who question skilfully,
In language gentle as thine own;
Whispering in enamoured tone
Sweet oracles of woods and dells,
And summer winds in sylvan° cells;   *woodland*
65   For it had learnt all harmonies
Of the plains and of the skies,
Of the forests and the mountains,
And the many-voicèd fountains;
The clearest echoes of the hills,
70   The softest notes of falling rills,
The melodies of birds and bees,
The murmuring of summer seas,
And pattering rain, and breathing dew,
And airs of evening; and it knew
75   That seldom-heard mysterious sound,
Which, driven on its diurnal° round   *daily*
As it floats through boundless day,
Our world enkindles on its way—
All this it knows, but will not tell
80   To those who cannot question well
The spirit that inhabits it;
It talks according to the wit°   *learning, skill*
Of its companions; and no more
Is heard than has been felt before,
85   By those who tempt it to betray[8]
These secrets of an elder day:

6. Mountain chain running the length of Italy.
7. Venus, named for the Roman goddess of Love.

8. A range of meanings: reveal, disclose against trust, desert,
prove false to.

But, sweetly as its answers will
Flatter hands of perfect skill,
It keeps its highest holiest tone
90   For our belovèd Jane alone.
1822   1840

To Jane

I sate down to write some words for an ariette which might be profane—but it was in vain to struggle with the ruling spirit, who compelled me to speak of things sacred to yours & Wilhelmeister's indulgence—I commit them to your secrecy & your mercy & will try & do better another time.[1]

    The keen stars were twinkling,
  And the fair moon was rising among them,
      Dear Jane!
    The guitar was tinkling
5 But the notes were not sweet till you sung them
      Again.

    As the moon's soft splendour
  O'er the faint cold starlight of heaven
      Is thrown,
10   So your voice most tender
  To the strings without soul had then given
      Its own.

    The stars will awaken,
  Though the moon sleep a full hour later,
15   To-night;
    No leaf will be shaken
  Whilst the dews of your melody scatter
      Delight.

    Though the sound overpowers,
20 Sing again, with your dear voice revealing
      A tone
    Of some world far from ours,
  Where music and moonlight and feeling
      Are one.
1822   1840

A DEFENCE OF POETRY Shelley was called to the *Defence* by an extravagant essay published in 1820 by his friend Thomas Love Peacock. Peacock described a fall from the grandeur of former ages into a modern poetry of triviality, vulgarity, and a studious ignorance "of history, society, and human nature": Wordsworth gives the "phantastical parturition of the

1. This note is part of the whole text, and with "profane" / "in vain" even sets up the third rhyme of stanza 1. Wilhelmeister ("William master") is Edward Williams, with a glance at the hero of Goethe's famous, semiautobiographical novel *Wilhelm Meister* (1795–1796).

moods of his own mind"; "Scott digs up the poachers and cattle-stealers of the ancient border. Lord Byron cruises for thieves and pirates," and Coleridge "superadds the dreams of crazy theologians and the mysticisms of German metaphysics." Replete with "obsolete customs, and exploded superstitions . . . the whine of exaggerated feeling, and the cant of factitious sentiment," such poetry, Peacock argued, lacks relevance to the modern world being shaped by the intellectual power of "mathematicians, astronomers, chemists, moralists, metaphysicians, historians, politicians, and political economists." Even as Shelley recognized the comedy of Peacock's essay, he also knew that such views had currency in contemporary Utilitarian philosophies. He began his *Defence* early the next year, but put it aside in the distraction of other projects and a tumultuous personal life. Left unfinished at his death, the fragment did not appear until Mary Shelley published it in 1840.

"Poets are the unacknowledged legislators of the world," Shelley famously concluded his defense, designating the poet as visionary lawgiver. Yet what makes *A Defence* so compelling is not any legal argumentation toward this verdict, but its welter of impassioned, often conflicting assertions and its evocative, often contradictory images for poetic authority and value. On the one hand, a radical dualism invests all truth in "the eternal, the infinite, and the one"— a transcendent realm to which the poet's imagination has visionary access. This is a theme elaborated throughout Shelley's career, with some of its most succinct expressions in *Adonais* (lines 343–69 and 460–95). Shelley concedes that "the mind in creation is as a fading coal. . . . when composition begins, inspiration is already on the decline, and the most glorious poetry that has ever been communicated to the world is probably a feeble shadow of the original conception." On the other hand, this inevitability has not thwarted poets, Shelley among them, from laboring to make beautiful poems in order to awaken readers' minds to higher values—a precondition for effective political action. In this line of defense, poetry is not just a weak record of truths beyond the reach of words but a force of revelation and vital creation. Many of the *Defence*'s sentences, including the celebration of the "electric life" of inspired words and of poets as "unacknowledged legislators," were ones Shelley first drafted for his political pamphlet (also unfinished), *A Philosophical Review of Reform*.

from A Defence of Poetry
or Remarks Suggested by an Essay Entitled "The Four Ages of Poetry"

According to one mode of regarding those two classes of mental action which are called reason and imagination, the former may be considered as mind contemplating the relations borne by one thought to another, however produced; and the latter as mind acting upon those thoughts so as to color them with its own light, and composing from them, as from elements, other thoughts, each containing within itself the principle of its own integrity. The one is the τὸ ποιεῖν,[1] or the principle of synthesis, and has for its object those forms which are common to universal nature and existence itself; the other is the τὸ λογίζειν,[2] or principle of analysis, and its action regards the relations of things simply as relations; considering thoughts not in their integral unity, but as the algebraical representations which conduct to certain general results. Reason is the enumeration of quantities already known; imagination is the perception of the value of those quantities, both separately and as a whole. Reason respects the differences, and imagination the similitudes of things. Reason is to

---

1. "Making something," the etymology of "poet." Sir Philip Sidney refers to the poet as "maker" in his late 16th-century *Defense of Poesie*.
2. The logic or reason.

imagination as the instrument to the agent, as the body to the spirit, as the shadow to the substance.

Poetry, in a general sense, may be defined to be "the expression of the imagination"; and poetry is connate with the origin of man. Man is an instrument over which a series of external and internal impressions are driven, like the alternations of an ever-changing wind over an Aeolian lyre,[3] which move it by their motion to ever-changing melody. But there is a principle within the human being (and perhaps within all sentient beings) which acts otherwise than in the lyre, and produces not melody alone, but harmony, by an internal adjustment of the sounds and motions thus excited to the impressions which excite them. It is as if the lyre could accommodate its chords to the motions of that which strikes them, in a determined proportion of sound—even as the musician can accommodate his voice to the sound of the lyre. A child at play by itself will express its delight by its voice and motions, and every inflection of tone and every gesture will bear exact relation to a corresponding antitype in the pleasurable impressions which awakened it. It will be the reflected image of that impression; and as the lyre trembles and sounds after the wind has died away, so the child seeks, by prolonging in its voice and motions the duration of the effect, to prolong also a consciousness of the cause. In relation to the objects which delight a child, these expressions are what poetry is to higher objects.

The savage (for the savage is to ages what the child is to years) expresses the emotions produced in him by surrounding objects in a similar manner; and language and gesture, together with plastic[4] or pictorial imitation, become the image of the combined effect of those objects and his apprehension of them. Man in society, with all his passions and his pleasures, next becomes the object of the passions and pleasures of man; an additional class of emotions produces an augmented treasure of expression; and language, gesture, and the imitative arts become at once the representation and the medium, the pencil and the picture, the chisel and the statue, the chord and the harmony. The social sympathies, or those laws from which, as from its elements, society results, begin to develop themselves from the moment that two human beings coexist; the future is contained within the present as the plant within the seed; and equality, diversity, unity, contrast, mutual dependence, become the principles alone capable of affording the motives according to which the will of a social being is determined to action (inasmuch as he is social), and constitute pleasure in sensation, virtue in sentiment, beauty in art, truth in reasoning, and love in the intercourse of kind. Hence men, even in the infancy of society, observe a certain order in their words and actions distinct from that of the objects and the impressions represented by them, all expression being subject to the laws of that from which it proceeds.

But let us dismiss those more general considerations which might involve an inquiry into the principles of society itself, and restrict our view to the manner in which the imagination is expressed upon its forms.

In the youth of the world, men dance and sing and imitate natural objects, observing[5] in these actions (as in all others) a certain rhythm or order. And, although all men observe a similar, they observe not the same order in the motions of the

---

3. Wind harp.
4. Shaping (cf. *Adonais*, line 381, page 906).

5. Seeing and following.

dance, in the melody of the song, in the combinations of language, in the series of their imitations of natural objects. For there is a certain order or rhythm belonging to each of these classes of mimetic representation, from which the hearer and the spectator receive an intenser and purer pleasure than from any other. The sense of an approximation to this order has been called taste by modern writers. Every man in the infancy of art observes an order which approximates more or less closely to that from which this highest delight results. But the diversity is not sufficiently marked as that its gradations should be sensible, except in those instances where the predominance of this faculty of approximation to the beautiful (for so we may be permitted to name the relation between this highest pleasure and its cause) is very great. Those in whom it exists to excess are poets, in the most universal sense of the word; and the pleasure resulting from the manner in which they express the influence of society or nature upon their own minds, communicates itself to others, and gathers a sort of reduplication from the community. Their language is vitally metaphorical; that is, it marks the before unapprehended relations of things, and perpetuates their apprehension, until words which represent them, become through time signs for portions or classes of thought instead of pictures of integral thoughts; and then, if no new poets should arise to create afresh the associations which have been thus disorganized, language will be dead to all the nobler purposes of human intercourse.

These similitudes or relations are finely said by Lord Bacon to be "the same footsteps of nature impressed upon the various subjects of the world"—and he considers the faculty which perceives them as the storehouse of axioms common to all knowledge.[6] In the infancy of society every author is necessarily a poet, because language itself is poetry; and to be a poet is to apprehend the true and the beautiful, in a word, the good which exists in the relation subsisting, first between existence and perception, and secondly between perception and expression. Every original language near to its source is in itself the chaos of a cyclic poem:[7] the copiousness of lexicography and the distinctions of grammar are the works of a later age, and are merely the catalogue and the form of the creations of poetry.

But Poets, or those who imagine and express this indestructible order, are not only the authors of language and of music, of the dance and architecture and statuary and painting; they are the institutors of laws, and the founders of civil society, and the inventors of the arts of life, and the teachers who draw into a certain propinquity with the beautiful and the true that partial apprehension of the agencies of the invisible world which is called religion. Hence all original religions are allegorical, or susceptible of allegory, and like Janus have a double face of false and true. Poets, according to the circumstances of the age and nation in which they appeared, were called in the earlier epochs of the world, legislators or prophets. A poet essentially comprises and unites both these characters. For he not only beholds intensely the present as it is, and discovers those laws according to which present things ought to be ordered, but he beholds the future in the present, and his thoughts are the germs of the flower and the fruit of latest time. Not that I assert poets to be prophets in the gross sense of the word, or that they can foretell the form as surely as they foreknow

6. In a note, Shelley cites Francis Bacon's *Of the Advancement of Learning* (1605), bk. 3, ch. 1.
7. An extended set of poems, not necessarily by the same author, with a common subject, event, or character, first

applied to a series of Greek epic poems supplementing Homer's *Iliad*; the most famous example of the genre in British literature is "the Arthurian Cycle," dealing with the court of King Arthur.

the spirit of events; such is the pretence of superstition, which would make poetry an attribute of prophecy, rather than prophecy an attribute of poetry.[8]

A Poet participates in the eternal, the infinite, and the one; as far as relates to his conceptions, time and place and number are not. The grammatical forms which express the moods of time, and the difference of persons and the distinction of place are convertible with respect to the highest poetry without injuring it as poetry and the choruses of Aeschylus, and the Book of Job, and Dante's Paradise would afford, more than any other writings, examples of this fact, if the limits of this essay did not forbid citation.[9] The creations of sculpture, painting, and music, are illustrations still more decisive.

Language, colour, form, and religious and civil habits of action are all the instruments and materials of poetry; they may be called poetry[1] by that figure of speech which considers the effect as a synonym of the cause. But poetry in a more restricted sense expresses those arrangements of language, and especially metrical language, which are created by that imperial faculty whose throne is curtained within the invisible nature of man. And this springs from the nature itself of language, which is a more direct representation of the actions and passions of our internal being, and is susceptible of more various and delicate combinations, than colour, form, or motion, and is more plastic and obedient to the control of that faculty of which it is the creation. For language is arbitrarily produced by the imagination, and has relation to thoughts alone; but all other materials, instruments and conditions of art have relations among each other which limit and interpose between conception and expression. The former is as a mirror which reflects, the latter as a cloud which enfeebles, the light of which both are mediums of communication. Hence the fame of sculptors, painters and musicians (although the intrinsic powers of the great masters of these arts may yield in no degree to that of those who have employed language as the hieroglyphic of their thoughts) has never equalled that of poets in the restricted sense of the term, as two performers of equal skill will produce unequal effects from a guitar and a harp. The fame of legislators and founders of religions (so long as their institutions last) alone seems to exceed that of poets in the restricted sense; but it can scarcely be a question whether, if we deduct the celebrity which their flattery of the gross opinions of the vulgar usually conciliates, together with that which belonged to them in their higher character of poets, any excess will remain. * * *

Poetry is ever accompanied with pleasure: all spirits on which it falls, open themselves to receive the wisdom which is mingled with its delight. * * * it acts in a divine and unapprehended manner, beyond and above consciousness; and it is reserved for future generations to contemplate and measure the mighty cause and effect in all the strength and splendour of their union. * * * no living poet ever arrived at the fulness of his fame; the jury which sits in judgement upon a poet, belonging as he does to all time, must be composed of his peers: it must be impanelled by Time from the selectest of the wise of many generations. A Poet is a nightingale, who sits in darkness and sings to cheer its own solitude with sweet sound; his auditors are as men entranced by the melody of an unseen musician, who feel that they are moved and softened, yet know not whence or why.[2] * * *

---

8. Sidney's *Defence* observes that the Roman word for poet, *vates*, means "prophet" or "oracle."
9. In addition to Job, referring to the Greek tragedian (525–456 B.C.E.), and *Paradiso*, the third and final part of

Dante's epic *Divina Commedia* (completed 1321).
1. Creative imagination and creative arts.
2. Compare *To a Sky-Lark*, especially lines 36–40 and 101–105.

The whole objection * * * of the immorality of poetry rests upon a misconception of the manner in which poetry acts to produce the moral improvement of man.[3] Ethical science[4] arranges the elements which poetry has created, and propounds schemes and proposes examples of civil and domestic life. Nor is it for want of admirable doctrines that men hate, and despise, and censure, and deceive, and subjugate one another. But poetry acts in another and diviner manner. It awakens and enlarges the mind itself by rendering it the receptacle of a thousand unapprehended combinations of thought. Poetry lifts the veil from the hidden beauty of the world, and makes familiar objects be as if they were not familiar; it re-produces all that it represents, and the impersonations clothed in its Elysian light[5] stand thenceforward in the minds of those who have once contemplated them as memorials of that gentle and exalted content[6] which extends itself over all thoughts and actions with which it co-exists. The great secret of morals is love, or a going out of our own[7] nature, and an identification of ourselves with the beautiful which exists in thought, action, or person, not our own. A man, to be greatly good, must imagine intensely and comprehensively; he must put himself in the place of another and of many others; the pains and pleasures of his species must become his own. The great instrument of moral good is the imagination; and poetry administers to the effect by acting upon the cause.

Poetry enlarges the circumference of the imagination by replenishing it with thoughts of ever new delight, which have the power of attracting and assimilating to their own nature all other thoughts, and which form new intervals and interstices whose void forever craves fresh food. Poetry strengthens the faculty which is the organ of the moral nature of man, in the same manner as exercise strengthens a limb. A poet therefore would do ill to embody his own conceptions of right and wrong (which are usually those of his place and time) in his poetical creations (which participate in neither). By this assumption of the inferior office of interpreting the effect, in which perhaps after all he might acquit himself but imperfectly, he would resign a glory in the participation of the cause. There was little danger that Homer, or any of the eternal poets, should have so far misunderstood themselves as to have abdicated this throne of their widest dominion. Those in whom the poetical faculty, though great, is less intense (as Euripides, Lucan, Tasso, Spenser) have frequently affected a moral aim, and the effect of their poetry is diminished in exact proportion to the degree in which they compel us to advert to this purpose.[8] * * *

---

3. Shelley has just defended poetry from the charge of immorality (leveled famously by Plato in *The Republic*, renewed by the English Puritans of the 17th century and the Evangelicals of Shelley's own age) for depicting characters "remote from moral perfection" and thus offering no "edifying pattern for general imitation" by their readers. Throughout, A *Defence* also counters Plato's other charge, that all art is only representation, and thus a diminishment of Ideal Truth.
4. Moral philosophy.
5. In Greek myth, Elysium is the abode of the blessed after death.

6. Noun: both "content" and "contentment."
7. In the argument of Plato's *Symposium*, a key sentence reads, "Love, therefore, and every thing else that desires anything, desires that which is absent and beyond his reach, that which it has not, that which is not itself, that which it wants" (Shelley's translation); "wants" means both "desires" and "lacks."
8. Euripides: Greek tragedian, 5th century B.C.E.; Lucan: Roman epic poet, 1st century C.E. (see *Adonais* 404); Torquato Tasso: Italian epic poet, 16th century; Edmund Spenser: 16th-century English poet, best known for the romance epic, *The Faerie Queene*.

Milton's poem contains within itself a philosophical refutation of that system, of which, by a strange and natural antithesis, it has been a chief popular support.[9] Nothing can exceed the energy and magnificence of the character of Satan as expressed in Paradise Lost. It is a mistake to suppose that he could ever have been intended for the popular personification of evil. Implacable hate, patient cunning, and a sleepless refinement of device to inflict the extremest anguish on an enemy, these things are evil; and, although venial[1] in a slave, are not to be forgiven in a tyrant; although redeemed by much that ennobles his defeat in one subdued, are marked by all that dishonors his conquest in the victor. Milton's Devil as a moral being is as far superior to his God, as one who perseveres in some purpose which he has conceived to be excellent, in spite of adversity and torture, is to one who in the cold security of undoubted triumph inflicts the most horrible revenge upon his enemy, not from any mistaken notion of inducing him to repent of a perseverance in enmity, but with the alleged design of exasperating him to deserve new torments. Milton has so far violated the popular creed (if this shall be judged to be a violation) as to have alleged no superiority of moral virtue to his God over his Devil. And this bold neglect of a direct moral purpose is the most decisive proof of the supremacy of Milton's genius.* * *

We have more moral, political and historical wisdom than we know how to reduce into practice; we have more scientific and economical knowledge than can be accommodated to the just distribution of the produce which it multiplies. The poetry in these systems of thought is concealed by the accumulation of facts and calculating processes. There is no want of knowledge respecting what is wisest and best in morals, government, and political economy, or at least what is wiser and better than what men now practise and endure. But we let "*I dare not wait upon I would, like the poor cat i' the adage.*"[2] We want the creative faculty to imagine that which we know; we want the generous impulse to act that which we imagine; we want the poetry of life:[3] our calculations have outrun conception; we have eaten more than we can digest. The cultivation of those sciences which have enlarged the limits of the empire of man over the external world, has, for want of the poetical faculty, proportionally circumscribed those of the internal world; and man, having enslaved the elements, remains himself a slave. To what but a cultivation of the mechanical arts in a degree disproportioned to the presence of the creative faculty (which is the basis of all knowledge) is to be attributed the abuse of all invention for abridging and combining labour, to the exasperation of the inequality of mankind? From what other cause has it arisen that these inventions, which should have lightened, have added a weight to the curse imposed on Adam?[4] Poetry, and the principle of Self (of which money is the visible incarnation) are the God and Mammon of the world.[5]

9. That is, the "great Argument" to "justify the ways of God to men" and Satan's punishment for the "Pride." "Envy and Revenge" by which he cast himself "th' Arch-Enemy" both of God and man (1.24–83).
1. Forgivable.
2. *Macbeth* 1.7.44–45. So Lady Macbeth taunts her reluctant husband, referring to the cat that has a taste for fish but won't get its paws wet.
3. In these declarations, "want" means "lack" and "need," shaded by a sense of "desire," "wish for."
4. The Lord says to Adam, in punishment for his sin, "cursed is the ground for thy sake; in sorrow shalt thou eat of it all the days of thy life; thorns also and thistles shall it bring forth.... In the sweat of thy face shalt thou eat bread, till thou return unto the ground;...dust thou art, and unto dust shalt thou return" (Genesis 3.17–19).
5. Mammon is the false idol of money and worldly goods, against whom Jesus cautions, "Ye cannot serve God and mammon" (Luke 16.13). Keats told Shelley the year before he wrote his *Defence*, "A modern work it is said must have a purpose, which may be the God—*an artist* must serve Mammon—he must have 'self concentration' selfishness perhaps. You I am sure will forgive me for sincerely remarking that you might curb your magnanimity and be more of an artist" (see page 1059).

The functions of the poetical faculty are twofold: by one it creates new materials of knowledge and power and pleasure; by the other it engenders in the mind a desire to reproduce and arrange them according to a certain rhythm and order which may be called the beautiful and the good. The cultivation of poetry is never more to be desired than in periods when, from an excess of the selfish and calculating principle, the accumulation of the materials of external life exceed the quantity of the power of assimilating them to the internal laws of human nature. The body has then become too unwieldy for that which animates it.

Poetry is indeed something divine. It is at once the centre and circumference of knowledge;[6] it is that which comprehends all science, and that to which all science must be referred. It is at the same time the root and blossom of all other systems of thought. It is that from which all spring, and that which adorns all; and that which, if blighted, denies the fruit and the seed, and withholds from the barren world the nourishment and the succession of the scions of the tree of life. It is the perfect and consummate surface and bloom of all things; it is as the odour and the colour of the rose to the texture of the elements which compose it, as the form and splendour of unfaded beauty to the secrets of anatomy and corruption. What were [would be] Virtue, Love, Patriotism, Friendship, etc., what were the scenery of this beautiful Universe which we inhabit; what were our consolations on this side of the grave, and what were our aspirations beyond it,—if Poetry did not ascend to bring light and fire from those eternal regions where the owl-winged faculty of calculation dare not ever soar? Poetry is not like reasoning, a power to be exerted according to the determination of the will. A man cannot say, "I will compose poetry." The greatest poet even cannot say it: for the mind in creation is as a fading coal which some invisible influence, like an inconstant wind, awakens to transitory brightness. This power arises from within, like the colour of a flower which fades and changes as it is developed, and the conscious portions of our natures are unprophetic either of its approach or its departure. Could this influence be durable in its original purity and force, it is impossible to predict the greatness of the results; but when composition begins, inspiration is already on the decline, and the most glorious poetry that has ever been communicated to the world is probably a feeble shadow of the original conceptions of the poet. I appeal to the greatest poets of the present day whether it is not an error to assert that the finest passages of poetry are produced by labour and study. The toil and the delay recommended by critics can be justly interpreted to mean no more than a careful observation of the inspired moments, and an artificial connection of the spaces between their suggestions by the intertexture of conventional expressions—a necessity only imposed by a limitedness of the poetical faculty itself. For Milton conceived the Paradise Lost as a whole before he executed it in portions. We have his own authority also for the muse having "dictated" to him the "unpremeditated song."[7] And let this be an answer to those who would allege the fifty-six various readings of the first line of the Orlando Furioso.[8] Compositions so produced are to poetry what mosaic is to painting. The instinct and intuition of the poetical faculty is still more observable in the plastic and pictorial arts: a great statue or picture grows under the

---

6. A description of God often attributed to St. Augustine (4th–5th century), as the circle whose center is everywhere and circumference nowhere.

7. In Paradise Lost, Milton says that his celestial muse "dictates to me slumb'ring, or inspires / Easy my unpremeditated verse" (9.23–24); compare To a Sky-Lark, 5.

8. Epic poem by Italian poet Ariosto (1632).

power of the artist as a child in the mother's womb, and the very mind which directs the hands in formation is incapable of accounting to itself for the origin, the gradations, or the media of the process.

Poetry is the record of the best and happiest moments of the happiest and best minds. We are aware of evanescent visitations of thought and feeling sometimes associated with place or person, sometimes regarding our own mind alone, and always arising unforeseen and departing unbidden, but elevating and delightful beyond all expression; so that even in the desire and the regret they leave, there cannot but be pleasure, participating as it does in the nature of its object. It is, as it were, the interpenetration of a diviner nature through our own, but its footsteps are like those of a wind over a sea, which the morning calm erases, and whose traces remain only as on the wrinkled sand which paves it. These and corresponding conditions of being are experienced principally by those of the most delicate sensibility and the most enlarged imagination; and the state of mind produced by them is at war with every base desire. The enthusiasm of virtue, love, patriotism, and friendship is essentially linked with emotions; and whilst they last, self appears as what it is, an atom to a Universe. Poets are not only subject to these experiences as spirits of the most refined organization, but they can colour all that they combine with the evanescent hues of this etherial world; a word or a trait in the representation of a scene or a passion will touch the enchanted chord, and reanimate, in those who have ever experienced these emotions, the sleeping, the cold, the buried image of the past. Poetry thus makes immortal all that is best and most beautiful in the world; it arrests the vanishing apparitions which haunt the interlunations[9] of life, and veiling them or [either] in language or in form, sends them forth among mankind, bearing sweet news of kindred joy to those with whom their sisters abide— abide, because there is no portal of expression from the caverns of the spirit which they inhabit into the universe of things.[1] Poetry redeems from decay the visitations of the divinity in man.

Poetry turns all things to loveliness: it exalts the beauty of that which is most beautiful, and it adds beauty to that which is most deformed; it marries exultation and horror, grief and pleasure, eternity and change; it subdues to union under its light yoke all irreconcilable things.[2] It transmutes all that it touches, and every form moving within the radiance of its presence is changed by wondrous sympathy to an incarnation of the spirit which it breathes; its secret alchemy turns to potable gold the poisonous waters which flow from death through life; it strips the veil of familiarity from the world, and lays bare the naked and sleeping beauty which is the spirit of its forms.

All things exist as they are perceived: at least in relation to the percipient. "The mind is its own place, and of itself can make a heaven of hell, a hell of heaven."[3] But poetry defeats the curse which binds us to be subjected to the accident of surrounding impressions. And whether it spreads its own figured curtain or withdraws life's dark veil from before the scene of things,[4] it equally creates for us a being within our

9. The dark intervals between the old and new moons.
1. Poetry is valuable because it articulates not only what the poet apprehends—those "vanishing apparitions"— but also their "sisters" in the spiritual selves of ordinary mankind, who would lack connection to what is "best and most beautiful in the world" and "the universe of things," were it not for poetry. In his *Defense*, Sidney calls the inner potential for understanding the "foreconceit," and grants poets similar power.

2. Coleridge's description of imagination, *Biographia Literaria* (1817), the end of ch. 14 (see page 692).
3. A small but significant misquotation of Satan's boast in Hell, *Paradise Lost* 1.254–55; Milton wrote "in itself" (not "of"), in order to set up, along with the second half of the chiasmus that Shelley goes on to deflect, the horribly ironic return of this boast of mind over place when Satan beholds Eve and Eden in the morning (9.467–70).
4. See "Lift not the painted veil" and *Mont Blanc* 53–54.

being. It makes us the inhabitant of a world to which the familiar world is a chaos. It reproduces the common universe of which we are portions and percipients, and it purges from our inward sight the film of familiarity which obscures from us the wonder of our being. It compels us to feel that which we perceive, and to imagine that which we know. It creates anew the universe after it has been annihilated in our minds by the recurrence of impressions blunted by reiteration. It justifies that bold and true word of Tasso: *Non merita nome di creatore, se non Iddio ed il Poeta.*[5]

A Poet, as he is the author to others of the highest wisdom, pleasure, virtue, and glory, so he ought personally to be the happiest, the best, the wisest, and the most illustrious of men. As to his glory, let time be challenged to declare whether the fame of any other institutor of human life be comparable to that of a poet. That he is the wisest, the happiest, and the best, inasmuch as he is a poet, is equally incontrovertible: the greatest poets have been men of the most spotless virtue, of the most consummate prudence, and (if we would look into the interior of their lives) the most fortunate of men. And the exceptions, as they regard those who possessed the poetic faculty in a high yet inferior degree, will be found on consideration to confirm rather than destroy the rule. Let us for a moment stoop to the arbitration of popular breath, and usurping and uniting in our own persons the incompatible characters of accuser, witness, judge and executioner, let us decide without trial, testimony, or form, that certain motives of those who are "there sitting where we dare not soar,"[6] are reprehensible. Let us assume that Homer was a drunkard, that Virgil was a flatterer, that Horace was a coward, that Tasso was a madman, that Lord Bacon was a peculator, that Raphael was a libertine, that Spenser was a Poet Laureate.[7] It is inconsistent with this division of our subject to cite living poets, but posterity has done ample justice to the great names now referred to. Their errors have been weighed and found to have been dust in the balance; if their sins "were as scarlet, they are now white as snow"; they have been washed in the blood of the mediator and redeemer, Time.[8] Observe in what a ludicrous chaos the imputations of real or fictitious crime have been confused in the contemporary calumnies against poetry and poets; consider how little is as it appears—or appears as it is; look to your own motives, and judge not, lest ye be judged.[9]

5. *None merits the name of creator except God and the Poet;* from Serassi's *Life of Torquato Tasso* (1785). Sidney's *Defense* refers to God as the "Maker of [the] maker" (punning on the Greek word root for "poet").

6. Poets whose reprehensible motives Shelley is willing to concede for the sake of argument. His quotation adapts Satan's sneering reminder to his former peers of his former state in Heaven: "ye knew me once no mate / For you, there sitting where ye durst not soar" (*Paradise Lost* 4.428–29); recall this phrase in *Adonais* 337 (page 905).

7. All charges made against these poets. Homer: epic poet of ancient Greece; Horace: Roman lyric poet and satirist, 1st century B.C.E.; Virgil: Roman pastoral and epic poet, 1st century B.C.E., sometimes accused of being an apologist for Roman imperialism; Bacon: English Renaissance philosopher, essayist, statesman, and scientist, whose public career was ruined by a conviction for accepting bribes (a peculator is an embezzler); Raphael: 16th-century Italian painter (a libertine is given to immoral sensual indulgence); for Tasso and Spenser, see n. 8, page 924. The first Poet Laureate, a royally bestowed office and honor, was Dryden (1670–1689), but because the

position is associated with royal patronage and devotion to the monarchy, other court poets, including Spenser, have been retroactively accorded the title. Shelley uses the charge against Spenser to sneer at one particular "living poet," the current Laureate, Robert Southey (see also Preface to *Adonais* and Byron's Dedication to *Don Juan*).

8. See Isaiah: "Come now, and let us reason together, saith the Lord: though your sins be as scarlet, they shall be as white as snow" (1.18); and Revelation: those in white robes at the throne of God "came out of great tribulation, and have washed their robes, and made them white in the blood of the Lamb" (i.e., Christ; 7.14).

9. Christ admonishes: "Judge not, that ye be not judged. For with what judgment ye judge, ye shall be judged" (Matthew 7.1–2); by "contemporary calumnies," slanders and lies intended to ruin reputations, Shelley refers to attacks on himself and others in Tory journals, especially *The Quarterly* (see Preface to *Adonais*). In the Preface of his panegyric on the death of King George III (1820), Poet Laureate Southey described Shelley and Byron as "the Satanic School"; see page 762.

Poetry, as has been said, differs in this respect from logic: that it is not subject to the controul of the active power of the mind, and that its birth and recurrence has no necessary connection with the consciousness or will. It is presumptuous to determine that these are the necessary conditions of all mental causation, when mental effects are experienced insusceptible of being referred to them.[1] The frequent recurrence of the poetical power, it is obvious to suppose, may produce in the mind a habit of order and harmony correlative with its own nature and with its effects upon other minds. But in the intervals of inspiration (and they may be frequent without being durable) a poet becomes a man, and is abandoned to the sudden reflux of the influences under which others habitually live. But as he is more delicately organized than other men, and sensible to pain and pleasure (both his own and that of others), in a degree unknown to them,[2] he will avoid the one [pain] and pursue the other [pleasure] with an ardor proportioned to this difference. And he renders himself obnoxious to calumny, when he neglects to observe the circumstances under which these objects of universal pursuit and flight have disguised themselves in one another's garments.

But there is nothing necessarily evil in this error, and thus cruelty, envy, revenge, avarice, and the passions purely evil, have never formed any portion of the popular imputations on the lives of poets.

I have thought it most favourable to the cause of truth to set down these remarks according to the order in which they were suggested to my mind by a consideration of the subject itself, instead of following that of the treatise that excited me to make them public. Thus although devoid of the formality of a polemical reply, if the views which they contain be just, they will be found to involve a refutation of the doctrines of "The Four Ages of Poetry" so far at least as regards the first division of the subject. I can readily conjecture what should have moved the gall of the learned and intelligent author of that paper; I confess myself like him unwilling to be stunned by the *Theseids* of the hoarse Codri of the day. Bavius and Maevius undoubtedly are, as they ever were, insufferable persons. But it belongs to a philosophical critic to distinguish rather than confound.[3]

The first part of these remarks has related to poetry in its elements and principles; and it has been shown, as well as the narrow limits assigned them would permit, that what is called poetry in a restricted sense has a common source with all other forms of order and of beauty according to which the materials of human life are susceptible of being arranged, and which is poetry in a universal sense.

The second part will have for its object an application of these principles to the present state of the cultivation of poetry, and a defense of the attempt to idealize the modern forms of manners and opinions, and compel them into a subordination to the imaginative and creative faculty.[4] For the literature of England, an energetic development of which has ever preceded or accompanied a great and free development of the national will, has arisen, as it were, from a new birth. In spite of the low-thoughted envy which would undervalue contemporary merit, our own will be a memorable age in intellectual achievements, and we live among such philosophers

---

1. "Consciousness and will" in the previous sentence.
2. An echo of Wordsworth's Preface to *Lyrical Ballads*; see page 439.
3. Theseids are epic poems about Theseus, hero of ancient Greek legend; one of the worst and longest, by Roman poet Codrus (*Codri*, the plural, names poems of this type), was savaged by Juvenal and other satirists. Two other

inferior Roman poets, Bavius and Maevius, were satirized by Virgil and Horace; the names became bywords for bad poetry. In the 1790s William Gifford (who would go on to edit *The Anti-Jacobin* and *The Quarterly*) gave the titles *The Baviad* and *The Maeviad* to his devastating mock-heroic satires of the sentimental-aesthetic poetry of the day.
4. Never drafted.

and poets as surpass beyond comparison any who have appeared since the last national struggle for civil and religious liberty.[5] The most unfailing herald, companion, and follower of the awakening of a great people to work a beneficial change in opinion or institution, is poetry. At such periods there is an accumulation of the power of communicating and receiving intense and impassioned conceptions respecting man and nature. The persons in whom this power resides may often (as far as regards many portions of their nature) have little apparent correspondence with that spirit of good of which they are the ministers. But even whilst they deny and abjure, they are yet compelled to serve the power which is seated on the throne of their own soul. It is impossible to read the compositions of the most celebrated writers of the present day[6] without being startled with the electric life which burns within their words. They measure the circumference and sound the depths of human nature with a comprehensive and all-penetrating spirit, and they are themselves perhaps the most sincerely astonished at its manifestations, for it is less their spirit than the spirit of the age. Poets are the hierophants[7] of an unapprehended inspiration, the mirrors of the gigantic shadows which futurity casts upon the present, the words which express what they understand not; the trumpets which sing to battle, and feel not what they inspire; the influence which is moved not, but moves.[8] Poets are the unacknowledged legislators of the world.

✦

Felicia Hemans
1793–1835

A best-selling poet in England and America through most of the nineteenth century, Felicia Hemans (née Browne) was prolific. In addition to numerous publications in magazines and gift-books, she produced nineteen volumes of poems and plays between 1808 and 1834. Lord Byron, with whom she shared the publisher John Murray, was sensitive to the competition. In letters to Murray, he tags her "your feminine *He-Man*" or "Mrs. Hewoman's," his punning turning her commercial prowess into a sexual monstrosity. Byron preferred women in their place, not his. "I do not despise Mrs. Heman—but if [she] knit blue stockings instead of wearing them it would be better," he declared to Murray, referring to the "bluestockings," a derisive term for learned women.

Born in Liverpool in 1793, the year of the Terror in France and the execution of its king and queen, Felicia Browne was raised in the distant calms of North Wales. Under the devoted tutelage of her mother, she became a child prodigy, learning Latin, German, French, and Italian, devouring Shakespeare, and quickly developing a talent for writing; when she was fourteen, her parents underwrote the publication of her first volume. Learning of her talents and beauty, Percy Shelley ventured a correspondence, but (fortunately for the young poet) her mother intervened and nothing came of his overture. The romance that did blossom was with Captain Alfred Hemans, a veteran of the Peninsular Campaign in Spain in which her brothers also served. They married in 1812, the year of her nineteenth birthday and third volume, *The Domestic Affections*. By 1818, she had produced three more volumes to favorable reviews, as well as five sons. Just before the birth of the last, the Captain left for Italy; the "story" was ill health. They never saw each other again, the breach mirroring her father's desertion of his wife and children in 1810, for

---

5. The Civil Wars of the 1640s, concluding in the execution of Charles I, and the Glorious Revolution of the late 1680s, unseating James II. Among "philosophers and poets," Shelley has Byron in mind.
6. Implicitly, himself and Byron.

7. Ancient priests who interpret sacred mysteries; oracles of revelation.
8. Aristotle (Greek philosopher, 4th century B.C.E.) described God as the "Unmoved Mover" of the universe.

Edward Smith, after a painting
by Edward Robertson, *Portrait of
Felicia Hemans*, 1831. Robertson's
portrait captures the melancholy
beauty that was the poet's
hallmark.

a fresh start in Canada. The collapse of her own and her mother's marriages haunts the idealism
of home for which "Mrs. Hemans" was becoming famous, shadowing it with repeated stories of
men's unreliability or treachery and the necessity of maternal responsibility.

Determined to support herself and her sons with her writing, Hemans returned to her
mother's home in Wales. With no wifely obligations or husband to "obey," and with sisters,
mother, and brothers to help care for her boys and run the home, Hemans had considerable
time to read, study, write, and publish. Moreover, as a daughter under "the maternal wing"
and an "affectionate, tender, and vigilant mother" herself (as prefaces to her works later in the
century put it), the professional writer was immunized against the stigma of "unfeminine" independence. The death of her mother in 1827 was a deep and devastating grief, aggravated by
the disintegration of her home as sons grew up and brothers and sisters married or moved away.
Her health suffered, and after a long decline, she died in Dublin in 1835, a few months before
her forty-second birthday. William Wordsworth warmly honored her in the memorial verses
of his *Extempore Effusion*, even as he indicated his discomfort with her ignorance of household
skills and her affectation of being a "literary lady."

Among Hemans's most successful volumes, both critically and commercially, were *Tales,
and Historic Scenes in Verse* (1819), *The Forest Sanctuary* (1825), *Records of Woman* (1828),
which she dedicated to Joanna Baillie, and *Songs of the Affections* (1830). She was popular well
into the Victorian age, especially among women. By the middle of the twentieth century, she
was remembered only by a few favorite poems, including *The Homes of England, The Landing of
the Pilgrim Fathers* ("The breaking waves dashed high, / On a stern and rockbound coast") and
Casabianca ("The boy stood on the burning deck")—this last a parlor-recitation and school-
assembly favorite, as well as the subject of multiple parodies. By the 1980s, she was virtually
forgotten. In the subsequent recovery of the "lost" women writers of the Romantic era, her work

has received fresh attention, especially for its reflection of many key social, psychological, and emotional concerns for women in her day. These involve not only woman's celebrated roles as a patient, devoted, and often long-suffering lover, wife, and mother, but also tensions within these definitions. Some still read her poetry as primers of traditional gender values: women's place at home and upholding "domestic affections," religious faith, and patriotic sentiment. But others find this same poetry haunted by the futility and vulnerability of the ideals it celebrates, invaded by sadness, melancholy, betrayal, suffering, and violence, and repeatedly staging women's heroism in scenes of defeat and death. Hemans was particularly tuned to conflicts besetting women who achieve fame in nontraditional roles, especially as artists, typically at great cost in personal happiness. Poetry by Hemans also appears in "*Manfred* and Its Time," page 759.

from TALES, AND HISTORIC SCENES, IN VERSE

The Wife of Asdrubal

"This governor, who had braved death when it was at a distance, and protested that the sun should never see him survive Carthage,[1] this fierce Asdrubal, was so mean-spirited, as to come alone, and privately throw himself at the conqueror's feet. The general, pleased to see his proud rival humbled, granted his life, and kept him to grace his triumph. The Carthaginians in the citadel no sooner understood that their commander had abandoned the place, than they threw open the gates, and put the proconsul in possession of Byrsa. The Romans had now no enemy to contend with but the nine hundred deserters, who, being reduced to despair, retired into the temple of Esculapius, which was a second citadel within the first: there the proconsul attacked them; and these unhappy wretches, finding there was no way to escape, set fire to the temple. As the flames spread, they retreated from one part to another, till they got to the roof of the building: there Asdrubal's wife appeared in her best apparel, as if the day of her death had been a day of triumph; and after having uttered the most bitter imprecations against her husband, whom she saw standing below with Emilianus,[2]—'Base coward!' said she, 'the mean things thou hast done to save thy life shall not avail thee; thou shalt die this instant, at least in thy two children.' Having thus spoken, she drew out a dagger, stabbed them both, and while they were yet struggling for life, threw them from the top of the temple, and leaped down after them into the flames."—*Ancient Universal History* [London, 1736–1744]

> The sun sets brightly—but a ruddier glow
> O'er Afric's heaven the flames of Carthage throw;
> Her walls have sunk, and pyramids of fire
> In lurid splendor from her domes aspire;
> 5   Sway'd by the wind, they wave—while glares the sky   *desert wind*
> As when the desert's red Simoom° is nigh;
> The sculptured altar, and the pillar'd hall,
> Shine out in dreadful brightness ere they fall;
> Far o'er the seas the light of ruin streams,
> 10   Rock, wave, and isle, are crimson'd by its beams;
> While captive thousands, bound in Roman chains,
> Gaze in mute horror on their burning fanes;°   *temples*

---

1. A powerful city-state on Africa's northern coast; its control of the western Mediterranean was challenged by the Roman empire, which finally destroyed it in the Third Punic War (149–146 B.C.E.).

2. Scipio Africanus Minor, the Roman general (son of Aemilius Paullus). The surviving Carthaginians were sold into slavery, and Asdrubal lived comfortably as a state prisoner in Italy.

And shouts of triumph, echoing far around,
Swell from the victor's tents with ivy crown'd.[3]

15   But mark! from yon fair temple's loftiest height
     What towering form bursts wildly on the sight,
     All regal in magnificent attire,
     And sternly beauteous in terrific ire?
     She might be deem'd a Pythia[4] in the hour
20   Of dread communion and delirious power;
     A being more than earthly, in whose eye
     There dwells a strange and fierce ascendancy.
     The flames are gathering round—intensely bright,
     Full on her features glares their meteor-light,
25   But a wild courage sits triumphant there,
     The stormy grandeur of a proud despair;
     A daring spirit, in its woes elate,
     Mightier than death, untameable by fate.
     The dark profusion of her locks unbound,
30   Waves like a warrior's floating plumage round;
     Flush'd is her cheek, inspired her haughty mien,
     She seems th' avenging goddess of the scene.
     Are those *her* infants, that with suppliant-cry
     Cling round her, shrinking as the flame draws nigh,
35   Clasp with their feeble hands her gorgeous vest,
     And fain would rush for shelter to her breast?
     Is that a mother's glance, where stern disdain,
     And passion awfully vindictive, reign?

     Fix'd is her eye on Asdrubal, who stands,
40   Ignobly safe, amidst the conquering bands;
     On him, who left her to that burning tomb,
     Alone to share her children's martyrdom;
     Who when his country perish'd, fled the strife,
     And knelt to win the worthless boon of life.
45   "Live, traitor, live!" she cries, "since dear to thee,
     E'en in thy fetters, can existence be!
     Scorn'd and dishonour'd, live!—with blasted name,
     The Roman's triumph° not to grace, but shame.   *victory parade*
     O slave in spirit! bitter be thy chain
50   With tenfold anguish to avenge my pain!
     Still may the manès° of thy children rise   *avenging spirits*
     To chase calm slumber from thy wearied eyes;
     Still may their voices on the haunted air
     In fearful whispers tell thee to despair,
55   Till vain remorse thy wither'd heart consume,
     Scourged by relentless shadows of the tomb!
     E'en now my sons shall die—and thou, their sire,

3. It was a Roman custom to adorn the tents of victors
with ivy [Hemans's note].
4. Priestess and medium of Apollo at the oracle of Delphi,
whose entranced, frenzied communications required interpretation by male priests.

In bondage safe, shalt yet in them expire.
Think'st thou I love them not?—'Twas thine to fly—
60 'Tis mine with these to suffer and to die.
Behold their fate!—the arms that cannot save
Have been their cradle, and shall be their grave."

Bright in her hand the lifted dagger gleams,
Swift from her children's hearts the life-blood streams;
65 With frantic laugh she clasps them to the breast
Whose woes and passions soon shall be at rest;
Lifts one appealing, frenzied glance on high,
Then deep midst rolling flames is lost to mortal eye.

1819

The Last Banquet of Antony and Cleopatra[1]

"Antony, concluding that he could not die more honourably than in battle, determined to attack Cæsar at the same time both by sea and land. The night preceding the execution of this design, he ordered his servants at supper to render him their best services that evening, and fill the wine round plentifully, for the day following they might belong to another master, whilst he lay extended on the ground, no longer of consequence either to them or to himself. His friends were affected, and wept to hear him talk thus; which, when he perceived, he encouraged them by assurances that his expectations of a glorious victory were at least equal to those of an honourable death. At the dead of night, when universal silence reigned through the city, a silence that was deepened by the awful thought of the ensuing day, on a sudden was heard the sound of musical instruments, and a noise which resembled the exclamations of Bacchanals.[2] This tumultuous procession seemed to pass through the whole city, and to go out at the gate which led to the enemy's camp. Those who reflected on this prodigy concluded that Bacchus, the god whom Antony affected to imitate, had then forsaken him." —*Langhorne's Plutarch* [The Life of Marc Antony][3]

Thy foes had girt thee with their dread array,
    O stately Alexandria![4]—yet the sound
Of mirth and music, at the close of day,
    Swell'd from thy splendid fabrics,° far around   *buildings*
5 O'er camp and wave. Within the royal hall,
    In gay magnificence the feast was spread;
And, brightly streaming from the pictured wall,
    A thousand lamps their trembling lustre shed
O'er many a column, rich with precious dyes,
10   That tinge the marble's vein, 'neath Afric's burning skies.

1. After avenging the assassination of Julius Caesar in 44 B.C.E. Octavius Caesar and Marc Antony consolidated power; Antony took command of the east, where he became enamored of Cleopatra of Egypt; this led to tensions with Octavius, whose sister Antony had married. Antony spurned her and Rome together, married Cleopatra (36 B.C.E.), and declared joint rule. Octavius then declared war, and defeated the two in 31 B.C.E. at the Battle of Actium (its eve is Hemans's setting). Rather than be taken captive, they committed suicide, Antony by falling on his sword and Cleopatra by poisonous snake bite.

2. Festivals held in ancient Greece in which women celebrated Bacchus, the god of wine.
3. Plutarch's (46–120) great work is *Lives* of famous Greeks and Romans, translated in 1779 by poet John Langhorne and his brother William. Shakespeare based several plays, including *Antony and Cleopatra*, on Plutarch.
4. Major city in northern Egypt, home of Cleopatra's palace. The last line of Hemans's stanza is Alexandrine meter, named for its use in medieval French romances about Alexander the Great, founder of Alexandria.

And soft and clear that wavering radiance play'd
    O'er sculptured forms, that round the pillar'd scene,
Calm and majestic rose, by art array'd
    In godlike beauty, awfully° serene.   *awesomely*
15 Oh! how unlike the troubled guests, reclined
    Round that luxurious board!°—in every face,   *table*
Some shadow from the tempest of the mind,
    Rising by fits, the searching eye might trace,
Though vainly mask'd in smiles which are not mirth,
20 But the proud spirit's veil thrown o'er the woes of earth.

Their brows are bound with wreaths, whose transient bloom
    May still survive the wearers—and the rose
Perchance may scarce be wither'd, when the tomb
    Receives the mighty to its dark repose!
25 The day must dawn on battle—and may set
    In death—but fill the mantling° wine-cup high!   *blushing*
Despair is fearless, and the Fates[5] e'en yet
    Lend her one hour for parting revelry.
They who the empire of the world possess'd,
30 Would taste its joys again, ere all exchanged for rest.

Its joys! oh! mark yon proud triumvir's mien,[6]
    And read their annals° on that brow of care!   *histories*
'Midst pleasure's lotus-bowers[7] his steps have been;
    Earth's brightest pathway led him to despair.
35 Trust not the glance that fain would yet inspire
    The buoyant energies of days gone by;
There is delusion in its meteor-fire,
    And all within is shame, is agony!
Away! the tear in bitterness may flow,
40 But there are smiles which bear a stamp of deeper woe.

Thy cheek is sunk, and faded as thy fame,
    O lost, devoted° Roman! yet thy brow   *enrapt, doomed*
To that ascendant and undying name,
    Pleads with stern loftiness thy right e'en now.
45 Thy glory is departed—but hath left
    A lingering light around thee—in decay
Not less than kingly, though of all bereft,
    Thou seem'st as empire had not pass'd away.
Supreme in ruin! teaching hearts elate,
50 A deep, prophetic dread of still mysterious fate!

But thou, enchantress-queen! whose love hath made
    His desolation—thou art by his side,
In all thy sovereignty of charms array'd,
    To meet the storm with still unconquer'd pride.

5. The three goddesses of classical mythology who control the length and course of human life.
6. With Octavius and Lepidus, Antony was triumvir (Latin *trium virum*, rule "of three men") of the Roman Empire after the defeat of the republicans who had assassinated Julius Caesar.
7. The narcotic lotus flower is a byword for easeful forgetfulness.

55 Imperial being! e'en though many a stain
        Of error be upon thee, there is power
    In thy commanding nature, which shall reign
        O'er the stern genius° of misfortune's hour;   *presiding spirit*
    And the dark beauty of thy troubled eye
60 E'en now is all illumed with wild sublimity.

    Thine aspect, all impassion'd, wears a light
        Inspiring and inspired—thy cheek a dye,
    Which rises not from joy, but yet is bright
        With the deep glow of feverish energy.
65 Proud siren of the Nile! thy glance is fraught
        With an immortal fire—in every beam
    It darts, there kindles some heroic thought,
        But wild and awful as a sybil's° dream;   *female oracle's*
    For thou with death hast communed, to attain
70 Dread knowledge of the pangs that ransom from the chain.[8]

    And the stern courage by such musings lent,
        Daughter of Afric! o'er thy beauty throws
    The grandeur of a regal spirit, blent
        With all the majesty of mighty woes!
75 While he, so fondly, fatally adored,
        Thy fallen Roman, gazes on thee yet,
    Till scarce the soul, that once exulting soar'd,
        Can deem the day-star° of its glory set;   *sun*
    Scarce his charm'd heart believes that power can be
80 In sovereign fate, o'er him, thus fondly loved by thee.

    But there is sadness in the eyes around,
        Which mark that ruin'd leader, and survey
    His changeful mien, whence oft the gloom profound,
        Strange triumph chases haughtily away.
85 "Fill the bright goblet, warrior guests!" he cries,
        "Quaff, ere we part, the generous nectar° deep!   *wine*
    Ere sunset gild once more the western skies,
        Your chief, in cold forgetfulness, may sleep,
    While sounds of revel float o'er shore and sea,
90 And the red bowl again is crown'd—but not for me."

    "Yet weep not thus—the struggle is not o'er,
        O victors of Philippi![9] many a field
    Hath yielded palms° to us:—one effort more,   *victory wreaths*
        By one stern conflict must our doom be seal'd!
95 Forget not, Romans! o'er a subject world

---

8. Cleopatra made a collection of poisonous drugs, and being desirous to know which was least painful in the operation, she tried them on the capital convicts. Such poisons as were quick in their operation, she found to be attended with violent pain and convulsions; such as were milder were slow in their effect: she therefore applied herself to the examination of venomous creatures; and at length she found that the bite of the asp was the most eligible kind of death; for it brought on a gradual kind of lethargy.—See *Plutarch* ["The Life of Marc Antony"; Hemans's note]. "Chain" is the tie to mortal life; "capital convicts" are those condemned to death.
9. Where the republican forces were defeated in 42 B.C.E.

How royally your eagle's wing hath spread,
Though from his eyrie° of dominion hurl'd,   *eagle's nest*
     Now bursts the tempest on his crested head![1]
Yet sovereign still, if banish'd from the sky,
100 The sun's indignant bird, he must not droop—but die."

The feast is o'er. 'Tis night, the dead of night—
     Unbroken stillness broods o'er earth and deep;
From Egypt's heaven of soft and starry light
     The moon looks cloudless o'er a world of sleep:
105 For those who wait the morn's awakening beams,
     The battle signal to decide their doom,
Have sunk to feverish rest and troubled dreams;
     Rest, that shall soon be calmer in the tomb,
Dreams, dark and ominous, but *there* to cease,
110 When sleep the lords of war in solitude and peace.

Wake, slumberers, wake! Hark! heard ye not a sound
     Of gathering tumult?—Near and nearer still
Its murmur swells. Above, below, around,
     Bursts a strange chorus forth, confused and shrill.
115 Wake, Alexandria! through thy streets the tread
     Of steps unseen is hurrying, and the note
Of pipe, and lyre, and trumpet, wild and dread,
     Is heard upon the midnight air to float;
And voices, clamorous as in frenzied mirth,
120 Mingle their thousand tones, which are not of the earth.

These are no mortal sounds—their thrilling strain
     Hath more mysterious power, and birth more high;
And the deep horror chilling every vein
     Owns them of stern, terrific augury.°   *prophecy*
125 Beings of worlds unknown! ye pass away,
     O ye invisible and awful throng!
Your echoing footsteps and resounding lay
     To Cæsar's camp exulting move along.
Thy gods forsake thee, Antony! the sky
130 By that dread sign reveals—thy doom—"Despair and die!"[2]

                                                                    1819

Evening Prayer, at a Girls' School[1]

Now in thy youth, beseech of Him
     Who giveth, upbraiding not,
That his light in thy heart becomes not dim,
     And his love be unforgot;

---

1. The eagle was a symbol of the Roman empire, adopted by Napoleon for imperial France.
2. "To-morrow in the battle think on me, / And fall thy edgeless sword; despair and die!" Shakespeare, *Richard III* [5.3.135–36; Hemans's note]. The voice in Shakespeare's play is the ghost of Richard's brother, one of several he murdered to get to the throne—all of whom haunt him the night before the battle in which he is killed.
1. First published in *Forget Me Not*, a gift-book annual, this poem was an anthology favorite in the 19th century.

And thy God, in the darkest of days, will be
Greenness, and beauty, and strength to thee.

—Bernard Barton[2]

Hush! 'tis a holy hour—the quiet room
   Seems like a temple, while yon soft lamp sheds
A faint and starry radiance, through the gloom
   And the sweet stillness, down on bright young heads,
5   With all their clustering locks, untouch'd by care,
   And bowed, as flowers are bowed with night, in prayer.

Gaze on—'tis lovely! childhood's lip and cheek,
   Mantling° beneath its earnest brow of thought!   *blushing*
Gaze, yet what seest thou in those fair and meek
10   And fragile things, as but for sunshine wrought?
Thou seest what grief must nurture for the sky,
What Death must fashion for eternity!

O joyous creatures! that will sink to rest,
   Lightly, when those pure orisons° are done,   *prayers*
15   As birds with slumber's honey-dew oppres'd,
   Midst the dim folded leaves, at set of sun—
Lift up your hearts! though yet no sorrow lies
Dark in the summer-heaven of those clear eyes.

Though fresh within your breasts th' untroubled springs
20   Of hope make melody where'er ye tread,
And o'er your sleep bright shadows, from the wings
   Of spirits visiting but youth, be spread—
Yet in those flute-like voices, mingling low,
Is woman's tenderness—how soon her wo!

25 Her lot° is on you!—silent tears to weep,   *fate*
   And patient smiles to wear through suffering's hour,
And sumless riches, from affection's deep,
   To pour on broken reeds—a wasted shower!
And to make idols, and to find them clay,[3]
30   And to bewail that worship—therefore pray!

Her lot is on you!—to be found untir'd,
   Watching the stars out by the bed of pain,
With a pale cheek, and yet a brow inspir'd,
   And a true heart of hope, though hope be vain;
35   Meekly to bear with wrong, to cheer decay,
And, oh! to love through all things—therefore pray!

And take the thought of this calm vesper-time,°   *evening prayer*
   With its low murmuring sounds and silvery light,
On through the dark days fading from their prime,

---

2. From *The Ivy, Addressed to a Young Friend.* Barton, "the Quaker poet," first sponsored by Quakers, would later secure a pension after he dedicated *Household Verses* (1845) to Queen Victoria.

3. Stock metaphors: "suffering's hour" is any affliction and particularly childbirth; "broken reeds" are those who die; "idols" of "clay" are those (probably husbands) who prove unworthy of the worship they court.

40   As a sweet dew to keep your souls from blight!
Earth will forsake—Oh! happy to have given
Th'unbroken heart's first fragrance unto Heaven.

1826

CASABIANCA   Hemans's most famous (and most scurrilously parodied) poem is based on an episode from the British campaign against Napoleon in Egypt. Ten-year-old Giacomo Jocante Casabianca was a boy-sailor on *L'Orient*, the admiral ship of Napoleon's fleet, commanded by fellow Corsican Louis de Casabianca (Giacomo's father) and destroyed in the Battle of the Nile, August 1798, by the British fleet, commanded by Horatio Nelson. Widely celebrated for this crucial victory, Nelson lost his life in 1805 in the Battle of Trafalgar, his even more celebrated victory over the restored French fleet. The coffin that conveyed him home was crafted from the iron and wrecked mainmast of *L'Orient*, a strange trophy for his future burial presented to him by one of his captains just after the Battle of the Nile. It did not serve this ultimate purpose, but, famously, "was cut in pieces, which were distributed as relics," so Southey writes in *Life of Horatio, Lord Nelson* (1813, much reissued). This *Life* was Hemans's likely source, but one she noticeably alters. Southey reports that "Casa-Bianca, and his son, a brave boy, only ten years old...were seen floating on a shattered mast when the ship blew up"—"a tremendous explosion...followed by a silence not less awful"; "the first sound which broke the silence was the dash of her shattered masts and yards, falling into the water from the vast height to which they had been exploded....no incident in war...has ever equalled the sublimity of this co-instantaneous pause, and all its circumstances." One of Southey's sources reports that the mast to which the Casabiancas clung was the mainmast used for Nelson's trophy-coffin.

Casabianca[1]

The boy stood on the burning deck
    Whence all but he had fled;
The flame that lit the battle's wreck,
    Shone round him o'er the dead.

5   Yet beautiful and bright he stood,
    As born to rule the storm;
A creature of heroic blood,
    A proud, though child-like form.

The flames rolled on—he would not go,
10   Without his Father's word;
That Father, faint in death below,
    His voice no longer heard.

He called aloud:—"Say, Father, say
    If yet my task is done?"
15   He knew not that the chieftain lay
    Unconscious of his son.

"Speak, Father!" once again he cried,
    "If I may yet be gone!
And"—but the booming shots replied,
20   And fast the flames rolled on.

1. Young Casabianca, a boy about thirteen years old, son to the Admiral of the Orient, remained at his post (in the Battle of the Nile) after the ship had taken fire, and all the guns had been abandoned; and perished in the explosion of the vessel, when the flames had reached the powder [Hemans's note; Hemans makes the boy older].

Upon his brow he felt their breath,
    And in his waving hair,
And looked from that lone post of death,
    In still, yet brave despair.

25   And shouted but once more aloud,
        "My Father! must I stay?"
While o'er him fast, through sail and shroud,
    The wreathing fires made way.

They wrapt the ship in splendour wild,
30   They caught the flag on high,
And streamed above the gallant child,
    Like banners in the sky.

There came a burst of thunder sound—
    The boy—oh! where was he?
35   Ask of the winds that far around
    With fragments strewed the sea!—

With mast, and helm, and pennon° fair,   *pennant*
    That well had borne their part—
But the noblest thing which perished there
40   Was that young faithful heart!

1826   1829

from Records of Woman, with Other Poems[1]
The Bride of the Greek Isle[2]

Fear!—I'm a Greek, and how should I fear death?
A slave, and wherefore should I dread my freedom?

        * * * * * *

I will not live degraded.   *Sardanapalus*[3]

Come from the woods with the citron-flowers,
Come with your lyres for the festal hours,
Maids of bright Scio!° They came, and the breeze   *Greek island*
Bore their sweet songs o'er the Grecian seas;—
5   They came, and Eudora° stood rob'd and crown'd,   *"Good Gift"*
The bride of the morn, with her train around.
Jewels flash'd out from her braided hair,
Like starry dews midst the roses there;
Pearls on her bosom quivering shone,
10   Heav'd by her heart thro' its golden zone;

---

1. Hemans's most popular volume was published in 1828, with a dedication to Joanna Baillie; as in Wollstonecraft, *Woman* identifies a universal category. A subsection of *Miscellaneous Poems* included *The Graves of a Household* and *The Homes of England*.
2. Founded on a circumstance related in the Second Series of the Curiosities of Literature [Hemans's note]—a popular collection of literary and historical anecdotes,

with some original material, by Isaac D'Israeli (1823).
3. Byron's play (1821), about the last days of Assyrian king Sardanapalus and his lover, his Greek slave Myrrha. The first quotation (1.2.479–80) is her pledge to die with him if he is defeated by his enemies (he is); the second (1.2.629) is his commitment to suicide over captivity, exile, or worse, enslavement.

But a brow, as those gems of the ocean pale,
Gleam'd from beneath her transparent veil;
Changeful and faint was her fair cheek's hue,
Tho' clear as a flower which the light looks through;
15   And the glance of her dark resplendent eye,
For the aspect of woman at times too high,
Lay floating in mists, which the troubled stream
Of the soul sent up o'er its fervid beam.
She look'd on the vine at her father's door,
20   Like one that is leaving his native shore;
She hung o'er the myrtle once call'd her own,
As it greenly wav'd by the threshold stone;
She turn'd—and her mother's gaze brought back
Each hue of her childhood's faded track.
25   Oh! hush the song, and let her tears
Flow to the dream of her early years!
Holy and pure are the drops that fall
When the young bride goes from her father's hall;
She goes unto love yet untried and new,
30   She parts from love which hath still been true;
Mute be the song and the choral strain,
Till her heart's deep well-spring is clear again!
She wept on her mother's faithful breast,
Like a babe that sobs itself to rest;
35   She wept—yet laid her hand awhile
In *his* that waited her dawning smile,
Her soul's affianced, nor cherish'd less
For the gush of nature's tenderness!
She lifted her graceful head at last—
40   The choking swell of her heart was past;
And her lovely thoughts from their cells found way
In the sudden flow of a plaintive lay.[4]

THE BRIDE'S FAREWELL

Why do I weep?—to leave the vine
    Whose clusters o'er me bend,—
45   The myrtle—yet, oh! call it mine!—
    The flowers I lov'd to tend.
A thousand thoughts of all things dear,
    Like shadows o'er me sweep,
I leave my sunny childhood here,
50   Oh, therefore let me weep!

I leave thee, sister! we have play'd
    Thro' many a joyous hour,
Where the silvery green of the olive shade
    Hung dim o'er fount and bower.
55   Yes, thou and I, by stream, by shore,

---

4. A Greek Bride, on leaving her father's house, takes leave of her friends and relatives frequently in extemporaneous verse.—See [Claude] Fauriel's *Chants Populaires de la Grèce Moderne* [1824–1825; Hemans's note].

In song, in prayer, in sleep,
Have been as we may be no more—
    Kind sister, let me weep!

I leave thee, father! Eve's bright moon
60   Must now light other feet,
With the gather'd grapes, and the lyre in tune,
    Thy homeward step to greet.
Thou in whose voice, to bless thy child,
    Lay tones of love so deep,
65 Whose eye o'er all my youth hath smiled—
    I leave thee! let me weep!

Mother! I leave thee! on thy breast,
    Pouring out joy and wo,
I have found that holy place of rest
70   Still changeless,—yet I go!
Lips, that have lull'd me with your strain,
    Eyes, that have watch'd my sleep!
Will earth give love like *yours* again?
    Sweet mother! let me weep!

75 And like a slight young tree, that throws
The weight of rain from its drooping boughs,
Once more she wept. But a changeful thing
Is the human heart, as a mountain spring,
That works its way, thro' the torrent's foam,
80 To the bright pool near it, the lily's home!
It is well!—the cloud, on her soul that lay,
Hath melted in glittering drops away.
Wake again, mingle, sweet flute and lyre!
She turns to her lover, she leaves her sire.
85 Mother! on earth it must still be so,
Thou rearest the lovely to see them go!

They are moving onward, the bridal throng,
Ye may track their way by the swells of song;
Ye may catch thro' the foliage their white robes' gleam,
90 Like a swan midst the reeds of a shadowy stream.
Their arms bear up garlands, their gliding tread
Is over the deep-vein'd violet's bed;
They have light leaves around them, blue skies above,
An arch for the triumph of youth and love!

2

95 Still and sweet was the home that stood
In the flowering depths of a Grecian wood,
With the soft green light o'er its low roof spread,
As if from the glow of an emerald shed,
Pouring thro' lime-leaves that mingled on high,
100 Asleep in the silence of noon's clear sky.
Citrons amidst their dark foliage glow'd,

Making a gleam round the lone abode;
Laurels o'erhung it, whose faintest shiver
Scatter'd out rays like a glancing river;
105   Stars of the jasmine its pillars crown'd,
Vine-stalks its lattice and walls had bound,
And brightly before it a fountain's play
Flung showers thro' a thicket of glossy bay,
To a cypress which rose in that flashing rain,
110   Like one tall shaft of some fallen fane.°   *temple*

And thither Ianthis had brought his bride,
And the guests were met by that fountain-side;
They lifted the veil from Eudora's face,
It smiled out softly in pensive grace,
115   With lips of love, and a brow serene,
Meet for the soul of the deep wood-scene.—
Bring wine, bring odours!—the board is spread—
Bring roses! a chaplet° for every head!   *wreath*
The wine-cups foam'd, and the rose was shower'd
120   On the young and fair from the world embower'd,
The sun look'd not on them in that sweet shade,
The winds amid scented boughs were laid;
But there came by fits, thro' some wavy tree,
A sound and a gleam of the moaning sea.

125   Hush! be still!—was that no more
        Than the murmur from the shore?
        Silence!—did thick rain-drops beat
        On the grass like trampling feet?—
        Fling down the goblet, and draw the sword!
130   The groves are filled with a pirate-horde!
        Thro' the dim olives their sabres shine;—
        Now must the red blood stream for wine!

The youths from the banquet to battle sprang,
The woods with the shriek of the maidens rang;
135   Under the golden-fruited boughs
There were flashing poniards,°and darkening brows,   *daggers*
Footsteps, o'er garland and lyre that fled;
And the dying soon on a greensward bed.

Eudora, Eudora! *thou* dost not fly!—
140   She saw but Ianthis before her lie,
With the blood from his breast in a gushing flow,
Like a child's large tears in its hour of wo,
And a gathering film in his lifted eye,
That sought his young bride out mournfully.—
145   She knelt down beside him, her arms she wound,
Like tendrils, his drooping neck around,
As if the passion of that fond grasp
Might chain in life with its ivy-clasp.

But they tore her thence in her wild despair,

150 The sea's fierce rovers—they left him there;
 They left to the fountain a dark-red vein,
 And on the wet violets a pile of slain,
 And a hush of fear thro' the summer-grove,—
 So clos'd the triumph of youth and love!

3

155 Gloomy lay the shore that night,
  When the moon, with sleeping light,
  Bath'd each purple Sciote° hill,—   *of Scio*
  Gloomy lay the shore, and still.
  O'er the wave no gay guitar
160 Sent its floating music far;
  No glad sound of dancing feet
  Woke, the starry hours to greet.
  But a voice of mortal wo,
  In its changes wild or low,
165 Thro' the midnight's blue repose,
  From the sea-beat rocks arose,
  As Eudora's mother stood
  Gazing o'er th' Egean flood,°   *Aegean Sea*
  With a fix'd and straining eye—
170 Oh! was the spoilers' vessel nigh?
  Yes! there, becalm'd in silent sleep,
  Dark and alone on a breathless deep,°   *sea*
  On a sea of molten silver dark,
  Brooding it frown'd that evil bark!°   *ship*
175 There its broad pennon° a shadow cast,   *flag*
  Moveless and black from the tall still mast,
  And the heavy sound of its flapping sail,
  Idly and vainly wooed the gale.
  Hush'd was all else—had ocean's breast
180 Rock'd e'en Eudora that hour to rest?

To rest?—the waves tremble!—what piercing cry
Bursts from the heart of the ship on high?
What light through the heavens, in a sudden spire,
Shoots from the deck up? Fire! 'tis fire!
185 There are wild forms hurrying to and fro,
Seen darkly clear on that lurid glow;
There are shout, and signal-gun, and call,
And the dashing of water,—but fruitless all!
Man may not fetter, nor ocean tame
190 The might and wrath of the rushing flame!
It hath twined the mast like a glittering snake,
That coils up a tree from a dusky brake;
It hath touch'd the sails, and their canvass rolls
Away from its breath into shrivell'd scrolls;
195 It hath taken the flag's high place in air,
And redden'd the stars with its wavy glare,
And sent out bright arrows, and soar'd in glee,

To a burning mount midst the moonlight sea.
The swimmers are plunging from stern and prow—
200   Eudora, Eudora! where, where art thou?
The slave and his master alike are gone.—
Mother! who stands on the deck alone?
The child of thy bosom!—and lo! a brand°   *torch*
Blazing up high in her lifted hand!
205   And her veil flung back, and her free dark hair
Sway'd by the flames as they rock and flare;
And her fragile form to its loftiest height
Dilated, as if by the spirit's might,
And her eye with an eagle-gladness fraught,—
210   Oh! could this work be of woman wrought?
Yes! 'twas her deed!—by that haughty smile
It was her's!—She hath kindled her funeral pile!
Never might shame on that bright head be,
Her blood was the Greek's, and hath made her free.

215   Proudly she stands, like an Indian bride
On the pyre with the holy dead beside;[5]
But a shriek from her mother hath caught her ear,
As the flames to her marriage-robe draw near,
And starting, she spreads her pale arms in vain
220   To the form they must never infold again.

One moment more, and her hands are clasp'd,
Fallen is the torch they had wildly grasp'd,
Her sinking knee unto Heaven is bow'd,
And her last look rais'd thro' the smoke's dim shroud,
225   And her lips as in prayer for her pardon move—
Now the night gathers o'er youth and love!

1825   1828

Properzia Rossi

Properzia Rossi, a celebrated female sculptor of Bologna, possessed also of talents for poetry and music, died in consequence of an unrequited attachment.—A painting by Ducis, represents her showing her last work, a basso-relievo of Ariadne, to a Roman Knight, the object of her affection, who regards it with indifference.[1]

5. A reference to the *suttee* (from the Sanskrit for "faithful wife"), a suicide rite, culturally compelled and enforced, and still prevalent in 1828, performed as a second marriage, whereby an Indian widow immolates herself on her husband's funeral pyre, ostensibly to unite the couple beyond the grave. In temporal terms, such suicide reflects a cultural attitude about the worthlessness of widows; it also was security against unhappy or ambitious wives conspiring in the murder of their husbands; it was abolished by British law in 1829. In *Sardanapalus* Myrrha declares her superiority to the suttee when she willingly joins the

king in a suicide conflagration.
1. Hemans's headnote refers to Properzia de'Rossi (c. 1491–1530) and Louis Ducis, a French painter (1775–1847). The subject of Rossi's sculpture, Ariadne, was the daughter of King Minos of Crete, who imprisoned the Greek prince Theseus in his labyrinth, there to be killed by the Minotaur. In love with Theseus, Ariadne told him how to slay the monster and escape the labyrinth. He married her, but after they left Crete, he abandoned her on the Greek isle of Naxos, where she pined away for him.

————Tell me no more, no more
Of my soul's lofty gifts! Are they not vain
To quench its haunting thirst for happiness?
Have I not lov'd, and striven, and fail'd to bind
One true heart unto me, whereon my own
Might find a resting-place, a home for all
Its burden of affections? I depart,
Unknown, tho' Fame goes with me; I must leave
The earth unknown. Yet it may be that death
Shall give my name a power to win such tears
As would have made life precious.[2]

1

One dream of passion and of beauty more!
And in its bright fulfilment let me pour
My soul away! Let earth retain a trace
Of that which lit my being, tho' its race
5   Might have been loftier far.—Yet one more dream!
From my deep spirit one victorious gleam
Ere I depart! For thee alone, for thee!
May this last work, this farewell triumph be,
Thou, lov'd so vainly! I would leave enshrined
10   Something immortal of my heart and mind,
That yet may speak to thee when I am gone,
Shaking thine inmost bosom with a tone
Of lost affection;—something that may prove
What she hath been, whose melancholy love
15   On thee was lavish'd; silent pang and tear,
And fervent song, that gush'd when none were near,
And dream by night, and weary thought by day,
Stealing the brightness from her life away,—
While thou————Awake! not yet within me die,
20   Under the burden and the agony
Of this vain tenderness,—my spirit, wake!
Ev'n for thy sorrowful affection's sake,
Live! in thy work breathe out!—that he may yet,
Feeling sad mastery there, perchance regret
25   Thine unrequited gift.

2

It comes,—the power
Within me born, flows back; my fruitless dower
That could not win me love. Yet once again
I greet it proudly, with its rushing train
Of glorious images:—they throng—they press—
30   A sudden joy lights up my loneliness,—
I shall not perish all!

2. The epigraph is also by Hemans.

The bright work grows
Beneath my hand, unfolding, as a rose,
Leaf after leaf, to beauty; line by line,
I fix my thought, heart, soul, to burn, to shine,
35   Thro' the pale marble's veins. It grows—and now
I give my own life's history to thy brow,
Forsaken Ariadne! thou shalt wear
My form, my lineaments; but oh! more fair,
Touch'd into lovelier being by the glow
40   Which in me dwells, as by the summer-light
All things are glorified. From thee my wo
        Shall yet look beautiful to meet his sight,
When I am pass'd away. Thou art the mould
Wherein I pour the fervent thoughts, th' untold,
45   The self-consuming! Speak to him of me,
Thou, the deserted by the lonely sea,
With the soft sadness of thine earnest eye,
Speak to him, lorn one! deeply, mournfully,
Of all my love and grief! Oh! could I throw
50   Into thy frame a voice, a sweet, and low,
And thrilling voice of song! when he came nigh,
To send the passion of its melody
Thro' his pierc'd bosom—on its tones to bear
My life's deep feeling, as the southern air
55   Wafts the faint myrtle's breath,—to rise, to swell,
To sink away in accents of farewell,
Winning but one, *one* gush of tears, whose flow
Surely my parted spirit yet might know,
If love be strong as death!

3
Now fair thou art,
60   Thou form, whose life is of my burning heart!
Yet all the vision that within me wrought,
    I cannot make thee! Oh! I might have given
Birth to creations of far nobler thought,
    I might have kindled, with the fire of heaven,
65   Things not of such as die! But I have been
Too much alone; a heart whereon to lean,
With all these deep affections, that o'erflow[3]
My aching soul, and find no shore below;
An eye to be my star, a voice to bring
70   Hope o'er my path, like sounds that breathe of spring,
These are denied me—dreamt of still in vain,—
Therefore my brief aspirings from the chain,
Are ever but as some wild fitful song,
Rising triumphantly, to die ere long
75   In dirge-like echoes.

3. The verb, reflected in Hemans's enjambment, evokes both "flow over from" and "overwhelm."

4
Yet the world will see
Little of this, my parting work, in thee,
    Thou shalt have fame! Oh, mockery! give the reed
From storms a shelter,—give the drooping vine
Something round which its tendrils may entwine,—
80   Give the parch'd flower a rain-drop, and the meed
Of love's kind words to woman! Worthless fame!
That in *his* bosom wins not for my name
Th' abiding-place it ask'd! Yet how my heart,
In its own fairy world of song and art,
85   Once beat for praise!—Are those high longings o'er?
That which I have been can I be no more?—
Never, oh! never more; tho' still thy sky
Be blue as then, my glorious Italy!
And tho' the music, whose rich breathings fill
90   Thine air with soul, be wandering past me still,
And tho' the mantle of thy sunlight streams,
Unchang'd on forms, instinct° with poet-dreams;   *inspired*
Never, oh! never more! Where'er I move,
The shadow of this broken-hearted love
95   Is on me and around! Too well *they* know,
    Whose life is all within, too soon and well,
When there the blight hath settled;—but I go
    Under the silent wings of peace to dwell;
From the slow wasting, from the lonely pain,
100   The inward burning of those words—"*in vain,*"
    Sear'd on the heart—I go. 'Twill soon be past.
Sunshine, and song, and bright Italian heaven,
    And thou, oh! thou, on whom my spirit cast
Unvalued wealth,—who know'st not what was given
105   In that devotedness,—the sad, and deep,
And unrepaid—farewell! If I could weep
Once, only once, belov'd one! on thy breast,
Pouring my heart forth ere I sink to rest!
But that were happiness, and unto me
110   Earth's gift is *fame*. Yet I was form'd to be
So richly blest! With thee to watch the sky,
Speaking not, feeling but that thou wert nigh;
With thee to listen, while the tones of song
Swept ev'n as part of our sweet air along,
115   To listen silently;—with thee to gaze
On forms, the deified of olden days,
This had been joy enough;—and hour by hour,
From its glad well-springs drinking life and power,
How had my spirit soar'd, and made its fame
120   A glory for thy brow!—Dreams, dreams!—the fire
Burns faint within me. Yet I leave my name—
    As a deep thrill may linger on the lyre
When its full chords are hush'd—awhile to live,

125
And one day haply in thy heart revive
Sad thoughts of me:—I leave it, with a sound,
A spell o'er memory, mournfully profound,
I leave it, on my country's air to dwell,—
Say proudly yet—"'Twas her's who lov'd me well!"

Indian Woman's Death-Song

An Indian woman, driven to despair by her husband's desertion of her for another wife, entered a canoe with her children, and rowed it down the Mississippi towards a cataract. Her voice was heard from the shore singing a mournful death-song, until overpowered by the sound of the waters in which she perished. The tale is related in Long's Expedition to the source of St Peter's River.[1]

Non, je ne puis vivre avec un coeur brisé. Il faut que je
retrouve la joie, et que je m'unisse aux esprits libres de l'air.

Bride of Messina, Translated by Madame de Staël[2]

Let not my child be a girl, for very sad is the life of a woman.

The Prairie[3]

Down a broad river of the western wilds,
Piercing thick forest glooms, a light canoe
Swept with the current: fearful was the speed
Of the frail bark, as by a tempest's wing
5
Borne leaf-like on to where the mist of spray
Rose with the cataract's thunder.—Yet within,
Proudly, and dauntlessly, and all alone,
Save that a babe lay sleeping at her breast,
A woman stood: upon her Indian brow
10
Sat a strange gladness, and her dark hair wav'd
As if triumphantly. She press'd her child,
In its bright slumber, to her beating heart,
And lifted her sweet voice, that rose awhile
Above the sound of waters, high and clear,
15
Wafting a wild proud strain, her song of death.

Roll swiftly to the Spirit's land, thou mighty stream and free!
Father of ancient waters,[4] roll! and bear our lives with thee!
The weary bird that storms have toss'd, would seek the sunshine's calm,
And the deer that hath the arrow's hurt, flies to the woods of balm.

1. William Hippolytus Keating, *Narrative of an Expedition to the Source of St. Peter's River* (1824) which includes notes from Stephen Long's narrative of his explorations in the American plains states in the 1820s.
2. "No, I cannot live with a broken heart. I must regain joy and join the free spirits of the air"; de Staël's translation of Friedrich Schiller's verse in *De L'Allemagne* (1810).
3. From Chapter 26 of the novel by American James

Fenimore Cooper (1827), spoken by the third wife of a Sioux Chief, who has proposed a fourth marriage to a "white" Mexican woman captured by his tribe, promising her status as favorite. The third wife never fully recovers from this betrayal and her sense of inferiority to the white woman.
4. "Father of waters," the Indian name for the Mississippi [Hemans's note].

20   Roll on!—my warrior's eye hath look'd upon another's face,
     And mine hath faded from his soul, as fades a moonbeam's trace;
     My shadow comes not o'er his path, my whisper to his dream,
     He flings away the broken reed—roll swifter yet, thou stream!

     The voice that spoke of other days is hush'd within *his* breast,
25   But *mine* its lonely music haunts, and will not let me rest;
     It sings a low and mournful song of gladness that is gone,
     I cannot live without that light—Father of waves! roll on!

     Will he not miss the bounding step that met him from the chase?°   *hunt*
     The heart of love that made his home an ever sunny place?
30   The hand that spread the hunter's board, and deck'd his couch of yore?—
     He will not!—roll, dark foaming stream, on to the better shore!

     Some blessed fount amidst the woods of that bright land must flow,
     Whose waters from my soul may lave the memory of this wo;
     Some gentle wind must whisper there, whose breath may waft away
35   The burden of the heavy night, the sadness of the day.

     And thou, my babe! tho' born, like me, for woman's weary lot,
     Smile!—to that wasting of the heart, my own! I leave thee not;
     Too bright a thing art *thou* to pine in aching love away,
     Thy mother bears thee far, young Fawn! from sorrow and decay.

40   She bears thee to the glorious bowers where none are heard to weep,
     And where th' unkind one hath no power again to trouble sleep;
     And where the soul shall find its youth, as wakening from a dream,—
     One moment, and that realm is ours—On, on, dark rolling stream!

Joan of Arc, in Rheims

Jeanne d'Arc avait eu la joie de voir à Chalons quelques amis de son enfance. Une joie plus ineffable encore l'attendait à Rheims, au sein de son triomphe: Jacques d'Arc, son père y se trouva, aussitôt que de troupes de Charles VII y furent entrées; et comme les deux frères de notre Héroïne l'avaient accompagnés, elle se vit, pour un instant au milieu de sa famille, dans les bras d'un père vertueux. *Vie de Jeanne d'Arc*.[1]

     Thou hast a charmed cup, O Fame!
       A draught that mantles° high,   *froths*
     And seems to lift this earth-born frame
       Above mortality:
     Away! to me—a woman—bring
     Sweet waters from affection's spring.[2]

1. Joan of Arc had the pleasure of seeing at Chalons some childhood friends. A still more exquisite pleasure awaited her at Rheims in the scene of her triumph: Jacques d'Arc, her father, arrived there just as the troops of Charles VII made their entry; and as the two brothers of our Heroine had accompanied him, she found herself for a moment, in the midst of her family, in the arms of a good father (*Almanach de Gotha*, 1822). French national heroine, Jeanne d'Arc (1412–1431), inspired by what she took to be holy voices, encouraged the Dauphin (prince and claimant to the throne) to throw off the English claim to France. She led his troops against the siege of Orleans and conducted him to the cathedral at Rheims, where he was crowned Charles VII and she received acclaim. She continued to lead the war against the English but suffered defeats and was taken prisoner in 1430; with Charles's cowardly acquiescence, she was turned over to the French ecclesiastical court, which tried her for witchcraft, blasphemy, and dressing in male armor; uneasy about punishing so popular a heroine, however, they handed her over to the English, who burned her at the stake in the marketplace at Rouen. 2. The first stanza of Hemans's *Woman and Fame*.

That was a joyous day in Rheims of old,
When peal on peal of mighty music roll'd
Forth from her throng'd cathedral; while around,
A multitude, whose billows made no sound,
5   Chain'd to a hush of wonder, tho' elate
With victory, listen'd at their temple's gate.
And what was done within?—within, the light
      Thro' the rich gloom of pictured windows flowing,
Tinged with soft awfulness a stately sight,
10   The chivalry of France, their proud heads bowing
In martial vassalage!—while midst that ring,
And shadow'd by ancestral tombs, a king
Receiv'd his birthright's crown. For this, the hymn
      Swell'd out like rushing waters, and the day
15   With the sweet censer's misty breath grew dim,
      As thro' long aisles it floated o'er th' array
Of arms and sweeping stoles. But who, alone
And unapproach'd, beside the altar-stone,
With the white banner, forth like sunshine streaming,
20   And the gold helm, thro' clouds of fragrance gleaming,
Silent and radiant stood?—the helm was rais'd,
And the fair face reveal'd, that upward gaz'd,
      Intensely worshipping:—a still, clear face,
Youthful, but brightly solemn!—Woman's cheek
25   And brow were there, in deep devotion meek,
      Yet glorified with inspiration's trace
On its pure paleness; while, enthron'd above,
The pictur'd virgin, with her smile of love,
Seem'd bending o'er her votaress.—That slight form!
30   Was that the leader thro' the battle storm?
Had the soft light in that adoring eye,
Guided the warrior where the swords flash'd high?
'Twas so, even so!—and thou, the shepherd's child,
Joanne,[3] the lowly dreamer of the wild!
35   Never before, and never since that hour,
Hath woman, mantled° with victorious power,   *flushed, covered*
Stood forth as *thou* beside the shrine didst stand,
Holy amidst the knighthood of the land;
And beautiful with joy and with renown,
40   Lift thy white banner o'er the olden crown,
Ransom'd for France by thee!

                              The rites are done.
Now let the dome with trumpet-notes be shaken,
And bid the echoes of the tombs awaken,
      And come thou forth, that Heaven's rejoicing sun
45   May give thee welcome from thine own blue skies,
      Daughter of victory!—A triumphant strain,

---

3. A hybrid of French "Jeanne" and English "Joan."

A proud rich stream of warlike melodies,
   Gush'd thro' the portals of the antique fane,°   *temple*
And forth she came.—Then rose a nation's sound—
50   Oh! what a power to bid the quick heart bound,
The wind bears onward with the stormy cheer
Man gives to glory on her high career!
Is there indeed such power?—far deeper dwells
In one kind household voice, to reach the cells
55   Whence happiness flows forth!—The shouts that fill'd
The hollow heaven tempestuously, were still'd
One moment; and in that brief pause, the tone,
As of a breeze that o'er her home had blown,
Sank on the bright maid's heart.—"Joanne!"—Who spoke
60   Like those whose childhood with *her* childhood grew
Under one roof?—"Joanne!"—*that* murmur broke
      With sounds of weeping forth!—She turn'd—she knew
Beside her, mark'd from all the thousands there,
In the calm beauty of his silver hair,
65   The stately shepherd; and the youth, whose joy
From his dark eye flash'd proudly; and the boy,
The youngest-born, that ever lov'd her best:
"Father! and ye, my brothers!"—On the breast
Of that grey sire she sank—and swiftly back,
70   Ev'n in an instant, to their native track
Her free thoughts flowed.—She saw the pomp no more—
The plumes, the banners:—to her cabin-door,
And to the Fairy's fountain in the glade,[4]
Where her young sisters by her side had play'd,
75   And to her hamlet's chapel, where it rose
Hallowing the forest unto deep repose,
Her spirit turn'd.—The very wood-note, sung
      In early spring-time by the bird, which dwelt
Where o'er her father's roof the beech-leaves hung,
80   Was in her heart; a music heard and felt,
Winning her back to nature.[5]—She unbound
      The helm of many battles from her head,
And, with her bright locks bow'd to sweep the ground,
      Lifting her voice up, wept for joy, and said,—
85   "Bless me, my father, bless me! and with thee,
To the still cabin and the beechen-tree,
Let me return!"[6]
                Oh! never did thine eye
Thro' the green haunts of happy infancy
Wander again, Joanne!—too much of fame
90   Had shed its radiance on thy peasant-name;
And bought alone by gifts beyond all price,[7]

---

4. A beautiful fountain near Domremi, believed to be haunted by fairies, and a favourite resort of Jeanne d'Arc in her childhood [Hemans's note].
5. The world of nature and also her deepest female "nature" as daughterly maid, before her days of fame.

6. Evoking Jesus's parable of the prodigal son, Luke 15.11–32.
7. Salvation through Christ is a promise "great beyond price" (2 Peter).

The trusting heart's repose, the paradise
Of home with all its loves, doth fate allow
The crown of glory unto woman's brow.[8]

1826

1828

The Homes of England

"Where's the coward that would not dare
To fight for such a land?"   —*Marmion*[1]

The stately Homes of England,
    How beautiful they stand!
Amidst their tall ancestral trees,
    O'er all the pleasant land.
5   The deer across their greensward bound
    Through shade and sunny gleam,
And the swan glides past them with the sound
    Of some rejoicing stream.

The merry Homes of England!
10   Around their hearths by night,
What gladsome looks of household love
    Meet, in the ruddy light!
There woman's voice flows forth in song,
    Or childhood's tale is told,
15 Or lips move tunefully along
    Some glorious page of old.

The blessed Homes of England!
    How softly on their bowers
Is laid the holy quietness
20   That breathes from Sabbath-hours!
Solemn, yet sweet, the church-bell's chime
    Floats through their woods at morn;
All other sounds, in that still time,
    Of breeze and leaf are born.

25   The Cottage Homes of England!
    By thousands on her plains,
They are smiling o'er the silvery brooks,
    And round the hamlet-fanes.
Thro' glowing orchards forth they peep,
30   Each from its nook of leaves,
And fearless there the lowly° sleep,   *the poor*
    As the bird beneath their eaves.

---

8. "Thou never from that hour in Paradise / Found'st either sweet repast, or sound repose," Milton writes of Eve
as she leaves Adam's side (*Paradise Lost* 9.406–407).
1. A poetic romance (1808) by Walter Scott.

The free, fair Homes of England!
    Long, long, in hut and hall,
35   May hearts of native proof be rear'd
        To guard each hallowed wall!
And green for ever be the groves,
        And bright the flowery sod,
Where first the child's glad spirit loves
40   Its country and its God!

1827   1828

The Graves of a Household

They grew in beauty, side by side,
    They filled one home with glee;—
Their graves are sever'd, far and wide,
    By mount, and stream, and sea.[1]

5   The same fond mother bent at night
      O'er each fair sleeping brow;
She had each folded flower in sight,—
      Where are those dreamers now?

One, midst the forest of the west,
10   By a dark stream is laid—
The Indian knows his place of rest,
    Far in the cedar shade.

The sea, the blue lone sea, hath one,
    He lies where pearls lie deep;
15   *He* was the lov'd of all, yet none
      O'er his low bed may weep.

One sleeps where southern vines are drest
    Above the noble slain:
He wrapt his colours round his breast
20   On a blood-red field of Spain.[2]

And one—o'er *her* the myrtle showers
    Its leaves, by soft winds fann'd;
She faded midst Italian flowers,—
    The last of that bright band.

25   And parted thus they rest, who play'd
    Beneath the same green tree;
Whose voices mingled as they pray'd
    Around one parent knee!

They that with smiles lit up the hall,
30   And cheer'd with song the hearth,—

---

1. Hemans's younger brother died in Canada in 1821.
2. Hemans's brothers and husband had served in the war in Spain against Napoleon; her first long poem was *England and Spain, or Valour and Patriotism* (1808).

Alas, for love! if *thou* wert all,
And naught beyond, oh, earth!

1825   1828

Corinne at the Capitol[1]

"Les femmes doivent penser [...] qu'il est dans cette carrière
bien peu de sorts qui puissent valoir la plus obscure vie d'une
femme aimée et d'une mère heureuse."   —*Madame de Staël*[2]

Daughter of th' Italian heaven!
Thou, to whom its fires are given,
Joyously thy car hath roll'd
Where the conqueror's pass'd of old;
5   And the festal sun that shone,
O'er three hundred triumphs gone,[3]
Makes thy day of glory bright,
With a shower of golden light.

Now thou tread'st th' ascending road,
10   Freedom's foot so proudly trode;
While, from tombs of heroes borne,
From the dust of empire shorn,
Flowers upon thy graceful head,
Chaplets° of all hues, are shed,   head-wreaths
15   In a soft and rosy rain,
Touch'd with many a gemlike stain.

Thou hast gain'd the summit now!
Music hails thee from below;—
Music, whose rich notes might stir
20   Ashes of the sepulchre;
Shaking with victorious notes
All the bright air as it floats.

1. Hemans's title is that of Book 2 of Germaine de Staël's *Corinne, ou l'Italie* (1807). Quickly translated into English, this novel was immensely popular, especially with women, not only Hemans, but also Jane Austen, Mary Godwin (Shelley), Elizabeth Barrett (Browning), George Eliot, and Harriet Beecher (Stowe). It was read as the definitive story of female "genius"—an inspirational and cautionary tale about artistic celebrity at the cost of domestic happiness. De Staël was famous for her intellect, her social charm, her essays, her forthright conversation (including blunt criticism of Napoleon), and her salons, attended by political and literary celebrities. Her heroine, Corinne, half English and half Italian, is a famous performing poet living in Italy, where she meets English Lord Nelvil. With him, we see her for the first time, at the Roman Capitol, celebrated in all her glorious genius. De Staël elaborates her triumph, transcribing "Corinne's Improvisation at the Capitol," and concluding in apotheosis: "No longer a fearful woman, she was an inspired priestess, joyously devoting herself to the cult of genius." Corinne and Nelvil fall in love, but she declines his proposal of marriage, fearing a too-constrained life as an English wife. He returns to England and marries her half-sister, a fully proper English maid. When Corinne learns of this, she dies of grief.

2. *De L'influence des Passions* (1796): "Women should consider that in this career there are very few destinies equal in worth to the most obscure life of a beloved wife and a happy mother." *Femme* means both *wife* and *woman*.

3. The trebly hundred triumphs.—Byron [Hemans's note] referring to *Childe Harold's Pilgrimage*, 4.731, a comment on the number of triumphs (victory parades), in ancient Rome.

Well may woman's heart beat high
Unto that proud harmony!

25   Now afar it rolls—it dies—
And thy voice is heard to rise
With a low and lovely tone
In its thrilling power alone;
And thy lyre's deep silvery string,
30   Touch'd as by a breeze's wing,
Murmurs tremblingly at first,
Ere the tide of rapture burst.

All the spirit of thy sky
Now hath lit thy large dark eye,
35   And thy cheek a flush hath caught
From the joy of kindled thought;
And the burning words of song
From thy lip flow fast and strong,
With a rushing stream's delight
40   In the freedom of its might.

Radiant daughter of the sun!
Now thy living wreath is won.
Crown'd of Rome!—Oh! art thou not
Happy in that glorious lot?—
45   Happier, happier far than thou,
With the laurel on thy brow,[4]
She that makes the humblest hearth
Lovely but to one on earth!

1827   1830

Woman and Fame[1]

Happy—happier far than thou,
With the laurel on thy brow;
She that makes the humblest hearth,
Lovely but to one on earth.

Thou hast a charmed cup, O Fame!
    A draught° that mantles° high,   *drink / blushes*
And seems to lift this earthly frame
    Above mortality.
5   Away! to me—a woman—bring
Sweet waters from affection's spring.[2]

---

4. The laurel wreath is a public honor for glorious accomplishment; laurel is the badge of Apollo, classical god of poetry (whence "Poet Laureate").

1. Published in *The Amulet*, an annual. The epigraph is a self-quotation from the end of *Corinne at the Capitol*.
2. The epigraph for *Joan of Arc, in Rheims.*

Thou hast green laurel-leaves that twine
    Into so proud a wreath;[3]
For that resplendent gift of thine,
10   Heroes have smiled in death.
Give *me* from some kind hand a flower,
    The record of one happy hour!

Thou hast a voice, whose thrilling tone
    Can bid each life-pulse beat,
15 As when a trumpet's note hath blown,
    Calling the brave to meet:
But mine, let mine—a woman's breast,
    By words of home-born love be bless'd.

A hollow sound is in thy song,
20   A mockery in thine eye,
To the sick heart that doth but long
    For aid, for sympathy;
For kindly looks to cheer it on,
For tender accents that are gone.

25 Fame, Fame! thou canst not be the stay
    Unto the drooping reed,
The cool fresh fountain, in the day
    Of the soul's feverish need;
Where must the lone one turn or flee?—
30 Not unto thee, oh! not to thee!

1827–1829   1829

RESPONSES

Francis Jeffrey: from *A review of Felicia Hemans's Poetry*[1]

Women we fear, cannot do every thing; nor even every thing they attempt. But what they can do, they do, for the most part, excellently—and much more frequently with an absolute and perfect success, than the aspirants of our rougher and more ambitious sex. They cannot, we think, represent naturally the fierce and sullen passions of men—nor their coarser vices—nor even scenes of actual business or contention—and the mixed motives, and strong and faulty characters, by which affairs of moment are usually conducted on the great theatre of the world. For much of this they are disqualified by the delicacy of their training and habits, and the still more disabling delicacy which pervades their conceptions and feelings; and from

---

3. See n. 4 to *Corinne at the Capitol.*

1. Francis Jeffrey cofounded the quarterly *Edinburgh Review* in 1802 and was its editor and chief literary reviewer until 1829. Appearing in one of the most influential periodicals of these decades, his essay on Hemans is relevant

not just to her popularity (it was generously excerpted by publishers of her collected works), but also for its comments about women writers and its sense of which contemporary male writers seemed destined for posterity.

much they are excluded by their actual inexperience of the realities they might wish to describe—by their substantial and incurable ignorance of business—of the way in which serious affairs are actually managed—and the true nature of the agents and impulses that give movement and direction to the stronger currents of ordinary life. Perhaps they are also incapable of long moral or political investigations, where many complex and indeterminate elements are to be taken into account, and a variety of opposite probabilities to be weighed before coming to a conclusion. They are generally too impatient to get at the ultimate results, to go well through with such discussions; and either stop short at some imperfect view of the truth, or turn aside to repose in the shadow of some plausible error. This, however, we are persuaded, arises entirely from their being seldom set on such tedious tasks. Their proper and natural business is the practical regulation of private life, in all its bearings, affections, and concerns; and the questions with which they have to deal in that most important department, though often of the utmost difficulty and nicety, involve, for the most part, but few elements; and may generally be better described as delicate than intricate;—requiring for their solution rather a quick tact and fine perception than a patient or laborious examination. For the same reason, they rarely succeed in long works, even on subjects the best suited to their genius; their natural training rendering them equally averse to long doubt and long labour.

For all other intellectual efforts, however, either of the understanding or the fancy, and requiring a thorough knowledge either of man's strength or his weakness, we apprehend them to be, in all respects, as well qualified as their brethren of the stronger sex; while, in their perceptions of grace, propriety, ridicule—their power of detecting artifice, hypocrisy, and affectation—the force and promptitude of their sympathy, and their capacity of noble and devoted attachment, and of the efforts and sacrifices it may require, they are, beyond all doubt, our superiors.

Their business being, as we have said, with actual or social life, and the colours it receives from the conduct and dispositions of individuals, they unconsciously acquire, at a very early age, the finest perception of character and manners, and are almost as soon instinctively schooled in the deep and dangerous learning of feeling and emotion; while the very minuteness with which they make and meditate on these interesting observations, and the finer shades and variations of sentiment which are thus treasured and recorded, trains their whole faculties to a nicety and precision of operation, which often discloses itself to advantage in their application to studies of a very different character. When women, accordingly, have turned their minds—as they have done but too seldom—to the exposition or arrangement of any branch of knowledge, they have commonly exhibited, we think, a more beautiful accuracy, and a more uniform and complete justness of thinking, than their less discriminating brethren. There is a finish and completeness about every thing they put out of their hands, which indicates not only an inherent taste for elegance and neatness, but a habit of nice observation, and singular exactness of judgment.

It has been so little the fashion, at any time, to encourage women to write for publication, that it is more difficult than it should be, to prove these truths by examples. Yet there are enough, within the reach of a very careless and superficial glance over the open field of literature, to enable us to explain, at least, and illustrate, if not entirely to verify, our assertions. No *man*, we will venture to say, could have written the Letters of Madame de Sevigné, or the Novels of Miss Austin, or the Hymns and

Early Lessons of Mrs Barbauld, or the Conversations of Mrs Marcet.[2] These performances, too, are not only essentially and intensely feminine, but they are, in our judgment, decidedly more perfect than any masculine productions with which they can be brought into comparison. They accomplish more completely all the ends at which they aim, and are worked out with a gracefulness and felicity of execution which excludes all idea of failure, and entirely satisfies the expectations they may have raised. We might easily have added to these instances. There are many parts of Miss Edgeworth's earlier stories, and of Miss Mitford's sketches and descriptions, and not a little of Mrs Opie's, that exhibit the same fine and penetrating spirit of observation, the same softness and delicacy of hand, and unerring truth of delineation, to which we have alluded as characterising the purer specimens of female art.[3] * * *

We think the poetry of Mrs Hemans a fine exemplification of Female Poetry—and we think it has much of the perfection which we have ventured to ascribe to the happier productions of female genius.

It may not be the best imaginable poetry, and may not indicate the very highest or most commanding genius; but it embraces a great deal of that which gives the very best poetry its chief power of pleasing; and would strike us, perhaps, as more impassioned and exalted, if it were not regulated and harmonized by the most beautiful taste. It is infinitely sweet, elegant, and tender—touching, perhaps, and contemplative, rather than vehement and overpowering; and not only finished throughout with an exquisite delicacy, and even serenity of execution, but informed with a purity and loftiness of feeling, and a certain sober and humble tone of indulgence and piety, which must satisfy all judgments, and allay the apprehensions of those who are most afraid of the passionate exaggerations of poetry. The diction is always beautiful, harmonious, and free—and the themes, though of infinite variety, uniformly treated with a grace, originality and judgment, which mark the same master hand. These themes she has borrowed, with the peculiar interest and imagery that belong to them, from the legends of different nations, and the most opposite states of society; and has contrived to retain much of what is interesting and peculiar in each of them, without adopting, along with it, any of the revolting or extravagant excesses which may characterise the taste or manners of the people or the age from which it has been derived. She has thus transfused into her German or Scandinavian legends the imaginative and daring tone of the originals, without the mystical exaggerations of the one, or the painful fierceness and coarseness of the other—she has preserved the clearness and elegance of the French, without their coldness or affectation—and the tenderness and simplicity of the early Italians, without their diffuseness or languor. Though occasionally expatiating, somewhat fondly and at large, amongst the sweets of her own planting, there is, on the whole, a great condensation and brevity in most of her pieces, and, almost without exception, a most judicious and vigorous conclusion. The great merit, however, of her poetry, is undoubtedly in its tenderness and its beautiful imagery. * * *

---

2. Marie de Rabutin-Chantal, Marquise de Sévigné (1626–1696), French lady of fashion, famous for her lively letters to her daughter and friends describing life in the court, the city, the country, and at home. "Austin" is Jane Austen. For Barbauld, see her principal listing (page 65); her *Hymns in Prose for Children* (1781) was translated into several European languages. Jane Marcet (1769–1858) was famous for her educational series *Conversations on Chemistry, intended especially for the Female*

Sex (1806; 15 later editions), *Conversations on Natural Philosophy* (1815), science for children; and her especially admired *Conversations on Political Economy* (1816; much reprinted).

3. Maria Edgeworth (1767–1829), best-selling Irish novelist; Mary Russell Mitford (1787–1859), woman of letters, whose sketches, *Our Village*, began to appear in 1824; Amelia Opie (1769–1853), fiction writer, poet, and abolitionist.

We have seen too much of the perishable nature of modern literary fame, to venture to predict to Mrs Hemans that hers will be immortal, or even of very long duration. Since the beginning of our critical career, we have seen a vast deal of beautiful poetry pass into oblivion, in spite of our feeble efforts to recall or retain it in remembrance. The tuneful quartos of Southey are already little better than lumber:—And the rich melodies of Keats and Shelley,—and the fantastical emphasis of Wordsworth,—and the plebeian pathos of Crabbe, are melting fast from the fields of our vision. The novels of Scott have put out his poetry. Even the splendid strains of Moore are fading into distance and dimness, except where they have been married to immortal music; and the blazing star of Byron himself is receding from its place of pride. We need say nothing of Milman, and Croly, and Atherstone, and Hood, and a legion of others, who, with no ordinary gifts of taste and fancy, have not so properly survived their fame, as been excluded by some hard fatality from what seemed their just inheritance. The two who have the longest withstood this rapid withering of the laurel, and with the least marks of decay on their branches, are Rogers and Campbell; neither of them, it may be remarked, voluminous writers, and both distinguished rather for the fine taste and consummate elegance of their writings, than for that fiery passion, and disdainful vehemence, which seemed for a time to be so much more in favour with the public.[4]

If taste and elegance, however, be titles to enduring fame, we might venture securely to promise that rich boon to the author before us; who adds to those great merits a tenderness and loftiness of feeling, and an ethereal purity of sentiment, which could only emanate from the soul of a woman. She must beware of becoming too voluminous; and must not venture again on any thing so long as the "Forest Sanctuary."[5] But, if the next generation inherits our taste for short poems, we are persuaded it will not readily allow her to be forgotten. For we do not hesitate to say, that she is, beyond all comparison, the most touching and accomplished writer of occasional verses that our literature has yet to boast of.

William Wordsworth: from *Prefatory Note to* Extempore Effusion[1]

Mrs Hemans was unfortunate as a poetess in being obliged by circumstances to write for money, and that so frequently and so much, that she was compelled to look out for subjects wherever she could find them, and to write as expeditiously as possible. As a woman, she was to a considerable degree a spoilt child of the world. She had been early in life distinguished for talent, and poems of hers were published while she was a girl. She had also been handsome in her youth, but her education had been most unfortunate. She was totally ignorant of housewifery, and could as easily have managed the spear of Minerva as her needle.[2] It was from observing these deficiencies, that, one day while she was under my roof, I *purposely* directed her attention to household

4. For Keats, Shelley, Byron (all dead by this time), Wordsworth, Southey, Scott, and Moore, see their listings. Other writers mentioned are George Crabbe (1754–1832), Thomas Campbell (1777–1844), Thomas Hood (1799–1845)—all read through the 19th century and beyond—and Samuel Rogers (1763–1855), George Croly (1780–1860), Edwin Atherstone (1788–1872), and Henry Hart Milman (1791–1868).
5. Jeffrey's article takes as occasion the second editions

of *Records of Woman* and *The Forest Sanctuary*, an epic romance that Hemans regarded as "almost, if not altogether, the best" of her works.
1. For the stanza on Hemans, see page 592.
2. Roman counterpart of Athena, Greek goddess of wisdom, Minerva is fabled to have sprung, in full armor and battle cry, from Jupiter's forehead; she is typically represented as stern and regal, clad in armor and holding a spear.

economy, and told her I had purchased *Scales*, which I intended to present to a young lady[3] as a wedding present; pointed out their utility (for her especial benefit), and said that no *ménage* [household] ought to be without them. Mrs Hemans, not in the least suspecting my drift, reported this saying, in a letter to a friend at the time, as a proof of my simplicity. Being disposed to make large allowances for the faults of her education and the circumstances in which she was placed, I felt most kindly disposed towards her, and took her part upon all occasions, and I was not a little affected by learning that after she withdrew to Ireland, a long and severe sickness raised her spirit as it depressed her body. This I heard from her most intimate friends, and there is striking evidence of it in a poem written and published not long before her death. These notices of Mrs Hemans would be very unsatisfactory to her intimate friends, as indeed they are to myself, not so much for what is said, but what for brevity's sake is left unsaid. Let it suffice to add, there was much sympathy between us, and, if opportunity had been allowed me to see more of her, I should have loved and valued her accordingly; as it is, I remember her with true affection for her amiable qualities, and, above all, for her delicate and irreproachable conduct during her long separation from an unfeeling husband, whom she had been led to marry from the romantic notions of inexperienced youth. Upon this husband I never heard her cast the least reproach, nor did I ever hear her even name him, though she did not wholly forbear to touch upon her domestic position; but never so as that any fault could be found with her manner of adverting to it.

1835

John Clare
1793–1864

The horizon of John Clare's world was defined by the village of Helpston, Northamptonshire, in which he was born to a barely literate farmhand and an illiterate mother. His formal education was sparse, though his poetry shows his knowledge of Milton and Thomson, and he read Wordsworth, Coleridge, Keats, and Byron (two late long poems are titled *Childe Harold* and *Don Juan*). By the "indefatigable savings of a penny and a half-penny," young Clare purchased fairy tales from hawkers, recalling, "I firmly believed every page I read and considerd I possessd in these the chief learning and literature of the country." His own writing was produced swiftly and with few revisions in time seized from agricultural labor, then hid "with all secresy possible" in "an old unused cubbard" or hole in the wall.

Clare's condition placed him in the line of those "natural geniuses" eagerly sought by eighteenth-century primitivism: Stephen Duck "The Thresher Poet" (1705–1756), Robert Bloomfield (*The Farmer's Boy*, 1800), Ann Yearsley "The Milkmaid Poet" (1752–1806), and Robert Burns (1759–1796) had all been fit into the stereotype of the peasant poet. In 1817 John Taylor saw Clare's proposal to publish a volume of poetry by subscription; in 1820 his firm brought out *Poems Descriptive of Rural Life and Scenery*, marketing it as the work of a young "Northamptonshire Peasant," a description that fixed Clare's regional and class identity.

---

3. According to Hemans, a poet's daughter.

The book enjoyed critical and popular success, with four editions in a year. The vogue that brought Clare attention quickly came to constrain him: his Evangelical patron disapproved of his social criticism and "vulgar" manner, while Taylor sought to broaden his appeal by standardizing his language and cutting his poems. Clare's pungent dialect usages—which illustrate by contrast how thoroughly Wordsworth "purified" the "language really used by men" in *Lyrical Ballads*—and belief "that what ever is intellig[i]ble to others is grammer and what ever is commonsense is not far from correctness" offended the norms of polite literature. "Grammer in learning," Clare adamantly insisted to Taylor in a phrase that by linking style and politics makes clear the twin offenses he posed to the urban book-buying public, "is like Tyranny in government—confound the bitch Ill never be her slave." Taylor found himself in the awkward position of intermediary between an audience for poetry increasingly represented by genteel women and a prickly lower-class male writer: "*false delicasy* damn it I hate it beyond every thing those prompt up misses brought up in those seminaries of mysterious wickedness (Boarding Schools) what will please 'em? why we well know—but while their heart & soul loves to extravagance (what we dare not mention) false delicasy's seriousness muscles [muzzles] up the mouth & condemns it." If that explosion reminds one of the "rhodomontade" with which Keats defended his sexually more explicit revisions to *The Eve of St. Agnes*, the distance between the literariness of Keats, whom Clare admired, and Clare's plainness is manifest in his objection that Keats "keeps up a constant alusion or illusion to the grecian mythology & there I cannot follow . . . the frequency of such classical accompaniment makes it wearisome to the reader where behind every rose bush he looks for a Venus & under every laurel a thrumming Appollo."

Before long, readers lost interest in Clare's rough independence from their expectations of verse. *The Village Minstrel* (1821) sold badly and *The Shepherd's Calendar* (1827) even worse; *The Rural Muse* (1835) got good reviews but not a readership. By then Clare had left Helpston for Northborough, where he moved to a cottage provided by another patron, hoping to set himself up as a farmer. Though the move measured only a few miles, it broke his firm sense of place. In 1837 Clare was admitted to an asylum for the mentally ill in southeast England, from which he escaped in 1841, walking back the eighty miles to Northborough. He was recommitted to an asylum in Northampton, where he spent the remaining years of his life. Yet Clare never ceased to write. His early poetry depicts with marked individuality a rural existence threatened by enclosure and by widening difference between classes; long and close observation of the landscape, of animals and birds, produced sharply detailed images in "a language that is ever green" (*Pastoral Poesy*) and far removed from the "egotistical sublime" to which Wordsworth's experience of nature gives rise. Clare once proclaimed of *Composed Upon Westminster Bridge* "I think it (& woud say it to the teeth of the critic in spite of his rule & compass) that it owns no equal in the English language," but he mocked Wordsworth's "affectations of simplicity." The delusions and instabilities of Clare's identity in the asylum period led to a poetry of fantasized memory and loss that possesses a strange and often visionary power.

New editions of Clare's writings have freed his texts from the emendations of their first publication and have brought unpublished materials to view, winning him the audience he missed in his own time. As illustration, we print two versions of *Written in November*, the first from the manuscripts edited by Eric Robinson and David Powell, the source of our texts, the second as the poem appeared in *The Village Minstrel* (1821).

Written in November (manuscript)

Autumn I love thy latter end to view
In cold novembers day so bleak & bare
When like lifes dwindled thread worn nearly thro

Wi lingering pottering° pace & head bleached bare   *dawdling, uncertain*
5   Thou like an old man bids the world adieu
I love thee well & often when a child
Have roamd the bare brown heath a flower to find
& in the moss clad vale & wood bank wild
Have cropt the little bell flowers paley blue
10   That trembling peept the sheltering bush behind
When winnowing north winds cold & blealy° blew   *coldly, bleakly*
How have I joyd wi dithering° hands to find   *shivering*
Each fading flower & still how sweet the blast
Would bleak novembers hour Restore the joy thats past

Written in November

Autumn, I love thy parting look to view
   In cold November's day, so bleak and bare,
When, thy life's dwindled thread worn nearly thro',
   With ling'ring pott'ring pace, and head bleach'd bare,
5   Thou, like an old man, bidd'st the world adieu.
   I love thee well: and often, when a child,
Have roam'd the bare brown heath a flower to find;
   And in the moss-clad vale, and wood-bank wild
Have cropt the little bell-flowers, pearly blue,
10   That trembling peep the shelt'ring bush behind.
When winnowing north-winds cold and bleaky blew,
   How have I joy'd, with dithering hands, to find
Each fading flower; and still how sweet the blast,
   Would bleak November's hour restore the joy that's past.

c. 1812   1821

Songs Eternity

What is songs eternity
Come and see
Can it noise and bustle be
Come and see
5   Praises sung or praises said
Can it be
Wait awhile and these are dead
Sigh sigh
Be they high or lowly bred
10   They die

What is songs eternity
Come and see
Melodys of earth and sky
Here they be
15   Songs once sung to adams ears

Can it be
—Ballads of six thousand years
Thrive thrive
Songs awakened with the spheres
20   Alive

Mighty songs that miss decay
What are they
Crowds and citys pass away
Like a day
25   Books are writ and books are read
What are they
Years will lay them with the dead
Sigh sigh
Trifles unto nothing wed
30   They die

Dreamers list the honey be[e]
Mark the tree
Where the blue cap tootle tee
Sings a glee
35   Sung to adam and to eve
Here they be
When floods covered every bough
Noahs ark
Heard that ballad singing now
40   Hark hark

Tootle tootle tootle tee
Can it be
Pride and fame must shadows be
Come and see
45   Every season own her own
Bird and be[e]
Sing creations music on
Natures glee
Is in every mood and tone
50   Eternity

The eternity of song
Liveth here
Natures universal tongue
Singeth here
55   Songs Ive heard and felt and seen
Everywhere
Songs like the grass are evergreen
The giver
Said live and be and they have been
60   For ever

1812–1831

[The Lament of Swordy Well]¹

Pe[ti]tioners are full of prayers
To fall in pitys way
But if her hand the gift forbears
Theyll sooner swear then pray
5   They're not the worst to want who lurch
On plenty with complaints
No more then those who go to church
Are eer the better saints

I hold no hat to beg a mite
10   Nor pick it up when thrown
Nor limping leg I hold in sight
But pray to keep my own
Where profit gets his clutches in
Theres little he will leave
15   Gain stooping for a single pin
Will stick it on his sleeve

For passers bye I never pin
No troubles to my breast
Nor carry round some names
20   More money from the rest
Im swordy well a piece of land
Thats fell upon the town
Who worked me till I couldnt stand
And crush me now Im down

25   In parish bonds I well may wail
Reduced to every shift
Pity may grieve at troubles tale
But cunning shares the gift
Harvests with plenty on his brow
30   Leaves losses taunts with me
Yet gain comes yearly with the plough
And will not let me be

Alas dependance thou'rt a brute
Want only understands
35   His feelings wither branch and root
That falls in parish hands
The muck that clouts the ploughmans shoe
The moss that hides the stone
Now Im become the parish due
40   Is more then I can own

---

1. Usually known as Swaddy Well, an ancient stone quarry used by the Romans. During Clare's childhood alive with flowers, birds, and animals, it had been enclosed, and given by the parish to the overseers of the roads for mending-stone. The speaker of the poem is the land itself.

Though Im no man yet any wrong
Some sort of right may seek
And I am glad if een a song
Gives me the room to speak
45 Ive got among such grubbing geer[2]
And such a hungry pack
If I brought harvests twice a year
They'd bring me nothing back

When war their tyrant prices got
50 I trembled with alarms
They fell and saved my little spot
Or towns had turned to farms
Let profit keep an humble place
That gentry may be known
55 Let pedigrees their honours trace
And toil enjoy its own

The silver springs grown naked dykes
Scarce own a bunch of rushes
When grain got high the tasteless tykes°   *bumpkins*
60 Grubbed up trees banks and bushes
And me they turned me inside out
For sand and grit and stones
And turned my old green hills about
And pickt my very bones

65 These things that claim my own as theirs
Where born but yesterday
But ere I fell to town affairs
I were as proud as they
I kept my horses cows and sheep
70 And built the town below
Ere they had cat or dog to keep
And then to use me so

Parish allowance gaunt and dread
Had it the earth to keep
75 Would even pine° the bees to dead   *torment*
To save an extra keep
Prides workhouse[3] is a place that yields
From poverty its gains
And mines a workhouse for the fields
80 A starving the remains

The bees flye round in feeble rings
And find no blossom bye

---

2. That is, those who dig the land for gain.   3. Able-bodied poor supported by the parish were con-
                        fined to the workhouse to labor.

Then thrum° their almost weary wings   *beat monotonously*
Upon the moss and die
85 Rabbits that find my hills turned oer
Forsake my poor abode
They dread a workhouse like the poor
And nibble on the road

If with a clover bottle° now   *bundle*
90 Spring dares to lift her head
The next day brings the hasty plough
And makes me miserys bed
The butterflyes may wir and come·
I cannot keep em now
95 Nor can they bear my parish home
That withers on my brow

No now not een a stone can lie
Im just what eer they like
My hedges like the winter flye
100 And leave me but the dyke
My gates are thrown from off the hooks
The parish thoroughfare
Lord he thats in the parish books
Has little wealth to spare

105 I couldnt keep a dust of grit
Nor scarce a grain of sand
But bags and carts claimed every bit
And now theyve got the land
I used to bring the summers life
110 To many a butterflye
But in oppressions iron strife
Dead tussocks° bow and sigh   *tufts of grass*

Ive scarce a nook to call my own
For things that creep or flye
115 The beetle hiding neath a stone
Does well to hurry bye
Stock[4] eats my struggles every day
As bare as any road
He's sure to be in somethings way
120 If eer he stirs abroad

I am no man to whine and beg
But fond of freedom still
I hing° no lies on pitys peg   *hang*
To bring a gris° to mill   *grain for grinding*
125 On pitys back I neednt jump
My looks speak loud alone

4. Generic name for a dull person.

My only tree they've left a stump
And nought remains my own

My mossy hills gains greedy hand
130   And more then greedy mind
Levels into a russet land
Nor leaves a bent° behind   *stalk of coarse grass*
In summers gone I bloomed in pride
Folks came for miles to prize
135   My flowers that bloomed no where beside
And scarce believed their eyes

Yet worried with a greedy pack
They rend and delve and tear
The very grass from off my back
140   Ive scarce a rag to wear
Gain takes my freedom all away
Since its dull suit I wore
And yet scorn vows I never pay
And hurts me more and more

145   And should the price of grain get high
Lord help and keep it low
I shant possess a single flye
Or get a weed to grow
I shant possess a yard of ground
150   To bid a mouse to thrive
For gain has put me in a pound
I scarce can keep alive

I own Im poor like many more
But then the poor mun° live   *must*
155   And many came for miles before
For what I had to give
But since I fell upon the town
They pass me with a sigh
Ive scarce the room to say sit down
160   And so they wander bye

Though now I seem so full of clack°   *chatter*
Yet when yer' riding bye
The very birds upon my back
Are not more fain to flye
165   I feel so lorn° in this disgrace   *forlorn*
God send the grain to fall
I am the oldest in the place
And the worst served of all

Lord bless ye I was kind to all
170   And poverty in me
Could always find a humble stall
A rest and lodging free
Poor bodys with an hungry ass

I welcomed many a day
175   And gave him tether room and grass
And never said him nay

There was a time my bit of ground
Made freemen of the slave
The ass no pindard[5] dare to pound
180   When I his supper gave
The gipseys camp was not affraid
I made his dwelling free
Till vile enclosure came and made
A parish slave of me

185   The gipseys further on sojourn
No parish bounds they like
No sticks I own and would earth burn
I shouldnt own a dyke
I am no friend to lawless work
190   Nor would a rebel be
And why I call a christian turk[6]
Is they are turks to me

And if I could but find a friend
With no deciet to sham
195   Who'd send me some few sheep to tend
And leave me as I am
To keep my hills from cart and plough
And strife of mongerel men
And as spring found me find me now
200   I should look up agen

And save his Lordships woods that past
The day of danger dwell
Of all the fields I am the last
That my own face can tell
205   Yet what with stone pits delving holes
And strife to buy and sell
My name will quickly be the whole
Thats left of swordy well

c. 1821–1824   1935

[The Mouse's Nest]

I found a ball of grass among the hay
And proged° it as I passed and went away   *prodded*
And when I looked I fancied somthing stirred
And turned agen and hoped to catch the bird
5   When out an old mouse bolted in the wheat
With all her young ones hanging at her teats
She looked so odd and so grotesque to me
I ran and wondered what the thing could be

---

5. A man employed to impound stray animals.   6. A long-standing term for traitor.

And pushed the knapweed° bunches where I stood   *purple flower*
10   When the mouse hurried from the crawling brood
The young ones squeaked and when I went away
She found her nest again among the hay
The water oer the pebbles scarce could run
And broad old cesspools° glittered in the sun   *pools of standing water*

c. 1835–1837   1935

Clock a Clay°   *ladybug*

In the cowslips peeps° I lye[1]   *primrose blossoms*
Hidden from the buzzing fly
While green grass beneath me lies
Pearled wi' dew like fishes eyes
5   Here I lye a Clock a clay
Waiting for the time o' day[2]

While grassy forests quake surprise
And the wild wind sobs and sighs
My gold home rocks as like to fall
10   On its pillars green and tall
When the pattering rain drives bye
Clock a Clay keeps warm and dry

Day by day and night by night
All the week I hide from sight
15   In the cowslips peeps I lye
In rain and dew still warm and dry
Day and night and night and day
Red black spotted clock a clay

My home it shakes in wind and showers
20   Pale green pillar top't wi' flowers
Bending at the wild winds breath
Till I touch the grass beneath
Here still I live lone clock a clay
Watching for the time of day

c. 1848   1873

"I Am"

I am—yet what I am, none cares or knows;
    My friends forsake me like a memory lost:—
I am the self-consumer of my woes;—
    They rise and vanish in oblivion's host,
5   Like shadows in love's frenzied stifled throes:—
And yet I am, and live—like vapours tost

Into the nothingness of scorn and noise,—
    Into the living sea of waking dreams,

1. Echoing Ariel's song in Shakespeare, *The Tempest,*   2. Refers to the children's game of counting the taps
5.1.89: "In a cowslip's bell I lie."   needed to make the ladybug fly away home.

Where there is neither sense of life or joys,
10   But the vast shipwreck of my lifes esteems;
Even the dearest, that I love the best
Are strange—nay, rather stranger than the rest.

I long for scenes, where man hath never trod
     A place where woman never smiled or wept
15   There to abide with my Creator, God;
     And sleep as I in childhood, sweetly slept,
Untroubling, and untroubled where I lie,
The grass below—above the vaulted sky.

c. 1842   1848

The Mores[1]

Far spread the moorey ground a level scene
Bespread with rush and one eternal green
That never felt the rage of blundering plough
Though centurys wreathed springs blossoms on its brow
5   Still meeting plains that stretched them far away
In uncheckt shadows of green brown and grey
Unbounded freedom ruled the wandering scene
Nor fence of ownership crept in between
To hide the prospect of the following eye
10 Its only bondage was the circling sky
One mighty flat undwarfed by bush and tree
Spread its faint shadow of immensity
And lost itself which seemed° to eke its bounds
In the blue mist the orisons° edge surrounds   *horizon's*
15 Now this sweet vision of my boyish hours
Free as spring clouds and wild as summer flowers
Is faded all—a hope that blossomed free
And hath been once no more shall ever be
Inclosure[2] came and trampled on the grave
20 Of labours rights and left the poor a slave
And memorys pride ere want to wealth did bow
Is both the shadow and the substance now
The sheep and cows were free to range as then
Where change might prompt nor felt the bonds of men
25 Cows went and came with evening morn and night
To the wild pasture as their common right
And sheep unfolded° with the rising sun   *unpenned*
Heard the swains shout and felt their freedom won
Tracked the red fallow field and heath and plain
30 Then met the brook and drank and roamed again
The brook that dribbled on as clear as glass
Beneath the roots they hid among the grass
While the glad shepherd traced their tracks along

---

1. The moors around Helpston.   2. For enclosure, see period introduction, pages 21–22.

Free as the lark and happy as her song
35 But now alls fled and flats of many a dye
That seemd to lengthen with the following eye
Moors loosing from the sight far smooth and blea°   *wild*
Where swopt the plover in its pleasure free
Are vanished now with commons wild and gay
40 As poets visions of lifes early day
Mulberry bushes where the boy would run
To fill his hands with fruit are grubbed and done
And hedgrow briars—flower lovers overjoyed
Came and got flower pots—these are all destroyed
45 And sky bound mores in mangled garbs are left
Like mighty giants of their limbs bereft
Fence now meets fence in owners little bounds
Of field and meadow large as garden grounds
In little parcels little minds to please
50 With men and flocks imprisoned ill at ease
Each little path that led its pleasant way
As sweet as morning leading night astray
Where little flowers bloomed round a varied host
That travel felt delighted to be lost
55 Nor grudged the steps that he had taen as vain
When right roads traced his journeys end again
Nay on a broken tree hed sit awhile
To see the mores and fields and meadows smile
Sometimes with cowslaps° smothered—then all white   *cowslip, primrose*
60 With daiseyes—then the summers splendid sight
Of corn fields crimson oer the "headach"° bloomd   *poppy*
Like splendid armys for the battle plumed
He gazed upon them with wild fancys eye
As fallen landscapes from an evening sky
65 These paths are stopt—the rude philistines thrall
Is laid upon them and destroyed them all
Each little tyrant with his little sign
Shows where man claims earth glows no more divine
On paths to freedom and to childhood dear
70 A board sticks up its notice "no road here"
And on the tree with ivy overhung
The hated sign by vulgar taste is hung
As tho the very birds should learn to know
When they go there they must no further go
75 This with the poor scared freedom bade good bye
And much the[y] feel it in the smothered sigh
And birds and trees and flowers without a name
All sighed when lawless laws enclosure came
And dreams of plunder in such rebel schemes
80 Have found too truly that they were but dreams

c. 1820–1825   1935

John Keats
1795–1821

"A thing of beauty is a joy for ever"; "tender is the night"; "Beauty is truth; truth Beauty"—
these phrases are so well known that we may forget that they were unheard before John
Keats. Keats's brief career ran only from 1814, when he wrote his first poem, to 1820, when
he revised his sonnet *Bright Star* on board a ship to Italy. "Oh, for ten years, that I may overwhelm / Myself in poesy," he said in 1816. Not even getting this decade, his active life as a
writer stopped around his twenty-fourth birthday. At age twenty-four, Chaucer had yet to
write anything, and if Shakespeare had died at twenty-four, he would be known only (if at
all) by a few early works. What if Keats had lived until 1881, like that Victorian sage Thomas
Carlyle, also born in 1795?

The drama of Keats is not just the poignancy of genius cut off in youth but also his
humble origins—a focus of ridicule during and after his lifetime by class-conscious reviewers
and aristocratic poets. Son of a livery-stable keeper who had married the owner's daughter
and inherited the suburban London business, Keats attended the progressive Enfield School.
Here he was tutored and befriended by Charles Cowden Clarke, the headmaster's son, who
introduced him to literature, music, the theater. When Keats was nine years old, his father
died in a riding accident and his mother remarried immediately; her commitment to her
children was as erratic as it was doting, and her presence at home was inconstant. Keats was
deeply attached to her and devastated when she disappeared for four years, leaving them all
with his grandmother. When she returned sick and consumptive, he nursed her, and she
died when he was fourteen; the welter of emotions she left in him is reflected in the series
of adored, inconstant women around which so much of his poetry revolves. The children
were remanded to the guardianship of a practical businessman whose chief concern was to
apprentice the boys to some viable trade. Unimaginative himself and unsympathetic to any
passion for learning and poetry, he apprenticed Keats to a London hospital surgeon in the
grim days before anesthesia. Keats stayed with this training long enough to be licensed as an
apothecary (more a general practitioner than a druggist), but he frequently took time off to
read and to write poetry. When he came of age in 1816, he gave up medicine and set out to
make a living as a poet.

Keats was already enjoying the society of Clarke and his circle of politically progressive
thinkers, artists, poets, journalists, and publishers, many of whom became close friends—
among them Leigh Hunt, also a poet as well as a radical journalist. Hunt launched Keats's
career, publishing him in his weekly paper, *The Examiner*, and advertising him as one of
the rising "Young Poets." It was through Hunt that Keats met some of the chief nonestab-
lishment writers of the day—William Wordsworth, William Hazlitt, Charles Lamb, Percy
Shelley—and the controversial painter Benjamin Robert Haydon. His inaugural volume,
published in 1817, included twenty sonnets, a favorite form for him, as well as Spenserian
stanzas, odes, verse epistles, romance fragments, and meditative long poems on the subject
of poetry itself. The writers that mattered most to him were Spenser (his first poem, written
in 1814, was a deft "Imitation of Spenser" in Spenserian stanzas), Shakespeare, and am-
bivalently, Milton, and among his contemporaries, Wordsworth and Byron, though again
with intelligent ambivalence. Keats warmly dedicated the 1817 *Poems* to Hunt and in a
long concluding piece (*Sleep and Poetry*) voiced sharp criticism of what he saw as the arid
formalism of eighteenth-century neoclassical poetry, which still had prestige with conservative or aristocratic writers, including Byron. Byron never forgave Keats for this tirade, and it

Charles Brown, *Portrait of John Keats*, 1819. Brown, Keats's friend, and traveling companion in the summer of 1818, invited Keats to move in with him after the death of his brother Tom in December. Keats remained at Wentworth Place until the end of summer 1820, when he left for Italy. This charcoal sketch, which was unknown in the 19th century, presents Keats in a stylish Regency mode: handsome, contemplative, rakishly "poetic."

immediately provoked the Tory journalists, who were only too eager to jab at their political enemy Hunt through his protégé. Published in a year when civil rights were weakened and the radical publisher William Hone brought to trial, *Poems* was viciously ridiculed in reviews marked by social snobbery and political prejudice, and Keats was indelibly tagged "the Cockney Poet"—one of Hunt's suburban radicals. He was stung, but determined to prove himself with his next effort, *Endymion*, initiated as part of a contest with Hunt and Shelley to see who could write a 4,000-line poem by the end of 1817. The only one to complete the challenge, Keats set off with a sense that it would be "a test" or "trial" of his talents. "A thing of beauty is a joy for ever" begins this tale of a shepherd-prince who dreams of a goddess, and on waking is profoundly alienated from ordinary life in the world. Book I narrates this episode; over the course of the next three books, Endymion dreams of her again, loses her, searches high (more dreams) and low (underground to the Bower of Venus and Adonis and several other labyrinthine terrains), and finally gives up, falling for a maid he finds abandoned in the woods. She turns out to be his goddess in disguise, and his dream comes true. This is the last time in Keats's poetry that dreams are so happily realized.

The same reviewers who had hooted at Keats's debut were waiting to savage *Endymion*, which they did with glee in the summer of 1818. But Keats himself had already grown weary of this poem, calling it "slipshod," and coming to feel that the most powerful poets did not write escapist, "golden-tongued Romance" but embraced the "fierce dispute" of life in the world. In 1818 he was attending Hazlitt's London lectures on English poetry, rereading *Paradise Lost*, *Hamlet*, *King Lear*, and Henry Cary's recent translation of Dante's *Divine Comedy*.

He was also acknowledging that Wordsworth, whose didacticism and egotism he disliked, had a profoundly modern sense of the "dark passages" of life—the misfortunes, miseries, and griefs that could not be dispelled by simple romance or explained away by simplistic moral philosophies. It was in this temper that Keats began a revisionary Miltonic epic, *Hyperion*, whose hero was intended to be Apollo, the god of knowledge, poetry, and medicine—a linkage dear to Keats. Its most deeply felt poetry, however—in the two books that Keats completed—involved the sorrows and anxieties of gods suffering their ejection from heaven, and the plight of the sun god Hyperion, not yet fallen but sensing his fate. When Keats turned to Apollo in Book 3, he lost inspiration, in part because he was feeling acutely the very mortal pain of nursing his beloved brother Tom, dying of tuberculosis, the disease that had killed their mother and that would kill Keats himself three years later (already he was suffering from a chronically sore throat).

Tom died at the end of 1818, and Keats sought relief in his poetry. In a burst of inspiration that lasted well into the fall of 1819 (when he revised *Hyperion*), he produced the work that established his fame: *The Eve of St. Agnes* (a part serious, part ironic romance), *La Belle Dame sans Mercy* (a romance with a vengeance), *Lamia* (a wickedly satirical, bitter romance), all the Great Odes, and a clutch of brilliant sonnets, including *Bright Star*. Although (unlike most of his contemporaries) he wrote no prefaces, defenses, self-promoting polemics, or theoretical essays, his letters display a critical intelligence as brilliant as the poetic talent. A number of their off-the-cuff formulations—the "finer tone" of repetition, "negative capability," "the camelion Poet," "the egotistical sublime," truth "proved upon our pulses"—have become standard terms in literary criticism and theory, and his letters from their first publication, after his death, have been admired for their generosity and playfulness, their insight, their candor, and their critical penetration.

His health worsening over the course of 1819, Keats suffered a major lung hemorrhage early in 1820; with the accuracy of his medical training, he read his "death warrant" and was devastated. For despite the shaky reception of *Poems* and *Endymion*, he was hopeful about his forthcoming volume and full of plans for new writing (journalism or plays); he was also deeply in love with the girl next door, Fanny Brawne, whom he secretly betrothed and hoped to marry once he was financially capable. He sailed to Italy in September, seeking health in a warmer climate, but died at the end of the next February, four months after his twenty-fifth birthday—far from Fanny and his friends and in such despair of fame that he asked his tombstone to be inscribed "Here lies one whose name was writ in water." Yet he did live long enough to see some favorable reviews of his 1820 volume. Shelley's fable in *Adonais* of Keats killed by hostile reviewers, though often credited, could not have been more out of tune with Keats's own resilience. "This is a mere matter of the moment," he assured his brother George of the first bad reviews; "I think I shall be among the English Poets after my death."

ON FIRST LOOKING INTO CHAPMAN'S HOMER   (from its publication in an article in *The Examiner*, 1 December 1816, by editor Leigh Hunt).

Leigh Hunt (1784–1859), poet, political journalist, and man of letters, was one of Keats's earliest, warmest and most devoted champions, and cherished by a wide circle, including Byron and Shelley. His radical politics, both on questions of government policy and literary taste, however, made Keats an unlucky target for John Gibson Lockhart's essays in *Blackwood's*. Advertising a rising generation of new poets, represented by Keats, Shelley, and J. H. Reynolds, Hunt's essay appeared on 1 December 1816 in *The Examiner*, the weekly newspaper he edited. This was the first publication of the sonnet Keats wrote after staying up all night with his friend Clarke reading George Chapman's vibrant, early seventeenth-century translation of Homer; in Keats's day, Alexander Pope's rendering in polished heroic couplets was the prestigious version (see our samples from both, in the Companion Readings below). The sonnet was only Keats's second publication, but it was Hunt's advertisement of him that encouraged Keats to attempt a career as a poet and to give up surgery.

YOUNG POETS

In sitting down to this subject, we happen to be restricted by time to a much shorter notice than we could wish: but we mean to take it up again shortly. Many of our readers however have perhaps observed for themselves, that there has been a new school of poetry rising of late, which promises to extinguish the French one that has prevailed among us since the time of Charles the 2d.[1] It began with something excessive, like most revolutions, but this gradually wore away; and an evident aspiration after real nature and original fancy remained, which called to mind the finer times of the English Muse. In fact it is wrong to call it a new school, and still more so to represent it as one of innovation, it's only object being to restore the same love of Nature, and of *thinking* instead of mere *talking,* which formerly rendered us real poets, and not merely versifying wits, and bead-rollers of couplets.

We were delighted to see the departure of the old school acknowledged in the number of the *Edinburgh Review* just published,—a candour more generous and spirited, inasmuch as that work has hitherto been the greatest surviving ornament of the same school in prose and criticism, as it is now destined, we trust, to be still the leader in the new.[2]

We also felt the same delight at the third canto of Lord Byron's *Child Harolde* [sic], in which, to our conceptions at least, he has fairly renounced a certain leaven of the French style, and taken his place where we always said he would be found,—among the poets who have a real feeling for numbers, and who go directly to Nature for inspiration. * * *

The object of the present article is merely to notice three young writers, who appear to us to promise a considerable addition of strength to the new school. Of the first who came before us, we have, it is true, yet seen only one or two specimens, and these were no sooner sent us than we unfortunately mislaid them; but we shall procure what he has published, and if the rest answer to what we have seen, we shall have no hesitation in announcing him for a very striking and original thinker. His name is PERCY BYSSHE SHELLEY, and he is the author of a poetical work entitled *Alastor, or the Spirit of Solitude.*[3]

The next with whose name we became acquainted, was JOHN HENRY REYNOLDS, author of a tale called *Safie,* written, we believe in imitation of Lord Byron, and more lately of a small set of poems published by Taylor and Hessey,[4] the principal of which is called the *Naiad.* [quotes lines 1–27] * * * The author's style is too artificial, though

---

1. For Keats's rejection of the influence of French neoclassicism on 18th-century British poets, see *Sleep and Poetry* 181–206.

2. A long essay in the September 1816 issue on 18th-century poet and satirist Jonathan Swift's *Works* declared that "the writers who adorned the beginning of the last century have been eclipsed by those of our own time . . . a revolution in our literature."

3. Published March 1816, this 720-line poem in heroic blank verse is a tale of visionary quest fulfilled in death. Keats's *Endymion* (1818) is an oblique quarrel with its metaphysics.

4. After the publishers of Keats's first volume dropped him, this firm would publish *Endymion* and the 1820 volume. The poet's middle name is actually Hamilton.

he is evidently an admirer of Mr. Wordsworth. Like all young poets too, properly so called, his love of detail is too over-wrought and indiscriminate; but still he is a young poet, and only wants a still closer attention to things as opposed to the seduction of words, to realize all that he promises. His nature seems very true and amiable.

The last of these young aspirants, whom we have met with, and who promises to help the new school to revive Nature and

"To put a spirit of youth in every thing,"[5]—

is, we believe, the youngest of them all, and just of age. His name is JOHN KEATS. He has not yet published any thing except in a newspaper;[6] but a set of his manuscripts was handed us the other day, and fairly surprised us with the truth of their ambition, and ardent grappling with Nature. In the following Sonnet there is one incorrect rhyme, which might be easily altered, but which shall serve in the mean time as a peace-offering to the rhyming critics. The rest of the composition, with the exception of a little vagueness in calling the regions of poetry "the realms of gold," we do not hesitate to pronounce excellent, especially the first six lines. The word *swims* is complete; and the conclusion is equally powerful and quiet:—

On First Looking into Chapman's Homer.

Much have I travel'd in the realms of Gold,[7]
    And many goodly states and Kingdoms seen;
Round many western Islands have I been,
    Which Bards in fealty to Apollo[8] hold
But of one wide expanse had I been told
    That deep-brow'd Homer ruled as his demesne;[9]
    Yet could I never judge what men could mean,[1]
Till I heard CHAPMAN speak out loud and bold,
Then felt I like some watcher of the skies,
    When a new planet swims into his ken;[2]
Or like stout CORTEZ, when with eagle eyes
He stared at the Pacific,—and all his men
Looked at each other with a wild surmise,—
    Silent, upon a peak in Darien.[3]

Oct. 1816   JOHN KEATS.

We have spoken with the less scruple of these poetical promises, because we really are not in the habit of lavishing praises and announcements, and because we have no fear of any pettier vanity on the part of young men, who promise to understand human nature so well.

5. Shakespeare, Sonnet 98, describing April.
6. The sonnet *To Solitude* in *The Examiner* 5 May 1816 was Keats's first (and thus far, only) publication.
7. In *A Defence of Poesie* (1595), Sir Philip Sidney wrote that poets "deliver a golden" world from the "brazen" one of nature; Keats's metaphor also involves early modern explorations for gold by new-world adventurers such as Cortez, conquistador of Mexico.
8. God of poetry.

9. Domain or realm.
1. *Poems* 1817] Yet did I never breathe its pure serene. (serene: expanse of clear sky.)
2. Range of apprehension; Uranus was discovered in 1781.
3. Panama. There is no reason to agree with Tennyson that "Cortez" is a mistake for Balboa (the first European to see the Pacific Ocean), and a sign of Keats's inferior education.

≪∾

COMPANION READINGS

Alexander Pope: from *Homer's* Iliad[1]

[THE ARMOR OF DIOMEDES]

5   High on his helm celestial lightnings play,
       His beamy shield emits a living ray;
       Th' unwearied blaze incessant streams supplies,
       Like the red star that fires th' autumnal skies,
       When fresh he rears his radiant orb to sight,
10   And bath'd in Ocean, shoots a keener light.
       Such glories Pallas[2] on the chief bestow'd,
       Such, from his arms, the fierce effulgence flow'd:
       Onward she drives him, furious to engage,
       Where the fight burns, and where the thickest rage.

George Chapman: from *Homer's* Iliad[3]

5   From his bright helme and shield did burne a most unwearied fire,
       Like rich Autumnus' golden lampe, whose brightnesse men admire
       Past all the other host of starres, when, with his cheaerfull face
       Fresh washt in loftie ocean waves he doth the skies enchase.
            To let whose glory lose no sight, still Pallas made him turne
10   Where tumult most expresst his powre, and where the fight did burne.

Alexander Pope: from *Homer's* Odyssey[4]

[ULYSSES COMES ASHORE]

       He pray'd, and straight the gentle stream subsides,
       Detains the rushing current of his tides,
       Before the wand'rer smooths the wat'ry way,
       And soft receives him from the rolling sea.
580   That moment, fainting as he touch'd the shore,
       He dropp'd his sinewy arms; his knees no more
       Perform'd their office, or his weight upheld;
       His swoln heart heav'd; his bloated body swell'd;
       From mouth and nose the briny torrent ran;
585   And lost in lassitude lay all the man,
       Deprived of voice, of motion, and of breath,
       The soul scarce waking in the arms of death.

1726

1. From Book 5. When Books 1–4 of Pope's *Iliad* were
published in 1715 (Book 5 in 1716), he was acclaimed
the greatest poet of the age; the successful sale inaugurated the first poetic career in England able to sustain
itself independent of political or aristocratic patronage.
This passage from Book 5 describes a Greek warrior's dazzling armor. Pope's version is followed by George Chapman's translation of the same passage.
2. Pallas Athene, an epithet of Athena, Greek goddess
of war.

3. From Book 5. Chapman uses the fourteener, an iambic seven-beat line, most common in ballad verse (as
two lines of four and three beats). Although both Pope
and Chapman turn Homer's unrhymed lines into couplets, Keats preferred Chapman's rougher lines and direct
language.
4. Pope followed the success of the *Iliad* with an incomplete *Odyssey*. In this passage from Book 5, having prayed
to a river god for relief, a shipwrecked, tempest-tossed
Ulysses staggers ashore at Phæacia.

George Chapman: from *Homer's Odyssey*

This (though but spoke in thought) the Godhead heard,
605   Her Current strait staid, and her thicke waves cleard
Before him, smooth'd her waters, and just where
He praied, halfe drownd, entirely sav'd him there.
     Then forth he came, his both knees faltring, both
His strong hands hanging downe, and all with froth
610   His cheeks and nosthrils flowing, voice and breath
Spent to all use; and downe he sunke to Death.
The sea had soakt his heart through:[5] all his vaines
His toiles had rackt t'a labouring woman's paines.
Dead wearie was he.

1611   1614–1615

"To one who has been long in city pent"

To one who has been long in city pent,[1]
    'Tis very sweet to look into the fair
    And open face of heaven,—to breathe a prayer
Full in the smile of the blue firmament.
5   Who is more happy, when, with hearts content,
     Fatigued he sinks into some pleasant lair
     Of wavy grass, and reads a debonair
And gentle tale of love and languishment?
Returning home at evening, with an ear
10   Catching the notes of Philomel,[2]—an eye
     Watching the sailing cloudlet's bright career,
     He mourns that day so soon has glided by:
E'en like the passage of an angel's tear
That falls through the clear ether° silently.   *upper air*

1816   1817

On the Grasshopper and Cricket[1]

The poetry of earth is never dead:
    When all the birds are faint with the hot sun,
    And hide in cooling trees, a voice will run

---

5. Keats was reportedly "delighted" by this line.
1. An allusion to *Paradise Lost* 9.445ff, an extended simile for Satan, on his first morning in the Garden of Eden (he is there to seduce Eve): "As one who long in populous city pent, / Where houses thick and sewers annoy the air, / Forth issuing on a summer's morn to breathe / Among the pleasant villages and farms. . . ." Keats's alignment instances a Romantic embrace of Milton's Satan as a psychological ally rather than moral antagonist.

2. Literally, "lover of song." The poetic name for nightingale evokes the Philomel of Ovid's *Metamorphoses*, a maiden raped, tortured, and ultimately turned by the gods into a nightingale, who sings in pain. See n. 8 on page 994.
1. The result of a competition with Hunt to write a sonnet on this subject in 15 minutes. Of Keats's first line, Hunt exclaimed, "Such a prosperous opening!" and of 10–11 (up to "silence"), "Ah! that's perfect! Bravo Keats!" In the 1817 *Poems*, the date is inscribed.

From hedge to hedge about the new-mown mead;°   *meadow*
5 That is the Grasshopper's—he takes the lead
  In summer luxury,—he has never done
  With his delights; for when tired out with fun
He rests at ease beneath some pleasant weed.
The poetry of earth is ceasing never:
10 On a lone winter evening, when the frost
   Has wrought a silence, from the stove there shrills
The Cricket's song, in warmth increasing ever,
  And seems to one in drowsiness half lost,
  The Grasshopper's among some grassy hills.

December 30, 1816   1817

from Sleep and Poetry[1]

O for ten years, that I may overwhelm
Myself in poesy; so I may do the deed
That my own soul has to itself decreed.
Then will I pass the countries that I see
100 In long perspective, and continually
Taste their pure fountains. First the realm I'll pass
Of Flora, and old Pan:[2] sleep in the grass,
Feed upon apples red, and strawberries,
And choose each pleasure that my fancy[3] sees;
105 Catch the white-handed nymphs in shady places,
To woo sweet kisses from averted faces,—
Play with their fingers, touch their shoulders white
Into a pretty shrinking with a bite
As hard as lips can make it: till agreed,
110 A lovely tale of human life we'll read.
And one will teach a tame dove how it best
May fan the cool air gently o'er my rest;
Another, bending o'er her nimble tread,
Will set a green robe floating round her head,
115 And still will dance with ever varied ease,
Smiling upon the flowers and the trees:
Another will entice me on, and on
Through almond blossoms and rich cinnamon;
Till in the bosom of a leafy world

---

1. This last piece in the 1817 *Poems* opens with praise of sleep and dreaming, then celebrates "Poesy" as "higher." Its statement of poetic aims, principles, and values was greeted enthusiastically by Keats's friends but despised by conservative reviewers and Byron, especially for the cheeky attack on 18th-century neoclassical poetics.
2. Flora is the goddess of flowers and gardens, Pan the god of universal nature and shepherds; his favored haunt is Arcadia, a place akin to Paradise. The imagery of frisky play with nymphs draws on his identity as a lustful satyr and, more specifically, of his attempted rape of nymph Syrinx, in part an allegory of poetic inspiration: when she eluded him by changing into a reed, he used the reed to make musical pipes (panpipes).
3. Generally regarded as a lesser faculty than "imagination"; see Coleridge, *Biographia Literaria*, ch. 13 (page 689).

120   We rest in silence, like two gems upcurl'd
      In the recesses of a pearly shell.

      And can I ever bid these joys farewell?
      Yes, I must pass them for a nobler life,
      Where I may find the agonies, the strife
125   Of human hearts.[4]

* * *

              Is there so small a range
      In the present strength of manhood, that the high
      Imagination cannot freely fly
165   As she was wont of old? prepare her steeds,
      Paw up against the light, and do strange deeds
      Upon the clouds?[5] Has she not shewn us all?
      From the clear space of ether, to the small
      Breath of new buds unfolding? From the meaning
170   Of Jove's large eye-brow, to the tender greening
      Of April meadows? Here her altar shone,
      E'en in this isle; and who could paragon°   *match, surpass*
      The fervid choir that lifted up a noise
      Of harmony, to where it aye° will poise   *forever*
175   Its mighty self of convoluting sound,
      Huge as a planet, and like that roll round,
      Eternally around a dizzy void?[6]
      Ay, in those days the Muses were nigh cloy'd
      With honors; nor had any other care
180   Than to sing out and sooth their wavy hair.

      Could all this be forgotten? Yes, a scism°   *schism, sect*
      Nurtured by foppery and barbarism,
      Made great Apollo° blush for this his land.   *god of poetry*
      Men were thought wise who could not understand
185   His glories: with a puling infant's force
      They sway'd about upon a rocking horse,
      And thought it Pegasus.[7] Ah dismal soul'd!
      The winds of heaven blew, the ocean roll'd
      Its gathering waves—ye felt it not. The blue
190   Bared its eternal bosom,[8] and the dew
      Of summer nights collected still to make
      The morning precious: beauty was awake!
      Why were ye not awake? But ye were dead

---

4. This aspiration traces a development reminiscent of Wordsworth's in *Tintern Abbey*, 72–93. For Keats's reading of this poem in relation to the curriculum here, see letter of 3 May 1818 (pages 1049–51).

5. Keats's critique of the present state of poetry, still dominated by 18th-century principles; the imagery alludes to Pegasus, the mythic winged horse that lived on Mount Helicon, sacred to the Muses, and thus an emblem of soaring imagination. Jove (170) or Jupiter is the king of the gods of Roman mythology.

6. English poetry before the neoclassical era, imaged as a heavenly planet that contributes to the music of the spheres (a traditional image of cosmic harmony).

7. An allusion to Hazlitt's remark (*Examiner* 1815) that the two chief upholders of neoclassical standards, Dr. Johnson and Pope, "would have converted [Milton's] vaulting Pegasus into a rocking horse."

8. For 188–90, see Wordsworth's "The world is too much with us" (page 475.)

<pre>
195   To things ye knew not of,—were closely wed
      To musty laws lined out with wretched rule
      And compass vile: so that ye taught a school
      Of dolts to smooth, inlay, and clip, and fit,
      Till, like the certain wands of Jacob's wit,
200   Their verses tallied.⁹ Easy was the task:
      A thousand handicraftsmen wore the mask
      Of Poesy. Ill-fated, impious race!
      That blasphemed the bright Lyrist° to his face,   Apollo
      And did not know it,—no, they went about,
      Holding a poor, decrepid standard out
205   Mark'd with most flimsy mottos, and in large
      The name of one Boileau!¹
</pre>

late 1816   1817

❦

RESPONSES

Z. *[John Gibson Lockhart]:* from *On the Cockney School of Poetry*¹

While the whole critical world is occupied with balancing the merits, whether in theory or in execution, of what is commonly called THE LAKE SCHOOL,² it is strange that no one seems to think it at all necessary to say a single word about another new school of poetry which has of late sprung up among us. This school has not, I believe, as yet received any name; but if I may be permitted to have the honour of christening it, it may henceforth be referred to by the designation of THE COCKNEY SCHOOL.³ Its chief Doctor and Professor is Mr Leigh Hunt, a man certainly of some talents, of extravagant pretensions both in wit, poetry, and politics, and withal of exquisitely bad taste, and extremely vulgar modes of thinking and manners in all respects. He is a man of little education. * * *

One feels the same disgust at the idea of opening Rimini,⁴ that impresses itself on the mind of a man of fashion, when he is invited to enter, for a second time, the gilded drawing-room of a little mincing boarding-school mistress, who would fain have an At

---

9. Tallied: achieved the desired number (of metrical feet); Jacob's wit was to deploy speckled wands to get Laban's herds to conceive speckled issue, which by agreement would become his (Genesis 30.27–43); "certain wands" is from Shylock's self-interested reference to this stratagem in *The Merchant of Venice* (1.3.81).
1. Nicolas Boileau-Despréaux, French poet and literary critic whose verse-treatise *L'Art poétique* (1674) was a neoclassic primer.
1. *Blackwood's Edinburgh Magazine*, which hosted this essay, was founded as a conservative Tory antidote to the liberal *Edinburgh Review*. In 1817 Lockhart (1794–1854), a Scots-born, Oxford-educated lawyer, inaugurated a series of articles over the signature "Z." on a literary culture he dubbed "The Cockney School of Poetry," led by Hunt and joined by Keats, Hazlitt, and even Shelley, who qualified by radical politics (aristocratic lineage notwithstanding). To attract readers, Z. was caustic and derisive.

Lockhart married Sir Walter Scott's daughter in 1820, became his official biographer, and from 1826 to 1853 edited *The Quarterly Review*, the leading Tory journal of London.
2. The catchy name given in 1807 by *Blackwood's* rival, the *Edinburgh*, to Wordsworth, Coleridge, and Southey (in his youth), all residents of the Lake District of northwest England.
3. "Cockney" is a politically inflected class slur, implying vulgarity, lack of classical education, immature masculinity, even effeminacy.
4. Hunt's first serious poem, *Story of Rimini* (1816), elaborates a story made famous in Dante's *Inferno*: Francesca's adulterous affair with her husband's brother Paolo, of the powerful family of Rimini. Her husband killed them both. Hunt's extravagant sympathy with the lovers outraged the Tory reviews, already primed by antipathy to his politics, and his sensuous poetic style was reviled as moral depravity.

Home in her house.[5] Every thing is pretence, affectation, finery, and gaudiness. The beaux are attorneys' apprentices, with chapeau bras and Limerick gloves[6]—fiddlers, harp teachers, and clerks of genius: the belles are faded fan-twinkling spinsters, prurient vulgar misses from school, and enormous citizens' wives. The company are entertained with lukewarm negus,[7] and the sounds of a paltry piano forte.

All the great poets of our country have been men of some rank in society, and there is no vulgarity in any of their writings; but Mr Hunt cannot utter a dedication, or even a note, without betraying the *Shibboleth*[8] of low birth and low habits. He is the ideal of a Cockney Poet. He raves perpetually about "green fields," "jaunty streams," and "o'er-arching leafiness," exactly as a Cheapside shop-keeper does about the beauties of his box on the Camberwell road.[9] Mr Hunt is altogether unacquainted with the face of nature in her magnificent scenes; he has never seen any mountain higher than Highgate-hill,[1] nor reclined by any stream more pastoral than the Serpentine River. But he is determined to be a poet eminently rural, and he rings the changes—till one is sick of him, on the beauties of the different "high views" which he has taken of God and nature, in the course of some Sunday dinner parties, at which he has assisted in the neighbourhood of London. His books are indeed not known in the country; his fame as a poet (and I might almost say, as a politician too) is entirely confined to the young attorneys and embryo-barristers about town. In the opinion of these competent judges, London is the world—and Hunt is a Homer. * * *

The poetry of Mr Hunt is such as might be expected from the personal character and habits of its author. As a vulgar man is perpetually labouring to be genteel—in like manner, the poetry of this man is always on the stretch to be grand. He has been allowed to look for a moment from the antichamber into the saloon, and mistaken the waving of feathers and the painted floor for the *sine qua non's* [essentials] of elegant society. He would fain be always tripping and waltzing, and is sorry that he cannot be allowed to walk about in the morning with yellow breeches and flesh-coloured silk stockings. He sticks an artificial rosebud into his button hole in the midst of winter. He wears no neckcloth, and cuts his hair in imitation of the Prints of Petrarch.[2] In his verses he is always desirous of being airy, graceful, easy, courtly, and ITALIAN. If he had the smallest acquaintance with the great demi-gods of Italian poetry, he could never fancy that the style in which he writes, bears any, even the most remote resemblance to the severe and simple manner of Dante—the tender stillness of the lover of Laura—or the sprightly and good-natured unconscious elegance of the inimitable Ariosto. * * *

The extreme moral depravity of the Cockney School is another thing which is for ever thrusting itself upon the public attention, and convincing every man of sense who looks into their productions, that they who sport such sentiments can never be great poets. How could any man of high original genius ever stoop publicly, at the present day, to dip his fingers in the least of those glittering and rancid obscenities which

5. Upper-class term for a social reception. An attack in 1811 in *The Examiner* on the Prince Regent as a spendthrift libertine earned Leigh Hunt and his brother John a two-year sentence in prison; Leigh rose to the occasion by applying flowered wallpaper to his cell, bringing in rugs, a piano, busts, books, and furniture, and receiving visitors in the manner of a salon.
6. Inexpensive hats and gloves.
7. An inexpensive mixture of wine, hot water, sugar, and flavorings—a drink for nondrinkers (by implication,

feminine, childish).
8. Identifying accent.
9. Such Huntian phrases appear in Keats's early poems; Cheapside is a London market district; Camberwell road is in the suburbs; box: a small country house.
1. A suburb, where Coleridge lived, in his doctor's home.
2. Arty affectations of aristocratic privilege; prints of Italian Renaissance poet Petrarch show him with longish curly hair.

float on the surface of Mr Hunt's Hippocrene?[3] His poetry resembles that of a man who has kept company with kept-mistresses. His muse talks indelicately like a tea-sipping milliner girl.[4] Some excuse for her there might have been, had she been hurried away by imagination or passion; but with her, indecency seems a disease, she appears to speak unclean things from perfect inanition. Surely they who are connected with Mr Hunt by the tender relations of society, have good reason to complain that his muse should have been so prostituted. In Rimini a deadly wound is aimed at the dearest confidences of domestic bliss. The author has voluntarily chosen—a subject not of simple seduction alone—one in which his mind seems absolutely to gloat over all the details of adultery and incest.

The unhealthy and jaundiced medium through which the Founder of the Cockney School views every thing like moral truth, is apparent, not only from his obscenity, but also from his want of respect for all that numerous class of plain upright men, and unpretending women, in which the real worth and excellence of human society consists. Every man is, according to Mr Hunt, a dull potato-eating blockhead—of no greater value to God or man than any ox or drayhorse—who is not an admirer of Voltaire's *romans*, a worshipper of Lord Holland and Mr Haydon, and a quoter of John Buncle and Chaucer's Flower and Leaf.[5] Every woman is useful only as a breeding machine, unless she is fond of reading Launcelot of the Lake, in an antique summer-house.[6]

How such an indelicate writer as Mr Hunt can pretend to be an admirer of Mr Wordsworth, is to us a thing altogether inexplicable. One great charm of Wordsworth's noble compositions consists in the dignified purity of thought, and the patriarchal simplicity of feeling, with which they are throughout penetrated and imbued. We can conceive a vicious man admiring with distant awe the spectacle of virtue and purity; but if he does so sincerely, he must also do so with the profoundest feeling of the error of his own ways, and the resolution to amend them. * * *

The Founder of the Cockney School would fain claim poetical kindred with Lord Byron. * * * Lord Byron! How must the haughty spirit of Lara and Harold contemn the subaltern sneaking of our modern tuft-hunter.[7] The insult which he offered to Lord Byron in the dedication of Rimini,—in which he, a paltry cockney newspaper scribbler, had the assurance to address one of the most nobly-born of English Patricians, and one of the first geniuses whom the world ever produced, as "My dear Byron," although it may have been forgotten and despised by the illustrious person whom it most nearly concerned,—excited a feeling of utter loathing and disgust in the public mind, which will always be remembered whenever the name of Leigh Hunt is mentioned. We dare say Mr Hunt has some fine dreams about the true nobility being the nobility of talent, and flatters himself, that with those who acknowledge

---

3. The fountain from Mount Helicon, sacred to the Muses.
4. Hat-maker; a stereotype of such girls as morally loose.
5. French author and philosopher Voltaire had spent time in prison for insulting a (French) Regent; his "*romans*" are anonymous anti-establishment novels. Lord Holland was a leading Whig (opposition) politician, and Haydon (1786–1846), a controversial painter. *The Life of John Buncle, Esq.* (1756–1766), by Irish novelist Thomas Amory, recounts the successive marriages of its freethinking but virtuous hero. *The Flower and Leaf* is a romantic allegory, then attributed to Chaucer; Keats used lines 17–21 as his epigraph for *Sleep and Poetry*, and his sonnet

Written on a Blank Space at the End of Chaucer's Tale of 'The Floure and the Lefe' was published by Hunt in *The Examiner*, March 1817, the same month *Poems* appeared.
6. Where Paolo and Francesca were reading the medieval legend of Sir Launcelot's adulterous love for Queen Guinevere, when, overcome by sympathetic passion, they put their book down and, famously, "read no more that day."
7. *Lara* is a popular poetic romance by Byron (1814; see pages 749–50); Harold is the hero of his *Childe Harold's Pilgrimage*; a subaltern is a subordinate in the military; a tuft-hunter is a social climber.

only that sort of rank, he himself passes for being the *peer* of Byron. He is sadly mistaken. He is as completely a Plebeian in his mind as he is in his rank and station in society. * * *

Z.

October 1817

Z. [John Gibson Lockhart]: from *The Cockney School of Poetry* No. IV[1]

————of Keats,
The Muses' son of promise, and what feats
He yet may do, &c.

Cornelius Webb[2]

Of all the manias of this mad age, the most incurable, as well as the most common, seems to be no other than the *Metromanie*.[3] The just celebrity of Robert Burns and Miss Baillie has had the melancholy effect of turning the heads of we know not how many farm-servants and unmarried ladies; our very footmen compose tragedies, and there is scarcely a superannuated governess in the island that does not leave a roll of lyrics behind her in her band-box. To witness the disease of any human understanding, however feeble, is distressing; but the spectacle of an able mind reduced to a state of insanity is of course ten times more afflicting. It is with such sorrow as this that we have contemplated the case of Mr John Keats. This young man appears to have received from nature talents of an excellent, perhaps even of a superior order—talents which, devoted to the purposes of any useful profession, must have rendered him a respectable, if not an eminent citizen. His friends, we understand, destined him to the career of medicine, and he was bound apprentice some years ago to a worthy apothecary in town. But all has been undone by a sudden attack of the malady to which we have alluded. Whether Mr John had been sent home with a diuretic or composing draught[4] to some patient far gone in the poetical mania, we have not heard. This much is certain, that he has caught the infection, and that thoroughly. For some time we were in hopes, that he might get off with a violent fit or two; but of late the symptoms are terrible. The phrenzy of the "Poems" was bad enough in its way; but it did not alarm us half so seriously as the calm, settled, imperturbable drivelling idiocy of "Endymion." We hope, however, that in so young a person, and with a constitution originally so good, even now the disease is not utterly incurable. Time, firm treatment, and rational restraint, do much for many apparently hopeless invalids; and if Mr Keats should happen, at some interval of reason, to cast his eye upon our pages, he may perhaps be convinced of the existence of his malady, which, in such cases, is often all that is necessary to put the patient in a fair way of being cured.

The readers of the Examiner newspaper were informed, some time ago, by a solemn paragraph, in Mr Hunt's best style, of the appearance of two new stars of glorious magnitude and splendour in the poetical horizon of the land of Cockaigne.[5] One of these turned out, by and by, to be no other than Mr John Keats. This precocious

---

1. In addition to *Poems*, Keats by now had published *Endymion* (April 1818)—a long poem undertaken in a self-conscious bid for poetic fame.
2. Either a serious eulogy, now lost, by Cornelius Webb (?1790–?1848), or verse invented by Z. and satirically

attributed to Webb, a member of the Hampstead set.
3. French coinage for a mad passion for writing poetry.
4. Sleeping potion.
5. Satirically punning on "Cockney," a country in medieval fable famed for luxury and idleness.

adulation confirmed the wavering apprentice in his desire to quit the gallipots,[6] and at the same time excited in his too susceptible mind a fatal admiration for the character and talents of the most worthless and affected of all the versifiers of our time. One of his first productions was the following sonnet, "*written on the day when Mr Leigh Hunt left prison.*"[7] It will be recollected, that the cause of Hunt's confinement was a series of libels against his sovereign, and that its fruit was the odious and incestuous "Story of Rimini." * * *

Mr Keats classes together WORDSWORTH, HUNT, and HAYDON, as the three greatest spirits of the age,[8] and that he alludes to himself, and some others of the rising brood of Cockneys, as likely to attain hereafter an equally honourable elevation. Wordsworth and Hunt! what a juxta-position! The purest, the loftiest, and, we do not fear to say it, the most classical of living English poets, joined together in the same compliment with the meanest, the filthiest, and the most vulgar of Cockney poetasters. No wonder that he who could be guilty of this should class Haydon with Raphael, and himself with Spencer. * * * At the period when these sonnets were published, Mr Keats had no hesitation in saying, that he looked on himself as "*not yet a glorious denizen of the wide heaven of poetry,*"[9] but he had many fine soothing visions of coming greatness, and many rare plans of study to prepare him for it. The following we think is very pretty raving. [Quotes *Sleep and Poetry*, lines 96–121.] Having cooled a little from this "fine passion," our youthful poet passes very naturally into a long strain of foaming abuse against a certain class of English Poets, whom, with Pope at their head, it is much the fashion with the ignorant unsettled pretenders of the present time to undervalue. Begging these gentlemens' pardon, although Pope was not a poet of the same high order with some who are now living, yet, to deny his genius, is just about as absurd as to dispute that of Wordsworth, or to believe in that of Hunt. Above all things, it is most pitiably ridiculous to hear men, of whom their country will always have reason to be proud, reviled by uneducated and flimsy striplings, who are not capable of understanding either their merits, or those of any other *men of power*—fanciful dreaming tea-drinkers, who, without logic enough to analyse a single idea, or imagination enough to form one original image, or learning enough to distinguish between the written language of Englishmen and the spoken jargon of Cockneys, presume to talk with contempt of some of the most exquisite spirits the world ever produced, merely because they did not happen to exert their faculties in laborious affected descriptions of flowers seen in window-pots, or cascades heard at Vauxhall;[1] in short, because they chose to be wits, philosophers, patriots, and poets, rather than to found the Cockney school of versification, morality, and politics, a century before its time. After blaspheming himself into a fury against Boileau, &c. Mr Keats comforts himself and his readers with a view of the present more promising aspect of affairs; above all, with the ripened glories of the poet of Rimini. [a lengthy abuse of *Endymion* follows.] We had almost forgot to mention, that Keats belongs to the Cockney School of Politics, as well as the Cockney School of Poetry.

---

6. Apothecaries' pots; also the apothecaries.

7. In *Poems*, the volume itself dedicated to Hunt, honoring his political courage; Z. quotes the sonnet, ridiculing the "absurdity" of its praise.

8. Another sonnet in *Poems*, "Great spirits now on earth are sojourning."

9. "O Poesy! for thee I hold my pen / That am not yet a glorious denizen / Of thy wide heaven" (*Sleep and Poetry* 47–49).

1. Musical concerts at the public gardens on the south bank of the Thames.

It is fit that he who holds Rimini to be the first poem, should believe the Examiner to be the first politician of the day. We admire consistency, even in folly. Hear how their bantling has already learned to lisp sedition.[2] * * * We venture to make one small prophecy, that his bookseller will not a second time venture £50 upon any thing he can write. It is a better and a wiser thing to be a starved apothecary than a starved poet; so back to the shop Mr John, back to "plasters, pills, and ointment boxes," &c. But, for Heaven's sake, young Sangrado, be a little more sparing of extenuatives and soporifics in your practice than you have been in your poetry.[3]

Z.

August 1818

❧

On Seeing the Elgin Marbles[1]

My spirit is too weak—Mortality
   Weighs heavily on me like unwilling sleep,
   And each imagined pinnacle and steep
Of godlike hardship, tells me I must die
5   Like a sick Eagle looking at the sky.
   Yet 'tis a gentle luxury to weep
   That I have not the cloudy winds to keep,
Fresh for the opening of the morning's eye.
Such dim-conceived glories of the brain
10   Bring round the heart an undescribable feud;
So do these wonders a most dizzy pain,
   That mingles Grecian grandeur with the rude
Wasting of old time—with a billowy main°—   *sea*
   A sun—a shadow of a magnitude.

1817   J.K.   1817

On sitting down to read King Lear once again[1]

O golden-tongued Romance, with serene lute!
Fair plumed Syren![2] Queen of far-away!
Leave melodizing on this wintry day,
Shut up thine olden pages, and be mute:

2. Z. quotes the attack on monarchies at the opening of *Endymion* III, a passage, like the one from *Sleep and Poetry*, that courted animosity. Bantling: baby, and in its German origin, bastard; sedition: illegal incitement of resistance to established authority.
3. Sangrado is a medical quack in Le Sage's novel *Gil Blas* (1715–1735); extenuatives are pain-easers; soporifics are sleep-inducers.
1. Keats viewed these sculptural fragments from the Athenian Parthenon with Haydon, a champion of Lord Elgin's purchase of them in 1806 from the Turks, then occupying Greece. Elgin (hard g) was motivated both by admiration for their powerful beauty and a desire to preserve them from erosion and the further peril of being turned into mortar or used for target practice by Turkish soldiers. Their aesthetic value was debated (some found

them crude and even inauthentic), and their purchase by the government in 1816 for deposit in the British Museum (they are still there) was (and still is) controversial. Keats's sonnet appeared in *The Examiner* in 1817 (our text) and in Haydon's *Annals of the Fine Arts* in 1818. For Haydon's enthusiasm, see page 38.
1. The emphasis on reading is critical, for Keats would not have been able to see Shakespeare's play. The stage was held by Nahum Tate's "romance" revision (1681): Lear doesn't die but regains the throne, then abdicates to newlyweds Edgar and Cordelia (she doesn't die either), and happily retires with Gloucester (ditto) and Kent.
2. Temptress and seductress; the Sirens of myth seemed women above the waist but were really birds of prey, whose singing lured men to destruction.

5   Adieu! for, once again, the fierce dispute,
         Betwixt damnation and impassion'd clay[3]
         Must I burn through; once more assay[4]
     The bitter sweet of this Shakesperean fruit:
     Chief Poet! and ye clouds of Albion,[5]
10   Begetters of our deep eternal theme!
     When through the old oak forest I am gone,
         Let me not wander in a barren dream,
     But when I am consumed in the Fire,
     Give me new Phoenix-wings to fly at my desire.[6]

January 1818   (1838, 1848), 1899

Sonnet: When I have fears

     When I have fears that I may cease to be[1]
         Before my pen has glean'd my teeming brain,
     Before high piled books, in charact'ry,°   *written symbols*
         Hold like rich garners the full-ripened grain;
5   When I behold, upon the night's starr'd face,
         Huge cloudy symbols of a high romance,
     And think that I may never live to trace
         Their shadows, with the magic hand of chance;
     And when I feel, fair creature of an hour!
10   That I shall never look upon thee more,
     Never have relish in the faery power
         Of unreflecting love!—then on the shore
     Of the wide world I stand alone, and think
     Till Love and Fame to nothingness do sink.

January 1818   1848

THE EVE OF ST. AGNES   Keats began this poem in the winter months of early 1819, setting it on St. Agnes' Eve, when, according to legend, a young virgin who has performed certain
rituals may dream of her future husband. The story of this patron saint of virgins is quite violent. A thirteen-year-old Christian martyr in early fourth-century Rome, she was condemned
to a night of rape in the brothels before execution. This preliminary torture was prevented
by a miraculous storm of thunder and lightning, a climate that Keats writes into the end of
his poem. Working in the intricate form of Spenserian stanzas, popularized by Byron's *Childe
Harold's Pilgrimage* (1812–1818), Keats spins an ironic romance—at once indulging the traditional pleasures of the genre (love, imagination, gorgeous sensuality with a spiritual aura)
and bringing a playful, sometimes satiric, sometimes darkly shaded perspective to its illusions.
With *Romeo and Juliet* in mind, Keats portrayed the sexual desire of his hero and heroine, but

3. The body and its mortal limitations; in *Childe Harold III* (1816), Byron described man as "clay" that inevitably "will sink / Its spark immortal" (14). In a letter-draft, Keats wrote "Hell-torment" instead of "Damnation."
4. Analyze the contents of, more specifically, the gold content of ore.
5. Old Celtic name for England, frequent in Romance; *King Lear* is set in the Celtic era.
6. Phoenix: bird fabled to rejuvenate itself with cyclical

self-immolation and rebirth from its ashes.
1. Several allusive echoes: Shakespeare's "When I do count the clock that tells the time"; Wordsworth's "few could know / When Lucy ceased to be" ("She dwelt among th'untrodden ways"; see page 447); Shelley's lament that by 1816 the radical Wordsworth should "cease to be" (*To Wordsworth*; see page 870); Milton's sonnet, "When I consider how my light is spent / Ere half my days, in this dark world and wide…"

his publishers, worried about indecency, forced him to revise. Though he complied with angry reluctance, the imagery of stars and flowers in stanza 36 shows his skill in retaining some of the original pulsation. We give some of his original draft in our footnotes.

The Eve of St. Agnes

I

St. Agnes' Eve—Ah, bitter chill it was!
The owl, for all his feathers, was a-cold;
The hare limp'd trembling through the frozen grass,
And silent was the flock in woolly fold:
5   Numb were the Beadsman's fingers, while he told
His rosary,[1] and while his frosted breath,
Like pious incense from a censer old,
Seem'd taking flight for heaven, without a death,
Past the sweet Virgin's picture, while his prayer he saith.

II

10   His prayer he saith, this patient, holy man;
Then takes his lamp, and riseth from his knees,
And back returneth, meagre, barefoot, wan,
Along the chapel aisle by slow degrees:
The sculptur'd dead, on each side, seem to freeze,
15   Emprison'd in black, purgatorial rails:
Knights, ladies, praying in dumb orat'ries,°   *chapels*
He passeth by; and his weak spirit fails
To think how they may ache in icy hoods and mails.°   *armor*

III

Northward he turneth through a little door,
20   And scarce three steps, ere Music's golden tongue
Flatter'd to tears this aged man and poor;
But no—already had his deathbell rung;
The joys of all his life were said and sung:
His was harsh penance on St. Agnes' Eve:
25   Another way he went, and soon among
Rough ashes sat he for his soul's reprieve,
And all night kept awake, for sinners' sake to grieve.

IV

That ancient Beadsman heard the prelude soft;
And so it chanc'd, for many a door was wide,
30   From hurry to and fro. Soon, up aloft,
The silver, snarling trumpets 'gan to chide:
The level chambers, ready with their pride,
Were glowing to receive a thousand guests:
The carved angels, ever eager-eyed,

---

1. A pensioner paid to say prayers, this beadsman is saying a rosary in the estate's cold chapel for the salvation of the ancestors.

35 Star'd, where upon their heads the cornice rests,
    With hair blown back, and wings put cross-wise on their breasts.

                    V

    At length burst in the argent° revelry,   silvery
    With plume, tiara, and all rich array,
    Numerous as shadows haunting fairily
40 The brain, new stuff'd, in youth, with triumphs gay
    Of old romance.[2] These let us wish away,
    And turn, sole-thoughted, to one Lady there,
    Whose heart had brooded, all that wintry day,
    On love, and wing'd St. Agnes' saintly care,
45 As she had heard old dames full many times declare.

                    VI

    They told her how, upon St. Agnes' Eve,
    Young virgins might have visions of delight,
    And soft adorings from their loves receive
    Upon the honey'd middle of the night,
50 If ceremonies due they did aright;
    As, supperless to bed they must retire,
    And couch supine their beauties, lily white;
    Nor look behind, nor sideways, but require°   beseech
    Of Heaven with upward eyes for all that they desire.[3]

                    VII

55 Full of this whim was thoughtful Madeline:[4]
    The music, yearning like a God in pain,
    She scarcely heard: her maiden eyes divine,
    Fix'd on the floor, saw many a sweeping train°   long skirt
    Pass by—she heeded not at all: in vain
60 Came many a tiptoe, amorous cavalier,
    And back retir'd; not cool'd by high disdain,
    But she saw not: her heart was otherwhere:
    She sigh'd for Agnes' dreams, the sweetest of the year.

                    VIII

    She danc'd along with vague, regardless eyes,
65 Anxious her lips, her breathing quick and short:[5]
    The hallow'd hour was near at hand: she sighs
    Amid the timbrels,° and the throng'd resort   tambourines
    Of whisperers in anger, or in sport;
    'Mid looks of love, defiance, hate, and scorn,

---

2. The literary genre; see the sonnet on *Lear*, page 987.
3. Keats's publishers forced him to cancel as too explicitly erotic a stanza that followed this one, recounting the
fable of a maid's "future lord" appearing in her dreams,
bringing "delicious food even to her lips": "Viands, and
wine, and fruit, and sugared cream, / To touch her palate
with the fine extreme / Of relish; the soft music heard;
and then / More pleasures followed in a dizzy stream, /

Palpable almost; then to wake again / Warm in the virgin
morn, no weeping Magdalen"—i.e., Mary Magdalen, the
prostitute befriended by Jesus; in Keats's day hospitals for
unwed mothers were called Magdalens.
4. A name derived from Magdalen.
5. Originally: "Her anxious lips mouth full pulp'd with
rosy thoughts."

70   Hoodwink'd° with faery fancy; all amort,°   *blinded / dead*
            Save to St. Agnes and her lambs unshorn,
     And all the bliss to be before to-morrow morn.[6]

                              IX

            So, purposing each moment to retire,
            She linger'd still. Meantime, across the moors,
75   Had come young Porphyro,[7] with heart on fire
            For Madeline. Beside the portal doors,
            Buttress'd from moonlight,[8] stands he, and implores
            All saints to give him sight of Madeline,
            But for one moment in the tedious hours,
80   That he might gaze and worship all unseen;
     Perchance speak, kneel, touch, kiss—in sooth such things have been.

                              X

            He ventures in: let no buzz'd whisper tell:
            All eyes be muffled, or a hundred swords
            Will storm his heart,[9] Love's fev'rous citadel:
85   For him, those chambers held barbarian hordes,
            Hyena foemen, and hot-blooded lords,
            Whose very dogs would execrations howl
            Against his lineage: not one breast affords
            Him any mercy, in that mansion foul,
90   Save one old beldame,[1] weak in body and in soul.

                              XI

            Ah, happy chance! the aged creature came,
            Shuffling along with ivory-headed wand,°   *staff*
            To where he stood, hid from the torch's flame,
            Behind a broad hall-pillar, far beyond
95   The sound of merriment and chorus bland:°   *soft*
            He startled her; but soon she knew his face,
            And grasp'd his fingers in her palsied hand,
            Saying, "Mercy, Porphyro! hie thee from this place;
     They are all here to-night, the whole blood-thirsty race!

                              XII

100   Get hence! get hence! there's dwarfish Hildebrand;
            He had a fever late, and in the fit
            He cursed thee and thine, both house and land:
            Then there's that old Lord Maurice, not a whit
            More tame for his grey hairs—Alas me! flit!

6. It was a custom at St. Agnes' Day mass, during the singing of Agnus Dei (Lamb of God), to bless two white unshorn lambs, whose wool nuns then spun and wove.
7. From porphyra, "purple," a precious dye for garments of the nobility; "purple blood" signifies royalty and nobility; a porphyre is a purple-colored serpent. Moreover, Porphyry (3rd century C.E.), famous antagonist of Christianity, instituted Neoplatonism throughout the Roman Empire a few decades before the martyrdom of St. Agnes.
8. Hidden in the shadow of a buttress (the external architecture that supports the castle walls).
9. An echo of Burke's famous account of the arrest of Marie Antoinette: "A band of cruel ruffians and assassins ... rushed into the chamber of the queen, and pierced with a hundred strokes of bayonets and poniards the bed, from whence this persecuted woman had but just time to fly almost naked" (see *Reflections*, page 117).
1. Grandmother or old nurse; Angela evokes Juliet's nurse Angelica in *Romeo and Juliet*, also a go-between for the lovers.

105 Flit like a ghost away."—"Ah, Gossip° dear,   *confidant*
We're safe enough; here in this arm-chair sit,
And tell me how"—"Good Saints! not here, not here;
Follow me, child, or else these stones will be thy bier."°   *coffin-platform*

XIII

He follow'd through a lowly arched way,
110 Brushing the cobwebs with his lofty plume,
And as she mutter'd "Well-a—well-a-day!"
He found him in a little moonlight room,
Pale, lattic'd, chill, and silent as a tomb.
"Now tell me where is Madeline," said he,
115 "O tell me, Angela, by the holy loom
Which none but secret sisterhood may see,
When they St. Agnes' wool are weaving piously."

XIV

"St. Agnes! Ah! it is St. Agnes' Eve—
Yet men will murder upon holy days:
120 Thou must hold water in a witch's sieve,
And be liege-lord of all the Elves and Fays,°   *fairies*
To venture so: it fills me with amaze
To see thee, Porphyro!—St. Agnes' Eve!
God's help! my lady fair the conjuror plays
125 This very night: good angels her deceive!
But let me laugh awhile, I've mickle° time to grieve."   *much*

XV

Feebly she laugheth in the languid moon,
While Porphyro upon her face doth look,
Like puzzled urchin on an aged crone
130 Who keepeth clos'd a wond'rous riddle-book,
As spectacled she sits in chimney nook.
But soon his eyes grew brilliant, when she told
His lady's purpose; and he scarce could brook°   *hold back*
Tears, at the thought of those enchantments cold,
135 And Madeline asleep in lap of legends old.

XVI

Sudden a thought came like a full-blown rose,
Flushing his brow, and in his pained heart
Made purple riot:[2] then doth he propose
A stratagem, that makes the beldame start:
140 "A cruel man and impious thou art:
Sweet lady, let her pray, and sleep, and dream
Alone with her good angels, far apart
From wicked men like thee. Go, go!—I deem
Thou canst not surely be the same that thou didst seem."

---

2. Originally: Heated his Brow / Made riot fierce.

XVII

145   "I will not harm her, by all saints I swear,"
    Quoth Porphyro: "O may I ne'er find grace
    When my weak voice shall whisper its last prayer,
    If one of her soft ringlets I displace,
150   Good Angela, believe me by these tears;
    Or I will, even in a moment's space,
    Awake, with horrid shout, my foemen's ears,
And beard° them, though they be more fang'd than wolves and bears."   *defy*

XVIII

    "Ah! why wilt thou affright a feeble soul?
155   A poor, weak, palsy-stricken, churchyard thing,
    Whose passing-bell° may ere the midnight toll;   *death knell*
    Whose prayers for thee, each morn and evening,
    Were never miss'd."—Thus plaining,° doth she bring   *lamenting*
    A gentler speech from burning Porphyro;
160   So woful, and of such deep sorrowing,
    That Angela gives promise she will do
Whatever he shall wish, betide her weal or woe.

XIX

    Which was, to lead him, in close secrecy,
    Even to Madeline's chamber, and there hide
165   Him in a closet,° of such privacy   *private room*
    That he might see her beauty unespied,
    And win perhaps that night a peerless bride,
    While legion'd fairies pac'd the coverlet,
    And pale enchantment held her sleepy-eyed.
170   Never on such a night have lovers met,
Since Merlin paid his Demon all the monstrous debt.[3]

XX

    "It shall be as thou wishest," said the Dame:
    "All cates° and dainties shall be stored there   *delicacies*
    Quickly on this feast-night: by the tambour frame[4]
175   Her own lute thou wilt see: no time to spare,
    For I am slow and feeble, and scarce dare
    On such a catering trust my dizzy head.
    Wait here, my child, with patience; kneel in prayer
    The while: Ah! thou must needs the lady wed,
180 Or may I never leave my grave among the dead."

XXI

    So saying, she hobbled off with busy fear.
    The lover's endless minutes slowly pass'd;
    The dame return'd, and whisper'd in his ear

3. In Arthurian legend, magician Merlin had his powers turned against him by enchantress Vivien, who repaid his love by imprisoning him in a cave, where he died.
4. Frame for embroidering, shaped like a tambourine.

To follow her; with aged eyes aghast
185   From fright of dim espial.[5] Safe at last,
Through many a dusky gallery, they gain
The maiden's chamber, silken, hush'd, and chaste;
Where Porphyro took covert,[6] pleas'd amain.°   *fully*
His poor guide hurried back with agues° in her brain.   *trembling*

XXII

190   Her falt'ring hand upon the balustrade,°   *bannister*
Old Angela was feeling for the stair,
When Madeline, St. Agnes' charmed maid,
Rose, like a mission'd spirit,[7] unaware:
With silver taper's° light, and pious care,   *candle's*
195   She turn'd, and down the aged gossip led
To a safe level matting. Now prepare,
Young Porphyro, for gazing on that bed;
She comes, she comes again, like ring-dove fray'd° and fled.   *frightened*

XXIII

Out went the taper° as she hurried in;   *candle*
200   Its little smoke, in pallid moonshine, died:
She clos'd the door, she panted, all akin
To spirits of the air, and visions wide:
No uttered syllable, or, woe betide!
But to her heart, her heart was voluble,
205   Paining with eloquence her balmy side;
As though a tongueless nightingale should swell
Her throat in vain, and die, heart-stifled, in her dell.[8]

XXIV

A casement° high and triple-arch'd there was,   *window*
All garlanded with carven imag'ries
210   Of fruits, and flowers, and bunches of knot-grass,
And diamonded with panes of quaint device,
Innumerable of stains and splendid dyes,
As are the tiger-moth's deep-damask'd wings;
And in the midst, 'mong thousand heraldries,°   *genealogical emblems*
215   And twilight saints, and dim emblazonings,
A shielded scutcheon° blush'd with blood of queens and kings.[9]   *coat of arms*

XXV

Full on this casement shone the wintry moon,
And threw warm gules° on Madeline's fair breast,   *red*
As down she knelt for heaven's grace and boon;°   *favor*

---

5. Being espied, even in dim light.
6. Originally: where he in panting covert.
7. Commissioned, as if an angel-messenger.
8. In a story in Ovid's *Metamorphoses*, Tereus, after raping his wife's sister Philomela, cut out her tongue to prevent her report; but she wove its imagery, which her sister understood, and was so enraged that she butchered her

and Tereus's son and fed him a dinner of the flesh. With Tereus on the verge of violent revenge, all three were turned into birds, Philomela into a nightingale; her name means "lover of honey, sweetness, song."
9. Although "blood" evokes bloodshed, here it refers to Madeline's royal bloodline.

220 Rose-bloom fell on her hands, together prest,
     And on her silver cross soft amethyst,
     And on her hair a glory,° like a saint: *halo*
     She seem'd a splendid angel, newly drest,
     Save wings, for heaven:—Porphyro grew faint:
225 She knelt, so pure a thing, so free from mortal taint.

                          XXVI
     Anon his heart revives: her vespers done,
     Of all its wreathed pearls her hair she frees;
     Unclasps her warmed jewels one by one;
     Loosens her fragrant bodice;[1] by degrees
230 Her rich attire creeps rustling to her knees:
     Half-hidden, like a mermaid in sea-weed,
     Pensive awhile she dreams awake, and sees,
     In fancy, fair St. Agnes in her bed,
     But dares not look behind, or all the charm is fled.[2]

                          XXVII
235 Soon, trembling in her soft and chilly nest,
     In sort of wakeful swoon, perplex'd she lay,
     Until the poppied° warmth of sleep oppress'd   *fragrant, narcotic*
     Her soothed limbs, and soul fatigued away;
     Flown, like a thought, until the morrow-day;
240 Blissfully haven'd both from joy and pain;
     Clasp'd like a missal where swart Paynims pray;[3]
     Blinded alike from sunshine and from rain,
     As though a rose should shut, and be a bud again.

                          XXVIII
     Stol'n to this paradise,[4] and so entranced,
245 Porphyro gazed upon her empty dress,
     And listen'd to her breathing, if it chanced
     To wake into a slumberous tenderness;
     Which when he heard, that minute did he bless,
     And breath'd himself: then from the closet crept,
250 Noiseless as fear in a wide wilderness,
     And over the hush'd carpet, silent, stept,
     And 'tween the curtains peep'd, where, lo!—how fast she slept.

                          XXIX
     Then by the bed-side, where the faded moon
     Made a dim, silver twilight, soft he set

---

1. Keats's drafts: her bosom jewels / loosens her bursting
boddice / her Boddice lace string / her Boddice and her
bosom bar[e] / Loosens her fragrant boddice and does bare
her.
2. Evoking the myth of Orpheus and Eurydice, with Madeline in the male role of the lover who wins the opportunity to lead his dead beloved back to life from Hades,
on the condition that he not look back at her until they

reach the upper world. Orpheus violated this injunction
and lost Eurydice forever.
3. Clasped shut and held like a prayer-book concealed
from the sight of hostile, dark-skinned pagans (Muslims);
"clasped" also suggests "arrested," with "pray" punning as
"prey" (on), or persecute.
4. Alluding to Satan's entry into the Garden of Eden to
corrupt Eve (*Paradise Lost*, bk. 9).

255   A table, and, half anguish'd, threw thereon
      A cloth of woven crimson, gold, and jet:—
      O for some drowsy Morphean amulet![5]
      The boisterous, midnight, festive clarion,
      The kettle-drum, and far-heard clarionet,
260   Affray° his ears, though but in dying tone:—   *frighten*
      The hall door shuts again, and all the noise is gone.

                            XXX

      And still she slept an azure-lidded sleep,
      In blanched linen, smooth, and lavender'd,
      While he from forth the closet brought a heap
265   Of candied apple, quince, and plum, and gourd;°   *melon*
      With jellies soother[6] than the creamy curd,
      And lucent syrops, tinct° with cinnamon;   *clear syrups, tinged*
      Manna° and dates, in argosy° transferr'd   *rare food / merchant fleet*
      From Fez; and spiced dainties, every one,
270   From silken Samarcand to cedar'd Lebanon.[7]

                            XXXI

      These delicates he heap'd with glowing hand
      On golden dishes and in baskets bright
      Of wreathed silver: sumptuous they stand
      In the retired quiet of the night,
275   Filling the chilly room with perfume light.—
      "And now, my love, my seraph° fair, awake!   *angel*
      Thou art my heaven, and I thine eremite:°   *worshipper*
      Open thine eyes, for meek St. Agnes' sake,
      Or I shall drowse beside thee, so my soul doth ache."

                            XXXII

280   Thus whispering, his warm, unnerved arm
      Sank in her pillow. Shaded was her dream
      By the dusk curtains:—'twas a midnight charm
      Impossible to melt as iced stream:
      The lustrous salvers° in the moonlight gleam;   *trays*
285   Broad golden fringe upon the carpet lies:
      It seem'd he never, never could redeem
      From such a stedfast spell his lady's eyes;
      So mus'd awhile, entoil'd in woofed° phantasies.   *woven*

                            XXXIII

      Awakening up, he took her hollow lute,—
290   Tumultuous,—and, in chords that tenderest be,
      He play'd an ancient ditty, long since mute,

---

5. Charm; Morpheus is the divine agent of sleep.
6. A Keats-coinage: smoother and more soothing.
7. All major places in the British trade in exotic goods, the luxuries of the feudal aristocracy: Fez in northern

Morocco was a source of sugar; the ancient Persian city of Samarkand was famous for its silk markets, and Lebanon for its fine cedar timber.

In Provence call'd, "La belle dame sans mercy":[8]
Close to her ear touching the melody;—
Wherewith disturb'd, she utter'd a soft moan:
295 He ceased—she panted quick—and suddenly
Her blue affrayed° eyes wide open shone: *frightened*
Upon his knees he sank, pale as smooth-sculptured stone.

XXXIV

Her eyes were open, but she still beheld,
Now wide awake, the vision of her sleep:
300 There was a painful change, that nigh expell'd
The blisses of her dream so pure and deep
At which fair Madeline began to weep,
And moan forth witless° words with many a sigh;   *uncomprehending*
While still her gaze on Porphyro would keep;
305 Who knelt, with joined hands and piteous eye,
Fearing to move or speak, she look'd so dreamingly.

XXXV

"Ah, Porphyro!" said she, "but even now
Thy voice was at sweet tremble in mine ear,
Made tuneable with every sweetest vow;
310 And those sad eyes were spiritual and clear:
How chang'd thou art! how pallid, chill, and drear!
Give me that voice again, my Porphyro,
Those looks immortal, those complainings° dear!   *laments*
Oh leave me not in this eternal woe,
315 For if thou diest, my Love, I know not where to go."

XXXVI

Beyond a mortal man impassion'd far
At these voluptuous accents, he arose,
Ethereal, flush'd, and like a throbbing star
Seen mid the sapphire heaven's deep repose;
320 Into her dream he melted, as the rose
Blendeth its odour with the violet,[9]—
Solution° sweet: meantime the frost-wind blows   *fusion*
Like Love's alarum,° pattering the sharp sleet   *Cupid's warning*
Against the window-panes; St. Agnes' moon hath set.

XXXVII

325 'Tis dark: quick pattereth the flaw-blown° sleet: *storm-driven*
"This is no dream, my bride, my Madeline!"
'Tis dark: the iced gusts still rave and beat:

8. Provence is a region of southern France famed for troubadours; in the poem by Alain Chartier (1424; translated
by Chaucer), a lady earns this title for refusing a suitor. In
a few months, Keats would write his own ballad of a lady
"sans mercy" / "sans merci."

9. Keats's publishers refused his revision of 314–22, in
which Porphyro's "arms encroaching slow … zon'd her,
heart to heart" as he spoke into "her burning ear," and
then "with her wild dream … mingled as a rose / Mar-
ryeth its odour to a violet."

      "No dream, alas! alas! and woe is mine!
      Porphyro will leave me here to fade and pine.—
330   Cruel! what traitor could thee hither bring?
      I curse not, for my heart is lost in thine,
      Though thou forsakest a deceived thing;—
A dove forlorn and lost with sick unpruned° wing."   *bedraggled*

XXXVIII

      "My Madeline! sweet dreamer! lovely bride!
335   Say, may I be for aye° thy vassal blest?[1]   *ever*
      Thy beauty's shield, heart-shaped and vermeil° dyed?   *vermillion*
      Ah, silver shrine, here will I take my rest
      After so many hours of toil and quest,
      A famish'd pilgrim,—saved by miracle.
340   Though I have found, I will not rob thy nest
      Saving of thy sweet self; if thou think'st well
To trust, fair Madeline, to no rude infidel.°   *unbeliever*

XXXIX

      Hark! 'tis an elfin-storm from faery land,
      Of haggard° seeming, but a boon indeed: *wild, bewitched*
345   Arise—arise! the morning is at hand;—
      The bloated wassaillers will never heed:—
      Let us away, my love, with happy speed;
      There are no ears to hear, or eyes to see,—
      Drown'd all in Rhenish and the sleepy mead:°   *sweet wine*
350   Awake! arise! my love, and fearless be,
For o'er the southern moors I have a home for thee."

XL

      She hurried at his words, beset with fears,
      For there were sleeping dragons all around,
      At glaring watch, perhaps, with ready spears—
355   Down the wide stairs a darkling° way they found.—   *dark, in the dark*
      In all the house was heard no human sound.
      A chain-droop'd lamp was flickering by each door;
      The arras,° rich with horseman, hawk, and hound,   *tapestry*
      Flutter'd in the besieging wind's uproar;
360   And the long carpets rose along the gusty floor.

XLI

      They glide, like phantoms, into the wide hall;
      Like phantoms to the iron porch they glide;
      Where lay the Porter,° in uneasy sprawl,   *gate-keeper*
      With a huge empty flagon by his side:
365   The wakeful bloodhound rose, and shook his hide,
      But his sagacious eye an inmate owns:[2]

---

1. Keats would tell Fanny Brawne (25 July 1819): "the very first week I knew you I wrote myself your vassal" (page 1058). Vassal: devoted servant.
2. Recognizes a resident (i.e., Madeline).

By one, and one, the bolts full easy slide:—
The chains lie silent on the footworn stones;—
The key turns, and the door upon its hinges groans.

XLII

370 And they are gone: ay, ages long ago
These lovers fled away into the storm.
That night the Baron dreamt of many a woe,
And all his warrior-guests, with shade and form
Of witch, and demon, and large coffin-worm,
375 Were long be-nightmar'd. Angela the old
Died palsy-twitch'd, with meagre face deform;
The Beadsman, after thousand aves told,[3]
For aye unsought for slept among his ashes cold.

1819   1820

La belle dame sans merci / LA BELLE DAME SANS MERCY

The title, French for "The beautiful lady without mercy," names her refusal to satisfy a lover's desire. Derived from the medieval word *merces*, price or wages, both *merci* and *mercy* involve an erotic economy: granting sexual favor for gifts and service. Women who did not honor this tacit contract suffered the charge of "sans merci." Keats's literary ballad joins a long lore of "femmes fatales," women whose allure is fatal to the men they enchant. We annotate the publication of 1819; our first text is transcribed from Keats's long journal letter to George and Georgiana Keats, 21 April 1819. When it was published, tidied up, in 1848, it became the preferred version, in part because it could be shorn of association with Leigh Hunt.

La belle dame sans merci—

O what can ail thee Knight at arms
    Alone and palely loitering?
The sedge has wither'd from the Lake
    And no birds sing!

5 O what can ail thee Knight at arms
    So haggard and so woe begone?
The squirrel's granary is full
    And the harvest's done.

                a
I see death's lilly on thy brow
10   With anguish moist and fever dew,
                a
And on thy cheeks death's fading rose
Fast Withereth too-

I met a Lady in the Wilds Meads
    Full beautiful, a faery's child,

15   Her hair was long, her foot was light
            And her eyes were wild-

      I made a Garland for her head,
            And bracelets too, and fragrant Zones
      She look'd at me as she did love
20   And made sweet moan-

      I set her on my pacing steed
            And nothing else saw all day long
      For sidelong would she bend, and sing
            A faerys song-
25   She found me roots of relish sweet,
                              manna
            And honey wild, and ~~honey~~ dew
      And sure in language strange she said
            I love thee true-
      She took me to her elfin grot,
                              and sigh'd full sore
30   And there she wept ~~and there she sighed fill sore~~
      And there I shut her wild wild eyes
            With kisses four.

      And there she lulled me asleep,
            And there I dream'd Ah woe betide!
35   The latest dream I ever dreamt
                  On the cold hill side

      I saw pale Kings and Princes too
            Pale warriors death pale were they all
      They cried-La belle dame sans merci
40   Thee hath in thrall-

      I saw their starv'd lips in the gloam
      ~~All tremble~~   gaped
            With horrid warning ^ wide ~~agape~~
      And I awoke and found me here
            On the cold hill's side.

45   And this is why I ~~wither~~ sojourn here,
            Alone and palely loitering,
      Though the sedge is wither'd from the lake,
            And no birds sing — - ....

Why four Kisses - you will say - why four because I wish to restrain the headlong
impetuosity of my Muse - she would have fain said 'score' without hurting the
rhyme—but we must temper the Imagination as the Critics say with Judgment. I
was obliged to choose an even number that both eyes might have fair play: and to
speak truly I think two a piece quite sufficient—Suppose I had said seven; there
would have been three and a half a piece—a very awkward affair-and well got out
of on my side–

From *The Indicator* 31 (10 May 1820), pp. 246–248. This is Leigh Hunt's aesthetic (as opposed to political) periodical. Keats's ballad appears at the end of an article titled

LA BELLE DAME SANS MERCY.

Among the pieces printed at the end of Chaucer's works, and attributed to him, is a translation, under this title, of a poem of the celebrated Alain Chartier, Secretary to Charles the Sixth and Seventh. It was the title which suggested to a friend the verses at the end of our present number. We wish Alain could have seen them. He would have found a Troubadour air for them, and sung them to La Belle Dame Agnes Sorel, who was however not Sans Mercy. The union of the imaginative and the real is very striking throughout, particularly in the dream. The wild gentleness of the rest of the thoughts and of the music are alike old; and they are also alike young; for love and imagination are always young, let them bring with them what times and accompaniments they may. If we take real flesh and blood with us, we may throw ourselves, on the facile wings of our sympathy, into what age we please. It is only by trying to feel, as well as to fancy, through the medium of a costume, that writers become mere fleshless masks and cloaks,—things like the trophies of the ancients, when they hung up the empty armour of an enemy. A hopeless lover would still feel these verses, in spite of the introduction of something unearthly. Indeed any lover, truly touched, or any body capable of being so, will feel them; because love itself resembles a visitation; and the kindest looks, which bring with them an inevitable portion of happiness because they seem happy themselves, haunt us with a spell-like power, which makes us shudder to guess at the suffering of those who can be fascinated by unkind ones.

People however need not be much alarmed at the thought of such sufferings now-a-days; not at least in some countries. Since the time when ladies, and cavaliers, and poets, and the lovers of nature, felt that humanity was a high and not a mean thing, love in general has become either a grossness or a formality. The modern systems of morals would ostensibly divide women into two classes, those who have no charity, and those who have no restraint; while men, poorly conversant with the latter, and rendered indifferent to the former, acquire bad ideas of both. Instead of the worship of Love, we have the worship of Mammon; and all the difference we can see between the sufferings attending on either is, that the sufferings from the worship of Love exalt and humanize us, and those from the worship of Mammon debase and brutalize. Between the delights there is no comparison.—Still our uneasiness keeps our knowledge going on. . . .

LA BELLE DAME SANS MERCY.

Ah, what can ail thee, wretched wight,°   *fellow*
 Alone and palely loitering;
The sedge° is wither'd from the lake,   *marsh grass*
  And no birds sing.

5 Ah, what can ail thee, wretched wight,
  So haggard and so woe-begone?
The squirrel's granary is full,
  And the harvest's done.

I see a lily on thy brow,
10 With anguish moist and fever dew;

And on thy cheek a fading rose
    Fast withereth too.[1]

I met a Lady in the meads°   *meadows*
    Full beautiful, a fairy's child;
15   Her hair was long, her foot was light,
    And her eyes were wild.[2]

I set her on my pacing steed,
    And nothing else saw all day long;
For sideways would she lean, and sing
20   A fairy's song.

I made a garland for her head,
    And bracelets too, and fragrant zone;°   *belt*
She look'd at me as° she did love,   *while; as if*
    And made sweet moan.

25   She found me roots of relish sweet,
    And honey wild, and manna dew;[3]
And sure in language strange she said,
    I love thee true.

She took me to her elfin grot,°   *grotto*
30   And there she gaz'd and sighed deep,
And there I shut her wild sad eyes—
    So kiss'd to sleep.

And there we slumber'd on the moss,
    And there I dream'd ah woe betide,
35   The latest° dream I ever dream'd   *last, most recent*
    On the cold hill side

I saw pale kings, and princes too,
    Pale warriors, death-pale were they all;
Who cried "La belle Dame sans mercy
40   Hath thee in thrall!"°   *enslaved*

I saw their starv'd lips in the gloom
    With horrid warning gaped wide,
And I awoke, and found me here
    On the cold hill side.

45   And this is why I sojourn here
    Alone and palely loitering,
Though the sedge is wither'd from the lake,
    And no birds sing.

                                                  CAVIARE.[4]

---

1. Traditional emblems: the lily, death; the rose, love.
2. This stanza seems to begin the wight's reply, but the lack of discriminating punctuation suggests that the questioner may be telling his own story to himself.
3. In Exodus 16, God feeds the Israelites in the wilderness with a miraculous dew that hardens into manna. Keats may also have in mind a passage he marked in *Paradise Lost*

describing fallen angel Belial's oratory: "all was false and hollow, though his Tongue / Dropt Manna" (2.112–13). See also *The Eve of St. Agnes*, line 268.
4. Keats's signature signifies a court delicacy; it is also an allusion to Hamlet's defense of the Player's speech as "caviary to the general": too refined for general playgoers, who like a jig or a tale of bawdry (2.2).

Incipit altera Sonneta[1]

I have been endeavouring to discover a better Sonnet Stanza than we have. The legitimate does not suit the language over-well from the pouncing rhymes – the other kind appears too elegaic[2] – and the couplet at the end of it has seldom a pleasing effect – I do not pretend to have succeeded – it will explain itself—

> If by dull rhymes our english° must be chaind   *English language*
> And, like Andromeda,[3] the Sonnet sweet
> Fetterd in spite of pained Loveliness . .
> Let us find out, if we must be constrain'd,
> 5 Sandals more interwoven and complete
> To fit the naked foot of Poesy.[4]
> Let us inspect the Lyre,[5] and weigh the stress
> Of every chord and see what may be gain'd
> By ear industrious and attention meet.°   *appropriate*
> 10 Misers of sound and syllable, no less
> Than Midas of his coinage,[6] let us be
> Jealous of dead leaves in the bay wreath crown;[7]
> So if we may not let the Muse be free,
> She will be bound with garlands of her own.

1819

THE ODES OF 1819   In Keats's career of ode-writing (from *Ode to Apollo*, 1814, to *Ode to Fanny*, 1820), the remarkable group composed in a burst of inspiration between April and September 1819 is regarded as his highest achievement. Except for *Ode on Indolence*, first published in 1848, all appeared, though not as a sequence, in Keats's 1820 volume (our text). *Ode to Psyche* was written in April, the others probably in May, and *To Autumn* the last, in September. The odes reflect personal, cultural, and political contexts of 1819, having to do with everything from the Elgin Marbles controversy, to the widespread use of opium as a painkiller, to social misery and political unrest, to Keats's grief over one brother's death and the other's emigration to America, to his nagging sensation that he was doomed to die young. Their language is enriched by literary allusion, as dense as it is casual, ranging through the Bible, Keats's earlier poetry and the hostile reviews of it, and favorite writers: Spenser, Shakespeare, Milton, Thomson, Collins, Chatterton, Coleridge, and Wordsworth. Even so, the odes also have an independent appeal that has made them, like Shakespeare's sonnets, general primers of the pleasure of reading poetry—of how verbal nuance and reverberation, and complex interplays of imagery, shape a dynamic process of thought. Nineteenth-century readers admired the beautiful phrases and sensuous language—the tactile, auditory, visual qualities, even sensations

---

1. Latin: "Here begins another Sonnet"; Keats's heading for this poem in the journal-letter (30 April 1819), containing this sonnet (our text). Although every sonnet implicitly comments on sonnet tradition, Keats's *Incipit*, like Wordsworth's "Nuns fret not" (pages 474 and 591), is an explicit reading of the tradition and his relation to it. Keats had written more than 60 sonnets by this point (not counting ones embedded in longer poems), but he would write only a few more after. Several allusions to Ovid's *Metamorphoses* reflect his concern with formal transformation. First published 1836.
2. The Petrarchan ("legitimate") sonnet has an octave of "pouncing rhymes": *abbaabba*; the "other" kind, the

Shakespearean sonnet, deploys three "elegiac" stanzas (quatrains rhymed *abab; cdcd; efef*).
3. In Ovid's fable, beautiful Andromeda was fettered to a rock to be ravaged by a sea serpent; she was rescued by Perseus on his winged horse, Pegasus, an emblem of poetic inspiration.
4. Alluding to "poetic feet"—that is, meter.
5. The instrument of Apollo, god of poetry.
6. When Ovid's miserly king got his wish that all he touched would turn to gold, he found he was unable to eat.
7. A head-wreath of bay laurel signifying poetic fame (hence, "poet laureate"); in *Metamorphoses*, when the nymph Daphne escapes Apollo's amorous pursuit by turning into a laurel, he takes the laurel as his emblem.

of smell and taste. Later readers have added an enthusiasm for the intellectual complexity and mental drama, variously described as a poetry of "internal debate," a structure of "paradox" and "contradiction," a "rhetoric of irony" or a poetics of "indeterminacy."

Keats once suggested that "a Question is the best beacon toward a little Speculation," and that knowledge was less a matter of "seeming sure points of Reasoning" than of "question and answer—a little pro and con." The key questions in his odes—"Was it a vision, or a waking dream?"; "What leaf-fringed legend haunts about thy shape ...?"; "Where are the songs of spring?"—are met less with answers than with pro and con: a poet's mind as a "rosy sanctuary" and a place of mere "shadowy thought"; a bird-song that evokes "full-throated ease" and "easeful death"; a world of art in which human figures are both "for ever young" and a "cold pastoral"; an intensity of "Beauty" that is always a "Beauty that must die"; a sensuous "indolence" that cannot stay "sheltered from annoy" of busy thoughts; an autumn that is inextricably a season of ripe fruition and of death.

Ode to Psyche[1]

	O GODDESS! hear these tuneless numbers,° wrung	*meters*
	By sweet enforcement and remembrance dear,	
	And pardon that thy secrets should be sung	
	Even into thine own soft-conched° ear:	*shell-shaped*
5	Surely I dreamt to-day, or did I see	
	The winged Psyche with awaken'd eyes?	
	I wander'd in a forest thoughtlessly,	
	And, on the sudden, fainting with surprise,	
	Saw two fair creatures, couched side by side	
10	In deepest grass, beneath the whisp'ring roof	
	Of leaves and trembled blossoms, where there ran	
	A brooklet, scarce espied:[2]	
	'Mid hush'd, cool-rooted flowers, fragrant-eyed,	
	Blue, silver-white, and budded Tyrian,°	*deep purple*
15	They lay calm-breathing on the bedded grass;	
	Their arms embraced, and their pinions° too;	*wings*
	Their lips touch'd not, but had not bade adieu	
	As if disjoined by soft-handed slumber,	
	And ready still past kisses to outnumber	
20	At tender eye-dawn of aurorean° love:	*dawning*
	The winged boy° I knew;	*Cupid*
	But who wast thou, O happy, happy dove?	
	His Psyche true!	

1. "Psyche" means *soul* or *mind* and *butterfly* in Greek; in Greek myth the nymph Psyche personified soul, sometimes in the form of a butterfly. In Apuleius's *The Golden Ass* (2nd century), she is a mortal loved by Cupid, who visited her only at night, to keep his identity secret and prevent discovery by his mother Venus, jealous of Psyche's beauty. "Psyche was not embodied as a goddess before the time of Apul[ei]us the Platonist who lived afte[r] the Augustan age, and consequently the goddess was never worshipped or sacrificed to with any of the ancient fervour—and perhaps never thought of in the old religion—I am more orthodox tha[n] let a hethan Goddess be so neglected," wrote Keats, who knew Mary

Tighe's *Psyche* (1805), a romance in Spenserian stanzas also based on Apuleius, which his ode echoes in several places. Keats was reflecting at this time on the development of the soul through suffering; see his journal-letter, 21 April 1819 (page 1056).

2. The scene evokes Satan's view of Adam and Eve in Eden: "the loveliest pair...Under a tuft of shade that on a green / Stood whispering soft, by a fresh Fountain side / They sat them down" (*Paradise Lost* 4.321–27); and later, the epic narrator's account of the pair "side by side" in "thir inmost bower" making "connubial Love" (4.742–43), then as "two fair Creatures...asleep secure of harm" (4.790–91).

O latest born and loveliest vision far
    Of all Olympus' faded hierarchy![3]
Fairer than Phœbe's sapphire-region'd star,
    Or Vesper, amorous glow-worm of the sky;[4]
Fairer than these, though temple thou hast none,
       Nor altar heap'd with flowers;
Nor virgin-choir to make delicious moan
       Upon the midnight hours;
No voice, no lute, no pipe, no incense sweet
    From chain-swung censer teeming;
No shrine, no grove, no oracle, no heat
    Of pale-mouth'd prophet dreaming.[5]

O brightest! though too late for antique vows,
    Too, too late for the fond believing lyre,°   *religious worship*
When holy were the haunted° forest boughs,   *spirit-filled*
    Holy the air, the water, and the fire;
Yet even in these days so far retir'd
    From happy pieties, thy lucent fans,°   *wings*
    Fluttering among the faint° Olympians,   *weak, faded*
I see, and sing, by my own eyes inspired.
So let me be thy choir, and make a moan
       Upon the midnight hours;
Thy voice, thy lute, thy pipe, thy incense sweet
    From swinged censer teeming;
Thy shrine, thy grove, thy oracle, thy heat
    Of pale-mouth'd prophet dreaming.

Yes, I will be thy priest, and build a fane°   *temple*
    In some untrodden region of my mind,[6]
Where branched thoughts, new grown with pleasant pain,
    Instead of pines shall murmur in the wind:
Far, far around shall those dark-cluster'd trees
    Fledge° the wild-ridged mountains steep by steep;   *feather*
And there by zephyrs,° streams, and birds, and bees,   *breezes*
    The moss-lain Dryads° shall be lull'd to sleep;   *wood-nymphs*
And in the midst of this wide quietness
A rosy sanctuary will I dress
With the wreath'd trellis of a working brain,

---

3. The gods who lived on Mount Olympus in classical mythology, now eclipsed by Christianity.
4. Phoebe is the moon-goddess whose "star" is the moon; Vesper: Venus, the evening star, and in the fable of Psyche, Cupid's jealous mother.
5. Alluding to the rout by Christianity of the pagan Greek deities in Milton's *On the Morning of Christ's Nativity* (1629): "The Oracles are dumb, / No voice ... No

nightly trance, or breathed spell, / Inspires the pale-ey'd priest from the prophetic cell" (19).
6. Echoing Spenser's *Amoretti* 22: "Her temple fayre is built within my mind, / In which her glorious ymage placèd is, / On which my thoughts doo day and night attend / Like sacred priests" (5–8). See letter of 3 May 1818 on the Chamber of Maiden-thought (pages 1050–51).

With buds, and bells, and stars without a name,
With all the gardener Fancy[7] e'er could feign,
   Who breeding flowers, will never breed the same:
And there shall be for thee all soft delight
65   That shadowy thought can win,
A bright torch, and a casement ope at night,
   To let the warm Love in!

Ode to a Nightingale[1]

1

My heart aches, and a drowsy numbness pains
   My sense, as though of hemlock I had drunk,
Or emptied some dull opiate to the drains
   One minute past, and Lethe-wards had sunk:[2]
5 'Tis not through envy of thy happy lot,
   But being too happy in thine happiness,—
     That thou, light-winged Dryad° of the trees,   *wood-nymph*
      In some melodious plot
Of beechen green, and shadows numberless,
10   Singest of summer in full-throated ease.

2

O, for a draught of vintage!° that hath been   *wine*
   Cool'd a long age in the deep-delved earth,
Tasting of Flora and the country green,
   Dance, and Provençal song, and sunburnt mirth![3]
15 O for a beaker full of the warm South,
   Full of the true, the blushful Hippocrene,[4]
     With beaded bubbles winking at the brim,
      And purple-stained mouth;
That I might drink, and leave the world unseen,[5]
20   And with thee fade away into the forest dim:

3

Fade far away, dissolve, and quite forget
   What thou among the leaves hast never known,

---

7. Fancy is often represented in literary tradition as a gardener who improves nature. Feign: invent, dissemble, with Shakespearean punning on *fain* and *fane* (50). Keats's language is allusively embedded in a stanza of Spenser's *Hymne in Honour of Love* (1596), about a jealous lover whose fears "to his fayning fansie represent / Sights never seene, and thousand shadowes vaine, / To break his sleepe, and waste his ydle braine" (254–56).

1. First published in *Annals of the Fine Arts*, 1819. Keats's stanza incorporates sonnet elements: a Shakespearean quatrain (*abab*) followed by a Petrarchan sestet (*cdecde*), also the form of the odes on "Melancholy" and "Indolence." The nightingale in literary tradition (including Milton, Charlotte Smith, Wordsworth, Coleridge) often evokes Ovid's story of Philomela; see page 994, n. 8.

Keats was also inspired by an actual nightingale's song at the house where he was living.

2. In small doses hemlock is a sedative; in large doses, such as Socrates's, it is fatal; an opiate is any sense-duller, particularly opium, widely used as a painkiller; Lethe is the mythic river of the underworld whose waters produce forgetfulness of previous life.

3. Magician Merlin dwells "in a deep delve, farre from the view of day, / That of no living wight he mote be found" (*Faerie Queene* 3.3.7). Flora: Roman goddess of flowers; see *Sleep and Poetry* 102. Provence: region in southern France famed for troubadours.

4. The fountain of the muses on Mount Helicon.

5. "Unseen" can modify both "I" and "world."

The weariness, the fever, and the fret
   Here, where men sit and hear each other groan;
25 Where palsy shakes a few, sad, last gray hairs,
   Where youth grows pale, and spectre-thin, and dies;[6]
     Where but to think is to be full of sorrow
      And leaden-eyed despairs,
     Where Beauty cannot keep her lustrous eyes,
30   Or new Love pine at them beyond to-morrow.

4

Away! away! for I will fly to thee,
   Not charioted by Bacchus and his pards,[7]
But on the viewless wings of Poesy,
   Though the dull brain perplexes and retards:
35 Already with thee! tender is the night,
   And haply° the Queen-Moon is on her throne,   *happily, perhaps*
     Cluster'd around by all her starry Fays;°   *fairies*
      But here there is no light,
   Save what from heaven is with the breezes blown
40   Through verdurous glooms and winding mossy ways.

5

I cannot see what flowers are at my feet,
   Nor what soft incense hangs upon the boughs,
But, in embalmed darkness, guess each sweet
   Wherewith the seasonable month endows
45 The grass, the thicket, and the fruit-tree wild;
   White hawthorn, and the pastoral eglantine;
     Fast fading violets cover'd up in leaves;
      And mid-May's eldest child,
   The coming musk-rose, full of dewy wine,
50   The murmurous haunt of flies on summer eves.[8]

6

Darkling° I listen; and, for many a time   *in the dark*
   I have been half in love with easeful Death,
Call'd him soft names in many a mused rhyme,
   To take into the air my quiet breath;
55 Now more than ever seems it rich to die,
   To cease upon the midnight with no pain,
     While thou art pouring forth thy soul abroad
      In such an ecstasy!

---

6. An echo of Wordsworth's memory in *Tintern Abbey* of himself in "darkness, and amid the many shapes / Of joyless day-light; when the fretful stir / Unprofitable, and the fever of the world, / Have hung upon the beatings of my heart" (52–55); see Keats's remarks on *Tintern Abbey* in the letter of 3 May 1818 (page 1051). Both poets recall Macbeth's envy of Duncan "in his grave; / After life's fitful fever he sleeps well" (*Macbeth* 3.322–323). Also echoed is Wordsworth's image of an ideal life "from diminution safe and weakening age; / While man grows old, and dwindles, and decays" (*Excursion* 4.759–60).

7. Bacchus, god of wine and revelry, whose chariot is drawn by leopards.

8. This guessing of flowers echoes Oberon's description in *A Midsummer Night's Dream* of a verdant bank where one may find a snakeskin whose juices make a sleeper fall in love with whatever is first seen on waking (2.1.249–58).

Still wouldst thou sing, and I have ears in vain—
60   To thy high requiem° become a sod.   *funeral mass*

7

Thou wast not born for death, immortal Bird!
No hungry generations tread thee down;
The voice I hear this passing night was heard
In ancient days by emperor and clown:°   *rustic, peasant*
65 Perhaps the self-same song that found a path
Through the sad heart of Ruth, when, sick for home,
She stood in tears amid the alien corn;[9]
The same that oft-times hath
Charm'd magic casements, opening on the foam
70   Of perilous seas, in faery lands forlorn.

8

Forlorn! the very word is like a bell
To toll me back from thee to my sole self!
Adieu! the fancy cannot cheat so well[1]
As she is fam'd to do, deceiving elf.
75 Adieu! adieu! thy plaintive anthem fades
Past the near meadows, over the still stream,
Up the hill-side; and now 'tis buried deep
In the next valley-glades:
Was it a vision, or a waking dream?
80 Fled is that music:—Do I wake or sleep?

Ode on a Grecian Urn[1]

1

THOU still unravish'd bride of quietness,
Thou foster-child of silence and slow time,
Sylvan° historian, who canst thus express   *woodland*
A flowery tale more sweetly than our rhyme:
5   What leaf-fring'd legend haunts about thy shape
Of deities or mortals, or of both,
In Tempe or the dales of Arcady?[2]
What men or gods are these? What maidens loth?

9. See Ruth 1–2: compelled by famine to leave her home, Ruth eked out a living as a gleaner in faraway fields.
1. The adieu echoes the opening line of Charlotte Smith's *On the Departure of the Nightingale* (1784), "Sweet poet of the woods!—a long adieu!" The closing question bears several echoes: *Psyche* 5–6; the opening of Spenser's *Amoretti* 77: "Was it a dreame, or did I see it playne?"; Hazlitt's remark that "Spenser was the poet of our waking dreams," his "music...lulling the senses into a deep oblivion of the jarring noises of the world from which we have no wish ever to be recalled" (*On Chaucer and Spenser*, 1818); a spellbound lover's confusion in *Midsummer Night's Dream*: "Are you sure / That we are awake? It seems to me / That yet we sleep, we dream" (4.1.194–96); Wordsworth's lament in the "Intimations"

Ode, "Whither is fled the visionary gleam? / Where is it now, the glory and the dream?" (56–57), and his phrase "waking dream" in *Yarrow Visited* (pub. 1815).
1. First published in *Annals of the Fine Arts*. Keats describes three scenes on an imaginary urn. The first is an image of revelry and sexual pursuit; the second (stanzas 2–3) is either a detail of this or another: a piper, and a lover in pursuit of a fair maid; in both, the story of Pan is implied (see n. 2 to *Sleep and Poetry*, page 980). The third (stanza 4) is a sacrificial ritual, perhaps inspired by one of the Elgin Marble friezes.
2. A design of leaves frames a "legend" or caption on some vases; Tempe and Arcadia are districts of ancient Greece famed for beauty and serenity, where the gods often frolicked.

What mad pursuit? What struggle to escape?
10   What pipes and timbrels?° What wild ecstasy?   *tambourines*

2

Heard melodies are sweet, but those unheard
      Are sweeter; therefore, ye soft pipes, play on;
Not to the sensual° ear, but, more endear'd,   *physical*
      Pipe to the spirit ditties of no tone:
15 Fair youth, beneath the trees, thou canst not leave
      Thy song, nor ever can those trees be bare;
          Bold Lover, never, never canst thou kiss,
Though winning near the goal—yet, do not grieve;
      She cannot fade, though thou hast not thy bliss,
20   For ever wilt thou love, and she be fair!

3

Ah, happy, happy° boughs! that cannot shed   *joyous, fortunate*
      Your leaves, nor ever bid the Spring adieu;
And, happy melodist, unwearied,
      For ever piping songs for ever new;
25 More happy love! more happy, happy love!
      For ever warm and still to be enjoy'd,
          For ever panting, and for ever young;
All breathing human passion far above,
      That leaves a heart high-sorrowful and cloy'd,
30   A burning forehead, and a parching tongue.

4

Who are these coming to the sacrifice?
      To what green altar, O mysterious[3] priest,
Lead'st thou that heifer lowing at the skies,
      And all her silken flanks with garlands drest?
35 What little town by river or sea shore,
      Or mountain-built with peaceful citadel,°   *fortress*
          Is emptied of this folk, this pious morn?
And, little town, thy streets for evermore
      Will silent be; and not a soul to tell
40   Why thou art desolate, can e'er return.

5

O Attic shape! Fair attitude!° with brede°   *pose / intricate design*
      Of marble men and maidens overwrought,[4]
With forest branches and the trodden weed;
      Thou, silent form, dost tease us out of thought
45 As doth eternity: Cold Pastoral!

---

3. Unknown; also denoting religious rites.
4. The urn, made in Attica (where Athens is located), is "overwrought" (overlaid) with its design; Keats may be implying "over-elaborated," with a hint of psychological or emotional anguish in the frozen figures; thus "brede" puns on what cannot happen, "breed."

When old age shall this generation waste,
   Thou shalt remain, in midst of other woe
Than ours, a friend to man, to whom thou say'st,
   "Beauty is truth, truth beauty,"[5]—that is all
50   Ye know on earth, and all ye need to know.

Ode on Indolence[1]

"They toil not, neither do they spin"[2]

I

One morn before me were three figures seen,
   With bowed necks, and joined hands, side-faced;
And one behind the other stepp'd serene,
   In placid sandals, and in white robes graced;
5   They pass'd, like figures on a marble urn,
   When shifted round to see the other side;
They came again; as when the urn once more
     Is shifted round, the first seen shades return;
   And they were strange to me, as may betide
10   With vases, to one deep in Phidian lore.[3]

II

How is it, Shadows!° that I knew ye not?   *shady figures, phantoms*
   How came ye muffled in so hush a mask?[4]
Was it a silent deep-disguised plot
   To steal away, and leave without a task
15   My idle days? Ripe was the drowsy hour;
   The blissful cloud of summer-indolence
Benumb'd my eyes; my pulse grew less and less;
     Pain had no sting, and pleasure's wreath no flower:
   O, why did ye not melt, and leave my sense
20   Unhaunted quite of all but—nothingness?

III

A third time pass'd they by, and, passing, turn'd
   Each one the face a moment whiles to me;

---

5. The quotation marks do not appear in any manuscript of the ode. Keats ponders the relation between beauty and truth throughout his career: see his letters of 22 November 1817, 21–27 December 1817, and 19 March 1819, pages 1045–47 and 1053.
1. Indolence is usually seen as a laxity boding moral dissolution; James Thomson's *Castle of Indolence* (1748) begins, however, by detailing its lush pleasures before the moral is applied. Keats mentions this poem in the journal-letter of 19 March 1819 in which he recounts the mood that inspires this ode. Our text is the first publication, in 1848.
2. In the Sermon on the Mount, Jesus advises: "Take no thought for your life, what ye shall eat, or what ye shall

drink; nor yet for your body, what ye shall put on. Is not the life more than meat, and the body than raiment . . . why take ye thought for raiment? Consider the lilies of the field, how they grow; they toil not, neither do they spin: And yet I say unto you, That even Solomon in all his glory was not arrayed like one of these" (Matthew 6.26–29). The spinning of garments obliquely relates to textuality (and writing) through the tacit pun on *textum* ("woven" in Latin).
3. The famous Athenian sculptor Phidias (5th century B.C.E.) created the Elgin Marbles.
4. Another manuscript has "masque," a theatrical ritual; Keats allows the puns.

Then faded, and to follow them I burn'd
   And ached for wings, because I knew the three;
25   The first was a fair Maid, and Love her name;
     The second was Ambition, pale of cheek,
And ever watchful with fatigued eye;
      The last, whom I love more, the more of blame
   Is heap'd upon her, maiden most unmeek,—
30 I knew to be my demon Poesy.[5]

IV

They faded, and, forsooth! I wanted° wings: *lacked and ached for*
   O folly! What is Love? and where is it?
And for that poor Ambition! it springs
   From a man's little heart's short fever-fit;
35   For Poesy!—no,—she has not a joy,—
   At least for me,—so sweet as drowsy noons,
And evenings steep'd in honeyed indolence;
     O, for an age so shelter'd from annoy,°   *annoyance, harm*
   That I may never know how change the moons,
40 Or hear the voice of busy common-sense!

V

And once more came they by;—alas! wherefore?
   My sleep had been embroider'd with dim dreams;
My soul had been a lawn besprinkled o'er
   With flowers, and stirring shades, and baffled beams:
45   The morn was clouded, but no shower fell,
   Tho' in her lids hung the sweet tears of May;
The open casement press'd a new-leaved vine,
   Let in the budding warmth and throstle's lay;[6]
     O Shadows! 'twas a time to bid farewell!
50 Upon your skirts had fallen no tears of mine.

VI

So, ye three Ghosts, adieu! Ye cannot raise
   My head cool-bedded in the flowery grass;
For I would not be dieted with praise,
   A pet-lamb in a sentimental farce![7]
55   Fade softly from my eyes, and be once more
   In masque-like figures on the dreamy urn;
Farewell! I yet have visions for the night,
   And for the day faint visions there is store;

---

5. In Greek myth, a "demon" or "daemon" is a semi-divine
spirit; the word also carries a Christian sense of "evil
spirit." The image hints at the kind of "unmeek" ("vulgar," "sensuous," "immodest") poetry for which Keats was
criticized in the reviews of 1817–1818.
6. Thrush's song, but with a possible pun related to the

epigraph, on "throstle" as a frame for spinning.
7. In a letter of June 1819, Keats claimed to be disenchanted with the idea of fame: "I hope I am a little more
of a Philosopher than I was, consequently a little less of a
versifying Pet-lamb."

Vanish, ye Phantoms! from my idle spright,[8]
60   Into the clouds, and never more return!

1848

Ode on Melancholy[1]

1

No, no, go not to Lethe,° neither twist   *river of forgetfulness*
     Wolf's-bane, tight-rooted, for its poisonous wine;
Nor suffer thy pale forehead to be kiss'd
     By nightshade, ruby grape of Proserpine;[2]
5   Make not your rosary of yew-berries,[3]
          Nor let the beetle, nor the death-moth be
          Your mournful Psyche,[4] nor the downy owl
A partner in your sorrow's mysteries;°   *secret rites*
     For shade to shade will come too drowsily,
10   And drown the wakeful anguish of the soul.

2

But when the melancholy fit shall fall
     Sudden from heaven like a weeping cloud,
That fosters the droop-headed flowers all,
     And hides the green hill in an April shroud;
15   Then glut thy sorrow on a morning rose,
          Or on the rainbow of the salt sand-wave,
          Or on the wealth of globed peonies;
Or if thy mistress some rich anger shows,
     Emprison her soft hand, and let her rave,
20   And feed deep, deep upon her peerless eyes.

3

She[5] dwells with Beauty—Beauty that must die;
     And Joy, whose hand is ever at his lips
Bidding adieu; and aching Pleasure nigh,

---

8. Old term for spirit or soul but also denoting a diminutive: ghost, elf, fairy.
1. In May 1819, Keats paraphrased a couplet from Wordsworth's "Intimations" Ode: "Nothing can bring back the hour / Of splendour in the grass and glory in the flower" (177–78), commenting, "I once thought this a Melancholist's dream." "Melancholy" is a traditional term for "the blues," or even "black" moods; Hamlet is famously "The Melancholy Dane." Robert Burton's treatise, *Anatomy of Melancholy* (1621), which Keats studied, offers an elaborate medical analysis as well as an anthology of notable remarks. Taking a stock subject for poets in the 18th century (see Charlotte Smith's sonnet *To Melancholy*, page 88), Keats prizes Melancholy as a sensibility that accepts, even relishes, evanescence. He originally began the ode with a macabre, mock-heroic stanza about the quest for the goddess Melancholy: "Though you should build a bark of dead men's bones, / And rear a phantom gibbet for a mast, / Stitch creeds together for a

sail, with groans / To fill it out, bloodstained and aghast; / Although your rudder be a Dragon's tail, / Long sever'd, yet still hard with agony, / Your cordage large uprootings from the skull / Of bald Medusa: certes you would fail / To find the Melancholy, whether she / Dreameth in any isle of Lethe dull..."
2. Wolfsbane and nightshade are poisons; Proserpine was abducted to the underworld by its ruler, Hades, but an appeal by her mother Ceres (goddess of grain) allowed her to return to the upper world from spring to fall—a seasonal flux relevant to the aesthetic of Melancholy.
3. Yew is an emblem of death; rosary: prayer beads.
4. In Greek, "psyche" means both "soul" and "butterfly" (its emblem); the markings on the death's-head moth resemble a human skull; the beetle may be the scarab, a jewel-bug placed in tombs by the ancient Egyptians as a portent of resurrection.
5. A double reference, to the mistress and to Melancholy.

25   Turning to poison while the bee-mouth sips:[6]
Ay, in the very temple of Delight
Veil'd Melancholy has her sovran shrine,
Though seen of none save him whose strenuous tongue
Can burst Joy's grape against his palate fine;°   *sensitive, refined*
His soul shall taste the sadness of her might,
30   And be among her cloudy trophies hung.

To Autumn[1]

1

SEASON of mists and mellow fruitfulness,
Close bosom-friend of the maturing sun;
Conspiring with him how to load and bless
With fruit the vines that round the thatch-eves[2] run;
5   To bend with apples the moss'd cottage-trees,
And fill all fruit with ripeness to the core;
To swell the gourd, and plump the hazel shells
With a sweet kernel; to set budding more,
And still more, later flowers for the bees,
10   Until they think warm days will never cease,
For Summer has o'er-brimm'd their clammy cells.

2

Who hath not seen thee oft amid thy store?
Sometimes whoever seeks abroad may find
Thee sitting careless on a granary floor,
15   Thy hair soft-lifted by the winnowing wind;
Or on a half-reap'd furrow sound asleep,
Drows'd with the fume of poppies, while thy hook°   *scythe*
Spares the next swath and all its twined flowers:
And sometimes like a gleaner thou dost keep
20   Steady thy laden head across a brook;
Or by a cyder-press, with patient look,
Thou watchest the last oozings hours by hours.

3

Where are the songs of Spring? Ay, where are they?[3]
Think not of them, thou hast thy music too,—
25   While barred clouds bloom the soft-dying day,

---

6. See letter on inevitable transformations, 19 March 1819, page 1054.
1. Composed 19–21 September 1819 in Winchester, a tranquil town in southern England, from which Keats wrote to a friend: "How beautiful the season is now— How fine the air. A temperate sharpness about it....I never lik'd stubble fields so much as now—Aye better than the chilly green of the spring. Somehow a stubble plain looks warm—in the same way that some pictures look warm—this struck me so much in my sunday's walk that I composed upon it." The ode evokes two competing but related senses of autumn: the social context of harvest bounty; and the symbolic association with death—the reaper as grim reaper, autumn as the presage of winter (see Shakespeare's Sonnet 73, "That time of year may'st in me behold"). Among other poems echoed are Thomson's *Autumn* in *The Seasons* (1740) and the last stanza of Coleridge's *Frost at Midnight* (page 630).
2. The eaves of thatched cottage roofs.
3. The "Ubi sunt" trope ("where are they now?") traditionally prefaces a lament for lost worlds, the implied answer being "gone"; cf. Wordsworth's "Intimations" Ode, stanza 4 (page 557).

And touch the stubble-plains with rosy hue;
Then in a wailful choir the small gnats mourn
    Among the river sallows,[4] borne aloft
    Or sinking as the light wind lives or dies;
30 And full-grown lambs loud bleat from hilly bourn;°   *boundary, region*
    Hedge-crickets sing; and now with treble soft°   *faint high pitch*
    The red-breast whistles from a garden-croft;°   *enclosure*
    And gathering swallows twitter in the skies.

LAMIA   Keats wrote this dark romance in the summer of 1819, hoping for commercial success: "I am certain there is that sort of fire in it which must take hold of people in some way— give them either pleasant or unpleasant sensation. What they want is sensation of some sort" (he reported to his brother and sister-in-law). His publishers were confident enough to feature it in the title of Keats's last lifetime volume: *Lamia, Isabella, The Eve of St. Agnes* (1820)— with the great odes of 1819 at the back. *Lamia* was not only the first but also the volume's longest work: of 200 pages, it commanded 46. Keats's previous volume was *Endymion* (1818), his longest poem ever, and one that left him, well before the savaging of the reviews, soured on the romance of a dreaming poet who wins the goddess of his desires. He even thought *The Eve of St. Agnes* "too smokeable" (open to ridicule), and invested *Lamia* as his antidote. "I have great hopes of success, because I make use of my Judgment more deliberately than I yet have done," he confided in July to friend and fellow poet J. H. Reynolds. He was enjoying Dryden's verse fables and legends, their heroic couplets spiced with triple rhymes and alexandrine extravagances (six-beat lines in the five-beat pattern). Not just in these poetic measures but also in key characterizations and circumstances, Keats saturates *Lamia* with corrosives to "golden Romance": Corinth was a well known site of slavery and erotic hedonism; philosopher Apollonius is no Apollo; Keats-age Lycius is a deluded visionary, then a tyrant, then a subject of catastrophic discipline; and Lamia is an unsolved question. Her name indicates the fabled sisterhood of African-descended she-vampires: seeming modest women above the waist, but below, serpents who thus tempt, then strangle and devour their victims. Is the enchantress herself also a victim? Keats was deeply and complexly in love with Fanny Brawne (see his letter to her, 25 July 1819). The vignette in Robert Burton's baroque seventeenth-century treatise *Anatomy of Melancholy* that Keats gave as his source and inspiration is set as an endnote in 1820, and here, too.

Lamia

PART I.

UPON a time, before the faery broods
Drove Nymph and Satyr from the prosperous woods,
Before King Oberon's bright diadem,°   *crown*
Sceptre, and mantle, clasp'd with dewy gem,
5 Frighted away the Dryads and the Fauns
From rushes green, and brakes,° and cowslip'd lawns,[1]   *thickets*
The ever-smitten Hermes[2] empty left
His golden throne, bent warm on amorous theft:

---

4. Willows (an emblem of death).
1. This vignette of faeryland-war involves nymphs (female deities), tree-nymphs (dryads), half-men half-goat lusty satyrs, fauns (junior satyrs), and a king who shares a name with the tyrant of fairyland in Shakespeare's

A Midsummer Night's Dream.
2. Lustful, foot-and-hat-winged messenger of Jove, king of the gods (all lived on Mount Olympus in Greece), Hermes is the patron of orators, merchants, thieves, pickpockets, and liars.

From high Olympus had he stolen light,
10   On this side of Jove's clouds, to escape the sight
Of his great summoner, and made retreat
Into a forest on the shores of Crete.
For somewhere in that sacred island dwelt
A nymph, to whom all hoofed Satyrs knelt;
15   At whose white feet the languid Tritons° poured   sea gods or mermen
Pearls, while on land they wither'd° and adored.   for lack of water
Fast by the springs where she to bathe was wont,
And in those meads° where sometime she might haunt,   meadows
Were strewn rich gifts, unknown to any Muse,
20   Though Fancy's casket were unlock'd to choose.
Ah, what a world of love was at her feet!
So Hermes thought, and a celestial heat
Burnt from his winged heels to either ear,
That from a whiteness, as the lily clear,
25   Blush'd into roses 'mid his golden hair,
Fallen in jealous curls about his shoulders bare.[3]
From vale to vale, from wood to wood, he flew,
Breathing upon the flowers his passion new,
And wound with many a river to its head,
30   To find where this sweet nymph prepar'd her secret bed:
In vain; the sweet nymph might nowhere be found,
And so he rested, on the lonely ground,
Pensive, and full of painful jealousies
Of the Wood-Gods, and even the very trees.
35   There as he stood, he heard a mournful voice,
Such as once heard, in gentle heart, destroys
All pain but pity: thus the lone voice spake:
"When from this wreathed tomb shall I awake!
When move in a sweet body fit for life,
40   And love, and pleasure, and the ruddy strife
Of hearts and lips! Ah, miserable me!"
The God, dove-footed, glided silently
Round bush and tree, soft-brushing, in his speed,
The taller grasses and full-flowering weed,
45   Until he found a palpitating snake,
Bright, and cirque-couchant[4] in a dusky brake.

She was a gordian shape[5] of dazzling hue,
Vermilion-spotted, golden, green, and blue;
Striped like a zebra, freckled like a pard,°   leopard
50   Eyed like a peacock,° and all crimson barr'd;   peacock's tail
And full of silver moons, that, as she breathed,
Dissolv'd, or brighter shone, or interwreathed

3. The first of many alexandrine or otherwise hypermetri-
cal lines (often thematically relevant).
4. Keats-invented faux-heraldic word for *lying in circular
coils.*

5. Like the famously intricate Gordian knot, impossible
to unravel; Keats uses this metaphor for his feelings about
women (page 1052).

Their lustres with the gloomier tapestries—
So rainbow-sided, touch'd with miseries,
55   She seem'd, at once, some penanced lady elf,
Some demon's mistress, or the demon's self.
Upon her crest she wore a wannish fire
Sprinkled with stars, like Ariadne's tiar:[6]
Her head was serpent, but ah, bitter-sweet!
60   She had a woman's mouth with all its pearls° complete: teeth
And for her eyes: what could such eyes do there
But weep, and weep, that they were born so fair?
As Proserpine still weeps for her Sicilian air.[7]
Her throat was serpent, but the words she spake
65   Came, as through bubbling honey, for Love's sake,
And thus; while Hermes on his pinions lay,
Like a stoop'd° falcon ere he takes his prey.   ready to swoop

"Fair Hermes, crown'd with feathers, fluttering light,
I had a splendid dream of thee last night:
70   I saw thee sitting, on a throne of gold,
Among the Gods, upon Olympus old,
The only sad one; for thou didst not hear
The soft, lute-finger'd Muses chaunting clear,
Nor even Apollo when he sang alone,
75   Deaf to his throbbing throat's long, long melodious moan.[8]
I dreamt I saw thee, robed in purple flakes,
Break amorous through the clouds, as morning breaks,
And, swiftly as a bright Phoebean dart,[9]
Strike for the Cretan isle; and here thou art!
80   Too gentle Hermes, hast thou found the maid?"
Whereat the star of Lethe[1] not delay'd
His rosy eloquence, and thus inquired:
"Thou smooth-lipp'd serpent, surely high inspired!
Thou beauteous wreath, with melancholy eyes,
85   Possess whatever bliss thou canst devise,
Telling me only where my nymph is fled,—
Where she doth breathe!" "Bright planet, thou hast said,"
Return'd the snake, "but seal with oaths, fair God!"
"I swear," said Hermes, "by my serpent rod,[2]
90   And by thine eyes, and by thy starry crown!"
Light flew his earnest words, among the blossoms blown.

---

6. King Minos of Crete imprisoned warrior Greek prince and serial rapist Theseus in his labyrinth for certain death from its monster Minotaur. His love-smitten daughter Ariadne helped him escape, on his vow to marry her. Scarcely honoring his vow, Theseus soon ditched her. She became a byword for heartbreaking betrayal. Her next suitor Bacchus gave her a crown (tiar) of seven stars (later, the constellation Pleiades); see Renaissance painter Titian's *Bacchus and Ariadne*.
7. From the fields of Enna in Sicily, Proserpine was abducted by Pluto to the underworld of Hades, allowed to

return to the upper earth for only half the year (hence, the seasons).
8. An extraordinarily long metrical line—to evoke the moan.
9. Ray from sun god Phoebus Apollo.
1. One of Hermes's offices, as the star psychopomp, was to guide the souls of the dead across Lethe, the river of forgetfulness in Hades.
2. The caduceus, Hermes's rod of two entwined (lythe) snakes, with two wings at the top, and as Keats knew, the emblem of the physician.

Then thus again the brilliance feminine:
"Too frail of heart! for this lost nymph of thine,
Free as the air, invisibly, she strays
95 About these thornless wilds; her pleasant days
She tastes unseen; unseen her nimble feet
Leave traces in the grass and flowers sweet;
From weary tendrils, and bow'd branches green,
She plucks the fruit unseen, she bathes unseen:
100 And by my power is her beauty veil'd
To keep it unaffronted, unassail'd
By the love-glances of unlovely eyes,
Of Satyrs, Fauns, and blear'd Silenus' sighs.[3]
Pale grew her immortality, for woe
105 Of all these lovers, and she grieved so
I took compassion on her, bade her steep
Her hair in weïrd syrops,° that would keep   *magical syrups*
Her loveliness invisible, yet free
To wander as she loves, in liberty.
110 Thou shalt behold her, Hermes, thou alone,
If thou wilt, as thou swearest, grant my boon!"
Then, once again, the charmed God began
An oath, and through the serpent's ears it ran
Warm, tremulous, devout, psalterian.[4]
115 Ravish'd, she lifted her Circean head,[5]
Blush'd a live damask,° and swift-lisping said, *big pink rose of Asia Minor*
"I was a woman, let me have once more
A woman's shape, and charming as before.
I love a youth of Corinth—O the bliss!
120 Give me my woman's form, and place me where he is.
Stoop, Hermes, let me breathe upon thy brow,
And thou shalt see thy sweet nymph even now."
The God on half-shut feathers sank serene,
She breath'd upon his eyes, and swift was seen
125 Of both the guarded nymph near-smiling on the green.
It was no dream; or say a dream it was,
Real are the dreams of Gods, and smoothly pass
Their pleasures in a long immortal dream.
One warm, flush'd moment, hovering, it might seem
130 Dash'd by the wood-nymph's beauty, so he burn'd;
Then, lighting on the printless verdure, turn'd
To the swoon'd serpent, and with languid arm,
Delicate, put to proof the lythe Caducean° charm. *medicinal, magical*
So done, upon the nymph his eyes he bent
135 Full of adoring tears and blandishment,
And towards her stept: she, like a moon in wane,

---

3. A satyr, usually depicted drunk, who tutored Bacchus, god of wine.
4. Like a psalm; sound like a psaltery (a stringed instrument,

like a zither).
5. Circe, enchantress of Homer's *Odyssey*, turns men, including Ulysses and his crew, into beasts.

Faded before him, cower'd, nor could restrain
Her fearful sobs, self-folding like a flower
That faints into itself at evening hour:
140   But the God fostering her chilled hand,
She felt the warmth, her eyelids open'd bland,°   *unperturbed*
And, like new flowers at morning song of bees,
Bloom'd, and gave up her honey to the lees.°   *depths*
Into the green-recessed woods they flew;
145   Nor grew they pale, as mortal lovers do.

Left to herself, the serpent now began
To change; her elfin blood in madness ran,
Her mouth foam'd, and the grass, therewith besprent,°   *sprinkled*
Wither'd at dew so sweet and virulent;°   *poisonous*
150   Her eyes in torture fix'd, and anguish drear,
Hot, glaz'd, and wide, with lid-lashes all sear,°   *scorched*
Flash'd phosphor and sharp sparks, without one cooling tear.
The colours all inflam'd throughout her train,
She writh'd about, convuls'd with scarlet pain:
155   A deep volcanian yellow took the place
Of all her milder-mooned body's grace;
And, as the lava ravishes the mead,
Spoilt all her silver mail,° and golden brede;°   *metal-mesh coat / embroidery*
Made gloom of all her frecklings, streaks and bars,
160   Eclips'd her crescents, and lick'd up her stars:
So that, in moments few, she was undrest
Of all her sapphires, greens, and amethyst,
And rubious-argent:° of all these bereft,   *silver*
Nothing but pain and ugliness were left.
165   Still shone her crown; that vanish'd, also she
Melted and disappear'd as suddenly;
And in the air, her new voice luting soft,
Cried, "Lycius! gentle Lycius!"—Borne aloft
With the bright mists about the mountains hoar
170   These words dissolv'd: Crete's forests heard no more.

Whither fled Lamia, now a lady bright,
A full-born beauty new and exquisite?
She fled into that valley they pass o'er
Who go to Corinth from Cenchreas' shore;[6]
175   And rested at the foot of those wild hills,
The rugged founts of the Peræan rills,
And of that other ridge whose barren back
Stretches, with all its mist and cloudy rack,
South-westward to Cleone.° There she stood   *a village*
180   About a young bird's flutter from a wood,
Fair, on a sloping green of mossy tread,
By a clear pool, wherein she passioned

---

6. Harbor of the southern Greek city of Corinth.

To see herself escap'd from so sore ills,
While her robes flaunted with the daffodils.

185   Ah, happy Lycius!—for she was a maid
More beautiful than ever twisted braid,
Or sigh'd, or blush'd, or on spring-flowered lea°   *meadow*
Spread a green kirtle° to the minstrelsy: *dress*
A virgin purest lipp'd, yet in the lore
190   Of love deep learned to the red heart's core:
Not one hour old, yet of sciential° brain   *knowing*
To unperplex bliss from its neighbour pain;
Define their pettish° limits, and estrange   *contested*
Their points of contact, and swift counterchange;
195   Intrigue with the specious° chaos, and dispart   *manipulate the seeming*
Its most ambiguous atoms with sure art;
As though in Cupid's college she had spent
Sweet days a lovely graduate, still unshent,°   *unspoiled*
And kept his rosy terms° in idle languishment.   *subjects; periods of study*

200   Why this fair creature chose so fairily
By the wayside to linger, we shall see;
But first 'tis fit to tell how she could muse
And dream, when in the serpent prison-house,[7]
Of all she list,° strange or magnificent: *wished*
205   How, ever, where she will'd, her spirit went;
Whether to faint Elysium, or where
Down through tress-lifting waves the Nereids fair
Wind into Thetis' bower by many a pearly stair;[8]
Or where God Bacchus drains his cups divine,
210   Stretch'd out, at ease, beneath a glutinous pine;
Or where in Pluto's gardens palatine
Mulciber's columns gleam in far piazzian line.[9]
And sometimes into cities she would send
Her dream, with feast and rioting to blend;
215   And once, while among mortals dreaming thus,
She saw the young Corinthian Lycius
Charioting foremost in the envious race,
Like a young Jove with calm uneager face,
And fell into a swooning love of him.
220   Now on the moth-time of that evening dim
He would return that way, as well she knew,
To Corinth from the shore; for freshly blew
The eastern soft wind, and his galley now
Grated the quaystones with her brazen prow

7. Next to the verse in *Paradise Lost* in which Milton describes Satan insinuating himself into a serpent's body for disguise (9.179–91), Keats marveled: "Whose spirit does not ache at the smothering and confinement . . . Whose head is not dizzy at the prosiable speculations of satan in the serpent prison—no passage of poetry ever can give a greater pain of suffocations."

8. Elysium is the abode of dead heroes; Nereid (seanymph) Thetis is the mother of Achilles, the semidivine but vulnerable hero on the Greek side of the Trojan War.
9. A piazza is an open courtyard with rows of columns; Mulciber, the Vulcan god of metalwork, was the architect of Pandemonium in hell (*Paradise Lost*). Pluto's gardens are in the underworld of classical mythology.

225   In port Cenchreas, from Egina isle
        Fresh anchor'd; whither he had been awhile
        To sacrifice to Jove, whose temple there
        Waits with high marble doors for blood and incense rare.
        Jove heard his vows, and better'd his desire;
230   For by some freakful chance he made retire
        From his companions, and set forth to walk,
        Perhaps grown wearied of their Corinth talk:
        Over the solitary hills he fared,
        Thoughtless at first, but ere eve's star appeared
235   His phantasy was lost, where reason fades,
        In the calm'd twilight of Platonic shades.[1]
        Lamia beheld him coming, near, more near—
        Close to her passing, in indifference drear,
        His silent sandals swept the mossy green;
240   So neighbour'd to him, and yet so unseen
        She stood: he pass'd, shut up in mysteries,°   *enigmas of religion*
        His mind wrapp'd like his mantle, while her eyes
        Follow'd his steps, and her neck regal white
        Turn'd—syllabling thus, "Ah, Lycius bright,
245   And will you leave me on the hills alone?
        Lycius, look back! and be some pity shown."
        He did; not with cold wonder fearingly,
        But Orpheus-like at an Eurydice;[2]
        For so delicious were the words she sung,
250   It seem'd he had lov'd them a whole summer long:
        And soon his eyes had drunk her beauty up,
        Leaving no drop in the bewildering cup,
        And still the cup was full,—while he, afraid
        Lest she should vanish ere his lip had paid
255   Due adoration, thus began to adore;
        Her soft look growing coy, she saw his chain so sure:
        "Leave thee alone! Look back! Ah, Goddess, see
        Whether my eyes can ever turn from thee!
        For pity do not this sad heart belie°—   *be untrue to*
260   Even as thou vanishest so I shall die.
        Stay! though a Naiad of the rivers, stay!
        To thy far wishes will thy streams obey:
        Stay! though the greenest woods be thy domain,
        Alone they can drink up the morning rain:
265   Though a descended Pleiad,[3] will not one
        Of thine harmonious sisters keep in tune
        Thy spheres, and as thy silver proxy shine?

---

1. The otherwordly ideals of Greek philosopher Plato's metaphysics. In Plato's "Allegory of the Cave," human cognition tends to mistake mere shadows for these truths. 2. Grief-stricken Orpheus descended to Hades and charmed Pluto into letting him reclaim his beloved wife Eurydice to the living, on the condition that he not look back at her during their ascent. He resisted the impulse almost to the end, then relented and lost her forever. 3. One of the seven daughters of Atlas, all constellated as the Pleiades after their death.

So sweetly to these ravish'd ears of mine
Came thy sweet greeting, that if thou shouldst fade
270　Thy memory will waste me to a shade:—
For pity do not melt!"—"If I should stay,"
Said Lamia, "here, upon this floor of clay,
And pain my steps upon these flowers too rough,
What canst thou say or do of charm enough
275　To dull the nice° remembrance of my home?　　　　　*highly detailed*
Thou canst not ask me with thee here to roam
Over these hills and vales, where no joy is,—
Empty of immortality and bliss!
Thou art a scholar, Lycius, and must know
280　That finer spirits cannot breathe below
In human climes, and live: Alas! poor youth,
What taste of purer air hast thou to soothe
My essence? What serener palaces,
Where I may all my many senses please,
285　And by mysterious sleights a hundred thirsts appease?
It cannot be—Adieu!" So said, she rose
Tiptoe with white arms spread. He, sick to lose
The amorous promise of her lone complain,°　　　　　*lament*
Swoon'd, murmuring of love, and pale with pain.
290　The cruel lady, without any show
Of sorrow for her tender favourite's woe,
But rather, if her eyes could brighter be,
With brighter eyes and slow amenity,
Put her new lips to his, and gave afresh
295　The life she had so tangled in her mesh:
And as he from one trance was wakening
Into another, she began to sing,
Happy in beauty, life, and love, and every thing,
A song of love, too sweet for earthly lyres,
300　While, like held breath, the stars drew in their panting fires.
And then she whisper'd in such trembling tone,
As those who, safe together met alone
For the first time through many anguish'd days,
Use other speech than looks; bidding him raise
305　His drooping head, and clear his soul of doubt,
For that she was a woman, and without
Any more subtle fluid in her veins
Than throbbing blood, and that the self-same pains
Inhabited her frail-strung heart as his.
310　And next she wonder'd how his eyes could miss
Her face so long in Corinth, where, she said,
She dwelt but half retir'd, and there had led
Days happy as the gold coin could invent
Without the aid of love; yet in content
315　Till she saw him, as once she pass'd him by,
Where 'gainst a column he leant thoughtfully

At Venus' temple porch, 'mid baskets heap'd
Of amorous herbs and flowers, newly reap'd
Late on that eve, as 'twas the night before
320   The Adonian feast;[4] whereof she saw no more,
But wept alone those days, for why should she adore?
Lycius from death awoke into amaze,
To see her still, and singing so sweet lays;
Then from amaze into delight he fell
325   To hear her whisper woman's lore so well;
And every word she spake entic'd him on
To unperplex'd delight and pleasure known.
Let the mad poets say whate'er they please
Of the sweets of Fairies, Peris,° Goddesses,   *good fairies of Persian myth*
330   There is not such a treat among them all,
Haunters of cavern, lake, and waterfall,
As a real woman, lineal indeed
From Pyrrha's pebbles[5] or old Adam's seed.
Thus gentle Lamia judg'd, and judg'd aright,
335   That Lycius could not love in half a fright,
So threw the goddess off, and won his heart
More pleasantly by playing woman's part,
With no more awe than what her beauty gave,
That, while it smote, still guaranteed to save.
340   Lycius to all made eloquent reply,
Marrying to every word a twinborn sigh;
And last, pointing to Corinth, ask'd her sweet,
If 'twas too far that night for her soft feet.
The way was short, for Lamia's eagerness
345   Made, by a spell, the triple league decrease
To a few paces; not at all surmised
By blinded Lycius, so in her comprized.°   *enrapt*
They pass'd the city gates, he knew not how,
So noiseless, and he never thought to know.

350   As men talk in a dream, so Corinth all,
Throughout her palaces imperial,
And all her populous streets and temples lewd,[6]
Mutter'd, like tempest in the distance brew'd,
To the wide-spreaded night above her towers.
355   Men, women, rich and poor, in the cool hours,
Shuffled their sandals o'er the pavement white,
Companion'd or alone; while many a light

---

4. Annual fertility rite, named for Venus's beloved Adonis, killed during a hunt; Proserpine (another maid Pluto abducted to the underworld) restored him to life, that he might be her lover for half the year, and Venus's, in the upper world, for the other half. The feast celebrates his return to Venus.
5. In the Greek-myth analogue to Noah, Jupiter punishes mankind with a flood, survived only by Deucalion (a son

of Prometheus) and his wife Pyrrha, who repopulate the earth by scattering life-engendering pebbles.
6. Of Corinth, Burton reports in *Anatomy of Melancholy:* "every day strangers came in, at each gate, from all quarters. In that one temple of Venus a thousand whores did prostitute themselves . . . all nations resorted thither as to a school of Venus."

Flared, here and there, from wealthy festivals,
And threw their moving shadows on the walls,
360 Or found them cluster'd in the corniced shade
Of some arch'd temple door, or dusky colonnade.°   *row of columns*

Muffling his face, of greeting friends in fear,
Her fingers he press'd hard, as one came near
With curl'd gray beard, sharp eyes, and smooth bald crown,
365 Slow-stepp'd, and robed in philosophic gown:
Lycius shrank closer, as they met and past,
Into his mantle, adding wings to haste,
While hurried Lamia trembled: "Ah," said he,
"Why do you shudder, love, so ruefully?
370 Why does your tender palm dissolve in dew?"—
"I'm wearied," said fair Lamia: "tell me who
Is that old man? I cannot bring to mind
His features:—Lycius! wherefore did you blind
Yourself from his quick eyes?" Lycius replied,
375 "'Tis Apollonius sage, my trusty guide
And good instructor; but to-night he seems
The ghost of folly haunting my sweet dreams."

While yet he spake they had arrived before
A pillar'd porch, with lofty portal door,
380 Where hung a silver lamp, whose phosphor glow
Reflected in the slabbed steps below,
Mild as a star in water; for so new,
And so unsullied was the marble hue,
So through the crystal polish, liquid fine,
385 Ran the dark veins, that none but feet divine
Could e'er have touch'd there. Sounds Æolian[7]
Breath'd from the hinges, as the ample span
Of the wide doors disclos'd a place unknown
Some time to any, but those two alone,
390 And a few Persian mutes, who that same year
Were seen about the markets: none knew where
They could inhabit; the most curious
Were foil'd, who watch'd to trace them to their house:
And but° the flitter-winged verse must tell,   *but for the fact that*
395 For truth's sake, what woe afterwards befel,
'Twould humour many a heart to leave them thus,
Shut from the busy world of more incredulous.

PART II.

LOVE in a hut, with water and a crust,
Is—Love, forgive us!—cinders, ashes, dust;
Love in a palace is perhaps at last
More grievous torment than a hermit's fast:—

7. Aeolus is the god of the winds.

That is a doubtful tale from faery land,
Hard for the non-elect to understand.
Had Lycius liv'd to hand his story down,
He might have given the moral a fresh frown,
Or clench'd it quite:° but too short was their bliss   *fully proved*
To breed distrust and hate, that make the soft voice hiss.
Besides, there, nightly, with terrific glare,
Love,° jealous grown of so complete a pair,   *Cupid*
Hover'd and buzz'd his wings, with fearful roar,
Above the lintel° of their chamber door,   *weight-bearing beam*
And down the passage cast a glow upon the floor.

    For all this came a ruin: side by side
They were enthroned, in the even tide,
Upon a couch, near to a curtaining
Whose airy texture, from a golden string,
Floated into the room, and let appear
Unveil'd the summer heaven, blue and clear,
Betwixt two marble shafts:—there they reposed,
Where use had made it sweet, with eyelids closed,
Saving a tythe° which love still open kept,   *tithe, tenth part*
That they might see each other while they almost slept;
When from the slope side of a suburb hill,
Deafening the swallow's twitter, came a thrill
Of trumpets—Lycius started—the sounds fled,
But left a thought, a buzzing in his head.
For the first time, since first he harbour'd in
That purple-lined palace of sweet sin,
His spirit pass'd beyond its golden bourn
Into the noisy world almost forsworn.
The lady, ever watchful, penetrant,
Saw this with pain, so arguing a want
Of something more, more than her empery°   *empire*
Of joys; and she began to moan and sigh
Because he mused beyond her, knowing well
That but a moment's thought is passion's passing bell.°   *death knell*
"Why do you sigh, fair creature?" whisper'd he:
"Why do you think?" return'd she tenderly:
"You have deserted me;—where am I now?
Not in your heart while care weighs on your brow:
No, no, you have dismiss'd me; and I go
From your breast houseless: ay, it must be so."
He answer'd, bending to her open eyes,
Where he was mirror'd small in paradise,
"My silver planet, both of eve and morn!⁸
Why will you plead yourself so sad forlorn,
While I am striving how to fill my heart
With deeper crimson, and a double smart?

8. The planet Venus, both the morning and the evening star.

How to entangle, trammel up and snare
Your soul in mine, and labyrinth[9] you there
Like the hid scent in an unbudded rose?
55 Ay, a sweet kiss—you see your mighty woes.
My thoughts! shall I unveil them? Listen then!
What mortal hath a prize, that other men
May be confounded and abash'd withal,
But lets it sometimes pace abroad majestical,
60 And triumph, as in thee I should rejoice
Amid the hoarse alarm of Corinth's voice.
Let my foes choke, and my friends shout afar,
While through the thronged streets your bridal car
Wheels round its dazzling spokes."—The lady's cheek
65 Trembled; she nothing said, but, pale and meek,
Arose and knelt before him, wept a rain
Of sorrows at his words; at last with pain
Beseeching him, the while his hand she wrung,
To change his purpose. He thereat was stung,
70 Perverse, with stronger fancy to reclaim
Her wild and timid nature to his aim:
Besides, for all his love, in self despite,
Against his better self, he took delight
Luxurious in her sorrows, soft and new.
75 His passion, cruel grown, took on a hue
Fierce and sanguineous as 'twas possible
In one whose brow had no dark veins to swell.
Fine was the mitigated fury, like
Apollo's presence when in act to strike
80 The serpent[1]—Ha, the serpent! certes,° she   *certainly*
Was none. She burnt, she lov'd the tyranny,[2]
And, all subdued, consented to the hour
When to the bridal he should lead his paramour.
Whispering in midnight silence, said the youth,
85 "Sure some sweet name thou hast, though, by my truth,
I have not ask'd it, ever thinking thee
Not mortal, but of heavenly progeny,
As still I do. Hast any mortal name,
Fit appellation for this dazzling frame?
90 Or friends or kinsfolk on the cited earth,
To share our marriage feast and nuptial mirth?"
"I have no friends," said Lamia, "no, not one;
My presence in wide Corinth hardly known:
My parents' bones are in their dusty urns
95 Sepulchred, where no kindled incense burns,
Seeing all their luckless race are dead, save me,

9. OED gives this instance as the first use as an active verb.
1. The monstrous sea-serpent Python, engendered from the mud left after the great flood (see n. 5, page 1022), was slain by Apollo at Delphi.

2. "Women love to be forced to do a thing, by a fine fellow- such as this," Keats smirked of Lycius (so his friend Woodhouse told his publisher in September 1819).

And I neglect the holy rite for thee.
Even as you list invite your many guests;
But if, as now it seems, your vision rests
100   With any pleasure on me, do not bid
Old Apollonius—from him keep me hid."
Lycius, perplex'd at words so blind and blank,
Made close inquiry; from whose touch she shrank,
Feigning a sleep; and he to the dull shade
105   Of deep sleep in a moment was betray'd.

      It was the custom then to bring away
The bride from home at blushing shut of day,
Veil'd, in a chariot, heralded along
By strewn flowers, torches, and a marriage song,
110   With other pageants: but this fair unknown
Had not a friend. So being left alone,
(Lycius was gone to summon all his kin)
And knowing surely she could never win
His foolish heart from its mad pompousness,
115   She set herself, high-thoughted, how to dress
The misery in fit magnificence.
She did so, but 'tis doubtful how and whence
Came, and who were her subtle servitors.
About the halls, and to and from the doors,
120   There was a noise of wings, till in short space
The glowing banquet-room shone with wide-arched grace.
A haunting music, sole perhaps and lone
Supportress of the faery-roof, made moan
Throughout, as fearful the whole charm might fade.
125   Fresh carved cedar, mimicking a glade
Of palm and plantain, met from either side,
High in the midst, in honour of the bride:
Two palms and then two plantains, and so on,
From either side their stems branch'd one to one
130   All down the aisled place; and beneath all
There ran a stream of lamps straight on from wall to wall.
So canopied, lay an untasted feast
Teeming with odours. Lamia, regal drest,
Silently paced about, and as she went,
135   In pale contented sort of discontent,
Mission'd her viewless° servants to enrich   *invisible*
The fretted° splendour of each nook and niche.   *intricately carved*
Between the tree-stems, marbled plain at first,
Came jasper pannels; then, anon, there burst
140   Forth creeping imagery of slighter trees,
And with the larger wove in small intricacies.
Approving all, she faded at self-will,
And shut the chamber up, close, hush'd and still,
Complete and ready for the revels rude,
145   When dreadful guests would come to spoil her solitude.

The day appear'd, and all the gossip rout.
O senseless Lycius! Madman! wherefore flout
The silent-blessing fate, warm cloister'd hours,
And show to common eyes these secret bowers?
150   The herd approach'd; each guest, with busy brain,
Arriving at the portal, gaz'd amain,°   *fully, eagerly*
And enter'd marveling: for they knew the street,
Remember'd it from childhood all complete
Without a gap, yet ne'er before had seen
155   That royal porch, that high-built fair demesne;°   *domain, realm*
So in they hurried all, maz'd, curious and keen:
Save one, who look'd thereon with eye severe,
And with calm-planted steps walk'd in austere;
'Twas Apollonius: something too he laugh'd,
160   As though some knotty problem, that had daft°   *thwarted, teased*
His patient thought, had now begun to thaw,
And solve and melt:—'twas just as he foresaw.

He met within the murmurous vestibule°   *lobby*
His young disciple. "'Tis no common rule,
165   Lycius," said he, "for uninvited guest
To force himself upon you, and infest
With an unbidden presence the bright throng
Of younger friends; yet must I do this wrong,
And you forgive me." Lycius blush'd, and led
170   The old man through the inner doors broad-spread;
With reconciling words and courteous mien
Turning into sweet milk the sophist's spleen.

Of wealthy lustre was the banquet-room,
Fill'd with pervading brilliance and perfume:
175   Before each lucid pannel fuming stood
A censer° fed with myrrh and spiced wood,   *incense-burner*
Each by a sacred tripod held aloft,
Whose slender feet wide-swerv'd upon the soft
Wool-woofed carpets: fifty wreaths of smoke
180   From fifty censers their light voyage took
To the high roof, still mimick'd as they rose
Along the mirror'd walls by twin-clouds odorous.
Twelve sphered tables, by silk seats insphered,
High as the level of a man's breast rear'd
185   On libbard's° paws, upheld the heavy gold   *leopard's*
Of cups and goblets, and the store thrice told
Of Ceres' horn,[3] and, in huge vessels, wine
Come from the gloomy tun° with merry shine.   *cask*
Thus loaded with a feast the tables stood,
190   Each shrining in the midst the image of a God.

---

3. Cornucopia; harvest-goddess Ceres is the mother of Proserpine.

When in an antichamber° every guest   *front room*
Had felt the cold full sponge to pleasure press'd,
By minist'ring slaves, upon his hands and feet,
And fragrant oils with ceremony meet
195   Pour'd on his hair, they all mov'd to the feast
In white robes, and themselves in order placed
Around the silken couches, wondering
Whence all this mighty cost and blaze of wealth could spring.

   Soft went the music the soft air along,
200   While fluent Greek a vowel'd undersong
Kept up among the guests, discoursing low
At first, for scarcely was the wine at flow;
But when the happy vintage touch'd their brains,
Louder they talk, and louder come the strains
205   Of powerful instruments:—the gorgeous dyes,
The space, the splendour of the draperies,
The roof of awful richness, nectarous cheer,
Beautiful slaves, and Lamia's self, appear,
Now, when the wine has done its rosy deed,
210   And every soul from human trammels freed,
No more so strange; for merry wine, sweet wine,
Will make Elysian shades not too fair, too divine.
Soon was God Bacchus at meridian° height;   *highest*
Flush'd were their cheeks, and bright eyes double bright:
215   Garlands of every green, and every scent
From vales deflower'd, or forest-trees branch-rent,
In baskets of bright osier'd° gold were brought   *woven of willow*
High as the handles heap'd, to suit the thought
Of every guest; that each, as he did please,
220   Might fancy-fit° his brows, silk-pillow'd at his ease.   *make a headwreath for*

   What wreath for Lamia? What for Lycius?
What for the sage, old Apollonius?
Upon her aching forehead be there hung
The leaves of willow and of adder's tongue,[4]
225   And for the youth, quick, let us strip for him
The thyrsus,[5] that his watching eyes may swim
Into forgetfulness; and, for the sage,
Let spear-grass and the spiteful thistle wage
War on his temples. Do not all charms fly
230   At the mere touch of cold philosophy?°   *scientific analysis*
There was an awful° rainbow once in heaven: *awesome*
We know her woof, her texture; she is given
In the dull catalogue of common things.
Philosophy will clip an Angel's wings,
235   Conquer all mysteries by rule and line,
Empty the haunted air, and gnomed mine—

---

4. Fern with leaves that look like snakes' tongues,   emblem of grief.
supposed to be medicinally soothing; the willow is an   5. Bacchus's vine-entwined staff, an emblem of inebriation.

Unweave a rainbow, as it erewhile made
The tender-person'd Lamia melt into a shade.[6]

    By her glad Lycius sitting, in chief place,
240   Scarce saw in all the room another face,
Till, checking his love trance, a cup he took
Full brimm'd, and opposite sent forth a look
'Cross the broad table, to beseech a glance
From his old teacher's wrinkled countenance,
245   And pledge° him. The bald-head philosopher   *drink a toast to*
Had fix'd his eye, without a twinkle or stir
Full on the alarmed beauty of the bride,
Brow-beating her fair form, and troubling her sweet pride.
Lycius then press'd her hand, with devout touch,
250   As pale it lay upon the rosy couch:
'Twas icy, and the cold ran through his veins;
Then sudden it grew hot, and all the pains
Of an unnatural heat shot to his heart.
"Lamia, what means this? Wherefore dost thou start?°   *Why are you startled?*
255   Know'st thou that man?" Poor Lamia answer'd not.
He gaz'd into her eyes, and not a jot
Own'd° they the lovelorn piteous appeal: *recognized*
More, more he gaz'd: his human senses reel:
Some hungry spell that loveliness absorbs;
260   There was no recognition in those orbs.
"Lamia!" he cried—and no soft-toned reply.
The many heard, and the loud revelry
Grew hush; the stately music no more breathes;
The myrtle[7] sicken'd in a thousand wreaths.
265   By faint degrees, voice, lute, and pleasure ceased;
A deadly silence step by step increased,
Until it seem'd a horrid presence there,
And not a man but felt the terror in his hair.
"Lamia!" he shriek'd; and nothing but the shriek
270   With its sad echo did the silence break.
"Begone, foul dream!" he cried, gazing again
In the bride's face, where now no azure vein
Wander'd on fair-spaced temples; no soft bloom
Misted the cheek; no passion to illume
275   The deep-recessed vision:—all was blight;
Lamia, no longer fair, there sat a deadly white.
"Shut, shut those juggling° eyes, thou ruthless man!   *magic-working*
Turn them aside, wretch! or the righteous ban
Of all the Gods, whose dreadful images

6. B. R. Haydon's *Autobiography* records a party at which Keats and Charles Lamb toasted to "Newton's confusion"—a light curse on the scientist whose optics "had destroyed all the poetry of the rainbow by reducing it to the prismatic colours." The "progress of knowledge," remarked Hazlitt in his lecture *On Poetry in General* (1818), tends to limit "the imagination, and to clip the wings of poetry." The gnomes of folklore guarded the precious ore of their underground world. In his essay in *The Champion*, 21 December 1817, Keats sighed, "romance lives but in the books. The goblin is driven from the hearth, and the rainbow is robbed of its mystery."
7. Plant sacred to Venus, an emblem of love-constancy.

280   Here represent their shadowy presences,
       May pierce them on the sudden with the thorn
       Of painful blindness; leaving thee forlorn,
       In trembling dotage to the feeblest fright
       Of conscience, for their long offended might,
285   For all thine impious proud-heart sophistries,°   *verbal trickery*
       Unlawful magic, and enticing lies.
       Corinthians! look upon that gray-beard wretch!
       Mark how, possess'd, his lashless eyelids stretch
       Around his demon eyes! Corinthians, see!
290   My sweet bride withers at their potency."
       "Fool!" said the sophist, in an under-tone
       Gruff with contempt; which a death-nighing moan
       From Lycius answer'd, as heart-struck and lost,
       He sank supine° beside the aching ghost.   *lying stupefied*
295   "Fool! Fool!" repeated he, while his eyes still
       Relented not, nor mov'd; "from every ill
       Of life have I preserv'd thee to this day,
       And shall I see thee made a serpent's prey?"
       Then Lamia breath'd death breath; the sophist's eye,
300   Like a sharp spear, went through her utterly,
       Keen, cruel, perceant,° stinging: she, as well   *piercing (archaism)*
       As her weak hand could any meaning tell,
       Motion'd him to be silent; vainly so,
       He look'd and look'd again a level—No!
305   "A Serpent!" echoed he; no sooner said,
       Than with a frightful scream she vanished:
       And Lycius' arms were empty of delight,
       As were his limbs of life, from that same night.
       On the high couch he lay!—his friends came round—
310   Supported him—no pulse, or breath they found,
       And, in its marriage robe, the heavy body wound.*

*"Philostratus, in his fourth book *de Vita Apollonii*,[8] hath a memorable instance in this kind, which I may not omit, of one Menippus Lycius, a young man twenty-five years of age, that going betwixt Cenchreas and Corinth, met such a phantasm in the habit of a fair gentlewoman, which taking him by the hand, carried him home to her house, in the suburbs of Corinth, and told him she was a Phoenician by birth, and if he would tarry with her, he should hear her sing and play, and drink such wine as never any drank, and no man should molest him; but she, being fair and lovely, would live and die with him, that was fair and lovely to behold. The young man, a philosopher, otherwise staid and discreet, able to moderate his passions, though not this of love, tarried with her a while to his great content, and at last

8. Greek philosopher Flavius Philostratus (c. 170–244) wrote the life of Apollonius of Tyana (in Asia Minor), 1st-century Pythagorean philosopher, known for moral and religious probity, and also "well skilled in magic, and thoroughly acquainted with those arts which can captivate and astonish the vulgar" (this from *Lemprière's Classical Dictionary*, used by Keats). Oxford scholar and lifelong bachelor Robert Burton first published *The Anatomy of Melancholy* in 1620, and added to it successively for the rest of his life. It is an eccentric work reflecting vast reading and erudition, rendered in extravagant prose. "Melancholy" is the pathological effect of an intense devotion to books and reading, both the subject and the cause of Burton's obsessive masterpiece.

married her, to whose wedding, amongst other guests, came Apollonius; who, by some probable conjectures, found her out to be a serpent, a lamia; and that all her furniture was, like Tantalus' gold, descried by Homer, no substance but mere illusions. When she saw herself descried, she wept, and desired Apollonius to be silent, but he would not be moved, and thereupon she, plate, house, and all that was in it, vanished in an instant: many thousands took notice of this fact, for it was done in the midst of Greece."

Burton's 'Anatomy of Melancholy.' Part 3. Sect. 2. Memb. 1. Subs. 1.

THE FALL OF HYPERION: A DREAM   Keats began this epic project in fall 1818, attracted to the grandeur of Miltonic blank verse but not the Miltonic "balance of good and evil" constantly measured in *Paradise Lost.* As his letter of 3 May 1818 shows (see pages 1049–51), he was interested in the struggle with irremediable pain and suffering, without having this darkness explained as the wages of sin. He turned to pre-Christian mythology, the story of the Titans' dethronement and expulsion from heaven by the next generation, their children the Olympians. Surpassing the Titan sun-god Hyperion, Olympian Apollo, nurtured by Mnemosyne, goddess of memory and mother of the muses, would be symbolic light, a god of poetry, learning, medicine. Yet by April 1819, Keats had become more occupied with the stunned agony of the fallen gods and the anxious apprehensions of the yet-to-fall Hyperion, brother to the already fallen Titan king, Saturn. He put the poem aside. When he returned to it later that year, after the death of his own brother, it was to recast it as a Dantean dream vision: a poet's dream of his fall from paradise into a wide wasteland (involving many echoes of and allusions to Dante's *Purgatorio*), where he experiences near death. He meets Moneta (her name evoking "admonition"), sole remnant of the Titans and bearer of their world in her memory. There is no god of poetry in this dream, only a human poet whom she accuses of being no poet at all, merely a fevered dreamer of no use to humanity. When he protests, she offers him a test, taking him into the theater of her memory (and back to the text of Keats's first *Hyperion*), to be immersed in the misery of the fallen Titans; then, with the burden of this foreknowledge (and his own near death), she challenges him to witness Hyperion's anxious apprehensions of his doom.

Keats abandoned this attempt, too. In the letter in which he recounts his inspiration by another "fall," *To Autumn*, he reports that he has "given up" on the project, feeling that its language was still affecting "Miltonic intonation" and syntax, mannerisms that produced a "false beauty proceeding from art" rather than "the true voice of feeling": "Miltonic verse cannot be written but in an artful or rather artist's humour. I wish to give myself up to other sensations." Yet like Milton, Keats indulged the art of inventing words for the sensations he wished to convey: "faulture" to convey "fault" and "failure" (1.70); "sooth" for "smooth," "soothing," "truthful" (1.155); "mourn" as a noun (1.231); "immortal sickness" (1.258), a paradox played against the medical term, "mortal sickness"; the negatives, "nerveless," "unsceptered," "realmless," to describe fallen Saturn (1.234); "adorant" (1.283) for prayerful and adoring. The first fragment, *Hyperion*, published over Keats's objections in the 1820 volume, was admired by Percy Shelley and even by Byron. When *The Fall of Hyperion* was published in 1857, it spoke to the critical Victorian debate about the relevance of poets, poetic vision, and poetic idealism to the modern age.

The Fall of Hyperion: A Dream

Canto I

Fanatics° have their dreams, wherewith they weave   *cultists*
A paradise for a sect; the savage too
From forth the loftiest fashion of his sleep

Guesses at Heaven; pity these have not
5   Trac'd upon vellum° or wild Indian leaf   *parchment*
The shadows of melodious utterance.
But bare of laurel they live, dream, and die;[1]
For Poesy alone can tell her dreams,
With the fine spell of words alone can save
10   Imagination from the sable charm
And dumb° enchantment. Who alive can say,   *mute*
"Thou art no Poet; mayst not tell thy dreams"?
Since every man whose soul is not a clod
Hath visions, and would speak, if he had lov'd,
15   And been well nurtured in his mother tongue.
Whether the dream now purposed to rehearse
Be poet's or Fanatic's will be known
When this warm scribe my hand is in the grave.[2]

Methought I stood[3] where trees of every clime,
20   Palm, Myrtle, oak, and sycamore, and beech,
With plantane, and spice blossoms, made a screen;
In neighbourhood of fountains, by the noise
Soft showering in mine ears; and, by the touch
Of scent, not far from roses. Turning round,
25   I saw an arbour with a drooping roof
Of trellis vines, and bells, and larger blooms,
Like floral-censers swinging light in air;
Before its wreathed doorway, on a mound
Of moss, was spread a feast of summer fruits,
30   Which nearer seen, seem'd refuse of a meal
By Angel tasted, or our Mother Eve;[4]
For empty shells were scattered on the grass,
And grapestalks but half bare, and remnants more,
Sweet smelling, whose pure kinds I could not know.
35   Still was more plenty than the fabled horn[5]
Thrice emptied could pour forth, at banqueting
For Proserpine return'd to her own fields,
Where the white heifers low. And appetite
More yearning than on earth I ever felt
40   Growing within, I ate deliciously;
And, after not long, thirsted, for thereby
Stood a cool vessel of transparent juice,

1. The laurel wreath, bestowed as a public honor, is the emblem of poetic fame and associated in classical mythology with Apollo, god of poetry. Keats echoes Thomas Gray's surmise in *Elegy Written in a Country Churchyard* (1751) that "some mute inglorious Milton here may rest" (59); he is also thinking of Wordsworth's reference in Book 1 of *The Excursion* (1814) to those "Poets" who lack "the accomplishment of verse" (80).
2. In a letter, Keats called this paragraph "the induction" to the dream; for the last image, see *This Living Hand*.
3. The first dreamscape (19–46), cued by the language of medieval dream allegory ("Methought"), evokes the realm of "Flora, and old Pan" in *Sleep and Poetry* (101–121) and the "Chamber of Infant Thought" in the letter of 3 May 1818 (see page 1051).
4. Alluding to the meal Eve served to Adam and the angel who visits Eden to tutor him (*Paradise Lost* 5.303–307 and 326–28), lines Keats marked in his copy.
5. The cornucopia, emblem of Ceres, goddess of grain and the mother of Proserpine, doomed to spend half the year in the underworld and half in the fields above.

Sipp'd by the wander'd bee, the which I took,
And, pledging all the Mortals of the World,
45   And all the dead whose names are in our lips,°   *still spoken of*
Drank. That full draught is parent of my theme.[6]
No Asian poppy,° nor Elixir fine°   *opium / subtle potion*
Of the soon fading jealous Caliphat;
No poison gender'd in close Monkish cell
50   To thin the scarlet conclave of old Men,[7]
Could so have rapt unwilling life away.
Among the fragrant husks and berries crush'd,
Upon the grass, I struggled hard against
The domineering potion, but in vain:
55   The cloudy swoon came on, and down I sunk
Like a Silenus on an antique vase.[8]
How long I slumber'd 'tis a chance to guess.
When sense of life return'd, I started up
As if with wings; but the fair trees were gone,
60   The mossy mound and arbour were no more;
I look'd around upon the carved sides
Of an old sanctuary with roof august,
Builded so high, it seem'd that filmed clouds
Might spread beneath, as o'er the stars of heaven;
65   So old the place was, I remembered none
The like upon the earth; what I had seen
Of gray Cathedrals, buttress'd walls, rent towers,
The superannuations° of sunk realms,   *remnants*
Or Nature's Rocks toil'd hard in waves and winds,
70   Seem'd but the faulture of decrepit things
To° that eternal domed Monument.   *compared to*
Upon the marble at my feet there lay
Store of strange vessels, and large draperies,
Which needs had been of dyed asbestus° wove,   *incombustible fiber*
75   Or° in that place the moth could not corrupt,[9]   *or else*
So white the linen; so, in some, distinct
Ran imageries from a sombre loom.
All in a mingled heap confus'd there lay
Robes, golden tongs, censer and chafing dish,
80   Girdles, and chains, and holy jewelries[1]—

     Turning from these with awe, once more I rais'd
My eyes to fathom the space every way;
The embossed roof, the silent massy range
Of columns north and South, ending in mist

---

6. The drink engenders the dream-within-a-dream that constitutes the rest of the fragment.
7. Stock figures of intrigue in "gothic" fiction: a caliph is a Muslim ruler, here poisoning a rival (that "elixir") but doomed ("soon fading") himself; the scarlet conclave is the red-robed College of Cardinals in the Vatican, who convene on the Pope's death to elect a successor.

8. A jolly old satyr (half god, half goat), tutor of Bacchus, god of wine and revelry.
9. "Lay up for yourselves treasures in heaven, where neither moth nor rust doth corrupt," preaches Jesus (Matthew 6.20).
1. Remnants of Greek and Hebrew rituals.

85 Of nothing; then to Eastward, where black gates
  Were shut against the sunrise evermore.
  Then to the West I look'd, and saw far off
  An Image, huge of feature as a cloud,
  At level of whose feet an altar slept,
90 To be approach'd on either side by steps,
  And marble balustrade, and patient travail
  To count with toil the innumerable degrees.
  Towards the altar sober-pac'd I went,
  Repressing haste, as too unholy there;
95 And, coming nearer, saw beside the shrine
  One minist'ring; and there arose a flame.
  When in mid-May[2] the sickening East Wind
  Shifts sudden to the South, the small warm rain
  Melts out the frozen incense from all flowers,
100 And fills the air with so much pleasant health
  That even the dying man forgets his shroud;
  Even so that lofty sacrificial fire,
  Sending forth Maian incense,[3] spread around
  Forgetfulness of everything but bliss,
105 And clouded all the altar with soft smoke,
  From whose white fragrant curtains thus I heard
  Language pronounc'd: "If thou canst not ascend
  These steps, die on that marble where thou art.
  Thy flesh, near cousin to the common dust,
110 Will parch for lack of nutriment—thy bones
  Will wither in few years, and vanish so
  That not the quickest eye could find a grain
  Of what thou now art on that pavement cold.
  The sands of thy short life are spent this hour,
115 And no hand in the Universe can turn
  Thy hour glass, if these gummed° leaves be burnt   *aromatic*
  Ere thou canst mount up these immortal steps."
  I heard, I look'd: two senses both at once
  So fine, so subtle, felt the tyranny
120 Of that fierce threat and the hard task proposed.
  Prodigious seem'd the toil; the leaves were yet
  Burning,—when suddenly a palsied chill
  Struck from the paved level up my limbs,
  And was ascending quick to put cold grasp
125 Upon those streams° that pulse beside the throat: *arteries*
  I shriek'd; and the sharp anguish of my shriek
  Stung my own ears—I strove hard to escape
  The numbness; strove to gain the lowest step.
  Slow, heavy, deadly was my pace: the cold

---

2. Woodhouse's transcript (our basis) has "midway." Poet and textual scholar A. E. Housman proposed the correction to "mid-May" (*TLS* 8 May 1924).

3. Maia is the Greek goddess of May. Keats borrows language from the end of Canto 24 of Dante's *Purgatorio*, about the enrichment and nourishment of the soul.

130 Grew stifling, suffocating, at the heart;
And when I clasp'd my hands I felt them not.
One minute before death, my iced foot touch'd
The lowest stair; and as it touch'd, life seem'd
To pour in at the toes: I mounted up,
135 As once fair Angels on a ladder flew
From the green turf to heaven.[4]—"Holy Power,"
Cried I, approaching near the horned shrine,[5]
"What am I that should so be saved from death?
What am I, that another death come not
140 To choak my utterance, sacrilegious, here?"
Then said the veiled shadow—"Thou hast felt
What 'tis to die and live again before
Thy fated hour. That thou hadst power to do so
Is thine own safety; thou hast dated on°   postponed
145 Thy doom."°—"High Prophetess," said I, "purge off   fate
Benign, if so it please thee, my mind's film."[6]—
"None can usurp this height," returned that shade,
"But those to whom the miseries of the world
Are misery, and will not let them rest[7]
150 All else who find a haven in the world,
Where they may thoughtless sleep away their days,
If by a chance into this fane° they come,   temple
Rot on the pavement where thou rotted'st half."—
"Are there not thousands in the world," said I,
155 Encouraged by the sooth° voice of the shade,   soothing, trustworthy
"Who love their fellows even to the death;
Who feel the giant agony of the world;[8]
And more, like slaves to poor humanity,
Labour for mortal good? I sure should see
160 Other men here: but I am here alone."
"They whom thou spak'st of are no vision'ries,"
Rejoin'd that voice—"They are no dreamers weak,
They seek no wonder but the human face;
No music but a happy-noted voice—
165 They come not here, they have no thought to come—
And thou art here, for thou art less than they—

---

4. Just before God promises Jacob that his descendants will claim the earth, Jacob dreams of a ladder from earth to heaven and "the angels of God ascending and descending on it" (Genesis 28.12); Milton alludes to this dream in describing Satan's view of the stairs to Heaven's Gate (*Paradise Lost* 3.510–11).
5. Horns often embellish ancient altars (Exodus 27.2); the image may also involve a Keatsian symbolism, the "horn-book" of instruction in the "vale of Soul-making" (letter, 21 April 1819; see page 1056).
6. Echoing blind Milton's plea for "Celestial Light" to "irradiate" his mind: "all mist from thence / Purge and disperse, that I may see and tell / Of things invisible to mortal sight" (*Paradise Lost* 3.51–55).

7. In tension with a staging in the poetry of a dream, lines 147–210 unfold a set of distinctions across which the status of the "I" (dreamer and present poet) is negotiated: visionary dreamers who feel "the miseries" of the world versus mere sleepers; the poet is "half" of each (147–53); those who feel miseries: humanitarian doers versus visionary dreamers (154–60); weak, fevered dreamers who cannot bear misery versus humanitarian benefactors (161–71); those who can accept joy and pain versus the self-poisoning dreamer (171–81); poets of wisdom and healing versus novice poets (187–92); healing poets versus merely impotent dreamers (188–202); true poets versus pretenders and braggarts (202–10).
8. The agenda of *Sleep and Poetry* 122–25 (page 981).

What benefit canst thou do, or all thy tribe,
To the great World? Thou art a dreaming thing;
A fever of thyself—think of the Earth;
170 What bliss even in hope is there for thee?
What haven? Every creature hath its home;
Every sole man hath days of joy and pain,
Whether his labours be sublime or low—
The pain alone; the joy alone; distinct:
175 Only the dreamer venoms all his days,
Bearing more woe than all his Sins deserve.
Therefore, that happiness be somewhat shar'd,
Such things as thou art are admitted oft
Into like gardens thou didst pass erewhile,
180 And suffer'd° in these Temples; for that cause   *allowed entry*
Thou standest safe beneath this statue's knees."
"That I am favoured for unworthiness,
By such propitious parley medicin'd
In sickness not ignoble, I rejoice,
185 Aye, and could weep for love of such award."
So answer'd I, continuing, "If it please,
Majestic shadow,[9] tell me: sure not all
Those melodies sung into the world's ear
Are useless: sure a poet is a sage;
190 A humanist,° Physician to all Men.   *humanitarian*
That I am none I feel, as Vultures feel
They are no birds when Eagles are abroad.
What am I then? Thou spakest of my tribe:
What tribe?"—The tall shade veil'd in drooping white
195 Then spake, so much more earnest, that the breath
Mov'd the thin linen folds that drooping hung
About a golden censer from the hand
Pendent.—"Art thou not of the dreamer tribe?
The poet and the dreamer are distinct,
200 Diverse, sheer opposite, antipodes.°   *exact opposites*
The one pours out a balm upon the world,
The other vexes it." Then shouted I
Spite of myself, and with a Pythia's spleen[1]
"Apollo! faded, far flown Apollo!
205 Where is thy misty pestilence[2] to creep
Into the dwellings, through the door crannies,
Of all the mock lyrists, large self worshippers,

9. The epithets "shade" and "shadow" evoke Dante's use of these terms throughout *Purgatorio* and the veiled Beatrice of *Paradiso*, as well as the veiled goddess Isis of Egyptian mythology. In Woodhouse's manuscript, 187–210 are canceled, with a note that this was Keats's intention (187 is repeated at 211, and 194–98 at 216–20), and in 1857 *The Fall* appeared without them; editorial tradition has restored them to document Keats's compositional process and pressing concerns; see the comparison of poetry and philosophy in the letters, 22 November 1817 and 19 March 1819 (pages 1045, 1054).
1. The Pythia is the priestess of Delphi who delivered the oracles of Apollo, god of poetry and medicine.
2. In the *Iliad*, Apollo is also the agent of plagues; the diatribe against modern poets is aimed, variously, at Byron, Wordsworth, and Hunt.

And careless Hectorers° in proud bad verse?   *bullies, braggarts*
Though I breathe death with them it will be life
210 To see them sprawl before me into graves.
Majestic shadow, tell me where I am:
Whose altar this; for whom this incense curls:
What Image this, whose face I cannot see,
For the broad marble knees; and who thou art,
215 Of accent feminine, so courteous."
Then the tall shade, in drooping linen veil'd
Spake out, so much more earnest, that her breath
Stirr'd the thin folds of gauze that drooping hung
About a golden censer from her hand
220 Pendent; and by her voice I knew she shed
Long treasured tears. "This temple sad and lone
Is all° spar'd from the thunder of a war   *all that is*
Foughten long since by giant hierarchy
Against rebellion: this old image here,
225 Whose carved features wrinkled as he fell,
Is Saturn's; I, Moneta, left supreme
Sole Priestess of his desolation."³—
I had no words to answer; for my tongue,
Useless, could find about its roofed home
230 No syllable of a fit Majesty
To make rejoinder to Moneta's mourn.
There was a silence while the altar's blaze
Was fainting for sweet food: I look'd thereon,
And on the paved floor, where nigh were pil'd
235 Faggots° of cinnamon, and many heaps   *bundles*
Of other crisped spice-wood—then again
I look'd upon the altar and its horns
Whiten'd with ashes, and its lang'rous flame,
And then upon the offerings again;
240 And so by turns—till sad Moneta cried,
"The sacrifice is done, but not the less
Will I be kind to thee for thy good will.
My power, which to me is still a curse,
Shall be to thee a wonder; for the scenes
245 Still swooning vivid through my globed brain
With an electral changing misery
Thou shalt with those dull mortal eyes behold,
Free from all pain, if wonder pain thee not."
As near as an immortal's sphered words
250 Could to a Mother's soften, were these last:
And yet I had a terror of her robes,

---

3. Saturn, king of the Titans, was displaced by his son Jupiter. The shattered statue evokes Shelley's *Ozymandias* (see page 877). Moneta is an alternative name for Mnemosyne, originally a Titan, then, by Jupiter, mother of the Muses, and in the first *Hyperion* the tutor of Apollo, Hyperion's successor. In some accounts Jupiter's wife Juno was called "Moneta" ("she who warns") after she warned the Romans of the invading Gauls.

And chiefly of the veils, that from her brow
Hung pale, and curtain'd her in mysteries
That made my heart too small to hold its blood.
255   This saw that Goddess, and with sacred hand
Parted the veils. Then saw I a wan face,
Not pin'd° by human sorrows, but bright blanch'd   *wasted, pained*
By an immortal sickness which kills not;
It works a constant change, which happy death
260   Can put no end to; deathwards progressing
To no death was that visage; it had pass'd
The lily and the snow; and beyond these
I must not think now, though I saw that face—
But for her eyes I should have fled away.
265   They held me back with a benignant light,
Soft mitigated by divinest lids
Half closed, and visionless entire they seem'd
Of all external things—they saw me not,
But in blank splendour beam'd like the mild moon,
270   Who comforts those she sees not, who knows not
What eyes are upward cast. As I had found
A grain of gold upon a mountain's side,
And twing'd with avarice strain'd out my eyes
To search its sullen entrails rich with ore,
275   So at the view of sad Moneta's brow,
I ached to see what things the hollow brain
Behind enwombed: what high tragedy
In the dark secret Chambers of her skull
Was acting, that could give so dread a stress
280   To her cold lips, and fill with such a light
Her planetary eyes, and touch her voice
With such a sorrow—"Shade of Memory!"[4]
Cried I, with act adorant at her feet,
"By all the gloom hung round thy fallen house,
285   By this last Temple, by the golden age,[5]
By great Apollo, thy dear foster child,
And by thy self, forlorn divinity,
The pale Omega[6] of a wither'd race,
Let me behold, according as thou said'st,
290   What in thy brain so ferments to and fro."—
No sooner had this conjuration pass'd
My devout Lips, than side by side we stood
(Like a stunt bramble by a solemn Pine)
Deep in the shady sadness of a vale,[7]
295   Far sunken from the healthy breath of morn,

4. "Memory" evokes Moneta's alternative name, "Mnemosyne" ("Memory"); see lines 1.331 and 2.50.
5. After his defeat by Jupiter, Saturn fled to Italy, to preside over a "Golden Age" of serenity and peace.
6. Last letter of the Greek alphabet.

7. The first line of *Hyperion*; from here on, Keats incorporates this first attempt, revising it to make the poet not just the epic narrator but a witness, feeling and suffering the burden of what he beholds.

Far from the fiery noon and Eve's one star.
Onward I look'd beneath the gloomy boughs,
And saw, was first I thought an Image huge,
Like to the Image pedestal'd so high
300   In Saturn's Temple. Then Moneta's voice
Came brief upon mine ear,—"So Saturn sat
When he had lost his realms."—Whereon there grew
A power within me of enormous ken,
To see as a God sees, and take the depth
305   Of things as nimbly as the outward eye
Can size and shape pervade. The lofty theme
At those few words hung vast before my mind,
With half unravel'd web. I set myself
Upon an Eagle's watch, that I might see,
310   And seeing ne'er forget. No stir of life
Was in this shrouded vale, not so much air
As in the zoning° of a Summer's day   *course, range*
Robs not one light seed from the feather'd grass,
But where the dead leaf fell there did it rest.
315   A stream went voiceless by, still deaden'd more
By reason of the fallen Divinity
Spreading more shade: the Naiad° mid her reeds   *water nymph*
Press'd her cold finger closer to her lips.
Along the margin sand large footmarks went
320   No further than to where old Saturn's feet
Had rested, and there slept, how long a sleep!
Degraded, cold, upon the sodden ground
His old right hand lay nerveless, listless, dead,
Unsceptred; and his realmless eyes were clos'd,
325   While his bow'd head seem'd listening to the Earth,
His antient mother, for some comfort yet.[8]

      It seem'd no force could wake him from his place;
But there came one who with a kindred hand
Touch'd his wide shoulders, after bending low
330   With reverence, though to one who knew it not.
Then came the griev'd voice of Mnemosyne,
And griev'd I hearken'd. "That divinity
Whom thou saw'st step from yon forlornest wood,
And with slow pace approach our fallen King,
335   Is Thea,[9] softest-natur'd of our Brood."
I mark'd the goddess in fair statuary°   *stature, statue*
Surpassing wan Moneta by the head,°   *a head taller*
And in her sorrow nearer woman's tears.
There was a listening fear in her regard,
340   As if calamity had but begun;

---

8. Heaven and Earth are the parents of Saturn and the
other Titans (cf. 357–58).

9. Hyperion's sister and wife.

As if the vanward clouds of evil days
Had spent their malice, and the sullen rear
Was with its stored thunder labouring up.[1]
One hand she press'd upon that aching spot
345   Where beats the human heart; as if just there,
Though an immortal, she felt cruel pain;
The other upon Saturn's bended neck
She laid, and to the level of his hollow ear
Leaning, with parted lips, some words she spake
350   In solemn tenor and deep organ tune;°   tone
Some mourning words, which in our feeble tongue
Would come in this-like accenting; how frail
To that large utterance of the early Gods!—
"Saturn, look up—and for what, poor lost King?[2]
355   I have no comfort for thee, no—not one—
I cannot cry, *Wherefore thus sleepest thou?*
For heaven is parted from thee, and the earth
Knows thee not, so afflicted, for a God;
And Ocean too, with all its solemn noise,
360   Has from thy sceptre pass'd and all the air
Is emptied of thy hoary Majesty.
Thy thunder, captious° at the new command,   quarrelsome
Rumbles reluctant o'er our fallen house;°   dynasty
And thy sharp lightning in unpracticed hands
365   Scorches and burns our once serene domain.
With such remorseless speed still come new woes
That unbelief has not a space to breathe.
Saturn, sleep on:—Me thoughtless, why should I
Thus violate thy slumbrous solitude?
370   Why should I ope thy melancholy eyes?
Saturn, sleep on, while at thy feet I weep.—"

        As when upon a tranced Summer Night,
Forests, branch-charmed by the earnest stars,
Dream, and so dream all night, without a noise,
375   Save from one gradual solitary gust,
Swelling upon the silence; dying off;
As if the ebbing air had but one wave;
So came these words, and went; the while in tears
She press'd her fair large forehead to the earth,
380   Just where her fallen hair might spread in curls,
A soft and silken mat for Saturn's feet.
Long, long, those two were postured motionless,
Like sculpture builded up upon the grave
Of their own power. A long awful time
385   I look'd upon them; still they were the same;

---

1. Military imagery; the "van" is the front line in battle.   2. Evoking both exiled King Lear and King George III, stripped of power.

The frozen God still bending to the Earth,
And the sad Goddess weeping at his feet.
Moneta silent. Without stay or prop
But my own weak mortality, I bore
390 The load of this eternal quietude,
The unchanging gloom and the three fixed shapes
Ponderous upon my senses a whole Moon.
For by my burning brain I measured sure
Her silver seasons shedded on the night,
395 And every day by day methought I grew
More gaunt and ghostly.—Oftentimes I pray'd
Intense, that Death would take me from the Vale
And all its burthens—Gasping with despair
Of change, hour after hour I curs'd myself:
400 Until old Saturn rais'd his faded eyes,
And look'd around, and saw his Kingdom gone,
And all the gloom and sorrow of the place,
And that fair kneeling Goddess at his feet.
As the moist scent of flowers, and grass, and leaves
405 Fills forest dells with a pervading air
Known to the woodland nostril, so the words
Of Saturn fill'd the mossy glooms around,
Even to the hollows of time-eaten oaks,
And to the windings of the foxes' hole,
410 With sad, low tones, while thus he spake, and sent
Strange musings to the solitary Pan.[3]

        "Moan, brethren, moan; for we are swallow'd up
And buried from all godlike exercise
Of influence benign on planets pale,
415 And peaceful sway upon man's harvesting,
And all those acts which Deity supreme
Doth ease its heart of love in. Moan and wail.
Moan, brethren, moan; for lo! the rebel spheres
Spin round, the stars their antient courses keep,
420 Clouds still with shadowy moisture haunt the earth,
Still suck their fill of light from Sun and Moon,
Still buds the tree, and still the sea-shores murmur.
There is no death in all the universe
No smell of Death—there shall be death—Moan, moan,
425 Moan, Cybele,[4] moan, for thy pernicious babes
Have chang'd a God into a shaking Palsy.
Moan, brethren, moan; for I have no strength left,
Weak as the reed—weak—feeble as my voice—
O, O, the pain, the pain of feebleness.
430 Moan, moan; for still I thaw—or give me help:
Throw down those Imps° and give me victory.   *rebel Titan sons*

3. "Solitary" because of the general desolation in nature,   4. Saturn's wife, mother of the rebellious gods.
and more particularly, his loss of the nymph Syrinx.

Let me hear other groans, and trumpets blown
Of triumph calm, and hymns of festival
From the gold peaks of Heaven's high piled clouds;
435   Voices of soft proclaim, and silver stir
Of strings in hollow shells; and let there be
Beautiful things made new for the surprize
Of the sky children."—So he feebly ceas'd,
With such a poor and sickly sounding pause,
440   Methought I heard some old Man of the earth
Bewailing earthly loss; nor could my eyes
And ears act with that unison of sense
Which marries sweet sound with the grace of form,
And dolorous accent from a tragic harp
445   With large limb'd visions—More I scrutinized:
Still fix'd he sat beneath the sable trees,
Whose arms spread straggling in wild serpent forms,
With leaves all hush'd: his awful presence there
(Now all was silent) gave a deadly lie
450   To what I erewhile heard: only his lips
Trembled amid the white curls of his beard.
They told the truth, though, round the snowy locks
Hung nobly, as upon the face of heaven
A midday fleece of clouds. Thea arose
455   And stretch'd her white arm through the hollow dark,
Pointing some whither: whereat he too rose
Like a vast giant seen by men at sea
To grow pale from the waves at dull midnight.
They melted from my sight into the woods:
460   Ere I could turn, Moneta cried—"These twain
Are speeding to the families of grief,
Where roof'd in by black rocks they waste in pain
And darkness, for no hope."—And she spake on,
As ye may read who can unwearied pass
465   Onward from the Antichamber° of this dream,   *entry room*
Where, even at the open doors awhile
I must delay, and glean my memory
Of her high phrase: perhaps no further dare.—

Canto II

"Mortal, that thou may'st understand aright,
I humanize my sayings to thine ear,
Making comparisons of earthly things;[5]
Or thou might'st better listen to the wind,
5   Whose language is to thee a barren noise,

5. The method Archangel Raphael uses—"lik'ning spiritual to corporal forms"—to relate to Adam the "exploits / Of warring Spirits" (the war in Heaven, fought between the legions of Satan and Christ; *Paradise Lost* 5.565ff.).

Though it blows legend-laden[6] through the trees—
In melancholy realms big tears are shed,
More sorrow like to this, and such-like woe,
Too huge for mortal tongue, or pen of scribe.
10 The Titans fierce, self-hid, or prison-bound,
Groan for the old allegiance once more,
Listening in their doom for Saturn's voice.
But one of our whole eagle-brood still keeps
His sov'reignty, and Rule, and Majesty;
15 Blazing Hyperion on his orbed fire
Still sits, still snuffs the incense teeming up
From man to the Sun's God: yet unsecure;
For as upon the Earth dire prodigies°   *ominous events*
Fright and perplex,[7] so also shudders he:
20 Not at dog's howl or gloom-bird's Even° screech,   *Evening*
Or the familiar visiting of one
Upon the first toll of his passing bell:°   *death knell*
But horrors, portion'd to a giant nerve
Make great Hyperion ache. His palace bright,
25 Bastion'd with pyramids of glowing gold,
And touch'd with shade of bronzed obelisks,
Glares a blood red through all the thousand Courts,
Arches, and domes, and fiery galleries:
And all its curtains of Aurorian[8] clouds
30 Flush angerly: when he would taste the wreaths
Of incense breath'd aloft from sacred hills,
Instead of sweets, his ample palate takes
Savour of poisonous brass and metals sick.[9]
Wherefore when harbour'd in the sleepy West,
35 After the full completion of fair day,
For rest divine upon exalted couch
And slumber in the arms of melody,
He paces through the pleasant hours of ease
With strides colossal,[1] on from Hall to Hall;
40 While, far within each aisle and deep recess,
His winged minions in close clusters stand
Amaz'd, and full of fear; like anxious men
Who on a wide plain gather in sad troops,
When earthquakes jar their battlements and towers.
45 Even now, while Saturn, rous'd from icy trance
Goes, step for step, with Thea from yon woods,

---

6. In a letter of 21 September 1819, Keats expressed his pleasure at the "fine sound" of this compound adjective (cf. "leaf-fringed legend" in *Ode on a Grecian Urn*).
7. Alluding to Milton's description of a lunar eclipse (*Paradise Lost* 1.594–600), underlined by Keats in his copy.
8. The goddess Aurora parts the curtains of the dawn when she leaves the bed of her husband, Night.
9. "The last two years taste like brass upon my Palate,"

Keats told Fanny Brawne in August 1820.
1. One of the seven wonders of the ancient world was the 100-foot "Colossus of Rhodes," a harbor-statue of the sun-god Helios, destroyed in antiquity. Keats is recalling Shelley's use of this adjective in *Ozymandias* and Shakespeare's depiction of about-to-be-assassinated Caesar: "he doth bestride the narrow world / Like a Colossus" (*Julius Caesar* 1.2.135–36).

Hyperion, leaving twilight in the rear,
Is sloping to the threshold of the west.—
Thither we tend."—Now in clear light I stood,
50   Reliev'd from the dusk vale. Mnemosyne
Was sitting on a square edg'd polish'd stone,
That in its lucid depth reflected pure
Her priestess-garments.[2] My quick eyes ran on
From stately nave to nave, from vault to vault,
55   Through bowers of fragrant and enwreathed light,
And diamond paved lustrous long arcades.[3]
Anon rush'd by the bright Hyperion;
His flaming robes stream'd out beyond his heels,
And gave a roar, as if of earthly fire,
60   That scar'd away the meek ethereal hours[4]
And made their dove-wings tremble: on he flared[5]—

"This living hand"[1]

This living hand, now warm and capable
Of earnest grasping, would, if it were cold
and in the icy silence of the tomb,
So haunt thy days and chill thy dreaming nights
5   That thou would wish thine own hea[r]t[2] dry of blood
So in my veins red life might stream again,
and thou be conscience-calm'd—see here it is—
I hold it towards you—

c. 1819   1898

"Bright star"[1]

Bright star! would I were steadfast as thou art—
    Not in lone splendour hung aloft the night,
And watching, with eternal lids apart,
    Like Nature's patient sleepless Eremite,°   *worshipper*
5   The moving waters at their priestlike task
    Of pure ablution° round earth's human shores,   *ritual washing*
Or gazing on the new soft fallen mask

2. Alluding to the steep stairs up the side of the Mount of Purgatory in which poet-dreamer Dante sees himself reflected: "The lowest stair was marble white, so smooth / And polish'd, that therein my mirror'd form / Distinct I saw" (*Purgatorio* 9.94–96; H. F. Cary's trans.).
3. In the first fragment, these actions were Hyperion's.
4. Nymphs attending the sun.
5. The sentence recalls Satan's motions through Chaos, "on he fares" (*Paradise Lost* 2.940) and nearing the border of Eden (4.131). Keats's manuscript ends here.
1. A mysterious fragment, context unknown; "hand" is also a term for "handwriting": for the relation of these two senses, see *Fall of Hyperion* 1.16–18.
2. Keats inserted "heat" as superscript between "thine" and "own"; his characteristic dropping of "r" in handwriting

makes it possible that he meant "heart," which best fits the context (although "heat" is relevant).
1. In summer 1818, Keats remarked that the scenery of the lake country "refine[s] one's sensual vision into a sort of north star which can never cease to be open lidded and stedfast over the wonders of the great Power"; sometime before summer 1819, he drafted this sonnet, then wrote this revised version in early autumn 1820 into the volume of Shakespeare's poems he took to Italy; perhaps the last poetry he wrote, it was titled in 19th-century editions "Keats's last sonnet." The opening recalls the heroic self-description of Julius Caesar: "I could be well moved...but I am constant as the Northern Star, / Of whose true-fixed and resting quality / There is no fellow in the firmament" (*Julius Caesar* 3.1.58–62).

Of snow upon the mountains and the moors—
No—yet still steadfast, still unchangeable,
10   Pillow'd upon my fair love's ripening breast,
To feel for ever its soft fall and swell,[2]
    Awake for ever in a sweet unrest,
Still, still to hear her tender-taken breath,
And so live ever—or else swoon to death.

1820   (1838), 1848

LETTERS[1]

To Benjamin Bailey[2]
["THE TRUTH OF IMAGINATION"]

My dear Bailey,   22 November 1817

* * * O I wish I was as certain of the end of all your troubles as that of your momentary start about the authenticity of the Imagination. I am certain of nothing but
of the holiness of the Heart's affections and the truth of Imagination – What the
imagination seizes as Beauty must be truth[3] – whether it existed before or not – for
I have the same Idea of all our Passions as of Love they are all in their sublime, creative of essential Beauty – In a Word, you may know my favorite Speculation by
my first Book and the little song I sent in my last[4] – which is a representation from
the fancy of the probable mode of operating in these Matters – The Imagination
may be compared to Adam's dream – he awoke and found it truth.[5] I am the more
zealous in this affair, because I have never yet been able to perceive how any thing
can be known for truth by consequitive[6] reasoning – and yet it must be – Can it
be that even the greatest Philosopher ever arrived at his goal without putting aside
numerous objections – However it may be, O for a Life of Sensations[7] rather than
of Thoughts! It is 'a Vision in the form of Youth' a Shadow of reality to come – and
this consideration has further convnced me for it has come as auxiliary to another
favorite Speculation of mine, that we shall enjoy ourselves here after by having what
we called happiness on Earth repeated in a finer tone and so repeated – And yet
such a fate can only befall those who delight in Sensation rather than hunger as
you do after Truth – Adam's dream will do here and seems to be a conviction that
Imagination and its empyreal[8] reflection is the same as
human Life and its Spiritual repetition.[9]
But as I was saying – the simple imaginative Mind
may have its rewards in the repetition of its own
silent Working coming continually on the Spirit with a fine Suddenness – to compare great

---

2. One draft has: swell and fall.

1. In order to convey the character of Keats's letter-writing, idiosyncrasies of spelling, punctuation, and capital-
ization are for the most part preserved. Our insertions for
clarity appear in square brackets [ ].

2. Keats met Bailey (1791–1853), a divinity student at
Oxford University, in spring 1817 and stayed with him in
September while he worked on *Endymion*.

3. Keats's persistent testing of the relation of these categories yields a statement of their equation at the end of
Ode on a Grecian Urn (1819).

4. Book 1 of *Endymion* and the lament of the Indian Maid

in Book 4.

5. In *Paradise Lost* Adam dreamed of "the Garden of
bliss," then "wak'd and found / Before mine Eyes all real,
as the dream / Had lively shadow'd" (8.292–311).

6. Keats-coinage, combining "consecutive" and
"consequent."

7. Truth sensed intuitively, by immediate sensation of
experience.

8. In medieval cosmology, the empyrean is the highest
sphere of the heavens.

9. Keats's letter insets this set of seven lines flush left, as if
he were almost drafting verse.

things with small – have you never by being
surprised with an old Melody – in a delicious
place – by a delicious voice, felt over again your very Speculations and Surmises at
the time it first operated on your Soul – do you not remember forming to yourself
the singer's face more beautiful that it was possible and yet with the elevation of the
Moment you did not think so – even then you were mounted on the Wings of Imagination so high – that the Prototype must be here after – that delicious face you will
see – What a time! I am continually running away from the subject – sure this cannot
be exactly the case with a complex Mind – one that is imaginative and at the same
time careful of its fruits – who would exist partly on sensation partly on thought – to
whom it is necessary that years should bring the philosophic Mind.[1] * * * you perhaps
at one time thought there was such a thing as Worldly Happiness to be arrived at, at
certain periods of time marked out – you have of necessity from your disposition been
thus led away – I scarcely remember counting upon any Happiness – I look not for it
if it be not in the present hour – nothing startles me beyond the Moment. The setting
sun will always set me to rights – or if a Sparrow come before my Window I take part
in its existence and pick about the Gravel. The first thing that strikes me on hea[r]ing
a Misfortune having befalled another is this. 'Well it cannot be helped. – he will have
the pleasure of trying the resourses of his spirit, and I beg now my dear Bailey that
hereafter should you observe any thing cold in me not to [put] it to the account of
heartlessness but abstraction – for I assure you I sometimes feel not the influence of
a Passion or Affection during a whole week – and so long this sometimes continues
I begin to suspect myself and the genuiness of my feelings at other times – thinking
them a few barren Tragedy-tears – My Brother Tom is much improved[2] * * *

Your affectionate friend
John Keats —

To George and Thomas Keats[1]
["INTENSITY" AND "NEGATIVE CAPABILITY"]

My dear Brothers   December 181[7]

[21 Dec.] * * * I saw Kean return to the public in Richard III,[2] & finely he did it.
* * * Hone the publisher's trial, you must find very amusing; & as Englishmen very
encouraging—his <u>Not Guilty</u> is a thing, which not to have been, would have dulled
still more Liberty's Emblazoning – Lord Ellenborough has been paid in his own coin—
Wooler & Hone have done us an essential service[3] * * * I spent Friday evening with

---

1. An allusion to Wordsworth's "Intimations" Ode (186); see page 557.

2. Keats's beloved youngest brother (b. 1799) was showing symptoms of tuberculosis by summer 1816; he died in
late 1818.

1. The brothers had lived together since 1816; George
(1797–1841) had taken Tom to Teignmouth, Devonshire for his health.

2. Edmund Kean (1787–1833), charismatic and scandal-
ridden actor who revolutionized the Shakespearean stage
with his passionate performances. Richard III was one of
his celebrated roles; Keats had just published an article
on him in The Champion.

3. Two notorious prosecutions. William Hone had just
been found not guilty on three counts of blasphemous libel for his parodies of the liturgy, of which nearly 100,000
copies had sold. Lord Chief Justice Ellenborough, who
had earlier sentenced John and Leigh Hunt for libel, presided at two of his trials and was humiliated by the loudly
applauded verdict. Thomas Wooler, politician, journalist,
and editor of the radical weekly The Black Dwarf, was acquitted on similar charges the previous June. The trials
were well attended and extremely amusing because the
"offenses" had to be read into the record, thus gaining
audience not only in the courtroom but also in reports in
the "legitimate" press.

Wells & went the next morning to see <u>Death on the Pale horse</u>.[4] It is a wonderful picture, when West's age is considered; But there is nothing to be intense upon; no women one feels mad to kiss; no face swelling into reality. the excellence of every Art is its intensity, capable of making all disagreeables evaporate, from their being in close relationship with Beauty & Truth – Examine King Lear[5] & you will find this examplified throughout; but in this picture we have unpleasantness without any momentous depth of speculation excited, in which to bury its repulsiveness. * * * [?27 Dec.] * * * I had not a dispute but a disquisition[6] with Dilke, on various subjects; several things dovetailed in my mind, & at once it struck me, what quality went to form a Man of Achievement especially in Literature & which Shakespeare posessed so enormously – I mean <u>Negative Capability</u>, that is when man is capable of being in uncertainties, Mysteries, doubts, without any irritable reaching after fact & reason[7]—Coleridge, for instance, would let go by a fine isolated verisimilitude caught from the Penetralium of mystery, from being incapable of remaining content with half knowledge.[8] This pursued through Volumes would perhaps take us no further than this, that with a great poet the sense of Beauty overcomes every other consideration, or rather obliterates all consideration.

Shelley's poem is out & there are words about its being objected too, as much as Queen Mab was. Poor Shelley I think he has his Quota of good qualities, in sooth la!![9]   Write soon to your most sincere friend & affectionate Brother

                                                                                John

To John Hamilton Reynolds[1]
[Wordsworth and "The Whims of an Egotist"]

My dear Reynolds,   3 February 1818

* * * It may be said that we ought to read our Contemporaries. that Wordsworth &c should have their due from us. but for the sake of a few fine imaginative or domestic passages, are we to be bullied into a certain Philosophy engendered in the whims of an Egotist – Every Man has his speculations, but every Man does not brood and peacock over[2] them till he makes a false coinage and deceives himself – Many a man can travel to the very bourne of Heaven,[3] and yet want confidence to put down his half seeing. Sancho[4] will invent a Journey heavenward as well as any body. We hate

---

4. Wells was a schoolmate of Tom; *Death on a Pale Horse*, by American painter Benjamin West, is based on the image in Revelation of the fourth horseman of the apocalypse.
5. West's painting of the storm scene in the play (Keats's rereading of the play the next month would provoke very different terms of description: see his sonnet, page 987).
6. Legalese for formal inquiry. Charles Dilke (1789–1864), government worker and amateur scholar, was a new friend.
7. <u>Negative Capability</u>, Keats's most famous formulation, is a self-conscious oxymoron; compare Keats's antipathy to egotistical assertions of "certain philosophy," "resting places and seeming sure points of Reasoning" (letters to Reynolds, 3 February and 3 May 1818).
8. In 1817, Coleridge published *Biographia Literaria* and *The Rime of the Ancient Mariner* with a marginal gloss. "Penetralium" is Keats's faux-Latin singular of "penetralia," the inmost chamber of a temple.
9. Shelley was forced to withdraw *Laon and Cythna* (1817), an epic featuring the incestuous love of its sibling

hero and heroine; the outcry was as heated as that against *Queen Mab* (1813), a visionary political epic attacking "Kingcraft, Priestcraft, and Statecraft." Keats's "sooth la!" ("the truth!") echoes Cleopatra as she tries, ineptly, to help Antony put on his armor after their night of debauchery (*Antony and Cleopatra* 4.4.8).
1. John Hamilton Reynolds (1794–1852), lawyer and poet, became one of Keats's closest friends; he introduced him to many others who would become friends, and to the publishers, Taylor and Hessey, who published *Endymion* and the 1820 volume.
2. Strut about ostentatiously; OED credits this as the first verb usage.
3. Hamlet describes the afterlife as the "undiscovered country, from whose bourn / No traveler returns" (*Hamlet* 3.1.79–80); bourn: region.
4. Down-to-earth squire to the idealistic hero of Cervantes's *Don Quixote*.

poetry that has a palpable design upon us – and if we do not agree, seems to put its hand in its breeches pocket.[5] Poetry should be great & unobtrusive, a thing which enters into one's soul, and does not startle it or amaze it with itself– but with its subject. – How beautiful are the retired flowers! how would they lose their beauty were they to throng into the highway crying out, "admire me I am a violet! –dote upon me I am a primrose! * * * I will cut all this – I will have no more of Wordsworth or Hunt in particular. * * * I don't mean to deny Wordsworth's grandeur & Hunt's merit, but I mean to say we need not be teazed with grandeur & merit – when we can have them uncontaminated & unobtrusive. Let us have the old Poets, & Robin Hood. Your letter and its sonnets gave me more pleasure than will the 4th Book of Childe Harold & the whole of any body's life & opinions.[6] * * *

Y[r] sincere friend and Coscribbler
John Keats.

To John Taylor[1]
["A Few Axioms"]

My dear Taylor,   27 February 1818

* * * In Poetry I have a few Axioms, and you will see how far I am from their Centre. 1st I think Poetry should surprise by a fine excess and not by Singularity – it should strike the Reader as a wording of his own highest thoughts, and appear almost a Remembrance — 2nd Its touches of Beauty should never be half way therby making the reader breathless instead of content: the rise, the progress, the setting of imagery should like the Sun come natural to him – shine over him and set soberly although in magnificence leaving him in the Luxury of twilight – but it is easier to think what Poetry should be than to write it — and this leads me on to another axiom. That if Poetry comes not as naturally as the Leaves to a tree it had better not come at all. However it may be with me I cannot help looking into new countries with 'O for a Muse of fire to ascend!'[2] – If Endymion serves me as a Pioneer perhaps I ought to be content.[3] I have great reason to be content, for thank God I can read and perhaps understand Shakspeare to his depths * * *

Your sincere and oblig[d] friend
John Keats —

To Benjamin Bailey[1]
["Ardent Pursuit"]

My dear Bailey,   13 March 1818

* * * You know my ideas about Religion – I do not think myself more in the right than other people and that nothing in this world is proveable. I wish I could enter

5. Refuse to engage; sulk.

6. Reynolds had just sent Keats some sonnets on Robin Hood; in response, Keats wrote *Robin Hood* and *Lines on the Mermaid Tavern*. The 4th canto of Byron's sensationally popular serial "Romaunt," *Childe Harold's Pilgrimage*, would be published in April.

1. Partner of the firm that published Keats after he was dumped by his first publishers, unhappy with the negative reviews and slow sales of the 1817 *Poems*. Taylor and Hessey were fond of Keats, and in 1820 raised the funds to send him to Rome.

2. The Prologue of Shakespeare's *Henry V*: "O for a Muse of fire, that would ascend / The brightest heaven of invention."

3. By this point, Keats was disenchanted with and somewhat embarrassed by *Endymion*, but eager to convey his sense of future accomplishment to his new publisher.

1. When much-loved Princess Charlotte died in childbirth in 1817, the nation mourned, and many in the clergy published memorial sermons, including Bailey, who was eager for Keats's response.

into all your feelings on the subject merely for one short 10 Minutes and give you a Page or two to your liking. I am sometimes so very sceptical as to think Poetry itself a mere Jack a lantern to amuse whoever may chance to be struck with its brilliance – As Tradesmen say every thing is worth what it will fetch, so probably every mental pursuit takes its reality and worth from the ardour of the pursuer – being in itself a nothing – Ethereal thing[s] may at least be thus real, divided under three heads– Things real – things semireal — and no things — Things real – such as existences of Sun Moon & Stars and passages of Shakspeare—Things semireal such as Love, the Clouds &c which require a greeting of the Spirit to make them wholly exist – and Nothings which are made Great and dignified by an ardent pursuit * * * Aye this may be carried — but what am I talking of – it is an old maxim of mine and of course must be well known that eve[r]y point of thought is the centre of an intellectual world – the two uppermost thoughts in a Man's mind are the two poles of his World he revolves on them and every thing is southward or northward to him through their means – We take but three steps from feathers to iron. Now my dear fellow I must once for all tell you I have not one Idea of the truth of any of my speculations – I shall never be a Reasoner because I care not to be in the right, when retired from bickering and in a proper philosophical temper * * * My Brother Tom desires to be remember'd to you – he has just this moment had a spitting of blood poor fellow * * *

Your affectionate friend

John Keats –

To John Hamilton Reynolds

[WORDSWORTH, MILTON, AND "DARK PASSAGES"]

My dear Reynolds.   Teignmouth May 3ᵈ 1818

What I complain of is that I have been in so an uneasy a state of Mind as not to be fit to write to an invalid. I cannot write to any length under a dis-guised feeling. I should have loaded you with an addition of gloom, which I am sure you do not want. I am now thank God in a humour to give you a good groats worth – for Tom, after a Night without a wink of sleep, and overburdened with fever, has got up after a refreshing day sleep and is better than he has been for a long time. * * * Were I to study physic or rather Medicine again, I feel it would not make the least difference in my Poetry; when the Mind is in its infancy a Bias is in reality a Bias, but when we have acquired more strength, a Bias becomes no Bias. Every department of Knowledge we see excellent and calculated towards a great whole. I am so convinced of this, that I am glad at not having given away my medical Books, which I shall again look over to keep alive the little I know thitherwards. * * * An extensive knowledge is needful to thinking people – it takes away the heat and fever; and helps, by widening speculation, to ease the Burden of the Mystery:[1] a thing I begin to understand a little, and which weighed upon you in the most gloomy and true sentence in your Letter. The differ-ence of high Sensations with and without knowledge appears to me this – in the latter case we are falling continually ten thousand fathoms deep and being blown up again without wings and with all horror of a bare shoulderd Creature – in the former case,

---

1. See Wordsworth's recollection in *Tintern Abbey* of that "blessed mood / In which the burthen of the mystery, / In which the heavy and the weary weight / Of all this unintelligible world, / Is lightened" (37–41).

our shoulders are fledge, and we go thro' the same air and space without fear.[2] This is running one's rigs[3] on the score of abstracted benefit – when we come to human Life and the affections it is impossible to know how a parallel of breast and head can be drawn—(you will forgive me for thus privately treading out my depth and take it for treading as schoolboys tread the water) – it is impossible to know how far Knowledge will console us for the death of a friend and the ill "that flesh is heir to"[4] * * *

My Branchings out therefrom have been numerous: one of them is the consideration of Wordsworth's genius and as a help, in the manner of gold being the meridian Line[5] of worldly wealth,–how he differs from Milton. – And here I have nothing but surmises, from an uncertainty whether Miltons apparently less anxiety for Humanity proceeds from his seeing further or no than Wordsworth: and whether Wordsworth has in truth epic passion, and martyrs himself to the human heart, the main region of his song[6] – In regard to his genius alone – we find what he says true as far as we have experienced and we can judge no further but by larger experience–for axioms in philosophy are not axioms until they are proved upon our pulses: We read fine — things but never feel them to thee full until we have gone the same steps as the Author. – I know this is not plain; you will know exactly my meaning when I say, that now I shall relish Hamlet more than I ever have done. Or, better—You are sensible no Man can set down Venery[7] as a bestial or joyless thing until he is sick of it and therefore all philosophizing on it would be mere wording. Until we are sick, we understand not;–in fine, as Byron says, "Knowledge is Sorrow"; and I go on to say that "Sorrow is Wisdom"–and further for aught we can know for certainty! "Wisdom is folly"[8]–So you see how I have run away from Wordsworth, and Milton. * * * I will return to Wordsworth – whether or no he has an extended vision or a circumscribed grandeur–whether he is an eagle in his nest, or on the wing –And to be more explicit and to show you how tall I stand by the giant, I will putdown a simile of human life as far as I now perceive it; that is, to the point to which I say we both have arrived at—' Well–I compare human life to a large Mansion of Many Apartments, two of which I can only describe, the doors of the rest being as yet shut upon me – The first we step into we call the infant or thoughtless Chamber, in which we remain as long as we do not think– We remain there along while, and notwithstanding the doors of the Second Chamber remain wide open, showing a bright appearance, we care not to hasten to it; but are at length imperceptibly impelled by the awakening of the thinking principle — within us – we no sooner get into the second Chamber, which I shall call the Chamber of Maiden-Thought, than we become intoxicated with the light and the atmosphere, we see nothing but pleasant wonders, and think of delaying there for ever in delight: However among the effects this breathing is father of is

---

2. Milton describes the angels in *Paradise Lost* as having "Shoulders fledge with wings" (3.627); even so, Satan is blown about in Chaos: "Flutt'ring his pennons vain plumb down he drops / Ten thousand fadom deep," then propelled "As many miles aloft" (2.933–38).
3. Going at top speed; Keats's next image of treading water suggests a shipwreck on this abstract value.
4. Hamlet longs for death as a way to "end / The heartache, and the thousand natural shocks / That flesh is heir to!" (*Hamlet* 3.1.61–63).
5. Reference point.
6. In the "Prospectus" to *The Excursion*, Wordsworth

aligned his epic with *Paradise Lost*, but declared "the Mind of Man" as the "haunt, and the main region of [his] song" (40–41).
7. Sexual debauchery; Keats may have indulged himself thus when he visited Bailey at Oxford.
8. A mismemory or reversing of the complaint of Byron's Manfred: "Sorrow is knowledge" (1.1.10); see page 712. Where Manfred alludes to Adam and Eve's gain of knowledge in tandem with a death sentence, Keats blends the phrase to echo the famous conclusion of Thomas Gray's *Ode on a Distant Prospect of Eton College* (1747): "where ignorance is bliss, / 'Tis folly to be wise."

that tremendous one of sharpening one's vision into the heart and nature of Man – of convincing ones nerves that the world is full of Misery and Heartbreak, Pain, Sickness and oppression – whereby This Chamber of Maiden Thought becomes gradually darken'd and at the same time on all sides of it many doors are set open – but all dark – all leading to dark passages – We see not the ballance of good and evil.[9] We are in a Mist – <u>We</u> are now in that state – We feel the "burden of the Mystery." To this point was Wordsworth come, as far as I can conceive when he wrote 'Tintern Abbey' and it seems to me that his Genius is explorative of those dark Passages. Now if we live, and go on thinking, we too shall explore them. he is a Genius and superior [to] us, in sofar as he can, more than we, make discoveries, and shed a light in them – Here I must think Wordsworth is deeper than Milton – though I think it has depended more upon the general and gregarious advance of intellect, than individual greatness of Mind – From the Paradise Lost and the other Works of Milton, I hope it is not too presuming, even between ourselves to say, his Philosophy, human and divine, may be tolerably understood by one not much advanced in years. In his time englishmen were just emancipated from a great superstition[1] and Men had got hold of certain points and resting places in reasoning which were too newly born to be doubted, and too much opposed by the Mass of Europe not to be thought etherial and authentically divine–who could gain say his ideas on virtue, vice, and Chastity in Comus, just at the time of the dismissal of Codpieces and a hundred other disgraces?[2] who would not rest satisfied with his hintings at good and evil in the Paradise Lost, when just free from the inquisition and burning in Smithfield? The Reformation[3] produced such immediate and great benefits, that Protestantism was considered under the immediate eye of heaven, and its own remaining Dogmas and superstitions, then, as it were, regenerated, constituted those resting places and seeming sure points of Reasoning–from that I have mentioned, Milton, whatever he may have thought in the sequel,[4] appears to have been content with these by his writings – He did not think into the human heart, as Wordsworth has done – Yet Milton as a Philosopher, had sure as great powers as Wordsworth – What is then to be inferr'd? O many things – It proves there is really a grand march of intellect—, It proves that a mighty providence subdues the mightiest Minds to the service of the time being, whether it be in human Knowledge or Religion * * *

Tom has spit a <u>leetle</u> blood this afternoon, and that is rather a damper – but I know – the truth is there is something real in the World Your third Chamber of Life shall be a lucky and a gentle one—stored with the wine of love – and the Bread of Friendship[5] * * *

Your affectionate friend
John Keats.

---

9. In the "Prospectus" to *The Excursion* Wordsworth stated his Miltonic "intent / To weigh the good and evil of our mortal state."

1. The teachings of the Catholic Church.

2. *Comus* (1634) depicts the temptation of a lady's virtue by the enchanter Comus. A codpiece is a bag, often quite prominent, worn over, to conceal, the "fly" opening in a man's breeches.

3. The medieval Church established the Inquisition to root out heretics, often burned at the stake. Smithfield,

northwest of London, was a notorious site of public executions in the 16th and 17th centuries, especially under the reign of Catholic ("Bloody") Queen Mary. The Reformation was a series of religious revolutions in the 16th century that resulted, often with violent warfare, in a variety of Protestant sects, including the Anglican Church.

4. *Paradise Regained.*

5. A consciously secular application of the emblems of the Christian Eucharist.

To Benjamin Bailey
["I HAVE NOT A RIGHT FEELING TOWARDS WOMEN"]

My dear Bailey,   18 July 1818

* * * I am certain I have not a right feeling towards Women — at this moment I am striving to be just to them. but I cannot — Is it because they fall so far beneath my Boyish imagination? When I was a Schoolboy I though[t] a fair Woman a pure Goddess, my mind was a soft nest in which some one of them slept though she knew it not — I have no right to expect more than their reality. I thought them etherial above Men — I find them perhaps equal — great by comparison is very small — Insult may be inflicted in more ways than by Word or action — one who is tender of being insulted does not like to think an insult against another — I do not like to think insults in a Lady's Company — I commit a Crime with her which absence would have not known — Is it not extraordinary? When among Men I have no evil thoughts, no malice, no spleen — I feel free to speak or to be silent — I can listen and from every one I can learn — my hands are in my pockets I am free from all suspicion and comfortable. When I am among Women I have evil thoughts, malice spleen — I cannot speak or be silent — I am full of Suspicions and therefore listen to nothing — I am in a hurry to be gone — You must be charitable and put all this perversity to my being disappointed since Boyhood — Yet with such feelings I am happier alone among Crowds of men, by myself or with a friend or two — With all this trust me — Bailey I have not the least idea that Men of different feelings and inclinations are more short sighted than myself — I never rejoiced more than at my Brother's Marriage and shall do so at that of any of my friends[1] —I must absolutely get over this — but how? The only way is to find the root of evil, and so cure it "with backward mutters of dissevering Power"[2] That is a difficult thing; for an obstinate Prejudice can seldom be produced but from a gordian complication of feelings, which must take time to unravell and care to keep unravelled.[3] I could say a good deal about this but I will leave it in hopes of better and more worthy dispositions — and also content that I am wronging no one, for after all I do think better of Womankind than to suppose they care whether Mister John Keats five feet high likes them or not. * * *

Your affectionate friend
John Keats —

To Richard Woodhouse[1]
[THE "CAMELION POET" VS. THE "EGOTISTICAL SUBLIME"]

My dear Woodhouse,   27 October 1818

            Your Letter gave me a great satisfaction; more on account of its friendliness, than any relish of that matter in it which is accounted so acceptable in the 'genus irritabile'[2] The best answer I can give you is in a clerklike manner to

---

1. George Keats had recently married.
2. From Milton's masque *Comus*, describing spells required to free a lady from the seductions of the enchanter Comus (816–817).
3. Gordias created a famously intricate knot.
1. Legal and literary adviser to Keats's second publishers, Woodhouse adored Keats and assiduously preserved or

transcribed his letters, manuscripts, and proof-sheets, as well as collected anecdotes. This is one of Keats's most famous letters, written after a summer of negative reviews in highly visible journals.
2. Horace's term for poets, "the irritable tribe" (*Epistles* 2.2.102).

make some observations on two principle points, which seem to point like indices into the midst of the whole pro and con, about genius, and views and atchievements and ambition and cœtera.[3] 1st As to the poetical Character itself, (I mean that sort of which, if I am any thing, I am a Member; that sort distinguished from the words-worthian or egotistical sublime;[4] which is a thing per se and stands alone[5]) it is not itself – it has no self – it is every thing and nothing – It has no character – it enjoys light and shade; it lives in gusto, be it foul or fair, high or low, rich or poor, mean or elevated – It has as much delight in conceiving an Iago as an Imogen.[6] What shocks the virtuous philosoper, delights the camelion[7] Poet. It does no harm from its relish of the dark side of things any more than from its taste for the bright one; because they both end in speculation. A Poet is the most unpoetical of any thing in existence; because he has no Identity – he is continually infor–[8] and filling some other Body – The Sun, the Moon, the Sea and Men and Women who are creatures of impulse are poetical and have about them an unchangeable attribute – the poet has none; no identity – he is certainly the most unpoetical of all God's Creatures. If then he has no self, and if I am a Poet, where is the Wonder that I should say I would ~~right~~ write no more? Might I not at that very instant been cogitating on the Characters of Saturn and Ops?[9] It is a wretched thing to confess; but is a very fact that not one word I ever utter can be taken for granted as an opinion growing out of my identical nature – how can it, when I have no nature? When I am in a room with People if I ever am free from speculating on creations of my own brain, then not myself goes home to myself: but the identity of every one in the room begins to so press upon me that, I am in a very little time anhilated – not only among Men; it would be the same in a Nursery of children: I know not whether I make myself wholly understood: I hope enough so to let you see that no dependence is to be placed on what I said that day. In the second place I will speak of my views, and of the life I purpose to myself – I am ambitious of doing the world some good: if I should be spared that may be the work of maturer years – in the interval I will assay to reach to as high a summit in Poetry as the nerve bestowed upon me will suffer. The faint conceptions I have of Poems to come brings the blood frequently into my forehead – All I hope is that I may not lose all interest in human affairs – that the solitary indifference I feel for applause even from the finest Spirits, will not blunt any acuteness of vision I may have. I do not think it will – I feel assured I should write from the mere yearning and fondness I have for the Beautiful even if my night's labours should be burnt every morning and no eye ever shine upon them. But even now I am perhaps not speaking from myself; but from some character in whose soul I now live – I am sure however that this next

---

3. The rest.
4. "Character" means not only a poet's personality but also the visibility of his identity, biases, philosophy, etc. in his work. In Keats's day, Shakespeare was admired, by Coleridge and others, for the invisibility of this "character"; in an influential lecture of 1818 (attended by Keats), Hazlitt called Shakespeare "the least of an egotist that it was possible to be. He was nothing in himself; but . . . all that others were" (see pages 706–07). Milton and Words-worth were typical contrasts, as poets of egotism.
5. A foolish soldier in Shakespeare's *Troilus and Cressida* is described as "a very man per se" who "stands alone" (1.2.15–16).
6. Hazlitt's *On Gusto* (see page 1099), begins, "Gusto in art is power or passion defining any object." Iago is the

scheming villain of *Othello*; Imogen is the virtuous heroine of *Cymbeline*.
7. A chameleon can change color according to circumstance.
8. At the bottom of the first letter-page, Keats writes "infor—" as if meaning to hyphenate, and complete the word on the next page. He began page 2 however with no such completion, but rather, "and filling."
9. Keats had remarked to Woodhouse that he felt pre-empted by the great poets of the past. In Greek mythology, Saturn is the king of the Titan gods and Ops a harvest goddess; cast out of heaven by the revolt of their children, the fallen Titans appear in the poem Keats was working on during these months, *Hyperion*.

sentence is from myself. I feel your anxiety, good opinion and friendliness in the highest degree, and am

Your's most sincerely
John Keats

To George and Georgiana Keats[1]
["INDOLENCE," "POETRY" VS. "PHILOSOPHY," THE "VALE OF SOUL-MAKING"]

My dear Brother & Sister—   Spring 1819

[19 March] Yesterday I got a black eye – the first time I took a Cricket bat. Brown who is always one's friend in a disaster applied a leech to the eyelid, and there is no inflammation this morning though the ball hit me directly on the sight – 't was a white ball – I am glad it was not a clout. This is the second black eye I have had since leaving school – during all my school days I never had one at all – we must eat a peck before we die – This morning I am in a sort of temper indolent and supremely careless: I long after a stanza or two of Thompson's Castle of indolence.[2] My passions are all asleep from my having slumbered till nearly eleven and weakened the animal fibre all over me to a delightful sensation about three degrees on this side of faintness – if I had teeth of pearl and the breath of lillies I should call it Langour – but as I am[3] I must call it Laziness – In this state of effeminacy the fibres of the brain are relaxed in common with the rest of the body, and to such a happy degree that pleasure has no show of enticement and pain no unbearable frown. Neither Poetry, nor Ambition, nor Love have any alertness of countenance as they pass by me: they seem rather like three figures on a greek vase – a Man and two women – whom no one but myself could distinguish in their disguisement. This is the only happiness; and is a rare instance of advantage in the body overpowering the Mind.[4] I have this moment received a note from Haslam in which he expects the death of his Father who has been for some time in a state of insensibility – his mother bears up he says very well – I shall go to twon tommorrow to see him. This is the world – thus we cannot expect to give way many hours to pleasure – Circumstances are like Clouds continually gathering and bursting – While we are laughing the seed of some trouble is put into the wide arable land of events – while we are laughing it sprouts is grows and suddenly bears a poison fruit which we must pluck[5] – Even so we have leisure to reason on the misfortunes of our friends; our own touch us too nearly for words. Very few men have ever arrived at a complete disinterestedness[6] of Mind: very few have been influenced by a pure desire of the benefit of others – in the greater part of the Benefactors of & to Humanity some meretricious motive has sullied their greatness – some melodramatic scenery has facinated them – From the manner in which I feel Haslam's misfortune I perceive how far I am from any humble standard of disinterestedness – Yet this

1. Between 14 February and 3 May 1819, Keats composed a long journal-letter to his brother George and wife Georgiana, emigrants to America; filling his pages with news and views, he also transcribed 11 poems, including *La belle dame sans merci*, *Ode to Psyche*, and *Incipit Altera Sonneta*.
2. In the first part of James Thomson's *The Castle of Indolence* (1748), a wizard named Indolence entices weary wayfarers into his castle, where they sink into idleness.
3. especially as I have a black eye. [Keats's footnote]
4. See *Ode on Indolence*, though it is not clear there that "Ambition" is a "man."
5. See *Ode on Melancholy*.
6. Not motivated by self-interest; the opposite of meretricious.

feeling ought to be carried to its highest pitch, as there is no fear of its ever injuring Society – which it would do I fear pushed to an extremity – For in wild nature the Hawk would loose his Breakfast of Robins and the Robin his of Worms The Lion must starve as well as the swallow – The greater part of Men make their way with the same instinctiveness, the same unwandering eye from their purposes, the same animal eagerness as the Hawk – The Hawk wants a Mate, so does the Man—look at them both they set about it and procure on in the same manner – They want both a nest and they both set about one in the same manner – they get their food in the same manner – The noble animal Man for his amusement smokes his pipe – the Hawk balances about the Clouds – that is the only difference of their leisures. This it is that makes the Amusement of Life – to a speculative Mind. I go among the Feilds and catch a glimpse of a stoat or a fieldmouse peeping out of the withered grass – the creature hath a purpose and its eyes are bright with it– I go amongst the buildings of a city and I see a Man hurrying along–to what? The Creature has a purpose and his eyes are bright with it. But then as Wordsworth says, "we have all one human heart"[7] – there is an ellectric fire in human nature tending to purify – so that among these human creatures there is continually some birth of new heroism – The pity is that we must wonder at it: as we should at finding a pearl in rubbish – I have no doubt that thousands of people never heard of have had hearts competely disinterested: I can remember but two – Socrates and Jesus – their Histories evince it – What I heard a little time ago, Taylor observe with respect to Socrates, may be said of Jesus – That he was so great as man that though he transmitted no writing of his own to posterity, we have his Mind and his sayings and his greatness handed to us by others. It is to be lamented that the history of the latter was written and revised by Men interested in the pious frauds of Religion. Yet through all this I see his splendour. Even here though I myself am pursueing the same instinctive course as the veriest human animal you can think of – I am however young writing at random – straining at particles of light in the midst of a great darkness – without knowing the bearing of any one assertion of any one opinion. Yet may I not in this be free from sin? May there not be superior beings amused with any graceful, though instinctive attitude my mind my fall into, as I am entertained with the alertness of a Stoat or the anxiety of a Deer? Though a quarrel in the streets is a thing to be hated, the energies displayed in it are fine; the commonest Man shows a grace in his quarrel – By a superior being our reasoning may take the same tone – though erroneous they may be fine – This is the very thing in which consists poetry; and if so it is not so fine a thing as philosophy – For the same reason that an eagle is not so fine a thing as a truth – Give me this credit – Do you not think I strive – to know myself? Give me this credit – and you will not think that on my own accou[n]t I repeat Milton's lines

> "How charming is divine Philosophy
> Not harsh and crabbed as dull fools suppose
> But musical as is Apollo's lute –"[8]

No – no for myself – feeling grateful as I do to have got into a state of mind to relish them properly – Nothing ever becomes real till it is experienced – Even a Proverb is no proverb to you till your Life has illustrated it– * * *

7. *The Old Cumberland Beggar* (1800) 146.   8. *Comus* 475–477.

[21 April] I have been reading lately two very different books Robertson's America and Voltaire's Siecle De Louis XIV It is like walking arm and arm between Pizzarro and the great little Monarch.[9] In How lementabl a case do we see the great body of the people in both instances: in the first, where Men might seem to inherit quiet of Mind from unsophisticated senses; from uncontamination of civilisation; and especially from their being as it were estranged from the mutual helps of Society and its mutual injuries – and thereby more immediately under the Protection of Providence – even there they had mortal pains to bear as bad; or even worse than Baliffs, Debts and Poverties of civilised Life – The whole appears to resolve into this – that Man is originally 'a poor forked creature'[1] subject to the same mischances as the beasts of the forest, destined to hardships and disquietude of some kind or other. If he improves by degrees his bodily accomodations and comforts – at each stage, at each accent there are waiting for him a fresh set of annoyances – he is mortal and there is still a heaven with its Stars abov his head. The most interesting question that can come before us is, How far by the persevering endeavours of a seldom appearing Socrates Mankind may be made happy – I can imagine such happiness carried to an extreme – but what must it end in? – Death – and who could in such a case bear with death – the whole troubles of life which are now frittered away in a series of years, would the[n] be accumulated for the last days of a being who instead of hailing its approach, would leave this world as Eve left Paradise – But in truth I do not at all believe in this sort of perfectibility – the nature of the world will not admit of it – the inhabitants of the world will correspond to itself. – Let the fish philosophise the ice away from the Rivers in winter time and they shall be at continual play in the tepid delight of summer. Look at the Poles and at the sands of Africa, Whirlpools and volcanoes – Let men exterminate them and I will say that they may arrive at earthly Happiness – The point at which Man may arrive is as far as the paralel state in inanimate nature and no further. – For instance suppose a rose to have sensation, it blooms on a beautiful morning it enjoys itself – but there comes a cold wind, a hot sun – it can not escape it, it cannot destroy its annoyances – they are as native to the world as itself: no more can man be happy in spite, the worldy elements will prey upon his nature – The common cognomen of this world among the misguided and superstitious is 'a vale of tears'[2] from which we are to be redeemed by a certain arbitary interposition of God and taken to Heaven – What a little circumscribe straightened notion! Call the world if you Please "The vale of Soul-making" Then you will find out the use of the world (I am speaking now in the highest terms for human nature admitting it to be immortal which I will here take for granted for the purpose of showing a thought which has struck me concerning it) I say 'Soul making' Soul as distinguished from an Intelligence – There may be intelligences or sparks of the divinity in millions – but they are not Souls the till they acquire identities,[3] till each

9. Scots minister William Robertson's *History of the Discovery and Settlement of America* (1777) was the first account in English to bring a sympathetic perspective to the Spanish conquistadors, including Cortez (see *On First Looking into Chapman's Homer*) and Pizarro (c. 1475–1541), conqueror of the Inca empire in Peru. Voltaire's *Le Siècle de Louis XIV* (1751) gave a new focus to culture and commerce as well as politics and war. "Le Grand Monarque" was one of the epithets of the Sun King, Louis XIV (1638–1715).
1. Lear's shocked realization as he looks at "Poor Tom" (*King Lear* 3.4.109–10).

2. This common term in theology for mortal life (implying salvation after death) was used by Shelley in *Hymn to Intellectual Beauty* (pub. *The Examiner* 1817), describing "our state" as a "dim vast vale of tears" (16–17).
3. Against the Platonic and later, Christian view of a preexisting, immortal soul (as in Wordsworth's "Intimations" Ode), Keats formulates a modern view of the soul as the identity shaped by the experiences, especially the adversities, of mortal life; see "the wakeful anguish of the soul" in *Ode on Melancholy*.

one is personally itself. Itelligences are atoms of perception – they know and they see and they are pure, in short they are God – how then are Souls to be made? How then are these sparks which are God to have identity given them – so as ever to possess a bliss peculiar to each ones individual existence? How, but by the medium of a world like this? This point I sincerely wish to consider because I think it a grander system of salvation than the chrystean religion – or rather it is a system of Spirit-creation – This is effected by three grand materials acting the one upon the other for a series of years – These theee Materials are the <u>Intelligence</u>—the <u>human heart</u> (as distinguished from intelligence or Mind) and the <u>World</u> or <u>Elemental space</u> suited for the proper action of <u>Mind and Heart</u> on each other for the purpose of forming the <u>Soul</u> or <u>Intelligence destined to possess the sense of Identity</u>. I can scarcely express what I but dimly perceive – and yet I think I perceive it – that you may judge the more clearly I will put it in the most homely form possible – I will call the <u>world</u> a School instituted for the purpose of teaching little children to read – I will call the <u>human heart</u> the <u>horn Book</u>[4] used in that School – and I will call the <u>Child able to read, the Soul</u> made from that <u>school</u> and its <u>hornbook</u>. Do you not see how necessary a World of Pains and troubles is to school an Intelligence and make it a Soul? A Place where the heart must feel and suffer in a thousand diverse ways! Not merely is the Heart a Hornbook, It is the Minds Bible, it is the Minds experience, it is the teat from which the Mind or intelligence sucks its identity – As various as the Lives of Men are – so various become their souls, and thus does God make individual beings, Souls, Identical Souls of the Sparks of his own essence. This appears to me a faint Sketch of a system of Salvation which does not affront our reason and humanity – I am convinced that many difficulties which christians labour under would vanish before it – There is one which even now Strikes me – the Salvation of Children – In them the Spark or intelligence returns to God without any identity – it having had no time to learn of, and be altered by, the heart – or seat of the human Passions[5]— * * * If what I have said should not be plain enough, as I fear it may not be, I will but you in the place where I began in this series of thoughts – I mean, I began by seeing how man was formed by circumstances – and what are circumstances?– but touchstones of his heart–? and what are touchstones? but proovings of his heart?–and what are proovings of his heart but fortifiers or alterers of his nature? and what is his altered nature but his Soul?— and what was his Soul before it came into the world and had these provings and alterations and perfectionings?—An intelligence – without Identity — and how is this Identity to be made? Through the medium of the Heart? and how is the heart to become this medium but in a world of Circumstances? There now I think what with Poetry and Theology you may thank your Stars that my pen is not very long winded * * *

    This is the 3rd of May and every thing is in delightful forwardness, the violets are not witherd before the peeping of the first rose * * * You must let me know every thing – how parcels come and go – what Papers Birtbecks[6] has and what newspaper you want and other things. God bless you, my dear Brother & Sister. Your ever affectionate Brother   John Keats

---

4. A child's primer for spelling, reading, and arithmetic.
5. Compare to Wordsworth's "Intimations" Ode, especially stanza 5.

6. Birbeck's Boltenhouse Prairie colony in the Illinois Territory; the Keatses went instead to Louisville, Kentucky.

To Fanny Brawne[1]
["You Take Possession of Me"]

My sweet Girl,   Sunday Night. [25 July 1819]

I hope you did not blame me much for not obeying your request of a Letter on Saturday: we have had four in our small room playing at cards night and morning leaving me no undisturb'd opportunity to write. [. . .] Brown to my sorrow confirms the account you give of your ill health. You cannot conceive how I ache to be with you: how I would die for one hour————for what is in the world? I say you cannot conceive; it is impossible you should look with such eyes upon me as I have upon you: it cannot be. Forgive me if I wander a little this evening, for I have been all day employ'd in a very abstr[a]ct Poem[2] and I am in deep love with you—two things which must excuse me. I have, believe me, not been an age in letting you take possession of me; the very first week I knew you I wrote myself your vassal; but burnt the Letter as the very next time I saw you I thought you manifested some dislike to me. If you should ever feel for Man at the first sight what I did for you, I am lost. Yet I should not quarrel with you, but hate myself if such a thing were to happen—only I should burst if the thing were not as fine as a Man as you are as a Woman. Perhaps I am too vehement, then fancy me on my knees, especially when I mention a part of you Letter which hurt me; you say speaking of Mr Severn[3] "but you must be satisfied in knowing that I admired you much more than your friend." My dear love, I cannot believe there ever was or ever could be any thing to admire in me especially as far as sight goes—I cannot be admired, I am not a thing to be admired. You are, I love you; all I can bring you is a swooning admiration of your Beauty. I hold that place among Men which snub-nos'd brunettes with meeting eyebrows do among women–they are trash to me–unless I should find one among them with a fire in her heart like the one that burns in mine. You absorb me in spite of myself—you alone: for I look not forward with any pleasure to what is call'd being settled in the world; I tremble at domestic cares–yet for you I would meet them, though if it would leave you the happier I would rather die than do so. I have two luxuries to brood over in my walks, your Loveliness and the hour of my death. O that I could have possession of them both in the same minute.[4] I hate the world: it batters too much the wings of my self-will, and would I could take a sweet poison from your lips to send me out of it. From no others would I take it. I am indeed astonish'd to find myself so careless of all cha[r]ms but yours–remembring as I do the time when even a bit of ribband was a matter of interest with me. What softer words can I find for you after this—what it is I will not read. Nor will I say more here, but in a Postscript answer any thing else you may have mentioned in your Letter in so many words—for I am distracted with a thousand thoughts. I will imagine you Venus tonight and pray, pray, pray to your star like a Hethen.

Your's ever, fair Star,

John Keats.

---

1. When Keats met Fanny Brawne (1800–1865) in the summer of 1818, he was charmed and vexed by her almost at once. They fell in love within a few months and became engaged at the end of the year, but kept it secret pending Keats's financial ability to make a formal offer. His first letters to her were written from a working vacation with Brown on the Isle of Wight in the summer of 1819. As a tenant in Brown's apartment in Hampstead, Keats lived next door to the Brawnes from October 1819 to May 1820, and they cared for him in their own quarters later that summer. He saw Fanny Brawne for the last time on 13 September 1820, just before he left for Italy. Her identity became public in 1878 when his surviving letters to her were first published, a sensational event that damaged both their reputations.
2. The remodeling of *Hyperion* into *The Fall of Hyperion*.
3. Joseph Severn (1793–1879), an artist; he went with Keats to Rome, and Keats died in his arms.
4. Compare "Bright star", page 1044.

To Percy Bysshe Shelley
["AN ARTIST MUST SERVE MAMMON"]

My dear Shelley,   16 August 1820

    I am very much gratified that you, in a foreign country, and with a mind almost overoccupied, should write to me in the strain of the Letter beside me. If I do not take advantage of your invitation it will be prevented by a circumstance I have very much at heart to prophesy.[1] - There is no doubt that an english winter would put an end to me, and do so in a lingering hateful manner. Therefore I must either voyage or journey to Italy as a soldier marches up to a battery. My nerves at present are the worst part of me, yet they feel soothed when I think that come what extreme may, I shall not be destined to remain in one spot long enough to take a hatred of any four particular bed-posts. I am glad you take any pleasure in my poor Poems;[2] – which I would willingly take the trouble to unwrite, if possible, did I care so much as I have done about Reputation. I received a copy of The Cenci, as from yourself from Hunt. There is only one part of it I am judge of, the Poetry, and dramatic effect, which by many spirits now a days is considered the mammon.[3] A modern work it is said must have a purpose, which may be the God—an artist must serve Mammon - he must have "self concentration" selfishness perhaps. You I am sure will forgive me for sincerely remarking that you might curb your magnanimity and be more of an artist, and 'load every rift' of your subject with ore.[4] The thought of such discipline must fall like cold chains upon you, who perhaps never sat with your wings furl'd for six Months together. And is not this extraordina[r]y talk for the writer of Endymion? whose mind was like a pack of scattered cards - I am pick'd up and sorted to a pip.[5] My Imagination is a Monastry and I am its Monk - you must explain my metap[hysics] to yourself. I am in expectation of Prometheus[6] every day. Could I have my own wish for its interest effected you would have it still in manuscript - or be but now putting an end to the second act. I remember you advising me not to publish my first-blights, on Hampstead Heath[7] - I am returning advice upon your hands. Most of the Poems in the volume I send you have been written above two years, and would never have been publish'd but from a hope of gain;[8] so you see I am inclined enough to take your advice now. I must express once more my deep sense of your kindness, adding my sincere thanks and respects for Mrs Shelley. In the hope of soon seeing you, remain

most sincerely,
John Keats –

---

1. Learning of Keats's grave ill health from Hunt, Shelley offered him hospitality in the warmer climate of Italy; Keats accepted the invitation, first going to Rome, where he died.
2. Sympathetic to the sting of negative reviews, Shelley had written some encouraging remarks about Endymion.
3. The false idol of money and worldly goods, against whom Jesus cautions, "Ye cannot serve God and mammon" (Matthew 6.24). In the Preface of The Cenci (1819), a tragedy of incestuous rape, tyranny, and parricide, Shelley proffered a moral judgment of its heroine Beatrice Cenci.

4. From the ceiling of the Palace of Mammon in Spenser's Faerie Queene hang stalactites "Embost with massy gold of glorious gift, / And with rich metall loaded every rift, / That heavy ruine they did seeme to threat" (2.7.28).
5. Arranged in order; pips are marks on playing cards.
6. Shelley's drama, Prometheus Unbound, just published.
7. Many of the pieces in Keats's 1817 Poems took inspiration from the landscape of Hampstead Heath; Keats met Shelley through Hunt, who lived there.
8. The 1820 volume; Keats was eager for financial "gain" as a requisite for marriage to Fanny Brawne.

To Charles Brown[1]
[Keats's Last Letter]

My Dear Brown,   Rome. 30th *November,* 1820.

'Tis the most difficult thing in the world to me to write a letter. My stomach continues so bad, that I feel it worse on opening any book,—yet I am much better than I was in quarantine.[2] Then I am afraid to encounter the pro-ing and con-ing of any thing interesting to me in England. I have an habitual feeling of my real life having passed, and that I am leading a posthumous existence. God knows how it would have been—but it appears to me—however, I will not speak of that subject. I must have been at Bedhampton nearly at the time you were writing to me from Chichester—how unfortunate—and to pass on the river too![3] There was my star predominant! I cannot answer any thing in your letter, which followed me from Naples to Rome, because I am afraid to look it over again. I am so weak (in mind) that I cannot bear the sight of any handwriting of a friend I love so much as I do you. Yet I ride the little horse,[4] and, at my worst, even in quarantine, summoned up more puns, in a sort of desperation, in one week than in any year of my life. There is one thought enough to kill me; I have been well, healthy, alert, &c., walking with her,[5] and now—the knowledge of contrast, feeling for light and shade, all that information (primitive sense) necessary for a poem are great enemies to the recovery of the stomach. There, you rogue, I put you to the torture; but you must bring your philosophy to bear, as I do mine, really, or how should I be able to live? Dr Clarke is very attentive to me; he says, there is very little the matter with my lungs,[6] but my stomach, he says, is very bad. I am well disappointed in hearing good news from George, for it runs in my head we shall all die young.[7] I have not written to Reynolds yet, which he must think very neglectful; being anxious to send him a good account of my health, I have delayed it from week to week. If I recover, I will do all in my power to correct the mistakes made during sickness; and if I should not, all my faults will be forgiven. Severn is very well, though he leads so dull a life with me. Remember me to all friends, and tell Haslam I should not have left London without taking leave of him, but from being so low in body and mind. Write to George as soon as you receive this, and tell him how I am, as far as you can guess: and also a note to my sister—who walks about my imagination like a ghost—she is so like Tom. I can scarcely bid you good-bye, even in a letter. I always made an awkward bow.

God bless you!
John Keats.

---

1. Charles Brown (1787–1842), a man of various literary and amorous pursuits, was a close friend, traveling companion, and housemate. He cared assiduously for Keats after his first major hemorrhage in February 1820, then left for his usual summer vacation in May. Keats earnestly hoped Brown would accompany him to Italy, but he could not be located. Our text of this letter is the one published in 1848.
2. The ship on which Keats sailed was held for quarantine outside Naples, in oppressive summer weather.

3. The towns are near Portsmouth harbor, from which Keats would sail.
4. Recommended by Keats's doctor in Rome as exercise.
5. Fanny Brawne; Brown deleted her name, as well as those of Keats's friends, when he included the letter in a biography of Keats.
6. Actually, Keats's lungs were nearly destroyed.
7. Tom died at 19, George lived to his mid-forties, and the youngest, Fanny, lived into her eighties.

Sir Walter Scott
1771–1832

Scott was born in Edinburgh but, lame and in ill health, was sent to his grandparents' farm, which was located just north of England. In this "Border country," he heard stories of the warfare between the Scots and the English, as ancient as the middle ages and as recent as the Jacobite rebellion of 1745, the Stuarts' last attempt at the throne of England. Against such romantic tales stands Scott's training as a lawyer. The son of a lawyer, he became a county judge in 1799, and in 1806 clerk to the highest civil court in Scotland. He was already a literary figure by then: he began by translating contemporary German ballad-imitations in vogue in the 1790s, then wrote imitations himself, then in *Minstrelsy of the Scottish Border* (1802–1803), appeared as the scholarly editor of the ballads he delighted to collect. Scott's passionate engagement with a romantic past and his antiquarian learning tugged against his trust in progress. If his heart was in the Highlands (to echo a nostalgic lyric), his intellect was in Scots common-sense philosophy and historiography. This tension enlivens *The Lay of the Last Minstrel* (1805), a six-canto romance that sets a sixteenth-century Border legend, complete with goblin and magical effects, in a complex chronological frame. The Minstrel, the last of his race, addresses a group of seventeenth-century ladies, a mirror of Scott and his nineteenth-century audience. The fantastic materials, paced in an irregular meter inspired by Coleridge's then-unpublished *Christabel* (see page 652) are counterpointed in the measured, often witty and skeptical voice of the extensive historical notes.

Other verse romances followed, notably *Marmion* (1808) and *The Lady of the Lake* (1810), but they failed to match the popularity of Byron's still more exotic *Eastern Tales*. A Lord or respectable lawyer might publish elegant volumes of poetry with authoritative critical apparatus, but a novel might injure the "solemnity of walk and conduct" required by the law. Scott tried a novel, *Waverley*, which appeared anonymously in 1814. Though the ruse was soon penetrated, he maintained it for all his novels; the issue was less secrecy than status and fictional freedom. While Scott did not invent "the historical novel," *Waverley* (about the adventures of a young Englishman caught up in that Jacobite rebellion) launched a prodigious series, including *Old Mortality* (1816), *Rob Roy* (1817), *The Heart of Midlothian* (1818), and *Ivanhoe* (1819), fixed its mode, and anticipated the appeal of nationalism and rational stability that spoke powerfully to a Britain recovering from the Napoleonic wars.

In 1811 Scott embarked on the construction of his estate, Abbotsford, a castle filled with armor and heraldic devices, where he could fashion himself benevolent lord of the manor. Made a baronet in 1820, and so now "Sir Walter Scott," the persona paradoxically depended on tireless labor. This most gifted, admired writer, Thomas Carlyle murmured, "must kill himself that he may be a country gentleman, the founder of a race of Scottish lairds." A friend was dismayed at the sight, in 1814, of Scott's hand in his study-window: "it fascinates my eye—it never stops—page after page is finished and thrown on that heap of MS., and still it goes on unwearied—and so it will be until the candles are brought in, and God knows how long after that. It is the same every night." Poet, novelist, sheriff, and clerk, Scott was also editor, historian, and biographer, and (covertly) investor in the printing house that brought his tireless production to market. When the book trade crashed in 1826, he was ruined. Determined to clear his debts, he kept writing. Resolute in spirit but broken in health and facing another harsh northern winter, in October 1831 Scott left for the warm Mediterranean. Recovery did not come. He returned the next fall to die at Abbotsford, as he wished.

The Author of Waverley.
Frontispiece to
*Illustrations of the Author
of Waverley,* by Robert
Chambers.

LORD RANDAL   "An eager student" of ballads in his youth, Scott remembered the tree under which he had first read Percy's "enchanting" *Reliques*. In 1795 Anna Letitia Barbauld visited Edinburgh and "electrified" audiences by reading a translation of the German Gottfried Bürger's *Lenore*; Scott's translations of two of Bürger's ballads (including *Lenore*) made up his first publication in 1796. In 1799 he lead a team to collect the "raiding" ballads, culminating in the two-volume *Minstrelsy of the Scottish Border* (1802), to which a third was added in 1803. *Lord Randal*, transcribed in the eighteenth century from oral tradition, was first published here, in Scott's own rendition, our text.

Lord Randal

"O where hae ye been, Lord Randal, my son?
"O where hae ye been, my handsome young man?"
"I hae been to the wild wood; mother, make my bed soon,
"For I'm weary wi' hunting, and fain wald lie down."

5   "Where gat ye your dinner, Lord Randal, my son?
"Where gat ye your dinner, my handsome young man?"

"I din'd wi' my true-love; mother, make my bed soon,
"For I'm weary wi' hunting, and fain wald lie down."

10
"What gat ye to your dinner, Lord Randal my son?
"What gat ye to your dinner, my handsome young man?"
"I got eels boil'd in broo'; mother, make my bed soon,
"For I'm weary wi' hunting, and fain wald lie down."

"What became of your bloodhounds, Lord Randal, my son?
"What became of your bloodhounds, my handsome young man?"
15
"O they swell'd and they died; mother, make my bed soon,
"For I'm weary wi' hunting, and fain wald lie down."

"O I fear ye are poison'd, Lord Randal, my son!
"O I fear ye are poison'd, my handsome young man!"
"O yes! I am poison'd; mother, make my bed soon,
20
"For I'm sick at the heart, and I fain wald lie down."

                                                          1802

The Two Drovers

Appearing in *Chronicles of the Canongate*, *The Two Drovers* was Scott's first work after the financial crash of 1826. Its frame-narrator, Chrystal Croftangry, has returned to the Canongate, once his sanctuary in debt. Though he has recovered his wealth, a fresh start is more difficult, and the subject matter a problem: "the Highlands, though formerly a rich mine for original matter, is . . . in some degree worn out by the incessant labour of modern romancers and novelists, who, finding in those remote regions primitive habits and manners, have vainly imagined that the public can never tire of them." But he hopes, in a desperation matching Scott's, that there is something left to do: "without calling in imagination to aid the impressions of juvenile recollection, I may just attempt to embody one or two scenes illustrative of the Highland character, and which belong peculiarly to the Chronicles of the Canongate. . . . Yet I will not go back to the days of clanship and claymores. Have at you, gentle reader, with a tale of Two Drovers. An oyster may be crossed in love, says the gentle Tilburina*—and a drover may be touched on a point of honour, says the Chronicler of the Canongate." The title page reads by the "Author of Waverley," but the autobiographical introduction discloses Scott himself as this author, for the first time. In February 1827 he allowed a friend to declare at a public dinner, "the *darkness visible* has been cleared away—and the Great Unknown—the minstrel of our native land . . . stands revealed." Scott modestly replied that the Great Unknown was the "small known now," and in *Chronicles* he confessed that the change of circumstances had undone his secrecy: "my mask, like my Aunt Dinah's in 'Tristram Shandy,' having begun to wax a little threadbare about the chin, it became time to lay it aside with a good grace, unless I desired it should fall in pieces from my face, which was now become likely."

Scott gleaned *The Two Drovers* tale from a friend who attended the trial recounted at its end. The business of cattle-driving, involving drovers from various cultures and crossing various national terrains, simmers with potential conflict: between Highland and Lowland Scots, between Scots and English, between codes of honor and systems of law. From his childhood, Scott was familiar with Lowland Scots language, akin to northern English dialect; but the

---

* The character in Richard Brinsley Sheridan's *The Critic* (1779) who utters this phrase.

Highland Celtic-Gaelic was almost foreign. The linguistic texturing of his tale (which also involves French and Latin terms) not only gives an aura of authenticity but also reflects cultural dissonance and differences. Scott translates some terms in parentheses; others we footnote, or gloss in square brackets.

The Two Drovers
Chapter 1

It was the day after the Doune Fair[1] when my story commences. It had been a brisk market, several dealers had attended from the northern and midland counties in England, and the English money had flown so merrily about as to gladden the hearts of the Highland farmers. Many large droves were about to set off for England, under the protection of their owners, or of the topsmen[2] whom they employed in the tedious, laborious, and responsible office of driving the cattle for many hundred miles, from the market where they had been purchased to the fields or farm-yards where they were to be fattened for the shambles.[3]

The Highlanders in particular are masters of this difficult trade of driving, which seems to suit them as well as the trade of war. It affords exercise for all their habits of patient endurance and active exertion. They are required to know perfectly the drove-roads, which lie over the wildest tracts of the country, and to avoid as much as possible the highways, which distress the feet of the bullocks, and the turnpikes,[4] which annoy the spirit of the drover; whereas on the broad green or grey track, which leads across the pathless moor, the herd not only move at ease and without taxation, but, if they mind their business, may pick up a mouthful of food by the way. At night, the drovers usually sleep along with their cattle, let the weather be what it will; and many of these hardy men do not once rest under a roof during a journey on foot from Lochaber to Lincolnshire.[5] They are paid very highly, for the trust reposed is of the last importance, as it depends on their prudence, vigilance and honesty, whether the cattle reach the final market in good order, and afford a profit to the grazier.[6] But as they maintain themselves at their own expense, they are especially economical in that particular. At the period we speak of, a Highland drover was victualled for his long and toilsome journey with a few handfulls of oatmeal and two or three onions, renewed from time to time, and a ram's horn filled with whisky, which he used regularly, but sparingly, every night and morning. His dirk, or *skene-dhu* (*i.e.* black-knife), so worn as to be concealed beneath the arm, or by the folds of the plaid,[7] was his only weapon, excepting the cudgel with which he directed the movements of the cattle. A Highlander was never so happy as on these occasions. There was a variety in the whole journey, which exercised the Celt's curiosity and natural love of motion; there were the constant change of place and scene, the petty adventures incidental to the traffic, and the intercourse with the various farmers, graziers, and traders, intermingled with occasional merry-makings, not the less acceptable to Donald[8] that they were void of expense;—and there was the consciousness of superior skill; for the

---

1. Held every November in Doune, Perthshire, where drovers would meet before driving their herds south for slaughter.
2. The topsman was the chief drover.
3. Slaughterhouses.
4. Toll-roads.

5. Lochaber is a mountain district in north-central Scotland; Lincolnshire is an east-central county in England.
6. Grazier, one who is grazing his herds.
7. Tartan kilt; plaids signified family.
8. A generic name for a Scotsman.

Highlander, a child amongst flocks, is a prince amongst herds, and his natural habits induce him to disdain the shepherd's slothful life, so that he feels himself nowhere more at home than when following a gallant drove of his country cattle in the character of their guardian.

Of the number who left Doune in the morning, and with the purpose we have described, not a *Glunamie*[9] of them all cocked his bonnet more briskly, or gartered his tartan hose under knee over a pair of more promising *spiogs* [legs], than did Robin Oig M'Combich, called familiarly Robin Oig, that is young, or the Lesser, Robin. Though small of stature, as the epithet Oig implies, and not very strongly limbed, he was as light and alert as one of the deer of his mountains. He had an elasticity of step, which, in the course of a long march, made many a stout fellow envy him; and the manner in which he busked[1] his plaid and adjusted his bonnet, argued a consciousness that so smart a John Highlandman as himself would not pass unnoticed among the Lowland lasses. The ruddy cheek, red lips, and white teeth, set off a countenance which had gained by exposure to the weather a healthful and hardy rather than a rugged hue. If Robin Oig did not laugh, or even smile frequently, as indeed is not the practice among his countrymen, his bright eyes usually gleamed from under his bonnet with an expression of cheerfulness ready to be turned into mirth.

The departure of Robin Oig was an incident in the little town, in and near which he had many friends, male and female. He was a topping person in his way, transacted considerable business on his own behalf, and was intrusted by the best farmers in the Highlands, in preference to any other drover in that district. He might have increased his business to any extent had he condescended to manage it by deputy; but except a lad or two, sister's sons of his own, Robin rejected the idea of assistance, conscious, perhaps, how much his reputation depended upon his attending in person to the practical discharge of his duty in every instance. He remained, therefore, contented with the highest premium given to persons of his description, and comforted himself with the hopes that a few journeys to England might enable him to conduct business on his own account, in a manner becoming his birth. For Robin Oig's father, Lachlan M'Combich (or *son of my friend,* his actual clan-surname being M'Gregor,) had been so called by the celebrated Rob Roy, because of the particular friendship which had subsisted between the grandsire of Robin and that renowned cateran.[2] Some people even say, that Robin Oig derived his Christian name[3] from one as renowned in the wilds of Loch Lomond as ever was his namesake Robin Hood, in the precincts of merry Sherwood. "Of such ancestry," as James Boswell says, "who would not be proud?"[4] Robin Oig was proud accordingly; but his frequent visits to England and to the Lowlands had given him tact enough to know that pretensions, which still gave him a little right to distinction in his own lonely glen, might be both obnoxious and ridiculous if preferred elsewhere. The pride of birth, therefore, was like the miser's treasure, the secret subject of his contemplation, but never exhibited to strangers as a subject of boasting.

---

9. Highlander.
1. Arrayed.
2. The folk hero Robert ("Rob Roy") McGregor (1671–1734), cattle-trader and cattle-thief (*cateran*), a traditional occupation in the Highlands. He is the title-figure of Scott's novel *Rob Roy* (1817), and he is also celebrated in Wordsworth's poem *Rob Roy's Grave* (1807), which treats the outlaw as a hero and champion of liberty.
3. First name (given at the church ritual of christening);

"Robin Oig" was also the name of one of Rob Roy's sons. Robin Hood is the 12th-century English outlaw-hero.
4. Scots man of letters James Boswell (1740–1795) toured Scotland with Dr. Samuel Johnson in 1773, the era of this story, and published his *Journal of a Tour of the Hebrides* in 1784. The phrase is from the first footnote to the first chapter, in which Boswell recounts his own ancestry, which includes the medieval Scots king Robert the Bruce.

Many were the words of gratulation and good-luck which were bestowed on Robin Oig. The judges commended his drove, especially the best of them, which were Robin's own property. Some thrust out their snuff-mulls[5] for the parting pinch—others tendered the *doch-an-dorrach*, or parting cup. All cried—"Good-luck travel out with you and come home with you.—Give you luck in the Saxon market—brave notes in the *leabhar-dhu* (black pocketbook,) and plenty of English gold in the *sporran* (pouch of goat-skin)."

The bonny lasses made their adieus more modestly, and more than one, it was said, would have given her best brooch to be certain that it was upon her that his eye last rested as he turned towards his road.

Robin Oig had just given the preliminary "Hoo-hoo!" to urge forward the loiterers of the drove, when there was a cry behind him.

"Stay, Robin—bide a blink. Here is Janet of Tomahourich—auld Janet, your father's sister."

"Plague on her, for an auld Highland witch and spaewife,"[6] said a farmer from the Carse of Stirling;[7] "she'll cast some of her cantrips[8] on the cattle."

"She canna do that," said another sapient of the same profession—"Robin Oig is no the lad to leave any of them, without tying Saint Mungo's knot on their tails, and that will put to her speed the best witch that ever flew over Dimayet upon a broomstick."[9]

It may not be indifferent to the reader to know that the Highland cattle are peculiarly liable to be taken, or infected, by spells and witchcraft, which judicious people guard against by knitting knots of peculiar complexity on the tuft of hair which terminates the animal's tail.

But the old woman who was the object of the farmer's suspicion seemed only busied about the drover, without paying any attention to the flock. Robin, on the contrary, appeared rather impatient of her presence.

"What auld-world fancy," he said, "has brought you so early from the ingle[1]-side this morning, Muhme?[2] I am sure I bid you good-even, and had your God-speed, last night."

"And left me more siller[3] than the useless old woman will use till you come back again, bird of my bosom," said the sibyl.[4] "But it is little I would care for the food that nourishes me, or the fire that warms me, or for God's blessed sun itself, if aught but weal should happen to the grandson of my father. So let me walk the *deasil* round you,[5] that you may go safe out into the far foreign land, and come safe home."

Robin Oig stopped, half embarrassed, half laughing, and signing to those around that he only complied with the old woman to soothe her humour. In the meantime, she traced around him, with wavering steps, the propitiation, which some have thought has been derived from the Druidical mythology.[6] It consists, as is well known, in the person who makes the *deasil*, walking three times round the person who is the object of the ceremony, taking care to move according to the course of the sun. At once, however, she stopped short, and exclaimed, in a voice of alarm and horror, "Grandson of my father, there is blood on your hand."

---

5. Boxes for pulverized tobacco, inhaled through the nose.
6. Fortune-teller.
7. A fertile valley near the river Forth.
8. Spells.
9. St. Mungo is the patron saint of Glasgow and in folklore the protector of herds; Dimayet is a hill near Stirling.

1. Hearth.
2. Foster-mother, nurse.
3. Silver coins.
4. Oracles and prophetesses of the ancient world.
5. For good luck (*weal*).
6. The Druids were ancient Celtic priests.

"Hush, for God's sake, aunt," said Robin Oig; "you will bring more trouble on yourself with this *Taishataragh*" (second sight) "than you will be able to get out of for many a day."

The old woman only repeated, with a ghastly look, "There is blood on your hand, and it is English blood. The blood of the Gael is richer and redder. Let us see— let us————"

Ere Robin Oig could prevent her, which, indeed, could only have been by positive violence, so hasty and peremptory were her proceedings, she had drawn from his side the dirk which lodged in the folds of his plaid, and held it up, exclaiming, although the weapon gleamed clear and bright in the sun, "Blood, blood—Saxon blood again. Robin Oig M'Combich, go not this day to England!"

"Prutt, trutt," answered Robin Oig, "that will never do neither—it would be next thing to running the country. For shame, Muhme—give me the dirk. You cannot tell by the colour the difference betwixt the blood of a black bullock and a white one, and you speak of knowing Saxon from Gaelic blood. All men have their blood from Adam, Muhme. Give me my skene-dhu, and let me go on my road. I should have been half way to Stirling brig[7] by this time—Give me my dirk, and let me go."

"Never will I give it to you," said the old woman—"Never will I quit my hold on your plaid, unless you promise me not to wear that unhappy weapon."

The women around him urged him also, saying few of his aunt's words fell to the ground; and as the Lowland farmers continued to look moodily on the scene, Robin Oig determined to close it at any sacrifice.

"Well, then," said the young drover, giving the scabbard of the weapon to Hugh Morrison, "you Lowlanders care nothing for these freats.[8] Keep my dirk for me. I cannot give it you, because it was my father's; but your drove follows ours, and I am content it should be in your keeping, not in mine.—Will this do, Muhme?"

"It must," said the old woman—"that is, if the Lowlander is mad enough to carry the knife."

The strong westlandman laughed aloud.

"Goodwife," said he, "I am Hugh Morrison from Glenae, come of the Manly Morrisons of auld langsyne,[9] that never took short weapon against a man in their lives. And neither needed they: They had their broadswords, and I have this bit supple,"[1] showing a formidable cudgel—"for dirking ower the board, I leave that to John Highlandman.—Ye needna snort, none of you Highlanders, and you in especial, Robin. I'll keep the bit knife, if you are feared for the auld spaewife's tale, and give it back to you whenever you want it."

Robin was not particularly pleased with some part of Hugh Morrison's speech; but he had learned in his travels more patience than belonged to his Highland constitution originally, and he accepted the service of the descendant of the Manly Morrisons, without finding fault with the rather depreciating manner in which it was offered.

"If he had not had his morning in his head, and been but a Dumfries-shire hog[2] into the boot, he would have spoken more like a gentleman. But you cannot have more of a sow but a grumph.[3] It's shame my father's knife should ever slash a haggis[4] for the like of him,"

7. Bridge.
8. Superstitions.
9. Long ago times; see Robert Burns's famous song (page 406).
1. A small cudgel.

2. Young sheep.
3. Grunt.
4. Pudding made of oatmeal and the minced organs of calf or sheep.

Thus saying (but saying it in Gaelic), Robin drove on his cattle, and waved fare-well to all behind him. He was in the greater haste, because he expected to join at Falkirk[5] a comrade and brother in profession, with whom he proposed to travel in company.

Robin Oig's chosen friend was a young Englishman, Harry Wakefield by name, well known at every northern market, and in his way as much famed and honoured as our Highland driver of bullocks. He was nearly six feet high, gallantly formed to keep the rounds at Smithfield,[6] or maintain the ring at a wrestling match; and although he might have been overmatched, perhaps, among the regular professors of the Fancy, yet, as a chance customer, he was able to give a bellyful to any amateur of the pu-gilistic art. Doncaster races saw him in his glory, betting his guinea,[7] and generally successfully; nor was there a main fought in Yorkshire, the feeders being persons of celebrity, at which he was not to be seen if business permitted. But though a *sprack*[8] lad, and fond of pleasure and its haunts, Harry Wakefield was steady, and not the cautious Robin Oig M'Combich himself was more attentive to the main chance. His holidays were holidays indeed; but his days of work were dedicated to steady and persevering labour. In countenance and temper, Wakefield was the model of Old England's merry yeomen, whose clothyard shafts,[9] in so many hundred battles, as-serted her superiority over the nations, and whose good sabres, in our own time, are her cheapest and most assured defence. His mirth was readily excited; for, strong in limb and constitution, and fortunate in circumstances, he was disposed to be pleased with every thing about him; and such difficulties as he might occasionally encounter, were, to a man of his energy, rather matter of amusement than serious annoyance. With all the merits of a sanguine temper, our young English drover was not without its defects. He was irascible, and sometimes to the verge of being quarrelsome; and perhaps not the less inclined to bring his disputes to a pugilistic decision, because he found few antagonists able to stand up to him in the boxing ring.

It is difficult to say how Harry Wakefield and Robin Oig first became intimates; but it is certain a close acquaintance had taken place betwixt them, although they had apparently few common subjects of conversation or of interest, so soon as their talk ceased to be of bullocks. Robin Oig, indeed, spoke the English language rather imperfectly upon any other topics but stots and kyloes,[1] and Harry Wakefield could never bring his broad Yorkshire tongue to utter a single word of Gaelic. It was in vain Robin spent a whole morning, during a walk over Minch Moor, in attempting to teach his companion to utter, with true precision, the shibboleth[2] *Llhu*, which is the Gaelic for a calf. From Traquair to Murder-cairn, the hill rung with the discor-dant attempts of the Saxon upon the unmanageable monosyllable, and the heartfelt laugh which followed every failure. They had, however, better modes of awaken-ing the echoes; for Wakefield could sing many a ditty to the praise of Moll, Susan, and Cicely, and Robin Oig had a particular gift at whistling interminable pibrochs[3] through all their involutions, and what was more agreeable to his companion's south-ern ear, knew many of the northern airs, both lively and pathetic, to which Wake-field learned to pipe a bass. Thus, though Robin could hardly have comprehended his

5. Another fair-site, to the south.
6. London's meat-market district, also a site for boxing ("the Fancy") and wrestling.
7. A pound and a shilling (a fairly extravagant bet for a drover); Doncaster, in Yorkshire, in northern England, was the site of famous horse races.
8. Lively, spirited.

9. Yard-long arrows.
1. Bulls and small cattle.
2. A word difficult for nonnative speakers to pronounce, hence a test-word (from *shibboleth* in Judges 12.4–6, where mispronunciation could be fatal).
3. Bagpipe tunes.

companion's stories about horse-racing, cock-fighting, or fox-hunting, and although his own legends of clan-fights and *creaghs*,[4] varied with talk of Highland goblins and fairy folk, would have been caviare to his companion,[5] they contrived nevertheless to find a degree of pleasure in each other's company, which had for three years back induced them to join company and travel together, when the direction of their journey permitted. Each, indeed, found his advantage in this companionship; for where could the Englishman have found a guide through the Western Highlands like Robin Oig M'Combich? and when they were on what Harry called the *right* side of the Border, his patronage, which was extensive, and his purse, which was heavy, were at all times at the service of his Highland friend, and on many occasions his liberality did him genuine yeoman's service.

Chapter 2

Were ever two such loving friends—
  How could they disagree?
O thus it was, he loved him dear,
  And thought how to requite him,
And having no friend left but he,
  He did resolve to fight him.

Duke upon Duke.[6]

The pair of friends[7] had traversed with their usual cordiality the grassy wilds of Liddesdale, and crossed the opposite part of Cumberland, emphatically called The Waste.[8] In these solitary regions, the cattle under the charge of our drovers subsisted themselves cheaply, by picking their food as they went along the drove-road, or sometimes by the tempting opportunity of a *start and overloup*, or invasion of the neighbouring pasture, where an occasion presented itself. But now the scene changed before them; they were descending towards a fertile and enclosed country,[9] where no such liberties could be taken with impunity, or without a previous arrangement and bargain with the possessors of the ground. This was more especially the case, as a great northern fair was upon the eve of taking place, where both the Scotch and English drover expected to dispose of a part of their cattle, which it was desirable to produce in the market, rested and in good order. Fields were therefore difficult to be obtained, and only upon high terms. This necessity occasioned a temporary separation betwixt the two friends, who went to bargain, each as he could, for the separate accommodation of his herd. Unhappily it chanced that both of them, unknown to each other, thought of bargaining for the ground they wanted on the property of a country gentleman of some fortune, whose estate lay in the neighbourhood. The English drover applied to the bailiff on the property, who was known to him. It chanced that the Cumbrian Squire, who had entertained some suspicions of his manager's honesty, was taking occasional measures to ascertain how far they were

---

4. Raids.
5. Wasted delicacy; Hamlet describes a play that he has seen as "caviary to the general" (too specialized or refined for popular taste) (Hamlet 2.2.455–56).
6. *Duke upon Duke, an Excellent New Ballad*, a topical satiric ballad published in 1720. It was included in the Pope-Swift *Miscellanies* (1742), and claimed by Alexander Pope. In the pseudo-medieval world of the poem "A

Word and Blow was then enough / (Such Honour did them prick)" (13–14) to provoke a duel.
7. Line 39 of the ballad, in a variant, is "Was ever such a loving Pair?"
8. They are now in northern England.
9. Across the 18th century, a series of parliamentary enclosure acts ceded formally public land, on which anyone could graze herds or farm, to private ownership.

well founded, and had desired that any enquiries about his enclosures, with a view to occupy them for a temporary purpose, should be referred to himself. As, however, Mr. Ireby had gone the day before upon a journey of some miles distance to the northward, the bailiff chose to consider the check upon his full powers as for the time removed, and concluded that he should best consult his master's interest, and perhaps his own, in making an agreement with Harry Wakefield. Meanwhile, ignorant of what his comrade was doing, Robin Oig, on his side, chanced to be overtaken by a well-looked smart little man upon a pony, most knowingly hogged and cropped,[1] as was then the fashion, the rider wearing tight leather breeches, and long-necked bright spurs. This cavalier asked one or two pertinent questions about markets and the price of stock. So Donald,[2] seeing him a well-judging civil gentleman, took the freedom to ask him whether he could let him know if there was any grass-land to be let in that neighbourhood, for the temporary accommodation of his drove. He could not have put the question to more willing ears. The gentleman of the buckskins was the proprietor, with whose bailiff Harry Wakefield had dealt, or was in the act of dealing.

"Thou art in good luck, my canny Scot," said Mr Ireby, "to have spoken to me, for I see thy cattle have done their day's work, and I have at my disposal the only field within three miles that is to be let in these parts."

"The drove can pe gang two, three, four miles very pratty weel indeed"—said the cautious Highlander; "put what would his honour pe axing for the peasts pe the head, if she was to tak the park for twa or three days?"[3]

"We wont differ, Sawney,[4] if you let me have six stots for winterers, in the way of reason."

"And which peasts wad your honour pe for having?"

"Why—let me see—the two black—the dun one—yon doddy—him with the twisted horn—the brockit—How much by the head?"

"Ah," said Robin, "your honour is a shudge—a real shudge—I couldna have set off the pest six peasts petter mysell, me that ken them as if they were my pairns,[5] puir things."

"Well, how much per head, Sawney," continued Mr Ireby.

"It was high markets at Doune and Falkirk," answered Robin.

And thus the conversation proceeded, until they had agreed on the *prix juste*[6] for the bullocks, the Squire throwing in the temporary accommodation of the enclosure for the cattle into the boot, and Robin making, as he thought, a very good bargain, provided the grass was but tolerable. The Squire walked his pony alongside of the drove, partly to show him the way, and see him put into possession of the field, and partly to learn the latest news of the northern markets.

They arrived at the field, and the pasture seemed excellent. But what was their surprise when they saw the bailiff quietly inducting the cattle of Harry Wakefield into the grassy Goshen[7] which had just been assigned to those of Robin Oig M'Combich by the proprietor himself! Squire Ireby set spurs to his horse, dashed up to his servant, and learning what had passed between the parties, briefly informed the English drover

---

1. Cut short.
2. A common Highland name: Robin as type-character (changed to Robin in later texts).
3. Robin's Gaelic pronounces *b* as *p*, and uses *she* for *I*; "take the park" means *graze the land*.
4. Nickname for Alexander (another generic Scots-name);

Squire Ireby asks to buy six cows in consideration (the doddy has a striped face; the bockit is hornless).
5. *bairns*: children.
6. Fair price (French).
7. Fertile land (where the Israelites live in Egypt; Genesis 47. 27).

that his bailiff had let the ground without his authority, and that he might seek grass for his cattle wherever he would, since he was to get none there. At the same time he rebuked his servant severely for having transgressed his commands, and ordered him instantly to assist in ejecting the hungry and weary cattle of Harry Wakefield, which were just beginning to enjoy a meal of unusual plenty, and to introduce those of his comrade, whom the English drover now began to consider as a rival.

The feelings which arose in Wakefield's mind would have induced him to resist Mr Ireby's decision; but every Englishman has a tolerably accurate sense of law and justice, and John Fleecebumpkin, the bailiff, having acknowledged that he had exceeded his commission, Wakefield saw nothing else for it than to collect his hungry and disappointed charge, and drive them on to seek quarters elsewhere. Robin Oig saw what had happened with regret, and hastened to offer to his English friend to share with him the disputed possession. But Wakefield's pride was severely hurt, and he answered disdainfully, "Take it all, man—take it all—never make two bites of a cherry—thou canst talk over the gentry, and blear a plain man's eye—Out upon you, man—I would not kiss any man's dirty latchets[8] for leave to bake in his oven."

Robin Oig, sorry but not surprised at his comrade's displeasure, hastened to entreat his friend to wait but an hour till he had gone to the Squire's house to receive payment for the cattle he had sold, and he would come back and help him to drive the cattle into some convenient place of rest, and explain to him the whole mistake they had both of them fallen into. But the Englishman continued indignant: "Thou hast been selling, hast thou? Ay, ay—thou is a cunning lad for kenning[9] the hours of bargaining. Go to the devil with thyself, for I will neer see thy fause loon's visage again—thou should be ashamed to look me in the face."

"I am ashamed to look no man in the face," said Robin Oig, something moved; "and, moreover, I will look you in the face this blessed day, if you will bide at the Clachan[1] down yonder."

"Mayhap you had as well keep away," said his comrade; and turning his back on his former friend, he collected his unwilling associates, assisted by the bailiff, who took some real and some affected interest in seeing Wakefield accommodated.

After spending some time in negotiating with more than one of the neighbouring farmers, who could not, or would not, afford the accommodation desired, Henry Wakefield at last, and in his necessity, accomplished his point by means of the landlord of the alehouse at which Robin Oig and he had agreed to pass the night, when they first separated from each other. Mine host was content to let him turn his cattle on a piece of barren moor, at a price little less than the bailiff had asked for the disputed enclosure; and the wretchedness of the pasture, as well as the price paid for it, were set down as exaggerations of the breach of faith and friendship of his Scottish crony. This turn of Wakefield's passions was encouraged by the bailiff, (who had his own reasons for being offended against poor Robin, as having been the unwitting cause of his falling into disgrace with his master,) as well as by the innkeeper, and two or three chance guests, who stimulated the drover in his resentment against his quondam associate,—some from the ancient grudge against the Scots, which, when it exists anywhere, is to be found lurking in the Border counties, and some from the general love of mischief, which characterises mankind in all ranks of life, to the honour of Adam's children be it spoken. Good John Barleycorn[2] also, who always

---

8. Leather shoe-thongs.
9. Knowing (with a pun on the etymologically related *cunning*).

1. Village; Robin is challenging him to a duel of honor.
2. Whiskey (made from barley).

heightens and exaggerates the prevailing passions, be they angry or kindly, was not wanting in his offices on this occasion; and confusion to false friends and hard masters, was pledged in more than one tankard.

In the meanwhile Mr Ireby found some amusement in detaining the northern drover at his ancient hall. He caused a cold round of beef to be placed before the Scot in the butler's pantry, together with a foaming tankard of home-brewed, and took pleasure in seeing the hearty appetite with which these unwonted[3] edibles were discussed by Robin Oig M'Combich. The Squire himself lighting his pipe, compounded between his patrician dignity and his love of agricultural gossip, by walking up and down while he conversed with his guest.

"I passed another drove," said the Squire, "with one of your countrymen behind them—they were something less beasts than your drove, doddies most of them—a big man was with them—none of your kilts though, but a decent pair of breeches[4]— D'ye know who he may be?"

"Hout aye—that might, could, and would be Hughie Morrison—I didna think he could hae peen sae weel up. He has made a day on us; but his Argyleshires will have wearied shanks. How far was he pehind?"

"I think about six or seven miles," answered the Squire, "for I passed them at the Christenbury Cragg, and I overtook you at the Hollan Bush. If his beasts be leg-weary, he will be maybe selling bargains."

"Na, na, Hughie Morrison is no the man for pargains—ye maun come to some Highland body like Robin Oig hersell[5] for the like of these—put I maun pe wishing you goot night, and twenty of them let alane ane, and I maun down to the Clachan to see if the lad Harry Waakfelt is out of his humdudgeons[6] yet."

The party at the alehouse were still in full talk, and the treachery of Robin Oig still the theme of conversation, when the supposed culprit entered the apartment. His arrival, as usually happens in such a case, put an instant stop to the discussion of which he had furnished the subject, and he was received by the company assembled with that chilling silence, which, more than a thousand exclamations, tells an intruder that he is unwelcome. Surprised and offended, but not appalled by the reception which he experienced, Robin entered with an undaunted and even a haughty air, attempted no greeting, as he saw he was received with none, and placed himself by the side of the fire, a little apart from a table, at which Harry Wakefield, the bailiff, and two or three other persons, were seated. The ample Cumbrian kitchen would have afforded plenty of room, even for a larger separation.

Robin thus seated, proceeded to light his pipe, and call for a pint of twopenny.

"We have no twopence ale," answered Ralph Heskett the landlord; "but as thou find'st thy own tobacco, it's like thou mayst find thy own liquor too—it's the wont of thy country, I wot."

"Shame, goodman," said the landlady, a blithe bustling housewife, hastening herself to supply the guest with liquor—"Thou knowest well enow what the strange man wants, and it's thy trade to be civil, man. Thou shouldst know, that if the Scot likes a small pot, he pays a sure penny."

Without taking any notice of this nuptial dialogue, the Highlander took the flagon in his hand, and addressing the company generally, drank the interesting toast of "Good markets," to the party assembled.

---

3. Unfamiliar.
4. Not highland, but lowland. (Breeches are pants.)
5. Himself.
6. Low-spirits.

"The better that the wind blew fewer dealers from the north," said one of the farmers, "and fewer Highland runts[7] to eat up the English meadows."

"Saul of my pody, put you are wrang there, my friend," answered Robin, with composure; "it is your fat Englishmen that eat up our Scots cattle, puir things."

"I wish there was a summat to eat up their drovers," said another; "a plain Englishman canna make bread within a kenning of them."

"Or an honest servant keep his master's favour but they will come sliding in between him and the sunshine," said the bailiff.

"If these pe jokes," said Robin Oig, with the same composure, "there is ower mony[8] jokes upon one man."

"It is no joke, but downright earnest," said the bailiff. "Harkye, Mr Robin Ogg, or whatever is your name, it's right we should tell you that we are all of one opinion, and that is, that you, Mr Robin Ogg, have behaved to our friend Mr Harry Wakefield here, like a raff and a blackguard."

"Nae doubt, nae doubt," answered Robin, with great composure; "and you are a set of very pretty judges, for whose prains or pehaviour I wad not gie a pinch of sneeshing.[9] If Mr Harry Waakfelt kens where he is wranged, he kens where he may be righted."[1]

"He speaks truth," said Wakefield, who had listened to what passed, divided between the offence which he had taken at Robin's late behaviour, and the revival of his habitual feelings of regard. He now rose, and went towards Robin, who got up from his seat as he approached, and held out his hand.

"That's right, Harry—go it—serve him out," resounded on all sides—"tip him the nailer—show him the mill."[2]

"Hold your peace all of you, and be ———," said Wakefield; and then addressing his comrade, he took him by the extended hand, with something alike of respect and defiance. "Robin," he said, "thou hast used me ill enough this day; but if you mean, like a frank fellow, to shake hands, and take a tussle for love on the sod, why I'll forgie thee, man, and we shall be better friends than ever."

"And would it not pe petter to pe cood friends without more of the matter?" said Robin; "we will be much petter friendships with our panes[3] hale than proken."

Harry Wakefield dropped the hand of his friend, or rather threw it from him. "I did not think I had been keeping company for three years with a coward."

"Coward pelongs to none of my name," said Robin, whose eyes began to kindle, but keeping the command of his temper. "It was no coward's legs or hands, Harry Waakfelt, that drew you out of the fords of Frew, when you was drifting ower the plack rock, and every eel in the river expected his share of you."

"And that is true enough, too," said the Englishman, struck by the appeal.

"Adzooks!"[4] exclaimed the bailiff—"sure Harry Wakefield, the nattiest lad at Whitson Tryste, Wooler Fair, Carlisle Sands, or Stagshaw Bank, is not going to show white feather?[5] Ah, this comes of living so long with kilts and bonnets—men forget the use of their daddles."[6]

"I may teach you, Master Fleecebumpkin, that I have not lost the use of mine," said Wakefield and then went on. "This will never do, Robin. We must have a

---

7. Poor-quality herds.
8. Over-many.
9. Sneezing (snuff).
1. Another reference to a duel of honor.
2. Terms of pugilistic strategy. (Harry is a boxer.)

3. Bones.
4. An oath, shortened from *Gadzooks* (God's hooks: the nails used to crucify Jesus).
5. Be a coward (flee).
6. Fists.

turn-up, or we shall be the talk of the country-side. I'll be d——d if I hurt thee—I'll put on the gloves gin[7] thou like. Come, stand forward like a man."

"To be peaten like a dog," said Robin; "is there any reason in that? If you think I have done you wrong, I'll go before your shudge, though I neither know his law nor his language."

A general cry of "No, no—no law, no lawyer! a bellyful[8] and be friends," was echoed by the bystanders.

"But," continued Robin, "if I am to fight, I have no skill to fight like a jacka-napes, with hands and nails."

"How would you fight then?" said his antagonist; "though I am thinking it would be hard to bring you to the scratch[9] anyhow."

"I would fight with proadswords, and sink point on the first plood drawn—like a gentlemans."

A loud shout of laughter followed the proposal, which indeed had rather escaped from poor Robin's swelling heart, than been the dictate of his sober judgment.

"Gentleman, quotha!" was echoed on all sides, with a shout of unextinguishable laughter; "a very pretty gentleman, God wot—Canst get two swords for the gentle-man to fight with, Ralph Heskett?"

"No, but I can send to the armoury at Carlisle, and lend them two forks, to be making shift with in the meantime."

"Tush, man," said another, "the bonny Scots come into the world with the blue bonnet on their heads, and dirk and pistol at their belt."

"Best send post," said Mr Fleecebumpkin, "to the Squire of Corby Castle, to come and stand second to the *gentleman*."[1]

In the midst of this torrent of general ridicule, the Highlander instinctively griped[2] beneath the folds of his plaid, "But it's better not," he said in his own lan-guage. "A hundred curses on the swine-eaters, who know neither decency nor civility!"

"Make room, the pack of you," he said advancing to the door.

But his former friend interposed his sturdy bulk, and opposed his leaving the house; and when Robin Oig attempted to make his way by force, he hit him down on the floor, with as much ease as a boy bowls down a nine-pin.

"A ring, a ring!" was now shouted, until the dark rafters, and the hams that hung on them, trembled again, and the very platters on the *bink*[3] clattered against each other. "Well done, Harry"—"Give it him home Harry"—"Take care of him now—he sees his own blood!"

Such were the exclamations, while the Highlander, starting from the ground, all his coldness and caution lost in frantic rage, sprung at his antagonist with the fury, the activity, and the vindictive purpose of an incensed tiger-cat. But when could rage encounter science and temper? Robin Oig again went down in the unequal contest; and as the blow was necessarily a severe one, he lay motionless on the floor of the kitchen. The landlady ran to offer some aid, but Mr Fleecebumpkin would not permit her to approach.

"Let him alone," he said, "he will come to within time, and come up to the scratch again. He has not got half his broth yet."

---

7. If.
8. Of drink.
9. The line drawn across the ring, to which boxers are brought for an encounter (*OED*).

1. Take his place in a duel should he be injured or killed (the language taunts Robin's honor).
2. Groped.
3. Shelf.

"He has got all I mean to give him, though," said his antagonist, whose heart began to relent towards his old associate; "and I would rather by half give the rest to yourself, Mr Fleecebumpkin, for you pretend to know a thing or two, and Robin had not art enough even to peel[4] before setting to, but fought with his plaid dangling about him.—Stand up, Robin, my man! all friends now; and let me hear the man that will speak a word against you, or your country, for your sake."

Robin Oig was still under the dominion of his passion, and eager to renew the onset; but being withheld on the one side by the peace-making Dame Heskett, and on the other, aware that Wakefield no longer meant to renew the combat, his fury sunk into gloomy sullenness.

"Come, come, never grudge so much at it, man," said the brave-spirited Englishman, with the placability of his country, "shake hands, and we will be better friends than ever."

"Friends!" exclaimed Robin Oig with strong emphasis—"friends!—Never. Look to yourself,[5] Harry Waakfelt."

"Then the curse of Cromwell[6] on your proud Scots stomach, as the man says in the play, and you may do your worst, and be d———d; for one man can say nothing more to another after a tussle, than that he is sorry for it."

On these terms the friends parted; Robin Oig drew out, in silence, a piece of money, threw it on the table, and then left the alehouse. But turning at the door, he shook his hand at Wakefield, pointing with his forefinger upwards, in a manner which might imply either a threat or a caution. He then disappeared in the moonlight.

Some words passed after his departure, between the bailiff, who piqued himself on being a little of a bully, and Harry Wakefield, who, with generous inconsistency, was now not indisposed to begin a new combat in defence of Robin Oig's reputation, "although he could not use his daddles like an Englishman, as it did not come natural to him." But Dame Heskett prevented this second quarrel from coming to a head by her peremptory interference. "There should be no more fighting in her house," she said; "there had been too much already.—And you, Mr. Wakefield, may live to learn," she added, "what it is to make a deadly enemy out of a good friend."

"Pshaw, dame! Robin Oig is an honest fellow, and will never keep malice."

"Do not trust to that—you do not know the dour temper of the Scots, though you have dealt with them so often. I have a right to know them, my mother being a Scot."

"And so is well seen on her daughter," said Ralph Heskett.

This nuptial sarcasm gave the discourse another turn; fresh customers entered the tap-room or kitchen, and others left it. The conversation turned on the expected markets, and the report of prices from different parts both of Scotland and England—treaties were commenced, and Harry Wakefield was lucky enough to find a chap for part of his drove, and at a very considerable profit; an event of consequence more than sufficient to blot out all remembrances of the unpleasant scuffle in the earlier part of the day. But there remained one party from whose mind that recollection could not have been wiped away by the possession of every head of cattle betwixt Esk and Eden.[7]

---

4. Strip down.
5. Watch out; be warned.
6. In a brutal nine-month campaign in 1649–1650 Protestant Oliver Cromwell and his army were so remorseless to the rebellious Irish Catholics that "The curse of Cromwell on you" became a popular Irish oath.
7. Rivers in Scotland.

This was Robin Oig M'Combich.—"That I should have had no weapon," he said, "and for the first time in my life!—Blighted be the tongue that bids the High-lander part with the dirk—the dirk—ha! the English blood!—My muhme's word—when did her word fall to the ground?"

The recollection of the fatal prophecy confirmed the deadly intention which instantly sprang up in his mind.

"Ha! Morrison cannot be many miles behind; and if it were an hundred, what then!"

His impetuous spirit had now a fixed purpose and motive of action, and he turned the light foot of his country towards the wilds, through which he knew, by Mr Ireby's report, that Morrison was advancing. His mind was wholly engrossed by the sense of injury—injury sustained from a friend; and by the desire of vengeance on one whom he now accounted his most bitter enemy. The treasured ideas of self-importance and self-opinion—of ideal birth and quality, had become more precious to him, (like the hoard to the miser,) because he could only enjoy them in secret. But that hoard was pillaged, the idols which he had secretly worshipped had been desecrated and profaned. Insulted, abused, and beaten, he was no longer worthy, in his own opinion, of the name he bore, or the lineage which he belonged to—nothing was left to him—nothing but revenge; and as the reflection added a galling spur to every step, he determined it should be as sudden and signal as the offence.

When Robin Oig left the door of the alehouse, seven or eight English miles at least lay betwixt Morrison and him. The advance of the former was slow, limited by the slug-gish pace of his cattle; the last left behind him stubble-field and hedge-row, crag and dark heath, all glittering with frost-rhime in the broad November moonlight, at the rate of six miles an hour. And now the distant lowing of Morrison's cattle is heard; and now they are seen creeping like moles in size and slowness of motion on the broad face of the moor; and now he meets them—passes them, and stops their conductor.

"May good betide us," said the Southlander—"Is this you, Robin M'Combich, or your wraith?"[8]

"It is Robin Oig M'Combich," answered the Highlander, "and it is not.—But never mind that, put pe giving me the skene-dhu."

"What! you are for back to the Highlands—The devil!—Have you selt all off before the fair? This beats all for quick markets!"

"I have not sold—I am not going north—May pe I will never go north again.—Give me pack my dirk, Hugh Morrison, or there will pe words petween us."

"Indeed, Robin, I'll be better advised before I gie it back to you—it is a wan-chancy[9] weapon in a Highlandman's hand, and I am thinking you will be about some barns-breaking."

"Prutt, trutt! let me have my weapon," said Robin Oig impatiently.

"Hooly and fairly,"[1] said his well-meaning friend. "I'll tell you what will do better than these dirking doings—Ye ken Highlander and Lowlander, and Border-men, are a' ae man's bairns[2] when you are over the Scots dyke. See, the Eskdale callants,[3] and fighting Charlie of Liddesdale, and the Lockerby lads, and the four Dandies of Lus-truther, and a wheen mair[4] grey plaids, are coming up behind; and if you are wronged, there is the hand of a Manly Morrison, we'll see you righted, if Carlisle and Stanwix baith took up the feud."

8. Ghost.
9. Unlucky.
1. Slowly and gently.
2. All are one man's children (all the same) when you

cross the border.
3. Gallants.
4. Great many.

"To tell you the truth," said Robin Oig, desirous of eluding the suspicions of his friend, "I have enlisted with a party of the Black Watch,[5] and must march off to-morrow morning."

"Enlisted! Were you mad or drunk?—You must buy yourself off—I can lend you twenty notes, and twenty to that, if the drove sell."

"I thank you—thank ye, Hughie; but I go with good will the gate[6] that I am going,—so the dirk—the dirk!"

"There it is for you then, since less wunna[7] serve. But think on what I was saying.—Waes me, it will be sair news in the braes of Balquidder,[8] that Robin Oig M'Combich should have run an ill gate, and ta'en on."

"Ill news in Balquidder, indeed!" echoed poor Robin: "but Cot speed you, Hughie, and send you good marcats.[9] Ye winna meet with Robin Oig again, either at tryste or fair."[1]

So saying, he shook hastily the hand of his acquaintance, and set out in the direction from which he had advanced, with the spirit of his former pace.

"There is something wrang with the lad," muttered the Morrison to himself; "but we will maybe see better into it the morn's morning."

But long ere the morning dawned, the catastrophe[2] of our tale had taken place. It was two hours after the affray had happened, and it was totally forgotten by almost every one, when Robin Oig returned to Heskett's inn. The place was filled at once by various sorts of men, and with noises corresponding to their character. There were the grave, low sounds of men engaged in busy traffic, with the laugh, the song, and the riotous jest of those who had nothing to do but to enjoy themselves. Among the last was Harry Wakefield, who, amidst a grinning group of smock-frocks, hobnailed shoes, and jolly English physiognomies, was trolling forth the old ditty,

> "What though my name be Roger,
> Who drives the plough and cart——"[3]

when he was interrupted by a well-known voice saying in a high and stern voice, marked by the sharp Highland accent, "Harry Waakfelt—if you be a man stand up!"[4]

"What is the matter?—what is it?" the guests demanded of each other.

"It is only a d——d Scotsman," said Fleecebumpkin, who was by this time very drunk, "whom Harry Wakefield helped to his broth to-day, who is now come to have *his cauld kail* het again."

"Harry Waakfelt," repeated the same ominous summons, "stand up, if you be a man!"

There is something in the tone of deep and concentrated passion, which attracts attention and imposes awe, even by the very sound. The guests shrunk back on every side, and gazed at the Highlander as he stood in the middle of them, his brows bent, and his features rigid with resolution.

"I will stand up with all my heart, Robin, my boy, but it shall be to shake hands with you, and drink down all unkindness. It is not the fault of your heart, man, that you don't know how to clench your hands."

5. Highland regiment of the regular British army, (go off to war).
6. Way.
7. Would not.
8. Rob-Roy country, Robin's home district.
9. Markets.
1. In private or public.
2. A term from Greek tragedy ("from the stars"), a genre

in which revenge is prominent.
3. In *Young Roger of the Mill*, a traditional English ballad (Lancashire area) published in broadside 1820–1824, Roger courts a woman reluctant to marry a mere ploughman; when he indicates he has "other fish to fry," she relents, they marry, pool their funds, and buy a cow.
4. A challenge to a duel of honor.

By this time he stood opposite to his antagonist; his open and unsuspecting look strangely contrasted with the stern purpose, which gleamed wild, dark, and vindictive in the eyes of the Highlander.

"'Tis not thy fault, man, that, not having the luck to be an Englishman, thou canst not fight more than a school-girl."

"I *can* fight," answered Robin Oig sternly, but calmly, "and you shall know it. You, Harry Waakfelt, showed me to-day how the Saxon churls fight—I show you now how the Highland Dunniewassel[5] fights."

He seconded the word with the action, and plunged the dagger, which he suddenly displayed, into the broad breast of the English yeoman, with such fatal certainty and force, that the hilt made a hollow sound against the breast-bone, and the double-edged point split the very heart of his victim. Harry Wakefield fell, and expired with a single groan. His assassin next seized the bailiff by the collar, and offered the bloody poniard to his throat, whilst dread and surprise rendered the man incapable of defence.

"It were very just to lay you beside him," he said, "but the blood of a base pick-thank[6] shall never mix on my father's dirk, with that of a brave man."

As he spoke, he cast the man from him with so much force that he fell on the floor, while Robin, with his other hand, threw the fatal weapon into the blazing turf-fire.

"There," he said, "take me who likes—and let fire cleanse blood if it can."

The pause of astonishment still continuing, Robin Oig asked for a peace-officer, and a constable having stepped out, he surrendered himself to his custody.

"A bloody night's work you have made of it," said the constable.

"Your own fault," said the Highlander. "Had you kept his hands off me twa hours since, he would have been now as well and merry as he was twa minutes since."

"It must be sorely answered," said the peace-officer.

"Never you mind that—death pays all debts; it will pay that too."

The horror of the bystanders began now to give way to indignation; and the sight of a favourite companion murdered in the midst of them, the provocation being, in their opinion, so utterly inadequate to the excess of vengeance, might have induced them to kill the perpetrator of the deed even upon the very spot. The constable, however, did his duty on this occasion, and with the assistance of some of the more reasonable persons present, procured horses to guard the prisoner to Carlisle, to abide his doom at the next assizes.[7] While the escort was preparing, the prisoner neither expressed the least interest, nor attempted the slightest reply. Only, before he was carried from the fatal apartment, he desired to look at the dead body, which, raised from the floor, had been deposited upon the large table (at the head of which Harry Wakefield had presided but a few minutes before, full of life, vigour, and animation,) until the surgeons should examine the mortal wound. The face of the corpse was decently covered with a napkin. To the surprise and horror of the bystanders, which displayed itself in a general *Ah!* drawn through clenched teeth and half-shut lips, Robin Oig removed the cloth, and gazed with a mournful but steady eye on the lifeless visage, which had been so lately animated, that the smile of good-humoured confidence in his own strength, of conciliation at once, and contempt towards his enemy, still curled his lip. While those present expected that the wound, which had so lately flooded the apartment with gore, would send forth fresh streams at the touch of the homicide, Robin Oig replaced the covering with the brief exclamation—"He was a pretty man!"

My story is nearly ended. The unfortunate Highlander stood his trial at Carlisle. I was myself present, and as a young Scottish lawyer, or barrister at least, and reputed

---

5. Clansman of rank and esteem.
6. Flatterer, sycophant.

7. Seasonal court-sessions.

a man of some quality, the politeness of the Sheriff of Cumberland offered me a place on the bench. The facts of the case were proved in the manner I have related them; and whatever might be at first the prejudice of the audience against a crime so un-English as that of assassination from revenge, yet when the rooted national prejudices of the prisoner had been explained, which made him consider himself as stained with indelible dishonour, when subjected to personal violence; when his previous patience, moderation, and endurance, were considered, the generosity of the English audience was inclined to regard his crime as the wayward aberration of a false idea of honour rather than as flowing from a heart naturally savage, or perverted by habitual vice. I shall never forget the charge of the venerable Judge to the jury, although not at that time liable to be much affected either by that which was eloquent or pathetic.

"We have had," he said, "in the previous part of our duty," (alluding to some former trials,) "to discuss crimes which infer disgust and abhorrence, while they call down the well-merited vengeance of the law. It is now our still more melancholy task to apply its salutary though severe enactments to a case of a very singular character, in which the crime (for a crime it is, and a deep one) arose less out of the malevolence of the heart, than the error of the understanding—less from any idea of committing wrong, than from an unhappily perverted notion of that which is right. Here we have two men, highly esteemed, it has been stated, in their rank of life, and attached, it seems, to each other as friends, one of whose lives has been already sacrificed to a punctilio,[8] and the other is about to prove the vengeance of the offended laws; and yet both may claim our commiseration at least, as men acting in ignorance of each other's national prejudices, and unhappily misguided rather than voluntarily erring from the path of right conduct.

"In the original cause of the misunderstanding, we must in justice give the right to the prisoner at the bar. He had acquired possession of the inclosure, which was the object of competition, by a legal contract with the proprietor Mr Ireby; and yet, when accosted with reproaches undeserved in themselves, and galling doubtless to a temper at least sufficiently susceptible of passion, he offered notwithstanding to yield up half his acquisition, for the sake of peace and good neighbourhood, and his amicable proposal was rejected with scorn. Then follows the scene at Mr Heskett the publican's, and you will observe how the stranger was treated by the deceased, and, I am sorry to observe, by those around, who seem to have urged him in a manner which was aggravating in the highest degree. While he asked for peace and for com-position, and offered submission to a magistrate, or to a mutual arbiter, the prisoner was insulted by a whole company, who seem on this occasion to have forgotten the national maxim of 'fair play;' and while attempting to escape from the place in peace, he was intercepted, struck down, and beaten to the effusion of his blood.

"Gentlemen of the Jury, it was with some impatience that I heard my learned brother, who opened the case for the crown,[9] give an unfavourable turn to the pris-oner's conduct on this occasion. He said the prisoner was afraid to encounter his an-tagonist in fair fight, or to submit to the laws of the ring; and that therefore, like a cowardly Italian, he had recourse to his fatal stiletto, to murder the man whom he dared not meet in manly encounter. I observed the prisoner shrink from this part of the accusation with the abhorrence natural to a brave man; and as I would wish to make my words impressive, when I point his real crime, I must secure his opinion of my impartiality, by rebutting every thing that seems to me a false accusation. There can be no doubt that the prisoner is a man of resolution—too much resolution—I wish to Heaven that he had less, or rather that he had had a better education to regulate it.

8. Fine point (of honor).   9. The government (the prosecution).

"Gentlemen, as to the laws my brother talks of, they may be known in the Bull-ring, or the Bear-garden, or the Cockpit, but they are not known here.[1] Or, if they should be so far admitted as furnishing a species of proof that no malice was intended in this sort of combat, from which fatal accidents do sometimes arise, it can only be so admitted when both parties are in pari casu,[2] equally acquainted with, and equally will-ing to refer themselves to, that species of arbitrement. But will it be contended that a man of superior rank and education is to be subjected, or is obliged to subject himself, to this coarse and brutal strife, perhaps in opposition to a younger, stronger, or more skilful opponent? Certainly even the pugilistic code, if founded upon the fair play of Merry Old England, as my brother alleges it to be, can contain nothing so preposter-ous. And, gentlemen of the jury, if the laws would support an English gentleman, wearing, we will suppose, his sword, in defending himself by force against a violent personal aggression of the nature offered to this prisoner, they will not less protect a foreigner and a stranger, involved in the same unpleasing circumstances. If, therefore, gentlemen of the jury, when thus pressed by a vis major,[3] the object of obloquy to a whole company, and of direct violence from one at least, and, as he might reasonably apprehend, from more, the panel had produced the weapon which his countrymen, as we are informed, generally carry about their persons, and the same unhappy cir-cumstance had ensued which you have heard detailed in evidence, I could not in my conscience have asked from you a verdict of murder. The prisoner's personal defence might indeed, even in that case, have gone more or less beyond the moderamen incul-patae tutelae,[4] spoken of by lawyers, but the punishment incurred would have been that of manslaughter, not of murder. I beg leave to add, that I should have thought this milder species of charge was demanded in the case supposed, notwithstanding the statute of James I. cap. 8, which takes the case of slaughter by stabbing with a short weapon, even without malice prepense, out of the benefit of clergy.[5] For this statute of stabbing, as it is termed, arose out of a temporary cause; and as the real guilt is the same, whether the slaughter be committed by the dagger, or by sword or pistol, the benignity of the modern law places them all on the same, or nearly the same footing.

"But, gentlemen of the jury, the pinch of the case lies in the interval of two hours interposed betwixt the reception of the injury and the fatal retaliation. In the heat of affray and chaude mêlée,[6] law, compassionating the infirmities of humanity, makes allowance for the passions which rule such a stormy moment——for the sense of present pain, for the apprehension of further injury, for the difficulty of ascertain-ing with due accuracy the precise degree of violence which is necessary to protect the person of the individual, without annoying or injuring the assailant more than is absolutely necessary. But the time necessary to walk twelve miles, however speedily performed, was an interval sufficient for the prisoner to have recollected himself; and the violence with which he carried his purpose into effect, with so many circum-stances of deliberate determination, could neither be induced by the passion of anger, nor that of fear. It was the purpose and the act of predetermined revenge, for which law neither can, will, nor ought to have sympathy or allowance.

---

1. Bear-fighting and cockfighting were popular English sports in the 17th century, and though some English were appalled at Spanish bullfighting, others enjoyed the tour-ist attraction.
2. In the same case (Latin).
3. Greater force (Latin).
4. Moderation of blameless protection (Latin), self-defense.

5. In English law, initially a provision that allowed cler-gymen exemption from secular jurisdiction and trial in-stead under canon law; this gradually became a plea for leniency for first-time convicts of some lesser crimes.
6. Heated conflict (French).

"It is true, we may repeat to ourselves, in alleviation of this poor man's unhappy action, that his case is a very peculiar one. The country which he inhabits was, in the days of many now alive, inaccessible to the laws, not only of England, which have not even yet penetrated thither, but to those to which our neighbours of Scotland are subjected, and which must be supposed to be, and no doubt actually are, founded upon the general principles of justice and equity which pervade every civilized country. Amongst their mountains, as among the North American Indians, the various tribes were wont to make war upon each other, so that each man was obliged to go armed for his own protection and for the offence of his neighbour. These men, from the ideas which they entertained of their own descent and of their own consequence, regarded themselves as so many cavaliers or men-at-arms, rather than as the peasantry of a peaceful country. Those laws of the ring, as my brother terms them, were unknown to the race of warlike mountaineers; that decision of quarrels by no other weapons than those which nature has given every man, must to them have seemed as vulgar and as preposterous as to the Noblesse[7] of France. Revenge, on the other hand, must have been as familiar to their habits of society as to those of the Cherokees or Mohawks. It is indeed, as described by Bacon, at bottom a kind of wild untutored justice;[8] for the fear of retaliation must withhold the hands of the oppressor where there is no regular law to check daring violence. But though all this may be granted, and though we may allow that, such having been the case of the Highlands in the days of the prisoner's fathers, many of the opinions and sentiments must still continue to influence the present generation, it cannot, and ought not, even in this most painful case, to alter the administration of the law, either in your hands, gentlemen of the jury, or in mine. The first object of civilisation is to place the general protection of the law, equally administered, in the room of that wild justice, which every man cut and carved for himself, according to the length of his sword and the strength of his arm. The law says to the subjects, with a voice only inferior to that of the Deity, 'Vengeance is mine.'[9] The instant that there is time for passion to cool, and reason to interpose, an injured party must become aware, that the law assumes the exclusive cognizance of the right and wrong betwixt the parties, and opposes her inviolable buckler[1] to every attempt of the private party to right himself. I repeat, that this unhappy man ought personally to be the object rather of our pity than our abhorrence, for he failed in his ignorance, and from mistaken notions of honour. But his crime is not the less that of murder, gentlemen, and, in your high and important office, it is your duty so to find. Englishmen have their angry passions as well as Scots; and should this man's action remain unpunished, you may unsheath, under various pretences, a thousand daggers betwixt the Land's-end and the Orkneys."[2]

The venerable Judge thus ended what, to judge by his apparent emotion, and by the tears which filled his eyes, was really a painful task. The jury, according to his instructions, brought in a verdict of Guilty; and Robin Oig M'Combich, *alias* McGregor, was sentenced to death, and left for execution, which took place accordingly. He met his fate with great firmness, and acknowledged the justice of his sentence. But he repelled indignantly the observations of those who accused him of attacking an unarmed man. "I give a life for the life I took," he said, "and what can I do more?"[3]

1827   1827

7. Nobility.
8. Francis Bacon opens his famous essay *Of Revenge* (1625): "Revenge is a kind of wild justice, which the more man's nature runs to, the more ought law to weed it out."
9. Peter's Epistle to the Romans (12.19), recalling God's warning that He alone may take vengeance on cursed Cain (Genesis 4.15).
1. Shield.

2. Southernmost England to northernmost Scottish isles.
3. In a later publication, Scott added a long note on the poems of "drover poet" Robert Mackay, who wrote under the name of Rob Donn (i.e., Brown Robert), some published in the *Quarterly Review*, July 1831; Scott's note gives two songs, in order to dispel the prejudice of Highlanders as people of "wild superstition and rude manners."

INTRODUCTION TO TALES OF MY LANDLORD Having succeeded as "the author of *Waverley*," Scott cannily decided in 1816 to multiply his authorial identity, and began a four-volume series, *Tales of My Landlord*, supposedly told to a Scots preacher by the landlord of a Scottish inn. Taken all together the profusion of memorable pseudonyms and nested narratives in the prefaces to Scott's novels turn questions of transmission and fictional truth every which way, forming not a systematic theory of fiction but an exuberant testimony to the working author's artful exploitation of his medium.

Introduction to *Tales of My Landlord*

Collected and Reported by Jedediah Cleishbotham,
School Master and Parish-Clerk of Gandercleugh

As I may, without vanity, presume that the name and official description prefixed to this Proem will secure it, from the sedate and reflecting part of mankind, to whom only I would be understood to address myself, such attention as is due to the sedulous instructor of youth, and the careful performer of my Sabbath duties, I will forbear to hold up a candle to the daylight, or to point out to the judicious those recommendations of my labours which they must necessarily anticipate from the perusal of the title-page. Nevertheless, I am not unaware, that, as Envy always dogs Merit at the heels, there may be those who will whisper, that albeit my learning and good principles cannot (lauded be the heavens) be denied by any one, yet that my situation at Gandercleugh hath been more favourable to my acquisitions in learning than to the enlargement of my views of the ways and works of the present generation. To the which objection, if, peradventure, any such shall be started, my answer shall be threefold:

First, Gandercleugh is, as it were, the central part—the navel (*si fas sit dicere* [if it may be said]) of this our native realm of Scotland; so that men, from every corner thereof, when travelling on their concernments of business, either towards our metropolis of law, by which I mean Edinburgh, or towards our metropolis and mart of gain, whereby I insinuate Glasgow, are frequently led to make Gandercleugh their abiding stage and place of rest for the night. And it must be acknowledged by the most sceptical, that I, who have sat in the leathern arm-chair, on the left-hand side of the fire, in the common room of the Wallace Inn, winter and summer, for every evening in my life, during forty years bypast, (the Christian Sabbaths only excepted,) must have seen more of the manners and customs of various tribes and people, than if I had sought them out by my own painful travel and bodily labour. Even so doth the tollman at the well-frequented turnpike on the Wellbrae-head, sitting at his ease in his own dwelling, gather more receipt of custom, than if, moving forth upon the road, he were to require a contribution from each person whom he chanced to meet in his journey, when, according to the vulgar adage, he might possibly be greeted with more kicks than halfpence.

But, secondly, supposing it again urged, that Ithacus [Odysseus], the most wise of the Greeks, acquired his renown, as the Roman poet [Virgil] hath assured us, by visiting states and men, I reply to the Zoilus[1] who shall adhere to this objection, that, *de facto*, I have seen states and men also; for I have visited the famous cities of Edinburgh and Glasgow, the former twice, and the latter three times, in the course of my earthly pilgrimage. And, moreover, I had the honour to sit in the General Assembly[2] (meaning, as an auditor, in the galleries thereof,) and have heard as much goodly speaking on the law of patronage, as, with the fructification thereof in mine own

---

1. A censorious critic of the 4th century B.C.E.   2. The highest court of the Church of Scotland.

understanding, hath made me be considered as an oracle upon that doctrine ever since my safe and happy return to Gandercleugh.

Again—and thirdly, if it be nevertheless pretended that my information and knowledge of mankind, however extensive, and however painfully acquired, by constant domestic enquiry, and by foreign travel, is, natheless, incompetent to the task of recording the pleasant narratives of my Landlord, I will let these critics know, to their own eternal shame and confusion, as well as to the abashment and discomfiture of all who shall rashly take up a song against me, that I am NOT the writer, redactor, or compiler, of the Tales of my Landlord; nor am I, in one single iota, answerable for their contents, more or less. And now, ye generation of critics, who raise yourselves up as if it were brazen serpents,[3] to hiss with your tongues, and to smite with your stings, bow yourselves down to your native dust, and acknowledge that yours have been the thoughts of ignorance, and the words of vain foolishness. Lo! ye are caught in your own snare, and your own pit hath yawned for you. Turn, then, aside from the task that is too heavy for you; destroy not your teeth by gnawing a file; waste not your strength by spurning [kicking] against a castle wall; nor spend your breath in contending in swiftness with a fleet steed; and let those weigh the Tales of my Landlord, who shall bring with them the scales of candour cleansed from the rust of prejudice by the hands of intelligent modesty. For these alone they were compiled, as will appear from a brief narrative which my zeal for truth compelled me to make supplementary to the present Proem.

It is well known that my Landlord was a pleasing and a facetious man, acceptable unto all the parish of Gandercleugh, excepting only the Laird, the Exciseman, and those for whom he refused to draw liquor upon trust.[4] Their causes of dislike I will touch separately, adding my own refutation thereof.

His honour, the Laird, accused our Landlord, deceased, of having encouraged, in various times and places, the destruction of hares, rabbits, fowls black and grey, partridges, moor-pouts, roe-deer, and other birds and quadrupeds, at unlawful seasons, and contrary to the laws of this realm, which have secured, in their wisdom, the slaughter of such animals for the great of the earth, whom I have remarked to take an uncommon (though to me, an unintelligible) pleasure therein. Now, in humble deference to his honour, and in justifiable defence of my friend deceased, I reply to this charge, that howsoever the form of such animals might appear to be similar to those so protected by the law, yet it was a mere *deceptio visus* [deceptive appearance]; for what resembled hares were, in fact, *hill-kids*, and those partaking of the appearance of moor-fowl, were truly *wood pigeons*, and consumed and eaten *eo nomine* [in their own name], and not otherwise.[5]

Again, the Exciseman pretended, that my deceased Landlord did encourage that species of manufacture called distillation, without having an especial permission from the Great, technically called a license, for doing so. Now, I stand up to confront this falsehood; and in defiance of him, his gauging-stick, and pen and ink-horn, I tell him, that I never saw, or tasted, a glass of unlawful aqua vitae in the house of my Landlord; nay, that, on the contrary, we needed not such devices, in respect of a pleasing and somewhat seductive liquor, which was vended and consumed

3. A parody of John the Baptist's rant at unrepentant hypocrites: "O generation of vipers" (Matthew 3.7).
4. The Laird was the landed proprietor, the Exciseman the tax collector (there was a special tax on alcohol); to draw upon trust is to buy on credit.
5. By simply renaming the game, the Landlord is evading the protections the Laird has placed on it.

at the Wallace Inn, under the name of *mountain dew*. If there is a penalty against manufacturing such a liquor, let him show me the statute; and when he does, I'll tell him if I will obey it or no.

Concerning those who came to my Landlord for liquor, and went thirsty away, for lack of present coin, or future credit, I cannot but say it has grieved my bowels as if the case had been mine own. Nevertheless, my Landlord considered the necessities of a thirsty soul, and would permit them, in extreme need, and when their soul was impoverished for lack of moisture, to drink to the full value of their watches and wearing apparel, exclusively of their inferior habiliments, which he was uniformly inexorable in obliging them to retain, for the credit of the house. As to mine own part, I may well say, that he never refused me that modicum of refreshment with which I am wont to recruit nature after the fatigues of my school. It is true, I taught his five sons English and Latin, writing, book-keeping, with a tincture of mathematics, and that I instructed his daughter in psalmody. Nor do I remember me of any fee or *honorarium* received from him on account of these my labours, except the compotations aforesaid. Nevertheless this compensation suited my humour well, since it is a hard sentence to bid a dry throat wait till quarter-day.[6]

But, truly, were I to speak my simple conceit and belief, I think my Landlord was chiefly moved to waive in my behalf the usual requisition of a symbol, or reckoning, from the pleasure he was wont to take in my conversation, which, though solid and edifying in the main, was, like a well-built palace, decorated with facetious narratives and devices, tending much to the enhancement and ornament thereof. And so pleased was my Landlord of the Wallace in his replies during such colloquies, that there was no district in Scotland, yea, and no peculiar, and, as it were, distinctive custom therein practised, but was discussed betwixt us; insomuch, that those who stood by were wont to say, it was worth a bottle of ale to hear us communicate with each other. And not a few travellers, from distant parts, as well as from the remote districts of our kingdom, were wont to mingle in the conversation, and to tell news that had been gathered in foreign lands, or preserved from oblivion in this our own.

Now I chanced to have contracted for teaching the lower classes with a young person called Peter, or Patrick, Pattieson, who had been educated for our Holy Kirk, yea, had, by the license of presbytery,[7] his voice opened therein as a preacher, who delighted in the collection of olden tales and legends, and in garnishing them with the flowers of poesy, whereof he was a vain and frivolous professor. For he followed not the example of those strong poets whom I proposed to him as a pattern, but formed versification of a flimsy and modern texture, to the compounding whereof was necessary small pains and less thought. And hence I have chid him as being one of those who bring forward the fatal revolution prophesied by Mr Robert Carey, in his Vatication[8] on the Death of the celebrated Dr John Donne:

> Now thou art gone, and thy strict laws will be
> Too hard for libertines in poetry;
> Till verse (by thee refined) in this last age
> Turn ballad rhyme.

I had also disputations with him touching his indulging rather a flowing and redundant than a concise and stately diction in his prose exercitations. But notwithstanding these symptoms of inferior taste, and a humour of contradicting his betters

---

6. Payday once every quarter-year.
7. Ordained by the Church (Kirk) of Scotland.

8. Prophetic utterance.

upon passages of dubious construction in Latin authors, I did grievously lament when Peter Pattieson was removed from me by death, even as if he had been the offspring of my own loins. And in respect his papers had been left in my care, (to answer funeral and death-bed expenses,) I conceived myself entitled to dispose of one parcel thereof, entitled, "Tales of my Landlord," to one cunning in the trade (as it is called) of bookselling. He was a mirthful man, of small stature, cunning in counterfeiting of voices, and in making facetious tales and responses, and whom I have to laud for the truth of his dealings towards me.

Now, therefore, the world may see the injustice that charges me with incapacity to write these narratives, seeing, that though I have proved that I could have written them if I would, yet, not having done so, the censure will deservedly fall, if at all due, upon the memory of Mr Peter Pattieson; whereas I must be justly entitled to the praise, when any is due, seeing that, as the Dean of St. Patrick's[9] wittily and logically expresseth it, "That without which a thing is not, /Is *Causa sine qua non*." The work, therefore, is unto me as a child is to a parent; in the which child, if it proveth worthy, the parent hath honour and praise; but, if otherwise, the disgrace will deservedly attach to itself alone.

I have only further to intimate, that Mr Peter Pattieson, in arranging these Tales for the press, hath more consulted his own fancy than the accuracy of the narrative; nay, that he hath sometimes blended two or three stories together for the mere grace of his plots. Of which infidelity, although I disapprove and enter my testimony against it, yet I have not taken upon me to correct the same, in respect it was the will of the deceased, that his manuscript should be submitted to the press without diminution or alteration. A fanciful nicety it was on the part of my deceased friend, who, if thinking wisely, ought rather to have conjured me, by all the tender ties of our friendship and common pursuits, to have carefully revised, altered, and augmented, at my judgment and discretion. But the will of the dead must be scrupulously obeyed, even when we weep over their pertinacity and self-delusion. So, gentle reader, I bid you farewell, recommending you to such fare as the mountains of your own country produce; and I will only farther premise, that each Tale is preceded by a short introduction, mentioning the persons by whom, and the circumstances under which, the materials thereof were collected.

Jedediah Cleishbotham.

---

9. Poet and satirist Jonathan Swift (1667–1745); Scott had done an edition of Donne's works.

⇥ PERSPECTIVES ⇥

Popular Prose and the Problems of Authorship

In his essay *Of Persons One Would Wish to Have Seen* William Hazlitt records a friend saying: "I suppose the two first persons . . . would be the two greatest names in English literature, Sir Isaac Newton and Mr. Locke." It may surprise a modern reader to see the scientist Newton and the philosopher John Locke placed in "English literature," but Hazlitt's choice tellingly demonstrates how the category covered the entire realm of learned writing. In Hazlitt's age, "literature" was just beginning to differentiate its essays, fiction, and poetry from the professional fields of science and philosophy. This nascent division took energy from the new idea of a "national" literature, underscored by Blake when he wrote in *The Marriage of Heaven and Hell* that "the sayings used in a nation mark its character." There was a new interest in the local and particular, in colloquial speech and regional dialect, in the eccentricities of conduct that bespoke the variety of sturdy individuals who composed the nation. A literature popular in aim, addressing a growing and diversely educated reading public, burst forth in an array of prose forms that ruptured the polite realm of "high" literature.

Foremost was the novel, climbing toward respectability from the suspect territory of romance but still a lower genre than poetry. A prime figure in the raising of the novel's status in these years was Walter Scott, whose many Waverley novels set the standard for historical fiction for the whole nineteenth century; yet Scott published his novels anonymously, partly because he feared that novelistic notoriety would lower his reputation as a serious poet. Scott contrasted his "Big Bow-wow strain" of broad comedy with the "exquisite touch" of Jane Austen, "which renders ordinary commonplace things and characters interesting"; but the two share with Wordsworth a concern with the typical life and language of unremarkable folk. Austen defined her ideal material as "3 or 4 Families in a Country Village"—a domestic English counterpart to Scott's Highlanders, exotic to English readers but taken by Scott's countrymen as true to life, or at least as memorials to a familiar but vanishing culture. Conversely, to Scott, Austen's "talent for describing the involvements and feelings and characters of ordinary life" was "the most wonderful I ever met with," and "wonderful" is a term charged with Romantic associations. If Austen's ironic comedy seems worlds away from Scott's earthy amplitude, their contemporaries appreciated both of them for their humor.

The magazines, joined by weekly newspapers such as *The Examiner* (founded 1808), represented the urban scene, giving employment to writers and making the bustling world of the city, its arts, its commerce, and its politics, available for discussion in coffeehouses, over tea, and at breakfast tables. Essays by Hazlitt and Lamb appeared in *London Magazine* (founded 1820), mixed amid regular items such as abstracts of foreign and domestic occurrences, a monthly register of agriculture and commerce, and a list of ecclesiastical and other preferments. *London* published De Quincey's *Confessions of an English Opium-Eater* in September and October 1821, over the signature XYZ. Such pseudonyms functioned not so much to ensure anonymity as to tease readers' curiosity: the recurrence from issue to issue of Lamb's *Elia* and T. G. Wainewright's *Janus Weathercock* generated a world to be found only within the pages of the magazine. At its heart were the characters that the pseudonyms brought into being, imagined persons modeled on real ones, yet untrammeled by actuality. The period produced a theater of personalities, a literature experienced as the extension of a fascinating author and fixed by his image. The connotation of copyright began to shift accordingly, from the claims of the publisher to certification of the author's original genius. In 1753 Thomas Gray had rejected with horror his publisher's idea of using his portrait as a frontispiece: "to appear in proper Person at the head of my works, would be worse than the Pillory." In contrast, Byron's publisher sold engravings of his best-selling poet—in Albanian costume (see Color Plate 3), in various postures, heroic or poetic—for purchasers to insert in their volumes. The pseudonym inverted and confirmed the public's enthrallment by the author. "The Great Unknown," the title bestowed on the anonymous author of the Waverley novels, could even have his—veiled—portrait engraved (see page 1062).

Even newspapers became the images of titans: T. J. Wooler's radical *Black Dwarf* and William Cobbett's *Political Register* bore the stamps of their conductors as vividly as the Byronic hero bore Byron's. "Whatever a man's talents, whatever a man's opinions, he sought the *Register* on the day of its appearance with eagerness, and read it with amusement," Edward Bulwer-Lytton wrote after Cobbett's death. To read Cobbett each week had become an addiction: "his loss was not merely that of a man, but of a habit—of a dose of strong drink, which all of us had been taking for years, most of us during our whole lives, and which it was impossible for any one again to concoct so strongly, so strangely, with so much spice and flavour, or with such a variety of ingredients."

Such flamboyance was not permissible for women of proper "feminine" modesty. Even when encouraged, Dorothy Wordsworth declined to step forward as author (see her letter to Mrs. Thomas Clarkson, page 616). To transgress was to risk male scorn, typified by Hazlitt's denunciation in 1821: "I have an aversion to Bluestockings. I do not care a fig for any woman that even knows what *an author* means." To publish was to be public, and "a public woman" was a prostitute. Despite the success of many women writers, the stigma signaled by a seventeenth-century couplet persisted: "Punk and Poesie agree so pat, / You cannot well be *this*, and not be *that*." Novelist Frances Burney, author of *Evelina* (1778), *Cecilia* (1782), and *The Wanderer* (1814), voiced the fear of indecent exposure that shadowed a woman writer's professional achievements: "I have an exceeding odd sensation, when I consider that it is now in the power of *any* and *every*body to read what I so carefully hoarded even from my best friends, till this last month or two,—and that a work which was so lately lodged, in all the privacy of my bureau, may now be seen by every butcher and baker, cobbler and tinker, throughout the three kingdoms." Pseudonymous or anonymous publication—Austen did not put her name to her novels—shielded the modesty of the woman writer from the notoriety inseparable from popularity, even as prose writers began to speak with increasing authority from behind their fictional veils.

✦ ✦❖✦ ✦

Charles Lamb
1775–1834

"Mr Lamb, from the peculiarity of his exterior and address as an author, would probably never have made his way by detached and independent efforts," wrote Hazlitt, "but fortunately for himself and others, he has taken advantage of the Periodical Press, where he has been stuck into notice, and the texture of his compositions is assuredly fine enough to bear the broadest glare of popularity that has hitherto shone upon them." Charles Lamb was born in London, the son of a legal clerk; his brother John and sister Mary, his literary collaborator and companion (see page 366), were more than a decade older. Lamb gives affectionate portraits of both, Mary as "Bridget" in *Old China*, and John in *Dream Children*. At seven he entered Christ's Hospital, a charity school where he became a lifelong friend of Coleridge, to whose *Poems on Various Subjects* he contributed in 1796–1797. Unlike Coleridge, Lamb, a stammerer, did not distinguish himself academically or go on to university. Shortly after leaving school he joined his brother briefly as a clerk at the South Sea House, moving in 1792 to the East India House, where he remained until his retirement in 1825. His early writings had little success, but Lamb persevered with a self-mocking resilience; when his farce *Mr H—* failed when staged at Drury Lane in 1806, Lamb joined in hissing his own play.

In 1796, in a fit of the insanity that ran through the family, Mary fatally stabbed their mother and wounded their father. To prevent her being committed to an asylum, Charles assumed responsibility for her care. Though her derangements periodically recurred, the weekly suppers that they hosted gathered a diverse group of London artists and intellectuals. Radicals such as Thomas Holcroft, Godwin, Hazlitt, and Leigh Hunt mixed with Wordsworth, Coleridge, and Southey, as Charles moved among them, smoking, drinking, and making outrageous puns. Such evenings concentrated the delights of city life that Lamb celebrated in his essays and letters. Not counting on future fame, Lamb declared, "I will write for Antiquity." He developed his essayistic voice from the Elizabethan and seventeenth-century models in which he luxuriated. In 1807 he and his sister jointly produced *Tales from Shakespear* (see page 702); the following year he published *Specimens of English Dramatic Poets Who Lived About the Time of Shakespeare*, an anthology that restored, with incisive commentary, Webster, Ford, Middleton, and other virtually forgotten playwrights, significantly impelling the Elizabethan revival that marks the era. In his defense of Restoration comedy against charges of indecency, Lamb shrewdly called the theater "a speculative scene," a "happy breathing-place from the burthen of a perpetual moral questioning." The sly stylistic inventions of his own essays affirm the "privileges" of art to escape "the exclusive and all devouring drama of common life."

Essays signed "Elia" began to appear in *London Magazine* in 1820. The second, *Oxford in the Vacation*, anticipated in its first paragraph the curiosity the pseudonym was meant to provoke: "methinks I hear you exclaim, reader, *Who is Elia?*" The name, Lamb told his publisher, belonged to an Italian clerk now "no more than a name, for he died of consumption," but the pseudonym established a self that could not be consumed in the market. Even as the essays made Lamb the most highly paid contributor to the *London*, Elia remained an enigma (or the useful fiction of an enigma; in London literary circles Lamb's authorship was known). "Elia," Lamb himself remarked, is anagrammatically "a lie." As he put it in *A Character of the Late Elia, by a Friend* (January 1823), the "first person" rather than the pseudonym was "his favorite figure." Lamb's achievement was to make the "person" emerge from the rhetorical figure; as Hazlitt saw, the response to the accumulating essays in the periodical conferred an identity on their peculiarly absent (minded) author. The popularity of the essays led to their republication in 1823 as *Essays which have appeared under that signature in the London Magazine; The Last Essays of Elia*, collected from various magazines, appeared in 1833.

Additional works by Lamb are included in Responses to Wordsworth (page 472), and Coleridge (page 703).

Oxford in the Vacation

Casting a preparatory glance at the bottom of this article—as the wary connoisseur in prints, with cursory eye, (which, while it reads, seems as though it read not,) never fails to consult the *quis sculpsit* [engraver's name] in the corner, before he pronounces some rare piece to be a Vivares or a Woollet—methinks I hear you exclaim, reader, *Who is Elia?*

Because in my last I tried to divert thee with some half-forgotten humours of some old clerks defunct, in an old house of business, long since gone to decay, doubtless you have already set me down in your mind as one of the self-same college, a votary of the desk, a notched and cropt scrivener,[1] one that sucks his sustenance, as certain sick people are said to do, through a quill.

Well, I do agnize[2] something of the sort. I confess that it is my humour, my fancy, in the fore part of the day, when the mind of your man of letters requires some relaxation, (and none better than such as at first sight seems most abhorrent from his beloved studies,) to while away some good hours of my time in the contemplation of

---

1. A copyist or clerk.
2. Acknowledge, a comic echo of *Othello* 1.3.228 (of a disposition to war, Othello says, "I do agnize").

indigos, cottons, raw silks, piece-goods, flowered or otherwise. In the first place * * *[3] and then it sends you home with such increased appetite to your books * * * not to say, that your outside sheets and waste wrappers of foolscap do receive into them, most kindly and naturally, the impression of sonnets, epigrams, *essays*—so that the very parings of a counting-house are, in some sort, the settings up of an author. The enfranchised quill, that has plodded all the morning among the cart-rucks of figures and ciphers, frisks and curvets so at its ease over the flowery carpet ground of a midnight dissertation. It feels its promotion. * * * So that you see, upon the whole, the literary dignity of *Elia* is very little, if at all, compromised in the condescension.

Not that, in my anxious detail of the many commodities incidental to the life of a public office, I would be thought blind to certain flaws, which a cunning carper might be able to pick in this Joseph's vest.[4] And here I must have leave, in the fulness of my soul, to regret the abolition, and doing-away-with altogether, of those consolatory interstices and sprinklings of freedom, through the four seasons—the *red-letter days*, now become, to all intents and purposes, *dead-letter days*.[5] There was Paul, and Stephen, and Barnabas, "Andrew, and John, men famous in old times,"[6] we were used to keep all their days holy as long back as I was at school at Christ's. I remember their effigies, by the same token, in the old Basket Prayer Book. There hung Peter in his uneasy posture, holy Bartlemy in the troublesome act of flaying, after the famous Marsyas by Spagnoletti.[7] I honoured them all, and could almost have wept the defalcation of Iscariot,—so much did we love to keep holy memories sacred:—only methought I a little grudged at the coalition of the better Jude with Simon[8]—clubbing (as it were) their sanctities together, to make up one poor gaudy day between them—as an economy unworthy of the dispensation.

These were bright visitations in a scholar's and a clerk's life—"far off their coming shone."[9] I was as good as an almanack in those days. I could have told you such a saint's day falls out next week, or the week after. Peradventure the Epiphany, by some periodical infelicity, would, once in six years, merge in a Sabbath. Now am I little better than one of the profane. Let me not be thought to arraign the wisdom of my civil superiors, who have judged the further observation of these holy tides to be papistical, superstitious. Only in a custom of such long standing, methinks if their Holinesses the Bishops had, in decency, been first sounded,—but I am wading out of my depths. I am not the man to decide the limits of civil and ecclesiastical authority; I am plain Elia—no Selden, nor Archbishop Usher—though at present in the thick of their books, here in the heart of learning, under the shadow of the mighty Bodley.[1]

I can here play the gentleman, enact the student. To such a one as myself, who has been defrauded in his young years of the sweet food of academic institution, nowhere is so pleasant, to while away a few idle weeks at, as one or other of the Universities. Their vacation, too, at this time of the year, falls in so pat with *ours*. Here I can take my walks unmolested, and fancy myself of what degree or standing I please. I seem admitted *ad eundem* [among them]. I fetch up past opportunities. I can rise at the chapel bell, and dream that it rings for *me*. In moods of humility I can be a

3. From the first printing in *London Magazine* through all reprintings supervised by Lamb, ellipses are indicated by asterisks; that this is *London's* own sign for its editor's elisions suggests Lamb's gentle, ironic wit about Elia's indulgences.
4. Joseph's coat of many colors (Genesis 37.3).
5. Red-letter days were holy days marked in the church calendar; "dead-letter days" because these days were no longer observed as holidays.
6. All saints; recalling "Andrew and Simon, famous after known" (*Paradise Regained*, 2.7).

7. St. Peter was crucified upside-down. St. Bartholomew was flayed alive, as was the mythological figure Marsyas; "Spagnoletti" is painter Jusepe José Ribera (1590–1652).
8. Because Judas Iscariot betrayed Jesus, no holiday commemorates him. St. Jude and St. Simon are commemorated on the same day.
9. Echoing *Paradise Lost* (6.768), Christ armed for battle.
1. John Selden (1584–1652), English jurist and antiquarian; James Ussher (1581–1656), Irish archbishop; the Bodleian Library of Oxford University was founded by Sir Thomas Bodley (1545–1613).

Sizar, or a Servitor. When the peacock vein rises I strut a Gentleman Commoner.[2] In graver moments I proceed Master of Arts. Indeed I do not think I am much unlike that respectable character. I have seen your dim-eyed vergers,[3] and bed-makers in spectacles, drop a bow or a curtsy as I pass, wisely mistaking me for something of the sort. I go about in black, which favours the notion. Only in Christ Church reverend quadrangle I can be content to pass for nothing short of a Seraphic Doctor.

The walks at these times are so much one's own—the tall trees of Christ's, the groves of Magdalen![4] The halls deserted, and with open doors inviting one to slip in unperceived, and pay a devoir[5] to some Founder, or noble or royal Benefactress, (that should have been ours,) whose portrait seems to smile upon their over-looked beadsman,[6] and to adopt me for their own. Then, to take a peep in by the way at the butteries and sculleries, redolent of antique hospitality: the immense caves of kitchens, kitchen fireplaces, cordial recesses; ovens whose first pies were baked four centuries ago; and spits which have cooked for Chaucer! Not the meanest minister among the dishes but is hallowed to me through his imagination, and the Cook goes forth a Manciple.[7]

Antiquity! thou wondrous charm, what art thou? that, being nothing, art every thing! When thou *wert*, thou wert not antiquity—then thou wert nothing, but hadst a remoter *antiquity*, as thou calledst it, to look back to with blind veneration; thou thyself being to thyself flat, jejune, *modern*! What mystery lurks in this retroversion? or what half Januses[8] are we, that cannot look forward with the same idolatry with which we for ever revert! The mighty future is as nothing, being every thing: the past is every thing, being nothing!

What were thy *dark ages?* Surely the sun rose as bright then as now, and man got him to his work in the morning. Why is it we can never hear mention of them without an accompanying feeling, as though a palpable obscure[9] had dimmed the face of things, and that our ancestors wandered to and fro groping!

Above all thy rarities, old Oxenford, what do most arride [amuse] and solace me are thy repositories of mouldering learning, thy shelves.

What a place to be in is an old library! It seems as though all the souls of all the writers, that have bequeathed their labours to these Bodleians, were reposing here, as in some dormitory, or middle state. I do not want to handle, to profane the leaves, their winding-sheets. I could as soon dislodge a shade. I seem to inhale learning, walking amid their foliage; and the odour of their old moth-scented coverings is fragrant as the first bloom of those sciential apples[1] which grew amid the happy orchard.

Still less have I curiosity to disturb the elder repose of MSS. Those *variae lectiones* [variant readings], so tempting to the more erudite palates, do but disturb and unsettle my faith. I am no Herculanean[2] raker. The credit of the three witnesses might have slept unimpeached for me. I leave these curiosities to Porson, and to G. D.———— whom, by the way, I found busy as a moth over some rotten archive,

2. Sizars and Servitors were scholarship students; Gentleman Commoners were wealthy students.
3. Minor church officials.
4. Two colleges at Oxford University.
5. Ritual of respect.
6. Beneficiary; originally, someone hired to say prayers for his patron.
7. The purchaser of provisions. Among Chaucer's Canterbury tale-tellers are a Cook and a Manciple.
8. Januses of one face—Sir Thomas Browne [Lamb's note]; Janus was the two-faced Roman god who looks

both backward and forward. Lamb's essays were influenced by Browne, enrolled at Oxford in the 17th century.
9. Satan's phrase for the expanse of chaos between Hell and Earth (*Paradise Lost* 2.406).
1. "Sciential" knowledge, from experience, is what Adam and Eve gain from eating the apple (*Paradise Lost* 9.680).
2. Referring to the archaeological excavations at Herculaneum, buried with Pompeii in the eruption of Vesuvius. One of Hercules's labors was to clean out the Augean stables.

rummaged out of some seldom explored press, in a nook at Oriel.[3] With long poring, he is grown almost into a book. He stood as passive as one by the side of the old shelves. I longed to new coat him in russia,[4] and assign him his place. He might have mustered for a tall Scapula.[5]

D. is assiduous in his visits to these seats of learning. No inconsiderable portion of his moderate fortune, I apprehend, is consumed in journeys between them and Clifford's Inn,[6] where, like a dove on the asp's nest, he has long taken up his unconscious abode, amid an incongruous assembly of attorneys, attorneys' clerks, apparitors, promoters, vermin of the law, among whom he sits "in calm and sinless peace."[7] The fangs of the law pierce him not; the winds of litigation blow over his humble chambers; the hard sheriff's officer moves his hat as he passes; legal nor illegal discourtesy touches him; none thinks of offering violence or injustice to him; you would as soon "strike an abstract idea."

D—— has been engaged, he tells me, through a course of laborious years, in an investigation into all curious matter connected with the two Universities; and has lately lit upon a MS. collection of charters relative to C———, by which he hopes to settle some disputed points, particularly that long controversy between them as to priority of foundation. The ardour with which he engages in these liberal pursuits, I am afraid, has not met with all the encouragement it deserved, either here or at C———. Your caputs[8] and heads of colleges care less than any body else about these questions.—Contented to suck the milky fountains of their Alma Maters, without inquiring into the venerable gentlewomen's years, they rather hold such curiosities to be impertinent—unreverend. They have their good glebe[9] lands *in manu* [in hand], and care not much to rake into the title-deeds. I gather at least so much from other sources, for D. is not a man to complain.

D. started like an unbroke heifer when I interrupted him. A *priori* it was not very probable that we should have met in Oriel. But D. would have done the same, had I accosted him on the sudden in his own walks in Clifford's Inn, or in the Temple. In addition to a provoking short-sightedness (the effect of late studies and watchings at the midnight oil) D. is the most absent of men. He made a call the other morning at our friend M.'s[1] in Bedford Square; and, finding nobody at home, was ushered into the hall, where, asking for pen and ink, with great exactitude of purpose he enters me his name in the book—which ordinarily lies about in such places, to record the failures of the untimely or unfortunate visitor—and takes his leave with many ceremonies and professions of regret. Some two or three hours after, his walking destinies returned him into the same neighbourhood again, and again the quiet image of the fire-side circle at M.'s—Mrs M. presiding at it like a Queen Lar,[2] with pretty A. S. at her side—striking irresistibly on his fancy, he makes another call, (forgetting that they were "certainly not to return from the country before that day week,") and disappointed a second time, inquires for pen and paper as before; again the book is brought, and in the line just above that in which he is about to print his second name (his re-script)—his first name (scarce dry) looks out upon him like

---

3. Another college; "G.D." was George Dyer, a schoolmate of Lamb who later attended Cambridge, where Richard Porson taught Greek. Porson had demonstrated the spuriousness of a passage in 1 John 5.7, taken as supporting Trinitarian doctrine.
4. Leather used in bookbinding.
5. Scapula's Graeco-Latin lexicon.
6. A residential college for members of the bar.

7. As Milton describes Christ facing Satan (*Paradise Regained*, 4.422).
8. Former ruling body of Cambridge University.
9. Revenue-producing.
1. Basil Montagu, a wealthy friend. Bedford Square is a fashionable London area. Like Clifford's Inn, the Temple was a residential college for members of the bar.
2. The queen of the Roman household gods.

another Sosia,[3] or as if a man should suddenly encounter his own duplicate!—The effect may be conceived. D. made many a good resolution against any such lapses in future. I hope he will not keep them too rigorously.

For with G. D., to be absent from the body is sometimes (not to speak it profanely) to be present with the Lord. At the very time when, personally encountering thee, he passes on with no recognition—or, being stopped, starts like a thing surprised,—at that moment, reader, he is on Mount Tabor,—or Parnassus—or co-sphered with Plato—or, with Harrington,[4] framing "immortal commonwealths"—devising some plan of amelioration to thy country, or thy species,—peradventure meditating some individual kindness or courtesy, to be done to *thee thyself*, the returning consciousness of which made him to start so guiltily at thy obtruded personal presence.

D. is delightful anywhere, but he is at the best in such places as these. He cares not much for Bath. He is out of his element at Buxton, at Scarborough, or Harrowgate.[5] The Cam and the Isis[6] are to him "better than all the waters of Damascus."[7] On the Muses' hill he is happy, and good, as one of the Shepherds on the Delectable Mountains; and when he goes about with you to show you the halls and colleges, you think you have with you the Interpreter at the House Beautiful.[8]

London Magazine, October 1820   1823

Dream Children
A Reverie

Children love to listen to stories about their elders, when *they* were children; to stretch their imagination to the conception of a traditionary great-uncle or grandame whom they never saw. It was in this spirit that my little ones crept about me the other evening to hear about their great-grandmother Field, who lived in a great house in Norfolk,[1] (a hundred times bigger than that in which they and papa lived,) which had been the scene (so at least it was generally believed in that part of the country) of the tragic incidents which they had lately become familiar with from the ballad of the Children in the Wood.[2] Certain it is that the whole story of the children and their uncle was to be seen fairly carved out in wood upon the chimney-piece of the great hall, the whole story down to the Robin Redbreasts; till a foolish rich person pulled it down to set up a marble one of modern invention in its stead, with no story upon it. Here Alice put out one of her dear mother's looks, too tender to be called upbraiding. Then I went on to say how religious and how good their great-grandmother Field was, how beloved and respected by every body, though she was not indeed the mistress of this great house, but had only the charge of it (and yet in some respects she might be said to be the mistress of it too) committed to her by the owner, who preferred living in a newer and more fashionable mansion which he had purchased somewhere in the adjoining county; but still she lived in it in a manner as if it had been her own, and kept up the dignity of the great house in a sort while she lived, which afterwards came to decay, and was nearly

---

3. In Dryden's *Amphitryon*, a servant whom the god Mercury impersonates.
4. Mount Tabor in Israel, the site of the Transfiguration of Jesus (Mark 9.2–8); Mount Parnassus in ancient Greece was sacred to Apollo and the muses. In *The Commonwealth of Oceana* (1656), James Harrington promoted the ideal of an English republic.
5. Various resorts.
6. The rivers that flow through Cambridge and Oxford.

7. Recalling 2 Kings 5.12. "Are not Abana and Pharpar, rivers of Damascus, better than all the waters of Israel?"
8. In Bunyan's *Pilgrim's Progress* (1678) Christian travels over the Delectable Mountains and visits the House Beautiful on his way to the Celestial City.
1. Where Lamb's grandmother was a housekeeper for over 50 years.
2. A play by Thomas Morton (1793).

pulled down, and all its old ornaments stripped and carried away to the owner's other house, where they were set up, and looked as awkward as if some one were to carry away the old tombs they had seen lately at the Abbey, and stick them up in Lady C.'s tawdry gilt drawing-room. Here John smiled, as much as to say, "that would be foolish indeed." And then I told how, when she came to die, her funeral was attended by a concourse of all the poor, and some of the gentry too, of the neighbourhood for many miles round, to show their respect for her memory, because she had been such a good and religious woman; so good indeed that she knew all the Psaltery by heart, ay, and a great part of the Testament besides. Here little Alice spread her hands. Then I told what a tall, upright, graceful person their great-grandmother Field once was; and how in her youth she was esteemed the best dancer, (here Alice's little right foot played an involuntary movement, till, upon my looking grave, it desisted,) the best dancer, I was saying, in the county, till a cruel disease, called a cancer, came, and bowed her down with pain; but it could never bend her good spirits, or make them stoop, but they were still upright, because she was so good and religious. Then I told how she was used to sleep by herself in a lone chamber of the great lone house; and how she believed that an apparition of two infants was to be seen at midnight gliding up and down the great staircase near where she slept, but she said "those innocents would do her no harm"; and how frightened I used to be, though in those days I had my maid to sleep with me, because I was never half so good or religious as she; and yet I never saw the infants. Here John expanded all his eyebrows and tried to look courageous. Then I told how good she was to all her grandchildren, having us to the great house in the holidays, where I in particular used to spend many hours by myself, in gazing upon the old busts of the twelve Cæsars, that had been Emperors of Rome, till the old marble heads would seem to live again, or I to be turned into marble with them; how I never could be tired with roaming about that huge mansion, with its vast empty rooms, with their worn-out hangings, fluttering tapestry, and carved oaken panels, with the gilding almost rubbed out; sometimes in the spacious old-fashioned gardens, which I had almost to myself, unless when now and then a solitary gardening man would cross me; and how the nectarines and peaches hung upon the walls, without my ever offering to pluck them, because they were forbidden fruit, unless now and then; and because I had more pleasure in strolling about among the old melancholy-looking yew-trees, or the firs, and picking up the red berries, and the fir-apples, which were good for nothing but to look at—or in lying about upon the fresh grass with all the fine garden smells around me—or basking in the orangery, till I could almost fancy myself ripening too along with the oranges and the limes in that grateful warmth—or in watching the dace that darted to and fro in the fish-pond at the bottom of the garden, with here and there a great sulky pike hanging midway down the water in silent state, as if it mocked at their impertinent friskings,—I had more pleasure in these busy-idle diversions than in all the sweet flavours of peaches, nectarines, oranges, and such-like common baits for children. Here John slyly deposited back upon the plate a bunch of grapes, which, not unobserved by Alice, he had meditated dividing with her, and both seemed willing to relinquish them for the present as irrelevant. Then, in somewhat a more heightened tone, I told how, though their great-grandmother Field loved all her grandchildren, yet in an especial manner she might be said to love their uncle, John L[3]——, because he was so handsome and spirited a youth, and a king to the rest of us; and, instead of moping about in solitary corners, like some of us, he would mount the most mettlesome horse he could get, when

---

3. Lamb's brother John had just died, in October 1821.

but an imp no bigger than themselves, and make it carry him half over the county in a morning, and join the hunters when there were any out; (and yet he loved the old great house and gardens too, but had too much spirit to be always pent up within their boundaries;) and how their uncle grew up to man's estate as brave as he was handsome, to the admiration of every body, but of their great-grandmother Field most especially; and how he used to carry me upon his back when I was a lame-footed boy, (for he was a good bit older than I,) many a mile when I could not walk for pain; and how in after life he became lame-footed too, and I did not always, I fear, make allowances enough for him when he was impatient, and in pain, nor remember sufficiently how considerate he had been to me when I was lame-footed; and how when he died, though he had not been dead an hour, it seemed as if he had died a great while ago, such a distance there is betwixt life and death; and how I bore his death as I thought pretty well at first, but afterwards it haunted and haunted me; and though I did not cry or take it to heart as some do, and as I think he would have done if I had died, yet I missed him all day long, and knew not till then how much I had loved him. I missed his kindness, and I missed his crossness, and wished him to be alive again, to be quarrelling with him, (for we quarrelled sometimes,) rather than not have him again, and was as uneasy without him as he, their poor uncle, must have been when the doctor took off his limb.—Here the children fell a crying, and asked if their little mourning which they had on was not for Uncle John, and they looked up, and prayed me not to go on about their uncle, but to tell them some stories about their pretty dead mother. Then I told how for seven long years, in hope sometimes, sometimes in despair, yet persisting ever, I courted the fair Alice W———n; and, as much as children could understand, I explained to them what coyness, and difficulty, and denial, meant in maidens—when suddenly, turning to Alice, the soul of the first Alice looked out at her eyes with such a reality of representment, that I became in doubt which of them stood there before me, or whose that bright hair was; and while I stood gazing, both the children gradually grew fainter to my view, receding, and still receding, till nothing at last but two mournful features were seen in the uttermost distance, which, without speech, strangely impressed upon me the effects of speech: "We are not of Alice, nor of thee, nor are we children at all. The children of Alice call Bartrum father. We are nothing; less than nothing, and dreams. We are only what might have been, and must wait upon the tedious shores of Lethe[4] millions of ages before we have existence and a name"————and immediately awaking, I found myself quietly seated in my bachelor arm-chair, where I had fallen asleep, with the faithful Bridget[5] unchanged by my side; but John L. (or James Elia) was gone for ever.

January 1822

Old China

I have an almost feminine partiality for old china. When I go to see any great house I inquire for the china closet, and next for the picture gallery. I cannot defend the order of preference but by saying that we have all some taste or other, of too ancient a date to admit of our remembering distinctly that it was an acquired one. I can call to mind the first play and the first exhibition that I was taken to; but I am not conscious of a time when china jars and saucers were introduced into my imagination.

4. In ancient mythology, the river of oblivion, from which the dead must drink.

5. Pseudonym for Mary.

I had no repugnance then (why should I now have?) to those little, lawless, azure-tinctured grotesques, that under the notion of men and women float about, uncircumscribed by any element, in that world before perspective—a china tea-cup.

I like to see my old friends—whom distance cannot diminish—figuring up in the air (so they appear to our optics), yet on *terra firma* [solid earth] still, for so we must in courtesy interpret that speck of deeper blue which the decorous artist, to prevent absurdity, had made to spring up beneath their sandals.

I love the men with women's faces, and the women, if possible, with still more womanish expressions.

Here is a young and courtly Mandarin, handing tea to a lady from a salver, two miles off. See how distance seems to set off respect! And here the same lady, or another, (for likeness is identity on tea-cups,) is stepping into a little fairy boat, moored on the hither side of this calm garden river, with a dainty mincing foot, which in a right angle of incidence (as angles go in our world) must infallibly land her in the midst of a flowery mead a furlong off on the other side of the same strange stream!

Farther on—if far or near can be predicated of their world—see horses, trees, pagodas, dancing the hays.

Here a cow and rabbit couchant[1] and co-extensive; so objects show, seen through the lucid atmosphere of fine Cathay.[2]

I was pointing out to my cousin last evening, over our Hyson [tea], (which we are old-fashioned enough to drink unmixed still of an afternoon,) some of these *speciosa miracula* [beautiful miracles] upon a set of extraordinary old blue china (a recent purchase) which we were now for the first time using; and could not help remarking how favourable circumstances had been to us of late years, that we could afford to please the eye sometimes with trifles of this sort, when a passing sentiment seemed to overshade the brows of my companion. I am quick at detecting these Summer clouds in Bridget.

"I wish the good old times would come again," she said, "when we were not quite so rich. I do not mean that I want to be poor; but there was a middle state" (so she was pleased to ramble on,) "in which I am sure we were a great deal happier. A purchase is but a purchase, now that you have money enough and to spare. Formerly it used to be a triumph. When we coveted a cheap luxury (and Oh, how much ado I had to get you to consent in those times!)—we were used to have a debate two or three days before, and to weight the *for* and *against*, and think what we might spare it out of, and what saving we could hit upon, that should be an equivalent. A thing was worth buying then, when we felt the money that we paid for it.

Do you remember the brown suit, which you made to hang upon you till all your friends cried shame upon you, it grew so thread-bare, and all because of that folio Beaumont and Fletcher,[3] which you dragged home late at night from Barker's, in Covent Garden? Do you remember how we eyed it for weeks before we could make up our minds to the purchase, and had not come to a determination till it was near ten o'clock of the Saturday night, when you set off from Islington,[4] fearing you should be too late,—and when the old bookseller with some grumbling opened his shop, and by the twinkling taper (for he was setting bedwards) lighted out the relic from his dusty treasures,—and when you lugged it home, wishing it were twice as cumbersome,—and when you presented it to me,—and when we were exploring the perfectness of it

1. Reclining as if in heraldic display.
2. Old European name for China.

3. A rare and early edition of the works of Elizabethan dramatists Sir Francis Beaumont and John Fletcher.
4. North London district where the Lambs lived.

(*collating* you called it),—and while I was repairing some of the loose leaves with paste, which your impatience would not suffer to be left till day-break,—was there no pleasure in being a poor man? Or can those neat black clothes which you wear now, and are so careful to keep brushed, since we have become rich and finical, give you half the honest vanity with which you flaunted it about in that overworn suit—your old corbeau—for four or five weeks longer than you should have done, to pacify your conscience for the mighty sum of fifteen shillings—or sixteen was it?—a great affair we thought it then—which you had lavished on the old folio. Now you can afford to buy any book that pleases you, but I do not see that you ever bring me home any nice old purchases now.

When you came home with twenty apologies for laying out a less number of shillings upon that print after Lionardo, which we christened the 'Lady Blanch';[5] when you looked at the purchase, and thought of the money—and looked again at the picture, and thought of the money—was there no pleasure in being a poor man? Now you have nothing to do but to walk into Colnaghi's,[6] and buy a wilderness of Lionardos. Yet do you?

Then do you remember our pleasant walks to Enfield, and Potter's Bar, and Waltham,[7] when we had a holyday, (holydays and all other fun are gone now we are rich,) and the little hand-basket in which I used to deposit our day's fare of savoury cold lamb and salad—and how you would pry about at noon-tide for some decent house, where we might go in and produce our store, only paying for the ale that you must call for, and speculate upon the looks of the landlady, and whether she was likely to allow us a table-cloth,—and wish for such another honest hostess as Izaak Walton has described many a one on the pleasant banks of the Lea, when he went a fishing; and sometimes they would prove obliging enough, and sometimes they would look grudgingly upon us; but we had cheerful looks still for one another, and would eat our plain food savourily, scarcely grudging Piscator his Trout Hall.[8] Now, when we go out a day's pleasuring, which is seldom moreover, we *ride* part of the way, and go into a fine inn, and order the best of dinners, never debating the expense, which, after all, never has half the relish of those chance country snaps, when we were at the mercy of uncertain usage and a precarious welcome.

You are too proud to see a play anywhere now but in the pit. Do you remember where it was we used to sit, when we saw the *Battle of Hexham*, and the *Surrender of Calais*, and Bannister and Mrs Bland in the *Children in the Wood*,[9]—when we squeezed out our shillings a-piece to sit three or four times in a season in the one-shilling gallery, where you felt all the time that you ought not to have brought me, and more strongly I felt obligation to you for having brought me,—and the pleasure was the better for a little shame,—and when the curtain drew up, what cared we for our place in the house, or what mattered it where we were sitting, when our thoughts were with Rosalind in Arden, or with Viola at the Court of Illyria?[1] You used to say that the gallery was the best place of all for enjoying a play socially; that the relish of such exhibitions must be in proportion to the infrequency of going; that the company we met there, not being in general readers of plays, were obliged to attend the more, and did attend, to what was going on on the stage, because a word lost would have been a chasm, which it was impossible for them to fill up. With such reflections we consoled

---

5. Mary Lamb wrote a poem on this picture ("Modesty and Vanity") by Leonardo da Vinci (1452–1519).
6. A famous print shop.
7. Various northern suburbs.
8. Piscator (Latin for "fisherman") is a character in Izaak Walton's *Complete Angler* (1653). Trout Hall is his favorite pub.

9. Comedies by George Colman (1762–1836). John Bannister was a popular comic actor; Maria Teresa Bland, a singer, performed regularly from 1789 to 1824.
1. Rosalind is the heroine of Shakespeare's *As You Like It*, and Viola is the heroine of his *Twelfth Night*.

our pride then; and I appeal to you whether, as a woman, I met generally with less attention and accommodation than I have done since in more expensive situations in the house? Getting in indeed, and crowding up those inconvenient staircases, was bad enough; but there was still a law of civility to woman recognised to quite as great an extent as we ever found in the other passages; and how a little difficulty overcome heightened the snug seat and the play, afterwards! Now we can only pay our money and walk in. You cannot see, you say, in the galleries now. I am sure we saw, and heard too, well enough then; but sight and all, I think, is gone with our poverty.

There was pleasure in eating strawberries before they became quite common; in the first dish of pease while they were yet dear;[2] to have them for a nice supper, a treat. What treat can we have now? If we were to treat ourselves now—that is, to have dainties a little above our means, it would be selfish and wicked. It is the very little more that we allow ourselves beyond what the actual poor can get at, that makes what I call a treat—when two people living together, as we have done, now and then indulge themselves in a cheap luxury, which both like; while each apologizes, and is willing to take both halves of the blame to his single share. I see no harm in people making much of themselves, in that sense of the word. It may give them a hint how to make much of others. But now, what I mean by the word—we never do make much of ourselves. None but the poor can do it. I do not mean the veriest poor of all, but persons as we were, just above poverty.

I know what you were going to say, that it is mighty pleasant at the end of the year to make all meet; and much ado we used to have every Thirty-first Night of December to account for our exceedings; many a long face did you make over your puzzled accounts, and in contriving to make it out how we had spent so much, or that we had not spent so much, or that it was impossible we should spend so much next year; and still we found our slender capital decreasing; but then,—betwixt ways, and projects, and compromises of one sort or another, and talk of curtailing this charge, and doing without that for the future, and the hope that youth brings, and laughing spirits, (in which you were never poor till now,) we pocketed up our loss, and in conclusion, with 'lusty brimmers,' (as you used to quote it out of *hearty cheerful Mr Cotton*,[3] as you called him,) we used to welcome in 'the coming guest.' Now we have no reckoning at all at the end of the Old Year,—no flattering promises about the New Year doing better for us."

Bridget is so sparing of her speech on most occasions, that when she gets into a rhetorical vein I am careful how I interrupt it. I could not help, however, smiling at the phantom of wealth which her dear imagination had conjured up out of a clear income of poor——hundred pounds a year. "It is true we were happier when we were poorer, but we were also younger, my cousin. I am afraid we must put up with the excess, for if we were to shake the superflux into the sea we should not much mend ourselves.[4] That we had much to struggle with, as we grew up together, we have reason to be most thankful. It strengthened and knit our compact closer. We could never have been what we have been to each other if we had always had the sufficiency which you now complain of. The resisting power—those natural dilations of the youthful spirit which circumstances cannot straiten—with us are long since passed away. Competence to age is supplementary youth; a sorry supplement indeed, but I fear the best that is to be had. We must ride where we formerly walked: live better and lie softer—and shall be wise to do so—than we had means to do in those good old days you speak of. Yet could those

---

2. Expensive.
3. A lusty brimmer is a glass filled to the brim; quoting *The New Year* by Charles Cotton (1630–1687).

4. "Expose thyself to feel what wretches feel, / That thou mayst shake the superflux to them." *King Lear*, 3.4.34–35.

days return; could you and I once more walk our thirty miles a day; could Bannister and Mrs Bland again be young, and you and I be young to see them; could the good old one-shilling gallery days return, (they are dreams, my cousin, now,) but could you and I at this moment, instead of this quiet argument, by our well-carpeted fireside, sitting on this luxurious sofa, be once more struggling up those inconvenient staircases, pushed about, and squeezed, and elbowed by the poorest rabble of poor gallery scramblers; could I once more hear those anxious shrieks of yours, and the delicious *Thank God, we are safe*, which always followed when the topmost stair, conquered, let in the first light of the whole cheerful theatre down beneath us, I know not the fathom-line that ever touched a descent so deep as I would be willing to bury more wealth in than Croesus had, or the great Jew R——— is supposed to have,[5] to purchase it. And now do just look at that merry little Chinese waiter holding an umbrella, big enough for a bed-tester,[6] over the head of that pretty insipid half Madonna-ish chit of a lady in that very blue summer-house."

1823

⊷ ⊷⬥⊷ ⊶

William Hazlitt
1778–1830

"Well, I've had a happy life," were William Hazlitt's famous last words—words that could seem surprising at the end of a life marked by short and unhappy marriages and by Hazlitt's vocal and even truculent criticisms of friends and enemies alike. "Brow-hanging, shoe-contemplative, *strange*," as Coleridge once described him, Hazlitt made his mark as a dynamic public lecturer and penetrating writer on the subject of English literature (see page 706), famous for his impatience with Wordsworth and his defense of Keats against the Tory political bias of negative reviews. Lamb and Coleridge were among his closest friends. His father was a Unitarian minister and political radical—a supporter of the American Revolution and the principles of the French Revolution. Hazlitt upheld these principles right through the decades of Tory reaction; his antipathy to political tyranny was so vehement that he defended Napoleon to the end of his life as "the crusher of kings who crushed the people"—commitments that made him a target for the Tory journals, especially the *Quarterly* and *Blackwood's*.

As a student at a Unitarian college in London, Hazlitt was drawn both to painting and philosophy but turned to political journalism to make a living. He began writing essays for the periodicals, on subjects ranging across literature, painting and sculpture, boxing and other sports, politics, economics, travel, and the personalities of the day. He was dauntingly prolific, his collected works occupying twenty-one volumes. His *Characters of Shakespear's Plays* (1817), his essay *On Gusto*, and his series of lectures in London in 1818 on English poets from Chaucer to the present impressed many, including Keats, who thought Hazlitt's "depth of taste" one of the "things to rejoice at in this Age." With an antipathy to Wordsworth's egotism sharpening his points, Hazlitt praised Shakespeare for being "the least of an egotist that it was possible to be," a poet whose dramatic imagination emanated instead from a genius of sympathy for his subject: "when he conceived of a character," Shakespeare "entered into all its thoughts and feelings." Within months, Keats was describing his ideal of the poet as a "camelion" who abjures "the wordsworthian or egotistical sublime" and instead "lives in gusto . . . continually

---

5. Croesus (d. 547 B.C.E.) was the last king of Lydia, legendary for his wealth. Nathan Mayer Rothschild (1777–1836) was the founder of the Anglo-French banking dynasty. 6. Canopy.

in for and filling some other Body." Such imaginative sympathy vividly animates the characters of Hazlitt's father, Lamb, Wordsworth, and especially Coleridge in *My First Acquaintance with Poets*, among the most memorable, most radiant depictions of personality in English letters. The recollection is also tinged with elegy in its portraits of Wordsworth and Coleridge, for Hazlitt regretted their falling away from their political idealism in the 1790s, the historical moment of this first acquaintance. Like so much of his writing, Hazlitt's wealth of familiar essays, such as *On Going on a Journey*, are frankly autobiographical, infused with opinions and enthusiasms, brisk conversational spontaneity, sly wit, and sparkling intelligence.

On Gusto[1]

Gusto in art is power or passion defining any object. It is not so difficult to explain this term in what relates to expression (of which it may be said to be the highest degree) as in what relates to things without expression, to the natural appearances of objects, as mere colour or form. In one sense, however, there is hardly any object entirely devoid of expression, without some character of power belonging to it, some precise association with pleasure or pain: and it is in giving this truth of character from the truth of feeling, whether in the highest or the lowest degree, but always in the highest degree of which the subject is capable, that gusto consists.

There is a gusto in the colouring of Titian.[2] Not only do his heads seem to think—his bodies seem to feel. This is what the Italians mean by the *morbidezza* [softness] of his flesh-colour. It seems sensitive and alive all over; not merely to have the look and texture of flesh, but the feeling in itself. For example, the limbs of his female figures have a luxurious softness and delicacy, which appears conscious of the pleasure of the beholder. As the objects themselves in nature would produce an impression on the sense, distinct from every other object, and having something divine in it, which the heart owns and the imagination consecrates, the objects in the picture preserve the same impression, absolute, unimpaired, stamped with all the truth of passion, the pride of the eye, and the charm of beauty. Rubens makes his flesh-colour like flowers; Albano's is like ivory; Titian's is like flesh, and like nothing else. It is as different from that of other painters, as the skin is from a piece of white or red drapery thrown over it. The blood circulates here and there, the blue veins just appear, the rest is distinguished throughout only by that sort of tingling sensation to the eye, which the body feels within itself. This is gusto. Vandyke's flesh-colour, though it has great truth and purity, wants gusto. It has not the internal character, the living principle in it. It is a smooth surface, not a warm, moving mass. It is painted without passion, with indifference. The hand only has been concerned. The impression slides off from the eye, and does not, like the tones of Titian's pencil [paintbrush], leave a sting behind it in the mind of the spectator! The eye does not acquire a taste or appetite for what it sees. In a word, gusto in painting is where the impression made on one sense excites by affinity those of another.

Michael Angelo's forms are full of gusto. They everywhere obtrude the sense of power upon the eye. His limbs convey an idea of muscular strength, of moral grandeur, and even of intellectual dignity: they are firm, commanding, broad, and massy, capable of executing with ease the determined purposes of the will. His faces have no other expression than his figures, conscious power and capacity. They appear only to think what they shall do, and to know that they can do it. This is what is

---

1. Published in Leigh Hunt's radical weekly *The Examiner*, May 1816, signed W. H. "Gusto," Italian for "taste," means both physical appetite and refined sensibility. See

Keats's use of the term, page 1053.
2. Italian painter (1477–1576). Hazlitt goes on to discuss a series of early modern European painters.

meant by saying that his style is hard and masculine. It is the reverse of Correggio's, which is effeminate. That is, the gusto of Michael Angelo consists in expressing energy of will without proportionable sensibility, Correggio's in expressing exquisite sensibility without energy of will. In Correggio's faces as well as figures we see neither bones nor muscles, but then what a soul is there, full of sweetness and of grace—pure, playful, soft, angelical! There is sentiment enough in a hand painted by Correggio to set up a school of history painters. Whenever we look at the hands of Correggio's women or of Raphael's, we always wish to touch them.

Again, Titian's landscapes have a prodigious gusto, both in the colouring and forms. We shall never forget one that we saw many years ago in the Orleans Gallery of Acteon hunting.[3] It had a brown, mellow, autumnal look. The sky was of the colour of stone. The winds seemed to sing through the rustling branches of the trees, and already you might hear the twanging of bows resound through the tangled mazes of the wood. Mr West,[4] we understand, has this landscape. He will know if this description of it is just. The landscape back-ground of the St Peter Martyr is another well known instance of the power of this great painter to give a romantic interest and an appropriate character to the objects of his pencil, where every circumstance adds to the effect of the scene—the bold trunks of the tall forest trees, the trailing ground plants, with that tall convent spire rising in the distance, amidst the blue sapphire mountains and the golden sky.

Rubens has a great deal of gusto in his Fauns and Satyrs, and in all that expresses motion, but in nothing else. Rembrandt has it in everything; everything in his pictures has a tangible character. If he puts a diamond in the ear of a burgomaster's wife, it is of the first water; and his furs and stuffs are proof against a Russian winter. Raphael's gusto was only in expression; he had no idea of the character of anything but the human form. The dryness and poverty of his style in other respects is a phenomenon in the art. His trees are like sprigs of grass stuck in a book of botanical specimens. Was it that Raphael never had time to go beyond the walls of Rome? That he was always in the streets, at church, or in the bath? He was not one of the Society of Arcadians.[5]

Claude's[6] landscapes, perfect as they are, want gusto. This is not easy to explain. They are perfect abstractions of the visible images of things; they speak the visible language of nature truly. They resemble a mirror or a microscope. To the eye only they are more perfect than any other landscapes that ever were or will be painted; they give more of nature, as cognisable by one sense alone; but they lay an equal stress on all visible impressions. They do not interpret one sense by another; they do not distinguish the character of different objects as we are taught, and can only be taught, to distinguish them by their effect on the different senses. That is, his eye wanted imagination: it did not strongly sympathise with his other faculties. He saw the atmosphere, but he did not feel it. He painted the trunk of a tree or a rock in the foreground as smooth—with as complete an abstraction of the gross, tangible impression, as any other part of the picture. His trees are perfectly beautiful, but quite

---

3. Exhibited in London in 1798.
4. Benjamin West, president of the Royal Academy of Art. Keats criticized his work for its lack of gusto (see page 1047).
5. Lovers of nature. "Raphael could not paint a landscape; he could not paint people in a landscape....His figures have always an *in-door* look, that is, a set, determined,

voluntary, dramatic character, arising from their own passions, or a watchfulness of those of others, and want that wild uncertainty of expression, which is connected with the accidents of nature and the changes of the elements. He has nothing *romantic* about him" [Hazlitt's note].
6. Claude Lorrain (1600–1682), French landscape painter.

immovable; they have a look of enchantment. In short, his landscapes are unequalled imitations of nature, released from its subjection to the elements, as if all objects were become a delightful fairy vision, and the eye had rarefied and refined away the other senses.

The gusto in the Greek statues is of a very singular kind. The sense of perfect form nearly occupies the whole mind, and hardly suffers it to dwell on any other feeling. It seems enough for them *to be*, without acting or suffering. Their forms are ideal, spiritual. Their beauty is power. By their beauty they are raised above the frailties of pain or passion; by their beauty they are deified.

The infinite quantity of dramatic invention in Shakspeare takes from his gusto. The power he delights to show is not intense, but discursive. He never insists on anything as much as he might, except a quibble. Milton has great gusto. He repeats his blows twice; grapples with and exhausts his subject. His imagination has a double relish of its objects, an inveterate attachment to the things he describes, and to the words describing them.

> ———Or where Chineses drive
> With sails and wind their *cany* waggons *light*.
> . . . .
> Wild above rule or art, *enormous* bliss.[7]

There is a gusto in Pope's compliments, in Dryden's satires, and Prior's tales; and among prose writers Boccacio and Rabelais had the most of it.[8] We will only mention one other work which appears to us to be full of gusto, and that is the *Beggar's Opera*.[9] If it is not, we are altogether mistaken in our notions on this delicate subject.

My First Acquaintance with Poets[1]

My father was a Dissenting Minister at W—m in Shropshire; and in the year 1798 (the figures that compose that date are to me like the "dreaded name of Demogorgon"[2]) Mr Coleridge came to Shrewsbury, to succeed Mr Rowe in the spiritual charge of a Unitarian Congregation there. He did not come till late on the Saturday afternoon before he was to preach; and Mr Rowe, who himself went down to the coach in a state of anxiety and expectation, to look for the arrival of his successor, could find no one at all answering the description but a round-faced man in a short black coat (like a shooting jacket) which hardly seemed to have been made for him, but who seemed to be talking at a great rate to his fellow-passengers. Mr Rowe had scarce returned to give an account of his disappointment, when the round-faced man in black entered, and dissipated all doubts on the subject, by beginning to talk. He did not cease while he staid; nor has he since, that I know of. He held the good town of Shrewsbury in delightful suspense for three weeks that he remained there, "fluttering the *proud Salopians* like an eagle in a dove-cote";[3] and the Welch mountains that skirt the horizon with their tempestuous confusion, agree to have heard no such mystic sounds since the days of

---

7. *Paradise Lost*, 3.438–39, 5.297.
8. Authors known for wit, satiric, bawdy, or both.
9. A popular comic opera (1728) by John Gay, dealing with criminals and prison.
1. First published in Byron and Leigh Hunt's short-lived journal *The Liberal*, 1823, 25 years after Hazlitt's first

acquaintance with Coleridge and Wordsworth.
2. Spirit of primeval chaos in *Paradise Lost*, 2.964–965.
3. Shakespeare's Coriolanus taunts his assassins: "like an eagle in a dovecote, I / Fluttered your Volscians" (*Coriolanus* 5.6.118–19). Salopians are residents of Shropshire.

High-born Hoel's harp or soft Llewellyn's lay![4]

As we passed along between W——m and Shrewsbury, and I eyed their blue tops seen through the wintry branches, or the red rustling leaves of the sturdy oak-trees by the road-side, a sound was in my ears as of a Siren's song; I was stunned, startled with it, as from deep sleep; but I had no notion then that I should ever be able to express my admiration to others in motley imagery or quaint allusion, till the light of his genius shone into my soul, like the sun's rays glittering in the puddles of the road. I was at that time dumb, inarticulate, helpless, like a worm by the way-side, crushed, bleeding, lifeless; but now, bursting from the deadly bands that "bound them,

With Styx nine times round them,"[5]

my ideas float on winged words, and as they expand their plumes, catch the golden light of other years. My soul has indeed remained in its original bondage, dark, obscure, with longings infinite and unsatisfied; my heart, shut up in the prison-house of this rude clay, has never found, nor will it ever find, a heart to speak to; but that my understanding also did not remain dumb and brutish, or at length found a language to express itself, I owe to Coleridge. But this is not to my purpose.

My father lived ten miles from Shrewsbury, and was in the habit of exchanging visits with Mr Rowe, and with Mr Jenkins of Whit-church (nine miles farther on) according to the custom of Dissenting Ministers in each other's neighbourhood. A line of communication is thus established, by which the flame of civil and religious liberty is kept alive, and nourishes its smouldering fire unquenchable, like the fires in the Agamemnon of Æschylus, placed at different stations, that waited for ten long years to announce with their blazing pyramids the destruction of Troy. Coleridge had agreed to come over to see my father, according to the courtesy of the country, as Mr Rowe's probable successor; but in the meantime I had gone to hear him preach the Sunday after his arrival. A poet and a philosopher getting up into a Unitarian pulpit to preach the Gospel, was a romance in these degenerate days, a sort of revival of the primitive spirit of Christianity, which was not to be resisted.

It was in January, 1798, that I rose one morning before daylight, to walk ten miles in the mud, and went to hear this celebrated person preach. Never, the longest day I have to live, shall I have such another walk as this cold, raw, comfortless one, in the winter of the year 1798. *Il y a des impressions que ni le tems ni les circonstances peuvent effacer. Dusse-je vivre des siècles entiers, le doux tems de ma jeunesse ne peut renaître pour moi, ni s'effacer jamais dans ma mémoire.*[6] When I got there, the organ was playing the 100th psalm, and, when it was done, Mr Coleridge rose and gave out his text, "And he went up into the mountain to pray, HIMSELF, ALONE."[7] As he gave out his text, his voice "rose like a steam of rich distilled perfumes,"[8] and when he came to the two last words, which he pronounced loud, deep, and distinct, it seemed to me, who was then young, as if the sounds had echoed from the bottom of the

---

4. The Bard's evocation of the inspired singers of the past; Thomas Gray, *The Bard*, line 28.

5. Alexander Pope, *Ode for Music on St. Cecilia's Day* (1708); Orpheus pleads for the release of his beloved Eurydice from Hell: "Though fate had fast bound her, / With Styx nine times round her, / Yet music and love were victorious" (90–92).

6. Adapted from J-J. Rousseau, *La Nouvelle Heloise* (1761), part 6, letter 7. "There are impressions that neither

time nor circumstances can efface. Were I to live entire centuries, the sweet time of my youth could not be reborn for me, or ever be effaced from my memory."

7. Jesus does thus, fearing that some would make him king in consequence of his miracles (John 6.15). The 100th Psalm begins, "Make a joyful noise unto the Lord, all ye lands."

8. A sound in the Sorcerer's woods in Milton's *Comus*, line 556.

human heart, and as if that prayer might have floated in solemn silence through the universe. The idea of St John came into mind, "of one crying in the wilderness, who had his loins girt about, and whose food was locusts and wild honey."[9] The preacher then launched into his subject, like an eagle dallying with the wind. The sermon was upon peace and war; upon church and state—not their alliance, but their separation— on the spirit of the world and the spirit of Christianity, not as the same, but as opposed to one another. He talked to those who had "inscribed the cross of Christ on banners dripping with human gore." He made a poetical and pastoral excursion—and to shew the fatal effects of war, drew a striking contrast between the simple shepherd boy, driving his team afield, or sitting under the hawthorn, piping to his flock, "as though he should never be old,"[1] and the same poor country-lad, crimped,[2] kidnapped, brought into town, made drunk at an alehouse, turned into a wretched drummer-boy, with his hair sticking on end with powder and pomatum, a long cue at his back, and tricked out in the loathsome finery of the profession of blood.

> Such were the notes our once-lov'd poet sung.[3]

And for myself, I could not have been more delighted if I had heard the music of the spheres. Poetry and Philosophy had met together. Truth and Genius had embraced, under the eye and with the sanction of Religion. This was even beyond my hopes. I returned home well satisfied. The sun that was still labouring pale and wan through the sky, obscured by thick mists, seemed an emblem of the *good cause*; and the cold dank drops of dew that hung half melted on the beard of the thistle, had something genial and refreshing in them; for there was a spirit of hope and youth in all nature, that turned every thing into good. The face of nature had not then the brand of JUS DIVINUM[4] on it:

> Like to that sanguine flower inscrib'd with woe.[5]

On the Tuesday following, the half-inspired speaker came. I was called down into the room where he was, and went half-hoping, half-afraid. He received me very graciously, and I listened for a long time without uttering a word. I did not suffer in his opinion by my silence. "For those two hours," he afterwards was pleased to say, "he was conversing with W. H.'s forehead!" His appearance was different from what I had anticipated from seeing him before. At a distance, and in the dim light of the chapel, there was to me a strange wildness in his aspect, a dusky obscurity, and I thought him pitted with the small-pox. His complexion was at that time clear, and even bright—

> As are the children of yon azure sheen.[6]

His forehead was broad and high, light as if built of ivory, with large projecting eyebrows, and his eyes rolling beneath them like a sea with darkened lustre. "A certain tender bloom his face o'erspread,"[7] a purple tinge as we see it in the pale thoughtful complexions of the Spanish portrait-painters, Murillo and Velasquez. His mouth was gross,

---

9. Matthew 3.3–4. The prophet of Christ.
1. Sir Philip Sidney (1554–1586), *Arcadia*, 1.2. Pastoral Arcadia stands in contrast to neighboring Laconia, devastated by war.
2. Forced into military service. Pomatum: scented hair oil; cue: pigtail.
3. Pope, *Epistle to Robert, Earl of Oxford*, line 1.

4. Divine Law.
5. Milton, *Lycidas*, line 106; the hyacinth has marks resembling the Greek word for "woe"; sanguine: bloody.
6. James Thomson, *The Castle of Indolence* (1748), 2.33.295.
7. *Castle of Indolence*, 1.57.507. Hazlitt changes "gloom" to "bloom."

voluptuous, open, eloquent; his chin good-humoured and round; but his nose, the rudder of the face, the index of the will, was small, feeble, nothing—like what he has done. It might seem that the genius of his face as from a height surveyed and projected him (with sufficient capacity and huge aspiration) into the world unknown of thought and imagination, with nothing to support or guide his veering purpose, as if Columbus had launched his adventurous course for the New World in a scallop,[8] without oars or compass. So at least I comment on it after the event. Coleridge in his person was rather above the common size, inclining to the corpulent, or like Lord Hamlet, "somewhat fat and pursy."[9] His hair (now, alas! grey) was then black and glossy as the raven's, and fell in smooth masses over his forehead. This long pendulous hair is peculiar to enthusiasts, to those whose minds tend heavenward; and is traditionally inseparable (though of a different colour) from the pictures of Christ. It ought to belong, as a character, to all who preach *Christ crucified*, and Coleridge was at that time one of those!

It was curious to observe the contrast between him and my father, who was a veteran in the cause, and then declining into the vale of years. He had been a poor Irish lad, carefully brought up by his parents, and sent to the University of Glasgow (where he studied under Adam Smith)[1] to prepare him for his future destination. It was his mother's proudest wish to see her son a Dissenting Minister. So if we look back to past generations (as far as eye can reach) we see the same hopes, fears, wishes, followed by the same disappointments, throbbing in the human heart; and so we may see them (if we look forward) rising up for ever, and disappearing, like vapourish bubbles, in the human breast! After being tossed about from congregation to congregation in the heats of the Unitarian controversy, and squabbles about the American war,[2] he had been relegated to an obscure village, where he was to spend the last thirty years of his life, far from the only converse that he loved, the talk about disputed texts of Scripture and the cause of civil and religious liberty. Here he passed his days, repining but resigned, in the study of the Bible, and the perusal of the Commentators,—huge folios, not easily got through, one of which would outlast a winter! Why did he pore on these from morn to night (with the exception of a walk in the fields or a turn in the garden to gather broccoli-plants or kidney-beans of his own rearing, with no small degree of pride and pleasure)?—Here were "no figures nor no fantasies"[3]—neither poetry nor philosophy—nothing to dazzle, nothing to excite modern curiosity; but to his lack-lustre eyes there appeared, within the pages of the ponderous, unwieldy, neglected tomes, the sacred name of JEHOVAH in Hebrew capitals: pressed down by the weight of the style, worn to the last fading thinness of the understanding, there were glimpses, glimmering notions of the patriarchal wanderings, with palm-trees hovering in the horizon, and processions of camels at the distance of three thousand years; there was Moses with the Burning Bush, the number of the Twelve Tribes, types, shadows, glosses on the law and the prophets; there were discussions (dull enough) on the age of Methuselah, a mighty speculation! there were outlines, rude guesses at the shape of Noah's Ark and of the riches of Solomon's Temple; questions as to the date of the creation, predictions of the end of all things; the great lapses of time, the strange mutations of the globe were unfolded with the voluminous leaf, as it turned over; and though the soul might slumber with

---

8. A small boat, or the shell itself.
9. Hazlitt transfers "the fatness of these pursy [bloated] times" to Hamlet himself (*Hamlet*, 3.4.154).
1. Author of *The Theory of Moral Sentiments*, his first published work (1759).

2. The Revolutionary War.
3. Shakespeare, *Julius Caesar*, 2.1.231; tormented conspirator Brutus admires the untroubled mind of his servant boy.

an hieroglyphic veil of inscrutable mysteries drawn over it, yet it was in a slumber ill-exchanged for all the sharpened realities of sense, wit, fancy, or reason. My father's life was comparatively a dream; but it was a dream of infinity and eternity, of death, the resurrection, and a judgment to come!

No two individuals were ever more unlike than were the host and his guest. A poet was to my father a sort of nondescript: yet whatever added grace to the Unitarian cause was to him welcome. He could hardly have been more surprised or pleased, if our visitor had worn wings. Indeed, his thoughts had wings; and as the silken sounds rustled round our little wainscoted parlour, my father threw back his spectacles over his forehead, his white hairs mixing with its sanguine hue; and a smile of delight beamed across his rugged cordial face, to think that Truth had found a new ally in Fancy![4] Besides, Coleridge seemed to take considerable notice of me, and that of itself was enough. He talked very familiarly, but agreeably, and glanced over a variety of subjects. At dinner-time he grew more animated, and dilated in a very edifying manner on Mary Wol[l]stonecraft and Mackintosh.[5] The last, he said, he considered (on my father's speaking of his *Vindiciae Gallicae* as a capital performance) as a clever scholastic man—a master of the topics,—or as the ready warehouseman of letters, who knew exactly where to lay his hand on what he wanted, though the goods were not his own. He thought him no match for Burke, either in style or matter. Burke was a meta-physician, Mackintosh a mere logician. Burke was an orator (almost a poet) who reasoned in figures, because he had an eye for nature: Mackintosh, on the other hand, was a rhetorician, who had only an eye to common-places. On this I ventured to say that I had always entertained a great opinion of Burke, and that (as far as I could find) the speaking of him with contempt might be made the test of a vulgar democratical mind. This was the first observation I ever made to Coleridge, and he said it was a very just and striking one. I remember the leg of Welsh mutton and the turnips on the table that day had the finest flavour imaginable. Coleridge added that Mackintosh and Tom Wedgwood[6] (of whom, however, he spoke highly) had expressed a very indifferent opinion of his friend Mr Wordsworth, on which he remarked to them—"He strides on so far before you, that he dwindles in the distance!" Godwin[7] had once boasted to him of having carried on an argument with Mackintosh for three hours with dubious success; Coleridge told him—"If there had been a man of genius in the room, he would have settled the question in five minutes." He asked me if I had ever seen Mary Wolstonecraft, and I said, I had once for a few moments, and that she seemed to me to turn off Godwin's objections to something she advanced with quite a playful, easy air. He replied, that "this was only one instance of the ascendancy which people of imagination exercised over those of mere intellect." He did not rate Godwin very high (this was caprice or prejudice, real or affected)[8] but he had a great idea of Mrs Wolstonecraft's powers of conversation,

---

4. My father was one of those who mistook his talent after all. He used to be very much dissatisfied that I preferred his Letters to his Sermons. The last were forced and dry; the first came naturally from him. For ease, half-plays on words, and a supine, monkish, indolent pleasantry, I have never seen them equalled [Hazlitt's note].

5. Sir James Mackintosh's *Vindiciae Gallicae* (1791) supported the French Revolution as did Wollstonecraft's *Vindication of the Rights of Man* (1790), against Edmund Burke's critical *Reflections*.

6. Son of Josiah Wedgwood, founder of the famous

potteries, who endowed Coleridge with the annuity that freed him from having to preach for a living.

7. William Godwin, anarchist philosopher and author, was Wollstonecraft's husband.

8. He complained in particular of the presumption of his attempting to establish the future immortality of man, "without . . . knowing what Death was, or what Life was"—and the tone in which he pronounced these two words seemed to convey a complete image of both [Hazlitt's note]. Hazlitt may have met Wollstonecraft in late 1796.

none at all of her talent for book-making. We talked a little about Holcroft.[9] He had been asked if he was not much struck *with* him, and he said, he thought himself in more danger of being struck *by* him. I complained that he would not let me get on at all, for he required a definition of every the commonest word, exclaiming, "What do you mean by a *sensation,* Sir? What do you mean by an *idea?*" This, Coleridge said, was barricadoing the road to truth:—it was setting up a turnpike-gate at every step we took. I forget a great number of things, many more than I remember; but the day passed off pleasantly, and the next morning Mr Coleridge was to return to Shrewsbury. When I came down to breakfast, I found that he had just received a letter from his friend T. Wedgwood, making him an offer of £150 a year if he chose to wa[i]ve his present pursuit, and devote himself entirely to the study of poetry and philosophy. Coleridge seemed to make up his mind to close with this proposal in the act of tying on one of his shoes. It threw an additional damp on his departure. It took the wayward enthusiast quite from us to cast him into Deva's winding vales, or by the shores of old romance. Instead of living at ten miles distance, of being the pastor of a Dissenting congregation at Shrewsbury, he was henceforth to inhabit the Hill of Parnassus, to be a shepherd on the Delectable Mountains.[1] Alas! I knew not the way thither, and felt very little gratitude for Mr Wedgwood's bounty. I was presently relieved from this dilemma; for Mr Coleridge, asking for a pen and ink, and going to a table to write something on a bit of card, advanced towards me with undulating step, and giving me the precious document, said that that was his address, *Mr Coleridge, Nether-Stowey, Somersetshire*; and that he should be glad to see me there in a few weeks' time, and, if I chose, would come half-way to meet me. I was not less surprised than the shepherd-boy (this simile is to be found in *Cassandra*)[2] when he sees a thunder-bolt fall close at his feet. I stammered out my acknowledgments and acceptance of this offer (I thought Mr Wedgwood's annuity a trifle to it) as well as I could; and this mighty business being settled, the poet-preacher took leave, and I accompanied him six miles on the road. It was a fine morning in the middle of winter, and he talked the whole way. The scholar in Chaucer is described as going

—Sounding on his way.[3]

So Coleridge went on his. In digressing, in dilating, in passing from subject to subject, he appeared to me to float in air, to slide on ice. He told me in confidence (going along) that he should have preached two sermons before he accepted the situation at Shrewsbury, one on Infant Baptism, the other on the Lord's Supper, shewing that he could not administer either, which would have effectually disqualified him for the object in view. I observed that he continually crossed me on the way by shifting from one side of the foot-path to the other. This struck me as an odd movement; but I did not at that time connect it with any instability of purpose or involuntary change of principle, as I have done since. He seemed unable to keep on in a strait line. He spoke slightingly of Hume (whose Essay on Miracles he said was stolen from

---

9. Thomas Holcroft (1745–1809), radical thinker, playwright, and friend of Godwin; Hazlitt edited and completed the autobiography left unfinished at his death.
1. Mount Parnassus in Greece was sacred to Apollo and the Muses; in John Bunyan's *Pilgrim's Progress*

(1678–1684) Christian passes through the Delectable Mountains on his way to the Celestial City.
2. A popular 17th-century French heroic romance.
3. Chaucer's Clerk of Oxford, Prologue to *The Canterbury Tales*.

an objection started in one of South's sermons—*Credat Judaeus Apella!*).[4] I was not very much pleased at this account of Hume, for I had just been reading, with infinite relish, that completest of all metaphysical *choke-pears*, his *Treatise on Human Nature*, to which the *Essays*, in point of scholastic subtlety and close reasoning, are mere elegant trifling, light summer-reading.[5] Coleridge even denied the excellence of Hume's general style, which I think betrayed a want of taste or candour. He however made me amends by the manner in which he spoke of Berkeley. He dwelt particularly on his *Essay on Vision* as a masterpiece of analytical reasoning.[6] So it undoubtedly is. He was exceedingly angry with Dr Johnson for striking the stone with his foot, in allusion to this author's Theory of Matter and Spirit, and saying, "Thus I confute him, Sir."[7] Coleridge drew a parallel (I don't know how he brought about the connection) between Bishop Berkeley and Tom Paine.[8] He said the one was an instance of a subtle, the other of an acute mind, than which no two things could be more distinct. The one was a shop-boy's quality, the other the characteristic of a philosopher. He considered Bishop Butler as a true philosopher, a profound and conscientious thinker, a genuine reader of nature and of his own mind. He did not speak of his *Analogy*, but of his *Sermons at the Rolls' Chapel*, of which I had never heard.[9] Coleridge somehow always contrived to prefer the *unknown* to the *known*. In this instance he was right. The *Analogy* is a tissue of sophistry, of wire-drawn, theological special-pleading; the *Sermons* (with the Preface to them) are in a fine vein of deep, matured reflection, a candid appeal to our observation of human nature, without pedantry and without bias. I told Coleridge I had written a few remarks, and was sometimes foolish enough to believe that I had made a discovery on the same subject (the *Natural Disinterestedness of the Human Mind*)[1]—and I tried to explain my view of it to Coleridge, who listened with great willingness, but I did not succeed in making myself understood. I sat down to the task shortly afterwards for the twentieth time, got new pens and paper, determined to make clear work of it, wrote a few meagre sentences in the skeleton-style of a mathematical demonstration, stopped half-way down the second page; and, after trying in vain to pump up any words, images, notions, apprehensions, facts, or observations, from that gulph of abstraction in which I had plunged myself for four or five years preceding, gave up the attempt as labour in vain, and shed tears of helpless despondency on the blank unfinished paper. I can write fast enough now. Am I better than I was then? Oh no! One truth discovered, one pang of regret at not being able to express it, is better than all the fluency and flippancy in the world. Would that I could go back to what I then was! Why can we not revive past times as we can revisit old places? If I had the quaint Muse of Sir Philip Sidney to assist me, I would write a *Sonnet to the Road between W—m and Shrewsbury*, and immortalise every step of it by some fond enigmatical conceit.[2]

4. David Hume (1711–1776), Scottish philosopher and historian; Robert South (1634–1716), English theologian. A skeptic's motto: "Let the Jew Apella believe it," from Horace's *Satires* (1.5.100), continues, "I shall not," implying that the Jew is more gullible than the Roman.
5. Hume's *Treatise* (1739–1740) was less popular than *Essays, Moral and Political* (1740–1742); choke-pears are bitter and astringent.
6. George Berkeley (1685–1753), philosopher and bishop. *Essay on Vision* was published in 1709.
7. Samuel Johnson (1709–1784), author and essayist. James Boswell records this incident in *Life of Johnson*,

"year 1763."
8. Thomas Paine (1737–1809), radical political theorist.
9. Joseph Butler (1692–1752), theologian and churchman who defended Christianity against Deism in *Analogy of Religion* (1736). The *Sermons* were published in 1706. Hazlitt admired his moral philosophy.
1. The premise of Hazlitt's *Principles of Human Action* (1805).
2. Sir Philip Sidney (1554–1586), Elizabethan poet. Hazlitt refers to the key metaphor of *Astrophil and Stella*, sonnet 84. Conceit: ingenious poetic image.

I would swear that the very milestones had ears, and that Harmer-hill stooped with all its pines, to listen to a poet, as he passed![3] I remember but one other topic of discourse in this walk. He mentioned Paley, praised the naturalness and clearness of his style, but condemned his sentiments, thought him a mere time-serving casuist, and said that "the fact of his work on Moral and Political Philosophy being made a text-book in our Universities was a disgrace to the national character."[4] We parted at the six-mile stone; and I returned homeward pensive but much pleased. I had met with unexpected notice from a person, whom I believed to have been prejudiced against me. "Kind and affable to me had been his condescension, and should be honoured ever with suitable regard."[5] He was the first poet I had known, and he certainly answered to that inspired name. I had heard a great deal of his powers of conversation, and was not disappointed. In fact, I never met with any thing at all like them, either before or since. I could easily credit the accounts which were circulated of his holding forth to a large party of ladies and gentlemen, an evening or two before, on the Berkeleian Theory, when he made the whole material universe look like a transparency of fine words; and another story (which I believe he has somewhere told himself) of his being asked to a party at Birmingham, of his smoking tobacco and going to sleep after dinner on a sofa, where the company found him to their no small surprise, which was increased to wonder when he started up of a sudden, and rubbing his eyes, looked about him, and launched into a three-hours' description of the third heaven, of which he had had a dream, very different from Mr Southey's *Vision of Judgment,* and also from that other *Vision of Judgment,* which Mr Murray, the Secretary of the Bridge-street Junto, has taken into his especial keeping![6]

On my way back, I had a sound in my ears, it was the voice of Fancy: I had a light before me, it was the face of Poetry. The one still lingers there, the other has not quitted my side! Coleridge in truth met me half-way on the ground of philosophy, or I should not have been won over to his imaginative creed. I had an uneasy, pleasurable sensation all the time, till I was to visit him. During those months the chill breath of winter gave me a welcoming; the vernal air was balm and inspiration to me. The golden sunsets, the silver star of evening, lighted me on my way to new hopes and prospects. *I was to visit Coleridge in the spring.* This circumstance was never absent from my thoughts, and mingled with all my feelings. I wrote to him at the time proposed, and received an answer postponing my intended visit for a week or two, but very cordially urging me to complete my promise then. This delay did not damp, but rather increased my ardour. In the meantime, I went to Llangollen Vale, by way of initiating myself in the mysteries of natural scenery; and I must say I was enchanted with it. I had been reading Coleridge's description of England in his fine *Ode on the Departing Year,* and I applied it, *con amore* [with love], to the objects before me. That valley was to me (in a manner) the cradle of a new existence: in the river that winds through it, my spirit was baptised in the waters of Helicon![7]

---

3. A comparison to mythic poet Orpheus.
4. In *Natural Theology* (1802), William Paley advanced the theory of God as watchmaker, who created the universe and left it to run itself out. Paley's *Moral and Political Philosophy* (1785) propounded the utilitarian theory that conduct is key to individual happiness and an awareness of ultimate judgment; a casuist is a slick moral reasoner.
5. Adam's praise of archangel Raphael, who instructs him in Eden (*Paradise Lost* 8.648–50).

6. Robert Southey's *A Vision of Judgement* (1821), written as Poet Laureate, depicts the entrance of George III into heaven. Byron's parody, *The Vision of Judgement* (published in *The Liberal*) was prosecuted for sedition by Charles Murray, whose offices were in Bridge Street in London.
7. The mountain of the Muses. Llangollen is in North Wales. Coleridge's *Ode* appeared in 1796.

I returned home, and soon after set out on my journey with unworn heart and untried feet. My way lay through Worcester and Gloucester, and by Upton, where I thought of Tom Jones and the adventure of the muff.[8] I remember getting completely wet through one day, and stopping at an inn (I think it was at Tewkesbury) where I sat up all night to read *Paul and Virginia*.[9] Sweet were the showers in early youth that drenched my body, and sweet the drops of pity that fell upon the books I read! I recollect a remark of Coleridge's upon this very book, that nothing could shew the gross indelicacy of French manners and the entire corruption of their imagination more strongly than the behaviour of the heroine in the last fatal scene, who turns away from a person on board the sinking vessel, that offers to save her life, because he has thrown off his clothes to assist him in swimming. Was this a time to think of such a circumstance? I once hinted to Wordsworth, as we were sailing in his boat on Grasmere lake, that I thought he had borrowed the idea of his *Poems on the Naming of Places*[1] from the local inscriptions of the same kind in *Paul and Virginia*. He did not own the obligation, and stated some distinction without a difference, in defence of his claim to originality. Any the slightest variation would be sufficient for this purpose in his mind; for whatever *he* added or omitted would inevitably be worth all that any one else had done, and contain the marrow of the sentiment. I was still two days before the time fixed for my arrival, for I had taken care to set out early enough. I stopped these two days at Bridgewater, and when I was tired of sauntering on the banks of its muddy river, returned to the inn, and read *Camilla*.[2] So have I loitered my life away, reading books, looking at pictures, going to plays, hearing, thinking, writing on what pleased me best. I have wanted only one thing to make me happy; but wanting that, have wanted everything!

I arrived, and was well received. The country about Nether Stowey is beautiful, green and hilly, and near the sea-shore. I saw it but the other day, after an interval of twenty years, from a hill near Taunton. How was the map of my life spread out before me, as the map of the country lay at my feet! In the afternoon, Coleridge took me over to All-Foxden, a romantic old family-mansion of the St. Aubins, where Wordsworth lived. It was then in the possession of a friend of the poet's who gave him the free use of it.[3] Somehow that period (the time just after the French Revolution) was not a time when *nothing was given for nothing*. The mind opened, and a softness might be perceived coming over the heart of individuals, beneath "the scales that fence" our self-interest. Wordsworth himself was from home, but his sister kept house, and set before us a frugal repast; and we had free access to her brother's poems, the *Lyrical Ballads*, which were still in manuscript, or in the form of *Sybilline Leaves*.[4] I dipped into a few of these with great satisfaction, and with the faith of a novice. I slept that night in an old room with blue hangings, and covered with the round-faced family-portraits of the age of George I and II, and from the wooded declivity of the adjoining park that overlooked my window, at the dawn of day, could

> —hear the loud stag speak.[5]

In the outset of life (and particularly at this time I felt it so) our imagination has a body to it. We are in a state between sleeping and waking, and have indistinct

---

8. Henry Fielding's *Tom Jones* (1749), bk. 10, chs. 5–7.
9. An idyllic romance by Bernardin de Saint Pierre, 1788.
1. A subsection of *Lyrical Ballads*, 1800 and after.
2. Popular novel by Frances Burney, 1796.
3. Wordsworth paid £23 for the year there.

4. The title of Coleridge's collected poems (1817). In Virgil, the Sybil scatters her prophecies, written on leaves.
5. Ben Jonson, *To Sir Robert Wroth*, line 22, naming one of the pleasures of Wroth's estate.

but glorious glimpses of strange shapes, and there is always something to come better than what we see. As in our dreams the fulness of the blood gives warmth and reality to the coinage of the brain, so in youth our ideas are clothed, and fed, and pampered with our good spirits; we breathe thick with thoughtless happiness, the weight of future years presses on the strong pulses of the heart, and we repose with undisturbed faith in truth and good. As we advance, we exhaust our fund of enjoyment and of hope. We are no longer wrapped in *lamb's-wool*, lulled in Elysium.[6] As we taste the pleasures of life, their spirit evaporates, the sense palls; and nothing is left but the phantoms, the lifeless shadows of what *has been*!

That morning, as soon as breakfast was over, we strolled out into the park, and seating ourselves on the trunk of an old ash-tree that stretched along the ground, Coleridge read aloud with a sonorous and musical voice, the ballad of *Betty Foy*.[7] I was not critically or sceptically inclined. I saw touches of truth and nature, and took the rest for granted. But in the *Thorn*, the *Mad Mother*, and the *Complaint of a Poor Indian Woman*, I felt that deeper power and pathos which have been since acknowledged,

> In spite of pride, in erring reason's spite,[8]

as the characteristics of this author; and the sense of a new style and a new spirit in poetry came over me. It had to me something of the effect that arises from the turning up of the fresh soil, or of the first welcome breath of Spring,

> While yet the trembling year is unconfirmed.[9]

Coleridge and myself walked back to Stowey that evening, and his voice sounded high

> Of Providence, foreknowledge, will, and fate,
> Fix'd fate, free-will, foreknowledge absolute,[1]

as we passed through echoing grove, by fairy stream or waterfall, gleaming in the summer moonlight! He lamented that Wordsworth was not prone enough to believe in the traditional superstitions of the place, and that there was a something corporeal, a *matter-of-fact-ness*, a clinging to the palpable, or often to the petty, in his poetry, in consequence. His genius was not a spirit that descended to him through the air; it sprung out of the ground like a flower, or unfolded itself from a green spray, on which the gold-finch sang. He said, however (if I remember right), that this objection must be confined to his descriptive pieces, that his philosophic poetry had a grand and comprehensive spirit in it, so that his soul seemed to inhabit the universe like a palace, and to discover truth by intuition, rather than by deduction. The next day Wordsworth arrived from Bristol at Coleridge's cottage. I think I see him now. He answered in some degree to his friend's description of him, but was more gaunt and Don Quixote-like. He was quaintly dressed (according to the *costume* of that unconstrained period) in a brown fustian jacket and striped pantaloons. There was something of a roll, a lounge in his gait, not unlike his own Peter Bell.[2] There was a severe, worn pressure of thought about his temples, a fire in his eye (as if he saw

---

6. Abode of the blessed in the afterlife.
7. Wordsworth's *The Idiot Boy*, in *Lyrical Ballads*, as are the other poems mentioned.
8. Pope, *Essay on Man*, Epistle I, line 293.
9. James Thomson, *The Seasons* (1726), "Spring," line 18.

1. Milton, *Paradise Lost*, 2.559–60; the topics debated in Hell by the fallen angels.
2. *Peter Bell* (pub. 1819) features an errant and fantastic potter; fustian: plain, heavy cotton.

something in objects more than the outward appearance), an intense high narrow forehead, a Roman nose, cheeks furrowed by strong purpose and feeling, and a convulsive inclination to laughter about the mouth, a good deal at variance with the solemn, stately expression of the rest of his face. Chantry's bust wants the marking traits; but he was teazed into making it regular and heavy: Haydon's head of him, introduced into the *Entrance of Christ into Jerusalem*, is the most like his drooping weight of thought and expression.[3] He sat down and talked very naturally and freely, with a mixture of clear gushing accents in his voice, a deep guttural intonation, and a strong tincture of the northern *burr*, like the crust on wine. He instantly began to make havoc of the half of a Cheshire cheese on the table, and said triumphantly that "his marriage with experience had not been so unproductive as Mr Southey's in teaching him a knowledge of the good things of this life." He had been to see the *Castle Spectre* by Monk Lewis, while at Bristol, and described it very well. He said "it fitted the taste of the audience like a glove."[4] This *ad captandum* [captivating] merit was however by no means a recommendation of it, according to the severe principles of the new school, which reject rather than court popular effect. Wordsworth, looking out of the low, latticed window, said, "How beautifully the sun sets on that yellow bank!" I thought within myself, "With what eyes these poets see nature!" and ever after, when I saw the sun-set stream upon the objects facing it, conceived I had made a discovery, or thanked Mr Wordsworth for having made one for me! We went over to All-Foxden again the day following, and Wordsworth read us the story of Peter Bell in the open air; and the comment made upon it by his face and voice was very different from that of some later critics! Whatever might be thought of the poem, "his face was as a book where men might read strange matters,"[5] and he announced the fate of his hero in prophetic tones. There is a *chaunt* in the recitation both of Coleridge and Wordsworth, which acts as a spell upon the hearer, and disarms the judgment. Perhaps they have deceived themselves by making habitual use of this ambiguous accompaniment. Coleridge's manner is more full, animated, and varied; Wordsworth's more equable, sustained, and internal. The one might be termed more *dramatic*, the other more *lyrical*. Coleridge has told me that he himself liked to compose in walking over uneven ground, or breaking through the straggling branches of a copse-wood; whereas Wordsworth always wrote (if he could) walking up and down a straight gravel-walk, or in some spot where the continuity of his verse met with no collateral interruption. Returning that same evening, I got into a metaphysical argument with Wordsworth,[6] while Coleridge was explaining the different notes of the nightingale to his sister, in which we neither of us succeeded in making ourselves perfectly clear and intelligible. Thus I passed three weeks at Nether Stowey and in the neighbourhood, generally devoting the afternoons to a delightful chat in an arbour made of bark by the poet's friend Tom Poole, sitting under two fine elm-trees, and listening to the bees humming round us, while we quaffed our *flip*.[7] It was agreed, among other things, that we should make a jaunt down the Bristol-Channel, as far as Linton. We set off together on foot, Coleridge, John Chester, and I. This Chester was a native of Nether Stowey, one of those who were attracted to

3. Sir Francis Chantrey's bust of Wordsworth was exhibited at the Royal Academy in 1821. Benjamin Robert Haydon had put Keats, Hazlitt, Lamb, and Wordsworth in this 1820 painting.
4. Matthew Gregory Lewis (1775–1818), author of Gothic novels and plays, was nicknamed for his most

famous work, *The Monk. Castle Spectre* was a big hit at London's Drury Lane theater in 1797 and then in Bristol.
5. Shakespeare, *Macbeth*, 1.5.62–63; Lady Macbeth to Macbeth, before they murder King Duncan.
6. See *The Tables Turned*, page 427.
7. Hot spiced sweet liquor.

Coleridge's discourse as flies are to honey, or bees in swarming-time to the sound of a brass pan. He "followed in the chase, like a dog who hunts, not like one that made up the cry."[8] He had on a brown cloth coat, boots, and corduroy breeches, was low in stature, bow-legged, had a drag in his walk like a drover, which he assisted by a hazel switch, and kept on a sort of trot by the side of Coleridge, like a running footman by a state coach, that he might not lose a syllable or sound that fell from Coleridge's lips. He told me his private opinion, that Coleridge was a wonderful man. He scarcely opened his lips, much less offered an opinion the whole way: yet of the three, had I to chuse during that journey, I would be John Chester. He afterwards followed Coleridge into Germany, where the Kantean philosophers[9] were puzzled how to bring him under any of their categories. When he sat down at table with his idol, John's felicity was complete; Sir Walter Scott's, or Mr Blackwood's, when they sat down at the same table with the King, was not more so.[1] We passed Dunster on our right, a small town between the brow of a hill and the sea. I remember eyeing it wistfully as it lay below us: contrasted with the woody scene around, it looked as clear, as pure, as *embrowned* and ideal as any landscape I have seen since, of Gaspar Poussin's or Domenichino's. We had a long day's march—(our feet kept time to the echoes of Coleridge's tongue)—through Mine-head and by the Blue Anchor, and on to Linton, which we did not reach till near midnight, and where we had some difficulty in making a lodgment. We however knocked the people of the house up at last, and we were repaid for our apprehensions and fatigue by some excellent rashers of fried bacon and eggs. The view in coming along had been splendid. We walked for miles and miles on dark brown heaths overlooking the Channel, with the Welsh hills beyond, and at times descended into little sheltered valleys close by the sea-side, with a smuggler's face scowling by us, and then had to ascend conical hills with a path winding up through a coppice to a barren top, like a monk's shaven crown, from one of which I pointed out to Coleridge's notice the bare masts of a vessel on the very edge of the horizon and within the red-orbed disk of the setting sun, like his own spectre-ship in the *Ancient Mariner*.[2] At Linton the character of the sea-coast becomes more marked and rugged. There is a place called the *Valley of Rocks* (I suspect this was only the poetical name for it) bedded among precipices overhanging the sea, with rocky caverns beneath, into which the waves dash, and where the sea-gull for ever wheels its screaming flight. On the tops of these are huge stones thrown transverse, as if an earthquake had tossed them there, and behind these is a fretwork of perpendicular rocks, something like the *Giant's Causeway*.[3] A thunder-storm came on while we were at the inn, and Coleridge was running out bare-headed to enjoy the commotion of the elements in the *Valley of Rocks*, but as if in spite, the clouds only muttered a few angry sounds, and let fall a few refreshing drops. Coleridge told me that he and Wordsworth were to have made this place the scene of a prose-tale, which was to have been in the manner of, but far superior to, the *Death of Abel*,[4] but they had relinquished the design. In the morning of the second day, we breakfasted luxuriously in an old-fashioned parlour, on tea, toast, eggs, and honey, in the very sight of the bee-hives from which it had been taken, and a garden full of thyme and wild flowers

8. Shakespeare, *Othello*, 2.3.363–64; in on the kill, rather than just howling.
9. Disciples of Immanuel Kant (1724–1804); see page 44.
1. Scott and William Blackwood (1776–1834), publisher of *Blackwood's Edinburgh Magazine*, both Tory monarchists,

attended a banquet for George IV, in Edinburgh, 1822.
2. Lines 177–80 from the 1817 text; see page 639.
3. Famous promontory off the northwest coast of Ireland.
4. Poem by Swiss poet Solomon Gessner (1758). Coleridge never finished his *Wanderings of Cain*.

that had produced it. On this occasion Coleridge spoke of Virgil's Georgics, but not well. I do not think he had much feeling for the classical or elegant. It was in this room that we found a little worn-out copy of the *Seasons*, lying in a window-seat, on which Coleridge exclaimed, "*That* is true fame!" He said Thomson was a great poet, rather than a good one; his style was as meretricious as his thoughts were natural. He spoke of Cowper as the best modern poet. He said the *Lyrical Ballads* were an experiment about to be tried by him and Wordsworth, to see how far the public taste would endure poetry written in a more natural and simple style than had hitherto been attempted; totally discarding the artifices of poetical diction, and making use only of such words as had probably been common in the most ordinary language since the days of Henry II.[5] Some comparison was introduced between Shakespear and Milton. He said "he hardly knew which to prefer. Shakespear appeared to him a mere stripling in the art; he was as tall and as strong, with infinitely more activity than Milton, but he never appeared to have come to man's estate; or if he had, he would not have been a man, but a monster." He spoke with contempt of Gray, and with intolerance of Pope. He did not like the versification of the latter. He observed that "the ears of these couplet-writers might be charged with having short memories, that could not retain the harmony of whole passages." He thought little of Junius as a writer; he had a dislike of Dr Johnson; and a much higher opinion of Burke as an orator and politician, than of Fox or Pitt.[6] He however thought him very inferior in richness of style and imagery to some of our elder prose-writers, particularly Jeremy Taylor.[7] He liked Richardson, but not Fielding; nor could I get him to enter into the merits of *Caleb Williams*.[8] In short, he was profound and discriminating with respect to those authors whom he liked, and where he gave his judgment fair play; capricious, perverse, and prejudiced in his antipathies and distastes. We loitered on the "ribbed sea-sands,"[9] in such talk as this, a whole morning, and I recollect met with a curious sea-weed, of which John Chester told us the country name! A fisherman gave Coleridge an account of a boy that had been drowned the day before, and that they had tried to save him at the risk of their own lives. He said "he did not know how it was that they ventured, but, Sir, we have a *nature* towards one another." This expression, Coleridge remarked to me, was a fine illustration of that theory of disinterestedness which I (in common with [Joseph] Butler) had adopted. I broached to him an argument of mine to prove that *likeness* was not mere association of ideas. I said that the mark in the sand put one in mind of a man's foot, not because it was part of a former impression of a man's foot (for it was quite new) but because it was like the shape of a man's foot. He assented to the justness of this distinction (which I have explained at length elsewhere, for the benefit of the curious) and John Chester listened; not from any interest in the subject, but because he was astonished that I should be able to suggest any thing to Coleridge that he did not already know. We returned

5. Reigned 1154–89. See Preface to *Lyrical Ballads*, pages 433–34.
6. Junius, the unknown author of a series of pamphlets attacking George III and the political establishment (1769–1772). Charles James Fox (1749–1806) and William Pitt (1759–1806) were statesmen and orators.
7. Religious writer famed for *Holy Living* (1650) and *Holy Dying* (1651).
8. Godwin's political novel; Samuel Richardson and Henry Fielding were famous 18th-century novelists. "He had no idea of pictures, of Claude or Raphael, and at this time I had as little as he. He sometimes gives a striking account at present of the Cartoons [sketches] at Pisa, by Buffamalco and others; or one in particular where Death is seen in the air brandishing his scythe, and the great and mighty of the earth shudder at his approach, while the beggars and the wretched kneel to him as their deliverer. He would of course understand so broad and fine a moral as this at any time" [Hazlitt's note, on Coleridge].
9. Part of a simile describing the Ancient Mariner (line 227; see page 640).

on the third morning, and Coleridge remarked the silent cottage-smoke curling up the valleys where, a few evenings before, we had seen the lights gleaming through the dark.

In a day or two after we arrived at Stowey, we set out, I on my return home, and he for Germany. It was a Sunday morning, and he was to preach that day for Dr Toulmin of Tauton. I asked him if he had prepared any thing for the occasion? He said he had not even thought of the text, but should as soon as we parted. I did not go to hear him,—this was a fault,—but we met in the evening at Bridgewater. The next day we had a long day's walk to Bristol, and sat down, I recollect, by a well-side on the road, to cool ourselves and satisfy our thirst, when Coleridge repeated to me some descriptive lines from his tragedy of *Remorse*; which I must say became his mouth and that occasion better than they, some years after, did Mr Elliston's and the Drury-lane boards,—

> Oh memory! shield me from the world's poor strife,
> And give those scenes thine everlasting life.[1]

I saw no more of him for a year or two, during which period he had been wandering in the Hartz Forest in Germany; and his return was cometary, meteorous, unlike his setting out. It was not till some time after that I knew his friends Lamb and Southey. The last always appears to me (as I first saw him) with a common-place book[2] under his arm, and the first with a *bon-mot* in his mouth. It was at Godwin's that I met him with Holcroft and Coleridge, where they were disputing fiercely which was the best—*Man as he was, or man as he is to be.* "Give me," says Lamb, "man as he is *not* to be." This saying was the beginning of a friendship between us, which I believe still continues.—Enough of this for the present.

> But there is matter for another rhyme,
> And I to this may add a second tale.[3]

The Liberal, 1823

Thomas De Quincey
1785–1859

Thomas De Quincey was born in the manufacturing town of Manchester, the fifth of eight children in the family of a wealthy textile merchant. Before he was ten, his grandmother, father, and two sisters died; he was devastated by the loss of his favorite Elizabeth. Sent to various schools, he was a precocious student but restless and frequently truant. Already adept in classical languages and literature, he entered Oxford in 1803 and left without a degree in the middle of final examinations in which he had been performing brilliantly. Having read *Lyrical Ballads* in 1799, he wrote Wordsworth an enthusiastic fan letter, and finally met him in 1807. Two years later, he moved to Grasmere, taking a lease on the Wordsworths' former home, Dove Cottage. Arriving with twenty-nine chests of books, he delighted the Wordsworths with this library and soon became an intimate, especially close to their daughter Kate, whose death in the summer of 1812 anguished him, reviving his grief for his sister.

---

1. *Remorse* (1797) was produced at Drury Lane in 1813, starring Robert William Elliston.
2. A notebook of personal reflections and favorite

quotations; *bon-mot*: witticism.
3. William Wordsworth, *Hart-Leap Well* (lines 95–96), first published in *Lyrical Ballads*, 1800.

He met Charles Lamb in 1804, and a few years later, Coleridge, who shared his enthusiasm for German metaphysics and addiction to opium. De Quincey first used opium while at Oxford for a toothache; it was a cheap, over-the-counter cure-all whose addictive powers were not understood. Like many, he developed a dependency as he relied on it to ease various ailments. By 1815 his addiction and his premarital housekeeping with a local farmer's daughter estranged him from the Wordsworths. Unable to make a living for his family (three small children) in the Lake District, De Quincey went to London in 1821 to join Lamb at the bustling *London Magazine*. His first contribution, *Confessions*, appeared anonymously and was an immediate hit, issued a year later as a book (still anonymous). Its income sustained De Quincey's addiction, and its widely admired dream-writing inspired others to opium adventures, including Edgar Allan Poe, Francis Thompson, and Charles Baudelaire. Tormented by his addiction, De Quincey was conventional, even conservative: known for social refinement and good manners, Tory politics and support of the Church of England. Versatile and prolific, he wrote over 200 essays on a wide range of subjects: political economy, history, philosophy, biography, translations, literature, and memoirs.

For De Quincey's essay on *Macbeth*, see page 1142.

from Confessions of an English Opium-Eater
Being an Extract from the Life of a Scholar

To the Reader.——I here present you, courteous reader, with the record of a remarkable period in my life: according to my application of it, I trust that it will prove, not merely an interesting record, but, in a considerable degree, useful and instructive. In *that* hope it is, that I have drawn it up: and *that* must be my apology for breaking through that delicate and honourable reserve, which, for the most part, restrains us from the public exposure of our own errors and infirmities. Nothing, indeed, is more revolting to English feelings, than the spectacle of a human being obtruding on our notice his moral ulcers or scars, and tearing away that "decent drapery,"[1] which time, or indulgence to human frailty, may have drawn over them: accordingly, the greater part of *our* confessions (that is, spontaneous and extra-judicial confessions) proceed from demireps,[2] adventurers, or swindlers: and for any such acts of gratuitous self-humiliation from those who can be supposed in sympathy with the decent and self-respecting part of society, we must look to French literature, or to that part of the German, which is tainted with the spurious and defective sensibility of the French. All this I feel so forcibly, and so nervously am I alive to reproach of this tendency, that I have for many months hesitated about the propriety of allowing this, or any part of my narrative, to come before the public eye, until after my death (when, for many reasons, the whole will be published): and it is not without an anxious review of the reasons, for and against this step, that I have, at last, concluded on taking it.

Guilt and misery shrink, by a natural instinct, from public notice: they court privacy and solitude: and, even in their choice of a grave, will sometimes sequester themselves from the general population of the church-yard, as if declining to claim fellowship with the great family of man, and wishing (in the affecting language of Mr Wordsworth)

——Humbly to express
A penitential loneliness.[3]

1. Quoting Burke's famous lament over the decline of chivalry in the French Revolution: "All the decent drapery of life is to be rudely torn off" (see page 119).

2. Disreputable women.

3. From *The White Doe of Rylstone* (1815) about a solitary grave (176–77).

It is well, upon the whole, and for the interest of us all, that it should be so: nor would I willingly, in my own person, manifest a disregard of such salutary feelings; nor in act or word do anything to weaken them. But, on the one hand, as my self-accusation does not amount to a confession of guilt, so, on the other, it is possible that, if it *did*, the benefit resulting to others, from the record of an experience purchased at so heavy a price, might compensate, by a vast overbalance, for any violence done to the feelings I have noticed, and justify a breach of the general rule. Infirmity and misery do not, of necessity, imply guilt. They approach, or recede from, the shades of that dark alliance, in proportion to the probable motives and prospects of the offender, and the palliations, known or secret, of the offence: in proportion as the temptations to it were potent from the first, and the resistance to it, in act or in effort, was earnest to the last. For my own part, without breach of truth or modesty, I may affirm, that my life has been, on the whole, the life of a philosopher: from my birth I was made an intellectual creature: and intellectual in the highest sense my pursuits and pleasures have been, even from my school-boy days. If opium-eating be a sensual pleasure, and if I am bound to confess that I have indulged in it to an excess, not yet *recorded* of any other man,[4] it is no less true, that I have struggled against this fascinating enthralment with a religious zeal, and have, at length, accomplished what I never yet heard attributed to any other man—have untwisted, almost to its final links, the accursed chain which fettered me. Such a self-conquest may reasonably be set off in counterbalance to any kind or degree of self-indulgence. Not to insist, that in my case, the self-conquest was unquestionable, the self-indulgence open to doubts of casuistry, according as that name shall be extended to acts aiming at the bare relief of pain, or shall be restricted to such as aim at the excitement of positive pleasure.

Guilt, therefore, I do not acknowledge: and, if I did, it is possible that I might still resolve on the present act of confession, in consideration of the service which I may thereby render to the whole class of opium-eaters. But who are they? Reader, I am sorry to say, a very numerous class indeed. Of this I became convinced some years ago, by computing, at that time, the number of those in one small class of English society (the class of men distinguished for talents, or of eminent station), who were known to me, directly or indirectly, as opium-eaters; such for instance, as the eloquent and benevolent——, the late dean of——; Lord——; Mr——, the philosopher; a late under-secretary of state (who described to me the sensation which first drove him to the use of opium, in the very same words as the dean of——, viz. "that he felt as though rats were gnawing and abrading the coats of his stomach"); Mr——; and many others, hardly less known, whom it would be tedious to mention.[5] Now, if one class, comparatively so limited, could furnish so many scores of cases (and *that* within the knowledge of one single inquirer), it was a natural inference, that the entire population of England would furnish a proportionable number. The soundness of this inference, however, I doubted, until some facts became known to me, which satisfied me, that it was not incorrect. I will mention two: 1. Three respectable London druggists, in widely remote quarters of London, from whom I happened lately to be purchasing small quantities of opium, assured me, that the number of *amateur*

---

4. "Not yet *recorded*," I say: for there is one celebrated man of the present day, who, if all be true which is reported of him, has greatly exceeded me in quantity [De Quincey's note, referring to Coleridge]. The term "opium-eater" is De Quincey's coinage.

5. In a footnote in 1856, De Quincey complains "some absurd coward" at the press saw to it that "all the names were struck out behind my back"; he now names abolitionist William Wilberforce; Isaac Milner, Dean of Carlisle; Lord Erskine; a Mr. Dash ("the philosopher"); under-secretary John H. Addington, and Coleridge.

opium-eaters (as I may term them) was, at this time, immense; and that the difficulty of distinguishing these persons, to whom habit had rendered opium necessary, from such as were purchasing it with a view to suicide, occasioned them daily trouble and disputes. This evidence respected London only. But, 2. (which will possibly surprise the reader more,) some years ago, on passing through Manchester, I was informed by several cotton-manufacturers, that their work-people were rapidly getting into the practice of opium-eating; so much so, that on a Saturday afternoon the counters of the druggists were strewed with pills of one, two, or three grains, in preparation for the known demand of the evening. The immediate occasion of this practice was the low-ness of wages, which, at that time, would not allow them to indulge in ale or spirits: and, wages rising, it may be thought that this practice would cease: but, as I do not readily believe that any man, having once tasted the divine luxuries of opium, will afterwards descend to the gross and mortal enjoyments of alcohol, I take it for granted,

> That those eat now, who never ate before;
> And those who always ate, now eat the more.[6]

Indeed the fascinating powers of opium are admitted, even by medical writers, who are its greatest enemies: thus, for instance, Awsiter, apothecary to Greenwich-hospital, in his "Essay on the Effects of Opium" (published in the year 1763), when attempting to explain, why Mead[7] had not been sufficiently explicit on the proper-ties, counteragents, &c. of this drug, expresses himself in the following mysterious terms (φωναντα συνετοισι [speaking to the wise]): "perhaps he thought the sub-ject of too delicate a nature to be made common; and as many people might then indiscriminately use it, it would take from that necessary fear and caution, which should prevent their experiencing the extensive power of this drug: *for there are many properties in it, if universally known, that would habituate the use, and make it more in re-quest with us than the Turks themselves*: the result of which knowledge," he adds, "must prove a general misfortune." In the necessity of this conclusion I do not altogether concur: but upon that point I shall have occasion to speak at the close of my confes-sions, where I shall present the reader with the *moral* of my narrative.

PRELIMINARY CONFESSIONS

These preliminary confessions, or introductory narrative of the youthful adventures which laid the foundation of the writer's habit of opium-eating in after-life, it has been judged proper to premise, for three several reasons:

1. As forestalling that question, and giving it a satisfactory answer, which else would painfully obtrude itself in the course of the Opium-Confessions—"How came any reasonable being to subject himself to such a yoke of misery, voluntarily to incur a captivity so servile, and knowingly to fetter himself with such a seven-fold chain?"—a question which, if not somewhere plausibly resolved, could hardly fail, by the indigna-tion which it would be apt to raise as against an act of wanton folly, to interfere with that degree of sympathy which is necessary in any case to an author's purposes.

2. As furnishing a key to some parts of that tremendous scenery which afterwards peopled the dreams of the Opium-eater.

3. As creating some previous interest of a personal sort in the confessing subject, apart from the matter of the confessions, which cannot fail to render the confessions

---

6. The opening lines of *The Vigil of Venus* by Thomas Par-nell (1679–1718).

7. Richard Mead (1673–1754), controversial physician and medical writer.

themselves more interesting. If a man "whose talk is of oxen," should become an Opium-eater, the probability is, that (if he is not too dull to dream at all)—he will dream about oxen:[8] whereas, in the case before him, the reader will find that the Opium-eater boasteth himself to be a philosopher; and accordingly, that the phantasmagoria of his dreams (waking or sleeping, day-dreams or night-dreams) is suitable to one who in that character,

Humani nihil a se alienum putat.[9]

For amongst the conditions which he deems indispensable to the sustaining of any claim to the title of philosopher, is not merely the possession of a superb intellect in its *analytic* functions (in which part of the pretension, however, England can for some generations show but few claimants; at least, he is not aware of any known candidate for this honour who can be styled emphatically a *subtle thinker*, with the exception of *Samuel Taylor Coleridge*, and in a narrower department of thought, with the recent illustrious exception of *David Ricardo*)[1]—but also on such a constitution of the *moral* faculties, as shall give him an inner eye and power of intuition for the vision and the mysteries of our human nature: *that* constitution of faculties, in short, which (amongst all the generations of men that from the beginning of time have deployed into life, as it were, upon this planet) our English poets have possessed in the highest degree—and Scottish Professors[2] in the lowest.

I have often been asked, how I first came to be a regular opium-eater; and have suffered, very unjustly, in the opinion of my acquaintance, from being reputed to have brought upon myself all the sufferings which I shall have to record, by a long course of indulgence in this practice purely for the sake of creating an artificial state of pleasurable excitement. This, however, is a misrepresentation of my case. True it is, that for nearly ten years I did occasionally take opium, for the sake of the exquisite pleasure it gave me: but, so long as I took it with this view, I was effectually protected from all material bad consequences, by the necessity of interposing long intervals between the several acts of indulgence, in order to renew the pleasurable sensations. It was not for the purpose of creating pleasure, but of mitigating pain in the severest degree, that I first began to use opium as an article of daily diet. In the twenty-eighth year of my age, a most painful affection of the stomach, which I had first experienced about ten years before, attacked me in great strength. This affection had originally been caused by extremities of hunger, suffered in my boyish days. During the season of hope and redundant happiness which succeeded (that is, from eighteen to twenty-four) it had slumbered: for the three following years it had revived at intervals: and now, under unfavourable circumstances, from depression of spirits, it attacked me

---

8. *Ecclesiasticus* 38.25: "How can a man become wise who . . . is absorbed in the task of driving oxen, / and talks only of cattle?"
9. He deems nothing human alien to him; from *The Self-Punisher* by Terence, Roman comic poet, 2nd century B.C.E.
1. In 1817 Ricardo published his landmark *Principles of Political Economy and Taxation*. De Quincey adds a note referring to Hazlitt: "A third exception might perhaps have been added: and my reason for not adding that exception is chiefly because it was only in his juvenile efforts that the writer whom I allude to, expressly addressed himself to philosophical themes; his riper powers having been all dedicated (on very excusable and very intelligent grounds, under the present direction of the popular mind in England) to criticism and the Fine Arts. This reason apart, however, I doubt whether he is not rather to be

considered an acute thinker than a subtle one. It is, besides, a great drawback on his mastery over philosophical subjects, that he has obviously not had the advantage of a regular scholastic education: he has not read Plato in his youth (which most likely was only his misfortune); but neither has he read Kant in his manhood (which is his fault)." The juvenile effort is *Essay on the Principles of Human Action* (1805).
2. I disclaim any allusion to *existing* professors, of whom indeed I know only one [De Quincey's note]. At this time, prominent philosophers taught at the universities in Edinburgh and Glasgow. De Quincey knew John Wilson (1785–1854), Professor of Moral Philosophy at Edinburgh, who wrote for *Blackwood's* under the name of "Christopher North."

with a violence that yielded to no remedies but opium. As the youthful sufferings, which first produced this derangement of the stomach, were interesting in themselves, and in the circumstances that attended them, I shall here briefly retrace them.

My father died, when I was about seven years old, and left me to the care of four guardians. I was sent to various schools, great and small; and was very early distinguished for my classical attainments, especially for my knowledge of Greek. At thirteen, I wrote Greek with ease; and at fifteen my command of that language was so great, that I not only composed Greek verses in lyric metres, but could converse in Greek fluently, and without embarrassment—an accomplishment which I have not since met with in any scholar of my times, and which, in my case, was owing to the practice of daily reading off the newspapers into the best Greek I could furnish *extempore*: for the necessity of ransacking my memory and invention, for all sorts and combinations of periphrastic expressions, as equivalents for modern ideas, images, relations of things, &c. gave me a compass of diction which would never have been called out by a dull translation of moral essays, &c. "That boy," said one of my masters, pointing the attention of a stranger to me, "that boy could harangue an Athenian mob, better than you or I could address an English one."

[SUFFERING IN LONDON; ANN THE PROSTITUTE][3]

And now began the latter and fiercer stage of my long-sufferings; without using a disproportionate expression I might say, of my agony. For I now suffered, for upwards of sixteen weeks, the physical anguish of hunger in various degrees of intensity; but as bitter, perhaps, as ever any human being can have suffered who has survived it. I would not needlessly harass my reader's feelings, by a detail of all that I endured: for extremities such as these, under any circumstances of heaviest misconduct or guilt, cannot be contemplated, even in description, without a rueful pity that is painful to the natural goodness of the human heart. Let it suffice, at least on this occasion, to say, that a few fragments of bread from the breakfast-table of one individual (who supposed me to be ill, but did not know of my being in utter want), and these at uncertain intervals, constituted my whole support. During the former part of my sufferings (that is, generally in Wales, and always for the first two months in London) I was houseless, and very seldom slept under a roof. To this constant exposure to the open air I ascribe it mainly, that I did not sink under my torments. Latterly, however, when colder and more inclement weather came on, and when, from the length of my sufferings, I had begun to sink into a more languishing condition, it was, no doubt, fortunate for me, that the same person to whose breakfast-table I had access, allowed me to sleep in a large unoccupied house, of which he was tenant. Unoccupied, I call it, for there was no household or establishment in it; nor any furniture, indeed, except a table, and a few chairs. But I found, on taking possession of my new quarters, that the house already contained one single inmate, a poor friendless child, apparently ten years old; but she seemed hunger-bitten; and sufferings of that sort often make children look older than they are. From this forlorn child I learned, that she had slept and lived there alone, for some time before I came: and great joy the poor creature expressed, when she found that I was, in future, to be her companion through the hours of darkness. The house was large; and, from the want of furniture, the noise of the rats made a prodigious echoing on the spacious stair-case and hall; and, amidst the real fleshly ills of cold, and, I fear, hunger, the forsaken child had found leisure to suffer still more (it appeared) from the self-created one of ghosts. I promised her protection against

3. At 16, De Quincey ran away from Manchester Grammar School, planning to head north to meet Wordsworth, but a series of "accidents" took him to North Wales. He then decided to go to London.

all ghosts whatsoever: but, alas! I could offer her no other assistance. We lay upon the floor, with a bundle of cursed law papers for a pillow: but with no other covering than a sort of large horseman's cloak: afterwards, however, we discovered, in a garret, an old sopha-cover, a small piece of rug, and some fragments of other articles, which added a little to our warmth. The poor child crept close to me for warmth, and for security against her ghostly enemies. When I was not more than usually ill, I took her into my arms, so that, in general, she was tolerably warm, and often slept when I could not: for, during the last two months of my sufferings, I slept much in the day-time, and was apt to fall into transient dozings at all hours. But my sleep distressed me more than my watching: for, besides the tumultuousness of my dreams (which were only not so awful as those which I shall have to describe hereafter as produced by opium), my sleep was never more than what is called *dog-sleep*; so that I could hear myself moaning, and was often, as it seemed to me, wakened suddenly by my own voice; and, about this time, a hideous sensation began to haunt me as soon as I fell into a slumber, which has since returned upon me, at different periods of my life, viz. a sort of twitching (I know not where, but apparently about the region of the stomach), which compelled me violently to throw out my feet for the sake of relieving it. This sensation coming on as soon as I began to sleep, and the effort to relieve it constantly awaking me, at length I slept only from exhaustion; and from increasing weakness (as I said before) I was constantly falling asleep, and constantly awaking. Meantime, the master of the house sometimes came in upon us suddenly, and very early, sometimes not till ten o'clock, sometimes not at all. He was in constant fear of bailiffs: improving on the plan of Cromwell, every night he slept in a different quarter of London;[4] and I observed that he never failed to examine, through a private window, the appearance of those who knocked at the door, before he would allow it to be opened. He breakfasted alone: indeed, his tea equipage would hardly have admitted of his hazarding an invitation to a second person—any more than the quantity of esculent *matériel*, which, for the most part, was little more than a roll, or a few biscuits, which he had bought on his road from the place where he had slept. Or, if he *had* asked a party, as I once learnedly and facetiously observed to him—the several members of it must have *stood* in the relation to each other (not *sate* in any relation whatever) of succession, as the metaphysicians have it, and not of co-existence; in the relation of the parts of time, and not of the parts of space. During his breakfast, I generally contrived a reason for lounging in; and, with an air of as much indifference as I could assume, took up such fragments as he had left—sometimes, indeed, there were none at all. In doing this, I committed no robbery except upon the man himself, who was thus obliged (I believe) now and then to send out at noon for an extra biscuit; for, as to the poor child, *she* was never admitted into his study (if I may give that name to his chief depository of parchments, law writings, &c.); that room was to her the Blue-beard room of the house,[5] being regularly locked on his departure to dinner, about six o'clock, which usually was his final departure for the night. Whether this child were an illegitimate daughter of Mr——, or only a servant, I could not ascertain; she did not herself know; but certainly she was treated altogether as a menial servant. No sooner did Mr——make his appearance, than she went below stairs, brushed his shoes, coat, &c.; and, except when she was summoned to run an errand, she never emerged from the dismal Tartarus[6] of the kitchens, &c. to the

---

4. According to one Royalist historian, Oliver Cromwell so feared for his life after the dissolution of his last Parliament that he "rarely lodged two nights" in one place.
5. In the popular 18th-century tale, the successive wives

of a wealthy blue-bearded man disappear; his most recent wife discovers their bodies in a secret room.
6. The most dismal region of Hell.

upper air, until my welcome knock at night called up her little trembling footsteps to the front door. Of her life during the day-time, however, I knew little but what I gathered from her own account at night; for, as soon as the hours of business commenced, I saw that my absence would be acceptable; and, in general, therefore, I went off and sate in the parks, or elsewhere, until night-fall.

But who, and what, meantime, was the master of the house himself? Reader, he was one of those anomalous practitioners in lower departments of the law, who—what shall I say?—who, on prudential reasons, or from necessity, deny themselves all indulgence in the luxury of too delicate a conscience: (a periphrasis which might be abridged considerably, but *that* I leave to the reader's taste:) in many walks of life, a conscience is a more expensive incumbrance, than a wife or a carriage; and just as people talk of "laying down" their carriages, so I suppose my friend, Mr—— had "laid down" his conscience for a time; meaning, doubtless, to resume it as soon as he could afford it. The inner economy of such a man's daily life would present a most strange picture, if I could allow myself to amuse the reader at his expense. Even with my limited opportunities for observing what went on, I saw many scenes of London intrigues, and complex chicanery, "cycle and epicycle, orb in orb,"[7] at which I sometimes smile to this day—and at which I smiled then, in spite of my misery. My situation, however, at that time, gave me little experience, in my own person, of any qualities in Mr——'s character but such as did him honour; and of his whole strange composition, I must forget every thing but that towards me he was obliging, and, to the extent of his power, generous.

That power was not, indeed, very extensive; however, in common with the rats, I sate rent free; and, as Dr. Johnson has recorded, that he never but once in his life had as much wall-fruit as he could eat, so let me be grateful, that on that single occasion I had as large a choice of apartments in a London mansion as I could possibly desire. Except the Blue-beard room, which the poor child believed to be haunted, all others, from the attics to the cellars, were at our service; "the world was all before us"; and we pitched our tent for the night in any spot we chose.[8] This house I have already described as a large one; it stands in a conspicuous situation, and in a well-known part of London. Many of my readers will have passed it, I doubt not, within a few hours of reading this. For myself, I never fail to visit it when business draws me to London; about ten o'clock, this very night, August 15, 1821, being my birth-day—I turned aside from my evening walk, down Oxford-street, purposely to take a glance at it: it is now occupied by a respectable family; and, by the lights in the front drawing-room, I observed a domestic party, assembled perhaps at tea, and apparently cheerful and gay. Marvellous contrast in my eyes to the darkness—cold—silence—and desolation of that same house eighteen years ago, when its nightly occupants were one famishing scholar, and a neglected child.——Her, by the bye, in after years, I vainly endeavoured to trace. Apart from her situation, she was not what would be called an interesting child: she was neither pretty, nor quick in understanding, nor remarkably pleasing in manners. But, thank God! even in those years I needed not the embellishments of novel-accessaries to conciliate my affections; plain human nature, in its humblest and most homely apparel, was enough for me: and I loved the child because she was my partner in wretchedness. If she is now living, she is probably a mother, with children of her own; but, as I have said, I could never trace her.

This I regret, but another person there was at that time, whom I have since sought to trace with far deeper earnestness, and with far deeper sorrow at my failure. This person was a young woman, and one of that unhappy class who subsist upon

---

7. The architecture of Heaven in *Paradise Lost* (8.84).
8. A wry comparison to Adam and Eve departing from Eden at the end of *Paradise Lost* (12.646).

the wages of prostitution. I feel no shame, nor have any reason to feel it, in avowing, that I was then on familiar and friendly terms with many women in that unfortunate condition. The reader needs neither smile at this avowal, nor frown. For, not to remind my classical readers of the old Latin proverb—"*Sine Cerere,*" &c.,[9] it may well be supposed that in the existing state of my purse, my connexion with such women could not have been an impure one. But the truth is, that at no time of my life have I been a person to hold myself polluted by the touch or approach of any creature that wore a human shape: on the contrary, from my very earliest youth it has been my pride to converse familiarly, *more Socratico* [in the manner of Socrates], with all human beings, man, woman, and child, that chance might fling in my way: a practice which is friendly to the knowledge of human nature, to good feelings, and to that frankness of address which becomes a man who would be thought a philosopher. For a philosopher should not see with the eyes of the poor limitary creature calling himself a man of the world, and filled with narrow and self-regarding prejudices of birth and education, but should look upon himself as a Catholic[1] creature, and as standing in an equal relation to high and low—to educated and uneducated, to the guilty and the innocent. Being myself at that time of necessity a peripatetic, or a walker of the streets, I naturally fell in more frequently with those female peripatetics who are technically called Street-walkers. Many of these women had occasionally taken my part against watchmen who wished to drive me off the steps of houses where I was sitting. But one amongst them, the one on whose account I have at all introduced this subject—yet no! let me not class thee, Oh noble minded Ann——, with that order of women; let me find, if it be possible, some gentler name to designate the condition of her to whose bounty and compassion, ministering to my necessities when all the world had forsaken me, I owe it that I am at this time alive.—For many weeks I had walked at nights with this poor friendless girl up and down Oxford Street, or had rested with her on steps and under the shelter of porticos. She could not be so old as myself: she told me, indeed, that she had not completed her sixteenth year. By such questions as my interest about her prompted, I had gradually drawn forth her simple history. Her's was a case of ordinary occurrence (as I have since had reason to think), and one in which, if London beneficence had better adapted its arrangements to meet it, the power of the law might oftener be interposed to protect, and to avenge. But the stream of London charity flows in a channel which, though deep and mighty, is yet noiseless and underground; not obvious or readily accessible to poor houseless wanderers:[2] and it cannot be denied that the outside air and frame-work of London society is harsh, cruel, and repulsive. In any case, however, I saw that part of her injuries might easily have been redressed: and I urged her often and earnestly to lay her complaint before a magistrate: friendless as she was, I assured her that she would meet with immediate attention; and that English justice, which was no respecter of persons, would speedily and amply avenge her on the brutal ruffian who had plundered her little property. She promised me often that she would; but she delayed taking the steps I pointed out from time to time: for she was timid and dejected to a degree which showed how deeply sorrow had taken hold of her young heart: and perhaps she thought justly that the most upright judge, and the most righteous tribunals, could do nothing to repair her heaviest wrongs.[3] Something, however, would perhaps have been done: for it had been settled between us at length, but unhappily on the very

9. Without bread and wine love goes hungry.
1. Broad in sympathies and interests.
2. Echoing King Lear's shocked recognition, on the

heath, of a world of human misery (*King Lear* 3.4.28ff).
3. Wrongs done to her.

last time but one that I was ever to see her, that in a day or two we should go together before a magistrate, and that I should speak on her behalf. This little service it was destined, however, that I should never realise. Meantime, that which she rendered to me, and which was greater than I could ever have repaid her, was this:—One night, when we were pacing slowly along Oxford Street, and after a day when I had felt more than usually ill and faint, I requested her to turn off with me into Soho Square: thither we went; and we sate down on the steps of a house, which, to this hour, I never pass without a pang of grief, and an inner act of homage to the spirit of that unhappy girl, in memory of the noble action which she there performed. Suddenly, as we sate, I grew much worse: I had been leaning my head against her bosom; and all at once I sank from her arms and fell backwards on the steps. From the sensations I then had, I felt an inner conviction of the liveliest kind that without some powerful and reviving stimulus, I should either have died on the spot—or should at least have sunk to a point of exhaustion from which all reäscent under my friendless circumstances would soon have become hopeless. Then it was, at this crisis of my fate, that my poor orphan companion—who had herself met with little but injuries in this world—stretched out a saving hand to me. Uttering a cry of terror, but without a moment's delay, she ran off into Oxford Street, and in less time than could be imagined, returned to me with a glass of port wine and spices, that acted upon my empty stomach (which at that time would have rejected all solid food) with an instantaneous power of restoration: and for this glass the generous girl without a murmur paid out of her own humble purse at a time—be it remembered!—when she had scarcely wherewithal to purchase the bare necessaries of life, and when she could have no reason to expect that I should ever be able to reimburse her.——Oh! youthful benefactress! how often in succeeding years, standing in solitary places, and thinking of thee with grief of heart and perfect love, how often have I wished that, as in ancient times the curse of a father was believed to have a supernatural power, and to pursue its object with a fatal necessity of self-fulfilment,—even so the benediction of a heart oppressed with gratitude, might have a like prerogative; might have power given to it from above to chace—to haunt—to way-lay—to overtake—to pursue thee into the central darkness of a London brothel, or (if it were possible) into the darkness of the grave[4]—there to awaken thee with an authentic message of peace and forgiveness, and of final reconciliation!

* * *

Meantime, what had become of poor Anne?[5] For her I have reserved my concluding words: according to our agreement, I sought her daily, and waited for her every night, so long as I staid in London, at the corner of Titchfield-street. I inquired for her of every one who was likely to know her; and, during the last hours of my stay in London, I put into activity every means of tracing her that my knowledge of London suggested, and the limited extent of my power made possible. The street where she had lodged I knew, but not the house; and I remembered at last some account which she had given me of ill treatment from her landlord, which made it probable that she had quitted those lodgings before we parted. She had few acquaintance; most people, besides, thought that the earnestness of my inquiries arose from motives which moved their laughter, or their slight regard; and others, thinking I was in chase of a girl who had robbed me of some trifles, were naturally and excusably indisposed to give me any clue to her, if, indeed, they had any to give. Finally, as my despairing resource, on

---

4. Echoing Wordsworth, *She was a Phantom of delight* (1807): "an Image gay, / To haunt, to startle, and way-lay" (9–10); and "Immortality" Ode: "those truths . . . / Which we are toiling all our lives to find, / In darkness

lost, the darkness of the grave" (115–17).
5. De Quincey left London for several months, first to get a loan, then to attend university. He arranged to meet Anne on his return.

the day I left London I put into the hands of the only person who (I was sure) must know Anne by sight, from having been in company with us once or twice, an address to —— in —— shire, at that time the residence of my family. But, to this hour, I have never heard a syllable about her. This, amongst such troubles as most men meet with in this life, has been my heaviest affliction.——If she lived, doubtless we must have been sometimes in search of each other, at the very same moment, through the mighty labyrinths of London; perhaps, even within a few feet of each other—a barrier no wider in a London street, often amounting in the end to a separation for eternity! During some years, I hoped that she did live; and I suppose that, in the literal and unrhetorical use of the word *myriad* [ten thousand], I may say that on my different visits to London, I have looked into many, many myriads of female faces, in the hope of meeting her. I should know her again amongst a thousand, if I saw her for a moment; for, though not handsome, she had a sweet expression of countenance, and a peculiar and graceful carriage of the head.——I sought her, I have said, in hope. So it was for years; but now I should fear to see her; and her cough, which grieved me when I parted with her, is now my consolation. I now wish to see her no longer; but think of her, more gladly, as one long since laid in the grave; in the grave, I would hope, of a Magdalen;[6] taken away, before injuries and cruelty had blotted out and transfigured her ingenuous nature, or the brutalities of ruffians had completed the ruin they had begun.

London Magazine, September 1821

Part II [1]

So then, Oxford-street, stony-hearted step-mother! thou that listenest to the sighs of orphans, and drinkest the tears of children, at length I was dismissed from thee: the time was come at last that I no more should pace in anguish thy never-ending terraces; no more should dream, and wake in captivity to the pangs of hunger. Successors, too many, to myself and Ann, have, doubtless, since then trodden in our footsteps—inheritors of our calamities: other orphans than Ann have sighed: tears have been shed by other children: and thou, Oxford-street, hast since, doubtless, echoed to the groans of innumerable hearts. For myself, however, the storm which I had outlived seemed to have been the pledge of a long fair-weather; the premature sufferings which I had paid down, to have been accepted as a ransom for many years to come, as a price of long immunity from sorrow: and if again I walked in London, a solitary and contemplative man (as oftentimes I did), I walked for the most part in serenity and peace of mind. And, although it is true that the calamities of my noviciate in London had struck root so deeply in my bodily constitution that afterwards they shot up and flourished afresh, and grew into a noxious umbrage that has overshadowed and darkened my latter years, yet these second assaults of suffering were met with a fortitude more confirmed, with the resources of a maturer intellect, and with alleviations from sympathising affection—how deep and tender!

Thus, however, with whatsoever alleviations, years that were far asunder were bound together by subtle links of suffering derived from a common root. And herein I notice an instance of the short-sightedness of human desires, that oftentimes on moonlight nights, during my first mournful abode in London, my consolation was

6. A repentant prostitute, from Mary Magdalene, follower of Jesus.
1. The first part was the 13th item in the September issue;

Part II was the opening piece in the next *London Magazine,* October 1821.

(if such it could be thought) to gaze from Oxford-street up every avenue in succession which pierces through the heart of Marylebone to the fields and the woods; for *that*, said I, travelling with my eyes up the long vistas which lay part in light and part in shade, "*that* is the road to the North, and therefore to ——, and if I had the wings of a dove, *that* way I would fly for comfort."[2] Thus I said, and thus I wished, in my blindness; yet, even in that very northern region it was, even in that very valley, nay, in that very house to which my erroneous wishes pointed, that this second birth of my sufferings began; and that they again threatened to besiege the citadel of life and hope. There it was, that for years I was persecuted by visions as ugly, and as ghastly phantoms as ever haunted the couch of an Orestes:[3] and in this unhappier than he, that sleep, which comes to all as a respite and a restoration, and to him especially, as a blessed[4] balm for his wounded heart and his haunted brain, visited me as my bitterest scourge. Thus blind was I in my desires; yet, if a veil interposes between the dim-sightedness of man and his future calamities, the same veil hides from him their alleviations; and a grief which had not been feared is met by consolations which had not been hoped. I, therefore, who participated, as it were, in the troubles of Orestes (excepting only in his agitated conscience), participated no less in all his supports: my Eumenides, like his, were at my bed-feet, and stared in upon me through the curtains: but, watching by my pillow, or defrauding herself of sleep to bear me company through the heavy watches of the night, sate my Electra: for thou, beloved M.,[5] dear companion of my later years, thou wast my Electra! and neither in nobility of mind nor in long-suffering affection, wouldst permit that a Grecian sister should excel an English wife. For thou thoughtst not much to stoop to humble offices of kindness, and to servile[6] ministrations of tenderest affection;—to wipe away for years the unwholesome dews upon the forehead, or to refresh the lips when parched and baked with fever; nor, even when thy own peaceful slumbers had by long sympathy become infected with the spectacle of my dread contest with phantoms and shadowy enemies that oftentimes bade me "sleep no more!"[7]—not even then, didst thou utter a complaint or any murmur, nor withdraw thy angelic smiles, nor shrink from thy service of love more than Electra did of old. For she too, though she was a Grecian woman, and the daughter of the king[8] of men, yet wept sometimes, and hid her face[9] in her robe.

But these troubles are past: and thou wilt read these records of a period so dolorous to us both as the legend of some hideous dream that can return no more. Meantime, I am again in London:[1] and again I pace the terraces of Oxford-street by night: and

---

2. Echoing David's Psalm 55, a plea for escape from the wicked city. The road north leads to Wordsworth.

3. Incited by his sister Electra, Orestes murders their mother, who conspired in the murder of their father; he was haunted by the Furies (the Eumenides).

4. φίλον ὕπνη θελητρον ἐπικερον νοσω [De Quincey's note]; "Dear spell of sleep, assuager of disease," Euripides *Orestes*, 211.

5. Margaret Simpson, with whom De Quincey lived before their marriage in 1817 (the first of their eight children was born in 1816). Electra was also a comforter and protector of Orestes.

6. ἡδὺ δλευμα. *Eurip. Orest.* [De Quincey's note]; "sweet slavery," paraphrasing *Orestes* 221.

7. After murdering King Duncan in his sleep, Macbeth tells Lady Macbeth, "Methought I heard a voice cry 'Sleep no more! / Macbeth does murder sleep'" (2.2.34–35).

8. ἄναξ ἀνδρων Ἀγαμεμνων [De Quincey's note]; "king of men, Agamemnon," is a frequent phrase in Homer's *Iliad*. A Greek general in the Trojan War, he is father of Orestes and Electra.

9. ὄμμα θεις᾽ ἐισω πεπλων ["covering her face with her robe," paraphrasing *Orestes* 280]. The scholar will know that throughout this passage I refer to the early scenes of the Orestes; one of the most beautiful exhibitions of the domestic affections which even the dramas of Euripides can furnish. To the English reader, it may be necessary to say, that the situation at the opening of the drama is that of a brother attended only by his sister during the demoniacal possession of a suffering conscience (or, in the mythology of the play, haunted by the furies), and in circumstances of immediate danger from enemies, and of desertion or cold regard from nominal friends [De Quincey's note].

1. Summer 1821, when De Quincey wrote *Confessions*.

oftentimes, when I am oppressed by anxieties that demand all my philosophy and the comfort of thy presence to support, and yet remember that I am separated from thee by three hundred miles, and the length of three dreary months,—I look up the streets that run northwards from Oxford-street, upon moonlight nights, and recollect my youthful ejaculation of anguish;—and remembering that thou art sitting alone in that same valley, and mistress of that very house to which my heart turned in its blindness nineteen years ago, I think that, though blind indeed, and scattered to the winds of late, the promptings of my heart may yet have had reference to a remoter time, and may be justified if read in another meaning:—and, if I could allow myself to descend again to the impotent wishes of childhood, I should again say to myself, as I look to the north, "Oh, that I had the wings of a dove—" and with how just a confidence in thy good and gracious nature might I add the other half of my early ejaculation—"And *that* way I would fly for comfort."

The Pleasures of Opium

It is so long since I first took opium, that if it had been a trifling incident in my life, I might have forgotten its date: but cardinal events are not to be forgotten; and from circumstances connected with it, I remember that it must be referred to the autumn of 1804. During that season I was in London, having come thither for the first time since my entrance at college. And my introduction to opium arose in the following way. From an early age I had been accustomed to wash my head in cold water at least once a day: being suddenly seized with tooth-ache, I attributed it to some relaxation caused by an accidental intermission of that practice; jumped out of bed; plunged my head into a bason of cold water; and with hair thus wetted went to sleep. The next morning, as I need hardly say, I awoke with excruciating rheumatic pains of the head and face, from which I had hardly any respite for about twenty days. On the twenty-first day, I think it was, and on a Sunday, that I went out into the streets; rather to run away, if possible, from my torments, than with any distinct purpose. By accident I met a college acquaintance who recommended opium. Opium! dread agent of unimaginable pleasure and pain! I had heard of it as I had of manna or of Ambrosia,[2] but no further: how unmeaning a sound was it at that time! what solemn chords does it now strike upon my heart! what heart-quaking vibrations of sad and happy remembrances! Reverting for a moment to these, I feel a mystic importance attached to the minutest circumstances connected with the place and the time, and the man (if man he was) that first laid open to me the Paradise of Opium-eaters. It was a Sunday afternoon, wet and cheerless: and a duller spectacle this earth of ours has not to show[3] than a rainy Sunday in London. My road homewards lay through Oxford-street; and near "the *stately* Pantheon," (as Mr Wordsworth has obligingly called it)[4] I saw a druggist's shop. The druggist—unconscious minister of celestial pleasures!—as if in sympathy with the rainy Sunday, looked dull and stupid, just as any mortal druggist might be expected to look on a Sunday: and, when I asked for the tincture of opium,[5] he gave it to me as any other man might do: and furthermore, out of my shilling, returned me what seemed to be real copper halfpence, taken out of a real wooden drawer. Nevertheless, in spite

---

2. Manna was food miraculously bestowed on the Israelites wandering in the wilderness (Exodus 16); ambrosia was food of the gods in Greek myth.
3. A parodic echo of Wordsworth's sonnet on London (see page 475).

4. Wordsworth, *The Power of Music* (3), pub. 1807; the Pantheon on Oxford Street hosted concerts, balls, exhibitions, and assemblies.
5. In this solution in alcohol, opium was called "laudanum" (Latin: "to be praised").

of such indications of humanity, he has ever since existed in my mind as the beatific vision of an immortal druggist, sent down to earth on a special mission to myself. And it confirms me in this way of considering him, that, when I next came up to London, I sought him near the stately Pantheon, and found him not:[6] and thus to me, who knew not his name (if indeed he had one) he seemed rather to have vanished from Oxford-street than to have removed in any bodily fashion. The reader may choose to think of him as, possibly, no more than a sublunary[7] druggist: it may be so: but my faith is better: I believe him to have evanesced,[8] or evaporated. So unwillingly would I connect any mortal remembrances with that hour, and place, and creature, that first brought me acquainted with the celestial drug.

Arrived at my lodgings, it may be supposed that I lost not a moment in taking the quantity prescribed. I was necessarily ignorant of the whole art and mystery of opium-taking: and, what I took, I took under every disadvantage. But I took it:— and in an hour, oh! Heavens! what a revulsion! what an upheaving, from its lowest depths, of the inner spirit! what an apocalypse of the world within me! That my pains had vanished, was now a trifle in my eyes:—this negative effect was swallowed up in the immensity of those positive effects which had opened before me—in the abyss of divine enjoyment thus suddenly revealed. Here was a panacea—a φαρμακον νη 'πενθες for all human woes:[9] here was the secret of happiness, about which philosophers had disputed for so many ages, at once discovered: happiness might now be bought for a penny, and carried in the waistcoat pocket: portable ecstacies might be had corked up in a pint bottle: and peace of mind could be sent down in gallons by the mail coach.

[THE LIVERPOOL REVERIE]

I often fell into these reveries upon taking opium; and more than once it has happened to me, on a summer-night, when I have been at an open window, in a room from which I could overlook the sea at a mile below me, and could command a view of the great town of L——, at about the same distance, that I have sate, from sun-set to sun-rise, motionless, and without wishing to move.

I shall be charged with mysticism, Behmenism,[1] quietism, &c. but *that* shall not alarm me. Sir H. Vane, the younger,[2] was one of our wisest men: and let my readers see if he, in his philosophical works, be half as unmystical as I am.—I say, then, that it has often struck me that the scene itself was somewhat typical of what took place in such a reverie. The town of L—— represented the earth, with its sorrows and its graves left behind, yet not out of sight, nor wholly forgotten. The ocean, in everlasting but gentle agitation, and brooded over by a dove-like calm,[3] might not

---

6. A parody of the Preacher's lament in Ecclesiastes over his futile search for earthly satisfaction (chs. 7 and 8).

7. Earthly (under the moon).

8. *Evanesced*:—this way of going off the stage of life appears to have been well known in the 17th century, but at that time to have been considered a peculiar privilege of blood-royal, and by no means allowed to druggists. For about the year 1686, a poet of rather ominous name (and who, by the bye, did ample justice to his name), viz. Mr *Flat-man*, in speaking of the death of Charles II, expresses his surprise that any prince should commit so absurd an act as dying; because, says he, "Kings should disdain to die, and only *disappear.*" They should *abscond*, that is, into the other world [De Quincey, paraphrasing *On the*

Death of King Charles II, a Pindaresque Ode, by Thomas Flatman (1637–1688)].

9. Nepenthe ("no grief," a "medicine of heartsease, free of gall, to make one forget all sorrows" (Homer, *Odyssey* 4.220–21), taken by Telemachus to ease his grief for his father Odysseus, presumed dead.

1. Jakob Boehme (1575–1624) argued that existence is defined by a conflict of opposites, ultimately resolved into unity.

2. Sir Henry Vane (1613–1662), Puritan and parliamentary leader during the English Civil Wars, wrote several works of mystical philosophy.

3. In *Paradise Lost*, Milton invokes the Spirit that at the Creation "dove-like satst brooding on the vast Abyss" (1.21).

unfitly typify the mind and the mood which then swayed it. For it seemed to me as if then first I stood at a distance, and aloof from the uproar of life; as if the tumult, the fever, and the strife, were suspended; a respite granted from the secret burthens of the heart; a sabbath of repose; a resting from human labours. Here were the hopes which blossom in the paths of life, reconciled with the peace which is in the grave; motions of the intellect as unwearied as the heavens, yet for all anxieties a halcyon calm:[4] a tranquillity that seemed no product of inertia, but as if resulting from mighty and equal antagonisms; infinite activities, infinite repose.

Oh! just, subtle, and mighty opium! that to the hearts of poor and rich alike, for the wounds that will never heal, and for "the pangs that tempt the spirit to rebel,"[5] bringest an assuaging balm; eloquent opium! that with thy potent rhetoric stealest away the purposes of wrath; and to the guilty man, for one night givest back the hopes of his youth, and hands washed pure from blood; and to the proud man, a brief oblivion for "Wrongs unredress'd, and insults unavenged";[6] that summonest to the chancery of dreams, for the triumphs of suffering innocence, false witnesses; and confoundest perjury; and dost reverse the sentences of unrighteous judges:—thou buildest upon the bosom of darkness, out of the fantastic imagery of the brain, cities and temples, beyond the art of Phidias and Praxiteles—beyond the splendour of Babylon and Hekatómpylos:[7] and "from the anarchy of dreaming sleep,"[8] callest into sunny light the faces of long-buried beauties, and the blessed household countenances, cleansed from the "dishonours of the grave."[9] Thou only givest these gifts to man; and thou hast the keys of Paradise, oh, just, subtle, and mighty opium!

[INTRODUCTION TO THE PAINS OF OPIUM]

Courteous, and, I hope, indulgent reader (for all *my* readers must be indulgent ones, or else, I fear, I shall shock them too much to count on their courtesy), having accompanied me thus far, now let me request you to move onwards, for about eight years; that is to say, from 1804 (when I have said that my acquaintance with opium first began) to 1812. The years of academic life are now over and gone—almost forgotten:— * * *

I am 250 miles away from it, and buried in the depth of mountains.[1] And what am I doing amongst the mountains? Taking opium. Yes, but what else? Why, reader, in 1812, the year we are now arrived at, as well as for some years previous, I have been chiefly studying German metaphysics, in the writings of Kant, Fichte, Schelling, &c.[2] And how, and in what manner, do I live? in short, what class or description of men do I belong to? I am at this period, viz. in 1812, living in a cottage; and with a single female servant (*honi soit qui mal y pense*[3]), who, amongst my neighbours, passes by the name of my "house-keeper." And, as a scholar and a man of learned education,

---

4. A blessed calm amid tumult; from the fable in Ovid's *Metamorphoses*: when Alcyone's husband perished in a shipwreck, she threw herself into the sea; the pitying gods changed them to halcyon birds and calmed the seas for a month each year so that they could nest. This paragraph has numerous echoes of *Tintern Abbey's* "city" paragraph.
5. Echoing the conclusion of Sir Walter Ralegh's *History of the World* (1614) ("O eloquent, just, and mighty Death!") and quoting the Dedication of Wordsworth's *White Doe of Rylstone* (line 36).
6. Part of a catalogue of the ills that drive one into retreat from the world, in Wordsworth's *Excursion* (3.374).
7. Phidias and Praxiteles: ancient Greek sculptors; Hekatómpylos was a name for Thebes, in Egypt.

8. In *The Excursion*, the Wanderer praises the "dread source" of everything, "Who from the anarchy of dreaming sleep . . . Restor'st us, daily, to the powers of sense / And reason's stedfast rule" (4.87–91).
9. A biblical phrase for the body, before the soul's release to Heaven (1 Corinthians 15.43).
1. In Dove Cottage, Grasmere, in the Lake District.
2. Leading German philosophers of the day, admired by De Quincey and Coleridge.
3. Shame to him who thinks (any) evil (of this), the motto of the knightly Order of the Garter, founded when a garter fell off a countess's leg as she was dancing with Edward III, who tied it to his leg, with this proclamation.

and in that sense a gentleman, I may presume to class myself as an unworthy member of that indefinite body called *gentlemen*. Partly on the ground I have assigned, perhaps; partly because, from my having no visible calling or business, it is rightly judged that I must be living on my private fortune; I am so classed by my neighbours: and, by the courtesy of modern England, I am usually addressed on letters, &c. *esquire*, though having, I fear, in the rigorous construction of heralds, but slender pretensions to that distinguished honour: yes, in popular estimation, I am X. Y. Z.,[4] esquire, but not Justice of the Peace, nor Custos Rotulorum.[5] Am I married? Not yet.[6] And I still take opium? On Saturday nights. And, perhaps, have taken it unblushingly ever since "the rainy Sunday," and "the stately Pantheon," and "the beatific druggist" of 1804?—Even so. And how do I find my health after all this opium-eating? in short, how do I do? Why, pretty well, I thank you, reader: in the phrase of ladies in the straw,[7] "as well as can be expected." In fact, if I dared to say the real and simple truth, though, to satisfy the theories of medical men, I *ought* to be ill, I never was better in my life than in the spring of 1812; and I hope sincerely, that the quantity of claret, port, or "particular Madeira," which, in all probability, you, good reader, have taken, and design to take, for every term of eight years, during your natural life, may as little disorder your health as mine was disordered by the opium I had taken for the eight years, between 1804 and 1812. * * *

But now comes a different era. Move on, if you please, reader, to 1813. In the summer of the year we have just quitted, I had suffered much in bodily health from distress of mind connected with a very melancholy event. This event, being no ways related to the subject now before me, further than through the bodily illness which it produced, I need not more particularly notice. Whether this illness of 1812 had any share in that of 1813, I know not: but so it was, that in the latter year, I was attacked by a most appalling irritation of the stomach, in all respects the same as that which had caused me so much suffering in youth, and accompanied by a revival of all the old dreams. This is the point of my narrative on which, as respects my own self-justification, the whole of what follows may be said to hinge. And here I find myself in a perplexing dilemma: Either, on the one hand, I must exhaust the reader's patience, by such a detail of my malady, and of my struggles with it, as might suffice to establish the fact of my inability to wrestle any longer with irritation and constant suffering: or, on the other hand, by passing lightly over this critical part of my story, I must forego the benefit of a stronger impression left on the mind of the reader, and must lay myself open to the misconstruction of having slipped by the easy and gradual steps of self-indulging persons, from the first to the final stage of opium-eating (a misconstruction to which there will be a lurking predisposition in most readers, from my previous acknowledgments.)

[A MALAY KNOCKS AT THE DOOR]

Strange as it may sound, I had a little before this time descended suddenly, and without any considerable effort, from 320 grains of opium (i.e. eight[8] thousand drops of

4. De Quincey's signature for essays in *London Magazine*.
5. "Keeper of the rolls."
6. He married Margaret in 1817.
7. In late pregnancy, a woman took to bed (straw mattress).
8. I here reckon twenty-five drops of laudanum as equivalent to one grain of opium, which, I believe, is the common estimate. However, as both may be considered variable

quantities (the crude opium varying much in strength, and the tincture still more), I suppose that no infinitesimal accuracy can be had in such a calculation. Tea-spoons vary as much in size as opium in strength. Small ones hold about 100 drops: so that 8000 drops are about eighty times a tea-spoonful. The reader sees how much I kept within Dr Buchan's indulgent allowance [De Quincey, citing Buchan's *Domestic Medicine*, a standard household text].

laudanum) per day, to forty grains, or one eighth part. Instantaneously, and as if by magic, the cloud of profoundest melancholy which rested upon my brain, like some black vapours that I have seen roll away from the summits of mountains, drew off in one day (νυχθη 'μερον [twenty-four hours]); passed off with its murky banners as simultaneously as a ship that has been stranded, and is floated off by a spring tide—

That moveth altogether, if it move at all.[9]

Now, then, I was again happy: I now took only 1000 drops of laudamum per day: and what was that? A latter spring had come to close up the season of youth: my brain performed its functions as healthily as ever before: I read Kant again; and again I understood him, or fancied that I did. Again my feelings of pleasure expanded themselves to all around me: and if any man from Oxford or Cambridge, or from neither had been announced to me in my unpretending cottage, I should have welcomed him with as sumptuous a reception as so poor a man could offer. Whatever else was wanting to a wise man's happiness,—of laudanum I would have given him as much as he wished, and in a golden cup. And, by the way, now that I speak of giving laudanum away, I remember, about this time, a little incident, which I mention, because, trifling as it was, the reader will soon meet it again in my dreams, which it influenced more fearfully than could be imagined. One day a Malay knocked at my door. What business a Malay could have to transact amongst English mountains, I cannot conjecture: but possibly he was on his road to a seaport about forty miles distant.

The servant who opened the door to him was a young girl born and bred amongst the mountains, who had never seen an Asiatic dress of any sort: his turban, therefore, confounded her not a little: and, as it turned out, that his attainments in English were exactly of the same extent as hers in the Malay, there seemed to be an impassable gulph fixed between all communication of ideas, if either party had happened to possess any. In this dilemma, the girl, recollecting the reputed learning of her master (and, doubtless, giving me credit for a knowledge of all the languages of the earth, besides, perhaps, a few of the lunar ones), came and gave me to understand that there was a sort of demon below, whom she clearly imagined that my art could exorcise from the house. I did not immediately go down: but, when I did, the group which presented itself, arranged as it was by accident, though not very elaborate, took hold of my fancy and my eye in a way that none of the statuesque attitudes exhibited in the ballets at the Opera House, though so ostentatiously complex, had ever done. In a cottage kitchen, but panelled on the wall with dark wood that from age and rubbing resembled oak, and looking more like a rustic hall of entrance than a kitchen, stood the Malay—his turban and loose trowsers of dingy white relieved upon the dark panelling: he had placed himself nearer to the girl than she seemed to relish; though her native spirit of mountain intrepidity contended with the feeling of simple awe which her countenance expressed as she gazed upon the tiger-cat before her. And a more striking picture there could not be imagined, than the beautiful English face of the girl; and its exquisite fairness, together with her erect and independent attitude, contrasted with the sallow and bilious skin of the Malay, enamelled or veneered with mahogany, by marine air, his small, fierce, restless eyes, thin lips, slavish gestures and adorations. Half-hidden by the ferocious looking Malay, was a

9. Wordsworth, *Resolution and Independence* (77).

little child from a neighbouring cottage who had crept in after him, and was now in the act of reverting its head, and gazing upwards at the turban and the fiery eyes beneath it, whilst with one hand he caught at the dress of the young woman for protection. My knowledge of the Oriental tongues is not remarkably extensive, being indeed confined to two words—the Arabic word for barley, and the Turkish for opium (madjoon), which I have learnt from Anastasius.[1] And, as I had neither a Malay dictionary, nor even Adelung's *Mithridates*,[2] which might have helped me to a few words, I addressed him in some lines from the Iliad; considering that, of such languages as I possessed, Greek, in point of longitude, came geographically nearest to an Oriental one. He worshipped[3] me in a most devout manner, and replied in what I suppose was Malay. In this way I saved my reputation with my neighbours: for the Malay had no means of betraying the secret. He lay down upon the floor for about an hour, and then pursued his journey. On his departure, I presented him with a piece of opium. To him, as an Orientalist, I concluded that opium must be familiar: and the expression of his face convinced me that it was. Nevertheless, I was struck with some little consternation when I saw him suddenly raise his hand to his mouth, and (in the school-boy phrase) bolt the whole, divided into three pieces, at one mouthful. The quantity was enough to kill three dragoons and their horses: and I felt some alarm for the poor creature: but what could be done? I had given him the opium in compassion for his solitary life, on recollecting that if he had travelled on foot from London, it must be nearly three weeks since he could have exchanged a thought with any human being. I could not think of violating the laws of hospitality, by having him seized and drenched with an emetic, and thus frightening him into a notion that we were going to sacrifice him to some English idol. No: there was clearly no help for it:—he took his leave: and for some days I felt anxious: but as I never heard of any Malay being found dead, I became convinced that he was used to opium:[4] and that I must have done him the service I designed, by giving him one night of respite from the pains of wandering.

This incident I have digressed to mention, because this Malay (partly from the picturesque exhibition he assisted to frame, partly from the anxiety I connected with his image for some days) fastened afterwards upon my dreams, and brought other Malays with him worse than himself, that ran "a-muck"[5] at me, and led me into a world of troubles.—

["A Picture of the Opium-Eater at Home"]

Paint me, then, a room seventeen feet by twelve, and not more than seven and a half feet high. This, reader, is somewhat ambitiously styled, in my family, the

1. Popular novel by Thomas Hope (1819), which De Quincey said promulgated a "grievous misrepresentation" of the effects of opium.
2. *Mithridate, or The Universal Table of Languages*, a dictionary and treatise on Asiatic languages, by German philologist J. C. Adelung (1732–1806).
3. Bowed to.
4. This, however, is not a necessary conclusion; the varieties of effect produced by opium on different constitutions are infinite. A London Magistrate (Harriott's *Struggles through Life*, vol. iii, p. 391, Third Edition), has recorded that, on the first occasion of his trying laudanum for the gout, he took *forty* drops, the next night

sixty, and on the fifth night *eighty*, without any effect whatever: and this at an advanced age. I have an anecdote from a country surgeon, however, which sinks Mr Harriott's case into a trifle; and in my projected medical treatise on opium, which I will publish, provided the College of Surgeons will pay me for enlightening their benighted understandings upon this subject, I will relate it; but it is far too good a story to be published gratis [De Quincey's note].
5. See the common accounts in any Eastern traveller or voyager of the frantic excesses committed by Malays who have taken opium, or are reduced to desperation by ill luck at gambling [De Quincey's note].

drawing-room: but, being contrived "a double debt to pay"[6] it is also, and more justly, termed the library; for it happens that books are the only article of property in which I am richer than my neighbours. Of these, I have about five thousand, collected gradually since my eighteenth year. Therefore, painter, put as many as you can into this room. Make it populous with books: and, furthermore, paint me a good fire; and furniture, plain and modest, befitting the unpretending cottage of a scholar. And near the fire, paint me a tea-table; and (as it is clear that no creature can come to see one such a stormy night,) place only two cups and saucers on the tea-tray; and, if you know how to paint such a thing symbolically or otherwise, paint me an eternal tea-pot—eternal à *parte ante* [from the part before] and à *parte post* [after]; for I usually drink tea from eight o'clock at night to four o'clock in the morning. And, as it is very unpleasant to make tea, or to pour it out for oneself, paint me a lovely young woman, sitting at the table. Paint her arms like Aurora's, and her smiles like Hebe's:—But not, dear M.,[7] not even in jest let me insinuate that thy power to illuminate my cottage rests upon a tenure so perishable as mere personal beauty; or that the witchcraft of angelic smiles lies within the empire of any earthly pencil. Pass, then, my good painter, to something more within its power: and the next article brought forward should naturally be myself—a picture of the Opium-eater, with his "little golden receptacle of the pernicious drug,"[8] lying beside him on the table. As to the opium, I have no objection to see a picture of *that*, though I would rather see the original: you may paint it, if you choose; but I apprize you, that no "little" receptacle would, even in 1816, answer my purpose, who was at a distance from the "stately Pantheon," and all druggists (mortal or otherwise). No: you may as well paint the real receptacle, which was not of gold, but of glass, and as much like a wine-decanter as possible. Into this you may put a quart of ruby-colored laudanum: that, and a book of German metaphysics placed by its side, will sufficiently attest my being in the neighbourhood; but, as to myself,—there I demur. I admit that, naturally, I ought to occupy the foreground of the picture; that being the hero of the piece, or (if you choose) the criminal at the bar, my body should be had into court. This seems reasonable: but why should I confess, on this point, to a painter? or why confess at all? If the public (into whose private ear I am confidentially whispering my confessions, and not into my painter's) should chance to have framed some agreeable picture for itself, of the Opium-eater's exterior,—should have ascribed to him, romantically, an elegant person, or a handsome face, why should I barbarously tear from it so pleasing a delusion—pleasing both to the public and to me? No: paint me, if at all, according to your own fancy: and, as a painter's fancy should teem with beautiful creations, I cannot fail, in that way, to be a gainer. And now, reader, we have run through all the ten categories of my condition, as it stood about 1816–17: up to the middle of which latter year I judge myself to have been a happy man: and the elements of that happiness I have endeavoured to place before you, in the above sketch of the interior of a scholar's library, in a cottage among the mountains, on a stormy winter evening.

But now farewell—a long farewell to happiness—winter or summer! farewell to smiles and laughter! farewell to peace of mind! farewell to hope and to tranquil dreams, and to the blessed consolations of sleep![9] for more than three years and a half

---

6. Oliver Goldsmith, *The Deserted Village* (1770): the schoolmaster's chest "contrived a double debt to pay, / A bed by night, a chest of drawers by day" (229–30).
7. Margaret; Aurora is the Roman goddess of the dawn;

Hebe is the Greek goddess of youth.
8. A mocking quotation from Hope's *Anastasius*.
9. Echoing Macbeth's "Sleep no more!" (2.2.35) and Othello's farewell to peace of mind (3.3.344–54).

I am summoned away from these: I am now arrived at an Iliad of woes: for I have now to record

THE PAINS OF OPIUM

—as when some great painter dips
His pencil in the gloom of earthquake and eclipse.

Shelley's Revolt of Islam[1]

Reader, who have thus far accompanied me, I must request your attention to a brief explanatory note on three points:

1. For several reasons, I have not been able to compose the notes for this part of my narrative into any regular and connected shape. I give the notes disjointed as I find them, or have now drawn them up from memory. Some of them point to their own date; some I have dated; and some are undated. Whenever it could answer my purpose to transplant them from the natural or chronological order, I have not scrupled to do so. Sometimes I speak in the present, sometimes in the past tense. Few of the notes, perhaps, were written exactly at the period of time to which they relate; but this can little affect their accuracy; as the impressions were such that they can never fade from my mind. Much has been omitted. I could not, without effort, constrain myself to the task of either recalling, or constructing into a regular narrative, the whole burthen of horrors which lies upon my brain. This feeling partly I plead in excuse, and partly that I am now in London, and am a helpless sort of person, who cannot even arrange his own papers without assistance; and I am separated from the hands which are wont to perform for me the offices of an amanuensis.[2]

2. You will think, perhaps, that I am too confidential and communicative of my own private history. It may be so. But my way of writing is rather to think aloud, and follow my own humours, than much to consider who is listening to me; and, if I stop to consider what is proper to be said to this or that person, I shall soon come to doubt whether any part at all is proper. The fact is, I place myself at a distance of fifteen or twenty years ahead of this time, and suppose myself writing to those who will be interested about me hereafter; and wishing to have some record of a time, the entire history of which no one can know but myself, I do it as fully as I am able with the efforts I am now capable of making, because I know not whether I can ever find time to do it again.

3. It will occur to you often to ask, why did I not release myself from the horrors of opium, by leaving it off, or diminishing it? To this I must answer briefly: it might be supposed that I yielded to the fascinations of opium too easily; it cannot be supposed that any man can be charmed by its terrors. The reader may be sure, therefore, that I made attempts innumerable to reduce the quantity. I add, that those who witnessed the agonies of those attempts, and not myself, were the first to beg me to desist. But could not I have reduced it a drop a day, or by adding water, have bisected or trisected a drop? A thousand drops bisected would thus have taken nearly six years to reduce; and that way would certainly not have answered. But this is a common mistake of those who know nothing of opium experimentally; I appeal to those who

1. Describing the face of a scornful king (5.23).   2. Secretary.

do, whether it is not always found that down to a certain point it can be reduced with ease and even pleasure, but that, after that point, further reduction causes intense suffering.

[OPIUM DREAMS]

I now pass to what is the main subject of these latter confessions, to the history and journal of what took place in my dreams; for these were the immediate and proximate cause of my acutest suffering.

The first notice I had of any important change going on in this part of my physical economy, was from the re-awakening of a state of eye generally incident to childhood, or exalted states of irritability. I know not whether my reader is aware that many children, perhaps most, have a power of painting, as it were, upon the darkness, all sorts of phantoms; in some, that power is simply a mechanic affection of the eye; others have a voluntary, or a semi-voluntary power to dismiss or to summon them; or, as a child once said to me when I questioned him on this matter, "I can tell them to go, and they go; but sometimes they come, when I don't tell them to come." Whereupon I told him that he had almost as unlimited a command over apparitions, as a Roman centurion over his soldiers.—In the middle of 1817, I think it was, that this faculty became positively distressing to me: at night, when I lay awake in bed, vast processions passed along in mournful pomp; friezes of never-ending stories, that to my feelings were as sad and solemn as if they were stories drawn from times before Oedipus or Priam—before Tyre—before Memphis. And, at the same time, a corresponding change took place in my dreams; a theatre seemed suddenly opened and lighted up within my brain, which presented nightly spectacles of more than earthly splendour. And the four following facts may be mentioned, as noticeable at this time:

1. That, as the creative state of the eye increased, a sympathy seemed to arise between the waking and the dreaming states of the brain in one point—that whatsoever I happened to call up and to trace by a voluntary act upon the darkness was very apt to transfer itself to my dreams; so that I feared to exercise this faculty; for, as Midas turned all things to gold, that yet baffled his hopes and defrauded his human desires, so whatsoever things capable of being visually represented I did but think of in the darkness, immediately shaped themselves into phantoms of the eye; and, by a process apparently no less inevitable, when thus once traced in faint and visionary colours, like writings in sympathetic ink,[3] they were drawn out by the fierce chemistry of my dreams, into insufferable splendour that fretted my heart.

2. For this, and all other changes in my dreams, were accompanied by deep-seated anxiety and gloomy melancholy, such as are wholly incommunicable by words. I seemed every night to descend, not metaphorically, but literally to descend, into chasms and sunless abysses, depths below depths, from which it seemed hopeless that I could ever re-ascend. Nor did I, by waking, feel that I *had* re-ascended. This I do not dwell upon; because the state of gloom which attended these gorgeous spectacles, amounting at last to utter darkness, as of some suicidal despondency, cannot be approached by words.

3. The sense of space, and in the end, the sense of time, were both powerfully affected. Buildings, landscapes, &c. were exhibited in proportions so vast as the bodily

---

3. A clear ink that colors when heated.

eye is not fitted to receive. Space swelled, and was amplified to an extent of unutterable infinity. This, however, did not disturb me so much as the vast expansion of time; I sometimes seemed to have lived for 70 or 100 years in one night; nay, sometimes had feelings representative of a millennium passed in that time, or, however, of a duration far beyond the limits of any human experience.

4. The minutest incidents of childhood, or forgotten scenes of later years, were often revived: I could not be said to recollect them; for if I had been told of them when waking, I should not have been able to acknowledge them as parts of my past experience. But placed as they were before me, in dreams like intuitions, and clothed in all their evanescent circumstances and accompanying feelings. I *recognised* them instantaneously. I was once told by a near relative of mine,[4] that having in her childhood fallen into a river, and being on the very verge of death but for the critical assistance which reached her, she saw in a moment her whole life, in its minutest incidents, arrayed before her simultaneously as in a mirror; and she had a faculty developed as suddenly for comprehending the whole and every part. This, from some opium experiences of mine, I can believe; I have, indeed, seen the same thing asserted twice in modern books,[5] and accompanied by a remark which I am convinced is true; viz. that the dread book of account, which the Scriptures speak of,[6] is, in fact, the mind itself of each individual. Of this at least, I feel assured, that there is no such thing as forgetting possible to the mind; a thousand accidents may, and will interpose a veil between our present consciousness and the secret inscriptions on the mind; accidents of the same sort will also rend away this veil; but alike, whether veiled or unveiled, the inscription remains for ever; just as the stars seem to withdraw before the common light of day, whereas, in fact, we all know that it is the light which is drawn over them as a veil—and that they are waiting to be revealed when the obscuring daylight shall have withdrawn.

[PIRANESI'S DREAMS]

Many years ago, when I was looking over Piranesi's Antiquities of Rome, Mr. Coleridge, who was standing by, described to me a set of plates by that artist, called his *Dreams*,[7] and which record the scenery of his own visions during the delirium of a fever. Some of them (I describe only from memory of Mr. Coleridge's account) represented vast Gothic halls: on the floor of which stood all sorts of engines and machinery, wheels, cables, pulleys, levers, catapults, &c. &c. expressive of enormous power put forth, and resistance overcome. Creeping along the sides of the walls, you perceived a staircase; and upon it, groping his way upwards, was Piranesi himself: follow the stairs a little further, and you perceive it come to a sudden abrupt termination, without any balustrade, and allowing no step onwards to him who had reached the extremity, except into the depths below. Whatever is to become of poor Piranesi, you suppose, at least, that his labours must in some way terminate here. But raise your eyes, and behold a second flight of stairs still higher: on which again Piranesi is perceived, but this time standing on the very brink of the abyss. Again elevate your

4. His mother.
5. Coleridge's *Biographia Literaria* (1817), and *Arcana Coelestria* (Heavenly Mysteries), 8 vols. 1749–1756, by Emanuel Swedenborg, 18th-century philosopher, mystic, and theologian.

6. The book of life from which final judgments are determined (Revelation 20.12).
7. The print-series *Carceri d'Invenzione* (Imaginary Prisons), pub. 1745 and 1761.

The gothic phantasmagoria described by Coleridge and dreamt of in De Quincey's opiumnightmares. Giovanni Battista Piranesi, Imaginary Prison No. 7 ("The Drawbridge"), 1761.

eye, and a still more aerial flight of stairs is beheld: and again is poor Piranesi busy on his aspiring labours: and so on, until the unfinished stairs and Piranesi both are lost in the upper gloom of the hall.—With the same power of endless growth and self-reproduction did my architecture proceed in dreams. In the early stage of my malady, the splendours of my dreams were indeed chiefly architectural: and I beheld such pomp of cities and palaces as was never yet beheld by the waking eye, unless in the clouds. From a great modern poet I cite part of a passage which describes, as an appearance actually beheld in the clouds, what in many of its circumstances I saw frequently in sleep:

> The appearance, instantaneously disclosed,
> Was of a mighty city—boldly say
> A wilderness of building, sinking far
> And self-withdrawn into a wondrous depth,
> Far sinking into splendor—without end!
> Fabric it seem'd of diamond, and of gold,
> With alabaster domes, and silver spires,
> And blazing terrace upon terrace, high
> Uplifted; here, serene pavilions bright
> In avenues disposed; there towers begirt

With battlements that on their restless fronts
Bore stars—illumination of all gems!
By earthly nature had the effect been wrought
Upon the dark materials of the storm
Now pacified; on them, and on the coves,
And mountain-steeps and summits, where unto
The vapours had receded,—taking there
Their station under a cerulean sky. &c. &c.[8]

The sublime circumstance—"battlements that on their *restless* fronts bore stars,"—might have been copied from my architectural dreams, for it often occurred.—We hear it reported of Dryden, and of Fuseli in modern times, that they thought proper to eat raw meat for the sake of obtaining splendid dreams: how much better for such a purpose to have eaten opium, which yet I do not remember that any poet is recorded to have done, except the dramatist Shadwell: and in ancient days, Homer is, I think, rightly reputed to have known the virtues of opium.[9]

To my architecture succeeded dreams of lakes—and silvery expanses of water:— these haunted me so much, that I feared (though possibly it will appear ludicrous to a medical man) that some dropsical state[1] or tendency of the brain might thus be making itself (to use a metaphysical word) *objective*; and the sentient organ *project* itself as its own object.—For two months I suffered greatly in my head,—a part of my bodily structure which had hitherto been so clear from all touch or taint of weakness (physically, I mean), that I used to say of it, as the last Lord Orford[2] said of his stomach, that it seemed likely to survive the rest of my person.—Till now I had never felt a head-ach even, or any the slightest pain, except rheumatic pains caused by my own folly. However, I got over this attack, though it must have been verging on something very dangerous.

The waters now changed their character,—from translucent lakes, shining like mirrors, they now became seas and oceans. And now came a tremendous change, which, unfolding itself slowly like a scroll, through many months, promised an abiding torment; and, in fact, it never left me until the winding up of my case. Hitherto the human face had mixed often in my dreams, but not despotically, nor with any special power of tormenting. But now that which I have called the tyranny of the human face began to unfold itself. Perhaps some part of my London life might be answerable for this. Be that as it may, now it was that upon the rocking waters of the ocean the human face began to appear: the sea appeared paved with innumerable faces, upturned to the heavens: faces, imploring, wrathful, despairing, surged upwards by thousands, by myriads, by generations, by centuries:—my agitation was infinite,— my mind tossed—and surged with the ocean.

May, 1818.

The Malay has been a fearful enemy for months. I have been every night, through his means, transported into Asiatic scenes. I know not whether others share in my

---

8. Wordsworth, *The Excursion* 2.834–51.
9. The passage about nepenthe in *The Odyssey*, to which he referred earlier. Dryden believed that diet was important to mental life. John Henry Fuseli (1741–1825), famous for his nightmare paintings, reportedly ate raw porkchops in hopes of inspiration. Thomas Shadwell,

Restoration dramatist and Poet Laureate, was chiefly remembered as the butt of Dryden's satires.
1. Bloating of tissues.
2. T. Horace Walpole, novelist, most famous for *The Castle of Otranto* (1764).

feelings on this point; but I have often thought that if I were compelled to forego England, and to live in China, and among Chinese manners and modes of life and scenery, I should go mad. The causes of my horror lie deep; and some of them must be common to others. Southern Asia, in general, is the seat of awful images and associations. As the cradle of the human race, it would alone have a dim and reverential feeling connected with it. But there are other reasons. No man can pretend that the wild, barbarous, and capricious superstitions of Africa, or of savage tribes elsewhere, affect him in the way that he is affected by the ancient, monumental, cruel, and elaborate religions of Indostan, &c. The mere antiquity of Asiatic things, of their institutions, histories, modes of faith, &c. is so impressive, that to me the vast age of the race and name overpowers the sense of youth in the individual. A young Chinese seems to me an antediluvian man renewed. Even Englishmen, though not bred in any knowledge of such institutions, cannot but shudder at the mystic sublimity of *castes* that have flowed apart, and refused to mix, through such immemorial tracts of time; nor can any man fail to be awed by the names of the Ganges, or the Euphrates. It contributes much to these feelings, that southern Asia is, and has been for thousands of years, the part of the earth most swarming with human life; the great *officina gentium* [workshop of nations]. Man is a weed in those regions. The vast empires also, into which the enormous population of Asia has always been cast, give a further sublimity to the feelings associated with all oriental names or images. In China, over and above what it has in common with the rest of southern Asia, I am terrified by the modes of life, by the manners, and the barrier of utter abhorrence, and want of sympathy, placed between us by feelings deeper than I can analyze. I could sooner live with lunatics, or brute animals. All this, and much more than I can say, or have time to say, the reader must enter into before he can comprehend the unimaginable horror which these dreams of oriental imagery, and mythological tortures, impressed upon me. Under the connecting feeling of tropical heat and vertical sun-lights, I brought together all creatures, birds, beasts, reptiles, all trees and plants, usages and appearances, that are found in all tropical regions, and assembled them together in China or Indostan. From kindred feelings, I soon brought Egypt and all her gods under the same law. I was stared at, hooted at, grinned at, chattered at, by monkeys, by paroquets, by cockatoos. I ran into pagodas: and was fixed, for centuries, at the summit, or in secret rooms; I was the idol; I was the priest; I was worshipped; I was sacrificed. I fled from the wrath of Brama through all the forests of Asia: Vishnu hated me: Seeva laid wait for me. I came suddenly upon Isis and Osiris:[3] I had done a deed, they said, which the ibis and the crocodile trembled at. I was buried, for a thousand years, in stone coffins, with mummies and sphynxes, in narrow chambers at the heart of eternal pyramids. I was kissed, with cancerous kisses, by crocodiles; and laid, confounded with all unutterable slimy things, amongst reeds and Nilotic mud.

I thus give the reader some slight abstraction of my oriental dreams, which always filled me with such amazement at the monstrous scenery, that horror seemed absorbed, for a while, in sheer astonishment. Sooner or later, came a reflux of feeling that swallowed up the astonishment, and left me, not so much in terror, as in hatred and abomination of what I saw. Over every form, and threat, and punishment, and dim sightless incarceration, brooded a sense of eternity and infinity that drove me

---

3. Brahma, Vishnu, and Shiva are Hindu deities; Isis and Osiris are ancient Egyptian deities.

into an oppression as of madness. Into these dreams only, it was, with one or two slight exceptions, that any circumstances of physical horror entered. All before had been moral and spiritual terrors. But here the main agents were ugly birds, or snakes, or crocodiles; especially the last. The cursed crocodile became to me the object of more horror than almost all the rest. I was compelled to live with him; and (as was always the case almost in my dreams) for centuries. I escaped sometimes, and found myself in Chinese houses, with cane tables, &c. All the feet of the tables, sophas, &c. soon became instinct with life: the abominable head of the crocodile, and his leering eyes, looked out at me, multiplied into a thousand repetitions: and I stood loathing and fascinated. And so often did this hideous reptile haunt my dreams, that many times the very same dream was broken up in the very same way: I heard gentle voices speaking to me (I hear every thing when I am sleeping); and instantly I awoke: it was broad noon; and my children were standing, hand in hand, at my bed-side; come to show me their coloured shoes, or new frocks, or to let me see them dressed for going out. I protest that so awful was the transition from the damned crocodile, and the other unutterable monsters and abortions of my dreams, to the sight of innocent *human* natures and of infancy, that, in the mighty and sudden revulsion of mind, I wept, and could not forbear it, as I kissed their faces.

June, 1819.

I have had occasion to remark, at various periods of my life, that the deaths of those whom we love, and indeed the contemplation of death generally, is (*caeteris paribus* [other things being equal]) more affecting in summer than in any other season of the year. And the reasons are these three, I think: first, that the visible heavens in summer appear far higher, more distant, and (if such a solecism may be excused) more infinite; the clouds, by which chiefly the eye expounds the distance of the blue pavilion stretched over our heads, are in summer more voluminous, massed, and accumulated in far grander and more towering piles: secondly, the light and the appearances of the declining and the setting sun are much more fitted to be types and characters of the Infinite: and, thirdly, (which is the main reason) the exuberant and riotous prodigality of life naturally forces the mind more powerfully upon the antagonist thought of death, and the wintry sterility of the grave. For it may be observed, generally, that wherever two thoughts stand related to each other by a law of antagonism, and exist, as it were, by mutual repulsion, they are apt to suggest each other. On these accounts it is that I find it impossible to banish the thought of death when I am walking alone in the endless days of summer; and any particular death, if not more affecting, at least haunts my mind more obstinately and besiegingly in that season. Perhaps this cause, and a slight incident which I omit, might have been the immediate occasions of the following dream; to which, however, a predisposition must always have existed in my mind; but having been once roused, it never left me, and split into a thousand fantastic varieties, which often suddenly reunited, and composed again the original dream.

I thought that it was a Sunday morning in May, that it was Easter Sunday, and as yet very early in the morning. I was standing, as it seemed to me, at the door of my own cottage. Right before me lay the very scene which could really be commanded from that situation, but exalted, as was usual, and solemnized by the power of dreams. There were the same mountains, and the same lovely valley at their feet; but the mountains were raised to more than Alpine height, and there was interspace far larger between them of meadows and forest lawns; the hedges were rich with white roses; and no living creature was to be seen, excepting that in the green church-yard there were cattle tranquilly reposing upon the verdant graves, and particularly round about the grave of a child whom I had tenderly loved,[4] just as I had really beheld them, a little before sun-rise in the same summer, when that child died. I gazed upon the well-known scene, and I said aloud (as I thought) to myself, "it yet wants much of sun-rise; and it is Easter Sunday; and that is the day on which they celebrate the first fruits of resurrection. I will walk abroad; old griefs shall be forgotten to-day; for the air is cool and still, and the hills are high, and stretch away to Heaven; and the forest-glades are as quiet as the church-yard; and, with the dew, I can wash the fever from my forehead, and then I shall be unhappy no longer." And I turned, as if to open my garden gate; and immediately I saw upon the left a scene far different; but which yet the power of dreams had reconciled into harmony with the other. The scene was an oriental one; and there also it was Easter Sunday, and very early in the morning. And at a vast distance were visible, as a stain upon the horizon, the domes and cupolas of a great city—an image or faint abstraction, caught perhaps in child-hood from some picture of Jerusalem. And not a bow-shot from me, upon a stone, and shaded by Judean palms, there sat a woman; and I looked; and it was—Ann! She fixed her eyes upon me earnestly; and I said to her at length: "So then I have found you at last." I waited: but she answered me not a word. Her face was the same as when I saw it last, and yet again how different! Seventeen years ago, when the lamp-light fell upon her face, as for the last time I kissed her lips (lips, Ann, that to me were not polluted), her eyes were streaming with tears: the tears were now wiped away; she seemed more beautiful than she was at that time, but in all other points the same, and not older. Her looks were tranquil, but with unusual solemnity of expression; and I now gazed upon her with some awe, but suddenly her countenance grew dim, and, turning to the mountains, I perceived vapours rolling between us; in a moment, all had vanished; thick darkness came on; and, in the twinkling of an eye,[5] I was far away from mountains, and by lamp-light in Oxford-street, walking again with Ann—just as we walked seventeen years before, when we were both children.

As a final specimen, I cite one of a different character, from 1820.

The dream commenced with a music which now I often heard in dreams—a music of preparation and of awakening suspense; a music like the opening of the Coronation Anthem,[6] and which, like *that*, gave the feeling of a vast march—of in-finite cavalcades filing off—and the tread of innumerable armies. The morning was come of a mighty day—a day of crisis and of final hope for human nature, then suf-fering some mysterious eclipse, and labouring in some dread extremity. Somewhere, I knew not where—somehow, I knew not how—by some beings, I knew not whom—a battle, a strife, an agony, was conducting,—was evolving like a great drama, or piece of music; with which my sympathy was the more insupportable from my confusion as to its place, its cause, its nature, and its possible issue. I, as is usual in dreams (where, of necessity, we make ourselves central to every movement), had the power, and yet had not the power, to decide it. I had the power, if I could raise myself, to will it; and yet again had not the power, for the weight of twenty Atlantics was upon me, or the oppression of inexpiable guilt. "Deeper than ever plummet sounded,"[7] I lay inactive.

---

4. Catherine Wordsworth, the poet's daughter and sub-ject of *Surprized by Joy* (page 590); De Quincey was es-pecially fond of her and devastated by her sudden death at age 4.
5. Paul's promise of the Resurrection: "In a moment, in the twinkling of an eye . . . the dead shall be raised incor-ruptible, and we shall be changed" (1 Corinthians 15.52).

6. Composed by Handel for George II's coronation in 1727 and used thereafter.
7. In Shakespeare's *Tempest*, King Alonso, believing his son perished in a shipwreck, feels driven to "seek him deeper than e'er plummet [plumb line] sounded / And with him there lie mudded" (3.3.101–2).

Then, like a chorus, the passion deepened. Some greater interest was at stake; some mightier cause than ever yet the sword had pleaded, or trumpet had proclaimed. Then came sudden alarms: hurryings to and fro: trepidations of innumerable fugitives, I knew not whether from the good cause or the bad: darkness and lights: tempest and human faces; and at last, with the sense that all was lost, female forms, and the features that were worth all the world to me, and but a moment allowed,—and clasped hands, and heart-breaking partings, and then—everlasting farewells! and with a sigh, such as the caves of hell sighed when the incestuous mother uttered the abhorred name of death,[8] the sound was reverberated—everlasting farewells! and again, and yet again reverberated—everlasting farewells!

And I awoke in struggles, and cried aloud—"I will sleep no more!"[9]

But I am now called upon to wind up a narrative which has already extended to an unreasonable length. Within more spacious limits, the materials which I have used might have been better unfolded; and much which I have not used might have been added with effect. Perhaps, however, enough has been given. It now remains that I should say something of the way in which this conflict of horrors was finally brought to its crisis. The reader is already aware (from a passage near the beginning of the introduction to the first part) that the opium-eater has, in some way or other, "unwound, almost to its final links, the accursed chain which bound him." By what means? To have narrated this, according to the original intention, would have far exceeded the space which can now be allowed. It is fortunate, as such a cogent reason exists for abridging it, that I should, on a maturer view of the case, have been exceedingly unwilling to injure, by any such unaffecting details, the impression of the history itself, as an appeal to the prudence and the conscience of the yet unconfirmed opium-eater—or even (though a very inferior consideration) to injure its effect as a composition. The interest of the judicious reader will not attach itself chiefly to the subject of the fascinating spells, but to the fascinating power. Not the opium-eater, but the opium, is the true hero of the tale; and the legitimate centre on which the interest revolves. The object was to display the marvellous agency of opium, whether for pleasure or for pain: if that is done, the action of the piece has closed.

However, as some people, in spite of all laws to the contrary, will persist in asking what became of the opium-eater, and in what state he now is, I answer for him thus: The reader is aware that opium had long ceased to found its empire on spells of pleasure; it was solely by the tortures connected with the attempt to abjure it, that it kept its hold. Yet, as other tortures, no less it may be thought, attended the non-abjuration of such a tyrant, a choice only of evils was left; and *that* might as well have been adopted, which, however terrific in itself, held out a prospect of final restoration to happiness. This appears true; but good logic gave the author no strength to act upon it. However, a crisis arrived for the author's life, and a crisis for other objects still dearer to him—and which will always be far dearer to him than his life, even now that it is again a happy one.—I saw that I must die if I continued the opium: I determined, therefore, if that should be required, to die in throwing it off. How much I was at that time taking I cannot say; for the opium which I used had been purchased for me by a friend who afterwards refused to let me pay him; so that I could not ascertain even what quantity I had used within the year. I apprehend, however, that I took it very irregularly: and that I varied from about fifty or sixty grains, to 150 a-day. My first task was to reduce it to forty, to thirty, and, as fast as I could, to twelve grains.

8. Milton's description of Sin in *Paradise Lost* (10.602).   9. Macbeth's guilty conscience (2.2.32–33).
Death is the son she conceived with her father Satan.

I triumphed: but think not, reader, that therefore my sufferings were ended; nor think of me as of one sitting in a *dejected* state. Think of me as of one, even when four months had passed, still agitated, writhing, throbbing, palpitating, shattered; and much, perhaps, in the situation of him who has been racked, as I collect the torments of that state from the affecting account of them left by a most innocent sufferer[1] (of the times of James I.). Meantime, I derived no benefit from any medicine, except one prescribed to me by an Edinburgh surgeon of great eminence, viz. ammoniated tincture of Valerian.[2] Medical account, therefore, of my emancipation I have not much to give: and even that little, as managed by a man so ignorant of medicine as myself, would probably tend only to mislead. At all events, it would be misplaced in this situation. The moral of the narrative is addressed to the opium-eater; and therefore, of necessity, limited in its application. If he is taught to fear and tremble, enough has been effected. But he may say, that the issue of my case is at least a proof that opium, after a seventeen years' use, and an eight years' abuse of its powers, may still be renounced: and that he may chance to bring to the task greater energy than I did, or that with a stronger constitution than mine he may obtain the same results with less. This may be true: I would not presume to measure the efforts of other men by my own: I heartily wish him more energy: I wish him the same success. Nevertheless, I had motives external to myself which he may unfortunately want: and these supplied me with conscientious supports which mere personal interests might fail to supply to a mind debilitated by opium.

Jeremy Taylor conjectures that it may be as painful to be born as to die:[3] I think it probable: and, during the whole period of diminishing the opium, I had the torments of a man passing out of one mode of existence into another. The issue was not death, but a sort of physical regeneration: and I may add, that ever since, at intervals, I have had a restoration of more than youthful spirits, though under the pressure of difficulties, which, in a less happy state of mind, I should have called misfortunes.

One memorial of my former condition still remains: my dreams are not yet perfectly calm: the dread swell and agitation of the storm have not wholly subsided: the legions that encamped in them are drawing off, but not all departed: my sleep is still tumultuous, and, like the gates of Paradise to our first parents when looking back from afar, it is still (in the tremendous line of Milton)

With dreadful faces throng'd and fiery arms.[4]

On the Knocking at the Gate in Macbeth[1]

From my boyish days I had always felt a great perplexity on one point in *Macbeth*: it was this: the knocking at the gate, which succeeds to the murder of Duncan, produced to my feelings an effect for which I never could account: the effect was—that it reflected back upon the murder a peculiar awfulness and a depth of solemnity: yet, however obstinately I endeavoured with my understanding to comprehend this, for many years I never could see *why* it should produce such an effect.——

---

1. William Lithgow: his book (Travels, &c.) is ill and pedantically written: but the account of his own sufferings on the rack at Malaga is overpoweringly affecting [De Quincey, referring to *Discourse of a Peregination in Europe, Asia and Affricke* (1614)].
2. An herbal sedative.
3. Jeremy Taylor, Anglican theologian; in 1856, De Quincey corrected the reference to the essay *Of Death* by

Francis Bacon (1561–1626): "to a little infant, perhaps, the one is as painful as the other."
4. Adam and Eve's last hellish view of the gates of Eden after their expulsion, *Paradise Lost* 12.641 ff.
1. This famous meditation on *Macbeth* 2.2–3, the morning after the Macbeths' murder of the king, appeared in *London Magazine*, 1823, titled, *Notes from the Pocket-Book of a Late Opium-Eater*, signed "X.Y.Z."

Here I pause for one moment to exhort the reader never to pay any attention to his understanding when it stands in opposition to any other faculty of his mind. The mere understanding, however useful and indispensable, is the meanest[2] faculty in the human mind and the most to be distrusted: and yet the great majority of people trust to nothing else; which may do for ordinary life, but not for philosophic purposes. Of this, out of ten thousand instances that I might produce, I will cite one. Ask of any person whatsoever, who is not previously prepared for the demand by a knowledge of perspective, to draw in the rudest way the commonest appearance which depends upon the laws of that science—as for instance, to represent the effect of two walls standing at right angles to each other, or the appearance of the houses on each side of a street, as seen by a person looking down the street from one extremity. Now in all cases, unless the person has happened to observe in pictures how it is that artists produce these effects, he will be utterly unable to make the smallest approximation to it. Yet why?—For he has actually seen the effect every day of his life. The reason is—that he allows his understanding to overrule his eyes. His understanding, which includes no intuitive knowledge of the laws of vision, can furnish him with no reason why a line which is known and can be proved to be a horizontal line, should not *appear* a horizontal line: a line, that made any angle with the perpendicular less than a right angle, would seem to him to indicate that his houses were all tumbling down together. Accordingly he makes the line of his houses a horizontal line, and fails of course to produce the effect demanded. Here then is one instance out of many, in which not only the understanding is allowed to overrule the eyes, but where the understanding is positively allowed to obliterate the eyes as it were: for not only does the man believe the evidence of his understanding in opposition to that of his eyes, but (which is monstrous!) the idiot is not aware that his eyes ever gave such evidence. He does not know that he has seen (and therefore *quoad* [as concerns] his consciousness has *not* seen) that which he *has* seen every day of his life.

But, to return from this digression,—my understanding could furnish no reason why the knocking at the gate in Macbeth should produce any effect direct or reflected: in fact, my understanding said positively that it could *not* produce any effect. But I knew better: I felt that it did: and I waited and clung to the problem until further knowledge should enable me to solve it.—At length, in 1812, Mr. Williams made his *début* on the stage of Ratcliffe Highway, and executed those unparalleled murders which have procured for him such a brilliant and undying reputation.[3] On which murders, by the way, I must observe, that in one respect they have had an ill effect, by making the connoisseur in murder very fastidious in his taste, and dissatisfied with any thing that has been since done in that line. All other murders look pale by the deep crimson of his: and, as an amateur[4] once said to me in a querulous tone. "There has been absolutely nothing *doing* since his time, or nothing that's worth speaking of." But this is wrong: for it is unreasonable to expect all men to be great artists, and born with the genius of Mr. Williams.—Now it will be remembered that in the first of these murders (that of the Marrs) the same incident (of a knocking at the door soon after the work of extermination was complete) did actually occur which the genius of Shakspeare had invented: and all good judges and the most eminent dilettanti [devotees] acknowledged the felicity of Shakspeare's suggestion as soon as it was actually realized. Here then

2. Lowest.

3. John Williams's series of lurid "hammer" murders at 29 Ratcliffe Highway, in a disreputable district of London, inspired De Quincey's darkly brilliant essay, *On Murder*

Considered as One of the Fine Arts (*Blackwood's Magazine*, 1827).

4. In the sense of devotee, admirer of an art.

was a fresh proof that I had been right in relying on my own feeling in opposition to my understanding; and again I set myself to study the problem: at length I solved it to my own satisfaction; and my solution is this. Murder in ordinary cases, where the sympathy is wholly directed to the case of the murdered person, is an incident of coarse and vulgar horror; and for this reason—that it flings the interest exclusively upon the natural but ignoble instinct by which we cleave to life; an instinct which, as being indispensable to the primal law of self-preservation, is the same in kind (though different in degree) amongst all living creatures; this instinct therefore, because it annihilates all distinctions, and degrades the greatest of men to the level of "the poor beetle that we tread on,"[5] exhibits human nature in its most abject and humiliating attitude. Such an attitude would little suit the purposes of the poet. What then must he do? He must throw the interest on the murderer: our sympathy must be with *him;* (of course I mean a sympathy of comprehension, a sympathy by which we enter into his feelings, and are made to understand them,—not a sympathy of pity or approbation).[6] In the murdered person all strife of thought, all flux and reflux of passion and of purpose, are crushed by one overwhelming panic: the fear of instant death smites him "with its petrific mace."[7] But in the murderer, such a murderer as a poet will condescend to, there must be raging some great storm of passion,—jealousy, ambition, vengeance, hatred,—which will create a hell within him; and into this hell we are to look.[8]

In *Macbeth*, for the sake of gratifying his own enormous and teeming faculty of creation, Shakspeare has introduced two murderers; and, as usual in his hands, they are remarkably discriminated: but, though in Macbeth the strife of mind is greater than in his wife, the tiger spirit not so awake, and his feelings caught chiefly by contagion from her,—yet, as both were finally involved in the guilt of murder, the murderous mind of necessity is finally to be presumed in both. This was to be expressed; and on its own account, as well as to make it a more proportionable antagonist to the unoffending nature of their victim, "the gracious Duncan," and adequately to expound "the deep damnation of his taking off,"[9] this was to be expressed with peculiar energy. We were to be made to feel that the human nature, *i.e.*, the divine nature of love and mercy, spread through the hearts of all creatures, and seldom utterly withdrawn from man,—was gone, vanished, extinct; and that the fiendish nature had taken its place. And, as this effect is marvellously accomplished in the dialogues and soliloquies themselves, so it is finally consummated by the expedient under consideration; and it is to this that I now solicit the reader's attention. If the reader has ever witnessed a wife, daughter, or sister, in a fainting fit, he may chance to have observed that the most affecting moment in such a spectacle, is *that* in which a sigh and a stirring announce the recommencement of suspended life. Or, if the reader has ever been present in a vast metropolis on the day when some great national idol was carried in funeral pomp to his grave, and chancing to walk near to the course through which it passed, has felt powerfully, in the silence and desertion of the streets and in the stagnation of ordinary business, the deep interest which at that moment was possessing the heart of man,—if all at once he should hear the death-like stillness broken up by the sound of wheels rattling away from the scene, and making known that the transitory vision was dissolved, he will be aware that at no moment was his sense of the complete suspension and pause in ordinary human concerns so full and affecting as at that moment when

5. *Measure for Measure*, 3.1.79–80, everyone "in corporeal sufferance finds a pang."
6. De Quincey later added a note to say that he means "the act of reproducing in our minds the feelings of another, whether for hatred, indignation, love, pity, or approbation."
7. Death scents his prey (*Paradise Lost*, 10.294; petrific: petrifying).
8. Satan's torment (*Paradise Lost* 4.75).
9. Macbeth's horror at his crime (3.1.66; 1.7.20).

the suspension ceases, and the goings-on of human life are suddenly resumed. All action in any direction is best expounded, measured, and made apprehensible, by reaction. Now apply this to the case in Macbeth. Here, as I have said, the retiring of the human heart and the entrance of the fiendish heart was to be expressed and made sensible. Another world has stepped in; and the murderers are taken out of the region of human things, human purposes, human desires. They are transfigured: Lady Macbeth is "unsexed";[1] Macbeth has forgot that he was born of woman;[2] both are conformed to the image of devils; and the world of devils is suddenly revealed. But how shall this be conveyed and made palpable? In order that a new world may step in, this world must for a time disappear. The murderers, and the murder, must be insulated—cut off by an immeasurable gulph from the ordinary tide and succession of human affairs—locked up and sequestered in some deep recess: we must be made sensible that the world of ordinary life is suddenly arrested—laid asleep—tranced—racked into a dread armistice: time must be annihilated; relation to things without abolished; and all must pass self-withdrawn into a deep syncope and suspension of earthly passion. Hence it is that when the deed is done—when the work of darkness is perfect, then the world of darkness passes away like a pageantry in the clouds: the knocking at the gate is heard; and it makes known audibly that the reaction has commenced: the human has made its reflux upon the fiendish: the pulses of life are beginning to beat again: and the re-establishment of the goings-on of the world in which we live, first makes us profoundly sensible of the awful parenthesis that had suspended them.

Oh! mighty poet!—Thy works are not as those of other men, simply and merely great works of art; but are also like the phenomena of nature, like the sun and the sea, the stars and the flowers,—like frost and snow, rain and dew, hail-storm and thunder, which are to be studied with entire submission of our own faculties, and in the perfect faith that in them there can be no too much or too little, nothing useless or inert—but that, the further we press in our discoveries, the more we shall see proofs of design and self-supporting arrangement where the careless eye had seen nothing but accident!

N.B. In the above specimen of psychological criticism, I have purposely omitted to notice another use of the knocking at the gate, viz. the opposition and contrast which it produces in the porter's comments to the scenes immediately preceding; because this use is tolerably obvious to all who are accustomed to reflect on what they read.

X. Y. Z.

["What is it that we mean by *literature*?"][1]

* * * In that great social organ, which collectively we call literature, there may be distinguished two separate offices that may blend and often *do* so, but capable severally of a severe insulation, and naturally fitted for reciprocal repulsion. There is first the literature of *knowledge,* and secondly, the literature of *power.* The function of the first is—to *teach;* the function of the second is—to *move:* the first is a rudder, the second an oar or a sail. The first speaks to the *mere* discursive understanding; the second speaks ultimately, it may happen, to the higher understanding or reason, but always *through* affections of pleasure and sympathy. * * * There is a rarer thing than truth, namely, *power* or deep sympathy with truth. A purpose of the same nature is answered by the higher literature, viz., the literature of power. What do you learn from Paradise Lost?

---

1. To harden herself to murder, Lady Macbeth invokes the spirits to "unsex" her (1.5.39).
2. The witches have promised that "none of woman born / Shall harm" him (4.1.80–81).

1. From a review (1848) of an edition of Pope's works published in 1847.

Nothing at all. What do you learn from a cookery-book? Something new, something that you did not know before, in every paragraph. But would you therefore put the wretched cookery-book on a higher level of estimation than the divine poem? What you owe to Milton is not any knowledge, of which a million separate items are still but a million of advancing steps on the same earthly level; what you owe, is *power*, that is, exercise and expansion to your own latent capacity of sympathy with the infinite, where every pulse and each separate influx is a step upwards—a step ascending as upon a Jacob's ladder from earth to mysterious altitudes above the earth.[2] *All* the steps of knowledge, from first to last, carry you further on the same plane, but could never raise you one foot above your ancient level of earth: whereas, the very *first* step in power is a flight—is an ascending into another element where earth is forgotten.

Were it not that human sensibilities are ventilated and continually called out into exercise by the great phenomena of infancy, or of real life as it moves through chance and change, or of literature as it recombines these elements in the mimicries of poetry, romance, &c., it is certain that, like any animal power or muscular energy falling into disuse, all such sensibilities would gradually droop and dwindle. It is in relation to these great *moral* capacities of man that the literature of power, as contradistinguished from that of knowledge, lives and has its field of action. It is concerned with what is highest in man: for the Scriptures themselves never condescended to deal by suggestion or co-operation, with the mere discursive understanding: when speaking of man in his intellectual capacity, the Scriptures speak not of the understanding, but of "*the understanding heart*,"—making the heart, *i.e.* the great *intuitive* (or non-discursive) organ, to be the interchangeable formula for man in his highest state of capacity for the infinite.[3] Tragedy, romance, fairy tale, or epopee [epic], all alike restore to man's mind the ideals of justice, of hope, of truth, of mercy, of retribution, which else (left to the support of daily life in its realities) would languish for want of sufficient illustration. What is meant, for instance, by *poetic justice?*[4]—It does not mean a justice that differs by its object from the ordinary justice of human jurisprudence; for then it must be confessedly a very bad kind of justice; but it means a justice that differs from common forensic justice by the degree in which it *attains* its object, a justice that is more omnipotent over its own ends, as dealing—not with the refractory elements of earthly life—but with elements of its own creation, and with materials flexible to its own purest preconceptions. It is certain that, were it not for the literature of power, these ideals would often remain amongst us as mere arid notional forms; whereas, by the creative forces of man put forth in literature, they gain a vernal life of restoration, and germinate into vital activities. The commonest novel by moving in alliance with human fears and hopes, with human instincts of wrong and right, sustains and quickens those affections. Calling them into action, it rescues them from torpor. And hence the pre-eminence over all authors that merely *teach*, of the meanest that *moves*; or that teaches, if at all, indirectly by moving. The very highest work that has ever existed in the literature of knowledge, is but a *provisional* work: a book upon trial and sufferance, and *quamdiu bene se gesserit* [as long as it

2. Jacob's dream in Genesis 28.12.
3. God grants Solomon's prayer for "an understanding heart" with which to rule his people (1 Kings 3.9–12); in *The Prelude* (which De Quincey had read), Wordsworth speaks of "occupation for the soul, / Whether discursive or intuitive" (13.111–12), echoing Raphael's lesson to Adam that "the soul" is animated by "reason, . . . Discursive, or

Intuitive" (*Paradise Lost* 5.486–88).
4. A term formulated by Thomas Rymer in the 17th century, for the obligation of literature to reward virtue and punish vice; by the 19th century, it had come to mean "merely fictional." De Quincey wants to resuscitate the ethical "ideal."

behaves itself]. Let its teaching be even partially revised, let it be but expanded, nay, even let its teaching be but placed in a better order, and instantly it is superseded. Whereas the feeblest works in the literature of power, surviving at all, survive as finished and unalterable amongst men. For instance, the *Principia* of Sir Isaac Newton was a book *militant* on earth from the first.[5] In all stages of its progress it would have to fight for its existence: 1st, as regards absolute truth; 2dly, when that combat is over, as regards its form or mode of presenting the truth. And as soon as a La Place,[6] or anybody else, builds higher upon the foundations laid by this book, effectually he throws it out of the sunshine into decay and darkness; by weapons won from this book he superannuates and destroys this book, so that soon the name of Newton remains, as a mere *nominis umbra* [shadow of a name], but his book, as a living power, has transmigrated into other forms. Now, on the contrary, the Iliad, the Prometheus of Æschylus,—the Othello or King Lear,—the Hamlet or Macbeth,—and the Paradise Lost, are not militant but triumphant for ever as long as the languages exist in which they speak or can be taught to speak. They never *can* transmigrate into new incarnations. To reproduce *these* in new forms, or variations, even if in some things they should be improved, would be to plagiarize. A good steam-engine is properly superseded by a better. But one lovely pastoral valley is not superseded by another, nor a statue of Praxiteles by a statue of Michael Angelo.[7]

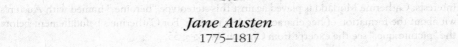

Jane Austen
1775–1817

Jane Austen was born the sixth of seven children; their father was an Anglican clergyman of a small village in Hampshire, where she lived until she was twenty-six. Aside from four years in Bath, she would spend her entire life in such a world. Her formal education (like that of most girls) ended at age nine, but her father continued to tutor her; by her teens, she was writing in earnest. She began a "History of England" and during the 1790s she drafted three novels. She had trouble getting a publisher, and had to issue *Sense and Sensibility* in 1811 at her own expense. She was to receive only modest sums thereafter—between £110 and £150. Before her publishing career emerged, she declined two proposals of marriage, choosing to stay at home and write. Aware of the strictures on women writers, Austen remained anonymous. The title page of *Sense and Sensibility* properly said "By a Lady"; *Pride and Prejudice* (1813) a little more pridefully said "By the Author of 'Sense and Sensibility,'" and both *Mansfield Park* (1814) and *Emma* (1816) were more proudly signed "By the Author of 'Pride and Prejudice,' &c. &c." The title-pages of the two novels published together posthumously in 1818, *Northanger Abbey* and *Persuasion,* were similarly signed. As the dates show, Austen's career of publication was scarcely longer than Keats's. Her international readership and ever new audiences through television and movies would have astonished Austen, whose idiom, by her own admission, was rather confined: "the little bit (two Inches wide) of Ivory on which I work with so fine a Brush" is "3 or 4 families in a Country Village . . . the very thing to work on."

5. *Philosophiae naturalis principia mathematica* (*Mathematical principles of natural philosophy*—i.e., science), by Isaac Newton (1687).
6. French astronomer and mathematician Pierre Simon La Place (1749–1827) confirmed Newton's hypothesis of gravitation.
7. Praxiteles: Greek sculptor, 4th century B.C.E.; Michelangelo (1475–1564): celebrated Florentine sculptor, painter, poet, and architect.

This "thing" is vividly presented by Austen: a world run on gossip and finely calibrated social codes—punctuated by dinners, teas, and suppers; dances and recitals; evenings of back-gammon and quadrille; afternoons of reading, letter writing, needlework; outings in chaises and barouche landaus. Its preoccupations are social status, land, property, and money; its residents seem full of leisure; in its parishes, manses, and estates, servants and laborers are nearly invisible and never complain. But this idiom is only deceptively narrow, for the deeper pulse is youth emerging into adulthood, surrounded by Austen's keen, critical, sometimes satirical commentary.

Austen vividly establishes these characters in broad social outlines and subtly revealing traits and tics, showing the world in which they move, act and desire, and the pressure points from which dramatic tensions and key developments will emerge. In the same way that some of *Paradise Lost* can be grasped in excerpts, Austen's first chapters are brief and finely nuanced narratives. Her famous first sentences bristle with deftly compacted signals: "It is a truth universally acknowledged, that a single man in possession of a good fortune must be in want of a wife"; "Emma Woodhouse, handsome, clever, and rich, with a comfortable home and happy disposition, seemed to unite some of the best blessings of existence; and had lived nearly twenty-one years in the world with very little to distress or vex her." Such sentences resemble poetic writing, in their concision, wit, and phrasing. Syntax, word choice, and authorial tone, often sift the seeds of future developments.

Not published until after Austen's death, *Northanger Abbey* was drafted between 1798 and 1803, at the height of the popularity of the gothic novel. Spoofing this genre, Austen is also working out what would become her own genre: a wry turn on the novel of female manners, a young woman finding her way in the world, choosing and mischoosing friends and romantic interests. Catherine Morland is played against this stereotype "heroine," framed with Austen's wit about the formation of her character by her reading. For Catherine's befuddlement before the "picturesque," see the excerpt from Chapter 14, page 55.

from Northanger Abbey, Chapter 1

No one who had ever seen Catherine Morland in her infancy would have supposed her born to be an heroine. Her situation in life, the character of her father and mother, her own person and disposition, were all equally against her. Her father was a clergyman, without being neglected, or poor, and a very respectable man, though his name was Richard—and he had never been handsome. He had a considerable independence besides two good livings—and he was not in the least addicted to locking up his daughters.[1] Her mother was a woman of useful plain sense, with a good temper, and, what is more remarkable, with a good constitution. She had three sons before Catherine was born; and instead of dying in bringing the latter into the world, as anybody might expect, she still lived on—lived to have six children more—to see them growing up around her, and to enjoy excellent health herself.[2] A family of ten children will be always called a fine family, where there are heads and arms and legs enough for the number; but the Morlands had little other right to the word, for they were in general very plain, and Catherine, for many years of her life, as plain as any. She had a thin awkward figure, a sallow skin without colour, dark lank hair, and strong features—so much for her person; and not less unpropitious for heroism seemed her mind. She was fond of all boy's plays, and greatly preferred cricket[3] not

1. A "living" is the residence and income from attached land, granted to a clergyman in exchange for his services. A daughter locked up by a father to prevent romantic escapades is a staple of 18th-century fiction, gothic and sentimental alike, famously in Samuel Richardson's *Clarissa* (1747–1748).

2. Death in childbirth, especially after bearing several children, was not uncommon in real life, and frequent in gothic novels.
3. A field game.

merely to dolls, but to the more heroic enjoyments of infancy, nursing a dormouse, feeding a canary-bird, or watering a rose-bush. Indeed she had no taste for a garden; and if she gathered flowers at all, it was chiefly for the pleasure of mischief—at least so it was conjectured from her always preferring those which she was forbidden to take. Such were her propensities—her abilities were quite as extraordinary. She never could learn or understand anything before she was taught; and sometimes not even then, for she was often inattentive, and occasionally stupid. Her mother was three months in teaching her only to repeat the "Beggar's Petition";[4] and after all, her next sister, Sally, could say it better than she did. Not that Catherine was always stupid— by no means; she learnt the fable of "The Hare and Many Friends"[5] as quickly as any girl in England. Her mother wished her to learn music; and Catherine was sure she should like it, for she was very fond of tinkling the keys of the old forlorn spinnet;[6] so, at eight years old she began. She learnt a year, and could not bear it; and Mrs Morland, who did not insist on her daughters being accomplished in spite of incapacity or distaste, allowed her to leave off. The day which dismissed the music-master was one of the happiest of Catherine's life. Her taste for drawing was not superior; though whenever she could obtain the outside of a letter[7] from her mother or seize upon any other odd piece of paper, she did what she could in that way, by drawing houses and trees, hens and chickens, all very much like one another. Writing and accounts[8] she was taught by her father; French by her mother: her proficiency in either was not remarkable, and she shirked her lessons in both whenever she could. What a strange, unaccountable character!—for with all these symptoms of profligacy at ten years old, she had neither a bad heart nor a bad temper, was seldom stubborn, scarcely ever quarrelsome, and very kind to the little ones, with few interruptions of tyranny; she was moreover noisy and wild, hated confinement and cleanliness, and loved nothing so well in the world as rolling down the green slope at the back of the house.

Such was Catherine Morland at ten. At fifteen, appearances were mending; she began to curl her hair and long for balls; her complexion improved, her features were softened by plumpness and colour, her eyes gained more animation, and her figure more consequence. Her love of dirt gave way to an inclination for finery, and she grew clean as she grew smart; she had now the pleasure of sometimes hearing her father and mother remark on her personal improvement. "Catherine grows quite a good-looking girl—she is almost pretty today," were words which caught her ears now and then; and how welcome were the sounds! To look almost pretty is an acquisition of higher delight to a girl who has been looking plain the first fifteen years of her life than a beauty from her cradle can ever receive.

Mrs Morland was a very good woman, and wished to see her children everything they ought to be; but her time was so much occupied in lying-in[9] and teaching the little ones, that her elder daughters were inevitably left to shift for themselves; and it was not very wonderful that Catherine, who had by nature nothing heroic about her, should prefer cricket, baseball,[1] riding on horseback, and running about the country at the age of fourteen, to books—or at least books of information—for, provided that nothing like useful knowledge could be gained from them, provided they were all

---

4. A poem by the Reverend Thomas Moss (1769).
5. A popular tale from John Gay's *Fables* (1727), about a hare deserted by his friends when pursued by hounds.
6. A common instrument (comparable to the harpsichord) popular in home parlors. Modest skill on such keyboard instruments was a prized female "accomplishment."

7. Instead of an envelope, a letter was sent in a paper wrapper, bearing the address.
8. Computation; minding a budget.
9. The last weeks of pregnancy.
1. Not yet the American pastime, but a forerunner.

story and no reflection, she had never any objection to books at all. But from fifteen to seventeen she was in training for a heroine; she read all such works as heroines must read to supply their memories with those quotations which are so serviceable and so soothing in the vicissitudes of their eventful lives.

From Pope, she learnt to censure those who

"bear about the mockery of woe."[2]

From Gray, that

"Many a flower is born to blush unseen,
And waste its fragrance on the desert air."[3]

From Thompson, that

———"It is a delightful task
To teach the young idea how to shoot."[4]

And from Shakespeare she gained a great store of information—amongst the rest, that

———"Trifles light as air,
Are, to the jealous, confirmation strong,
As proofs of Holy Writ."[5]

That

"The poor beetle, which we tread upon,
In corporal sufferance feels a pang as great
As when a giant dies."[6]

And that a young woman in love always looks

———"like Patience on a monument
Smiling at Grief."[7]

So far her improvement was sufficient—and in many other points she came on exceedingly well; for though she could not write sonnets, she brought herself to read them; and though there seemed no chance of her throwing a whole party into raptures by a prelude on the pianoforte, of her own composition, she could listen to other people's performance with very little fatigue. Her greatest deficiency was in the pencil—she had no notion of drawing—not enough even to attempt a sketch of her lover's profile, that she might be detected in the design. There she fell miserably short of the true heroic height. At present she did not know her own poverty, for she had no lover to portray. She had reached the age of seventeen, without having seen one amiable youth who could call forth her sensibility,[8] without having inspired one real passion, and without

2. Alexander Pope, *Elegy to the Memory of an Unfortunate Lady* (1717) 57. This and the following quotations parody a young lady's commonplace book (collections of extracts copied from books, for browsing and sharing).
3. Thomas Gray, *Elegy Written in a Country Churchyard* (1751) 55–56 (slightly miscopied).
4. James Thomson, *Spring* 1149–50, from *The Seasons* (1728).
5. Villain Iago, plotting to arouse Othello's jealousy; *Othello* 3.2.322–24.
6. Virtuous Isabella, comforting her imprisoned brother,

condemned to die for the "crime" of impregnating his fiancée before marriage; *Measure for Measure* 3.1.78–80.
7. Viola, disguised as a young man, telling the man for whom she has fallen of the plight of a young woman who "never told her love"; *Twelfth Night* 2.4.114–15.
8. Amiable youth: a sentimentalist's term (like "dreamboat"); the 18th-century cult of "sensibility" (excoriated by Wollstonecraft and Hannah More alike) promoted emotional sensitivity and expressiveness as a sign of refinement unsuited for, and implicitly superior to, what was needed to negotiate worldly life.

having excited even any admiration but what was very moderate and very transient. This was strange indeed! But strange things may be generally accounted for if their cause be fairly searched out. There was not one lord in the neighbourhood; no—not even a baronet. There was not one family among their acquaintance who had reared and supported a boy accidentally found at their door—not one young man whose origin was unknown.[9] Her father had no ward, and the squire of the parish no children.

But when a young lady is to be a heroine, the perverseness of forty surrounding families cannot prevent her. Something must and will happen to throw a hero in her way.

Mr Allen, who owned the chief of the property about Fullerton, the village in Wiltshire where the Morlands lived, was ordered to Bath for the benefit of a gouty constitution[1]—and his lady, a good-humoured woman, fond of Miss Morland, and probably aware that if adventures will not befall a young lady in her own village, she must seek them abroad, invited her to go with them. Mr and Mrs Morland were all compliance, and Catherine all happiness.[2]

✦ ═✧═ ✦

Maria Jane Jewsbury
1800–1833

Although Maria Jane Jewsbury herself was an aspiring young author, this sketch from her debut volume, *Phantasmagoria; or Sketches of Life and Literature* (1825), signed "M. J. J." (whom some reviewers took to be male), deftly satirizes the culture and its calculating aspirants. For more about Jewsbury, and another satire from *Phantasmagoria*, see Perspectives: The Sublime, the Beautiful and the Picturesque (page 56).

The Young Author[1]

Go! to your desks and counters all return!
Your sonnets scatter, your acrostics burn;
.   .   .   .
Alas what years you thus consume in vain,
Ruled by this wretched bias of the brain.

CRABBE.[2]

---

9. Stock situations in romance novels.
1. Gout is a painful inflammation of the small joints. Bath, a popular resort west of London dating back to Roman times, was famed for its curative waters. In Austen's day, it was a fashionable site for health, recreation, and romantic adventure; the Austen family lived there from 1801 to 1805. By 1818, however, it was losing its prestige as a high-end resort to Brighton.
2. For the rest of the novel, see the Longman Cultural Edition, edited by Marilyn Gaull.
1. This paper, as also the Arria, the Military Spectacle, and the Song of the Hindoo women, contained in these volumes appeared originally in Mr Alaric Watts's *Literary Souvenir* [MJJ's note; referring to the two-volume *Phantasmagoria*]. *Literary Souvenir*, edited by her friend

and encourager, Alaric Watts, was one of many annuals (elaborate, mass produced anthologies for gift-giving) to appear in the 1820s.
2. George Crabbe, *The Newspaper* (1785) 459–60, 457–58, with this headnote: "This not a Time favourable to poetical Composition: and why—Newspapers enemies to Literature, and their general Influence—Their Numbers—The Sunday Monitor—Their general Character—Their Effect upon Individuals—Society—in the Country—The Village Freeholder—What Kind of Composition a Newspaper is; and the Amusement it affords—Of what Parts it is chiefly composed—Articles of Intelligence: Advertisements: The Stage: Quacks: Puffing—The Correspondents to a Newspaper, political and poetical—Advice to the latter—Conclusion."

The young gentleman to whose performances this paper will be devoted, had the misfortune, in very early life, to discover that he was a genius (a piece of knowledge which most of us acquire *before*, and lose *after* we arrive at years of discretion); and, in consequence of this discovery, he very soon began to *train* as a literary character. "Link by link the mail was made,"[3] appears to have been his governing motto; for he wisely determined to be great amongst little things and little people, before he made his *début* among great ones. He accordingly commenced his career by reading every new novel—sporting every new opinion—circulating the cant of the most common-place critics—and adopting the pet phrases of the worst periodicals. He wrote in all the Albums, far and near, original verses on those original subjects, "Forget me not," and "Remember me";— recommended books to very young ladies, (kindly aiding their judgments in the discovery of fine passages);—quoted whole lines of Moore, and half lines of Byron,[4] during the intervals of a ball supper;—spoke Italian, knew a little of Spanish, and played on the German flute;—was a regular lounger at librar-ies;—could recognise authors by their style:—

> Had seen Sir Walter's head, Lord Byron's hat,
> And once with Southey's wife's third cousin sat;[5]—

was the oracle of the tea-table on every tea-table subject; and the arbitrator of all feminine disputes, respecting flowers and ribbons. The ladies (peculiarly happy in their efforts when any thing is to be spoiled) flattered him without mercy; some for his pretty face, and others for his pretty verses; whilst he, not to be outdone in folly and affectation, wrote acrostics for them, collected seals, invented mottos, drew pat-terns, cut out likenesses, made interest with his bookseller for the loan of the last new novel,[6]—and proved himself, in all points, "a more interesting young man."

These, it is true, were follies, but follies nevertheless, which a youth of even *real* talent might give into for two years, and be none the worse, if at the end of those two years he discarded them for ever. But it was not so with our present hero. Tired of the confined sphere in which he had hitherto moved, and the *little* great-nesses by which he had hitherto distinguished himself—from the bud of his former insignificance he suddenly burst forth into the glories of full-blown authorship. In an evil hour[7] (for his publisher) he favoured the world with a small volume of ama-tory poems, which by no means raised his fame with that large portion of society, who think that human life was intended for more important purposes than kiss-ing and crying; and that rational beings have something else to do than frisk like lambs, or coo like doves. As a "young author," he would have considered it very wrong to have been reasonable, or, to use his mother's phrase, "like other people"; and he accordingly adopted, all those eccentricities and affectations by which *little* geniuses endeavour to make themselves appear *great*. He became possessed (as if by magic) of nerves and sensibilities, and "thoughts too deep for tears," and "feelings all too delicate for use,"[8] and, unable of course, to endure any society but that of

---

3. The warrior's suit of linked metal; the quotation is from an old ballad.

4. Albums are blank-page books for collecting autographs and, if one were lucky, inscriptions of poetry or prose by authors of note. Byron was one of many poets to use the sentimental titles *Forget me not* and *Remember me*. *Forget Me Not* was also the name of another popular annual, first published in 1823. The sentimental poetry of Thomas Moore was often set to music (see page 408).

5. Referring to Sir Walter Scott, Lord Byron (whose portraits never show a hat), and the Poet Laureate, Robert Southey.

6. All female hobbies, of the sort lamented by Wollstone-craft; an acrostic is a rhyme in which the first letters of the lines, read vertically, spell out a name.

7. "her rash hand in evil hour / Forth reaching to the Fruit, she pluck'd, she eat" (*Paradise Lost* 9.780–81).

8. The last words of Wordsworth's "Intimations" Ode and a phrase from Coleridge's *Reflections on Having Left a Place of Retirement* (1795): "Was it right, / While my unnumber'd brethren toil'd and bled, / That I should dream away the entrusted hours / On rose-leaf beds, pampering the coward heart / With feelings all too delicate for use?" (44–48).

persons as refined and intellectual as himself. Then came "my study":—a repository of litter and literature, studiously *disarranged* for effect! Books, plays, pictures, newspapers, magazines, &c. covering the table and chairs, in most elaborate confusion! The large massy business-like looking desk, not merely loaded, but stuffed beyond the power of shutting, with MSS.;—"my proofs"[9] so *accidentally* scattered about the floor;—and letters from "my literary friends," left open on the table with so much *careless care:*—and the heaps of well-worn pens;—and the spattered inkstand;—and the busts of Milton and Shakspeare;—and the real skull stuck between bouquets of artificial flowers—and the pea-green walls hung round with portraits of living poets;—and the chimney-piece[1] covered with "contributions from my female friends"; and all the thousand theatrical affectations, by which the Tom Thumbs of literature strive to hide their native diminutiveness! And then the late hours,—(because Milton recommends lonely watching, and Schiller wrote his tragedies in the night,)—as our "young author" can do nothing in the day-time for "domestic annoyances," and he never joins the dinner-table, because the "children are so disgusting," but dines upon "one dry biscuit and a single glass of wine"; and drinks coffee for three hours afterwards, because it is "the only intellectual beverage";—and "composes aloud in his own room," (when he has any neighbours in the next); and "prepares himself for conversation"; and dislikes "feminine babble"; and "endures mirth rather than enjoys it," as his "dancing days are over," etc. etc. etc. Then comes the climax:—the pale and languid looks in public;—the "melancholy smile";—the little dry delicate cough, just to indicate "consumptive tendencies";—the alarm of mothers and matrons lest "his genius should kill him"; and the declarations of the young ladies, that he is "more inter*est*ing than ever!" Well! it is certainly a fine thing to be a "young author"! But he shall now speak for himself, in his own memoranda, a few of which are here transcribed from his pocket-book; and to those who may think this sketch of ineffable puppyism a caricature, I only say—*lisez et croyez!*[2]

"Mem:—'Determined,' as Bubb Dodington[3] says, 'to make some sort of figure in life'; what it will be I cannot pretend to say; I must look round me a little and consult my friends, but some figure I am resolved to make."

"Mem:—Miserable thing for genius to be born either after or before the age capable of appreciating it, as the chances of distinction diminish in exact proportion to the numbers who have already acquired, and the numbers who are now seeking to acquire it.—Eminent dead authors ought decidedly to be forgotten, and eminent living ones to give over writing, to leave room for rising 'men.' Young authors generally treated with gross injustice by their elder contemporaries, who dread being eclipsed. Public a great tyrant—unable to discover the violets of promise for the leaves of obscurity (to introduce this figure in conversation to-night); determined to distinguish myself in some way or other immediately."

"Mem;—To read over the Old Essayists, in order to see whether something may not be stolen from them and dressed up again—perfectly benevolent, since no one reads them now—have been most dreadfully overpraised. Pray what are the 'Specta-

9. Manuscripts and printed pages to be proofread.
1. Mantelpiece and chimney-covering.
2. *Read and believe!*
3. Bubb Dodington (1691–1762) was satirized by

Alexander Pope for his tasteless wealth and patronage in *Epistle to Dr. Arbuthnot* (1735) and *Epistle to Burlington* (1731).

tors,' the 'Tatlers,' the 'Idlers,' the 'Ramblers,'[4] and all the rest of those old-world things, but collections—

> Of tame trite truths, correct and common-place?

The present, decidedly, the golden age of intellect. Heard yesterday there were six poets in · · · · · · besides myself; the eldest not twenty-one!"

"Mem:—Agreed to contribute all the poetry for the · · · Magazine; to write theatrical critiques for the New Whig Paper; and employ the odds and ends of my time on a Tragedy-subject, either the Burning of Rome, or the Siege of Gibraltar.—Z. says I have very tragical turn of thought.—Astonishing how Z. improves upon acquaintance."[5]

"Mem:—Wrote yesterday six Sonnets in imitation of Milton's best—found it very easy. Parodied 'Auld Robin Gray'; and gave the 'Improvisatrice' a regular cutting up[6]—perfectly infamous for a woman to write, and write well; ought to be satisfied with reading what men write. Shall make a point of abusing every clever book written by a woman.

> Shut, shut the door, good John, fatigued, I said,
> Tie up the knocker, say I'm sick, I'm dead![7]

Wearied and overwhelmed with interruptions. Alas! the pains and penalties of a literary life! Must positively make some regulations to prevent such encroachments. Like Alfieri, open no letters of which I do not know the hand-writing. Write over my study door, 'Time is my estate';[8] deny myself to morning callers; and make my sister answer all notes."

"Mem:—Luncheons, except of dry biscuits, fatal to intellectual exertions; bottled porter the best beverage for a literary man; roasted mutton, taken in small portions, the best food to compose after."

"Mem:—Pensive, a good epithet to apply to the evening star."[9]

"Mem:—To beware of praising too much or too often: risked my character the other day by speaking well of B.'s poems. Must remember that it is more creditable to a person's taste to discover a fault than a beauty. Shenstone[1] said, good taste and good-nature were always united—meant fastidiousness."

"Mem:—To appear at Monday's ball without a neckcloth; to order an amethyst-coloured waistcoat; wear my arm in a sling, and sport bad spirits during the next week."

"Mem:—To fall in love without loss of time: deep blue downcast-looking eyes, not vulgarly happy,—'fond faint smile,'—'brow of alabaster';—must celebrate her under the name of Laura; my own (of course) Petrarch."[2]

"Mem:—'Wood-wail';—'wifeless';—'doubled echoes';—'my heart's queen';— 'last benefit last sorrow';—&c. &c. Phrases culled from old poems, to introduce

---

4. All prominent 18th-century periodicals.

5. Z is the signature of J. G. Lockhart, notorious scourge of "The Cockney School of Poetry" in *Blackwood's Edinburgh Magazine* (see page 982).

6. *Auld Robin Gray* is Anne Lindsay's widely admired ballad of love and longing (1776). *The Improvisatrice* (1824) was such a sensation that poet and novelist Laetitia E. Landon (already famed as L.E.L.) won this nickname, designating someone gifted with spontaneous and seemingly inexhaustible powers of poetic utterance—a performative mode popular in Italy.

7. The opening lines of *Epistle to Dr. Arbuthnot*.

8. Count Vittorio Alfieri (1749–1803) was a popular Italian

tragedian, champion of political liberty in America and Italy. The motto is from Goethe's fame-launching novel of the 1790s, *Wilhelm Meister's Apprenticeship*, recently translated by Thomas Carlyle (1824), whose life of Schiller (the dramatist mentioned above) appeared in *London Magazine* in 1823.

9. Already done by Milton, Wordsworth, and Walter Savage Landor, among many others.

1. William Shenstone, famously frustrated 18th-century poet, published only one juvenile volume, and left a manuscript unpublished at his death.

2. Italian Renaissance poet Francesco Petrarch addressed a famous set of sonnets and songs to his beloved Laura.

judiciously in my own. To bear this in mind whilst reading the old poets, in order to read them to profit."

"Mem:—Mrs. Radcliffe's 'Italian,'[3] vol. i. p. 173, contains a passage which may be turned into some touching Stanzas."

"Mem:—To annihilate Wordsworth in an article,[4] and offer my Autograph to Mr. ——— for his collection."

"Mem:—To get a 'Walker's Rhyming Dictionary';—no degradation:—Byron used one constantly. His 'Dream,' by the way, strikingly resembles my 'Vision,' received with so much applause at our 'Juvenile Literary Society,' myself in the chair."[5]

"Mem:—Determined to send Blackwood no more articles, particularly as he has inserted none of the last six; and told Z. it would be better to bind me to some good thriving *trade!*[6] A trade! bind myself to some little, low, paltry, sordid, shilling-scraping, penny-saving occupation, which would be as a benumbing blight upon all the powers of my mind! There is madness in the thought! Suppose Shakspeare had taken his relation's advice, and continued a wool-comber, where had been the world's poet? No! fired by this glorious example, I will calmly and proudly pursue the bent of my genius and inclination; the morning sun, and the midnight lamp, shall find me at my studies! I will write, though none may read; I will print, though none may purchase; and if the world's neglect canker my young spirit, and studious days and sleepless nights, 'sickly my brow with the pale cast of thought,' till, like 'Chatterton, the marvellous boy,'[7] I sink into an early and untimely grave!—how small the sacrifice: How glorious the reward! when the world for which I toiled becomes sensible of its injustice! and the marble monument and laurelled bust———"

"Mem:—Though prevented finishing the above peroration by the forcible entrance of two villanous duns[8]—a tailor and a washerwoman—may, nevertheless, introduce it as a soliloquy in my tragedy; for it possesses much of the sweep and swell of Burke."[9]

But trusting that the reader is more than satisfied with the foregoing specimens of folly and foppery, I here close the Young Author's Memorandum-book.

William Cobbett
1763–1835

William Cobbett was born in a rural district south of London, his father the proprietor of a tavern named "The Jolly Farmer." When he took his own son to see a sand-hill he had tumbled down as a boy, emerging with "hair, eyes, ears, nose, and mouth" full of sand, he declared, "if I had not received such an education . . . I should have been at this day as great

---

3. Extremely popular, best-selling gothic novel (1797), by Ann Radcliffe (1764–1823).

4. A bit belated; Wordsworth's sales fell off in the 1820s, though Jewsbury was a warm admirer, dedicating *Phantasmagoria* to him, and sending him a complimentary copy—a gesture that inaugurated their friendship.

5. The report about Byron's use of John Walker's *Rhyming Dictionary* (1775) is accurate; Byron jests about it in *Beppo* (1818): "I . . . take for rhyme, to hook my rambling verse on. / The first that Walker's Lexicon unravels" (52). *The Dream* is his poem on a lost love and a doomed marriage, published in 1816, in the wake of the scandal of his separation from Lady Byron and his permanent departure from England.

6. William Blackwood edited and published *Blackwood's Edinburgh Magazine*, which hosted poetry by Hemans and Jewsbury, among others. Z's ridicule of Keats's poetry ended with the advice that he was better off as an apothecary's apprentice (see page 987).

7. A phrase from Hamlet's famous suicide soliloquy (3.1.84) attached to Wordsworth's epithet for the young 18th-century poet who killed himself in despair of success (*Resolution and Independence* 43).

8. Bill collectors.

9. Edmund Burke (see page 113) was renowned for his oratory and rhetorical flourish.

a fool, as inefficient a mortal, as any of those frivolous idiots that are turned out from Winchester and Westminster School, or from any of those dens of dunces called Colleges and Universities." At fourteen Cobbett ran away from home; at twenty he enlisted as a soldier and went to Novia Scotia. He rose to sergeant-major but his protest against mismanagement in the army ended with his flight to France in 1792 and then to America, where he lived until 1800.

Cobbett's name is inseparable from his *Political Register*, founded in 1802 as a reactionary (anti-Jacobin) journal. While repeated experience of government corruption and a widening knowledge of laboring-class misery drove him to the forefront of the reformers, he was also prejudiced against Quakers, Jews, Methodists, Utilitarians, and the mercantile economy. Committed to the family as the center of personal and national happiness, Cobbett was conservative even in his unceasing demands for reform. He inveighed against the plight of industrial workers and was finally elected to Parliament from the manufacturing town of Oldham, but he insisted in the first issue of the *Register*, "We want *great alteration*, but we want *nothing new*." It was newness that was eroding the agrarian England Cobbett held dear. He furiously denounced THE THING, his term for the political monster of centralizing economy and expanding national debt, feeding the investors while heavily taxing the poor to whom it denied the vote. THE WEN, as Cobbett called London, was visible proof of this monster's triumph.

Cobbett was "not only unquestionably the most powerful political writer of the present day, but one of the best writers in the language," said Hazlitt, who deemed him a one-man "fourth estate." Francis Jeffrey admitted that the *Register*, which Cobbett produced single-handedly from 1802 to 1835, had acquired more influence than any previous journal upon "that most important and most independent class of society, which stands just above the lowest." When in 1816 Cobbett produced a two-penny version (to avoid the stamp tax), he reached "the lowest" as well. With a weekly circulation soaring to 50,000, the *Register* virtually brought into being the political consciousness of the working classes. Cobbett thus fruitfully contradicted the vision of a stable society he upheld. A self-made man, he owed his influence to his writing. At his death the London *Times* pronounced him "by far the most voluminous writer that has lived for centuries." Cobbett realized the potential of the new audiences, means of production, and systems of distribution that characterized the early nineteenth-century market. The era that literary historians denote as "English Romanticism" is one that social historians name "Cobbett's England"—at once the modern world of this market and the idealized rural society to which Cobbett appealed against modern corruptions and misery. In *Rural Rides* (1830), Cobbett the writer is Cobbett the rider, describing the landscape and transforming it into political argument.

Rural Rides
from Reigate (Surrey)

Friday, 8th August

At the end of a long, twisting-about ride, but a most delightful ride, I got to this place about nine o'clock in the evening. From Thursley I came to Brook, and there crossed the turnpike-road from London to Chichester through Godalming and Midhurst. Thence I came on, turning upon the left upon the sandhills of Hambledon (in Surrey, mind). On one of these hills is one of those precious jobs, called "*Semaphores*."[1] For what reason this pretty name is given to a sort of Telegraph house, stuck up at public expense upon a high hill; for what reason this outlandish name is given to the thing, I must leave the reader to guess; but as to the thing itself; I know that it

---

1. A network of towers built during the Napoleonic wars, permitting military communication by flag signals.

means this: a pretence for giving a good sum of the public money away every year to some one that the Borough-system has condemned this labouring and toiling nation to provide for. The Dead Weight of nearly about six millions sterling a year; that is to say, this curse entailed upon the country on account of the late wars against the liberties of the French people,[2] this Dead Weight is, however, falling, in part, at least, upon the landed jolterheads[3] who were so eager to create it, and who thought that no part of it would fall upon themselves. Theirs has been a grand mistake. They saw the war carried on without any loss or any cost to themselves. By the means of paper-money and loans, the labouring classes were made to pay the whole of the expenses of the war.[4] When the war was over, the jolterheads thought they would get gold back again to make all secure; and some of them really said, I am told, that it was high time to put an end to the gains of the paper-money people. The jolterheads quite overlooked the circumstance, that, in returning to gold, they doubled and trebled what they had to pay on account of the debt, and that, at last, they were bringing the burden upon themselves. Grand, also, was the mistake of the jolterheads, when they approved of the squanderings upon the Dead Weight. They thought that the labour-ing classes were going to pay the whole of the expenses of the Knights of Waterloo, and of the other heroes of the war. The jolterheads thought that they should have none of this to pay. Some of them had relations belonging to the Dead Weight, and all of them were willing to make the labouring classes toil like asses for the support of those who had what was called fought and bled for Gatton and Old Sarum.[5] The jolterheads have now found, however, that a pretty good share of the expense is to fall upon themselves. Their mortgagees are letting them know that *Semaphores* and such pretty things cost something, and that it is unreasonable for a loyal country gentleman, a friend of social order and of the "blessed comforts of religion" to expect to have Semaphores and to keep his estate too. This Dead Weight is, unquestionably, a thing, such as the world never saw before. Here are not only a tribe of pensioned naval and military officers, commissaries, quarter-masters, pursers, and God knows what besides; not only these, but their wives and children are to be pensioned, after the death of the heroes themselves. Nor does it signify, it seems, whether the hero were married, before he became part of the Dead Weight, or since. Upon the death of the man, the pension is to begin with the wife, and a pension for each child; so that, if there be a large family of children, the family, in many cases, *actually gains by the death of the father!* Was such a thing as this ever before heard of in the world? Any man that is going to die has nothing to do but to marry a girl to give her a pension for life to be paid out of the sweat of the people; and it was distinctly stated, during the Session of Parliament before the last, that the widows and children of insane of-ficers were to have the same treatment as the rest! Here is the envy of surrounding nations and the admiration of the world! In addition, then, to twenty thousand par-sons, more than twenty thousand stock-brokers and stock-jobbers perhaps; forty or fifty thousand tax-gatherers; thousands upon thousands of military and naval officers in full pay; in addition to all these, here are the thousands upon thousands of pairs of this Dead Weight, all busily engaged in breeding gentlemen and ladies; and all, while Malthus[6] is wanting to put a check upon the breeding of the labouring classes; all

---

2. The Napoleonic Wars.
3. Blockheads.
4. The Bank of England had gone off the gold standard in 1797. Laborers were paid in paper money that was subject to pernicious inflation, depressing both wages and pur-chasing power.

5. Notorious "rotten" (depopulated) boroughs, with pa-tronage-controlled seats in Parliament.
6. In *An Essay on the Principle of Population* (1798) and in essays in the *Edinburgh Review*, Thomas Malthus had argued that population was growing faster than the food supply.

receiving a *premium for breeding!* Where is Malthus? Where is this check-population parson? Where are his friends, the Edinburgh Reviewers? Faith, I believe they have given him up. They begin to be ashamed of giving countenance to a man who wants to check the breeding of those who labour, while he says not a word about those two hundred thousand breeding pairs, whose offspring are necessarily to be maintained at the public charge. Well may these fatteners upon the labour of others rail against the radicals! Let them once take the fan to their hand, and they will, I warrant it, thoroughly purge the floor. However, it is a consolation to know, that the jolterheads who have been the promoters of the measures that have led to these heavy charges; it is a consolation to know that the jolterheads have now to bear part of the charges, and that they cannot any longer make them fall exclusively upon the shoulders of the labouring classes. The disgust that one feels at seeing the whiskers and hearing the copper heels rattle, is in some measure compensated for by the reflection, that the expense of them is now beginning to fall upon the malignant and tyrannical jolterheads who are the principal cause of their being created.

Bidding the *Semaphore* good bye, I came along by the church at Hambledon, and then crossed a little common and the turnpike-road from London to Chichester through Godalming and Petworth; not Midhurst, as before. The turnpike-road here is one of the best that ever I saw. It is like the road upon Horley Common, near Worth, and like that between Godstone and East Grinstead; and the cause of this is, that it is made of precisely the same sort of stone, which, they tell me, is brought, in some cases, even from Blackdown Hill, which cannot be less, I should think, than twelve miles distant. This stone is brought in great lumps and then cracked into little pieces.

The next village I came to after Hambledon was Hascomb, famous for its *Beech*, insomuch that it is called HASCOMB BEECH. There are two lofty hills here, between which you go out of the sandy country down into the Weald. Here are hills of all height and forms. Whether they came in consequence of a boiling of the earth, I know not; but, in form, they very much resemble the bubbles upon the top of the water of a pot which is violently boiling. The soil is a beautiful loam upon a bed of sand. Springs start here and there at the feet of the hills; and little rivulets pour away in all directions. The roads are difficult merely on account of their extreme unevenness. The bottom is everywhere sound; and every thing that meets the eye is beautiful; trees, coppices, corn-fields, meadows; and then the distant views in every direction.

━◈━

Mary Wollstonecraft Shelley
1797–1851

"My husband was, from the first, very anxious that I should prove myself worthy of my parentage, and enrol myself on the page of fame. He was for ever inciting me to obtain literary reputation." Though she was less anxious for this consequence than he, Mary Shelley succeeded with a vengeance with *Frankenstein*, a sensational novel that has been in print since its publication in 1818 (now a Longman Cultural Edition). Her parentage was no small burden. It was not just that they were two leading intellectuals of the 1790s, William Godwin and Mary Wollstonecraft, whose social and political writing made them both famous and infamous. It was also that her mother died in giving birth to her, a tragedy that made her a monster in her father's eyes, and which she later invoked in the famous story of the creature whose creator can regard only as a monster. Mary Godwin never felt loved by her father, though she was passionately attached to him. When she was fourteen he sent her to live with the family of an admirer in Scotland, feeling that he could not support her along with his family by his second wife, Mary Jane Clairmont (who also wanted to distance Mary from her father). On a six-month visit to the Godwin home in 1812–1813, she met an ardent disciple of his, Percy Shelley, and resumed the acquaintance when she returned in spring 1814. She was sixteen; he was twenty-one and unhappily married. They fell in love, courted secretly, and Mary was soon pregnant. At the end of July, they eloped to France, taking along Mary's stepsister, Claire Clairmont. Godwin was furious, and scarcely warmer when they returned a few months later and married at the end of 1816, even as he continued to pester Percy for loans. The journey across the natural beauties and war-ravaged landscapes of Europe was recorded in Mary's first book, *History of a Six Weeks' Tour*, published anonymously in 1817.

Mary's life with Percy was exciting, tempestuous, and fraught with pain. Their first child, born prematurely, died within weeks. Percy had lost custody of his two children by his first wife, and from 1814 to 1822, Mary was almost continuously pregnant or nursing. Their second child, William, born in 1816, died in 1819; her third child, born in 1817, died even sooner, in 1818. She suffered a nearly fatal miscarriage in 1822, and a few weeks later Percy, who had been increasingly distant from her, drowned in a storm at sea.

Devastated, impoverished, and with one surviving child (Percy Florence) to support, Shelley returned to London at age twenty-four, longing for anonymity and propriety. Though she had admired her mother's writing, she felt the stigma of her notoriety and radical political views. Godwin, declined from his celebrity in the 1790s, was regarded as an eccentric thinker wedded to radical ideas. The scandals of Percy's life and opinions and their unconventional life together were acute social embarrassments—even as she devoted herself to rehabilitating his reputation with editions of his writings that downplayed his politics and idealized (and idolized) his character. Though never matching the success of *Frankenstein*, Shelley developed a career as a writer, supplementing the small annuity (£100) from her father-in-law that was contingent on her agreeing not to publish a biography of her husband.

Shelley published poems, a mythological drama, some two dozen short tales, many placed in handsomely paying gift-book annuals (see page 27), as well as encyclopedia articles, essays, reviews, travel books, and six novels. *The Swiss Peasant* appeared in the 1831 *Keepsake*, the annual that published most of Mary Shelley's tales. The volume included another of her tales, *Transformation*, and a poem, all of which were ascribed in the Table of Contents to "The Author of *Frankenstein*." Also included, in a mixture of the popular, the fashionable, and the aristocratic that characterized the annual, were poems by Letitia Landon and contributions from Lords Morpeth and Nugent, Archdeacon Spencer, the Hon. George Agar Ellis, two Members of Parliament, Lady Blessington, the journalist and fiction-writer Theodore Hook, and Shelley's stepmother, Mrs. Godwin. The narrator who introduces Fanny's story is little more than a device—the frame is never completed—yet his Byronic posturing sets the postwar perspective of the tale. If the attitudes of Monsieur and Madame de Marville are criticized, so also are the impulses and the events of the French Revolution represented without radical glamor and subordinated to the tangled history of the love between Fanny and Louis. The political engagements of earlier decades yield to the ideology of faith and domesticity.

For other writing by Mary Shelley, see pages 757, 561–62.

The Swiss Peasant
By the Author of "Frankenstein"

Why is the mind of man so apt to be swayed by contraries? why does the imagination for ever paint the impossible in glittering tints, and the hearts of wayward mortals cling, with the greatest tenacity, to what, eel-like, is bent on escaping from their grasp? Why—to bring the matter home—is solitude abhorrent to me, now that I enjoy it in perfection? I have apostrophised the coy nymph in ball-rooms, when the bright lamps of heaven were shamed by brighter earth-stars, and lamented her absence at a picnic party, where the nightingale was silenced by the fiddle, and the flowery turf was strewed with the impertinent finery of ugly old women, and the greenwood shade made redolent with the fumes of roasted fowls.

And now, O solitude! I abjure thee, in thy fitting temple—in Switzerland—among cloud-piercing mountains, by the resounding waves of the isle-surrounding lake. I am beside the waters of Uri—where Tell lived—in Brunen, where the Swiss patriots swore to die for freedom.[1] It rains—magic word to destroy the spell to which these words give rise—the clouds envelop the hills—the white mists veil the ravines—there is a roar and a splash in my ears—and now, and then, the vapours break and scatter themselves, and I see something dark between, which is the hoar side of a dark precipice, but which might as well be the turf stack or old wall that bounded Cumberland's view as he wrote the "Wheel of Fortune."[2]

The sole book that I possess is the *Prisoner of Chillon*.[3] I have read it through three times within an hour.—Its noble author composed it to beguile weary hours like these when he remained rain-bound for three days in a little inn on the shores of the Lake of Geneva; and cannot I, following with unequal steps, so cheat the minutes in this dim spot? I never, by the by, could invent the commonest incident. As a man of honour, of course I never lie; but, as a nursery child and schoolboy, I never did; simply, as I remember, because I never could concoct one—but a true tale was lately narrated to me by its very heroine, the incidents of which haunt my memory, adorned as they were, by her animated looks and soft silvery accent. Let me try to record them, stripped though they must be of their greatest charm.

I was, but a week ago, travelling with my friend Ashburn in a coupée, in the district of Soubiaco, in the ecclesiastical territory.[4] We were jolted along a rough ravine, through which the river Anio sped, and beetling mountains and shady trees, a distant convent and a picturesque cell on a hill, formed a view which so awoke the pictorial propensities of my friend, that he stopped the coupée (though we were assured that we should never reach our inn by nightfall, and that the road was dangerous in the dark), took out his portfolio, and began to sketch. As he drew I continued to speak in support of an argument we had entered upon before. I had been complaining of the commonplace and ennui of life. Ashburn insisted that our existence was only too full of variety and change—tragic variety and wondrous incredible change.—"Even," said the painter, "as sky, and earth, and water seem for ever the same to the vulgar eye, and yet to the gifted one assume a thousand various guises and hues—now robed in purple—now shrouded in black—now resplendent with living gold—and anon sinking into sober and unobtrusive gray, so do our mortal lives change and vary. No living being among us but could tell a tale of soul-subduing joys and heart-consuming woes, worthy, had they their poet, of the imagination of Shakspeare or Goëthe. The veriest weather-worn cabin is a study for colouring, and the meanest peasant will offer all the acts of a drama in the apparently dull routine of his humble life."

1. William Tell, the legendary peasant-hero of the 14th century, lived in Brunnen; tradition credited his exploits, such as shooting an apple off the head of his son, with inspiring Swiss resistance to Austrian domination.
2. The melodrama (1795) by Richard Cumberland (1732–1811) centers on the gloomy hermit Penruddock, a part in which John Philip Kemble won great acclaim.

3. Byron's poem, published in 1816, tells of the imprisonment of the 16th-century Swiss patriot Bonivard in the dungeon of the Castle of Chillon, on Lake Geneva.
4. Under the control of the Roman Catholic church (as opposed to the free states, mentioned below). Subiaco, in Italy, is the site of a celebrated Benedictine abbey.

"This is pure romance," I replied; "put it to the test. Let us take, for example, yonder woman descending the mountain-path."

"What a figure!" cried Ashburn; "oh that she would stay thus but one quarter of an hour!—she has come down to bathe her child—her upturned face—her dark hair—her picturesque costume—the little plump fellow bestriding her—the rude scenery around—"[5]

"And the romantic tale she has to tell."

"I would wager a louis that hers has been no common fate. She steps a goddess— her attitude—her looks, are all filled with majesty."

I laughed at his enthusiasm, and accepted his bet. We hurried to join our fair peasantess, and thus formed acquaintance with Fanny Chaumont. A sudden storm, as we were engaged conversing with her, came, driven down from the tempest-bearing hills, and she gave us a cordial invitation to her cottage.

It was situated on a sunny slope, yet sheltered from the winds. There was a look of cheerfulness and *aisance* about it, beyond what is usually met in that part of Switzerland, reminding me of the cottages of the inhabitants of the free states. There, also, we found her husband. I always feel curious to know on whom a woman, who bears the stamp of superior intellect; who is beautiful and refined—for peasant as she was, Fanny was both—has been induced to bestow herself.

Louis Chaumont was considerably older than his wife; he was handsome, with brown lively eyes, curly chestnut hair, a visage embrowned by the sun, bearing every mark of having led an active, even an adventurous life; there was, besides, an expression which, if it were not ferocity, resembled it nearly, in his vivacious glances, and in the sternness of his deeply-lined forehead; while she, in spite of her finely-formed brow, her majestic person, and her large expressive eyes, looked softness and patience itself. There was something incongruous in the pair, and more strangely matched they seemed when we heard their story. It lost me my louis, but proved Fanny at once to be a fitting heroine for romance, and was a lesson, moreover, to teach the strange pranks love can play with us, mingling fire and water, blending in one harmonious concord the harsh base, and melodious tenor of two differently stringed instruments. Though their child was five years old, Fanny and her husband were attached to each other with the tenderness and passion of early love; they were happy—his faults were tempered by her angel disposition, and her too melancholy and feeling-fraught spirit was enlivened and made plastic to the purposes of this world by his energy and activity.

Fanny was a Bernese[6] by birth: she was the child of humble cottagers, one among a large family. They lived on the brow of one summit and at the foot of another. The snowy mountains were piled about them; thaw-fed torrents brawled around; during the night a sound like thunder, a crash among the tempest-beaten pines would tell of an avalanche; or the snow-drift, whirring past the lattice, threatened to bury the little fabric [structure]. Winter was the season of peace in the deep vales, not so in the higher district. The peasant was often kept waking by the soft-falling snow which threatened insidiously to encroach on, and to overwhelm his habitation; or a straying cow would lead him far into the depths of the stormy hills, and his fearful family would count in agony the hours of his absence. Perpetual hardship and danger, however, rather brutify than exalt the soul of man; and those of the Swiss who are most deeply planted among the rocky wilds are often stultified and sullen.

5. In *The Keepsake* the story is accompanied by an engraving of this vignette.

6. Of the canton of Bern, one of the 13 federated states that make up Switzerland.

Fanny opened her youthful eyes and observation on this scene. She was one of those lovely children only to be seen in Switzerland, whose beauty is heartfelt but indescribable: hers was the smooth candid brow, the large hazel eyes, half soft, half wild; the round dimpled cheek, the full sensitive mouth, the pointed chin, and (as framework to the picture) the luxuriant curly chesnut hair, and voice which is sweetest music. The exceeding beauty of little Fanny gained her the observation of the wife of the governor of the chateau [castle] which overlooked and commanded the district, and at ten years of age she became a frequent visitor there. Fanny's little soul was love, so she soon twined herself round the kind lady's heart, became a pet with the governor, and the favourite playmate of their only son.

One fête day Fanny had dined at the chateau. It had been fine warm spring weather, but wind and storm came on with the setting sun; the snow began to fall thickly, and it was decided that Fanny must pass the night in the chateau. She had been unusually eager to return home; and when the tempest came on, she crept near her protectress, and begged to be sent to her mother. C'est impossible [It is impossible]—Fanny pressed no further, but she clambered to a window, and looked out wistfully to where, hidden by the hills, her parents' cottage stood. It was a fatal night for her: the thunders of frequent avalanches, the roaring of torrents, the crash of trees, spoke of devastation, and her home was its chief prey. Father, mother, brothers, and sisters, not one survived. Where, the day before, cottage and outhouse and flower-adorned garden had stood, the little lawn where she played, and the grove that sheltered her, there was now a monumental pile of snow, and the rocky path of a torrent; no trace remained, not one survivor to tell the tale. From that night Fanny became a constant inmate of the chateau.

It was Madame de Marville's project to give her a bourgeois education, which would raise her from the hardships of a peasant's life, and yet not elevate her above her natural position in society. She was brought up kindly, but humbly; it was the virtues of her disposition which raised her in the eyes of all around her, not any ill-judged favour of her benefactress. The night of the destruction of her family never passed away from her memory; it set a seal of untimely seriousness on her childish brow, awoke deep thoughts in her infant heart, and a strong resolve that while she lived, her beloved friends should find her, as far as her humble powers admitted, a source of good alone—a reason to rejoice that they had saved her from the destruction that had overwhelmed her family.

Thus Fanny grew up in beauty and in virtue. Her smiles were as the rainbows of her native torrents: her voice, her caresses, her light step, her unalterable sweetness and ceaseless devotion to the wishes of others, made her the idol of the family. Henry, the only child of her protectors, was of her own age, or but a few months her senior. Every time Henry returned from school to visit his parents, he found Fanny more beautiful, more kind, more attractive than before; and the first passion his youthful heart knew was for the lovely peasant girl, whose virtues sanctified his home. A look, a gesture betrayed his secret to his mother; she turned a hasty glance on Fanny, and saw on her countenance innocence and confidence alone. Half reassured, yet still fearful, Madame de Marville began to reflect on some cure for the threatened evil. She could not bear to send away Fanny; she was solicitous that her son should for the present reside in his home. The lovely girl was perfectly unconscious of the sentiments of the young seigneur [master]; but would she always continue so? and was the burning heart that warmed her gentle bosom to be for ever insensible to the despotic and absorbing emotions of love?

It was with wonder, and a curious mixture of disappointed maternal pride and real gladness, that the lady, at length, discovered a passion dawning in fair Fanny's heart for Louis Chaumont, a peasant some ten years older than herself. It was natural that one with such high wrought feelings as our heroine should love one to whom she could look up, and on whom to depend, rather than her childhood's playmate—the gay thoughtless Henry. Louis's family had been the victim of a moral ruin, as hers of a physical one. They had been oppressed, reduced to poverty, driven from their homes by some feudal tyrant, and had come poor and forlorn from a distant district. His mother, accustomed to a bourgeois' life, died broken-hearted: his father, a man of violent passions, nourished in his own and in his son's heart, sentiments of hatred and revenge against the "proud oppressors of the land." They were obliged to labour hard, yet in the intervals of work, father and son would read or discourse concerning the ills attendant on humanity, and they traced all to the social system, which made the few, the tyrants of the many.

Louis was handsome, bold, and active; he excelled his compeers in every hardy exercise; his resolution, his eloquence, his daring, made him, in spite of his poverty, a kind of leader among them. He had many faults: he was too full of passion, of the spirit of resistance and revenge; but his heart was kind; his understanding, when not thwarted, strong; and the very depth of his feelings made him keenly suscep-tible to love. Fanny, in her simple but majestic beauty, in her soft kindness of man-ner, mingled with the profoundest sensibility, made a deep impression on the young man's heart. His converse, so different and so superior to those of his fellows, won her attention.

Hitherto Fanny had never given utterance to the secrets of her soul. Habitual respect held her silent with Madame, and Henry, as spirited and as heedless as a chamois [native antelope], could ill understand her; but Louis became the depositary of the many feelings which, piled up in secresy and silence, were half awful to herself; he brought reason, or what he deemed such, to direct her heart-born conclusions. To have heard them talk of life and death, and all its shows, you would have wondered by what freak, philosophy had dressed herself in youth and a peasant's garb, and wan-dered from the schools to these untaught wilds.

Madame de Marville saw and encouraged this attachment. Louis was not exactly the person she would have selected for Fanny; but he was the only being for whom she had ever evinced a predilection; and, besides, the danger of a misalliance which threatened her own son, rendered her eager to build an insurmountable wall between him and the object of his affections. Thus Fanny enjoyed the heart-gladdening pride of hearing her choice applauded and praised by the person she most respected and loved in the world. As yet, however, love had been covert; the soul but not the ap-parent body of their intercourse. Louis was kept in awe by this highminded girl, and Fanny had not yet learned her own secret. It was Henry who made the discovery for them;—Henry, who, with all the impetuosity of his vivacious character, contrived a thousand ways to come between them; who, stung by jealousy to injustice, reviled Louis for his ruin, his poverty, his opinions, and brought the spirit of dissension to disquiet a mind entirely bent, as she imagined, on holy and pure thoughts.

Under this clash of passion, the action of the drama rapidly developed itself, and, for nearly a year, a variety of scenes were acted among these secluded moun-tains of no interest save to the parties themselves, but to them fateful and engrossing. Louis and Fanny exchanged vows; but that sufficed not. Fanny insisted on the right of treating with uniform kindness the son of her best friend, in spite of his injustice and insolence. The young men were often, during the rural festivals, brought into angry collision. Fanny was the peace-maker: but a woman is the worst possible mediator between her rival lovers. Henry was sometimes irritated to complain to his father of Louis' presumption. The spirit of the French revolution then awakening, rendered a peasant's assumptions peculiarly grating; and it required Madame de Marville's impartial gentleness to prevent Fanny's betrothed, as now he was almost considered, from being farther oppressed.

At length it was decided that Henry should absent himself for a time, and visit Paris. He was enraged in the extreme by what he called his banishment. Noble and generous as he naturally was, love was the tyrant of his soul, and drove him almost to crime. He entered into a fierce quarrel with his rival on the very eve of his departure: it ended in a scene of violence and bloodshed. No great real harm was done; but Monsieur de Marville, hitherto scarcely kept back from such a measure by his wife, suddenly obtained an order for Louis (his father had died a year before) to quit the territory within twelve hours. Fanny was commanded, as she valued the favour of her friends, to give him up. The young men were both gone before any intercession could avail; and that kind of peace which resembles desolation[7] took possession of the chateau.

Aware of the part she had taken in encouraging Fanny's attachment to her peasant-lover, Madame de Marville did not make herself a party to the tyranny of her husband; she requested only of her protégée to defer any decisive step, and not to quit her guardianship until the return of her son, which was to take place the following year. Fanny consented to such a delay, although in doing so, she had to resist the angry representations of her lover, who exacted that she should quit the roof of his oppressors. It was galling to his proud spirit that she should continue to receive benefits from them, and injurious to his love that she should remain where his rival's name was the constant theme of discourse and the object of interest. Fanny in vain represented her debt of gratitude, the absence of Henry, the impossibility that she could feel any undue sentiment towards the young seigneur; not to hate him was a crime in Louis's eyes; yet how, in spite of his ill conduct, could Fanny hate her childhood's playmate—her brother? His violent passions excited to their utmost height—jealousy and the sense of impotent indignation raging in his heart—Louis swore to revenge himself on the Marvilles—to forget and to abhor his mistress!—his last words were a malediction on them, and a violent denunciation of scorn upon her.

"It will all be well yet," thought Fanny, as she strove to calm the tumultuous and painful emotions to which his intemperate passion gave rise. "Not only are storms the birth of the wild elements, but of the heart of man, and we can oppose patience and fortitude alone to their destructive violence. A year will pass—I shall quit the chateau; Louis will acknowledge my truth, and retract his frightful words."

She continued, therefore, to fulfil her duties cheerfully, not permitting her thoughts to dwell on the idea, that, in spite of her struggles, too painfully occupied her—the probability that Louis would in the end renounce or forget her; but committing her cause to the spirit of good, she trusted that its influence would in the end prevail.

She had, however, much to endure; for months passed, and no tidings reached her of Louis. Often she felt sick at heart; often she became the prey of the darkest despair; above all, her tender heart missed the fond attentions of love, the bliss of

7. Echoing a well-known phrase of the Roman historian Tacitus.

knowing that she bestowed happiness, and the unrestrained intercourse to which mutual affection had given rise. She cherished hope as a duty, and faith in love, rather than in her unjust and cruelly neglectful lover. It was a hard task, for she had nowhere to turn for consolation or encouragement. Madame de Marville marked with gladness the total separation between them. Now that the danger that threatened her son was averted, she repented having been influential in producing an attachment between Fanny and one whom she deemed unworthy of her. She redoubled her kindness, and, in the true continental fashion, tried to get up a match between her and some one among her many and more prosperous admirers. She failed, but did not despair, till she saw the poor girl's cheek grow pale and her vivacity desert her, as month after month passed away, and the very name of Louis appeared to be forgotten by all except herself.

The stirring and terrible events that took place at this time in France added to Fanny's distress of mind. She had been familiarized to the discussion of the theories, now attempted to be put in practice, by the conversations of Chaumont. As each fresh account brought information of the guilty and sanguinary acts of men whose opinions were the same as those of her lover, her fears on his account increased. In a few words I shall hurry over this part of her story. Switzerland became agitated by the same commotions as tore the near kingdom. The peasantry rose in tumult; acts of violence and blood were committed; at first at a distance from her retired valley, but gradually approaching its precincts, until at last the tree of liberty was set up in the neighbouring village. Monsieur de Marville was an aristocrat of the most bigoted species. In vain was the danger represented to him, and the unwarlike state of his retinue. He armed them—he hurried down—he came unawares on the crowd who were proclaiming the triumph of liberty, rather by feasting than force. On the first attack, they were dispersed, and one or two among them were wounded; the pole they had gathered round was uprooted, the emblematic cap trampled to the earth.[8] The governor returned victorious to his chateau.

This act of violence on his part seemed the match to fire a train of organized resistance to his authority, of which none had dreamt before. Strangers from other cantons thronged into the valley; rustic labours were cast aside; popular assemblies were held, and the peasants exercised in the use of arms. One was coming to place himself at their head, it was said, who had been a party in the tumults at Geneva. Louis Chaumont was coming—the champion of liberty, the sworn enemy of M. de Marville. The influence of his presence soon became manifest. The inhabitants of the chateau were, as it were, besieged. If one ventured beyond a certain limit he was assailed by stones and knives. It was the resolve of Louis that all within its walls should surrender themselves to his mercy. What that might be, the proud curl of his lip and the fire that glanced from his dark eyes rendered scarcely problematic. Fanny would not believe the worst of her lover, but Monsieur and Madame de Marville, no longer restrained by any delicacy, spoke of the leveller in unmeasured terms of abhorrence, comparing him to the monsters who then reigned in France, while the danger they incurred through him added a bitter sting to their words. The peril grew each day; famine began to make its appearance in the chateau; while the intelligence which some of the more friendly peasants brought was indicative of preparations for a regular attack of the most formidable nature. A summons at last came from the insurgents. They were resolved to destroy the emblem of their slavery—the feudal halls

---

8. The Maypole and the cap of liberty were the emblems of the revolutionaries.

of their tyrants. They declared their intention of firing the chateau the next day, and called on all within to deliver themselves up, if they would not be buried in its ruins. They offered their lives and free leave to depart to all, save the governor himself, who must place himself unconditionally at the mercy of their leader—"The wretch," exclaimed his lady, "who thirsts for your blood! Fly! if there is yet time for flight; we, you see, are safe. Fly! nor suffer these cruel dastards to boast of having murdered you."

M. de Marville yielded to these entreaties and representations. He had sent for a military force to aid him—it had been denied; he saw that he himself, as the detested person, was the cause of danger to his family. It was therefore agreed that he should seek a chalêt [cabin] situated on a mountain ten leagues [about 30 miles] distant, where he might lie concealed till his family joined him. Accordingly, in a base disguise, he quitted at midnight the walls he was unable to defend; a miserable night for the unfortunate beings left behind. The coming day was to witness the destruction of their home; and they, beggars in the world, were to wander through the inhospitable mountains, till, with caution and terror, they could unobserved reach the remote and miserable chalêt, and learn the fate of the unhappy fugitive. It was a sleepless night for all. To add to Madame's agony, she knew that her son's life was in danger in Paris—that he had been denounced[9]—and though yet untaken, his escape was still uncertain. From the turret of the castle, that, situated high on a rock, commanded the valley below, she sat the livelong night watching for every sound—fearful of some shout, some report of fire-arms, which would announce the capture of her husband. It was September; the nights were chill; pale and trembling, she saw day break over the hills. Fanny had busied herself during these anxious hours by preparing for their departure; the terrified domestics had already fled; she, the lady, and the old lame gardener were all that remained. At dawn she brought forth the mule, and harnessed him to the rude vehicle which was to convey them to their place of refuge. Whatever was most valuable in the chateau had already been sent away long before, or was secreted; a few necessaries alone she provided. And now she ascended the turret stairs, and stood before her protectress, announcing that all was ready, and that they must depart. At this last moment, Madame de Marville appeared deprived of strength; she strove to rise—she sank to the ground in a fit. Forgetful of her deserted state, Fanny called aloud for help, and then her heart beat wildly, as a quick, youthful step was heard on the stairs. Who could he be? would *he* come to insult their wretchedness—he, the author of their wo? The first glance changed the object of her terror. Henry flew to his mother's side, and, with broken exclamations and agitated questions, demanded an explanation of what he saw. He had fled for safety to the habitation of his parents—he found it deserted; the first voice he heard was that of Fanny crying for help—the first sight that presented itself was his mother, to all appearance dead, lying on the floor of the turret. Her recovery was followed by brief explanations, and a consultation of how his safety was to be provided for. The name of Chaumont excited his bitterest execrations. With a soldier's haughty resolve, he was darting from the castle, to meet and to wreak vengeance on his rival. His mother threw herself at his feet, clasping his knees, calling wildly on him not to desert her. Fanny's gentle, sweet voice was of more avail to calm his passion. "Chevalier," she said, "it is not thus that you must display your courage or protect the helpless. To encounter yonder infuriated mob would be to run on certain death; you must preserve yourself for your family—you must have pity on your mother, who cannot survive you. Be guided by me, I beseech you."

---

9. Identified as an aristocratic enemy of the Revolution by the Jacobins.

Henry yielded to her voice, and a more reasonable arrangement took place. The departure of Madame de Marville and Fanny was expected at the village, and a pledge had been given that they should proceed unmolested. But deeply had the insurgents sworn, that if the governor or his son (whose arrival in the chateau had been suspected) attempted to escape with them, they should be immediately sacrificed to *justice*. No disguise would suffice—the active observation of their enemies was known. Every inhabitant of the castle had been numbered—the fate of each ascertained, save that of the two most detested—the governor, whose flight had not been discovered, and his son, whose arrival was so unexpected and ill-timed. As still they consulted, a beat to arms was heard in the valley below: it was the signal that the attack on the empty castle walls would soon begin. There was no time for delay or hesitation; Henry placed himself at the bottom of the *charrette* [wagon]; straw and a variety of articles were heaped upon him; the two women ascended in trepidation; and the old gardener sat in front and held the reins.

In consequence of the disturbed state of the districts through which they were to pass,—where the appearance of one of the upper classes excited the fiercest enmity, and frightful insult, if not death, was their sure welcome,—Madame and her friend assumed a peasant's garb. And thus they wound their way down the steep; the unhappy lady weeping bitterly—Fanny, with tearless eyes, but with pale cheek and compressed lips, gazing for the last time on the abode which had been her refuge when, in helpless infancy, she was left an orphan—where kindness and benevolence had waited on her, and where her days had passed in innocence and peace. "And he drives us away!—him, whom I loved—whom I love!—O misery!"

They reached the foot of the eminence on which the chateau was placed, and proceeded along the road which led directly through the village. With the approach of danger, vain regrets were exchanged for a lively sense of fear in the bosom of the hapless mother, and for the exertion of her courage and forethought in Fanny's more energetic mind. They passed a peasant or two, who uttered a malediction or imprecation on them as they went; then groups of two or three, who were even more violent in gesture and menace; when suddenly the sound of many steps came on their ears, and, at a turn of the road, they met Chaumont with a band of about twenty disciplined men.

"Fear not," he said to Madame de Marville; "I will protect you from danger till you are beyond the village."

With a shriek, the lady, in answer, threw herself in Fanny's arms, crying, "He is here!—save me!—he will murder us."

"Fear not, Madame—he dares not injure you. Begone, Louis! insult us not by your presence. Begone! I say."

Fanny spoke angrily. She had not adopted this tone, but that the lady's terror, and the knowledge that even then the young soldier crouched at their feet, burnt to spring up and confront his enemy, made her use an authority which a woman always imagines that a lover dare not resist.

"I do not insult you," repeated Chaumont—"I save you. I have no quarrel with the lady; tyrants alone need fear me. You are not safe without my escort. Do not you, false girl, irritate me. I have ensured her escape; but yours—you are in my power."

A violent movement at the bottom of the charrette called forth all Fanny's terrors.

"Take me!" she cried; "do with me what you please; but you dare not, you cannot raise a finger against the innocent. Begone, I say! let me never see you more!"

"You are obeyed. On you fall the consequences."

Thus, after many months of separation, did Fanny and her lover meet. She had purposed when she should see him to make an appeal to his better nature—his reason; she had meant to use her all-persuasive voice to recall him from the dangerous path he was treading. Several times, indeed, since his arrival in the valley, she had endeavoured to obtain an interview with him, but he dreaded her influence: he had resolved on revenge, and he feared to be turned back. But now the unexpected presence of his rival robbed her of her self-possession, and forced her to change her plans. She saw frightful danger in their meeting, and all her endeavours were directed to the getting rid of her lover.

Louis and his companions proceeded towards the chateau, while the *charrette* of the fugitives moved on in the opposite direction. They met many a ferocious group, who were rushing forward to aid in the destruction of their home; and glad they were, in that awful hour, that any object had power to divert the minds of their enemies from attention to themselves. The road they pursued wound through the valley; the precipitous mountain on one side, a brawling stream on the other. Now they ascended higher and now again descended in their route, while the road, broken by the fall of rocks, intersected by torrents, which tore their way athwart it, made their progress slow. To get beyond the village was the aim of their desires; when, lo! just as they came upon it, and were in the very midst of its population, which was pouring towards the castle, suddenly the *charrette* sank in a deep rut; it half upset, and every spoke in the wheel giving way rendered the vehicle wholly useless.

"*Mais, descendez donc, mesdames,*" said a peasant; "*il faut bien marcher.*" ["Get down then, ladies . . . it is necessary to walk."]

Fanny had indeed, already sprung to the ground to examine what hope remained: there was none. "*Grand Dieu! nous sommes perdues!*" ["Good God! we are lost!"] were the first words that escaped her, while her friend stood aghast, trembling, almost insensible, knowing that the hope of her life, the existence of her son, depended on these miserable moments.

A peasant who owed Fanny some kindness now advanced, and in a kind of cavalier way, as if to blemish as much as he could the matter of his offer by its manner, told them, that, for the pleasure of getting rid of the aristocrats, he would lend his car—there it was, let them quickly bestow their lading in it and pursue their way. As he spoke, he caught up a box, and began the transfer from one car to the other.

"No, no!" cried Madame de Marville, as, with a scream, she sprang forward and grasped the arm of the man as he was in the very act of discovering her son's hiding-place. "We will accept nothing from our base enemies!—Begone with your offers! we will die here, rather than accept any thing from such *canaille.*" [rabble]

The word was electric. The fierce passions of the mob, excited by the mischief they were about to perpetrate, now burst like a stream into this new channel. With violent execrations they rushed upon the unfortunate woman: they would have torn her from the car, but already her son had sprung from his hiding-place, and striking a violent blow at the foremost assailant, checked for a moment their brutal outrages. Then again, with a yell, such as the savage Indians alone could emulate, they rushed on their prey. Mother and son were torn asunder, and cries of "A *bas les aristocrats!"*—*"A la lanterne!"* ["Down with the aristocrats."—"To the lamp-post!"] declared too truly their sanguinary designs.[1]

At this moment, Louis appeared—Louis, whose fears for Fanny had overcome his indignation, and who returned to guard her; while she, perceiving him, with a burst of joy, called on him to rescue her friends. His cry of *"Arretez-vous!"* ["Stop!"] was loud and distinct amidst the uproar. It was obeyed; and then first he beheld his rival, his oppressor, his enemy in his power. At first, rage inflamed every feature, to be replaced by an expression of triumph and implacable hatred. Fanny caught the fierce glance of his eye, and grew pale. She trembled as, trying to be calm, she said, "Yes, you behold he is here.—And you must save him—and your own soul. Rescue him from death, and be blest that your evil career enables you at least to perform this one good action."

For a moment Louis seemed seeking for a word, as a man, meaning to stab, may fumble for his dagger's hilt, unable in his agitation to grasp his weapon.

"My friends," at length he said, "let the women depart—we have promised it. Ye may deal with the young aristocrat according to his merits."

"A la lanterne!" burst in response from a hundred voices.

"Let his mother first depart!"

Could it be Louis that spoke these words, and had she loved this man? To appeal to him was to rouse a tiger from his lair. Another thought darted into Fanny's mind; she scarcely knew what she said or did: but already knives were drawn; already, with a thrill of horror, she thought she saw the blood of her childhood's playmate spilt like water on the earth. She rushed forward—she caught the uplifted arm of one—"He is no aristocrat!" she cried; "he is my husband!—Will you murder one who, forgetting his birth, his duty, his honour, has married a peasant girl—one of yourselves?"

Even this appeal had little effect upon the mob; but it strangely affected her cruel lover. Grasping her arm with iron fingers, he cried, "Is this tale true? Art thou married to that man—his wife?"

"Even so!"—the words died on her lips as she strove to form them, terrified by their purport, and the effect they might produce. An inexplicable expression passed over Chaumont's face; the fierceness that jealousy had engendered for a moment was exalted almost to madness, and then faded wholly away. The stony heart within him softened at once. A tide of warm, human, and overpowering emotion flowed into his soul: he looked on her he had loved even to guilt and crime, on her whom he had lost for ever; and tears rushed into his eyes, as he saw her gasping, trembling before him—at his mercy.

"Fear not," at last he said; "fear neither for him nor yourself.—Poor girl! so young, you shall not lose all—so young, you shall not become a widow.—He shall be saved!"

Yet it was no easy task, even for him, to stem the awakened passions of the bloodthirsty mob. He had spent many an hour in exciting them against their seigneurs, and now at once to control the violence to which he had given rise seemed impossible. Yet his energy, his strong will overcame all opposition. They should pierce the chevalier's heart, he swore, through his alone. He prevailed—the fugitives were again seated in their car. He took the rein of their mule, and saying to his comrades *"Attendez moi,"* ["Wait for me"] he led them out of the village. All were silent; Fanny knew not what to say, and surprise held the others mute. Louis went with them until a turn in the road hid them from the view of the village. What his thoughts were, none could guess: he looked calm, as resigning the rein into the chevalier's hands, he

---

1. Lamp-posts were used for lynchings during the Reign of Terror that followed the French Revolution.

gently wished them "*Bon voyage*" ["a good trip"], touching his hat in reply to their sal-
utations. They moved on, and Fanny looked back to catch a last view of her lover: he
was standing where they left him, when suddenly, instead of returning on his steps
into the village, she saw him with rapid strides ascend the mountain side, taking a
well-known path that conducted him away from the scene of his late exploits. His
pace was that of a man flying from pursuers—soon he was lost to sight.

Astonishment still kept the fugitives silent, as they pursued their way; and
when at last joy broke forth, and Madame de Marville, rejoicing in their escape,
embraced again and again her son, he with the softest tenderness thanked Fanny
for his life: she answered not, but withdrawing to the furthest part of the *charrette*,
wept bitterly.

Late that night, they reached the destined chalêt, and found Monsieur de Marville arrived. It was a half-ruined miserable habitation perched among the snows,
cold and bare; food was ill to be obtained, and danger breathed around them. Fanny
attended on them with assiduous care, but she never spoke of the scene in the village; and though she strove to look the same, Henry never addressed her but her
cheeks grew white, and her voice trembled. She could not divine her distant lover's
thoughts, but she knew that he believed her married to another; and that other,
earnestly though she strove to rule her feelings, became an object of abhorrence to
her.

Three weeks they passed in this wretched abode; three weeks replete with alarm,
for the district around was in arms, and the life of Monsieur de Marville loudly
threatened. They never slept but they dreaded the approach of the murderers; food
they had little, and the inclement season visited them roughly. Fanny seemed to
feel no inconvenience; her voice was cheerful: to console, encourage, and assist her
friends appeared to occupy her whole heart. At length one night they were roused
by a violent knocking at the door of their hut: Monsieur de Marville and Henry
were on their feet in a moment, seizing their weapons as they rose. It was a domestic
of their own, come to communicate the intelligence that the troubles were over,
that the legal government had reasserted its authority, and invited the governor to
return to Berne.

They descended from their mountain refuge, and the name of Louis hovered on
Fanny's lips, but she spoke it not. He seemed everywhere forgotten. It was not until
some time afterwards that she ascertained the fact, that he had never been seen or
heard of, since he had parted from her on the morning of their escape. The villagers
had waited for him in vain; they suspended their designs, for they all depended upon
him; but he came not.

Monsieur and Madame de Marville returned to their chateau with their son, but
Fanny remained behind. She would not inhabit the same roof as Henry; she recoiled
even from receiving further benefits from his parents. What could she do? Louis would
doubtless discover the falsehood of her marriage, but he dared not return; and even if
he communicated with her, even though yet she loved him, could she unite herself
with one accused too truly of the most frightful crimes? At first, these doubts agitated
her, but by degrees they faded as oblivion closed over Chaumont's name—and he
came not and she heard not of him, and he was as dead to her. Then the memory of
the past revived in her heart; her love awoke with her despair; his mysterious flight
became the sole occupation of her thoughts: time rolled on and brought its changes.
Madame de Marville died—Henry was united to another—Fanny remained, to her

own thoughts, alone in the world. A relation, who lived at Soubiaco, sent for her, and there she went to take up her abode. In vain she strove to wean herself from the memory of Louis—her love for him haunted her soul.

There was war in Europe, and every man was converted into a soldier; the country was thinned of its inhabitants, and each victory or defeat brought a new conscription. At length peace came again, and its return was celebrated with rejoicing. Many a soldier returned to his home—and one came back who had no home. A man, evidently suffering from recent wounds, way-worn, and sick, asked for hospitality at Fanny's cottage; it was readily afforded, and he sat at her cottage fire, and removed his cap from his brows. His person was bent—his cheeks fallen in—yet those eyes of fire, that quick animated look, which almost brought the bright expression of youth back into his face, could never be forgotten. Fanny gazed almost in alarm, and then in joy, and at last, in her own sweet voice, she said, "*Et toi, Louis—tu aussi es de retour.*" ["And you also, Louis—you also have returned."][2]

Louis had endured many a sorrow and many a hardship, and, most of all, he had been called on to wage battle with his own fierce spirit. The rage and hate which he had sedulously nourished suddenly became his tormentors and his tyrants—at the moment that love, before too closely allied to them, emancipated itself from their control. Love, which is the source of all that is most generous and noble in our nature, of self-devotion and of high intent, separated from the alloy he had blended with it, asserted its undivided power over him—strange that it should be so, at the moment that he believed that he had lost her he loved for ever!

All his plans had been built for revenge. He would destroy the family that oppressed him—unbuild, stone by stone, the proud abode of their inheritance—he would be the sole refuge and support of his mistress in exile and in poverty. He had entered upon his criminal career with this design alone, and with the anticipation of ending all by heaping benefits and the gifts of fortune upon Fanny. The very steps he had taken, he now believed to be those that occasioned his defeat. He had lost her— the lovely and the good—he had lost her by proving unworthy—yet not so unworthy was he as to make her the victim of his crimes. The family he had vowed to ruin was now hers, and every injury that befel them visited her; to save her he must unweave his pernicious webs—to keep her scatheless [unharmed], his dearest designs must fall to the ground.

A veil seemed rent before his eyes—he had fled, for he would not assist in the destruction of her fortunes—he had not returned, for it was torture to him to know that she lived, the wife of another. He entered the French army—but in every change his altered feelings pursued him, and to prove himself worthy of her he had lost, was the constant aim of his ambition. His excellent conduct led to his promotion, and yet mishap still waited on him. He was wounded, even dangerously, and became so incapable of service as to be forced to solicit his dismission. This had occurred at the end of a hard campaign in Germany, and his intention was to pass into Italy, where a friend, with whom he had formed an intimacy in the army, promised to procure him some employment under government. He passed through Soubiaco in his way, and, ignorant of its occupiers, had asked for hospitality in his mistress's cottage.

---

2. *Toi* and *tu* are intimate forms of second-person address.

If guilt can be expiated by repentance and reform, as is the best lesson of religion, Louis had expiated his. If constancy in love deserve reward, these lovers deserved that, which they reaped, in the happiness consequent on their union. Her image, side by side with all that is good in our nature, had dwelt in his heart; which thus became a shrine at which he sacrificed every evil passion. It was a greater bliss than he had ever dared to anticipate, to find, that in so doing, he had at the same time been conducing the welfare of her he loved, and that the lost and idolized being whom he worshipped founded the happiness of her life upon his return to virtue, and the constancy of his affection.

⇥ END OF PERSPECTIVES: POPULAR PROSE AND THE PROBLEMS OF AUTHORSHIP ⇥

LITERARY AND CULTURAL TERMS*

Absolutism. In criticism, the belief in irreducible, unchanging values of form and content that underlie the tastes of individuals and periods and arise from the stability of an absolute hierarchical order.

Accent. Stress or emphasis on a syllable, as opposed to the syllable's length of duration, its quantity. *Metrical accent* denotes the metrical pattern ($\smile$ $-$) to which writers fit and adjust accented words and rhetorical emphases, keeping the meter as they substitute word-accented feet and tune their rhetoric.

Accentual Verse. Verse with lines established by counting accents only, without regard to the number of unstressed syllables. This was the dominant form of verse in English until the time of Chaucer.

Acrostic. Words arranged, frequently in a poem or puzzle, to disclose a hidden word or message when the correct combination of letters is read in sequence.

Aestheticism. Devotion to beauty. The term applies particularly to a 19th-century literary and artistic movement celebrating beauty as independent from morality, and praising form above content; art for art's sake.

Aesthetics. The study of the beautiful; the branch of philosophy concerned with defining the nature of art and establishing criteria of judgment.

Alexandrine. A six-foot iambic pentameter line.

Allegorical Meaning. A secondary meaning of a narrative in addition to its primary meaning or literal meaning.

Allegory. A story that suggests another story. The first part of this word comes from the Greek *allos*, "other." An allegory is present in literature whenever it is clear that the author is saying, "By this I also mean that." In practice, allegory appears when a progression of events or images suggests a translation of them into conceptual language. Allegory is thus a technique of aligning imaginative constructs, mythological or poetic, with conceptual or moral models. During the Romantic era a distinction arose between allegory and symbol. With Coleridge, symbol took precedence: "an allegory is but a translation of abstract notions into picture-language," but "a symbol always partakes of the reality which it makes intelligible."

Alliteration. "Adding letters" (*Latin ad + littera,* "letter"). Two or more words, or accented syllables, chime on the same initial letter (lost love alone; after apple-picking) or repeat the same consonant.

Alliterative Revival. The outburst of alliterative verse that occurred in the second half of the 14th century in west and northwest England.

Alliterative Verse. Verse using alliteration on stressed syllables for its fundamental structure.

Allusion. A meaningful reference, direct or indirect, as when William Butler Yeats writes, "Another Troy must rise and set," calling to mind the whole tragic history of Troy.

Amplification. A restatement of something more fully and in more detail, especially in oratory, poetry, and music.

Analogy. A comparison between things similar in a number of ways; frequently used to explain the unfamiliar by the familiar.

Anapest. A metrical foot: $\smile$ $\smile$ $-$.

Anaphora. The technique of beginning successive clauses or lines with the same word.

Anatomy. Greek for "a cutting up": a dissection, analysis, or systematic study. The term was popular in titles in the 16th and 17th centuries.

* Adapted from *The Harper Handbook to Literature* by Northrop Frye, Sheridan Baker, George Perkins, and Barbara M. Perkins, 2nd edition (Longman, 1997).

Anglo-Norman (Language). The language of upper-class England after the Norman Conquest in 1066.

Anglo-Saxon. The people, culture, and language of three neighboring tribes—Jutes, Angles, and Saxons—who invaded England, beginning in 449, from the lower part of Denmark's Jutland Peninsula. The Angles, settling along the eastern seaboard of central and northern England, developed the first literate culture of any Germanic people. Hence England (Angle-land) became the dominant term.

Antagonist. In Greek drama, the character who opposes the protagonist, or hero: therefore, any character who opposes another. In some works, the antagonist is clearly the villain (Iago in *Othello*), but in strict terminology an antagonist is merely an opponent and may be in the right.

Anthropomorphism. The practice of giving human attributes to animals, plants, rivers, winds, and the like, or to such entities as Grecian urns and abstract ideas.

Antithesis. (1) A direct contrast or opposition. (2) The second phase of dialectical argument, which considers the opposition—the three steps being *thesis, antithesis, synthesis*. (3) A rhetorical figure sharply contrasting ideas in balanced parallel structures.

Aphorism. A pithy saying of known authorship, as distinguished from a folk proverb.

Apology. A justification, as in Sir Philip Sidney's *The Apology for Poetry* (1595).

Apostrophe. (Greek, "a turning away"). An address to an absent or imaginary person, a thing, or a personified abstraction.

Archaism. An archaic or old-fashioned word or expression—for example, *o'er, ere,* or *darkling*.

Archetype. (1) The first of a genre, like Homer's *Iliad*, the first heroic epic. (2) A natural symbol imprinted in human consciousness by experience and literature, like dawn symbolizing hope or an awakening; night, death, or repose.

Assonance. Repetition of middle vowel sounds: *fight, hive; pane, make*. Assonance, most effective on stressed syllables, is often found within a line of poetry; less frequently it substitutes for end rhyme.

Aubade. Dawn song, from French *aube*, for dawn. The aubade originated in the Middle Ages as a song sung by a lover greeting the dawn, ordinarily expressing regret that morning means parting.

Avant-Garde. Experimental, innovative, at the forefront of a literary or artistic trend or movement. The term is French for *vanguard*, the advance unit of an army. It frequently suggests a struggle with tradition and convention.

Ballad. A narrative poem in short stanzas, with or without music. The term derives by way of French *ballade* from Latin *ballare*, "to dance," and once meant a simple song of any kind, lyric or narrative, especially one to accompany a dance. As ballads evolved, most lost their association with dance, although they kept their strong rhythms. Modern usage distinguishes three major kinds: the anonymous *traditional ballad* (popular ballad or *folk ballad*), transmitted orally; the *broadside ballad*, printed and sold on single sheets; and the *literary ballad* (or art ballad), a sophisticated imitation of the traditional ballad.

Ballad Stanza. The name for common meter as found in ballads: a quatrain in iambic meter, alternating tetrameter and trimeter lines, usually rhyming *abcb*.

Bard. An ancient Celtic singer of the culture's lore in epic form; a poetic term for any poet.

Baroque. (1) A richly ornamented style in architecture and art. Founded in Rome by Frederigo Barocci about 1550, and characterized by swirling allegorical frescoes on ceilings and walls, it flourished throughout Europe until 1700. (2) A chromatic musical style with strict forms containing similar exuberant ornamentation, flourishing from 1600 to 1750. In literature, Richard Crashaw's bizarre imagery and the conceits and rhythms of John Donne and other metaphysical poets are sometimes called baroque, sometimes mannerist. Some literary historians designate a Baroque Age from 1580 to 1680, between the Renaissance and the Enlightenment.

Bathos. (1) A sudden slippage from the sublime to the ridiculous. (2) Any anticlimax. (3) Sentimental pathos. (4) Triteness or dullness.

Blank Verse. Unrhymed iambic pentameter. *See also* Meter. In the 1540s Henry Howard, Earl of Surrey, seems to have originated it in English as the equivalent of Virgil's unrhymed dactylic hexameter. In *Gorboduc* (1561), Thomas Sackville and Thomas Norton introduced blank verse into the drama, whence it soared with Marlowe and Shakespeare in the 1590s. Milton forged it anew for the epic in *Paradise Lost* (1667).

Bloomsbury Group. An informal social and intellectual group associated with Bloomsbury, a London residential district near the British Museum, from about 1904 until the outbreak of World War II. Virginia Woolf was a principal member. With her husband, Leonard Woolf, she established the Hogarth Press, which published works by many of their friends. The group was loosely knit, but famed, especially in the 1920s, for its exclusiveness, aestheticism, and social and political freethinking.

Broadside. A sheet of paper printed on one side only. Broadsides containing a ballad, a tract, a criminal's gallows speech, a scurrilous satire, and the like were once commonly sold on the streets like newspapers.

Burden. (1) A refrain or set phrase repeated at intervals throughout a song or poem. (2) A bass accompaniment, the "load" carried by the melody, the origin of the term.

Burlesque. (1) A ridicule, especially on the stage, treating the lofty in low style, or the low in grandiose style. (2) A bawdy vaudeville, with obscene clowning and stripteasing.

Caesura. A pause in a metrical line, indicated by punctuation, momentarily suspending the beat (from Latin "a cutting off"). Caesuras are *masculine* at the end of a foot, and *feminine* in midfoot.

Canon. The writings accepted as forming a part of the Bible, of the works of an author, or of a body of literature. Shakespeare's canon consists of works he wrote, which may be distinguished from works attributed to him but written by others. The word derives from Greek *kanon,* "rod" or "rule," and suggests authority. Canonical authors and texts are those taught most frequently, noncanonical are those rarely taught, and in between are disputed degrees of canonicity for authors considered minor or marginalized.

Canto. A major division in a long poem. The Italian expression is from Latin *cantus,* "song," a section singable in one sitting.

Caricature. Literary cartooning, depicting characters with exaggerated physical traits such as huge noses and bellies, short stature, squints, tics, humped backs, and so forth. Sir Thomas Browne seems to have introduced the term into English in 1682 from the Italian *caricatura.*

Catalog. In literature, an enumeration of ancestors, of ships, of warriors, of a woman's beauties, and the like; a standard feature of the classical epic.

Celtic Revival. In the 18th century, a groundswell of the Romantic movement in discovering the power in ancient, primitive poetry, particularly Welsh and Scottish Gaelic, as distinct from that of the classics.

Chiasmus. A rhetorical balance created by the inversion of one of two parallel phrases or clauses; from the Greek for a "placing crosswise," as in the Greek letter χ (chi).

Chronicle. A kind of history, with the emphasis on *time* (Greek *chronos*). Events are described in order as they occurred. The chronicles of the Middle Ages provided material for later writers and serve now as important sources of knowledge about the period. Raphael Holinshed's *Chronicles* (1577) is especially famous as the immediate source of much of Shakespeare's knowledge of English history.

Chronicle Play. A play dramatizing historical events, as from a chronicle. Chronicle plays tend to stress time order, presenting the reign of a king, for example, with much emphasis on pageantry and little on the unity of action and dramatic conflict necessary for a tragedy.

Classical Literature. (1) The literature of ancient Greece and Rome. (2) Later literature reflecting the qualities of classical Greece or Rome. *See also* Classicism; Neoclassicism.

(3) The classic literature of any time or place, as, for example, classical American literature or classical Japanese literature.

Classicism. A principle in art and conduct reflecting the ethos of ancient Greece and Rome: balance, form, proportion, propriety, dignity, simplicity, objectivity, rationality, restraint, unity rather than diversity. In English literature, classicism emerged with Erasmus (1466–1536) and his fellow humanists. In the Restoration and 18th century, classicism, or neoclassicism, expressed society's deep need for balance and restraint after the shattering Civil War and Puritan commonwealth. Classicism continued in the 19th century, after the Romantic period, particularly in the work of Matthew Arnold. T. E. Hulme, Ezra Pound, and T. S. Eliot expressed it for the 20th century.

Cliché. An overused expression, once clever or metaphorical but now trite and timeworn.

Closed Couplet. The heroic couplet, especially when the thought and grammar are complete in the two iambic pentameter lines.

Closet Drama. A play written for reading in the "closet," or private study. Closet dramas were usually in verse, like Percy Shelley's *Prometheus Unbound* (1820) and Robert Browning's *Pippa Passes* (1841).

Cockney. A native of the East End of central London. The term originally meant "cocks' eggs," a rural term of contempt for city softies and fools. Cockneys are London's ingenious street peddlers, speaking a dialect rich with an inventive rhyming slang, dropping and adding aitches.

Comedy. One of the typical literary structures, originating as a form of drama and later extending into prose fiction and other genres as well. Comedy, as Susanne Langer says, is the image of Fortune; tragedy, the image of Fate. Each sorts out for attention the different facts of life. Comedy sorts its pleasures. It pleases our egos and endows our dreams, stirring at once two opposing impulses, our vindictive lust for superiority and our wishful drive for success and happiness ever after. The dark impulse stirs the pleasure of laughter; the light, the pleasure of wish fulfillment.

Comedy of Humors. Comedy based on the ancient physiological theory that a predominance of one of the body's four fluids (humors) produces a comically unbalanced personality: (1) blood—sanguine, hearty, cheerful, amorous; (2) phlegm—phlegmatic, sluggish; (3) choler (yellow bile)—angry, touchy; (4) black bile—melancholic.

Comedy of Manners. Suave, witty, and risqué satire of upper-class manners and immorals, particularly that of Restoration masters like George Etherege and William Congreve.

Common Meter. The ballad stanza as found in hymns and other poems: a quatrain (four-line stanza) in iambic meter, alternating tetrameter and trimeter, rhyming *abcb* or *abab*.

Complaint. A lyric poem, popular in the Middle Ages and the Renaissance, complaining of unrequited love, a personal situation, or the state of the world.

Conceit. Any fanciful, ingenious expression or idea, but especially one in the form of an extended metaphor.

Concordia Discors. "Discordant harmony," a phrase expressing for the 18th century the harmonious diversity of nature, a pleasing balance of opposites.

Concrete Poetry. Poetry that attempts a concrete embodiment of its idea, expressing itself physically apart from the meaning of the words. A recent relative of the much older *shaped poem*, the concrete poem places heavy emphasis on the picture and less on the words, so that the visual experience may be more interesting than the linguistic.

Connotation. The ideas, attitudes, or emotions associated with a word in the mind of speaker or listener, writer or reader. It is contrasted with the *denotation*, the thing the word stands for, the dictionary definition, an objective concept without emotional coloring.

Consonance. (1) Repetition of inner or end consonant sounds, as, for example, the r and s sounds from Gerard Manley Hopkins's *God's Grandeur*: "broods with warm breast." (2) In a broader sense, a generally pleasing combination of sounds or ideas; things that sound well together.

Couplet. A pair of rhymed metrical lines, usually in iambic tetrameter or pentameter. Sometimes the two lines are of different length.

Covenanters. Scottish Presbyterians who signed a covenant in 1557 as a "godly band" to stand together to resist the Anglican church and the English establishment.

Cynghanedd. A complex medieval Welsh system of rhyme, alliteration, and consonance, to which Gerard Manley Hopkins alluded to describe his interplay of euphonious sounds, actually to be heard in any rich poet, as in the Welsh Dylan Thomas: "The force that through the green fuse drives the flower / Drives my green age."

Dactyl. A three-syllable metrical foot: $-\smile\smile$. It is the basic foot of dactylic hexameter, the six-foot line of Greek and Roman epic poetry.

Dactylic Hexameter. The classical or heroic line of the epic. A line based on six dactylic feet, with spondees substituted, and always ending $-\smile\smile\mid--$.

Dead Metaphor. A metaphor accepted without its figurative picture: "a jacket," for the paper around a book, with no mental picture of the human coat that prompted the original metaphor.

Decasyllabic. Having ten syllables. An iambic pentameter line is decasyllabic.

Deconstruction. The critical dissection of a literary text's statements, ambiguities, and structure to expose its hidden contradictions, implications, and fundamental instability of meaning. Jacques Derrida originated deconstruction in *Of Grammatology* (1967) and *Writing and Difference* (1967). Because no understanding of any text is stable, as each new reading is subject to the deconstruction of any meaning it appears to have established, it follows that criticism can be a kind of game, either playful or serious, as each critic ingeniously deconstructs the meanings established by others.

Decorum. Propriety, fitness, the quality of being appropriate. George Puttenham, in his *Arte of English Poesie* (1589), chides a translator of Virgil for his indecorum of having Aeneas "trudge," like a beggar, from Troy.

Defamiliarization. Turning the familiar to the strange by disrupting habitual ways of perceiving things. Derived from the thought of Victor Shklovsky and other Russian formalists, the idea is that art forces us to see things differently as we view them through the artist's sensibility, not our own.

Deism. A rational philosophy of religion, beginning with the theories of Lord Herbert of Cherbury, the "Father of Deism," in his *De Veritate* (1624). Deists generally held that God, the supreme Artisan, created a perfect clock of a universe, withdrew, and left it running, not to return to intervene in its natural works or the life of humankind; that the Bible is a moral guide, but neither historically accurate nor divinely authentic; and that reason guides human beings to virtuous conduct.

Denotation. The thing that a word stands for, the dictionary definition, an objective concept without emotional coloring. It is contrasted with the *connotation*, ideas, attitudes, or emotions associated with the word in the mind of user or hearer.

Dénouement. French for "unknotting": the unraveling of plot threads toward the end of a play, novel, or other narrative.

Determinism. The philosophical belief that events are shaped by forces beyond the control of human beings.

Dialect. A variety of language belonging to a particular time, place, or social group, as, for example, an 18th-century Cockney dialect, a New England dialect, or a coal miner's dialect. A language other than one's own is for the most part unintelligible without study or translation; a dialect other than one's own can generally be understood, although pronunciation, vocabulary, and syntax seem strange.

Dialogue. Conversation between two or more persons, as represented in prose fiction, drama, or essays, as opposed to *monologue*, the speech of one person. Good dialogue characterizes each speaker by idiom and attitude as it advances the dramatic conflict. The dialogue as a form of speculative exposition, or dialectical argument, is often less careful to distinguish the diction and character of the speakers.

Diatribe. Greek for "a wearing away": a bitter and abusive criticism or invective, often lengthy, directed against a person, institution, or work.

Diction. Word choice in speech or writing, an important element of style.

Didactic. Greek for "teaching": instructive, or having the qualities of a teacher. Since ancient times, literature has been assumed to have two functions, instruction and entertainment, with sometimes one and sometimes the other dominant. Literature intended primarily for instruction or containing an important moralistic element is didactic.

Dirge. A lamenting funeral song.

Discourse. (1) A formal discussion of a subject. (2) The conventions of communication associated with specific areas, in usages such as "poetic discourse," "the discourse of the novel," or "historical discourse."

Dissenter. A term arising in the 1640s for a member of the clergy or a follower who dissented from the forms of the established Anglican church, particularly Puritans. Dissenters generally came from the lower middle classes, merchants who disapproved of aristocratic frivolity and ecclesiastical pomp.

Dissonance. (1) Harsh and jarring sound; discord. It is frequently an intentional effect, as in the poems of Robert Browning. (2) Occasionally a term for half rhyme or slant rhyme.

Distich. A couplet, or pair of rhymed metrical lines.

Dithyramb. A frenzied choral song and dance to honor Dionysus, Greek god of wine and the power of fertility. Any irregular, impassioned poetry may be called *dithyrambic*. The irregular ode also evolved from the dithyramb.

Doggerel. (1) Trivial verse clumsily aiming at meter, usually tetrameter. (2) Any verse facetiously low and loose in meter and rhyme.

Domesday Book. The recorded census and survey of landholders that William the Conqueror ordered in 1085; from "Doomsday," the Last Judgment.

Dramatic Irony. A character in drama or fiction unknowingly says or does something in ironic contrast to what the audience or reader knows or will learn.

Dramatic Monologue. A monologue in verse. A speaker addresses a silent listener, revealing, in dramatic irony, things about himself or herself of which the speaker is unaware.

Eclogue. A short poem, usually a pastoral, and often in the form of a dialogue or soliloquy. During the Renaissance, in the works of Spenser and others, the eclogue became a major form of verse, with shepherds exchanging verses of love, lament, or eulogy.

Edition. The form in which a book is published, including its physical qualities and its content. A *first edition* is the first form of a book, printed and bound; a *second edition* is a later form, usually with substantial changes in content. Between the two, there may be more than one printing or impression of the first edition, sometimes with minor corrections. The term *edition* also refers to the format of a book. For example, an *illustrated edition* or a *two-volume edition* may be identical in verbal content to one without pictures or bound in a single volume.

Edwardian Period (1901–1914). From the death of Queen Victoria to the outbreak of World War I, named for the reign of Victoria's son, Edward VII (1901–1910), a period generally reacting against Victorian propriety and convention.

Elegiac Stanza. An iambic pentameter quatrain rhyming *abab*. Taking its name from Thomas Gray's *Elegy Written in a Country Churchyard* (1751), it is identical to the heroic quatrain.

Elegy. Greek for "lament": a poem on death or on a serious loss; characteristically a sustained meditation expressing sorrow and, frequently, an explicit or implied consolation.

Elision. Latin for "striking out": the omission or slurring of an unstressed vowel at the end of a word to bring a line of poetry closer to a prescribed metrical pattern, as in John Milton's *Lycidas:* "Tempered to th'oaten flute." *See also* Meter; Syncope.

Elizabethan Drama. English drama of the reign of Elizabeth I (1558–1603). Strictly speaking, drama from the reign of James I (1603–1625) belongs to the Jacobean period and that from the reign of Charles I (1625–1642) to the Caroline period, but the term *Elizabethan* is sometimes extended to include works of later reigns, before the closing of the theaters in 1642.

Elizabethan Period (1558–1603). The years marked by the reign of Elizabeth I; the "Golden Age of English Literature," especially as exemplified by the lyric poetry and dramas of Christopher Marlowe, Edmund Spenser, Sir Philip Sidney, and William Shakespeare, as well as the early Ben Jonson and John Donne.

Ellipsis. The omission of words for rhetorical effect: "*Drop dead*" for "You drop dead."

Emblem. (1) A didactic pictorial and literary form consisting of a word or phrase (*mot* or *motto*), a symbolic woodcut or engraving, and a brief moralistic poem (*explicatio*). Collections of emblems in book form were popular in the 16th and 17th centuries. (2) A type or symbol.

Emendation. A change made in a literary text to remove faults that have appeared through tampering or by errors in reading, transcription, or printing from the manuscript.

Empathy. Greek for "feeling with": identification with the feelings or passions of another person, natural creature, or even an inanimate object conceived of as possessing human attributes. Empathy suggests emotional identification, whereas sympathy may be largely an intellectual appreciation of another's situation.

Emphasis. Stress placed on words, phrases, or ideas to show their importance, by *italics*, **boldface,** and punctuation "!!!"; by figurative language, meter, and rhyme; or by strategies of rhetoric, like climactic order, contrast, repetition, and position.

Empiricism. Greek for "experience": the belief that all knowledge comes from experience, that human understanding of general truth can be founded only on observation of particulars. Empiricism is basic to the scientific method and to literary naturalism. It is opposed to rationalism, which discovers truth through reason alone, without regard to experience.

Enclosed Rhyme. A couplet, or pair of rhyming lines, enclosed in rhyming lines to give the pattern *abba*.

Encomium. Originally a Greek choral song in praise of a hero; later, any formal expression of praise, in verse or prose.

End Rhyme. Rhyme at the end of a line of verse (the usual placement), as distinguished from *initial rhyme*, at the beginning, or *internal rhyme*, within the line.

Enjambment. Run-on lines in which grammatical sense runs from one line of poetry to the next without pause or punctuation. The opposite of an end-stopped line.

Enlightenment. A philosophical movement in the 17th and 18th centuries, particularly in France, characterized by the conviction that reason could achieve all knowledge, supplant organized religion, and ensure progress toward happiness and perfection.

Envoy (or Envoi). A concluding stanza, generally shorter than the earlier stanzas of a poem, giving a brief summary of theme, address to a prince or patron, or return to a refrain.

Epic. A long narrative poem, typically a recounting of history or legend or of the deeds of a national hero. During the Renaissance, critical theory emphasized two assumptions: (1) the encyclopedic knowledge needed for major poetry, and (2) an aristocracy of genres, according to which epic and tragedy, because they deal with heroes and ruling-class figures, were reserved for major poets. Romanticism revived both the long mythological poem and the verse romance, but the prestige of the encyclopedic epic still lingered. In his autobiographical poem *The Prelude*, Wordsworth self-consciously internalized the heroic argument of the epic.

Epic Simile. Sometimes called a *Homeric simile:* an extended simile, comparing one thing with another by lengthy description of the second, often beginning with "as when" and concluding with "so" or "such."

Epicurean. Often meaning hedonistic (*see also* Hedonism), devoted to sensual pleasure and ease. Actually, Epicurus (c. 341–270 B.C.E.) was a kind of puritanical Stoic, recommending detachment from pleasure and pain to avoid life's inevitable suffering, hence advocating serenity as the highest happiness, intellect over the senses.

Epigram. (1) A brief poetic and witty couching of a home truth. (2) An equivalent statement in prose.

Epigraph. (1) An inscription on a monument or building. (2) A quotation or motto heading a book or chapter.

Epilogue. (1) A poetic address to the audience at the end of a play. (2) The actor performing the address. (3) Any similar appendage to a literary work, usually describing what happens to the characters in the future.

Epiphany. In religious tradition, the revelation of a divinity. James Joyce adapted the term to signify a moment of profound or spiritual revelation, when even the stroke of a clock or a noise in the street brings sudden illumination, and "its soul, its whatness leaps to us from the vestment of its appearance." For Joyce, art was an epiphany.

Episode. An incident in a play or novel; a continuous event in action and dialogue. Originally the term referred to a section in Greek tragedy between two choric songs.

Episodic Structure. In narration, the incidental stringing of one episode upon another, as in *Don Quixote* or *Moll Flanders*, in which one episode follows another with no necessary causal connection or plot.

Epistle. (1) A letter, usually a formal or artistic one, like Saint Paul's Epistles in the New Testament, or Horace's verse *Epistles*, widely imitated in the late 17th and 18th centuries, most notably by Alexander Pope. (2) A dedication in a prefatory epistle to a play or book.

Epitaph. (1) An inscription on a tombstone or monument memorializing the person, or persons, buried there. (2) A literary epigram or brief poem epitomizing the dead.

Epithalamium (or Epithalamion). A lyric ode honoring a bride and groom.

Epithet. A term characterizing a person or thing: e.g., *Richard the Lion-Hearted*.

Epitome. (1) A summary, an abridgment, an abstract. (2) One that supremely represents an entire class.

Essay. A literary composition on a single subject; usually short, in prose, and nonexhaustive. The word derives from French *essai* "an attempt," first used in the modern sense by Michel de Montaigne, whose *Essais* (1580–1588) are classics of the genre. Francis Bacon's *Essays* (1597) brought the term and form to English.

Estates. The "three estates of the realm," recognized from feudal times onward: the clergy (Lords Spiritual), the nobility (Lords Temporal), and the burghers (the Commons). In *Heroes and Hero-Worship*, Thomas Carlyle says that Edmund Burke (member of Parliament from 1766 to 1794) added to Parliament's three estates "the Reporters' Gallery" where "sat a fourth Estate more important than they all" (Lecture V). The Fourth Estate is now the press and other media.

Eulogy. A speech or composition of praise, especially of a deceased person.

Euphemism. Greek for "good speech": an attractive substitute for a harsh or unpleasant word or concept; figurative language or circumlocution substituting an indirect or oblique reference for a direct one.

Euphony. Melodious sound, the opposite of cacophony. A major feature of verse, but also a consideration in prose, euphony results from smooth-flowing meter or sentence rhythm as well as attractive sounds.

Euphuism. An artificial, highly elaborate affected style that takes its name from John Lyly's *Euphues: The Anatomy of Wit* (1578). Euphuism is characterized by the heavy use of rhetorical devices such as balance and antithesis, by much attention to alliteration and other sound patterns, and by learned allusion.

Excursus. (1) A lengthy discussion of a point, appended to a literary work. (2) A long digression.

Exegesis. (1) A detailed analysis, explanation, and interpretation of a difficult text, especially the Bible. (2) A rhetorical figure, also called *explicatio*, which clarifies a thought.

Exemplum. Latin for "example": a story used to illustrate a moral point. *Exempla* were a characteristic feature of medieval sermons. Chaucer's *Pardoner's Tale* and *Nun's Priest's Tale* are famous secular examples.

Existentialism. A philosophy centered on individual existence as unique and unrepeatable, hence rejecting the past for present existence and its unique dilemmas. Existentialism rose to prominence in the 1930s and 1940s, particularly in France after World War II in the work of Jean-Paul Sartre.

Expressionism. An early 20th-century movement in art and literature, best understood as a reaction against conventional realism and naturalism, and especially as a revolt against conventional society. The expressionist looked inward for images, expressing in paint, on stage, or in prose or verse a distorted, nightmarish version of reality, things dreamed about rather than actually existing.

Eye Rhyme. A rhyme of words that look but do not sound the same: *one, stone; word, lord; teak, break*.

Fable. (1) A short, allegorical story in verse or prose, frequently of animals, told to illustrate a moral. (2) The story line or plot of a narrative or drama. (3) Loosely, any legendary or fabulous account.

Falling Meter. A meter beginning with a stress, running from heavy to light.

Farce. A wildly comic play, mocking dramatic and social conventions, frequently with satiric intent.

Feminine Ending. An extra unstressed syllable at the end of a metrical line, usually iambic.

Feminine Rhyme. A rhyme of both the stressed and the unstressed syllables of one feminine ending with another.

Feudalism. The political and social system prevailing in Europe from the ninth century until the 1400s. It was a system of independent holdings (*feud* is Germanic for "estate") in which autonomous lords pledged fealty and service to those more powerful in exchange for protection, as did villagers to the neighboring lord of the manor.

Fiction. An imagined creation in verse, drama, or prose. Fiction is a thing made, an invention. It is distinguished from nonfiction by its essentially imaginative nature, but elements of fiction appear in fundamentally nonfictional constructions such as essays, biographies, autobiographies, and histories. Fictional anecdotes and illustrations abound in the works of politicians, business leaders, the clergy, philosophers, and scientists. Although any invented person, place, event, or condition is a fiction, the term is now most frequently used to mean "prose fiction," as distinct from verse or drama.

Figurative Language. Language that is not literal, being either metaphorical or rhetorically patterned.

Figure of Speech. An expression extending language beyond its literal meaning, either pictorially through metaphor, simile, allusion, and the like, or rhetorically through repetition, balance, antithesis, and the like. A figure of speech is also called a *trope*.

Fin de Siècle. "The end of the century," especially the last decade of the 19th. The term, acquired with the French influence of the symbolists Stéphane Mallarmé and Charles Baudelaire, connotes preciosity and decadence.

First-Person Narration. Narration by a character involved in a story.

Flyting. Scottish for "scolding": a form of invective, or violent verbal assault, in verse; traditional in Scottish literature, possibly Celtic in origin. Typically, two poets exchange scurrilous and often exhaustive abuse.

Folio. From Latin for "leaf." (1) A sheet of paper, folded once. (2) The largest of the book sizes, made from standard printing sheets, folded once before trimming and binding.

Folk Song. A song forming part of the folklore of a community. Like the folktale and the legend, a folk song is a traditional creative expression, characteristically shaped by oral tradition into the form in which it is later recorded in manuscript or print.

Folktale. A story forming part of the folklore of a community, generally less serious than the stories called *myths*. In preliterate societies, virtually all narratives were either myths or folktales: oral histories of real wars, kings, heroes, great families, and the like accumulating large amounts of legendary material.

Foot. The metrical unit; in English, an accented syllable with accompanying light syllable or syllables.

Foreshadowing. The technique of suggesting or prefiguring a development in a literary work before it occurs.

Formula. A plot outline or set of characteristic ingredients used in the construction of a literary work or applied to a portion of one. Formula fiction is written to the requirements of a particular market, usually undistinguished by much imagination or originality in applying the formula.

Foul Copy. A manuscript that has been used for printing, bearing the marks of the proofreader, editor, and printer, as well as, frequently, the author's queries and comments.

Four Elements. In ancient and medieval cosmology, earth, air, fire, and water—the four ultimate, exclusive, and eternal constituents that, according to Empedocles (c. 493–c. 433 B.C.E.) made up the world.

Four Senses of Interpretation. A mode of medieval criticism in which a work is examined for four kinds of meaning. The *literal meaning* is related to fact or history. The *moral* or *tropological meaning* is the lesson of the work as applied to individual behavior. The *allegorical meaning* is the particular story in its application to people generally, with emphasis on their beliefs. The *anagogical meaning* is its spiritual or mystical truth, its universal significance. After the literal, each of the others represents a broader form of what is usually called allegory, moving from individual morality to social organization to God.

Fourteeners. Lines of 14 syllables—7 iambic feet, popular with the Elizabethans.

Frame Narrative. A narrative enclosing one or more separate stories. Characteristically, the frame narrative is created as a vehicle for the stories it contains.

Free Verse. French *vers libre*; poetry free of traditional metrical and stanzaic patterns.

Genre. A term often applied loosely to the larger forms of literary convention, roughly analogous to "species" in biology. The Greeks spoke of three main genres of poetry—lyric, epic, and drama. Within each major genre, there are subgenres. In written forms dominated by prose, for example, there is a broad distinction between works of fiction (e.g., the novel) and thematic works (e.g., the essay). Within the fictional category, we note a distinction between novel and romance, and other forms such as satire and confession. The object of making these distinctions in literary tradition is not simply to classify but to judge authors in terms of the conventions they themselves chose.

Georgian. (1) Pertaining to the reigns of the four Georges—1714–1830, particularly the reigns of the first three, up to the close of the 18th century. (2) The literature written during the early years (1910–1914) of the reign of George V.

Georgic. A poem about farming and annual rural labors, after Virgil's *Georgics*.

Gloss. An explanation (from Greek *glossa* "tongue, language"); originally, Latin synonyms in the margins of Greek manuscripts and vernacular synonyms in later manuscripts as scribes gave the reader some help.

Glossary. A list of words, with explanations or definitions. A glossary is ordinarily a partial dictionary, appended to the end of a book to explain technical or unfamiliar terms.

Gothic. Originally, pertaining to the Goths, then to any Germanic people. Because the Goths began warring with the Roman empire in the 3rd century C.E., eventually sacking Rome itself, the term later became a synonym for "barbaric," which the 18th century next applied to anything medieval, of the Dark Ages.

Gothic Novel. A type of fiction introduced and named by Horace Walpole's *Castle of Otranto, A Gothic Story* (1764). Walpole introduced supernatural terror, with a huge mysterious helmet, portraits that walk abroad, and statues with nosebleeds. Matthew Gregory Lewis, "Monk Lewis," added sexual depravity to the murderous supernatural mix (*The Monk*, 1796). Mary Shelley's *Frankenstein* (1818) transformed the Gothic into moral science fiction.

Grotesque. Anything unnaturally distorted, ugly, ludicrous, fanciful, or bizarre; especially, in the 19th century, literature exploiting the abnormal.

Hedonism. A philosophy that sees pleasure as the highest good.

Hegelianism. The philosophy of G. W. F. Hegel (1770–1831), who developed the system of thought known as Hegelian dialectic, in which a given concept, or *thesis*, generates its opposite, or *antithesis*, and from the interaction of the two arises a *synthesis*. The synthesis then forms a thesis for a new cycle. Hegelian dialectic suggests that history is not static but contains a rational progression, an idea influential on many later thinkers.

Heroic Couplet. The closed and balanced iambic pentameter couplet typical of the heroic plays of John Dryden; hence, any closed couplet.

Heroic Quatrain. A stanza in four lines of iambic pentameter, rhyming *abab* (see also Meter). Also known as the *heroic stanza* and the *elegiac stanza*.

Hexameter. Six-foot lines.

Historicism. (1) Historical relativism. (2) An approach to literature that emphasizes its historical environment, the climate of ideas, belief, and literary conventions surrounding and influencing the writer.

Homily. A religious discourse or sermon, especially one emphasizing practical spiritual or moral advice.

Hubris. From Greek *hybris*, "pride": prideful arrogance or insolence of the kind that causes the tragic hero to ignore the warnings that might turn aside the action that leads to disaster.

Humors. The *cardinal humors* of ancient medical theory: blood, phlegm, yellow bile (choler), black bile (melancholy). From ancient times until the 19th century, the humors were believed largely responsible for health and disposition. Hippocrates (c. 460–c. 370 B.C.E.) thought an imbalance produced illness. Galen (c. 130–300 C.E.) suggested that character types are produced by dominance of fluids: *sanguine*, or kindly, cheerful, amorous; *phlegmatic*, or sluggish, unresponsive; *choleric*, or quick-tempered; and *melancholic*, or brooding, dejected. In literature, especially during the early modern period, characters were portrayed according to the humors that dominated them, as in the comedy of humors.

Hyperbole. Overstatement to make a point, as when a parent tells a child "I've told you a thousand times."

Iambus (or Iamb). A metrical foot: ⌣ –.

Idealism. (1) In philosophy and ethics, an emphasis on ideas and ideals, as opposed to the sensory emphasis of materialism. (2) Literary idealism follows from philosophical precepts, emphasizing a world in which the most important reality is a spiritual or transcendent truth not always reflected in the world of sense perception.

Idyll. A short poem of rustic pastoral serenity.

Image. A concrete picture, either literally descriptive, as in "Red roses covered the white wall," or figurative, as in "She is a rose," each carrying a sensual and emotive connotation. A figurative image may be an analogy, metaphor, simile, personification, or the like.

Impressionism. A literary style conveying subjective impressions rather than objective reality, taking its name from the movement in French painting in the mid–19th century, notably in the works of Manet, Monet, and Renoir. The Imagists represented impressionism in poetry; in fiction, writers like Virginia Woolf and James Joyce.

Industrial Revolution. The accelerated change, beginning in the 1760s, from an agricultural-shopkeeping society, using hand tools, to an industrial-mechanized one.

Influence. The apparent effect of literary works on subsequent writers and their work, as in Robert Browning's influence on T. S. Eliot.

Innuendo. An indirect remark or gesture, especially one implying something derogatory; an insinuation.

Interlocking Rhyme. Rhyme between stanzas; a word unrhymed in one stanza is used as a rhyme for the next, as in terza rima: *aba bcb cdc* and so on.

Internal Rhyme. Rhyme within a line, rather than at the beginning (*initial rhyme*) or end (*end rhyme*); also, rhyme matching sounds in the middle of a line with sounds at the end.

Intertextuality. (1) The relations between one literary text and others it evokes through such means as quotation, paraphrase, allusion, parody, and revision. (2) More broadly, the relations between a given text and all other texts, the potentially infinite sum of knowledge within which any text has its meaning.

Inversion. A reversal of sequence or position, as when the normal order of elements within a sentence is inverted for poetic or rhetorical effect.

Irony. In general, irony is the perception of a clash between appearance and reality, between *seems* and *is*, or between *ought* and *is*. The myriad shadings of irony seem to fall into three categories: (1) *Verbal irony*—saying something contrary to what it means; the appearance is what the words say, the reality is their contrary meaning. (2) *Dramatic irony*—saying or doing something while unaware of its ironic contrast with the whole truth; named for its frequency in drama, dramatic irony is a verbal irony with the speaker's awareness erased. (3) *Situational irony*—events turning to the opposite of what is expected or what should be. The ironic situation turns the speaker's unknowing words ironic. Situational irony is the essence of both comedy and tragedy: the young lovers run into the worst possible luck, until everything clears up happily; the most noble spirits go to their death, while the featherheads survive.

Italian Sonnet (or Petrarchan Sonnet). A sonnet composed of an octave and sestet, rhyming *abbaabba cdecde* (or *cdcdcd* or some variant, without a closing couplet).

Italic (or Italics). Type slanting upward to the right. *This sentence is italic.*

Jacobean Period (1603–1625). The reign of James I, *Jacobus* being the Latin for "James." A certain skepticism and even cynicism seeped into Elizabethan joy. The Puritans and the court party, the Cavaliers, grew more antagonistic. But it was in the Jacobean period that Shakespeare wrote his greatest tragedies and tragicomedies, and Ben Jonson did his major work.

Jargon. (1) Language peculiar to a trade or calling, as, for example, the jargon of astronauts, lawyers, or literary critics. (2) Confused or confusing language. This kind of jargon does not communicate to anybody.

Jeremiad. A lament or complaint, especially one enumerating transgressions and predicting destruction of a people, of the kind found in the Book of Jeremiah.

Juvenilia. Youthful literary products.

Kenning. A compound figurative metaphor, a circumlocution, in Old English and Old Norse poetry: "whale-road," for the sea.

Lament. A grieving poem, an elegy, in Anglo-Saxon or Renaissance times. *Deor's Lament* (c. 980) records the actual grief of a scop, or court poet, at being displaced in his lord's hall.

Lampoon. A satirical, personal ridicule in verse or prose. The term probably derives from the French *lampons*, "Let's guzzle," a refrain in 17th-century drinking songs.

Lay (or Lai). (1) A ballad or related metrical romance originating with the Breton lay of French Brittany and retaining some of its Celtic magic and folklore.

Lexicon. A word list, a vocabulary, a dictionary.

Libretto. "The little book" (Italian): the text of an opera, cantata, or other musical drama.

Litany. A prayer with phrases spoken or sung by a leader alternated with responses from congregation or choir. *The Litany* is a group of such prayers in the Book of Common Prayer.

Literal. According to the letter (of the alphabet): the precise, plain meaning of a word or phrase in its simplest, original sense, considered apart from its sense as a metaphor or other figure of speech. Literal language is the opposite of figurative language.

Literature. Strictly defined, anything written. Therefore the oral culture of a people—its folklore, folk songs, folktales, and so on—is not literature until it is written down. The movies are not literature except in their printed scripts. By the same strict meaning, historical records, telephone books, and the like are all literature because they are written in letters of the alphabet, although they are not taught as literature in schools. In contrast to this strict, literal meaning, literature has come to be equated with *creative writing* or works of the imagination: chiefly poetry, prose fiction, and drama.

Lollards. From Middle Dutch, literally, "mumblers": a derisive term applied to the followers of John Wyclif (c. 1328–1384), the reformer behind the Wyclif Bible (1385), the first in English. Lollards preached against the abuses of the medieval church, setting up a standard of poverty and individual service as against wealth and hierarchical privilege.

Lyric. A poem, brief and discontinuous, emphasizing sound and pictorial imagery rather than narrative or dramatic movement.

Macaronic Verse. (1) Strictly, verse mixing words in a writer's native language with endings, phrases, and syntax of another language, usually Latin or Greek, creating a comic or burlesque effect. (2) Loosely, any verse mingling two or more languages.

Mannerism, Mannerist. (1) In architecture and painting, a style elongating and distorting human figures and spaces, deliberately confusing scale and perspective. (2) Literary or artistic affectation; a stylistic quality produced by excessively peculiar, ornamental, or ingenious devices.

Manners. Social behavior. In usages like comedy of manners and novel of manners, the term suggests an examination of the behavior, morals, and values of a particular time, place, or social class.

Manuscript. Literally, "written by hand": any handwritten document, as, for example, a letter or diary; also, a work submitted for publication.

Marginalia. Commentary, references, or other material written by a reader in the margins of a manuscript or book.

Masculine Ending. The usual iambic ending, on the accented foot: ⏑ –.

Masculine Rhyme. The most common rhyme in English, on the last syllable of a line.

Masque. An allegorical, poetic, and musical dramatic spectacle popular in the English courts and mansions of the 16th and early 17th centuries. Figures from mythology, history, and romance mingled in a pastoral fantasy with fairies, fauns, satyrs, and witches, as masked amateurs from the court (including kings and queens) participated in dances and scenes.

Materialism. In philosophy, an emphasis upon the material world as the ultimate reality. Its opposite is *idealism*. Thomas Hobbes was an early materialist in 17th-century England. In the 19th century, materialism had evolved into naturalism, which emerged as an especially materialistic form of realism.

Melodrama. A play with dire ingredients—the mortgage foreclosed, the daughter tied to the railroad tracks—but with a happy ending. The typical emotions produced here result in romantic tremors, pity, and terror.

Menippean Satire. Satire on pedants, bigots, rapacious professional people, and other persons or institutions perceiving the world from a single framework. The focus is on intellectual limitations and mental attitudes. Typical ingredients include a rambling narrative; unusual settings; displays of erudition; and long digressions.

Metaphor. Greek for "transfer" (*meta* and *trans* meaning "across"; *phor* and *fer* meaning "carry"): to carry something across. Hence a metaphor treats something as if it were something else. Money becomes a *nest egg*; a sandwich, a *submarine*.

Metaphysical Poetry. Seventeenth-century poetry of wit and startling extended metaphor.

Meter. The measured pulse of poetry. English meters derive from four Greek and Roman quantitative meters (*see also* Quantitative Verse), which English stresses more sharply, although the patterns are the same. The unit of each pattern is the *foot*, containing one stressed syllable and one or two light ones. *Rising meter* goes from light to heavy; *falling* *meter*, from heavy to light. One meter—iambic—has dominated English poetry, with the three others lending an occasional foot, for variety, and producing a few poems.

Rising Meters

Iambic: ˘ ¯ (the iambus)
Anapestic: ˘ ˘ ¯ (the anapest)

Falling Meters

Trochaic: ¯ ˘ (the trochee)
Dactylic: ¯ ˘ ˘ (the dactyl)

The number of feet in a line also gives the verse a name:

1 foot: monometer
2 feet: dimeter
3 feet: trimeter
4 feet: tetrameter
5 feet: pentameter
6 feet: hexameter
7 feet: heptameter

All meters show some variations, and substitutions of other kinds of feet, but three variations in iambic writing are virtually standard:

Inverted foot: ¯ ˘ (a trochee)
Spondee: ¯ ¯
Ionic double foot: ˘ ˘ ¯ ¯

The *pyrrhic foot* of classical meters, two light syllables (˘ ˘), lives in the English line only in the Ionic double foot, although some prosodists scan a relatively light iambus as pyrrhic. Examples of meters and scansion:

Iabic Tetrameter

An-ni-| hil-a-| ting all | that's made |
To a | green thought| in a | green shade. |

Andrew Marvell, "The Garden"

Iambic Tetrameter
(with two inverted feet)
Close to | the sun | in lone-| ly lands, |
Ringed with | the az- | ure world, | he stands. |

Alfred, Lord Tennyson, "The Eagle"

Iambic Pentameter
Love's not | Time's fool, | though ros- | y lips | and cheeks |
Within | his bend- | ing sick- | le's com-| pass come |

William Shakespeare, Sonnet 116

When to| the ses-| sions of | sweet si -| lent thought |

William Shakespeare, Sonnet 30

Anapestic Tetrameter
(trochees substituted)
The pop- | lars are felled; | farwell | to the shade |
And the whis- | pering sound | of the cool | colonnade |

   William Cowper, "The Poplar Field"

Trochaic Tetrameter
Tell me | not in | mournful | numbers |

   Henry Wadsworth Longfellow, "A Psalm of Life"

Dactylic Hexameter
This is the | forest prim- | eval. The | murmuring | pines and the | hemlocks |
Bearded with | moss. . . .

   Henry Wadsworth Longfellow, "Evangeline"

Metonymy. "Substitute naming." A figure of speech in which an associated idea stands in for the actual item: "The *pen* is mightier than the *sword*" for "Literature and propaganda accomplish more and survive longer than warfare," or "The *White House* announced" for "The President announced." *See also* Synecdoche.

Metrics. The analysis and description of meter; also called *prosody*.

Middle English. The language of England from the middle of the 12th century to approximately 1500. English began to lose its inflectional endings and accepted many French words into its vocabulary, especially terms associated with the new social, legal, and governmental structures (*baron, judge, jury, marshal, parliament, prince*), and those in common use by the French upper classes (*mansion, chamber, veal, beef*).

Mimesis. A term meaning "imitation." It has been central to literary criticism since Aristotle's *Poetics*. The ordinary meaning of *imitation* as creating a resemblance to something else is clearly involved in Aristotle's definition of dramatic plot as *mimesis praxeos*, the imitation of an action. But there are many things that a work of literature may imitate, and hence many contexts of imitation. Works of literature may imitate other works of literature: this is the aspect of literature that comes into such conceptions as convention and genre. In a larger sense, every work of literature imitates, or finds its identity in, the entire "world of words," in Wallace Stevens's phrase, the sense of the whole of reality as potentially literary, as finding its end in a book, as Stéphane Mallarmé says.

Miracle Play. A medieval play based on a saint's life or story from the Bible.

Miscellany. A collection of various things. A literary miscellany is therefore a book collecting varied works, usually poems by different authors, a kind of anthology. The term is applied especially to the many books of this kind that appeared in the Elizabethan period.

Mock Epic. A poem in epic form and manner ludicrously elevating some trivial subject to epic grandeur.

Modernism. A collective term, generally associated with the first half of the 20th century, for various aesthetic and cultural attempts to place a "modern" face on experience. Modernism arose from a sense that the old ways were worn out. The new century opened with broad social, philosophical, religious, and cultural discussion and reform. For creative artists, the challenges of the new present meant that art became subject to change in every way, that the content, forms, and techniques inherited from the 19th century existed to be challenged, broken apart, and re-formed.

Monodrama. (1) A play with one character. (2) A closet drama or dramatic monologue.

Monody. (1) A Greek ode for one voice. (2) An elegiac lament, a dirge, in poetic soliloquy.

Monologue. (1) A poem or story in the form of a soliloquy. (2) Any extended speech.

Motif (or Motive). (1) A recurrent thematic element—word, image, symbol, object, phrase, action. (2) A conventional incident, situation, or device like the unknown knight of mysterious origin and low degree in the romance, or the baffling riddle in fairy tales.

Muse. The inspirer of poetry, on whom the poet calls for assistance. In Greek mythology the Muses were the nine daughters of Zeus and Mnemosyne ("Memory") presiding over the arts and sciences.

Mystery Play. Medieval religious drama; eventually performed in elaborate cycles of plays acted on pageant wagons or stages throughout city streets, with different guilds of artisans and merchants responsible for each.

Mysticism. A spiritual discipline in which sensory experience is expunged and the mind is devoted to deep contemplation and the reaching of a transcendental union with God.

Myth. From Greek *mythos,* "plot" or "narrative." The verbal culture of most if not all human societies began with stories, and certain stories have achieved a distinctive importance as being connected with what the society feels it most needs to know: stories illustrating the society's religion, history, class structure, or the origin of peculiar features of the natural environment.

Narrative Poem. One that tells a story, particularly the epic, metrical romance, and shorter narratives, like the ballad.

Naturalism. (1) Broadly, according to nature. In this sense, naturalism is opposed to idealism, emphasizing things accessible to the senses in this world in contrast to permanent or spiritual truths presumed to lie outside it. (2) More specifically, a literary movement of the late 19th century; an extension of realism, naturalism was a reaction against the restrictions inherent in the realistic emphasis on the ordinary, as naturalists insisted that the extraordinary is real, too.

Neoclassical Period. Generally, the span of time from the restoration of Charles II to his father's throne in 1660 until the publication of William Wordsworth and Samuel Taylor Coleridge's *Lyrical Ballads* (1798). Writers hoped to revive something like the classical Pax Romana, an era of peace and literary excellence.

Neologism. A word newly coined or introduced into a language, or a new meaning given to an old word.

New Criticism. An approach to criticism prominent in the United States after the publication of John Crowe Ransom's *New Criticism* (1941). Generally, the New Critics were agreed that a poem or story should be considered an organic unit, with each part working to support the whole. They worked by close analysis, considering the text as the final authority, and were distrustful, though not wholly neglectful, of considerations brought from outside the text, as, for example, from biography or history.

New Historicism. A cross-disciplinary approach fostered by the rise of feminist and multicultural studies as well as a renewed emphasis on historical perspective. Associated in particular with work on the early modern and the romantic periods in the United States and England, the approach emphasizes analysis of the relationship between history and literature, viewing writings in both fields as "texts" for study. New Historicism has tended to note political influences on literary and historical texts, to illuminate the role of the writer against the backdrop of social customs and assumptions, and to view history as changeable and interconnected instead of as a linear progressive evolution.

Nocturne. A night piece; writing evocative of evening or night.

Nominalism. In the Middle Ages, the belief that universals have no real being, but are only names, their existence limited to their presence in the minds and language of humans. This belief was opposed to the beliefs of medieval realists, who held that universals have an independent existence, at least in the mind of God.

Norman Conquest. The period of English history in which the Normans consolidated their hold on England after the defeat of the Saxon King Harold by William, Duke of Normandy, in 1066. French became the court language and Norman lords gained control of English lands, but Anglo-Saxon administrative and judicial systems remained largely in place.

Novel. The extended prose fiction that arose in the 18th century to become a major literary expression of the modern world. The term comes from the Italian *novella*, the short "new" tale of intrigue and moral comeuppance most eminently disseminated by Boccaccio's *Decameron* (1348–1353). The terms *novel* and *romance*, from the French *roman*, competed interchangeably for most of the 18th century.

Novella. (1) Originally, a short tale. (2) In modern usage, a term sometimes used interchangeably with short novel or for a fiction of middle length, between a short story and a novel. *See* Novel.

Octave. (1) The first unit in an Italian sonnet: eight lines of iambic pentameter, rhyming *abbaabba*. (2) A stanza in eight lines. *See also* Meter.

Octavo (Abbreviated 8vo). A book made from sheets folded to give signatures of eight leaves (16 pages), a book of average size.

Octet. An octastich or octave.

Octosyllabic. Eight-syllable.

Ode. A long, stately lyric poem in stanzas of varied metrical pattern.

Old English. The language brought to England, beginning in 449, by the Jute, Angle, and Saxon invaders from Denmark; the language base from which modern English evolved.

Old English Literature. The literature of England from the Anglo-Saxon invasion of the mid-5th century until the beginning of the Middle English period in the mid-12th century.

Omniscient Narrative. A narrative account untrammeled by constraints of time or space. An omniscient narrator perspective knows about the external and internal realities of characters as well as incidents unknown to them, and can interpret motivation and meaning.

Onomatopoeia. The use of words formed or sounding like what they signify—*buzz, crack, smack, whinny*—especially in an extensive capturing of sense by sound.

Orientalism. A term denoting Western portrayals of Oriental culture. In literature it refers to a varied body of work beginning in the 18th century that described for Western readers the history, language, politics, and culture of the area east of the Mediterranean.

Oxford Movement. A 19th-century movement to reform the Anglican church according to the high-church and more nearly Catholic ideals and rituals of the later 17th-century church.

Oxymoron. A pointed stupidity: *oxy*, "sharp," plus *moron*. One of the great ironic figures of speech—for example, "a fearful joy," or Milton's "darkness visible."

Paleography. The study and interpretation of ancient handwriting and manuscript styles.

Palimpsest. A piece of writing on secondhand vellum, parchment, or other surface carrying traces of erased previous writings.

Panegyric. A piece of writing in praise of a person, thing, or achievement.

Pantheism. A belief that God and the universe are identical, from the Greek words *pan* ("all") and *theos* ("god"). God is all; all is God.

Pantomime. A form of drama presented without words, in a dumb show.

Parable. (1) A short tale, such as those of Jesus in the gospels, encapsulating a moral or religious lesson. (2) Any saying, figure of speech, or narrative in which one thing is expressed in terms of another.

Paradox. An apparently untrue or self-contradictory statement or circumstance that proves true upon reflection or when examined in another light.

Paraphrase. A rendering in other words of the sense of a text or passage, as of a poem, essay, short story, or other writing.

Parody. Originally, "a song sung beside" another. From this idea of juxtaposition arose the two basic elements of parody, comedy and criticism. As comedy, parody exaggerates or distorts the prominent features of style or content in a work. As criticism, it mimics the work, borrowing words or phrases or characteristic turns of thought in order to highlight weaknesses of conception or expression.

Passion Play. Originally a play based on Christ's Passion; later, one including both Passion and Resurrection. Such plays began in the Middle Ages, performed from the 13th century onward, often as part of the pageants presented for the feast of Corpus Christi.

Pastiche. A literary or other artistic work created by assembling bits and pieces from other works.

Pastoral. From Latin *pastor*, a shepherd. The first pastoral poet was Theocritus, a Greek of the 3rd century B.C.E. The pastoral was especially popular in Europe from the 14th through the 18th centuries, with some fine examples still written in England in the 19th century. The pastoral mode is self-reflexive. Typically the poet echoes the conventions of earlier pastorals in order to put "the complex into the simple," as William Empson observed in *Some Versions of Pastoral* (1935). The poem is not really about shepherds, but about the complex society the poet and readers inhabit.

Pathetic Fallacy. The attribution of animate or human characteristics to nature, as, for example, when rocks, trees, or weather are portrayed as reacting in sympathy to human feelings or events.

Pathos. The feeling of pity, sympathy, tenderness, compassion, or sorrow evoked by someone or something that is helpless.

Pedantry. Ostentatious book learning: an accusation frequently hurled in scholarly disagreements.

Pentameter. A line of five metrical feet. *See also* Meter.

Peripeteia (or Peripetia, Peripety). A sudden change in situation in a drama or fiction, a reversal of luck for good or ill.

Periphrasis. The practice of talking around the point; a wordy restatement; a circumlocution.

Peroration. (1) The summative conclusion of a formal oration. (2) Loosely, a grandiloquent speech.

Persona. A mask (in Latin); in poetry and fiction, the projected speaker or narrator of the work—that is, a mask for the actual author.

Personification. The technique of treating abstractions, things, or animals as persons. A kind of metaphor, personification turns abstract ideas, like love, into a physical beauty named Venus, or conversely, makes dumb animals speak and act like humans.

Petrarchan Sonnet. Another name for an Italian sonnet.

Philology. The study of ancient languages and literatures; also more broadly interpreted from its basic meaning, "love of the word," to include all literary studies. In the 19th century, the field of historical linguistics.

Phoneme. In linguistics, the smallest distinguishable unit of sound. Different for each language, phonemes are defined by determining which differences in sound function to signal a difference in meaning.

Phonetics. (1) The study of speech sounds and their production, transmission, and reception. (2) The phonetic system of a particular language. (3) Symbols used to represent speech sounds.

Picaresque Novel. A novel chronicling the adventures of a rogue (Spanish: *picaro*), typically presented as an autobiography, episodic in structure and panoramic in its coverage of time and place.

Picturesque, the. A quality in landscape, and in idealized landscape painting, admired in the second half of the 18th century and featuring crags, flaring and blasted trees, a torrent or winding stream, ruins, and perhaps a quiet cottage and cart, with contrasting light and shadow. It was considered an aesthetic mean between the poles of Edmund Burke's *A Philosophical Inquiry into the Sublime and the Beautiful* (1756).

Plagiarism. Literary kidnapping (Latin *plagiarius*, "kidnapper")—the seizing and presenting as one's own the ideas or writings of another.

Plain Style. The straightforward, unembellished style of preaching favored by 17th-century Puritans as well as by reformers within the Anglican church, as speaking God's word directly from the inspired heart as opposed to the high style of aristocratic oratory and courtliness, the vehicle of subterfuge. Plain style was simultaneously advocated for scientific accuracy by the Royal Society.

Platonism. Any reflection of Plato's philosophy, particularly the belief in the eternal reality of ideal forms, of which the diversities of the physical world are but transitory shadows.

Poetics. The theory, art, or science of poetry. Poetics is concerned with the nature and function of poetry and with identifying and explaining its types, forms, and techniques.

Poet Laureate. Since the 17th century, a title conferred by the monarch on English poets. At first, the laureate was required to write poems to commemorate special occasions, such as royal birthdays, national celebrations, and the like, but since the early 19th century the appointment has been for the most part honorary.

Poetry. Imaginatively intense language, usually in verse. Poetry is a form of fiction—"the supreme fiction," said Wallace Stevens. It is distinguished from other fictions by the compression resulting from its heavier use of figures of speech and allusion and, usually, by the music of its patterns of sounds.

Postmodernism. A term first used in relation to literature in the late 1940s by Randall Jarrell and John Berryman to proclaim a new sensibility arising to challenge the reigning assumptions and practices of modernism. The attitudes and literary devices of the modernists— stream of consciousness, for example—had taken on the patina of tradition. For many of the postmodernists, disillusionment seemed to have reached its fullest measure. Life had little meaning, art less, and a neat closure to expectations raised by the artist seemed impossible. Intruding into one's own fiction to ponder its powers became a hallmark of the 1960s and 1970s.

Poststructuralism. A mode of literary criticism and thought centered on Jacques Derrida's concept of deconstruction. Structuralists see language as the paradigm for all structures. Poststructuralists see language as based on differences—hence the analytical deconstruction of what seemed an immutable system. What language expresses is already absent. Poststructuralism challenges the New Criticism, which seeks a truth fixed within the "verbal icon," the text, in W. K. Wimsatt's term. Poststructuralism invites interpretations through the spaces left by the way words operate.

Pragmatism. In philosophy, the idea that the value of a belief is best judged by the acts that follow from it—its practical results.

Preciosity. Since the 19th century, a term for an affected or overingenious refinement of language.

Predestination. The belief that an omniscient God, at the Creation, destined all subsequent events, particularly, in Calvinist belief, the election for salvation and the damnation of individual souls.

Pre-Raphaelite. Characteristic of a small but influential group of mid-19th-century painters who hoped to recapture the spiritual vividness they saw in medieval painting before Raphael (1483–1520).

Presbyterianism. John Calvin's organization of ecclesiastical governance not by bishops representing the pope but by elders representing the congregation.

Proscenium. Originally, in Greece, the whole acting area ("in front of the scenery"); now, that part of the stage projecting in front of the curtain.

Prose. Ordinary writing patterned on speech, as distinct from verse.

Prose Poetry. Prose rich in cadenced and poetic effects like alliteration, assonance, consonance, and the like, and in imagery.

Prosody. The analysis and description of meters; metrics (*see also* Meter). Linguists apply the term to the study of patterns of accent in a language.

Protagonist. The leading character in a play or story; originally the leader of the chorus in the agon ("contest") of Greek drama, faced with the antagonist, the opposition.

Pseudonym. A fictitious name adopted by an author for public use, like George Eliot (Mary Ann/Marian Evans), and George Orwell (Eric Arthur Blair).

Psychoanalytic Criticism. A form of criticism that uses the insights of Freudian psychology to illuminate a work.

Ptolemaic Universe. The universe as perceived by Ptolemy, a Greco-Egyptian astronomer of the 2nd century C.E., whose theories were dominant until the Renaissance produced the Copernican universe. In Ptolemy's system, the universe was world-centered, with the sun, moon, planets, and stars understood as rotating around the earth in a series of concentric spheres, producing as they revolved the harmonious "music of the spheres."

Puritanism. A Protestant movement arising in the mid-16th century with the Reformation in England. Theocracy—the individual and the congregation governed directly under God through Christ—became primary, reflected in the centrality of the Scriptures and their exposition, direct confession through prayer and public confession to the congregation rather than through priests, and the direct individual experience of God's grace.

Quadrivium. The more advanced four of the seven liberal arts as studied in medieval universities: arithmetic, geometry, astronomy, and music.

Quantitative Verse. Verse that takes account of the quantity of the syllables (whether they take a long or short time to pronounce) rather than their stress patterns.

Quarto (Abbreviated 4to, 4o). A book made from sheets folded twice, giving signatures of four leaves (eight pages). Many of Shakespeare's plays were first printed individually in quarto editions, designated First Quarto, Second Quarto, etc.

Quatrain. A stanza of four lines, rhymed or unrhymed. With its many variations, it is the most common stanzaic form in English.

Rationalism. The theory that reason, rather than revelation or authority, provides knowledge, truth, the choice of good over evil, and an adequate understanding of God and the universe.

Reader-Response Theory. A form of criticism that arose during the 1970s; it postulates the essential active involvement of the reader with the text and focuses on the effect of the process of reading on the mind.

Realism (in literature). The faithful representation of life. Realism carries the conviction of true reports of phenomena observable by others.

Realism (in philosophy). (1) In the Middle Ages, the belief that universal concepts possess real existence apart from particular things and the human mind. They exist either as entities like Platonic forms or as concepts in the mind of God. Medieval realism was opposed to nominalism. (2) In later epistemology, the belief that things exist apart from our perception of them. In this sense, realism is opposed to idealism, which locates all reality in our minds.

Recension. (1) A process of editorial revision based on an examination of the various versions and sources of a literary text. (2) The text produced as a result of reconciling variant readings.

Recto. The right-hand page of an open book; the front of a leaf as opposed to the *verso* or back of a leaf.

Redaction. (1) A revised version. (2) A rewriting or condensing of an older work.

Refrain. A set phrase, or chorus, recurring throughout a song or poem, usually at the end of a stanza or other regular interval.

Relativism. The philosophical belief that nothing is absolute, that values are relative to circumstances. In criticism, relativism is either personal or historical.

Revenge Tragedy. The popular Elizabethan mode, initiated by Thomas Kyd's *Spanish Tragedy* (c. 1586), wherein the hero must revenge a ruler's murder of father, son, or lover.

Reversal. The thrilling change of luck for the protagonist at the last moment in comedy or tragedy—the *peripeteia*, which Aristotle first described in his *Poetics*, along with the discovery that usually sparks it.

Rhetoric. From Greek *rhetor*, "orator": the art of persuasion in speaking or writing. Since ancient times, rhetoric has been understood by some as a system of persuasive devices divorced from considerations of the merits of the case argued.

Rhetorical Figure. A figure of speech employing stylized patterns of word order or meaning for purposes of ornamentation or persuasion.

Rhetorical Question. A question posed for rhetorical effect, usually with a self-evident answer.

Rhyme (sometimes Rime, an older spelling). The effect created by matching sounds at the ends of words. The functions of rhyme are essentially four: pleasurable, mnemonic, structural, and rhetorical. Like meter and figurative language, rhyme provides a pleasure derived from fulfillment of a basic human desire to see similarity in dissimilarity, likeness with a difference.

Rhyme Royal. A stanza of seven lines of iambic pentameter, rhyming *ababbcc*. *See also* Meter.

Rhythm. The measured flow of repeated sound patterns, as, for example, the heavy stresses of accentual verse, the long and short syllables of quantitative verse, the balanced syntactical arrangements of parallelism in either verse or prose.

Romance. A continuous narrative in which the emphasis is on what happens in the plot, rather than on what is reflected from ordinary life or experience. Thus a central element in romance is adventure; at its most primitive, romance is an endless sequence of adventures.

Romanticism. A term describing qualities that colored most elements of European and American intellectual life in the late 18th and early 19th centuries, from literature, art, and music, through architecture, landscape gardening, philosophy, and politics. Within the social, political, and intellectual structures of society, the Romantics stressed the separateness of the person, celebrated individual perception and imagination, and embraced nature as a model for harmony in society and art. Their view was an egalitarian one, stressing the value of expressive abilities common to all, inborn rather than developed through training.

Roundheads. Adherents of the Parliamentary, or Puritan, party in the English Civil War, so called from their short haircuts, as opposed to the fashionable long wigs of the Cavaliers, supporters of King Charles I.

Rubric. From Latin *rubrica*, "red earth" (for coloring): in a book or manuscript, a heading, marginal notation, or other section distinguished for special attention by being printed in red ink or in distinctive type.

Run-on Line. A line of poetry whose sense does not stop at the end, with punctuation, but runs on to the next line.

Satire. Poking corrective ridicule at persons, types, actions, follies, mores, and beliefs.

Scop. An Anglo-Saxon bard, or court poet, a kind of poet laureate.

Semiotics. In anthropology, sociology, and linguistics, the study of signs, including words, other sounds, gestures, facial expressions, music, pictures, and other signals used in communication.

Senecan Tragedy. The bloody and bombastic tragedies of revenge inspired by Seneca's nine closet dramas, which had been discovered in Italy in the mid-16th century and soon thereafter translated into English.

Sensibility. Sensitive feeling, emotion. The term arose early in the 18th century to denote the tender undercurrent of feeling in the neoclassical period, continuing through Jane Austen's *Sense and Sensibility* (1811) and afterward.

Sequel. A literary work that explores later events in the lives of characters introduced elsewhere.

Serial. A narration presented in segments separated by time. Novels by Charles Dickens and other 19th-century writers were first serialized in magazines.

Seven Liberal Arts. The subjects studied in medieval universities, consisting of the *trivium* (grammar, logic, and rhetoric), for the B.A., and the *quadrivium* (arithmetic, geometry, astronomy, and music), for the M.A.

Shakespearean Sonnet (or English Sonnet). A sonnet in three quatrains and a couplet, rhyming *abab cdcd efef gg.*

Signified, Signifier. In structural linguistics, the *signified* is the idea in mind when a word is used, an entity separate from the *signifier,* the word itself.

Simile. A metaphor stating the comparison by use of *like, as,* or *as if.*

Slang. The special vocabulary of a class or group of people (as, for example, truck drivers, jazz musicians, salespeople, drug dealers), generally considered substandard, low, or offensive when measured against formal, educated usage.

Sonnet. A verse form of 14 lines, in English characteristically in iambic pentameter and most often in one of two rhyme schemes: the *Italian* (or *Petrarchan)* or *Shakespearean* (or *English).* An Italian sonnet is composed of an octave, rhyming *abbaabba,* and a sestet, rhyming *cdecde* or *cdcdcd,* or in some variant pattern, but with no closing couplet. A Shakespearean sonnet has three quatrains and a couplet, and rhymes *abab cdcd efef gg.* In both types, the content tends to follow the formal outline suggested by rhyme linkage, giving two divisions to the thought of an Italian sonnet and four to a Shakespearean one.

Sonnet Sequence. A group of sonnets thematically unified to create a longer work, although generally, unlike the stanza, each sonnet so connected can also be read as a meaningful separate unit.

Spondee. A metrical foot of two long, or stressed, syllables: – –.

Sprung Rhythm. Gerard Manley Hopkins's term to describe his variations of iambic meter to avoid the "same and tame." His feet, he said, vary from one to four syllables, with one stress per foot, on the first syllable.

Stanza. A term derived from an Italian word for "room" or "stopping place" and used, loosely, to designate any grouping of lines in a separate unit in a poem: a verse paragraph. More strictly, a stanza is a grouping of a prescribed number of lines in a given meter, usually with a particular rhyme scheme, repeated as a unit of structure. Poems in stanzas provide an instance of the aesthetic pleasure in repetition with a difference that also underlies the metrical and rhyming elements of poetry.

Stereotype. A character representing generalized racial or social traits repeated as typical from work to work, with no individualizing traits.

Stichomythia. Dialogue in alternate lines, favored in Greek tragedy and by Seneca and his imitators among the Elizabethans—including William Shakespeare.

Stock Characters. Familiar types repeated in literature to become symbolic of a particular genre, like the strong, silent hero of the western or the hard-boiled hero of the detective story.

Stoicism. (1) Generally, fortitude, repression of feeling, indifference to pleasure or pain. (2) Specifically, the philosophy of the Stoics, who, cultivating endurance and self-control, restrain passions such as joy and grief that place them in conflict with nature's dictates.

Stress. In poetry, the accent or emphasis given to certain syllables, indicated in scansion by a *macron* (–). In a trochee, for example, the stress falls on the first syllable: *sŭmmĕr. See also* Meter.

Structuralism. The study of social organizations and myths, of language, and of literature as structures. Each part is significant only as it relates to others in the total structure, with nothing meaningful by itself.

Structural Linguistics. Analysis and description of the grammatical structures of a spoken language.

Sublime. In literature, a quality attributed to lofty or noble ideas, grand or elevated expression, or (the ideal of sublimity) an inspiring combination of thought and language. In nature or art, it is a quality, as in a landscape or painting, that inspires awe or reverence.

Subplot. A sequence of events subordinate to the main story in a narrative or dramatic work.

Syllabic Verse. Poetry in which meter has been set aside and the line is controlled by a set number of syllables, regardless of stress.

Symbol. Something standing for its natural qualities in another context, with human meaning added: an eagle, standing for the soaring imperious dominance of Rome.

Symbolism. Any use of symbols, especially with a theoretical commitment, as when the French Symbolists of the 1880s and 1890s stressed, in Stéphane Mallarmé's words, not the thing but the effect, the subjective emotion implied by the surface rendering.

Syncopation. The effect produced in verse or music when two stress patterns play off against one another.

Synecdoche. The understanding of one thing by another—a kind of metaphor in which a part stands for the whole, or the whole for a part: *a hired hand* meaning "a laborer."

Synesthesia. Greek for "perceiving together": close association or confusion of sense impressions. The result is essentially a metaphor, transferring qualities of one sense to another, as in common phrases like "blue note" and "cold eye."

Synonyms. Words in the same language denoting the same thing, usually with different connotations: *female, woman, lady, dame; male, masculine, macho.*

Synopsis. A summary of a play, a narrative, or an argument.

Tenor and Vehicle. I. A. Richards's terms for the two aspects of metaphor, *tenor* being the actual thing projected figuratively in the *vehicle.* "She [tenor] is a rose [vehicle]."

Tercet (or Triplet). A verse unit of three lines, sometimes rhymed, sometimes not.

Terza Rima. A verse form composed of tercets with interlocking rhyme (*aba bcb cdc,* and so on), usually in iambic pentameter. Invented by Dante for his *Divine Comedy.*

Third-Person Narration. A method of storytelling in which someone who is not involved in the story, but stands somewhere outside it in space and time, tells of the events.

Topos. A commonplace, from Greek *topos* (plural *topoi*), "place." (1) A topic for argument, remembered by the classical system of placing it, in the mind's eye, in a place within a building and then proceeding mentally from one place to the next. (2) A rhetorical device, similarly remembered as a commonplace.

Tragedy. Fundamentally, a serious fiction involving the downfall of a hero or heroine. As a literary form, a basic mode of drama. Tragedy often involves the theme of isolation, in which a hero, a character of greater than ordinary human importance, becomes isolated from the community. Then there is the theme of the violation and reestablishment of order, in which the neutralizing of the violent act may take the form of revenge. Finally, a character may embody a passion too great for the cosmic order to tolerate, such as the passion of sexual love. Renaissance tragedy seems to be essentially a mixture of the heroic and the ironic. It tends to center on heroes who, though they cannot be of divine parentage in Christianized Western Europe, are still of titanic importance, with an articulateness and social authority beyond anything in our normal experience.

Tragic Irony. The essence of tragedy, in which the most noble and most deserving person, because of the very grounds of his or her excellence, dies in defeat. *See also* Irony.

Tragicomedy. (1) A tragedy with a happy ending, frequently with penitent villain and romantic setting, disguises, and discoveries.

Travesty. Literally a "cross-dressing": a literary work so clothed, or presented, as to appear ludicrous; a grotesque image or likeness.

Trivium. The first three of the seven liberal arts as studied in medieval universities: grammar, logic, and rhetoric (including oratory).

Trochee. A metrical foot going – ‿ .

Trope. Greek *tropos* for "a turn": a word or phrase turned from its usual meaning to an unusual one; hence, a figure of speech, or an expression turned beyond its literal meaning.

Type. (1) A literary genre. (2) One of the type characters. (3) A symbol or emblem. (4) In theology and literary criticism, an event in early Scriptures or literatures that is seen as prefiguring an event in later Scriptures or in history or literature generally.

Type Characters. Individuals endowed with traits that mark them more distinctly as representatives of a type or class than as standing apart from a type: the typical doctor or rakish aristocrat, for example. Type characters are the opposite of individualized characters.

Typology. The study of types. Typology springs from a theory of literature or history that recognizes events as duplicated in time.

Utopia. A word from two Greek roots (*outopia*, meaning "no place," and *eutopia*, meaning "good place"), pointing to the idea that a utopia is a nonexistent land of social perfection.

Verisimilitude (*vraisemblance* in French). The appearance of actuality.

Verso. The left-hand page of an open book; the back of a leaf of paper.

Vice. A stock character from the medieval morality play, a mischief-making tempter.

Vignette. (1) A brief, subtle, and intimate literary portrait, named for *vignette* portraiture, which is unbordered, shading off into the surrounding color at the edges, with features delicately rendered. (2) A short essay, sketch, or story, usually fewer than five hundred words.

Villanelle. One of the French verse forms, in five tercets, all rhyming *aba*, and a quatrain, rhyming *abaa*. The entire first and third lines are repeated alternately as the final lines of tercets 2, 3, 4, and 5, and together to conclude the quatrain.

Virgule. A "little rod"—the diagonal mark or slash used to indicate line ends in poetry printed continuously in running prose.

Vulgate. (1) A people's common vernacular language (Latin *vulgus*, "common people"). (2) The Vulgate Bible, translated by St. Jerome c. 383–405; the official Roman Catholic Bible.

Wit and Humor. *Wit* is intellectual acuity; *humor*, an amused indulgence of human deficiencies. Wit now denotes the acuity that produces laughter. It originally meant mere understanding, then quickness of understanding, then, beginning in the 17th century, quick perception coupled with creative fancy. Humor (British *humour*, from the four bodily humors) was simply a disposition, usually eccentric. In the 18th century, *humour* came to mean a laughable eccentricity and then a kindly amusement at such eccentricity.

Zeugma. The technique of using one word to yoke two or more others for ironic or amusing effect, achieved when at least one of the yoked is a misfit, as in Alexander Pope's "lose her Heart, or Necklace, at a Ball."

BIBLIOGRAPHY
The Romantics and Their Contemporaries

Bibliographies, General Collections, General Reference • Annual bibliographies are published by the Modern Language Association of America, the Modern Humanities Research Association, the *Keats-Shelley Journal*, *The Romantic Movement*, and *The Year's Work in English Studies* • *Encyclopedia of the Romantic Era, 1760–1860* (Fitzroy, Dearborn), 2002. • Stuart Curran, ed., *The Cambridge Companion to British Romanticism*, 1993. • Frank Jordan, ed., *The English Romantic Poets: A Review of Research and Criticism*, 4th ed. 1985 [covers Blake, W. Wordsworth, Coleridge, Byron, P. B. Shelley, Keats]. • Karl Kroeber and Gene Ruoff, eds., *Romantic Poetry: Recent Revisionary Criticism*, 1993. • Iain McCalman, *An Oxford Companion to The Romantic Age: British Culture 1176–1832*, 1999. • Jerome McGann, ed., *The New Oxford Book of Romantic Period Verse*, 1993. • Anne K. Mellor and Richard Matlak, eds., *British Literature 1780–1830*, 1996. • Michael O'Neill, ed., *Literature of the Romantic Period: A Bibliographical Guide*, 1998. • David Perkins, ed., *English Romantic Writers*, 2nd ed., 1995. • Duncan Wu, ed., *A Companion to Romanticism*, 1997. • Duncan Wu, ed., *Romanticism, An Anthology*, 1994. • Duncan Wu, ed., *Romanticism, A Critical Reader*, 1995 [essays on Blake, W. Wordsworth, Coleridge, P. B. Shelley, Byron, Keats, Clare, M. Shelley, Austen]. • Several volumes in the series *Approaches to Teaching World Literature* published by the Modern Language Association are devoted to writers in our period: among others, Blake (ed. Robert Gleckner and Mark Greenberg); Byron (ed. F. W. Shilstone); Coleridge (ed. Richard Matlak); Keats (ed. Walter Evert and Jack Rhodes); Mary Shelley (ed. Stephen Behrendt); Percy Shelley (ed. Spencer Hall); and Wordsworth (ed. Spencer Hall and Jonathan Ramsey). • *Studies in English Literature* publishes an annual omnibus review in each fall issue: "Recent Studies in the Nineteenth Century." • Website hub for a wealth of resources on authors, issues, as well as visual images is the award-winning *Romantic Circles*, ed. Stephen Jones and Neil Fraistat. http://www.rc.umd.edu

History and Literary History • M. H. Abrams "English Romanticism: The Spirit of the Age," 1963; repr. in *Romanticism and Consciousness: Essays in Criticism*, ed. Harold Bloom, 1970. • Derek Beales, *From Castlereagh to Gladstone 1815-85*, 1969. • Marilyn Butler, *Romantics, Rebels, and Reactionaries: English Literature and Its Background, 1760–1830*, 1981. • Marilyn Butler, "Romanticism in England," *Romanticism in National Context*, eds. Roy Park and Mikulá Teich, 1988. • James Chandler, *England in 1819*, 1998. • James Chandler, ed., *The Cambridge History of Romanticism*, 2002. • Ian R. Christie, *Wars and Revolutions*, in *New History of England*, vol. 7, 1982. • J. C. D. Clark, *English Society 1688–1832*, 1985. • Linda Colley, *Britons: Forging the Nation 1707–1837*, 1992. • Jeffrey N. Cox, *Poetry and Politics in the Cockney School: Keats, Shelley, Hunt and their Circle*, 1998. • M. J. Daunton, *Progress and Poverty: An Economic and Social History of Britain 1700–1850*, 1995. • Lee Erickson, *The Economy of Literary Form: English Literature and the Industrialization of Publishing 1800–1850*, 1996. • Norman Gash, *Aristocracy and People: Britain 1815-1865*, 1979. • Kevin Goodman, *Georgic Modernity and British Romanticism: Poetry and the Mediation of History*, 2004. • Marilyn Gaull, *English Romanticism: The Human Context*, 1988. • Élie Halévy, *A History of the English People in 1815*, trans. 1924, repr. 1987. • Ian Jack, *English Literature, 1815–1832*, 1963. • Jon Klancher, *The Making of English Reading Audiences, 1790–1832*, 1987. • John B. Owen, *The Eighteenth Century 1714–1815*, 1974. • Harold Perkin, *Origins of Modern English Society*, 1969. • Roy Porter, *English Society in the Eighteenth Century*, 1982. • W. L. Renwick, *English Literature, 1789–1815*, 1963. • Alan Richardson, *Literature, Education, and Romanticism*, 1994. • Clifford Siskin, *The Historicity of Romantic Discourse*, 1988; *The Work of Writing: Literature and Social Change in Britain, 1700–1830*, 1998. • E. P. Thompson, *The Making of the English Working Class*, 1963. • E. P. Thompson, *Customs in Common*, 1991. • R. J. White, *Waterloo to Peterloo*, 1957. • Raymond Williams,

Culture and Society 1780–1950, 1960. • Raymond Williams, *The Country and The City*, 1973. • Susan J. Wolfson and William H. Galperin, eds., "The Romantic Century," *European Romantic Review* 11, 2000. • Susan J. Wolfson, "Our Puny Boundaries: Why the Craving to Carve Up the Nineteenth Century?" *PMLA* 116, 2001. • Carl Woodring, *Politics in English Romantic Poetry*, 1970.

Contemporary Reception • John O. Hayden, *The Romantic Reviewers 1802–24*, 1969. • Theodore Redpath, ed., *The Young Romantics and Critical Opinion, 1807–1824: Poetry of Byron, Shelley, and Keats as Seen by Their Contemporary Critics*, 1973. • Donald H. Reiman, *The Romantics Reviewed: Contemporary Reviews of British Romantic Writers*, 1972.

Poetic Form and Genres • M. H. Abrams, "Structure and Style in the Greater Romantic Lyric," 1965, repr. in *Romanticism and Consciousness*, ed. Harold Bloom 1970. • M. H. Abrams, *Natural Supernaturalism: Tradition and Revolution in Romantic Literature*, 1971. • Harold Bloom, "The Internalization of Questromance," 1969, repr. in *Romanticism and Consciousness*, ed. Harold Bloom, 1970. • Harold Bloom, *The Anxiety of Influence: A Theory of Poetry*, 1973. • Douglas Bush, *Mythology and the Romantic Tradition in English Poetry*, 1937. • Stuart Curran, *Poetic Form and British Romanticism*, 1986. • Geoffrey Hartman, *Beyond Formalism*, 1970. • John Hollander, "Romantic Verse Form and the Metrical Contract," 1965, repr. in *Romanticism and Consciousness*, ed. Harold Bloom, 1970. • David Perkins, "The Construction of 'The Romantic Movement' as a Literary Classification," *Nineteenth-Century Literature*, 1990. • Thomas Vogler, *Preludes to Vision: On the Epic Venture in Blake, Wordsworth, Keats, and Hart Crane*, 1971. • Brian Wilkie, *Romantic Poets and Epic Tradition*, 1965. • W. K. Wimsatt, "The Structure of Romantic Nature Imagery," in *The Verbal Icon*, 1954; repr. in *Romanticism and Consciousness*, ed. Harold Bloom, 1970.

Literary Ballads • Bertrand Bronson, *The Ballad as Song*, 1969. • David Fowler, *A Literary History of the Popular Ballad*, 1968. • Albert Friedman, *The Ballad Revival*, 1961. • Nick Groom, *The Making of Percy's Reliques*, 1999. • Peter T. Murphy, *Poetry as an Occupation and an Art in Great Britain 1769–1830*, 1993.

Criticism. • Maureen McLane, "Ballads and Bards: British Romantic Orality," *Modern Philology*, 2001; "Tuning the Multi-Media Nation; or, Minstrelsy of the Afro-Scottish Border ca. 1800," *European Romantic Review*, 2004; and "The Figure Minstrelsy Makes: Poetry and Historicity," *Critical Inquiry*, 2003. • Susan Stewart, "Scandals of the Ballad," *Representations*, 1990. • David Vincent, "The Decline of the Oral Tradition in Popular Culture," in *Popular Culture and Custom in 19th-Century England*, ed. Robert Storch, 1982.

Theory and Criticism • M. H. Abrams, *The Mirror and the Lamp: Romantic Theory and Critical Tradition*, 1953. • M. H. Abrams, *Natural Supernaturalism*, 1971. • M. H. Abrams, *The Correspondent Breeze: Essays on English Romanticism*, 1984. • John Beer, ed., *Questioning Romanticism*, 1995. • Edward E. Bostetter, *The Romantic Ventriloquists: Wordsworth, Coleridge, Shelley, Keats, Byron*, 1963. • Marshall Brown, ed., *The Cambridge History of Literary Criticism*, vol. 5, *Romanticism*, 2000. • Paul de Man, *The Rhetoric of Romanticism*, 1984. • Paul de Man, "The Rhetoric of Temporality," in his *Blindness and Insight*, 2nd ed., 1983. • William H. Galperin, *The Return of the Visible in British Romanticism*, 1993. • William Keach, *Arbitrary Power: Romanticism, Language, Politics*, 2004. • Karl Kroeber, *British Romantic Art*, 1986. • Jerome McGann, *The Romantic Ideology: A Critical Investigation*, 1983. • Jerome McGann, *The Poetics of Sensibility: A Revolution in Literary Style*, 1996. • Anne K. Mellor, *English Romantic Irony*, 1980. • David Perkins, *The Quest for Permanence: The Symbolism of Wordsworth, Shelley, and Keats*, 1959. • Tilottama Rajan, *Dark Interpreter: The Discourse of Romanticism*, 1980. • Alan Richardson, *British Romanticism and the Science of the Mind*, 2001. • Charles R. Rzepka, *The Self as Mind: Vision and Identity in Wordsworth, Coleridge, and Keats*, 1986. • David Simpson, *Irony and Authority in Romantic Poetry*, 1979. • Stuart M. Sperry, "Towards a Definition of Romantic Irony," in *Romantic and Modern: Revaluations of Literary Tradition*, ed. George Bornstein, 1977. • Willard Spiegelman, *Majestic Indolence: English Romantic Poetry and the Work of Art*, 1995. • Earl R. Wasserman, "The English Romantics: The Grounds of Knowledge," *Studies in Romanticism*, 1964. • Susan J. Wolfson, *Formal Charges: The Shaping of Poetry in British Romanticism*, 1997. • Susan J. Wolfson, ed.,

"Ideology and Romantic Aesthetics: a Forum," *Studies in Romanticism* 37, 1998: essays on P. B. Shelley, Keats, Barbauld, Coleridge, the Elgin Marbles, Wollstonecraft.

The Rights of Man and the Revolution Controversy • *Headnote:* Coleridge is quoted from *Table Talk,* 4 January 1823; Wordsworth is quoted from a letter of 30 March 1835.

Criticism. • Simon Bainbridge, *Napoleon and English Romanticism,* 1996. • Stephen Blakemore, *Crisis in Representation: Thomas Paine, Mary Wollstonecraft, Helen Maria Williams, and the Rewriting of the French Revolution,* 1997; and *Intertextual War: Edmund Burke and the French Revolution in the Writings of Mary Wollstonecraft, Thomas Paine, and James Mackintosh,* 1997. • Marilyn Butler, ed., *Burke, Paine, Godwin, and the Revolution Controversy,* 1984. • Ceri Crossley and Ian Small, eds., *The French Revolution and British Culture,* 1989. • Seamus Deane, *The French Revolution and Enlightenment England 1789–1832,* 1988. • H. T. Dickinson, *British Radicalism and the French Revolution,* 1985. • Clive Emsley, *British Society and the French Wars 1793–1815,* 1979. • Burton R. Friedman, *Fabricating History: English Writers and the French Revolution,* 1988. • Kevin Gilmartin, *Print Politics: The Press and Radical Opposition in Early Nineteenth-Century England,* 1996. • Albert Goodwin, *The Friends of Liberty,* 1979. • E. J. Hobsbawm, *The Age of Revolution 1789–1848,* 1962. • Howard Mumford Jones, *Revolution and Romanticism,* 1974. • Anne K. Mellor, "English Women Writers and the French Revolution," in *Rebel Daughters: Women and the French Revolution,* eds. Sara Melzer and Leslie Rabine, 1992. • Ronald Paulson, *Representations of Revolution, 1789–1820,* 1983. • Mark Philp, ed., *The French Revolution and British Popular Politics,* 1991. • Mark Philp, "Vulgar Conservatism, 1792-1793," *English Historical Review,* 1995. • Esther Schor, *Bearing the Dead: The British Culture of Mourning from the Enlightenment to Victoria,* 1994. • David Simpson, *Romanticism, Nationalism, and the Revolt Against Theory,* 1993. • Olivia Smith, *The Politics of Language 1791–1819,* 1984. • Bruce Woodcock and John Coates. *Combative Styles: Romantic Writing and Ideology,* 1995.

The Anti-Jacobin • *Context.* • M. Dorothy George, *English Political Caricature: A Study of Opinion and Propaganda, 1793–1832,* 1959.

Text. • Charles Edmonds, ed., *Poetry of the Anti-Jacobin* 1890.

The Abolition of Slavery and the Slave Trade • *General Studies.* • Roger Anstey, *The Atlantic Slave Trade and British Abolition, 1760–1810,* 1975. • Joan Baum, *Mind-forg'd Manacles: Slavery and the English Romantic Poets,* 1994. • Robin Blackburn, *The Overthrow of Colonial Slavery, 1776–1848,* 1988. • Reginald Coupland, *The British Anti-Slavery Movement,* 1933. • Michael Craton, *Sinews of Empire: A Short History of British Slavery,* 1974. • Michael Craton, James Walvin, and David Wright, eds., *Slavery, Abolition and Emancipation: Black Slaves and the British Empire,* 1976 [an anthology of important documents, including the "Mansfield decision" (Somerset v. Stewart, June 1772), and a succinct history]. • David Brion Davis, *The Problem of Slavery in the Age of Revolution,* 1975. • Eva Dyke, *The Negro in English Romantic Thought,* 1942. • Moira Ferguson, *Subject to Others: British Women Writers and Colonial Slavery, 1670–1834,* 1992 [including a massive bibliography]. • Tim Fulford and Peter J. Kitson, eds., *Romanticism and Colonialism,* 1998. • Sonia Hofkosh and Alan Richardson, eds., *Romanticism, Race and Imperial Culture,* 1996. • Edith F. Hurwitz, *Politics and Public Conscience: Slave Emancipation and the Abolitionist Movement in Britain,* 1973. • Margaret Kirkham, *Jane Austen, Feminism and Fiction,* 1983 [on the Mansfield Decision and *Mansfield Park*]. • Frank Joseph Klingberg, *The Anti-Slavery Movement in England: A Study in English Humanitarianism,* 1926. • Debbie Lee, *Slavery and the Romantic Imagination,* 2002. • Gordon K. Lewis, *Slavery, Imperialism, and Freedom Studies in English Radical Thought,* 1978. • Dale H. Porter, *The Abolition of the Slave Trade in England, 1784–1807,* 1970. • Alan Richardson, ed. vol. 4 (verse), *Slavery, Abolition, and Emancipation: Writings in the British Romantic Period,* 1999. • Helen Thomas, *Romanticism and Slave Narratives,* 2000. • James Walvin, *Black and White: The Negro and English Society, 1555–1945,* 1973. • James Walvin, *Slavery and British Society, 1776–1846,* 1982. • James Walvin, *England, Slaves, and Freedom 1776–1838,* 1986. • Eric Williams, *Capitalism and Slavery,* 1944.

Specific Figures. • Reginald Coupland, *Wilberforce: A Narrative,* 1923. • E. L. Griggs, *Thomas Clarkson: The Friend of the Slaves,*

1938. • Edmund Heward, *Lord Mansfield*, 1979. • Robert Isaac and Samuel Wilberforce, *The Life of William Wilberforce*, 1835. • C. L. R. James, *The Black Jacobins: Toussaint L'Ouverture and the San Domingo Rebellion*, 1938; repr. 1963. • Oliver M. Warner, *William Wilberforce and His Times*, 1962. *See also* the entries on Olaudah Equiano and Mary Prince.

Gender, Women Writers, The Rights of Woman
• *Editions*. • Paula Feldman, ed., *British Women Poets of the Romantic Era, An Anthology*, 1997. • Duncan Wu, ed., *Romantic Women Poets, An Anthology*, 1997.

Criticism. • Stephen C. Behrendt and Harriet Kramer Linkin, eds., *Approaches to Teaching British Women Poets of the Romantic Period*, 1997. • Stuart Curran, "Romantic Poetry: The 'I' Altered," in *Romanticism and Feminism*, ed. Anne Mellor • Paula Feldman and Theresa M. Kelley, eds., *Romantic Women Writers: Voices and Countervoices*, 1995. • Harriet Guest, *Small Change: Women, Patriotism, Learning, 1750–1810*, 2000. • Harriet Kramer Linkin and Stephen C. Behrendt, eds., *Romanticism and Women Poets: Opening the Doors of Reception*, 1999. • Diane Long Hoeveler, *Romantic Androgyny: The Women Within*, 1990. • Sonia Hofkosh, *Sexual Politics and the Romantic Author*, 1998. • Jerome McGann, *The Poetics of Sensibility*, 1996. • Anne K. Mellor, *Mothers of the Nation: Women's Political Writing in England, 1780–1830*, 2000. • Anne K. Mellor, ed., *Romanticism and Feminism*, 1988. • Anne K. Mellor, *Romanticism and Gender*, 1993. • Judith Pascoe, *Romantic Theatricality: Gender, Poetry, and Spectatorship*. 1997. • Marlon Ross, *The Contours of Masculine Desire: Romanticism and the Rise of Women's Poetry*, 1989. • Irene Tayler and Gina Luria, "Women in British Romantic Literature," in *What Manner of Woman*, ed. Marlene Springer, 1977. • Carol Shiner Wilson and Joel Haefner, eds., *Revisioning Romanticism: British Women Writers, 1776–1837*, 1994. • Susan Wolfson, *Borderlines: The Shiftings of Gender in British Romanticism*, 2006: Wollstonecraft, Hemans, Jewsbury, Keats, Byron. • Jonathan Wordsworth, *The Bright Work Grows: Women Writers of the Romantic Age*, 1997.

The Wollstonecraft Controversy and the Rights of Women • *Textual Reference*. • Anna Laeti-tia Le Breton, *Memoir of Mrs. Barbauld*, 1874 [Barbauld's letter to Edgeworth, 4 September 1804].

General Studies. • Leonore Davidoff and Catherine Hall, *Family Fortunes: Men and Women of the English Middle Class, 1780–1850*, 1987. • Bridget Hill, *Women, Work, and Sexual Politics in Eighteenth-Century England*, 1989. • Gary Kelly, *Women, Writing, and Revolution, 1790–1827*, 1993. • Anne K. Mellor, *Romanticism and Gender*, 1993. • Mitzi Myers, "Reform or Ruin: 'A Revolution in Female Manners,'" in *Studies in Eighteenth-Century Culture*, 1982. • Mary Poovey, *The Proper Lady and the Woman Writer*, 1984. • Katharine Rogers, *Feminism in Eighteenth-Century England*, 1982. • For Barbauld, Southey, Blake, and More, see the main entries under their names.

Aesthetics: The Sublime, the Beautiful, and the Picturesque • *General Criticism*. • Malcolm Andrews, *The Search for the Picturesque*, 1989. • Andrew Ashfield and Peter de Bolla, eds., *The Sublime: A Reader in British Eighteenth-Century Aesthetic Theory*, 1996. • John Barrell, *The Idea of Landscape and a Sense of Place*, 1972; and *The Dark Side of the Landscape: The Rural Poor in English Painting 1730–1840*, 1980. • Ann Bermingham, *Landscape and Ideology*, 1986. • Stephen Copley and Peter Garside, eds., *The Politics of the Picturesque*, 1994. • Peter de Bolla, *The Discourse of the Sublime*, 1989. • Frances Ferguson, *Solitude and the Sublime*, 1992. • Neil Hertz, *The End of the Line*, 1985. • Walter John Hipple, Jr., *The Beautiful, the Sublime, and the Picturesque in Eighteenth-Century British Aesthetic Theory*, 1957. • Christopher Hussey, *The Picturesque*, 1927. • Elizabeth W. Manwaring, *Italian Landscape in Eighteenth-Century England*, 1925. • Samuel H. Monk, *The Sublime*, 1935. • Thomas Weiskel, *The Romantic Sublime*, 1976. • Gillen D'Arcy Wood, *The Shock of the Real: Romanticism and Visual Culture, 1760–1860*, 2000.

The Writers Surveyed. • Donald Greene, "The Original of Pemberley," *Eighteenth-Century Fiction*, 1998 (on Austen's *Pride and Prejudice*). • J. T. Boulder, ed., *Burke's Sublime and Beautiful*, 1968. • W. D. Templeman, *The Life and Work of William Gilpin*, 1937. • C. P. Barbier, *William Gilpin*, 1963. • René Wellek, *Immanuel Kant in England 1793-1838*, 1938. • Giuseppe Micheli, *The Early Reception of Kant's Thought in England 1785–1805*, 1990. • For more on Austen and Wollstonecraft, see the main author entries, and Ruskin in the Victorian era.

Our Texts. • Jane Austen, *Pride and Prejudice,* 1813. • *Edmund Burke, A Philosophical Enquiry into the Origin of Our Ideas of the Sublime and Beautiful,* 1757; 1812 ed. • William Gilpin, *Three Essays,* 2nd ed., 1794. • Immanuel Kant, *The Critique of Judgement,* trans. James Creed Meredith, 1952. • John Ruskin, *Modern Painters,* 1968. • Mary Wollstonecraft, *A Vindication of the Rights of Men,* 1790.

Popular Prose and the Problems of Authorship
• Josephine Bauer, The *London Magazine,* 1953. • Marilyn Butler, "Culture's Medium: The Role of the Review," in *Cambridge Companion to British Romanticism,* ed. Stuart Curran, 1993. • Kevin Gilmartin, *Print Politics,* 1996. • Ian Jack, "The Literary Scene in 1815," in his *English Literature 1815-32,* 1963. • Gary Kelly, *English Fiction of the Romantic Period,* 1989. • Jon P. Klancher, *The Making of English Reading Audiences, 1780–1832,* 1987. • Peter T. Murphy, "Impersonation and Authorship in Romantic Britain," *ELH,* 1992. • Lucy Newlyn, *Reading, Writing, and Romanticism: The Anxiety of Reception,* 2000. • Mark Parker, *Literary Magazines and British Romanticism,* 2000. • Mark Schoenfield, "Voices Together: Lamb, Hazlitt, and the *London Magazine,*" *Studies in Romanticism,* 1990. • Kim Wheatley, ed., *Romantic Periodicals and Print Culture,* 2003. • Duncan Wu and Massimiliano Demata, *British Romanticism and the Edinburgh Review,* 2002. • For other essays on the literary milieu, see the entries for Francis Jeffrey and the individual authors in this section.

Criticism • Mark Parker, *Literary Magazines and British Romanticism,* 2000.

Jane Austen • *Letters.* • Deirdre Le Faye, ed., *Jane Austen's Letters,* 1997.

Life and Background. • Park Honan, *Jane Austen: Her Life,* 1987. • David Nokes, *Jane Austen,* 1997. • Clare Tomalin, *Jane Austen: A Life,* 1997.

Edition. • Marilyn Gaull, ed. *Northanger Abbey,* a Longman Cultural Edition, 2004. • Frances Ferguson, ed. *Emma,* a Longman Cultural Edition, 2005. • Claudia L. Johnson and Susan J. Wolfson, eds., *Pride and Prejudice,* a Longman Cultural Edition, 2002.

Criticism. • Wayne Booth, *The Rhetoric of Fiction,* 1961. • Marilyn Butler, *Jane Austen and the War of Ideas,* 1975.

Criticism and Reference. • Edward Copeland and Juliet McMaster, eds., *The Cambridge Companion to Jane Austen,* 1997. • Alistair Duckworth, *The Improvement of the Estate, A Study of Jane Austen's Novels,* 1971 • William H. Galperin, *The Historical Austen,* 2002. • Sandra Gilbert and Susan Gubar, *The Madwoman in the Attic: The Woman Writer and the Nineteenth-Century Literary Imagination,* 1979. • Claudia Johnson, *Jane Austen: Women, Politics, and the Novel,* 1988. • Claudia Johnson, *Equivocal Beings: Politics, Gender, and Sentimentality in the 1790s,* 1995. • Arnold Kettle, *An Introduction to the English Novel,* 1951. • Margaret Kirkham, *Jane Austen, Feminism, and Fiction,* 1983. • U. C. Knoepflmacher, "The Importance of Being Frank: Character and Letter-Writing in Emma," *SEL* 1967. • A. Walton Litz, *Jane Austen: A Study of Her Artistic Development,* 1965. • Susan Morgan, *In the Meantime: Character and Perception in Jane Austen's Fiction,* 1980. • Judith Lowder Newton, *Women, Power and Subversion: Social Strategies in British Fiction, 1778–1860,* 1981. • Warren Roberts, *Jane Austen and the French Revolution,* 1979. • Tony Tanner, *Jane Austen,* 1986. • Sir Walter Scott, review of *Emma, Quarterly Review,* 1815.

Our Texts. • *Northanger Abbey,* 1817.

Joanna Baillie • *Biography and Criticism.* • Catherine Burroughs, "English Romantic Women Writers and Theatre Theory: Joanna Baillie's Prefaces to Plays on the Passions," in *Revisioning Romanticism,* eds. Carol Shiner Wilson and Joel Haefner, 1994. • Margaret S. Carhart, *The Life and Work of Joanna Baillie,* 1923. • Julie Carlson, *In the Theatre of Romanticism,* 1994. • Andrea Henderson, "Passion and Fashion in Joanna Baillie's 'Introductory Discourse,'" *PMLA,* 1997. • Jonathan Wordsworth, *The Bright Work Grows: Women Writers of the Romantic Age,* 1997. • Paul Zall, "The Question of Joanna Baillie," *The Wordsworth Circle,* 1982.

Our Texts. • *The Dramatic and Poetical Works of Joanna Baillie,* 1853; *Byron's Letters and Journals,* ed. Leslie A. Marchand (1973–82): 6 Sept. 1813 and 2 Apr. 1817; the comparison to Byron from "Celebrated Female Writers: Joanna Baillie," *Blackwood's Edinburgh Magazine,* August 1824.

Anna Letitia Barbauld • *Biography and Editions.* • Lucy Aikin, "Memoir" in *The Works of Anna*

Letitia Barbauld, 1825. • William McCarthy and Elizabeth Kraft, eds., *The Poems of Anna Letitia Barbauld*, 1994.

Edition. • William McCarthy and Elizabeth Kraft, eds., *Anna Letitia Barbauld, Selected Poetry and Prose*, 2002. • Betsy Rodgers, *Georgian Chronicle: Mrs. Barbauld and Her Family*, 1958.

Criticism. • Isobel Armstrong, "The Gush of the Feminine: How Can We Read Women's Poetry of the Romantic Period?" in *Romantic Women Writers*, eds. Theresa Kelley and Paula Feldman, 1995. • William Keach, "A Regency Prophecy and the End of Anna Barbauld's Career," *Studies in Romanticism*, 1994. • William McCarthy, "'We Hoped the Woman Was Going to Appear': Repression, Desire, and Gender in Anna Letitia Barbauld's Early Poems," in *Romantic Women Writers*, eds. Kelley and Feldman, 1995. • William McCarthy, "The Posthumous Reception of Anna Letitia Barbauld," in Linkin and Behrendt, *Romanticism and Women Poets*, 1999. • Marlon B. Ross, "Configurations of Feminine Reform: The Woman Writer and the Tradition of Dissent," in *Revisioning Romanticism*, eds. Carol Shiner Wilson and Joel Haefner, 1994. • Jonathan Wordsworth, *The Bright Work Grows: Women Writers of the Romantic Age*, 1997.

Our Texts. • "The Mouse's Petition," "On a Lady's Writing," "Washing Day," and "Eighteen Hundred and Eleven" from *A Selection From the Poems . . . of Anna Letitia Barbauld*, ed. Grace Ellis, 1874; "Inscription for an Ice-House," "The First Fire," from *The Works of Anna Laetitia Barbauld*, ed. Lucy Aikin, 1825; "To the Poor" and "To A Little Invisible Being" from *The Poems of Anna Laetitia Barbauld*, eds. McCarthy and Kraft, 1994.

William Blake • *Biography*. • Peter Ackroyd, *Blake*, 1996. • Alexander Gilchrist, *The Life of William Blake, Pictor Ignotus*, 1863. • Mona Wilson, *The Life of William Blake*, 1927.

Illuminations. • Oxford University Press: paperback color-plate editions, with commentary by Geoffrey Keynes, of *The Songs of Innocence and of Experience*, 1967; *The Marriage of Heaven and Hell*, 1975; *Visions of the Daughters of Albion*, 1980. • Princeton University Press, of the *Songs*, 1991. All plates are reproduced in

black and white photographs, with commentary, in David V. Erdman, *The Illuminated Blake*, 1974. http://www.blakearchive.org • *See also* "Romantic Circles" for guidance: http://www.rc.umd.edu

Criticism. • Harold Bloom, *The Visionary Company*, 1961, rev. 1971. • Harold Bloom, *Blake's Apocalypse*, 1963, rev. 1970. • Leopold Damrosch, *Symbol and Truth in Blake's Myth*, 1980. • Jackie DiSalvo, *War of the Titans: Blake's Critique of Milton and the Politics of Religion*, 1984. • Vincent Arthur de Luca, *Words of Eternity: Blake and the Poetics of the Sublime*, 1991. • Morris Eaves, *William Blake's Theory of Art*, 1982. • Morris Eaves, *The Counter-Arts Conspiracy: Art and Industry in the Age of Blake*, 1992. • Morris Eaves, ed., *The Cambridge Companion to William Blake*, 2002. • David V. Erdman, *Blake: Prophet Against Empire*, 1969. • Robert Essick, *William Blake, Printmaker*, 1980. • Robert Essick, *William Blake and the Language of Adam*, 1989. • Michael Ferber, "'London' and Its Politics," *ELH*, 1981. • Michael Ferber, *The Poetry of William Blake*, 1981. • Northrop Frye, *Fearful Symmetry*, 1947. • Robert Gleckner, *The Piper and the Bard*, 1959. • Heather Glen, *Vision and Disenchantment: Blake's "Songs" and Wordsworth's "Lyrical Ballads,"* 1983. • Nancy Moore Goslee, "Slavery and Sexual Character: Questioning the Master Trope in *Visions of the Daughters of Albion*," *ELH*, 1990. • Jean H. Hagstrum, *William Blake: Poet and Painter*, 1964. • Zachary Leader, *Reading Blake's Songs*, 1981. • John Mee, *Dangerous Enthusiasm: William Blake and the Culture of Radicalism in the 1790s*, 1992. • W. J. T. Mitchell, *Blake's Composite Art*, 1978. • Martin K. Nurmi, "Fact and Symbol in 'The Chimney Sweeper' of Blake's *Songs of Innocence*," *Bulletin of the New York Public Library*, 1964. • Morton Paley, *Energy and the Imagination: A Study of the Development of Blake's Thought*, 1970. • Mark Schorer, *William Blake: the Politics of Vision*, 1946. • Irene Tayler, "The Woman Scaly" [on *Visions of the Daughters of Albion*], 1973; repr. Norton Critical Edition of *Blake's Poetry and Designs*. • E. P. Thompson, *Witness Against the Beast: William Blake and Moral Law*, 1993. • Joseph Viscomi, *Blake and the Idea of the Book*, 1993. • Thomas Vogler, "'In Vain the Eloquent Tongue': An Un-Reading of *Visions of the Daughters of Albion*," in *Blake and the Argument of Method*, eds. Dan Miller, Mark Bracher, and Donald Ault, 1987.

Our Texts. • Edited for this volume with reference to the design of Blake's illuminated plates.

Edmund Burke • *Biographical Studies.* • Carl B. Cone, *Burke and the Nature of Politics,* 2 vols., 1957, 1964. • C. B. Macpherson, *Burke,* 1980. • Conor Cruise O'Brien, *The Great Melody: A Thematic Biography and Commented Anthology of Edmund Burke,* 1992.

Criticism and Context. • James T. Boulton, *The Language of Politics in the Age of Wilkes and Burke,* 1963. • Alfred Cobban, *Edmund Burke and the Revolt Against the Eighteenth Century,* 1929, repr. 1962. • Tom Furniss, *Edmund Burke's Aesthetic Ideology: Language, Gender, and Political Economy in Revolution,* 1993. • J. G. A. Pocock, "Burke and the Ancient Constitution: A Problem in the History of Ideas," in *Politics, Language, and Time,* 1971. • J. G. A. Pocock "The Political Economy of Burke's Analysis of the French Revolution," in *Virtue, Commerce, and History,* 1985.

Our Text. • *The Works of Edmund Burke,* 1894.

Robert Burns • *Biographical Studies.* • Raymond Bentman, *Robert Burns,* 1987. • David Daiches, *Robert Burns and His World,* 1971. • John Delancey Ferguson, *Pride and Passion: Robert Burns,* 1939. • James Mackay, *A Biography of Robert Burns,* 1992.

Editions. • John Delancey Ferguson, ed., *The Letters of Robert Burns,* 2 vols., rev. ed. by G. Ross Roy, 1985. • James Kinsley, ed., *The Poems and Songs of Robert Burns,* 3 vols., 1968.

Criticism. • Thomas Crawford, *Burns: A Study of the Poems and Songs,* 1960. • Thomas Crawford, ed., *Robert Burns and Cultural Authority,* 1997. • Leopold Damrosch, "Burns, Blake, and the Recovery of Lyric," *Studies in Romanticism,* 1982. • R. D. S. Jack and Andrew Noble, eds., *The Art of Robert Burns,* 1982. • Donald A. Low, ed., *Critical Essays on Robert Burns,* 1975. • Carol McGuirk, *Robert Burns and the Sentimental Era,* 1985.

Our Texts. • *The Centenary Burns,* eds. Ernest Henley and Thomas F. Henderson, 1896–1897; the second version of "Comin' Thro' the Rye" and "The Fornicator" from *The Merry Muses of Caledonia,* 1799-1800.

George Gordon, Lord Byron • *Biography.* • Benita Eisler, *Byron: Child of Passion, Fool of Fame,* 1999. • Leslie A. Marchand, *Byron: A Biography,* 3 vols., 1957; abridged and revised in one volume as *Byron: A Portrait,* 1970.

Editions. • E. H. Coleridge and R. E. Prothero, eds., *The Works of Lord Byron,* 13 vols., 1898–1904. • Leslie A. Marchand, ed., *Byron's Letters and Journals,* 12 vols., 1973–82. • Jerome J. McGann, ed., *Lord Byron: The Complete Poetical Works,* 7 vols., 1980–93. • Susan J. Wolfson and Peter J. Manning, eds., *Lord Byron: Selected Poems,* 1998.

Criticism. • Bernard Beatty, *Byron's Don Juan,* 1985. • Drummond Bone, ed., *The Cambridge Companion to Byron,* 2004. • Jerome Christensen, *Lord Byron's Strength: Romantic Writing and Commercial Society,* 1993. • Michael G. Cooke, *The Blind Man Traces the Circle: On the Patterns and Philosophy of Byron's Poetry,* 1969. • Louis Crompton, *Byron and Greek Love,* 1985. • Charles Donelan, *Romanticism and Male Fantasy in Byron's "Don Juan,"* 2000. • Gary Dyer, "Being Flash to Don Juan," *PMLA* 116, 2001. • Andrew Elfenbein, *Byron and the Victorians,* 1995. • W. Paul Elledge, *Byron and the Dynamics of Metaphor,* 1968. • W. Paul Elledge, "Parting Shots: Byron Ending Don Juan I," *Studies in Romanticism,* 1988. • Caroline Franklin, *Byron's Heroines,* 1992. • Robert F. Gleckner, *Byron and the Ruins of Paradise,* 1967. • Robert F. Gleckner, ed., *Critical Essays on Lord Byron,* 1991. • Peter W. Graham, *Don Juan and Regency England,* 1990. • Peter Graham, *Lord Byron,* 1998. • Sonia Hofkosh, "Women and the Romantic Author: The Example of Byron," in *Romanticism and Feminism,* ed. Anne Mellor, 1988. • M. K. Joseph, *Byron the Poet,* 1964. • Malcolm Kelsall, *Byron's Politics,* 1987. • Alice Levine and Robert N. Keane, eds., *Rereading Byron,* 1993. • Peter J. Manning, *Byron and His Fictions,* 1978. • Peter J. Manning, "Don Juan and Byron's Imperceptiveness to the English Word," *Studies in Romanticism,* 1979; repr. in his *Reading Romantics,* 1990. • Peter J. Manning, "Don Juan and the Revisionary Self," in *Romantic Revisions,* eds. Robert Brinkley and Keith Hanley, 1992. • Jerome J. McGann, *Fiery Dust: Byron's Poetic Development,* 1968. • Jerome J. McGann, *Don Juan in Context,* 1976. • Jerome J. McGann, "The Book of Byron and the Book of a World," in his *The Beauty of Inflections,* 1988.

• Jerome McGann, *Byron and Wordsworth*, 1999.
• Donald H. Reiman, "*Don Juan* in Epic Context," in *Studies in Romanticism*, 1977, repr. in his *Romantic Texts and Contexts*, 1987 • Alan Richardson, on *Manfred*, in *A Mental Theater: Poetic Drama and Consciousness in the Romantic Age*, 1988. • George M. Ridenour, *The Style of Don Juan*, 1960. • Andrew Rutherford, *Byron: A Critical Study*, 1961. • Frederick W. Shilstone, *Byron and the Myth of Tradition*, 1988. • Stuart M. Sperry, "Byron and the Meaning of *Manfred*," *Criticism* 16, 1974. • Jane Stabler, ed., *Byron, A Longman Critical Reader*, 1998; *Byron, Poetics, and History*, 2002. • Peter L. Thorslev, *The Byronic Hero: Types and Prototypes*, 1962. • Francis Wilson, ed., *Byromania*, 1999. • Susan J. Wolfson, "Hemans and the Romance of Byron," in Sweet and Melnyck, eds., *Felicia Hemans: Reimagining Poetry in the Nineteenth Century*.

Our Texts. • *Childe Harold's Pilgrimage III*, from the 1816 edition, *IV* from the 1818 edition. • *The Works of Lord Byron, with his Letters and Journals, and His Life*, by Thomas Moore, 1832–34; *Byron's Letters and Journals*, ed. Leslie A. Marchand, 1973–1982.

John Clare • *Biography.* • Jonathan Bate, *John Clare: A Biography*, 2003. • William J. Howard, *John Clare*, 1981. • Edward Storey, *A Right to Song: The Life of John Clare*, 1982. • J. W. Tibble and Anne Tibble, *John Clare: A Life*, rev. 1972.

Criticism. • John Barrell, *The Idea of Landscape and the Sense of Place, 1730–1840: An Approach to the Poetry of John Clare*, 1972. • John Goodridge and Simon Kövesi, eds., *John Clare: New Approaches*, 2000 (with complete bibliography, several essays; and a bibliography of the copyright dispute). • Hugh Haughton, Adam Phillips, and Geoffrey Summerfield, eds., *John Clare in Context*, 1994. • Elizabeth Helsinger, "Clare and the Place of the Peasant Poet," *Critical Inquiry*, 1987. • James C. McKusick, "'A Language that is Ever Green': The Ecological Vision of John Clare," *University of Toronto Quarterly*, 1991–92. • James McCusick, *Green Writing: Romanticism and Ecology*, 2000 • James C. McKusick, "John Clare and The Tyranny of Grammar," *Studies in Romanticism*, 1994. • David Simpson, "A Speaking Place: The Matter of Genre in 'The Lament of Swordy Well,'" *The Wordsworth Circle*, 2003. • Mark Storey, *The Poetry of John Clare: A Critical Introduction*, 1974. • L. J. Swingle, "Stalking the Essential John Clare: Clare in Relation to His Romantic Contemporaries," *Studies in Romanticism*, 1975. • Anne Wallace, "Farming on Foot: Tracking Georgic in Clare and Wordsworth," *Texas Studies in Language and Literature*, 1992. • Sarah Zimmerman, *Romanticism, Lyricism, and History*, 1999.

Our Texts. • Eric Robinson and David Powell, eds., *John Clare*, 1984; "Written in November" also from *The Village Minstrel*, 1821.

William Cobbett • *Biography.* • George Spater, *William Cobbett: The Poor Man's Friend*, 1982.

Critical Studies. • Asa Briggs, *William Cobbett*, 1967. • John Charles Clarke, *The Price of Progress: Cobbett's England*, 1977.

Criticism. • Kevin Gilmartin, *Print Politics: The Press and Radical Opposition in Early Nineteenth-Century England*, 1996. • Leonora Nattrass, *William Cobbett: The Politics of Style*, 1995. • James Sambrook, *William Cobbett*, 1973. • Raymond Williams, *Cobbett*, 1983.

Our Text. • *Rural Rides*, 1830.

Samuel Taylor Coleridge • *Biography.* • Rosemary Ashton, *The Life of Samuel Taylor Coleridge*, 1996. • Walter Jackson Bate, *Coleridge*, 1968. • Richard Holmes, *Coleridge: Early Visions*, 1990.

Editions. • Kathryn Coburn, ed., *The Collected Works of Samuel Taylor Coleridge*, Bollingen Series 75, 1969—. Includes (among others): *Essays on His Times*, ed. David V. Erdman, 3 vols., 1978; *Lectures 1808–19 On Literature*, ed. R. A. Foakes, 2 vols., 1987; *Lay Sermons*, ed. R. J. White, 1972; *Biographia Literaria*, ed. James Engell and Walter Jackson Bate, 2 vols., 1983; *Poetical Works*, ed. J. C. C. Mays, 3 vols. (forthcoming). • E. H. Coleridge, ed., *Complete Poetical Works*, 2 vols., 1912. • R. A. Foakes, ed., *Coleridge on Shakespeare: The Text of the Lectures of 1811–12*, 1971. • Paul H. Fry, ed., *The Rime of the Ancient Mariner*, ed. 1999 (texts and critical contexts). • E. L. Griggs, ed., *Collected Letters of Samuel Taylor Coleridge*, 6 vols., 1956–71. • William Keach, ed., *Samuel Taylor Coleridge: The Complete Poems*, 1997. • Thomas M. Raysor, ed.,

Coleridge's Shakespearian Criticism, 2 vols., 1960. • Martin Wallen, ed., *Coleridge's Ancient Mariner: An Experimental Edition of Texts and Revisions 1798-1828*, 1993.

Criticism. • M. H. Abrams, *The Mirror and the Lamp*, 1953. • J. A. Appleyard, *Coleridge's Philosophy of Literature*, 1965. • John Beer, *Coleridge the Visionary*, 1959. • John Beer, *Coleridge's Poetic Intelligence*, 1977. • Frederick Burwick, ed., *Coleridge's Biographia Literaria: Text and Meaning*, 1989. • Jerome Christensen, *Coleridge's Blessed Machine of Language*, 1981. • George Dekker, *Coleridge and the Literature of Sensibility*, 1978. • Susan Eilenberg, *Strange Power of Speech: Wordsworth, Coleridge, and Literary Possession*, 1992. • Kelvin Everest, *Coleridge's Secret Ministry: The Context of the Conversation Poems*, 1979. • Frances Ferguson, "Coleridge and the Deluded Reader: 'The Rime of the Ancient Mariner,'" *Georgia Review*, 1977. • Norman Fruman, *Coleridge: The Damaged Archangel*, 1971. • Christine Gallant, ed., *Coleridge's Theory of Imagination Today*, 1989. • William H. Galperin, "'Desynonymizing' the Self in Wordsworth and Coleridge," *Studies in Romanticism*, 1987. • Paul Hamilton, *Coleridge's Poetics*, 1984. • Anthony John Harding, *Coleridge and the Inspired Word*, 1985. • Alethea Hayter, *Opium and the Romantic Imagination*, 1968. • William Heath, *Wordsworth and Coleridge: A Study of Their Literary Relations in 1801-02*, 1972. • Patrick Keane, *Coleridge's Submerged Politics: The Ancient Mariner and Robinson Crusoe*, 1994. • John Livingston Lowes, *The Road to Xanadu*, 1927. • Paul Magnuson, *Coleridge's Nightmare Poetry*, 1974. • Paul Magnuson, *Coleridge and Wordsworth: A Lyrical Dialogue*, 1989. • Thomas McFarland, *Coleridge and the Pantheist Tradition*, 1969. • Thomas McFarland, *Romanticism and The Forms of Ruin*, 1981. • Jerome J. McGann, "The Ancient Mariner: The Meaning of Meanings," in *The Beauty of Inflections*, 1985. • James C. McKusick, *Coleridge's Philosophy of Language*, 1986. • Raimonda Modiano, *Coleridge and the Concept of Nature*, 1985. • Raimonda Modiano, "Word and 'Languageless' Meaning: Limits of Expression in *The Rime of the Ancient Mariner*," *Modern Language Quarterly*, 1977. • John Morrow, *Coleridge's Political Thought: Property, Morality, and the Limits of Traditional Discourse*, 1990. • Roy Park, "Coleridge's Two Voices as a Critic of Wordsworth," *ELH*, 1969.

• Reeve Parker, *Coleridge's Meditative Art*, 1975. • Arden Reed, *Romantic Weather*, 1983. • Nicholas Roe, *Wordsworth and Coleridge: The Radical Years*, 1988. • Gene W. Ruoff, *Wordsworth and Coleridge: The Making of the Major Lyrics, 1802–1804*, 1989. • Elizabeth Schneider, *Coleridge, Opium, and Kubla Khan*, 1953. • Max F. Schuli, *The Poetic Voices of Coleridge*, 1963. • Elinor Shaffer, *Coleridge, Kubla Khan, and the Fall of Jerusalem*, 1985. • Karen Swann, "Christabel: The Wandering Mother and the Enigma of Form," *Studies in Romanticism*, 1984. • Karen Swann, "Literary Gentlemen and Lovely Ladies: The Debate on the Character of *Christabel*," *ELH*, 1985. • Kathleen M. Wheeler, *Sources, Processes, and Methods in Coleridge's* Biographia Literaria, 1980.

Our Texts. • *Poems*, 1796; *Lyrical Ballads*, 1798; *Christabel c*, 1816; *Sibylline Leaves*, 1817; *Poems*, 1834.

Coleridge's Lectures in Context: Shakespeare in the Nineteenth Century

• Jonathan Bate, *Shakespeare and the English Romantic Imagination*, 1986. • Jonathan Bate, *Shakespearean Constitutions: Politics, Theatre, Criticism, 1730–1830*, 1989. • Jonathan Bate, ed., *The Romantics on Shakespeare*, 1992. • Michael Bristol, *Big-Time Shakespeare*, 1996. • Julie Carlson, *In the Theatre of Romanticism: Coleridge, Nationalism, Women*, 1994. • Margreta De Grazia, *Shakespeare Verbatim: The Reproduction of Authenticity and the 1790 Apparatus*, 1991. • Marilyn Gaull, *English Romanticism: The Human Context*, ch. 4, 1988. • Jean E. Howard and Marion F. O'Connor, eds., *Shakespeare Reproduced: The Text in History and Ideology*, 1987. • Loren Kruger, *The National Stage*, 1992. • Antony Kubiak, *The Stages of Terror: Terrorism, Ideology, and Coercion as Theatre History*, 1991. • Jean I. Marsden, ed., *The Appropriation of Shakespeare: Post-Renaissance Reconstructions of the Works and the Myth*, 1991. • George C. D. Odell, *Shakespeare from Betterton to Irving*, vol. 2, 1920, repr. 1966. • Samuel Schoenbaum, *Shakespeare's Lives*, 1991. • Susan J. Wolfson, "'Explaining to Their Sisters': Mary Lamb's *Tales from Shakespeare*," in *Women's (Re)visions of Shakespeare*, ed. Marianne Novy, 1990. • Susan J. Wolfson, "Shakespeare and the Romantic Girl Reader," *Nineteenth-Century Contexts* 21, 1999.

William Cowper • *Biography.* • David Cecil, *The Stricken Deer*, 1929. • M. J. Quinlan, *Cowper: A Critical Life*, 1953. • Charles Ryskamp, *William Cowper of the Inner Temple*, 1959.

Editions. • John D. Baird and Charles Ryskamp, eds., *Poems of William Cowper*, 3 vols., 1980. • James King and Charles Ryskamp, eds., *Letters and Prose Writings of William Cowper*, 5 vols., 1979-86.

Criticism. • Morris Golden, *In Search of Stability: The Poetry of William Cowper*, 1960. • Vincent Newey, *Cowper's Poetry*, 1982.

Our Texts. • *Poems*, 1851.

Thomas De Quincey • *Biography and Background.* • Horace A. Eaton, *Thomas De Quincey*, 1936, repr. 1972. • Alethea Hayter, *Opium and the Romantic Imagination*, 1970. • Grevel Lindop, *The Opium-Eater: A Life of Thomas De Quincey*, 1981. • Judson S. Lyon, *Thomas De Quincey*, 1969.

Criticism. • John Barrell, *The Infection of Thomas De Quincey: A Psychopathology of Imperialism*, 1991. • Elizabeth Bruss, *Autobiographical Acts: The Changing Situation of a Literary Genre*, 1976. • Alina Clej, *A Genealogy of the Modern Self: Thomas De Quincey and the Intoxication of Writing*, 1995. • Vincent De Luca, *Thomas De Quincey: The Prose of Vision*, 1980. • Nigel Leask, "Toward a Universal Aesthetic: De Quincey on Murder as Carnival and Tragedy," in *Questioning Romanticism*, ed. John Beer, 1995. • J. Hillis Miller, *The Disappearance of God*, 1973. • Arden Reed, *Romantic Weather*, Part III, 1983. • Margaret Russett, *De Quincey's Romanticism: Canonical Minority and the Forms of Transmission*, 1997. • Charles Rzepka, *Sacramental Commodities: Gift, Text, and the Sublime in De Quincey*, 1995. • Stephen J. Spector, "Thomas De Quincey: Self-Effacing Autobiographer," *Studies in Romanticism*, 1979. • Eve Kosofsky Sedgwick, *The Coherence of Gothic Conventions*, 1980. • Robert L. Snyder, ed., *Thomas De Quincey: Bicentenary Studies*, 1985. • Joshua Wilner, "Autobiography and Addiction: The Case of De Quincey," *Genre*, 1991.

Our Texts. • *Confessions* from the *London Magazine*, 1821; "On the Knocking at the Gate in *Macbeth*" from the *London Magazine*, 1823; "Alexander Pope" from the *North British Review*, 1848.

Maria Edgeworth • *Biography.* • Marilyn Butler, *Maria Edgeworth: A Literary Biography*, 1972. • Elizabeth Harden, *Maria Edgeworth*, 1984. • A. J. C. Hare, *The Life and Letters of Maria Edgeworth*, 1894.

Criticism. • Elizabeth Kowaleski-Wallace, *Their Fathers' Daughters: Hannah More, Maria Edgeworth and Patriarchal Complicity*, 1991. • Alan Richardson, *Literature, Education, and Romanticism*, ch. 2 [on *Practical Education*], 1994.

Our Text. • *Practical Education*, 1798.

Olaudah Equiano • *Editions.* • Angelo Costanzo, ed., *The Interesting Narrative of the Life of Olaudah Equiano* (with contextual materials), 2001. • Werner Sollors, ed., *Narrative of the Life of Olaudah Equiano* (with contextual materials and critical essays), 2001.

Criticism. • William L. Andrews, *To Tell a Free Story: The First Century of Afro-American Autobiography*, 1986. • Vincent Carretta, "Olaudah Equiano or Gustavus Vassa? New Light on an Eighteenth-Century Question of Identity," *Slavery and Abolition*, 1999. • Angelo Costanzo, *Surprizing Narrative: Olaudah Equiano and the Beginnings of Black Autobiography*, 1987. • Srinivas Aravamudan, *Tropicopolitans*, 1999. • Henry L. Gates, Jr., *The Signifying Monkey: A Theory of Afro-American Literary Criticism*, 1988. • Sonia Hofkosh, "Capitalism, Abolition, and the Romantic Individual," in *Romanticism, Race, and Imperial Culture*, ed. Hofkosh and Richardson. • Susan M. Marren, "Between Slavery and Freedom: The Transgressive Self in Olaudah Equiano's Autobiography," *PMLA*, 1993. • Dwight McBride, *Impossible Witnesses: Truth, Abolitionism, and Slave Testimony*, 2001. • Geraldine Murphy, "Olaudah Equiano, Accidental Tourist," *Eighteenth-Century Studies*, 1994. • Adam Potkay, "Olaudah Equiano and the Art of Spiritual Autobiography," *Eighteenth-Century Studies*, 1994.

Our Text. • *The Life of Olaudah Equiano*, 1814.

William Godwin • John P. Clarke, *The Philosophical Anarchism of William Godwin*, 1977.

• R. G. Grylls, *William Godwin and His World*, 1953. • Don Locke, *A Fantasy of Reason: The Life and Thought of William Godwin*, 1980. • Peter H. Marshall, *William Godwin*, 1984. • E. E. Smith and E. G. Smith, *William Godwin*, 1966. • William St. Clair, *The Godwins and the Shelleys*, 1989.

Our Text. • *An Enquiry Concerning Political Justice, and Its Influence on General Virtue and Happiness*, 1793.

William Hazlitt. • *Biography:* Herschel Baker, *William Hazlitt*, 1962. • Stanley Jones, *Hazlitt: A Life: From Winterslow to Frith Street*, 1989. • Ralph Wardle, *Hazlitt*, 1971.

Criticism. • David Bromwich, *Hazlitt; The Mind of a Critic*, 1984. • John Kinnaird, *William Hazlitt: Critic of Power*, 1978. • John L. Mahoney, *The Logic of Passion: The Literary Criticism of William Hazlitt*, 1981. • Tom Paulin, *The Day-Star of Liberty: William Hazlitt's Radical Style*, 1998. • Bill Ruddick, "Recollecting Coleridge: The Internalization of Radical Energies in Hazlitt's Political Prose," *Yearbook of English Studies*, 1989.

Our Text. • P. P. Howe, ed., *The Complete Works of William Hazlitt*, 21 vols., 1930–34.

Felicia Hemans • *Editions:* Paula R. Feldman, *Records of Woman with Other Poems*, 1999. • Susan J. Wolfson, ed., *Felicia Hemans: Selected Poems, Letters, & Reception Materials*, 2000.

Biography. • Henry F. Chorley, *Memorials of Mrs. Hemans, with Illustrations of Her Literary Character from Her Private Correspondence*, 1836. • [Harriett Mary Hughes {Browne}; later Owen], *Memoir of the Life and Writings of Felicia Hemans: By Her Sister*, 1845. • Peter W. Trinder, *Mrs. Hemans*, 1984.

Criticism. • Isobel Armstrong, *Victorian Poetry: Poetry, Poetics and Politics*, 1993. • Norma Clarke, *Ambitious Heights: Writing, Friendship, Love*, 1990. • George Gilfillan, "Female Authors. No. I–Mrs. Hemans," *Tait's Edinburgh Magazine*, 1847. • Anthony John Harding, "Felicia Hemans and the Effacement of Woman," in *Romantic Women Writers*, eds. Theresa Kelley and Paula Feldman, 1995. • Angela Leighton, *Victorian Woman Poets:*

Writing Against the Heart, 1993. • Tricia Lootens, "Hemans and Home: Victorianism, Feminine 'Internal Enemies,' and the Domestication of National Identity," *PMLA*, 1994. • Jerome J. McGann, "Literary History, Romanticism, and Felicia Hemans," in *Revisioning Romanticism*, eds. Carol Shiner Wilson and Joel Haefner, 1994. • Anne Mellor, *Romanticism and Gender*, 1993. • Nanora Sweet and Julie Melnyck, eds., *Felicia Hemans: Reimagining Poetry in the Nineteenth Century*, 2001. • Herbert F. Tucker, "House Arrest: The Domestication of English Poetry in the 1820s," *ELH*, 1994. • Susan J. Wolfson, "'Domestic Affections' and 'the Spear of Minerva': Felicia Hemans and the Dilemma of Gender," in *Revisioning Romanticism*, eds. Wilson and Haefner, 1994. • Susan J. Wolfson, "Gendering the Soul," in *Romantic Women Writers*, eds. Kelley and Feldman, 1995. • Jonathan Wordsworth, *The Bright Work Grows: Women Writers of the Romantic Age*, 1997.

Our Texts. • All lifetime editions, for which see *Felicia Hemans*, ed. Wolfson.

Francis Jeffrey • *Biography.* • Henry Cockburn, *Life of Lord Jeffrey*, 2 vols., 1852.

Editions. • Francis Jeffrey, *Contributions to the Edinburgh Review*, 4 vols., 1844.

Criticism. • David Bromwich, "Romantic Poetry and the *Edinburgh* Ordinances," *Yearbook of English Studies*, 1986. • Jerome Christensen, "The Detection of the Romantic Conspiracy in Britain," *South Atlantic Quarterly*, 1996. • John Clive, *Scotch Reviewers: The Edinburgh Review 1802–1815*, 1957. • Philip Flynn, *Francis Jeffrey*, 1978. • Peter F. Morgan, *Literary Critics and Reviewers in Early 19th Century Britain*, 1983. • Mark Schoenfield, "Regulating Standards: The *Edinburgh Review* and the Circulations of Judgement," *The Wordsworth Circle*, 1993. • Kim Wheatley, "Paranoid Politics: The *Quarterly* and *Edinburgh* Reviews," *Prose Studies*, 1992.

Our Texts. • *Edinburgh Review*, 1 (October 1802), and 24 (November 1814).

Maria Jane Jewsbury • *Criticism.* • Norma Clarke, *Ambitious Heights*, 1990. • Joanne Wilkes, "'Only the Broken Music'? The Critical Writings of Maria Jane Jewsbury," *Women's Writing* (2000). • Susan Wolfson, *Borderlines*, 2006.

Our Texts. • *A Rural Excursion* and *The Young Author* both from *Phantasmagoria*, 1825.

John Keats • *Biography and Reception.* • Walter Jackson Bate, *John Keats*, 1963. • George H. Ford, *Keats and the Victorians: A Study of His Influence and Rise to Fame 1821–1895*, 1944. • G. M. Matthews, ed., *Keats: The Critical Heritage*, 1971. • Andrew Motion, *Keats*, 1998. • James Najarian, *Manliness, Sexuality, and Desire*, 2002. • Aileen Ward, *John Keats: The Making of a Poet*, 1963. • Susan J. Wolfson, "Feminizing Keats," in *Critical Essays on John Keats*, ed. Hermione de Almeida, 1990.

Criticism. • John Barnard, *John Keats*, 1987. • Walter Jackson Bate, *The Stylistic Development of Keats*, 1945. • John Bayley, "Keats and Reality," *Proceedings of the British Academy*, 1962. • Cleanth Brooks, "Keats's Sylvan Historian: History without Footnotes," in *The Well Wrought Urn: Studies in the Structure of Poetry*, 1947. • Douglas Bush, *John Keats: His Life and Writings*, 1966. • Morris Dickstein, *Keats and His Poetry*, 1971. • Stuart Ende, *Keats and the Sublime*, 1976. • Geoffrey Hartman, "Spectral Symbolism and Authorial Self," in *The Fate of Reading*, 1975. • Wolf Z. Hirst, *John Keats*, 1981. • Margaret Homans, "Keats Reading Women, Women Reading Keats," *Studies in Romanticism*, 1990. • John Jones, *John Keats's Dream of Truth*, 1969. • William Keach, "Cockney Couplets: Keats and the Politics of Style," *Studies in Romanticism*, 1986. • Robert Kern, "Keats and the Problem of Romance," *Philological Quarterly*, 1979. • Marjorie Levinson, *Keats's Life of Allegary*, 1988. • Jerome J. McGann, "Keats and the Historical Method in Literary Criticism," 1979, repr. in *The Beauty of Inflections*, 1985. • Christopher Ricks, *Keats and Embarrassment*, 1976. • Jeffrey Robinson, *Reception and Poetics in Keats*, 1998. • Nicholas Roe, *John Keats and the Culture of Dissent*, 1997. • Stuart M. Sperry, *Keats the Poet*, 1973. • Jack Stillinger, "Imagination and Reality in the Odes" and "The Hoodwinking of Madeline," in *"The Hoodwinking of Madeline" and Other Essays on Keats's Poems*, 1971; *Reading "The Eve of St. Agnes": The Multiples of Complex Literary Transaction*, 1999. • Karen Swann, "Harrassing the Muse," in *Romanticism and Feminism*, Anne Mellor, ed. 1988. • Helen Vendler, *The Odes of John Keats*, 1983; "John Keats: Perfecting the Sonnet,"

in *Coming of Age as a Poet*, 2003. • Leon Waldoff, *Keats and the Silent Work of Imagination*, 1985. • Daniel P. Watkins, *Keats's Poetry and the Politics of the Imagination*, 1989. • Susan J. Wolfson, "Keats and the Manhood of the Poet," *European Romantic Review*, 1995. • Susan J. Wolfson, *The Questioning Presence: Wordsworth, Keats, and the Interrogative Mode in Romantic Poetry*, 1986. • Susan J. Wolfson, ed., *The Cambridge Companion to John Keats*, 2001.

Our Texts. • Poems published in Keats's lifetime are from first editions; posthumous publications are from Houghton's *Poetical Works*, 1891, checked against *The Poems of John Keats*, ed. Jack Stillinger, 1978, the best modern edition. • Letters edited from manuscripts, or from M. Buxton Forman's edition. Posthumous poems from various manuscript and print sources indicated, or otherwise [etc.].

Caroline Lamb • H. Blyth, *Caro: The Fatal Passion: The Life of Lady Caroline Lamb*, 1972. • John Clubbe, "Glenarvon Revised—and Revisited," *The Wordsworth Circle*, 1979. • Peter Graham, *Don Juan and Regency England*, 1990. • Malcolm Kelsall, "The Byronic Hero and Revolution in Ireland," *Byron Journal*, 1981. • James Soderholm, "Lady Caroline Lamb: Byron's Miniature Writ Large," *Keats-Shelley Journal*, 1991.

Charles Lamb • *Biography.* • David Cecil, *A Portrait of Charles Lamb*, 1983. • Winifred F. Courtney, *Young Charles Lamb 1775–1802*, 1982. • E. V. Lucas, *Life of Charles Lamb*, rev. ed., 2 vols., 1921.

Editions. • E. V. Lucas, ed., *The Works of Charles and Mary Lamb*, 1903–1905. • E. W. Marrs, ed., *The Letters of Charles and Mary Anne Lamb*, 3 vols., 1975—.

Critical Studies. • Jane Aaron, *A Double Singleness: Gender and the Writing of Charles and Mary Lamb*, 1991. • George L. Barnett, *Charles Lamb*, 1976. • Robert Frank, *Don't Call Me Gentle Charles!*, 1976. • Richard Haven, "The Romantic Art of Charles Lamb," *ELH*, 1963. • Alison Hickey, "Double Bonds: Charles Lamb's Romantic Collaborations," *ELH*, 1996. • Gerald Monsman, *Confessions of a Prosaic Dreamer: Charles Lamb's Art of Autobiography*, 1984. • John Nabholtz, *"My Reader My Fellow-Labourer": A Study of English Romantic Prose*,

1986. • Roy Park, "Lamb, Shakespeare, and the Stage," *Shakespeare Quarterly*, 1982. • Mark Parker, "'A Piece of Autobiography'; Reference in Charles Lamb's Essays," *Auto/Biography Studies*, 1986–1987. • Mark Parker, "Ideology and Editing: The Political Context of the Elia Essays," *Studies in Romanticism*, 1991. • F. V. Randel, *The World of Elia*, 1975. • See also the entry for Mary Lamb.

Our Texts. • *The Works of Charles and Mary Lamb*, ed. E. V. Lucas, 1903–1905.

Mary Lamb • Criticism. • Jane Aaron, "'On Needle-Work': Protest and Contradiction in Mary Lamb's Essay," in *Romanticism and Feminism*, ed. Anne K. Mellor, 1988. • Jean I. Marsden, "Shakespeare for Girls: Mary Lamb and *Tales from Shakespeare*," *Children's Literature*, 1989. See also the entry for Charles Lamb.

Our Text. • *The Works of Charles and Mary Lamb*, ed. E. V. Lucas, 1903–1905.

Catharine Macaulay • Criticism. • Bridget Hill, *Republican Virago: The Life and Times of Catharine Macaulay*, 1992. • Jonathan Wordsworth, *The Bright Work Grows: Women Writers of the Romantic Age*, 1997.

Our Text. • *Letters on Education, With Observations on Religious and Metaphysical Subjects* (1790). Reprinted in *Feminist Controversy in England, 1788–1810*, ed. Gina Luria, 1974; excerpts from letters 4 and 21, and all of letters 22 and 23 are included in *A Vindication of the Rights of Woman*, ed. Carol Poston, 2nd ed. 1988.

Thomas Moore • Leith Davis, "Irish Bards and English Consumers: Thomas Moore's 'Irish Melodies' and the Colonized Nation," *Ariel*, 1993. • Miriam A. DeFord, *Thomas Moore*, 1967. • Howard Mumford Jones, *The Harp That Once: A Chronicle of Thomas Moore*, 1937. • Thérèse Tessier, *The Bard of Erin: A Study of Thomas Moore's Irish Melodies*, 1981. • Terence de Vere White, *Thomas Moore: The Irish Poet*, 1977.

Our Text. • *Poetical Works of Thomas Moore*, 1875.

Hannah More • Biography. • M. G. Jones, *Hannah More*, 1952. • W. Roberts, *Memoirs of the Life and Correspondence of Mrs. Hannah More*, 1834. • Mary Alden Hopkins, *Hannah More and Her Circle*, 1947.

Criticism. • Elizabeth Kowaleski-Wallace, *Their Fathers' Daughters: Hannah More, Maria Edgeworth and Patriarchal Complicity*, 1991. • Anne K. Mellor, *Mothers of the Nation*, 2001. • Mitzi Myers, "Hannah More's Tracts for the Times: Social Fiction and Female Ideology," *Fetter'd or Free: British Women Novelists, 1670–1815*, eds. Mary Anne Schofield and Cecelia Macheski, 1986. • Alan Richardson, *Literature, Education, and Romanticism*, 1994. • G. H. Spinney, "Cheap Repository Tracts," in *The Library*, 1939. • Jonathan Wordsworth, *The Bright Work Grows: Women Writers of the Romantic Age*, 1997.

Our Texts. • *Village Politics*, 1792; *The Works of Hannah More*, 1830.

Thomas Paine • A. J. Ayer, *Thomas Paine*, 1988. • Eric Foner, *Thomas Paine and Revolutionary America*, 1976. • David F. Hawke, *Thomas Paine*, 1974. • John Keane, *Thomas Paine: A Political Life*, 1995. • Edward Larkin, *Thomas Paine and the Literature of Revolution*, 2005. • Mark Philp, *Paine*, 1989.

Our Text. • *The Rights of Man*, 1790.

Thomas Percy • Biographical Studies. • Bertram H. Davis, *Thomas Percy*, 1981. • Bertram H. Davis, *Thomas Percy: A Scholar-Cleric in the Age of Johnson*, 1989.

Criticism. • William H. Matchett, "The Integrity of 'Sir Patrick Spence,'" *Modern Philology*, 1970. • Kathryn Sutherland, "The Native Poet: The Influence of Percy's Minstrel from Beattie to Wordsworth," *Review of English Studies*, 1982.

Our Text. • *Reliques of Ancient English Poetry*, 2 vols., 1906.

Mary Prince • Moira Ferguson, ed., *The History of Mary Prince*, 1987. • Moira Ferguson, *Subject to Others: British Women Writers and Colonial Slavery, 1670–1834*, 1992. • Jenny Sharpe, "'Something Akin to Freedom': The Case of Mary Prince," in *Differences*, 1996.

Our Text. • *History of Mary Prince*, 1831.

Mary Anne Radcliffe • Criticism. • Jonathan Wordsworth, *The Bright Work Grows*, 1997.

Our Text. • The Female Advocate; Or an Attempt to Recover the Rights of Women from Male Usurpation, 1799.

Mary Robinson • Edition. • Judith Pascoe, ed., Mary Robinson, Selected Poems, 2000; with reception materials.

Biography. • Robert D. Bass, The Green Dragoon: The Lives of Banastre Tarleton and Mary Robinson, 1957. • Paula Byrne, Perdita: The Life of Mary Robinson, 2004. • Mary Robinson, Memoirs of the Late Mrs. Robinson, Written by Herself: With Some Posthumous Pieces, 1801. • Marguerite Steen, The Lost One: A Biography of Mary (Perdita) Robinson, 1937.

Criticism. • Stuart Curran, "Mary Robinson's Lyrical Tales in Context," in Revisioning Romanticism, ed. Carol Shiner Wilson and Joel Haefner, 1994. • Jerome McGann, The Poetics of Sensibility (chs. 10), 1996. • Judith Pascoe, Romantic Theatricality (chs. 5 and 6), 1995. • Daniel Robinson, "From 'Mingled Measure' to 'Ecstatic Measures': Mary Robinson's Poetic Reading of 'Kubla Khan,'" The Wordsworth Circle, 1995. • Jonathan Wordsworth, The Bright Work Grows: Women Writers of the Romantic Age, 1997.

Our Texts. • "The Haunted Beach," Lyrical Tales (1800); repr. Woodstock Press. Other poems: Sappho and Phaon, 1796; "The Camp" repr. in Jerome McGann, ed., The New Oxford Book of Romantic Period Verse, 1993; Poetical Works of the Late Mrs. Mary Robinson, 1806 (repr. 1824); "To the Poet Coleridge" (1801).

Sir Walter Scott • Biography. • Edgar Johnson, Sir Walter Scott: The Great Unknown, 1970. • John Sutherland, The Life of Walter Scott, 1995.

Criticism. • David Daiches, Sir Walter Scott and His World, 1971. • Ian Duncan, Modern Romance and the Transformations of the Novel, 1992. • Ina Ferris, The Achievement of Literary Authority: Gender, History, and the Waverley Novels, 1991. • Alexander Welsh, The Hero of the Waverley Novels, 1963.

Our Texts. • The Black Dwarf and a Legend of Montrose, 1879; "Lord Randal" from Minstrelsy of the Scottish Border, 1802–1803.

Mary Wollstonecraft Shelley • Biography. • William St. Clair, The Godwins and the Shelleys,

1989. • Emily Sunstein, Mary Wollstonecraft Shelley: Romance and Reality, 1989. • William Walling, Mary Shelley, 1972.

General Criticism. • Anne K. Mellor, Mary Shelley: Her Life, Her Fiction, Her Monsters, 1988. • Mary Poovey, The Proper Lady and the Woman Writer: Ideology as Style in the Works of Mary Wollstonecraft, Mary Shelley, and Jane Austen, 1984. • Esther Schor, ed., The Cambridge Companion to Mary Shelley, 2003.

Edition. • Charles E. Robinson, ed., Mary Shelley: Collected Tales and Stories with Original Engravings, 1976.

Our Text. • The Keepsake for MDCCCXXXI.

Criticism. • Sonia Hofkosh, "Mary Shelley's Gift-Book Stories," in Sexual Politics and the Romantic Author, 1998. • Peter J. Manning, "Wordsworth in the Keepsake, 1829," in Literature in the Marketplace, eds. John O. Jordan and Robert L. Patten, 1995. • Judith Pascoe, "Mary Shelley in the Annuals," Mary Shelley in Her Times, ed. Betty T. Bennett and Stuart Curran, 1999.

Percy Bysshe Shelley • Biography. • Kenneth Neill Cameron, The Young Shelley, 1950. • Richard Holmes, Shelley: The Pursuit, 1974. • Newman Ivey White, Shelley, 1940.

Editions. • Kelvin Everest and Geoffrey Matthews, The Poems of Shelley, 1989, 1999. • Donald Reiman and Neil Fraistat, eds., The Complete Poetry of Percy Bysshe Shelley, v. 1, 2000; more volumes to follow. • Donald Reiman and Neil Fraistat, eds., Shelley's Poetry and Prose. 2nd ed., 2002; texts and critical essays.

Reception. • Mark Kipperman, "Absorbing a Revolution: Shelley Becomes a Romantic, 1889–1903," in Nineteenth-Century Literature, 1992. • Sylva Norman, The Flight of the Skylark, 1954. • N. I. White, The Unextinguish'd Hearth, 1938.

General Criticism. • Stephen C. Behrendt, Shelley and His Audiences, 1989. • Harold Bloom, Shelley's Mythmaking, 1959. • Judith Chernaik, The Lyrics of Shelley, 1972. • Frances Ferguson, "Shelley's Mont Blanc: What the Mountain Said," in Romanticism and Language, ed. Arden Reed, 1984. • Paul Foot, Red Shelley,

1980. • Jerrold Hogle, *Shelley's Process*, 1988.
• William C. Keach, *Shelley's Style*, 1984.
• Angela Leighton, *Shelley and the Sublime*,
984. • Donald H. Reiman, *Percy Bysshe
Shelley*, 1990. • Hugh Roberts, *Shelley and the
Chaos of History*, 1997. • Michael Henry
Scrivener, *Radical Shelley*, 1982. • Stuart
Sperry, *Shelley's Major Verse*, 1988. • Earl R.
Wasserman, *Shelley: A Critical Reading*,
1981. • Milton Wilson, *Shelley's Later Poetry*,
1959. • Ross G. Woodman, *The Apocalyptic
Vision in the Poetry of Shelley*, 1964.

On The Mask of Anarchy. • *The Masque
of Anarchy, A Poem*, with Preface by
Leigh Hunt (1832), facsimile repr. ed.
Jonathan Wordsworth, 1990. • Stuart
Curran, *Shelley's Annus Mirabilis: The
Maturing of an Epic Vision*, 1975. • Tho-
mas R. Edwards, *Imagination and Power:
A Study of Poetry on Public Themes*, 1971.
• Stephen Goldsmith, *Unbinding Jerusalem:
Apocalypse and Romantic Imagination*, 1993.
• Donald H. Reiman, *"The Mask of Anarchy":
A Facsimile Edition, with Scholarly Introduc-
tions, Bibliographical Descriptions, and Anno-
tations*, 1985. • E. P. Thompson, *The Making
of the English Working Class*, 1964. • Susan J.
Wolfson, *Formal Charges*, 1997.

On Adonais. • James A. W. Heffernan,
"Adonais: Shelley's Consumption of Keats,"
Studies in Romanticism, 1984. • Susan J. Wolfson, "Keats Enters History: Autopsy, Adonais,
and the Fame of Keats," in *Keats and History*,
ed. Nicholas Roe, 1994.

Our Texts. • *The Complete Poetical Works of
Percy Bysshe Shelley*, ed. William Michael Ros-
setti, 1881, checked against modern editions;
The Mask of Anarchy is checked against Rei-
man's 1985 facsimile edition of the 1819 *The
Mask of Anarchy*.

Charlotte Smith • *Biography*. • Lorraine Fletcher,
Charlotte Smith: A Critical Biography, 1998.

Editions. • *The Poems of Charlotte Smith*,
ed. Stuart Curran, 1993. • *The Collected
Letters of Charlotte Smith*, ed. Judith Phillips
Stanton, 2003.

Criticism. • Stuart Curran, "Charlotte Smith
and British Romanticism," *South Central Review* 11.2, 1994. • Paula Feldman, headnote in
British Women Poets of the Romantic Era, 1997.

• Bishop C. Hunt, "Wordsworth and Char-
lotte Smith," *The Wordsworth Circle*, 1970.
• Theresa M. Kelley, "Romantic Nature Bites
Back: Adorno and Romantic Natural History,"
European Romantic Review, 2004. • Judith Pas-
coe, "Female Botanists and the Poetry of Char-
lotte Smith," in *Revisioning Romanticism*, eds.
Carol Shiner Wilson and Joel Haefner, 1994.
• Adela Pinch, *Strange Fits of Passion*, 1996.
• Sarah Zimmerman, *Romanticism, Lyricism,
and History*, 1999; and "Charlotte Smith and
the Lyric's Audience," in Linkin and Behrendt,
Romanticism and Women Poets, 1999.

Our Text. • *Elegiac Sonnets*, 5th ed., 1789.

Robert Southey • *Biographical Studies*. • Ernest
Bernhardt-Kabisch, *Robert Southey*, 1977.
• Geoffrey Carnall, *Robert Southey and His
Age*, 1960. • Kenneth Curry, *Southey*, 1975.
• Mark Storey, *Robert Southey: A Life*, 1997.

Criticism. • Marilyn Butler, *Literature as a
Heritage, or Reading Other Ways*, 1988. • Li-
onel Madden, ed., *Robert Southey: The Critical
Heritage*, 1972.

Our Texts. • *Poetical Works of Robert
Southey*, 1837.

Priscilla Wakefield • *Criticism*. • Katherine
M. Rogers, *Feminism in Eighteenth-Century
England*, 1982.

Our Text. • *Reflections on the Present Condition of the Female Sex; with Suggestions for Its
Improvement*. London, 1798.

William Thompson and Anna Wheeler • *Text,
Biography*. • Richard Pankhurst's edition of
Appeal, 1983; Pankhurst has also written a
biography of Thompson, 1954.

Criticism (Wheeler). • Stephen Burke, "Let-
ter from a Pioneer Feminist," *Studies in Labour
History*, 1976. • Richard Pankhurst, "Anna
Wheeler; A Pioneer Socialist and Feminist,"
Philological Quarterly, 1954.

Helen Maria Williams • *Edition*. • Neil Fraistat and Susan S. Lanser, eds., *Helen Maria
Williams, Letters Written in France*, 2001 (with
reviews and other contextual materials).

Criticism. • M. Ray Adams, "Helen Maria
Williams and the French Revolution," in

Wordsworth and Coleridge, ed. Earl Leslie Griggs, 1939. • Mary Favret, *Romantic Correspondence: Women, Politics, and the Fiction of Letters,* 1993. • Chris Jones, "Helen Maria Williams and Radical Sensibility," *Prose Studies,* 1989. • Nicola Watson, *Revolution and the Form of the British Novel, 1790–1825,* 1994.

Our Texts. • *Letters from France,* 1790, 1796.

Mary Wollstonecraft • *Biography:* Pamela Clemit and Gina Luria Walker, *Memoirs of the Author of A Vindication of the Rights of Woman, by William Godwin,* 2001. • Caroline Franklin, *Mary Wollstonecraft: A Literary Life,* 2004. • William Godwin, *Memoirs of the Author of a Vindication of the Rights of Woman,* 1798 • Gary Kelly, *Revolutionary Feminism: The Mind and Career of Mary Wollstonecraft,* 1992. • Jennifer Lorch, *Mary Wollstonecraft: The Making of a Radical Feminist,* 1990. • Emily Sunstein, *A Different Face—The Life of Mary Wollstonecraft,* 1975. • Janet Todd, *Mary Wollstonecraft: A Revolutionary Life,* 2000. • Claire Tomalin, *The Life and Death of Mary Wollstonecraft,* 1974.

Criticism. • Claudia L. Johnson, ed., *The Cambridge Companion to Mary Wollstonecraft,* 2002. • Claudia Johnson, *Equivocal Beings: Politics, Gender, and Sentimentality in the 1790s,* 1995. • Anne K. Mellor, *Romanticism and Gender,* 1993. • Ellen Moers, *Literary Women: The Great Writers,* 1963. • Mary Poovey, *The Proper Lady and the Woman Writer,* 1984. • In Carol Poston's edition are included appreciations by George Eliot, 1855; Emma Goldman, c. 1910; and Virginia Woolf, 1932; as well as Ferdinand Lundberg and Marynia Farnham's notorious "Mary Wollstonecraft and the Psychopathology of Feminism," 1947; and helpful essays by (among others) Carolyn W. Korsmeyer, "Reason and Morals in the Early Feminist Movement," 1976; Elissa Guralnick on radical politics in *Rights of Woman,* 1977; R. M. Janes, on the reception of *Rights of Woman,* 1978; and Mitzi Myers, "Reform or Ruin," 1982. • Timothy J. Reiss, "Revolution in Bounds: Wollstonecraft, Women, and Reason," in *Gender and Theory: Dialogues on Feminist Criticism,* ed. Linda Kauffman, 1989. • Virginia Sapiro, *A Vindication of Political Virtue: The Political Theory of Mary Wollstonecraft,* 1992. • Nicola Trott, "Sexing the Critic: Mary Wollstonecraft at the Turn of the Century," in Richard Cronin, ed.,

1798: The Year of the "Lyrical Ballads," 1998. • Orrin Wang, "The Other Reasons," *Yale Journal of Criticism,* 1991.

On *Vindication of the Rights of Men* • Gary Kelly, "Mary Wollstonecraft as Vir Bonus," *English Studies in Canada,* 1979. • Mitzi Myers, "Politics from the Outside," *Studies in Eighteenth-Century Culture,* 1977.

On *The Wrongs of Woman, or Maria.* • Moira Ferguson, Introduction to the Norton Edition, 1975. • Gary Kelly, Introduction to the Oxford Edition, 1976; related remarks in *The English Jacobin Novel 1780–1805,* 1976, and *English Fiction of the Romantic Period 1789–1830,* 1989. • Anne K. Mellor, "Righting the Wrongs of Woman: Mary Wollstonecraft's *Maria,*" *Nineteenth-Century Contexts* 19, 1996. • Tilottama Rajan, "Wollstonecraft and Godwin: Reading the Secrets of the Political Novel," *Studies in Romanticism,* 1988.

Our Texts. • *A Vindication of the Rights of Men, in a Letter to the Right Honourable Edmund Burke; Occasioned by His "Reflections on the Revolution in France,"* 2nd ed., 1790; *Vindication of the Rights of Woman,* ed. Carol Poston, 2nd ed., 1988; *Maria or the Wrongs of Woman* and letter to Joseph Johnson from William Godwin's edition in *The Posthumous Works,* 1798; repr. Norton, 1975.

Dorothy Wordsworth • *Biographies.* • Catherine Macdonald Maclean, *Dorothy and William Wordsworth,* 1927. • Robert Gittings and Jo Manton, *Dorothy Wordsworth,* 1985.

Editions. • Susan Levin, *The Collected Poems of Dorothy Wordsworth,* in *Dorothy Wordsworth and Romanticism,* 1987. • Ernest de Selincourt, ed., *Journals of Dorothy Wordsworth,* 1941. • Mary Moorman, ed., *Journals of Dorothy Wordsworth* (Alfoxden and Grasmere), 1971. • Pamela Woof, ed., *The Grasmere Journals,* 1991. • Alan G. Hill, ed., *Letters of Dorothy Wordsworth,* 1981.

Criticism. • Rachael Brownstein, "The Private Life," *Modern Language Quarterly* 34, 1971. • Robert Con Davis, "The Structure of the Picturesque: Dorothy Wordsworth's Journals," *The Wordsworth Circle* 9, 1978. • Thomas De Quincey, "Recollections of Grasmere," *Tait's Edinburgh Magazine,* 1839, reprinted in various collected works. • Elizabeth Fay, *Becoming Wordsworthian*, 1995. • Kurt Heinzelman, "The Cult of Domesticity: Dorothy and William Wordsworth at Grasmere," in *Romanticism and Feminism*, ed. Mellor (above). • Margaret Homans, *Women Writers and Poetic Identity*, 1980; and *Bearing the Word: Language and Female Experience in Nineteenth-Century Women's Writing*, 1986. • Susan M. Levin, *Dorothy Wordsworth and Romanticism*, 1987. • Alan Liu, "On the Autobiographical Present: Dorothy Wordsworth's Grasmere Journals," *Criticism* 26, 1984. • Susan J. Wolfson, "Individual in Community," in *Romanticism and Feminism*, ed. Mellor (above). • Virginia Woolf, "Dorothy Wordsworth," *The Second Common Reader*, 1932.

Our Texts. • Levin's *Poems.* • Moorman's *Journals*, with reference to Woof's. • Hill's *Letters*.

William Wordsworth • *Biography and Reference.* • Stephen Gill, *Wordsworth: A Life*, 1989. • John L. Mahoney, *William Wordsworth: A Poetic Life*, 1997. • Mary Moorman, *William Wordsworth: A Biography*, 2 vols., 1957–1965. • Mark L. Reed, *Wordsworth: The Chronology of the Early Years, 1770–1799*, 1967. • Mark L. Reed, *Wordsworth: The Chronology of the Middle Years, 1800–1815*, 1975. • Duncan Wu, *Wordsworth's Reading 1779–1799*, 1993. • Duncan Wu, *Wordsworth's Reading 1800–1815*, 1995.

Biography and Criticism. • Kenneth R. Johnston, *The Hidden Wordsworth*, 1998. • Duncan Wu, *Wordsworth: An Inner Life*, 2002.

Editions. • R. L. Brett and A. R. Jones, eds., *Wordsworth and Coleridge: Lyrical Ballads*, 1968. • Beth Darlington, ed., *The Love Letters of William and Mary Wordsworth*, 1981. • Ernest de Selincourt, ed., *The Letters of William and Dorothy Wordsworth*, 2nd ed. rev.: *Early Years, 1787–1805*, ed. Chester L. Shaver, 1967; *Middle Years, Part 1, 1806–1811*, ed. Mary Moorman, 1969, *Part 2, 1812–1820*, ed. Alan G. Hill, 1970; *Later Years, Part 1, 1821–1828*, 1978, *Part 2, 1829–1834*, 1979, *Part 3, 1835–1839*, 1982, and *Part 4, 1840–1853*, 1988, all ed. Alan G. Hill. • Michael Mason, ed., *Lyrical Ballads*, 1992. • W. J. B. Owen and Jane Worthington Smyser, eds., *The Prose Works of William Wordsworth*, 3 vols., 1974. • Stephen Parrish, gen. ed., *The Cornell Wordsworth*, 1975–. This series, based on Wordsworth's earliest texts, thus far includes (among others): *The Prelude, 1798–1799*, ed. Stephen Parrish, 1977; *Poems, in Two Volumes and Other Poems 1800–1807*, ed. Jared Curtis, 1983; *The Fourteen-Book Prelude*, ed. W. J. B. Owen, 1985; *The Thirteen-Book Prelude*, ed. Mark L. Reed, 2 vols., 1991; *Shorter Poems, 1807–1820*, ed. Carl H. Ketcham, 1989; *Lyrical Ballads, and Other Poems, 1797–1800*, ed. James Butler and Karen Green, 1992. • Jonathan Wordsworth, M. H. Abrams, and Stephen Gill, eds., *The Prelude 1799, 1805, 1850*, 1979. • Ernest de Selincourt and Helen Darbishire, eds., *The Poetical Works of William Wordsworth*, 5 vols., 1940–1949. [Based on Wordsworth's final texts.]

Criticism. • Jonathan Arac, "Bounding Lines: *The Prelude* and Critical Revision," *boundary 2*, 1979. • James Averill, *Wordsworth and the Poetry of Human Suffering*, 1980. • Alan Bewell, *Wordsworth and the Enlightenment*, 1989. • Don Bialostosky, *Making Tales: The Poetics of Wordsworth's Narrative Experiments*, 1988. • James K. Chandler, *Wordsworth's Second Nature: A Study of the Poetry and Politics*, 1984. • David Collings, *Wordsworthian Errancies*, 1994. • Jared Curtis, *Wordsworth's Experiments with Tradition: The Lyric Poems of 1802*, 1971. • Paul de Man, "Time and History in Wordsworth," *Diacritics*, 1987. • David Ellis, *Wordsworth, Freud, and the Spots of Time*, 1985. • Elizabeth Fay, *Becoming Wordsworthian*, 1995. • Frances Ferguson, *Wordsworth: Language as Counter-Spirit*, 1977. • William H. Galperin, *Revision and Authority in Wordsworth*, 1989. • Frederick Garber, *Wordsworth and the Poetry of Encounter*, 1971. • George Gilpin, ed., *Critical Essays on William Wordsworth*, 1990. • Heather Glen, *Vision and Disenchantment: Blake's Songs and Wordsworth's Lyrical Ballads*, 1983. • Alan Grob, *The Philosophic Mind: A Study of Wordsworth's Poetry and Thought 1797–1805*, 1973. • Geoffrey Hartman, *Wordsworth's Poetry 1787–1814*, 1964; repr. rev. 1971. • Geoffrey Hartman, *The Unremarkable Wordsworth*, 1987. • James A. W. Heffernan, *Wordsworth's Theory of Poetry*, 1969. • James Heffernan, "Wordsworth's 'Levelling' Muse in 1798," in *1798: The Year of the "Lyrical Ballads,"* ed. Richard Cronin, 1998. • Mary Jacobus, *Romanticism, Writing, and Sexual Difference: Essays on The Prelude*, 1989.

• Mary Jacobus, *Tradition and Experiment in Wordsworth's Lyrical Ballads*, 1976. • Kenneth R. Johnston, *Wordsworth and The Recluse*, 1984. • Kenneth R. Johnston, "The Politics of 'Tintern Abbey,'" *The Wordsworth Circle*, 1983. • Kenneth R. Johnston and Gene W. Ruoff, eds., *The Age of William Wordsworth*, 1987. • John E. Jordan, *Why the Lyrical Ballads?*, 1976. • Theresa M. Kelley, *Wordsworth's Revisionary Aesthetics*, 1988. • J. Douglas Kneale, *Monumental Writing: Aspects of Rhetoric in Wordsworth's Poetry*, 1988. • Marjorie Levinson, *Wordsworth's Great Period Poems*, 1986. • Herbert Lindenberger, *On Wordsworth's Prelude*, 1963. • Alan Liu, *Wordsworth: The Sense of History*, 1989. • Peter J. Manning, *Reading Romantics*, 1990. • Richard J. Onorato, *The Character of the Poet: Wordsworth in The Prelude*, 1971. • Judith W. Page, *Wordsworth and the Cultivation of Women*, 1994. • Stephen M. Parrish, *The Art of the Lyrical Ballads*, 1973. • David Perkins, *The Quest for Permanence: The Symbolism of Wordsworth, Shelley, and Keats*, 1959. • Adela Pinch, "Female Chatter: Gender and Feeling in Wordsworth's Early Poetry," in *Strange Fits of Passion*, 1996. • Jeffrey C. Robinson, *Radical Literary Education: A Classroom Experiment with Wordsworth's 'Ode'*, 1987. • Nicholas Roe, *The Politics of Nature: William Wordsworth and Some Contemporaries*, 2002. • Paul D. Sheats, *The Making of Wordsworth's Poetry 1785–1798*, 1973. • David Simpson, *Wordsworth and the Figurings of the Real*, 1982. • David Simpson, *Wordsworth's Historical Imagination: The Poetry of Displacement*, 1987. • Gayatri C. Spivak, "Sex and History in *The Prelude* (1805): Books Nine to Thirteen," *Texas Studies in Language and Literature*, 1981. • Keith G. Thomas, *Wordsworth and Philosophy*, 1989. • Leon Waldoff, *Wordsworth in his Major Lyrics: The Art and Psychology of Self-Representation*, 2001. • Douglas B. Wilson, *The Romantic Dream: Wordsworth and the Poetics of the Unconscious*, 1993. • Susan J. Wolfson, *The Questioning Presence*, 1986. • Jonathan Wordsworth, *William Wordsworth: The Borders of Vision*, 1982. • For the relations of Wordsworth and Coleridge, see also the entry under Samuel Taylor Coleridge.

Our Texts. • *Lyrical Ballads*, 1798–1802; other poems from *Poems, in Two Volumes*, 1807; *Poems*, 1815; and *Poems*, 1849; *Complete Poetical Works*, 1892, 1898, and 1911; *The Thirteen-Book Prelude*, ed. Mark L. Reed; *The Excursion* (1814); letter to Mary Ann Rawson from *The Letters of William and Dorothy Wordsworth*, 2nd ed., *Later Years, Part 2*, ed. Alan G. Hill, 1979.

Ann Yearsley • *Criticism.* • Margaret Anne Doody, *The Daring Muse: Augustan Poetry Reconsidered*, 1985. • Moira Ferguson, "Resistance and Power in the Life and Writings of Ann Yearsley," *The Eighteenth Century: Theory and Interpretation*, 1986. • Moira Ferguson, *Subject to Others*, 1992 (for *Poem, on the Inhumanity of the Slave Trade*). • Donna Landry, *The Muses of Resistance: Laboring-Class Women's Poetry in Britain 1739–1796*, 1990. • Jerome McGann, *The Poetry of Sensibility*, 1996.

Our Texts. • *A Poem on the Inhumanity of the Slave Trade*, 1788. • *The Indifferent Shepherdess*, from *The Rural Muse*, 1796.

Arthur Young • *Biography.* • G. E. Mingay, *Arthur Young and His Times*, 1975.

Our Texts. • *Travels in France…1787, 1788, 1789*, ed. Matilda Betham-Edwards, 1892; *The Example of France*, 2nd ed., 1793.

CREDITS

ILLUSTRATION CREDITS

Page 2: Thomas Girtin, *Tintern Abbey*. Blackburn Museum and Art Galleries; 3 (top): Snark/Victoria and Albert Museum, London/Art Resource, NY; 4: Victoria & Albert Museum, London/Art Resource; 5 (top): Tate, London/Art Resource, NY; 5 (middle-top): HIP/Art Resource, NY; 5 (middle-bottom): William Beechey (1753–1839). *George IV (1762–1830), When Prince of Wales*. Oil on canvas, 56 1/4 x 44 1/2 in. (142.9 x 113 cm). Gift of Heathcote Art Foundation, 1986 (1986.264.3). The Metropolitan Museum of Art, New York, NY, U.S.A. Image copyright © The Metropolitan Museum of Art/Art Resource, NY; 5 (bottom): HIP/Art Resource, NY; 16: Thomas Rowlandson (1756–1827), English, *The Contrast 1793: British Liberty and French Liberty - Which is Best?* c. 1793. Colour engraving. Musee de la Revolution Francaise, Vizille, France/ Visual Arts Library/The Bridgeman Art Library; 20: National Portrait Gallery, London; 32: © The Trustees of the British Museum; 35: Victoria & Albert Museum, London, UK/The Bridgeman Art Library; 36: Passage of Mount St. Gotthard from the Devil's Bridge, 1804 (w/c on paper), Turner, Joseph Mallord William (1775–1851)/? Abbot Hall Art Gallery, Kendal, Cumbria, UK /The Bridgeman Art Library; 38: Thomas Landseer (after Benjamin Robert Haydon), Engraving after a drawing of 2 horses' heads. *Annals of the Fine Arts*, Vol III No. 9, 1819. Foldout at the front of the journal, unpaginated. General Research Division, The New York Public Library, Astor, Lenox and Tildon Foundations/Art Resource/The New York Public Library Photographic Services; 48: Edward Dayes, *Tintern Abbey from across the Wye*. Pencil and watercolor. The Whitworth Art Gallery, The University of Manchester; 51: Professor Peter Manning; 51: Professor Peter Manning; 83: Princeton University Library; 87: Princeton University Library; 114: © The Trustees of the British Museum; 151: © The Trustees of the British Museum; 177: The Rosenwald Collection. Reproduced from the Collections of the Library of Congress. Courtesy of the Library of Congress; 180: © Reproduced from the Collections of the Library of Congress; 182: The Rosenwald Collection, Reproduced from the Collections of the Library of Congress. Courtesy of the Library of Congress; 183: Courtesy of the Library of Congress; 195: Courtesy of the Library of Congress; 196: © Reproduced from the Collections of the Library of Congress; 201: Reproduced from the collection of the Library of Congress; 217: The Rosenwald Collecion/Courtesy of the Library of Congress; 223: The Rosenwald Collecion/Courtesy of the Library of Congress; 280: © Reproduced from the Collections of the Library of Congress; 302: Courtesy of Princeton University Library.

COLOR PLATE CREDITS

Color Plate 1: Laing Art Gallery, Tyne and Wear Museums; Color Plate 2: The Wallace Collection, London; Color Plate 3: Copyright © National Portrait Gallery, London; Color Plate 4: The Bridgeman Art Library International; Color Plate 5: Museum of Fine Arts, Boston. Henry Lillie Pierce Fund; 99.22. All Rights Reserved. Photograph © 2003, Museum of Fine Arts, Boston; Color Plates 6–8: The Bridgeman Art Library International; Color Plate 9: Courtesy of the Library of Congress; Color Plate 10: The Bridgeman Art Library International.

INDEX